x86 Instruction Set Architecture

Comprehensive 32/64-bit Coverage

First Edition

ASCENT: THE RISE OF CHINGGIS KHAN
BOOK ONE OF

HEAVEN'S FAVORITE
BY TOM SHANLEY

Also by Tom Shanley

HEAVEN'S FAVORITE
—A Novel of Genghis Khan—
Book 1, ASCENT: THE RISE OF CHINGGIS KHAN
Book 2, DOMINION: DAWN OF THE MONGOL EMPIRE

MINDSHARE TECHNICAL TRAINING

Please visit www.mindshare.com for a complete description of Mind-Share's technical offerings:

- Books
- eBooks
- eLearning modules
- Public courses
- On-site course
- On-line courses

Intel Core 2 Processor (Penryn)
Intel Nehalem Processor
Intel Atom Processor
AMD Opteron Processor (Barcelona)
Intel 32/64-bit x86 Software Architecture
AMD 32/64-bit x86 Software Architecture
x86 Assembly Language Programming
Protected Mode Programming
PC Virtualization
IO Virtualization (IOV)
Computer Architectures with Intel Chipsets
Intel QuickPath Interconnect (QPI)
PCI Express 2.0
USB 2.0
USB 3.0
Embedded USB 2.0 Workshop
PCI
PCI-X
Modern DRAM Architecture
SAS
Serial ATA
High Speed Design
EMI / EMC
Bluetooth Wireless Product Development
SMT Manufacturing
SMT Testing

x86 Instruction Set Architecture

Comprehensive 32/64-bit Coverage

First Edition

MINDSHARE, INC.

TOM SHANLEY

MindShare Press

Colorado Springs, USA

Refer to "Trademarks" on page 5 for trademark information.

The author and publisher have taken care in preparation of this book but make no expressed or implied warranty of any kind and assume no responsibility for errors or omissions. No liability is assumed for incidental or consequential damages in connection with or arising out of the use of the information or programs contained herein.

ISBN: 0-9770878-5-3

Copyright © 2009 by MindShare, Inc.

Cover Design: Michelle Petrie
Set in 10 point Palatino by MindShare, Inc.

First Printing, December 2009

MindShare Press books are available for bulk purchases by corporations, institutions, and other organizations. For more information please contact the Special Sales Department at (575)-373-0336.

Find MindShare Press on the World Wide Web at:
http://www.mindshare.com/

To Nancy, the strongest person I know.

With Love,

Tom

P. S. It's done. I'm back.

At-a-Glance
Table of Contents

Part 1: Introduction, intended as a back-drop to the detailed discussions that follow, consists of the following chapters:

Part 2: IA-32 Mode provides a detailed description of two IA-32 Mode sub-modes—Real Mode and Protected Mode—and consists of the following chapters:

Part 3: IA-32e OS Kernel Environment provides a detailed description of the IA-32e OS kernel environment and consists of the following chapters:

Part 4: Compatibility Mode provides a detailed description of the Compatibility submode of IA-32e Mode and consist of the following chapter:

Part 5: 64-bit Mode provides a detailed description of the 64-bit submode of IA-32e Mode and consists of the following chapters:

Part 6: Mode Switching Detail provides a detailed description of:

Part 7: Other Topics provides detailed descriptions of the following topics:

Contents

Part 1: Introduction

Chapter 1: Basic Terms and Concepts

Chapter 2: Mode/SubMode Introduction

Contents

Chapter 3: A (very) Brief History

Chapter 4: State After Reset

Part 2: IA-32 Mode

Chapter 5: Intro to the IA-32 Ecosystem

Contents

Contents

Chapter 7: 32-bit Machine Language Instruction Format

Contents

Contents

Contents

Contents

Contents

Chapter 10: Introduction to Multitasking

Chapter 11: Multitasking-Related Issues

Contents

Chapter 12: Summary of the Protection Mechanisms

Chapter 13: Protected Mode Memory Addressing

Chapter 14: Code, Calls and Privilege Checks

Contents

Chapter 15: Data and Stack Segments

Chapter 16: IA-32 Address Translation Mechanisms

Contents

Contents

Contents

Chapter 17: Memory Type Configuration

Contents

Contents

Chapter 18: Task Switching

Contents

Chapter 19: Protected Mode Interrupts and Exceptions

Contents

Contents

Contents

Contents

Contents

Chapter 20: Virtual 8086 Mode

Contents

Contents

Chapter 21: The MMX Facilities

Contents

Chapter 22: The SSE Facilities

Contents

Contents

Part 3: IA-32e OS Kernel Environment

Chapter 23: IA-32e OS Environment

Contents

Contents

Chapter 24: IA-32e Address Translation

Part 4: Compatibility Mode

Chapter 25: Compatibility Mode

Contents

Part 5: 64-bit Mode

Chapter 26: 64-bit Register Overview

Chapter 27: 64-bit Operands and Addressing

Contents

Chapter 28: 64-bit Odds and Ends

Contents

Part 6: Mode Switching Detail

Chapter 29: Transitioning to Protected Mode

Contents

Chapter 30: Transitioning to IA-32e Mode

Part 7: Other Topics

Chapter 31: Introduction to Virtualization Technology

Contents

Chapter 32: System Management Mode (SMM)

Contents

Chapter 33: Machine Check Architecture (MCA)

Contents

Contents

Chapter 34: The Local and IO APICs

Contents

Contents

Contents

Contents

Contents

Figures

Figures

Figures

Figures

Figures

Figures

Figures

Figures

Figures

Figures

Tables

Tables

Tables

Tables

Tables

About This Book

Is This the Book for You?

If you're looking for a book designed specifically for those who need to come up to speed on the 32-/64-bit x86 Instruction Set Architecture (ISA) as quickly and painlessly as possible, then consider this book.

On the other hand, the author fully realizes that a certain segment of the technical population rejects and is, indeed, deeply offended by any attempt to present arcane technical material in a learning-friendly manner. Having been exposed to the occasional criticism from such individuals, if you fall into this category I can only forewarn that this book is not for you. Do not waste your money or your time.

A Moving Target

The reader should keep in mind that MindShare books often deal with rapidly evolving technologies. This being the case, it should be recognized that this book is a *snapshot* of the state of the x86 programming environment at the time that the book was completed (November, 2009).

x86 Instruction Set Architecture (ISA)

Throughout this book, the term *ISA (Instruction Set Architecture)* refers to the current execution environment defined by the x86 ISA specification:

- Any reference to the term *IA-32 ISA* refers to the facilities visible to the programmer when the processor is operating in 32-bit mode (referred to by Intel as IA-32 Mode and by AMD as Legacy Mode).
- Any reference to the term *Intel 64 ISA* refers to the facilities visible to the programmer when the processor is operating in 64-bit Mode (referred to by Intel as Intel 64 Mode and by AMD as Long Mode).

Glossary of Terms

A comprehensive glossary may be found on page 1391.

32-/64-bit x86 Instruction Set Architecture Specification

As of this writing (February, 2009), the ISA specification is embodied in the *Intel 64 and IA-32 Architectures Software Developer's Manual* which currently consist of the following five volumes:

- *Basic Architecture*; order number 253665.
- *Instruction Set Reference A-M*; order number 253666.
- *Instruction Set Reference N-Z*; order number 253667.
- *System Programming Guide, Part 1*; order number 253668.
- *System Programming Guide, Part 2*; order number 253669.

Alternatively, the specification is also embodied in the equivalent manuals available from AMD.

While the specification does define the register and instruction sets, interrupt and software exception handling, and standard processor facilities such as memory address generation and translation, the processor modes of operation, multitasking and protection mechanisms, etc., it does *not* specify processor-specific features such as the following:

- Whether or not a processor design includes caches and, if so, the number of, size of, and architecture of the caches.
- Whether or not a processor design includes one or more TLBs (Translation Lookaside Buffers) and, if so, the number of, size of, and architecture of the TLBs.
- The type of interface that connects the processor to the system.
- The number and types of instruction execution units.
- The implementation-specific aspects of a processor's microarchitecture.
- Various other performance enhancement features (branch prediction mechanisms, etc.).

The Specification Is the Final Word

This book represents the author's interpretation of the Intel x86 ISA specification. When in doubt, the Intel specification is the final word.

Book Organization

This book is organized in seven parts:

"Part 1: Introduction", intended as a back-drop to the detailed discussions that follow, consists of the following chapters:

- Chapter 1, entitled "Basic Terms and Concepts," on page 11.
- Chapter 2, entitled "Mode/SubMode Introduction," on page 21.
- Chapter 3, entitled "A (very) Brief History," on page 41.
- Chapter 4, entitled "State After Reset," on page 63.

"Part 2: IA-32 Mode" provides a detailed description of two IA-32 Mode sub-modes—Real Mode and Protected Mode—and consists of the following chapters:

- Chapter 5, entitled "Intro to the IA-32 Ecosystem," on page 79.
- Chapter 6, entitled "Instruction Set Expansion," on page 109.
- Chapter 7, entitled "32-bit Machine Language Instruction Format," on page 155.
- Chapter 8, entitled "Real Mode (8086 Emulation)," on page 227.
- Chapter 9, entitled "Legacy x87 FP Support," on page 339.
- Chapter 10, entitled "Introduction to Multitasking," on page 361.
- Chapter 11, entitled "Multitasking-Related Issues," on page 367.
- Chapter 12, entitled "Summary of the Protection Mechanisms," on page 377.
- Chapter 13, entitled "Protected Mode Memory Addressing," on page 383.
- Chapter 14, entitled "Code, Calls and Privilege Checks," on page 415.
- Chapter 15, entitled "Data and Stack Segments," on page 479.
- Chapter 16, entitled "IA-32 Address Translation Mechanisms," on page 493.
- Chapter 17, entitled "Memory Type Configuration," on page 599.
- Chapter 18, entitled "Task Switching," on page 629.
- Chapter 19, entitled "Protected Mode Interrupts and Exceptions," on page 681.
- Chapter 20, entitled "Virtual 8086 Mode," on page 783.
- Chapter 21, entitled "The MMX Facilities," on page 835.
- Chapter 22, entitled "The SSE Facilities," on page 851.

"Part 3: IA-32e OS Kernel Environment" provides a detailed description of the IA-32e OS kernel environment and consists of the following chapters:

- Chapter 23, entitled "IA-32e OS Environment," on page 913.
- Chapter 24, entitled "IA-32e Address Translation," on page 983.

"Part 4: Compatibility Mode" provides a detailed description of the Compatibility submode of IA-32e Mode and consist of the following chapter:

- Chapter 25, entitled "Compatibility Mode," on page 1009.

"Part 5: 64-bit Mode" provides a detailed description of the 64-bit submode of IA-32e Mode and consists of the following chapters:

- Chapter 26, entitled "64-bit Register Overview," on page 1023.
- Chapter 27, entitled "64-bit Operands and Addressing," on page 1041.
- Chapter 28, entitled "64-bit Odds and Ends," on page 1075.

"Part 6: Mode Switching Detail" provides a detailed description of:

- Switching from Real Mode to Protected Mode. This topic is covered in Chapter 29, entitled "Transitioning to Protected Mode," on page 1113.
- Switching from Protected Mode to IA-32e Mode. This topic is covered in Chapter 30, entitled "Transitioning to IA-32e Mode," on page 1139.

"Part 7: Other Topics" provides detailed descriptions of the following topics:

- Chapter 31, entitled "Introduction to Virtualization Technology," on page 1147.
- Chapter 32, entitled "System Management Mode (SMM)," on page 1167.
- Chapter 33, entitled "Machine Check Architecture (MCA)," on page 1207.
- Chapter 34, entitled "The Local and IO APICs," on page 1239.

Topics Outside the Scope of This Book

The CPUID Instruction

The CPUID instruction is referred to numerous times in this book. For a detailed description of its usage, refer to the Intel publication entitled *Intel 64 and IA-32 Architectures Software Developer's Manual, Volume 2A, Instruction Set Reference A-M.*

Detailed Description of Hyper-Threading

The Intel Hyper-Threading facility is not covered in this book because it is not part of the x86 ISA. For a detailed description of this facility, refer to Chapter 39 in the MindShare book entitled *The Unabridged Pentium 4.*

Detailed Description of Performance Monitoring

The Intel Performance Monitoring facility is not covered in this book because it is not part of the x86 ISA. For a detailed description of this facility, refer to the section entitled *The Performance Monitoring Facility* in Chapter 56 of the Mind-Share book entitled *The Unabridged Pentium 4*.

Documentation Conventions

The conventions used in this book for numeric values are defined below:

- Hexadecimal Notation. All hex numbers are followed by an "h." Examples:
  — 9A4Eh
  — 0100h
- Binary Notation. All binary numbers are followed by a "b." Examples:
  — 0001 0101b
  — 01b
- Decimal Notation. Numbers without any suffix are decimal. When required for clarity, decimal numbers may be followed by a *d*. Examples:
  — 16
  — 255
  — 256d
  — 128d

Other commonly used designations are defined below:

- *lsb* refers to the least-significant bit.
- *LSB* refers to the least-significant byte.
- *msb* refers to the most-significant bit.
- *MSB* refers to the most-significant byte.
- Bit Fields. In many cases, bit fields are documented in the following manner: CR0[15:8] refers to Control Register 0 bits 8 - 15.
- Notations such as *CSDesc[BaseAddress]* are interpreted as the *Base Address field in the Code Segment Descriptor*.

Trademarks

Many of the designations used by manufacturers and sellers to distinguish their products are claimed as trademarks. Those trademark designations known to MindShare Press are listed in Table 1-1 on page 6.

Table 1-1: Trademarks

Trademarked Terms	Trademark Owner
AMD, AMD64, Opteron	AMD
Atom, Core, Core 2, Core 2 Duo, Core 2 Quad, Core 2 Solo, Core i7, Core Solo, Hyper-Threading, Intel, Itanium, MMX, NetBurst, Pentium, QPI or QuickPath Interconnect, SpeedStep, SSE, VTune, Xeon.	Intel
Apple, OS X	Apple Computer
FrameMaker	Adobe Systems
IBM, PC-AT, PS/2	IBM
Linux	Linus Torvalds
PCI, PCI Express, PCIe, PCI-X	PCI SIG
SIMD	?
Unix	The Open Group, SCO, ? (I'll leave this one to the lawyers; your guess is as good as mine)
Word	Microsoft

Visit Our Web Site

Our web site (*www.mindshare.com*) provides detailed descriptions of all of our products including:

- Books and ebooks.
- On-site classes.
- Public, open-enrollment classes.
- Virtual, instructor-led classes.
- Self-paced eLearning modules.
- Technical papers and the MindShare newsletter.

We Want Your Feedback

MindShare values your comments, questions and suggestions. You can contact us via mail, phone, fax or email.

Phone: (719) 487-1417 and in the U.S. (800) 633-1440
Fax: (719) 487-1434
Email: support@mindshare.com

Mailing Address:

MindShare, Inc.
4285 Slash Pine Drive
Colorado Springs, CO 80908

Part 1:
Introduction

Part 1

Part 1, intended as a back-drop to the detailed discussions that follow, consists of the following chapters:

The Next Part

Part 2 provides a detailed description of two submodes of IA-32 Mode: Real Mode and Protected Mode.

1 *Basic Terms and Concepts*

This Chapter

This chapter provides a basic definition of the Instruction Set Architecture (ISA), differentiates between the IA-32 and Intel 64 processor architectures, and defines some other important terms and concepts.

The Next Chapter

The next chapter introduces the execution modes and submodes as well as mode switching basics.

ISA Definition

Wikipedia Definition: The Instruction Set Architecture, or ISA, is defined as that part of the processor architecture related to programming, including the native data types, instructions, registers, addressing modes, memory architecture, interrupt and exception handling, and external IO.

This Book Focuses on the Common Intel/AMD ISA

With the exception of some small deviations and differences in terminology, the Intel and AMD x86 processors share a common ISA. This book focuses on their shared attributes and does not cover those areas where the two companies have chosen widely divergent, non-x86 ISA-compliant, solutions.

For Simplicity, Intel Terminology Is Used Throughout

Rather than confusing matters by using both Intel and AMD terminology throughout the book, the author has chosen to use only Intel terminology.

Some Terms in This Chapter May Be New To the Reader

Someone new to the x86 software environment will almost certainly encounter some unfamiliar terms in this chapter. Don't let it disturb you. Every term and concept *will* be described in detail at the appropriate place in the book. The important things to take away from this chapter are the broader concepts.

Two x86 ISA Architectures

All Intel x86-family processors introduced since the advent of the 386 can be divided into two categories (see Table 1-1 on page 13):

- Those that cannot execute 64-bit code—defined by Intel as *IA-32 Architecture* processors,
- and those that can—defined by Intel as *Intel 64 Architecture* processors.

This distinction is an important one but is not always referred to correctly—even in the vendor's own documentation. As an example, in section 3.2.1 of the *Intel 64 and IA-32 Architectures Software Developer's Manual Volume 1: Basic Architecture* manual, it states:

"A task or program running in 64-bit mode on an IA-32 processor can address linear address space of up to 2^{64} bytes (subject to the canonical addressing requirement described in Section 3.3.7.1) and physical address space of up to 2^{40} bytes."

There is no such thing as 64-bit Mode on an IA-32 processor. Consistent use of terms is critical to a clear understanding of any subject. For someone learning the fundamentals of the x86 programming environment, misleading statements such as this can lead to monumental confusion.

Table 1-1: x86 Software Architectures

Processor Family	Description
x86 Software Architectures All Intel x86-family processors introduced since the advent of the 386 can be divided into two categories:	
IA-32 Processor	Implements only the Intel IA-32 Architecture which supports the execution of 16- and 32-bit x86 code.
Intel 64 Processor	Implements the Intel 64 Architecture, a superset of the IA-32 Architecture: • When operating in IA-32 Mode, the processor supports the execution of 16- and 32-bit x86 code. • When operating in IA-32e Mode, the processor supports the execution of 16-, 32- and 64-bit x86 code.

Processors, Cores and Logical Processors

For many, many years, life was simple: a physical processor package contained a single *core*: i.e, the engine that fetched machine language instructions (i.e., a program) from memory, decoded them, dispatched them to the appropriate execution units and then committed their results to the core's register set. This required:

- A single register set.
- A single set of execution units.
- A set of facilities to handle things like:
  — Virtual-to-physical memory address translation.
  — Interrupts and exceptions.
  — Protection.
  — etc.

The advent of multi-core processors and Hyper-Threading (more in a moment) has inevitably led to a confusion of terminology. As an example, consider the case where a dual core processor contains two cores each of which represents a stand-alone fetch, decode, dispatch, execution engine. Each implements its own register set, instruction fetcher, decoders, dispatcher, and execution units. So, in this scenario, the term *processor* really refers to a package containing two cores, each of which represents a separate processing engine. In all likelihood, though, the two cores may share some resources (typically, one or more caches).

Refer to Figure 1-1 on page 15. To further muddy the waters, a core may implement Hyper-Threading capability, in which case, from a programmer's perspective, a single core would implement two or more independent execution engines (referred to as logical processors):

- Each of which implements its own register set and dedicated resources. This includes a dedicated Local APIC (see "APIC" on page 19) to handle interrupt and exception events for its associated logical processor.
- All of which, invisible to software, may share some resources.

As if that's not confusing enough, if the physical processor's Hyper-Threading capability is disabled, then the second logical processor in each core (referred to as the *secondary logical processor;* the first is referred to as the *primary logical processor*) is disabled and each core functions as a single logical processor.

To sum it up, a physical processor contains one or more cores and, if it implements Hyper-Threading *and* it has been enabled, each core appears to software as two or more separate processors (i.e., logical processors). During a given period of time, all of the logical processors could be executing separate program threads.

Fundamental Processing Engine: Logical Processor

Rather than sprinkling hundreds of references to processors, cores and logical processors throughout the remainder of the book, the fundamental processing engine will heretofore be referred to as a *logical processor* (unless, of course, I am specifically discussing the physical processor package or a core, rather than a logical processor).

Figure 1-1: Processor, Core, Logical Processor

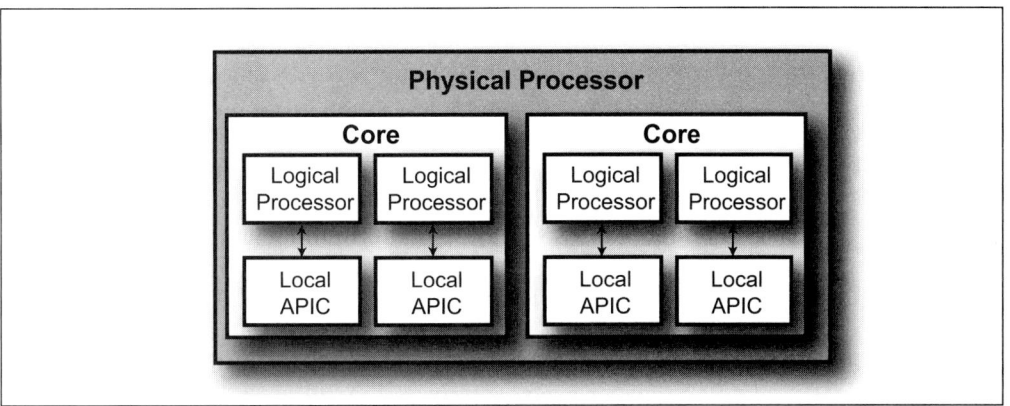

IA Instructions vs. Micro-ops

RISC Instructions Sets Are Simple

RISC (Reduced Instruction Set Computer) ISAs define an instruction set comprised of simple instructions each of which is the same length. As an example, the PowerPC ISA defines an environment wherein each instruction is 32-bits in length and each must reside in memory starting at an address divisible by four. This has the following advantages:

- Simplifies the logical processor's instruction fetch logic.
- Simplifies the logic necessary to parse the incoming instruction stream.
- Simplifies the design of the instruction decoders.
- Simplifies the logic associated with the instruction dispatch logic.
- Standardizes the width of the internal buses that interconnect functional units within the logical processor.

x86 Instruction Set Is Complex

The x86 ISA, on the other hand—a CISC (Complex Instruction Set Computer) architecture—defines a complex, variable-length instruction set. Depending on the type of instruction, the number of operands it specifies, and the operand types (memory- or register-based), a single instruction may be anywhere between one and fifteen bytes in length. This:

- Complicates the logical processor's instruction fetch logic.
- Greatly complicates the logic necessary to parse the incoming instruction stream.
- Complicates the design of the instruction decoders.
- Complicates the logic associated with the instruction dispatch logic.
- Dictates a multitude of varying widths regarding the internal buses that interconnect functional units within the logical processor.

But You Can't Leave It Behind

For all the problems associated with the x86 ISA, Intel would have been mad to design a new generation of processors using a new ISA. If they had done so, every x86 OS, application and driver ever written would have had to be rewritten or recompiled in order to run on a new, completely different type of computer. Very few customers would have bitten the bullet and Intel would now be a distant memory.

Complexity vs. Speed Dictated a Break With the Past

Nonetheless, in order to continue its relentless march towards ever faster processor speeds, Intel had to take action. The break with the past occurred with the advent of the Pentium Pro in 1995, a processor that employed an on-die instruction set translator. The variable-length x86 instructions were fetched from memory into the processor's cache. In strict program order, the complex x86 instructions comprising the program stream were then fed to an array of decoders that translated each x86 instruction into a set of one or more simple, fixed-length instructions (referred to as *micro-ops*) which, when executed, would accomplish the same function. In other words, the Pentium Pro *and all subsequent Intel processors* are, in fact, RISC machines.

Why Not Publish a Micro-Op ISA?

That raises an interesting question: why didn't Intel publish an ISA specification for the new instruction set and make compilers available to produce machine language object code that could be processed directly by the new breed of processors? It would be a simple matter to inform a processor that the code it is fetching from memory is comprised of x86 or micro-op object code and, in the case of the latter, the code translator logic (the instruction decoders) would then be bypassed.

The answer is simple. If Intel had, in fact, done this, they would then be obligated to support yet another instruction set going forward into the future. Furthermore, having made this new instruction set visible to the outside world, they would not have the freedom to switch to another, perhaps more efficient form of internal instruction set in future products.

Some Important Definitions

A basic understanding of the following terms will prove useful in the pages to come.

Virtual vs. Physical Memory

Table 1-2 on page 17 provides a basic definition of physical, virtual and linear memory addresses.

Table 1-2: Physical, Virtual and Linear Memory Address Space

Memory Address Terminology	Description
Physical memory address	The actual address used to address a memory location.
Virtual memory address	The information (both code and data) associated with the currently-running task frequently occupies widely-fragmented areas of physical memory. In order to simplify the task's view of memory, the OS kernel's memory manager assigns it a contiguous range of memory addresses to use when accessing its code and data. This is referred to as a virtual memory address range. When a logical processor is operating in 32-bit Protected Mode, Compatibility Mode or 64-bit Mode, the virtual memory addresses generated by the instruction fetcher or when a load or store must be performed are first submitted to the logical processor's address translation services (commonly referred to as the Paging unit) which translates the virtual address into the actual physical address before the memory read or write is performed.

Table 1-2: Physical, Virtual and Linear Memory Address Space (Continued)

Memory Address Terminology	Description
linear memory address	Because of the contiguous (or linear) nature of the virtual address space assigned to a task by the OS kernel, Intel refers to the virtual address as a linear address. *Although Intel tends to use the term **linear address** almost exclusively in its documentation, the author has chosen to standardize on the term **virtual address** because of its universal usage in other processor architectures.*

Other Important Terms

Table 1-3 on page 18 provides basic descriptions of a few other useful terms.

Table 1-3: Some Other Useful Terms

Term	Description
Privilege Levels	When operating in IA-32 Protected Mode, or the Compatibility or 64-bit SubModes of IA-32e Mode, x86 processors support the concept of the privilege level. At any given moment in time, the logical processor is fetching code from a region of memory whose characteristics are defined by a special descriptor (called a code segment descriptor). The logical processor assigns the currently-running program's privilege level (referred to as the Current Privilege Level, or CPL) from the 2-bit DPL (Descriptor Privilege Level) field of the code segment descriptor. There are four privilege levels: • **0** is the highest privilege level. Typically, only the OS kernel runs at privilege level 0 permitting it to perform any operation. • **1**, the next privilege level, is typically assigned to high-priority device drivers and OS services. It could also be assigned to debuggers to protect them from interference by less privileged device drivers and application programs. • **2** is typically assigned to less privileged device drivers. • **3** is the least privileged and is typically assigned to application programs. This prevents them from performing actions that would be injurious to the OS, debuggers, device drivers, or each other.

Table 1-3: Some Other Useful Terms (Continued)

Term	Description
APIC	**Advanced Programmable Interrupt Controller**. There are two versions of the APIC: • **IO APIC**. One or more IO APICs (the number is platform design-specific) are located external to the processors (typically, integrated into the chipset). The IO APIC: – Receives interrupt requests from device adapters (e.g., network adapters, disk controllers, etc.) and from the chipset (e.g., SMIs—System Management Interrupts, NMIs—Non-Maskable Interrupts, etc.). – Formulates interrupt message packets. – Delivers interrupt message packets to one or more Local APICs associated with the targeted logical processors that have been assigned to handle the respective interrupts. • **Local APIC**. Each core (or logical processor if Hyper-Threading is implemented and enabled) incorporates a dedicated Local APIC that receives interrupt messages from: – IO APIC(s). – The Local APICs associated with other cores or logical processors. – From internal sources (e.g., thermal interrupts, Local APIC Timer interrupts, etc.). Upon receipt of one or more types of interrupts, the Local APIC prioritizes them and delivers them to its associated core or logical processor.

Table 1-3: Some Other Useful Terms (Continued)

Term	Description
Intel Virtualization Technology (VT)	Much like a DOS task, an OS tends to be ego-centric. It assumes that it knows the overall system status and can do anything it wants: • What if you wanted to execute two or more OSs simultaneously? • The VMM (Virtual Machine Monitor; also referred to as the hypervisor) is the software entity that fulfills the role of the scheduler for multiple OSs. • When VT is enabled, the VMM creates a special data structure in memory (the VMCS—Virtual Machine Control Structure) for each OS that is to be run. In addition to other fields, the VMCS contains a series of fields that define the operations that are *sensitive* (i.e., that will trigger a suspension of the guest OS and a switch back to the hypervisor). • When a guest OS is running and the logical processor's VT hardware detects a guest OS attempt to execute a *sensitive* operation, the logical processor's VT hardware automatically saves the state of the logical processor (i.e., its register set contents) in the OS's VMCS and then transfers control back to the VMM.

2 *Mode/SubMode Introduction*

The Previous Chapter

The previous chapter provided a basic definition of the Instruction Set Architecture (ISA), differentiated between the IA-32 and Intel 64 processor architectures, and defined some other important terms and concepts.

This Chapter

This chapter introduces the execution modes and submodes and mode switching basics.

The Next Chapter

The next chapter introduces the evolution of the x86 ISA, as well as the basic operational characteristics of 8086 Real Mode, 286 Protected Mode, and 386 Protected Mode. It also introduces the Intel microarchitecture families including a product introduction timeline.

Basic Execution Modes

Figure 2-1 on page 22 illustrates the execution modes supported on processors based on the IA-32 architecture versus those based on the Intel 64 architecture. Table 2-1 on page 23 provides an elementary description of the two basic execution modes—IA-32 Mode and IA-32e Mode.

Figure 2-1: Execution Mode Diagram

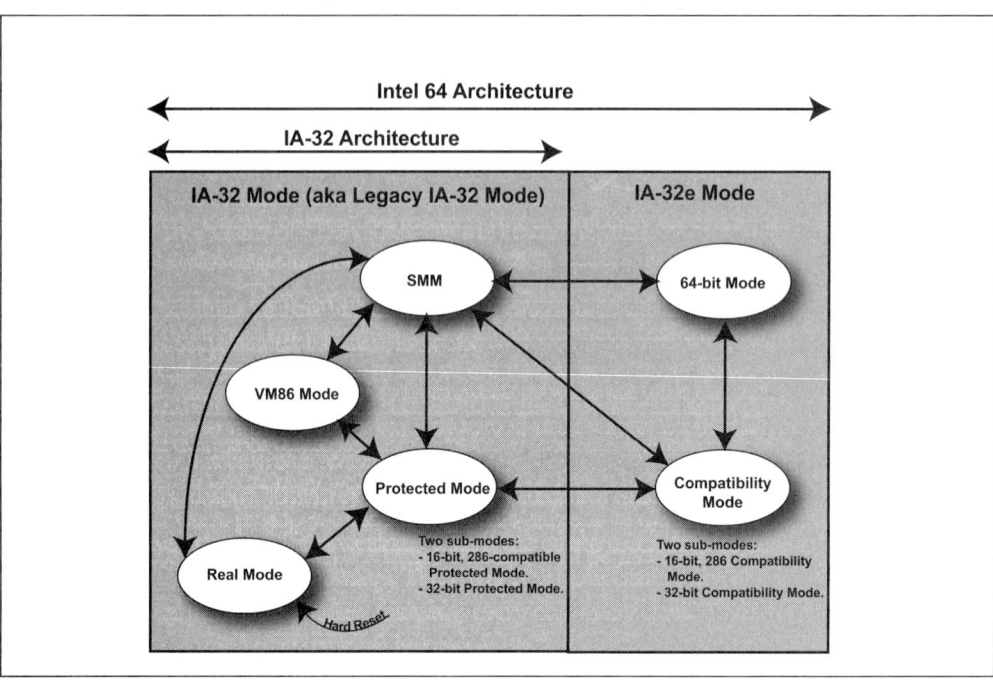

Table 2-1: Basic Execution Modes

Mode	Description
IA-32 Mode (also referred to as Legacy IA-32 Mode)	• IA-32 Architecture processors are always in IA-32 Mode which consists of the following SubModes: – Real Mode. – System Management Mode (SMM). – Protected Mode. – VM86 Mode. • At a given moment in time, an Intel 64 Architecture processor is operating in either: – IA-32 Mode, or – IA-32e (IA-32 Extended) Mode. "IA-32 SubModes" on page 25 describes the IA-32 execution Sub-Modes. **Problems associated with IA-32 Mode**: Some of the problems associated with IA-32 Mode are: • The instruction set syntax uses a 3-bit field to specify a source or destination register. As a result, there are only eight addressable General Purpose Registers (GPRs), Control registers, Debug registers, or XMM registers. • The maximum width of each GPR is 32-bits limiting the amount of data each can hold. • Virtual memory address space available for each application is limited to 4GB by the 32-bit width of the linear (i.e., virtual) address. • The virtual-to-physical memory address translation mechanism limits the maximum addressable physical memory address space to 64GB. • The 32-bit Extended Instruction Pointer (EIP) register limits each application's code space to 4GB. • The x86 family's segmented memory model is complex and difficult to work with. Virtually all of today's OSs utilize a Flat Memory Model that effectively disables the segmented memory model. • The hardware-assisted task switching mechanism defined by the IA-32 ISA is slow and cumbersome. • IA-32 Mode permits virus code to be loaded into a stack or data segment from which it can then be executed. • Lacks the ability to address code-local data by specifying an address relative to the current EIP value.

Table 2-1: Basic Execution Modes (Continued)

Mode	Description
IA-32e Mode	IA-32 Extended Mode is comprised of two submodes: – 64-bit Mode. – Compatibility Mode. • Must be enabled by a 64-bit capable OS. • Provides an environment for the execution of 64-bit applications, as well as existing 32- and 16-bit Protected Mode applications. • Doesn't support the execution of VM86 Mode applications (i.e., MS-DOS applications). • Provides a fast transition between a 32-bit environment (Compatibility Mode) and a 64-bit environment (64-bit Mode). • Implements the Intel 64 extensions (formerly known as x86-64 or EM64T). "IA-32e SubModes" on page 28 describes the IA-32e execution Sub-Modes. **Some benefits associated with IA-32e Mode**: The following are some of the benefits realized when the logical processor is executing in IA-32e Mode: • Backward compatible with the IA-32 code environment. Intel's earlier attempt at a 64-bit architecture (Itanium) is not. • Expands the size of the virtual memory address space from 2^{32} (4GB) to 2^{64} (16EB; EB = exabytes). • Expands the size of the physical memory address space to 2^{52} (4PB; PB = petabytes). • The larger number of data registers permits a greater number of data variables to be accessed/manipulated rapidly: – Yields faster data set accessibility. – Widening and increasing the number of registers diminishes the number of accesses to memory and translates into improved performance. – The degree of improvement in kernel code efficiency depends on a kernel rewrite to manage memory better and to utilize 64-bit (rather than 32-bit) data variables. – The degree of improvement in application code efficiency depends on utilization of 64-bit data variables and, for large scale applications, capitalizing on the enlarged virtual address space.

IA-32 SubModes

Table 2-2 on page 25 provides a basic introduction to the IA-32 execution Sub-Modes.

Table 2-2: IA-32 SubModes

IA-32 SubMode	Description

Real Mode	• After a hard reset, a logical processor always begins operation in Real Mode.
	• In Real Mode, the logical processor is emulating the behavior of the Intel 8088/8086 processors.
	• Memory address space is divided into 64KB segments (i.e., regions of memory):
	  – **CS**: the Code Segment contains the code to be executed.
	  – **SS**: the Stack Segment defines the area of RAM memory where register-based information can be temporarily saved and subsequently restored from.
	  – **DS**: the Data Segment defines the default area of memory containing data the currently-executing program operates upon.
	  – **ES, FS, and GS**: may be used to define additional areas of memory containing data the currently-executing program operates upon.
	• No mechanism exists to protect information within a specific segment of memory from unauthorized accesses.
	• The currently-executing program can access any IO port and thereby change the state of an IO device without the knowledge of the OS or any other program.
	• There is no concept of privilege level assignment to a program. The currently-executing program has unrestricted access to the entire instruction and register sets as well as to any area of memory.
	• In general, software is restricted to the first 1MB of memory. When in Real Mode, the logical processor is emulating the behavior of the Intel 8088/8086 processors which were restricted to a 1MB memory space due to an external address bus width of 20-bits.

Table 2-2: IA-32 SubModes (Continued)

IA-32 SubMode	Description
Protected Mode	Protected Mode implements an environment wherein the OS task scheduler permits the logical processor to execute a specific task for a given period of time (i.e., a timeslice; e.g. 10ms) while all other tasks are temporarily suspended. Protected Mode provides solutions to the problems commonly associated with such a multitasking environment: • Comprehensive memory protection. • Allows the OS kernel to police access to IO ports. • Prevents unauthorized access to OS services and resources. • Intercepts unauthorized attempts to disable/enable recognition of external interrupts. • Intercepts unauthorized attempts to access the BIOS or the MS-DOS OS services by way of software interrupt instructions. In order to handle such multitasking-related issues, several new features were introduced to the x86 architecture: • The ability of the OS scheduler to assign a privilege level to a program in order to restrict its ability to use certain logical processor facilities (e.g., certain instructions, registers, areas of memory, etc.). • Support for both 16-bit, 286 code as well as 32-bit code. • The concept of the segment descriptor data structure was added, permitting the OS kernel's memory manager to specify the following characteristics of each memory segment: – 32-bit base address. – 32-bit length. – The minimum privilege level a program must have in order to access it. – Its read/write access rights. • A hardware-based task switching mechanism. • Virtual-to-physical memory address translation services. • Interrupt descriptors.

Table 2-2: IA-32 SubModes (Continued)

IA-32 SubMode	Description

VM86 Mode	**Virtual 8086 Mode**. Due to their potentially disruptive behavior in a multitasking OS environment (i.e., a Protected Mode environment), the OS task scheduler switches the logical processor into VM86 Mode prior to initiating or resuming the execution of a Real Mode task. When operating in VM86 Mode, the logical processor activates hardware which monitors the behavior of the running task on an instruction-by-instruction basis and, when it attempts to execute one of those instructions defined as *sensitive*:
	• It suspends execution of the offending task,
	• and calls a special OS monitor program, referred to as a Virtual Machine Monitor (VMM).
	• The VMM examines the offending instruction and takes one of the following actions:
	  – permits the execution of the instruction.
	  – emulates the instruction in software in a manner that will not disrupt the proper operation of the overall software environment.
	  – forbids the operation and shuts down the offending task.
	While in VM86 Mode, the logical processor operates as if it is running in Real Mode (but with the intercept logic described above activated).

System Management Mode (SMM)	SMM is used to handle system design-specific events (e.g., platform-specific power management or thermal events) and is entered when a logical processor receives a System Management Interrupt (SMI) from the chipset. In response, the logical processor: • Automatically saves the state of the machine (i.e., the contents of the logical processor's entire register set), • Enters SMM, • Executes the SM handler which handles the event, • Restores the register set to its original state, • And then resumes execution of the interrupted program.

IA-32e SubModes

Table 2-3 on page 28 provides a basic introduction to the IA-32e execution Sub-Modes.

Table 2-3: IA-32e SubModes

IA-32e SubMode	Description

64-bit Mode	Assume that a logical processor is:
	• Currently operating in IA-32e Mode and
	• is currently fetching/executing code from a legacy 16- or 32-bit code segment and is therefore operating in the Compatibility SubMode of IA-32e Mode.
	• An instruction now causes a jump to a location in a different code segment, one wherein the L bit (Long Mode bit; AMD's name for IA-32e Mode) is set to one in its code segment descriptor.
	• As a result, the logical processor automatically switches from Compatibility Mode to 64-bit Mode.
	The logical processor remains in 64-bit Mode until either:
	• An SMI (System Management Interrupt) causes a temporary transition into SM Mode to handle a platform-specific event.
	• An instruction causes a jump to a location in a different code segment, one wherein the L bit is cleared to zero in its code segment descriptor. In this case, the logical processor automatically switches from 64-bit Mode to Compatibility Mode.
	While operating in 64-bit Mode, the following are true:
	• The logical processor supports substantially larger virtual and physical memory address spaces:
	  – Theoretically, up to a 64-bit virtual memory address space. Current Intel processors support 48-bits of virtual memory address space.
	  – Theoretically, up to a 52-bit physical memory address space. Current Intel processors implement a 40-bit physical memory address space, while some AMD processors support a 41- or 48-bit physical memory address space.
	• Allows software to use a greater number of wider registers that become available in 64-bit Mode:
	  – General Purpose Registers (GPRs) are expanded from 32- to 64-bits.
	  – Control and Debug registers are expanded from 32- to 64-bits.
	  – Eight additional 64-bit GPR registers (R8 - R15).
	  – Eight additional 64-bit Control registers (CR8 - CR15).
	  – Eight additional 64-bit Debug registers (DR8 - DR15).
	  – Eight additional 128-bit SIMD registers (XMM8 – XMM15).
	• Disables legacy mechanisms unused by modern OSs (e.g., segmentation and hardware-based task switch assist logic).
	• Flat Memory Model is hardware-enforced.

Table 2-3: IA-32e SubModes (Continued)

IA-32e SubMode	Description
Compatibil-ity Mode	**SubModes**. Compatibility Mode consists of two SubModes: • *16-bit Compatibility SubMode*. The logical processor operates in 16-bit Compatibility Mode whenever it is executing code from a legacy, 286-compatible 16-bit code segment. • *32-bit Compatibility SubMode*. The logical processor operates in 32-bit Compatibility Mode whenever it is executing code from a 32-bit code segment. **Entry**. The logical processor enters the Compatibility SubMode of IA-32e Mode under two circumstances: • *Initial Entry*. On the initial transition from Protected Mode to IA-32e Mode. • *Task Switch*. The logical processor is executing code from a 64-bit code segment and an instruction causes a jump to a location in a different code segment wherein the L bit is cleared to zero in its code segment descriptor. **Not Quite Protected Mode**. While in Compatibility Mode, the logical processor operates as if it is in Protected Mode with the following exceptions: • It does not support the execution of VM86 tasks. • While it is restricted to a 32-bit virtual memory address space, it is *not* restricted to a 32-bit physical memory address space. • Interrupt and exception events *always* cause the logical processor to transition into 64-bit Mode (it is a rule that handlers must reside in 64-bit code segments). Once the interrupt handler has completed execution, logical processor control is returned to the interrupted application running in Compatibility Mode. • Control registers are 64-bits wide. • TSS descriptors in the GDT are 16- rather than 8-bytes in size. • LDT descriptors in the GDT are 16- rather than 8-bytes in size. • Call Gate descriptors in the GDT and LDT are 16- rather than 8-bytes in size.

Mode Switching Basics

Initial Switch from IA-32 to IA-32e Mode

IA-32e Mode can only be entered by transitioning from legacy Protected Mode to Compatibility Mode. This transition is accomplished as follows (refer to Figure 2-2 on page 31 and to Table 2-4 on page 32 for a brief description of some of the terms used):

1a. If the virtual-to-physical address translation mechanism (i.e., Paging) has been enabled in Protected Mode, it must be disabled in preparation for the switch into IA-32e Mode.

1b. The special data structures utilized by an IA-32e OS kernel differ from those used in Protected Mode. Software creates the revised structures in memory. This includes the revised address translation tables that will be used in IA-32e Mode.

2a. CR4[PAE] is set to one (because IA-32e Mode uses a revised form of the PAE—Physical Address Extension—address translation mechanism).

2b. The LME (Long Mode Enable) bit in the EFER register is set to one. AMD refers to IA-32e Mode as Long Mode and Intel uses the same name for the bit). It should be noted, however, that even though LME = 1, IA-32e Mode is not yet active.

2c. Point CR3 to the top-level IA-32e Mode address translation table (i.e., the PML4 directory). Since CR3 is only 32-bits wide in Protected Mode, the initial PML4 directory's physical base address must be in the lower 4GB.

3. Setting CR0[PG] to one reenables Paging and simultaneously enables IA-32e Mode. The logical processor enters the Compatibility SubMode of IA-32e Mode and sets the EFER[LMA] (Long Mode Active) bit to one indicating that IA-32e Mode is now active.

4. Software now loads the logical processor's kernel data structure registers with the pointers to the IA-32e Mode data structures that were created in step 1b:
   — GDTR register is loaded with the base address and length of the Global Descriptor Table.
   — LDTR register is loaded with the base address and length of the Local Descriptor Table.
   — IDTR register is loaded with the base address and length of the Interrupt Descriptor Table.
   — TR (Task Register) is loaded with the base address and length of the OS kernel's TSS (Task State Segment data structure).

Figure 2-2: Switching to IA-32e Mode

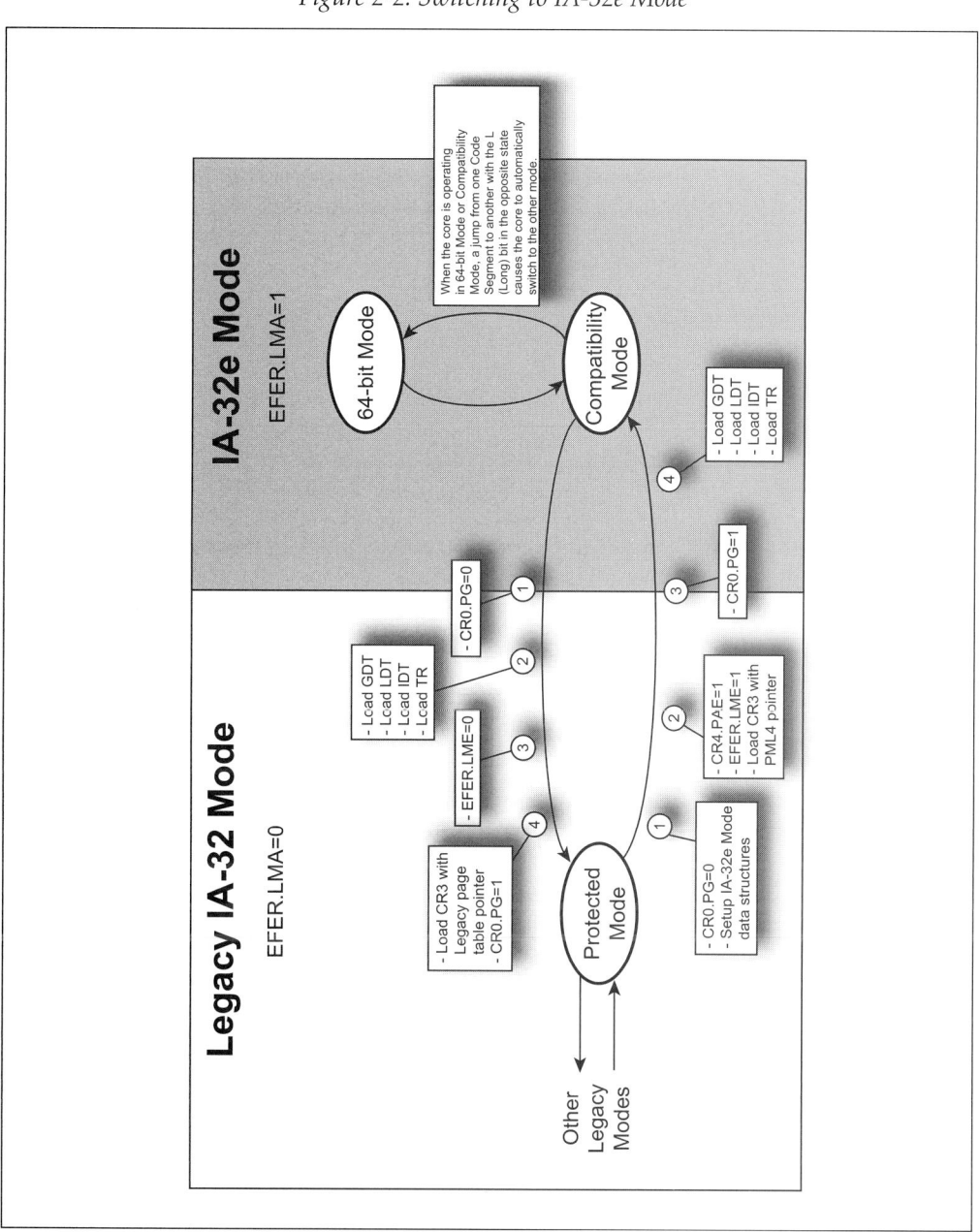

Table 2-4: Terminology

Term	Brief Description
Address Translation	When enabled, the logical processor's Paging logic translates the virtual memory address specified by the instruction fetch logic or by a load or a store instruction into the actual physical address of the location.
Code Segment	The code segment is the area of memory that contains the currently-executing program.
Code Segment Descriptor	In Protected Mode, Compatibility Mode, and 64-bit Mode, the 16-bit value loaded into the Code Segment (CS) register selects an 8-byte descriptor in memory that is read into the register. This descriptor describes the characteristics of the currently-active code segment.
CR0[PG]	Control Register 0, Paging Enable bit. When set to one, it enables the logical processor's virtual-to-physical address translation mechanism.
CR3	In order to translate the virtual address into a physical address, the logical processor must access a set of address translation tables created in memory by the OS kernel. Control Register 3 is programmed with the physical base address of the top-level table (i.e., the PML4 Table).
CR4[PAE]	Control Register 4, Physical Address Extension bit. When set to one, it enables the logical processor's second generation address translation mechanism (but it is not actually activated until CR0[PG] is subsequently set to one).
EFER[LMA]	Once CR0[PG] is set to one, the logical processor automatically sets the Long Mode Active bit indicating that it is now in IA-32e Mode.
EFER[LME]	Extended Features Enable Register, Long Mode Enable bit. The name can be misleading as it refers to AMD's rather than Intel's name for IA-32e Mode.

Table 2-4: Terminology (Continued)

Term	Brief Description
PML4 Table	Page Map Level 4 address translation table. When the logical processor is in IA-32e Mode it is using the 3rd generation address translation mechanism to translate virtual memory addresses into physical memory addresses. When using this mechanism, the PML4 Table is the top-level address translation table.
TSS	Task State Segment. A data structure created by the OS kernel and usually associated with a specific task.
Virtual Address	When address translation is enabled (CR0[PG] = 1), the logical processor treats memory addresses generated by the currently-running program as virtual rather than physical addresses. The virtual address is translated into the actual physical memory address before the location is accessed. Also referred to as the linear address.

IA-32e SubMode Selection

When the logical processor is in Protected Mode or IA-32e Mode, the contents of its Code Segment (CS) register (referred to as a CS descriptor) defines the characteristics of the currently-running program:

- Code segment's base address in memory.
- Its size.
- Its privilege level.
- Its type:
  — 16-bit, 286-style code segment. See Figure 2-3 on page 35.
  — 32-bit, 386-style code segment. See Figure 2-4 on page 36.
  — 64-bit code segment. See Figure 2-5 on page 37.
- Other code segment characteristics:
  — Contains only code or both code and read-only data.
  — Whether it's a conforming or non-conforming code segment (more on this later).

When the logical processor is in IA-32e Mode, the code segment type defines which submode the logical processor is in. The type is determined by two bits (L and D) in the CS register:

- **L = 0, D = 0**: The logical processor is executing code from a 16-bit, 286-style code segment and is therefore in the **16-bit Compatibility SubMode** of IA-32e Mode. See Figure 2-3 on page 35.
- **L = 0, D = 1**:The logical processor is executing code from a 32-bit, 386-style code segment and is therefore in the **32-bit Compatibility SubMode** of IA-32e Mode. See Figure 2-4 on page 36.
- **L = 1, D = 0**: The logical processor is executing code from a 64-bit code segment and is therefore in the **64-bit SubMode** of IA-32e Mode. See Figure 2-5 on page 37.
- **L = 1, D = 1**: Reserved.

Immediately after the switch into IA-32e Mode, the logical processor is in Compatibility Mode. It should be noted, however, that it is still fetching code from the same code segment (a legacy Protected Mode code segment). It is therefore operating in either the 16- or 32-bit Compatibility SubMode of IA-32e Mode.

A more detailed description may be found in "Transitioning to IA-32e Mode" on page 1139.

Figure 2-3: 16-bit, 286-style CS Descriptor Format

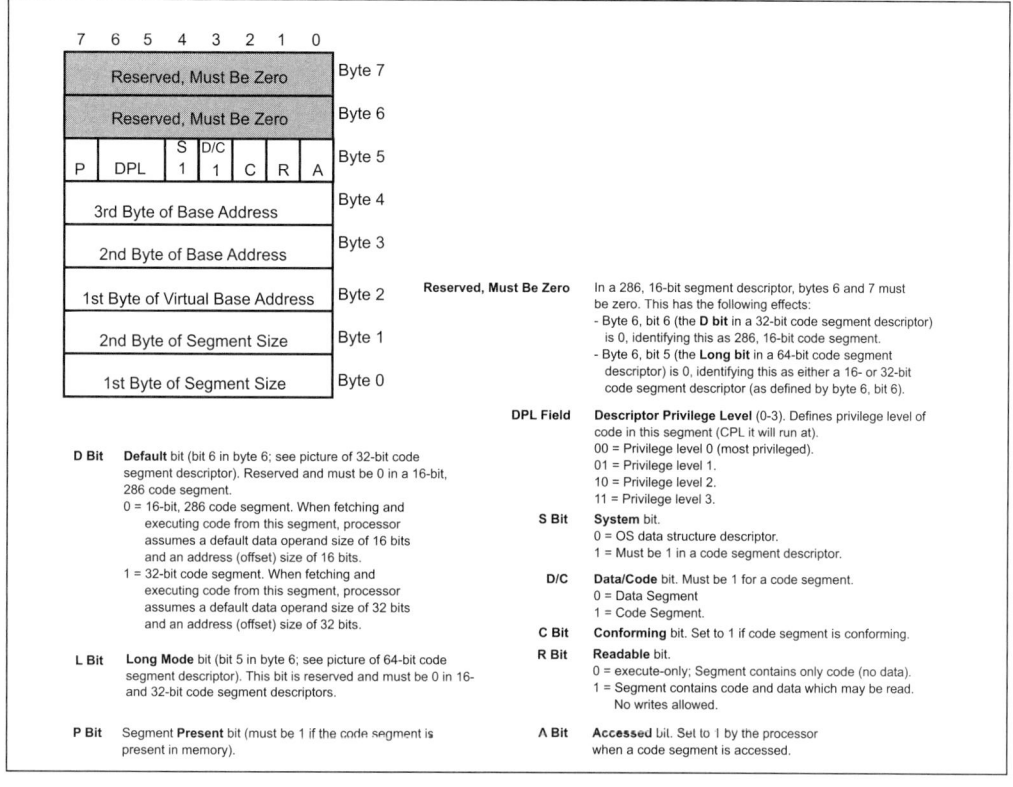

Reserved, Must Be Zero In a 286, 16-bit segment descriptor, bytes 6 and 7 must be zero. This has the following effects:
- Byte 6, bit 6 (the **D bit** in a 32-bit code segment descriptor) is 0, identifying this as 286, 16-bit code segment.
- Byte 6, bit 5 (the **Long bit** in a 64-bit code segment descriptor) is 0, identifying this as either a 16- or 32-bit code segment descriptor (as defined by byte 6, bit 6).

D Bit **Default** bit (bit 6 in byte 6; see picture of 32-bit code segment descriptor). Reserved and must be 0 in a 16-bit, 286 code segment.
0 = 16-bit, 286 code segment. When fetching and executing code from this segment, processor assumes a default data operand size of 16 bits and an address (offset) size of 16 bits.
1 = 32-bit code segment. When fetching and executing code from this segment, processor assumes a default data operand size of 32 bits and an address (offset) size of 32 bits.

L Bit **Long Mode** bit (bit 5 in byte 6; see picture of 64-bit code segment descriptor). This bit is reserved and must be 0 in 16- and 32-bit code segment descriptors.

P Bit Segment **Present** bit (must be 1 if the code segment is present in memory).

DPL Field **Descriptor Privilege Level** (0-3). Defines privilege level of code in this segment (CPL it will run at).
00 = Privilege level 0 (most privileged).
01 = Privilege level 1.
10 = Privilege level 2.
11 = Privilege level 3.

S Bit **System** bit.
0 = OS data structure descriptor.
1 = Must be 1 in a code segment descriptor.

D/C **Data/Code** bit. Must be 1 for a code segment.
0 = Data Segment
1 = Code Segment.

C Bit **Conforming** bit. Set to 1 if code segment is conforming.

R Bit **Readable** bit.
0 = execute-only; Segment contains only code (no data).
1 = Segment contains code and data which may be read. No writes allowed.

A Bit **Accessed** bit. Set to 1 by the processor when a code segment is accessed.

Figure 2-4: 32-bit Code Segment Descriptor Format

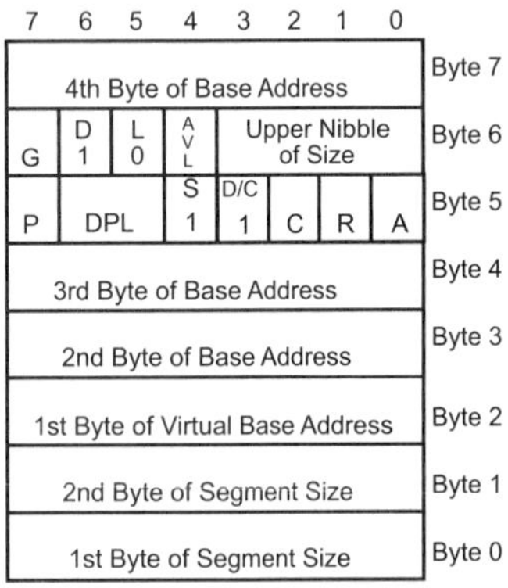

```
  7   6   5   4   3   2   1   0
┌───────────────────────────────┐
│    4th Byte of Base Address    │ Byte 7
├───┬───┬───┬───┬───────────────┤
│   │ D │ L │ A │  Upper Nibble │ Byte 6
│ G │ 1 │ 0 │ V │    of Size    │
│   │   │   │ L │               │
├───┼───┴───┼─S─┼D/C┬───┬───┬───┤
│ P │  DPL  │ 1 │ 1 │ C │ R │ A │ Byte 5
├───┴───────┴───┴───┴───┴───┴───┤
│    3rd Byte of Base Address    │ Byte 4
├───────────────────────────────┤
│    2nd Byte of Base Address    │ Byte 3
├───────────────────────────────┤
│ 1st Byte of Virtual Base Address│ Byte 2
├───────────────────────────────┤
│    2nd Byte of Segment Size    │ Byte 1
├───────────────────────────────┤
│    1st Byte of Segment Size    │ Byte 0
└───────────────────────────────┘
```

G Bit   **Granularity** bit defines interpretation of Size field.
0 = Segment size in bytes.
1 = Segment size in 4KB pages.

D Bit   **Default** bit:
0 = 16-bit, 286 code segment. When fetching and executing code from this segment, processor assumes a default data operand size of 16 bits and an address (offset) size of 16 bits.
1 = 32-bit code segment. When fetching and executing code from this segment, processor assumes a default data operand size of 32 bits and an address (offset) size of 32 bits.

L Bit   **Long Mode** bit. This bit is reserved and must be 0 in 16- and 32-bit code segment descriptors.

AVL Bit   Available for use by OS kernel.

P Bit   Segment **Present** bit (must be 1 if the code segment is present in memory).

DPL Field   **Descriptor Privilege Level** (0-3). Defines privilege level of code in this segment (CPL it will run at).
00 = Privilege level 0 (most privileged).
01 = Privilege level 1.
10 = Privilege level 2.
11 = Privilege level 3.

S Bit   **System** bit.
0 = OS data structure descriptor.
1 = Must be 1 in a code segment descriptor.

D/C   **Data/Code** bit. Must be 1 for a code segment.
0 = Data Segment
1 = Code Segment.

C Bit   **Conforming** bit. Set to 1 if code segment is conforming.

R Bit   **Readable** bit.
0 = execute-only; Segment contains only code (no data).
1 = Segment contains code and data which may be read. No writes allowed.

A Bit   **Accessed** bit. Set to 1 by the processor when a code segment is accessed.

Figure 2-5: 64-bit Code Segment Descriptor

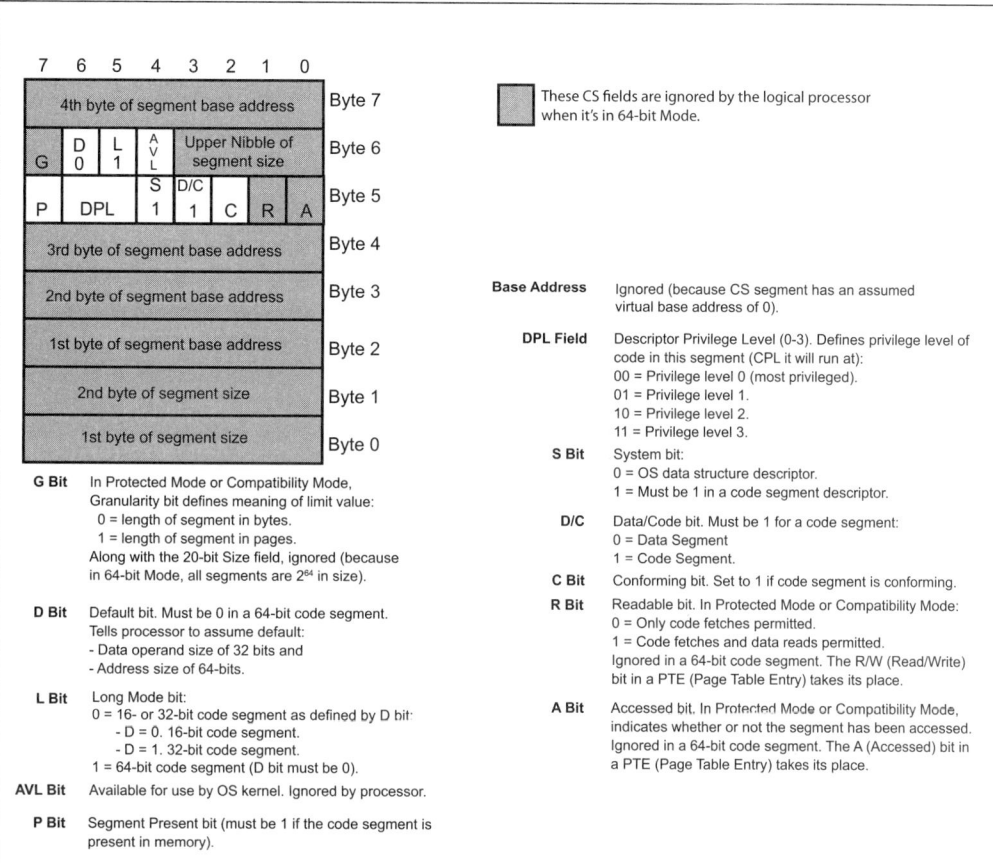

G Bit In Protected Mode or Compatibility Mode, Granularity bit defines meaning of limit value:
0 = length of segment in bytes.
1 = length of segment in pages.
Along with the 20-bit Size field, ignored (because in 64-bit Mode, all segments are 2^{64} in size).

D Bit Default bit. Must be 0 in a 64-bit code segment. Tells processor to assume default:
- Data operand size of 32 bits and
- Address size of 64-bits.

L Bit Long Mode bit:
0 = 16- or 32-bit code segment as defined by D bit·
- D = 0. 16-bit code segment.
- D = 1. 32-bit code segment.
1 = 64-bit code segment (D bit must be 0).

AVL Bit Available for use by OS kernel. Ignored by processor.

P Bit Segment Present bit (must be 1 if the code segment is present in memory).

These CS fields are ignored by the logical processor when it's in 64-bit Mode.

Base Address Ignored (because CS segment has an assumed virtual base address of 0).

DPL Field Descriptor Privilege Level (0-3). Defines privilege level of code in this segment (CPL it will run at):
00 = Privilege level 0 (most privileged).
01 = Privilege level 1.
10 = Privilege level 2.
11 = Privilege level 3.

S Bit System bit:
0 = OS data structure descriptor.
1 = Must be 1 in a code segment descriptor.

D/C Data/Code bit. Must be 1 for a code segment:
0 = Data Segment
1 = Code Segment.

C Bit Conforming bit. Set to 1 if code segment is conforming.

R Bit Readable bit. In Protected Mode or Compatibility Mode:
0 = Only code fetches permitted.
1 = Code fetches and data reads permitted.
Ignored in a 64-bit code segment. The R/W (Read/Write) bit in a PTE (Page Table Entry) takes its place.

A Bit Accessed bit. In Protected Mode or Compatibility Mode, indicates whether or not the segment has been accessed. Ignored in a 64-bit code segment. The A (Accessed) bit in a PTE (Page Table Entry) takes its place.

Protected/Compatibility 16-/32-bit SubModes

Excluding Real Mode and SMM (System Management Mode), there are five major modes of operation (refer to Figure 2-6 on page 39):

- **16-bit Protected Mode**. The logical processor is in this mode whenever it is in Protected Mode and is fetching and executing code from a code segment identified as a 286, first generation code segment.
- **32-bit Protected Mode**. The logical processor is in this mode whenever it is in Protected Mode and is fetching and executing code from a code segment identified as a 32-bit code segment (first introduced with the advent of the 386 processor).
- **16-bit Compatibility Mode**. The logical processor is in this mode whenever it is in IA-32e Mode and is fetching and executing code from a code segment identified as a 286, first generation code segment.
- **32-bit Compatibility Mode**. The logical processor is in this mode whenever it is in IA-32e Mode and is fetching and executing code from a code segment identified as a 32-bit code segment (first introduced with the advent of the 386 processor).
- **64-bit Mode**. The logical processor is in this mode whenever it is in IA-32e Mode and is fetching and executing code from a code segment identified as a third generation, 64-bit code segment.

Figure 2-6: Protected Mode and Compatibility Mode Consists of Two SubModes

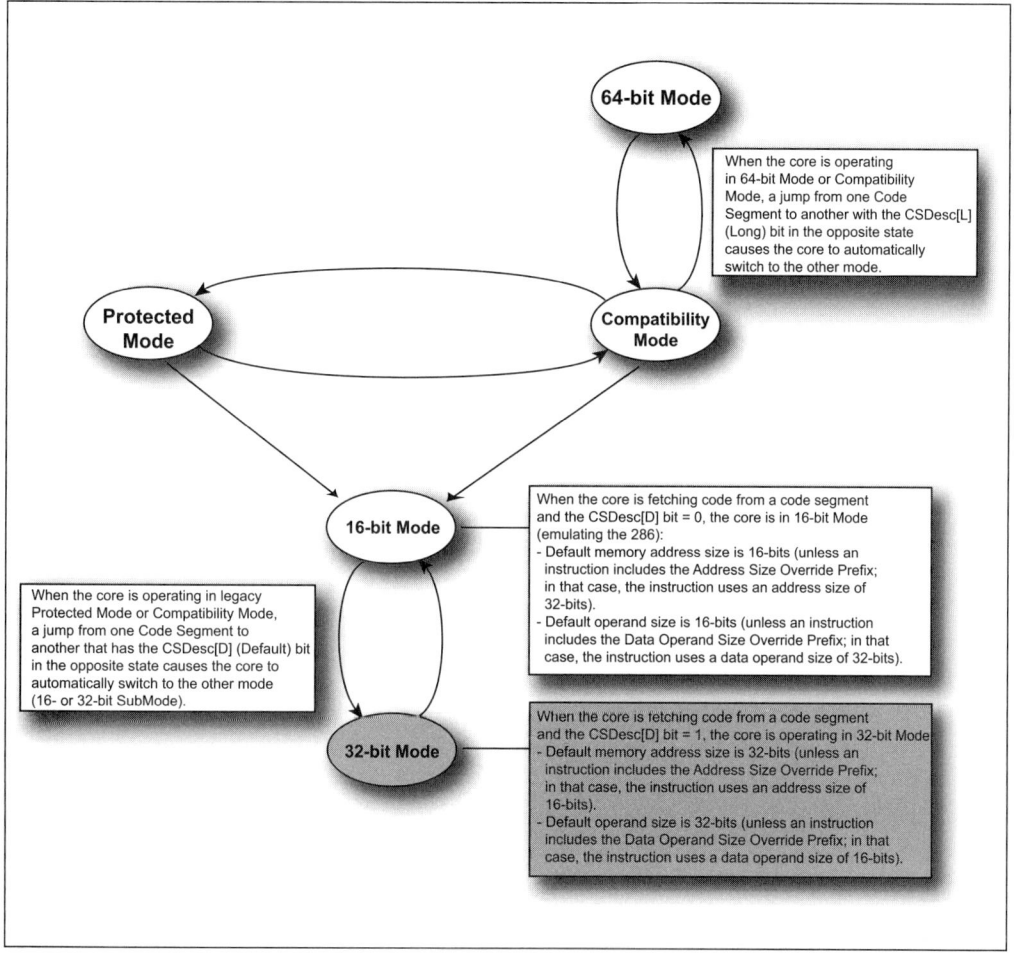

3 *A (very) Brief History*

The Previous Chapter

The previous chapter introduced the execution modes and submodes and mode switching basics.

This Chapter

This chapter introduces the evolution of the x86 ISA, as well as the basic operational characteristics of 8086 Real Mode, 286 Protected Mode, and 386 Protected Mode. It also introduces the Intel microarchitecture families including a product introduction timeline.

The Next Chapter

The next chapter defines the state of a logical processor immediately after the removal of reset and introduces the concept of a soft reset (also referred to as an INIT). It also describes the initial code fetches performed by the BootStrap Processor as well as the methodology utilized by software to discover and configure all of the logical processors in the system.

Major Evolutionary Developments

Through the years, the x86 software architecture has steadily evolved with the introduction of new x86 processors. Some changes were small, evolutionary ones while others made significant additions to the architecture. Figure 3-1 on page 42 illustrates (and Table 3-1 on page 43 describes) those that, in the author's opinion, fall into the latter category.

Figure 3-1: Major Milestones in Evolution of Software Environment

8086. Real Mode.

286. 1st generation, 16-bit Protected Mode added.

386. 2nd generation 32-bit Protected Mode + 1st generation Paging + SMM + VM86 Mode + 32-bit GP registers.

Pentium P55C. MMX/SIMD paradigm + MMX instruction and register sets added + Local APIC.

Pentium Pro. 2nd generation Paging (PAE-36) permits physical memory addressing above 4GB boundary.

Pentium III. Expansion of SIMD paradigm. SSE instruction set + XMM register set added.

Pentium 4. Netburst microarchitecture + Hyper-Threading.

Core Solo/Duo. Virtualization Technology added.

Core 2 Solo/Duo. 3rd generation Paging + IA-32e Mode (64-bit register set + 64-bit addressing added).

Core i7 (first Nehalem-based product). Hyper-Threading back + up to 8 cores + Integrated DRAM controller + QPI.

Note: Smaller, incremental evolutionary steps not included (e.g., SSE2, SSE3, SSSE3, SSE4.1, SSE4.2, etc.)

Table 3-1: Major Evolutionary Developments

Introduced In	Major Enhancements to the x86 Instruction Set Architecture
8086	At the root of the x86 family tree lies the 8086, a processor with the following characteristics: • Modes: **Real Mode**. • Addressable Memory: 1MB. • Data Transfer Width: 16-bits. • Programming Model: 16-bit.

286	Next, we have the 286, a processor with the following characteristics:
	• Modes: Real Mode and **first generation 16-bit Protected Mode.**
	• Missing three critical capabilities:
	  – It did not implement a virtual-to-physical address translation facility (i.e., the Paging mechanism).
	  – Could not address more than 16MB of physical memory.
	  – It did not implement Virtual 8086 (VM86) Mode, an exemption that effectively crippled the processor's ability to run ill-behaved DOS applications under a multi-tasking OS.
	• Addressable Physical Memory: 16MB.
	• Data Transfer Width: 16-bits.
	• Programming Model: 16-bit (16-bit GP registers and 16-bit addressing).

Table 3-1: Major Evolutionary Developments (Continued)

Introduced In	Major Enhancements to the x86 Instruction Set Architecture
386	The introduction of the 386 contributed the following major architectural changes: • **2nd generation 32-bit Protected Mode**. Permits 32-bit addressing (rather than the 16-bit addressing supported by the 286's first generation Protected Mode). • **1st generation virtual-to-physical address translation** mechanism (i.e., Paging). Permitted a 32-bit virtual memory address to be translated into a 32-bit physical memory address. • **System Management Mode (SMM)** first appeared in the 386SX processor. If the platform logic detects a platform-specific issue (e.g., a thermal zone is warming up), the chipset generates an SM Interrupt (SMI) to the processor which interrupts the currently-running program, saves the processor's register set and executes the SMM handler. The handler checks chipset status to determine the nature of the problem, handles the problem (e.g., by turning on a fan) and then restores the processor's register set and resumes execution of the interrupted program. • **VM86 Mode**. This mechanism permits the processor hardware to monitor the execution of ill-behaved DOS applications on an instruction-by-instruction basis. If an instruction that could destabilize the multi-tasking OS is detected, the DOS program is interrupted and a special program, the VMM (Virtual Machine Monitor), is executed to determine the nature of the problem and fix it. The OS then resumes execution of the DOS application. • Addressable Physical Memory: 4GB. • Data Transfer Width: 32-bits. • Programming Model: 32-bit (32-bit GP registers and 32-bit addressing).

Table 3-1: Major Evolutionary Developments (Continued)

Introduced In	Major Enhancements to the x86 Instruction Set Architecture
Pentium P55C	• Introduced the **MMX/SIMD** programming paradigm including 55 new instructions and a set of eight 64-bit pseudo-registers (rather than implementing a new set of discrete registers, the lower 64 bits of the x87 FPU's eight data registers are used as MMX registers when executing MMX code). • Computation on multiple data items can be sped up dramatically using the SIMD (**S**ingle **I**nstruction operating on **M**ultiple **D**ata items simultaneously) programming model wherein MMX instructions can perform simultaneous operations on bytes, words or dwords that are packed into the 64-bit MMX registers. • Integrated **Local APIC**.
Pentium Pro	**2nd generation virtual-to-physical address translation** facility (i.e., Paging mechanism). The 1st generation mechanism could not address physical memory above the 4GB boundary. The 2nd generation **PAE-36 feature** permits the processor to translate a 32-bit virtual memory address into a 36-bit (rather than a 32-bit) physical memory address, thereby allowing the processor to address up to 64GB of physical memory. Note, however, that the virtual address width is still 32 bits, limiting the application to a 4GB virtual address space.

Pentium III	Dramatically expanded the SIMD programming model by adding the **SSE** (**S**treaming **S**IMD **E**xtension) instruction and register sets consisting of:
	• 70 new instructions and
	• A set of nine new registers:
	  – Eight 128-bit XMM registers (XMM0 - XMM7). Unlike the MMX registers, this is a discrete register set.
	  – 32-bit control/status register (MXCSR).
	Note that later processors continued to add to the SSE capabilities (SSE2, SSE3, SSSE3, SSE4.1, SSE4.2). No new SSE registers were added, however, until the advent of 64-bit Mode.

Core Solo/ Duo	Added the **Virtualization Technology (VT)** feature that permits an executive with super-privileges to multi-task multiple operating systems.

Table 3-1: Major Evolutionary Developments (Continued)

Introduced In	Major Enhancements to the x86 Instruction Set Architecture
Core 2 Solo/Duo	• Added **64-bit Mode** which includes an expanded 64-bit register set and 64-bit addressing. • Permits application programs to address a 52-bit (rather than a 32-bit) virtual address space and the **3rd generation virtual-to-physical address translation mechanism** is capable of translating the 52-bit virtual address into a physical memory address up to 48-bits in width (rather than 32- or 36-bits). Supported physical address widths are implementation-specific.
Core i7	First product based on the Nehalem core: • Integrated DRAM controller. • Intel QPI interface. • Hyper-Threading.

16-bit Mode Background

8086 and Real Mode

In the beginning, there was the 8086 and only one mode of operation: Real Mode. The 8086 exhibited the basic operational characteristics listed in Table 3-2 on page 46.

Table 3-2: 8086 Real Mode Characteristics

Feature	Characteristic(s)
Memory Address Space	20-bit, 1MB memory address space.
Virtual (i.e., Linear) Memory	No such concept. The memory address created by adding a 16-bit offset to a segment's base address yielded the actual, physical memory address.

Table 3-2: 8086 Real Mode Characteristics (Continued)

Feature	Characteristic(s)
Memory Segments	The four segment registers—CS, DS, SS and ES—each defined the base address of a 64KB memory region: • **CS** defined the base address of the 64KB area of memory that holds the currently-executing program. • **DS** defined the base address of the 64KB area of memory containing the data that the program acted upon. • **ES** defined the base address of an optional, additional 64KB area of memory containing data that the program acted upon. • **SS** defined the base address of the 64KB area of memory used as scratchpad memory by the processor hardware as well as by the programmer. When necessary, the hardware and the programmer can temporarily store information (by pushing it onto the stack from one or more registers) and easily retrieve it (by popping it back off the stack).
Memory Address Calculation	**Instruction Fetch**. When fetching the next instruction from the code segment, the logical processor: 1. Extends the 16-bit segment base address in the CS register to 20-bits by adding the digit 0h to its lower end. 2. Adds the 16-bit IP (Instruction Pointer register) value to the base address to create the 20-bit physical start address of the next instruction to be fetched from memory. **Loads and Stores**. When performing a load (i.e., a memory data read into a GPR) or a store (i.e., a memory data write from a GPR), the logical processor: 1. Extends the 16-bit segment base address in the DS or ES register to 20-bits by adding the digit 0h to its lower end. 2. Adds the programmer-specified 16-bit offset to the 20-bit base address to create the 20-bit physical address of the data item (either an 8-bit or 16-bit item) in memory. **16-bit Offset**. It is important to note that, because segments are no more than 64KB in length, the programmer-supplied offset cannot be wider than 16-bits. Example: `add bx, [FE23]`; the offset provided within the brackets is, by definition, a 16-bit value.
GPRs	All of the General-Purpose Registers (GPRs) were either 8-bits or 16-bits in size.

Table 3-2: 8086 Real Mode Characteristics (Continued)

Feature	Characteristic(s)
Data Operand size	All accesses to store data from a GPR to memory or, conversely, to retrieve data from memory into a GPR, were, by definition, either **8-bit** (byte) or **16-bit** (word) accesses.
Protected Mode	No such concept.

286 Introduced 16-bit Protected Mode

While remaining backward-compatible with Real Mode, the 286 introduced Intel's first-generation Protected Mode which exhibits the characteristics listed in Table 3-3 on page 48. One of the important elements to note in this table is that, when the logical processor is operating in 286 Protected Mode (also referred to as 16-bit Protected Mode), it **assumes that the offset portion of a memory address is 16-bits in width and that the data operands operated on by instructions are either 8- or 16-bits in width.**

Table 3-3: 286 16-bit Protected Mode Characteristics (& short-comings)

Feature	Characteristic(s)
Memory Address Space	24-bit, **16MB physical memory address space**. The memory address created by adding a 16-bit offset to a segment's 24-bit base address yielded a 24-bit physical memory address (see next item).
Virtual (i.e., Linear) memory	**No such concept**. A virtual-to-physical address translation mechanism (i.e., Paging) was not implemented until the advent of the 386 processor.

Table 3-3: 286 16-bit Protected Mode Characteristics (& short-comings) (Continued)

Feature	Characteristic(s)
Memory Segments	When operating in **Real Mode**, the logical processor's treatment of the four segment registers and the segments of memory space they define is the same as the 8086 processor. When operating in **Protected Mode**, however, loading a new, 16-bit value into any of the segment registers causes the logical processor to read a 64-bit segment descriptor (see Figure 3-2 on page 51) from either the GDT (Global Descriptor Table) or the LDT (Local Descriptor Table). The descriptor defined the respective segment's characteristics: • The **24-bit base address** of the segment in a 16MB physical memory address space. • The 16-bit **size** of the segment (**1-byte to 64KB** in size). • The **privilege level** of the memory area. • **Segment type**: Whether it was a code segment, a data segment, or it contained a special data structure built and maintained by the OS kernel (e.g., a TSS or an LDT). • If it was a code segment, whether it also contained data that could be read (but not written). • Whether the logical processor had accessed any location(s) in the segment since it was set up by the OS.
Memory Address Calculation	• When **fetching the next instruction from the code segment**, the logical processor adds the 16-bit IP value to the 24-bit code segment base address to create the 24-bit physical start address of the next instruction to be fetched from memory. • When performing a **load** (i.e., a memory data read into a GPR) **or a store** (i.e., a memory data write from a GPR), the logical processor adds the programmer-specified 16-bit offset to the 24-bit base address of the DS or ES segment to create the 24-bit physical address of the data item (either an 8-bit or 16-bit item) in memory. It is important to note that, because segments are no more than 64KB in length, the **programmer-supplied offset is a 16-bit value**. **Example**: `add bx, [FE23]`; the offset provided within the brackets is, by definition, a 16-bit value. **The small size of segments is one of many severe limitations of 16-bit, 286 Protected Mode.**

Table 3-3: 286 16-bit Protected Mode Characteristics (& short-comings) (Continued)

Feature	Characteristic(s)
GPRs	All of the General-Purpose Registers (GPRs) were either 8-bits or 16-bits in size.
Data Operand size	All accesses to store data from a GPR to memory or, conversely, to retrieve data from memory into a GPR, were, by definition, either **8-bit** (byte) or **16-bit** (word) accesses.
VM86 Mode	Not implemented until the advent of the 386. Since Real Mode DOS applications do not play well with others, 286 Protected Mode, although purportedly designed to support multitasking OSs, offered little protection from the havoc that DOS applications might cause to other applications or to the OS.

Figure 3-2: 16-bit, 286-style Code Segment Descriptor

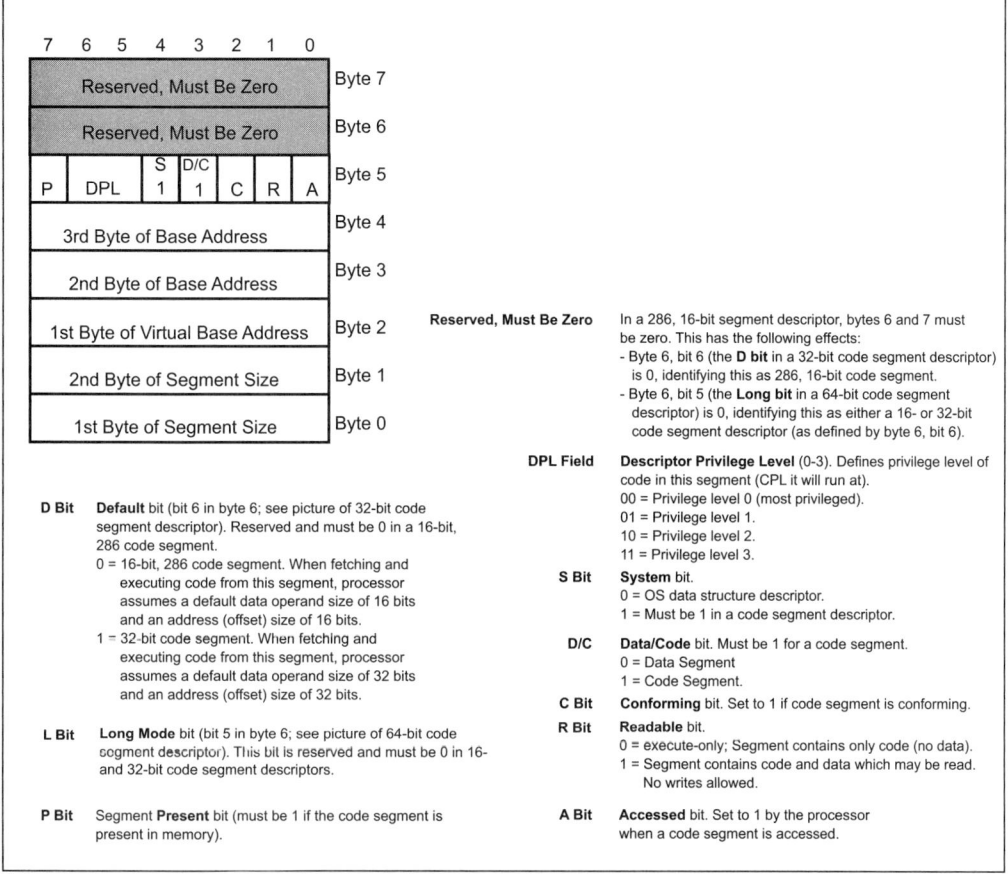

386 Supported Both 16- and 32-bit Protected Mode

The 386 (and all subsequent x86 processors), while maintaining the ability to execute code written for 16-bit, 286 Protected Mode, can also execute 32-bit code. Table 3-4 on page 52 lists the major improvements that were made to Protected Mode with the advent of the 386.

While the 386 did introduce a greatly-improved 32-bit Protected Mode, when fetching code from programs written for the 286's 16-bit Protected Mode environment, it must behave as if the code is executing on a 286. This means:

- When the logical processor is executing code from a 16-bit code segment, it assumes:
  — that the default memory address offset size is 16- rather than 32-bits.
  — that the default data operand size is 16-bits (not 32-bits).
- When the logical processor is executing code from a 32-bit code segment, it assumes:
  — that the default memory address offset size is 32- rather than 16-bits.
  — that the default data operand size is 32-bits (not 16-bits).

This raises the question: how does the logical processor know if it is currently fetching code from a 16-bit vs. a 32-bit code segment? This question was answered in the "Mode Switching Basics" on page 30.

Table 3-4: 386 32-bit Protected Mode Characteristics

Feature	Characteristic(s)
Memory Address Space	32-bit, **4GB linear (i.e. virtual) memory address space**. In Protected Mode, the memory address created by adding a 32-bit offset to a segment's 32-bit base address yields a 32-bit address. Assuming that the virtual-to-physical address translation mechanism (also known as Paging) is enabled, the address produced is referred to as the linear (virtual) address.
Virtual (i.e., Linear) memory	**In a major leap forward,** a virtual-to-physical address translation mechanism (i.e., Paging) was implemented. It permitted the application programmer to treat the memory assigned to their application as one contiguous (linear) space.

Table 3-4: 386 32-bit Protected Mode Characteristics (Continued)

Feature	Characteristic(s)
Memory Segments	When operating in **Real Mode**, the logical processor's treatment of the **six segment registers** (two new data segment registers, FS and GS, were added) and the segments of memory space they define is the same as the 8086 processor. When operating in **Protected Mode**, loading a new, 16-bit value into any of the segment registers causes the logical processor to read a 64-bit segment descriptor (see Figure 3-3 on page 55) from either the GDT or the LDT. The descriptor defines the respective segment's characteristics: • The **32-bit base address** of the segment in a 4GB virtual memory address space. • The 20-bit **size** of the segment (in bytes or 4KB pages; **1-byte to 4GB** in size). • The **privilege level** of the memory area. • **Segment type**: Whether it is a code segment, a data segment or it contains a special data structure built and maintained by the OS kernel (e.g., a TSS or an LDT). • If it is a code segment, whether it also contains data that can be read (but not written). • Whether the logical processor has accessed any location(s) in the segment since it was set by the OS.

Table 3-4: 386 32-bit Protected Mode Characteristics (Continued)

Feature	Characteristic(s)
Memory Address Calculation	• When **fetching the next instruction from the code segment**, the logical processor adds the 32-bit EIP (Extended Instruction Pointer) value to the 32-bit code segment base address to create the 32-bit virtual start address of the next instruction to be fetched from memory. • When performing a **load** (i.e., a memory data read into a GPR) **or a store** (i.e., a memory data write from a GPR), the logical processor adds the programmer-specified 32-bit offset to the 32-bit base address of the DS, ES, FS or GS segment to create the 32-bit virtual address of the data item (either an 8-, 16-, or 32-bit item) in memory. It is important to note that, because segments are now up to 4GB in length, the **programmer-supplied offset is a 32-bit value**. **Example**: `add bx, [C045FE23]`; the offset provided within the brackets can be a 32-bit value. **The small size of segments (max of 64KB) was a severe limitation (one of many) in 16-bit, 286 Protected Mode.**
GPRs	All of the General-Purpose Registers (GPRs) are 32-bits wide.
Data Operand size	All accesses to store data from a GPR to memory or, conversely, to retrieve data from memory into a GPR, are, by definition, either **8-bit** (byte), **16-bit** (word), or 32-bit (doubleword, or dword) accesses.
VM86 Mode	Not implemented until the advent of the 386. Since Real Mode DOS applications do not play well with others, 286 Protected Mode, although purportedly designed to support multitasking OSs, offered little protection from the havoc that DOS applications might cause to other applications or the OS. Automatically activated whenever a Real Mode task is started or resumed, VM86 Mode allows the logical processor to automatically call the kernel's VMM (Virtual Machine Monitor) program whenever the task attempts an operation that might cause problems for the multitasking OS environment.

Figure 3-3: 32-bit, 386-style Code Segment Descriptor

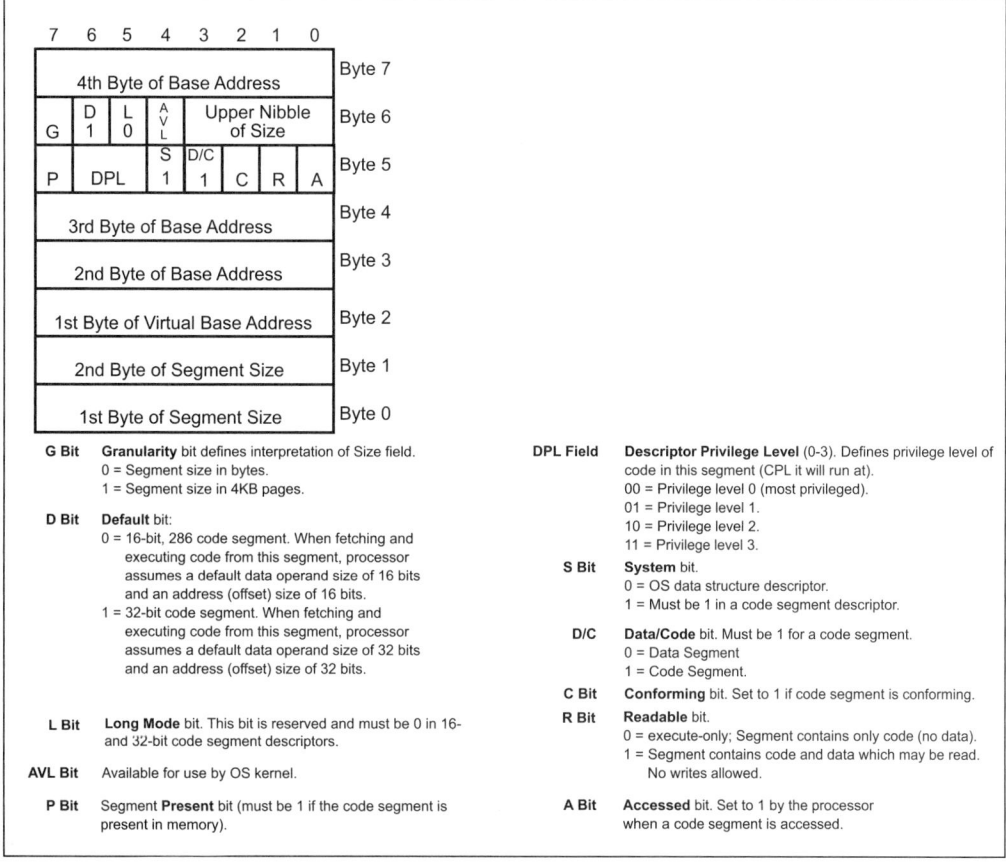

G Bit **Granularity** bit defines interpretation of Size field.
0 = Segment size in bytes.
1 = Segment size in 4KB pages.

D Bit **Default** bit:
0 = 16-bit, 286 code segment. When fetching and executing code from this segment, processor assumes a default data operand size of 16 bits and an address (offset) size of 16 bits.
1 = 32-bit code segment. When fetching and executing code from this segment, processor assumes a default data operand size of 32 bits and an address (offset) size of 32 bits.

L Bit **Long Mode** bit. This bit is reserved and must be 0 in 16- and 32-bit code segment descriptors.

AVL Bit Available for use by OS kernel.

P Bit Segment **Present** bit (must be 1 if the code segment is present in memory).

DPL Field **Descriptor Privilege Level** (0-3). Defines privilege level of code in this segment (CPL it will run at).
00 = Privilege level 0 (most privileged).
01 = Privilege level 1.
10 = Privilege level 2.
11 = Privilege level 3.

S Bit **System** bit.
0 = OS data structure descriptor.
1 = Must be 1 in a code segment descriptor.

D/C **Data/Code** bit. Must be 1 for a code segment.
0 = Data Segment
1 = Code Segment.

C Bit **Conforming** bit. Set to 1 if code segment is conforming.

R Bit **Readable** bit.
0 = execute-only; Segment contains only code (no data).
1 = Segment contains code and data which may be read. No writes allowed.

A Bit **Accessed** bit. Set to 1 by the processor when a code segment is accessed.

The Intel Microarchitecture Families

Table 3-5 on page 56 lists the microarchitecture families of the Intel x86 processors from the 386 through Nehalem (Core i7).

Table 3-5: Intel Processor Microarchitecture Families

Family	Description
386	The first Intel x86 processor to implement a full, 32-bit Protected Mode environment. The first implementation of SMM appeared in the 386SL processor. See page 57 for more information.
486	The first Intel x86 processor to implement an on-die cache and, starting with the 486DX, an on-die x87 FPU (Floating-Point Unit). SMM became standard in the later versions of the 486. See page 58 for more information.
P5	The Pentium processor family was based on the P5 core and its variants. See page 58 for more information.
P6	The processors based on the P6 processor core were the Pentium Pro, Pentium II, Pentium III and Pentium M. See page 59, page 59, and page 60 for more information.
Intel Netburst microarchitecture	The Pentium 4 processors and their Xeon derivatives were based on the NetBurst microarchitecture. See page 60 for more information.
Pentium M microarchitecture	An improved version of the Pentium III processor, the Pentium M was derived from the P6 microarchitecture. See page 60 for more information.
Core microarchitecture	In their initial incarnations, the Core Solo (single core) and Core Duo (dual core) processors were improved versions of the Pentium M design. See page 61 for more information.
Core 2 microarchitecture	An enhanced version of the Core microarchitecture. See Core 2 Duo on page 61 and Core 2 Quad on page 61 for more information.
Atom microarchitecture	See page 61 for more information.
Nehalem microarchitecture	See Core i7 on page 61 for more information.

A Brief Timeline

Table 3-6 on page 57 lists the Intel x86 processors from the 8086 through the present (as of this writing: March, 2009). It should be noted that specialty products such as Celerons and Xeons aren't listed because they are merely different flavors of the listed products.

Table 3-6: x86 Family Members (as of February 2009)

Product	Year	Description
8086	1978	<ul><li>Modes: Real Mode.</li><li>Addressable Memory: 1MB.</li><li>Data Transfer Width: 16-bits.</li><li>Programming Model: 16-bit.</li></ul>
8088	1979	<ul><li>Modes: Real Mode.</li><li>Addressable Memory: 1MB.</li><li>Data Transfer Width: 8-bits.</li><li>Programming Model: 16-bit.</li></ul>
286	1982	<ul><li>Modes: Real Mode, limited 16-bit Protected Mode.</li><li>Addressable Memory: 16MB.</li><li>Data Transfer Width: 16-bits.</li><li>Programming Model: 16-bit.</li></ul>
386	1985	<ul><li>Modes: Real Mode, 16-/32-bit Protected Mode, VM86 Mode, SMM (first introduced in 386SL).</li><li>32-bit physical-to-virtual memory address translation.</li><li>Addressable Memory: 4GB.</li><li>Data Transfer Width: 32-bits.</li><li>Programming Model: 32-bit.</li><li>Added Debug register set.</li></ul>

Table 3-6: x86 Family Members (as of February 2009) (Continued)

Product	Year	Description
486	1989	• SX version had no on-chip x87 FPU. • Since advent of 486DX, all subsequent processors include on-chip x87 FPU. • Modes: Real Mode, Protected Mode, VM86 Mode, SMM. • Addressable Memory: 4GB. • Data Transfer Width: 32-bits. • Programming Model: 32-bit. • First x86 processor with on-chip cache. • Added caching control bits in CR0. • Added a handful of new instructions (including CPUID). • Added Alignment Checking feature. • Minor additions to the physical-to-virtual memory address translation mechanism. • Deleted Exception 9 and added 17 (Alignment Check).
Pentium	1993	• Modes: Real Mode, Protected Mode, VM86 Mode, SMM. • Addressable Memory: 4GB. • Data Transfer Width: 64-bits. • Programming Model: 32-bit. • Instruction set additions including MMX instructions. • Added VM86 Mode performance-enhancement extensions. • Added Protected Mode Virtual Interrupts. • Added ability to set IO address breakpoints. • Added Time Stamp Counter MSR. • Added support for 4MB Pages to address translation mechanism. • First appearance of the Machine Check Architecture (MCA) register set (in a very primitive form). • First implementation of the Performance Monitoring facility. • Integrated Local APIC (Advanced Programmable Interrupt Controller). • First Model-Specific Registers (MSRs) added. • Enhanced exceptions 13 (GP exception) and 14 (Page Fault exception), and added exception 18 (Machine Check exception).

Table 3-6: x86 Family Members (as of February 2009) (Continued)

Product	Year	Description
Pentium Pro	1995	• Modes: Real Mode, Protected Mode, VM86 Mode, SMM. • Addressable Memory: 64GB. • Data Transfer Width: 64-bits. • Programming Model: 32-bit. • PAE-36 feature added, permitting a 32-bit virtual memory address to be translated into a 36-bit physical memory address. • Added support for Global pages to the address translation mechanism. • Various incremental enhancements to the on-chip Local APIC. • Small enhancement to SMM. • Memory Type and Range Register (MTRR) set added. • No support for the MMX instruction set. • Added a handful of new instructions. • Enhanced CPUID instruction. • Machine Check Architecture register set greatly enhanced and becomes part of the ISA definition. • Small enhancement to the Performance Monitoring facility. • MSR register set greatly expanded. • Debugging facilities greatly expanded. • Due to the complexity of the x86 variable-length instruction set, all processors from this point forward employed the dynamic translation of variable length x86 instructions into simple, fixed-length instructions referred to as micro-ops. Each x86 instruction is translated into a series of one or more micro-ops that, when executed, perform the equivalent operation.
Pentium II	1997	• Repackaging of the Pentium Pro. • Reintroduced the MMX registers and instruction sets (they weren't present in the Pentium Pro) and from that day forward they have been part of the x86 ISA specification. • Added the Fast System Call and Return instruction pair and three MSRs to support them. • Very first Xeon processor was a derivative of the Pentium II. It added the PSE-36 address translation feature.

Table 3-6: x86 Family Members (as of February 2009) (Continued)

Product	Year	Description
Pentium III	1999	• Added the SSE registers (XMM registers and MXCSR) and the SSE (i.e., SSE1) instruction set. • CPUID instruction enhanced. • Added Exception 19, the SSE floating-point exception. • The CPUID Serial Number feature was added, condemned around the globe, and subsequently removed never to appear again. • Added FXSAVE/FXRSTOR instruction pair. • The Pentium III Xeon added the PAT (Page Attribute Table) feature.
Pentium 4	2000	• Added 144 new SSE2 instructions. • The 11-bit x87 FPU's Fopcode register was added. • Enhanced the CPUID instruction. • Added 13 new SSE3 instructions. • Added thermal sensor interrupt capability to the Local APIC. • Expanded the Processor ID bit field width in the Local APIC ID register from 4- to 8-bits. • Introduced the Software Controlled Clock Modulation mechanism that allows software to decrease processor performance in order to lower the core temperature. • Added the Thermal Monitor feature. • Belying their name, many of the MSRs became part of the x86 ISA specification. • The MCA register set was enhanced. • The debugging facilities were enhanced. • The Performance Monitoring facilities were greatly enhanced. • Implemented Hyper-Threading technology.
Pentium M	2003	The advent of the Pentium M processor marks the point at which Intel left the Pentium 4 Netburst microarchitecture behind. The Pentium M was an improved version of the Pentium III microarchitecture (and was therefore based on the P6 core). • Eliminated Hyper-Threading.

Table 3-6: x86 Family Members (as of February 2009) (Continued)

Product	Year	Description
Products based on the Core Microarchitecture		
Core Solo/ Duo	2005	Based on the Pentium M technology, the Solo contained a single core while the Duo contained dual cores. • Enhanced SpeedStep technology. • Implemented the Execute Disable feature. • Implemented Virtualization Technology (VT). • Enhanced Digital Thermal Sensor. • Software-selectable frequency/voltage set points.
Core 2 Solo/ Duo	2006	• Implemented IA-32e Mode. • Added 16 new SSSE3 instructions as well 47 new SSE4.1 instructions. • Feature permits enable/disable of adjacent cache line prefetch. • Enhanced Thermal Monitoring logic. • Enhanced CPUID instruction. • Enhanced MCA error logging capability.
Core 2 Quad	2007	Quad-core version of the Core 2 processor.
Core i7	2008	The first x86 processor based on the technology code-named Nehalem. Products based on Nehalem may incorporate the following characteristics: • Hyper-Threading returns. • Up to eight cores, some of which may be special-purpose (e.g., graphic cores). • Integrated DRAM memory controller. • First appearance of the Intel QPI (QuickPath Interconnect) interconnect technology (which replaces the old Front Side Bus—FSB). • Introduces 7 new SSE4.2 instructions.
Emergence of the Atom Processor Family		
Atom	2008	• Focused on low-power applications (such as mobile handheld devices and netbook computers). • Supports Hyper-Threading. • Some models are Intel 64 Architecture processors (and therefore support IA-32e Mode) while others are IA-32 Architecture processors. • Supports Intel's Virtualization Technology. • Available in single and dual core models.

4 *State After Reset*

The Previous Chapter

The previous chapter introduced the evolution of the x86 ISA, as well as the basic operational characteristics of 8086 Real Mode, 286 Protected Mode, and 386 Protected Mode. It also introduced the Intel microarchitecture families including a product introduction timeline.

This Chapter

This chapter defines the state of a logical processor immediately after the removal of reset and introduces the concept of a soft reset (also referred to as an INIT). It also describes the initial code fetches performed by the BootStrap Processor and introduces the methodology utilized by software to discover and configure all of the logical processors in the system.

The Next Chapter

The next chapter provides a very basic introduction to the various facilities that support the IA-32 computing environment. These facilities include:

- Pre-386 Register Sets (this section is provided for historical background).
- IA-32 Register Set Overview.
- Control Registers.
- Status/Control Register (Eflags).
- Instruction Fetch Facilities.
- General Purpose Data Registers.
- Defining Memory Regions/Characteristics.
- Interrupt/Exception Facilities.
- Kernel Facilities.
- Address Translation Facilities.
- Legacy FP Facilities.
- MMX Facilities.

- SSE Facilities.
- Model-Specific Registers.
- Debug Facilities.
- Automatic Task Switching Mechanism.

State After Reset

Table 4-1 on page 66 defines the state of the logical processor's registers (the IA-32 register set is shown in Figure 4-1 on page 65) and resources immediately after the removal of reset. To summarize:

- The logical processor is in Real Mode (Protected Mode and Paging are disabled).
- Its caches are empty and caching is disabled.
- All of the feature bits in CR4 are cleared disabling most of the new features introduced after the advent of the 386.
- Recognition of external hardware interrupts is disabled.
- No instructions have been fetched from memory.
- The x87 FPU is disabled.
- All x87 FPU and SSE exceptions are disabled.
- The Machine Check and Alignment Check exceptions are disabled.
- The first instruction will be fetched from location FFFFFFF0h.

Figure 4-1: IA-32 Register Set

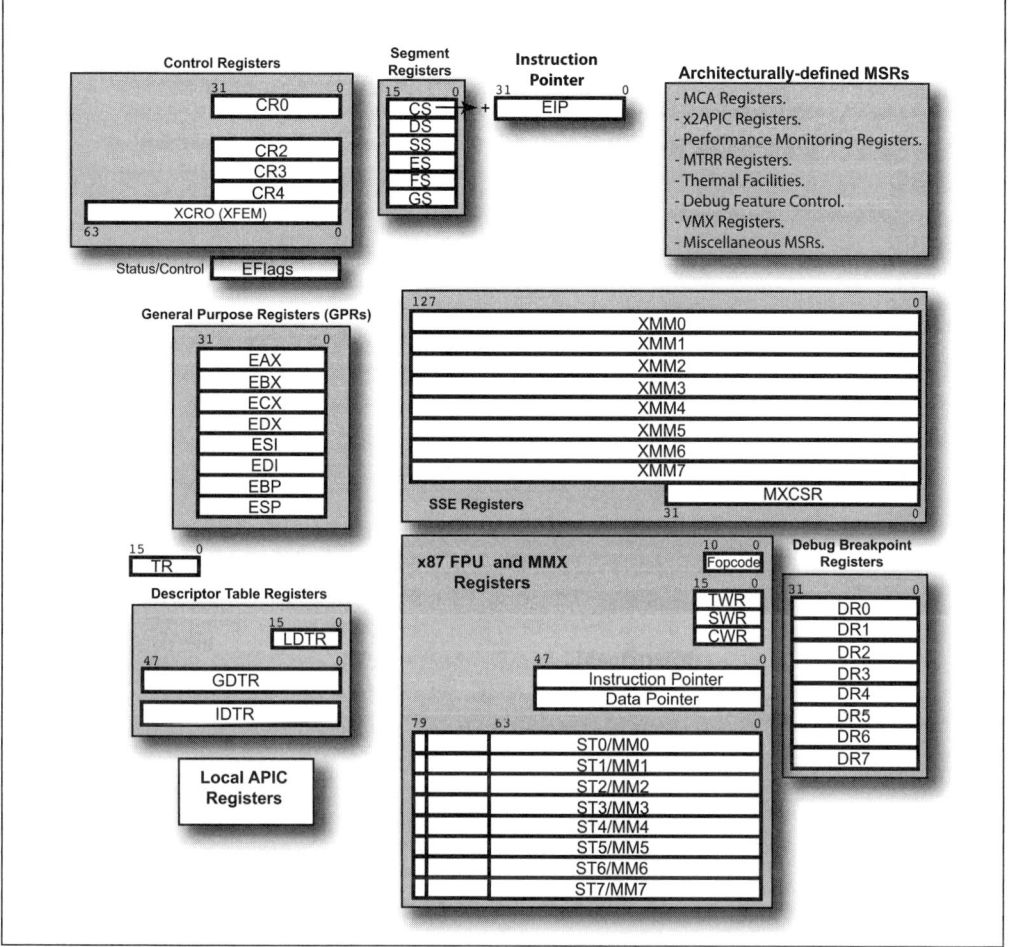

Table 4-1: Logical Processor State After Removal of Reset

Register or Resource	Effect(s)
Instruction Pipeline	No instructions have been fetched from memory yet.
ROB	Since no instructions have been fetched from memory yet to be translated into micro-ops, the Reorder Buffer is empty and the instruction dispatch logic is idle.
BTB Cache	The Branch Target Buffer maintains history on branch execution (i.e., whether branches were taken or not taken) is empty.
CR0 register	Contains 60000010h after reset: • CR0[PE] = 0, disabling Protected Mode. The logical processor is therefore in Real Mode. • CR0[PG] = 0, disabling Paging (virtual-to-physical address translation services). • CR0[CD&NW] = 11b, disabling the caching logic. • CR0[EM&MP] = 11b, indicating the x87 FPU isn't present and the logical processor should therefore permit software to emulate it (by executing integer-only code). • CR0[TS] = 0, indicating a task switch has not occurred. • CR0[ET] = 1, indicating that the integrated x87 FPU is compatible with the 387 FPU. • CR0[NE] = 0, disabling the logical processor's ability to generate an exception 16 if an x87 FP exception occurs. Instead, the logical processor signals the event using the DOS-compatible method (i.e., by asserting the processor's FERR# output which causes the assertion of IRQ13 to the 8259A PIC (Programmable Interrupt Controller). • CR0[WP] = 0. This has no effect at this time because Paging is disabled. When paging is enabled, setting this bit to a one prevents privilege level 0 software from writing to read-only pages. • CR0[AM] = 0. Clearing the Alignment Mask bit disables the logical processor's ability to generate the Alignment Check exception when a mis-aligned multi-byte memory access is detected.

Table 4-1: Logical Processor State After Removal of Reset (Continued)

Register or Resource	Effect(s)

CR4 register	New Feature Control register. Contains 00000000h after reset:
	• VME. VM86 Mode extensions are disabled.
	• PVI. Protected Mode Virtual Interrupt feature is disabled.
	• TSD. Time Stamp Disable is disabled.
	• DE. Debug extensions are disabled.
	• PSE. Page Size Extension is disabled.
	• PAE. Physical Address Extension (PAE-36 Mode) is disabled.
	• MCE. Machine Check Exception is disabled.
	• PGE. Global Page feature is disabled.
	• PCE. Performance Counter Enable is disabled.
	• OSFXSR. OS FX Save/Restore instruction pair support bit.
	  – FXSAVE and FXRSTOR save/restore the contents of FPU/MMX registers, but they may or may not (processor design-specific) save/restore SSE register set.
	  – Logical processor generates Invalid Opcode exception whenever it attempts to execute SSE instructions (except PREFETCHh or SFENCE).
	  – On any IA-32 processor (starting with Pentium 4) the logical processor generates the Invalid Opcode exception whenever it attempts to execute SSE2 instructions (except PAUSE, LFENCE, MFENCE, MOVNTI, and CLFLUSH).
	• OSXMMEXCPT. OS XMM Exception. The logical processor generates an Invalid Opcode exception whenever it detects an unmasked SIMD FP error.
	• VMXE. Virtual Mode Extension Enable. Disables the logical processor's virtualization technology feature.
	• SMXE. Safer Mode Extension Enable. Safer Mode is disabled.
	• OSXSAVE.
	  – Kernel doesn't support use of XGETBV, XSAVE and XRSTOR instructions by applications.
	  – Disables XSAVE/XRSTOR instructions ability to save/restore x87 FPU/MMX registers, SSE registers, and any other register sets enabled in XCR0.
	  – Disables logical processor's ability to read/ write XCR0 register using the XGETBV and XSETBV instructions.

Table 4-1: Logical Processor State After Removal of Reset (Continued)

Register or Resource	Effect(s)
Eflags register	Contains 00000002h after reset: • Eflags[TF] = 0, disabling debug single-step mode. • Eflags[IF] = 0, disabling recognition of external interrupts. • Eflags[DF] = 0 causes string instructions to process strings of information in memory starting at the start address and ascending through memory (i.e., ascending from the start address). • Eflags[IOPL] is don't care (because the logical processor is not in Protected Mode). • Eflags[NT] is don't care (because the logical processor is not in Protected Mode). • Eflags[RF] is don't care because the debug single-step feature is disabled. • Eflags[VM] = 0, disabling VM86 Mode. • Eflags[AC] is don't care because CR0[AM] = 0, disabling Alignment Checking. • Eflags[VIF] is don't care (because the logical processor is not in Protected Mode). • Eflags[VIP] is don't care (because the logical processor is not in Protected Mode). • Eflags[ID] = 0 and this has no effect on anything. • The remaining bits in Eflags are status bits that reflect the results of instruction execution.
MTRR register set	MTRRdefType register contains 0: • All of memory is set to the UC (Uncacheable) memory type. • The Fixed range MTRRs are disabled (because they have not yet been initialized by the BIOS). • The Variable range MTRRs are disabled (because they have not yet been initialized by the BIOS).
Caches	All of the logical processor's caches are empty (i.e., all lines are marked invalid). Furthermore, caching is disabled (CR0[CD&NW] = 11b) and all of memory is marked as uncacheable (MTRRdefType register contains 0). Result: performance will be terrible until caching is enabled and some information has been accumulated in the caches.

Table 4-1: Logical Processor State After Removal of Reset (Continued)

Register or Resource	Effect(s)
CS and EIP registers	**CS = F000h**. As a result, the Code Segment starts at memory location 000F0000h. Actually, it starts at FFFFF0000h (refer to "Initial Memory Reads" on page 74). The invisible part of the CS register (referred to as the CS cache register) is loaded with values that define the Code Segment as having the following characteristics: • Base address = FFFFF0000h. • Segment size = 0FFFFh (64KB). • The segment is present in memory. • It's a read/write segment. • The segment has been accessed. **EIP = 0000FFF0h**. The first instruction is fetched from location 0000FFF0h in the code segment which starts at memory location FFFF0000h (in other words, location 4GB-1).
DS, ES, FS and GS registers	All of the data segment registers contain **0000h**. The contents of the invisible part of the data segment registers (referred to as cache registers) define each of the data segments as having the following characteristics: • Base address = 00000000h. • Segment size = 0FFFFh (64KB). • The segment is present in memory. • It's a read/write segment. • The segment has been accessed.
SS and ESP registers	**SS = 0000h**. The contents of the invisible part of the SS register (referred to as the SS cache register) defines the Stack Segment as having the following characteristics: • Base address = 00000000h. • Segment size = 0FFFFh (64KB). • The segment is present in memory. • It's a read/write segment. • The segment has been accessed. • It's an expand-up stack segment. **ESP = 00000000h**. SS:ESP indicate that the stack's base address = 0 and the current TOS (top-of-stack) = 0; in other words, the stack is full (i.e., top = bottom).

Table 4-1: Logical Processor State After Removal of Reset (Continued)

Register or Resource	Effect(s)
EBX, ECX, EBP, ESI, EDI	These GPRs contain 00000000h.
EAX	• Contains 00000000h if BIST (Built-In Self-Test) wasn't run or if it was run and no errors were encountered. • If an error was encountered, EAX contains a non-zero, processor design-specific error code.
EDX	After reset is removed but before code fetching begins, the logical processor automatically deposits the processor type, family, model and stepping in the EDX register.
IDTR	IDTR (Interrupt Descriptor Table Register) = **0000h** and the Interrupt Table has the following characteristics: • Base address = 00000000h. • Size = FFFFh (64KB). • It is present in memory. • It is read/write accessible. The Real Mode interrupt table starts at physical memory address 00000000h.
GDTR	The 48-bit Global Descriptor Table Register contents after reset defines the GDT as follows: • Base address = 00000000h. • Size = FFFF (64KB). Since the GDTR and the GDT are only used in Protected Mode, this has no effect.
LDTR	The 16-bit Local Descriptor Table Register contains 0000h and the contents of the invisible portion of the LDT after reset defines the LDT as having the following characteristics: • Base address = 00000000h. • Size = FFFFh (64KB). Since the LDTR and the LDT are only used in Protected Mode, this has no effect.

Table 4-1: Logical Processor State After Removal of Reset (Continued)

Register or Resource	Effect(s)
TR register	The 16-bit Task Register contains 0000h and the contents of the invisible portion of the TR after reset defines the TSS (Task State Segment) of the currently-executing task as having the following characteristics: • Base address = 00000000h. • Size = FFFFh (64KB). Since the TR is only used in Protected Mode, this has no effect.
CR2 and CR3 registers	CR2 (Page Fault Address Register) and CR3 (Page Directory Base Address Register or PDBR) both contain 00000000h. Since these two registers are only used in Protected Mode when Paging (i.e., virtual-to-physical address translation) is enabled, this has no effect.
TLBs	The Translation Lookaside Buffers are special-purpose caches that cache copies of Page Table Entries (PTEs) to enable fast address translation. All entries are marked invalid after reset removal. Since the TLBs are only used in Protected Mode when Paging (i.e., virtual-to-physical address translation) is enabled, this has no effect.
XCR0 (XFEM) register	Only bit 1, the SSE bit, is currently implemented and it is cleared to zero.
Debug registers	DR7 (Debug Control register) contains **00000400h**, disabling the logical processor's breakpoint recognition logic. DR0-DR6 are therefore don't care.
Local APIC registers	Advanced Programmable Interrupt Controller has been assigned a unique APIC ID. It begins (after the BIST, if the BIST was executed) to negotiate with the Local APICs associated with the other logical processors to select the logical processor that will act as the bootstrap processor. Recognition of all external interrupts is disabled. The local APIC is in Virtual-Wire Mode (aka 8259A mode).

Table 4-1: Logical Processor State After Removal of Reset (Continued)

Register or Resource	Effect(s)
SSE register set	XMM data registers 0-7 all contain zero. MXCSR register contains 1F80h which has the following effects: • Flush-to-Zero mode is disabled. • Denormals As Zero mode is disabled. • Rounding Control bits = 00b. Round to nearest (even). Rounded result is the closest to the infinitely precise result. If two values are equally close, the result is the even value (i.e., the one with the lsb = 0). • All six types of SSE exceptions are disabled. • All six SSE error status bits are cleared.

x87 register set (and MMX data registers)	• Control register = 0040h.
	  – All six types of x87 FPU exceptions are disabled.
	  – Round to nearest (even). Rounded result is the closest to the infinitely precise result. If two values are equally close, the result is the even value (that is, the one with the lsb = 0). This is the default rounding mode.
	  – Precision = SP (Single-Precision).
	• Status register = 0000h.
	  – All status bits are cleared.
	  – Top-of-Stack pointer points to data register 0.
	• Tag Word register = 5555h. Indicating that all eight data register contain zero.
	• Data registers = 0.
	• Data Operand segment:offset registers = 0:0.
	• Instruction segment:offset registers = 0:0.

MCA register set	No hardware errors have been logged yet.
Performance Monitoring register set	All of the logical processor's Performance Monitoring counters are disabled, therefore no events of any type have been counted.
Thermal Monitoring facilities	None of the logical processor's thermal monitoring and control features are enabled.
Debug Feature Control registers	None of the debug features are enabled.

Table 4-1: Logical Processor State After Removal of Reset (Continued)

Register or Resource	Effect(s)
VMX capability	CR4[VMXE] = 0, disabling the logical processor's virtualization technology-related features.
TSC	The 64-bit Time Stamp Counter MSR is cleared to zero. After reset removal it begins counting logical processor clock cycles.

Soft Reset

As described in the previous section, a hard reset completely initializes the logical processor and its Local APIC, and clears its caches. A soft reset (known as an INIT) has the same effect but preserves the contents of the caches, MSRs, MTRRs, and the x87 FPU state (the contents of the BTB and the TLBs are cleared, however).

A soft reset may be delivered to a logical processor in one of two ways:

- The chipset can be commanded to assert the INIT# signal to the processor. See "286 DOS Extenders on Post-286 Processors" on page 313 for additional information.
- Software (typically kernel code) running on a logical processor may command its Local APIC to transmit an INIT IPI (Inter-Processor Interrupt) message to one or more other Local APICs in the system. See "SW-Initiated Interrupt Message Transmission" on page 1351.

Boot Strap Processor (BSP) Selection

Immediately after the removal of reset but before code fetches are initiated from the boot ROM, all of the logical processors in the system must negotiate among themselves to determine which of them will fulfill the role of the BootStrap Processor (BSP). The BSP is the logical processor responsible for system topology discovery and configuration, and for booting the OS. The manner in which the BSP is selected is processor design-specific.

- **FSB-based systems**. A description of the BSP selection method used in systems wherein the processor(s) communicate with each other and with the chipset via the Front-Side Bus (FSB) external interface can be found in "Boot Strap Processor (BSP) Selection" on page 1378.

- **Intel QPI-based systems**. Systems wherein the processor(s) communicate with each other and with the system via the Intel QuickPath Interconnect (QPI) utilize a different methodology. Immediately after reset removal and before initiating code fetches from the boot ROM, each of the physical processors must first execute the internal microcode responsible for:
  - Configuring their integrated memory controllers and transaction routing devices. This includes determination of the path to the chipset, the boot ROM, and to the remainder of the system.
  - Determining the number of logical processors present and configuration of the QPI paths that permit them to communicate with each other.
  - Selection of the logical processor that will play the role of the BSP.

  Intel has not yet officially released a detailed description of this process, but Intel Press has released (in Q3/2009) a book entitled *Weaving High Performance Multiprocessor Fabric* that provides a basic description.

AP Discovery and Configuration

The logical processors other than the one chosen as the BSP are referred to as Application Processors (APs). They remain in the halted, low-power state while the BSP begins to fetch and execute the boot ROM code responsible for system topology discovery and configuration, and for booting the OS. Among the BSP's responsibilities is the discovery and initial configuration of the APs. The boot ROM code accomplishes this by loading a configuration program in memory and then instructing its Local APIC to transmit a special message containing the program's start address to the Local APICs associated with all of the APs in the system. Receipt of this special message—referred to as the Startup Inter-Processor Interrupt (SIPI) message—causes all of the APs to exit the halt state and begin execution of the configuration program placed in memory by the boot ROM code. A detailed description of this process can be found in "How the APs are Discovered and Configured" on page 1381.

Initial Memory Reads

x86 processors always begin operation in Real Mode in which memory addresses are formed by adding the 20-bit segment base address specified in a 16-bit segment register ("Real Mode Memory Addressing" on page 288 explains how a 20-bit address is specified in a 16-bit segment register) to the 16-bit offset that is specified by:

- The 16-bit IP (Instruction Pointer) register when the logical processor is forming the memory address for a code fetch.

- The 16-bit SP (Stack Pointer) register when the logical processor is forming the memory address for a write into or a read from stack memory.
- The instruction when the logical processor is forming the memory address for a data access.

Since the offset is a 16-bit value, all segments are restricted to a length of 64KB.

After reset is deasserted, the CS register contains a segment start value of F000h and the EIP register contains an offset of 0000FFF0h. It would seem that the first instruction would therefore be fetched from memory location 000FFFF0h (i.e., base address F0000h + offset FFF0h = FFFF0h, or 1MB - 16). Immediately following power-up, however, the logical processor forms the memory addresses for the initial memory instruction reads differently than it does during normal Real Mode operation. The segment base address = FFFF0000h, rather than F0000h. When the EIP offset of 0000FFF0h is added to the segment base address, the result is therefore FFFFFFF0h (4GB - 1). This is the address that the logical processor uses in the initial memory instruction read transaction. The addresses for memory instruction reads continues to be formed in this manner until the programmer loads any value into the CS register (even if it's F000h, the same value that it already contains)—in other words, until a far jump (or a far call) instruction is executed. Very typically, the first instruction found at the power-on restart address (address FFFFFFF0h) *is* a far jump to the start of the system's Power-On Self-Test (POST) program in ROM. The 16-bit value loaded into the CS register is extended to the 20-bit base address of the code segment (the 16-bits from the CS register is extended to 20-bits by adding four bits of zero to the lower end of the 16-bit value). From this point forward until software switches the logical processor into Protected Mode, addresses are formed normally and accesses are therefore restricted to the first megabyte of physical memory address space. It should be noted, however, that while remaining in Real Mode it *is* possible to access extended memory—i.e., memory above the first megabyte—in two ways (see "Accessing Extended Memory in Real Mode" on page 307 and "Big Real Mode" on page 310).

Part 2:
IA-32 Mode

The Previous Part

Part 1 is intended as a back-drop to the detailed discussions that follow.

This Part

Part 2 provides a detailed description of two IA-32 Mode submodes—Real Mode and Protected Mode—and consists of the following chapters:

The Next Part

"Part 3: IA-32e OS Kernel Environment" on page 911 provides a detailed description of the IA-32e OS kernel environment.

5 *Intro to the IA-32 Ecosystem*

The Previous Chapter

The previous chapter defined the state of a logical processor immediately after the removal of reset and introduced the concept of a soft reset (also referred to as an INIT). It also described the initial code fetches performed by the BootStrap Processor and introduced the methodology utilized by software to discover and configure all of the logical processors in the system.

This Chapter

This chapter provides a very basic introduction to the various facilities that support the IA-32 computing environment. These facilities include:

- Pre-386 Register Sets (this section is provided for historical background).
- IA-32 Register Set Overview.
- Control Registers.
- Status/Control Register (Eflags).
- Instruction Fetch Facilities.
- General Purpose Data Registers.
- Defining Memory Regions/Characteristics.
- Interrupt/Exception Facilities.
- Kernel Facilities.
- Address Translation Facilities.
- Legacy FP Facilities.
- MMX Facilities.
- SSE Facilities.
- Model-Specific Registers.
- Debug Facilities.
- Automatic Task Switching Mechanism.

The Next Chapter

The next chapter highlights the dramatic expansion of the x86 instruction set since the advent of the 386 by listing both the 386 instruction set as well as the current-day instruction set.

The Pre-386 Register Sets

This section provides a little background regarding the baseline register set that was a precursor to the expanded register set found in today's x86 processors. Basic descriptions of these registers are included in this chapter.

8086 Register Set

The 8086 register set (see Figure 5-1 on page 80) consisted of the following registers:

- Eight General Purpose Registers (GPRs). See Figure 5-2 on page 81.
- Flags register. See Figure 5-3 on page 81.
- Four Segment registers.
- Instruction Pointer (IP) register.

Figure 5-1: 8086 Register Set

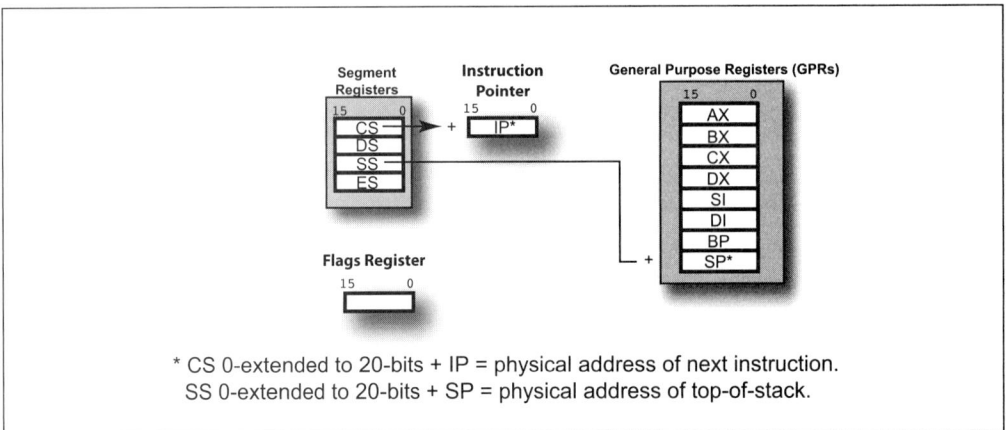

* CS 0-extended to 20-bits + IP = physical address of next instruction.
SS 0-extended to 20-bits + SP = physical address of top-of-stack.

Figure 5-2: 8086 GPRs

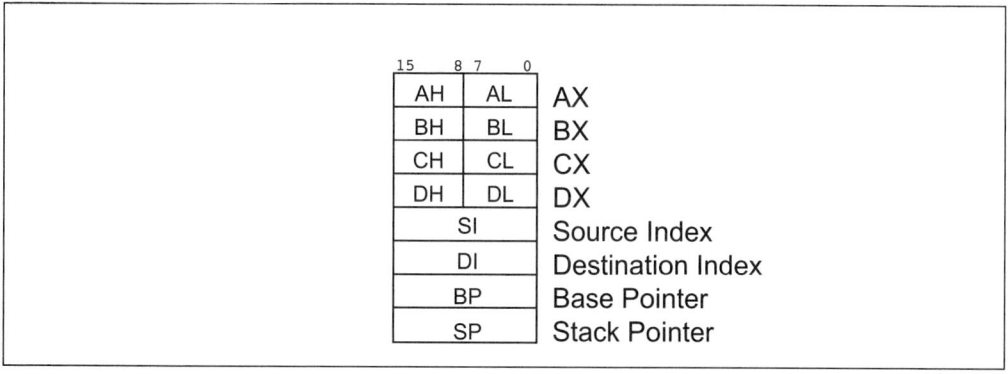

Figure 5-3: 8086 Flag Register

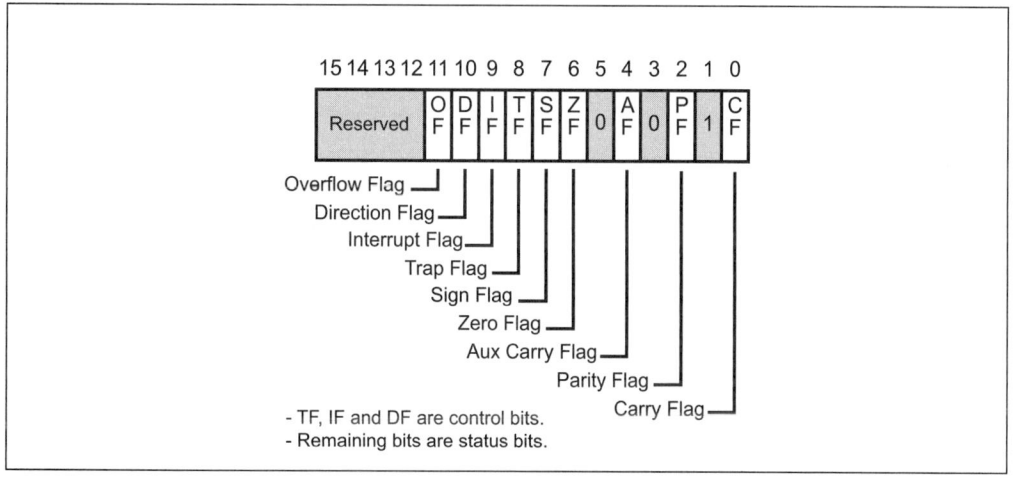

286 Register Set

The 286 added the following registers (see Figure 5-4 on page 82):

- Machine Status Word (MSW) register. See Figure 5-5 on page 83.
- Kernel-related registers:
  — Task Register (TR).
  — Interrupt Descriptor Table Register (IDTR).
  — Global Descriptor Table Register (GDTR).
  — Local Descriptor Table Register (LDTR).

It also added two additional bit fields (Nested Task and IO Privilege Level) to the Flags register (see Figure 5-6 on page 83).

Figure 5-4: 286 Register Set

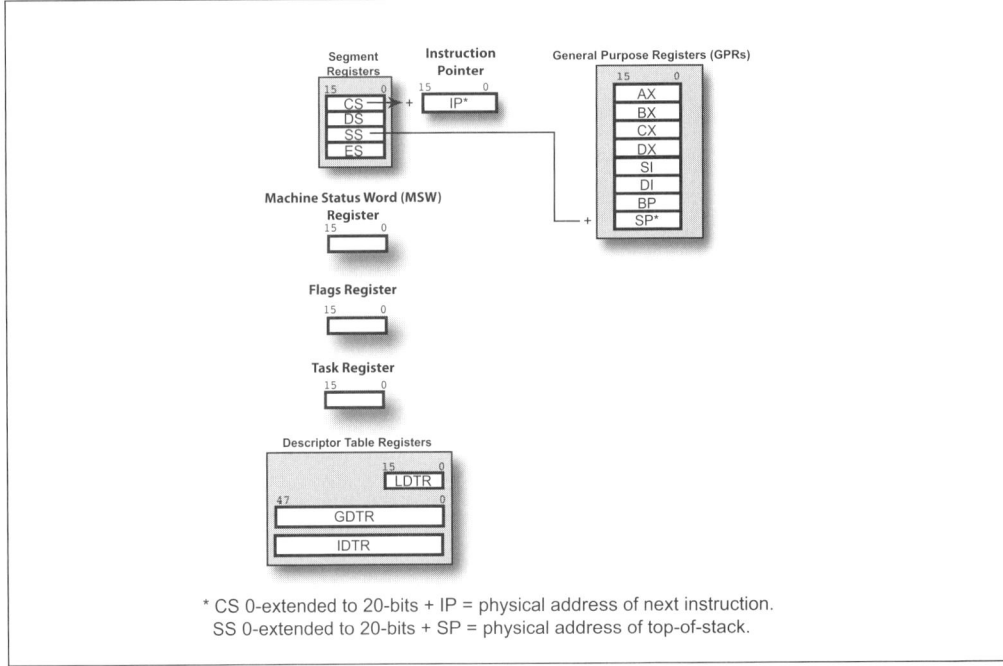

* CS 0-extended to 20-bits + IP = physical address of next instruction.
SS 0-extended to 20-bits + SP = physical address of top-of-stack.

Figure 5-5: 286 Machine Status Word Register (MSW)

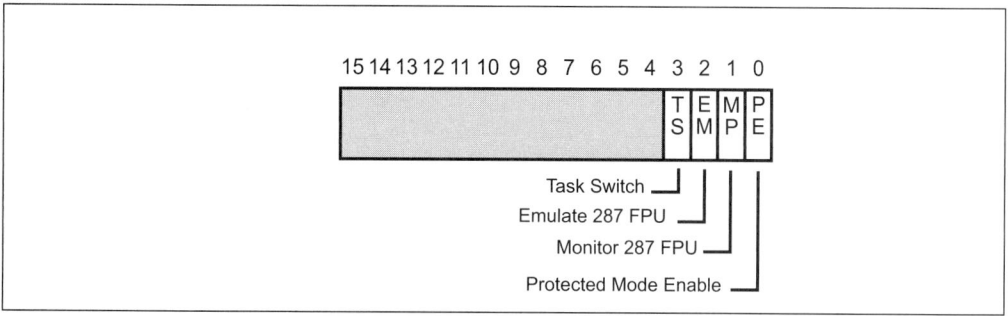

Figure 5-6: 286 Flags Register

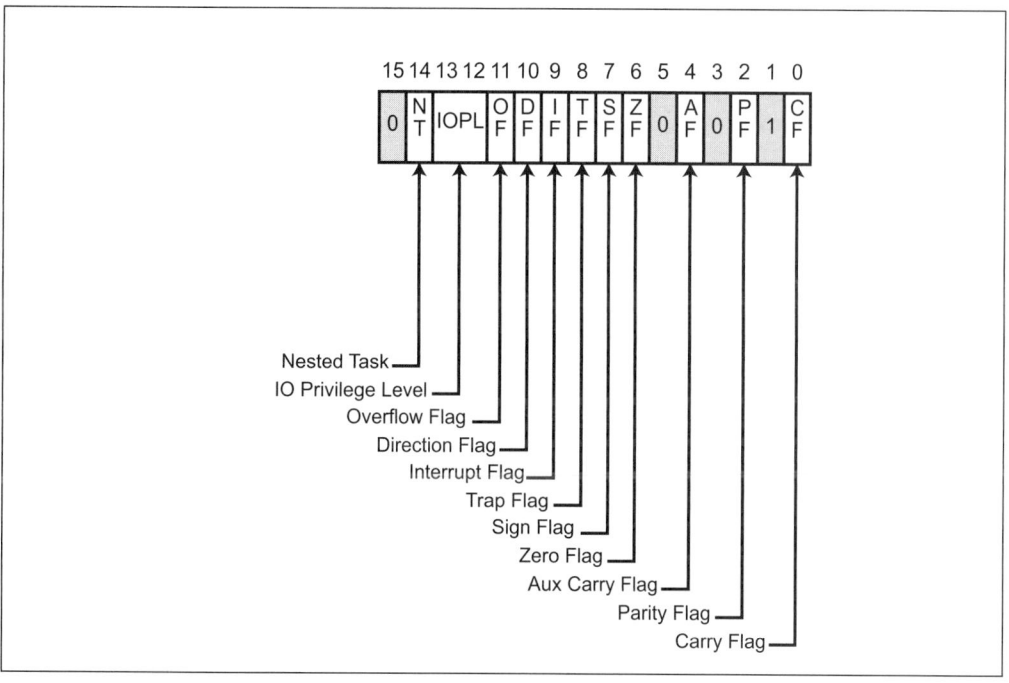

IA-32 Register Set Overview

Figure 5-7 on page 85 illustrates the 32-bit register set visible to the programmer when the logical processor is in one of the following modes (note: not all registers may be accessible in each of the listed modes):

- Real Mode.
- Protected Mode.
- System Management Mode.
- VM86 Mode.
- IA-32e Compatibility Mode.

A brief description of each block of registers can be found in this chapter. An introduction to the expanded register set available when the logical processor is operating in 64-bit Mode may be found in "64-bit Register Overview" on page 1023.

Figure 5-7: IA-32 Register Set

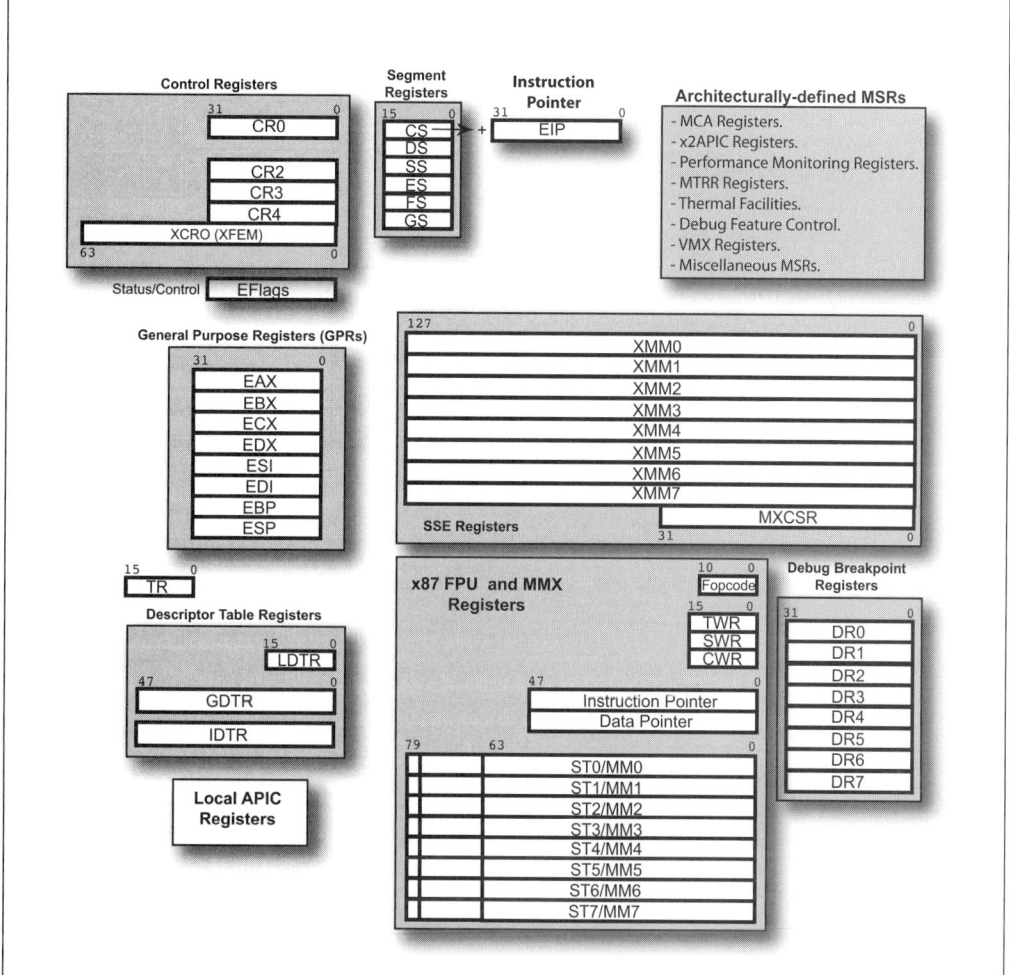

Control Registers

Contrary to the name, some Control Registers are not necessarily used to control various aspects of logical processor operation. Detailed descriptions of the Control Registers can be found in "Control Registers" on page 237:

- **CR0**. See Figure 5-8 on page 86. Controls a number of logical processor functions including enabling/disabling Protected Mode and virtual-to-physical address translation (i.e., Paging). *Not accessible in VM86 Mode.*
- **CR2**. When the logical processor fails to successfully translate a virtual address to a physical address, the offending virtual address is latched into this register and a Page Fault exception is generated. The exception handler obtains the virtual address from CR2, determines the nature of the problem, attempts to fix it and, if successful, retries the memory access. *Accessible in Protected Mode.*
- **CR3**. See Figure 5-9 on page 87. When the OS starts or resumes the execution of a task, it programs CR3 with the start physical memory address of the task's top-level address translation table. *Not accessible in Real Mode or SMM. Accessible in Protected Mode.*
- **CR4**. See Figure 5-10 on page 87. The author thinks of this as the New Feature Control Register as it contains a number of bits that the OS uses to enable/disable various logical processor features. *Not accessible in VM86 Mode.*
- **CR1 and CR5 - CR7**. Reserved for possible future expansion.

Figure 5-8: CR0

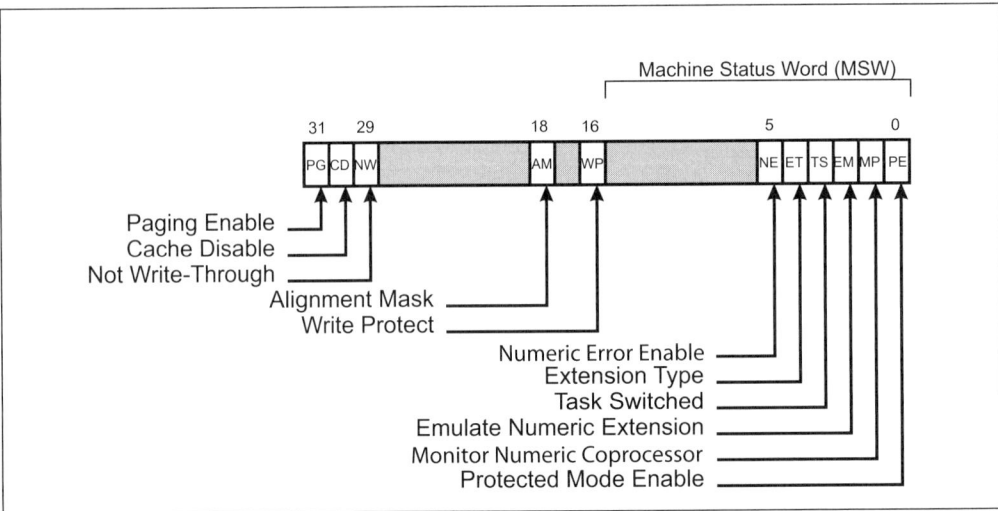

Figure 5-9: CR3

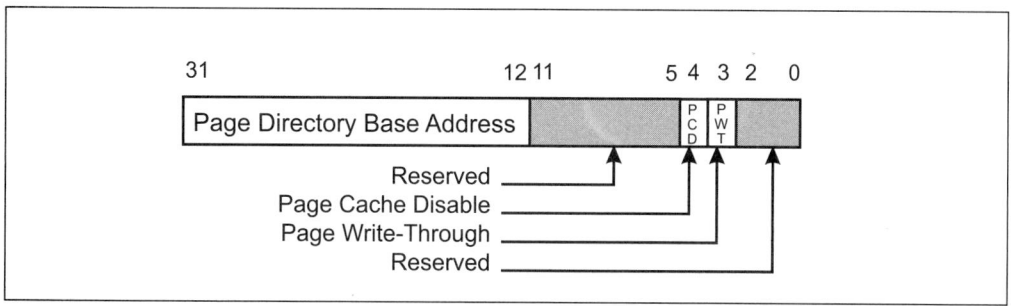

Figure 5-10: CR4

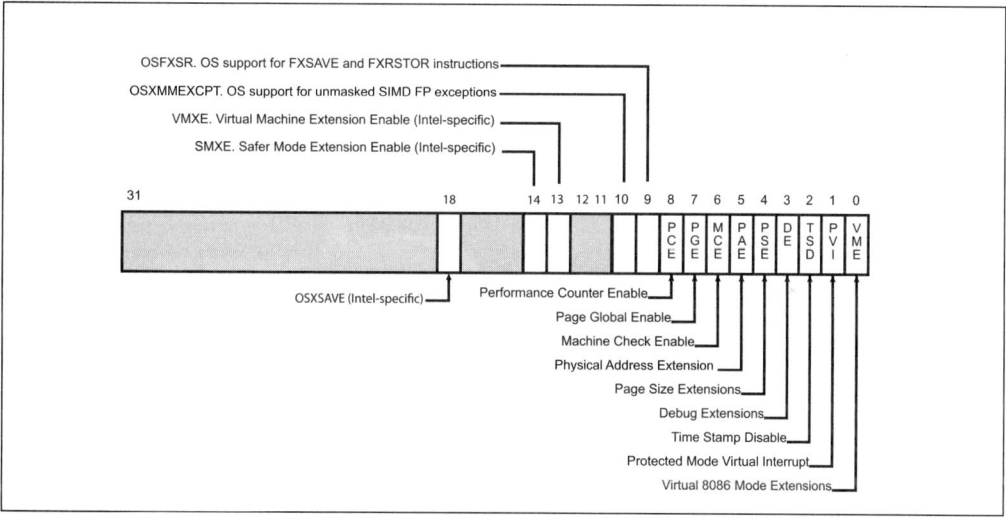

Status/Control Register (Eflags)

Accessible in: all modes.

The flags register contains two types of bit fields:

- **Status bits** that indicate the result of the previously-executed instruction.
- **Control bits**. Bits that control certain aspects of logical processor operation (e.g., the Interrupt Flag bit—IF—controls whether or not the logical processor recognizes maskable hardware interrupts).

The width of the flags register is determined by whether the logical processor is currently operating with an operand size of 16- or 32-bits:

- If the logical processor's current operand size is 16-bits, the flags register is backward-compatible with the 286 Flags register and is 16-bits in width (see Figure 5-6 on page 83).
- If the logical processor's current operand size is 32-bits, the flags register is referred to as the Eflags register and is 32-bits in width (see Figure 5-11 on page 88).

A detailed description of the Eflags register can be found in "Flags Register" on page 251.

Figure 5-11: 32-bit Eflags Register

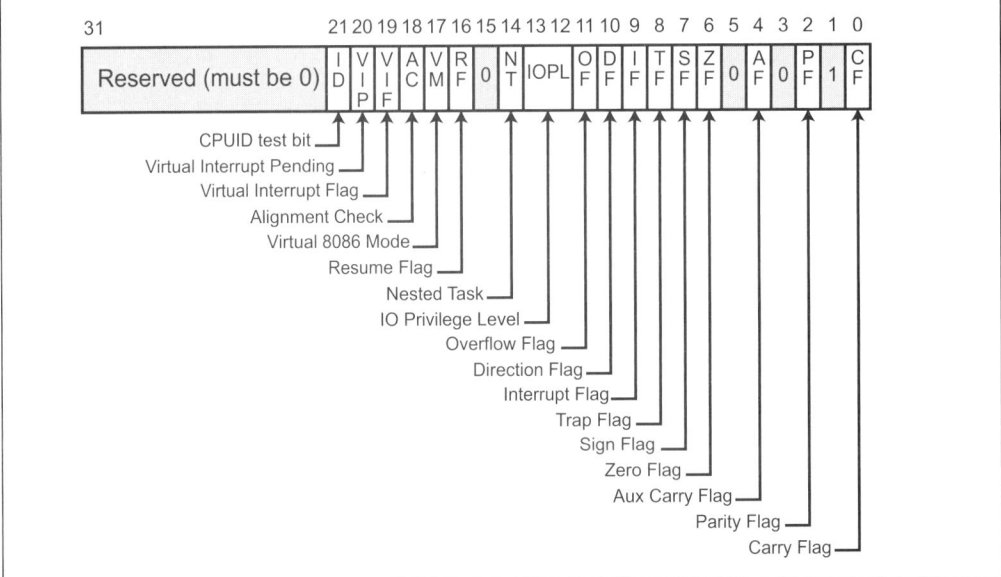

Instruction Fetch Facilities

Used in: all modes.

General

The logical processor's instruction fetch logic fetches the next instruction of the currently-executing program from the address formed by adding the contents of the Instruction Pointer register to the base address of the code segment pointed to by the CS register.

- **In-line code fetching**. If the currently-executing instruction does not cause a branch to a different location in the same or a different code segment, then the Instruction Pointer register is auto-incremented to point to the start address of the next sequential instruction.
- **Branching**. When, on the other hand, the currently-executing instruction does cause a branch to a different location, there are two possible cases:
  — **Case1**. If the branch is to a location in the same code segment, then the branch target address is loaded into the Instruction Pointer register and code fetching resumes at the new address (in the same code segment).
  — **Case 2**. If the branch is to a location in a different code segment, then the segment portion of the branch target address is loaded into the CS register and the offset portion is loaded into the Instruction Pointer register and code fetching resumes at the new address (in the new code segment).

The effective width of the Instruction Pointer register is determined by whether the logical processor is currently operating with an operand size of 16- or 32-bits:

- If the logical processor's current operand size is 16-bits (because it is executing code from a 286 style 16-bit code segment), the Instruction Pointer register (the IP register) is 16-bits in width (see Figure 5-4 on page 82).
- If the logical processor's current operand size is 32-bits (because it is executing code from a 386 style 32-bit code segment), the Instruction Pointer register (the EIP register) is 32-bits in width (see Figure 5-7 on page 85).

Branch Prediction Logic

The Pentium was the first x86 processor to include branch prediction logic. This consisted of the Branch Target Buffer, or BTB, a special, high speed look-aside cache that maintained history on the execution of branch instructions. Whenever a branch instruction entered the processor's instruction pipeline, the BTB used the memory address the branch was fetched from to perform a lookup:

- A BTB miss meant that the processor had no history on the branch. As a result, it would not predict the branch as taken and would continue fetching instructions sequentially.
- A BTB hit indicated that the BTB had seen the branch executed one or more times in the past and, each time, had recorded whether the branch was taken or not. The processor would therefore use the BTB history to predict whether or not the branch would be taken or not when it was executed later in the instruction pipeline:
  — If the branch was predicted as not taken, the processor would continue fetching instructions sequentially
  — If the branch was predicted to be taken, any instruction already in the pipeline that came after the branch instruction were flushed and the code fetcher would be instructed to start fetching instructions from the predicted branch target address.

All subsequent x86 processor implement BTBs.

General Purpose Data Registers

Accessible in: all modes.

See Figure 5-12 on page 91. In IA-32 Mode, eight 32-bit GPR data registers are available for use. Although any of them can be used as general purpose data registers, their typical usage is outlined below:

- **A, B, C and D registers**. General purpose data registers. Each of these registers may be addressed as a 32-bit register (e.g., EAX), a 16-bit register (e.g., AX), or an 8-bit register (e.g., AL or AH).
- **Index registers**. In concert with the C register, the Source Index and Destination Index registers can be used to automate operations that act on blocks of information in memory. Depending on the operand size used by the current instruction, these registers may be addressed as either 16- or 32-bit registers (SI or ESI; DI or EDI).

- **Base Pointer register.** Before making a procedure call, the caller typically pushes one or more parameters onto the stack. In many structured languages (e.g., C, or C++), the contents of the Stack Pointer register is then typically copied into the BP register before the call is made. The called procedure can then access the parameters in stack memory as if it were a data structure starting at the address in the BP register. Depending on the operand size used by the current instruction, this register may be addressed as either 16- or 32-bit register (BP or EBP).
- **Stack Pointer register.** The Stack Segment (SS) register contains the base address of stack memory while the offset in the Stack Pointer register points to the current top-of-stack (TOS). Depending on the operand size used by the current instruction, this register may be addressed as either a 16- or 32-bit register (SP or ESP).

It must be stressed that a number of these registers have special functions when used in concert with certain instructions; it should also be stressed that the contents of the BX, BP, SI and DI registers are frequently used as components in calculating the address of a memory-based operand. The A, B, C, and D registers can also be used as components in calculating the address of a memory-based operand.

A detailed discussion of the GPRs can be found in "General Purpose Registers (GPRs)" on page 255.

Figure 5-12: IA-32 GPRs

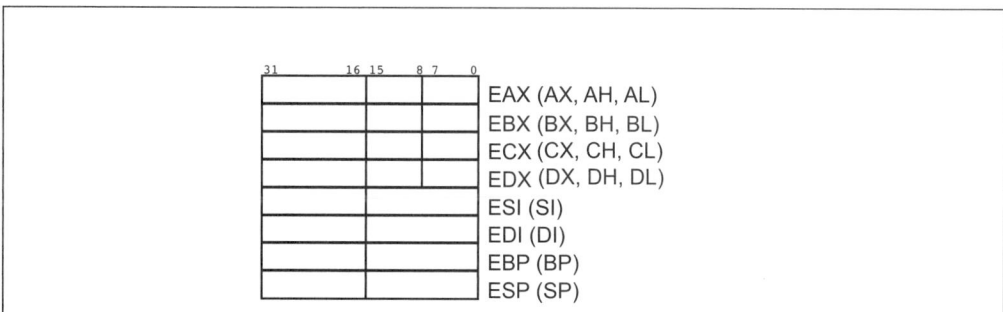

Defining Memory Regions/Characteristics

Two sets of registers are used to define the various regions of memory associated with the currently-executing program and the characteristics of each.

MTRRs

Accessible in: all modes.

The Memory Type and Range Registers (MTRRs) permit the programmer to define the cacheability and other characteristics of a block of memory space. These registers are implemented as Model-Specific Registers (MSRs) and are accessed using the RDMSR and WRMSR instructions. A detailed description of the MTRRs may be found in "Memory Type Configuration" on page 599.

Segment Registers

Accessible in: all modes.

The six segment registers are used to define a number of characteristics related to the various regions of memory associated with the currently-executing program:

- **CS register**. In Real Mode, VM86 Mode and SM Mode, the CS register defines the 16-byte aligned base address of the 64KB area of memory (in the first MB of memory space) that contains the currently-executing program. In Protected Mode, it defines the following characteristics of the area of memory that contains the currently-executing program:
  — Base address anywhere in a 4GB address space.
  — Size (from 1-byte to 4GB).
  — Whether the code segment contains 286-style 16-bit code or 32-bit code.
  — Privilege level of the program.
  — Type of code segment (Conforming or Non-Conforming).
  — Whether or not the code segment has been accessed.
  — Whether or not the code segment contains read-only data as well as code.
- **DS register**. In Real Mode, VM86 Mode and SM Mode, the DS register defines the base address of the 64KB area of memory (in the first MB of memory space) that contains the data the currently-executing program acts

upon. In Protected Mode, it defines the following characteristics of the data area:

— Base address anywhere in a 4GB address space.
— Size (from 1-byte to 4GB).
— Minimum privilege level a program must have in order to access the data segment.
— The Read/Writability of the data segment.
— Whether or not the data segment has been accessed.
— If it will be used as stack memory, the type of stack (Expand-Up or Expand-Down).

• **ES, FS, and GS registers**. Allow up to three additional data areas to be specified.

• **SS register**. In Real Mode, VM86 Mode and SM Mode, the SS register defines the base address of the 64KB read/writable data segment (in the first MB of memory space) that will be used as stack memory. In Protected Mode, it defines the following characteristics of the stack area:

— Base address anywhere in a 4GB address space.
— Size (from 1-byte to 4GB).
— Minimum privilege level a program must have in order to access the stack segment.
— Whether the Stack Pointer register is 16- or 32-bits wide.
— Whether or not the stack segment has been accessed.
— If it will be used as stack memory, the type of stack (Expand-Up or Expand-Down).

A detailed description of the segment registers may be found in:

• "Real Mode Memory Addressing" on page 288.
• "Protected Mode Memory Addressing" on page 383.
• "Code, Calls and Privilege Checks" on page 415.
• "Data and Stack Segments" on page 479.

Address Translation Facilities

Refer to "Address Translation Facilities" on page 97.

Interrupt/Exception Facilities

Used in: all modes.

The facilities associated with the handling of interrupts and exceptions are:

- **Interrupt Descriptor Table (IDT)**. A memory-based table containing pointers to up to 256 interrupt and exception event handlers. In Real Mode, sometimes referred to as the Interrupt Vector Table (IVT).
- **Interrupt Descriptor Table Register (IDTR)**. Refer to Figure 5-7 on page 85. Contains the base memory address and size of the IDT.
- **Interrupt Gate and Trap Gate Descriptors**. In Protected Mode, each IDT entry contains a gate that, in turn, contains the start address of an interrupt or exception handler as well as the minimum privilege level a program must have in order to call the handler using a software interrupt instruction.
- **Task Gate Descriptor**. If an interrupt or exception selects an IDT entry containing a Task Gate descriptor, the logical processor's hardware-based task switching mechanism is triggered. The logical processor suspends the interrupted task, switches to and executes the task which will handle the event, and then switches back to the interrupted task. It should be noted that no modern OSs use this mechanism.
- **Local APIC**. An on-die Local Advanced Programmable Interrupt Controller is associated with each logical processor. It handles the prioritization and delivery of interrupts to the logical processor.
- **IO APIC**. Although the IO APIC is external to the logical processor, it is included here for completeness. It receives interrupts from external device adapters and the chipset and routes them to the logical processors in the system. It is typically integrated into the chipset.
- **Eflags[IF], [VIF] and [VIP] bits** (see Figure 5-11 on page 88). These three bits are associated with the handling of maskable hardware interrupts.
- **IRET instruction**. At the conclusion of an interrupt or exception handler, the last instruction executed is the Interrupt Return instruction. The original contents of the CS:EIP register pair is restored from the stack, causing the logical processor to return to the interrupted program.

Complete descriptions related to interrupt and exception handling can be found in:

- "Real Mode Interrupt/Exception Handling" on page 316.
- "Protected Mode Interrupts and Exceptions" on page 681.

Kernel Facilities

Accessible in: Protected Mode. The facilities associated with the OS kernel are:

- Global Descriptor Table (GDT) and the GDT Register (GDTR).
- Local Descriptor Table (LDT) and the LDT Register (LDTR).

- Interrupt Descriptor Table (IDT) and the IDT Register (IDTR).
- Task State Segment (TSS) and the Task Register (TR).

Detailed descriptions of memory protection in Protected Mode may be found in:

- "Protected Mode Memory Addressing" on page 383.
- "Code, Calls and Privilege Checks" on page 415.
- "Data and Stack Segments" on page 479.

Real Mode Has No Memory Protection

The Real Mode execution environment was designed to run a single task at a time from start to completion. Because this is true, no mechanism is provided to prevent the currently-running task from accessing areas of memory that don't belong to it. As long as it doesn't corrupt itself or the single-task OS (e.g., DOS), no harm is done.

Memory Protection in Protected Mode

Introduction

Unlike the single-task environment, in any given period of time a multitasking OS permits the currently active task to run while one or more suspended tasks are also resident in memory. There must be a method to prevent the currently-running program from touching areas of memory that do not belong to it. The segment registers provide such protection.

Segment Selection in Protected Mode

When any of the six segment registers (see Figure 5-7 on page 85) are loaded with a 16-bit value:

- In Real Mode, it is treated as the upper 16-bits of the segment's 20-bit base address.
- In Protected Mode, it is treated as a selector. Selecting what, you may ask?

The 16-bit segment selector selects an entry in a segment descriptor table created by the OS kernel in memory. The logical processor reads the selected 8-byte entry into the invisible portion of the segment register. From that point forward until and if another selector is loaded into the segment register, whenever the currently-running program attempts an access within the respective segment of memory, the logical processor has rapid access to the following information:

- Base address.
- Size.
- Minimum privilege level a program must have in order to access the segment.
- The Read/Writability of the segment.

Access Rights Check

Before the currently-running program is permitted to access the respective segment of memory, the logical processor checks the following:

- Whether or not the currently-running program has sufficient privilege to access the segment of memory.
- Whether or not the location being accessed falls within the bounds of the segment of memory.
- If the currently-running program is attempting a write, whether or not writes are permitted within the segment of memory.

If it fails any of these checks, a software exception is generated and the OS kernel is called to handle the error.

The Descriptor Tables

There are two types of memory descriptor tables:

- **Global Descriptor Table, or GDT**. Generally speaking, the entries in this table describe segments of memory that are globally accessible by multiple tasks.
- **Local Descriptor Table, or LDT**. Generally speaking, the entries in this table describe segments of memory that are locally-accessible by the current task.

Descriptor Table Registers

It should be fairly obvious that when a 16-bit selector is loaded into any of the six segment registers it must specify two things:

- Which descriptor table to access (the GDT or the LDT).
- Which entry is to be read from the selected table.

It should also be obvious that in order to access the selected table, the logical processor must know the selected table's base memory address. Perhaps not so obvious, it must also know the length of the selected table in order to verify that the selected entry is, in fact, within the bounds of the table. These two items of information are provided to the logical processor by (refer to Figure 5-7 on page 85) the GDT Register (GDTR) and the LDT Register (LDTR) which are programmed by the OS kernel.

Task Data Structure

A multitasking OS associates each task with a task-specific data structure in memory that contains information about that task. The x86 architects intended that this role would be fulfilled by the Task State Segment (TSS) data structure. Whenever a task was started or resumed by the OS kernel's task scheduler, the Task Register (TR; see Figure 5-7 on page 85) would be programmed with a 16-bit selector that would select a special GDT entry containing a TSS descriptor that defined the base address and size of the task's associated TSS data structure. In reality, though, although modern OSs *do* use some of the TSS's functionality, it is *not* used as the Task Data Structure:

- Detailed descriptions of the Task Register (TR) and the originally intended usage of the TSS may be found in "Task Switching" on page 629.
- The manner in which the TSS is actually used by most modern OSs is covered in "Real World TSS Usage" on page 968.

Address Translation Facilities

Accessible in: Protected Mode.

A detailed description of virtual-to-physical address translation may be found in "IA-32 Address Translation Mechanisms" on page 493.

Effective/Virtual/Linear/Physical Addresses

Some very important terms:

- **Effective address = offset**. The Effective Address is defined as the 16-bit (if the logical processor is operating in Real Mode, 286 Protected Mode, VM86 Mode, or SM Mode) or 32-bit (if it is operating in 386 Protected Mode) offset portion of the address that selects a location within a code, data or stack segment.

- **Linear/Virtual address = segment base + offset**. When virtual-to-physical address translation is enabled, the address produced when the offset is added to the segment base address is referred to either as the virtual or linear memory address. Throughout the remainder of this book, the author has standardized on the term *virtual address*.
- In Real Mode, VM86 Mode and SM Mode, the effective address and the **physical memory address** are one and the same.
- In 386 Protected Mode, the virtual address is an intermediate address that must be translated into the physical memory address that has been associated with it by the OS kernel's memory manager. The **virtual-to-physical address translation services (i.e., the Paging logic)** uses the virtual address to perform a lookup in the Paging tables associated with the currently running task. The Page Table Entry (PTE) selected by the virtual address is used by the hardware to translate the virtual address into the physical memory address that is actually used to address memory.

Introduction to Address Translation (Paging)

Address translation is not supported in Real Mode, VM86 Mode, or SM Mode. It may or may not be used in Protected Mode (virtually all modern OSs use it), and it is required in IA-32e Mode.

RAM Is Finite and Can't Hold Everything

One of the most important tasks handled by the OS kernel is memory management. Any computer system obviously has a finite amount of RAM memory which invariably is insufficient to hold the entire OS (which is typically huge), let alone a series of application programs. At a given moment in time, system RAM contains:

- The **OS kernel**. In other words, the OS code that is most frequently utilized and should therefore be loaded from disk (which is slow) into RAM (which is significantly faster) at initialization time and *pinned* in memory (i.e., it should remain RAM-resident and not be swapped out to disk for the remainder of the power-up session). The remaining OS code remains on disk and is only read into RAM on demand (i.e., when it's needed).
- When the end-user requests the initiation of an application program, the OS kernel loads the **application's startup code** into RAM. The remainder of the application's code remains on disk and is only read into RAM on demand (i.e., when it's needed).
- The **data** associated with the applications currently in play.

- **Device drivers**. During the OS initialization process, the OS startup code determines what devices are currently installed in the system and loads the appropriate device drivers into RAM.

RAM and Mass Storage Are Managed on a Page Basis

The OS memory manager is responsible for tracking and efficiently managing RAM usage. RAM is managed as a series of fixed-length pages, each 4KB in size (in some few cases, special large memory buffers may be set up as 2MB or 4MB pages, but the majority of RAM is managed as 4KB pages). The OS views mass storage devices (e.g., disk drives) as a significantly larger but slower extension of its local memory (i.e., RAM) and, for consistency and simplicity, also typically manages the information on them in blocks (pages) of 4KB each.

This Requires a Series of Directories

It stands to reason that the OS memory manager must maintain directories indicating:

- The pages of RAM currently in use by applications as well as which applications they belong to.
- The pages of RAM currently in use by the OS kernel.
- The pages of RAM currently in use by other OS facilities (those that aren't part of the kernel and therefore aren't kept in RAM all the time).
- The pages of RAM that are currently free.
- The location of code and data pages on mass storage belonging to each application.
- The mass storage location of code (and, possibly, data) pages belonging to OS facilities that aren't part of the kernel and which are only loaded into RAM on demand (i.e., when they are needed).

Malloc Request

When an application requires the allocation of additional memory for some reason, it issues a request to *malloc* (the OS kernel's memory allocation manager). In response, malloc takes the following steps:

1. It examines its RAM page directories to locate a sufficient number of 4KB pages to fulfill the request. At a given moment in time, it is highly likely that these pages may not occupy a single, contiguous physical memory address range.
   — It should also be noted that, if the system has been running for a while, malloc may not be able to locate a sufficient number of free pages to ful-

fill the request. In that case, malloc must identify pages of information (code or data) that are in memory but haven't been accessed for a while (i.e., the least-recently used pages) and must reassign these pages to the requesting application. If any of these pages have been updated (i.e., written to) by their previous owner, before being reallocated they must be flushed back to disk so the changes are not lost.

2. The pages being allocated to the requester are removed from the free pool and allocated to the requesting application by creating an application-specific directory identifying the pages allocated for the application's use.

3. Malloc returns control to the requesting application.

Problem: Non-Contiguous Memory Allocation

As indicated in the previous section, it is highly-likely that the series of pages allocated to an application will not be contiguous. Rather, they may be highly fragmented and distributed throughout physical memory. How is this problem addressed? Do we hand the application a list of the 4KB-aligned start physical addresses of the various pages that have been set aside for its use? No.

Malloc Returns a Virtual Address to the Application

In fact, the only thing malloc returns to the application is the start address of a contiguous virtual address range (a sequential—or linear—address range; hence the term linear address which equates to virtual address) that it uses to access the requested memory buffer. In other words, the application is shielded from the messiness of the real world. To the application, the range of memory locations set aside for its use appears to be a range of sequential memory addresses. Life is simple. Unknown to the application, each time it generates a virtual memory address associated with a code read, data read (a load), or a data write (a store), that address is submitted to a hardware-based address translation facility (the logical processor's Paging logic) which uses the virtual address to perform a lookup in the set of address translation tables associated with the currently-running program. The Page Table Entry (PTE) selected by the virtual address indicates one of two things:

- **The page is currently present in physical memory**. In this case, the 4KB-aligned start physical address obtained from the selected PTE is substituted for the 4KB-aligned virtual page address and the correct physical RAM location is addressed.

- **The page is not currently in memory**. In this case, the logical processor generates a Page Fault exception causing it to jump to the Page Fault exception handler in the kernel. The handler locates a free page in physical memory, fills in the PTE with its start address, marks the page present and then returns to and re-executes the offending code read, load, or store which now translates correctly.

IA-32 Applications Have a 4GB Virtual Address Space

In IA-32 Protected Mode, instructions that access memory operands generate a 32-bit virtual memory address giving them the ability to access a 4GB virtual address space. The virtual address, in turn, is submitted to the logical processor's Paging logic which translates the address into either a 32- or 36-bit physical memory address (depending on which flavor of paging is supported by the OS kernel's memory manager; more on this later) within a 4GB or 64GB physical memory address space.

As will be seen later, in IA-32e Mode applications generate a 64-bit virtual address which can be translated into a significantly-larger physical memory address space than that available in IA-32 Protected Mode.

Legacy FP Facilities

Accessible in: all modes.

A detailed description of the x87 FPU (Floating-Point Unit) can be found in "Legacy x87 FP Support" on page 339.

In the Beginning, FPU Was External and Optional

The 8086, 8088, and 286 processors were general purpose processors and did not include a floating-point (FP) math execution unit. For those who felt the need for one, system boards typically provided an empty socket into which an FPU (FP Unit) chip could be installed. Once detected by the BIOS software, the Flags register was programmed to inform the logical processor of its presence. There were four flavors of FPU:

- The 8087 FPU was the companion chip for the 8088 and 8086 processors.
- The 80287 FPU was the companion chip for the 286.
- The 80387 FPU was the companion chip for the 386.
- The 80487SX was the companion chip for the 486SX.

It Was Slow...

The external FPU was treated as an IO device. Whenever the x86 processor fetched a FP instruction from memory, it forwarded it—and, if there was one, its memory data operand—to the x87 FPU by performing a series of one or IO writes to the x87. Since the x87 could only handle one instruction at a time, it would then immediately assert its BUSY signal to the x86 processor. Very slow stuff indeed.

486DX Integrated It

Since the advent of the 486DX processor, the x87 FPU has been integrated onto the processor die (sped things up considerably).

x87 Register Set

The x87 register set is shown in Figure 5-7 on page 85.

x87 FP Instruction Set

An x87 FP instruction is distinguished by the first of its two opcode bytes: a value between D8h and DFh. A listing of x87 FP instructions may be found in "X87 FPU INSTRUCTIONS" on page 127 and a detailed description of their structure in "x87 FP Opcodes Inhabit Opcode Mini-Maps" on page 187.

General Purpose Instruction Set

Building upon the earlier instruction sets (see Table 6-1 on page 111), today's processors implement a greatly expanded general purpose instruction set (see Table 6-2 on page 118).

MMX Facilities

Accessible in: all modes.

A detailed description may be found in "The MMX Facilities" on page 835.

Introduction

The MMX register set (see Figure 5-7 on page 85; the eight 64-bit MMX registers are aliased over the lower 64-bits of the x87 FPU's data registers) and the original 47 instructions (see "MMX INSTRUCTIONS" on page 131) were first introduced in the P55C version of the Pentium.

SIMD Programming Model

Refer to Figure 5-13 on page 103. MMX instructions can perform simultaneous operations on multiple bytes, words or dwords packed into 64-bit MMX registers. This is referred to as a **S**ingle **I**nstruction operating on **M**ultiple **D**ata items (SIMD) operation. The programmer can read 64-bits (8-bytes, 4-words, or 2-dwords) into an MMX register using one instruction. In the example illustrated, the programmer has loaded eight bytes packed into MMX register MM0, another eight bytes packed into MMX register MM1, and then executes a PADDB instruction (an add on packed bytes). Loading eight bytes into a register at a time substantially reduces the number of memory accesses that have to be performed. Furthermore, the MMX execution unit has eight independent adders that operate simultaneously on the eight bytes in each of the registers. This results in a dramatic reduction in compute time.

Figure 5-13: MMX SIMD Solution Increases Throughput

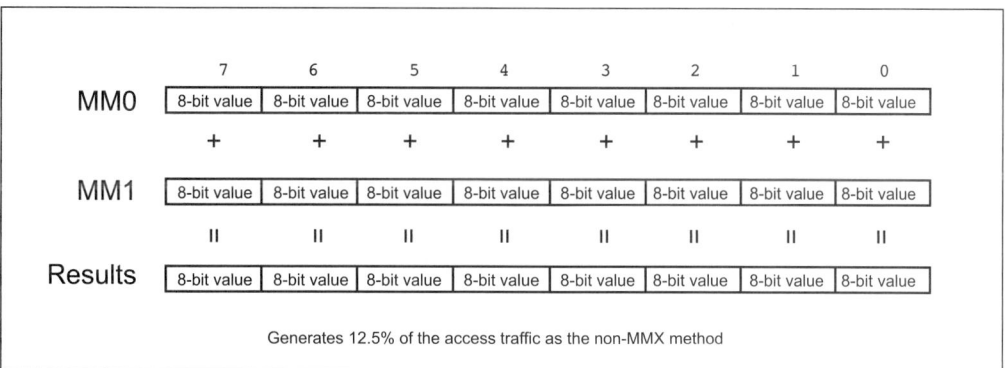

SSE Facilities

Accessible in: all modes.

A detailed description of the Streaming SIMD Extensions (SSE) can be found in "The SSE Facilities" on page 851.

Introduction

The Streaming SIMD Extensions (SSE) were first introduced in the Pentium III (with the addition of the original 70 SSE instructions and the SSE register set) and has been greatly expanded in subsequent x86 processor generations. The implementation of SSE was accomplished by adding the following elements to the processor architecture:

- **Instructions.** 70 new instructions (the SSE1 instruction set) were added to the instruction set.
- **Data registers.** Eight, 128-bit data registers (XMM - XMM7) were added to the architecture (see Figure 5-7 on page 85). Unlike the MMX registers which are aliased over the lower 64-bits of each of the x87 FPU's data registers, the XMM registers are implemented as a separate stand-alone register set.
- **Control/status register.** A control/status register (MXCSR; Figure 5-7 on page 85) which:
  — Controls the generation of SSE FP exceptions (via six FP exception masking bits).
  — Records the status of SSE FP operations (via six FP exception error status bits).
  — Enables/disables two SSE FP performance enhancement modes (FTZ and DAZ modes).
- **Exception.** A new SIMD FP exception (exception 19) was added to report SSE SIMD FP errors to the OS.

Motivation

Application performance enhancement has been steadily addressed over the years by the expanding role of the SIMD programming model utilized by both the MMX and SSE facilities. It would be incorrect, however, to describe the SSE facilities solely as an expansion of MMX's SIMD programming model. While many of the SSE instructions do, in fact, expand on the SIMD programming model, many other non-SIMD instructions were added to address application-specific performance issues.

The single most important motivation behind the implementation of both MMX and SSE was improved performance of multimedia applications.

- While MMX's SIMD capability supported the acceleration of integer-based applications, MMX did not extend the SIMD programming model into the realm of FP-intensive applications.
- SSE1 extended the SIMD model to include support for 32-bit SP FP math operations.
- SSE1 provided new instructions specifically tailored to boost the performance of multimedia applications.
- SSE1 enhanced certain types of memory write operations (i.e., stores) to make more efficient use of external interface bandwidth.

It should be noted that many applications outside the realm of multimedia applications can also realize significant benefit from utilization of the SSE feature set.

Instruction Set

The original 70-member SSE instruction set has steadily grown over the years with the addition of the SSE2 (144 instructions), SSE3 (13 instructions), SSSE3 (32 instructions), SSE4.1 (47 instructions), and SSE 4.2 (7 instructions) instruction sets.

Model-Specific Registers

Accessible in: all modes.

General

The class of registers referred to as Model-Specific Registers first appeared in the original Pentium and, at that time, were truly model-specific in nature. Later however, with the advent of the Pentium 4, a number of these registers—belying their name—were officially added to the ISA specification (their names are preceded by *IA32*) and the number of architecturally-defined MSRs has continued to grow ever since. Many others, however are truly model-specific in nature (their names are not preceded by *IA32*). These registers are used to control a myriad of logical processor features (too numerous to mention here).

Accessing the MSRs

The MSRs are accessed using the RDMSR and WRMSR instructions.

- **RDMSR**. When executed, this instruction loads the contents of the 64-bit MSR specified in ECX (a list of the currently-defined MSRs may be found in Appendix B of the Intel Software Developer's Manual, Volume 3B: System Programming Guide, Part 2) into the EDX:EAX register pair (EDX is loaded with the upper 32 MSR bits, and EAX is loaded with the lower 32-bits). It must be executed at privilege level 0 or in Real Mode (or it will result in the generation of a GP exception).
- **WRMSR**. When executed, this instruction writes the contents of the EDX:EAX register pair into the MSR specified by the MSR address specified in ECX. EDX is written to the upper 32-bits of the MSR and EAX into the lower 32-bits of the MSR. This instruction must be executed at privilege level 0 or in Real Mode (or a GP exception will be generated).

Debug Facilities

Accessible in: all modes.

Starting with the 386, all x86 processors provide hardware address breakpoint detection. This is implemented using the logical processor's Debug registers (see Figure 5-7 on page 85). Some other logical processor functions associated with debug include:

- The Debug exception (Exception 1). This exception is generated when the logical processor encounters a breakpoint address match on a condition specified in the Debug registers.
- The Breakpoint instruction exception (Exception 3). This exception is generated when the logical processor executes the breakpoint (INT3) instruction.
- The Trap bit in a task's TSS. Causes a debug exception when a task switch occurs to a task with this bit (the T bit) set to one.
- The Eflags[RF] bit. When the Resume Flag bit is set to one by the debugger, the subsequent execution of the IRETD instruction prevents the logical processor from generating a debug exception again when it returns to an instruction that already caused a debug exception.
- The Eflags[TF] bit. When the Trap Flag bit is set to one, the logical processor

generates a Debug exception before the execution of each instruction. This permits single-stepping through a program.

Automatic Task Switching Mechanism

Starting with the 386, all x86 processors support a hardware-based automatic task switching mechanism. Unfortunately, due to its inefficiency, no modern OSs use it and, in IA-32e Mode, it is disabled and any attempt to trigger it results in a software exception.

6 *Instruction Set Expansion*

The Previous Chapter

The previous chapter provided a very basic introduction to the various facilities that support the IA-32 computing environment. These facilities include:

- Pre-386 Register Sets (this section is provided for historical background).
- IA-32 Register Set Overview.
- Control Registers.
- Status/Control Register (Eflags).
- Instruction Fetch Facilities.
- General Purpose Data Registers.
- Defining Memory Regions/Characteristics.
- Interrupt/Exception Facilities.
- Kernel Facilities.
- Address Translation Facilities.
- Legacy FP Facilities.
- MMX Facilities.
- SSE Facilities.
- Model-Specific Registers.
- Debug Facilities.
- Automatic Task Switching Mechanism.

This Chapter

This chapter illustrates the expansion of the x86 instruction set since the advent of the 386 by listing both the 386 instruction set as well as the current-day instruction set.

The Next Chapter

The next chapter provides a detailed explanation of the structure of an IA-32 instruction and covers the following topics:

- Effective Operand Size.
- Instruction Composition.
- Instruction Format Basics.
- Opcode (Instruction Identification).
  - In the Beginning.
  - 1-byte Opcodes.
  - 2-byte Opcodes Use 2-Level Lookup.
  - 3-byte Opcodes Use 3-Level Lookup.
  - Opcode Micro-Maps (Groups).
  - x87 FP Opcodes Inhabit Opcode Mini-Maps.
  - Special Opcode Fields.
- Operand Identification.
  - Specifying Registers as Operands.
  - Addressing a Memory-Based Operand.
  - Specifying an Immediate Value As an Operand.
- Instruction Prefixes.
  - Operand Size Override Prefix (66h).
  - Address Size Override Prefix (67h).
  - Lock Prefix.
  - Repeat Prefixes.
  - Segment Override Prefix.
  - Branch Hint Prefix.
- Summary of Instruction Set Formats.

Why a Comprehensive Instruction Set Listing Isn't Included

Since the Intel and AMD x86 instruction set reference guides already do a fine job fulfilling this role, this chapter does not provide a comprehensive description of each instruction in the x86 instruction set. Rather, it is intended as an introduction to the instruction set. To lend historical perspective, it begins with a listing of the entire 386 instruction set (all 128 of them) and then continues with a listing of the current instruction set (well over 400 instructions as of March 2009) sorted by category. It should be stressed that the instruction set is constantly evolving, maintaining backward-compatibility even as successive generations of x86 processors continue to add new instructions—sometimes in small numbers; at other times, with substantial additions to the instruction repertoire (e.g., MMX and SSE).

386 Instruction Set

To lend historical perspective, Table 6-1 on page 111 lists the 386 processor's instruction set organized by category.

Table 6-1: 386 Instruction Set

Instruction	Description
Data Transfer—General Purpose	
MOV	Move operand
PUSH	Push operand onto stack
POP	Pop operand off stack
PUSHA	Push all registers on stack
POPA	Pop all registers off stack
XCHG	Exchange Operand, Register
XLAT	Translate
Data Transfer—Conversion	
MOVZX	Move byte or Word, DW, with zero extension
MOVSX	Move byte or Word, DW, sign extended
CBW	Convert byte to Word, or Word to DW
CWD	Convert Word to DW
CWDE	Convert Word to DW extended
CDQ	Convert DW to QW
Data Transfer—Input/Output	
IN	Input operand from I/O space

Table 6-1: 386 Instruction Set (Continued)

Instruction	Description
OUT	Output operand to I/O space
Data Transfer—Address Object	
LEA	Load effective address
LDS	Load pointer into D segment register
LES	Load pointer into E segment register
LFS	Load pointer into F segment register
LGS	Load pointer into G segment register
LSS	Load pointer into S (Stack) segment register
Data Transfer—Flag Manipulation	
LAHF	Load A register from Flags
SAHF	Store A register in Flags
PUSHF	Push flags onto stack
POPF	Pop flags off stack
PUSHFD	Push Eflags onto stack
POPFD	Pop Eflags off stack
CLC	Clear Carry Flag
CLD	Clear Direction Flag
CMC	Complement Carry Flag
STC	Set Carry Flag
STD	Set Direction Flag
Arithmetic Instructions - Addition	
ADD	Add operands
ADC	Add with carry

Table 6-1: 386 Instruction Set (Continued)

Instruction	Description
INC	Increment operand by 1
AAA	ASCII adjust for addition
DAA	Decimal adjust for addition
Arithmetic Instructions - Subtraction	
SUB	Subtract operands
SBB	Subtract with borrow
DEC	Decrement operand by 1
NEG	Negate operand
CMP	Compare operands
DAS	Decimal adjust for subtraction
AAS	ASCII Adjust for subtraction
Arithmetic Instructions - Multiplication	
MUL	Multiply Double/Single Precision
IMUL	Integer multiply
AAM	ASCII adjust after multiply
Arithmetic Instructions - Division	
DIV	Divide unsigned
IDIV	Integer Divide
AAD	ASCII adjust before division
String Instructions	
MOVS	Move byte or Word, DW string
INS	Input string from I/O space
OUTS	Output string to I/O space

Table 6-1: 386 Instruction Set (Continued)

Instruction	Description
CMPS	Compare byte or Word, DW string
SCAS	Scan Byte or Word, DW string
LODS	Load byte or Word, DW string
STOS	Store byte or Word, DW string
REP	Repeat
REPE/REPZ	Repeat while equal/zero
RENE/REPNZ	Repeat while not equal/not zero
Logical Instructions-Logical Operations	
NOT	``NOT" operands
AND	``AND" operands
OR	``Inclusive OR" operands
XOR	``Exclusive OR" operands
TEST	``Test" operands
Logical Instructions-Shifts	
SHL/SHR	Shift logical left or right
SAL/SAR	Shift arithmetic left or right
SHLD/SHRD	Double shift left or right
Logical Instructions-Rotates	
ROL/ROR	Rotate left/right
RCL/RCR	Rotate through carry left/right
Bit Manipulation Instructions	
BT	Bit Test
BTS	Bit Test and Set

Table 6-1: 386 Instruction Set (Continued)

Instruction	Description
BTR	Bit Test and Reset
BTC	Bit Test and Complement
BSF	Bit Scan Forward
BSR	Bit Scan Reverse
Program Control Instructions-Conditional Transfers	
SETCC	Set byte equal to condition code
JA/JNBE	Jump if above/not below nor equal
JAE/JNB	Jump if above or equal/not below
JB/JNAE	Jump if below/not above nor equal
JBE/JNA	Jump if below or equal/not above
JC	Jump if carry
JE/JZ	JE/JZ Jump if equal/zero
JG/JNLE	Jump if greater/not less nor equal
JGE/JNL	Jump if greater or equal/not less
JL/JNGE	Jump if less/not greater nor equal
JLE/JNG	Jump if less or equal/not greater
JNC	Jump if not carry
JNE/JNZ	Jump if not equal/not zero
JNO	Jump if not overflow
JNP/JPO	Jump if not parity/parity odd
JNS	Jump if not sign
JO	Jump if overflow
JP/JPE	Jump if parity/parity even

Table 6-1: 386 Instruction Set (Continued)

Instruction	Description
JS	Jump if Sign
Program Control Instructions-Unconditional Transfers	
CALL	Call procedure/task
RET	Return from procedure
JMP	Jump
Program Control Instructions-Iteration Controls	
LOOP	Loop
LOOPE/LOOPZ	Loop if equal/zero
LOOPNE/ LOOPNZ	Loop if not equal/not zero
JCXZ	JUMP if register CXe0
Program Control Instructions-Interrupts	
INT	Interrupt
INTO	Interrupt if overflow
IRET	Return from Interrupt/Task
CLI	Clear Interrupt Enable
STI	Set Interrupt Enable
High Level Language Instructions	
BOUND	Check Array Bounds
ENTER	Setup Parameter Block for Entering Procedure
LEAVE	Leave Procedure
Protection Model	
SGDT	Store Global Descriptor Table
SIDT	Store Interrupt Descriptor Table

Table 6-1: 386 Instruction Set (Continued)

Instruction	Description
STR	Store Task Register
SLDT	Store Local Descriptor Table
LGDT	Load Global Descriptor Table
LIDT	Load Interrupt Descriptor Table
LTR	Load Task Register
LLDT	Load Local Descriptor Table
ARPL	Adjust Requested Privilege Level
LAR	Load Access Rights
LSL	Load Segment Limit
VERR/VERW	Verify Segment for Reading or Writing
LMSW	Load Machine Status Word (lower 16 bits of CR0)
SMSW	Store Machine Status Word
Processor Control Instructions	
HLT	Halt
WAIT	Wait until BUSY negated
ESC	Escape
LOCK	Lock Bus

Instruction Set (as of March, 2009)

Table 6-2 on page 118 lists the current-day instruction set organized by category. Keep in mind that future generations of processors will continue to add to the instruction repertoire. The instructions are divided into the following categories:

- General purpose instructions.
- x87 FPU instructions.

- X87 FPU and SIMD state management instructions.
- MMX instructions.
- SSE instructions.
- SSE2 instructions.
- SSE3 instructions.
- SSSE3 instructions.
- SSE4.1 instructions.
- SSE4.2 instructions.
- System instructions.
- 64-bit Mode instructions.
- Virtual Mode Extensions (VMX) instructions.
- Safer Mode Extension (SMX) instruction.

Table 6-2: Current-Day Instruction Set

Instruction	Description
Abbreviations used in this table: • FPU—Floating-Point Unit • FP—Floating-Point • SP—32-bit Single-Precision FP number • DP—64-bit Double-Precision FP number • DW—Doubleword (32-bits) • QW—Quadword (64-bits)	
General Purpose Instructions	
Data Transfer Instructions	
MOV	Move data between general-purpose registers; move data between memory and general-purpose or segment registers; move immediates to general-purpose registers
CMOVE/ CMOVZ	Conditional move if equal/Conditional move if zero
CMOVNE/ CMOVNZ	Conditional move if not equal/Conditional move if not zero
CMOVA/ CMOVNBE	Conditional move if above/Conditional move if not below or equal

Table 6-2: Current-Day Instruction Set (Continued)

Instruction	Description
CMOVAE/ CMOVNB	Conditional move if above or equal/Conditional move if not below
CMOVB/CMOV-NAE	Conditional move if below/Conditional move if not above or equal
CMOVBE/ CMOVNA	Conditional move if below or equal/Conditional move if not above
CMOVG/ CMOVNLE	Conditional move if greater/Conditional move if not less or equal
CMOVGE/ CMOVNL	Conditional move if greater or equal/Conditional move if not less
CMOVL/ CMOVNGE	Conditional move if less/Conditional move if not greater or equal
CMOVLE/ CMOVNG	Conditional move if less or equal/Conditional move if not greater
CMOVC	Conditional move if carry
CMOVNC	Conditional move if not carry
CMOVO	Conditional move if overflow
CMOVNO	Conditional move if not overflow
CMOVS	Conditional move if sign (negative)
CMOVNS	Conditional move if not sign (non-negative)
CMOVP/ CMOVPE	Conditional move if parity/Conditional move if parity even
CMOVNP/ CMOVPO	Conditional move if not parity/Conditional move if parity odd
XCHG	Exchange
BSWAP	Byte swap
XADD	Exchange and add

Table 6-2: Current-Day Instruction Set (Continued)

Instruction	Description
CMPXCHG	Compare and exchange
CMPXCHG8B	Compare and exchange 8 bytes
PUSH	Push onto stack
POP	Pop off of stack
PUSHA/ PUSHAD	Push general-purpose registers onto stack
POPA/POPAD	Pop general-purpose registers from stack
CWD/CDQ	Convert word to DW/Convert DW to QW
CBW/CWDE	Convert byte to word/Convert word to DW in EAX register
MOVSX	Move and sign extend
MOVZX	Move and zero extend
Binary Arithmetic Instructions	
ADD	Integer add
ADC	Add with carry
SUB	Subtract
SBB	Subtract with borrow
IMUL	Signed multiply
MUL	Unsigned multiply
IDIV	Signed divide
DIV	Unsigned divide
INC	Increment
DEC	Decrement
NEG	Negate
CMP	Compare

Table 6-2: Current-Day Instruction Set (Continued)

Instruction	Description
Decimal Arithmetic Instructions	
DAA	Decimal adjust after addition
DAS	Decimal adjust after subtraction
AAA	ASCII adjust after addition
AAS	ASCII adjust after subtraction
AAM	ASCII adjust after multiplication
AAD	ASCII adjust before division
Logical Instructions	
AND	Perform bitwise logical AND
OR	Perform bitwise logical OR
XOR	Perform bitwise logical exclusive OR
NOT	Perform bitwise logical NOT
Shift and Rotate Instructions	
SAR	Shift arithmetic right
SHR	Shift logical right
SAL/SHL	Shift arithmetic left/Shift logical left
SHRD	Shift right double
SHLD	Shift left double
ROR	Rotate right
ROL	Rotate left
RCR	Rotate through carry right
RCL	Rotate through carry left

Table 6-2: Current-Day Instruction Set (Continued)

Instruction	Description
Bit and Byte Instructions	
BT	Bit test
BTS	Bit test and set
BTR	Bit test and reset
BTC	Bit test and complement
BSF	Bit scan forward
BSR	Bit scan reverse
SETE/SETZ	Set byte if equal/Set byte if zero
SETNE/SETNZ	Set byte if not equal/Set byte if not zero
SETA/SETNBE	Set byte if above/Set byte if not below or equal
SETAE/SETNB/ SETNC	Set byte if above or equal/Set byte if not below/Set byte if not carry
SETB/SETNAE/ SETC	Set byte if below/Set byte if not above or equal/Set byte if carry
SETBE/SETNA	Set byte if below or equal/Set byte if not above
SETG/SETNLE	Set byte if greater/Set byte if not less or equal
SETGE/SETNL	Set byte if greater or equal/Set byte if not less
SETL/SETNGE	Set byte if less/Set byte if not greater or equal
SETLE/SETNG	Set byte if less or equal/Set byte if not greater
SETS	Set byte if sign (negative)
SETNS	Set byte if not sign (non-negative)
SETO	Set byte if overflow
SETNO	Set byte if not overflow
SETPE/SETP	Set byte if parity even/Set byte if parity

Table 6-2: Current-Day Instruction Set (Continued)

Instruction	Description
SETPO/SETNP	Set byte if parity odd/Set byte if not parity
TEST	Logical compare
Control Transfer Instructions	
JMP	Jump
JE/JZ	Jump if equal/Jump if zero
JNE/JNZ	Jump if not equal/Jump if not zero
JA/JNBE	Jump if above/Jump if not below or equal
JAE/JNB	Jump if above or equal/Jump if not below
JB/JNAE	Jump if below/Jump if not above or equal
JBE/JNA	Jump if below or equal/Jump if not above
JG/JNLE	Jump if greater/Jump if not less or equal
JGE/JNL	Jump if greater or equal/Jump if not less
JL/JNGE	Jump if less/Jump if not greater or equal
JLE/JNG	Jump if less or equal/Jump if not greater
JC	Jump if carry
JNC	Jump if not carry
JO	Jump if overflow
JNO	Jump if not overflow
JS	Jump if sign (negative)
JNS	Jump if not sign (non-negative)
JPO/JNP	Jump if parity odd/Jump if not parity
JPE/JP	Jump if parity even/Jump if parity
JCXZ/JECXZ	Jump register CX zero/Jump register ECX zero

Table 6-2: Current-Day Instruction Set (Continued)

Instruction	Description
LOOP	Loop with ECX counter
LOOPZ/LOOPE	Loop with ECX and zero/Loop with ECX and equal
LOOPNZ/ LOOPNE	Loop on ECX count not = 0
CALL	Call procedure
RET	Return
IRET	Return from interrupt
INT	Software interrupt
INTO	Interrupt on overflow
BOUND	Detect value out of range
ENTER	High-level procedure entry
LEAVE	High-level procedure exit
String Instructions	
MOVS/MOVSB	Move string/Move byte string
MOVS/MOVSW	Move string/Move word string
MOVS/MOVSD	Move string/Move DW string
CMPS/CMPSB	Compare string/Compare byte string
CMPS/CMPSW	Compare string/Compare word string
CMPS/CMPSD	Compare string/Compare DW string
SCAS/SCASB	Scan string/Scan byte string
SCAS/SCASW	Scan string/Scan word string
SCAS/SCASD	Scan string/Scan DW string
LODS/LODSB	Load string/Load byte string
LODS/LODSW	Load string/Load word string

Table 6-2: Current-Day Instruction Set (Continued)

Instruction	Description
LODS/LODSD	Load string/Load DW string
STOS/STOSB	Store string/Store byte string
STOS/STOSW	Store string/Store word string
STOS/STOSD	Store string/Store DW string
REP instruction prefix	Repeat while ECX not zero
REPE/REPZ instruction prefix	Repeat while equal/Repeat while zero
REPNE/REPNZ instruction prefix	Repeat while not equal/Repeat while not zero
IO Instructions	
IN	Read from a port
OUT	Write to a port
INS/INSB	Input string from port/Input byte string from port
INS/INSW	Input string from port/Input word string from port
INS/INSD	Input string from port/Input DW string from port
OUTS/OUTSB	Output string to port/Output byte string to port
OUTS/OUTSW	Output string to port/Output word string to port
OUTS/OUTSD	Output string to port/Output DW string to port
Enter and Leave Instructions	
ENTER	High-level procedure entry
LEAVE	High-level procedure exit
Flag Control (Eflag) Instructions	
STC	Set carry flag

x86 Instruction Set Architecture

Table 6-2: Current-Day Instruction Set (Continued)

Instruction	Description
CLC	Clear the carry flag
CMC	Complement the carry flag
CLD	Clear the direction flag
STD	Set direction flag
LAHF	Load flags into AH register
SAHF	Store AH register into flags
PUSHF/PUSHFD	Push EFLAGS onto stack
POPF/POPFD	Pop EFLAGS from stack
STI	Set interrupt flag
CLI	Clear the interrupt flag
Segment Register Instructions	
LDS	Load far pointer using DS
LES	Load far pointer using ES
LFS	Load far pointer using FS
LGS	Load far pointer using GS
LSS	Load far pointer using SS
Miscellaneous Instructions	
LEA	Load effective address
NOP	No operation
UD2	Undefined instruction
XLAT/XLATB	Table lookup translation
CPUID	Processor identification
MOVBE	Move data after swapping data bytes

Table 6-2: Current-Day Instruction Set (Continued)

Instruction	Description
X87 FPU INSTRUCTIONS	
x87 FPU Data Transfer Instructions	
FLD	Load FP value
FST	Store FP value
FSTP	Store FP value and pop
FILD	Load integer
FIST	Store integer
FISTP1	Store integer and pop
FBLD	Load BCD
FBSTP	Store BCD and pop
FXCH	Exchange registers
FCMOVE	FP conditional move if equal
FCMOVNE	FP conditional move if not equal
FCMOVB	FP conditional move if below
FCMOVBE	FP conditional move if below or equal
FCMOVNB	FP conditional move if not below
FCMOVNBE	FP conditional move if not below or equal
FCMOVU	FP conditional move if unordered
FCMOVNU	FP conditional move if not unordered
x87 FPU Basic Arithmetic Instructions	
FADD	Add FP
FADDP	Add FP and pop
FIADD	Add integer

Table 6-2: Current-Day Instruction Set (Continued)

Instruction	Description
FSUB	Subtract FP
FSUBP	Subtract FP and pop
FISUB	Subtract integer
FSUBR	Subtract FP reverse
FSUBRP	Subtract FP reverse and pop
FISUBR	Subtract integer reverse
FMUL	Multiply FP
FMULP	Multiply FP and pop
FIMUL	Multiply integer
FDIV	Divide FP
FDIVP	Divide FP and pop
FIDIV	Divide integer
FDIVR	Divide FP reverse
FDIVRP	Divide FP reverse and pop
FIDIVR	Divide integer reverse
FPREM	Partial remainder
FPREM1	IEEE Partial remainder
FABS	Absolute value
FCHS	Change sign
FRNDINT	Round to integer
FSCALE	Scale by power of two
FSQRT	Square root
FXTRACT	Extract exponent and significand

Table 6-2: Current-Day Instruction Set (Continued)

Instruction	Description
x87 FPU Comparison Instructions	
FCOM	Compare FP
FCOMP	Compare FP and pop
FCOMPP	Compare FP and pop twice
FUCOM	Unordered compare FP
FUCOMP	Unordered compare FP and pop
FUCOMPP	Unordered compare FP and pop twice
FICOM	Compare integer
FICOMP	Compare integer and pop
FCOMI	Compare FP and set EFLAGS
FUCOMI	Unordered compare FP and set EFLAGS
FCOMIP	Compare FP, set EFLAGS, and pop
FUCOMIP	Unordered compare FP, set EFLAGS, and pop
FTST	Test FP (compare with 0.0)
FXAM	Examine FP
x87 FPU Transcendental Instructions	
FSIN	Sine
FCOS	Cosine
FSINCOS	Sine and cosine
FPTAN	Partial tangent
FPATAN	Partial arctangent
F2XM1	Compute $2^x - 1$
FYL2X	$y * \log_2 x$

Table 6-2: Current-Day Instruction Set (Continued)

Instruction	Description
FYL2XP1	$y * \log_2(x+1)$
x87 FPU Load Constants Instructions	
FLD1	Push +1.0 onto the FPU register stack.
FLDZ	Push +0.0 onto the FPU register stack.
FLDPI	Push pi onto the FPU register stack.
FLDL2E	Push $\log_2 e$ onto the FPU register stack.
FLDLN2	Push $\log_e 2$ onto the FPU register stack.
FLDL2T	Push $\log_2 10$ onto the FPU register stack.
FLDLG2	Push $\log_{10} 2$ onto the FPU register stack.
x87 FPU Control Instructions	
FINCSTP	Increment FPU register stack pointer
FDECSTP	Decrement FPU register stack pointer
FFREE	Free FP register
FINIT	Initialize FPU after checking error conditions
FNINIT	Initialize FPU without checking error conditions
FCLEX	Clear FP exception flags after checking for error conditions
FNCLEX	Clear FP exception flags without checking for error conditions
FSTCW	Store FPU control word after checking error conditions
FNSTCW	Store FPU control word without checking error conditions
FLDCW	Load FPU control word
FSTENV	Store FPU environment after checking error conditions
FNSTENV	Store FPU environment without checking error conditions
FLDENV	Load FPU environment

Table 6-2: Current-Day Instruction Set (Continued)

Instruction	Description
FSAVE	Save FPU state after checking error conditions
FNSAVE	Save FPU state without checking error conditions
FRSTOR	Restore FPU state
FSTSW	Store FPU status word after checking error conditions
FNSTSW	Store FPU status word without checking error conditions
WAIT/FWAIT	Wait for FPU
FNOP	FPU no operation
X87 FPU AND SIMD STATE MANAGEMENT INSTRUCTIONS	
FXSAVE	Save x87 FPU and SIMD state
FXRSTOR	Restore x87 FPU and SIMD state
MMX INSTRUCTIONS	
MMX Data Transfer Instructions	
MOVD	Move DW
MOVQ	Move QW
MMX Conversion Instructions	
PACKSSWB	Pack words into bytes with signed saturation
PACKSSDW	Pack DWs into words with signed saturation
PACKUSWB	Pack words into bytes with unsigned saturation.
PUNPCKHBW	Unpack high-order bytes
PUNPCKHWD	Unpack high-order words
PUNPCKHDQ	Unpack high-order DWs
PUNPCKLBW	Unpack low-order bytes
PUNPCKLWD	Unpack low-order words

Table 6-2: Current-Day Instruction Set (Continued)

Instruction	Description
PUNPCKLDQ	Unpack low-order DWs
MMX Packed Arithmetic Instructions	
PADDB	Add packed byte integers
PADDW	Add packed word integers
PADDD	Add packed DW integers
PADDSB	Add packed signed byte integers with signed saturation
PADDSW	Add packed signed word integers with signed saturation
PADDUSB	Add packed unsigned byte integers with unsigned saturation
PADDUSW	Add packed unsigned word integers with unsigned saturation
PSUBB	Subtract packed byte integers
PSUBW	Subtract packed word integers
PSUBD	Subtract packed DW integers
PSUBSB	Subtract packed signed byte integers with signed saturation
PSUBSW	Subtract packed signed word integers with signed saturation
PSUBUSB	Subtract packed unsigned byte integers with unsigned saturation
PSUBUSW	Subtract packed unsigned word integers with unsigned saturation
PMULHW	Multiply packed signed word integers and store high result
PMULLW	Multiply packed signed word integers and store low result
PMADDWD	Multiply and add packed word integers
MMX Comparison Instructions	
PCMPEQB	Compare packed bytes for equal
PCMPEQW	Compare packed words for equal

Table 6-2: Current-Day Instruction Set (Continued)

Instruction	Description
PCMPEQD	Compare packed DWs for equal
PCMPGTB	Compare packed signed byte integers for greater than
PCMPGTW	Compare packed signed word integers for greater than
PCMPGTD	Compare packed signed DW integers for greater than
MMX Logical Instructions	
PAND	Bitwise logical AND
PANDN	Bitwise logical AND NOT
POR	Bitwise logical OR
PXOR	Bitwise logical exclusive OR
MMX Shift and Rotate Instructions	
PSLLW	Shift packed words left logical
PSLLD	Shift packed DWs left logical
PSLLQ	Shift packed QW left logical
PSRLW	Shift packed words right logical
PSRLD	Shift packed DWs right logical
PSRLQ	Shift packed QW right logical
PSRAW	Shift packed words right arithmetic
PSRAD	Shift packed DWs right arithmetic
MMX State Management Instructions	
EMMS	Empty MMX state

Table 6-2: Current-Day Instruction Set (Continued)

Instruction	Description
SSE INSTRUCTIONS	
SSE SIMD SP FP Instructions: SSE Data Transfer Instructions	
MOVAPS	Move four aligned packed SP FP values between XMM registers or between and XMM register and memory
MOVUPS	Move four unaligned packed SP FP values between XMM registers or between and XMM register and memory
MOVHPS	Move two packed SP FP values to and from the high QW of an XMM register and memory
MOVHLPS	Move two packed SP FP values from the high QW of an XMM register to the low QW of another XMM register
MOVLPS	Move two packed SP FP values to and from the low QW of an XMM register and memory
MOVLHPS	Move two packed SP FP values from the low QW of an XMM register to the high QW of another XMM register
MOVMSKPS	Extract sign mask from four packed SP floating point values
MOVSS	Move scalar SP FP value between XMM registers or between an XMM register and memory
SSE SIMD SP FP Instructions: SSE Packed Arithmetic Instructions	
ADDPS	Add packed SP FP values
ADDSS	Add scalar SP FP values
SUBPS	Subtract packed SP FP values
SUBSS	Subtract scalar SP FP values
MULPS	Multiply packed SP FP values
MULSS	Multiply scalar SP FP values
DIVPS	Divide packed SP FP values
DIVSS	Divide scalar SP FP values

Table 6-2: Current-Day Instruction Set (Continued)

Instruction	Description
RCPPS	Compute reciprocals of packed SP FP values
RCPSS	Compute reciprocal of scalar SP FP values
SQRTPS	Compute square roots of packed SP FP values
SQRTSS	Compute square root of scalar SP FP values
RSQRTPS	Compute reciprocals of square roots of packed SP FP values
RSQRTSS	Compute reciprocal of square root of scalar SP FP values
MAXPS	Return maximum packed SP FP values
MAXSS	Return maximum scalar SP FP values
MINPS	Return minimum packed SP FP values
MINSS	Return minimum scalar SP FP values
SSE SIMD SP FP Instructions: SSE Comparison Instructions	
CMPPS	Compare packed SP FP values
CMPSS	Compare scalar SP FP values
COMISS	Perform ordered comparison of scalar SP FP values and set flags in EFLAGS register
UCOMISS	Perform unordered comparison of scalar SP FP values and set flags in EFLAGS register
SSE SIMD SP FP Instructions: SSE Logical Instructions	
ANDPS	Perform bitwise logical AND of packed SP FP values
ANDNPS	Perform bitwise logical AND NOT of packed SP FP values
ORPS	Perform bitwise logical OR of packed SP FP values
XORPS	Perform bitwise logical XOR of packed SP FP values
SSE SIMD SP FP Instructions: SSE Shuffle and Unpack Instructions	
SHUFPS	Shuffles values in packed SP FP operands

Table 6-2: Current-Day Instruction Set (Continued)

Instruction	Description
UNPCKHPS	Unpacks and interleaves the two high-order values from two SP FP operands
UNPCKLPS	Unpacks and interleaves the two low-order values from two SP FP operands
SSE SIMD SP FP Instructions: SSE Conversion Instructions	
CVTPI2PS	Convert packed DW integers to packed SP FP values
CVTSI2SS	Convert DW integer to scalar SP FP value
CVTPS2PI	Convert packed SP FP values to packed DW integers
CVTTPS2PI	Convert with truncation packed SP FP values to packed DW integers
CVTSS2SI	Convert a scalar SP FP value to a DW integer
CVTTSS2SI	Convert with truncation a scalar SP FP value to a scalar DW integer
SSE MXCSR State Management Instructions	
LDMXCSR	Load MXCSR register
STMXCSR	Save MXCSR register state
SSE 64-Bit SIMD Integer Instructions	
PAVGB	Compute average of packed unsigned byte integers
PAVGW	Compute average of packed unsigned word integers
PEXTRW	Extract word
PINSRW	Insert word
PMAXUB	Maximum of packed unsigned byte integers
PMAXSW	Maximum of packed signed word integers
PMINUB	Minimum of packed unsigned byte integers
PMINSW	Minimum of packed signed word integers

Table 6-2: Current-Day Instruction Set (Continued)

Instruction	Description
PMOVMSKB	Move byte mask
PMULHUW	Multiply packed unsigned integers and store high result
PSADBW	Compute sum of absolute differences
PSHUFW	Shuffle packed integer word in MMX register
SSE Cacheability Control, Prefetch, and Instruction Ordering Instructions	
MASKMOVQ	Non-temporal store of selected bytes from an MMX register into memory
MOVNTQ	Non-temporal store of QW from an MMX register into memory
MOVNTPS	Non-temporal store of four packed SP FP values from an XMM register into memory
PREFETCH*h*	Load 32 or more of bytes from memory to a selected level of the processor's cache hierarchy
SFENCE	Serializes store operations
SSE2 INSTRUCTIONS	
SSE2 Packed and Scalar DP FP Instructions: SSE2 Data Movement Instructions	
MOVAPD	Move two aligned packed DP FP values between XMM registers or between and XMM register and memory
MOVUPD	Move two unaligned packed DP FP values between XMM registers or between and XMM register and memory
MOVHPD	Move high packed DP FP value to an from the high QW of an XMM register and memory
MOVLPD	Move low packed SP FP value to an from the low QW of an XMM register and memory
MOVMSKPD	Extract sign mask from two packed DP FP values
MOVSD	Move scalar DP FP value between XMM registers or between an XMM register and memory

Table 6-2: Current-Day Instruction Set (Continued)

Instruction	Description
SSE2 Packed and Scalar DP FP Instructions: SSE2 Packed Arithmetic Instructions	
ADDPD	Add packed DP FP values
ADDSD	Add scalar double precision FP values
SUBPD	Subtract scalar DP FP values
SUBSD	Subtract scalar DP FP values
MULPD	Multiply packed DP FP values
MULSD	Multiply scalar DP FP values
DIVPD	Divide packed DP FP values
DIVSD	Divide scalar DP FP values
SQRTPD	Compute packed square roots of packed DP FP values
SQRTSD	Compute scalar square root of scalar DP FP values
MAXPD	Return maximum packed DP FP values
MAXSD	Return maximum scalar DP FP values
MINPD	Return minimum packed DP FP values
MINSD	Return minimum scalar DP FP values
SSE2 Packed and Scalar DP FP Instructions: SSE2 Logical Instructions	
ANDPD	Perform bitwise logical AND of packed DP FP values
ANDNPD	Perform bitwise logical AND NOT of packed DP FP values
ORPD	Perform bitwise logical OR of packed DP FP values
XORPD	Perform bitwise logical XOR of packed DP FP values
SSE2 Packed and Scalar DP FP Instructions: SSE2 Compare Instructions	
CMPPD	Compare packed DP FP values
CMPSD	Compare scalar DP FP values

Table 6-2: Current-Day Instruction Set (Continued)

Instruction	Description
COMISD	Perform ordered comparison of scalar DP FP values and set flags in EFLAGS register
UCOMISD	Perform unordered comparison of scalar DP FP values and set flags in EFLAGS register.
SSE2 Packed and Scalar DP FP Instructions: SSE2 Shuffle and Unpack Instructions	
SHUFPD	Shuffles values in packed DP FP operands
UNPCKHPD	Unpacks and interleaves the high values from two packed DP FP operands
UNPCKLPD	Unpacks and interleaves the low values from two packed DP FP operands
SSE2 Packed and Scalar DP FP Instructions: SSE2 Conversion Instructions	
CVTPD2PI	Convert packed DP FP values to packed DW integers.
CVTTPD2PI	Convert with truncation packed DP FP values to packed DW integers
CVTPI2PD	Convert packed DW integers to packed DP FP values
CVTPD2DQ	Convert packed DP FP values to packed DW integers
CVTTPD2DQ	Convert with truncation packed DP FP values to packed DW integers
CVTDQ2PD	Convert packed DW integers to packed DP FP values
CVTPS2PD	Convert packed SP FP values to packed DP FP values
CVTPD2PS	Convert packed DP FP values to packed SP FP values
CVTSS2SD	Convert scalar SP FP values to scalar DP FP values
CVTSD2SS	Convert scalar DP FP values to scalar SP FP values
CVTSD2SI	Convert scalar DP FP values to a DW integer
CVTTSD2SI	Convert with truncation scalar DP FP values to scalar DW integers

Table 6-2: Current-Day Instruction Set (Continued)

Instruction	Description
CVTSI2SD	Convert DW integer to scalar DP FP value
SSE2 Packed SP FP Instructions	
CVTDQ2PS	Convert packed DW integers to packed SP FP values
CVTPS2DQ	Convert packed SP FP values to packed DW integers
CVTTPS2DQ	Convert with truncation packed SP FP values to packed DW integers
SSE2 128-Bit SIMD Integer Instructions	
MOVDQA	Move aligned double QW.
MOVDQU	Move unaligned double QW
MOVQ2DQ	Move QW integer from MMX to XMM registers
MOVDQ2Q	Move QW integer from XMM to MMX registers
PMULUDQ	Multiply packed unsigned DW integers
PADDQ	Add packed QW integers
PSUBQ	Subtract packed QW integers
PSHUFLW	Shuffle packed low words
PSHUFHW	Shuffle packed high words
PSHUFD	Shuffle packed DWs
PSLLDQ	Shift double QW left logical
PSRLDQ	Shift double QW right logical
PUNPCKHQDQ	Unpack high QWs
PUNPCKLQDQ	Unpack low QWs
SSE2 Cacheability Control and Ordering Instructions	
LFENCE	Serializes load operations
MFENCE	Serializes load and store operations

Table 6-2: Current-Day Instruction Set (Continued)

Instruction	Description
PAUSE	Improves the performance of spin-wait loops (but MONITOR/MWAIT instruction pair better)
MASKMOVDQU	Non-temporal store of selected bytes from an XMM register into memory
MOVNTPD	Non-temporal store of two packed DP FP values from an XMM register into memory
CLFLUSH	Flushes and invalidates a memory operand and its associated cache line from all levels of the processor's cache hierarchy
LFENCE	Serializes load operations
SSE3 INSTRUCTIONS	
SSE3 x87-FP Integer Conversion Instruction	
FISTTP	Behaves like the FISTP instruction but uses truncation, irrespective of the rounding mode specified in the FP control word (FCW).
SSE3 Specialized 128-bit Unaligned Data Load Instruction	
LDDQU	Special 128-bit unaligned load designed to avoid cache line splits.
SSE3 SIMD FP Packed ADD/SUB Instructions	
ADDSUBPS	Performs SP addition on the second and fourth pairs of 32-bit data elements within the operands; SP subtraction on the first and third pairs.
ADDSUBPD	Performs DP addition on the second pair of QWs, and DP subtraction on the first pair.

Table 6-2: Current-Day Instruction Set (Continued)

Instruction	Description
SSE3 SIMD FP Horizontal ADD/SUB Instructions	
HADDPS	Performs a SP addition on contiguous data elements. The first data element of the result is obtained by adding the first and second elements of the first operand; the second element by adding the third and fourth elements of the first operand; the third by adding the first and second elements of the second operand; and the fourth by adding the third and fourth elements of the second operand.
HSUBPS	Performs a SP subtraction on contiguous data elements. The first data element of the result is obtained by subtracting the second element of the first operand from the first element of the first operand; the second element by subtracting the fourth element of the first operand from the third element of the first operand; the third by subtracting the second element of the second operand from the first element of the second operand; and the fourth by subtracting the fourth element of the second operand from the third element of the second operand.
HADDPD	Performs a DP addition on contiguous data elements. The first data element of the result is obtained by adding the first and second elements of the first operand; the second element by adding the first and second elements of the second operand.
HSUBPD	Performs a DP subtraction on contiguous data elements. The first data element of the result is obtained by subtracting the second element of the first operand from the first element of the first operand; the second element by subtracting the second element of the second operand from the first element of the second operand.
SSE3 SIMD FP LOAD/MOVE/DUPLICATE Instructions	
MOVSHDUP	Loads/moves 128 bits; duplicating the second and fourth 32-bit data elements.
MOVSLDUP	Loads/moves 128 bits; duplicating the first and third 32-bit data elements.

Table 6-2: Current-Day Instruction Set (Continued)

Instruction	Description
MOVDDUP	Loads/moves 64 bits (bits[63:0] if the source is a register) and returns the same 64 bits in both the lower and upper halves of the 128-bit result register; duplicates the 64 bits from the source.
SSE3 Agent Synchronization Instructions	
MONITOR	Sets up an address range used to monitor write-back stores.
MWAIT	Enables a logical processor to enter into an optimized state while waiting for a write-back store to the address range set up by the instruction.
SUPPLEMENTAL STREAMING SIMD EXTENSIONS 3 (SSSE3) INSTRUCTIONS	
Horizontal Addition/Subtraction	
PHADDW	Adds two adjacent, signed 16-bit integers horizontally from the source and destination operands and packs the signed 16-bit results to the destination operand.
PHADDSW	Adds two adjacent, signed 16-bit integers horizontally from the source and destination operands and packs the signed, saturated 16-bit results to the destination operand.
PHADDD	Adds two adjacent, signed 32-bit integers horizontally from the source and destination operands and packs the signed 32-bit results to the destination operand.
PHSUBW	Performs horizontal subtraction on each adjacent pair of 16-bit signed integers by subtracting the most significant word from the least significant word of each pair in the source and destination operands. The signed 16-bit results are packed and written to the destination operand.
PHSUBSW	Performs horizontal subtraction on each adjacent pair of 16-bit signed integers by subtracting the most significant word from the least significant word of each pair in the source and destination operands. The signed, saturated 16-bit results are packed and written to the destination operand.

Table 6-2: Current-Day Instruction Set (Continued)

Instruction	Description
PHSUBD	Performs horizontal subtraction on each adjacent pair of 32-bit signed integers by subtracting the most significant DW from the least significant double word of each pair in the source and destination operands. The signed 32-bit results are packed and written to the destination operand.
Packed Absolute Values	
PABSB	Computes the absolute value of each signed byte data element.
PABSW	Computes the absolute value of each signed 16-bit data element.
PABSD	Computes the absolute value of each signed 32-bit data element.
Multiply and Add Packed Signed and Unsigned Bytes	
PMADDUBSW	Multiplies each unsigned byte value with the corresponding signed byte value to produce an intermediate, 16-bit signed integer. Each adjacent pair of 16-bit signed values are added horizontally. The signed, saturated 16-bit results are packed to the destination operand.
Packed Multiply High with Round and Scale	
PMULHRSW	Multiplies vertically each signed 16-bit integer from the destination operand with the corresponding signed 16-bit integer of the source operand, producing intermediate, signed 32-bit integers. Each intermediate 32-bit integer is truncated to the 18 most-significant bits. Rounding is always performed by adding 1 to the least significant bit of the 18-bit intermediate result. The final result is obtained by selecting the 16 bits immediately to the right of the most significant bit of each 18-bit intermediate result and packed to the destination operand.
Packed Shuffle Bytes	
PSHUFB	Permutes each byte in place, according to a shuffle control mask. The least significant three or four bits of each shuffle control byte of the control mask form the shuffle index. The shuffle mask is unaffected. If the most significant bit (bit 7) of a shuffle control byte is set, the constant zero is written in the result byte.

Table 6-2: Current-Day Instruction Set (Continued)

Instruction	Description
Packed Sign	
PSIGNB/W/D	Negates each signed integer element of the destination operand if the sign of the corresponding data element in the source operand is less than zero.
Packed Align Right	
PALIGNR	Source operand is appended after the destination operand forming an intermediate value of twice the width of an operand. The result is extracted from the intermediate value into the destination operand by selecting the 128 bit or 64 bit value that are right-aligned to the byte offset specified by the immediate value.
SSE4.1 INSTRUCTIONS	
DW Multiply Instructions	
PMULLD	Returns four lower 32-bits of the 64-bit results of signed 32-bit integer multiplies.
PMULDQ	Returns two 64-bit signed result of signed 32-bit integer multiplies.
FP Dot Product Instructions	
DPPD	Perform DP dot product for up to 2 elements and broadcast.
DPPS	Perform SP dot products for up to 4 elements and broadcast.
Streaming Load Hint Instruction	
MOVNTDQA	Provides a non-temporal hint that can cause adjacent 16-byte items within an aligned 64-byte region (a streaming line) to be fetched and held in a small set of temporary buffers ("streaming load buffers"). Subsequent streaming loads to other aligned 16-byte items in the same streaming line may be supplied from the streaming load buffer and can improve throughput.

Table 6-2: Current-Day Instruction Set (Continued)

Instruction	Description
Packed Blending Instructions	
BLENDPD	Conditionally copies specified DP FP data elements in the source operand to the corresponding data elements in the destination, using an immediate byte control.
BLENDPS	Conditionally copies specified SP FP data elements in the source operand to the corresponding data elements in the destination, using an immediate byte control.
BLENDVPD	Conditionally copies specified DP FP data elements in the source operand to the corresponding data elements in the destination, using an implied mask.
BLENDVPD	Conditionally copies specified SP FP data elements in the source operand to the corresponding data elements in the destination, using an implied mask.
PBLENDVB	Conditionally copies specified byte elements in the source operand to the corresponding elements in the destination, using an implied mask.
PBLENDW	Conditionally copies specified word elements in the source operand to the corresponding elements in the destination, using an immediate byte control.
Packed Integer MIN/MAX Instructions	
PMINUW	Compare packed unsigned word integers.
PMINUD	Compare packed unsigned DW integers.
PMINSB	Compare packed signed byte integers.
PMINSD	Compare packed signed DW integers.
PMAXUW	Compare packed unsigned word integers.
PMAXUD	Compare packed unsigned DW integers.
PMAXSB	Compare packed signed byte integers.
PMAXSD	Compare packed signed DW integers.

Table 6-2: Current-Day Instruction Set (Continued)

Instruction	Description
FP Round Instructions with Selectable Rounding Mode	
ROUNDPS	Round packed single precision FP values into integer values and return rounded FP values.
ROUNDPD	Round packed double precision FP values into integer values and return rounded FP values.
ROUNDSS	Round the low packed single precision FP value into an integer value and return a rounded FP value.
ROUNDSD	Round the low packed double precision FP value into an integer value and return a rounded FP value.
Insertion and Extractions from XMM Registers	
EXTRACTPS	Extracts a SP FP value from a specified offset in an XMM register and stores the result to memory or a general-purpose register
INSERTPS	Inserts a SP FP value from either a 32-bit memory location or selected from a specified offset in an XMM register to a specified offset in the destination XMM register. In addition, INSERTPS allows zeroing out selected data elements in the destination, using a mask.
PINSRB	Insert a byte value from a register or memory into an XMM register.
PINSRD	Insert a DW value from 32-bit register or memory into an XMM register.
PINSRQ	Insert a QW value from 64-bit register or memory into an XMM register.
PEXTRB	Extract a byte from an XMM register and insert the value into a general-purpose register or memory.
PEXTRW	Extract a word from an XMM register and insert the value into a general-purpose register or memory.
PEXTRD	Extract a DW from an XMM register and insert the value into a general-purpose register or memory.

Table 6-2: Current-Day Instruction Set (Continued)

Instruction	Description
PEXTRQ	Extract a QW from an XMM register and insert the value into a general-purpose register or memory.
Packed Integer Format Conversions	
PMOVSXBW	Sign extend the lower 8-bit integer of each packed word element into packed signed word integers.
PMOVZXBW	Zero extend the lower 8-bit integer of each packed word element into packed signed word integers.
PMOVSXBD	Sign extend the lower 8-bit integer of each packed DW element into packed signed DW integers.
PMOVZXBD	Zero extend the lower 8-bit integer of each packed DW element into packed signed DW integers.
PMOVSXWD	Sign extend the lower 16-bit integer of each packed DW element into packed signed DW integers.
PMOVZXWD	Zero extend the lower 16-bit integer of each packed DW element into packed signed DW integers.
PMOVSXBQ	Sign extend the lower 8-bit integer of each packed QW element into packed signed QW integers.
PMOVZXBQ	Zero extend the lower 8-bit integer of each packed QW element into packed signed QW integers.
PMOVSXWQ	Sign extend the lower 16-bit integer of each packed QW element into packed signed QW integers.
PMOVZXWQ	Zero extend the lower 16-bit integer of each packed QW element into packed signed QW integers.
PMOVSXDQ	Sign extend the lower 32-bit integer of each packed QW element into packed signed QW integers.
PMOVZXDQ	Zero extend the lower 32-bit integer of each

Table 6-2: Current-Day Instruction Set (Continued)

Instruction	Description
Improved Sums of Absolute Differences (SAD) for 4-Byte Blocks	
MPSADBW	Performs eight 4-byte wide Sum of Absolute Differences operations to produce eight word integers.
Horizontal Search	
PHMINPOSUW	Finds the value and location of the minimum unsigned word from one of 8 horizontally packed unsigned words. The resulting value and location (offset within the source) are packed into the low DW of the destination XMM register.
Packed Test	
PTEST	Performs a logical AND between the destination with this mask and sets the ZF flag if the result is zero. The CF flag (zero for TEST) is set if the inverted mask AND'd with the destination is all zero
Packed QW Equality Comparisons	
PCMPEQQ	128-bit packed QW equality test.
DW Packing With Unsigned Saturation	
PACKUSDW	Packs DW to word with unsigned saturation.
SSE4.2 INSTRUCTION SET	
String and Text Processing Instructions	
PCMPESTRI	Packed compare explicit-length strings, return index in ECX/RCX.
PCMPESTRM	Packed compare explicit-length strings, return mask in XMM0.
PCMPISTRI	Packed compare implicit-length strings, return index in ECX/RCX.
PCMPISTRM	Packed compare implicit-length strings, return mask in XMM0.

Table 6-2: Current-Day Instruction Set (Continued)

Instruction	Description
Packed Comparison SIMD integer Instruction	
PCMPGTQ	Performs logical compare of greater-than on packed integer QWs.
Application-Targeted Accelerator Instructions	
CRC32	Provides hardware acceleration to calculate cyclic redundancy checks for fast and efficient implementation of data integrity protocols.
POPCNT	This instruction calculates of number of bits set to 1 in the second operand (source) and returns the count in the first operand (a destination register)
SYSTEM (OS kernel-related) INSTRUCTIONS	
LGDT	Load Global Descriptor Table Register (GDTR)
SGDT	Store Global Descriptor Table Register (GDTR)
LLDT	Load Local Descriptor Table Register (LDTR)
SLDT	Store Local Descriptor Table Register (LDTR)
LTR	Load Task Register (TR)
STR	Store Task Register (TR)
LIDT	Load Interrupt Descriptor Table Register (IDTR)
SIDT	Store Interrupt Descriptor Table Register (IDTR)
MOV	Load and store control registers
LMSW	Load Machine Status Word (MSW) register. MSW is the lower 16 bits of CR0.
SMSW	Store Machine Status Word (MSW) register
CLTS	Clear the Task Switch (TS) bit in CR0
ARPL	Adjust Requested Privilege Level field of segment selector

Table 6-2: Current-Day Instruction Set (Continued)

Instruction	Description
LAR	Load access rights from segment descriptor
LSL	Load segment limit from segment descriptor
VERR	Verify segment for reading
VERW	Verify segment for writing
MOV	Load and store debug registers
INVD	Invalidate cache without writing modified lines back to memory
WBINVD	Invalidate cache after writing modified lines back to memory
INVLPG	Invalidate TLB Entry
LOCK instruction prefix	Lock bus while performing locked read/modify/write on a memory-based semaphore
HLT	Halt logical processor
RSM	Return from System Management Mode (SMM)
RDMSR	Read MSR
WRMSR	Write MSR
RDPMC	Read Performance Monitoring Counters
RDTSC	Read Time Stamp Counter
RDTSCP	Read Time Stamp Counter and processor ID
SYSENTER	Fast System Call, transfers to a flat protected mode kernel at CPL = 0
SYSEXIT	Fast System return, transfers control back to a flat protected mode application at CPL = 3
XSAVE	Save logical processor extended states to memory
XRSTOR	Restore logical processor extended states from memory
XGETBV	Reads the state of an extended control register

Table 6-2: Current-Day Instruction Set (Continued)

Instruction	Description
XSETBV	Writes the state of an extended control register
64-BIT MODE INSTRUCTIONS	
CDQE	Convert DW to QW
CMPSQ	Compare string operands
CMPXCHG16B	Compare RDX:RAX with a 16-byte memory-based operand
LODSQ	Load QW at address (R)SI into RAX
MOVSQ	Move QW from address (R)SI to (R)DI
MOVZX	(64-bits) Move DW to QW, zero-extension
STOSQ	Store RAX at address RDI
SWAPGS	Exchanges current GS base register value with value in MSR address C0000102H
SYSCALL	Fast call to privilege level 0 system procedures
SYSRET	Return from fast system call
VIRTUAL-MACHINE EXTENSIONS (VMX)	
VMPTRLD	Loads the VMPTR register with the base address of a VMCS data structure in memory and makes the referenced VMCS active and current.
VMPTRST	Stores the pointer to the currently-active VMCS data structure to memory.
VMCLEAR	Takes a single 64-bit operand in memory. The instruction sets the launch state of the VMCS referenced by the operand to "clear", renders that VMCS inactive, and ensures that data for the VMCS have been written to the VMCS data structure in the referenced VMCS region.
VMREAD	Reads a component from the VMCS (the encoding of that field is given in a register operand) and stores it into a destination operand.

Table 6-2: Current-Day Instruction Set (Continued)

Instruction	Description
VMWRITE	Writes a component to the VMCS (the encoding of that field is given in a register operand) from a source operand.
VMCALL	Allows a guest OS executing in VMX non-root mode to call the VMM for service. A VM exit occurs, transferring control to the VMM.
VMLAUNCH	Launches the virtual machine associated with the currently-active VMCS. A VM entry occurs, transferring control to the VM.
VMRESUME	Resumes the virtual machine associated with the currently-active VMCS. A VM entry occurs, transferring control to the VM.
VMXOFF	Causes the logical processor to leave VMX mode.
VMXON	Takes a single 64-bit source operand in memory. It causes a logical processor to enter VMX root operation and to use the memory referenced by the operand to support VMX operation.
INVEPT	Invalidate cached Extended Page Table (EPT) mappings in the logical processor to synchronize address translation in virtual machines with memory-resident EPT pages.
INVVPID	Invalidate cached mappings of address translation based on the Virtual Processor ID (VPID).
SAFER MODE EXTENSIONS (SMX)	
GETSEC [CAPABILITIES]	Returns the available leaf functions of the GETSEC instruction.
GETSEC [ENTERACCS]	Loads an authenticated code chipset module and enters authenticated code execution mode.
GETSEC [EXITAC]	Exits authenticated code execution mode.
GETSEC [SENTER]	Establishes a Measured Launched Environment (MLE) which has its dynamic root of trust anchored to a chipset supporting Intel Trusted Execution Technology.

Table 6-2: Current-Day Instruction Set (Continued)

Instruction	Description
GETSEC [SEXIT]	Exits the MLE.
GETSEC [PARAMETERS]	Returns SMX related parameter information.
GETSEC [SMCRTL]	SMX mode control.
GETSEC [WAKEUP]	Wakes up sleeping logical processors inside an MLE.

7 *32-bit Machine Language Instruction Format*

The Previous Chapter

The previous chapter illustrated the expansion of the x86 instruction set since the advent of the 386 by listing both the 386 instruction set as well as the current-day instruction set.

This Chapter

This chapter provides a detailed explanation of the structure of an IA-32 instruction and covers the following topics:

- Effective Operand Size.
- Instruction Composition.
- Instruction Format Basics.
- Opcode (Instruction Identification).
  - In the Beginning.
  - 1-byte Opcodes.
  - 2-byte Opcodes Use 2-Level Lookup.
  - 3-byte Opcodes Use 3-Level Lookup.
  - Opcode Micro-Maps (Groups).
  - x87 FP Opcodes Inhabit Opcode Mini-Maps.
  - Special Opcode Fields.
- Operand Identification.
  - Specifying Registers as Operands.
  - Addressing a Memory-Based Operand.
  - Specifying an Immediate Value As an Operand.
- Instruction Prefixes.
  - Operand Size Override Prefix (66h).
  - Address Size Override Prefix (67h).
  - Lock Prefix.
  - Repeat Prefixes.

— Segment Override Prefix.
— Branch Hint Prefix.
• Summary of Instruction Set Formats.

The Next Chapter

The next chapter provides a detailed description of Real Mode operation and covers the following topics:

• 8086 Emulation.
• Unused Facilities.
• Real Mode OS Environment.
• Running Real Mode Applications Under a Protected Mode OS.
• Real Mode Applications Aren't Supported in IA-32e Mode.
• Real Mode Register Set.
• IO Space versus Memory Space.
• IO and Memory-Mapped IO Operations.
• Operand Size Selection.
• Address Size Selection.
• Real Mode Memory Addressing.
• Real Mode Interrupt/Exception Handling.
• Summary of Real Mode Limitations.

64-bit Machine Language Instruction Format

As its name implies, the current chapter provides a detailed description of the 32-bit machine language instruction format. The 64-bit extensions to the machine language instruction format are covered in:

• "64-bit Operands and Addressing" on page 1041.
• "64-bit Odds and Ends" on page 1075.

A Complex Instruction Set with Roots in the Past

As mentioned earlier in "IA Instructions vs. Micro-ops" on page 15, the x86 machine language instruction set is quite complex. Depending on the type of instruction, the number of operands it specifies, and the operand types (memory- and/or register-based), a single instruction may consist of anywhere between one and fifteen bytes. Beginning with the advent of the Pentium Pro processor, all x86 processors incorporate a translator that converts each IA-32 machine language instruction into a series of one or more simple, fixed-length micro-ops which are then executed by the logical processor.

Effective Operand Size

Introduction

In order to limit the number of opcodes, the same opcode is used for an instruction whether it operates on an 8-, 16- or 32-bit operand. As an example:

```
mov ax,dx
mov eax,edx
```

both use the same basic opcode. This naturally brings up a question: how, then, does the logical processor determine which registers are being referenced? The answer is simple and is described in the next two sections.

Operand Size in 16- and 32-bit Code Segments

Assuming that an instruction is not prefaced by a Operand Size Override prefix byte (66h), the logical processor behaves as outlined in Table 7-1 on page 157. Adding the prefix byte before the instruction's first opcode byte alters its behavior as defined in Table 7-2 on page 158.

Table 7-1: Effective Operand Size in 16- or 32-bit Mode (without prefix)

State of D-bit in active CS Descriptor	Effective Operand Size and Instruction Behavior
0: 16-bit, 286 CS descriptor.	**16-bits**. Instruction operates on 16-bits (a word) in a 16-bit register (e.g., AX) and either of the following: • Two sequential memory locations. • Another 16-bit register.
1: 32-bit, 386 CS descriptor.	**32-bits**. Instruction operates on 32-bits (a dword) in a 32-bit register (e.g., EAX) and either of the following: • Four sequential memory locations. • Another 32-bit register.

Table 7-1: Effective Operand Size in 16- or 32-bit Mode (without prefix) (Continued)

State of D-bit in active CS Descriptor	Effective Operand Size and Instruction Behavior
For some instructions, the opcode contains a width (W) bit: • W = 0. The operand size is 8- rather than 16- or 32-bits. • W = 1. The operand size is either 16- or 32-bits (based on the state of CSDesc[D] and the presence or absence of the Operand Size Override prefix).	

Table 7-2: Effective Operand Size in 16- or 32-bit Mode (with prefix)

State of D-bit in active CS Descriptor	Effective Operand Size and Instruction Behavior
0: 16-bit, 286 CS descriptor.	**Inclusion of the Operand Size Override prefix before the instruction flips the effective operand size from 16- to 32-bits.** Instruction operates on 32-bits (a dword) in a 32-bit register (e.g., EAX) and either of the following: • Four sequential memory locations. • Another 32-bit register.
1: 32-bit, 386 CS descriptor.	**Inclusion of the Operand Size Override prefix before the instruction flips the effective operand size from 32- to 16-bits.** Instruction operates on 16-bits (a word) in a 16-bit register (e.g., AX) and either of the following: • Two sequential memory locations. • Another 16-bit register.
For some instructions, the opcode contains a width (W) bit: • W = 0. The operand size is 8- rather than 16- or 32-bits. • W = 1. The operand size is either 16- or 32-bits (based on the state of CSDesc[D] and the presence or absence of the Operand Size Override prefix).	

Operand Size in 64-bit Code Segments

The default data operand size when executing code from a 64-bit code segment (code segment descriptor's L bit = 1) is 32-bits and its default address size is 64-bits. In other words, unless instructed otherwise, the logical processor assumes that an instruction's default data operand size is 32-bits (i.e., a dword) and the default address size of memory-based operands is 64-bits.

If an instruction references one of the newly-defined, extended registers (XMM8 - XMM15, a 64-bit GPR register, CR8 - CR15, or DR8 - DR15), a special prefix byte known as the REX prefix (more on this later) must be placed immediately before the instruction's first opcode byte in order to address the register.

— An exception: on AMD processors, CR8 (the Task Priority register) can be accessed in modes other than 64-bit Mode by prefacing the MOV CR8 instruction with the LOCK prefix (F0h).

When executing code from a 64-bit code segment (the CS descriptor's L bit = 1), three factors affect the logical processor's behavior relative to the operand size when executing an instruction:

- Some instructions default to an operand size of 64-bits.
- For those that don't, the effective operand size is determined by:
  — The presence or absence of the Operand Size Override prefix byte.
  — The presence or absence of the REX prefix byte and the state of the W bit within it.

Table 7-3 on page 159 outlines the logical processor's behavior relative to the effective operand size (for instructions that don't default to an operand size of 64-bits).

Table 7-3: Determination of Effective Operand Size in 64-bit Mode

State of D-bit in active 64-bit CS Descriptor	Operand Size Override prefix (66h) present?	State of W bit in REX prefix	Resultant Effective Operand Size
0 *	No	0	**32-bits**. Instruction operates on 32-bits (a dword) in a 32-bit register (e.g., EAX) and either of the following: • Four sequential memory locations. • Another 32-bit register.

Table 7-3: Determination of Effective Operand Size in 64-bit Mode (Continued)

State of D-bit in active 64-bit CS Descriptor	Operand Size Override prefix (66h) present?	State of W bit in REX prefix	Resultant Effective Operand Size
0	No	1	**64-bits**. Instruction operates on 64-bits (a qword) in a 64-bit register (e.g., RAX) and either of the following: • Eight sequential memory locations. • Another 64-bit register.
0	Yes	0	**16-bits**. Instruction operates on 16-bits (a word) in a 16-bit register (e.g., AX) and either of the following: • Two sequential memory locations. • Another 16-bit register.
0	Yes	1	**66h ignored. Size = 64-bits**. Instruction operates on 64-bits (a qword) in a 64-bit register (e.g., RAX) and either of the following: • Eight sequential memory locations. • Another 64-bit register.
0	N/A	N/A	For any byte-oriented instruction, 66h and W bit are ignored (and operand size = 8-bits).

* Note: The only allowable value for the D bit in a 64-bit CS descriptor is 0 indicating:
• Default operand size = 32-bits.
• Default address size = 64-bits.

Instruction Composition

Table 7-4 on page 161 introduces the type of information that comprise the typical IA-32 instruction.

Table 7-4: Information Related to an Instruction

Element	Brief Description
Type of operation	**Opcode**. One or more bytes (referred to as opcode bytes) that collectively define the instruction type and, in some cases, implicitly identifies an operand the instruction acts upon (as an example, the CLI instruction is a 1-byte instruction that by definition only affects one specific register: it causes the logical processor to clear the IF—Interrupt enable Flag—bit in the Eflags register).
Entity or entities to be operated on	**Operands**. In a few cases, a particular instruction only affects one specific register. In that case, the target register does not need to be identified. In all other cases, however, the instruction encoding must explicitly identify the entity or entities (referred to as the operands) to be acted upon by the instruction. The possible combinations are: • One register. • Two registers. • A register and a memory-based operand. • Just a memory-based operand.
Memory Address Calculation	**Memory Address Calculation**. If one of the operands specified is a memory-based operand, the instruction must direct the logical processor regarding how to calculate the effective memory address.

Is the programmer explicitly supplying a data item as an instruction operand?	**Immediate Data**. For some instruction types, the programmer explicitly supplies an 8-, 16-bit or 32-bit data value to be used as one of the operands. It is appended to the instruction.
	Examples:
	  – mov eax, 12ac4336
	  – add ax, 12
	  – adc [memadd], 9809451a

Table 7-4: Information Related to an Instruction (Continued)

Element	Brief Description
Any variations on normal execution?	**Prefixes.** Up to four optional instruction prefixes, each 1-byte long, may be included before the first opcode byte to alter the instruction's normal execution characteristics. The currently-defined prefixes are: • an optional Operand Size Override prefix. • an optional Address Size Override prefix. • an optional Lock prefix. • an optional Repeat prefix to define the extent of a memory string operation or an IO input or output string operation. • an optional Segment Override prefix to access a segment other than the data segment defined by the DS register. • An optional Branch Hint prefix to accompany a conditional branch (Jcc) instruction. • An optional REX (**R**egister **eX**tension) prefix that enables an instruction to access a 64-bit data operand (in memory or a 64-bit register). A detailed description of the prefixes and their usage may be found in "Instruction Prefixes" on page 210. Some prefixes have alternate usages described in "Special Use of Prefix Bytes" on page 177.

Instruction Format Basics

The previous section, "Instruction Composition", introduced the types of information that can be encoded as part of each instruction.

Figure 7-1 on page 163 illustrates the basic components of an IA-32 machine language instruction and Table 7-5 on page 164 provides a basic description of each element. Please note that the author has standardized on using the terms *Operand 1* and *Operand 2* to refer to the RM and Reg instructions fields of the ModRM byte, respectively. The Intel manuals are not always consistent in their usage of these two terms.

Figure 7-1: General Instruction Format

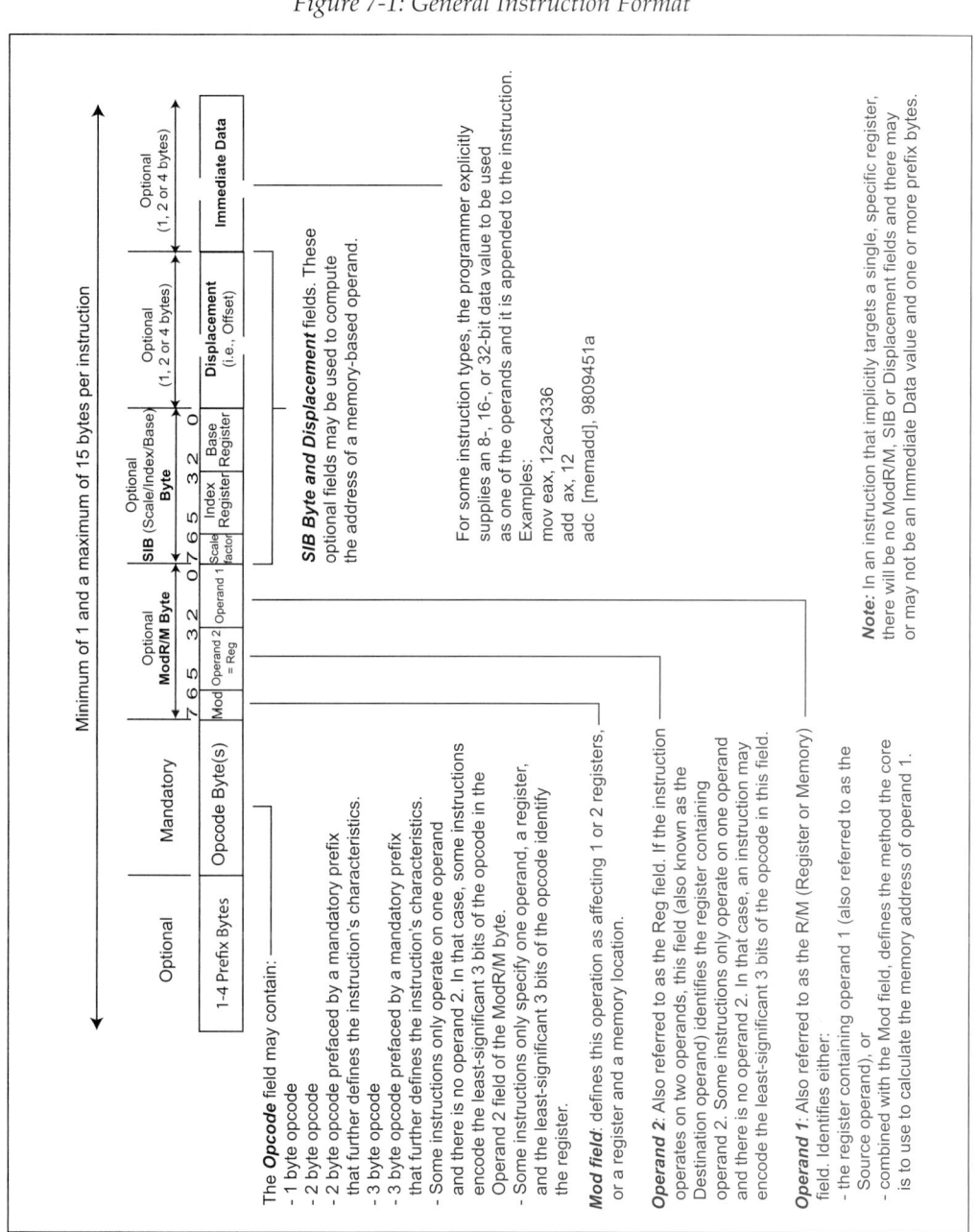

Table 7-5: Instruction Elements

Element	Basic Description
Opcode field	The **instruction type** is defined by: • A series of between 1 and 3 opcode bytes. • In some cases where the instruction only requires one operand, the Operand 2 field in the ModRM byte is appended as the least-significant three bits of the opcode. • In some cases, a 2- or 3-byte opcode is prefaced by a byte that normally fulfills the role of an instruction prefix, but, in this case, further defines the instruction's characteristics. • Some instructions only specify one operand, a register, and the least-significant 3 bits of the opcode identify the register.

	Examples:
	• **1-byte opcode**: 06h = push es
	• **2-byte opcode**: 0Fh 30h = wrmsr
	• **3-byte opcode**: 0Fh 38h 01h = phaddw
	• **2-byte opcode** prefaced by a mandatory **prefix** that further defines the instruction's characteristics:
	  – F2h 0Fh 7Ch = haddps
	• **3-byte opcode** prefaced by a mandatory **prefix** that further defines the instruction's characteristics:
	  – 66h 0Fh 38h 28h = pmuldq

Table 7-5: Instruction Elements (Continued)

Element	Basic Description

ModRM Byte	The **Mode, Register/Memory byte** is used in many (but not all) instructions to define an operand or a pair of operands that the instruction acts upon:
	• The 2-bit **Mode field** defines:
	  – whether the **operation involves one or two registers**,
	  – or that it involves **a register** (defined by the Operand 2 field) **and a memory address** (Operand 1), in which case the method used to calculate the address is defined by the combined Mod and RM fields.
	• The 3-bit **RM field** either:
	  – **defines a register** to act **as Operand 1**, or
	  – in combination with the Mod field, defines the method used to calculate the memory address of Operand 1.
	• The 3-bit **Reg field**:
	  – **defines the register** to act **as Operand 2**.
	  – In some cases where an instruction only acts upon one operand, the Operand 2 field is not used.
	  – In some cases when an instruction only uses one operand (Operand 1), these three bits provide the least-significant **three bits of the opcode**.
	A detailed description of the ModRM byte can be found in "Addressing Memory Using the ModRM Byte" on page 200.

	Examples:
	• 11**D0**h: adc edx,eax
	  – 11h: 1-byte opcode = adc instruction.
	  – D0 (1101 0000b) = ModRM Byte:
	    Mod: 11b = 2 register operands.
	    Operand 2: 010b = edx register.
	    Operand 1: 000b = eax register.
	• 39**1E**h: cmp ebx,[esi]
	  – 39h: 1-byte opcode = cmp instruction.
	  – 1Eh (0001 1110b) = ModRM Byte:
	    Mod: 00b = memory to register.
	    Operand 2: 011b = ebx register.
	    Operand 1: 110b = memory address is specified in esi.

Table 7-5: Instruction Elements (Continued)

Element	Basic Description
Instruction Prefixes	See **Instruction Prefixes** in Table 7-4 on page 161. A detailed description can be found in "Instruction Prefixes" on page 210.

	Example:
	 • **Without prefix**:
	 mov eax,[12345678]
	 Machine language: 8B0534127856h
	 – reads DS location 12345678h => eax
	 • **With** ES Segment Override **prefix (26h)**:
	 mov eax,*es*:[12345678]
	 Machine language: <u>26</u>8B0534127856h
	 – reads ES location 12345678h => eax

SIB Byte	**Scale/Index/Base Byte**. The contents of the Mode and RM fields in the ModRM byte may specify that the memory address of Operand 1 is to be calculated using these three fields together with a Displacement and, possibly, the contents of the EBP register. A detailed description of the SIB byte can be found in "Using the SIB Byte to Access a Data Structure" on page 203.
	Example: mov eax,[edx+ebx*4] Machine language: 8B04<u>9A</u>h – multiplies index value in ebx by 4, adds to base address in edx and reads dword from memory into eax register. – opcode (8Bh): move memory to register. – Mod = 00b, RM=100: SIB byte supplies mem address. – Reg = 000b: operand 2 is eax register. – SIB (1001 1010b): - **Base register** (010b): edx - **Index register** (011b): ebx - **Scale factor** (10b): 4

Table 7-5: Instruction Elements (Continued)

Element	Basic Description
Displacement field	If present, specifies an 8-, 16- or 32-bit displacement value to be used in calculating the memory address of Operand 1. There are two cases:

	Direct or Absolute Address:
	An unsigned, 16-bit (when using 16-bit addressing) or 32-bit (when using 32-bit addressing) value can be specified as the one and only addressing component of a memory-based operand. In other words, the programmer specifies a hard-coded address (as an offset from a segment base address) which is encoded as part of the instruction itself. This is frequently referred to as direct or absolute addressing.
	Example:
	 mov eax,[*12345678*]
	 Machine language: 8B05*34127856*h
	  – reads DS location 12345678h => eax
	  – explicitly stated displacement follows the ModRM byte.

	A Signed Displacement:
	A signed, 8-, 16-, or 32-bit value that is encoded directly in the instruction itself and is added to (or subtracted from) the other components specified as part of the memory address calculation.
	Example:
	 move eax, [ebp - *122*]
	 Machine language: 8B45*86*h
	  – subtracts 122 from address in EBP register then reads dword from memory into EAX register.
	  – 86h = 8-bit negative displacement of 122.

Table 7-5: Instruction Elements (Continued)

Element	Basic Description

Immediate Data field	Rather than specifying a register or a memory location containing a data value to be used by an instruction, in some cases the programmer may explicitly specify an 8-, 16- or 32-bit data value as the source operand. In this case, it is encoded at the tail end of the instruction.
	Example:
	  mov eax, 00000023 ;move value 00000023 => eax
	  Machine language: C7C0*00002300*h
	    – Opcode (C7h) indicates immediate value => register
	    – Mod (11b): register-only operation (no memory)
	    – Reg (000b): don't care; operand 2 is not used.
	    – RM (000b): operand 1 = eax register.
	    – 00002300h: 32-bit immediate value.

Opcode (Instruction Identification)

In the Beginning

The 8088/8086 ISA defined the opcode field as a single byte, thereby limiting the maximum number of instructions to 256. Refer to Figure 7-2 on page 169 (each square in the grid represents an instruction with a 1-byte opcode). Clearly this constraint had to be addressed in future processor designs and it obviously was (current-day x86 processors support in excess of four hundred instructions).

Figure 7-2: 8086 Opcode Map

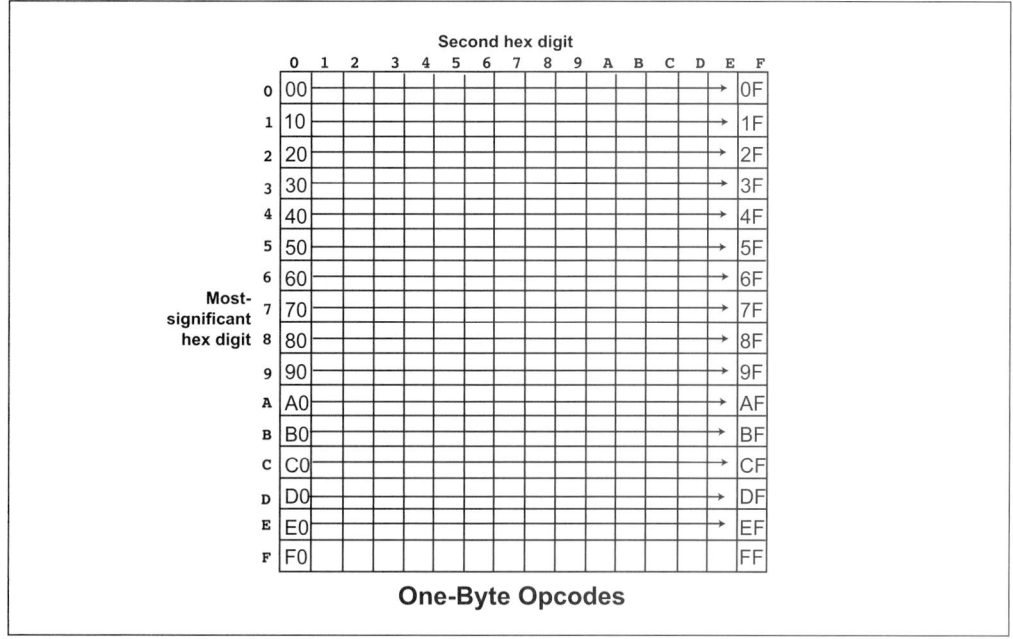

1-byte Opcodes

In today's x86 processors, instructions containing a single opcode byte come in seven forms (see Figure 7-3 on page 171):

Case 1. A **1-byte opcode with no operands** (and therefore no ModRM, SIB or displacement bytes; the operand is explicitly-defined by the instruction type):

— An example would be the STI (Set Interrupt Enable Flag) instruction where the operand is implied by the opcode type (the instruction sets the IF bit to one in the Eflags register).

— In some cases, a single-byte opcode incorporates a 3-bit register select field (see Figure 7-4 on page 172). Examples would be the INC (opcodes 40-47h) and DEC (opcodes 48-4Fh) instructions where the least-significant three bits identify the register to be incremented or decremented.

Case 2. A **1-byte opcode followed by a Displacement.** Examples:

— A conditional branch (Jcc) opcode followed by a positive or negative Displacement from the Instruction Pointer that identifies the branch target address.

— A move instruction to move a byte, word, or dword from memory to al, ax, or eax.

Case 3. In some cases, an instruction may consist of a **1-byte opcode followed by** a programmer-specified 1-, 2- or 4-byte **immediate data** item. Examples:

— adc ax, 1234h.

— In or Out instruction with the port address supplied as an immediate data item: e.g., IN AL, 61h.

Case 4. A **1-byte Far Jump opcode followed by** either a **4- or 6-byte branch target address** in segment:offset format:

— 16:16 (2-bytes + 2-bytes) if target is in 16-bit code segment.

— 16:32 (2-bytes + 4-bytes) if target is in 32-bit code segment.

Case 5. **1-byte opcode with** a **single register operand specified in** the **ModRM** byte. An example:

— An indirect jump instruction with the branch target address specified in a register. The ModRM byte specifies the register.

Case 6. A **1-byte opcode that operates on 2 operands**:

— Operand 1 is either memory or a register:

– It is a register if the 2-bit Mod field in the ModRM byte = 11b.

– It is a memory location if Mod = 00b, 01b, or 10b and the Mod and RM fields together define how the memory address is calculated.

— Operand 2 is a register and is defined by the 3-bit Operand 2 field of the ModRM byte.

A detailed description of the ModRM byte and the memory addressing modes can be found in "Addressing Memory Using the ModRM Byte" on page 200.

Case 7. **A 1-byte opcode that only operates on a memory-based operand.** In this case, since the 3-bit Operand 2 field in the ModRM byte (bits 5:3) are not required (because there is no second operand), some instructions append these three bits to the 8-bit opcode byte to pinpoint the instruction in what I choose to think of as a micro-map (Intel refers to it as a Group) consisting of up to eight types of instructions. In other words, the opcode byte identifies a group of up to eight instructions and the ModRM byte's Operand 2 field (in this case, it's really an extension of the opcode field) selects 1-of-8 instructions within the group.

If operand 1 is a memory-based operand (case 7, and possibly case 6), then the memory addressing mode indicated by the combination of the Mod and RM fields may require the inclusion of one or more of the following fields:

• The SIB byte.
• The 1-, 2-, or 4-byte Displacement field.
• The 1-, 2-, or 4-byte Immediate Data field.

Figure 7-3: Format of Instructions with Single Opcode Byte

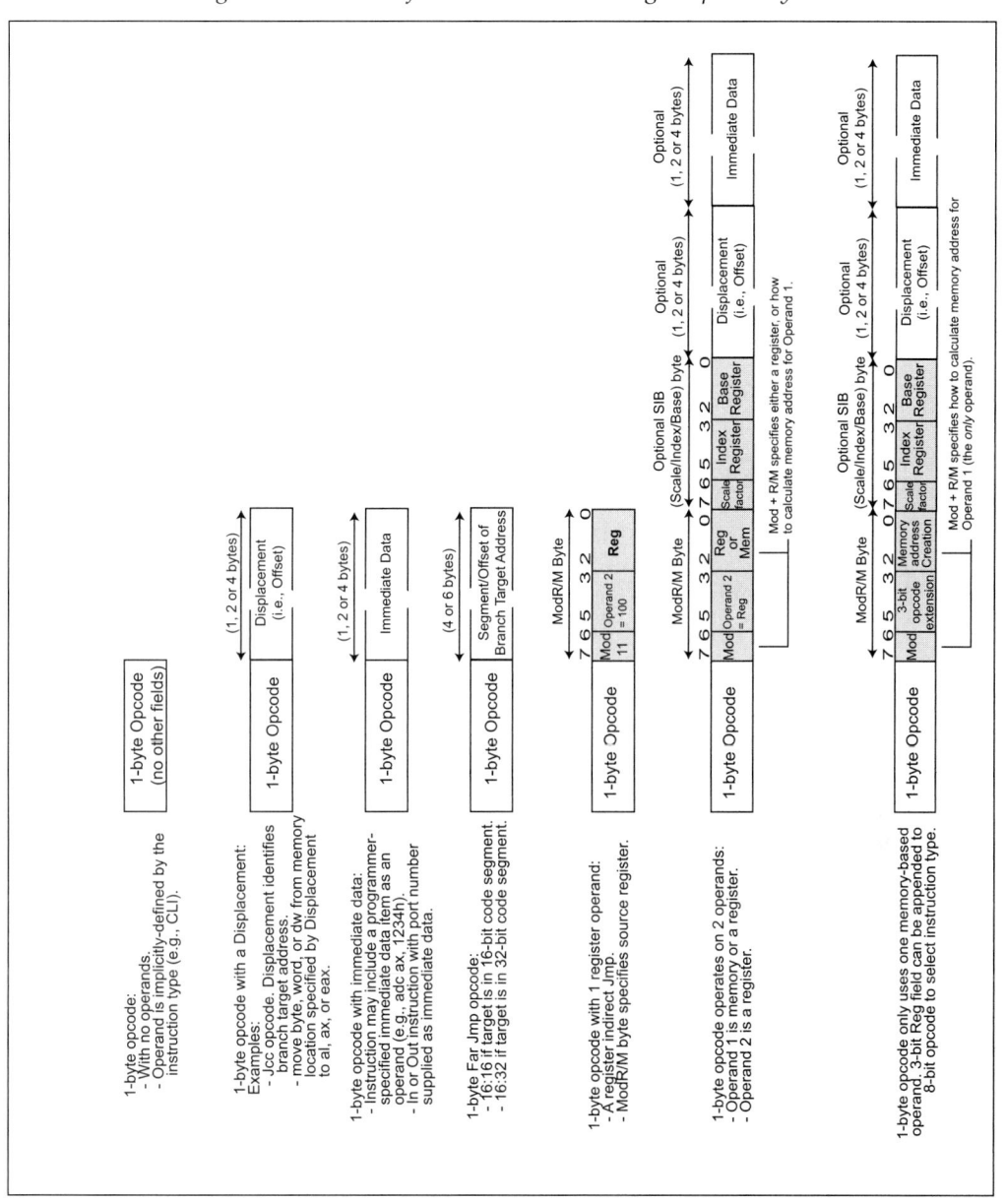

Figure 7-4: Reg Select Field in Primary Opcode Byte

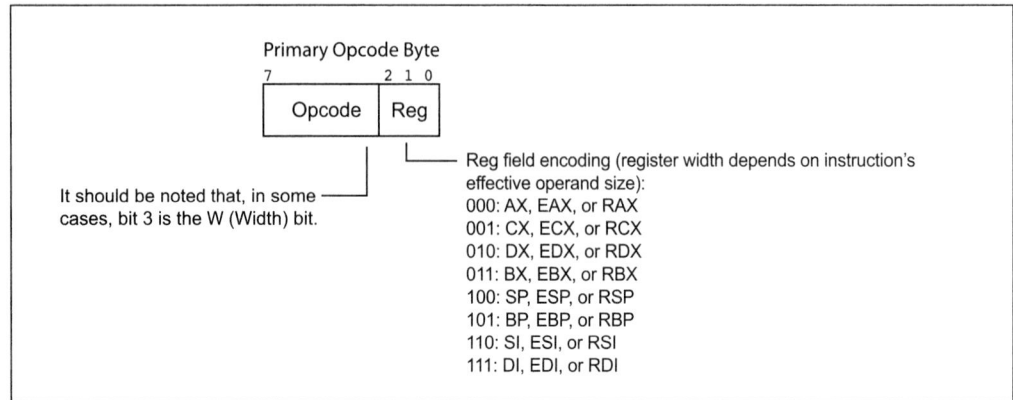

2-byte Opcodes Use 2-Level Lookup

2nd-Level Opcode Map Introduced in 286

With the advent of the 286 processor, Intel eliminated the 256 opcode limit. See Figure 7-5 on page 174. When used as the first byte of the newly-defined 2-byte opcodes, a previously-unused 1-byte opcode, 0Fh, indicates that the instruction resides in a 2nd-level opcode map and is identified by the second opcode byte.

In the example shown in the figure, the opcode field of the instruction consists of 0F32h:

- where 0Fh selects the 2nd-level map,
- and 32h selects row 3, column 2, the location of the RDMSR (Read Model-Specific Register) instruction.

Instructions with 2-byte Opcodes: Five Possible Forms

In today's x86 processors, instructions containing two opcode bytes come in four forms (see Figure 7-6 on page 175; note that cases 1 and 2 below are both illustrated by the first example in the illustration):

Case 1. A **2-byte opcode** (0Fxxh, where xxh is the selector in the 2nd-level opcode map) **with no operands** (and therefore no ModRM, SIB or Displacement bytes; the operand is explicitly-defined by the instruction type). There are currently no cases of a 2-byte opcode followed immediately by an immediate data value.

Case 2. A **2-byte opcode followed by a Displacement** value. Example:
— A conditional branch (Jcc) instruction followed by a positive or negative Displacement which is added to or subtracted from the offset currently in the Instruction Pointer register.

Case 3. A **2-byte opcode that operates on 2 operands** (and therefore requires the ModRM byte and, if Operand 1 is a memory operand, possibly the SIB byte and Displacement). It may also require the inclusion of an Immediate Data value:
— Operand 1 is either memory or a register:
  – It is a register if the 2-bit Mod field in the ModRM byte = 11b.
  – It is a memory location if Mod = 00b, 01b, or 10b and the Mod and RM fields together define how the memory address is calculated.
— Operand 2 is a register and is defined by the 3-bit Operand 2 field in the ModRM byte.

A detailed description of the ModRM byte and the memory addressing modes can be found in "Addressing Memory Using the ModRM Byte" on page 200.

Case 4. **A 2-byte opcode that only operates on one operand (in memory).** In this case, since the 3-bit Operand 2 field in the ModRM byte (bits 5:3) is not required (because there is no second operand), some instructions append these three bits to the opcode to pinpoint the instruction in what I choose to think of as a micro-map (Intel refers to it as a Group) consisting of up to eight types of instructions. In other words, the opcode identifies a group of eight instructions and the ModRM byte's Operand 2 field (in this case, it's really an extension of the opcode field) selects 1-of-8 instructions within the group.

Case 5. A **2-byte opcode preceded by a prefix byte** being used in a non-standard manner (see "Special Use of Prefix Bytes" on page 177) that alters the characteristics of the instruction. As in case 3, the instruction operates on two operands.

If operand 1 is a memory-based operand (case 4, and possibly case 3), then the memory addressing mode indicated by the combination of the Mod and RM fields may require the inclusion of one or more of the following fields:

• The SIB byte.
• The 1-, 2-, or 4-byte Displacement field.

Also refer to "Special Use of Prefix Bytes" on page 177.

Figure 7-5: Instructions With 2 Opcode Bytes Use 2-level Lookup

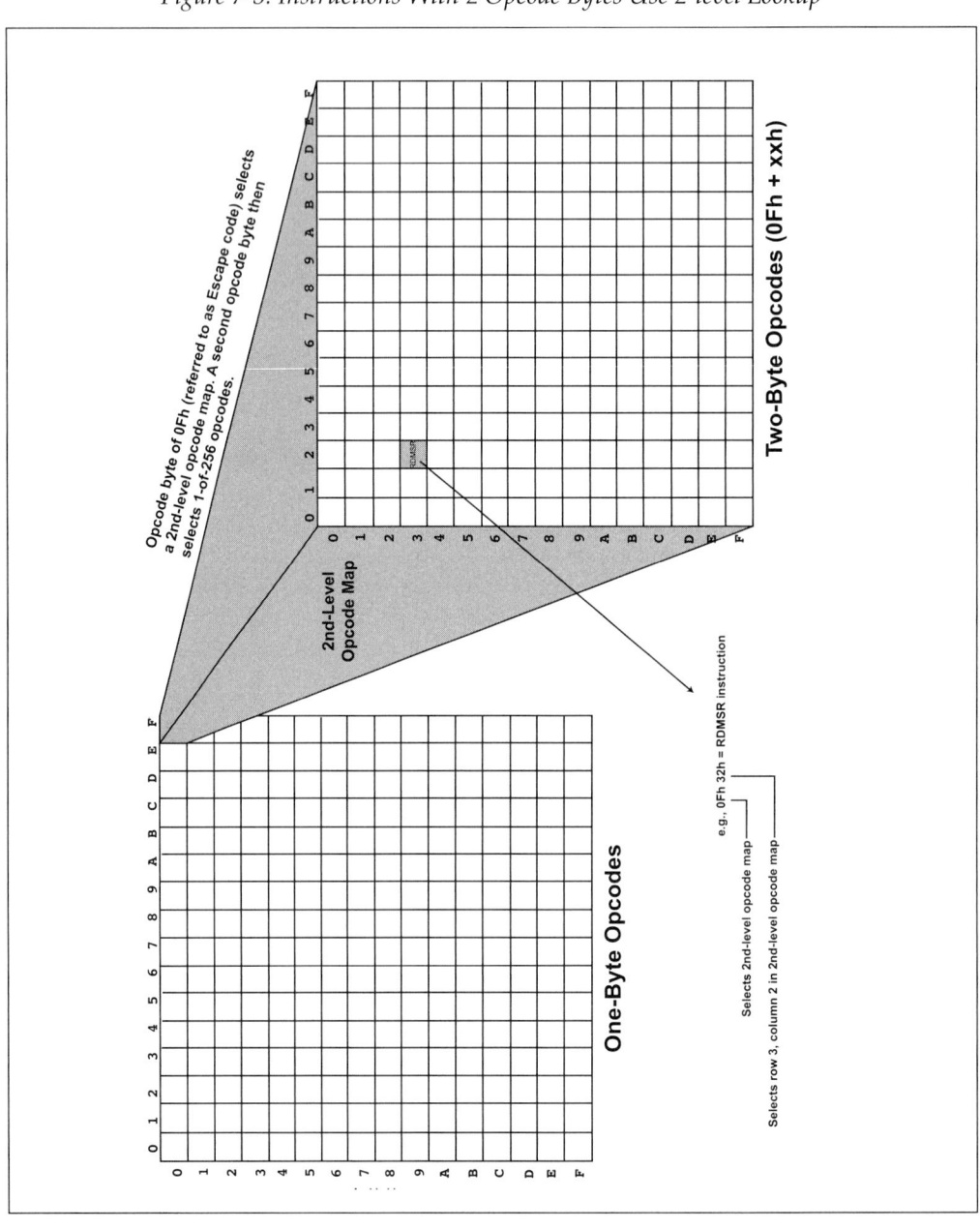

Figure 7-6: Format of Instructions With 2 Opcode Bytes

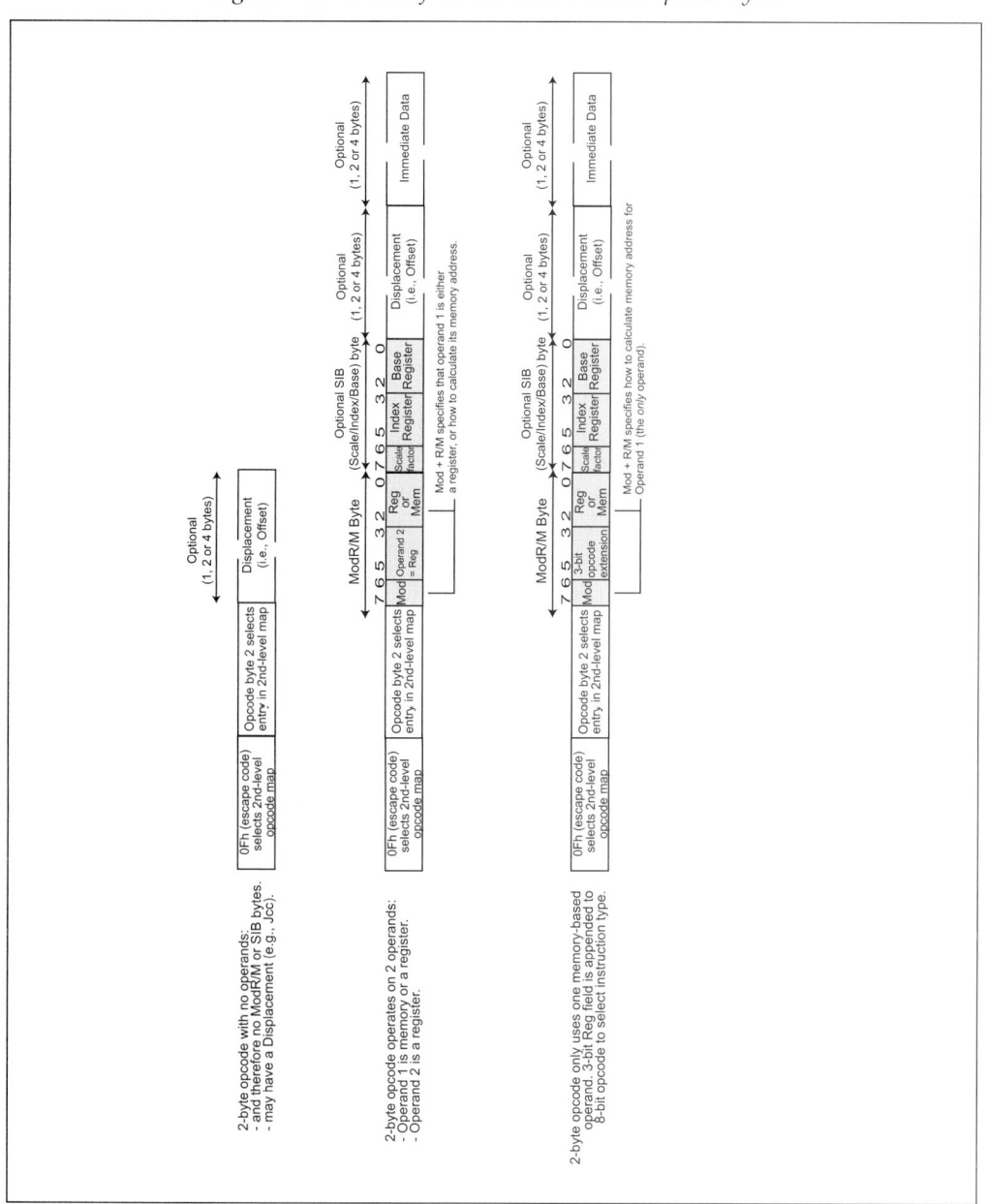

3-byte Opcodes Use 3-Level Lookup

3-Level Opcode Maps Introduced in Pentium 4 Prescott

The 286 processor made another 256 opcodes available by introducing a 2nd-level opcode map selected by prefacing an opcode byte with the value 0Fh. The advent of the Pentium 4 model—code-named *Prescott*—further expanded the available opcodes by introducing 3rd-level opcode maps.

Currently There Are Two 3rd-Level Maps Defined

As illustrated in Figure 7-7 on page 178, two 3rd-level opcode maps are currently implemented:

- 1st opcode byte of 0Fh selects a 2nd-level opcode map:
  — 2nd opcode byte of 38h selects one of the two new, 3rd-level opcode maps;
  — 2nd opcode byte of 3Ah selects the other new 3rd-level opcode map;
- and the 3rd opcode byte selects the instruction type within the selected 3rd-level map.

Currently, the two 3rd-level opcode maps are populated as follows:

- The 3rd-level map selected by the value 38h includes:
  — a couple of general-purpose instructions,
  — a lot of SSE3 and SSE4.1 instructions,
  — and a handful of SSE4.2 instructions.
- The 3rd-level map selected by the value 3Ah includes:
  — One SSSE3 instruction,
  — a lot of SSE4.1 instructions,
  — and about half of the SSE4.2 instructions.

Instructions with 3-byte Opcodes: Three Possible Forms

Case 1. A **3-byte opcode** (0Fxxyyh, where 0Fh selects the 2nd-level map, a 3rd-level map is selected by xxh = 38h or 3Ah, and yy is the selector in the 3rd-level opcode map) **with no operands** (and therefore no ModRM, SIB or Displacement bytes; the operand is explicitly-defined by the instruction type). There are currently no cases of a 3-byte opcode followed immediately by an immediate data value.

Case 2. A **3-byte opcode that operates on 2 operands** (and therefore requires the ModRM byte and, if Operand 1 is a memory operand, possibly the SIB byte, Displacement and/or Immediate Data fields):

— Operand 1 is either memory or a register:
 – It is a register if the 2-bit Mod field in the ModRM byte = 11b.
 – It is a memory location if Mod = 00b, 01b, or 10b and the Mod and RM fields together define how the memory address is calculated.
— Operand 2 is a register and is defined by the 3-bit Operand 2 field of the ModRM byte.

A detailed description of the ModRM byte and the memory addressing modes can be found in "Addressing Memory Using the ModRM Byte" on page 200.

Case 3. A 3-byte opcode preceded by a prefix byte being used in a non-standard manner (see "Special Use of Prefix Bytes" on page 177) that alters the characteristics of the instruction. As in case 2, the instruction operates on two operands.

If operand 1 is a memory-based operand (case 3, and possibly case 2), then the memory addressing mode indicated by the combination of the Mod and RM fields may require the inclusion of one or more of the following fields:

- The SIB byte.
- The 1-, 2-, or 4-byte Displacement field.

Special Use of Prefix Bytes

In normal usage, the optional prefix bytes placed in front of instructions have the purposes described in "Instruction Prefixes" on page 210. Three of these prefixes (the Operand Size Override prefix—66h—and the two Repeat prefixes—F2h and F3h), serve an alternate purpose when placed before certain 2- and 3-byte opcodes. The presence of one of these prefixes alters the size and type of the operand(s) operated upon by the instruction. Some examples:

- An instruction that operates on MMX register(s) can be altered to operate on XMM register(s) instead.
- An instruction that operates on packed single-precision floating-point values can be altered to operate on:
  — packed double-precision floating-point values.
  — scalar single-precision floating-point numbers.
  — scalar double-precision floating-point numbers.

The instructions in question are too numerous to list here (it would be counterproductive), but the reader can easily locate them in the appropriate Intel or AMD reference manuals.

Figure 7-7: Instructions With 3 Opcode Bytes Use 3-Level Lookup

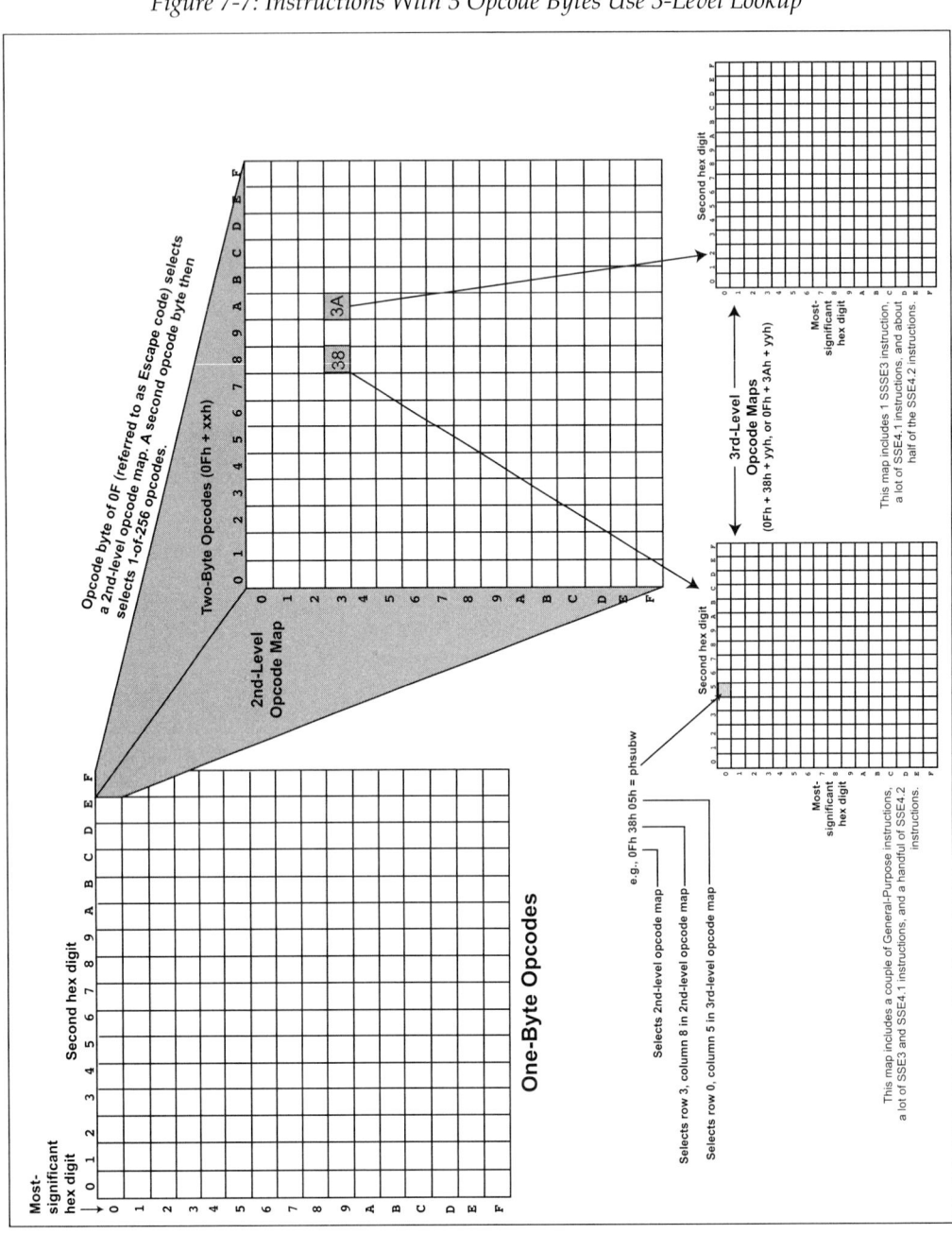

Figure 7-8: Format of Instructions With 3 Opcode Bytes

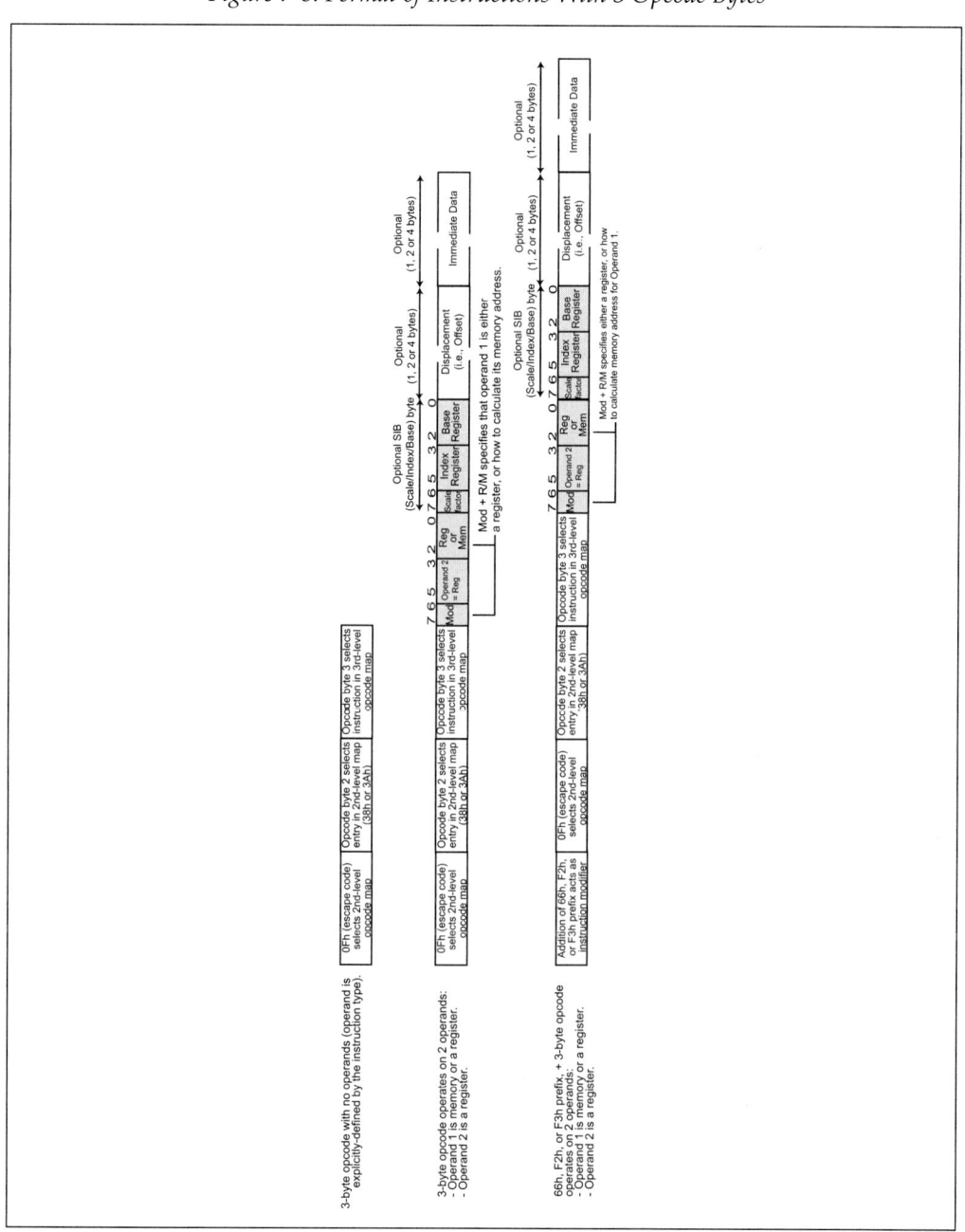

Opcode Micro-Maps (Groups)

Since some instructions only require a single operand specified by the ModRM byte's Operand 1 field (also referred to as the RM field), the 3-bit Operand 2 field in the ModRM byte is available for an alternative use. Intel chose to use it to expand the number of available opcodes.

Micro-Maps Associated with 1-byte Opcodes

Refer to Figure 7-10 on page 182 which illustrates the 1-byte opcode map. As an example, let's take an instruction that contains a 1-byte opcode plus a ModRM byte: F6E1h. This breaks down as follows:

- **1-byte opcode F6h**: Entry F6h in the 1-byte opcode map is shaded indicating that there is a very small opcode submap (Intel's Group; the author's micro-map) associated with this opcode and the ModRM byte's Operand 2 field (see Figure 7-9 on page 181) will be used to select the actual instruction from the group of eight instructions in the micro-map.
- **ModRM byte = E1h** which breaks down as follows:
    7 6| 5 4 3| 2 1 0
    1 1| 1 0 0| 0 0 1
- where:
    — Mod = 11b, indicating that RM field defines a register as operand 1 rather than a memory-based operand.
    — Operand 2 = 100b (4d), selecting the MUL instruction from the F6h micro-map.
    — RM = 001b, selecting CL as the source register. When executed, the following operation is performed:
        – the result placed in the destination register, AX (by definition, the Multiply instruction uses the AX register) = the contents of the AL register (once again, the MUL instruction uses this register by definition) multiplied by the contents of the CL register.

Some Opcodes Employ 2 x 8 Micro-Maps

In Figure 7-10 on page 182, note that the 1-byte opcode C7h is associated with a 2 x 8 micro-map where:

- The ModRM Operand 2 field selects the column and
- the value of the Mod field selects the row:
    — Mod 11b indicates the operand is a register (not memory).
    — Any other value in the Mod field indicates the operand is memory.

As defined in the next section, all but two of the 2-byte opcodes with micro-maps employ 2 x 8 (rather than 1 x 8) micro-maps.

Figure 7-9: The ModRM Byte

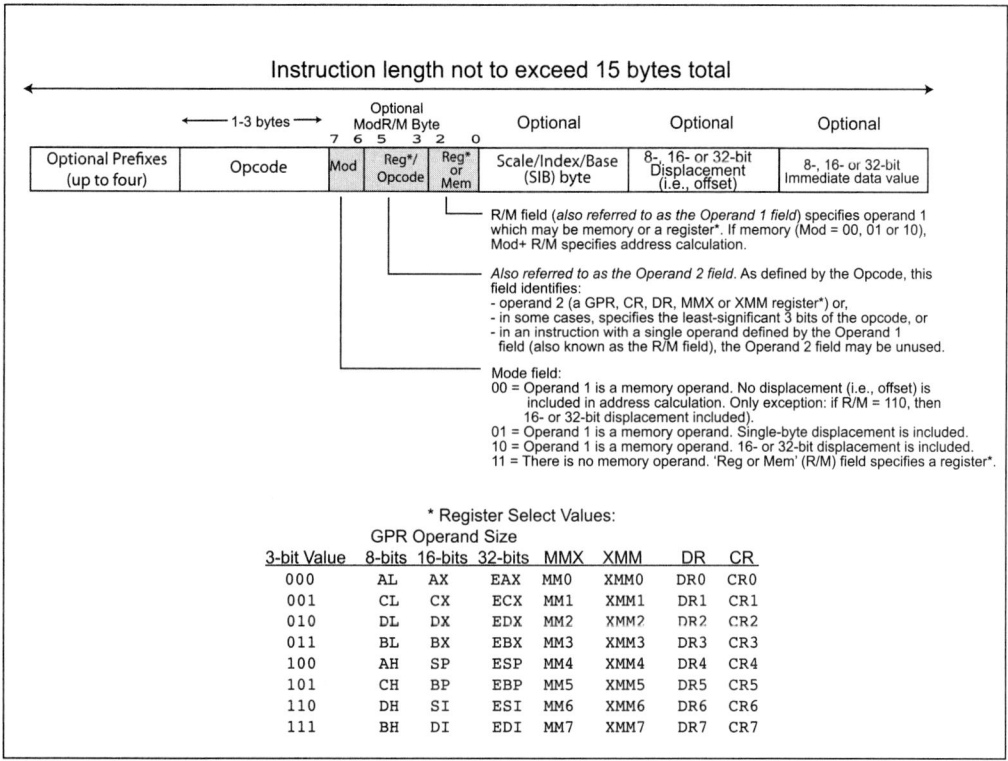

Figure 7-10: Micro-Maps (i.e., Groups) Associated with 1-byte Opcodes

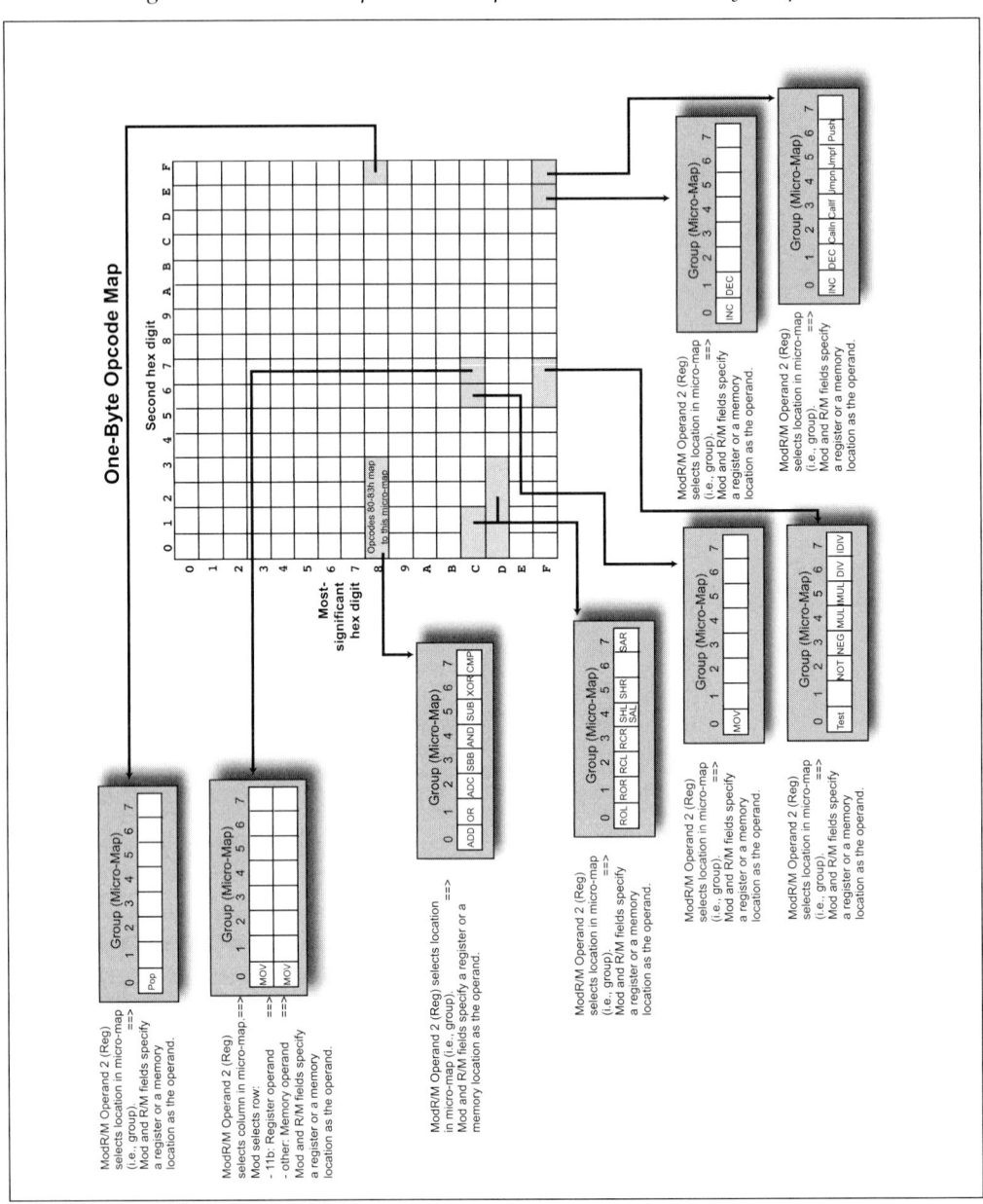

Micro-Maps Associated with 2-byte Opcodes

The 2-byte opcode map is shown in Figure 7-11 on page 183: the shaded entries are the opcodes associated with micro-maps (and the micro-maps are detailed in Table 7-6 through Table 7-12). As mentioned in the previous section, all but two of the 2-byte opcodes with micro-maps employ 2 x 8 micro-maps. The two exceptions (0F00h and 0FBAh; see Table 7-6 on page 183) employ 1 x 8 micro-maps.

Figure 7-11: Micro-Maps (i.e., Groups) Associated with 2-byte Opcodes

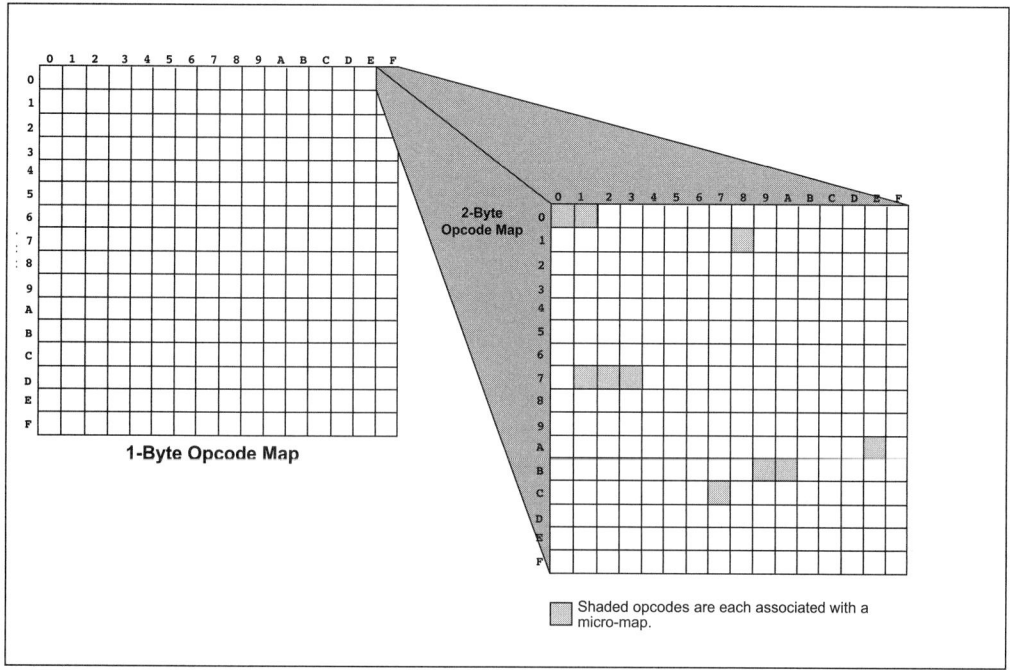

Table 7-6: 0F 00 Micro-Map

	ModRM Operand 2 Field (in binary)							
	000	001	010	011	100	101	110	111
Mod=any value	sldt	str	lldt	ltr	verr	verw		

Table 7-7: 0F 01 Micro-Map

	ModRM Operand 2 Field (in binary)							
	000	**001**	**010**	**011**	**100**	**101**	**110**	**111**
Mod: 00,01,10 (op=memory)	sgdt	sidt	lgdt	lidt				invlpg
Mod: 11 & Op 1: 0-> 1-> 2-> 3-> 4->	Rsvd vmcall vmlaunch vmresume vmxoff	monitor mwait	xgetbv xsetbv		smsw		lmsw	swapgs rdtscp

Table 7-8: 0F 18 Micro-Map

	ModRM Operand 2 Field (in binary)							
	000	001	010	011	100	101	110	111
Mod: 00,01,10 (op=memory)	prefetch nta	prefetch t0	prefetch t1	prefetch t2				
Mod: 11 (op=register)								

Table 7-9: 0F 71 Micro-Map

	ModRM Operand 2 Field (in binary)							
	000	001	010	011	100	101	110	111
Mod: 00,01,10 (op=memory)								

Table 7-9: 0F 71 Micro-Map

	ModRM Operand 2 Field (in binary)							
	000	001	010	011	100	101	110	111
Mod: 11 (op=register)			psrlw mmx +66=psrlw xmm		psraw mmx +66=psraw xmm		psllw mmx +66=psllw xmm	

Table 7-10: 0F 72 Micro-Map

	ModRM Operand 2 Field (in binary)							
	000	001	010	011	100	101	110	111
Mod: 00,01,10 (op=memory)								
Mod: 11 (op=register)			psrld mmx +66=psrld xmm		psrad mmx +66=psrad xmm		pslld mmx +66=pslld xmm	

Table 7-11: 0F 73 Micro-Map

	ModRM Operand 2 Field (in binary)							
	000	001	010	011	100	101	110	111
Mod: 00,01,10 (op=memory)								
Mod: 11 (op=register)			psrlq mmx +66= psrlq xmm	+66= psrldq xmm			psllq mmx +66= psllq xmm	+66 =pslldq xmm

Table 7-12: 0F AE Micro-Map

	ModRM Operand 2 Field (in binary)							
	000	001	010	011	100	101	110	111
Mod: 00,01,10 (op=memory)	fxsave	fxrstor	ldmxcsr	stmxcsr	xsave	xrstor		clflush
Mod: 11 (op=register)						lfence	mfence	sfence

Table 7-13: 0F B9 Micro-Map Is Reserved for Future Use

	ModRM Operand 2 Field (in binary)							
	000	001	010	011	100	101	110	111
Mod: 00,01,10 (op=memory)								
Mod: 11 (op=register)								

Table 7-14: 0F BA Micro-Map

	ModRM Operand 2 Field (in binary)							
	000	001	010	011	100	101	110	111
Mod=any value					bt	bts	btr	btc

Table 7-15: 0F C7 Micro-Map

	ModRM Operand 2 Field (in binary)							
	000	001	010	011	100	101	110	111
Mod: 00,01,10 (op=memory)		cmpxchg8b +rex.w=cmpxchg16b					no prefix=vmptrld +66=vmclear +F3=vmxon	vmptrst
Mod: 11 (op=register)								

3-byte Opcodes Don't Use Micro-Maps

None of the 3-byte opcodes currently employ micro-maps to achieve opcode expansion.

x87 FP Opcodes Inhabit Opcode Mini-Maps

Just as location 0Fh in the 1-byte opcode map acts as a window into the 256-location, 2nd-level opcode map inhabited by 2-byte opcodes, opcodes D8h - DFh, each of which is an x87 instruction with one opcode byte followed by a ModRM byte (and, possibly, a SIB byte), are windows (refer to Figure 7-12 on page 188) into 2nd-level opcode maps.

The opcode byte (e.g., D9h) selects a set of two 2nd-level maps, one a 1 x 8 map and the other a 4 x 16 map:

- **1 x 8 Map**. If the Mod field in the ModRM byte = 00b, 01b, or 10b (indicating the operand is a memory location), then the 1 x 8 map is selected and the 3-bit Operand 2 field of the ModRM byte selects one of the eight possible x87 FP instructions.
- **4 x 16 Map**. If the Mod field in the ModRM byte = 11b (indicating the operand is a register), then the 4 x 16 map is selected and the entire 8-bit ModRM byte (a value between C0h - FFh) selects one of the 64 possible x87 FP instructions.

Figure 7-12: x87 FP Instructions Inhabit Opcode Mini-Maps

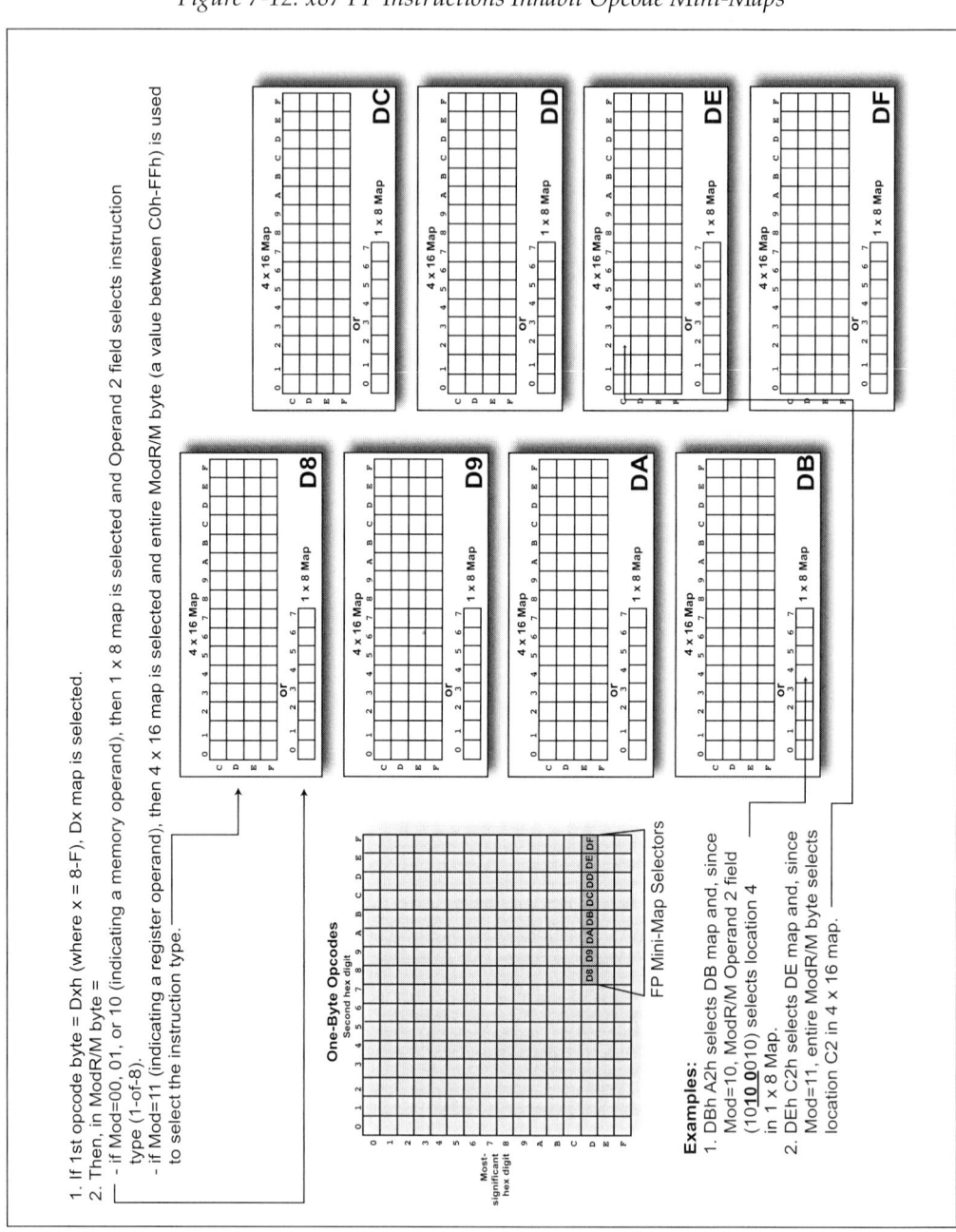

Special Opcode Fields

Refer to Figure 7-13 on page 192 and Figure 7-14 on page 192. The last opcode byte of an instruction is referred to as the primary opcode byte and, in some cases, one or more of its bit fields are used to define additional information related to the instruction. Additionally, special bit fields are sometimes defined within the ModRM byte associated with some instructions. Both categories of special fields are summarized in Table 7-16 on page 189.

Table 7-16: Fields in Primary Opcode or ModRM Byte of Some Instructions

Field	Found in	Basic Description
w	Bit 0 of opcode byte. In some cases, bit 3 is the w bit and bits 2:0 is the reg field.	**Width bit**. See Figure 7-14 on page 192. Also see Figure 7-15 on page 193.
d	Bit 1 of opcode byte.	**Direction bit**. • **D = 0**: – Source = Operand 2 (ModRM byte's REG field). – Destination = Operand 1 (ModRM byte's RM field). • **D = 1**: – Source = Operand 1 (ModRM byte's RM field). – Destination = Operand 2 (ModRM byte's REG field). See Figure 7-14 on page 192 and ModRM layout in Figure 7-9 on page 181.
s	Bit 1 of opcode byte.	**Sign extension bit**. See Figure 7-14 on page 192. • **S = 0**: No sign extension. • **S = 1**: Extend the sign bit.

Table 7-16: Fields in Primary Opcode or ModRM Byte of Some Instructions (Continued)

Field	Found in	Basic Description
reg	Opcode byte	The following instructions include a 3-bit REG field which is used to encode the register operand in the three lsbs of the primary opcode byte: • BSWAP • DEC • INC • MOV immediate-to-register • POP • PUSH • XCHG Figure 7-15 on page 193 illustrates the reg field encoding.
eee	ModRM byte	Operand 2 field identifies: • A Control register (CR0 - CR7), • A Debug register (DR0 - DR7), • Or a Test register (TR0 - TR7) as an operand.
sreg2	Opcode byte	On the 286 processor, this 2-bit field was used in bits 4:3 to define which of the four segment registers to use for a POP to segment register. Encoding: • 00: ES segment register. • 01: reserved. • 10: SS segment register. • 11: DS segment register.
sreg3	Opcode byte and ModRM	In the primary opcode or ModRM bytes, used to identify which of the six segment registers (this was introduced in the 386; 286 only had four segment registers) would act as an operand. Encoding: • 000: ES segment register. • 001: CS segment register. • 010: SS segment register. • 011: DS segment register. • 100: FS segment register. • 101: GS segment register. • 110: Reserved. • 111: Reserved.

Table 7-16: Fields in Primary Opcode or ModRM Byte of Some Instructions (Continued)

Field	Found in	Basic Description
gg	Opcode byte	**Granularity field**. Found in many MMX and SSE2 instructions as the least-significant two bits of the primary opcode byte. Defines the type of packed operands to be operated on. Encoding: • 00: Operation on packed bytes. • 01: Operation on packed words. • 10: Operation on packed doublewords (dwords). • 11: Operation on packed quadwords (qwords).
tttn	Opcode byte	For conditional instructions that test the state of condition code (cc) bits in the Eflags register: • *ttt* field defines the condition to be tested. • *n* field defines whether that condition is being tested for a true or false state. See Table 7-17 on page 193.
opcode	ModRM	In instructions that only operate on a single operand, the Operand 2 field (also referred to as the Reg field) of the ModRM byte is not required to define a second operand. In some instructions, this 3-bit field supplies the three least-significant bits of the opcode. For more information, see: • "Opcode Micro-Maps (Groups)" on page 180, and • "x87 FP Opcodes Inhabit Opcode Mini-Maps" on page 187.

Figure 7-13: The Primary Opcode Byte

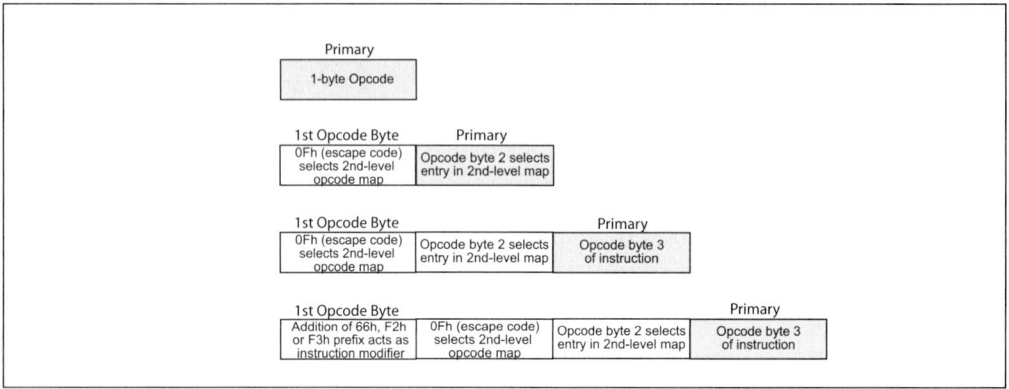

Figure 7-14: The Width, Sign-Extension and Direction Bits

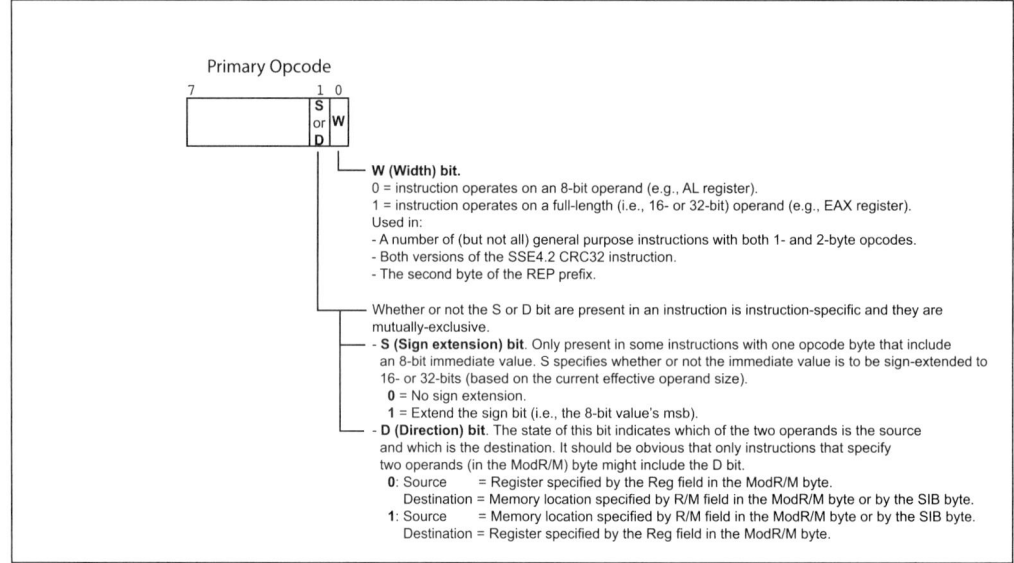

Figure 7-15: Reg Select Field in Primary Opcode Byte

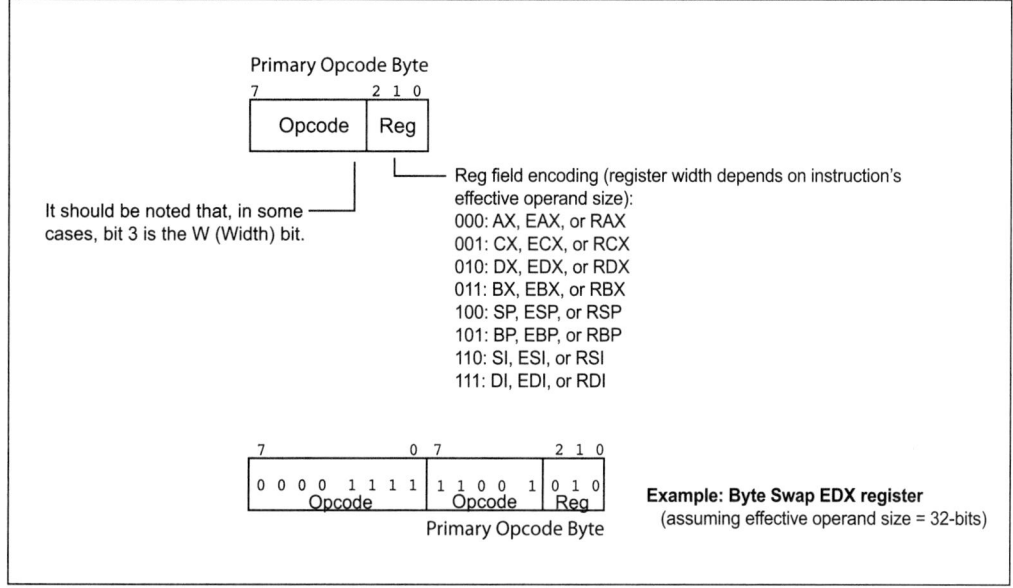

Table 7-17: tttn Condition Code Definition Field

ttt	n	Mnemonic	Condition Tested
000	0	O	Overflow.
000	1	NO	No overflow.
001	0	B, NAE	Below, Not above or equal
001	1	NB, AE	Not below, Above or equal
010	0	E, Z	Equal, Zero
010	1	NE, NZ	Not equal, Not zero
011	0	BE, NA	Below or equal, Not above
011	1	NBE, A	Not below or equal, Above

Table 7-17: tttn Condition Code Definition Field (Continued)

ttt	n	Mnemonic	Condition Tested
100	0	S	Sign
100	1	NS	Not sign
101	0	P, PE	Parity, Parity Even
101	1	NP, PO	Not parity, Parity Odd
110	0	L, NGE	Less than, Not greater than or equal to
110	1	NL, GE	Not less than, Greater than or equal to
111	0	LE, NG	Less than or equal to, Not greater than
111	1	NLE, G	Not less than or equal to, Greater than

Condition code test field (*tttn*) is found in the least-significant 4 bits of the primary opcode field of:
- Jcc (conditional jump) instructions.
- SETcc instructions.
- CMOV (conditional move) instructions.

Operand Identification

General

When executed, most instructions perform an operation on one or two data values (referred to as data operands). There are a number of possibilities:

- The contents of a single register.
- The contents of two registers.
- The contents of a register and a memory location.
- A data value provided as part of the instruction (referred to as an immediate data value) and the contents of a register.
- An immediate data value and the contents of a memory location.

This section describes the manner in which the data operand(s) are specified in an instruction.

Specifying Registers as Operands

When an instruction operates upon the contents of a register or registers, they are specified in one of the following ways:

- Implicitly by the instruction type.
- Explicitly by the programmer.

Some examples are shown in Table 7-18 on page 195. The sections that follow describe how register-based operands are encoded in the instruction.

Table 7-18: Examples of Register Operand Specification

Instruction	Operation	Implied Operand(s)	Explicitly-declared Operands
CLI or STI	Clear or set the IF bit in the Eflags register.	Eflags register.	None.
MUL	The unsigned multiply instruction takes one of the following basic forms: • MUL memory or • MUL register and performs the following operation: the contents of the EAX register is multiplied by the contents of the GPR register or memory location explicitly specified by the programmer and the result is stored in the EDX:EAX register pair.	EAX register. EDX register.	GPR register or memory location explicitly specified by the programmer.
MOV	ECX,EDX	None.	ECX register. EDX register.

Table 7-18: Examples of Register Operand Specification (Continued)

Instruction	Operation	Implied Operand(s)	Explicitly-declared Operands
ADC	Add with Carry: • ADC AX,1234	Carry bit in Eflags register.	• Immediate data value: 1234h • AX register.
	• ADC EBX, EDX	Carry bit in Eflags register.	• EDX register. • EBX register.

Implicit Register Specification

As demonstrated in Table 7-18 on page 195, by their very nature some instructions implicitly utilize one or more pre-defined registers as data operands.

Explicit Register Specification in Opcode

The following instructions include a 3-bit REG field that encodes the GPR register operand in the three lsbs of the primary opcode byte (see Figure 7-15 on page 193):

- BSWAP
- DEC
- INC
- MOV immediate-to-register
- POP
- PUSH
- XCHG

In most cases, however, the register(s) utilized by an instruction is specified in the ModRM byte (see the next section).

Explicit Register Specification in ModRM Byte

Refer to the ModRM byte in Figure 7-9 on page 181. Regarding register-based operands explicitly identified by the programmer, there are several cases:

Case 1. **Single register-based operand.** The instruction uses a single register-based operand explicitly identified by the programmer. In this case:
— The Mod field of the ModRM byte = 11b indicating that the instruction only utilizes register-based operands (and no memory-based operands).

— The register is identified by the 3-bit value in the Operand 1 field (also referred to as the RM field).

Case 2. **Two register-based operands.** The instruction uses two register-based operands explicitly identified by the programmer. In this case:

— The Mod field of the ModRM byte = 11b indicating that the instruction only utilizes register-based operands (and no memory-based operands).

— The two registers are identified by the Operand 1 and Operand 2 fields.

Case 3. **Memory-based operand and a register-based operand.** The instruction uses a memory-based operand and a register-based operand, both of which are explicitly identified by the programmer. In this case:

— The Mod field of the ModRM byte = 00b, 01b, or 10b, indicating that the instruction does include a memory-based operand.

— The method used to calculate the address of the memory-based operand is identified by the combination of the Mod and RM (i.e., Operand 1) fields.

— The register operand is identified by the value in the Operand 2 field.

The binary-weighted value encoded in the 3-bit Operand 1 or Operand 2 field identifies one of the following:

- **1-of-8 GPR registers.** When the instruction type is one that operates strictly on GPR registers, the 3-bit value selects 1 of 8 GPR registers. The effective operand size in force when the instruction is executed defines the size of the selected GPR register (e.g., AL, AX or EAX). The effective operand size is dependent on the following factors:

  — Whether the instruction was fetched from a 16- or 32-bit code segment.

  — If the instruction's primary opcode byte includes a W bit (Width bit; refer to Figure 7-14 on page 192), then the state of the W bit is taken into account.

  — Whether or not the programmer has included an Operand Size Override prefix in front of the instruction.

  Assuming the programmer has not prefaced the instruction with the Operand Size Override prefix, the ModRM byte's register select fields (each 3-bits wide) are interpreted as shown in Table 7-19 on page 198.

- **1-of-8 MMX registers** (MM0 - MM7).

  — When the instruction type is one that operates strictly on MMX registers, the 3-bit value selects 1 of 8 MMX registers (MM0 - MM7).

  — When the instruction type is one that operates on a GPR register and an MMX register:

    – The 3-bit value in the Operand 1 field selects 1 of 8 GPR registers (see Table 7-19 on page 198).

    – The 3-bit value in the Operand 2 field selects 1 of 8 MMX registers (MM0 - MM7).

- **1-of-8 XMM registers** (XMM0 - XMM7).
  — When the instruction type is one that operates strictly on XMM registers, the 3-bit value selects 1 of 8 XMM registers (XMM0 - XMM7).
  — When the instruction type is one that operates on a GPR register and an XMM register:
    – The 3-bit value in the Operand 1 field selects 1 of 8 GPR registers (see Table 7-19 on page 198).
    – The 3-bit value in the Operand 2 field selects 1 of 8 XMM registers (XMM0 - XMM7).
- **1-of-8 Debug Registers** (DR0 - DR7).
  — In this case, the 3-bit Operand 2 field selects 1 of 8 Debug registers (DR0 - DR7).
- **1-of-8 Control Registers** (CR0 - CR7).
  — In this case, the 3-bit Operand 2 field selects 1 of 8 Control registers (CR0 - CR7).

Table 7-19: Register Is Selected Based on Reg Value (plus Opcode's W bit if present)

Effective Operand Size	W bit?	ModRM Byte's Reg (Operand 2) Field Value							
		0	**1**	**2**	**3**	**4**	**5**	**6**	**7**
16-bit	No	AX	CX	DX	BX	SP	BP	SI	DI
16-bit	0	AL	CL	DL	BL	AH	CH	DH	BH
16-bit	1	AX	CX	DX	BX	SP	BP	SI	DI
32-bit	No	EAX	ECX	EDX	EBX	ESP	EBP	ESI	EDI
32-bit	0	AL	CL	DL	BL	AH	CH	DH	BH
32-bit	1	EAX	ECX	EDX	EBX	ESP	EBP	ESI	EDI

Addressing a Memory-Based Operand

Instruction Can Specify Only One Memory-Based Operand

An instruction may explicitly specify one or two operands (although some have no explicitly-specified operands) but only one of them may be based in memory. *x86 vendor documentation refers to there being twenty-four (or more) different* *memory addressing modes. In truth, there are **really only the four modes** summarized in Table 7-20 on page 199.*

Table 7-20: Summary of Memory Addressing Modes

Method	Effective Address Computed?	Effective Address Derivation
1	No	Effective address is contained in the specified register. Symbolically shown as: *[reg]*. Referred to as a **register-indirect address**.
2	No	Effective address is **hard-coded** in the instruction as a Displacement from the base address of a segment. Referred to as **direct addressing**.
3	Yes	Effective address = **[reg] +/- a hard-coded 8- or 32-bit value** (i.e., an 8- or 32-bit signed displacement).
4	Yes	Target memory item resides in a **data structure** and the effective address computation is defined by one of four calculation methods: 1. [base] + [index * SF]. 2. [base] + [index * SF] +/- hard-coded 8- or 32-bit value. 3. [index * SF] +/- hard-coded 8- or 32-bit value. 4. [ebp] + [index * SF] +/- hard-coded 8- or 32-bit value. **where:** • **base** = a register defined in the SIB byte containing the data structure's base address. • **index** = a register defined in the SIB byte containing the target record number in the data structure. • **SF** = the Scaling Factor (record length in bytes) to be multiplied by the value in the Index register. • The signed, 8- or 32-bit value is a **Displacement** that is hard-coded as part of the instruction. • **[ebp]** is the contents of the EBP register.

The instruction specifies how the logical processor is to calculate the memory address using one of two methods:

- **Just ModRM**. For methods 1 - 3 in Table 7-20 on page 199, the memory address calculation is fully-specified using the Mod and RM fields of the ModRM byte. In this case, the instruction does not include the SIB byte. "Addressing Memory Using the ModRM Byte" on page 200 describes this address calculation method.
- **ModRM + SIB**. For method 4 in Table 7-20 on page 199, the memory address calculation is specified using the combination of:
  — The Mod field in the ModRM byte.
  — The RM field in the ModRM byte.
  — The full SIB (Scale/Index/Base) byte.
  "Using the SIB Byte to Access a Data Structure" on page 203 describes this method of address calculation.

Addressing Memory Using the ModRM Byte

A Mod field value of 00b, 01b, or 10b indicates that Operand 1 is a memory-based operand while 11b indicates the operand (or operands) are contained in register(s) and there is no memory-based operand (register addressing was covered in "Specifying Registers as Operands" on page 195). There are eight possible RM field values associated with each 2-bit Mod value, yielding 24 possible methods for calculating the address of the memory operand.

When Effective Address Size = 16-Bits. Table 7-21 on page 201 defines the 24 memory address calculation methods available when an instruction is executed with an effective address size of 16 bits either because:
  — the instruction was fetched from a 16-bit code segment and was not prefaced by the Address Size Override prefix,
  — or the instruction was fetched from a 32-bit code segment and was prefaced by the Address Size Override prefix.

Note 1 (Table 7-21): If the Mod = 00b and RM = 110b, then the ModRM byte is followed by a programmer-specified 16-bit offset which is added to the Data Segment base address to yield the address of the memory operand.

Note 2 (Table 7-21): **When the effective address size is 16 bits, *there will not be a SIB byte* included in the instruction (because the 286 processor did not support the SIB byte).**

Table 7-21: ModRM Interpretation When Effective Address Size = 16-bits

• Opcode selects GPR, MMX or XMM • If GPRs, effective operand size selects 16- or 32-bit GPR (Width bit can select 8-bit GPR). Operand 2 (Reg field) ==>			AL AX EAX MM0 XMM0 **000**	CL CX ECX MM1 XMM1 **001**	DL DX EDX MM2 XMM2 **010**	BL BX EBX MM3 XMM3 **011**	AH SP ESP MM4 XMM4 **100**	CH BP EBP MM5 XMM5 **101**	DH SI ESI MM6 XMM6 **110**	BH DI EDI MM7 XMM7 **111**
Mod	**RM**	Calculation Components	\	\	\	Resultant ModRM Hex Value	\	\	\	\
00 Mem	000	[BX+SI]	00	08	10	18	20	28	30	38
	001	[BX+DI]	01	09	11	19	21	29	31	39
	010	[BP+SI]	02	0A	12	1A	22	2A	32	3A
	011	[BP+DI]	03	0B	13	1B	23	2B	33	3B
	100	[SI]	04	0C	14	1C	24	2C	34	3C
	101	[DI]	05	0D	15	1D	25	2D	35	3D
	110	DS:16-bit disp	06	0E	16	1E	26	2E	36	3E
	111	[BX]	07	0F	17	1F	27	2F	37	3F
01 Mem	000	[BX+SI]+8-bit disp	40	48	50	58	60	68	70	78
	001	[BX+DI]+8-bit disp	41	49	51	59	61	69	71	79
	010	[BP+SI]+8-bit disp	42	4A	52	5A	62	6A	72	7A
	011	[BP+DI]+8-bit disp	43	4B	53	5B	63	6B	73	7B
	100	[SI]+8-bit disp	44	4C	54	5C	64	6C	74	7C
	101	[DI]+8-bit disp	45	4D	55	5D	65	6D	75	7D
	110	[BP]+8-bit disp	46	4E	56	5E	66	6E	76	7E
	111	[BX]+8-bit disp	47	4F	57	5F	67	6F	77	7F
10 Mem	000	[BX+SI]+16-bit disp	00	88	90	98	A0	A8	B0	B8
	001	[BX+DI]+16-bit disp	81	89	91	99	A1	A9	B1	B9
	010	[BP+SI]+16-bit disp	82	8A	92	9A	A2	AA	B2	BA
	011	[BP+DI]+16-bit disp	83	8B	93	9B	A3	AB	B3	BB
	100	[SI]+16-bit disp	84	8C	94	9C	A4	AC	B4	BC
	101	[DI]+16-bit disp	85	8D	95	9D	A5	AD	B5	BD
	110	[BP]+16-bit disp	86	8E	96	9E	A6	AE	B6	BE
	111	[BX]+16-bit disp	87	8F	97	9F	A7	AF	B7	BF
11 Reg only	000	EAX/AX/AL/MM0/XMM0	C0	C8	D0	D8	E0	E8	F0	F8
	001	ECX/CX/CL/MM1/XMM1	C1	C9	D1	D9	E1	E9	F1	F9
	010	EDX/DX/DL/MM2/XMM2	C2	CA	D2	DA	E2	EA	F2	FA
	011	EBX/BX/BL/MM3/XMM3	C3	CB	D3	DB	E3	EB	F3	FB
	100	ESP/SP/AH/MM4/XMM4	C4	CC	D4	DC	E4	EC	F4	FC
	101	EBP/BP/CH/MM5/XMM5	C5	CD	D5	DD	E5	ED	F5	FD
	110	ESI/SI/DH/MM6/XMM6	C6	CE	D6	DE	E6	EE	F6	FE
	111	EDI/DI/BH/MM7/XMM7	C7	CF	D7	DF	E7	EF	F7	FF

When Effective Address Size = 32-Bits. Table 7-22 on page 202 defines the 24 memory address calculation methods available when an instruction is executed with an effective address size of 32-bits either because:
— the instruction was fetched from a 16-bit code segment and was prefaced by the Address Size Override prefix,
— or the instruction was fetched from a 32-bit code segment and was not prefaced by the Address Size Override prefix.

Note 1 (Table 7-22): If RM = 100b for any of the three Mod values associated with a memory operand (i.e., 00b, 01b, or 10b), then the instruction includes the SIB byte and the address is formed according to the rules shown in Table 7-23 on page 205. See "Using the SIB Byte to Access a Data Structure" on page 203.

Note 2 (Table 7-22): If Mod = 00b and RM = 101b, then the instruction includes the SIB byte and a 32-bit displacement (i.e., offset) and the memory address is formed as follows:

[Index Reg x Scale Factor] + 32-bit displacement.

Table 7-22: ModRM Interpretation When Effective Address Size = 32-bits

• Opcode selects GPR, MMX or XMM
• If GPRs, effective operand size selects
  16- or 32-bit GPR (Width bit can select
  8-bit GPR).
			AL
			AX
			EAX
			MM0
			XMM0
				CL
				CX
				ECX
				MM1
				XMM1
					DL
					DX
					EDX
					MM2
					XMM2
						BL
						BX
						EBX
						MM3
						XMM3
							AH
							SP
							ESP
							MM4
							XMM4
								CH
								BP
								EBP
								MM5
								XMM5
									DH
									SI
									ESI
									MM6
									XMM6
										BH
										DI
										EDI
										MM7
										XMM7

		Operand 2 (Reg field) ==>	**000**	**001**	**010**	**011**	**100**	**101**	**110**	**111**
Mod	**RM**	**Calculation Components**	Resultant ModRM Hex Value							
00 Mem	000	[EAX]	00	08	10	18	20	28	30	38
	001	[ECX]	01	09	11	19	21	29	31	39
	010	[EDX]	02	0A	12	1A	22	2A	32	3A
	011	[EBX]	03	0B	13	1B	23	2B	33	3B
	100	**address = SIB**	04	0C	14	1C	24	2C	34	3C
	101	32-bit Displacement	05	0D	15	1D	25	2D	35	3D
	110	[ESI]	06	0E	16	1E	26	2E	36	3E
	111	[EDI]	07	0F	17	1F	27	2F	37	3F

Table 7-22: ModRM Interpretation When Effective Address Size = 32-bits (Continued)

01 Mem	000	[EAX]+8-bit disp	40	48	50	58	60	68	70	78
	001	[ECX]+8-bit disp	41	49	51	59	61	69	71	79
	010	[EDX]+8-bit disp	42	4A	52	5A	62	6A	72	7A
	011	[EBX]+8-bit disp	43	4B	53	5B	63	6B	73	7B
	100	**SIB + 8-bit disp**	44	4C	54	5C	64	6C	74	7C
	101	[EBP]+8-bit disp	45	4D	55	5D	65	6D	75	7D
	110	[ESI]+8-bit disp	46	4E	56	5E	66	6E	76	7E
	111	[EDI]+8-bit disp	47	4F	57	5F	67	6F	77	7F
10 Mem	000	[EAX]+32-bit disp	80	88	90	98	A0	A8	B0	B8
	001	[ECX]+32-bit disp	81	89	91	99	A1	A9	B1	B9
	010	[EDX]+32-bit disp	82	8A	92	9A	A2	AA	B2	BA
	011	[EBX]+32-bit disp	83	8B	93	9B	A3	AB	B3	BB
	100	**SIB + 32-bit disp**	84	8C	94	9C	A4	AC	B4	BC
	101	[EBP]+32-bit disp	85	8D	95	9D	A5	AD	B5	BD
	110	[ESI]+32-bit disp	86	8E	96	9E	A6	AE	B6	BE
	111	[EDI]+32-bit disp	87	8F	97	9F	A7	AF	B7	BF
11 Reg only	000	EAX/AX/AL/MM0/XMM0	C0	C8	D0	D8	E0	E8	F0	F8
	001	ECX/CX/CL/MM/XMM1	C1	C9	D1	D9	E1	E9	F1	F9
	010	EDX/DX/DL/MM2/XMM2	C2	CA	D2	DA	E2	EA	F2	FA
	011	EBX/BX/BL/MM3/XMM3	C3	CB	D3	DB	E3	EB	F3	FB
	100	ESP/SP/AH/MM4/XMM4	C4	CC	D4	DC	E4	EC	F4	FC
	101	EBP/BP/CH/MM5/XMM5	C5	CD	D5	DD	E5	ED	F5	FD
	110	ESI/SI/DH/MM6/XMM6	C6	CE	D6	DE	E6	EE	F6	FE
	111	EDI/DI/BH/MM7/XMM7	C7	CF	D7	DF	E7	EF	F7	FF

Using the SIB Byte to Access a Data Structure

The introduction of the 386 saw the addition of a new memory addressing feature designed to facilitate access to fixed-length records in memory-based data structures. The idea is a simple one (see Figure 7-16 on page 204):
- The record number to be accessed (referred to as the Index)
- Is multiplied by the record length (referred to as the Scaling Factor). The defined record lengths (i.e., scaling factors) are 1, 2, 4 and 8 bytes (2^{Scale}).
- The resultant offset (the address of the target record within the data structure) is added to the base address of the data structure in memory.

Refer to Table 7-22 on page 202. This feature is only available when the effective address size is 32-bits and its use (and the presence of the SIB byte; see Figure 7-17 on page 205) is indicated when the ModRM byte's:
- **Mod = 00b and**
  — RM = 100b. In this case, the address is formed using the Index and Base registers and the Scale Factor specified in the SIB byte.
  — RM = 101b. In this case, the address is formed using the Index register

and the Scale Factor specified in the SIB byte and the base address specified as a 32-bit displacement encoded in the instruction.

- **Mod = 01b and**
  — RM = 100b. In this case, the address is formed using the Index and Base registers and the Scale Factor specified in the SIB byte and then adding the 8-bit displacement value encoded in the instruction.
- **Mod = 10b and**
  — RM = 100b. In this case, the address is formed using the Index and Base registers and the Scale Factor specified in the SIB byte and then adding the 32-bit displacement value encoded in the instruction.

Table 7-23 on page 205 details the encoding of the SIB byte and the resultant addressing modes available.

Figure 7-16: SIB Byte Usage

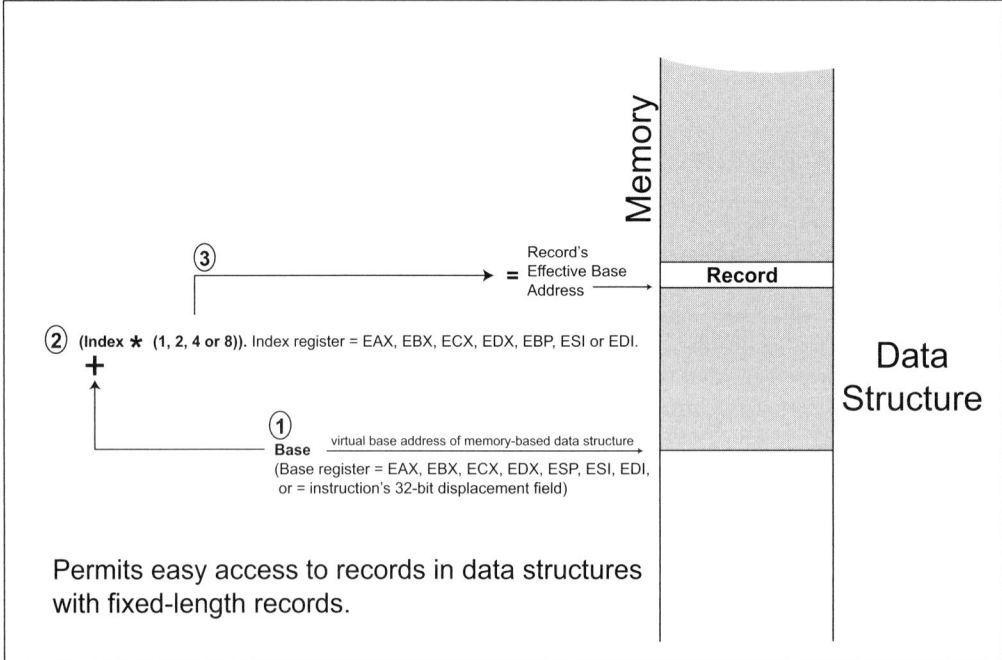

③ = Record's Effective Base Address

② **(Index ✱ (1, 2, 4 or 8)).** Index register = EAX, EBX, ECX, EDX, EBP, ESI or EDI.

+

① **Base**   virtual base address of memory-based data structure
(Base register = EAX, EBX, ECX, EDX, ESP, ESI, EDI,
or = instruction's 32-bit displacement field)

Record

Memory

Data Structure

Permits easy access to records in data structures with fixed-length records.

Figure 7-17: The Scale/Index/Base (SIB) Byte

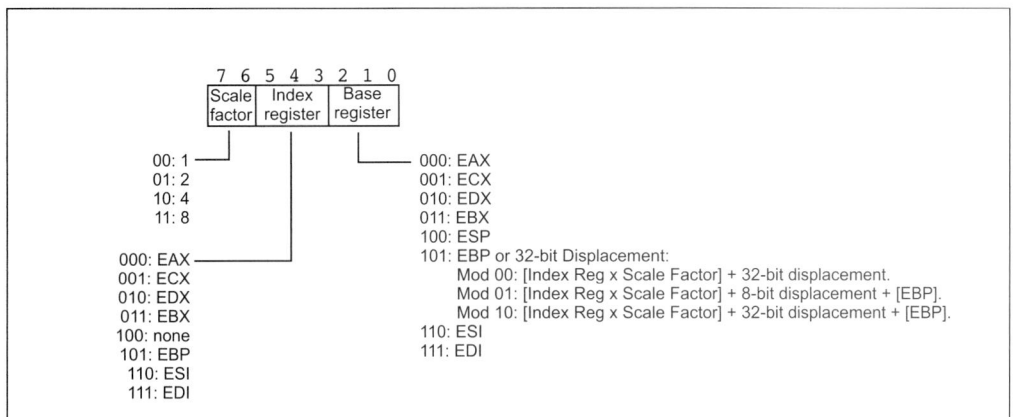

*Table 7-23: Effective Address = Base + (Index * Scale Factor)*

Base Register ==>		EAX 000	ECX 001	EDX 010	EBX 011	ESP 100	Note1 101	ESI 110	EDI 111
Index Register	Scale Factor (Index * SF)	Hex Value of SIB Byte							
000 [EAX]	00	00	01	02	03	04	05	06	07
001 [ECX]		08	09	0A	0B	0C	0D	0E	0F
010 [EDX]	x 1	10	11	12	13	14	15	16	17
011 [EBX]		18	19	1A	1B	1C	1D	1E	1F
100 Note2		20	21	22	23	24	25	26	27
101 [EBP]		28	29	2A	2B	2C	2D	2E	2F
110 [ESI]		30	31	32	33	34	35	36	37
111 [EDI]		38	39	3A	3B	3C	3D	3E	3F
000 [EAX]	01	40	41	42	43	44	45	46	47
001 [ECX]		48	49	4A	4B	4C	4D	4E	4F
010 [EDX]	x 2	50	51	52	53	54	55	56	57
011 [EBX]		58	59	5A	5B	5C	5D	5E	5F
100 Note2		60	61	62	63	64	65	66	67
101 [EBP]		68	69	6A	6B	6C	6D	6E	6F
110 [ESI]		70	71	72	73	74	75	76	77
111 [EDI]		78	79	7A	7B	7C	7D	7E	7F

*Table 7-23: Effective Address = Base + (Index * Scale Factor) (Continued)*

000	[EAX]	10	80	81	82	83	84	85	86	87
001	[ECX]		88	89	8A	8B	8C	8D	8E	8F
010	[EDX]	x 4	90	91	92	93	94	95	96	97
011	[EBX]		98	99	9A	9B	9C	9D	9E	9F
100	Note2		A0	A1	A2	A3	A4	A5	A6	A7
101	[EBP]		A8	A9	AA	AB	AC	AD	AE	AF
110	[ESI]		B0	B1	B2	B3	B4	B5	B6	B7
111	[EDI]		B8	B9	BA	BB	BC	BD	BE	BF
000	[EAX]	11	C0	C1	C2	C3	C4	C5	C6	C7
001	[ECX]		C8	C9	CA	CB	CC	CD	CE	CF
010	[EDX]	x 8	D0	D1	D2	D3	D4	D5	D6	D7
011	[EBX]		D8	D9	DA	DB	DC	DD	DE	DF
100	Note2		E0	E1	E2	E3	E4	E5	E6	E7
101	[EBP]		E8	E9	EA	EB	EC	ED	EE	EF
110	[ESI]		F0	F1	F2	F3	F4	F5	F6	F7
111	[EDI]		F8	F9	FA	FB	FC	FD	FE	FF

Note 1: Base register value = 101b provides the following address modes for the three memory-related values of ModRM[Mod]:

Mod	Effective Address
00	[Index Reg x Scale Factor] + 32-bit displacement.
01	[Index Reg x Scale Factor] + 8-bit displacement + [EBP].
10	[Index Reg x Scale Factor] + 32-bit displacement + [EBP].

Note 2: When SIB[Index] field = 100b, the effective memory address = the address contained in the Base register defined by the SIB[Base] field. In other words, there is no index value and the Scale Factor is don't care.

Near and Far Branch Target Addressing

Branches come in a number of forms. Table 7-24 on page 207 lists the manner in which the branch target address is specified.

Table 7-24: Branch Forms in 32-bit Mode

Type	Branch Form
Conditional Branch	• **Short Jump**. Forward or backward from offset in EIP register. Distance of up to 128 bytes backward or 127 forward is specified via an 8-bit, signed displacement which is sign-extended to 32-bits. • **Near Jump 16**. Forward or backward from offset in EIP register. Signed 16-bit displacement (sign-extended to 32-bits) permits jump up to 32K backward or 32K-1 forward of address in EIP register. • **Near Jump 32**. Forward or backward from offset in EIP register. Signed 32-bit displacement permits jump up to 2G backward or 2G-1 forward of address in EIP register.
Unconditional branch within same segment (i.e., a **near Jump**)	• **Short Jump, EIP-Relative**. Forward or backward from offset in EIP register (EIP + 127 to -128), specified via an 8-bit, signed displacement sign-extended to 32-bits. • **Near Jump, 16-bit EIP-Relative**. Forward or backward from offset in EIP register (EIP + [32K-1] to -32K), specified via a 16-bit, signed displacement sign-extended to 32-bits. • **Near Jump, 32-bit EIP-Relative**. Forward or backward from offset in EIP register (EIP + [2G-1] to - 2G), specified via a 32-bit, signed displacement. • **Near Jump, Register or Memory Indirect**. The 16- or 32-bit branch target address is specified in a 16- or 32-bit register or by a 16- or 32-bit address pointer stored in memory.

Table 7-24: Branch Forms in 32-bit Mode (Continued)

Type	Branch Form
Unconditional branch to different segment (i.e., a **far Jump**)	**Far Jump, new CS:IP or CS:EIP values specified in instruction.** The new selector and offset values to be placed in the CS:EIP register pair are encoded in the instruction itself: • in four byte CS:IP form if performing a far jump to a 16-bit code segment. • in six byte CS:EIP form if performing a far jump to a 32-bit code segment. **Far Jump, Memory Indirect**. The new selector and off-set values to be placed in the CS:EIP register pair are specified in memory in one of two forms: • When performing a **far jump to a 16-bit code segment**, four bytes are read from memory: a new 16-bit CS selector value and a new 16-bit IP value. • When performing a **far jump to a 32-bit code segment,** six bytes are read from memory: a new 16-bit CS selector value and a new 32-bit EIP value.
Procedure Call within same segment (i.e., a **near Call**)	• **Near Call, 16-bit EIP-Relative**. Forward or backward from offset in EIP register (EIP + [32K-1] to - 32K), specified via a 16-bit, signed displacement sign-extended to 32-bits. • **Near Call, 32-bit EIP-Relative**. Forward or backward from offset in EIP register (EIP + [2G-1] to - 2G), specified via a 32-bit, signed displacement. • **Near Call, Register or Memory Indirect**. The 16- or 32-bit branch target address is specified in a 16- or 32-bit register or by a 16- or 32-bit address pointer stored in memory.

Table 7-24: Branch Forms in 32-bit Mode (Continued)

Type	Branch Form
Procedure Call to different segment (i.e., a **far Call**)	**Far Call, new CS:IP or CS:EIP values specified in instruction.** The new selector and offset values to be placed in the CS:EIP register pair are encoded in the instruction itself: • in four byte CS:IP form if performing a far call to a 16-bit code segment. • in six byte CS:EIP form if performing a far call to a 32-bit code segment. **Far Call, Memory Indirect.** The new selector and offset values to be placed in the CS:EIP register pair are specified in memory in one of two forms: • When performing a **far call to a 16-bit code segment**, four bytes are read from memory: a new 16-bit CS selector value and a new 16-bit IP value. • When performing a **far call to a 32-bit code segment**, six bytes are read from memory: a new 16-bit CS selector value and a new 32-bit EIP value.

Specifying an Immediate Value As an Operand

Some instructions include an immediate data value supplied by the programmer to be used in the operation. In all cases, the immediate data value is located at the end of the instruction. There are four scenarios:

Case 1. **Immediate value + register encoded in opcode.** One operand is the immediate data value specified by the programmer. The other operand, a register, is implicitly identified by the 3 lsbs of the instruction opcode. In this case, there are no ModRM or SIB bytes (because no programmer-specified register or memory operands need be identified). The instruction consists of: opcode + immediate data value. Example: ADC AL,3A.

Case 2. **Two operands: immediate value and register encoded in ModRM.** The programmer specifies an immediate data value and a register as operands. In this case, the instruction consists of: opcode + ModRM + immediate data value. The ModRM byte is encoded as follows:

— Mod = 11b, indicating that no memory operand is involved.

— Operand 2 = xxxb, where xxx = three additional opcode bits indicating that the instruction acts upon one operand and a programmer-supplied immediate data value.

— Operand 1 = yyyb, where yyy identifies the register operand.

Case 3. **Two operands: immediate value and a memory operand**. The programmer specifies a memory location and an immediate data value as the operands. In this case, the instruction consists of: opcode + ModRM (+ SIB byte, possibly) + immediate data value. The ModRM byte is encoded as follows:

— Mod = 00b, 01b, or 10b indicating that a memory operand is involved.

— Operand 2 = xxxb, where xxx = three additional opcode bits indicating that the instruction acts upon one operand and a programmer-supplied immediate data value.

— Operand 1, the RM field, combined with the Mod field (and, possibly, the SIB byte), identifies the address of the memory-based operand.

Case 4. **Three operands: immediate value + two registers or a register and a memory operand**. The programmer specifies two operands (two registers or a memory address and a register) and an immediate data value as operands. The opcode defines the instruction as having three operands. In this case, the instruction consists of: opcode + ModRM (+ SIB byte, possibly) + immediate data value. The ModRM byte is encoded as follows:

— Mod =
   – 11b if both operands are registers.
   – 01b, 01b, or 10b if one operand is memory-based.

— Operand 2 = xxxb, where xxx identifies a register as an operand.

— Operand 1, the RM field indicates either:
   – Another register as an operand (if Mod = 11b).
   – Or, combined with the Mod field (and, possibly, the SIB byte), identifies the address of the memory-based operand (if Mod = 00b, 01b, or 10b).

Instruction Prefixes

Up to four optional instruction prefixes, each one byte long, may be included before the first opcode byte to alter the instruction's normal execution characteristics. The currently-defined IA-32 instruction prefixes are:

• an optional **Operand Size Override** prefix.
• an optional **Address Size Override** prefix.
• an optional **Lock** prefix.
• an optional **Repeat** prefix to define the extent of a memory string operation or an IO input or output string operation.
• an optional **Segment Override** prefix to access a segment other than the data segment defined by the DS register.

- An optional **Branch Hint** prefix to accompany a conditional branch (Jcc) instruction.
- An optional **REX** (**R**egister **ex**tension) prefix that enables an instruction to access a 64-bit data operand (in memory or a 64-bit register) and to access the new registers introduced with the advent of 64-bit Mode. The REX prefix is only valid in 64-bit Mode and is covered in "The REX Prefix" on page 1043.

Operand Size Override Prefix (66h)

In order to limit the number of opcodes, the same opcode is used for an instruction whether it operates on an 8-, 16- or 32-bit operand. As an example:

```
mov al,dl
mov ax,dx
mov eax,edx
```

all use the same base opcode. This naturally brings up a question: how does the logical processor determine which registers are being referenced? The answer is simple and is described in the next two sections.

In 32-bit Mode

The logical processor is operating in 32-bit Mode whenever it is fetching code from a 32-bit code segment (the code segment descriptor's L bit = 0 and D bit = 1; see Figure 14-2 on page 421). Unless instructed otherwise when executing an instruction (by prefacing an instruction with the Operand Size Override prefix), the logical processor assumes that the default data operand size is 32-bits. Some instruction opcodes also use the Width bit (bit 0 or 3 of the primary opcode byte, depending on the instruction type) to indicate whether to use an 8-bit or a full-width operand (in 32-bit Mode, full-width is 32-bits). If an instruction executing in 32-bit Mode is prefaced by the Operand Size Override prefix (66h), full-width is considered to be 16-bits rather than 32-bits. Some examples are shown in Table 7-25 on page 212.

Table 7-25: Example Instruction Execution in 32-bit Mode (with and without Operand Size Override prefix)

Instruction	Operand Size Override Prefix?	Opcode Byte		ModRM Byte			Description
		Opcode	W bit	Mod	Reg 1	Reg 2	
mov al,dl	No	1000 100	0	11	000 al	010 dl	W=0, so 1-byte operand registers.
88C2 ==>	**Description:** • **Opcode** = 1000 1000b (88h): – bit 1 (Direction bit) = 0 indicating Operand 2 to Operand 1. – bit 0 (Width bit) = 0 indicating 1-byte operands. • **ModRM** = 1100 0010b (C2h): – Mod = 11b, operation on two registers: – Operand 2 = 000, AL register. – Operand 1 = 010, DL register							
mov eax,edx	No	1000 100	1	11	000 eax	010 edx	Same opcode, but W=1, so full-width, 32-bit register operands.
89C2 ==>	**Description:** • **Opcode** = 1000 1001b (89h): – bit 1 (Direction bit) = 0 indicating Operand 2 to Operand 1. – bit 1 (Width bit) = 0 indicating full-width operands (32-bits). • **ModRM** = 1100 0010b (C2h): – Mod = 11b, operation on two registers: – Operand 2 = 000, EAX register. – Operand 1 = 010, EDX register.							

Table 7-25: Example Instruction Execution in 32-bit Mode
(with and without Operand Size Override prefix) (Continued)

Instruction	Operand Size Override Prefix?	Opcode Byte		ModRM Byte			Description
		Opcode	W bit	Mod	Reg 1	Reg 2	
mov ax,dx	Yes (66h)	1000 100	1	11	000 ax	010 dx	Same opcode with prefix, so full width = 16, not 32.
6689C2 ==>	**Description:** • **66 = Operand Size Override prefix**. Normal full-width operands are 16-bits for this instruction's execution. • **Opcode** = 1000 1001b (89h): – bit 1 (Direction bit) = 0 indicating Operand 2 to Operand 1. – bit 0 (Width bit) = 1 indicating full-width operand (16-bits). • **ModRM** = 1100 0010b (C2h): – Mod = 11b, operation on two registers: – Operand 2 = 000, AL register. – Operand 1 = 010, DL register.						

In 16-bit Mode

The logical processor is operating in 16-bit Mode whenever:

- It is fetching code from a 16-bit code segment (the code segment descriptor's L bit = 0 and D bit = 0; see Figure 14-3 on page 422).
- It is in Real Mode or VM86 Mode.

Unless instructed otherwise when executing an instruction (by prefacing an instruction with the Operand Size Override prefix), the logical processor assumes that the default data operand size is 16-bits. Some instruction opcodes also use the Width bit (bit 0 or 3 of the primary opcode byte, depending on the instruction type) to indicate whether to use an 8-bit or a full-width operand (in 16-bit Mode, full-width is 16-bits). If an instruction executing in 16-bit Mode is prefaced by the Operand Size Override prefix (66h), full-width is considered to be 32-bits rather than 16-bits. Some examples are shown in Table 7-26 on page 214.

Special Usage of 66h Prefix

Refer to "Special Use of Prefix Bytes" on page 177.

Table 7-26: Example Instruction Execution in 16-bit Mode (with and without override)

Instruction	Operand Size Override Prefix?	Opcode Byte		ModRM Byte			Description
		Opcode	W bit	Mod	Reg 1	Reg 2	
mov al,dl 88C2	No	1000 100	0	11	000 al	010 dl	W=0, so 1-byte operand registers.
mov ax,dx 89C2	No	1000 100	1	11	000 ax	010 dx	Same opcode, but W=1, so full-width, 16-bit register operands.
mov eax,edx 6689C2	Yes (66h)	1000 100	1	11	000 eax	010 edx	Same opcode with prefix, so full width = 32, not 16.

Address Size Override Prefix (67h)

The logical processor is operating in 32-bit Mode whenever it is fetching code from a 32-bit code segment (the code segment descriptor's L bit = 0 and D bit = 1; see Figure 14-2 on page 421). Unless instructed otherwise when executing an instruction that accesses a memory operand (by prefacing an instruction with the Address Size Override prefix), it assumes that the default memory address size is 32-bits.

Likewise, the logical processor is operating in 16-bit Mode whenever it is fetching code from a 16-bit code segment (the code segment descriptor's L bit = 0 and D bit = 0; see Figure 14-3 on page 422). Unless instructed otherwise when executing an instruction that accesses a memory operand (by prefacing an instruction with the Address Size Override prefix), it assumes that the default memory address size is 16-bits (because 286 segments were a maximum of 64KBs in size).

In 32-Bit Mode

Consider the following example and assume that the logical processor is operating in 32-bit Mode:

```
MOV  EAX,[EBX]  ;without Address Size Override prefix (67h), displacement
                ; in brackets is assumed to be 32-bits (and EBX—not BX—
                ;is therefore used).
MOV  EAX,[BX]   ;if the same instruction is preceded by the Address Size
                ;Override prefix (67h), displacement in brackets is 16-bits
                ;(and BX is therefore used).
```

In 16-Bit Mode

The logical processor is operating in 16-bit Mode whenever:

- It is fetching code from a 16-bit code segment (the code segment descriptor's L bit = 0 and D bit = 0; see Figure 14-3 on page 422).
- It is in Real Mode or VM86 Mode.

Consider the following example and assume that the logical processor is operating in 16-bit Mode:

```
MOV  EAX,[BX]   ;without Address Size Override prefix (67h), displacement
                ; in brackets is assumed to be 16-bits (and BX is therefore
                ;used).
MOV  EAX,[EBX]  ;if the same instruction is preceded by the Address Size
                ;Override prefix (67h), displacement in brackets is 32-bits
                ;(and EBX is therefore used).
```

Lock Prefix

Shared Resource Concept

Assume that the OS sets aside an area of memory to be used by tasks executing on multiple logical processors (or even by different tasks executed by the same logical processor) as a shared memory buffer. It is intended to be used as follows:

1. Before using the buffer (i.e., reading from or writing to it), a task must first test a memory-based semaphore to ensure that the buffer isn't currently owned by another task. If the buffer is currently unavailable (semaphore value is non-zero), the task wishing to gain ownership should periodically check back to see when it becomes available.
2. When the semaphore indicates that the buffer is available (semaphore value = 0), the task sets it, indicating that it has exclusive ownership of the buffer. The buffer is then unavailable if any other task should attempt to gain ownership of it.

3. Having gained exclusive ownership of the buffer, the task can now read and write the buffer.
4. If the buffer is in an area of memory designated as WT, WC, or UC memory (refer to "Memory Type Configuration" on page 599), memory writes are absorbed into the logical processor's Posted Memory Write Buffer (PMWB). *These buffers are not snooped* when other agents access memory. In this case, when the task is done using the buffer, it should ensure that all of its updates (i.e., memory writes) have been flushed all the way to memory.
5. After ensuring that the buffer has received all updates, the task should release ownership of the buffer (by clearing the semaphore location to 0) so it can be accessed by other tasks.

Race Condition Can Present Problem

Consider the following possibility:

1. The task executing on logical processor 0 reads the semaphore to determine the buffer's availability. The task tests the semaphore's value and determines that the buffer is available (semaphore value is zero).
2. After the task on logical processor 0 has completed the memory read to obtain and test the semaphore value, a task executing on logical processor 1 initiates a memory read request to test the state of the same semaphore. It completes the read and begins testing the value.
3. The logical processor 0 task initiates a memory write to update the semaphore to a non-zero value to mark the shared buffer as unavailable. After it completes the write, it considers itself the sole owner of the buffer.
4. The logical processor 1 task also determines that the buffer is available and it now also performs a memory write to update the semaphore to a non-zero value to mark the shared buffer as unavailable. It completes the write and, like the task executing on logical processor 0, considers itself the sole owner of the buffer.

Two tasks executing on two separate logical processors now each believe that they have exclusive ownership of the buffer.

Guaranteeing Atomicity of Read/Modify/Write

The problem cited in the previous section came about because logical processor 1 was able to read the semaphore immediately after logical processor 0 read it (but before it updated it). The two logical processors were in a race condition. Logical processor 0 then wrote to it, followed by logical processor 1 writing to it. The tasks on the two logical processors each ended up believing they had sole ownership of the buffer.

The problem can be averted if logical processor 0 could prevent other initiator's from accessing memory (either all of memory or just the affected area of memory) from the time it initiates its read until the time it performs the write to update the semaphore to a non-zero value. In other words, it should lock access to memory while it performs the read/modify/write (frequently referred to as a RMW) of the semaphore.

To do this, the programmer uses an instruction (e.g., CMPXCHG) prefixed by the Lock prefix (F0h) to perform the RMW operation. When executing such an instruction, the logical processor:

1. Asserts the LOCK# signal when it initiates the memory read, keeps LOCK# asserted while it performs the internal semaphore test, and performs the memory write to update the semaphore before releasing the LOCK# signal. The assertion of LOCK# prevents a priority agent (e.g., the chipset) from obtaining bus ownership during this period.
2. It also prevents any of the other logical processors from initiating a memory transaction by continuously asserting its bus ownership request signal for the duration of the read and subsequent write.

Please note that the locking method described above is specific to Intel processors that communicate with the chipset and each other via the FSB. The hardware locking mechanism is processor design-specific. For example, the method used by processors that communicate via the Intel QPI interface is different (but the goal and the result is the same).

Use Locked RMW to Obtain and Give Up Semaphore Ownership

The programmer should always:

*   Use a locked RMW instruction to obtain ownership of the semaphore, and
*   Use a locked instruction to release ownership (in other words, perform a locked RMW to clear the semaphore back to zero).

Locked instructions are *serializing, synchronizing* operations. All x86 processors subsequent to the Pentium Pro perform out-of-order execution. This means that if the programmer used an unlocked RMW to release the semaphore, it could be executed before all of the code that precedes it has been executed. Using a locked RMW instruction ensures that the logical processor will execute all instructions before the locked instruction prior to executing it (i.e., it is serializing). In addition, the locked instruction is synchronizing—it forces all posted writes within the logical processor to be flushed to external memory before executing the next instruction. This ensures that the buffer has received all updates before it ownership is released.

Instructions That Accept Lock Prefix

By their very nature, some instructions result in a memory read followed by a memory write (to the same location). The following instructions may be preceded by the LOCK prefix to force the assertion of LOCK# for the duration of the resultant read and write:

*   The bit test and modify instructions: BTS, BTR, and BTC.
*   The exchange instructions: XADD, CMPXCHG, CMPXCHG8B, and CMPXCHG16B.
*   The following single-operand arithmetic and logical operations: INC, DEC, NOT, and NEG.
*   The following two-operand arithmetic and logical operations: ADD, ADC, SUB, SBB, AND, OR, and XOR.

The XCHG instruction doesn't require the LOCK prefix to assert LOCK#.

Repeat Prefixes

Normal Usage

A string instruction is one that, based on an initial count loaded into the CX or ECX register processes a string of bytes, words or dwords. As an example, the following code fragment moves 128 dwords from the source buffer in memory to the destination buffer in memory:

```
mov esi, 10000000h ;set up source buffer address
mov edi, 20000000h ;set up destination buffer address
mov ecx, 128d      ;count in ecx register
rep movsd          ;loop until done
```

*   The first three instructions set up the start address of the source and destination buffers in the ESI and EDI registers and the number of dwords to move in the ECX register.
*   The fourth instruction, movsd, instructs the logical processor to:
    — read a dword from the address pointed to by ESI (into a temporary, unnamed holding register),
    — write it to the memory address pointed to by EDI,
    — increment or decrement (based on the state of Eflags[DF]) ESI and EDI by 4 (because we're moving dwords),

— decrement ECX by one (because we've moved one dword),

— and test for ECX = 0 to see if we're done yet.

Placing the REP prefix (F3h) before the `movsd` instruction tells the logical processor to loop on the instruction until the count has been exhausted, at which time it will fall through to the instruction immediately after the `movsd`.

The Repeat prefix comes in **two flavors**:

- **F3h**. **Terminate on count exhaustion**. When used with any of the following instructions, the logical processor is testing for ECX = 0 after each execution of the string instruction it prefaces and it is referred to simply as the REP prefix (repeat while ECX non-zero).
  - **INS: Input String**. Performs *n* repetitions of: IO Read, memory write, increment or decrement memory pointer in DI or EDI (based on state of Eflags[DF] bit), decrement Count register by one, test for Count register = 0.
  - **LODS: Load String**. Each time it's executed, this instruction loads the next operand (a byte, word, or dword) from the specified memory buffer into the AL, AX, or EAX register.
  - **MOVS: Move String**. Copies a block of bytes, words or dwords from one memory buffer to another. Performs *n* repetitions of: memory read from [SI] or [ESI], memory write to [DI] or [EDI], increment or decrement source and destination memory pointers (based on state of Eflags[DF] bit), decrement Count register by one, test for Count register = 0.
  - **OUTS: Output String**. Performs *n* repetitions of: memory read from [SI] or [ESI], IO write, increment or decrement memory pointer in SI or ESI (based on state of Eflags[DF] bit), decrement Count register by one, test for Count register = 0.
  - **STOS: Store String**. Each time it's executed, this instruction stores the byte, word, or dword in the AL, AX, or EAX register into the next location in a memory buffer.
  - **Terminate on count exhaustion or if Eflags[ZF] = 0**. When used before either of the following instructions, the logical processor is testing for either ECX = 0 or Eflags[ZF] = 0 after each execution of the string instruction it prefaces. In this context, it is referred to as the **REPE prefix** (Repeat while Eflags[ZF] = 1 and ECX is still non-zero).
    - CMPS: Compare String.
    - SCAS: Scan String.
- **F2h**. **Terminate on count exhaustion or if Eflags[ZF] = 1**. When used before either of the following instructions, the logical processor is testing for either ECX = 0 or Eflags[ZF] = 1 after each execution of the string instruction it

prefaces. In this context, it is referred to as the **REPNE prefix** (repeat while ECX is still non-zero and Eflags[ZF] = 0).
— CMPS: Compare String.
— SCAS: Scan String.

Special Usage

Refer to "Special Use of Prefix Bytes" on page 177.

Segment Override Prefix

General

Consider the following instruction:

```
mov eax, [00001000]
```

It instructs the logical processor to add the specified offset (00001000h) to the base address of the default data segment (the segment specified in the DS register) and then read four bytes into the EAX register. But what if the programmer wishes to read four bytes from memory starting at location 00001000h in a segment other than the one specified in the DS register? That's where the segment override prefix comes in:

```
mov eax,es:[00001000] ;ES prefix (26h) precedes instruction
mov eax,fs:[00001000] ;FS prefix (64h) precedes instruction
mov eax,gs:[00001000] ;GS prefix (65h) precedes instruction
mov eax,cs:[00001000] ;CS prefix (2Eh) precedes instruction
mov eax,ss:[00001000] ;SS prefix (36h) precedes instruction
```

Note: The segment override prefix to specify the DS segment is 3Eh.

There are some constraints:

* They may not be used with branch instructions.
* Instruction fetches must be made from the code segment.
* Destination strings (pointed to by the EDI register) in string instructions reside in the ES segment.
* Push and pop operations always reference the SS segment.

Usage In String Operations

With reference to string instructions:

- By default, the segment associated with the source string pointed to by the ESI register is the DS segment, but a segment override (e.g., `fs:[esi]`) can be used to access a source string in any other segment.
- With reference to the destination string pointed to by the EDI register, however, that string by definition resides in the ES segment and may not be overridden by a segment override.

Segment Override Use With MMX and SSE1 - 4 Instructions

It stands to reason that a segment override can only be used if an instruction accesses a memory-based operand.

Branch Hint Prefix

Starting with the Pentium, all x86 processors incorporate some form of branch prediction logic that maintains history on each conditional branch instruction executed and, based on that history, attempts to predict whether the branch will be taken or not taken the next time that branch is detected entering the instruction pipeline. Guided by the branch prediction logic, the instruction fetch logic attempts to fetch the instruction stream most likely to be executed as a result of the conditional branch's execution. If it predicts incorrectly, however, a performance hit is taken. The incorrect instruction stream must be deleted, creating a bubble in the pipeline which must then be refilled with the instruction stream from the correct path of execution.

The first time that a conditional branch enters the instruction pipeline, the branch prediction logic (a special form of cache) has no history on its previous execution and must therefore make a prediction based on default assumptions (a prediction that may prove to be incorrect). The programmer or compiler may increase the odds that the path to be taken by a conditional branch will be correctly predicted by prefacing the conditional branch with one of the two Branch Hint prefixes:

- **2Eh**: **predict** the branch as **not taken** and assume that the instructions immediately following the conditional branch are to be executed.
- **3Eh**: **predict** the branch as **taken** and assume that the instructions from the branch target address are to be executed.

x86 Instruction Set Architecture

Summary of Instruction Set Formats

Table 7-27: Format(s) Associated With Instruction Sets

Instruction Set	General Format(s)
General Purpose	**Format1:** 1-byte opcode **Format2:** 1-byte opcode + imm8 **Format3:** 1-byte opcode + Displacement **Format4:** 1-byte opcode + 16:16 or 16:32 **Format5:** 1-byte opcode + Port Number **Format6:** 1-byte opcode + Interrupt Vector **Format7:** 1-byte opcode + ModRM **Format8:** 1-byte opcode + ModRM + imm8 **Format9:** 2-byte opcode (0F xx) **Format10:** 2-byte opcode (0F xx) + Displacement **Format11:** 2-byte opcode (0F xx) + ModRM **Format12:** 2-byte opcode (0F xx) + ModRM + imm8 **Format13:** 3-byte opcode (0F 38 xx) **Format14:** 3-byte opcode (0F 38 xx) + ModRM Optionally, assuming that the ModRM byte's Mod field = 00b, 01b, or 10b (which means a memory operand is involved), there may also be a SIB byte and/or a Displacement field included. Some instructions also include an 8-bit immediate data value.
x87 FP	**Format: 1-byte opcode + ModRM** **(optionally, + SIB + Displacement)** All x87 FP instructions consists of at least two bytes: • an opcode byte, the upper five bits of which are always 1101 1b, so the opcode byte falls within the range D8h-DFh. • A ModRM byte. Optionally, assuming that the ModRM byte's Mod field = 00b, 01b, or 10b (which means a memory operand is involved), there may also be a SIB byte and/or a Displacement field. See "x87 FP Opcodes Inhabit Opcode Mini-Maps" on page 187 for more information.

Table 7-27: Format(s) Associated With Instruction Sets (Continued)

Instruction Set	General Format(s)
MMX	**Format: 2-byte opcode (0F xx) + ModRM** **(optionally, + SIB + Displacement + 8-bit immediate data)** All MMX instructions are characterized by 2-byte opcodes (0F xx) and therefore reside in the 2nd-level opcode map pictured in Figure 7-5 on page 174. With one exception (the EMMS instruction), the ModRM byte is also included. If the Mod field = 00b, 01b, or 10b (which means a memory operand is involved), there may also be a SIB byte and/or a Displacement field. In two cases (both Shift instructions) a shift count is included as an 8-bit immediate data value.
SSE	**Format1: 2-byte opcode (0F xx) + ModRM** **(optionally, + SIB + Displacement + 8-bit immediate data)** **Format2: F3 + 2-byte opcode (0F xx) + ModRM** **(optionally, + SIB + Displacement + 8-bit immediate data)** All SSE instructions are characterized by 2-byte opcodes (0F xx) and therefore reside in the 2nd-level opcode map pictured in Figure 7-5 on page 174. In some cases, preceding the instruction with a special use of the F3h (Repeat) prefix alters the size of the operand(s). In all cases, the ModRM byte is included. If the Mod field = 00b, 01b, or 10b (which means a memory operand is involved), there may also be a SIB byte and/or a Displacement field. Some instructions also include an 8-bit immediate data value.

Table 7-27: Format(s) Associated With Instruction Sets (Continued)

Instruction Set	General Format(s)
SSE2	**Format1: 2-byte opcode (0F xx) + ModRM** 　　　　**(optionally, + SIB + Displacement + 8-bit immediate data)** **Format2: 66h + 2-byte opcode (0F xx) + ModRM** 　　　　**(optionally, + SIB + Displacement + 8-bit immediate data)** **Format3: F2h + 2-byte opcode (0F xx) + ModRM** 　　　　**(optionally, + SIB + Displacement + 8-bit immediate data)** **Format4: F3h + 2-byte opcode (0F xx) + ModRM** 　　　　**(optionally, + SIB + Displacement + 8-bit immediate data)** All SSE instructions are characterized by 2-byte opcodes (0F xx) and therefore reside in the 2nd-level opcode map pictured in Figure 7-5 on page 174. In some cases, preceding the instruction with a special use of the 66h, F2h or F3h prefix alters the size of the operand(s). In all cases, the ModRM byte is included. If the Mod field = 00b, 01b, or 10b (which means a memory operand is involved), there may also be a SIB byte and/or a Displacement field. Some instructions also include an 8-bit immediate data value. The PAUSE instruction is an odd case, consisting of the F3h prefix followed by an opcode byte of 90h.
SSE3	**Formats1-4: same as SSE2 (except no immediate values)** **Format5: DB, DD, DF (each an x87 opcode) + ModRM** 　　　　**(optionally, + SIB + Displacement)** See the description of SSE2 in this table.

Table 7-27: Format(s) Associated With Instruction Sets (Continued)

Instruction Set	General Format(s)
SSSE3	**Format1: 3-byte opcode (0F 38 xx) + ModRM** **(optionally, + SIB + Displacement)** **Format2: 3-byte opcode (0F 3A xx) + ModRM** **(optionally, + SIB + Displacement)** **Format3: 66 + 3-byte opcode (0F 38 xx) + ModRM** **(optionally, + SIB + Displacement)** **Format4: 66 + 3-byte opcode (0F 3A xx) + ModRM** **(optionally, + SIB + Displacement)** All SSSE3 instructions are characterized by 3-byte opcodes—0F 38 xx or 0F 3A xx—and therefore reside in one of the 3rd-level opcode maps as pictured in Figure 7-7 on page 178. In some cases, preceding the instruction with a special use of the 66h prefix alters the size of the operand(s). In all cases, the ModRM byte is included. If the Mod field = 00b, 01b, or 10b (which means a memory operand is involved), there may also be a SIB byte and/or a Displacement field.
SSE4.1	**Format1: 66 + 3-byte opcode (0F 38 xx) + ModRM** **(optionally, + SIB + Displacement)** **Format2: 66 + 3-byte opcode (0F 3A xx) + ModRM** **(optionally, + SIB + Displacement + 8-bit immediate data)** All SSE4.1 instructions are characterized by 3-byte opcodes—0F 38 xx or 0F 3A xx—and therefore reside in one of the 3rd-level opcode maps as pictured in Figure 7-7 on page 178. In all cases, the instructions are preceded by a special use of the 66h prefix. In all cases, the ModRM byte is included. If the Mod field = 00b, 01b, or 10b (which means a memory operand is involved), there may also be a SIB byte and/or a Displacement field. In some cases of format 2, an 8-bit immediate data value may also be included. **Note**: SSE4.1 instructions that include the REX byte have not been included here. "64-bit Operands and Addressing" on page 1041 covers the instruction format issues related to the 64-bit extensions.

Table 7-27: Format(s) Associated With Instruction Sets (Continued)

Instruction Set	General Format(s)
SSE4.2	**Format1: F2 + 3-byte opcode (0F 38 xx) + ModRM** **(optionally, + SIB + Displacement)** **Format2: 66 + 3-byte opcode (0F 3A xx) + ModRM** **(optionally, + SIB + Displacement + 8-bit immediate data)** **Format3: F3 + 2-byte opcode (0F xx) + ModRM** **(optionally, + SIB + Displacement)** All SSE4.1 instructions (except one: the POPCNT instruction) are characterized by 3-byte opcodes—0F 38 xx or 0F 3A xx—and therefore reside in one of the 3rd-level opcode maps as pictured in Figure 7-7 on page 178. In all cases, the instructions are preceded by a special use of the 66h, F2h or F3h prefix. In all cases, the ModRM byte is included. If the Mod field = 00b, 01b, or 10b (which means a memory operand is involved), there may also be a SIB byte and/or a Displacement field. Only one instruction, POPCNT, adheres to format 3. **Note**: SSE4.2 instructions that include the REX byte have not been included here. "64-bit Operands and Addressing" on page 1041 covers the instruction format issues related to the 64-bit extensions.

8 *Real Mode (8086 Emulation)*

The Previous Chapter

The previous chapter provided a detailed explanation of the structure of an IA-32 instruction and covered the following topics:

- Effective Operand Size.
- Instruction Composition.
- Instruction Format Basics.
- Opcode (Instruction Identification).
  — In the Beginning.
  — 1-byte Opcodes.
  — 2-byte Opcodes Use 2-Level Lookup.
  — 3-byte Opcodes Use 3-Level Lookup.
  — Opcode Micro-Maps (Groups).
  — x87 FP Opcodes Inhabit Opcode Mini-Maps.
  — Special Opcode Fields.
- Operand Identification.
  — Specifying Registers as Operands.
  — Addressing a Memory-Based Operand.
  — Specifying an Immediate Value As an Operand.
- Instruction Prefixes.
  — Operand Size Override Prefix (66h).
  — Address Size Override Prefix (67h).
  — Lock Prefix.
  — Repeat Prefixes.
  — Segment Override Prefix.
  — Branch Hint Prefix.
- Summary of Instruction Set Formats.

This Chapter

This chapter provides a detailed description of Real Mode operation and covers the following topics:

- 8086 Emulation.
- Unused Facilities.
- Real Mode OS Environment.
- Running Real Mode Applications Under a Protected Mode OS.
- Real Mode Applications Aren't Supported in IA-32e Mode.
- Real Mode Register Set.
- IO Space versus Memory Space.
- IO and Memory-Mapped IO Operations.
- Operand Size Selection.
- Address Size Selection.
- Real Mode Memory Addressing.
- Real Mode Interrupt/Exception Handling.
- Summary of Real Mode Limitations.

The Next Chapter

The next chapter provides a detailed description of the x87 FPU and covers the following topics:

- A Little History.
- x87 FP Instruction Format.
- FPU-Related CR0 Bit Fields.
- x87 FPU Register Set.
  — The FP Data Registers.
  — x87 FPU's Native Data Operand Format.
  — 32-bit SP FP Numeric Format.
  — DP FP Number Representation.
  — FCW Register.
  — FSW Register.
  — FTW Register.
  — Instruction Pointer Register.
  — Data Pointer Register.
  — Fopcode Register.
- FP Error Reporting.
  — Precise Error Reporting.
  — Imprecise (Deferred) Error Reporting.
  — Why Deferred Error Reporting Is Used.
  — The WAIT/FWAIT Instruction.
  — CR0[NE].
  — Ignoring FP Errors.

8086 Emulation

Real Mode was introduced with the advent of the 8086/8088 processors, and, due to the huge success of the IBM PC and the proliferation of software written for the Real Mode environment, Intel could ill-afford to leave it behind. Immediately after the removal of reset, all subsequent x86 processors emulate the operation of the 8086 by initiating operation in Real Mode. There are, of course, some differences (see Table 8-1 on page 229).

Table 8-1: Basic Differences Between 8086 Operation and Real Mode

Difference	Basic Description
Speed of execution	In the IBM PC, the processor clock ran at 4.77MHz. Today's processors execute Real Mode code hundreds of times faster.
Cache boost	Today's processors enjoy a substantial performance boost due to on-chip caches.
Accessing extended memory	While the 8086/8088 processors were strictly limited to a 1MB address space due to an address bus width of 20-bits, current-day x86 processors can, even in Real Mode, access significantly more memory: • See "Accessing Extended Memory in Real Mode" on page 307. • See "Big Real Mode" on page 310.
Operand and address size	**Operand Size.** While the default data operand size in Real Mode is 16-bits, 32-bit operands can be specified by prefacing an instruction with the Operand Size Override prefix. The logical processor can then access 32-bit operands in memory as well as the 32-bit GPR registers: EAX, EBX, ECX, EDX, ESP, EBP, ESI, and EDI. The 8086/8088 GPR registers were only 16-bits wide. **Address Size.** While the default address size for memory-based operands in Real Mode is 16-bits, a 32-bit address can be specified by prefacing an instruction with the Address Size Override prefix.

Table 8-1: Basic Differences Between 8086 Operation and Real Mode (Continued)

Difference	Basic Description
Number of memory data segments	Using the ES, FS and GS Segment Override prefixes, the programmer can access memory-based data operands in the E, F and G data segments. The 8086/8088 only implemented the DS data segment.
Integrated x87 FPU	Today's logical processors incorporate an integrated x87 FPU. The 8087 FPU was implemented as an optional, external companion device to the 8086/8088. Upon detection of a FP instruction, the processor had to forward the instruction to the x87 FPU by performing a series of IO write transactions on its external interface. Very slow, indeed.
Debug register set	The address breakpoint facility is available through the Debug register set (not implemented on the 8086/8088).
Additional instructions available	The instructions listed in Table 8-2 on page 230, although not available on the 8086/8088, can be used in Real Mode.

Table 8-2: Expanded/Enhanced Real Mode Instructions

Instructions Available (that weren't present in the 8086/8088)
The MMX instruction set as well as the MMX data registers (MM0 - MM7).
The SSE1, SSE2, SSE3, SSSE3, SSE4.1 and SSE4.2 instruction sets as well as the SSE register set and the SSE FP exception (exception 19).
MOV instructions that operate on the Control and Debug registers.
Load segment register instructions: LSS, LFS, and LGS.
Generalized multiply and multiply immediate data instructions.
Shift and rotate by immediate counts.
PUSHA, PUSHAD, POPA and POPAD, and PUSH immediate data stack instructions.
MOVSX and MOVZX Move with sign extension instructions.

Table 8-2: Expanded/Enhanced Real Mode Instructions (Continued)

Instructions Available (that weren't present in the 8086/8088)
Large displacement J*cc* instructions.
CMPXCHG, CMPXCHG8B, CMPXCHG16B, and XADD Exchange instructions.
MOVS, CMPS, SCAS, LODS, and STOS String instructions.
• Bit test and bit scan instructions: BT, BTS, BTR, BTC, BSF, and BSR. • Byte set-on condition instruction: SET*cc*. • Byte swap (BSWAP) instruction.
SHLD and SHRD Double shift instructions.
PUSHF and POPF Eflags control instructions.
ENTER and LEAVE control instructions.
BOUND instruction.
CPU identification (CPUID) instruction.
Kernel-related instructions: CLTS, INVD, WINVD, INVLPG, LGDT, SGDT, LIDT, SIDT, LMSW, SMSW, RDMSR, WRMSR, RDTSC, and RDPMC.

Unused Facilities

The following tables and registers associated with a Protected Mode OS kernel are *not used in Real Mode except when software initializes them in preparation for a switch to Protected Mode operation*:

- The Global Descriptor Table (GDT) and the GDT register (GDTR).
- The Local Descriptor Tables (LDTs) and the LDT register (LDTR). The LDT register is not accessible in Real Mode.
- The facilities associated with virtual-to-physical address translation (i.e., paging):
  — CR3 (Page Directory Address Register, or PDBR).
  — CR2 (Page Fault Address Register).
  — The memory-based Page Directory and Page Tables.
- CR4 (New Features Control Register). Some bits are applicable to Real Mode while others are not.
- XCR0 (XFEM) register.

- Task Register (TR). It is not accessible in Real Mode.
- Virtualization Technology register set and related memory-based tables (e.g., VMCS).

Real Mode OS Environment

This discussion focuses on an ancient OS (DOS). Antiquated terminology and processes are therefore described.

Single-Task OS Environment Overview

The 8086/8088 processors were not designed to support a multitasking OS. Rather, the intention was to run an OS (e.g., DOS) that permitted the end-user to specify a single application to be loaded into memory and executed. When it was terminated, control would return back to the OS which would then prompt the end-user for another selection.

A typical single-task OS (e.g., MS DOS) consists of the following basic components:

- The Command Line Interface (CLI).
- The program loader.
- The OS services.

Command Line Interface (CLI)

Once the OS has been loaded into memory by the startup firmware, control is passed to the OS initialization code which sets up any necessary data structures (e.g., the Interrupt Descriptor Table) in memory, loads and initializes device drivers, etc., and then passes control to the CLI.

The CLI issues a prompt requesting that the user enter a command (e.g., identify the program to be run). The exact form that the prompt takes and the method utilized to make a selection is OS-dependent. In the case of DOS's COMMAND.COM CLI, the prompt—consisting of >:—was not very user-friendly. In response to the prompt, the user keys in a command or the name of a program to be executed. In the case of DOS DOSSHELL, the user used the mouse to point and click on a file name.

Program Loader

Once the user selects a file name:

1. The OS reads the file's directory entry from disk and ascertains the amount of RAM memory necessary to hold the program. The OS locates a block of free (i.e., unused) memory sufficiently large enough into which it can load the program.
2. The OS either directly accesses the disk controller to initiate the read, or issues a disk read request to the disk BIOS routine in system memory or to the disk device driver. The BIOS routine or driver issues the request to the disk controller.
3. If the disk-to-memory transfer will be performed by the DMA controller, the BIOS routine or driver programs the disk controller's associated DMA channel to transfer the data into the target memory buffer. If the disk controller has bus master capability, the BIOS routine or the driver programs the disk controller to transfer the data directly into the target memory buffer.
4. The DMA controller or bus master-capable disk controller transfers the block of information into memory.
5. The disk controller then informs the BIOS or driver that the transfer has been completed. To do so, it generates its device-specific interrupt causing the logical processor to jump to the disk interrupt handler.
6. The handler checks the disk controller's completion status to ensure that no errors were incurred during the transfer of the information into memory.
7. The handler returns a good completion notification to the BIOS or driver and a good completion is, in turn, returned to the OS.
8. Upon ascertaining that the requested program has been transferred into memory, the OS executes a far jump instruction to the program's entry point (in a far jump instruction, the programmer specifies a target location in a different code segment; in a near jump instruction, the programmer specifies a target location in the same code segment). The application program then begins execution.

OS Services

In the course of accomplishing its task, the application program may have to communicate with a number of devices in the system. It may have to read/write disk files, perform data communications, interface with the display and keyboard, etc. Rather than force the author of each application program to write routines to interface with these entities, the OS provides a variety of services to the application program. When the application wishes to establish a communications channel that can be used to access a disk file, for instance, it issues a *file open* request to the OS. The OS performs this function for the programmer. When the programmer needs to change the appearance of the display, a request can be issued to the OS. In short, the OS provides a toolbox of services useful to the application program. This increases the productivity of the application programmer by lessening the amount of code to be written. It also renders the application program platform hardware-independent (because it doesn't communicate directly with the devices).

Direct IO Access

In the early PC environment, in order to avoid calling inefficient device drivers built into the BIOS or those supplied by the OS and thereby achieve better performance, application programs sometimes communicated with a device adapter directly by writing to its registers using IO read and write instructions (IN and OUT). As a negative side effect, this renders the program much more device-dependent. In addition, the OS is left out of the loop, so it doesn't always know the current state of an IO device. In a single-task OS environment this usually will not cause problems because the OS only starts one application program at a time and lets it run to completion before starting another.

Because an application program can manipulate IO ports directly, neither application programs nor the OS can make any assumptions about the current state of an IO device when they begin execution, but must always initialize all of the device's IO registers to a known state before attempting to use it.

Application Memory Usage

Because a single-task OS only runs one program at a time, there is no need to protect application programs from invading each other's memory space. As long as the currently running application program doesn't trash itself or the OS that spawned it, everything should be fine.

Task Initiation, Execution and Termination

Figure 8-1 on page 235 illustrates (in a rather simplified manner) the application program's dependence on the OS while it's executing. The OS loads the task (i.e., application program) into memory and executes it. While executing, the task may issue calls to the OS requesting the performance of various functions. Upon completion, the task returns control back to the OS. The OS then deallocates the memory used by the program and prompts the user for the name of another program to be executed.

Figure 8-1: Task/OS Relationship

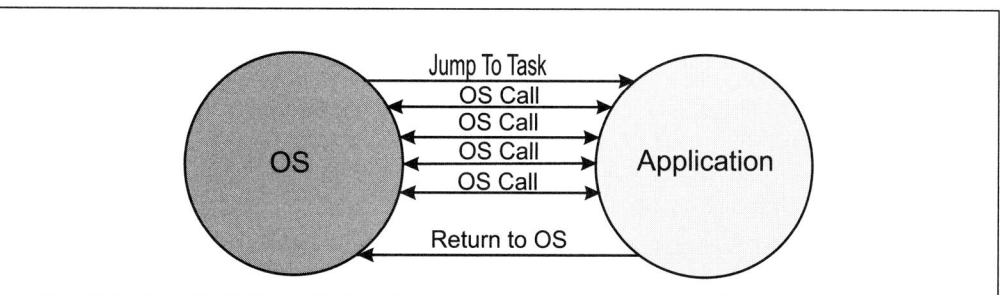

Running Real Mode Applications Under a Protected Mode OS

This subject is covered in "Virtual 8086 Mode" on page 783.

Real Mode Applications Aren't Supported in IA-32e Mode

Real Mode applications are not supported in IA-32e Mode and VM86 Mode (which allows Real Mode applications to be run under Protected Mode), is not supported in IA-32e Mode.

Real Mode Register Set

Introduction

Figure 8-2 on page 237 illustrates the Real Mode Register Set.

- A description of the Control Registers can be found in "Control Registers" on page 237.
  — CR1 is not implemented on any x86 processors.
  — CR2 and CR3 are only used with the virtual-to-physical address translation services (which are not supported in Real Mode, VM86 Mode, or SM Mode).

- A description of the Flags register can be found in "Flags Register" on page 251.
- A description of the Segment registers can be found in "Real Mode Memory Addressing" on page 288.
- A description of the Instruction Pointer register can be found in "Instruction Pointer Register" on page 259.
- A description of the General Purpose Registers can be found in "General Purpose Registers (GPRs)" on page 255.
- A description of the GDTR register can be found in "Protected Mode Memory Addressing" on page 383. Although the GDTR is not used in Real Mode, it must be programmed with the start address and size of the GDT in preparation for switching from Real Mode to Protected Mode.
- A description of the IDTR register can be found in:
  — "Real Mode Interrupt/Exception Handling" on page 316.
  — "Protected Mode Interrupts and Exceptions" on page 681.
- An introduction to the SSE registers can be found in "SSE Register Set" on page 262. A detailed description can be found in "The SSE Facilities" on page 851.
- An introduction to the x87 FPU registers can be found in "x87/MMX FPU Register Set" on page 260. A detailed description can be found in "Legacy x87 FP Support" on page 339.
- A detailed description of the MMX registers can be found in "The MMX Facilities" on page 835.
- A description of the Debug Registers can be found in "Debug Address Breakpoint Register Set" on page 262.

Figure 8-2: Real Mode Register Set

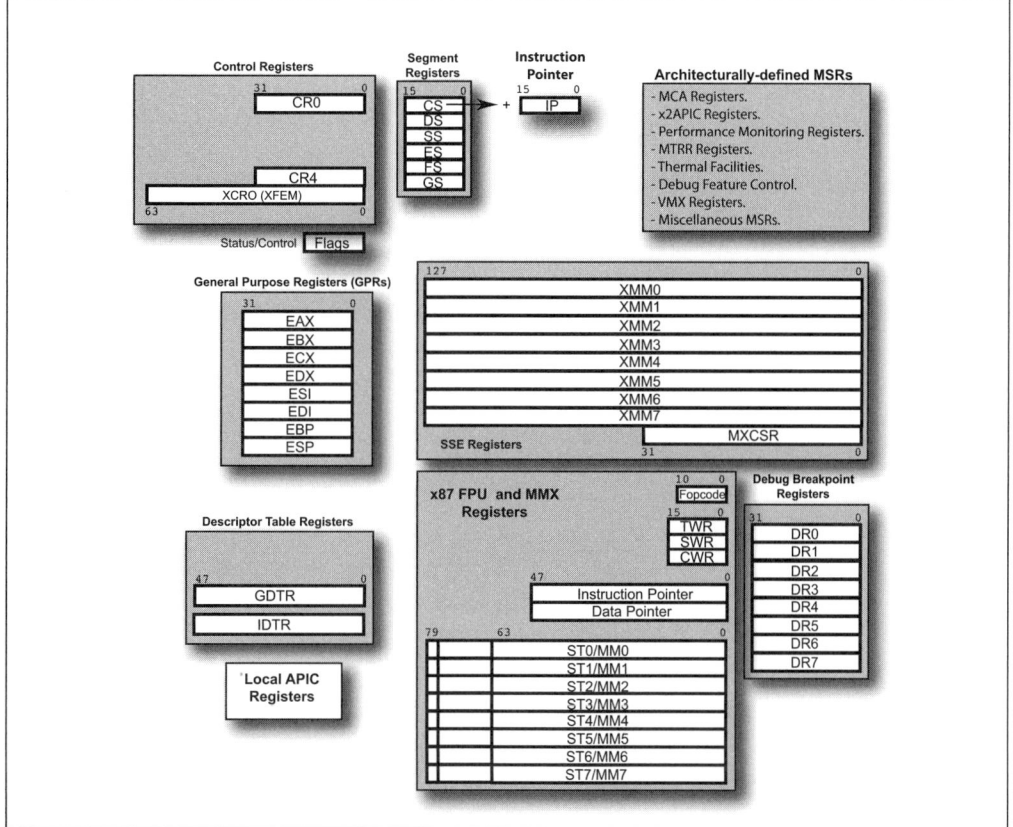

Control Registers

Figure 5-7 on page 85 illustrates the control registers currently-defined in the IA-32 ISA specification while Figure 8-2 on page 237 illustrates the Real Mode Control Registers.

- **CR1** is currently reserved (and has been since it was conceptually introduced with the advent of the 386).
- Although not currently-defined, **Control Registers 5 - 7** may be defined in later versions of the x86 ISA specification and may be implemented in future processors.

- Although only CR0, CR2, CR3, CR4 and, optionally, XCR0 are currently implemented, when operating in IA-32 Mode the instruction set format actually supports addressing up to eight Control Registers (CR0 - CR7).

A detailed description of the control register bit fields can be found in the this chapter and in the appropriate sections throughout the book.

CR0

Accessible in: all modes.

CR0 (see Figure 8-3 on page 238 and Table 8-3 on page 238) contains a diverse collection of bit fields that control various aspects of logical processor operation.

Figure 8-3: Control Register 0 (CR0) in IA-32 Mode

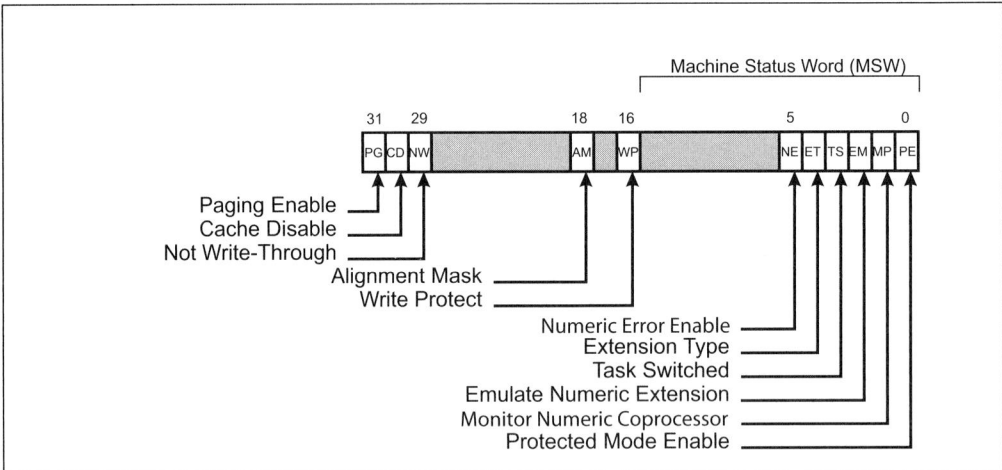

Table 8-3: CR0 Bit Assignment

Bit(s)	Name	Description
0	PE	**Protected Mode enable.** • 0 = Logical processor operates in Real Mode • 1 = Logical processor operates in Protected Mode.

Table 8-3: CR0 Bit Assignment (Continued)

Bit(s)	Name	Description
2:1	EM, MP	The OS uses these x87 FPU-related bits to indicate whether an x87 FPU is present and whether the logical processor is: • **running DOS**, • **running a multitasking OS**, • or **neither** of the above; in this case, a software exception is generated when the logical processor detects an x87 instruction and the X87 **FP instruction is emulated** in the exception handler. See Table 8-4 on page 241.
3	TS	**x87 Task Switch status bit**. The x87 FPU registers are not automatically saved on a task switch performed by the hardware-based task switch mechanism. When a task switch occurs in Protected Mode: • CR0[TS] is set to one. • Most but not all registers are automatically saved in the TSS (Task State Segment) associated with the currently-running task. • When an attempt is made to execute an x87 FP instruction or an MMX instruction while CR0[TS] = 1, a DNA (Device Not Available) Exception 7 is generated. • The DNA exception handler executes FSAVE or FXSAVE to save the x87 and, possibly, the SSE registers in the TSS of the task that last used the x87. This information is saved in an OS-designated area of the task's TSS data structure. • The DNA exception handler then clears CR0[TS] and executes an IRET instruction to return to the x87 instruction that caused the DNA exception. It now executes successfully.
4	ET	**x87 FPU type**. This bit is hardwired to one indicating that the logical processor incorporates a 387-style FPU.

Table 8-3: CR0 Bit Assignment (Continued)

Bit(s)	Name	Description
5	NE	**Numeric Exception**. Controls whether floating-point errors are reported using the DOS-compatible method (IRQ13; see "DOS-Compatible FP Error Reporting" on page 359) or by generating an exception 16. If the OS kernel sets NE = 1, a FPU error causes the logical processor to generate an internal exception 16.
16	WP	**Write-Protect** (WP). When set to one, protects read-only memory pages from supervisor (i.e., OS kernel) write access. • WP = 0 permits the OS to write to write-protected pages. • WP = 1. An exception is generated when the OS attempts to write to a write-protected memory page. For a detailed description, refer to "Write-Protection" on page 568 and "Example Usage: Unix Copy-on-Write Strategy" on page 569.
18	AM	**Alignment Mask** (AM). The alignment mask bit enables or disables alignment checking. • If AM = 0, Eflags[AC] is ignored and alignment checking isn't performed. • If AM = 1, allows Eflags[AC] to control alignment checking. See "Alignment Check Exception (17)" on page 774 for more information.
30:29	CD, NW	**Cache control**. These two bits (Cache Disable and Not Write-Through) control the logical processor's ability to cache information from memory. CD NW 0 0 Caching fully enabled. 0 1 Cache is locked. No new lines are read in. 1 0 Reserved. 1 1 Caching disabled (state after reset).

Table 8-3: CR0 Bit Assignment (Continued)

Bit(s)	Name	Description
31	PG	**Paging enable bit** (i.e., virtual-to-physical memory address translation). • 0 = Paging disabled. • 1 = Paging enabled. • See "IA-32 Address Translation Mechanisms" on page 493 for a detailed description of the virtual-to-physical memory address translation mechanism.

Table 8-4: CR0 FPU Control Bits

CR0[EM]	CR0[MP]	
0	0	**x87 FPU present and running DOS**: • CR0[EM] = 0 indicates that the x87 FPU is present and enables it to execute FP instructions. If an x86 processor incorporates MMX technology, this setting enables execution of MMX instructions. If an x86 processor incorporates SSE1/SSE2/SSE3/SSE4 technology, this setting enables execution of these instructions. The SSE1 and SSE2 instructions that are not affected by the EM flag are the PAUSE, PREFETCHh, SFENCE, LFENCE, MFENCE, MOVNTI, and CLFLUSH instructions. • CR0[MP] = 0 causes the logical processor to ignore the state of CR0[TS] when executing the FPU's WAIT/FWAIT instruction.

Table 8-4: CR0 FPU Control Bits (Continued)

CR0[EM]	CR0[MP]	
0	1	**x87 FPU present and running multitasking OS**: • CR0[EM] = 0 indicates that the x87 FPU is present and enables it to execute FP instructions. If an x86 processor incorporates MMX technology, this setting enables execution of MMX instructions. If an x86 processor incorporates SSE1/SSE2/SSE3/SSE4 technology, this setting enables execution of these instructions. The SSE and SSE2 instructions that are not affected by the EM flag are the PAUSE, PREFETCHh, SFENCE, LFENCE, MFENCE, MOVNTI, and CLFLUSH instructions. • CR0[MP] = 1 causes the logical processor to test the state of CR0[TS] when executing the FPU's WAIT/FWAIT instruction and to generate a DNA exception if CR0[TS] =1.
1	0	**x87 FPU not present.** This setting is used to emulate the execution of x87 FP, SSE1/SSE2/SSE3/SSE4 instructions:
1	1	• CR0[EM] = 1 indicates that the x87 FPU is not present. If the x87 FPU is present, its ability to execute FP instructions is disabled. When an x87 FP instruction is detected, a DNA exception is generated. If the logical processor is MMX-capable, the detection of an MMX instruction causes an invalid opcode exception. If the logical processor is SSE1/SSE2/SSE3/SSE4-capable, the detection of an SSE instruction causes an invalid opcode exception. The SSE1/SSE2/SSE3 instructions that are not affected by the EM bit are the PAUSE, PREFETCHh, SFENCE, LFENCE, MFENCE, MOVNTI, and CLFLUSH instructions. • CR0[MP]: - CR0[MP] = 0 causes the logical processor to ignore the state of CR0[TS] when executing the FPU's WAIT/FWAIT instruction. This setting would be used when running a single-task OS (e.g., **DOS**). - CR0[MP] = 1 causes the logical processor to test the state of CR0[TS] when executing the FPU's WAIT/FWAIT instruction and to generate a DNA exception if CR0[TS] =1. This setting would be used when running a **multitasking OS**.

Address Translation (Paging) Control Registers

CR2. Accessible in: Protected Mode. See Figure 8-4 on page 243. When a Page Fault exception occurs, upon entry to the OS kernel's Page Fault exception handler, CR2 contains a snapshot of the linear (i.e., virtual) memory address that caused the exception. Refer to "IA-32 Address Translation Mechanisms" on page 493 for a detailed description of the paging (i.e., the virtual-to-physical memory address translation) mechanism.

Figure 8-4: Control Register 2 (CR2) in IA-32 Mode

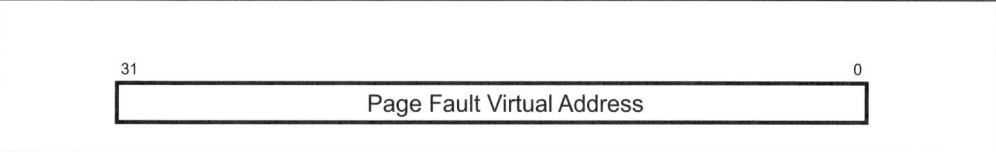

CR3. Accessible in: Real and Protected Modes. See Figure 8-5 on page 244. Whenever a task is initiated or resumed, CR3 (sometimes referred to as the Page Directory Base Address register, or PDBR) is initialized with the physical start memory address of the top-level address translation table associated with the task. The state of the PCD and PWT bits determine the cacheability of the entries in the top-level address translation table:

— **PCD:PWT = 00b**: The logical processor is permitted to cache entries from the top-level address translation table and writes to those entries are treated as writes to cacheable, write-back (WB) memory (i.e., the copy of the top-level address translation table entry in the cache is updated and marked modified, but the update is not forwarded through to the top-level address translation table in memory).
— **PCD:PWT = 01b**: The logical processor is permitted to cache entries from the top-level address translation table and writes to those entries are treated as writes to cacheable, write-through (WT) memory (i.e., the cache entry is updated and the update is also forwarded through to the top-level address translation table in memory).
— **PCD:PWT = 10b or 11b**: The logical processor is not permitted to cache copies of entries from the top-level address translation table.

Refer to "IA-32 Address Translation Mechanisms" on page 493 for detailed description of Paging (i.e., virtual-to-physical memory address translation).

Figure 8-5: Control Register 3 (CR3) in IA-32 Mode

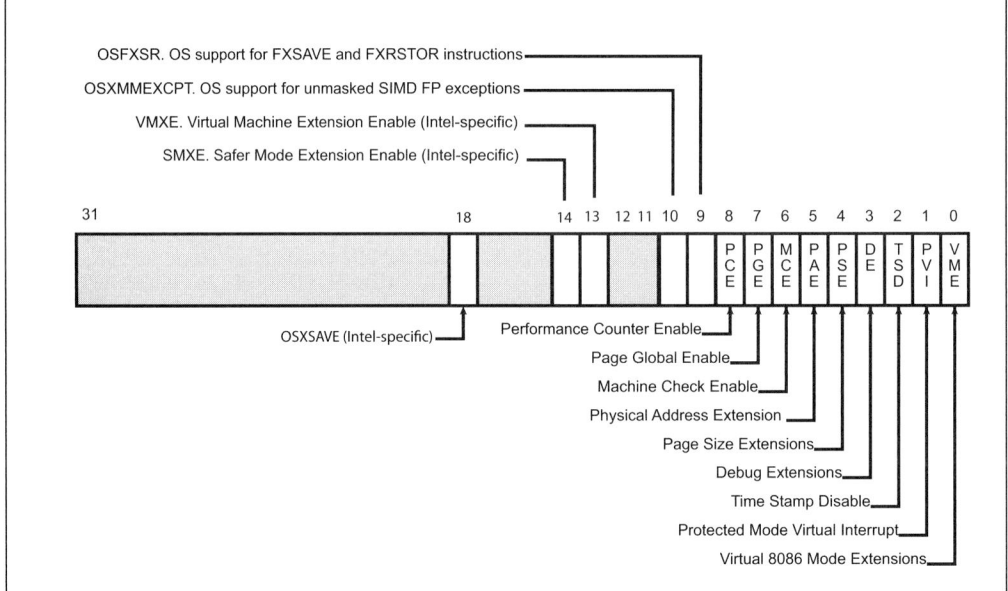

CR4 (Feature Control Register)

Accessible in: all modes.

See Figure 8-6 on page 244 and Table 8-5 on page 245. I like to think of this as the *Feature Control Register*. It contains a series of bits used by the OS kernel to enable/disable miscellaneous logical processor features.

Figure 8-6: Control Register 4 (CR4) in IA-32 Mode

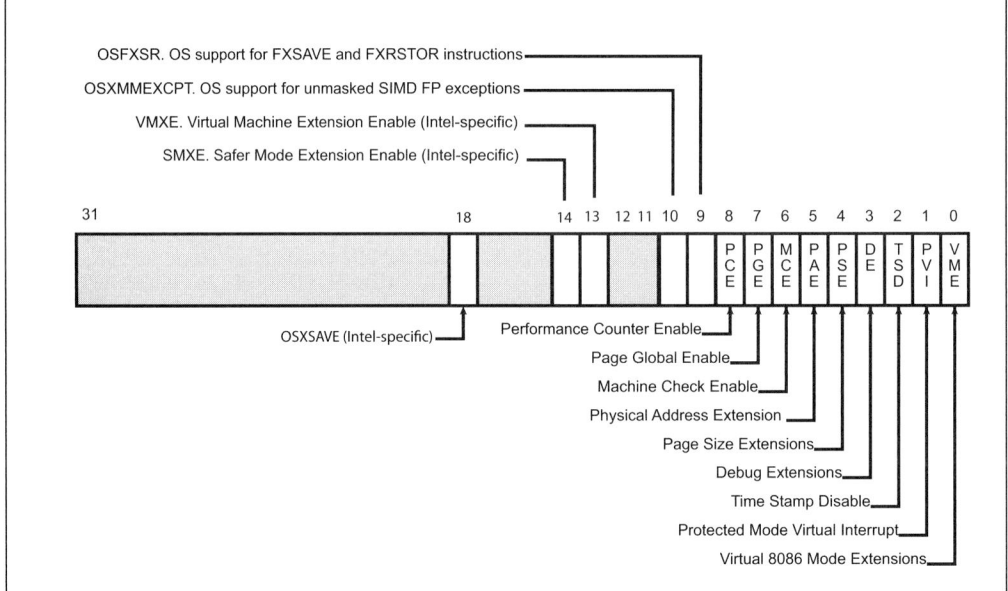

Table 8-5: CR4 Bit Assignment

Bit(s)	Name	Description
0	VME	**Virtual 8086 (VM86) Mode Extension Enable**. The Pentium introduced some improvements to VM86 Mode. Whether or not these improvements are activated is controlled by CR4[VME] (VM86 Mode Extensions). Refer to "Virtual 8086 Mode" on page 783 for a detailed description of VM86 Mode.
1	PVI	**Protected Mode Virtual Interrupt**. The PVI feature was first implemented in the Pentium. It was migrated into the later versions of the 486 and is present in all subsequent processors. • When CR4[PVI] = 1, if a Protected Mode application (i.e., with a CPL of 3) attempts the execution of a CLI or an STI instruction it is handled in the same manner as would a VM86 task's attempted execution of CLI or STI. See "Protected Mode Virtual Interrupt Feature" on page 832 for a detailed description.
2	TSD	**RDTSC (Read Time Stamp Counter) instruction permission.** When the logical processor is in Protected Mode or VM86 Mode, CR4[TSD] restricts use of the RDTSC (Read Time Stamp Counter) instruction as follows: • When CR4[TSD] = 0, RDTSC can be executed at any privilege level. • When CR4[TSD] = 1, RDTSC can only be executed by programs executing with a privilege level of 0. The RDTSC instruction can be executed when the logical processor is in Real Mode.

Table 8-5: CR4 Bit Assignment (Continued)

Bit(s)	Name	Description
3	DE	**Debug Extensions**. Setting CR4[DE] = 1 has the following effects: • It enables the ability to set IO as well as memory access breakpoints using the logical processor's Debug Breakpoint register set (see "Debug Address Breakpoint Register Set" on page 262). In DR7, the R/W fields associated with each of the four possible breakpoints are used as follows: – 00b: Break on instruction execution only. – 01b: Break on data writes only. – 10b: Break on IO reads or writes. When CR4[DE] = 0, this pattern is reserved. – 11b: Break on data reads or writes but not instruction fetches. • When CR4[DE] = 1, DR4 and DR5 are reserved and attempts to access them result in the generation of an Invalid Opcode exception. When CR4[DE] = 0, access attempts to DR4 and DR5 are aliased to DR6 and DR7, respectively.
4	PSE	**Page Size Extension (i.e., Big Page feature)**. Permits the OS kernel memory manager to designate some pages as either 2MB or 4MB in size rather than 4KB. See "4MB Pages" on page 550 and "Step 2b: PDE Points to a 2MB Physical Page" on page 563 for more information.
5	PAE	**Physical Address Extension**. Also referred to as PAE-36 Mode. • 0: The Paging mechanism can only map a 32-bit virtual address to a 32-bit physical memory address in the first 4GB of memory space. • 1: The Paging mechanism can map a 32-bit virtual memory address to a 36-bit physical memory address in the first 64GB of memory space. Refer to "Second-Generation Paging" on page 553 for a detailed description.

Table 8-5: CR4 Bit Assignment (Continued)

Bit(s)	Name	Description
6	MCE	**Machine Check Exception enable**. • 0: The OS kernel has disabled the MCE because it does not implement a MC exception handler. • 1: The OS kernel has enabled the MCE because it implements a MC exception handler. Refer to "Machine Check Architecture (MCA)" on page 1207 for a detailed description of the Machine Check Architecture.
7	PGE	**Enable Global Page feature**. When enabled by the OS kernel, using the G bit in a Page Table Entry (PTE) the OS memory manager can designate a page as one accessed by multiple applications. When CR3 is reloaded on a task switch and the TLB(s) are flushed, the logical processor will retain global PTEs. For more information, refer to "Global Pages" on page 526.
8	PCE	**RDPMC (Read Performance Counter) instruction permission**. The RDPMC instruction, if permitted by the state of CR4[PCE], can be used to read the contents of a performance counter: • When CR4[PCE] = 0, the RDPMC instruction can only be successfully executed (without causing a GP exception) by programs executing at privilege level 0. • When CR4[PCE] = 1, the RDPMC instruction can be successfully executed by programs executing at any privilege level. Refer to the MindShare book entitled *The Unabridged Pentium 4* for a detailed description of the Performance Monitoring logic.

Table 8-5: CR4 Bit Assignment (Continued)

Bit(s)	Name	Description
9	OSFXSR	**OS FX Save/Restore instruction pair support bit**. The OS will set CR4[OSFXSR] bit to one if it supports: • the use of the FXSAVE and FXRSTOR instructions to save and restore both the FPU and SSE register sets, and • it also supports the use of the SSE instruction set (and, if this is any x86 processor starting with the Pentium 4, supports the use of the SSE2/SSE3/SSE4 instruction sets). Setting CR4[OSFXSR] to one: • Enables the logical processor to execute the SSE (and, if this is any x86 processor starting with the Pentium 4, the SSE2/SSE3/SSE4) instruction set. *The following SSE instructions are always enabled: PREFETCHh or SFENCE. On any x86 processor starting with the Pentium 4, the following additional SSE instructions are always enabled: PAUSE, LFENCE, MFENCE, MOVNTI, and CLFLUSH.* • Enables the FXSAVE and FXRSTOR instructions to save and restore the contents of the SSE register set along with the contents of the x87 FPU/MMX register set. Clearing CR4[OSFXSR] to zero has the following effects: • When the FXSAVE and FXRSTOR instructions are executed, they save and restore the contents of the FPU/MMX register set, but they may or may not (processor design-specific) save and restore the contents of the SSE register set. • The logical processor generates the Invalid Opcode exception whenever it attempts to execute any of the SSE instructions with the exception of the PREFETCHh or SFENCE instructions. These two instructions are always enabled. • On any x86 processor (starting with the Pentium 4) the logical processor generates the Invalid Opcode exception whenever it attempts to execute any of the SSE2 instructions with the exception of the PAUSE, LFENCE, MFENCE, MOVNTI, and CLFLUSH instructions. These five instructions are always enabled.

Table 8-5: CR4 Bit Assignment (Continued)

Bit(s)	Name	Description
10	OSXMMEXCPT	**OS XMM Exception support bit**. SSE SIMD FP exceptions are only generated by SSE SIMD FP instructions. • 1: The OS will set CR4[OSXMMEXCPT] to one if it implements an SSE FP SIMD exception handler (i.e., the exception 19 handler). • 0: If CR4[OSXMMEXCPT] is cleared to zero, the logical processor generates an Invalid Opcode exception whenever it detects an unmasked (i.e., enabled) SIMD FP exception.
13	VMXE	**Virtual Machine Extension Enable**. For more information, refer to "Introduction to Virtualization Technology" on page 1147. When set to one, it enables the logical processor's VT feature.
14	SMXE	**Safer Mode Extension Enable**. This feature is covered in MindShare's Virtualization class.
18	OSXSAVE	When set to one by the OS kernel, this bit **has three effects**: 1. Indicates the kernel supports the use of the XGETBV, XSAVE and XRSTOR instructions by applications. 2. Enables the XSAVE and XRSTOR instructions to save and restore the x87 FPU/MMX register set, SSE register set, and any other register sets enabled in XCR0. 3. Enables the logical processor's ability to read and write the XCR0 register using the XGETBV and XSETBV instructions.

XCR0 (XFEM)

Accessible in: all modes.

XCR0 (also known as the XFEM—Extended Feature Enable Mask—register; see Figure 8-7 on page 250) is optional. Whether or not it is implemented in a particular processor design is determined by execution of a CPUID Request Type 1. If implemented, this register can only be accessed if CR4[OSXSAVE] = 1.

Each defined bit in XCR0 corresponds to a specific register set and is initialized by the OS kernel to reflect whether or not it supports saving the respective register set to the data structure in memory used by the XSAVE instruction. Prior to executing the XSAVE instruction, the programmer sets up a bit mask in the EDX:EAX register pair to indicate which register set(s) he or she wishes to save to the data structure in memory. Upon execution of XSAVE, the logical processor ANDs the request bits specified in EDX:EAX with the support bits in XCR0 and only saves the requested register sets if the respective request and support bits are both set to one.

For a detailed description of the memory-based data structure layout and additional information on the XRSTOR instruction, refer to the detailed description of the XSAVE and XRSTOR instructions in the *Intel Software Developer's Manual, Volume 2B, Instruction Set Reference, N-Z*.

Table 8-6: XCR0 Bit Assignment

Bit	Name	Description
0	X87	Hard-wired to a one because all processors support the X87/MMX register set.
1	SSE	Initialized to a one by the OS if the logical processor supports SSE and the OS kernel supports saving/restoring the SSE register set to or from a data structure in memory.
63	none	Reserved for XCR0 bit vector expansion. Insufficient information to determine its usage in the future.

Figure 8-7: XCR0 (also referred to XFEM)

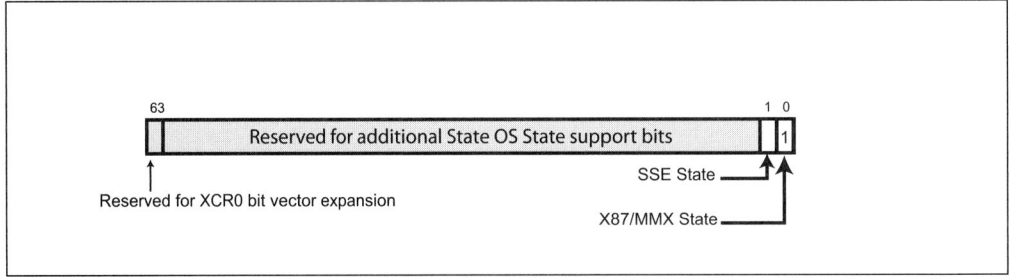

Flags Register

Accessible in: all modes.

While Figure 8-8 on page 251 illustrates the 32-bit Eflags register, only the lower 16-bits, referred to as the Flags register, are available in Real Mode. Table 8-7 on page 252 provides a description of all of the Eflags register bit fields. The bit fields within the Eflags register may be categorized as follows:

- **Status bits**. A series of status bits (referred to as *Condition Code—or cc—bits*) that indicate the results of the previously-executed instruction. These bits are tested by the Jcc (i.e., conditional jump) or Loop instructions to determine whether to jump to the branch target address or fall through to the next instruction.
- **Control bits**. A series of control bits that control various aspects of the logical processor's operation (e.g., the IF bit—set and cleared by the STI and CLI instructions, respectively—enables or disables the logical processor's ability to recognize interrupt requests from external devices).
- **Miscellaneous bits**. A series of **miscellaneous bits** related to other logical processor behaviors. They are described in Table 8-7 on page 252 and are covered at the appropriate points in the book.

Figure 8-8: Eflags Register in IA-32 Mode

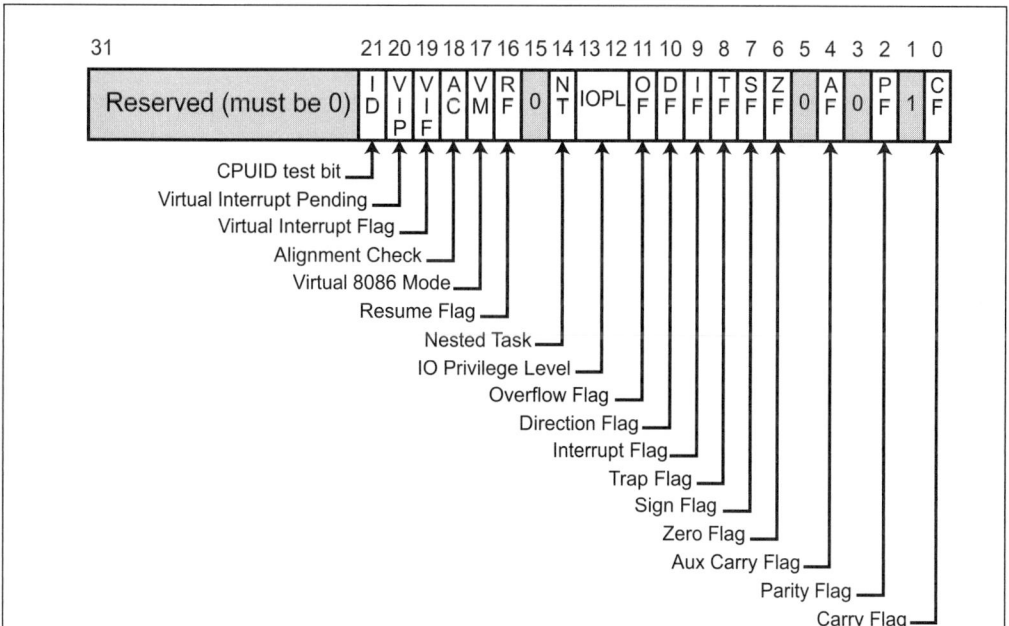

Table 8-7: Eflags Register Bit Assignment

Bit(s)	Name	Description
\multicolumn{3}{c}{**Status (i.e., Condition Code—cc) Bits**}		
0	CF	**Carry Flag**. • This bit is set to one if an arithmetic operation generates a carry or a borrow out of the msb of the result; • otherwise, it is cleared.
2	PF	**Parity Flag**. • If the LSB of the result contains an even number of one bits, PF = 1; • Otherwise, PF = 0.
4	AF	**Auxiliary Carry Flag**. This bit is used in binary-coded decimal (BCD) arithmetic. • AF = 1 if a BCD arithmetic operation generates a carry or a borrow out of bit 3 of the result. • Otherwise, AF = 0.
6	ZF	**Zero Flag**. • ZF = 1 if the result is zero. • Otherwise, ZF = 0.
7	SF	**Sign Flag**. SF = the value (1 or 0) of the result's msb (i.e., the sign bit of a signed integer). • 0 = a positive value. • 1 = a negative value.
11	OF	**Overflow Flag**. • OF = 1 if the integer result is too large a positive number or too small a negative number (excluding the sign-bit) to fit in the destination operand; it indicates an overflow condition for signed-integer (i.e., two's complement) arithmetic operations. • Otherwise, OF = 0.

Table 8-7: Eflags Register Bit Assignment (Continued)

Bit(s)	Name	Description
\multicolumn{3}{c}{Control Bits}		
8	TF	**Trap Flag**. When TF = 1, it enables the logical processor's single-step mode to facilitate program debug. Prior to the execution of each instruction in the program under debug, a Debug Exception is generated, causing the logical processor to jump to the program debugger.
9	IF	**Interrupt Flag**. • 0 = disables recognition of maskable external hardware interrupts. • 1 = enables recognition of maskable external hardware interrupts.
10	DF	**Direction Flag**. The state of the DF bit controls the actions taken by the string-oriented instructions (MOVS, CMPS, SCAS, LODS, and STOS). • DF = 1 causes the string instructions to process strings of information in memory starting at the start address and descending through memory (i.e., descending from the start address). • DF = 0 causes the string instructions to process strings of information in memory starting at the start address and ascending through memory (i.e., ascending from the start address). The STD and CLD instructions set and clear DF, respectively.
17	VM	**VM86 Mode Enable**. See "Virtual 8086 Mode" on page 783 for a detailed description of VM86 Mode. • 1 = VM86 mode is enabled. • 0 = VM86 mode is disabled.
18	AC	**Alignment Check Enable**. CR0[AM] is the master enable/disable for the alignment checking feature: • If AM = 0, Eflags[AC] is ignored and alignment checking isn't performed while the current application is running. • If AM = 1, allows Eflags[AC] to control alignment checking while the current application is running. See "Alignment Check Exception (17)" on page 774 for a discussion of alignment checking.

Table 8-7: Eflags Register Bit Assignment (Continued)

Bit(s)	Name	Description
16	RF	**Debugger Single-Step Resume Flag**. If Eflags[TF] = 1, the logical processor's single step mode is enabled. Prior to the execution of the next instruction of the program being debugged, the logical processor generates a Debug Exception and jumps to the debug program. Prior to exiting the debug program and returning to the program under debug, the programmer first sets Eflags[RF] to one and then executes the IRETD instruction to return to the program under debug. Upon return to the program under debug, Eflags[RF] = 1 prevents the logical processor from immediately generating another Debug Exception. Rather, the next instruction in the program under debug is executed before another Debug Exception is generated.
		Other Bit Fields
13:12	IOPL	**IO Privilege Level**. In Protected Mode, in order to successfully execute IO instructions, the Current Privilege Level (CPL) of the currently executing program must be numerically <= the application's IO privilege level. Eflags[IOPL] can only be modified by execution of the POPF and IRET instructions by a program executing at privilege level zero (i.e., the OS kernel). Refer to "Virtual 8086 Mode" on page 783.
14	NT	**Nested Task**. Controls the chaining of interrupted and called tasks: • Automatically set when the current task is linked to (i.e., is called from) another task or when the current task is interrupted and the handler is another task. • Automatically cleared if the current task is not linked to (i.e., is not called from) another task. See "Calling Another Task" on page 670 for more information.
19	VIF	**Virtual Interrupt Flag**. Refer to "Virtual 8086 Mode" on page 783.
20	VIP	**Virtual Interrupt Pending**. Refer to "Virtual 8086 Mode" on page 783.
21	ID	If this bit can be set to one, execution of the CPUID instruction is supported.

General Purpose Registers (GPRs)

Accessible in: all modes.

Figure 8-10 on page 259 illustrates the logical processor's 32-bit GP register set. Although all of them can be used as general purpose data registers, it should be noted that some have special usages related to certain instructions.

A, B, C and D Registers

Accessible in: all modes.

General Usage. Each of these four registers can hold 32-bits (4-bytes, 2 words, one dword) of information. As an example, the following instruction will move the 32-bit value 12345678h into the EAX register:

```
MOV EAX,12345678;move the value 12345678h into EAX
```

In addition, the programmer can individually address the 8- or 16-bit registers that comprise the lower half (e.g., AX) of each of these registers. The 16-bit AX register actually consists of two 8-bit registers:

— AL (lower half of AX register).
— AH (upper half of the AX register).

The same is true of the BX, CX and DX registers. To move only one byte of information, specify one of the 8-bit registers rather than a 16- or 32-bit register.

```
MOV AL,02;move value 02h into AL
OUT 60,AL;write AL contents to IO port 60h
```

This will cause an external IO write transaction with address 000060h as the address and 02h as the data. In general, the AX, BX, CX and DX registers are used for the following purposes:

— to temporarily hold values to be used in calculations.
— to receive data being read from an external memory or IO location.
— to provide the data to be written to an external memory or IO location.
— to hold values to be used in calculating a memory address.

Special Usage Examples. As mentioned earlier, in some cases, the A, B, C or D registers have a special use when certain instructions are executed. Some examples:

— IO read and write instructions (IN and OUT) always use the AL, AX, or EAX register as the source (on an IO write: OUT) or destination (on an IO read: IN) operation.
— The MSR read (RDMSR) and write (WRMSR) instructions always use the following registers:
   – The EDX:EAX register pair as the source (on a write) or destination (on a read).
   – The ECX register is used to specify the address of the MSR register.
— When a Move String (MOVS) instruction is executed to copy a block of data from one memory buffer to another, the logical processor always uses the following registers:
   – The Source Index register contains the address of the source memory buffer. This can, however, be overriden using a Segment Override prefix.
   – The Destination Index register contains the address of the destination memory buffer.
   – The CX register contains the number of bytes, words, or dwords to be copied.

EBP Register: Stack Frame Address Register

Accessible in: all modes.

The EBP (Extended Base Pointer) register can be used for any of the following purposes:

* **Method 1**. As a general purpose data register.
* **Method 2**. **Data Structure Access**. The programmer can address locations in a memory-based data structure by placing the base address in the BP or EBP register and specifying an offset from the base address. In response, the logical processor forms the memory address by adding the specified operand offset to the base address in the BP or EBP register.
* **Method 3**. **Stack Frame Access**. Its most common usage reflects that described in method 2. The logical processor automatically increments (on a push) or decrements (after a pop) the Stack Pointer register. Refer to Figure 8-9 on page 258.

1. In preparation for a call to another procedure, the programmer saves the current address in the SP register in the BP register. This is referred to as the caller's *stack frame pointer* and demarks the base address of the stack section containing the variables, register images, and dynamically-allocated buffers associated with the calling procedure.

2. Assume that two arguments (parameters) are then pushed onto the stack in preparation for the procedure call. At the conclusion of the second push, the address in the Stack Pointer register points to the location containing argument two (see A in the figure).

3. The Call instruction is then executed (assume it's a near call; i.e., the branch target address is a location in the same code segment). Before jumping to the called procedure's entry point, the logical processor pushes the current contents of the IP register onto the stack (this is the return address to the calling program).

4. On entry to the called procedure, the address in the Stack Pointer register points to the return address just saved on the stack (see B in the figure).

5. Having now entered the called procedure, the programmer obviously needs to access the two arguments that were passed on the stack. Rather than manipulating the Stack Pointer and using pops to access the arguments on the stack, the programmer will use the BP register.

   — In order to save it so it can be restored before returning back to the caller, the programmer pushes the current contents of the BP register (which contains the base address of the caller's stack frame) onto the stack.

   — It then copies the address currently in the SP register (C in the figure) into the BP register.

6. As indicated at the bottom of the figure, by supplying the appropriate positive or negative offsets, the programmer can then use the address in the BP register to access the passed parameters (by adding positive offsets of +8 or +10 to the address in the BP register). As an example:

`mov ax, [BP + 8]` can be used to access argument 2.

The BP register is often used to access the stack without affecting (i.e., incrementing or decrementing) the contents of the SP register. When using the contents of the BP register as the address in calculating a memory address, the logical processor automatically defaults to using the SS base address in the address calculation (e.g., SS base + BP + offset of a passed parameter).

Figure 8-9: Stack Usage in C Function Call

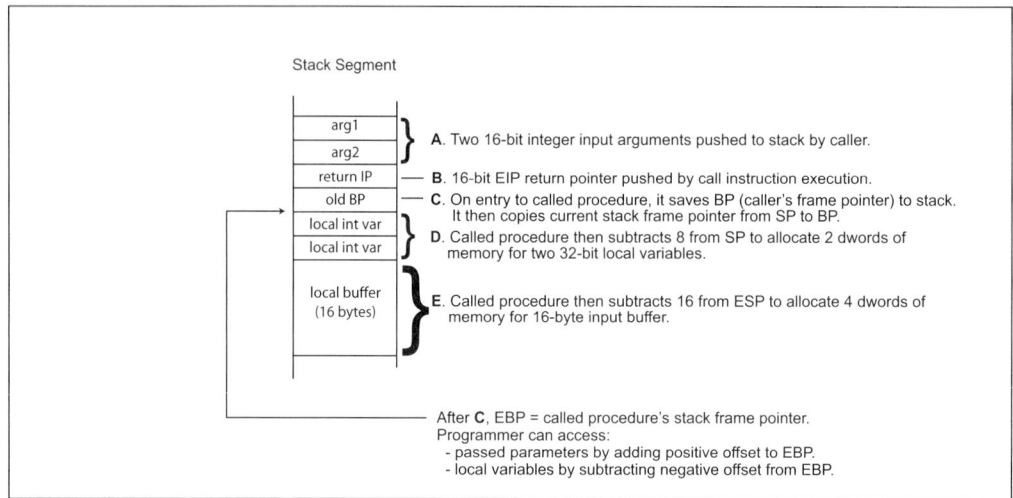

Index Registers

Accessible in: all modes.

The following are some example usages of the Source and Destination Index registers (SI and DI):

- As a general purpose data register.
- As a component in calculating the address of a memory-based operand:
  — Address = [BX + SI], or [BX + DI].
  — Address = [BP + SI], or [BP + DI].
  — Address = [BX + SI] + 8-, 16- or 32-bit displacement; or [BX + DI] + 8-, 16- or 32-bit displacement.
  — Address = [SI] + 8-, 16- or 32-bit displacement; or [DI] + 8-, 16- or 32-bit displacement.
- These two registers are frequently used when performing string operations (i.e., an operation that is performed on a series of locations, rather than just one). As an example, when a Move String (MOVS) instruction is executed to copy a block of data from one memory buffer to another, the logical processor always uses the following registers (see "String Operations" on page 315 for a more detailed description):
  — The Source Index register contains the offset of source memory buffer's base address in the DS segment. This can be overriden by preceding the instruction with a Segment Override prefix.

— The Destination Index register contains the offset of the destination memory buffer's base address in the ES segment.

— The CX register contains the number of bytes, words, or dwords to be copied.

Stack Pointer (SP) Register

Accessible in: all modes.

Although the Stack Pointer register is most frequently used to access stack memory, it can also be used as a general purpose data register. See "Accessing the Stack Segment" on page 297 for a detailed description of stack operation in Real Mode.

Figure 8-10: General Purpose Registers (GPRs) in IA-32 Mode

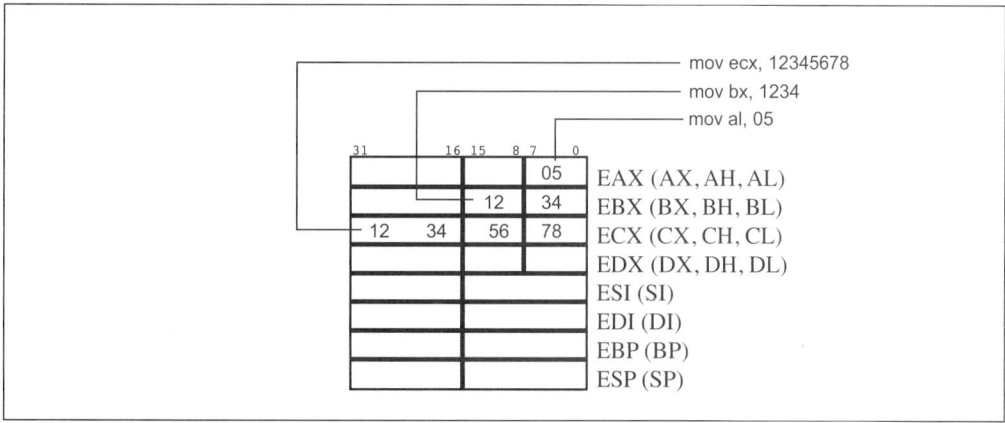

Instruction Pointer Register

Accessible in: all modes.

Refer to Figure 8-11 on page 260. In Real Mode, the logical processor 0-extends the 16-bit code segment base address in the CS register to 20-bits by adding the digit 0h as the least-significant hex digit. It then adds the 16-bit offset from the IP register to generate the 20-bit physical memory address from which the next instruction will be fetched. For a more detailed description of code fetching in Real Mode, refer to "Accessing the Code Segment" on page 293.

Figure 8-11: Instruction Pointer Register

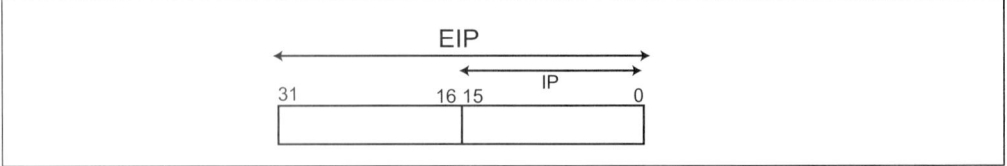

Kernel Registers

The following registers are only used by a Protected Mode OS kernel:

• Global Descriptor Table Register (GDTR). When preparing to switch the logical processor into Protected Mode, the programmer creates a GDT in memory and then uses the LGDT instruction to load the GDTR with the base address and size of the GDT.
• Local Descriptor Table Register (LDTR). This register is not accessible in Real Mode.
• Task Register (TR). This register is not accessible in Real Mode.

They are therefore not covered in this chapter. A detailed description may be found in the following sections:

• GDTR and LDTR. See "Protected Mode Memory Addressing" on page 383.
• TR. See "The Task Register (TR)" on page 637 and "The Task Register" on page 652.

The Interrupt Descriptor Table Register (IDTR), however, is used in both Real Mode and Protected Mode:

• For a detailed description of the IDT and the IDTR in Real Mode, refer to "The IDT" on page 317.
• For a detailed description of the IDT and the IDTR in Protected Mode Mode, refer to "Protected Mode Interrupts and Exceptions" on page 681.

x87/MMX FPU Register Set

Accessible in: all modes.

Figure 8-12 on page 261 illustrates the register set associated with the x87 FPU and the MMX facility. Note that the MMX facility does not have its own discrete register set. Rather, when the logical processor is executing MMX code the lower 64-bits of the x87 FPU's data registers (R0 - R7) fulfill the role of MMX registers MM0 - MM7. A detailed description of the x87 FPU can be found in "Legacy x87 FP Support" on page 339, and a description of MMX can be found in "The MMX Facilities" on page 835.

Figure 8-12: x87 FPU and MMX Registers

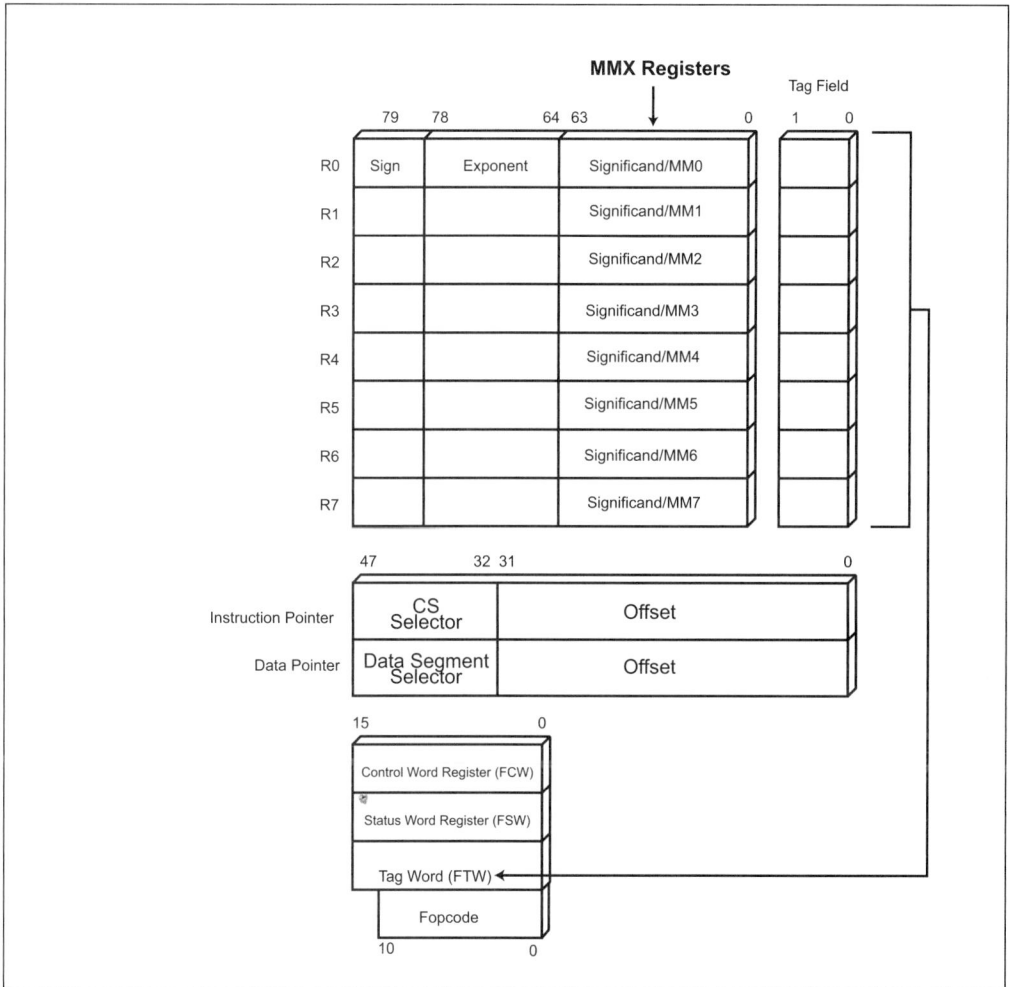

SSE Register Set

Accessible in: all modes.

Figure 8-13 on page 262 illustrates the SSE register set (**S**treaming **S**IMD Extensions; **S**ingle **I**nstruction operating on **M**ultiple **D**ata items). It consists of:

- Eight, 128-bit XMM data registers.
- 32-bit MX Control/Status Register (MXCSR).

A description of SSE can be found in "The SSE Facilities" on page 851.

Figure 8-13: SSE Register Set in IA-32 Mode

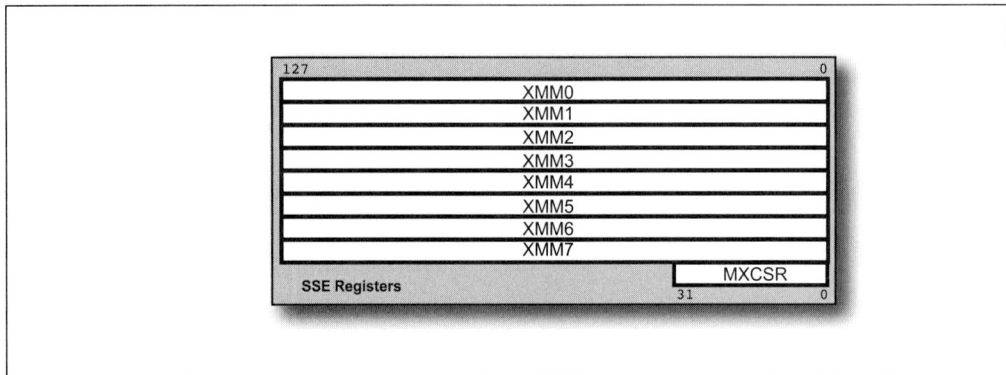

Debug Address Breakpoint Register Set

General

Accessible in: all modes.

Starting with the 386, all x86 processors provide hardware address breakpoint detection. This is implemented using the logical processor's Debug Registers (see Figure 8-14 on page 269). Other logical processor functions associated with debug include:

- The Debug exception (Exception 1). This exception is generated when the logical processor encounters a breakpoint match on a condition specified in the debug registers.
- The Breakpoint instruction exception (Exception 3). This exception is generated when the logical processor executes the breakpoint (INT3) instruction.
- TSS[T] (the Trap bit in a task's TSS). Causes a Debug exception when a task switch occurs to a task with this bit (the T bit) set to one in its TSS.
- Flags[RF] (Resume Flag). When set to one by the debugger, the subsequent execution of the IRETD (Interrupt Return from Debugger) instruction prevents the logical processor from generating a debug exception again when it returns to an instruction that already caused a debug exception.
- Flags[TF]. When set to one, the logical processor generates a Debug exception before the execution of each instruction. This permits single-stepping through a program.

The Debug Control register, DR7, is used to enable and configure one or more of the four address breakpoint comparators. Table 8-8 on page 264 describes the bits in DR7.

Using the logical processor's DR7, DR0, DR1, DR2 and DR3 registers, the programmer may enable the logical processor to detect any of four different types of accesses within four different memory or IO address ranges specified in DR0 - DR3. The Pentium added the capability to monitor for read or write accesses to IO ports. Earlier processors did not possess this capability.

When an access of a specified type within a specified address range is detected, the logical processor generates a Debug exception (Exception 1) and jumps to the debug exception handler. In addition, it sets the appropriate bits in the Debug Status register, DR6. Table 8-11 on page 268 describes the bits in DR6.

Defining Trigger Address Range

Two elements are involved in defining the address range to be monitored:

- The start virtual memory address or IO address (0-extended to 32-bits) is defined in the desired Breakpoint Address register (DR0 - DR3):
  — A 2-byte range must start at an address divisible by 2.
  — A 4-byte range must start at an address divisible by 4.
  — An 8-byte range must start at an address divisible by 8.
- The length of the address ranged to be monitored is defined in the DR7 LEN field (see Table 8-10 on page 268) that is associated with the selected Breakpoint Address register.

Defining Access Type

The access type is defined in the respective DR7 R/W field (see Table 8-9 on page 267).

Defining Scope (Current Task or All Tasks)

The DR7[L*n* & G*n*] bits associated with a breakpoint specification are used to define the scope of the breakpoint as being either local to the current task or global to all tasks.

Special Notes

- A data breakpoint for an unaligned operand can be constructed using two break- points, where each breakpoint is byte-aligned and the two breakpoints together cover the operand. The breakpoints generate exceptions only for the operand, not for neighboring bytes.
- Instruction breakpoint addresses must have a length specification of 1-byte. Code breakpoints for other operand sizes are undefined. The logical processor recognizes an instruction breakpoint address only when it points to the first byte of an instruction. If the instruction has prefixes, the breakpoint address must point to the first prefix.

Table 8-8: Definition of DR7 Bits Fields

Field	Description
DR7 fields associated with Breakpoint Address register 0 (DR0).	
R/W0	Defines the access type to be monitored for within the address range defined by the start address in DR0 and the range defined by DR7[LEN0]. Table 8-9 on page 267 defines the interpretation of the value in this field.
LEN0	Defines the size of the address range to be monitored. The interpretation of the value in this field is defined in Table 8-10 on page 268.
L0	Enable local breakpoint. When set to one, a Debug exception will be generated if the debug logic detects a match on an access of the type defined by R/W0 within the range defined by DR0 and LEN0 *while in the current task*. This bit is automatically cleared when a task switch occurs. This prevents the generation of a Debug exception on an access match while in another task.

Table 8-8: Definition of DR7 Bits Fields (Continued)

Field	Description
G0	Enable global breakpoint. When set to one, a Debug exception will be generated if the debug logic detects a match on an access of the type defined by R/W0 within the range defined by DR0 and LEN0 *in any task*. The processor does not clear this flag on a task switch, thereby defining the scope of the breakpoint as global to all tasks.
	DR7 fields associated with Breakpoint Address register 1 (DR1).
R/W1	Defines the access type to be monitored for within the address range defined by the start address in DR1 and the range defined by DR7[LEN1]. Table 8-9 on page 267 defines the interpretation of the value in this field.
LEN1	Defines the size of the address range to be monitored. The interpretation of the value in this field is defined in Table 8-10 on page 268.
L1	Enable local breakpoint. When set to one, a Debug exception will be generated if the debug logic detects a match on an access of the type defined by R/W1 within the range defined by DR1 and LEN1 *while in the current task*. This bit is automatically cleared when a task switch occurs. This prevents the generation of a Debug exception on an access match while in another task.
G1	Enable global breakpoint. When set to one, a Debug exception will be generated if the debug logic detects a match on an access of the type defined by R/W1 within the range defined by DR1 and LEN1 *in any task*. The processor does not clear this flag on a task switch, thereby defining the scope of the breakpoint as global to all tasks.
	DR7 fields associated with Breakpoint Address register 2 (DR2).
R/W2	Defines the access type to be monitored for within the address range defined by the start address in DR2 and the range defined by DR7[LEN2]. Table 8-9 on page 267 defines the interpretation of the value in this field.
LEN2	Defines the size of the address range to be monitored. The interpretation of the value in this field is defined in Table 8-10 on page 268.

Table 8-8: Definition of DR7 Bits Fields (Continued)

Field	Description
L2	Enable local breakpoint. When set to one, a Debug exception will be generated if the debug logic detects a match on an access of the type defined by R/W0 within the range defined by DR2 and LEN2 *while in the current task*. This bit is automatically cleared when a task switch occurs. This prevents the generation of a Debug exception on an access match while in another task.
G2	Enable global breakpoint. When set to one, a Debug exception will be generated if the debug logic detects a match on an access of the type defined by R/W2 within the range defined by DR2 and LEN2 *in any task*. The processor does not clear this flag on a task switch, thereby defining the scope of the breakpoint as global to all tasks.
DR7 fields associated with Breakpoint Address register 3 (DR3).	
R/W3	Defines the access type to be monitored for within the address range defined by the start address in DR3 and the range defined by DR7[LEN3]. Table 8-9 on page 267 defines the interpretation of the value in this field.
LEN3	Defines the size of the address range to be monitored. The interpretation of the value in this field is defined in Table 8-10 on page 268.
L3	Enable local breakpoint. When set to one, a Debug exception will be generated if the debug logic detects a match on an access of the type defined by R/W0 within the range defined by DR3 and LEN3 *while in the current task*. This bit is automatically cleared when a task switch occurs. This prevents the generation of a Debug exception on an access match while in another task.
G3	Enable global breakpoint. When set to one, a Debug exception will be generated if the debug logic detects a match on an access of the type defined by R/W3 within the range defined by DR3 and LEN3 *in any task*. The processor does not clear this flag on a task switch, thereby defining the scope of the breakpoint as global to all tasks.

Table 8-8: Definition of DR7 Bits Fields (Continued)

Field	Description
Other fields:	
LE and GE	Starting with the Pentium Pro, all x86 processors ignore the setting of the LE and GE bits. They are provided for backward compatibility. When set, these bits causes earlier processors to detect the exact instruction that caused a data breakpoint condition. For backward and forward compatibility with other Intel processors, Intel recommends that they be set to one if exact breakpoints are required.
GD	**General Detect**. When set to a one, the debug logic will generate a Debug exception if the next instruction to be executed will attempt to access one of the debug registers while it is in use by a debug tool (e.g., an ITP). In addition, the BD bit in the Debug Status register, DR6, will be set to one to indicate to the Debug exception handler the reason for the exception. This bit is automatically cleared when a Debug exception does occur so that the logical processor can freely access the debug registers in the exception handler.

Table 8-9: Interpretation of the R/W Field In DR7

R/W Value	Access Type To Monitor For
00b	Break on a memory instruction read.
01b	Break on a memory data write.
10b	Break on an IO read or write. Note that post-386 x86 processors only recognizes this selection if the Debug Extension bit, CR4[DE], is set to one. The 386 and early 486 processors did not support this feature.
11b	Break on a memory data read or write address match, but not on a memory instruction read.

Table 8-10: Interpretation of the LEN Field In DR7

LEN Value	Interpretation
00b	Defines a 1-byte address range starting at the virtual memory address or IO address specified in the associated Breakpoint Address register (DR0 - DR3).
01b	Defines a 2-byte address range starting at the virtual memory address or IO address specified in the associated Breakpoint Address register (DR0 - DR3).
10b	Defines an 8-byte address range starting at the virtual memory address or IO address specified in the associated Breakpoint Address register (DR0 - DR3). *Note: This setting is only valid in an Intel 64 processor.*
11b	Defines a 4-byte address range starting at the virtual memory address or IO address specified in the associated Breakpoint Address register (DR0 - DR3).

Table 8-11: Debug Status Register Bits

Bit	Description
B0	This bit is set if the logical processor had a match on an access of the type defined by DR7[R/W0] within the address range defined by DR0 and DR7[LEN0].
B1	This bit is set if the logical processor had a match on an access of the type defined by DR7[R/W1] within the address range defined by DR1 and DR7[LEN1].
B2	This bit is set if the logical processor had a match on an access of the type defined by DR7[R/W2] within the address range defined by DR2 and DR7[LEN2].
B3	This bit is set if the logical processor had a match on an access of the type defined by DR7[R/W3] within the address range defined by DR3 and DR7[LEN3].

Table 8-11: Debug Status Register Bits (Continued)

Bit	Description
BD	This bit is set to one when the GD bit in DR7 is set to one and the logical processor detects a software attempt to access one of the debug registers while they are being used by a debug tool (e.g., an ITP). This protects the debug registers from being altered by the program while they are in use by an ICE (In-Circuit Emulator) or some other debug tool.
BS	This status bit is set to one when the logical processor generates a Debug exception due to Flags[TF] = 1. This feature permits the logical processor to single-step through a program and allows the programmer to examine the state of the logical processor's registers after each instruction is executed.
BT	This status bit is set to one if a Debug exception occurred because the logical processor switched to a task that has the Trap bit = 1 in its TSS. This permits the programmer to detect when a task is about to begin (or resume) execution.

Figure 8-14: Debug Register Set (available in all modes)

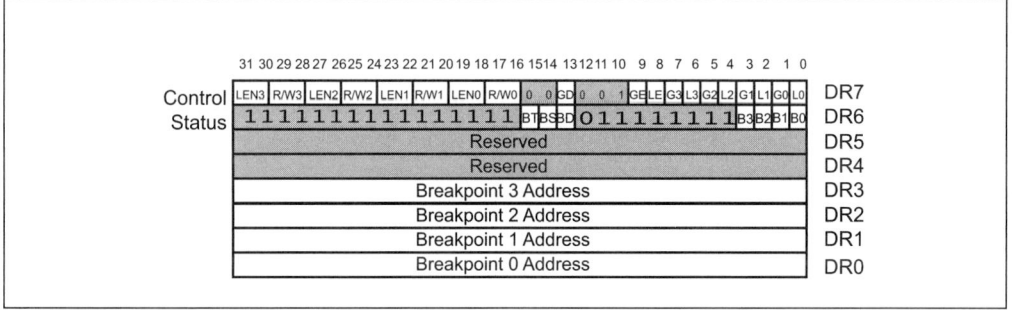

Local APIC Register Set

Accessible in: all modes.

A separate Local APIC (**A**dvanced **P**rogrammable **I**nterrupt **C**ontroller) is associated with each logical processor (each core if the processor doesn't support Hyper-Threading). The Local APIC receives interrupt messages from IO APIC(s) (typically integrated into the chipset), from the Local APICs associated with other logical processors, as well as interrupts from internal sources (e.g., thermal interrupts, Local APIC Timer interrupt, etc.), prioritizes them and delivers them to its associated logical processor. Software running on a logical processor can also command its Local APIC to transmit an interrupt message to one or more other Local APICs in the system.

The Local APIC's register set is implemented in memory-mapped IO space (in later processors that support the x2APIC architecture, they can be relocated to MSR register space). Pictured in Figure 8-15 on page 271, please note that all of the registers defined by the original APIC specification as well as those defined by the later xAPIC and x2APIC specifications are shown including those no longer used in today's products. A detailed description of the Local APIC's operation (and a discussion of APIC, xAPIC and x2APIC) can be found in "The Local and IO APICs" on page 1239.

Figure 8-15: Local APIC Register Set

		Offset from base address (MMIO/MSR)
Reserved		0000 03F0h/3Fh
	Timer Divide Config Register	0000 03E0h/3Eh
Reserved		0000 03D0h/3Dh
		0000 03C0h/3Ch
		0000 03B0h/3Bh
		0000 03A0h/3Ah
Reserved	Timer Current Count Register	0000 0390h/39h
Reserved	Timer Initial Count Register	0000 0380h38h
Reserved	LVT—Error	0000 0370h/37h
Reserved	LVT—LINT1	0000 0360h/36h
Reserved	LVT—LINT0	0000 0350h/35h
Reserved	LVT—Perf Counter OverFlow	0000 0340h/34h
Reserved	LVT—Thermal Sensor	0000 0330h/33h
Reserved	LVT—Timer	0000 0320h/32h
Reserved	Interrupt Command Register[63:32]	0000 0310h/**31h***
Reserved	Interrupt Command Register[31:0]	0000 0300h/**30h***
	LVT—CMC	0000 02F0h/2Fh
Reserved		0000 02E0h/2Eh
		0000 02D0h/2Dh
		0000 02C0h/2Ch
		0000 02B0h/2Bh
		0000 02A0h/2Ah
		0000 0290h/29H
Reserved	Error Status Register	0000 0280h/28h
Reserved	Interrupt Request Register (IRR) 256 bits	0000 0270h/27h
		0000 0260h/26h
		0000 0250h/25h
		0000 0240h/24h
		0000 0230h/23h
		0000 0220h/22h
		0000 0210h/21h
		0000 0200h/20h
Reserved	Trigger Mode Register (TMR) 256 bits	0000 01F0h/1Fh
		0000 01E0h/1Eh
		0000 01D0h/1Dh
		0000 01C0h/1Ch
		0000 01B0h/1Bh
		0000 01A0h/1Ah
		0000 0190h/19h
		0000 0180h/18h
Reserved	In Service Register (ISR) 256 bits	0000 0170h/17h
		0000 0160h/16h
		0000 0150h/15h
		0000 0140h/14h
		0000 0130h/13h
		0000 0120h/12h
		0000 0110h/11h
		0000 0100h/10h
Reserved	Spurious Interrupt Vector Register	0000 00F0h/0Fh
Reserved	Destination Format Register	0000 00E0h/0Eh
Reserved	Logical Destination Register	0000 00D0h/0Dh
Reserved	Remote Read Register	0000 00C0h/0Ch
Reserved	EOI Register	0000 00B0h/0Bh
Reserved	Processor Priority Register	0000 00A0h/0Ah
Reserved	Arbitration Priority Register	0000 0090h/09h
Reserved	Task Priority Register	0000 0080h/08h
Reserved		0000 0070h/07
		0000 0060h/06h
		0000 0050h/05h
		0000 0040h/04h
Reserved	Local APIC Version Register	0000 0030h/03h
Reserved	Local APIC ID Register	0000 0020h/02h
Reserved		0000 0010h/01h
Reserved		0000 0000h/00h

F E D C B A 9 8 7 6 5 4 3 2 1 0
Byte

Note: In x2APIC Mode, all registers are 32-bits except ICR. It is 64-bits at MSR address 30h.

Architecturally-Defined MSRs

Accessible in: all modes.

General

The class of registers referred to as Model-Specific Registers first appeared in the original Pentium and, at that time, were truly model-specific in nature. Later however, with the advent of the Pentium 4, a number of these registers—belying their names—were officially added to the ISA specification and the number of architecturally-defined MSRs has continued to grow since then (see Table 8-12 on page 273).

Determining MSR Support

CPUID request type 1 should be used to determine whether the MSRs are supported (EDX[5]=1) before executing the RDMSR or WRMSR instructions on a logical processor.

Accessing the MSRs

The MSRs are accessed using the RDMSR and WRMSR instructions.

- **RDMSR**. When executed, this instruction loads the contents of the 64-bit MSR specified in ECX (a list of the currently-defined MSRs may be found in Appendix B of the Software Developer's Manual, Volume 3B: System Programming Guide, Part 2) into the EDX:EAX register pair (EDX is loaded with the upper 32 MSR bits, and EAX is loaded with the lower 32-bits). It must be executed at privilege level 0 or in Real Mode (or a GP exception will be generated).
- **WRMSR**. When executed, this instruction writes the contents of the EDX:EAX register pair into the MSR specified by the MSR address specified in ECX. EDX is written to the upper 32-bits of the MSR and EAX to the lower 32-bits of the MSR. This instruction must be executed at privilege level 0 or in Real Mode (or a GP exception will be generated).

Table 8-12: List of Currently-Defined Architectural MSRs

Register(s)	Brief Description
IA32_P5_MC_ADDR and IA32_P5_MC_TYPE	**Pentium Machine Check Address and Machine Check Type registers**. When an error is detected in a transaction on the processor's FSB, the transaction's address and type are latched into this register pair. On later generation processors, the MCA (Machine Check Architecture) registers that record this type of error are aliased into these two registers.
IA32_MONITOR_FILTER_SIZE	Used by the MONITOR instruction (see "MONITOR/ MWAIT Instruction Pair" on page 907).
IA32_TIME_STAMP_ COUNTER (TSC)	**Time Stamp Counter register**. Starting with the Pentium, all x86 processors implement the 64-bit TSC register. It is cleared to zero on the assertion of reset to the processor. Upon deassertion of reset, the TSC is incremented once for each logical processor clock cycle.
IA32_PLATFORM_ID	**Platform ID register**. A Microcode Update image is appropriate to be uploaded into a processor if *both* of the following conditions are met: 1. The processor type, family, model, stepping returned by a CPUID request type 1 is the same as the type, family, model, stepping in the Microcode Image's header fields. 2. The bit in the header's Processor Flag field identified by the IA32_Platform_ID MSR Platform ID bit field = 1. To perform the check specified in step 2, the programmer uses the RDMSR instruction to obtain the contents of the IA32_PlatformID MSR. The BCD value specified in the 3-bit Platform ID field is used to select a bit in the header's 8-bit Processor Flag field. If the selected bit is set to one and the processor type, family, model and stepping fields returned by the CPUID request type 1 are the same as those fields in the image's header, then the image is intended for this processor. For more information on the Microcode Update feature, refer to the MindShare book entitled *The Unabridged Pentium 4*.

Table 8-12: List of Currently-Defined Architectural MSRs (Continued)

Register(s)	Brief Description
IA32_APIC_BASE	**Local APIC Base address register**. Used to set the base memory address for the logical processor's Local APIC register set. For more information, see "The Local and IO APICs" on page 1239.
IA32_FEATURE_CONTROL	**Virtual Mode Extentions**. Contains bits related to enabling VMX Mode. See "Introduction to Virtualization Technology" on page 1147 for more information.
BIOS Update registers	At the heart of Intel x86 processors, microcode instructions (referred to as µops or micro-ops) are executed to accomplish the logical processor's internal operations. The processor's microcode is contained in the integrated Microcode ROM. In earlier processors, this ROM was truly read-only—the microcode burned into it at the time of manufacture could not be changed. Starting with the Pentium Pro and using a special procedure, revised microcode that eliminates bugs can be automatically loaded into a processor each time the system is powered up (or even after it has been powered up). When a new revision of microcode is loaded into the processor after the machine is powered up, the silicon level, or stepping, of the processor is effectively raised to match a new silicon stepping that is currently being shipped from Intel manufacturing plants. For more information on the Microcode Update feature, refer to the MindShare book entitled *The Unabridged Pentium 4*.
IA32_SMM_MONITOR_CTL	**System Management Mode Monitor Control register**. Related to having separate VMMs to handle virtualization both within and outside of SMM.
Performance Monitoring registers	A set of counters that can be programmed to count the number of one or more internal event types that occur during a given period of time. Refer to refer to the MindShare book entitled *The Unabridged Pentium 4* for a detailed discussion of Performance Monitoring.

Table 8-12: List of Currently-Defined Architectural MSRs (Continued)

Register(s)	Brief Description
IA32_MPERF and IA32_APERF	**Maximum Performance** and **Average Performance registers**. Related to tracking the performance level at which a logical processor is currently operating. • **IA32_MPERF MSR**: increments in proportion to the maximum operating frequency indicated in the processor brand string (i.e., maximum performance level that the logical processor is capable of). • **IA32_APERF MSR**: increments in proportion to the logical processor's *actual* performance. The following are taken into account: – Hardware alteration of the P-state (i.e., the current freq/Vcc setting). – Activation of TM1 (Thermal Management 1) logic. – Activation of TM2 (Thermal Management 2) logic. – Software-initiated throttling (using On-Demand mode). • These two MSRs only measure performance when the logical processor is in the C0 state (i.e., when it's executing code). • While the ratio of this register pair is architecturally defined, no meaning should be placed on the content of them. OS power management software can use the ratio of these two registers to determine the amount of time that a logical processor is busy (i.e., productive) and may use this information to decide when to change a logical processor's freq/Vcc setpoint.
IA32_PERF_STATUS	**Current Performance Setting status register**. The logical processor's current freq/Vcc setpoint can be read from the Performance Status register.
IA32_PERF_CTL	**Current Performance Setting Control register**. Software uses the Performance Control register to set a logical processor's freq/Vcc setpoint.

Table 8-12: List of Currently-Defined Architectural MSRs (Continued)

Register(s)	Brief Description
MTRR registers	**Memory Type and Range registers**. Set up by the BIOS and possibly the OS to define the memory types occupying the various regions of memory. This is necessary so the logical processor knows the rules of conduct it must adhere to when performing memory reads and writes in order to ensure proper operation. See "Memory Type Configuration" on page 599.
SYSENTER/SYSRET registers	Parameter registers supporting the SYSENTER/SYSRET fast system call/return instruction pair.
MCA registers	**Machine Check Architecture register set**. Used to log various types of internal and external hardware errors. Refer to "Machine Check Architecture (MCA)" on page 1207 for a detailed description of the MCA facility.
IA32_MCi_CTL2	**Machine Check Control Register 2 for MC bank i (where i = the MCA error logging bank number).** This register is used to set a threshold count for correctable errors logged in a bank and to enable the delivery of an interrupt to the CMCI (Corrected Machine Check Interrupt) input of the logical processor's Local APIC when the correctable error count equals the threshold value.

Table 8-12: List of Currently-Defined Architectural MSRs (Continued)

Register(s)	Brief Description
IA32_CLOCK_MODULATION	• When bit 4 of this register = 1, the logical processor will, without regard to the processor temperature, immediately reduce its power consumption by using the internal Stop Clock signal to modulate the logical processor clock. This is referred to as **On-Demand Mode**. • The duty cycle of the clock modulation is program-mable using bits [3:1]. It can be programmed from 12.5% on/ 87.5% off, to 87.5% on/12.5% off in 12.5% increments. • This mode can be used along with the TM1 (Thermal Monitor 1) facility, but if software tries to enable On-Demand mode at the same time the TCC (Thermal Control Circuit; i.e., TM1) is engaged, the factory-configured TCC duty cycle will override that selected by On-Demand mode.
IA32_THERM_INTERRUPT	**Thermal Interrupt register**. The bits in this register are used to enable various types of thermal status conditions to generate a thermal interrupt to the logical processor's Local APIC. See "The Thermal Sensor Interrupt" on page 1370.
IA32_THERM_STATUS	**Thermal Status register**. The bits in this register indicate whether or not various types of thermal conditions have been detected by the logical processor.
IA32_MISC_ENABLE	The bits in this register are used to enable or disable miscellaneous logical processor features.
IA32_TEMPERATURE_TARGET	Permits the programmer to specify the minimum temperature at which the **PROCHOT#** signal will be asserted to the chipset. The value is in degrees Centigrade.
IA32_DEBUGCTL	**Debug Control register**. Also referred to as the Trace/Profile Resource Control register.

Table 8-12: List of Currently-Defined Architectural MSRs (Continued)

Register(s)	Brief Description
IA32_PLATFORM_DCA_CAP	**Platform DCA (Direct Cache Access) Capabilities register.** Related to a feature that permits the logical processor to prefetch data into its cache in advance of an overt request for the data.
IA32_CR_PAT	In a logical processor that supports the PAT feature, each of the following paging-related entries contains a bit referred to as the PAT*i* (PAT Index) bit: • Each PTE that maps to a 4KB page. • Each PDE that maps to a 2MB page. • Each PDE that maps to a 4MB page. The 3-bit field comprised of PATi, PCD, and PWT selects one of eight possible fields in the IA32_CR_PAT MSR. The value in the selected field of the MSR defines the memory type assigned to the page. See "PAT Feature (Page Attribute Table)" on page 587.
VMX registers	A series of read-only registers that report the logical processor's **VMX** (Virtual Machine Extensions; i.e., Virtualization Technology) **capabilities**.
IA32_DS_AREA	**Debug Store facility base address register.** Used to specify the base memory address of the memory-based data structure (referred to as the DS Save area) in which the logical processor will store branch (Branch Trace Store, or BTS) and PEBS (Precise Event Based Sampling) records. For more information, refer to the MindShare book entitled *The Unabridged Pentium 4.*

Table 8-12: List of Currently-Defined Architectural MSRs (Continued)

Register(s)	Brief Description
x2APIC registers	When x2APIC mode is enabled, the programmer can access all of the logical processor's Local APIC registers as MSRs (rather than as memory-mapped IO registers) using the RDMSR and WRMSR instructions. All of the Local APIC's registers are supported except for the following: • Arbitration Priority register (discontinued years ago). • Remote Read register (discontinued years ago). • Destination Format register (discontinued with the advent of the x2APIC architecture). In addition, one new register, the Self IPI (Inter-Processor Interrupt) MSR, is supported. A detailed description of the Local APIC may be found in "The Local and IO APICs" on page 1239.
IA32_EFER	**Extended Features Enable Register**. Contains the bit fields shown in Figure 26-2 on page 1026.
IA32_STAR_CS IA32_LSTAR IA32_FMASK	These three registers are **used when performing a Fast System Call** (via the SYSCALL/SYSRET instruction pair) to the OS kernel.
IA32_FS_BASE	**FS data segment base address register**. In 64-bit Mode, the programmer uses the WRMSR instruction to write the 64-bit base address of the FS data segment into this register.
IA32_GS_BASE	**GS data segment base address register**. In 64-bit Mode, the programmer uses the WRMSR instruction to write the 64-bit base address of the GS data segment into this register.

Table 8-12: List of Currently-Defined Architectural MSRs (Continued)

Register(s)	Brief Description
IA32_KERNEL_GS_BASE	• Only used in 64-bit Mode. • When using SYSCALL to call the OS kernel, there is no kernel stack at the kernel entry point. • When SYSCALL is executed, it automatically exchanges the privilege level 0 data pointer in the Kernel_GS_Base MSR with the GS base register. • The kernel can then use the GS segment override on memory references to access kernel data structures (e.g., mov rax,GS:[offset]). • When an interrupt or exception is generated, the kernel stack has already been set up and the SWAPGS instruction can be used to quickly obtain a pointer to the kernel data structures. See "SwapGS Instruction" on page 1076 for more information.
IA32_TSC_AUX	• Contains a 32-bit field initialized by kernel software with a signature value (e.g., a logical processor ID). • Using the RDTSCP instruction, software can read the 64-bit time stamp from the IA32_TSC register and the signature from the IA32_TSC_AUX register as a locked, atomic operation. The 64-bit time stamp is returned in EDX:EAX and the 32-bit TSC_AUX signature in ECX. • This locked operation ensures that no context switch can occur between the reads of the TSC and TSC_AUX registers (as could possibly occur if the two registers were read one after the other by two RDMSR instructions and an interrupt were to occur between the two reads). • Application software can use RDTSCP to detect if the application has been migrated from one logical processor to another between successive reads of the TSC. It can also be used to adjust for per-CPU differences in TSC values in a NUMA (Non-Uniform Memory Architecture) system.

IO Space versus Memory Space

A logical processor supports two address spaces:

- **IO space**. Consisting of IO addresses 0000h - FFFFh, the logical processor's 64KB IO space can only be addressed using dedicated IO instructions:
    — IN (IO Read).
    — OUT (IO Write).
    — INS (Input a string of IO data from an IO port to memory).
    — OUTS (Output a string of IO data from memory to an IO port).
  Originally, the intent was that device adapter IO ports would be implemented in this address space. Rather than expanding the size of the 64KB IO space to accommodate the ever-expanding array of device adapters, the vast majority of today's adapter control, status and data ports are implemented as memory-mapped IO ports (and are therefore accessed using memory loads and stores).
- **Memory space**. The 8086 processor implemented 20 address signal lines and was therefore restricted to a 1MB memory address space (locations 00000h - FFFFFh). Later generation x86 processors implement a significantly larger number of address lines and can therefore, in the appropriate mode, address appreciably larger memory areas (16MB for the 286, 4GB for later processors, 64GB starting with the Pentium Pro, and 1TB or larger for the latest processors).

IO Operations

IO operations fall into two categories:

- Accessing IO ports implemented in the logical processor's IO address space.
- Accessing IO ports implemented in the logical processor's memory space (i.e., memory-mapped IO, or MMIO, operations).

IO Operations in IO Address Space

IN and OUT Instructions

The x86 processor family is restricted to the 64K + 3 range of IO addresses from 0000h - 10002h. The programmer uses one of two instruction forms to identify the target of an IO read or write operation:

1. If the IO address is within the range 0000h - 00FFh, the following form may be used:

```
in ah, nn ;read data from io port nnh into ah
mov al, xx ;set up write data in al
out nn, al ;write data in al to io port nnh
```

where *nn* = the 8-bit target IO address.

2. When the IO address is within the range 0100h - FFFFh, the following form of register-indirect IO addressing must be used:

```
mov dx, nnnn;set up the 16-bit io address in dx
in al, dx  ;read data from address in dx into al

mov dx, nnnn;set up the io address in dx
mov al, xx ;set up the write data in al
out dx, al ;write data from al to io port in dx
```

The IO address—specified directly as an 8-bit immediate value embedded within the instruction (the first form) or indirectly in DX (the second form)—is used by the logical processor's external interface when it initiates the IO transaction.

Block (String) IO Operations

The instruction set also provides a mechanism that permits the transfer of a block of bytes, words, or dwords between an IO port and a buffer in memory.

Block Transfer from IO Port to Memory. This is accomplished in the following manner:

1. Set up the number of bytes, words or dwords to be transferred in the CX register.
2. Set up the offset of the destination memory buffer's base address in the DI or EDI register. The logical processor hardware assumes the buffer is in the ES memory segment (and this *cannot* be overridden with a Segment Override prefix).
3. Set up the IO port address in the DX register.
4. The transfer is then initiated by executing the INSB, INSW, or INSD instruction (Input a String of Bytes, Words, or Dwords) prefaced by the REP (Repeat) prefix. The logical processor then takes the following actions:
   a) Performs a byte, word, or dword IO read from the IO port and stores the data in an internal, temporary holding register.

b) Performs a memory data write (i.e., a store) to store the byte, word, or dword into the memory address pointed to by the ES:DI (or ES:EDI) register pair.

c) Dictated by the state of the Direction flag bit in the Flags register (Flags[DF]) the logical processor increments (if DF = 0) or decrements (if DF = 1) the memory address offset in the DI or EDI register. The magnitude of the increment or decrement is either one, two, or four bytes.

d) The logical processor then decrements the transfer count in the CX register by one and tests to determine if the count is now 0. If it isn't, then the REP prefix causes the logical processor to re-execute the INS instruction again. When the count is exhausted (0), the logical processor falls through to the next instruction.

Block Transfer from Memory to an IO Port. This is accomplished in the following manner:

1. Set up the number of bytes, words or dwords to be transferred in the CX register.
2. Set up the offset of the source memory buffer in the SI or ESI register. The logical processor hardware assumes the buffer is in the DS memory segment (this *can* be overridden with a Segment Override prefix).
3. Set up the IO port address in the DX register.
4. The transfer is then initiated by executing the OUTSB, OUTSW, or OUTSD instruction (Output a String of Bytes, Words, or Dwords) prefaced by the REP (Repeat) prefix. The logical processor then takes the following actions:

   a) Performs a memory data read (i.e., a load) to read the byte, word, or dword from the memory address pointed to by the DS:SI (or DS:ESI) register pair and stores the data in an internal, temporary holding register.

   b) Performs a byte, word, or dword IO write to the IO port specified in the DX register.

   c) Dictated by the state of the Direction flag bit in the Flags register (Flags[DF]) the logical processor increments (if DF = 0) or decrements (if DF = 1) the memory address offset in the SI or ESI register. The magnitude of the increment or decrement is either one, two, or four bytes.

   d) The logical processor then decrements the transfer count in the CX register by one and tests to determine if the count is now 0. If it isn't, then the REP prefix causes the logical processor to re-execute the OUTS instruction again. When the count is exhausted (0), the logical processor falls through to the next instruction.

IO Space is Limited and Crowded

The size of the logical processor's IO address space is constrained by the method of specifying an IO address (i.e., as an immediate 8-bit value, or indirectly in the 16-bit DX register). The IO address space is therefore 64KB in size (actually, 64KB + 3 because the programmer could specify a 4-byte IO read or write starting at IO address FFFFh). Considering the vast variety of device adapters available in the marketplace, this tiny address space very soon became impossibly crowded and the possibility of installing two or more device adapters whose register sets partially- or full-overlapped in IO address space became a very real problem. As a result, it wasn't very long before adapter designers began implementing adapter register sets in memory space rather than IO address space. This discussion continues in the next section.

Memory-Mapped IO (MMIO) Operations

Introduction

While implementing a device adapter's register set in memory space (which is vastly larger than IO address space) avoids the problems associated with the tiny, crowded IO address space, it also presents new problems. Software communicates with memory-mapped IO ports using memory data reads (loads) and memory data writes (stores).

Know the Characteristics of Your Target

When the logical processor must perform a memory access, it is important that it understand the operational characteristics of the device being accessed. If it does not, the manner in which the memory access is performed may result in improper operation of the device or of the program.

Why the Logical Processor Must Know the Memory Type

As an example, assume an area of memory is populated with a series of memory-mapped IO registers associated with one or more device adapters. Now assume that the program (e.g., a device driver) performs a 4-byte memory read to obtain the status of a device from its 32-bit, device-specific status register. If the logical processor were to assume that the region of memory being accessed is cacheable and the cache lookup resulted in a cache miss, it would not only read the targeted four locations from memory, but would read from *all* locations of the cache line within which the desired four locations reside. This could result in a serious problem. The contents of all of the memory-mapped IO ports within that line of memory space would be read and cached in the processor. If the program should subsequently issue a request to access any of those locations, it would result in a cache hit:

- **If it's a read**, the requested data is supplied from the cache and not from the actual IO device that implements that memory-mapped IO port. This means that the data or status obtained does not represent the current, up-to-date contents of the location read. This desynchronization between a device driver and its related device can result in erroneous operation.
- **If it's a write**, the line in the cache is updated but, if the memory area is designated as cacheable WB (Write Back) memory, the memory write is not performed to external physical memory (and, as a result, the actual memory-mapped IO device does not receive the write).

The example just described is but one case wherein the logical processor's lack of knowledge of a target device's operational characteristics can result in spurious operation. In a very limited sense, the 486 and the Pentium possessed a mechanism that permitted the OS programmer to define the characteristics of a region of memory. Each PTE (Page Table Entry) contained two bits, PTE[PCD] and PTE[PWT], that permitted the OS to define the 4KB memory page as cacheable Write Through (WT), cacheable Write Back (WB), or Uncacheable (UC) memory. This was insufficient for two reasons:

- The OS typically is not platform-specific and therefore doesn't necessarily know the characteristics of the various devices that populate memory space. The BIOS, on the other hand, is platform-specific but it is the OS and not the BIOS that sets up and maintains the Page Tables in memory.
- In order to ensure proper operation, some device types require that the logical processor behave in a manner other than those defined by the various possible bit settings of the PTE's PCD and PWT bits.

Uncacheable (UC) Memory

The rules that the logical processor follows when performing memory reads and writes in a memory range designated as UC (in the MTRR registers—see "Memory Type Configuration" on page 599—or in a Page Table Entry) are as follows:

- Cache lookups are performed and, in the event of a cache hit, the line is evicted from the cache (because the area is designated as UC).
- Read requests are not turned into line reads from memory. They are per-

formed as is (e.g., one, two, four, or eight bytes). The data returned is routed directly to the requester and is not placed in any cache.

- Memory writes are first posted in the logical processor's Posted Memory Write Buffer and are performed later on the processor's external interface in original program order.
- Speculative reads are not performed (as a result of out-of-order program execution; see "The Definition of a Speculatively Executed Load" on page 615 for more information).

In other words, the logical processor is very well-behaved within a UC memory area. For this reason, the UC type is well-suited to memory regions populated by memory-mapped IO devices. On the negative side, accesses within UC memory yield low performance due to lack of caching and speculative read constraining.

No IO Protection

In Real Mode there is no way to prevent or detect an application program attempt to access an IO or memory-mapped IO port. While this doesn't typically result in problems in a single-task OS environment, it most assuredly would in a multitasking environment.

Operand Size Selection

Consider the following two cases:

- `mov ax, bx`. Move 2-bytes (a word) from the BX register to the AX register.
- `mov eax, ebx`: Move 4-bytes (a dword) from the EBX register to the EAX register.

Both operations are accomplished using exactly the same machine language instruction—89D8h—which brings up the question, "How does the logical processor know which operation to perform?" Unless instructed otherwise, when the logical processor is operating in Real Mode it assumes that the operand size is 16-bits:

- **16-bit operation**. If it fetches and decodes the instruction 89D8h and is not instructed otherwise, it uses the default operand size of 16-bits and performs the following operation: `mov ax, bx`.

- **32-bit operation**. If, however, the same instruction is prefaced with the Operand Size Override prefix—6689D8h—it uses an operand size of 32-bits and performs the following operation: `mov eax, ebx`.

For more information on Operand Size Override prefix usage in Real Mode, refer to "In 16-bit Mode" on page 213.

Address Size Selection

Consider the following two cases:

- `mov ax, [bx]`. Move 2-bytes into the ax register from the two memory locations starting at the 16-bit address specified in the BX register (note: since the source segment is not specified, it assumes the location is in the DS data segment).
- `mov ax, [ebx]`. Move 2-bytes into the ax register from the two memory locations starting at the 32-bit address specified in the EBX register.

Both operations are accomplished using exactly the same machine language instruction—8B03h—which brings up the question, "How does the logical processor know which operation to perform?" Unless instructed otherwise, when the logical processor is operating in Real Mode it assumes that the size of a memory operand address is 16-bits:

- If it fetches and decodes the instruction 8B03h and is not instructed otherwise, it uses the default address size of 16-bits and performs the following operation: `mov ax, [bx]`. That is, it calculates the memory address by adding the 16-bit offset specified in the BX register to the 20-bit base address of the DS data segment.
- If, however, the same instruction is prefaced with the Address Size Override prefix—678B03h—it uses an address size of 32-bits and performs the following operation: `mov ax, [ebx]`. That is, it calculates the memory address by adding the 32-bit offset specified in the EBX register to the 20-bit base address of the DS data segment.

Although the programmer may specify a 32-bit memory address offset by using the Address Size Override prefix, it should be noted that, in Real Mode, segments are still only 64KB in size. Any attempt to access a location with an offset greater than 64KB will therefore cause an exception. This limitation can be addressed, however, by temporarily switching the logical processor into Protected Mode, changing the respective length to a value greater than 64KB (up to 4GB), and then switching it back into Real Mode. For more information, refer to "Big Real Mode" on page 310.

For more information on the Address Size Override prefix usage in Real Mode, refer to "In 16-Bit Mode" on page 215.

Real Mode Memory Addressing

No Address Translation

The 8086/8088 processors did not implement virtual-to-physical address translation (i.e., Paging). The 20-bit memory address formed by adding the 16-bit offset to the 20-bit segment base address *was* the physical memory address that would be accessed.

Introduction to Real Mode Segmentation

The 8088/8086/286 processors implemented a set of four segment registers:

*   CS, DS, ES, and SS.

The 386 and all subsequent x86 processors added two additional data segment registers: FS and GS.

In Real Mode, the programmer uses these registers to specify the base address of up to six different regions of memory to be utilized by the currently executing program as data, code and stack areas. Figure 8-16 on page 289 illustrates the segment registers.

Each segment register is 16-bits in size. When the programmer loads a 16-bit value into one of these registers in Real Mode, the logical processor automatically extends it to a 20-bit address by appending a least-significant digit (consisting of four bits of all zeros) to the lower end of the value contained in the segment register. As an example, if the following code is executed (see Figure 8-17 on page 289):

```
mov  ax, 2000
mov  ds, ax
mov  bx,[0100] ;when no segment specified, DS is assumed
```

the value 2000h is moved into the DS register. The logical processor extends it to a 20-bit base address by appending a 0d to the low end yielding a Data Segment base address of 20000h. The specified 16-bit memory operand address of 0100h is then added to the segment base address to yield an operand address of 20100h. Two bytes are read from memory locations 20100h and 20101h and are placed into the least-significant byte of the BX register and its upper byte, respectively.

Table 8-13 on page 290 describes how the physical memory address is formed when accesses are performed within each type of segment. A basic description of how the six segment registers are used can be found in defined in Table 8-14 on page 291.

Figure 8-16: Segment Registers

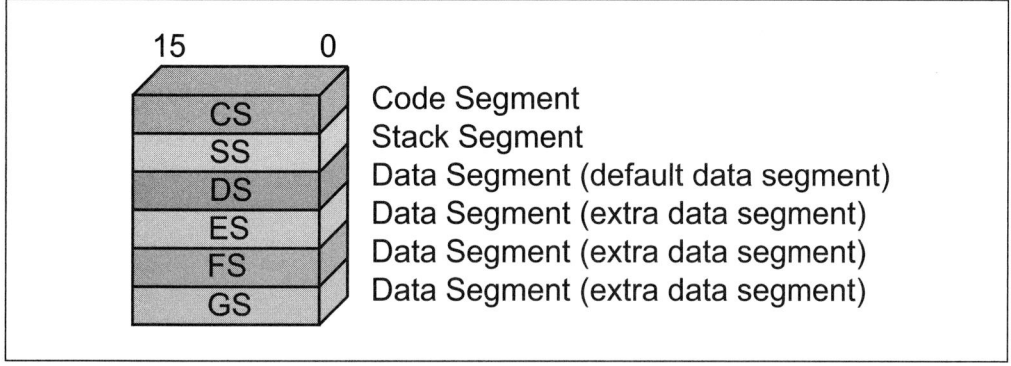

Figure 8-17: Example Data Segment Access

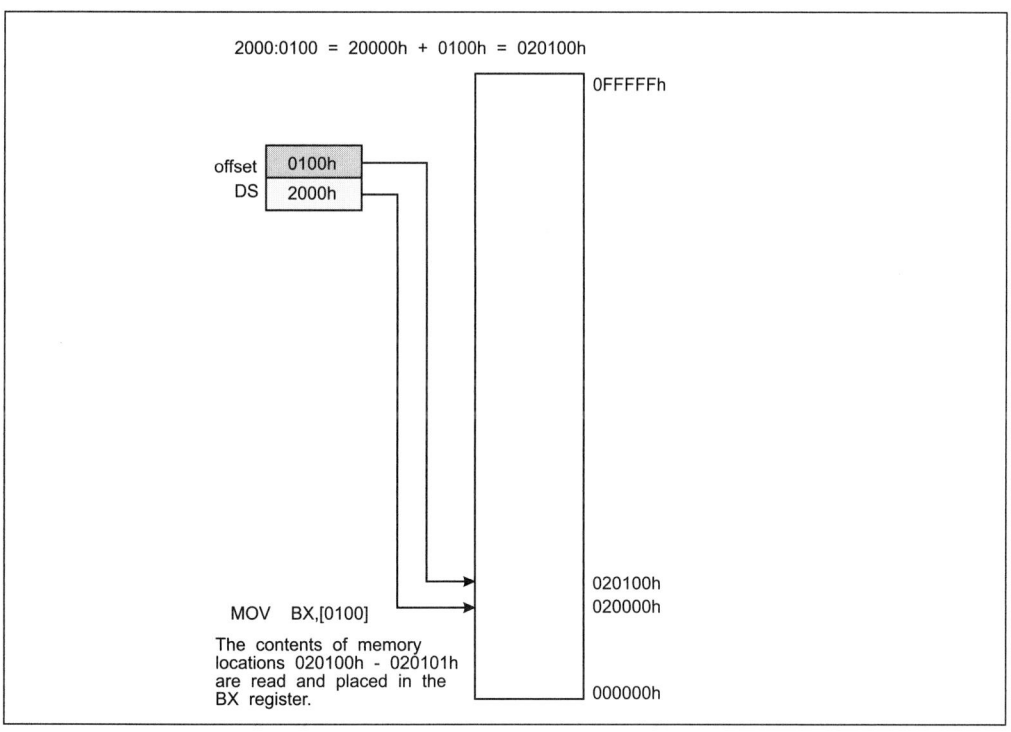

Table 8-13: Physical Memory Address Formation in Real Mode

Access in	4-digit offset supplied	is added to the 5-digit base address specified by	To yield

Code Segment	from 16-bit IP register	Least-significant digit of 0h appended to the 4 upper digits from CS register.	5-digit physical memory address from which next instruction will be read. **Example:**
			`CS = 1F00`
			`IP = 03A0`
			`Base address: 1F000`
			`    + Offset:  03A0`
			`Phys address: 1F3A0`

Data Segment	by the instruction accessing the memory-based data item	Least-significant digit of 0h appended to the 4 upper digits from DS, ES, FS or GS register.	5-digit physical memory address of the data item to be read or written. **Example 1:**
			`DS = 2A90`
			`  mov ax, [0040]`
			`Base address: 2A900`
			`    + Offset:  0040`
			`Phys address: 2A940`
			Note: when no data segment is specified, DS segment is assumed. **Example 2:**
			`ES = F715`
			`  mov al,es:[3023]`
			`Base address: F7150`
			`    + Offset:  3023`
			`Phys address: FA173`
			ES segment override used to override default (DS).

Table 8-13: Physical Memory Address Formation in Real Mode (Continued)

Access in	4-digit offset supplied	is added to the 5-digit base address specified by	To yield
Stack Segment	from 16-bit SP register	Least-significant digit of 0h appended to the 4 upper digits from SS register.	5-digit physical memory address of the stack location which will be read (on a pop operation) or written (on a push operation). **Example:** `SS = 4EA2` `SP = FF96` `push cx` `Base address: 4EA20` `   + Offset:  FF94` `Phys address: 5E9B4` On a push operation, the logical processor decrements SP by 2 before performing the 2-byte write to memory.

Table 8-14: Segment Register Usage in Real Mode

Segment Register	
SS	The **Stack Segment** register indicates the base address of the memory region used by the programmer and the logical processor to temporarily save data. It is loaded using a MOV or LSS (Load Stack Segment) instruction.
DS	The **Data Segment** register indicates the base address of the default memory region containing data the currently executing program acts upon. It is loaded using a MOV or LDS (Load Data Segment) instruction.
ES, FS and GS	The **other Data Segment** registers indicate the base addresses of the memory regions containing additional data that the currently executing program may act upon. They are loaded using the MOV, LES, LFS or LGS instructions.

Table 8-14: Segment Register Usage in Real Mode (Continued)

Segment Register	
CS	The **Code Segment** register indicates the base address of the memory region containing the currently running program. The base address can be changed in any of the following ways: • **Far Jump**. Executing a far Jump instruction loads the CS:IP register pair with the target code segment base address and the offset of the 16-bit branch target address within the target code segment. • **Far Call**. Executing a far Call instruction loads the CS:IP register pair with the target code segment base address and the offset of the 16-bit branch target address within the target code segment. • **External Interrupt**. Recognition of an external interrupt causes the logical processor to push the current contents of the CS:IP register pair (i.e., the address to return to after the interrupt handler has been executed and the IRET instruction is executed) onto the stack. It then reads the 4-byte IDT entry selected by the interrupt type (i.e., the 8-bit interrupt vector) and loads the CS:IP register pair with the target code segment base address and 16-bit branch target address (i.e., offset) of the handler to be executed. • **Software Exception**. Recognition of a software exception condition causes the processor to push the current contents of the CS:IP register pair (i.e., the address to return to after the exception handler has been executed and the IRET instruction is executed) onto the stack. It then reads the 4-byte IDT entry selected by the exception type and loads the CS:IP register pair with the target code segment base address and 16-bit branch target address (i.e., offset) of the exception handler to be executed. • **Software Interrupt Instruction**. Execution of a software interrupt instruction (INT nn, INTO, BOUND, or INT3) causes the logical processor to push the current contents of the CS:IP register pair (i.e., the address to return to after the handler has been executed and the IRET instruction is executed) onto the stack. It then reads the 4-byte IDT entry selected by the interrupt type (the vector—*nn*—supplied as the operand of the INT instruction, or the one associated with the INTO, INT3, or BOUND instruction) and loads the CS:IP register pair with the target code segment base address and 16-bit branch target address (i.e., offset) of the handler to be executed. • **Far Return**. Execution of a far Return (RET) instruction. The 4-byte return address is popped from the stack and placed in the CS:IP register pair. • **IRET**. Execution of an Interrupt Return instruction (IRET). The return address is popped from the stack and placed in the CS:IP register pair.

All Segments are 64KB in Size

While the 20-bit base address of a segment is specified in the respective segment register, all six segments are assumed to be 64KB in size. This constraint is enforced by the following:

- **Code Segment**. The logical processor's code fetch logic uses the 16-bit value in the IP register to select the location to fetch the next instruction from in the current code segment (20-bit base address in CS + 16-bit IP offset = start address of the next instruction to be fetched).
- **Stack Segment**. When accessing the stack segment, the logical processor uses the 16-bit value in the SP (Stack Pointer) register to select the location to access in the stack segment (20-bit base address in SS + 16-bit SP offset = start address of the location to be accessed in stack memory).
- **Data Segments**. When accessing a data operand in one of the four data segments, the offset specified by the programmer is constrained to a 16-bit value. Some examples:
  - `mov ax,[0100]`   `;load ax from DS locations 0100-0101h`
  - `mov bx,es:[FE32]`   `;load bx from ES locations FE32-FE33h`
  - `mov fs:[A1F4], al`   `;store al into FS location A1F4`
  - `mov gs:[92B3], bx`   `;store bx into GS locations 92B3-92B4h`

The limited size (64KB) of segments in Real Mode *represents one of the most severe Real Mode limitations.* If a Real Mode application is greater than 64KB in size, the programmer must break it up into separate 64KB code segments. Whenever the programmer wishes to transfer execution (i.e., branch) to an instruction within another code segment, a far Jump or a far Call must be executed. This causes the start address of the new code segment to be loaded into the CS register and the new offset to be loaded into the IP register.

Memory Address Representation

All memory addresses are formed by adding an offset to a segment base address. In documentation, the address is frequently represented in segment: offset form. Some examples:

- 0100:FE23 = Location FE23h in the segment that starts at location 01000h.
- F000:0045. Location 0045h in the segment that starts at location F0000h.
- 1234:5500. Location 5500h in the segment that starts at location 12340h.

Accessing the Code Segment

The Code Segment (CS) and Instruction Pointer (IP) registers comprise a register pair (note that the IP register consists of the lower 16-bits of the 32-bit EIP register; see Figure 8-18 on page 294). Together, CS:IP define the memory location the next instruction of the currently executing program is to be fetched from. This is their only purpose.

Figure 8-18: IP and EIP Registers

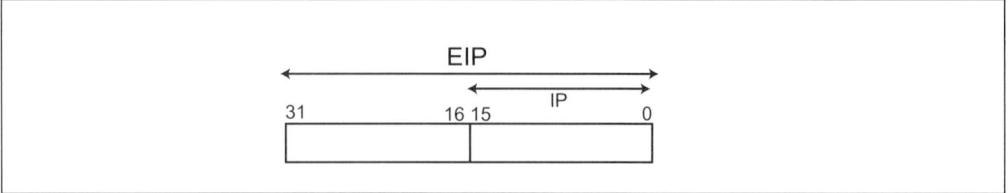

Jumping Between Code Segments

All of the events which can cause a jump from one code segment to another are listed in the CS row of Table 8-14 on page 291.

Far Jumps and Calls

Refer to Figure 8-19 on page 295. A far Jump or a far Call instruction tells the logical processor to fetch its next instruction from a location (the offset portion of the target address) within a different code segment. As an example, in Real Mode the following instruction,

```
jmp  8000:1000  ;far jump branches to location 81000h in
                ;the code segment starting at 80000h
```

tells the logical processor to fetch its next instruction from location 1000h in the code segment that starts at memory location 80000h. In order to execute this instruction, the logical processor loads the segment value, 8000h, into the CS register and the offset within the segment into the IP register. Then, in order to form the branch target address, it appends the trailing 0d (0000b) to the start address in the CS register and adds the offset to it, yielding the physical memory address of 81000h. This process is illustrated below:

```
CS value:80000h
IP value: 1000h
         81000h
```

The logical processor performs a read from memory starting at this location to fetch the next instruction (note that, depending on the instruction type and any optional prefixes that may precede it, an instruction may be anywhere from 1 - 15 bytes in length). The instruction is then decoded and executed.

Figure 8-19: Example Code Fetch in Real Mode

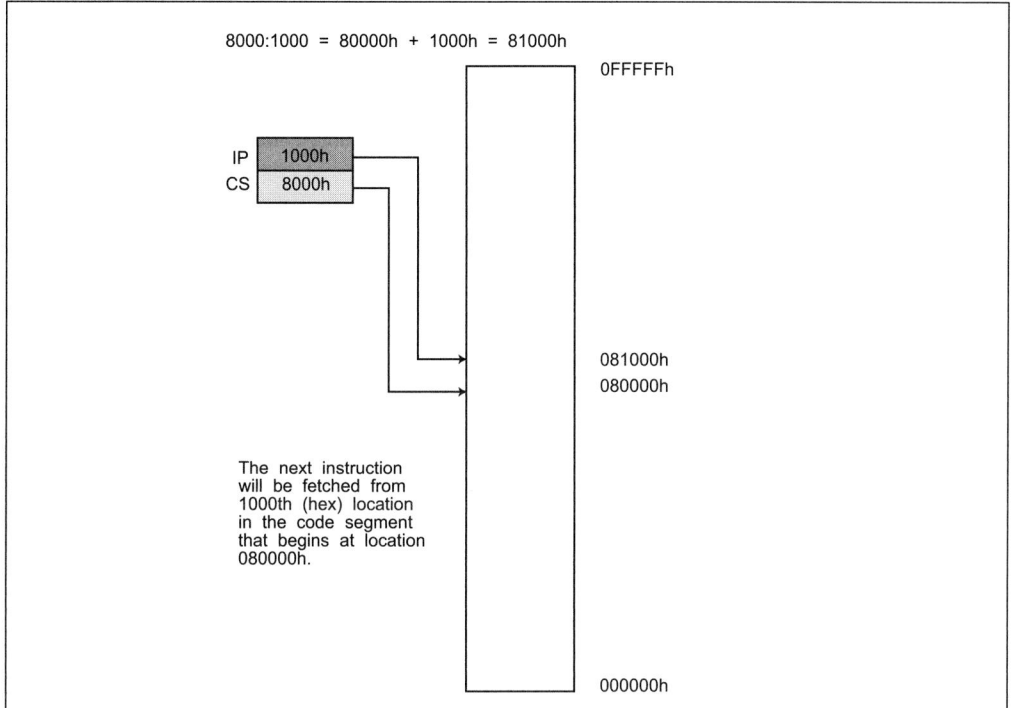

Near Jumps and Calls

Unlike the far Jump or far Call, a near jump or near Call instruction only specifies an offset within the current code segment. As an example,

```
jmp 0009
```

instructs the logical processor to jump to location 0009h in the current code segment. The logical processor places the value 0009h into the IP portion of the EIP register (and 0-fills the upper half). If it is assumed that the CS register currently contains the value 2000h, the logical processor will fetch the next instruction from location 20009h.

Jumps and Calls are two of the instructions that alter program flow. Each time that an instruction is fetched from memory, the logical processor automatically increments the Instruction Pointer register to point to the start address of the next instruction in the current code segment. Consider the following example:

```
mov  al, 33
out  63, al
add  ax, bx
sub  cx, bx
jmp  3400          ;near jump loads 3400 into IP register
```

The first four instructions are not branch instructions and therefore do not load new values into CS and/or IP. The logical processor just auto-increments IP to point to the start of the next instruction. This is referred to as *in-line code fetching*. When the logical processor fetches the fifth instruction, however, it loads the value 3400h into the IP register, altering program flow. Because this is only a near jump, the CS register isn't altered.

IP-Relative Branches

Two types of IP-relative branches are supported in Real Mode:

- If the branch target address is within -128 to +127 locations of the current IP address, then a **short jump** instruction is used (i.e., the signed 8-bit displacement value included in the instruction is added to or subtracted from the address currently in the IP register).
- If the branch target address is within -32K to +32K-1 locations of the current IP address, then a **near jump** instruction is used (i.e., the signed 16-bit displacement value included in the instruction is added to or subtracted from the address currently in the IP register).

Operations That Default to the Code Segment

Operations that, by default, utilize the code segment are:

- The logical processor's **code fetch mechanism** always fetches code from the active code segment using the CS:IP register pair.
- All forms of **short and near Jumps** load the 16-bit branch target address into IP and the logical processor then starts fetching code from the new offset in the current code segment.
- **Far Jumps** load new values into the CS:IP register pair and the logical processor then starts fetching code from the specified offset in the new code segment.
- **Near Calls** push the contents of IP onto the stack and then load the new 16-bit branch target address into IP.
- **Far Calls** push the contents of the CS:IP register pair onto the stack, load the branch target address into the CS:IP register pair, and the logical processor then starts fetching code from the specified offset in the new code segment.

- Execution of the **near RET** instruction causes the logical processor to pop a 16-bit offset from the stack into IP after which it resumes fetching code from the calling procedure.
- Execution of the **far RET or** the **IRET** instructions cause the logical processor to pop 4-bytes from the stack into the CS:IP register pair after which it resumes fetching code from the calling procedure (or, in the case of the IRET instruction, from the interrupted program; note that IRET also causes the Flags register to be reloaded from the stack).
- Detection of an **external hardware interrupt or a software exception** causes the logical processor to push the current contents of the CS:IP register pair onto the stack, load the branch target address specified in the selected IDT entry into the CS:IP register pair, after which it then starts fetching code from the interrupt or exception handler.
- Execution of a **software interrupt instruction** (INT nn, INTO, BOUND, or INT3) causes the logical processor to push the current contents of the CS:IP register pair (i.e., the address to return to after the handler has been executed and the IRET instruction is executed) onto the stack. It then reads the 4-byte IDT entry selected by the interrupt type (the vector specified as the operand of the INT instruction, or the one associated with the INTO, INT3, or BOUND instruction) and loads the CS:IP register pair with the target code segment base address and 16-bit branch target address (i.e., offset) of the handler to be executed.

Accessing the Stack Segment

Introduction

The area of memory designated as the stack is scratchpad memory set aside for the use of both the programmer and the processor hardware. It is most often used to temporarily save the contents of registers thus freeing them up for other use:

- **SS register.** Stack Segment register identifies the 20-bit base address of the area to be used as the stack. This can be thought of as the Bottom-of-Stack (BOS) pointer.
- **SP register.** The 16-bit Stack Pointer register provides the offset portion of the address and points to the location in the stack segment where the last item was stored. This can be thought of as the Top-of-Stack (TOS) pointer.

At the beginning of a program, the programmer places the base address of the program's stack segment in the SS register and the offset of the **Top-of-Stack (TOS)** in the SP register. As indicated earlier, since the SP register is only 16-bits in size, the stack cannot be greater than 64KB in size (i.e., the maximum offset is FFFFh). *This is a Real Mode limitation.* As data items are stored in the program's stack, the stack grows downward towards the stack segment base address specified in the SS register.

Stack Characteristics

The characteristics of the stack in Real Mode are:

- Stack length = **64KB**. Its size cannot be adjusted to less than or greater than 64KB.
- In Real Mode, there is no support for an alternative type of stack known as an *expand down stack*. This stack type is only available in Protected Mode and Compatibility Mode and is not supported in Real Mode, SM Mode, or 64-bit Mode (see "Expand-Down Stack" on page 487 for more information on this subject).
- Since the stack base address is essentially a 20-bit address (16-bits from SS zero-extended to 20-bits), the specified base address is, by definition, in the first megabyte of memory address space. Specifically, it is a paragraph-aligned address (i.e., an address divisible by 16) between 00000h and FFFF0h.
- Pushes and Pops (stack accesses) are always 2-byte writes or reads (i.e., SP ± 2).
- The logical processor doesn't check to ensure that the SP is aligned (i.e., to see if the address it contains is divisible by two). If the SP is not aligned on an address divisible by two, it can result in poor performance due to misalignment. For more information, see "Alignment Check Exception (17)" on page 774.

Pushing Data Onto the Stack

Refer to Figure 8-20 on page 299 and Figure 8-21 on page 299. When the programmer wishes to save the contents of a register on the stack, a PUSH instruction is executed. As an example, PUSH AX causes the contents of the AX register to be written into stack memory. Assume that SS = 8000h, SP = FFFFh and that the stack is currently empty. Also assume that the AX register currently contains 1234h and BX contains AA55h. Now consider the following:

1. When the PUSH AX is executed, the logical processor first *decrements* SP by two (FFFFh - 2 = FFFDh). It then writes the 2-bytes from AX—12h and 34h—into memory starting at 8FFFDh (80000h + FFFDh). AL is stored in memory location 8FFFDh and AH is stored in 8FFFEh.
2. If BX is now pushed onto the stack (PUSH BX), the SP is again decremented by two and the two bytes from BX (AAh and 55h) are stored in memory starting at location 8FFFBh (in 8FFFBh and 8FFFCh).

3. Each time the logical processor executes a subsequent PUSH operation, it first decrements SP by two and then stores the data in stack memory.

The stack grows downward in memory from the highest memory location in the stack (i.e., its top) towards the segment base address specified in SS.

Figure 8-20: Push Operation in Real Mode

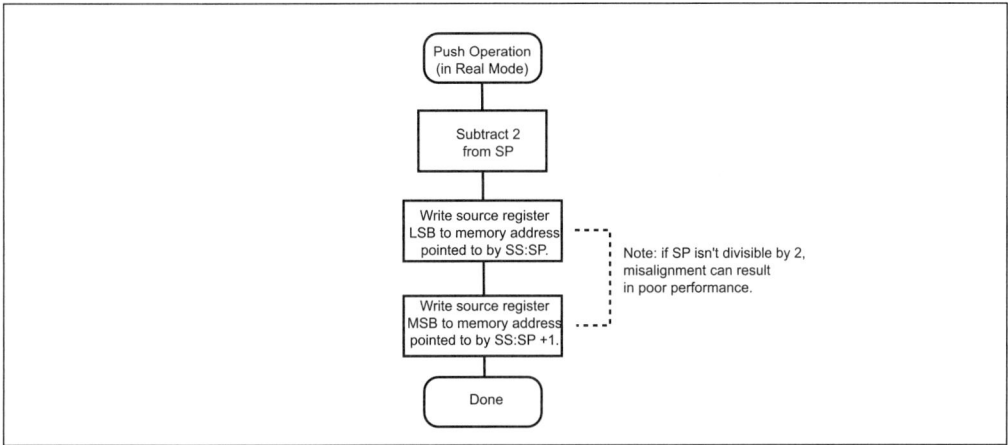

Figure 8-21: Stack Segment

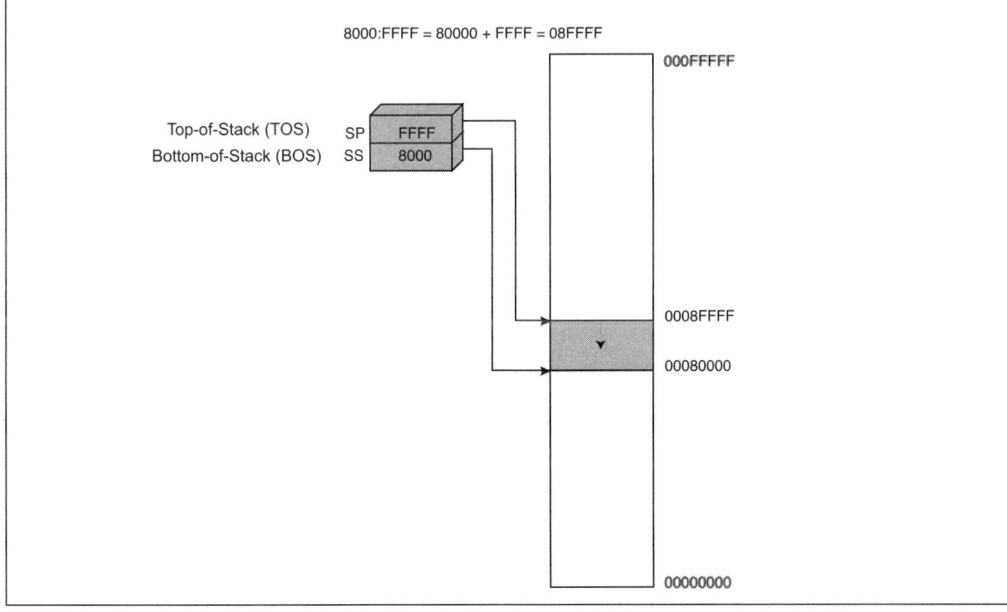

Popping Data From the Stack

Refer to Figure 8-22 on page 300. To restore data previously stored in the stack to a register, the programmer uses the POP instruction. When the logical processor executes a POP (e.g., POP BX), it reads 2-bytes from the stack using the current value in SS:SP to form the memory address:

1. Continuing the example used earlier, a POP BX causes the logical processor to read the two bytes (AAh and 55h) from locations 8FFFBh and 8FFFCh and place them in the BX register.
2. The logical processor then *increments* SP by two, so SS:SP now points to 8000:FFFD.
3. A subsequent POP AX causes the logical processor to read the 2-bytes (12h and 34h) from locations 8FFFDh and 8FFFEh and place them in the AX register.
4. The logical processor then increments SP by two, so SS:SP now point to 8000:FFFF, the Top of the Stack. The stack is now empty.

As implemented in x86 processors, the stack is a LIFO (Last In, First Out) buffer—the last object in is the first out.

Stack Underflow/Overflow

If the programmer attempts to pop more data from the stack than was pushed onto it (referred to as a *stack underflow*), the logical processor generates a Stack exception. Conversely, if the programmer continues pushing data onto the stack until the entire segment is full and then attempts to push one more item onto the stack (referred to as a *stack overflow*), the logical processor also generates a Stack exception.

Figure 8-22: Pop Operation in Real Mode

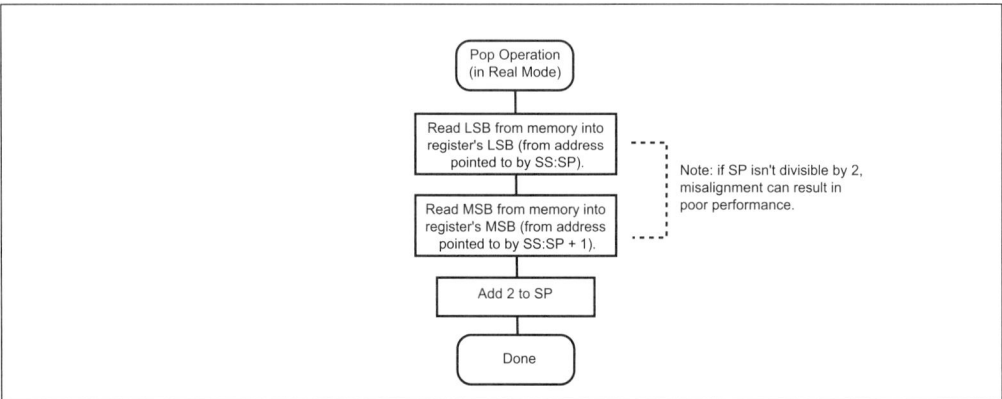

Processor Stack Usage

In addition to the programmer using the stack for temporary storage, the logical processor itself also uses it under certain circumstances. The following are some (but not all) of the cases where it implicitly uses the stack:

- When a software interrupt instruction is executed, the logical processor pushes the current CS:IP values onto the stack before jumping to the target interrupt handler.
- When a **hardware interrupt** occurs, the logical processor pushes the current CS:IP and Flags values onto the stack before jumping to the target interrupt handler.
- When a **software exception** occurs, the logical processor pushes the current CS:IP and Flags values onto the stack before jumping to the target exception handler. For some exception types, an error code is also pushed onto the stack (more on this can be found in "Exception Error Codes" on page 735).
- When the logical processor executes a **Call instruction**, it pushes the current IP (for a near Call) or CS:IP (for a far Call) values onto the stack before jumping to the target procedure.

Accessing Parameters Passed on the Stack

A convenient method of accessing data currently stored in stack memory without affecting the contents of the SP register involves the use of the BP (Base Pointer) register. Consider the following example scenario:

1. Before calling a procedure, the currently-executing program pushes a number of parameters onto the stack.
2. Just before executing the Call instruction, it then copies the current contents of the SP register into the BP (Base Pointer) register.
3. It then executes the Call instruction.
   — Before jumping to the target procedure, the logical processor first pushes the current contents of the IP register (if it's a near call) or CS:IP register pair (if it's a far call) onto the stack. This address is referred to as the *return instruction pointer*.
   — Next:
     – In the case of a **near Call**, it loads the IP register with the address of the called procedure and begins fetching it.
     – In the case of a **far Call**, it loads the CS:IP register pair with the address of the called procedure and begins fetching it.
4. Upon entry to the called procedure, the BP register contains the base address of the list of parameters which had been pushed onto the stack before the call was made. In the called procedure, the programmer can then

access the parameters on the stack by adding the appropriate offset values to the base address specified in the BP register (e.g., `mov ax, [bp +8]`). When using the contents of the BP register as the base address in calculating a memory address, the logical processor automatically defaults to using the SS base address in the address calculation (e.g., SS base + BP + offset of a passed parameter).

Operations That Default To the Stack Segment

The following operations, by default, access the stack segment:

- Obviously, **any form of the Push and Pop** instructions access the stack using the SS:SP register pair.
- Any instruction which accesses a memory-based operand and specifies the **SP or BP registers as the Base register** for the address computation defaults to the stack segment.
- Execution of a **near or far Call** instruction causes the logical processor to push the current contents of IP (in the case of a near Call) or the CS:IP register pair (in the case of a far Call) onto the stack.
- Execution of a **near or far RET** instruction causes the logical processor to pop 2-bytes into IP (in the case of a near RET) or 4-bytes into the CS:IP register pair (in the case of a far RET).
- Detection of an **external hardware interrupt or a software exception** causes the logical processor to:
  — Push the contents of the CS:IP register pair and the Flags register onto the stack.
  — Load the branch target address specified in the selected IDT entry into the CS:IP register pair.
  — Start fetching code from interrupt or exception handler.
- Execution of the **IRET** instruction cause the logical processor to pop 4-bytes from the stack into the CS:IP register pair after which it resumes fetching code from the interrupted program. Note that Flags register is also reloaded from the stack.
- Execution of a **software interrupt instruction** (INT nn, INTO, BOUND or INT3) causes the logical processor to push the current contents of the CS:IP register pair (i.e., the address to return to after the handler has been executed and the IRET instruction is executed) onto the stack. It then reads the 4-byte IDT entry selected by the interrupt type and loads the CS:IP register pair with the target code segment base address and 16-bit branch target address (i.e., offset) of the handler to be executed.

Accessing the DS Data Segment

General

Data in the DS data segment can be read and written using MOV instructions (as well as a number of other instructions that access memory-based data operands). The programmer first loads the DS register with the start address of the data segment in memory. This is accomplished using a MOV or LDS instruction. When loading the DS register using a MOV instruction, the data must first be moved into the AX register before being copied into the DS register:

```
mov  ax, 4500
mov  ds, ax
```

The data segment now starts at location 45000h. The data segment pointed to by the DS register is the default data segment. In this example (see Figure 8-23 on page 304),

```
mov  ax, 4500
mov  ds, ax
mov  ax, [0100]
```

the contents of locations 45100h and 45101h are copied into the lower and upper bytes of the AX register respectively by the last instruction. The 16-bit offset is enclosed within the brackets but the data segment to be accessed isn't explicitly specified in this instruction. The logical processor therefore uses the default data segment, DS, to calculate the physical memory address to be accessed. In Real Mode, it is illegal to specify an offset (the address within the brackets) greater than FFFFh (with one exception; see "Big Real Mode" on page 310). This means that the data segment is limited to 64KB in length in Real Mode. *This is one of the drawbacks to Real Mode.*

Operations That Default to the DS Data Segment

The following operations default to the DS data segment:

* In any form of string operation, the memory address offset specified in the SI or ESI register is added to the base address of the DS data segment (but this can be overridden by prefacing the instruction with a Segment Override prefix).
* Most forms of memory load and store operations default to the DS data segment (but this can be overridden by prefacing the instruction with a Segment Override prefix).

Figure 8-23: Example Data Segment Access

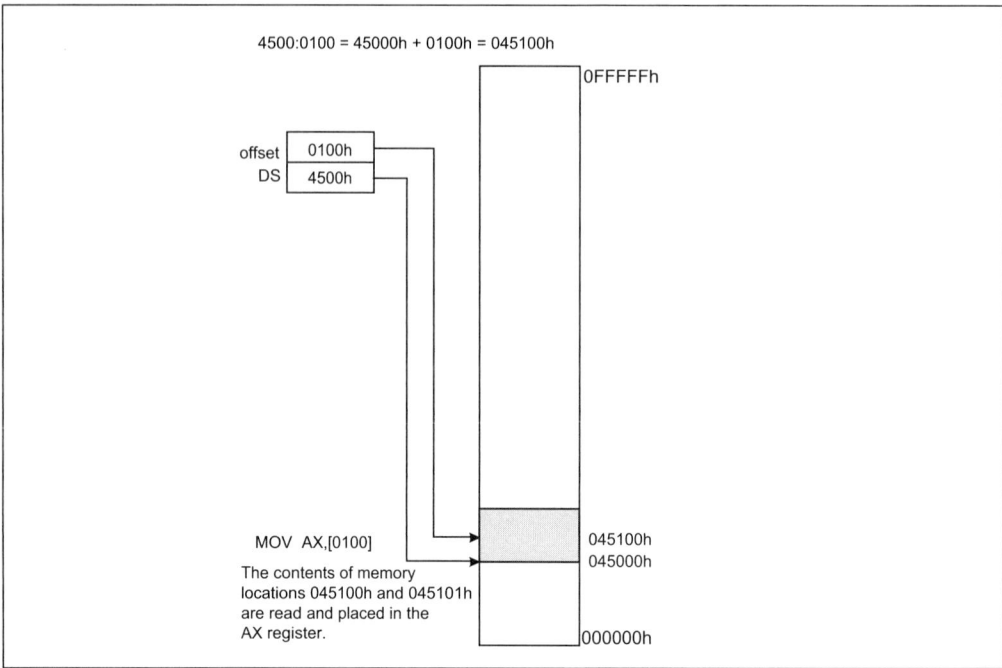

Accessing the ES/FS/GS Data Segments

General

The following code illustrates accessing data segments other than DS:

```
mov  ax, 1000
mov  ds, ax
mov  ax, 2000
mov  es, ax
mov  ax, 3000
mov  fs, ax
mov  ax, 4000
mov  gs, ax
mov  bl, [0002]    ;move from ds data segment
mov  bh, es:[0002] ;move from es data segment
mov  cl, fs:[0002] ;move from fs data segment
mov  ch, gs:[0002] ;move from gs data segment
```

The first memory read moves one byte from location 10002h (DS base address 10000h plus offset 0002h) into the BL register. The second memory read moves one byte from location 20002h (ES base address 20000h plus offset 0002h) into the BH register. The third memory read moves one byte from location 30002h (FS base address 30000h plus offset 0002h) into the CL register. The fourth memory read moves one byte from memory location 40002h (GS base address 40000h plus offset 0002h) into the CH register. The **ES:**, **FS:** and **GS: Segment Override prefix bytes** instruct the logical processor to access the specified segment rather than the default data segment (DS).

The offset specified within the brackets may not exceed FFFFh when in Real Mode (with one exception; see "Big Real Mode" on page 310).

Operations That Default to the ES Data Segment

The following operation defaults to the ES data segment:

* In any form of string operation, the memory address offset specified in the DI or EDI register is added to the base address of the ES data segment. No Segment Override prefix is permitted.

Segment Override Prefixes

Refer to "Segment Override Prefix" on page 220.

Example Segment Register Initialization

Figure 8-24 on page 306 illustrates the use of the segment registers in Real Mode. The figure assumes that the following far jump instruction residing at location 0600:0050 (i.e., location 0050h in the code segment that starts at location 06000h) has already been executed in Real Mode:

```
jmp f000:0100 ;jmp to address 0100h in CS starting at F0000h
```

Starting at the branch target address (F000:0100) the following instructions are then fetched and executed:

```
mov  ax, d000
mov  ds, ax    ;ds = d000
mov  ax, a320
mov  ss, ax    ;ss = a320
mov  ax, 7200
mov  es, ax    ;es = 7200
```

```
mov  ax, 3000
mov  fs, ax     ;fs = 3000
mov  ax, 1000
mov  gs, ax     ;gs = 1000
```

When the logical processor executes the far jump instruction fetched from memory location 0600:0050 (06050h), the CS register is loaded with F000h and the IP register with 0100h. As a result, it fetches its next instruction from memory location 000F0100h. The series of instructions starting at this location causes the values indicated in the figure to be moved into the stack and data segment registers. The figure illustrates how the logical processor then uses the segment registers to identify the six segments of memory space that are associated with the currently running program.

Figure 8-24: Example Usage of Segment Registers in Real Mode

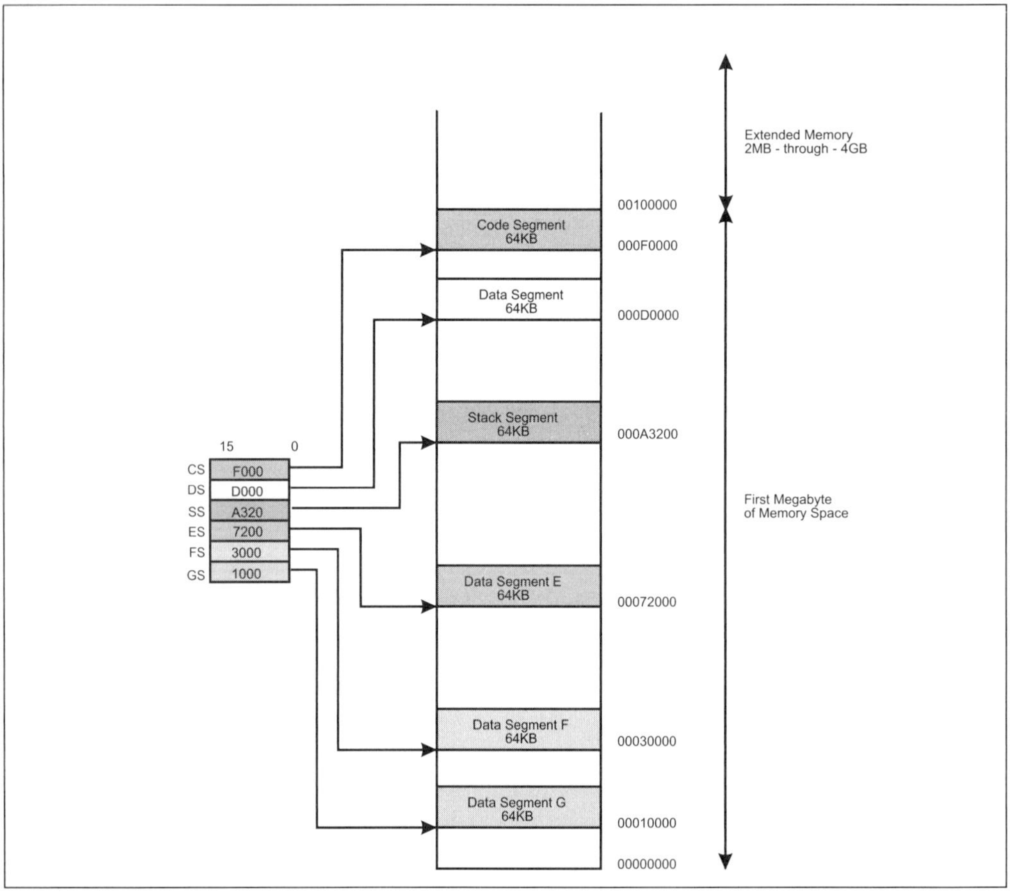

Accessing Extended Memory in Real Mode

It is possible to access a small amount of *extended memory* (memory above 1MB) while in Real Mode. Consider the following example:

```
mov  ax,ffff     ;ffffh to ax
mov  ds,ax       ;transfer ffffh to ds
mov  al,[0010]   ;load contents of memory
                 ;location ffff:0010 into al
```

In order to form the physical memory address when executing the final instruction, the logical processor appends the digit zero to the lower end of the DS data segment value (FFFFh) to point to the start address of the data segment (FFFF0h). It then adds the specified offset (0010h) to the data segment start address to create the physical memory address:

```
        DS + 0h =              FFFF0h
        Offset =                0010h
Physical memory address = 100000h
```

It then performs a memory read using the resultant physical memory address—00100000h—to address memory. Notice that the 21st address bit, A[20], is a one. The logical processor is addressing the first memory location of the second megabyte of memory address space. This is *extended memory* (i.e., memory above the first MB) and the logical processor is addressing it in Real Mode! If it were faithfully emulating the 8086/8088, this wouldn't be possible (because the 8086/8088 had no A20 address signal line).

Now consider this example:

```
mov  ax,ffff     ;ffffh to ax
mov  ds,ax       ;transfer ffffh to ds
mov  al,[ffff]   ;load byte from memory address
                 ;ffff:ffff into al
```

As before, in order to form the physical memory address when executing the third instruction, the logical processor appends a 0h on the lower end of the DS data segment value (FFFFh) to point to the start address of the data segment (000FFFF0h). It then adds the offset (FFFFh) to the data segment start address to create the physical memory address:

```
        DS + 0h =              FFFF0h
        Offset =                FFFFh
Physical memory address =   10FFEFh
```

It then performs a memory read using the resultant physical memory address—0010FFEFh—to address memory. With the value FFFFh in the segment register and by supplying any offset in the range 0010h - FFFFh, any extended memory location from 00100000h - 0010FFEFh can be accessed. A total of 65520d extended memory locations at the start of the second MB of memory space can be accessed while still in Real Mode.

This method was used by many DOS memory management programs running on x86 processors starting with the 286 to access extended memory while remaining in Real Mode. This memory area was usually referred to as the *High Memory Area* (*HMA*).

Note that the code fragments shown in this section can be executed on an 8088/8086 processor (these processors only had a 20-bit address bus consisting of A[19:0]). The results would be different, however, than if the code were executed on a later processor (one which has more than 20 address signal lines). If an 8088/8086 executed the code, address bit A[20] would not be high (because the 8088/8086 processors did not implement address lines above A[19]). The net result, therefore, would be that the 8088/8086 would produce an address that is between 00000000h - 0000FFEFh for the examples shown earlier. This is called *address* or *segment wraparound*.

Some programs written for the 8088/8086 depended on segment wraparound to access data in lower memory (e.g., in the IDT or the BIOS data area). If such programs are executed on a later processor, however, they would not operate correctly because they would end up addressing the HMA rather than the expected locations in lower memory. In order for machines based on later processors to be compatible with such legacy code, the processor's A[20] address output must be forced to zero to simulate the address generated by the 8088/8086.

Figure 8-25 on page 309 illustrates the 286 processor in an IBM PC-AT compatible machine. Note that address bit A[20] is set to one when a segment value of FFFFh and offsets larger than 000Fh are used. Therefore, only A[20] needs to be masked. A[23:21] are never set to one when executing the old code.

This discussion assumes that the system is a PC-compatible based on a later processor (286 or a subsequent processor). External to the processor on the system board, A[20] is connected to one input of an AND gate. The other input of the AND gate is supplied by a signal called A20MASK# supplied by the Keyboard Controller. The output of the AND gate becomes the A[20] address bit that is broadcast with the rest of the processor's address to the system. If the A20MASK# signal is asserted by the Keyboard Controller (i.e., it is driven to zero), the AND gate's output (i.e., the system's A[20] bit) is forced to zero, thereby simulating the truncated address generated by an 8088/8086. In early

PC-compatible machines, the A20MASK# signal was originated by the Keyboard Controller (the Keyboard Controller performed some non-keyboard-related functions) when commanded by software. Today, it is typically generated by intercept hardware (in the chipset) that watches for commands issued to the keyboard controller to raise or lower this line. The intercepted command is not delivered to the keyboard controller. Rather the intercept logic generates the A20MASK# signal much quicker (than would the Keyboard Controller's firmware routines).

Starting with the advent of the 486, the A20 gate is located on the processor die and the chipset's A20MASK# signal is tied to the A20MASK# input on the processor.

Figure 8-25: A20 Gate

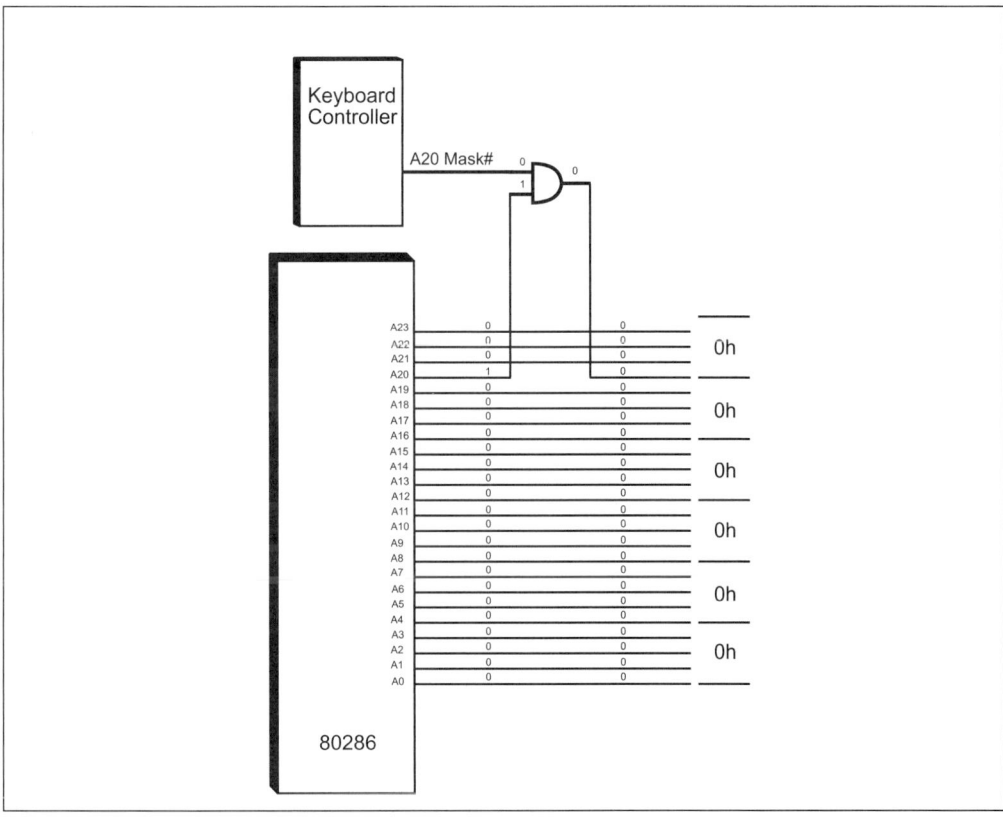

Big Real Mode

All x86 processors subsequent to the 286 can address up to 4GB of memory space in Real Mode, as long as they have (at least once) been switched to Protected Mode and back to Real Mode since the last reset. This is sometimes referred to as *Big Real Mode, Flat Real Mode, Real Big Mode* and *UnReal Mode*.

After temporarily switching to Protected Mode, software sets up a segment descriptor table entry (in the Global Descriptor Table—the GDT) that describes a data segment starting at location 0 and with a length (i.e., a limit) of 4GB (see "Segment Register—Selects Descriptor Table and Entry" on page 386). Software then loads one or more of the data segment registers (DS, ES, FS and GS) with a value that selects this descriptor, thereby causing the logical processor to load the invisible part of the segment register (i.e., its associated segment cache register) with the new start address and length. When the switch is made back to Real Mode, as long as the programmer doesn't load a new value into the respective data segment register(s), the previous segment definition holds true. This permits the programmer to access any location within the 4GB data segment (by prefacing an instruction with the Address Size Override prefix to permit the specification of a 32-bit rather than the default 16-bit offset). If a new value is loaded into a data segment register, the new base address goes into effect, but the limit (i.e., the segment size) that was loaded while in Protected Mode is not modified. The limit will only be changed under the following circumstances:

- If the logical processor is switched back into Protected Mode and the data segment register is loaded with a value that selects a descriptor defining a different length.
- If the logical processor is reset, all segment lengths (i.e., limits) revert back to 64KB.
- If the logical processor is placed in VM86 Mode, all segment lengths (i.e., limits) revert back to 64KB.

This method cannot be used for the code or stack segments, however. In Real Mode, code fetches from the code segment are performed using the CS:IP register pair and IP is a 16-bit register, thereby restricting the code segment to a length of 64KB. Likewise, stack accesses are performed using the SS:SP register pair and SP is a 16-bit register restricting the stack segment to a length of 64KB.

The 286 lacked this capability (it could only be switched from Protected back to Real Mode by resetting the logical processor, thus resetting the invisible part of the segment registers to values that restricted the logical processor to accesses in the first meg of memory space). See the next section for additional information.

286 DOS Extender Programs

Hot Reset and 286 DOS Extender Programs

MS-DOS was written specifically for the 8088 processor using 8088-specific instructions. Since the 8088 only implemented 20 address signal lines, it was incapable of generating a memory address greater than FFFFFh, or 1MB. Furthermore, Protected Mode wasn't introduced until the advent of the 286. Consequently, MS-DOS could only address the lower 1MB and had no concept of Protected Mode.

When a 286 was first powered up, it initially operated in Real Mode (as if it were an 8086/8088). Among other things this meant that although the 286 had 24 address signal lines and could therefore physically address up to 16MB of memory address space, it was limited to the lower 1MB when in Real Mode.

Many MS-DOS application programs required access to more memory space than allowed under MS-DOS. As an example, many Lotus 1-2-3 spreadsheets required very large amounts of memory space, well in excess of that allowed under MS-DOS and the 8088 processor.

On a system based on the 286, the application program accomplished an access to extended memory by calling a special device driver (typically referred to as a 286 *DOS Extender* program) that, when called, accomplished the following:

1. The driver prepared the segment descriptor tables in memory prior to switching the processor into Protected Mode.
2. The driver also saved the address of the next instruction to be executed when the processor was subsequently returned to Real Mode.
3. It then switched the 286 into Protected Mode (by setting CR0[PE] = 1) and accessed extended memory above 1MB on behalf of the application program that called it (for example, to store spreadsheet data).
4. Once the extended memory access was completed, the driver had to switch the processor back into Real Mode (and this is where the problem came in). Due to a feature (i.e., a bug) in the 286 design, although the processor could be programmatically switched into Protected Mode by setting CR0[PE] = 1, clearing the bit back to zero had no effect; the processor remained in Protected Mode.
5. In order to switch the 286 from Protected back to Real Mode, the processor had to be reset.

To accomplish this, the following actions had to be taken:

1. The programmer stored an address pointer in memory that pointed to the start address of a Real Mode procedure responsible for restoring the system

to its previous operating condition (prior to the calling of the DOS extender program). This far pointer was stored in locations 0040:0067 to 0040:006A in the *BIOS Data Area*.

2. A special value (05h or 0Ah) was stored in configuration CMOS RAM location 0Fh (sometimes referred to as the *Reset Code Byte* location) to indicate the reason for the reset. Refer to Table 8-15 on page 313 for the definition of the Reset Code Byte in CMOS RAM.

3. At this point, the system had been prepared for the return to Real Mode and resumption of the DOS application. The Hot Reset command was then issued to the Keyboard/Mouse interface. This is accomplished by writing a FEh to the Keyboard/Mouse interface's command port at IO port 0064h.

4. In response, the Keyboard/Mouse interface pulsed its Hot Reset output one time, causing the system board hardware to generate a reset to the 286.

5. When reset was asserted and then deasserted, the processor initiated Real Mode operation and began to fetch and execute instructions at the power-on restart address (FFFFF0h) exactly as if a power up had just occurred.

6. At the beginning of the POST (Power-On Self-Test program), the programmer reads the Reset Code Byte value from configuration RAM to ascertain the reset's cause. In this case, the value (05h or 0Ah) indicates that it was caused by a Hot Reset to get back to Real Mode and continue execution of the DOS application that had called the DOS extender program.

7. The POST code then retrieved the Real Mode address pointer previously stored in locations 0040:0067h-0040:006Ah of the BIOS Data Area, jumped to the indicated address and resumed execution of the DOS application that had called the DOS extender program.

Note that most system board vendors employ a Hot Reset *intercept* where logic residing between the processor and the Keyboard/Mouse Controller detects a FEh written to the Keyboard controller and immediately generates a Fast Hot Reset to the processor. This provides faster pulsing of the processor's reset signal compared to the slower generation via a command to the Keyboard controller. Later versions of Intel's microcontrollers (typically used as keyboard controllers) provide an internal intercept that results in the generation of Fast Hot Reset.

Alternate (Fast) Hot Reset

The Alternate or Fast Hot Reset command can be issued to System Control Port A at IO address 0092h (sometimes called the PS/2 compatibility port). Alternate Hot Reset performs the same function as the Hot Reset command. However, the processor is reset more quickly using this method than when using Hot Reset. If the Hot Reset command is issued to the Keyboard/Mouse Controller, it must be interpreted by the firmware inside of the controller, while the Alternate Hot

Reset signal is pulsed much more quickly by the hardware.

Alternate Hot Reset is generated by writing a one to bit 0 of System Control Port A. This generates a pulse on the Alternate Hot Reset signal line which, in turn, causes a pulse on the Hot Reset signal. This resets the processor.

286 DOS Extenders on Post-286 Processors

If a DOS Extender program written for the 286 is executed on a system with a later processor, things must be handled a little differently. The system board logic is designed so that the Hot Reset signal line is attached to the processor's INIT# input (the processor's soft reset input introduced with the advent of the Pentium) rather than to its RESET# input.

While the assertion of the INIT# signal does cause the processor to start fetching from the power-on restart address, it exhibits the following differences from the assertion of RESET#:

- The code cache retains its contents.
- The data cache retains its contents.
- The processor's posted memory write buffers retain their contents.
- The FP registers retain their contents.
- The Model-Specific Registers (MSRs) retain their contents.
- CR0[CD] and CR0[NW] remain unchanged (so caching remains enabled).
- The processor resets its GPR registers to their default values.
- The processor continues to handle the snooping of memory transactions initiated by other processor entities while INIT# is asserted.

In other words, the POST begins executing, but the processor does not lose any of the code or data that it worked so hard to collect in its caches, nor does it lose any data operands currently in its FP data registers.

Table 8-15: Reset Code Byte Values

Value	Description
00h	Normal Power-Up reset or Ctrl-Alt-Del reset depending on the value of the Reset flag in memory at locations 0040:0072h - 0040:0073h of the BIOS Data Area. When the Reset flag contains the value 1234h, the POST memory test is skipped.
04h	POST is skipped. Causes the OS to be loaded from disk.

Table 8-15: Reset Code Byte Values (Continued)

Value	Description
05h	POST is skipped and memory preserved. The 286 could only be switched from Protected Mode back into Real Mode by resetting the processor. This presented problems when the programmer wished to temporarily switch to Protected Mode to access extended memory and then switch back into Real Mode to continue execution. When a program had to temporarily leave Real Mode and enter Protected Mode, the programmer first stored a 4-byte memory address (a pointer) into memory starting at 0040:0067h. This pointer specifies the address at which Real Mode execution would resume. Having done so, the program could then switch the processor into Protected Mode and access extended memory. Upon completing the extended memory access, the programmer had to place the value 05h or 0Ah into the Reset Code byte in CMOS RAM and then reset the 286. When reset is deasserted, the processor is again in Real Mode and begins executing the POST. The POST code checks for a 05h or a 0Ah in the Reset Code Byte, and, if present, jumps to the memory address specified in memory starting at location 0040:0067h to resume execution. In addition, if the Reset Code byte value is 05h, an EOI (End-of-Interrupt; see "Overview of Level-Sensitive Interrupt Handling" on page 1321) command is issued to the Interrupt Controller.
09h	Block-move return. This value is placed in the reset code byte when a BIOS call uses INT 15h to move a block of information between conventional and extended memory. In order to accomplish this move, the processor must switch into Protected Mode. On a 286-based system, the INT 15h routine set the Reset Code Byte to 09h prior to resetting the processor to return to Real Mode after the block move. After being reset, the processor started executing the POST, checked the Reset Code Byte value, and then executed an interrupt return (IRET) instruction to return to the original program after completion of the call to the INT 15h BIOS routine.
0Ah	Jump to the Real Mode pointer stored in memory starting at 0040:0067h without issuing an EOI to the Interrupt Controller. See the explanation for Reset Code byte = 05h (in this table).

String Operations

The index registers are:

- The 32-bit Extended Source index (ESI) register and the 16-bit SI register.
- The 32-bit Extended Destination index (EDI) register and the 16-bit DI register.

While these two registers can be used as GPRs, they frequently used to perform operations on blocks of memory-based data.

A classic example of a string operation would be the copy string operation which performs a series of memory reads and writes to transfer a block of data of a specified length from one area of memory (the source buffer) to another (the destination buffer). To accomplish this, the programmer would code the following instructions (this example assumes a 32- rather than a 16-bit address size):

```
    mov esi,xxxx;esi=start address of source buffer
    mov edi,yyyy;edi=destination buffer start address
    mov ecx,zzzz;cx = the number bytes to move
rep movsb        ;move string of bytes & repeat til done
```

The programmer places the start address of the area of memory containing the source data into the ESI register and the start address of the destination memory buffer in the EDI register. The number of bytes to move is placed into ECX, which acts as the count register in this context. The programmer then executes the Move String of Bytes (MOVSB) instruction prefaced by the Repeat (REP) prefix. When executed, this instruction causes the logical processor to perform a memory read from the memory address specified in the ESI register. The byte received from this location is then written to the memory location specified in the EDI register. The ECX register is then decremented and the ESI and EDI registers are incremented by one (assumes that the Direction bit in the Flags register = 0; if it were 1, the registers would be decremented). When the count in the ECX register is exhausted, all of the bytes have been moved and the REP MOVSB instruction has completed execution. The next instruction is then executed. If the count is not exhausted, however, the REP MOVSB is repeated as many times as necessary until the block copy is completed.

- The size of the data operand can be specified as bytes (movsb), words, (movsw), or dwords (movsd):
  - If a byte operation is specified, then after each move, the source and destination buffer addresses are either incremented or decremented by one.

- If a word operation is specified, then after each move, the source and destination buffer addresses are either incremented or decremented by two.
- If a dword operation is specified, then after each move, the source and destination buffer addresses are either incremented or decremented by four.

- The direction of the operation in memory (and therefore whether the source and destination buffer addresses are incremented or decremented) is defined by the state of the Flags[DF] bit:
  - DF = 0: Increment (ascend through memory).
  - DF = 1: Decrement (descend through memory).
- The state of the Flags[DF] bit is controlled using the CLD and STD instructions.

x86 processors support the following types of string operations:

- **MOVS** (Move String). Copy string from source buffer to destination buffer.
- **CMPS** (Compare Strings). Compare two memory strings.
- **SCAS** (Scan String). Performs an operand-by-operand compare of the contents of a memory buffer with the value in the AL, AX, or EAX register.
- **LODS** (Load String). Each time it's executed, this instruction loads the next operand (a byte, word, or dword) from the specified memory buffer into the AL, AX, or EAX register. Typically used within a loop.
- **STOS** (Store String). Each time it's executed, this instruction stores the byte, word, or dword in the AL, AX, or EAX register into the next location in a memory buffer. Typically used within a loop.
- **INS** (IO Input String). Performs n repetitions of: IO Read, memory write, increment or decrement (based on state of Flags[DF] bit) memory pointer in DI or EDI, decrement Count register by one, test for Count register = 0.
- **OUTS** (IO Output String). Performs n repetitions of: memory read from [SI] or [ESI], IO write, increment or decrement (based on state of Flags[DF] bit) memory pointer in SI or ESI, decrement Count register by one, test for Count register = 0.

Real Mode Interrupt/Exception Handling

Events and Event Handlers

An event handler, otherwise referred to as a interrupt or exception service routine, is an event-specific procedure that is automatically invoked (i.e., executed) whenever the associated event occurs. Events may be divided into three basic categories:

- **Hardware interrupts**. These are device-specific events generated by device adapters, the chipset, or by logic internal to the processor itself.
- **Software exceptions**. These are error events associated with the attempted execution of an instruction.
- **Software interrupts**. These are non-error events generated by the following instructions (INT nn, BOUND, INT3 and INTO).

Events Are Recognized on an Instruction Boundary

Both exceptions and hardware interrupts are recognized on instruction boundaries (i.e., an instruction has just completed execution but the execution of the next one has not yet been initiated). As a result, on entry to a handler the CS:IP pointer that was pushed onto the stack points to the next instruction that would have been executed if the interrupt or exception had not been detected (it's important to note, however, that for some types of software exceptions, the pointer on the stack actually points to the offending instruction rather than the next one—refer to "Three Categories of Software Exceptions" on page 330.

When it is said that an interrupt or exception is recognized on an instruction boundary, this refers to the legacy, variable-length IA-32 instructions, not the more primitive micro-ops into which the IA-32 (and IA-64) instructions are translated by the logical processor before execution. If a legacy instruction decodes into a series of two or more micro-ops, *all* of those micro-ops must complete execution before a legacy instruction boundary is reached and an interrupt or exception may be recognized.

The IDT

Definition of the IDT

Refer to Figure 8-26 on page 318 and Table 8-16 on page 318. The Interrupt Descriptor Table, or IDT—sometimes referred to as the Interrupt Vector Table in Real Mode, is a memory-based data structure consisting of 256 entries, each of which, after the table has been initialized by system software, contains the start address of an event-specific handler. Each entry contains 4-bytes of information—the entry point of the handler in CS:IP format.

Figure 8-26: Real Mode Interrupt Table

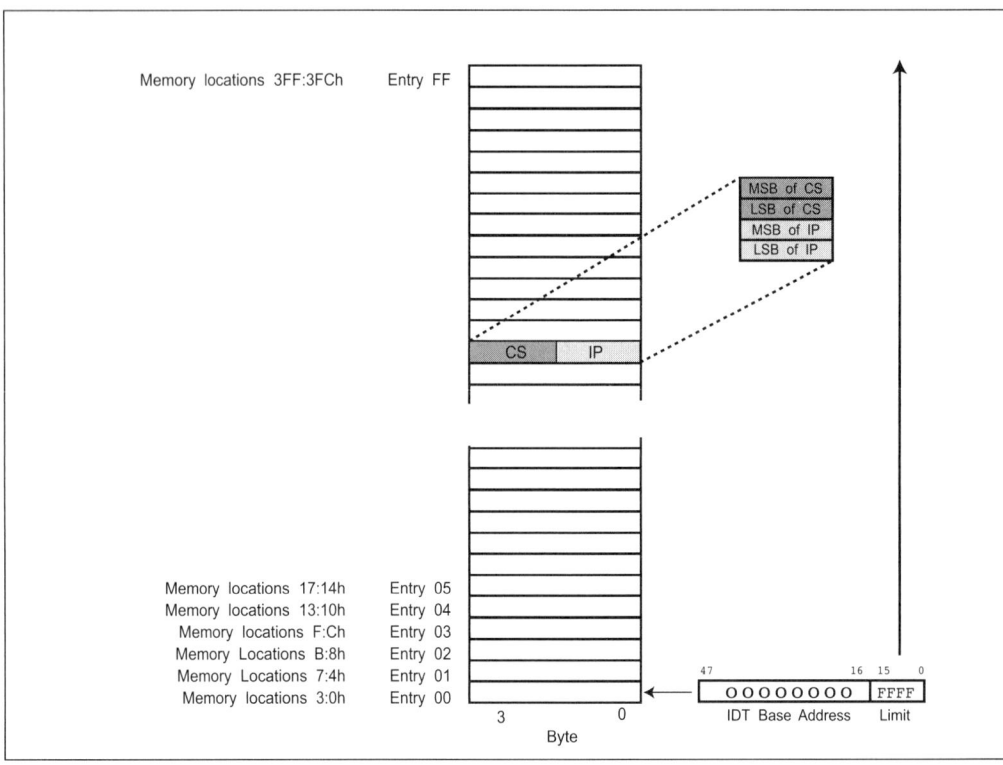

Table 8-16: IDT Entry Assignments

IDT Entry (decimal)	Real Mode ?	Description
0	Y	A Divide-By-Zero exception can be generated during execution of the DIV or IDIV instruction. A detailed description of this exception can be found in "Divide-by-Zero Exception (0)" on page 743.

Table 8-16: IDT Entry Assignments (Continued)

IDT Entry (decimal)	Real Mode ?	Description
1	Y	**A Debug exception** caused by the detection of an instruction address match. A detailed description of this exception can be found in "Debug Exception (1)" on page 744.
	Y	A Debug exception caused by the detection of a data address match.
	Y	A Debug exception caused by a General Detect condition. This occurs when a software attempt is made to use the logical processor's Debug registers when they are already in use by an In-Circuit Emulator (ICE) or an In-Target Probe (ITP) tool.
	Y	A Debug exception caused by the single-step interrupt.
	N	A Debug exception caused by a task-switch breakpoint.
2	Y	**NMI** (Non-Maskable Interrupt) is a form of hardware interrupt generated by the chipset, not a software exception. A detailed description of this interrupt can be found in "NMI" on page 332.
3	Y	The INT3 instruction is also referred to as the **Breakpoint** instruction. Unlike the 2-byte INT *03* instruction, it is one byte long. A detailed description of this software interrupt can be found in "Breakpoint Exception (3)" on page 746.
4	Y	Generated by the execution of the **INTO** (Interrupt on Overflow) instruction if Flags[OF] = 1. Useful because the signed and unsigned arithmetic instructions cannot detect a result overflow. A detailed description of this exception can be found in "Overflow Exception (4)" on page 748.
5	Y	Generated by the **BOUND** instruction if the specified array index is not within the bounds of the specified memory array. A detailed description of this software interrupt can be found in "Array Bounds Check Exception (5)" on page 748.

Table 8-16: IDT Entry Assignments (Continued)

IDT Entry (decimal)	Real Mode ?	Description
6	Y	• Generated when an **invalid opcode** is detected upon the attempted execution of an instruction (instruction prefetch cannot cause this exception). • Also generated when an invalid operand is used with an instruction (e.g., specifying a register as the target of a jump). • Use of the LOCK prefix with instructions for which locking is not supported also causes this exception. A detailed description of this exception can be found in "Invalid OpCode Exception (6)" on page 749.
7	Y	The **Device Not Available** (DNA) exception is generated under two circumstances: • CR0[EM] = 1 (indicating that FPU is not present) and a FP instruction is encountered. The exception handler can be used to emulate the execution of FP instructions. • CR0[TS] = 1, CR0[MP] = 1, and a WAIT or ESC instruction is encountered. The FPU is about to execute an instruction associated with a new task after a task switch has occurred (but the FPU registers were not automatically saved on a task switch). A detailed description of this exception can be found in "Device Not Available (DNA) Exception (7)" on page 751.
8	Y	**Double-Fault encountered**. The logical processor encountered a fault while attempting to call an exception handler for a previously-encountered fault. Most of the time this can be handled by servicing the two exceptions serially, but some combinations are unrecoverable. Such combinations result in a Double-Fault exception. If a third exception occurs while the logical processor is attempting to call the Double-Fault handler, the logical processor generates the Special transaction on its external interface to broadcast a Shutdown message to the chipset and then enters the Shutdown state. A detailed description of this exception can be found in "Double Fault Exception (8)" on page 752.

Table 8-16: IDT Entry Assignments (Continued)

IDT Entry (decimal)	Real Mode ?	Description
9	---	The **Coprocessor Segment Overrun abort** is reserved in post-286 processors. It was only generated by the 286 when a page or segment violation was detected during the transfer of a FP operand to or from memory. The later processors generate exception 13h instead (General Protection). A detailed description of this exception can be found in "Coprocessor Segment Overrun Exception (9)" on page 756.
10 *	N	**Invalid TSS fault**. Generated if a task switch is attempted to a task with an invalid TSS. A detailed description of this exception can be found in "Invalid TSS Exception (10)" on page 757.
11 *	N	**Segment Not Present**. Generated when the Present bit in the selected segment descriptor (CS, DS, ES, FS, GS) = 0. An SS descriptor with P = 0 results in a stack exception (number 12). A detailed description of this exception can be found in "Segment Not Present Exception (11)" on page 759.
12	Y	**Stack exception** occurs for one of two reasons: • A Stack Underflow or Overflow error (in other words, too many pops or pushes). • An attempt to load the SS register with a selector for a descriptor marked not present (P = 0). A detailed description of this exception can be found in "Stack Exception (12)" on page 761.
13	Y	**General Protection (GP)** exception. All protection violations that don't cause another exception result in a GP exception. A detailed description of this exception can be found in "General Protection (GP) Exception (13)" on page 763.

Table 8-16: IDT Entry Assignments (Continued)

IDT Entry (decimal)	Real Mode ?	Description
14 *	N	**Page Fault** exception. Occurs for one the following reasons: • The selected PDE's P bit = 0, indicating that the selected Page Table is not present in memory. • The selected PTE's P bit = 0, indicating that the target page is not present in memory. • An attempt to write to a read-only page. • Code running in user mode (privilege level 3) attempts to write to a read-only page. • If CR0[WP] = 1, a Page Fault also occurs on an attempt by code with supervisor privilege (0, 1, or 2) to write to a user page (i.e., PTE[U/S] = 1). • Insufficient page-level privilege to access the Page Table or the page. • A reserved bit set to one in the PDE or PTE. If the Page Fault occurs due to a page not present or a page privilege or access violation (insufficient privilege or writes not permitted), the A (Accessed) bit is affected in the PDE, but not in the PTE. The PTE's Accessed and Dirty (Modified) bits are only affected if the page access succeeds. A detailed description of this exception can be found in "Page Fault Exception (14)" on page 766. A detailed description of Paging can be found in "IA-32 Address Translation Mechanisms" on page 493.
15	---	Reserved.
16	Y	**FP error** exception. Error generated by the attempted execution of an x87 FP math instruction. It can only occur when CR0[NE] = 1. A detailed description of this exception can be found in "FPU Exception (16)" on page 770. Additional information can be found in "FP Error Reporting" on page 357.

Table 8-16: IDT Entry Assignments (Continued)

IDT Entry (decimal)	Real Mode ?	Description
17	Y	**Alignment Check** exception. The occurrence of this exception indicates that the logical processor detected an unaligned multi-byte memory access when alignment checking was enabled. Alignment checks are only carried out in data (or stack) segments (not in code or system segments—e.g., a TSS). An example of an alignment-check violation is a word (a 2-byte data object) stored in memory starting at an odd address, or a dword stored in memory starting at an address that is not divisible by four. A detailed description of this exception can be found in "Alignment Check Exception (17)" on page 774.
18	Y	**Machine Check** exception. If enabled to do so, this exception is generated when the logical processor detects unrecoverable hardware errors that generally fall within the following categories: • External interface transaction errors. • Both uncorrectable ECC errors detected on internal caches or on the external interface. • Parity errors detected on the external interface or on internal ROM devices (such as the logical processor's Microcode ROM). • Storage errors in the logical processor's internal caches or TLBs (Translation Lookaside Buffers; see "The TLBs" on page 523). A detailed description of this exception can be found in "Machine Check Exception (18)" on page 778. Additional information can be found in "Machine Check Architecture (MCA)" on page 1207.

Table 8-16: IDT Entry Assignments (Continued)

IDT Entry (decimal)	Real Mode ?	Description
19	Y	The SIMD FP exception (exception 19). Added with the advent of the Pentium III processor. SIMD FP exceptions are generated independently from the x87 FP exceptions. Generation of an SSE SIMD FP exception does not result in the assertion of the processor's FERR# output pin (regardless of the CR0[NE] setting), and the state of the processor's IGNNE# input pin has no effect on the SSE SIMD FP logic. A detailed description of this exception can be found in "SIMD Floating-Point Exception (19)" on page 779. Additional information can be found in "The SSE Facilities" on page 851.
20-31	---	**Intel reserved**. Do not use. These IDT entries are reserved for future software exceptions.
32-255	Y	Available for use by maskable hardware interrupts, the INT *nn* instruction, and in Inter-Processor Interrupt (IPI) messages sent from one Local APIC to another.

* Note: These exceptions do not occur in Real Mode, but may occur in VM86 mode.

IDT and IDTR Initialization

Please note that Intel documentation refers to the Interrupt Table by two names:

- In Real Mode, it is sometimes referred to as the Interrupt Vector Table (IVT).
- In Protected Mode, it is referred to as the Interrupt Descriptor Table (IDT).

Since having multiple names for the same entity only creates possible confusion, the author has chosen to refer to it as the IDT (no matter what mode the logical processor happens to be in).

While initializing the system, software creates the IDT in system RAM memory and, if the default base address and size aren't acceptable (see Figure 8-26 on page 318), programs the IDTR (IDT register) with a new base address and size. In x86 processors, the assertion of reset at power-up presets the IDTR with an IDT base address of 00000000h and a table length of FFFFh (64KB; although, in reality, the maximum size of the IDT in Real Mode is 1KB in length—256 entries x 4 bytes/entry). The programmer can use the LIDT (Load IDT Register) and

SIDT (Store IDT Register) instructions to access the IDTR. Note that while you can alter the base address of the IDT and relocate it elsewhere (to an address other the default base address of 00000000h), generally speaking this isn't a wise move. DOS applications, device drivers, etc., assuming that the IDT starts at location zero, frequently read IDT entries and make updates to them. If the table has been relocated somewhere else, this will obviously result in memory corruption.

If an interrupt vector indexes to an IDT entry beyond the length of the IDT, a General Protection exception is generated.

In Real Mode, the initialization software writes a CS:IP value (consisting of two 16-bit values; see Figure 8-26 on page 318) into each entry of the IDT. Each entry contains the entry point of either a device-specific or exception-specific handler (in CS:IP format). Unused entries are typically directed to a dummy handler that only contains an IRET instruction.

To be more specific, before the OS has been loaded into memory, the ROM-based BIOS code initializes the IDT and directs some entries to the interrupt handlers associated with the default devices that will be used to boot the OS (i.e., a display device, an input device—the keyboard, and the mass storage device from which the OS will be loaded). Other entries are directed to software exception handlers location within the ROM BIOS. When the OS is booted into memory, its startup and initialization code will load loadable device drivers for all of the devices discovered in the system and, as it does so, call the initialization code in each of them. This will cause additional entries to be made in the IDT, each one directed to a device-specific handler within the respective device driver. The OS initialization code will also set up the IDT entries associated with the exception handlers incorporated into the OS kernel.

Stack Initialization

Just a cautionary note: since the logical processor automatically pushes return information onto the stack in preparation for servicing an interrupt or exception, the programmer should ensure that RAM is allocated for the stack as quickly as possible after start-up and that the SS:SP register pair is initialized with the BOS (Bottom of Stack) and TOS (Top of Stack).

Event (Interrupt and Exception) Handling

Figure 8-27 on page 326 illustrates the actions taken by the logical processor when an interrupt or exception event is detected or a software interrupt instruction is executed. Figure 8-28 on page 327 illustrates the actions taken by the logical processor when the IRET instruction is executed at the completion of the handler.

Figure 8-27: Real Mode Event Handling

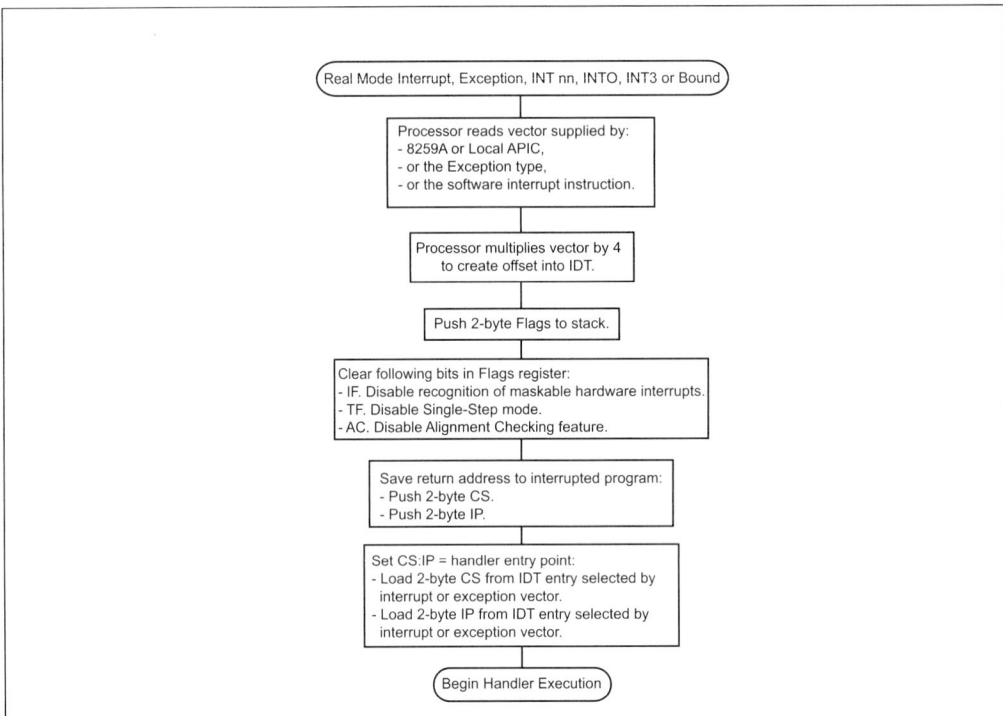

Figure 8-28: Return from Real Mode Handler to Interrupted Real Mode Application

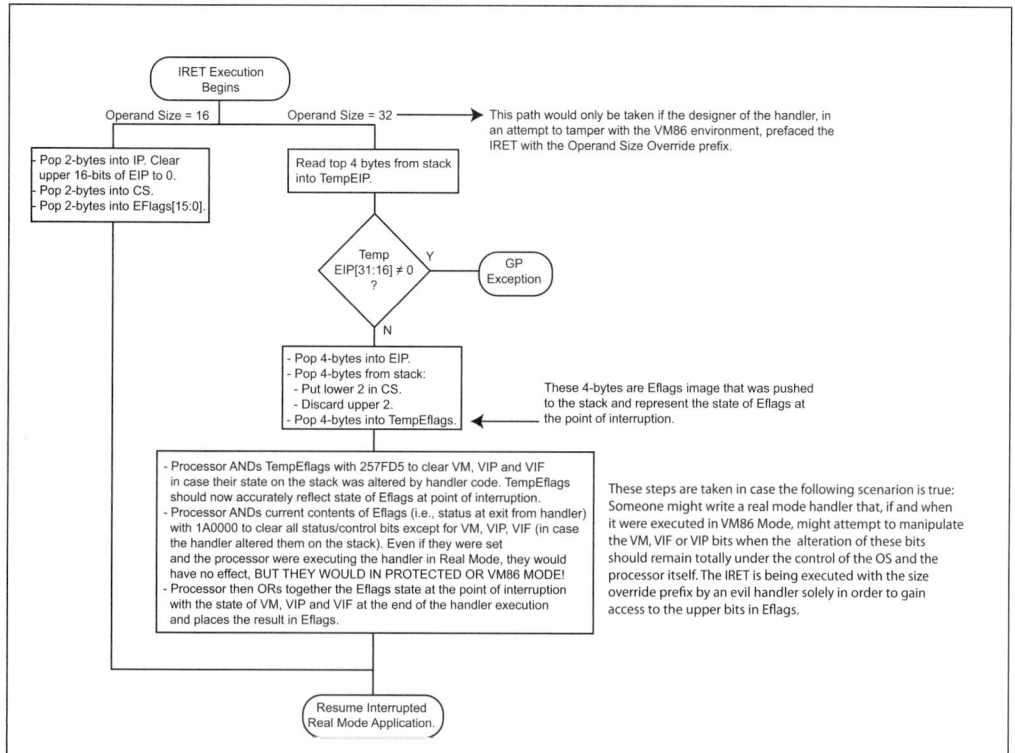

Software Event Types

Introduction

As noted earlier, software-related events may be divided into two categories:

- **Software exceptions**. Error events associated with the attempted execution of an instruction.
- **Software interrupt instructions**. These are non-error events generated by the following instructions (INT nn, BOUND, INT3 and INTO).

Software Exceptions

All of the currently-defined software exception events are listed in Table 8-16 on page 318. By design, each of these event types have a hard-wired association with their respective IDT entries.

Definition of an Exception. Exceptions can be divided into two categories:

— **Software exceptions**. These are error events associated with the attempted execution of an instruction.
— **Machine Check exception**. Although technically categorized as an exception, events generated by the logical processor's Machine Check logic are actually generated upon the detection of a hardware-related error that falls into one of the following categories:
  – An error detected during a transaction on the processor's external interface.
  – An error detected within the processor itself (e.g., an uncorrectable ECC error when accessing a cache, or a Microcode ROM checksum error).

Exception Handling. Refer to Figure 8-29 on page 329. Figure 8-30 on page 329 illustrates the contents of the stack upon entry to the handler. Upon entry into the exception handler, the programmer pushes the contents of any additional registers which will be modified in the course of handling the exception onto the stack. The body of the handler then performs the necessary series of actions to handle, and, hopefully fix, the problem encountered on the attempted execution of the offending instruction. It should be noted that some exception types can be caused by more than one type of instruction-oriented problem. In this case, an error code is also pushed onto the stack and the exception handler uses it to determine the exact cause of the exception.

Assuming that the problem was correctable, the programmer then restores the contents of any modified registers from the stack. The final instruction in the handler, the IRET (Interrupt Return), then causes the logical processor to pop the CS:IP and Flags register contents back into the CS:IP register pair and the Flag register after which the logical processor resumes normal operation: i.e., it resumes fetching instructions from the interrupted program using the restored pointer in the CS:IP register pair.

Figure 8-29: Exception Handling in Real Mode

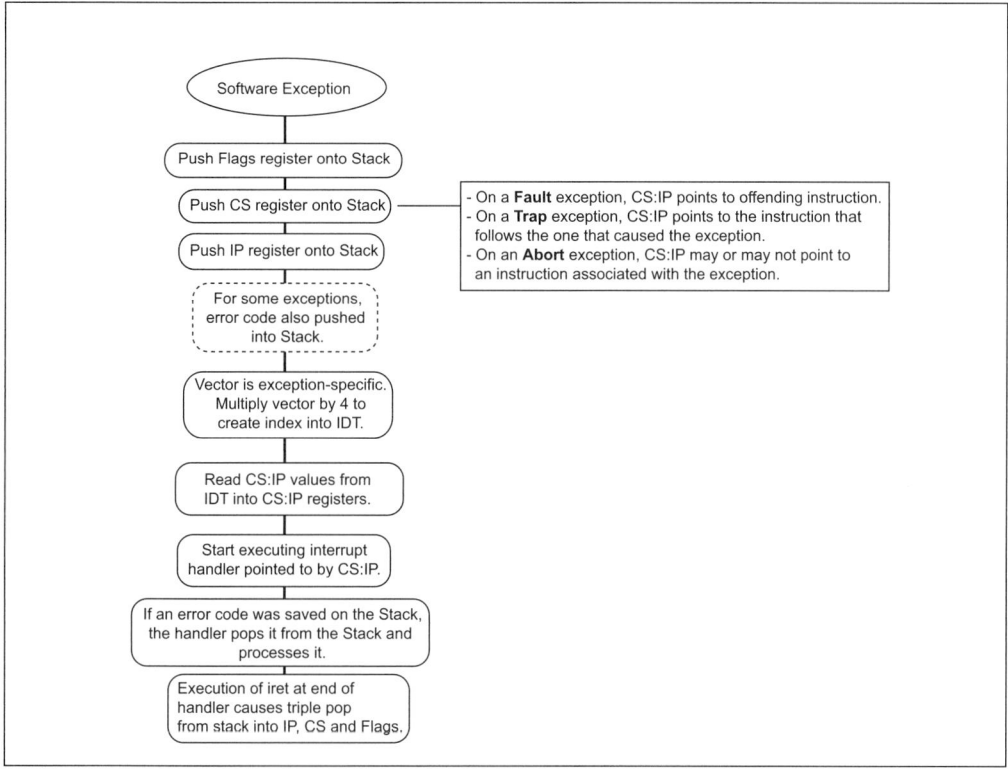

Figure 8-30: Real Mode Stack on Entry to Handler

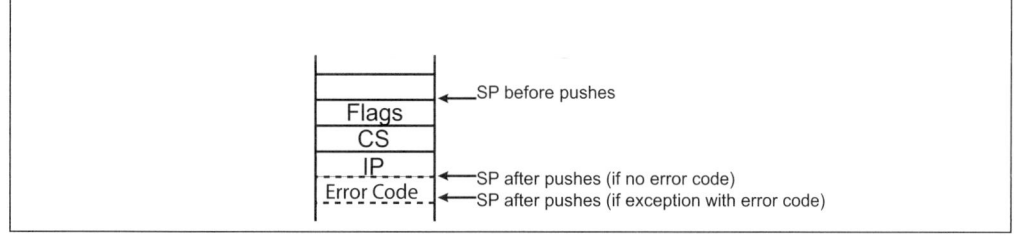

Three Categories of Software Exceptions. As described in Table 8-17 on page 330, software exception events may be divided into three categories: traps, faults, and aborts. See "Software Exceptions" on page 728 for a more detailed description.

Table 8-17: Software Exception Categories

Type	Definition
Fault	**Before being pushed onto the stack, the logical processor rewinds CS:IP (which had already incremented to point to the next instruction) to point to the instruction that caused the error event.** A fault is an exception reported with the address on the stack pointing to the offending instruction. The fault is reported with the logical processor restored to a state that permits the instruction to be restarted (i.e., all registers are restored to their original state prior to the attempted execution of the instruction).
Trap	**CS:IP pushed onto the stack points to the instruction after the one that caused the error event.** A trap is reported after the instruction that caused it has completed execution. If the trap occurs during execution of an instruction that alters program flow (e.g., a jump), the return address points to the branch target address (e.g., the address being jumped to). If the instruction is a string instruction and has a repeat prefix and the count has not been exhausted, the return address points to the same instruction and the values in the other registers related to the instruction contain the values for the next iteration.
Abort	**CS:IP on the stack may not be reliable.** An abort does not always reliably supply the address of the instruction that caused the exception. This makes it impossible for the exception handler to fix the problem and resume program execution.

Software Interrupt Instructions

When executed, the following four instructions emulate an interrupt or exception event.

INT *nn* Instruction. The currently executing program can use the software interrupt instruction, INT *nn* (where *nn* = an entry in the IDT), to call an interrupt or exception handler. Upon execution of the INT instruction, the logical processor suspends execution of the currently-executing program and takes the following actions:

1. If (nn x 4-bytes/entry) + 3 exceeds the size of the IDT, a GP exception is generated.
2. If the stack isn't large enough to hold the six bytes to be pushed onto it (i.e., CS:IP and Flags register), a Stack exception is generated.
3. The Flags register contents is pushed onto the stack.
4. Clears the following bits in the Flags register:
   - IF = 0. Disables recognition of maskable hardware interrupts.
   - TF = 0. Disables debug single-step mode (if it was enabled).
   - AC = 0. Disables the alignment checking feature (if it was enabled).
5. Pushes CS:IP onto the stack.
6. No error code is pushed onto the stack (because, unlike a software exception, there was no error). *Note*: If the *nn* value selects an IDT entry associated with an exception which expects an error code to have been pushed onto the stack along with CS:IP and Flag, no such error code was pushed in this case.
7. CS is loaded from the IDT entry selected by *nn*. This is the upper 16-bits of the 20-bit base address of the code segment containing the handler.
8. IP is loaded from the IDT entry selected by *nn*. The upper 16-bits of EIP are cleared to 0.
9. Using the CS:IP pointer, the logical processor begins execution of the selected handler.

The last instruction in the called procedure is the IRET instruction. When executed, it causes the logical processor to reload (i.e., pop) the previously-saved CS:IP value as well as the contents of the Flags register (note: restoring the Flags register from the stack restores the original setting of the IF, TF, and AC bits). The logical processor then resumes execution of the calling program at the instruction immediately following the INT *nn*.

BOUND Instruction. If the specified array index value falls outside the bounds of the specified memory-based array, the Bound exception is generated. This automatically selects IDT entry five which contains the start address of the Bound exception handler.

INTO Instruction. If, when the INTO (Interrupt on Overflow) instruction is executed, the Overflow bit (OF) in the Flags register is set to one, the INTO exception is generated. This automatically selects IDT entry four which contains the start address of the Overflow exception handler.

INT3 (Breakpoint) Instruction. When encountered in the program flow, the execution of this 1-byte instruction causes the generation of the Breakpoint exception. This automatically selects IDT entry three which contains the start address of the Breakpoint handler within the debugger.

Hardware Event Types

As with software exceptions, hardware interrupts are recognized on IA-32 legacy instruction boundaries. They fall into four categories:

- NMI.
- SMI.
- Maskable interrupts.
- Machine Check exception.

NMI

Definition of NMI and Delivery Mechanisms. Unlike maskable hardware interrupts, if an NMI (Non-Maskable Interrupt) is delivered to the logical processor, its recognition cannot be masked by software. NMI is issued to the logical processor by the chipset to signal that a serious hardware condition has been detected on the system board. An NMI can be delivered to the logical processor in any of the following ways:

— On a processor using an external interface other than Intel QPI:
  – If the logical processor's Local APIC is disabled, the chipset asserts the NMI signal to the processor.
  – If the logical processor's Local APIC is enabled, the chipset sends an NMI IPI (Inter-Processor Interrupt) message packet to the logical processor over the processor's external interface.
— On a processor using the Intel QPI external interface, the NMI is delivered in an interrupt message packet.

External NMI Masking Mechanism. Since the logical processor will recognize and attempt to handle an NMI if it is detected, it is important that the system designer provide an external hardware mechanism that will prevent the delivery of an NMI immediately after power-up before IDT entry two (the NMI entry) has been initialized with the NMI handler entry point. As an example, in the PC-compatible world, the programmer:

— May mask out the external hardware's ability to generate NMI by writing a zero to bit seven of IO port 70h (note this is the default state of the

NMI Mask bit).
— Conversely, the programmer may unmask it by writing a one to bit seven of IO port 70h.
Caution should be exercised, however, because bits [6:0] of this same IO port are assigned to the Real-Time Clock (RTC) chip's address port.

NMI Handling. When an NMI request is detected, the logical processor takes the following actions:

1. If the stack isn't large enough to hold the six bytes to be pushed onto it (i.e., CS:IP and Flags register), a Stack exception is generated.
2. The Flags register content is pushed onto the stack.
3. Clears the following bits in the Flags register:
   – TF = 0. Disables debug single-step mode (if it was enabled).
   – AC = 0. Disables the alignment checking feature (if it was enabled).
4. Pushes CS:IP onto the stack.
5. CS is loaded from IDT entry two. This is the upper 16-bits of the 20-bit code segment base address (the code segment containing the NMI handler).
6. IP is loaded from IDT entry two. The upper 16-bits of EIP are cleared to 0.
7. The logical processor automatically disables recognition of any additional NMI interrupts until the IRET instruction is executed at the end of the NMI handler.
8. Using the CS:IP pointer, the logical processor begins execution of the NMI handler.

It is recommended that, at the start of the handler, the programmer execute a CLI instruction to disable recognition of maskable hardware interrupts until the NMI has been handled. Once in the handler, the programmer polls the chipset to discover the source and type of failure. Upon discovering the source of the failure, in a PC environment a failure-specific message is typically output to the display, maskable interrupt recognition is disabled (if it wasn't already), and the HLT instruction is executed. In response to the HLT instruction, the logical processor broadcasts a halt message on its external interface (to inform the chipset of its intention to stop fetching and executing instructions) using the Special transaction and ceases to fetch and execute instructions. In the event that the NMI could be gracefully handled and its cause corrected, the last instruction is the IRET instruction. When executed, it causes the logical processor to:

— Reload (i.e., pop) the previously-saved CS:IP value as well as the contents of the Flags register from the stack (note: restoring the Flags register from the stack restores the original setting of the TF and AC bits).
— Reenable recognition of the NMI interrupt.

The logical processor then resumes execution of the interrupted program at the next instruction.

SMI

The chipset sends an SMI (System Management Interrupt) to inform software of a platform-specific event (e.g., a thermal or power management event). It can be sent in any of the following ways:

- On a processor using an external interface other than Intel QPI:
  — If the logical processor's Local APIC is disabled, the chipset asserts the processor's SMI input.
  — If the logical processor's Local APIC is enabled, the chipset sends an SMI IPI (Inter-Processor Interrupt) message packet to the logical processor's Local APIC over the processor's external interface.
- On a processor using the Intel QPI external interface, the SMI is sent to the logical processor's Local APIC in an interrupt message packet.

An SMI is not treated in the same manner as a normal interrupt or exception. Rather, it causes the logical processor to save all of its current state (i.e., its register set contents) and then switches it into SMM (System Management Mode) to handle the event. A complete description of SMM (System Management Mode) can be found in "System Management Mode (SMM)" on page 1167.

Maskable Interrupts

Maskable Interrupts Are Originated by Devices.
All device interrupts not delivered to the logical processor via the NMI or SMI mechanisms are categorized as maskable hardware interrupts. This includes external device adapters as well as several hardware devices embedded on the CPU die itself (e.g., the Local APIC Timer, CPU Thermal Sensor interrupts, Performance Counter Overflow interrupts, etc.).

Enabling/Disabling Maskable Interrupt Recognition.
Whether or not a maskable hardware interrupt is recognized by the logical processor depends on the current state of the Flags[IF] bit:

— IF = 0. Maskable interrupts are ignored as long as the IF bit remains cleared. The CLI instruction is used to clear IF to 0.
— IF = 1. Maskable interrupts are recognized when IF = 1. The STI instruction is used to set IF = 1.

Selective Masking of Maskable Interrupts. Software also has the ability to selectively enable or disable the recognition of maskable interrupts:

— If the logical processor's Local APIC is disabled and the legacy 8259A interrupt controller is in use, the programmer may selectively enable or disable the generation of maskable interrupts by programming the 8259A's IMR (Interrupt Mask Register) accordingly.

— If the logical processor's Local APIC is enabled, the programmer may selectively enable or disable the recognition of maskable interrupts by programming the IO APIC's register set accordingly.

Maskable Interrupt Delivery Mechanisms. A maskable interrupt can be delivered to the logical processor in any of the following ways:

— On a processor using an external interface other than Intel QPI:
  – If the logical processor's Local APIC is disabled, the chipset asserts the processor's INTR input.
  – If the logical processor's Local APIC is enabled, the chipset sends a User-Defined IPI (Inter-Processor Interrupt) message packet (also called a fixed interrupt) to the logical processor's Local APIC over the processor's external interface.

— On a processor using the Intel QPI external interface, the IPI is sent to the logical processor's Local APIC in an interrupt message packet.

IDT Entries Associated with Maskable Interrupts. IDT entries 0 - 31d are reserved for software exception conditions. IDT entries 32d - 255d are available for assignment to:

— Hardware devices that utilize the maskable interrupt mechanism.

— BIOS or OS function calls using the INT nn instruction.

— Any other function calls implemented using the INT nn instruction.

Handling Maskable Interrupts. On the detection of a maskable hardware interrupt request, the actions shown in Figure 8-31 on page 336 are taken.

Figure 8-31: Maskable Interrupt Handling in Real Mode

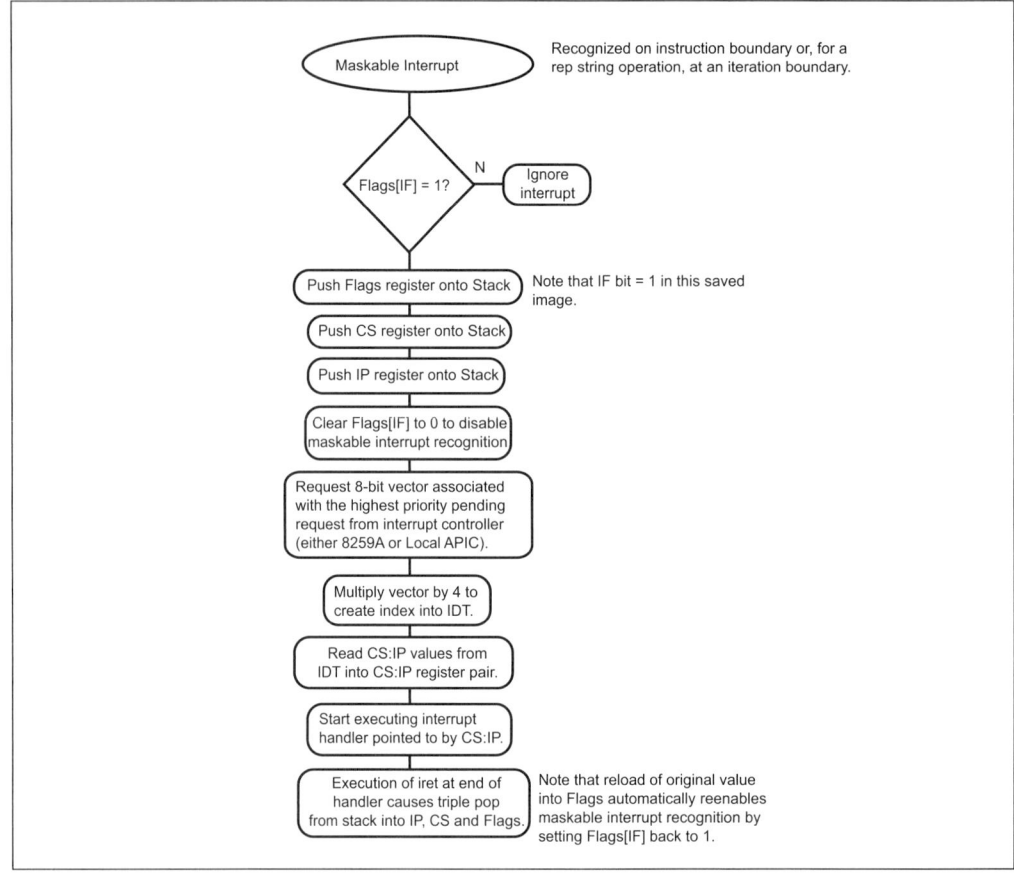

Machine Check Exception

Although technically categorized as an exception, events generated by the logical processor's Machine Check logic are actually generated upon the detection of a hardware-related error that falls into one of the following categories:

- An error detected during a transaction on the processor's external interface.
- An error detected within the logical processor itself (e.g., an uncorrectable ECC error when accessing a cache; or a Microcode ROM checksum error).

The ability of the logical processor to generate a Machine Check exception may be enabled or disabled via CR4[MCE]. A detailed description of the Machine Check exception may be found in "Machine Check Architecture (MCA)" on page 1207.

Summary of Real Mode Limitations

- No protection whatsoever. The currently-running program can touch any IO port, memory location, or register, and can execute any instruction.
- Does not support virtual-to-physical address translation (i.e., Paging).
- No support for multitasking.
- Segments have a fixed size of 64KB (not adjustable), forcing the programmer to segment larger applications (let's face it, virtually *all* applications) into multiple code and data segments.
- Segments are restricted to the first MB of memory space.
- All interrupt and exception handlers must reside in the 1st MB of memory space.

The net result: Real Mode is wholly unsuited to supporting a multitasking OS environment.

Transitioning to Protected Mode

This topic is covered in "Transitioning to Protected Mode" on page 1113.

9 *Legacy x87 FP Support*

The Previous Chapter

The previous chapter provided a detailed description of Real Mode operation and covered the following topics:

- 8086 Emulation.
- Unused Facilities.
- Real Mode OS Environment.
- Running Real Mode Applications Under a Protected Mode OS.
- Real Mode Applications Aren't Supported in IA-32e Mode.
- Real Mode Register Set.
- IO Space versus Memory Space.
- IO and Memory-Mapped IO Operations.
- Operand Size Selection.
- Address Size Selection.
- Real Mode Memory Addressing.
- Real Mode Interrupt/Exception Handling.
- Summary of Real Mode Limitations.

This Chapter

This chapter provides a detailed description of the x87 FPU and covers the following topics:

- A Little History.
- x87 FP Instruction Format.
- FPU-Related CR0 Bit Fields.
- x87 FPU Register Set.
  - The FP Data Registers.
  - x87 FPU's Native Data Operand Format.

- — 32-bit SP FP Numeric Format.
- — DP FP Number Representation.
- — FCW Register.
- — FSW Register.
- — FTW Register.
- — Instruction Pointer Register.
- — Data Pointer Register.
- — Fopcode Register.
- FP Error Reporting.
  - — Precise Error Reporting.
  - — Imprecise (Deferred) Error Reporting.
  - — Why Deferred Error Reporting Is Used.
  - — The WAIT/FWAIT Instruction.
  - — CR0[NE].
  - — Ignoring FP Errors.

The Next Chapter

The next chapter provides an introduction to the concept of multitasking and covers the following topics:

- Concept.
- An Example—Timeslicing.
- Another Example—Awaiting an Event.
  - — 1. Task Issues Call to OS for Disk Read.
  - — 2. Device Driver Initiates Disk Read.
  - — 3. OS Suspends Task.
  - — 4. OS Makes Entry in Event Queue.
  - — 5. OS Starts or Resumes Another Task.
  - — 6. Disk-Generated Interrupt Causes Jump to OS.
  - — 7. Interrupted Task Suspended.
  - — 8. Task Queue Checked.
  - — 9. OS Resumes Task.

A Little History

Prior to the advent of the 486DX processor, x86 processors did not include an on-die FPU. In order to perform floating-point (FP) math operations the end user had to add an external x87 FPU chip to the system which the processor treated as a specialized IO device. When the processor encountered a FP instruction in the currently-executing program, it would perform a series of one or more IO write transactions on its external bus to forward the instruction to the off-chip FPU for execution. Obviously, this was very inefficient.

The 486DX was the first x86 processor to integrate the x87 FPU (all subsequent x86 processors include it). The sections that follow provide a description of the FPU's register set and the format in which FP numbers are represented.

x87 FP Instruction Format

This topic is covered in "x87 FP Opcodes Inhabit Opcode Mini-Maps" on page 187.

FPU-Related CR0 Bit Fields

Refer to Figure 9-1 on page 341, Table 9-1 on page 341, and Table 8-4 on page 241 for a description of the CR0 bit fields related to the x87 FPU.

Figure 9-1: CR0

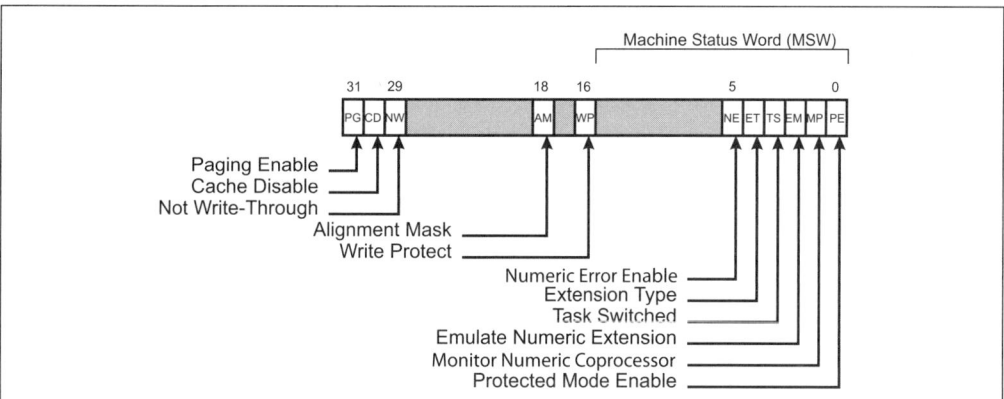

Table 9-1: CR0 x87 FPU-related Bit Fields

Bit(s)	Name	Description
2:1	EM, MP	The OS uses these x87 FPU-related bits to indicate whether the logical processor is: • **Running DOS**. • **Running a multitasking OS**. • **Neither** of the above (the FPU isn't present or is disabled); in this case, a software exception is generated when the logical processor detects an x87 instruction and software **emulates the x87 FPU**. See Table 8-4 on page 241.

Table 9-1: CR0 x87 FPU-related Bit Fields (Continued)

Bit(s)	Name	Description
3	TS	**x87 Task Switch status bit**. The x87 FPU registers are not saved on an automatic task switch. When a hardware-based task switch occurs: • CR0[TS] is set to one. • Most but not all registers are automatically saved in the TSS (Task State Segment) data structure associated with the currently-running task. • When an attempt is made to execute an x87 FP instruction or an MMX instruction while CR0[TS] = 1, a DNA (Device Not Available) Exception 7 is generated. • The DNA exception handler executes FSAVE or FXSAVE to save the x87 and, possibly, the SSE registers in the TSS of the task that last used the x87. This information is saved in an OS-designated area of the previous task's TSS. • The DNA exception handler then clears CR0[TS] and executes an IRET instruction to return to the x87 instruction in the current task that caused the DNA exception. It now executes successfully.
4	ET	**x87 FPU type**. In processors prior to the 486DX, CR0[ET] (ET = Extension Type) was a read/write bit used by software to indicate the type of numeric coprocessor installed on the system board (287 or 387 FPU-compatible). Since the advent of the 486DX this bit is hardwired to one indicating that the logical processor incorporates a 387-style FPU.
5	NE	**Numeric Exception**. Controls whether FP errors are reported using the DOS-compatible method (IRQ13; see "DOS-Compatible FP Error Reporting" on page 359) or by generating an exception 16. The OS kernel sets NE = 1 if it incorporates an x87 FP exception handler. Any x87 FPU error then causes the logical processor to generate an internal exception 16 (rather than using the DOS-compatible method and asserting its external FERR# signal).

x87 FPU Register Set

The x87 FP register set is pictured in Figure 9-2 on page 343 and described in the sections that follow.

Figure 9-2: The x87 FPU Register Set

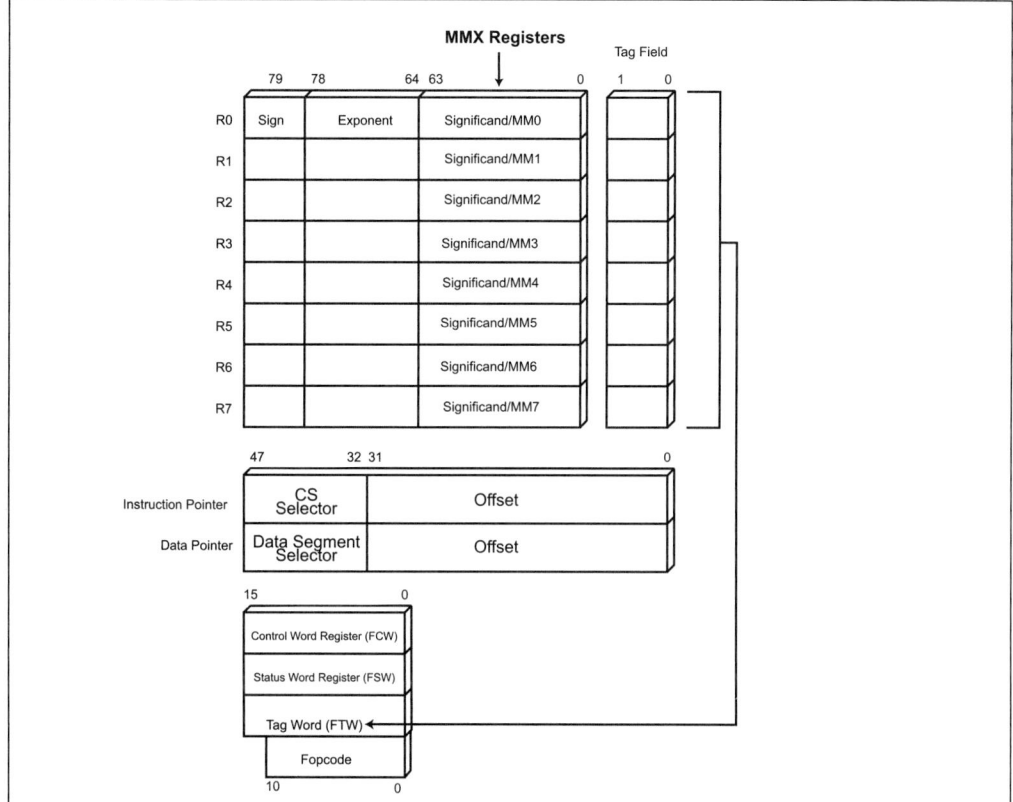

The FP Data Registers

Refer to Figure 9-2 on page 343. The FPU has eight, 80-bit data registers (R0 - R7) organized as a register stack. When executing x87 FP code, all addressing of the data registers is relative to the register currently pointed to by the 3-bit TOS (Top-of-Stack) field in the FSW (FP Status Word) register (see Figure 9-7 on page 354 and Table 9-6 on page 352):

- Load operations decrement the TOS field by one and then load (i.e., write) a value into the data register at the new TOS. This is the equivalent of a stack pop operation.
- Store operations store the value from the data register currently pointed to by the TOS field into memory and then increment the TOS field by one. This is the equivalent of a stack push operation.

Load and store operations are also available that do not push and pop the stack (i.e., they do not cause the TOS pointer to be incremented or decremented).

It should be noted that when executing MMX code (rather than x87 FP code), the lower 64-bits (the Significand field) of the eight FP data registers (R0 - R7) are used as the MMX data registers (MM0 - MM7). A complete description of MMX capability can be found in "The MMX Facilities" on page 835.

x87 FPU's Native Data Operand Format

All memory-based FP numeric operands that the x87 FPU deals with are stored in the 80-bit Double Extended Precision (DEP) format (see Figure 9-3 on page 345). Unless instructed otherwise, all x87 FP operations assume a number is represented in the x87's native DEP format.

A FP value represented in the 80-bit DEP FP format is represented as follows:

$$x.yyyyy * 2^{zth}$$

where:

- x = 0 or 1 (see bit 63 in Figure 9-3 on page 345).
- yyyyy = the decimal portion of the number (referred to as the significand or mantissa field).
- z = the exponent.
- Bit 79, the Sign bit, indicates whether the represented number is positive or negative.

When the x87 FPU is instructed to operate on an 80-bit DEP memory-based FP numeric value as a 64-bit DP (IEEE Double-Precision) FP number, it reads the 80-bit value from memory and converts it into the 64-bit DP format (see Figure 9-4 on page 345) before performing an operation on it. Likewise, when the FPU is instructed to treat an 80-bit DEP memory-based FP numeric value as a 32-bit SP (IEEE Single-Precision) FP number, it reads the 80-bit value from memory and converts it into the 32-bit SP format (see Figure 9-5 on page 345) before performing an operation on it. Conversely, when a FP number must be stored in memory, the FPU automatically converts it (if necessary) into the 80-bit DEP format before storing it to memory.

For a primer on the IEEE 32-bit SP FP numeric representation, see "A Brief IEEE FP Primer" on page 346.

Figure 9-3: The Double Extended Precision (DEP) FP Numeric Format

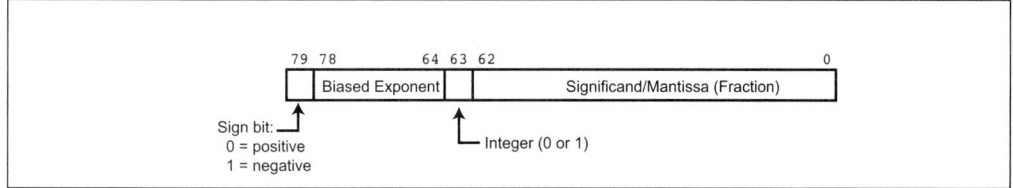

Figure 9-4: 64-bit DP FP Numeric Format

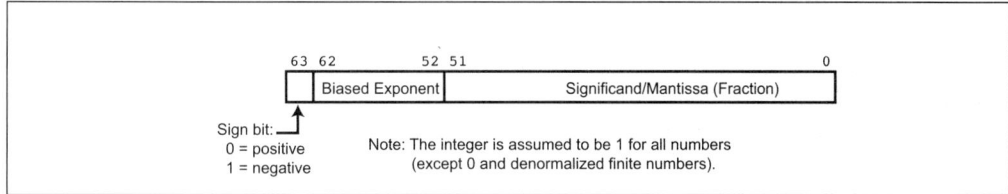

Figure 9-5: 32-bit SP FP Numeric Format

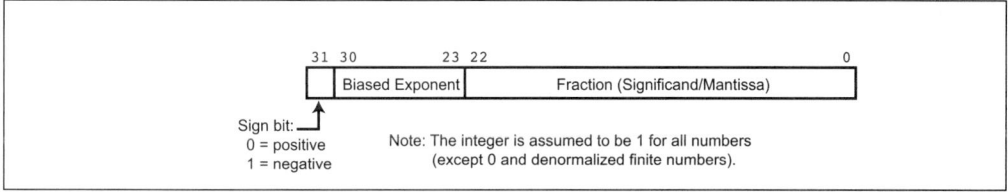

32-bit SP FP Numeric Format

Background

A new type of memory-based data operand introduced with the advent of SSE was the 32-bit SP FP numeric format which fully complies with the definition found in the IEEE Standard 754 for binary FP arithmetic. It should be noted that although this data type was new to the x86 SIMD (*S*ingle *I*nstruction operating on *M*ultiple *D*ata items) model, it was not new to the x86 processor. Rather, it was defined in the 1980s (by the IEEE 754 committee) and has been supported by the x87 FPU for many years. The x87 FPU, however, stores all FP numeric values in memory in the 80-bit (10-byte) DEP (Double-Extended Precision) format (see the previous section). On reading a value from memory, the x87 can perform computations on the value in its native DEP form or, prior to performing a computation, can internally convert it into the 32-bit SP or the 64-bit DP form (see "DP FP Number Representation" on page 350). When a numeric value is stored back to memory, however, the x87 FPU automatically converts it to the DEP form before storing it. The following is a brief tutorial on the 32-bit SP FP format.

A Brief IEEE FP Primer

The author would like to stress that this is not meant to be a comprehensive tutorial on the IEEE 754 FP specification. Rather, it is meant to familiarize the reader who is not conversant in the FP vernacular with the concepts and terms necessary to understand the basics.

A FP value in the IEEE FP format is represented as follows:

$$x.yyyyy * 2^{zth}$$

where the digit to the left of the decimal point (x) is implied and is assumed to be one for all numbers (positive or negative) except for:

- Zero and
- Numbers (irrespective of their sign, either positive or negative) that are less than 1 but greater than 0 (e.g., +0.1242, +0.98, -0.548, -0.13, etc.). These are referred to as *denormal* numbers (and are also referred to as *tiny* numbers).

In both of these cases, the implied digit is assumed to be 0.

The range of all possible real numbers that can be represented using this format are limited by the widths of the y field (referred to as the mantissa or significand field) and the z field (the exponent field). As shown in Figure 9-5 on page 345, the 32-bit format uses an 8-bit exponent field and a 23-bit mantissa field.

The IEEE specification defines the range of possible real numbers as falling into the following categories (ranging from most positive to most negative):

- $+ \infty$ (positive infinity).
- $+ 1.n$, where n is > 0 (referred to as positive normal numbers).
- $+ 0.n$, where n is > 0 (referred to as positive denormal, or tiny, numbers).
- $+ 0$.
- $- 0$.
- $- 0.n$, where n is > 0 (referred to as negative denormal, or tiny, numbers).
- $- 1.n$, where n is > 0 (referred to as negative normal numbers).
- $- \infty$ (negative infinity).

The specification also expresses the concept of values that are not real numbers (referred to as *NaNs* for *Not a Number*). They are categorized as follows:

- **SNaN (Signaling NaN).** A SNaN is a NaN with the most significant fraction (significand) bit cleared to zero. SNaNs generally signal a FP Invalid Operation exception whenever they appear as operands in arithmetic operations. SNaNs are typically used to cause a FP exception. The logical processor never generates an SNaN as a result of a FP operation. Rather, software would insert a SNaN operand to cause a FP exception.
- **QNaN (Quiet NaN).** A QNaN is a NaN with the most significant fraction bit set to one. The logical processor's FP execution units allow QNaNs to propagate through most arithmetic operations without causing a FP exception.

The 32-bit SP FP Format

As illustrated in Figure 9-5 on page 345, a 32-bit FP number is represented as follows:

- Bit 31 is the sign bit and indicates whether the value represented is a positive (0) or a negative (1) value.
- Bits [30:23] is the exponent field.
- Bits [22:0] is the mantissa field and represents the fractional part of the number that is to be multiplied by $2^{exponent}$.
- The digit to the left of the decimal point is implied and is assumed to be 1 (as mentioned earlier).

Representing Special Values

Table 9-2 on page 348 defines how special values are represented.

Table 9-2: Representation of Special Values

Special Value	Sign	Exponent	Mantissa/Significand
+ 0	0	0	0
- 0	1	0	0
+ ∞	0	all ones	0
- ∞	1	all ones	0
+QNaN	0	all ones	msb set to 1b and remaining bits represent the fractional part of the value.
-QNaN	1	all ones	
+SNaN	0	all ones	msb cleared to 0b and remaining bits represent the fractional part of the value.
-SNaN	1	all ones	
+denormal value	0	all ones	
-denormal value	1	all ones	

An Example

The following example presents the steps necessary to convert the base 10 number +100.25 into a 32-bit SP FP number.

1. Converting the whole number (100_{10}) to binary yields 1100100_2.
2. Converting the fractional part ($.25_{10}$) to binary yields $.01_2$. The first bit position to the right of the decimal place represents the value $.5_{10}$ (1 divided by 2), the 2nd bit the value $.25_{10}$ (1 divided by 4), the third the value $.125_{10}$ (1 divided by .8), etc.
3. Convert the full binary representation of the number to the normalized form (i.e., as in scientific notation):

    $+1100100.01_2 = +1.10010001_2 * 2^{6(\text{base }10)}$
4. Convert the exponent. When using the 32-bit SP FP format, the exponent is generated by adding a bias value of 127_{10} to the base 10 exponent generated in the previous step (6_{10}). In this case, $127_{10} + 6_{10} = 133_{10}$. That number is then converted to binary: $133_{10} = 10000101_2$.

5. Finally, assemble the components using the 32-bit SP FP template (see Table 9-3 on page 349). *If necessary, pad the exponent with zeros on the left so as to make it a full 8 bits in width. In addition, if necessary, pad the mantissa with zeros on the right to make it a full 23 bits in width.*

Table 9-3: The First Example

31	30	29	28	27	26	25	24	23	22	21	20	19	18	17	16	15	14	13	12	11	10	9	8	7	6	5	4	3	2	1	0
S	Exponent							Mantissa/Significand																							
0	1	0	0	0	0	1	1	1	1	0	0	1	0	0	0	1	0	0	0	0	0	0	0	0	0	0	0	0	0	0	0
	Exponent did not require 0-padding on the left.							Actual mantissa.								Mantissa 0-padded on the right to a full 23 bits.															

Another Example

The following example presents the steps necessary to convert the base 10 number +178.125 into a 32-bit SP FP number.

1. Converting the whole number (178_{10}) to binary yields 10110010_2.
2. Converting the fractional part ($.125_{10}$) to binary yields $.001_2$. The first bit position to the right of the decimal place represents the value $.5_{10}$ (1 divided by 2), the 2nd bit the value $.25_{10}$ (1 divided by 4), the third the value $.125_{10}$ (1 divided by .8), etc.
3. Convert the full binary representation of the number to the normalized form (i.e., as in scientific notation):
    $+10110010.001_2 = +1.0110010001_2 * 2^{7(\text{base }10)}$
4. Convert the exponent. When using the 32-bit SP FP format, the exponent is generated by adding a bias value of 127_{10} to the base 10 exponent generated in the previous step (7_{10}). In this case, $127_{10} + 7_{10} = 134_{10}$. That number is then converted to binary: $134_{10} = 10000110_2$.
5. Finally, assemble the components using the 32-bit SP FP template (see Table 9-4 on page 350). *If necessary, pad the exponent with zeros on the left so as to make it a full 8 bits in width. In addition, if necessary, pad the mantissa with zeros on the right to make it a full 23 bits in width.*

Table 9-4: The Second Example

| 3 | 3 | 2 | 2 | 2 | 2 | 2 | 2 | 2 | 2 | 2 | 1 | 1 | 1 | 1 | 1 | 1 | 1 | 1 | 1 | 1 | 0 | 0 | 0 | 0 | 0 | 0 | 0 | 0 | 0 | 0 |
1	0	9	8	7	6	5	4	3	2	1	0	9	8	7	6	5	4	3	2	1	0	9	8	7	6	5	4	3	2	1	0
S	Exponent								Mantissa/Significand																						
0	1	0	0	0	0	1	1	0	0	1	1	0	0	1	0	0	0	1	0	0	0	0	0	0	0	0	0	0	0	0	0
	Exponent did not require 0-padding on the left.								Actual mantissa.									Mantissa 0-padded on the right to a full 23 bits.														

DP FP Number Representation

Refer to Figure 9-4 on page 345. A primer on the representation of 32-bit SP FP numbers was covered in the previous section. In the DP FP format, like the 32-bit SP FP format, the digit to the left of the decimal point is assumed to be one. With wider significand (also referred to as the mantissa) and biased-exponent fields, a wider range of values can be represented (2.23×10^{-308} to 1.79×10^{308}, versus 1.18×10^{-38} to 3.40×10^{38} for SP FP numbers).

FCW Register

The FPU's Control Word register consists of the fields described in Table 9-5 on page 350 and illustrated in Figure 9-6 on page 352.

Table 9-5: FCW Register Fields

Field	Width (in bits)	Description
IM	1	When set to one (i.e., when it is masked), the FPU cannot generate a FP exception due to an **Invalid Operation**.
DM	1	When set to one, the FPU cannot generate a FP exception due to a **Denormal** Operand (i.e., when a tiny number is specified as an operand; see "A Brief IEEE FP Primer" on page 346).

Table 9-5: FCW Register Fields (Continued)

Field	Width (in bits)	Description
ZM	1	When set to one, the FPU cannot generate a FP exception due to a **Divide-by-Zero** attempt.
OM	1	When set to one, the FPU cannot generate a FP exception due to an **Overflow** error.
UM	1	When set to one, the FPU cannot generate a FP exception due to an **Underflow** error.
PM	1	When set to one, the FPU cannot generate a FP exception due to a **Precision** error.
PC	2	**Precision Control**. This 2-bit field controls the precision of the results produced by the FPU: • 00b = SP (Single-Precision). See "32-bit SP FP Numeric Format" on page 346. • 01b = Reserved. • 10b = DP (Double-Precision). See "DP FP Number Representation" on page 350. • 11b = DEP (Double Extended Precision). See "x87 FPU's Native Data Operand Format" on page 344.
RC	2	**Rounding Control**. This 2-bit field controls the rounding algorithm used by the FPU: • 00b = Round to **nearest (even)**. Rounded result is the closest to the infinitely precise result. If two values are equally close, the result is the even value (that is, the one with the lsb = 0). This is the default rounding mode. • 01b = **Round down** (toward $-\infty$). Rounded result is closest to but no greater than the infinitely precise result. • 10b = **Round up** (toward $+\infty$). Rounded result is closest to but no less than the infinitely precise result. • 11b = **Round toward zero** (Truncate). Rounded result is closest to but no greater in absolute value than the infinitely precise result.
IC	1	Infinity Control. Was used in the 287 and is now reserved.

Figure 9-6: The FPU's FCW Register

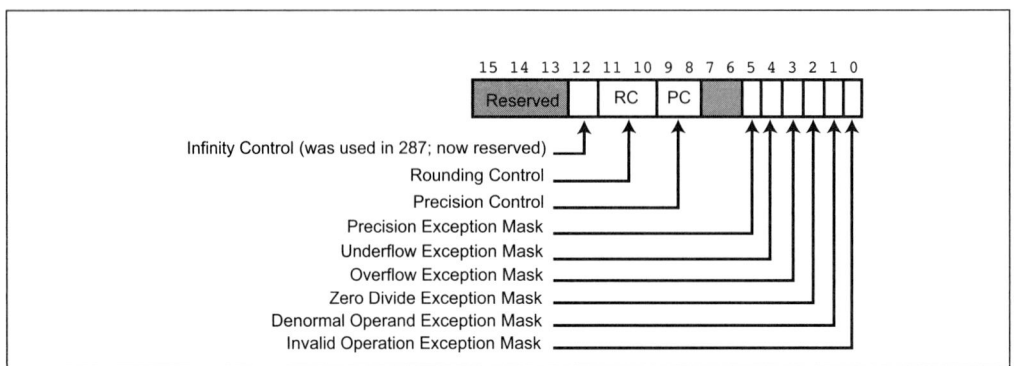

FSW Register

The FPU's Status Word register consists of the fields described in Table 9-6 on page 352 and illustrated in Figure 9-7 on page 354.

Table 9-6: FSW Register Fields

Field	Width (in bits)	Description
IE	1	Set to one when the FPU generates a FP exception due to an **Invalid Operation**.
DE	1	Set to one when the FPU generates a FP exception due to a **Denormal Operand** (see "A Brief IEEE FP Primer" on page 346).
ZE	1	Set to one when the FPU generates a FP exception due to a **Divide-by-Zero** attempt.
OE	1	Set to one when the FPU generates a FP exception due to an **Overflow error**.
UE	1	Set to one when the FPU generates a FP exception due to an **Underflow error**.

Table 9-6: FSW Register Fields (Continued)

Field	Width (in bits)	Description
PE	1	Set to one when the FPU generates a FP exception due to a **Precision error**.
SF	1	**Stack exception**. When set to one, indicates that a stack overflow or underflow has occurred with data in the x87 FPU data register stack. Condition code bit C1 (in FSW[CC] field) indicates the nature of the fault: • C1 = 1: Overflow. • C1 = 0: Underflow. SF is a "sticky" bit. After it is set to one, the logical processor does not clear it until explicitly instructed to do so (e.g., by executing an FINIT, FNINIT, FCLEX, FNCLEX, FSAVE, or FNSAVE instruction). *Intel documentation states "The FPU does not explicitly clear the flag when it detects an invalid-arithmetic operand condition." This statement doesn't make any sense to the author (perhaps this is a function of my advanced age or lack of intelligence).*
ES	1	**Error Summary Status**. ES is set when any of the exception status bits are set and a FPU exception is generated. If a specific exception type is currently masked (i.e., that error's mask bit is set to one in the FCW register), the FPU will still set the respective error bit in the FSW, but it will not set the ES bit, nor will it generate a FP exception.

Table 9-6: FSW Register Fields (Continued)

Field	Width (in bits)	Description
CC	3	**Condition Code bit field**. Indicates the results of FP comparison and arithmetic operations. It is used for conditional branching and for storage of information used in exception handling. **C1 is used for a variety of functions**: • When both IE and SF are set (indicating a stack overflow or underflow), the C1 flag distinguishes between overflow (C1 = 1) and underflow (C1 = 0). • When PE is set (indicating an inexact, rounded result), C1 is set to one if the last rounding by the instruction was upward. • The FXAM instruction sets C1 to the sign of the value being examined. **C2** is used by the FPREM and FPREM1 instructions to indicate an incomplete reduction (or partial remainder). When a successful reduction has been completed, C0, C3, and C1 are set to the three lsbs of the quotient (Q2, Q1, and Q0, respectively). The FPTAN, FSIN, FCOS, and FSINCOS instructions set C2 to 1 to indicate that the source operand is beyond the allowable range of $\pm 2^{63}$ and clears C2 if the source operand is within the allowable range.
TOP	3	**Top of Stack**. Points to the FP data register that is currently at the top of the stack.
B	1	**FPU Busy**. No longer used.

Figure 9-7: The FPU's FSW Register

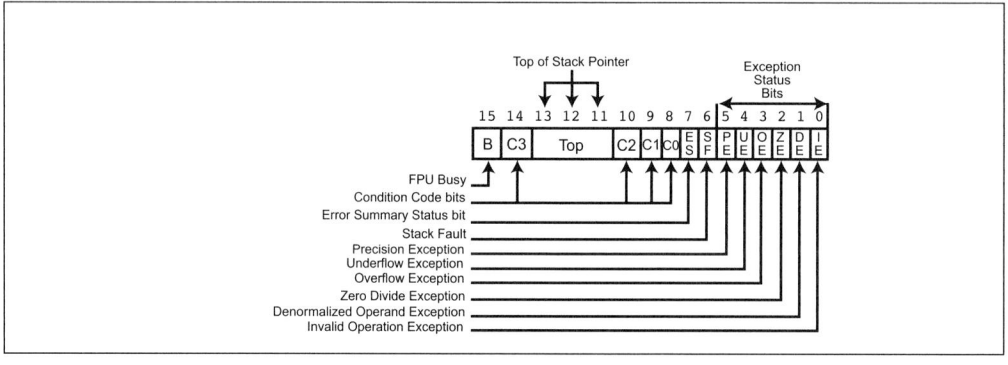

FTW Register

Refer to Figure 9-8 on page 355. The 16-bit Tag Word register is divided into eight 2-bit fields. Each of the eight fields corresponds to one of the FP data registers and indicates the current contents of the respective data register.

Figure 9-8: The FPU's FTW Register

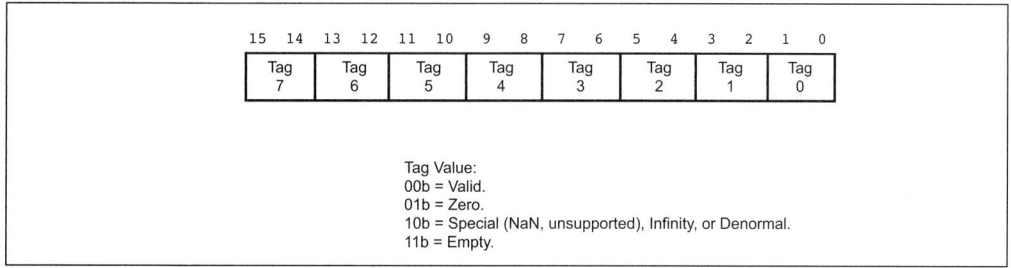

Instruction Pointer Register

The Instruction Pointer register is a 48-bit register consisting of a 16-bit portion (to hold the CS value) and a 32-bit portion (to hold the EIP value; when in Real Mode, only the lower 16-bits are used to hold the IP value). When a FP exception occurs, the FPU stores the pointer (in this register) to the last non-control (i.e., FP calculation) instruction that was executed. The FP exception handler can use this pointer to fetch the opcode of the instruction that caused the exception.

Data Pointer Register

The Data Pointer register is a 48-bit register consisting of a 16-bit portion (to hold the data segment value) and a 32-bit portion (to hold the offset value; in Real Mode, the 16-bit offset is stored in the lower 16-bits). When a FP exception occurs, if a memory-based data operand is associated with the instruction that caused the exception, the FPU stores the pointer to the data operand in this register. The FP exception handler can use this pointer to fetch the data operand so it can be examined.

Fopcode Register

General

The only new x87 FPU register added to x86 register set (added in the Pentium 4 processor) was the 11-bit OpCode register (also referred to as the Fopcode register; see Figure 9-9 on page 357). When an x87 FPU exception occurs, the opcode of the last computational (i.e., non-control) instruction executed is recorded in this register.

Only the opcode bytes (no prefixes) are stored in the x87 FP Opcode register. The upper five bits of the first opcode byte are the same for all x87 FP opcodes (11011b), so only the lower three bits of this byte plus all eight bits of the second opcode byte are stored in the Opcode register.

Fopcode Compatibility Mode

Bit 2 in the IA32_MISC_ENABLE MSR enables (1) or disables (0) Fopcode Compatibility Mode:

- **When enabled**, the Fopcode register contains the opcode of the last non-transparent FP instruction executed before the execution of the FSAVE, FSTENV, or FXSAVE instruction.
- **When disabled (the default)**, the contents of the Fopcode register is only valid if the last non-transparent FP instruction executed before the execution of the FSAVE, FSTENV, or FXSAVE instruction caused an unmasked exception.

Fopcode Compatibility Mode must be enabled only when the x87 FPU exception handlers are designed to use the fopcode to analyze program performance or to restart a program after an exception has been handled.

Figure 9-9: The x87 FPU's Opcode Register

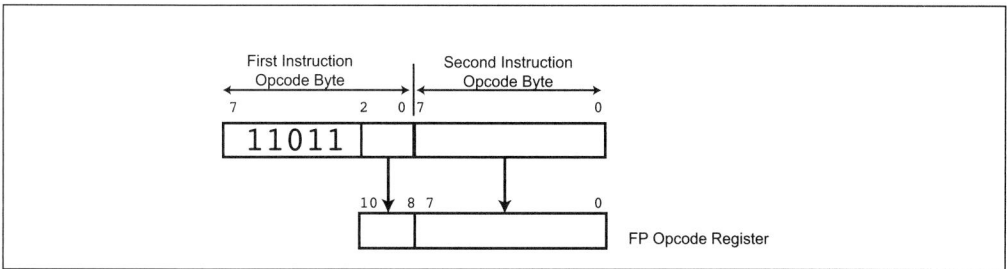

FP Error Reporting

Precise Error Reporting

A precise error is one that is reported (via an exception or interrupt) immediately upon the attempted execution of the offending instruction. A precise (i.e., immediate) error is reported when some x87 FPU instructions experience specific types of errors. In those cases, the FERR# output signal is asserted immediately (note: if CR0[NE] = 1, exception 16 is generated and FERR# is not asserted). Immediate error reporting is used for the x87 FPU Stack Fault, Invalid Operation and Denormal exceptions caused by all transcendental instructions, FSCALE, FXTRACT, FPREM, and all errors (with the exception of precision-related errors) caused by x87 FPU store instructions. After generating an immediate error, the x87 FPU freezes just before executing the next WAIT or x87 FPU instruction if the error condition has not yet been cleared.

Imprecise (Deferred) Error Reporting

In most error cases (other than those cited in the previous section), the x87 FPU uses imprecise error reporting. When the execution of a computational FP instruction results in the detection of an unmasked error, the x87 FPU sets the appropriate error bit in the FSW and also sets the FSW[ES] bit. An exception or interrupt is not generated immediately, however. Rather, the generation of the exception or interrupt is deferred until one of the following occurs:

- The execution of the next WAIT/FWAIT instruction.
- The detection of another computational FP instruction.

Before executing the instruction, the x87 FPU first tests the state of the FSW[ES] bit and generates an exception or interrupt if FSW[ES] = 1. In other words, an exception or interrupt is generated if the execution of the previous computational FP instruction caused an unmasked error to be generated and the FSW[ES] bit to be set to one.

Why Deferred Error Reporting Is Used

Back in the bad old days, the x87 FPU was implemented as a separate IO device. The processor would fetch an instruction from memory and decode it. If it was a FP instruction, the processor performed a series of one or more IO writes to send the instruction to the external FPU for execution. The FPU would then assert its BUSY output to the processor (because it could only handle one instruction at a time). Rather than stall non-FP program execution until the FPU completed the execution of the FP instruction, the processor would continue to fetch and execute non-FP instructions. If the execution of the FP instruction resulted in an error, the FPU set the appropriate error bit in its FSW register and also set FSW[ES] bit = 1. The error would not be reported however, until the processor encountered another computational FP instruction or the WAIT/ FWAIT instruction. At that time, the FPU checked the state of FSW[ES] and asserted its FERR# output if ES = 1.

The WAIT/FWAIT Instruction

The WAIT/FWAIT instruction (both names refer to the same opcode) is used to synchronize instruction execution between the x87 FPU and the logical processor's integer execution units. When executed, it causes the x87 FPU to check the FSW for pending unmasked x87 FPU exceptions (the ES bit is checked). If FSW[ES] = 1, an x87 FPU exception or interrupt is generated and all pending errors are handled before the logical processor resumes execution of the interrupted program.

CR0[NE]

The 486DX added the CR0[NE] (Numeric Exception) bit (see Figure 9-1 on page 341). It controls whether FP errors are reported using the DOS-compatible method (IRQ13; see the next section) or by generating an exception 16.

DOS-Compatible FP Error Reporting

When CR0[NE] = 0, FP errors are reported using the DOS-compatible method (via IRQ13). Figure 9-10 on page 359 illustrates the FP error reporting mechanism utilized in the IBM PC-AT. Starting with the 486DX, clearing this bit to 0 (when the system is running DOS) has the following effect: the next time the logical processor incurs a FP exception, it reports an internal FP exception by asserting the processor's FERR# output. On the system board, FERR# is routed to the legacy interrupt controller's IRQ13 input and the DOS OS's IRQ13 interrupt handler served as the FP error handler. The handler services the exception condition and then performs an IO write of 00h to IO port 00F0h, causing this system board IO port to assert the IGNNE# signal to the processor. When asserted, IGNNE# (Ignore Numeric Error) forces the logical processor to ignore a FP error and continue to execute non-control (i.e., computational) FP instructions. If the previously executed non-control FP instruction incurred an error and IGNNE# was deasserted, the processor asserts FERR# when it attempts the execution of the next non-control FP instruction. IGNNE# has no effect when CR0[NE] = 1.

FP Error Reporting Via Exception 16

When CR0[NE] = 1, the logical processor generates an internal exception 16 when an x87 FP error is detected. Much cleaner, indeed.

Figure 9-10: IBM PC-AT FP Error Reporting Mechanism

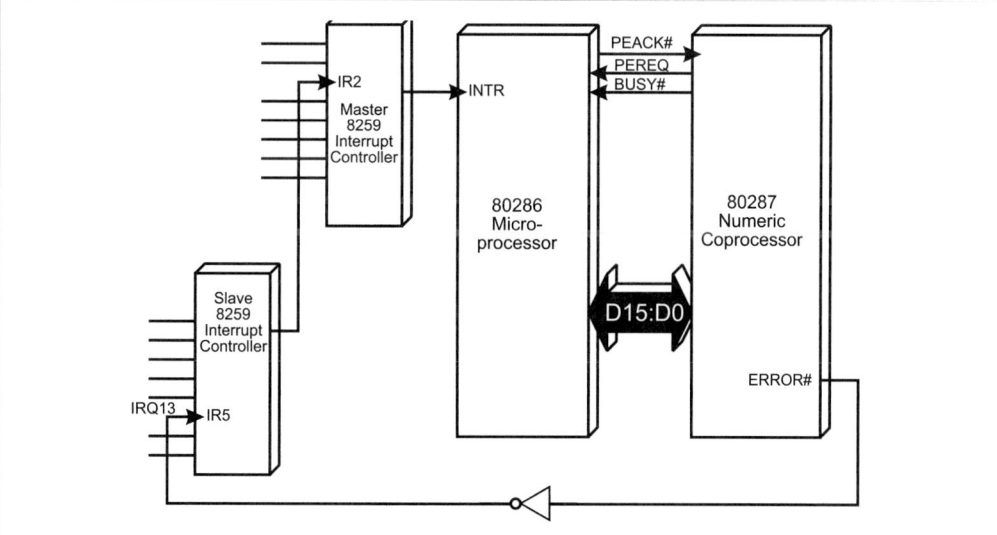

Ignoring FP Errors

Refer to Figure 9-11 on page 360. When an x87 FP error is detected and reported, the logical processor asserts its FERR# output (if CR0[NE] = 0; if CR0[NE] = 1, it generates exception 16 instead) and invokes the error handler. Until the error is handled, the x87 FPU remains busy with its error output asserted. While it remains in this state, the FPU cannot successfully execute any additional computational FP instructions. However, the programmer may wish to execute one or more computational instructions within the error handler in order to diagnose the nature of the original error and, possibly, to recover from it.

To do so, the programmer may cause the system logic to assert IGNNE# to the processor by writing a byte of all zeros to IO port 00F0h. The assertion of IGNNE# (Ignore Numeric Exception) is intended for use only inside the x87 FPU exception handler. The assertion of IGNNE# causes the x87 FPU to deassert its BUSY and FERR outputs thereby permitting the x87 FPU to execute non-control (i.e., computational) x87 FPU instructions within the handler. If IGNNE# is asserted while the exception handler is executing and a preceding x87 FPU exception had caused FERR# to be asserted, IGNNE# assertion prevents the x87 FPU from freezing at x87 FPU instructions. If IGNNE# remains asserted outside of the x87 FPU exception handler, additional x87 FPU instructions may be executed after a given instruction has caused an x87 FPU exception. In this case, if the x87 FPU exception handler ever did get invoked, it could not determine which instruction caused the exception.

Figure 9-11: Ignoring FP Errors

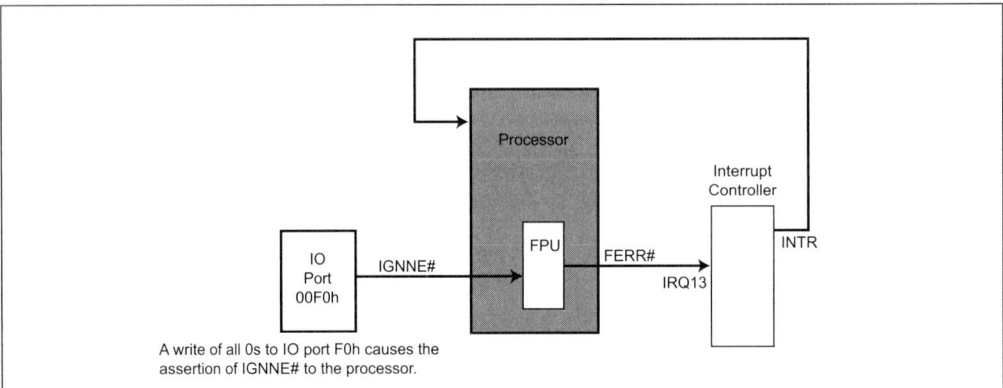

A write of all 0s to IO port F0h causes the
assertion of IGNNE# to the processor.

10 *Introduction to Multitasking*

The Previous Chapter

The previous chapter provided a detailed description of the x87 FPU and covered the following topics:

- A Little History.
- x87 FP Instruction Format.
- FPU-Related CR0 Bit Fields.
- x87 FPU Register Set.
  — The FP Data Registers.
  — x87 FPU's Native Data Operand Format.
  — 32-bit SP FP Numeric Format.
  — DP FP Number Representation.
  — FCW Register.
  — FSW Register.
  — FTW Register.
  — Instruction Pointer Register.
  — Data Pointer Register.
  — Fopcode Register.
- FP Error Reporting.
  — Precise Error Reporting.
  — Imprecise (Deferred) Error Reporting.
  — Why Deferred Error Reporting Is Used.
  — The WAIT/FWAIT Instruction.
  — CR0[NE].
  — Ignoring FP Errors.

This Chapter

This chapter provides an introduction to the concept of multitasking and covers the following topics:

- Concept.
- An Example—Timeslicing.
- Another Example—Awaiting an Event.
  - 1. Task Issues Call to OS for Disk Read.
  - 2. Device Driver Initiates Disk Read.
  - 3. OS Suspends Task.
  - 4. OS Makes Entry in Event Queue.
  - 5. OS Starts or Resumes Another Task.
  - 6. Disk-Generated Interrupt Causes Jump to OS.
  - 7. Interrupted Task Suspended.
  - 8. Task Queue Checked.
  - 9. OS Resumes Task.

The Next Chapter

The next chapter introduces the concepts of hardware-based task switching, global and local memory, privilege checking, read/write protection, IO port protection, interrupt masking, and BIOS call interception. The following topics are covered:

- Hardware-based Task Switching Is Slow!
- Private (Local) and Global Memory.
- Preventing Unauthorized Use of OS Code.
- With Privilege Comes Access.
  - Program Privilege Level.
    - The CPL.
    - Calling One of Your Equals.
    - Calling a Procedure to Act as Your Surrogate.
  - Data Segment Protection.
    - Data Segment Privilege Level.
    - Read-Only Data Areas.
- Some Code Segments Contain Data, Others Don't.
- IO Port Anarchy.
- No Interrupts, Please!
- BIOS Calls.

Concept

A multitasking OS does not run multiple programs (i.e., tasks) simultaneously. In reality, it loads a task into memory, permits it to run for a while and then suspends it. The program is suspended by creating a snapshot, or image, containing the contents of all or many of the logical processor's registers in memory (frequently referred to as the processor context). If the OS *were* using the hardware-based task switching mechanism included in the IA-32 architecture, (most modern OSs do not) the logical processor would automatically store the image in a special data structure in memory referred to as a Task State Segment (TSS) by performing an automated series of memory writes. In other words, the state of the logical processor at the point of suspension would be saved in memory. In reality, most modern OSs save the register contents (under software control) in an OS-specific data structure (rather than the TSS) which the author will refer to as the Task Data Structure. Some of the TSS's functionality is, in fact, used, however (this will be covered later).

Having effectively saved a snapshot that indicates the point of suspension and the logical processor's state at that time, the logical processor could then initiate another task by loading it into memory and jumping to its entry point, or it could resume a previously-suspended task by reloading its register set from that task's Task Data Structure. Based on OS-specific criteria, the OS could at some point decide to suspend this task as well. As before, the state of the logical processor would be saved in memory (in the Task Data Structure) as a snapshot of the task's state at its point of suspension.

When the OS decides to resume a previously-suspended task, the logical processor's registers would be restored from the Task Data Structure under software control by performing a series of memory reads. The logical processor would then use the address pointer stored in the CS:EIP register pair to fetch the next instruction, thereby resuming program execution at the point where it had been suspended earlier.

The circumstances under which an OS decides to suspend a task is specific to the OS. It may simply use *timeslicing* wherein each task is permitted to execute for a fixed amount of time (e.g., 10ms). At the end of that period of time, the currently executing task is suspended and the next task in the queue is started or resumed. The OS might be designed to suspend the currently executing program when it requests something that is not immediately available (e.g., when it attempts an access to a page of information that resides on a mass storage device and is currently not in memory). It starts or resumes another task and, when the event previously requested by the now-suspended task occurs, typically signaled by an interrupt, the current task is interrupted and suspended and the previously suspended task resumed. This is commonly referred to as *preemptive multitasking*.

An Example—Timeslicing

Prior to starting or resuming execution of a task:

1. The OS *task scheduler* would initialize a hardware timer (typically, the timer incorporated within the Local APIC associated with the logical processor) to interrupt program execution after a defined period of time (e.g., 10ms).
2. The scheduler then causes the logical processor to initiate or resume execution of the task.
3. The logical processor proceeds to fetch and execute the instructions comprising the task for 10ms.
4. When the hardware timer expires it generates an interrupt, causing the logical processor to suspend execution of the currently executing task and to switch back to the OS's task scheduler.
5. The scheduler then determines which task to initiate or resume next.

Another Example—Awaiting an Event

1. Task Issues Call to OS for Disk Read

The application program calls the OS requesting that a block of data be read from a disk drive into memory. The OS then forwards the request to the disk driver, and, having done so, suspends the task and either starts or resumes another one.

Rather than awaiting the completion of the disk read, the OS scheduler would better utilize the machine's resources by suspending the task that originated the request and transferring control to another program so work can be accomplished while the disk operation is in progress.

2. Device Driver Initiates Disk Read

The driver issues a call to malloc (the OS's memory allocation manager) requesting the allocation of a memory buffer to hold the requested data. After receiving the buffer start address, the driver issues a disk read command to the disk controller, supplying it with:

- The buffer start address.
- The disk start address.
- The amount of data to be read.

In response, the disk controller begins to seek the read/write head mechanism to the target cylinder. This is a lengthy mechanical process typically requiring milliseconds to complete. When the head mechanism has positioned the heads over the target cylinder, the disk interface must then wait for the surface to spin until the start sector of the requested block is present under the read head. The duration of this delay is defined by the rotational speed of the disk drive as well as the circumference of the cylinder. Once again, this is a lengthy delay that can be measured in milliseconds. Only then can the data transfer begin.

3. OS Suspends Task

As described earlier, the logical processor suspends the requesting task by saving its current state (i.e., its register image) in a special area of memory set aside for this purpose (e.g., the Task Data Structure). Once this series of memory writes is complete, the task has been suspended.

4. OS Makes Entry in Event Queue

The OS makes an entry in its event queue. This entry will be used to transfer control back to the suspended task when the disk interface signals the completion of the transfer by generating an interrupt.

5. OS Starts or Resumes Another Task

Rather than waiting for the completion of the disk read operation, the OS starts or resumes another task.

6. Disk-Generated Interrupt Causes Jump to OS

When the disk controller completes the transfer of the requested information into system memory, it generates an interrupt. This causes the logical processor to jump to the disk driver's interrupt handler which checks the completion status of the disk operation to ensure a good completion.

7. Interrupted Task Suspended

The OS suspends the interrupted task by making a snapshot of its register set in the Task Data Structure.

8. Task Queue Checked

The OS then scans the event queue to determine which previously-suspended task is awaiting this completion notification.

9. OS Resumes Task

The OS causes the logical processor to reload the task's stored register image (from its Task Data Structure) into the logical processor's registers. The logical processor then uses CS:EIP to determine what memory address to fetch its next instruction from. The resumed task then processes the data in memory that was read from the disk.

11 *Multitasking-Related Issues*

The Previous Chapter

The previous chapter provided an introduction to the concept of multitasking and covered the following topics:

- Concept.
- An Example—Timeslicing.
- Another Example—Awaiting an Event.
  - 1. Task Issues Call to OS for Disk Read.
  - 2. Device Driver Initiates Disk Read.
  - 3. OS Suspends Task.
  - 4. OS Makes Entry in Event Queue.
  - 5. OS Starts or Resumes Another Task.
  - 6. Disk-Generated Interrupt Causes Jump to OS.
  - 7. Interrupted Task Suspended.
  - 8. Task Queue Checked.
  - 9. OS Resumes Task.

This Chapter

This chapter introduces the concept of hardware-based task switching, global and local memory, privilege checking, read/write protection, IO port protection, interrupt masking, and BIOS call interception. The following topics are covered:

- Hardware-based Task Switching Is Slow!
- Private (Local) and Global Memory.
- Preventing Unauthorized Use of OS Code.

- With Privilege Comes Access.
  — Program Privilege Level.
    - The CPL.
    - Calling One of Your Equals.
    - Calling a Procedure to Act as Your Surrogate.
  — Data Segment Protection.
    - Data Segment Privilege Level.
    - Read-Only Data Areas.
- Some Code Segments Contain Data, Others Don't.
- IO Port Anarchy.
- No Interrupts, Please!
- BIOS Calls.

The Next Chapter

The next brief chapter summarizes various situations that can destabilize a multitasking OS environment and the x86 protection mechanisms that exist to address each of them.

Hardware-based Task Switching Is Slow!

The multitasking OS loads multiple tasks into different areas of memory and permits each to run for a slice of time. As described in the previous chapter, it permits a task to run for its assigned timeslice, suspends it, permits another task to run for a timeslice, suspends it, etc. If the OS is executing on a fast processor with fast access to memory, this task switching can be accomplished so quickly that all of the tasks *appear* to be executing simultaneously.

While the logical processor is executing a task, the OS kernel and all of the other dormant tasks are resident in memory. When each of the tasks (and the OS kernel's scheduler) were suspended earlier in time, the logical processor created a snapshot of its register image in memory at the moment of task suspension. In the IA-32 environment, the typical OS sets up a separate Task Data Structure for each task. If the OS designers had chosen to utilize the x86 processor's hardware-based task switching mechanism, the processor would automatically save its register set in and restore it from a task's TSS when suspending or resuming a task. *In fact, though, due to the inefficiency of this mechanism, no modern, mainstream OSs use the hardware-based task switch mechanism.* Rather, the OS task scheduler performs the register set save and restore in software using a task-specific data structure the author refers to as the Task Data Structure.

While x86 processors support the hardware-based mechanism in IA-32 Mode to ensure that any software that does use it will function correctly, *the hardware mechanism is not supported in IA-32e Mode.*

Private (Local) and Global Memory

The currently executing application is typically only aware of two entities—itself and the OS that manages it—and is unaware of the existence of any other tasks that, although partially or fully present in memory, are currently suspended. The currently executing application should only be permitted to access its own, private memory and, perhaps, one or more areas of memory that the OS has designated as globally-accessible by multiple applications to permit data and/or code sharing. If it were permitted to perform memory writes anywhere in memory, it is entirely probable that it will corrupt the code, stack or data areas of programs that are in memory but currently suspended. Consider what would happen when the OS resumes execution of a task that had been corrupted while in suspension. Its program and/or data would have been corrupted, causing it to behave unpredictably when it resumes execution. The OS must protect suspended tasks (including itself!) from the currently executing task. If it doesn't, multitasking will not work reliably.

When an application is loaded into memory, the OS memory manager designates certain areas of memory for its use:

- Some areas of memory are designated as private (i.e., local) to the application. These segments could be defined by entries (segment descriptors) in the application's Local Descriptor Table (LDT; see Figure 11-1 on page 373).
- The OS may also designate one or more areas of memory that are globally accessible by multiple applications (thereby permitting the sharing of data or code). These segments could be defined by entries in the Global Descriptor Table (GDT; Figure 11-1 on page 373).

In addition to defining the accessibility of memory areas using the logical processor's segmentation mechanism, the OS memory manager can also accomplish this using the virtual-to-physical address translation mechanism (i.e., Paging).

Preventing Unauthorized Use of OS Code

The OS maintains the integrity of the system. It manages all shared resources and decides what task will run next and for how long. It should be fairly obvious that the person in charge must have more authority (i.e., greater privileges) than the other tasks. It would be ill-conceived to permit normal tasks to access certain logical processor control registers, OS-related tables in memory, etc.

This form of protection can be accomplished in two ways: assignment of privilege levels to programs and assignment of ownership to areas of memory. IA-32 processors utilize both methods. There are four privilege levels:

- **Level zero**. Greatest amount of privilege. Assigned to the heart, or kernel, of the OS. It handles the task queues, memory management, etc.
- **Level one**. Typically assigned to OS services that provide services to the application programs and device drivers.
- **Level two**. Typically assigned to device drivers that the OS uses to communicate with peripheral devices.
- **Level three**. Least-privileged. Assigned to application programs.

The application program operates at the lowest privilege level (3) because its actions must be restricted. The OS kernel has the highest privilege level (0) so that it can accomplish its job of managing every aspect of the system. The integrity of the system would be compromised if an application program could call highly-privileged parts of the OS code to accomplish things it shouldn't be able to do. This implies that the logical processor must have some way of comparing the privilege level of the calling program to that of the program being called. To gain entry into the called program, the calling program's privilege level (CPL, or Current Privilege Level) must equal or exceed the privilege level of the program it is calling. IA-32 processors incorporate this feature.

With Privilege Comes Access

Privilege level 0 code has access to all of the logical processor's facilities: it can execute any instruction, access any register, and access all memory data segments. Privilege level 3 code (i.e., application code), on the other hand, only has access to a subset of the instruction set and register set.

Program Privilege Level

The CPL

Refer to Figure 11-1 on page 373. When a far jump or far call is performed, the new value loaded into the 16-bit CS register selects a segment descriptor in either the GDT or the LDT. The 2-bit DPL (Descriptor Privilege Level) field in the selected code segment descriptor becomes the logical processor's CPL (Current Privilege Level).

There are multiple cases where the OS wishes to restrict access to the code that resides in a code segment and they are introduced in the sections that follow.

Calling One of Your Equals

A code segment's descriptor may define it as a *non-conforming code segment*. In that case, procedures within that code segment can only be called by programs with the same privilege level.

Calling a Procedure to Act as Your Surrogate

A code segment's descriptor may define it as a *conforming code segment*. In that case, when a procedure within that code segment is called by code in another code segment, the logical processor executes the called procedure at the caller's assigned privilege level rather than that assigned to the target code segment.

As an example, assume that there is a conforming code segment with a DPL of 0. If a procedure within the code segment is called by a program running at privilege level 3, the code in the called procedure would then execute at privilege level 3 (and would therefore be bound by the same restrictions as the caller: limited instruction set use, register set use, and limited access to data in memory). If called by a program running at privilege level 0, on the other hand, the code in the called procedure would then execute at privilege level 0 and would have full access to all of the logical processor's facilities (and data residing in memory).

Data Segment Protection

Data Segment Privilege Level

The segment descriptors that describe each data segment also contain the 2-bit DPL field (see Figure 11-1 on page 373). In order to successfully perform a load from or a store to a data segment, the privilege level of the currently-executing program (i.e., the CPL) must be at least equal to the privilege level assigned to the target data segment.

Read-Only Data Areas

Refer to Figure 11-1 on page 373. The OS can define a data segment as read-only using the W bit in the data segment descriptor:

- W = 0 designates a data segment as read-only.
- W = 1 designates it as read-writable.

Some Code Segments Contain Data, Others Don't

In a code segment descriptor (note: the segment descriptor shown in Figure 11-1 on page 373 is a data segment descriptor; a code segment descriptor is shown in Figure 14-2 on page 421), the bit designated as the W bit in a data segment descriptor is re-assigned as the R, or data Read, bit.

- R = 0. Only code fetches are permitted within the code segment.
- R = 1. In addition to code fetches, the currently-running program is also permitted to perform data reads (i.e., loads) in order to read data variables that reside within the code segment.

Figure 11-1: Segment Descriptor Selection

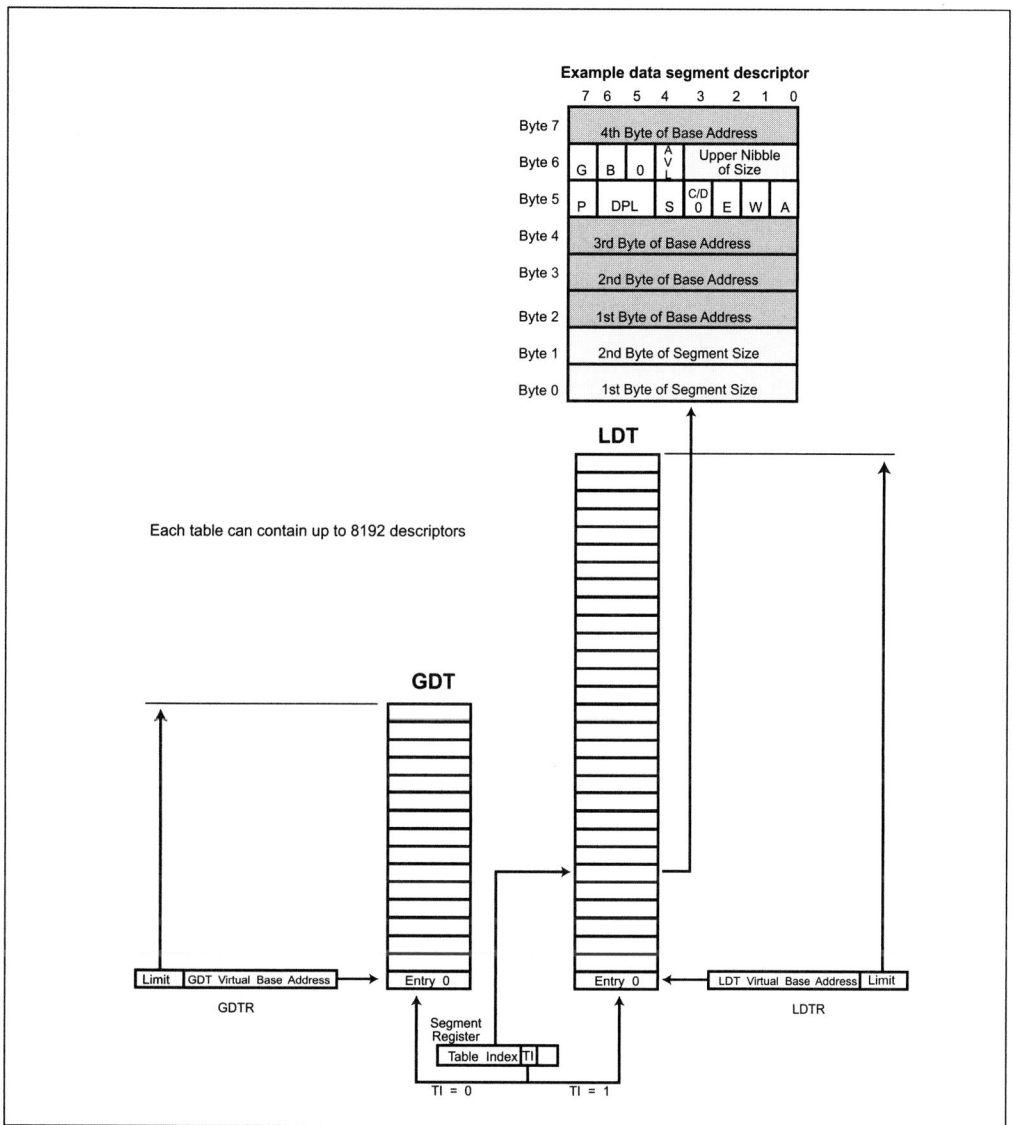

IO Port Anarchy

Assume that the currently-executing task needs to initiate a disk access.

1. To do this, it must program the disk controller's IO registers with the information defining the disk command type (e.g., disk read), the cylinder number, the head (or surface) number, the start sector number and the number of sectors to be transferred. This might be accomplished by executing a series of OUT instructions that cause the logical processor to perform a series of IO write transactions on its FSB to transfer the command and associated parameters to the disk controller.
2. Now assume that the task has programmed some, but not all of the disk controller's registers and the task's timeslice expires. The logical processor is interrupted, causing a switch back to the OS scheduler.
3. The scheduler suspends the current task and starts or resumes another task.
4. The new task, having no knowledge of the suspended task, may decide that it also wants to issue a command to the disk controller. Assume that it does so and that the operation completes without error.
5. Eventually, the OS suspends this task and reawakens the other task. This task doesn't know that it was put to sleep and resumes execution at the point of suspension.
6. It completes the series of IO writes to transfer the remainder of the request parameters to the disk controller. It has no idea that the initial parameters that it sent to the disk controller (before it was suspended) were overwritten by the other task while it was asleep.
7. The end result will be that the task's disk operation will not occur correctly.

Generally speaking, the system's IO devices should be treated as a pool of shared resources to be managed by a central entity (the OS). Having one entity perform all communications with IO devices ensures that there will be no contention for IO devices between multiple tasks.

To accomplish this, the OS typically does not permit tasks to talk directly to IO ports (at least, to critical ones). In other words, any attempt to execute an IN or OUT instruction (or INS or OUTS) would cause the logical processor to trap (i.e., jump) to the OS. The OS then communicates with the IO device for the task.

The OS and/or logical processor could be configured to permit a task to access certain IO ports directly, but restrict access to other ports.

No Interrupts, Please!

While it is executing, an application program written to run under a single-task OS considers itself master of all it surveys. It can communicate with any IO device, any memory location, disable interrupt recognition if it doesn't want to be interrupted, etc. In a single task environment, there is no reason why the only program running shouldn't be able to disable recognition of interrupts (by executing the CLI instruction) as long as it doesn't adversely affect its own operation.

If this same program is run under the management of a multitasking OS and no measures are taken to intercept its attempts to play with the Flags[IF] bit using the CLI and STI instructions, however, it can result in severe problems. If permitted to execute a CLI (Clear Interrupt Enable) instruction, the Flags[IF] bit is cleared to zero and, as result, the logical processor will no longer recognize interrupt requests originated by device adapters throughout the system. This means that these devices may not receive the servicing they require on a timely basis. As a result, they may, as an example, suffer from buffer overflow or underflow conditions. This can result in anything from poor performance of a subsystem to completely flawed operation (data may be lost due to insufficient temporary buffer space within the subsystem). It should be noted that a device adapter may generate an interrupt request to signal an event to a program that is currently suspended. The correct action may be for the logical processor to recognize the request, perform a task switch to the other program, service the request, and then return to the interrupted task.

To summarize, the logical processor and the OS should not permit an application (one written for a single-task OS environment) to execute the CLI (or, for that matter, the STI) instruction. An attempt to execute CLI or STI should cause the logical processor to trap out to the OS (due to an exception). The OS would then set a bit somewhere (in a table in memory or in a register) noting that this task prefers not to be interrupted. The Flags[IF] bit would not really be cleared, so the logical processor would still be able to recognize interrupt requests. The OS then resumes execution of the task at the next instruction. If an interrupt request is detected while this task is still executing, the logical processor is interrupted and jumps to a special routine to determine if this particular interrupt request is deemed important enough to interrupt the currently-executing program. If not, the OS marks this request (in a memory-based table or in a register) for subsequent servicing and resumes the interrupted task. The request is serviced *after* the current task has completed its timeslice and has been suspended.

If, on the other hand, the request is considered important enough to be serviced immediately, the OS permits the logical processor to execute the device adapter's interrupt handler (which services the device) and then resumes the interrupted task.

BIOS Calls

If an application program originally written to run under a single-task OS (e.g., DOS) needs to communicate with an IO device, it may do this in one of the following manners:

- It could communicate with the device's registers directly by executing an IN (IO read) or an OUT (IO write) instruction.
- It could communicate with the device's registers directly by executing a memory read or a memory write instruction (if the device's registers are mapped into memory rather than IO space).
- It could issue a request to the OS services.
- It could call the device's BIOS routine (which is nothing more than a firmware-based device driver). The BIOS routine, in turn, performs the necessary series of INs and OUTs to communicate the request to the IO device.

DOS programs call BIOS routines by executing software interrupt instructions. An example would be INT 13 to call the disk BIOS routine. In response, the logical processor indexes into entry 13h in the Interrupt Descriptor Table (IDT) in memory and jumps to the start address of the disk BIOS routine indicated in this entry.

In a multitasking OS environment, all or most accesses to IO devices should be routed through the OS. An attempt by an application program to call a BIOS routine (or DOS, for that matter) using the INT instruction should cause the logical processor to generate an exception. The OS can then use the IDT entry number specified by the INT instruction to determine what BIOS (or DOS) service the task is calling. The OS can then execute its own respective device driver to communicate the request to the target IO device.

12 *Summary of the Protection Mechanisms*

The Previous Chapter

The previous chapter introduced the concept of hardware-based task switching, global and local memory, privilege checking, read/write protection, IO port protection, interrupt masking, and BIOS call interception. The following topics were covered:

- Hardware-based Task Switching Is Slow!
- Private (Local) and Global Memory.
- Preventing Unauthorized Use of OS Code.
- With Privilege Comes Access.
  - Program Privilege Level.
    - The CPL.
    - Calling One of Your Equals.
    - Calling a Procedure to Act as Your Surrogate.
  - Data Segment Protection.
    - Data Segment Privilege Level.
    - Read-Only Data Areas.
- Some Code Segments Contain Data, Others Don't.
- IO Port Anarchy.
- No Interrupts, Please!
- BIOS Calls.

x86 Instruction Set Architecture

This Chapter

This chapter summarizes various situations that can destabilize a multitasking OS environment and the x86 protection mechanisms that exist to address each of them.

The Next Chapter

The next chapter introduces segment register usage in Protected Mode and the roles of segment descriptors, the GDT, the LDTs, the IDT, and the general segment descriptor format. It also introduces the concept of the flat memory model. The following topics are covered:

- Real Mode Segment Limitations.
- An Important Reminder: Segment Base + Offset = Virtual Address.
- Descriptor Contains Detailed Segment Description.
- Segment Register—Selects Descriptor Table and Entry.
- The Descriptor Tables.
- General Segment Descriptor Format.
- Goodbye to Segmentation.

Protection-Related Mechanisms

This chapter is not intended as a detailed discussion of the various protection mechanisms available in the x86 architecture. Rather, they've been collected here in one place for ease of reference and as an introduction to the various topics related to protection.

Some of the protection mechanisms were introduced in the previous chapter (privilege level assignment, local and global memory segments, data segment write protection, preventing data accesses to code segments, and guarding access to IO ports). All of the protection mechanisms are listed in Table 12-1 on page 379.

Table 12-1: Protection Mechanisms

Condition	Mechanism
Attempted access to a segment by a program with insufficient privilege	Some examples: • Currently-running program attempts to access a data segment with a higher privilege level (i.e., the data segment's descriptor[DPL] value is numerically less than the CPL of the program). • Currently-running program executes a far jump or a far call to a procedure in a code segment with a higher privilege level (e.g., a privilege level 3 program attempts to jump to or call a procedure in a privilege level 0 code segment). This would result in an exception.
Attempted write to a read-only data segment	The data segment descriptor's W bit = 0 indicating it is a read-only data segment. This would result in an exception.
Attempted data read from a code segment	The code segment descriptor's R bit = 0 indicating it's an execute-only code segment. This would result in an exception (if R = 1, then the code segment contains read-only data as well as code).
Out-of-range access to a segment	The offset address specified exceeds the segment size specified in the target segment's descriptor. This would result in an exception.
Attempted page access by an under-privileged program	A program with a privilege level of 3 attempted to access a page whose PTE[U/S] bit = 0. This would result in an exception. Note: U/S stands for User/Supervisor.

Table 12-1: Protection Mechanisms (Continued)

Condition	Mechanism
Attempted write to a read-only page	There are two possibilities: • A privilege level 3 program attempted to write to a page whose PTE[R/W] bit = 0 marking it as a read-only page. • A program with supervisor privileges (i.e., it has a privilege level of 0, 1 or 2) attempted to write to a user page (its PTE[U/S] bit = 1) with PTE[R/W] bit = 0 marking it as a read-only user page *and CR0[WP] = 1 (indicating supervisor programs are not permitted to write into read-only user pages).* This would result in an exception.
Access to an absent page	A virtual memory address selected a PTE with the Page Present bit (bit 0) = 0 indicating that the target physical page isn't currently in memory. This would result in an Page Fault exception.

Attempted direct access to an IO or memory-mapped IO port	• **Access to an IO port**:
	  – **By a Protected Mode task (other than a VM86 task)**. Any attempt by a program (other than a VM86 task) with a privilege level numerically greater than the Eflags[IOPL] threshold to execute the **IN, INS, OUT and OUTS** instructions will trigger a General Protection exception.
	  – **By a VM86 task**. When an IN, INS, OUT or OUTS instruction is executed, the logical processor uses the 16-bit IO port address to index into the IO Permission bit map in the task's TSS data structure. The state of the selected bit determines whether the IO instruction is executed or a General Protection exception is generated.
	• **Access to a memory-mapped IO port**. This form of protection can be provided by the virtual-to-physical address translation mechanism (i.e., Paging). The virtual addresses of memory-mapped IO ports could be grouped into a page and the virtual page address could select a PTE that indicates the page isn't present in memory. Any attempted access within the page would then result in a Page Fault exception.

Table 12-1: Protection Mechanisms (Continued)

Condition	Mechanism
Attempted execution of a software interrupt instruction	**Real Mode application**. There are two possible cases: • A Real Mode program running as a VM86 task under Protected Mode with CR4[VME] = 0 attempts to execute an INT instruction. This would result in an exception and the GP exception handler can then determine what action to take. • A Real Mode program running as a VM86 task under Protected Mode with CR4[VME] = 1 attempts to execute an INT instruction. The logical processor uses the interrupt vector to interrogate the Interrupt Redirection Bitmap in the task's TSS. The state of the selected bit instructs it to either call the respective Real Mode or Protected Mode interrupt handler. • **Protected Mode application**. A privilege level 3 application attempts to execute an INT instruction, but the Eflags[IOPL] threshold value is set to a value less than three. This would result in an exception and the GP exception handler can then determine what action to take.
Attempted execution of a sensitive instruction by a program with insufficient privilege	While a task is running, the value of the 2-bit Eflags[IOPL] field sets a threshold privilege level trigger to detect the attempted execution of a sensitive instruction: • **In Protected Mode**, any attempt by a program (other than a VM86 task) with a privilege level numerically greater than the IOPL threshold to execute the **IN, INS, OUT and OUTS** instructions will trigger a General Protection exception. • **In VM86 Mode**, any attempt by a program with a privilege level numerically greater than the IOPL threshold to execute the **CLI, STI, PUSHF, POPF, INT *n*, and IRET** instructions will trigger a General Protection exception.
Attempted access to the TSC (Time Stamp Counter MSR) by an application program	When CR4[PSD] = 1, any attempt by a program that is not a privilege level 0 program to execute the RDTSC (or RDTSCP) instruction results in an exception.

Table 12-1: Protection Mechanisms (Continued)

Condition	Mechanism
Attempted access to a Performance Counter by an application program	When CR4[PCE] = 0, any attempt by a program that is not a privilege level 0 program to execute the RDPMC instruction results in an exception.

13 *Protected Mode Memory Addressing*

The Previous Chapter

The previous chapter summarized various situations that can destabilize a multitasking OS environment and the x86 protection mechanisms that exist to address each of them.

This Chapter

This chapter introduces segment register usage in Protected Mode and the roles of segment descriptors, the GDT, the LDTs, the IDT, and the general segment descriptor format. It also introduces the concept of the flat memory model. The following topics are covered:

- Real Mode Segment Limitations.
- An Important Reminder: Segment Base + Offset = Virtual Address.
- Descriptor Contains Detailed Segment Description.
- Segment Register—Selects Descriptor Table and Entry.
- The Descriptor Tables.
- General Segment Descriptor Format.
- Goodbye to Segmentation.

The Next Chapter

The next chapter provides a detailed description of code segments (both Conforming and Non-Conforming), privilege checking, and Call Gates. The following topics are covered:

- Selecting the Active Code Segment.
- CS Descriptor.
- Accessing the Code Segment.
- Short/Near Jumps.
- Unconditional Far Jumps.
- Privilege Checking.
- Jumping from a Higher-to-Lesser Privileged Program.
- Direct Procedure Calls.
- Indirect Procedure Far Call Though a Call Gate.
- Automatic Stack Switch.
- Far Call From 32-bit CS to 16-bit CS.
- Far Call From 16-bit CS to 32-bit CS.
- Far Returns.

Real Mode Segment Limitations

Figure 13-1 on page 385 illustrates the contents of a segment register while operating in Real Mode; i.e., the upper 16 bits of the segment's 20-bit base address (aligned on a 16-byte address boundary) in the first megabyte of memory space. The logical processor automatically appends four bits of zero to the lower end to form the base address. As an example, if the programmer moves the value 1010h into the DS register

```
mov ax, 1010
mov ds, ax
```

this would set the start address of the data segment to 10100h.

As stated earlier in the book, when in Protected Mode the OS memory manager must be able to define a number of segment properties in addition to its base address (and this is not possible in a 16-bit register).

In Real Mode, a segment has the following characteristics:

- Its base address must be in the **first megabyte of memory space**. In order to have the maximum flexibility in memory allocation while operating in Protected Mode, the OS must be able to define a program's segments as residing anywhere within physical memory (above or below the 1MB address boundary).
- The **segment length is fixed at 64KB**. Unless they are incredibly small, programs and the data they manipulate virtually always occupy more than 64KB of memory space, but each segment has a fixed length of 64KB in Real

Mode. If the OS only requires a very small segment for a program's code, data or stack area, the only size available is still fixed at 64KB. This can waste memory space (albeit, not very much). If the code comprising a particular program is larger than 64KB, the programmer must set up and jump back and forth between multiple code segments. The data that a program acts upon may also occupy multiple data segments. This is a very inefficient memory organization model and one that forces the programmer to think in a very fragmented manner. It's one of the major things programmers dislike about Real Mode segmentation.

- The **segment can be read or written by any program**. In Real Mode, a segment can be accessed by any program. This is an invitation for one program to inadvertently trash another's code, data or stack area. In addition, any program can call procedures within any other program. There is no concept of restricting access to certain programs.

Figure 13-1: Segment Register Contents in Real Mode

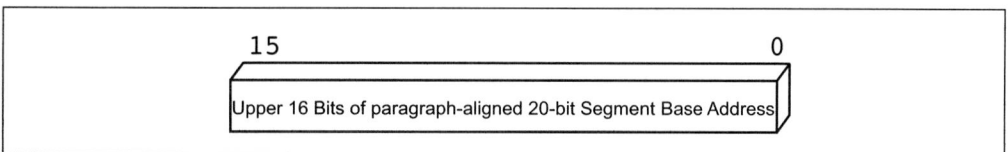

An Important Reminder: Segment Base + Offset = Virtual Address

While this chapter (along with the two chapters that follow) provides a detailed description of segmentation, keep in mind that the address produced by adding an offset to a segment base address may *not*, in fact, be the memory address that is used to access physical memory. If the virtual-to-physical address translation mechanism (i.e., paging) is enabled, it is treated as a *virtual* (also referred to as *linear*) memory address that is subsequently submitted to the virtual-to-physical address translation logic. Upon receipt of a virtual memory address, the Paging logic uses it to perform a lookup in special address translation tables created in memory by the OS kernel. The Page Table Entry (PTE) selected by the virtual address contains the information used to translate the virtual address into a physical memory address.

The two chapters immediately following this one provide detailed discussions of code, data and stack segments, after which the subsequent chapter provides a detailed description of the address translation mechanism.

x86 Instruction Set Architecture

Descriptor Contains Detailed Segment Description

In a Protected Mode environment, the OS programmer must be able to specify the following characteristics of each segment:

- The base address anywhere in a 4GB virtual address range.
- Segment length (anywhere from one byte to 4GB in length).
- How the segment may be accessed:
  — A read-only data segment.
  — An execute-only code segment (contains only code and no data).
  — A code segment that also contains read-only data.
  — A read/writable data segment (contains both code and read-only data).
- The minimum privilege level a program must have in order to access the segment.
- Whether it's a code or data segment, or a special segment used only by the OS kernel and the logical processor.
- Whether the segment of information is currently present in memory or not.

In Protected Mode, it requires eight bytes (64-bits) of information to describe all of these characteristics. The Protected Mode OS memory manager must create an eight byte descriptor for each memory segment to be used by each program (including those used by the OS itself). Obviously, it would consume a great deal of processor real estate to keep the descriptors of all segments in use by all tasks on the processor chip itself. For this reason, the descriptors are stored in special tables in memory. The next section provides a description of these descriptor tables.

Segment Register—Selects Descriptor Table and Entry

When a programmer wishes to gain access to an area of memory, the respective segment register (the CS, SS, or one the data segment registers: DS, ES, FS, or GS) must be loaded with a 16-bit value that identifies the area of memory. In Real Mode, the value loaded into the segment register represents the upper 16 bits of the 20-bit start address of the segment in memory. In Protected Mode, the value loaded into a segment register is referred to as the segment selector, illustrated in the upper part (i.e., the segment register's visible part) of Figure 13-3 on page 389:

- **RPL field**. The Requester Privilege Level (RPL) field is described in "RPL Definition" on page 439 and "RPL Definition" on page 439.

- **TI bit**. Bit [2] (the Table Indicator, or TI bit) of the segment register selects either the Global Descriptor Table (GDT) or the Local Descriptor Table (LDT). The descriptor tables are described in "Introduction to the Descriptor Tables" on page 390.
- **DT Index field**. The Descriptor Table Index field is used to select an entry (i.e., 1 of 8192 segment descriptors) in the indicated table.

Whenever a value is loaded into a segment register in Protected Mode, the logical processor multiplies the segment register's index field value by eight (because there are eight bytes per entry) to create the offset into the indicated table. It then adds this offset to the respective table's base address (supplied by either the GDT Register—GDTR, or the LDT Register—LDTR), yielding the start address of the selected segment descriptor in the specified table. The logical processor then fetches the 8-byte descriptor from memory and places it into the invisible part of the specified segment register (see Figure 13-3 on page 389). The invisible part is sometimes referred to as the segment register's cache register and is not program-accessible. There is a separate segment cache register for each of the six segment registers. Table 13-1 on page 389 defines the validity checks that the logical processor performs on a descriptor before it is loaded into the invisible portion of the respective segment register.

Figure 13-2 on page 388 illustrates the visible part of a segment register, the Global and Local Descriptor Tables (GDT and LDT), and the GDTR and the LDTR. Note that although there is only one GDT, there may be more than one LDT (but only one per task).

x86 Instruction Set Architecture

Figure 13-2: Relationship of a Segment Register and GDT, GDTR, LDT, and LDTR

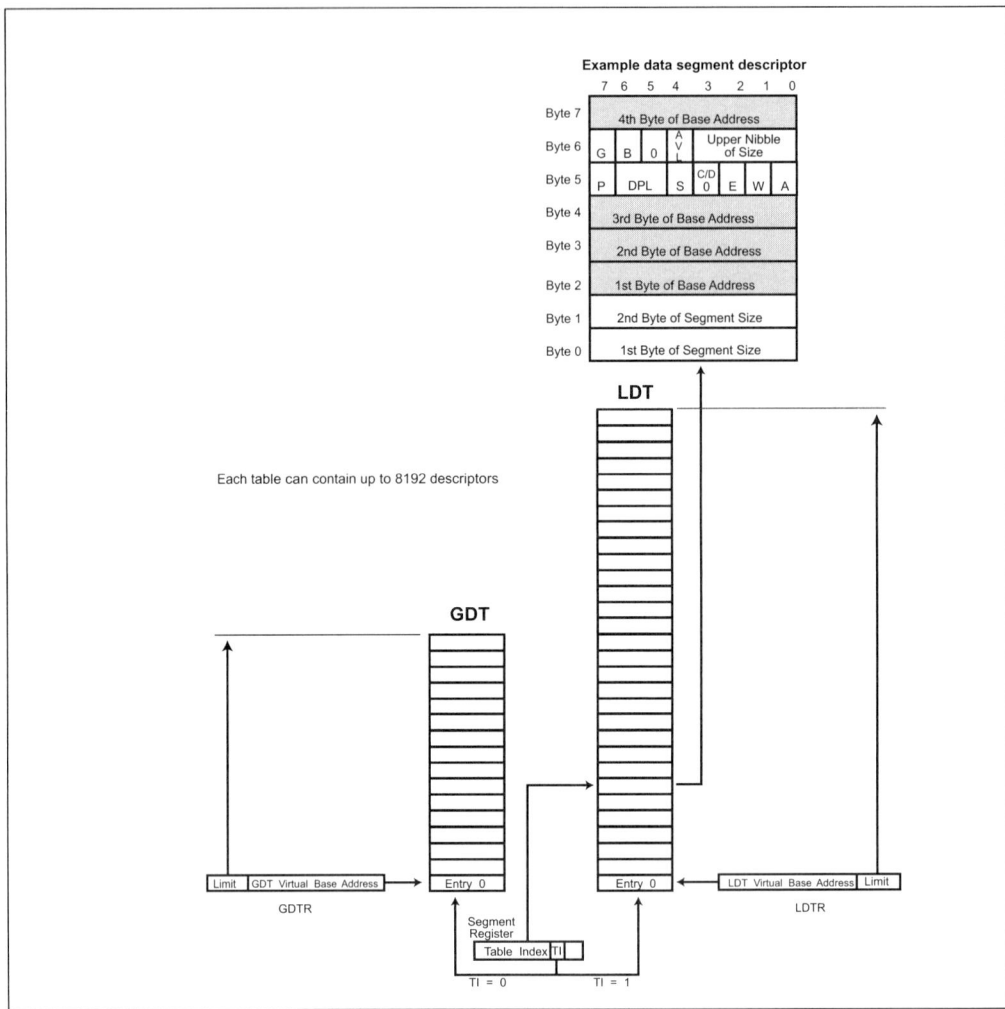

Figure 13-3: Segment Register's Visible and Invisible Elements

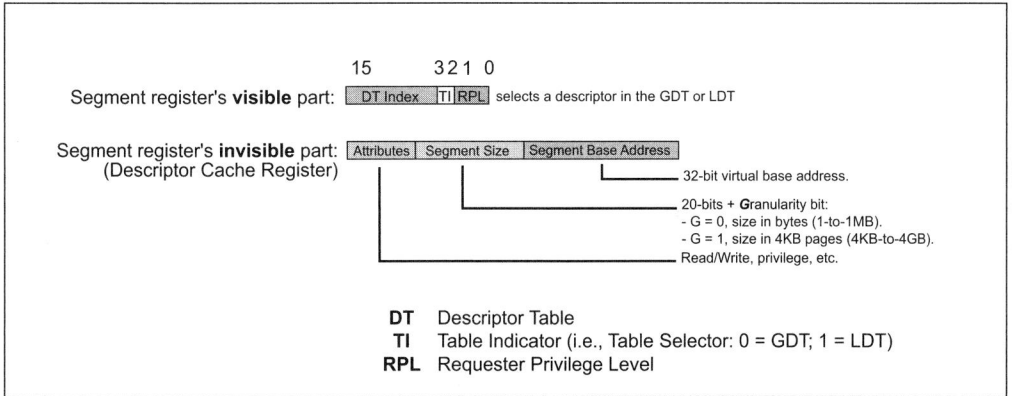

Table 13-1: Logical Processor Actions When a Segment Register Is Loaded

Segment Register Loaded	Basic Actions Taken by the Logical Processor
CS	1. Validates that the DT Index field doesn't select an entry beyond the end of the selected descriptor table: – GDT if the TI bit = 0. – LDT if the TI bit = 1. 2. Reads the selected descriptor from the indicated table (see Figure 13-2 on page 388). 3. Validates that the descriptor Type field (bits 3:0 of byte 5) indicates it is, in fact, a code segment descriptor. 4. Stores the code segment's base address, size and attributes in the CS cache register.

Table 13-1: Logical Processor Actions When a Segment Register Is Loaded (Continued)

Segment Register Loaded	Basic Actions Taken by the Logical Processor
SS	1. Validates that the DT Index field doesn't select an entry beyond the end of the selected descriptor table: – GDT if the TI bit = 0. – LDT if the TI bit = 1. 2. Reads the selected descriptor from the indicated table (see Figure 13-2 on page 388). 3. Validates that the descriptor Type field (bits 3:0 of byte 5) indicates that it is, in fact, a read/write data segment descriptor (because the area of memory designated as the stack must be read/writable). 4. Stores the stack segment's base address, size and attributes in the SS cache register.
DS, ES, FS or GS	1. Validates that the DT Index field doesn't select an entry beyond the end of the selected descriptor table: – GDT if the TI bit = 0. – LDT if the TI bit = 1. 2. Reads the selected descriptor from the indicated table (see Figure 13-2 on page 388). 3. Validates that the descriptor Type field (bits 3:0 of byte 5) indicates that it is, in fact, a data segment descriptor. 4. Stores the data segment's base address, size and attributes in the respective data segment register's cache register.

Introduction to the Descriptor Tables

Segment Descriptors Reside in Memory

Whenever the currently-running program attempts to define a new memory segment (by loading a value into a segment register: due to a far jump or far call, an access to one of the four data segment registers, or an access to the stack segment register), the logical processor reads the selected segment descriptor from the memory-based GDT or LDT into the invisible portion of the respective segment register. From that point forward, the logical processor has fast access to the base address, length and other attributes related to that segment.

There are three types of descriptor tables, all of which are created in memory by the OS kernel. They are described in Table 13-2 on page 391. While the GDT and LDTs are described in this chapter, the IDT is described in "Protected Mode Interrupts and Exceptions" on page 681 and in "The IDT" on page 317.

Table 13-2: Descriptor Table Types

Table Type	Description
GDT	**Global Descriptor Table (GDT).** There is only one GDT and it contains the following types of descriptors: • One descriptor for each code or data segment that is **shared** among more than one task (i.e., it is a globally-accessible segment). • **One TSS** (Task State Segment) **descriptor for each task** (but also refer to "Real World TSS Usage" on page 968). This descriptor defines the base address and size (as well as other attributes) associated with a task's TSS data structure. • If an OS utilizes one or more optional Local Descriptor Tables (LDTs) to describe the segments of memory that are private (local) to various tasks, it will create one **LDT descriptor** for each LDT defining its base address and size (as well as other attributes). • **Procedure Call Gates.** More on these later. These are gates that permit applications to call to OS kernel procedures. • If the OS utilizes the x86 processor's hardware-based task switching mechanism (*note that none of the major OSs use it*), it may create (for each task) a **Task Gate descriptor** in the GDT. If a far jump or a far call is executed and the 16-bit segment selector portion of the far address selects a Task Gate descriptor in the GDT, the logical processor's hardware-based task switching mechanism is triggered (and the logical processor suspends the current task and switches to the task associated with the TSS descriptor pointed to by the Task Gate descriptor).

Table 13-2: Descriptor Table Types (Continued)

Table Type	Description
LDT	**Local Descriptor Tables (LDTs).** A particular OS may not implement any LDTs, only one LDT for all tasks, or a separate LDT for each task. Ideally, if they are used, the OS would implement a separate LDT for each task. An LDT can contain the following types of descriptors: • One descriptor for each code or data segment that is **local to the current task** (i.e., it is a private segment). • **Procedure Call Gates**. These are gates that permit calls to OS kernel procedures. • If the OS utilizes the x86 processor's hardware-based task switching mechanism (*note that none of the major OSs use it*), it may create a **Task Gate descriptor** in a task's LDT. If a far jump or a far call is executed and the 16-bit segment selector portion of the far address selects a Task Gate descriptor in the current task's LDT, the logical processor's hardware-based task switching mechanism is triggered (and the logical processor switches to the task associated with the GDT-based TSS descriptor pointed to by the Task Gate descriptor).
IDT	**Interrupt Descriptor Table (IDT).** There is only one IDT and, like the Real Mode IDT, it can contain up to 256 entries (one associated with each type of interrupt or exception). Three types of descriptors may be found in the IDT: • **Interrupt Gate Descriptor**. When an interrupt or exception selects an IDT entry containing an Interrupt Gate, Eflags[IF] is cleared after Eflags is pushed onto the stack. This prevents the interrupt/exception handler from being interrupted by any subsequent maskable hardware interrupt. The logical processor then jumps to the handler pointed to by the CS:EIP value contained in the gate. • **Trap Gate Descriptor**. When an interrupt or exception selects an IDT entry containing a Trap Gate, Eflags[IF] is not cleared after Eflags is pushed onto the stack. If Eflags[IF] is set when the interrupt or exception is detected, the interrupt/exception handler will recognize any subsequent maskable interrupts. The logical processor then jumps to the handler pointed to by the CS:EIP value contained in the gate. • **Task Gate Descriptor**. When an interrupt or exception selects an IDT entry containing a Task Gate, a task switch occurs. *Note that none of the major OSs use the x86 processor's hardware-based task switching mechanism.*

Global Descriptor Table (GDT)

GDT Description

The OS creates and maintains one GDT (illustrated in Figure 13-4 on page 394) which may contain as many as 8192d entries (note that entry zero is not used).

Five different types of descriptors may reside in the GDT:

1. One Task State Segment (**TSS) descriptor** for each task (but refer to "Real World TSS Usage" on page 968). TSSs are described in the chapter entitled "Task Switching" on page 629.
2. One or more Local Descriptor Table (**LDT) descriptors**. LDTs are described in the section entitled "Local Descriptor Tables (LDTs)" on page 395.
3. Descriptors for **shared code or data/stack segments** of memory that may be accessed by multiple tasks.
4. **Procedure Call Gates** used to control access to OS kernel services. Procedure Call Gates are described in the section entitled "Indirect Procedure Far Call Through a Call Gate" on page 452.
5. **Task Gates** used to switch to other tasks. *Note that none of the major OSs use the x86 processor's hardware-based task switching mechanism.* Task Gates are described in the chapter entitled "Task Switching" on page 629.

- Code, data and stack segments are described in:
  — The chapter entitled "Code, Calls and Privilege Checks" on page 415.
  — The chapter entitled "Data and Stack Segments" on page 479.
  — The section entitled "Selecting and Accessing a Stack Segment" on page 484.

Setting the GDT Base Address and Size

The OS kernel is responsible for creating and maintaining the GDT in memory. Once created, the OS kernel obviously must inform the logical processor regarding the location and size of the GDT. This is accomplished using the LGDT (Load GDT Register) instruction. When the LGDT instruction is executed, the logical processor reads the GDT's virtual base address and size from memory into the GDTR (see Figure 13-4 on page 394). The size is always specified as a 16-bit value. Regarding the GDT base address, there are two possibilities:

- If the LGDT instruction is executed when the operand size is 16-bits (because the LGDT instruction is executed in Real Mode; or the LGDT instruction was fetched from a 16-bit code segment; or the instruction was fetched from a 32-bit code segment but was prefaced by the Operand Size

Override prefix), the logical processor emulates the 286 by loading the GDTR with a 24-bit base address. In actuality, a 32-bit address is read from memory, but the logical processor forces the upper 8-bits to 0.

- If the LGDT instruction is executed when the operand size is 32-bits (because the LGDT instruction was fetched from a 32-bit code segment; or the instruction was fetched from a 16-bit code segment but was prefaced by the Operand Size Override prefix), the logical processor loads the GDTR with a 32-bit base address.

At a maximum, the table can contain 8192d entries (minus one, because entry zero is unused), each eight bytes in size, for a maximum table length of 64KB.

GDT Entry 0

GDT entry 0 must contain a null descriptor (consisting of all 0s) for a good reason. This permits the programmer to place the null value of 0000h into any of the data segment registers without causing an exception (e.g., when initializing the register set). This selects entry zero in the GDT which must be initialized to a null descriptor value of 00000000h.

Figure 13-4: The Global Descriptor Table (GDT)

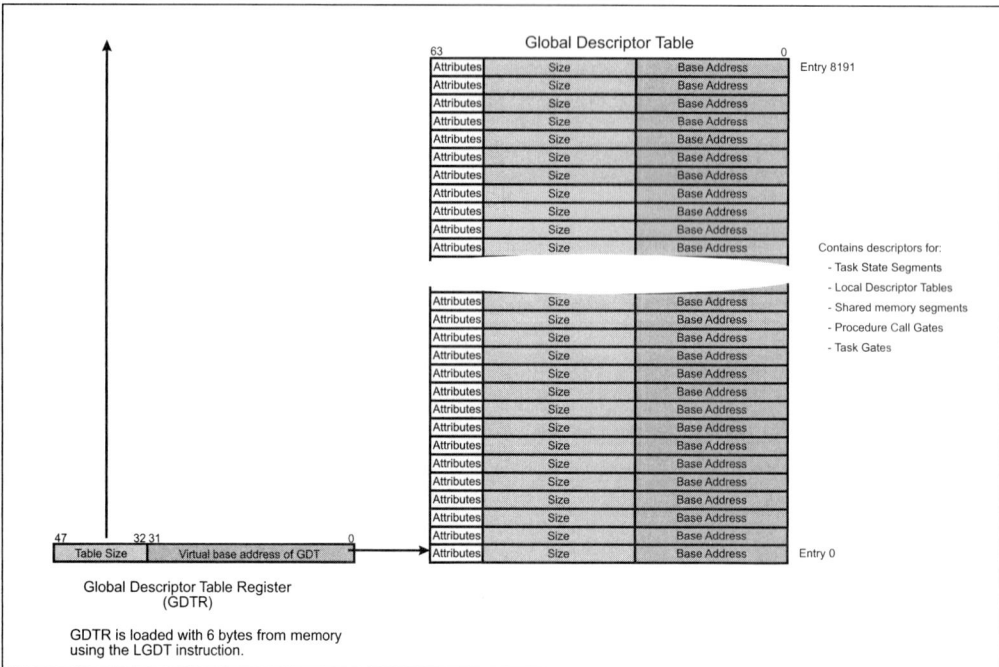

Local Descriptor Tables (LDTs)

General

Optimally, the OS memory manager may use Protected Mode's LDT functionality to define a set of private memory segments associated with each separate task—see Figure 13-5 on page 395—or it could create one LDT to be used by multiple tasks. The LDT for the currently executing task may contain:

- Code, data and stack segment descriptors for memory **segments local to this task**.
- **Procedure Call Gates** that permit the currently executing task to call procedures residing in code segments of a higher privilege level (i.e., OS kernel function calls).
- **Task Gates** that permit the currently executing task to trigger the execution of another task.

Figure 13-5: The GDT and the LDTs

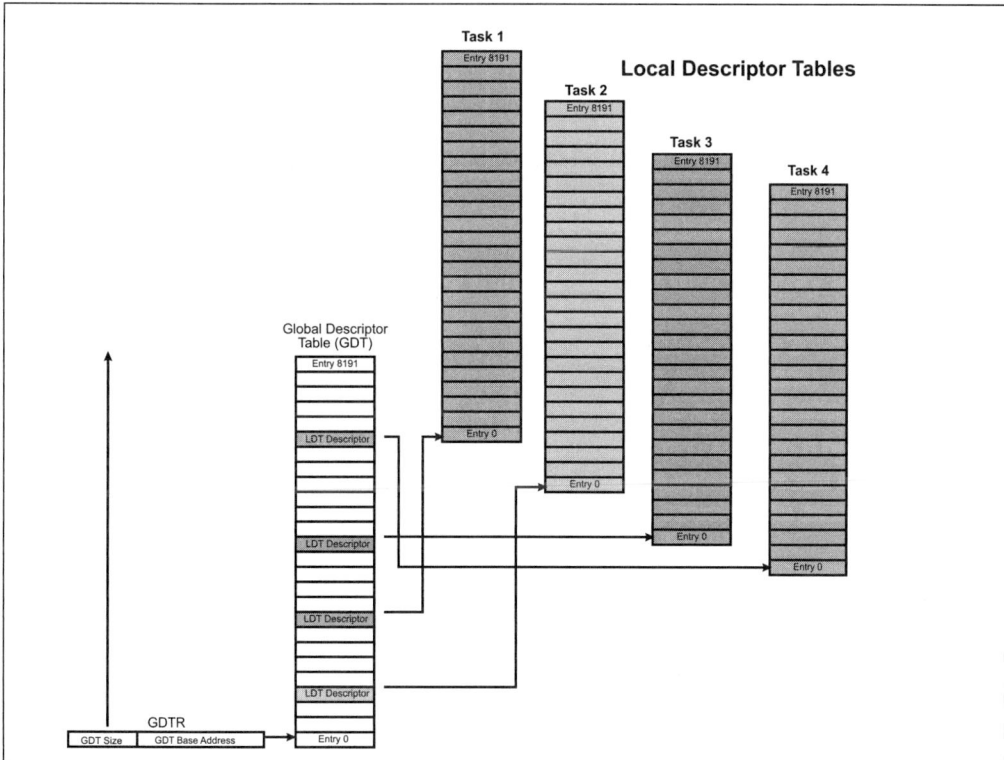

Creating and Selecting an LDT

Establishing an LDT and selecting it is accomplished as follows:

1. Create an LDT in memory (see Figure 13-6 on page 397) containing a set of descriptors defining the task's local segments and OS kernel Call Gates.
2. Create an LDT descriptor in the GDT. This descriptor (see Figure 13-7 on page 398; note that the RPL—Requester Privilege Level—field is described in "RPL Definition" on page 439) contains the base address and size of the LDT. The base address is the table's virtual, not physical, base address.
3. Whenever the task is initiated or resumed, the LLDT instruction is executed to load a 16-bit GDT selector value from memory into the LDTR (see Figure 13-8 on page 398; note that if the hardware-based task switching mechanism were being used, the LDTR is automatically loaded from the LDTR field in the task's TSS). Since it is a rule that LDT descriptors must reside in the GDT, the logical processor verifies that the TI bit = 0 to select the GDT.
4. The logical processor then:
   — Reads the descriptor selected by the 11-bit Descriptor Table Index field from the GDT into the invisible portion of the LDTR.
   — Verifies that the descriptor is, indeed, an LDT descriptor by validating the following (see Figure 13-7 on page 398):
      – System bit = 0 indicating that it is an OS-kernel related descriptor.
      – The descriptor type field (bits 3:0 of byte 5) = 0010b identifying this as an LDT descriptor.

From this point forward, the logical processor then has immediate on-chip access to the base address, size and attributes of the currently executing task's LDT.

Whenever the currently-running task loads a new selector value in any of the six segment registers with the TI bit set to 1 (selecting the LDT), the logical processor reads (from the LDT) the descriptor selected by the segment register's Descriptor Index field and loads it into the invisible part of the respective segment register.

Figure 13-6: LDT Structure

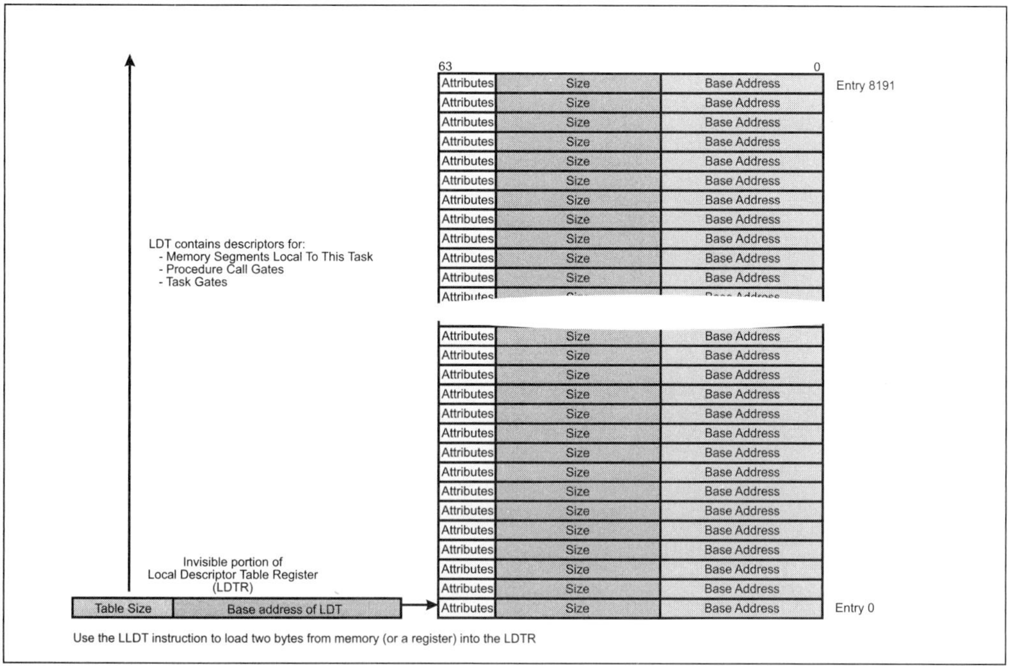

Figure 13-7: Format of an LDT Descriptor (must be in the GDT)

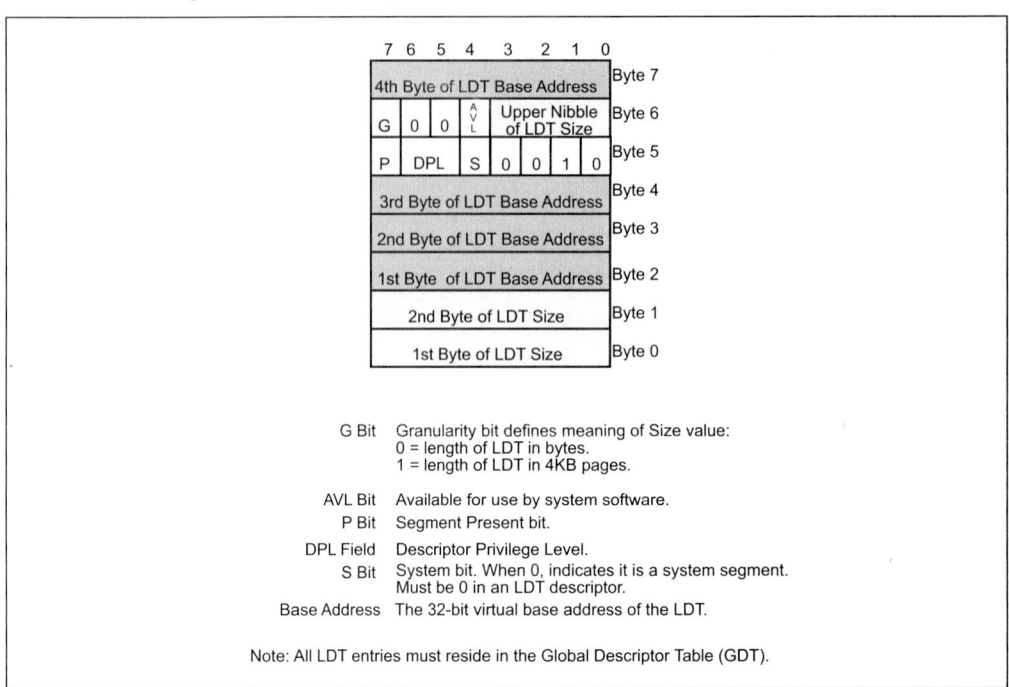

Figure 13-8: Local Descriptor Table Register (LDTR)

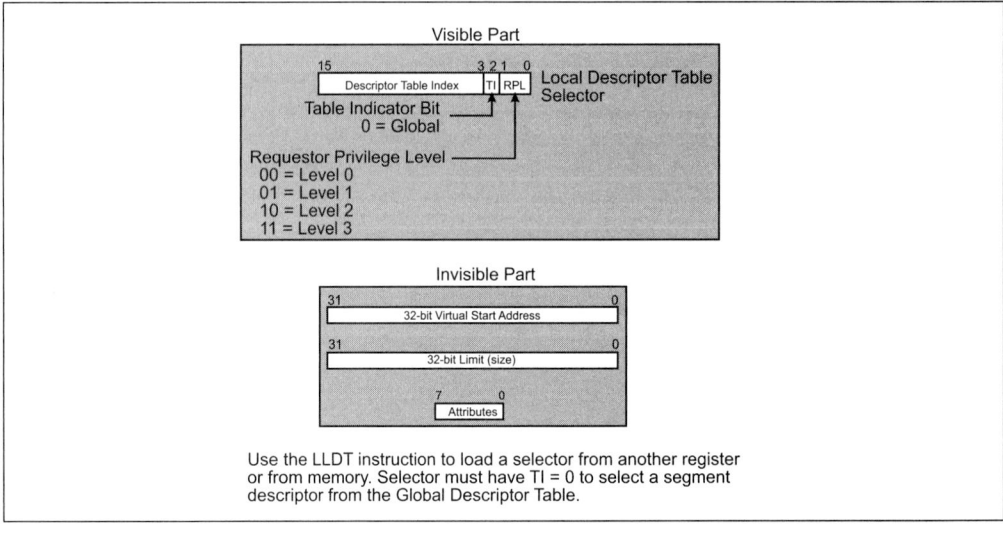

General Segment Descriptor Format

Figure 13-9 on page 399 illustrates the general format of a segment descriptor and the sections that follow provide a detailed description of each descriptor element. It should be noted, however, that there are a number of variations on the segment descriptor; they are covered in the chapters that follow.

Figure 13-9: General Format of a Segment Descriptor

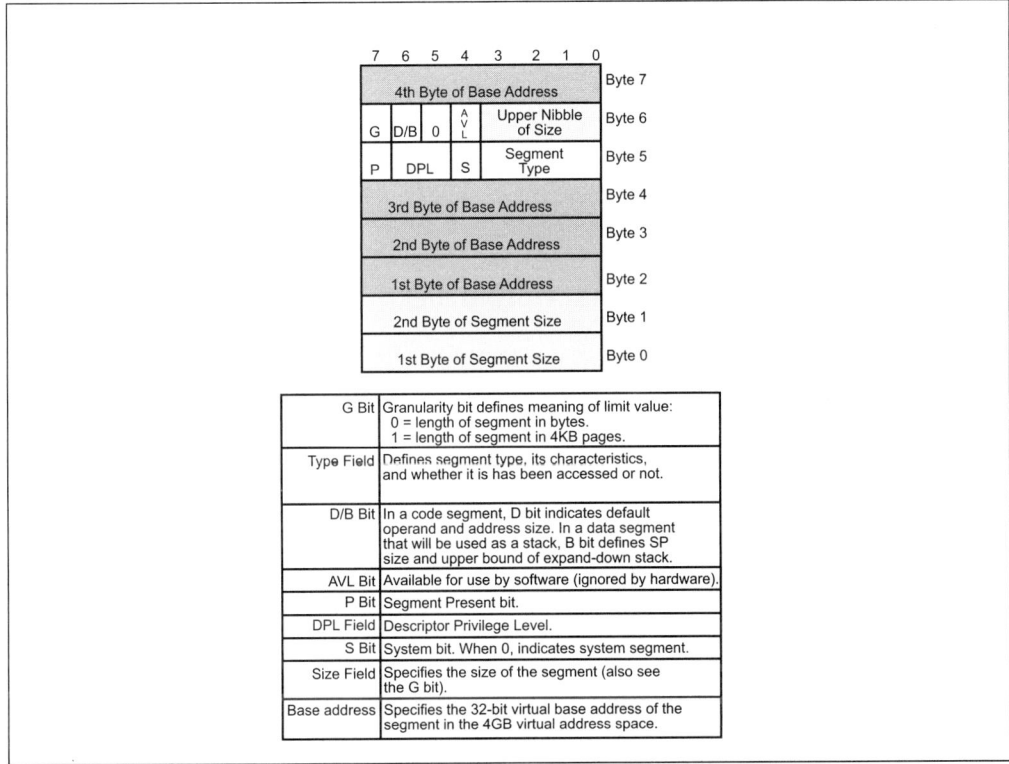

Granularity Bit and the Segment Size

The granularity bit tells the logical processor how to interpret the descriptor's size field (also referred to as the limit):

- G = 0 indicates that the size field specifies the segment size in bytes.
- G = 1 indicates that the size is specified in pages of 4KB each.

The size field is 20-bits wide. Depending on the state of the granularity bit, the segment's size may be defined in the range from one to 1,048,576d bytes (i.e., 1MB) or from one page (4KB) to 2^{20} pages (4GB) in size.

Segment Base Address Field

The 32-bit base address field is used to specify the start segment address within the 4GB virtual address space. It can start at any virtual address from 00000000h through FFFFFFFFh.

Default/Big Bit

The interpretation of the D/B bit depends on whether this is a code segment descriptor, or a data segment descriptor.

In a Code Segment Descriptor, D/B = "Default" Bit

In a code segment descriptor, the *D*/B bit is defined as the *D*efault size bit. It defines a code segment as either a 16-bit, 286 style code segment or a 32-bit, 386 style code segment:

- **D = 0 indicates that it is a 16-bit code segment** (see Figure 13-10 on page 401). Unless instructed otherwise (by prefacing an instruction with the Operand Size Override prefix and/or the Address Size Override prefix), the logical processor assumes that both of the following are true when instructions from a 16-bit code segment are executed:
  — All operands are 16-bits in size.
  — All memory offset addresses are 16-bits in size.
- **D = 1 indicates that it is a 32-bit code segment** (see Figure 13-11 on page 402). Unless instructed otherwise (by prefacing an instruction with the Operand Size Override prefix and/or the Address Size Override prefix), the logical processor assumes that both of the following are true when instructions from a 32-bit code segment are executed:
  — All operands are 32-bits in size.
  — All memory addresses are 32-bits in size.

Programs that execute in Real or VM86 Mode use 16-bit addresses and 16-bit operand size by default.

Override Prefixes

To override the logical processor's assumptions (regarding the address and/or operand size), an instruction must be preceded by the Address Size Override prefix (67h) and/or the Operand Size Override prefix (66h). When detected by a logical processor executing code from a 32-bit code segment (D = 1), this instructs the logical processor to treat this as a 16-bit instruction (regarding the interpretation of the fields within the instruction that change meaning in 32- versus 16-bit mode). Conversely, when detected by a logical processor executing code from a 16-bit code segment (D = 1), this instructs the logical processor to treat this as a 32-bit instruction.

Processors earlier than the 386 cannot execute code from 32-bit code segments. The address size and operand size prefixes were added in the 386 processor to permit it to execute both 16- and 32-bit code correctly.

Figure 13-10: 16-bit, 286-Style Code Segment Descriptor

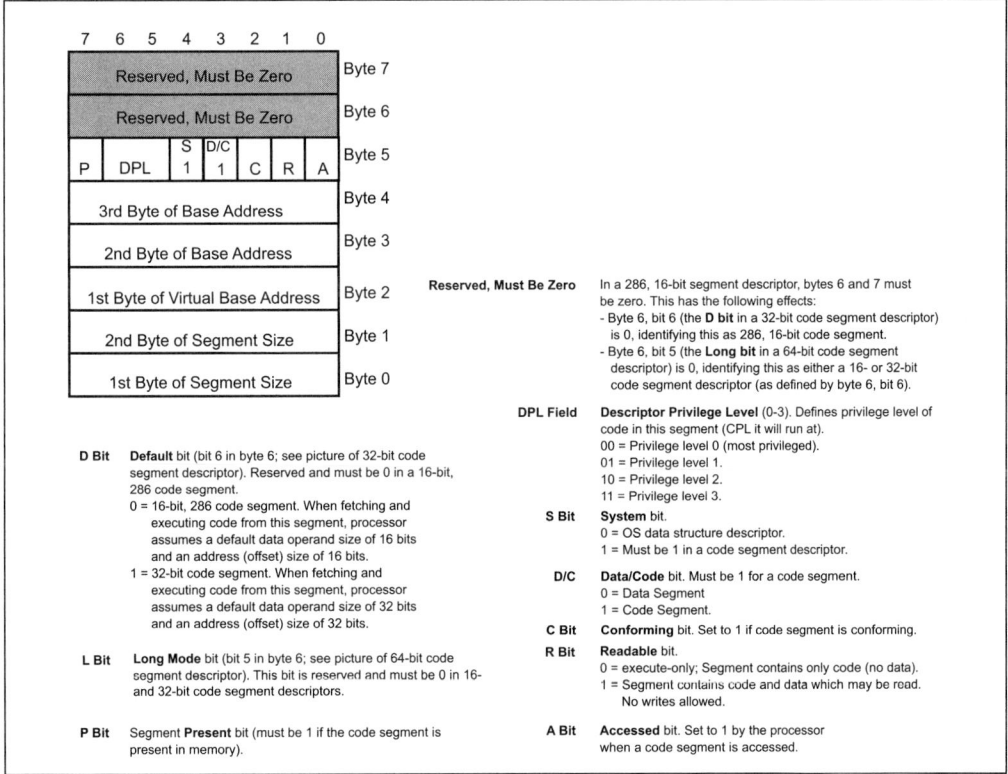

Figure 13-11: 32-bit Code Segment Descriptor

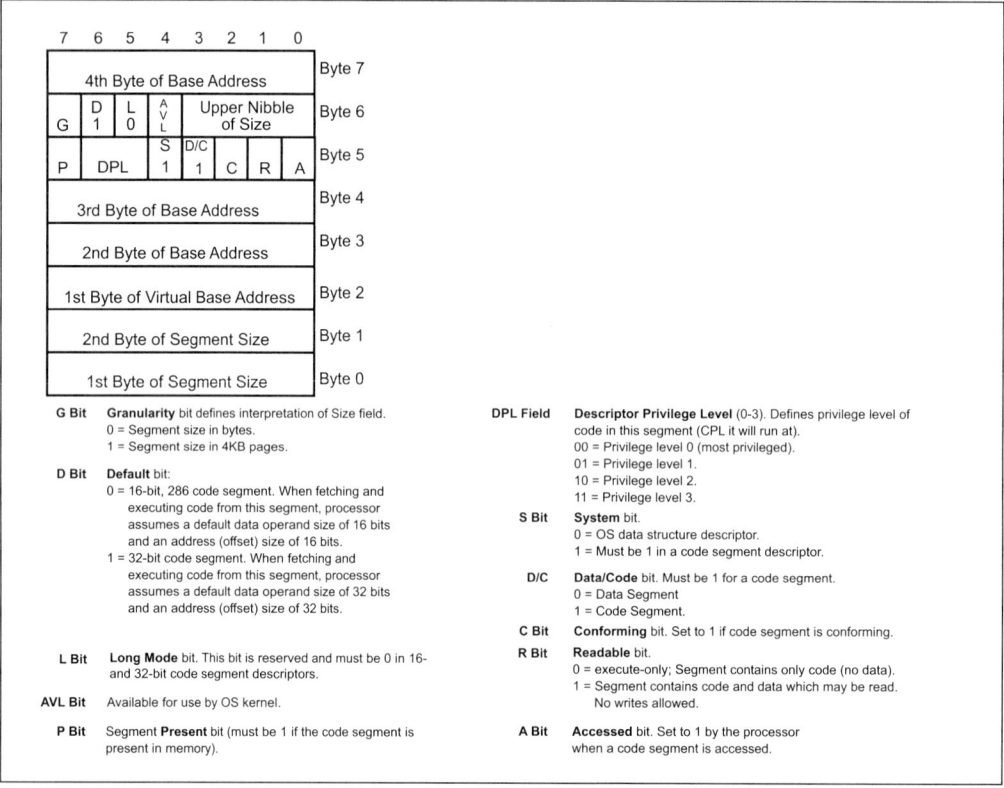

In a Stack Segment Descriptor, D/B = "Big" Bit

In a stack segment descriptor (a stack segment is nothing more than a read/writable data segment), the D/*B* bit is defined as the *B*ig bit. It defines the size of the Stack Pointer register (16-bit SP, or 32-bit ESP) and the upper bound of the stack (if it is an expand-down stack; see "Expand-Down Stack" on page 487):

- **B = 1** indicates that the **32-bit ESP** register is used as the Stack Pointer and, if the stack is implemented as an expand-down stack, its upper bound = FFFFFFFFh.

- **B = 0** indicates that the **16-bit SP** register is used as a Stack Pointer and, if the stack is implemented as an expand-down stack, its upper bound = 0000FFFFh.

For a description of both expand-up and expand-down stacks, refer to the section entitled "Selecting and Accessing a Stack Segment" on page 484.

Chapter 13: Protected Mode Memory Addressing

Segment Type Field

Introduction to the Type Field

The 4-bit segment Type field (see bits 3:0 in byte 5 of Figure 13-9 on page 399) defines the type of segment descriptor. The state of the descriptor's System (S) bit qualifies the interpretation of the Type field:

- **S = 0** indicates that segment is a special-purpose **OS (kernel) segment** and the Type field defines the type of OS segment (see "System Bit" on page 407).
- **S = 1** indicates that segment defined by the descriptor is not a System segment; rather it is either a **code segment, or a data/stack segment** (a stack segment is nothing more than a read/writable data segment). The Type field further defines whether it is a code segment, or a data/stack segment, as well as the segment's access rights and access history.

Non-System Segment Types

The segment Type field consists of bits [3:0] of byte five in the descriptor. Bit [3], the C/D (Code or Data) bit, defines whether it's a code segment, or a data/stack segment:

- **C/D = 1** indicates that it is a **code segment** (see Figure 13-10 on page 401 and Figure 13-11 on page 402).
- **C/D = 0** indicates that it is a **data/stack segment** (see Figure 13-12 on page 406).

Table 13-3 on page 404 and Table 13-4 on page 405 define the data segment types and code segment types, respectively. Note that the definition of bits [2:0] are different for code segments and data/stack segments.

Stack segments must be designated as read/write. The subject of expand-up versus expand-down stacks is covered under the heading "Selecting and Accessing a Stack Segment" on page 484.

The subject of Conforming versus Non-Conforming code segments is covered under the heading "Conforming and Non-Conforming Code Segments" on page 438. Code segments that are marked accessible for data reads (i.e., loads) as well as instruction fetch in Table 13-4 may, in addition to instruction fetches, be read using data access instructions (e.g., MOV instructions). This would be necessary if the code segment contains data constants that would be read as data (using data access instructions).

Table 13-3: Data/Stack Segment Types (C/D = 0)

Type Field Bits				Description
3	2	1	0	
C/D	E	W	A	Data/Stack Segment Attributes & Access History
0	0	0	0	Not yet accessed (A = 0), read-only (W = 0), data segment (stack segment must be read/writable).
0	0	0	1	Accessed (A = 1), read-only (W = 0), data segment (stack segment must be read/writable).
0	0	1	0	Not yet accessed (A = 0), read/write (W = 1), and it can be used as either an expand-up stack segment (E = 0) or a data segment.
0	0	1	1	Accessed (A = 1), read/write (W = 1), and it can be used as either an expand-up stack segment (E = 0) or a data segment.
0	1	0	0	Not yet accessed (A = 0), read-only (W = 0), data segment (stack segment must be read/writable).
0	1	0	1	Accessed (A = 1), read-only (W = 0), data segment (stack segment must be read/writable).
0	1	1	0	Not yet accessed (A = 0), read/write (W = 1), and it can be used as either an expand-down stack segment (E = 1) or a data segment.
0	1	1	1	Accessed (A = 1), read/write (W = 1), and it can be used as either an expand-down stack segment (E = 1) or a data segment.

Table 13-4: Code Segment Types (C/D = 1)

Type Field Bits				Description
3	2	1	0	
C/D	C	R	A	Code Segment Attributes & Access History
1	0	0	0	Not yet accessed (A = 0), accessible for instruction fetch only (R = 0), non-conforming (C = 0).
1	0	0	1	Accessed (A = 1), accessible for instruction fetch only (R = 0), non-conforming (C = 0).
1	0	1	0	Not yet accessed (A = 0), accessible for instruction fetch and for data reads (R = 1), non-conforming (C = 0).
1	0	1	1	Accessed (A = 1), accessible for instruction fetch and for data reads (R = 1), non-conforming (C = 0).
1	1	0	0	Not yet accessed (A = 0), accessible for instruction fetch only (R = 0), conforming (C = 1).
1	1	0	1	Accessed (A = 1), accessible for instruction fetch only (R = 0), conforming (C = 1).
1	1	1	0	Not yet accessed (A = 0), accessible for instruction fetch and data reads (R = 1), conforming (C = 1).
1	1	1	1	Accessed (A = 1), accessible for instruction fetch and data reads (R = 1), conforming (C = 1).

Figure 13-12: 32-bit Data Segment Descriptor Format

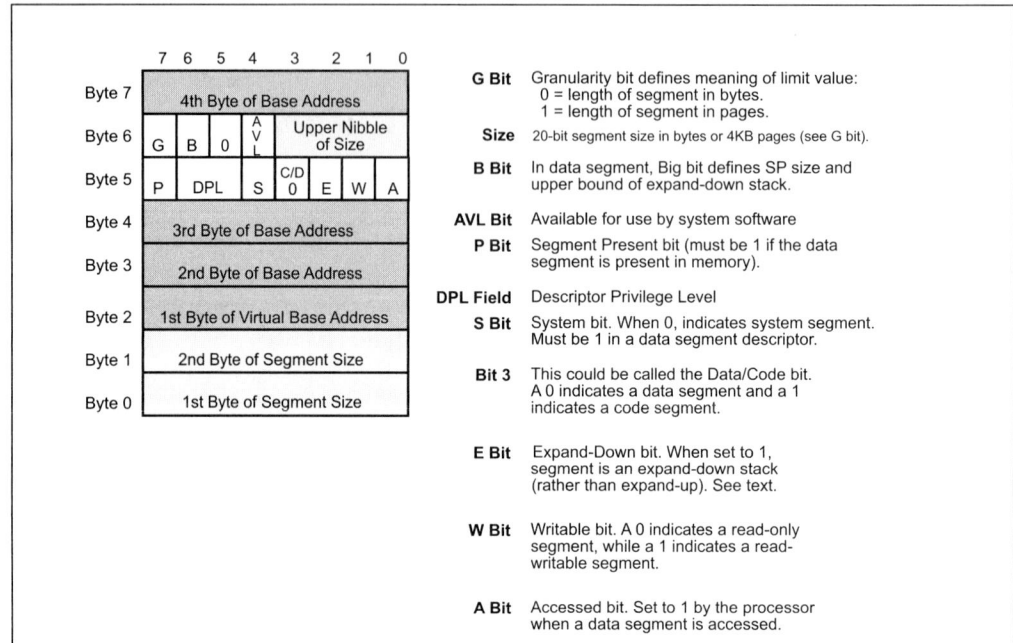

G Bit — Granularity bit defines meaning of limit value:
0 = length of segment in bytes.
1 = length of segment in pages.

Size — 20-bit segment size in bytes or 4KB pages (see G bit).

B Bit — In data segment, Big bit defines SP size and upper bound of expand-down stack.

AVL Bit — Available for use by system software

P Bit — Segment Present bit (must be 1 if the data segment is present in memory).

DPL Field — Descriptor Privilege Level

S Bit — System bit. When 0, indicates system segment. Must be 1 in a data segment descriptor.

Bit 3 — This could be called the Data/Code bit. A 0 indicates a data segment and a 1 indicates a code segment.

E Bit — Expand-Down bit. When set to 1, segment is an expand-down stack (rather than expand-up). See text.

W Bit — Writable bit. A 0 indicates a read-only segment, while a 1 indicates a read-writable segment.

A Bit — Accessed bit. Set to 1 by the processor when a data segment is accessed.

Segment Present Bit

The state of this bit indicates whether the code segment or data/stack segment is currently in memory:

- P = 1 indicates that the segment of information is currently memory-resident starting at the base address indicated in this descriptor.
- P = 0 indicates that the segment of information is not currently present in memory and descriptor bytes zero through four, six, and seven may be used by the OS (e.g., to store a mass storage address). Byte five is still the attribute byte and defines the privilege level and segment type.

Descriptor Privilege Level (DPL) Field

This two bit field defines the segment's privilege level. Generally speaking, the logical processor only permits a program to access a segment if the program attempting the access has a privilege level (CPL, or Current Privilege Level) that meets or exceeds the descriptor's privilege level (DPL). A detailed description of privilege checking can be found in "Privilege Checking" on page 436 and"Two-Step Permission Check" on page 481.

System Bit

A segment descriptor with S = 0 defines a special-purpose segment used by the OS kernel and the processor hardware. System segments are defined in detail in later sections of this book. Table 13-5 on page 407 identifies the system segment types.

Table 13-5: Types of System Segments

Type Field				Description
3	**2**	**1**	**0**	
0	0	0	0	Reserved.
0	0	0	1	This descriptor resides in the GDT and describes an **available 16-bit, 286 TSS** (Task State Segment).
0	0	1	0	This descriptor resides in the GDT and describes a **Local Descriptor Table** (LDT).
0	0	1	1	This descriptor resides in the GDT and describes a **busy** (bit 1 = 1) **16-bit, 286 TSS**.
0	1	0	0	This descriptor resides in the GDT or an LDT and describes a **16-bit, 286 Call Gate**. It may not reside in the IDT.
0	1	0	1	This descriptor resides in the GDT, an LDT, or the IDT and describes a **Task Gate**.
0	1	1	0	This descriptor resides in the IDT and describes a **16-bit, 286 Interrupt Gate**.
0	1	1	1	This descriptor resides in the IDT and describes a **16-bit, 286 Trap Gate**.
1	0	0	0	Reserved

Table 13-5: Types of System Segments (Continued)

Type Field				Description
3	**2**	**1**	**0**	
1	0	0	1	This descriptor resides in the GDT and describes an **available 32-bit, post-286 TSS**.
1	0	1	0	Reserved
1	0	1	1	This descriptor resides in the GDT and describes a **busy 32-bit, post-286 TSS**.
1	1	0	0	This descriptor resides in the GDT or an LDT and describes a **32-bit, post-286 Call Gate**. It may not reside in the IDT.
1	1	0	1	Reserved
1	1	1	0	This descriptor resides in the IDT and describes a **32-bit, post-286 Interrupt Gate**.
1	1	1	1	This descriptor resides in the IDT and describes a **32-bit, post-286 Trap Gate**.

Available Bit

This bit is ignored by the processor hardware and may be used by the OS to describe an additional, OS-specific segment attribute.

Goodbye to Segmentation

Introduction

With all due respect to the architects of the x86 segmented memory model, its complexity did not serve the programming community well. On most if not all non-x86 processors, an instruction such as the following

```
mov eax, [12345678]
```

would be interpreted as: load the EAX register with four bytes from memory starting at location 12345678h. Because of the x86 segmented memory model, however, this instruction actually loads the EAX register with four bytes from memory starting at location 12345678h *in the data segment* and, assuming that the data segment doesn't start at memory location 00000000h, the actual address to be read from is calculated by adding the data segment base address (whatever that may be) to the offset value of 12345678h. Not a very straight-forward programming model.

IA-32 Flat Memory Model

On an IA-32 processor (or an Intel 64 processor operating in IA-32 Mode or Compatibility Mode), there is no way to disable segmentation. In order to create a simpler programming environment wherein the offset portion of the address (the address specified by the application programmer) is the actual address of the item being addressed (i.e., the programmer doesn't have to worry about what segment the item resides in or where that segment starts in memory), modern 32-bit OS kernels written for the IA-32 processor define the base address of all segments as 00000000h and their size as 4GB. In other words, the logical processor acts as if there is only one, unified memory space encompassing all of virtual memory space (see Figure 13-13 on page 411). This can be accomplished by creating (at a minimum) three segment descriptors in the GDT (refer to Figure 13-14 on page 411):

- A Code Segment descriptor that describes a code segment with the following characteristics:
    - A base address of 00000000h.
    - 4GB in size.
    - Accessible by the code fetch logic as well as by data reads. Code can then be read from the segment as well as read-only data.
    - DPL = 3 indicating it is a User-level code segment containing a user-level application.
- A Code Segment descriptor that describes a code segment with the following characteristics:
    - A base address of 00000000h.
    - 4GB in size.
    - Accessible by the code fetch logic as well as by data reads. Code can then be read from the segment as well as read-only data.
    - DPL = 0 indicating it is a Supervisor-level code segment containing the OS kernel code, drivers, etc.

- One data segment descriptor that describes a data segment with the following characteristics:
  — A base address of 00000000h.
  — 4GB in size.
  — Read/writable.
  — By any program running at any privilege level.
  — Part of this segment can be used as the stack while the remainder contains the data the current task operates upon.

Before running any applications, the OS kernel first:

- Preloads the CS register with a pointer to either the User-level or Supervisor-level CS descriptor in the GDT (entry 1 or 2 in the figure).
- Preloads the remaining five segment registers with a pointer to the read/writable data segment descriptor (entry 3 in the figure).

Having done this and using the previous example,

```
mov eax, [12345678]
```

would be interpreted as: load the EAX register with four bytes from memory starting at location 12345678h. Since segmentation cannot be disabled, the logical processor will, in fact, add the offset (12345678h) to the data segment base address, but since the data segment (and all other segments) have been set up with a base address of 00000000h, the offset address *is* the virtual address.

As described later in the book, when the logical processor is operating in 64-bit Mode, segmentation is disabled and a hardware-enforced flat memory model takes its place.

Figure 13-13: The Flat Memory Model

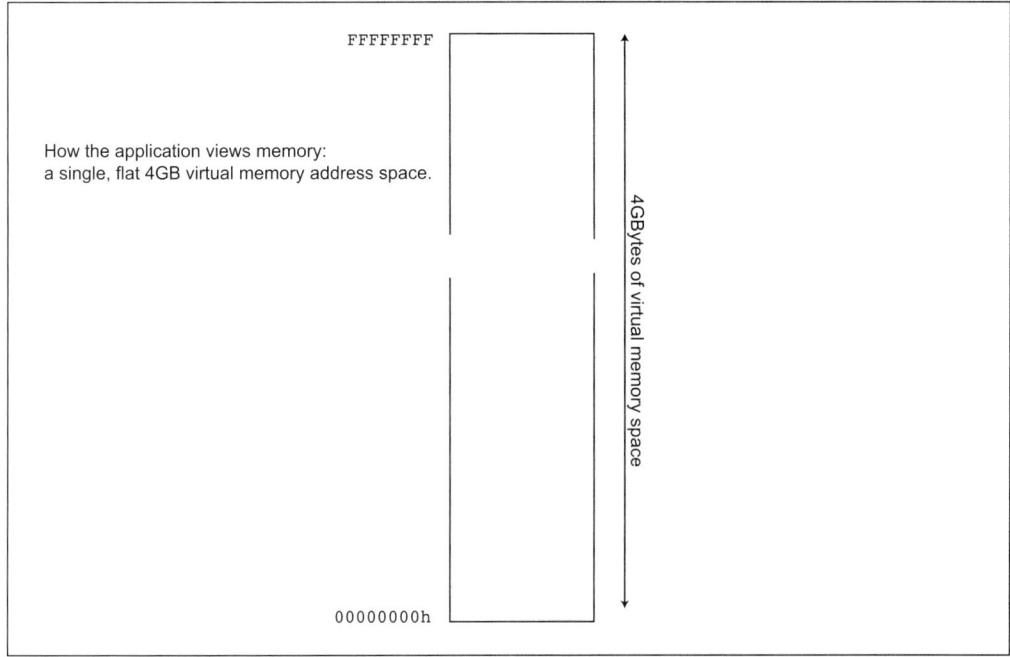

Figure 13-14: Creating a Flat Memory Model

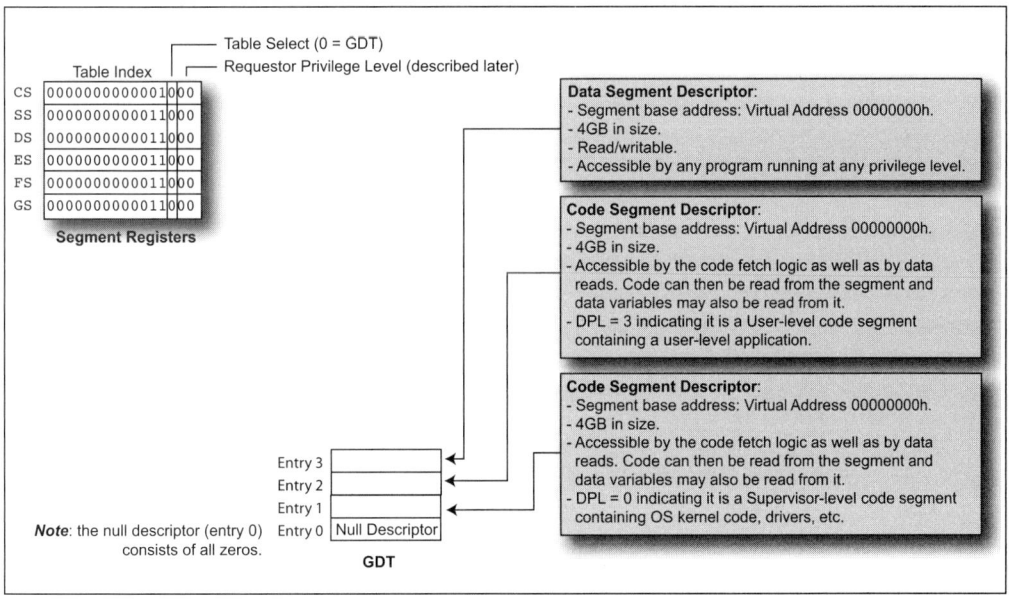

No Protection? Paging Takes Care of It

Although the flat memory model creates a simpler environment wherein the programmer-specified offset address is the address of the desired item in memory, we appear to have paid a heavy price:

- The code, data and stack areas—each 2^{32} (4GB) in size—now overlay each other.
- Most of the protection mechanisms pertaining to read/writability, privilege level checking, etc., have been eliminated.

The virtual-to-physical address translation services (i.e., the Paging logic) takes care of this. Before the OS kernel initiates the execution of an application, it creates a set of virtual-to-physical address mapping tables for that specific application. When the application is executing, the memory addresses it generates—the offset addresses, or virtual addresses—are submitted to the Paging logic for a lookup in the application's Page Tables. The Page Table Entry (PTE) selected by a virtual address is used to translate the virtual address into the address in physical memory. The selected Page Table Entry also contains attribute bits defining the privilege level the currently-executing program must meet or beat, the read/writability of the page, etc. In other words, the Paging logic directs the virtual addresses to the correct physical area of memory and also gives us back the protection lost by effectively crippling the segmentation logic.

The IA-32 address translation mechanism is described in "IA-32 Address Translation Mechanisms" on page 493.

A Reminder of Where We Are

At the risk of seeming repetitive, the following is a repeat of the reminder found at the beginning of this chapter.

Keep in mind that the address produced by adding an offset to a segment base address is *not* the memory address that is actually used to access physical memory (except if address translation is not used by the OS). Rather, it is a *virtual* (also referred to as *linear*) memory address that is subsequently submitted to the virtual-to-physical address translation logic (i.e., the Paging logic). Upon receipt of a virtual memory address, the Paging logic uses it to perform a lookup in special tables (Page Tables) maintained in memory by the OS kernel. The Page Table Entry (PTE) selected by the virtual address contains the information used to translate the virtual address into a physical memory address.

The two chapters immediately following this one complete the discussion of segmentation by providing detailed discussions of code, data and stack segments, after which the following chapter then provides a detailed description of the Paging mechanism.

14 Code, Calls and Privilege Checks

The Previous Chapter

The previous chapter introduced segment register usage in Protected Mode and the role of segment descriptors, the GDT, the LDTs, the IDT, and the general segment descriptor format. It also introduced the concept of the flat memory model. The following topics were covered:

- Real Mode Segment Limitations.
- An Important Reminder: Segment Base + Offset = Virtual Address.
- Descriptor Contains Detailed Segment Description.
- Segment Register—Selects Descriptor Table and Entry.
- The Descriptor Tables.
- General Segment Descriptor Format.
- Goodbye to Segmentation.

This Chapter

This chapter provides a detailed description of code segments (both Conforming and Non-Conforming), privilege checking, and Call Gates. The following topics are covered:

- Selecting the Active Code Segment.
- CS Descriptor.
- Accessing the Code Segment.
- Short/Near Jumps.
- Unconditional Far Jumps.
- Privilege Checking.
- Jumping from a Higher-to-Lesser Privileged Program.
- Direct Procedure Calls.

- Indirect Procedure Far Call Though a Call Gate.
- Automatic Stack Switch.
- Far Call From 32-bit CS to 16-bit CS.
- Far Call From 16-bit CS to 32-bit CS.
- Far Returns.

The Next Chapter

The next chapter provides a detailed description of Data and Stack segments (including Expand-Up and Expand-Down Stacks) and privilege checking. The following topics are covered:

- The Data Segments.
  — General.
  — Two-Step Permission Check.
  — An Example.
- Selecting and Accessing a Stack Segment.
  — Introduction.
  — Expand-Up Stack.
  — Expand-Down Stack.
    – The Problem.
    – Expand-Down Stack Description.
    – An Example.
    – Another Example.

Abbreviation Alert

In many cases in this chapter, the abbreviation *CS* is substituted for *code segment*.

Selecting the Active Code Segment

To execute code from a specific area of memory, the programmer must tell the logical processor what code segment the instructions are to be fetched from. This is accomplished by loading a 16-bit value (a selector) into the Code Segment (CS) register. In Real Mode, this value represents the upper 16-bits of the 20-bit zero-extended segment base address. In Protected Mode, the value loaded into the 16-bit visible portion of the CS register (see Figure 14-1 on page 418) selects an entry in either the GDT or the LDT. The selected 8-byte CS descriptor is automatically read from memory and stored in the invisible part of the CS register.

Any of the actions listed in Table 14-1 on page 417 loads a new selector into CS and causes the logical processor to begin fetching instructions from a new code segment in memory.

Table 14-1: Actions That Cause a Switch to a New CS

Action	Description
Execution of a **far jump** instruction	Loads the CS/Instruction Pointer register pair with new values.
Execution of a **far call** instruction	
A **hardware interrupt** or a **software exception**	In response, the logical processor loads new values into the CS/Instruction Pointer register pair from the IDT entry selected by the interrupt or exception vector.
Execution of a **software interrupt instruction**	• **INT nn**. In response, the logical processor loads new values into the CS/Instruction Pointer register pair from the IDT entry selected by the instruction's 8-bit operand. • **INT3**. In response, the logical processor loads new values into the CS/Instruction Pointer register pair from IDT entry 3. • **INTO**. In response, the logical processor loads new values into the CS/Instruction Pointer register pair from IDT entry 4. • **BOUND**. In response, the logical processor loads new values into the CS/Instruction Pointer register pair from IDT entry 5.
Initiation of a **new task or resumption** of a previously-**suspended task**	During a task switch by the x86 processor's hardware-based task switching mechanism (which most modern OSs do not use), the logical processor loads most of its registers, including CS:EIP, with values from the TSS associated with the task being started or resumed.
Execution of a **far RET** instruction	The far return address (CS and Instruction Pointer) is popped from the stack and loaded into the CS/Instruction Pointer register pair.

Table 14-1: Actions That Cause a Switch to a New CS (Continued)

Action	Description
Execution of an **Interrupt Return** instruction (IRET)	The far return address is popped from the stack and loaded into the CS/Instruction Pointer register pair.

Figure 14-1: Segment Register

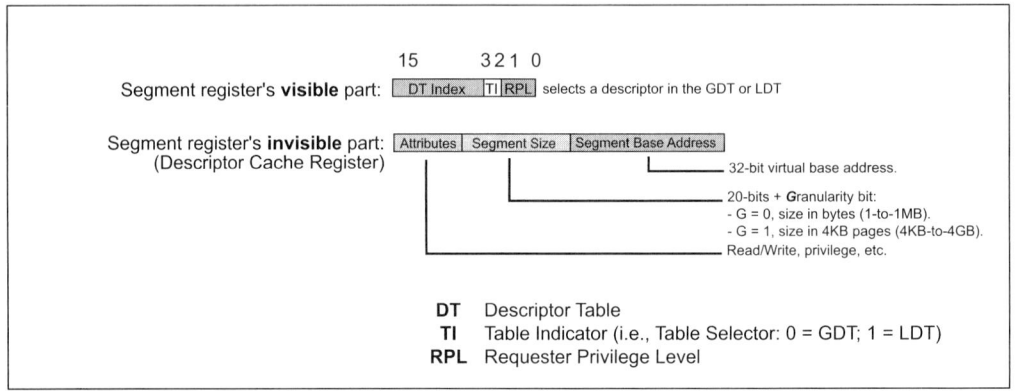

CS Descriptor

CS Descriptor Selector

The value loaded into the visible part of CS (Figure 14-1 on page 418) identifies:

- The descriptor table that contains the code segment descriptor:
  — TI = 0 selects the GDT.
  — TI = 1 selects the LDT.
- The entry in the specified descriptor table. The DT (Descriptor Table) Index field selects one of 8192d entries in the selected table.
- The privilege level of the program that created the selector in the CS register. This is referred to as the Requester Privilege Level (RPL).

Calculating the Descriptor's Memory Address

The logical processor multiplies the descriptor table index by eight (eight bytes per entry) to obtain the offset in the selected table. A check is performed to ensure that the offset is not beyond the indicated table's limit (the limit is stored in the invisible portion of the GDTR or LDTR register). Otherwise, an exception results. The offset is then added to the table base address (obtained from the invisible portion of the GDTR or LDTR register) to form the address of the descriptor in memory.

Descriptor Read and Privilege Checked

The logical processor reads the selected code segment descriptor from the descriptor table and checks to ensure that the currently executing program has sufficient privilege to access this code segment. A complete description of the privilege check can be found in "Privilege Checking" on page 436.

- If the privilege checks fails, a General Protection (GP) exception is generated.
- If the privilege test passes, the logical processor saves the descriptor information in the invisible portion of the CS register.

CS Descriptor Format

Table 14-2 on page 419 and Figure 14-2 on page 421 illustrate the format of a 32-bit code segment descriptor. For completeness, Figure 14-3 on page 422 illustrates the format of the 16-bit, 286-style CS descriptor.

Table 14-2: Code Segment Descriptor Format

Field	Description
D	The state of the Default bit identifies the segment as a first or second generation code segment: • 0 = 286-compliant 16-bit code segment. – Default operand size is 16-bits. – Default memory operand offset address size is 16-bits. • 1 = 386-compliant 32-bit code segment. – Default operand size is 32-bits. – Default memory operand offset address size is 32-bits.

Table 14-2: Code Segment Descriptor Format (Continued)

Field	Description
S	The System (S) bit must = 1 in a code or data segment descriptor.
C/D	**Code or Data** bit. 1 indicates that the descriptor defines a code segment, rather than a data/stack segment.
Conforming bit	Refer to the section entitled "Conforming and Non-Conforming Code Segments" on page 438 for a description of conforming versus non-conforming code segments. • 0 = Non-conforming code segment. • 1 = Conforming code segment.
R	• **R = 0**. Only the instruction prefetcher may access this code segment (in other words, the segment is **execute-only**). Any attempt to access the code segment using either a read or write data access instruction (e.g., a MOV) causes a GP exception. • **R = 1**. This segment may be read by the instruction prefetcher and by data access instructions. This is necessary if the code segment contains data items that must be read during the course of program execution. It may not be written to.
Other fields	The remaining bit fields in the code segment descriptor are defined in the section entitled "General Segment Descriptor Format" on page 399.

Figure 14-2: 32-bit Code Segment Descriptor Format

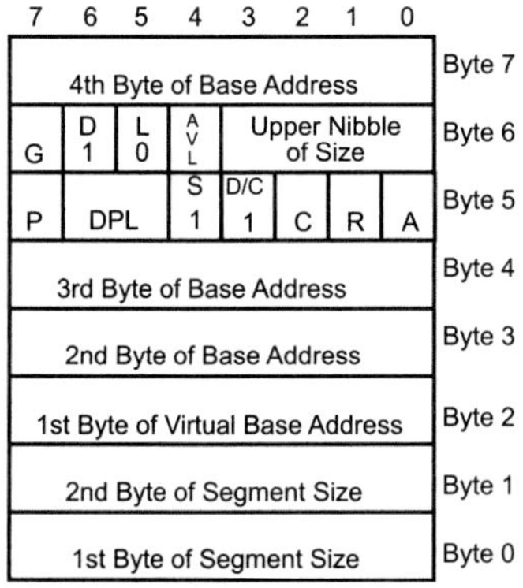

G Bit   **Granularity** bit defines interpretation of Size field.
0 = Segment size in bytes.
1 = Segment size in 4KB pages.

D Bit   **Default** bit:
0 = 16-bit, 286 code segment. When fetching and executing code from this segment, processor assumes a default data operand size of 16 bits and an address (offset) size of 16 bits.
1 = 32-bit code segment. When fetching and executing code from this segment, processor assumes a default data operand size of 32 bits and an address (offset) size of 32 bits.

L Bit   **Long Mode** bit. This bit is reserved and must be 0 in 16- and 32-bit code segment descriptors.

AVL Bit   Available for use by OS kernel.

P Bit   Segment **Present** bit (must be 1 if the code segment is present in memory).

DPL Field   **Descriptor Privilege Level** (0-3). Defines privilege level of code in this segment (CPL it will run at).
00 = Privilege level 0 (most privileged).
01 = Privilege level 1.
10 = Privilege level 2.
11 = Privilege level 3.

S Bit   **System** bit.
0 = OS data structure descriptor.
1 = Must be 1 in a code segment descriptor.

D/C   **Data/Code** bit. Must be 1 for a code segment.
0 = Data Segment
1 = Code Segment.

C Bit   **Conforming** bit. Set to 1 if code segment is conforming.

R Bit   **Readable** bit.
0 = execute-only; Segment contains only code (no data).
1 = Segment contains code and data which may be read. No writes allowed.

A Bit   **Accessed** bit. Set to 1 by the processor when a code segment is accessed.

Figure 14-3: 16-bit, 286-style CS Descriptor Format

7 6 5 4 3 2 1 0	
Reserved, Must Be Zero	Byte 7
Reserved, Must Be Zero	Byte 6
P DPL S 1 D/C 1 C R A	Byte 5
3rd Byte of Base Address	Byte 4
2nd Byte of Base Address	Byte 3
1st Byte of Virtual Base Address	Byte 2
2nd Byte of Segment Size	Byte 1
1st Byte of Segment Size	Byte 0

D Bit **Default** bit (bit 6 in byte 6; see picture of 32-bit code segment descriptor). Reserved and must be 0 in a 16-bit, 286 code segment.
0 = 16-bit, 286 code segment. When fetching and executing code from this segment, processor assumes a default data operand size of 16 bits and an address (offset) size of 16 bits.
1 = 32-bit code segment. When fetching and executing code from this segment, processor assumes a default data operand size of 32 bits and an address (offset) size of 32 bits.

L Bit **Long Mode** bit (bit 5 in byte 6; see picture of 64-bit code segment descriptor). This bit is reserved and must be 0 in 16- and 32-bit code segment descriptors.

P Bit Segment **Present** bit (must be 1 if the code segment is present in memory).

Reserved, Must Be Zero In a 286, 16-bit segment descriptor, bytes 6 and 7 must be zero. This has the following effects:
- Byte 6, bit 6 (the **D bit** in a 32-bit code segment descriptor) is 0, identifying this as 286, 16-bit code segment.
- Byte 6, bit 5 (the **Long bit** in a 64-bit code segment descriptor) is 0, identifying this as either a 16- or 32-bit code segment descriptor (as defined by byte 6, bit 6).

DPL Field **Descriptor Privilege Level** (0-3). Defines privilege level of code in this segment (CPL it will run at).
00 = Privilege level 0 (most privileged).
01 = Privilege level 1.
10 = Privilege level 2.
11 = Privilege level 3.

S Bit **System** bit.
0 = OS data structure descriptor.
1 = Must be 1 in a code segment descriptor.

D/C **Data/Code** bit. Must be 1 for a code segment.
0 = Data Segment
1 = Code Segment.

C Bit **Conforming** bit. Set to 1 if code segment is conforming.

R Bit **Readable** bit.
0 = execute-only; Segment contains only code (no data).
1 = Segment contains code and data which may be read. No writes allowed.

A Bit **Accessed** bit. Set to 1 by the processor when a code segment is accessed.

Accessing the Code Segment

Unless the logical processor is halted or in a non-execution low-power state its instruction fetch logic continually reads the predicted code stream from the currently-active code segment, translates it into the native instruction set (i.e., micro-ops) and feeds it into the instruction pipeline for probable execution (assuming branch instructions are predicted correctly).

In-Line Code Fetching

The majority of the instructions comprising a typical program do not cause a branch to another location in the same or a different CS. Unconditional branches are fairly rare and, due to the performance hit taken by a logical processor when a conditional branch's resolution is mispredicted, well-written programs contain a minimal number of conditional branches. As a result, most of the time the logical processor's instruction fetch logic performs in-line code fetching, repeatedly incrementing the instruction pointer to point to the next sequential instruction in the currently-active CS. While performing in-line code fetches, the logical processor's instruction fetch logic forms the address of the next instruction as follows:

1. Uses the address in the CS:IP or CS:EIP register pair to read the next instruction from memory.
2. Adjusts the pointer in IP or EIP to point to the start address of the next instruction.
3. Go back to step 1. Repeat until one of the following occurs:
   — An unconditional branch is encountered (this would include a branch due to the execution of a RET or IRET instruction at the end of a called procedure or an event handler).
   — A conditional branch is predicted to be taken.
   — An interrupt or exception is recognized (causing a far branch).
   — An automatic task switch occurs (but virtually no modern OSs utilize the x86 hardware-based task switching mechanism).

Short and Near Branches (Jumps and Calls)

General

When the logical processor encounters a short or near jump (conditional or unconditional), the CS selector in the CS register remains unchanged (because it is a branch within the currently-active CS). The specified branch target address consists solely of a new address (offset) within the current code segment and replaces the offset address currently in the IP or EIP register. The logical processor then, as always, uses the CS:IP or CS:EIP register pair to generate the virtual address of the next instruction (i.e., the instruction that resides at the branch target address).

Example Near Jump

Consider the following unconditional near jump instruction:

```
jmp 13A20009
```

The programmer has specified an offset—13A20009h—within the current code segment as the branch target address of this unconditional jump. In response:

1. The logical processor compares the specified offset to the size, or limit, of the currently-active CS to ensure that the branch target address is within the bounds of the currently active CS (the CS's base address, size and attributes are stored in the invisible portion of the CS register).
2. If the target location is within segment bounds, the logical processor loads the specified offset into the EIP register and adds it to the CS base address to yield the virtual address of the branch's target location.
3. It then resumes code fetching at the new location.

Far Branches (Far Jumps and Calls)

General

When the logical processor encounters a far Jump or a far Call instruction (a branch to a location in a different CS), the 16-bit selector in the CS register is replaced by the one specified in the far Jump's or Call's branch target address. As a result:

1. The logical processor reads the newly-selected CS descriptor from the GDT or LDT.
2. The privilege check is performed (see "Privilege Checking" on page 436) to determine that the code in the original CS has sufficient privilege to jump to or call code within the target CS.
3. The offset portion of the branch target address—i.e., the offset within the newly-specified CS—is compared to the size, or limit, specified in the target CS's descriptor to ensure that the branch target address is within the bounds of the target CS.

4. Assuming that both the privilege check and the bounds check succeed, the logical processor loads the target CS descriptor into the invisible portion of the CS register and the offset portion of the address into the IP or EIP register.

5. The logical processor then, as always, uses the CS:IP or CS:EIP register pair to generate the virtual address of the next instruction (i.e., the instruction that resides at the branch target address).

Example Far Jump

In the following example, the instruction is a far jump to a location within a different CS.

```
jmp 00d0:00000003
```

Since this is an attempt to transfer control to a different code segment, the logical processor must first verify that the currently executing program is permitted to access the location in the new code segment. To do this, it must read the new code segment descriptor from memory and compare its Descriptor Privilege Level (DPL) to the CPL of the currently running program. The 16-bit segment selector 00d0h is placed in the CS register (see Figure 14-5 on page 426) selecting GDT entry 26 (the index field is binarily-weighted). Figure 14-4 on page 426 illustrates an example code segment descriptor read from the GDT.

1. The logical processor verifies that the new segment is, in fact, a code segment (System bit = 1, and C/D = 1) and that it is present in memory (P = 1).

2. It must also determine if the currently executing program is sufficiently privileged to call or jump to the targeted code segment. This subject is covered in "Privilege Checking" on page 436.

3. It checks the specified target offset, 00000003h, to determine if it exceeds the limit (size) of the selected CS. The segment size is 126525d bytes (the Granularity bit = 0, indicating that the size is specified in bytes, rather than in 4KB pages).

4. If all tests pass, it loads the new segment descriptor into the invisible part of the CS register, adds the specified offset (00000003h) to the code segment's base address (00131BCCh) and fetches the next instruction from the target address—00131BCFh.

Figure 14-4: Sample Code Segment Descriptor

Upper byte of Base Address 0 0 0 0 0 0 0 0	Byte 7
G D Avl **Upper digit of Limit** 0 1 0 0 0 0 0 1	Byte 6
P DPL S D/C C R A 1 1 1 1 1 0 0 1	Byte 5
3rd byte of Base Address 0 0 0 1 0 0 1 1	Byte 4
2nd byte of Base Address 0 0 0 1 1 0 1 1	Byte 3
1st byte of Base Address 1 1 0 0 1 1 0 0	Byte 2
2nd byte of Limit 1 1 1 0 1 1 1 0	Byte 1
1st byte of Limit 0 0 1 1 1 1 0 1	Byte 0

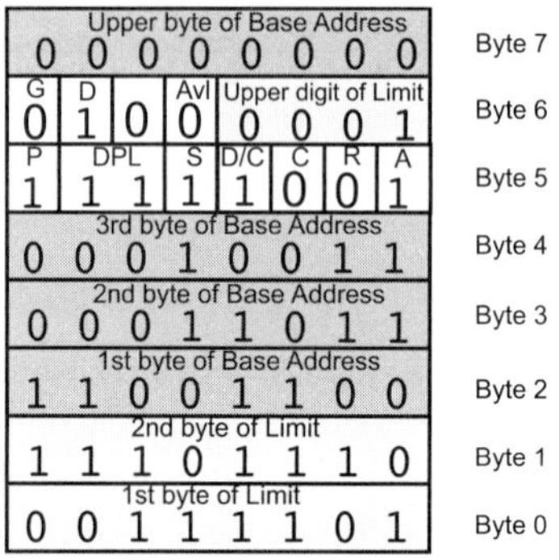

Segment Base Address   Segment base address = 00131BCCh.

Size   Limit = 1EE3Dh (126,525) and G = 0 indicating size is in bytes rather than 4KB pages.

D Bit   In code segment, *D*efault bit defines default size of operands and effective addresses.
1 = 32-bit default operand and address length.

AVL Bit   Available for use by system software.

P Bit   Segment Present bit (must be 1 if the code segment is present in memory).

DPL Field   Descriptor Privilege Level = 3.

S Bit   System bit. When 0, indicates system segment. Must be 1 in a code segment descriptor.

D/C   Data/Code bit: 1 = code segment.

C Bit   Conforming bit. 0 = code segment is non-conforming. Procedures in this segment can only be called by programs with same privilege or through a Call Gate.

R Bit   Readable bit. 0 = execute-only segment.

A Bit   Accessed bit. Set to 1 by the processor the first time the the code segment is accessed.

Figure 14-5: Example Value in CS Register

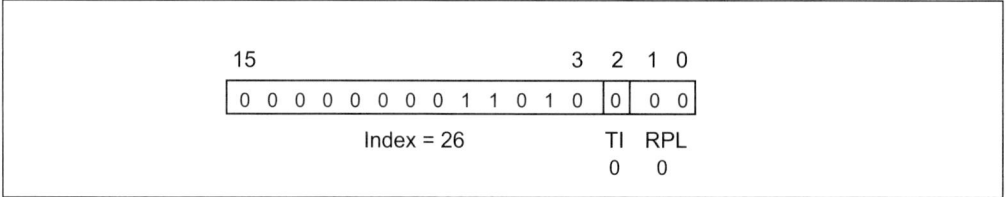

Short/Near Jumps

General

A short or near jump instruction cannot cause a jump to a location in another code segment (i.e., a far jump). Rather, it causes a branch to another location within the currently active code segment. There are two basic forms:

*   Unconditional short/near branches.
*   Conditional pointer-relative branches.

These two forms are described in the following sections.

No Privilege Check

A call or a jump to a location within the same code segment does not require a privilege check because, by definition, all code within a code segment runs at the same privilege level.

Unconditional Short/Near Branches

There are three forms of unconditional branches (see Table 14-3 on page 428) that branch to locations within the same code segment:

*   The **short instruction pointer-relative jump** unconditionally branches to the address calculated by adding the 8-bit positive or negative immediate value included as part of the instruction to the current address in the Instruction Pointer register. This permits a jump backwards -128 locations or forward 127 locations.
*   The **near instruction pointer-relative jump** unconditionally branches to the address calculated by adding the 16-bit or 32-bit positive or negative immediate value included as part of the instruction to the current address in the Instruction Pointer register.
*   The **near indirect jump** unconditionally branches to the address specified in a 16- or 32-bit register or memory-based operand.

Table 14-3: Short/Near Jump Forms

Jump Type	Opcode	Effective Operand Size	Description
Jmp *rel8*	EB	16-bit	Jump to IP ± 8-bit signed displacement included as part of the instruction.
		32-bit	Jump to EIP ± 8-bit signed displacement included as part of the instruction.
Jmp *rel16* or *rel32*	E9	16-bit	Jump to IP ± 32-bit signed displacement included as part of the instruction.
		32-bit	Jump to EIP ± 32-bit signed displacement included as part of the instruction.
Jmp *r/m*	FF /4	16-bit	Jump indirect to the location (in the current code segment) specified by the 2-byte offset in the indicated 16-bit register or memory operand.
		32-bit	Jump indirect to the location (in the current code segment) specified by the 4-byte offset in the indicated 32-bit register or memory operand.

Note: FF /4 represents the 1-byte opcode FF wherein the ModRM byte's Operand 2 field (i.e., the REG field) = 4 (100b) and acts as a 3-bit extension of the opcode to select the Jmp r/m instruction. Refer to Figure 7-10 on page 182.

Conditional Branches

General

Upon execution of a conditional branch instruction, the logical processor tests the state of one or more of the following status bits in the Eflags register:

- **CF**. Carry bit.
- **OF**. Overflow bit.

- **PF.** Parity bit.
- **SF.** Sign bit.
- **ZF.** Zero bit.

The bits to be tested and the overall condition to be tested for (true or false) are referred to as the *condition code* (cc) and are specified by the least-significant 4-bits (referred to as the *tttn* field; see Table 14-4 on page 429) in the primary (i.e., the last) opcode byte:

- If the condition is not satisfied, the jump is not performed and execution falls through to the next instruction.
- If the specified condition is met, the logical processor jumps to the address (in the current code segment) which is specified as a negative or positive displacement from the current address in the Instruction Pointer register. The displacement is included as either an 8- or 32-bit displacement encoded within the instruction.

Two conditional branch instructions differ from the others; rather than testing the flag bits, they test the contents of the ECX or CX register. If the register contains zero, the branch is taken, else it is not. This is useful at the beginning of a program loop that terminates with a conditional Loop instruction (such as LoopNE; see "Loop Instructions" on page 431). It can prevent the logical processor from entering a loop when the initial value of ECX or CX on entry to the loop is already at 0, thus erroneously causing the loop to execute 2^{32} or 2^{16} times (rather than 0 times).

All conditional branches cause a code fetch of one or two cache lines, regardless of the specified branch address or the cacheability of the target memory area (but the lines are not cached if the memory area is uncacheable).

Table 14-5 on page 430 provides a description of the various forms of the conditional branch instruction.

Table 14-4: Condition Code Encoding in Least-Significant Primary Opcode Byte

tttn	Mnemonic	Condition
0000	O	Overflow
0001	NO	No overflow
0010	B, NAE	Below, Not above or equal

Table 14-4: Condition Code Encoding in Least-Significant Primary Opcode Byte (Continued)

tttn	Mnemonic	Condition
0011	NB, AE	Not below, Above or equal
0100	E, Z	Equal, Zero
0101	NE, NZ	Not equal, Not zero
0110	BE, NA	Below or equal, Not above
0111	NBE, A	Not below or equal, Above
1000	S	Sign bit = negative
1001	NS	Sign bit = positive
1010	P, PE	Even parity
1011	NP, PO	Odd parity
1100	L, NGE	Less than, Not greater than or equal to
1101	NL, GE	Not less than, Greater than or equal to
1110	LE, NG	Less than or equal to, Not greater than
1111	NLE, G	Not less than or equal to, Greater than

Table 14-5: Conditional Branch Forms

Opcode(s)	Effective Operand Size	Branch Target Address Computation
70 to 7F Jump Short	16-bit	• Branch target address = IP + signed 8-bit displacement. • Upper 16-bits of EIP are cleared to 0.
	32-bit	Branch target address = EIP + signed 8-bit displacement.

Table 14-5: Conditional Branch Forms (Continued)

Opcode(s)	Effective Operand Size	Branch Target Address Computation
0F 80 to 0F 8F Jump Near	16-bit	• Branch target address = IP + signed 16-bit displacement. • It should be noted, however, that the displacement field encoded in the instruction is a 32-bit displacement (with the upper 16-bits cleared to 0).
	32-bit	Branch target address = EIP + signed 32-bit displacement.
E3	16-bit	• Jump if CX register = 0. • Branch target address = IP + signed 8-bit displacement. • Upper 16-bits of EIP cleared to 0.
	32-bit	• Jump if ECX register = 0. • Branch target address = EIP + signed 8-bit displacement.

Loop Instructions

The Loop instructions are a special form of conditional branch. There are three basic forms (see below and Table 14-6 on page 432):

- **Loop**. Consider the following code fragment (it assumes an effective operand size of 32-bits):

```
              mov   ecx, eax   ;move loop count to ecx
      begin:  sub   ebx, 5
              add   edx, ebx
              loop begin         ;ecx-1, loop if not 0
```

Each time the Loop instruction is executed, the logical processor decrements the count in the ECX register. If the count is not yet exhausted (not 0), it jumps back to the beginning of the loop. If exhausted, it exits the program loop and falls through to the next instruction. It should be noted that if the initial contents of ECX is 0, the Loop instruction will decrement it to FFFFFFFFh, test for 0 and loop back. The loop will be executed 2^{32} times before it is exited.

- **LoopE**. Operates the same as the Loop, except that it also tests the ZF flag. If ECX != 0 and the ZF flag = 1, it branches back to the start of the loop. If ECX = 0 OR the ZF flag = 0, it exits the loop and falls through to the next instruction.
- **LoopNE**. Operates the same as the LoopE, except it exits the loop if the ZF flag = 1.

Table 14-6: Loop Instruction Forms

Loop Type	Opcode	Effective *Address* Size	Description
			• In all forms, a GP exception is generated if the branch is taken and the effective branch target address < CS base address or > segment limit. • The effective address size chooses the count register width.
Loop *rel8*	E2	16-bit	Decrements the CX register. If CX = 0, it falls through to the next instruction, otherwise: • **If operand size = 16-bits**, branch target address (start of loop) = EIP ± (8-bit immediate value embedded in the instruction sign-extended to 16-bits) and then clear upper 16-bits of EIP to 0. • **If operand size = 32-bits**, branch target address (start of loop) = EIP ± (8-bit immediate value embedded in the instruction sign-extended to 32-bits).
		32-bit	Decrements the ECX register. If ECX = 0, it falls through to the next instruction, otherwise: • **If operand size = 16-bits**, branch target address (start of loop) = EIP ± (8-bit immediate value embedded in the instruction sign-extended to 16-bits) and then clear upper 16-bits of EIP to 0. • **If operand size = 32-bits**, branch target address (start of loop) = EIP ± (8-bit immediate value embedded in the instruction sign-extended to 32-bits).

Table 14-6: Loop Instruction Forms (Continued)

Loop Type	Opcode	Effective *Address* Size	Description
LoopE *rel8*	E1	16-bit	Decrements CX register. If CX != 0 *and* the ZF flag = 1, it branches back to the start of the loop. If CX = 0 *or* the ZF flag = 0, it exits the loop and falls through to the next instruction. • **If operand size = 16-bits**, branch target address (start of loop) = EIP ± (8-bit immediate value embedded in the instruction sign-extended to 16-bits) and then clear upper 16-bits of EIP to 0. • **If operand size = 32-bits**, branch target address (start of loop) = EIP ± (8-bit immediate value embedded in the instruction sign-extended to 32-bits).
		32-bit	Decrements ECX register. If ECX != 0 *and* the ZF flag = 1, it branches back to the start of the loop. If CX = 0 *or* the ZF flag = 0, it exits the loop and falls through to the next instruction. • **If operand size = 16-bits**, branch target address (start of loop) = EIP ± (8-bit immediate value embedded in the instruction sign-extended to 16-bits) and then clear upper 16-bits of EIP to 0. • **If operand size = 32-bits**, branch target address (start of loop) = EIP ± (8-bit immediate value embedded in the instruction sign-extended to 32-bits).

Table 14-6: Loop Instruction Forms (Continued)

Loop Type	Opcode	Effective *Address* Size	Description
LoopNE *rel8*	E0	16-bit	Decrements CX register. If CX != 0 *and* the ZF flag = 0, it branches back to the start of the loop. If CX = 0 *or* the ZF flag = 1, it exits the loop and falls through to the next instruction. • **If operand size = 16-bits**, branch target address (start of loop) = EIP ± (8-bit immediate value embedded in the instruction sign-extended to 16-bits) and then clear upper 16-bits of EIP to 0. • **If operand size = 32-bits**, branch target address (start of loop) = EIP ± (8-bit immediate value embedded in the instruction sign-extended to 32-bits).
		32-bit	Decrements ECX register. If ECX != 0 *and* the ZF flag = 0, it branches back to the start of the loop. If CX = 0 *or* the ZF flag = 1, it exits the loop and falls through to the next instruction. • **If operand size = 16-bits**, branch target address (start of loop) = EIP ± (8-bit immediate value embedded in the instruction sign-extended to 16-bits) and then clear upper 16-bits of EIP to 0. • **If operand size = 32-bits**, branch target address (start of loop) = EIP ± (8-bit immediate value embedded in the instruction sign-extended to 32-bits).

Unconditional Far Jumps

The Privilege Check

Unlike a short or near jump, a privilege check (see "Privilege Checking" on page 436) is performed before a far jump instruction is permitted to transfer control to a location in another code segment.

Far Jump Targets

The 16-bit CS portion of the branch target address specified as the far jump instruction's operand may select one of the following types of descriptors:

- **A CS descriptor in the GDT or LDT.** In this case, assuming the privilege test passes, the logical processor jumps to the location (offset) in the target code segment specified by the branch target address.
- **A Task Gate descriptor in the GDT or LDT.** In this case, the logical processor discards the offset portion of the branch target address and an automatic task switch is triggered to the task associated with the TSS descriptor pointed to by the selected Task Gate (note: most modern OSs do not use the automatic task switching mechanism).
- **A TSS descriptor in the GDT.** In this case, the logical processor discards the offset portion of the branch target address and an automatic task switch is triggered to the task associated with the selected TSS descriptor (note: most modern OSs do not use the automatic task switching mechanism).
- **A Call Gate descriptor in the GDT or LDT.** In this case, assuming the privilege tests pass, the logical processor discards the offset portion of the branch target address and jumps to the address contained in the Call Gate.

Far Jump Forms

There are two forms of unconditional far branches (see Table 14-7 on page 436) that branch to locations within a different code segment.

- The **Jmp ptr** instruction form causes the logical processor to jump to the branch target address (in another code segment) specified by the 4-byte (CS:IP) or 6-byte (CS:EIP) pointer embedded within the instruction itself.
- The **Jmp indirect memory** form causes the logical processor to jump to the branch target address (in another code segment) specified by the 4- or 6-byte pointer stored in the specified memory operand.

Table 14-7: Far Jump Forms

Call Type	Opcode	Effective Operand Size	Description
Jmp *ptr*	EA	16-bits	Jump to the 4-byte address embedded in the instruction: 2-bytes are loaded into the CS register and 2 are loaded into the IP register. The upper 16-bits of EIP are cleared to 0.
		32-bits	Jump to the 6-byte address embedded in the instruction: 2-bytes are loaded into the CS register and 4 are loaded into the EIP register.
Jmp *indirect memory*	FF /5	16-bits	Jump to the 4-byte address contained in the specified memory operand: 2-bytes are loaded into the CS register and 2 are loaded into the IP register. The upper 16-bits of EIP are cleared to 0.
		32-bits	Jump to the 6-byte address contained in the specified memory operand: 2-bytes are loaded into the CS register and 4 are loaded into the EIP register.

Note: FF /5 represents the 1-byte opcode FF wherein the ModRM byte's Operand 2 field (i.e., the REG field) = 5 (101b) and acts as a 3-bit extension of the opcode to select the Jmp mem instruction. Refer to Figure 7-10 on page 182.

Privilege Checking

No Check on Near Calls or Near Jumps

A call or a jump to a location within the same code segment does not require a privilege check because, by definition, all code within a code segment runs at the same privilege level.

General

The privilege checking mechanism ensures that the currently executing program cannot access a procedure in another code segment unless permitted to do so. Any attempt to do so results in a General Protection (GP) exception.

Definitions

Before permitting access to code in a different code segment, the logical processor must verify that the currently executing program has sufficient privilege. The three components involved in this comparison are:

- The CPL (Current Privilege Level) of the currently executing program.
- The RPL (Requester Privilege Level) field in the CS portion of the branch target address.
- The DPL (Descriptor Privilege Level) field in the code segment descriptor of the target code segment.

Definition of a Task

A task doesn't necessarily consist of just one set of code and data segments. At any time during task execution, the programmer can select a different code segment and/or data segments (by placing a new 16-bit segment selector value in the appropriate segment register). A task may consist of a number of program segments and data segments. Examples of tasks would be applications such as FrameMaker, Microsoft Word, etc. We tend to think of each of these as a program, when in fact each typically consists of a group of programs that interact with each other to accomplish the overall task. The programs that comprise an application may reside in the same code segment, or may be distributed throughout a number of code segments in memory.

Definition of a Procedure

The term *procedure* refers to a function or routine that may be called (using a near or far Call instruction).

CPL Definition

With one exception, the Current Privilege Level (CPL) is defined as the privilege level (i.e., the DPL) of the currently-active CS from which instructions are being fetched (i.e., the CPL = the DPL of the active code segment).

This is true unless the code currently executing resides in a Conforming code segment (the C bit in the CS descriptor = 1). In that case the logical processor's CPL while executing a procedure in a Conforming CS = the DPL of the code that called the procedure. Conforming and Non-Conforming code segments are described in the section entitled "Conforming and Non-Conforming Code Segments" on page 438.

CS DPL Definition

Each CS descriptor (see Figure 14-2 on page 421) contains:

- A 2-bit Descriptor Privilege Level (DPL) field,
- and a bit (the C bit) that identifies the code segment as either:
  — A Non-Conforming (C = 0) or
  — A Conforming (C = 1) code segment.

Together, these two fields define the minimum privilege level a program residing in another CS must have in order to successfully jump to or call code in a CS.

Conforming and Non-Conforming Code Segments

Definition. Non-Conforming code segments are far more common than Conforming code segments. The definitions of both follow:

— **Non-Conforming (can only be entered by an equal)**. A CS with C = 0 is a Non-Conforming CS. Code within it can only be jumped to or called successfully if the CPL of the code attempting the far call or far jump is the same as the target code segment's DPL (i.e., CPL = DPL).
— **Conforming (I'll lower myself to your level)**. A code segment with C = 1 is a Conforming code segment. Code in a Conforming code segment can be jumped to or called by programs whose CPL is the same as or less privileged than the target segment's DPL. Furthermore, the logical processor then executes the code in the conforming code segment at the same privilege level as that of the program that called it. In other words, the code in the conforming code segment "conforms to" or assumes the privilege level of the program that called it. The CPL remains the same as that of the calling program.

Examples. As an example, if the CPL of the currently active CS = 2, code within the active CS may successfully perform a direct call or jump to either of the following:

— Non-Conforming code segment with a DPL = 2.
— Conforming code segment with a privilege level (i.e., a DPL) of 0, 1 or 2.

It cannot jump to or call code in either of the following without causing a GP exception:

— A Non-Conforming code segment whose DPL != the CPL (CPL = 2).
— A Conforming code segment with a privilege level (i.e., a DPL) of 3.

RPL Definition

General. The RPL (Requester Privilege Level) consists of the lower 2-bits in the CS portion of a far branch target address and serves two purposes:

— It is used in the privilege level check to determine if the call or jump is allowed.
— It is also checked when a RET or IRET is executed.

These two topics are described in the next two sections.

RPL Usage in Privilege Check. When a far call or a far jump is executed, the RPL indicates the privilege level of the software that created the far branch target address:

— As an example, assume a privilege level 2 program creates a 6-byte pointer to a procedure (one in another CS) in CS:EIP form. It sets the RPL field in the CS portion of the pointer to its own privilege level (2) indicating that the pointer was created by a privilege level 2 entity and stores the pointer in memory.
— Assume that it then performs a far call to a different procedure in another CS (let's say a privilege level 3 CS) and passes the pointer to it as a parameter.
— The called privilege level 3 procedure may then, in turn, execute a far call using the 6-byte pointer that was passed to it. In this case, the CPL of the caller is 3 and the RPL in the called procedure's branch target address (the privilege level of the entity that created the pointer) is 2.
— Before permitting the procedure call to proceed, the privilege check logic must compare both of the following to the DPL of the target CS:
    – The CPL of the caller (3, in this case),
    – As well as the privilege level of the pointer creator (2, in this case; the RPL specified in the CS portion of the branch target address),
— A detailed description of this privilege check can be found in "Privilege Check on Far Call or Far Jmp" on page 440.

RPL Use on RET or IRET. When a RET (Return) or an IRET (Interrupt Return) instruction is executed at the end of a called procedure or an interrupt or exception handler, the logical processor must determine whether it is returning to the same or to a different privilege level.

— **Return to same privilege level**. If it's returning to code that executes at the same privilege level, the logical processor pops the return address from the current stack into the CS:IP or CS:EIP register pair.

— **Return to different privilege level**. If, on the other hand, it is returning to a different, less-privileged level, the logical processor must first restore the pointer to the caller's stack by popping the caller's SS:SP or SS:ESP from the current stack, after which it then pops the return address from the current stack into the CS:IP or CS:EIP register pair. More information can be found in "Automatic Stack Switch" on page 462.

When the RET or IRET is executed, the RPL field in the 16-bit value popped into the CS register indicates the privilege level being returned to. This is compared to the CPL in force when the RET or IRET is executed to make this determination.

Privilege Check on Far Call or Far Jmp

General

The privilege check is only performed when an attempt is made to jump to or call code in a different code segment. As mentioned earlier, no check is performed when the branch target address is within the same code segment. Refer to Figure 14-6 on page 441.

Example

1. Assume that the currently executing program's CPL = 2.
2. A far jump or call is executed specifying a new CS selector wherein the RPL = 3. In other words, the address of the procedure to be called or jumped to was passed to a procedure in the currently-active privilege level 2 CS by code residing in a privilege level 3 CS.
3. In this example, the target code segment of the jump or call is a Non-Conforming code segment with a DPL = 2 (so the call or jump will only succeed if the caller's *effective* privilege level = 2).
4. Refer to Figure 14-6 on page 441. While the caller's CPL (2) = the called procedure's DPL (2), the access attempt nevertheless results in a GP exception

because the RPL (3) specified in the branch target address indicates that branch target address was created by a privilege level 3 procedure (which is not privileged enough to have direct access to a Non-Conforming privilege level 2 procedure).

Figure 14-6: Privilege Check on Far Call or Jmp

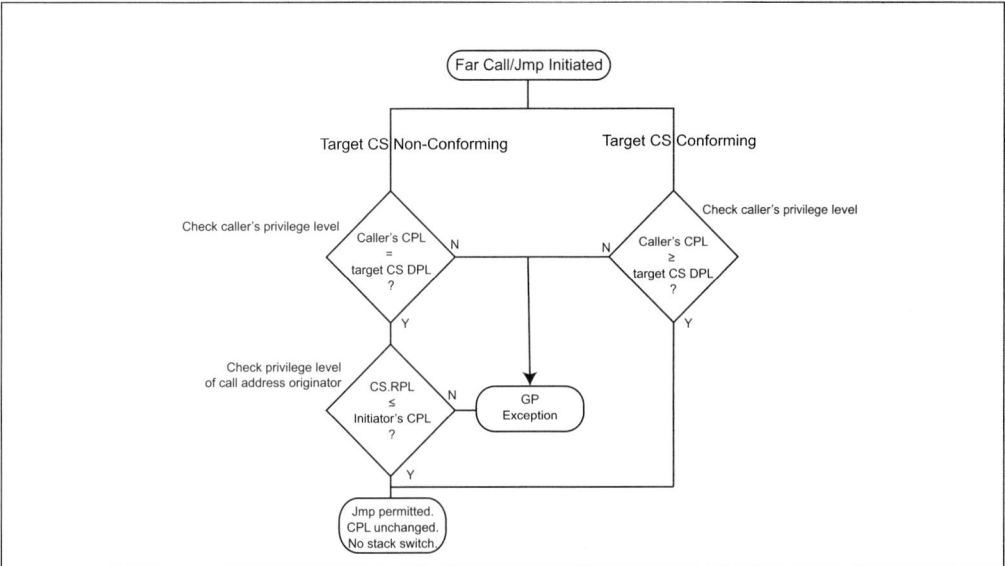

Jumping from a Higher-to-Lesser Privileged Program

The x86 processor architecture doesn't support jumping or calling from a more-privileged program to one that executes at a less-privileged level. It can, however, be done using the hardware-based task switching mechanism, but, due to the inefficiency of hardware-based task switching, modern OSs do not use it. So how does the OS scheduler (which executes at privilege level 0) start or resume an application program (which executes at privilege level 3)? It is accomplished by simulating a return from an exception handler using the following procedure:

1. Push the initial values to be loaded into the target application's CS:EIP, SS:ESP, and Eflags registers onto the kernel's stack. The CS and SS selector values pushed onto the stack must point to GDT entries that describe the application program's code and stack segments.

2. Execute the IRET (Interrupt Return) instruction. Note that the IRET instruction normally only pops CS:EIP and Eflags from the stack when executed at the end of an interrupt handler. However, if the RPL (Requester Privilege Level; see "RPL Definition" on page 439) of the CS selector value on the stack indicates that we are switching back to a lesser privilege level (3) than the CPL of the kernel task (0), SS:ESP are also loaded from the stack.
3. The new CS selector loaded into the CS register selects the application program's code segment descriptor which has a DPL of 3. As a result, the logical processor sets the CPL to 3. EIP is loaded from the stack as well.
4. The values loaded into the SS:ESP register pair from the kernel stack points to the top of the privilege level 3 stack pre-allocated by the OS for the use of the application program.

Direct Procedure Calls

Introduction

A *direct procedure call* refers to a call which specifies as its operand the branch target address of the called procedure. Alternatively, a far call may select as its target a Call Gate descriptor in the GDT or LDT. When this is the case, the actual branch target address of the called procedure (in segment:offset format) is contained within the selected Call Gate descriptor. This is, in effect, an indirect far call and is described in detail in "Indirect Procedure Far Call Through a Call Gate" on page 452.

General

When a Call instruction is executed, the logical processor:

1. First marks its place in the currently executing program by pushing the current Instruction Pointer (which at that point has already been incremented to point to the beginning of the instruction that immediately follows the Call) onto the stack.
2. It then loads the Instruction Pointer register with the start address of the called procedure and initiates execution at that address.
3. At the conclusion of the called procedure, the final instruction, a RET (Return), causes the logical processor to pop the return address from the stack back into the instruction pointer register. It then resumes execution at the instruction immediately following the Call.

Basically, there are two scenarios:

- **Near Call**. The called procedure resides in the same code segment as the caller. This is referred to as a near call. In this case, the return address pushed onto the stack consists only of the contents of the Instruction Pointer register.
- **Far Call**. The called procedure resides in a different code segment than the caller. This is referred to as a far call. In this case, the return address pushed onto the stack consists of the contents of both the CS register and the Instruction Pointer register.

The following two sections describe the various forms of near calls and far calls.

Near Calls/Returns

Description

A near Call instruction calls a procedure in the same code segment and, as such, need only specify the branch target address in the form of a new:

- 16-bit offset (if it's a 16-bit 286-compliant code segment) or
- 32-bit offset (if it's a 32-bit 386-compliant code segment) within the current code segment.

Since the target address is within the same code segment, there is no privilege check. The behavior of the Call instruction depends on the operand size in effect when the instruction is executed. There are four possibilities:

Case 1: Near 16-bit call within a 16-bit CS. The near Call instruction resides in a 16-bit, 286-compliant code segment (the D bit in the CS descriptor = 0) and the instruction is not preceded by the Operand Size Override prefix. In this case, the effective operand size is 16-bits:
- **The Push**. Since the effective operand size is 16-bits, the logical processor performs a 2-byte push to save the contents of the IP register (the return address) to the stack.
- **The Jump**. The 16-bit branch target address is loaded into the IP register and the upper 16-bits of the EIP register are cleared to 0. The logical processor initiates execution of the called procedure.
- **The Return**. At the end of the called procedure, the RET instruction (without the Operand Size Override prefix) is executed, causing the logical processor to pop the 2-byte return address from the stack into the IP register. The upper 16-bits of the EIP register are cleared to 0.

Case 2: Near 32-bit call within a 16-bit CS. The near Call instruction resides in a 16-bit, 286-compliant code segment (the D bit in the CS descriptor = 0) and the instruction is preceded by the Operand Size Override prefix. In this case, the effective operand size (i.e., the size of the branch target address) is 32-bits:

— **The Push**. Since the effective operand size is 32-bits, the logical processor performs a 4-byte push to save the contents of the EIP register (the return address) to the stack.

— **The Jump**. The 32-bit branch target address is loaded into the EIP register and the logical processor initiates execution of the called procedure.

— **The Return**. At the end of the called procedure, the RET instruction (with the Operand Size Override prefix) is executed, causing the logical processor to pop the 4-byte return address from the stack into the EIP register.

It should be stressed that, in this case, due to the 64KB size limitation of 16-bit code segments, the 32-bit branch target address must not be greater than FFFFh.

Case 3: Near 32-bit call within 32-bit CS. The near Call instruction resides in a 32-bit code segment (the D bit in the CS descriptor = 1) and the instruction is not preceded by the Operand Size Override prefix. In this case, the effective operand size is 32-bits:

— **The Push**. Since the effective operand size is 32-bits, the logical processor performs a 4-byte push to save the contents of the EIP register (the return address) to the stack.

— **The Jump**. The 32-bit branch target address is loaded into the EIP register. The logical processor initiates execution of the called procedure.

— **The Return**. At the end of the called procedure, the RET instruction (without the Operand Size Override prefix) is executed, causing the logical processor to pop the 4-byte return address from the stack into the EIP register.

Case 4: Near 16-bit call within 32-bit CS. The near Call instruction resides in a 32-bit code segment (the D bit in the CS descriptor = 1) and the instruction is preceded by the Operand Size Override prefix. In this case, the effective operand size is 16-bits:

— **The Push**. Since the effective operand size is 16-bits, the logical processor performs a 2-byte push to save the contents of the IP register (the return address) to the stack.

— **The Jump**. The 16-bit branch target address is loaded into the IP register and the upper 16-bits of the EIP register are cleared to 0. The logical processor initiates execution of the called procedure.

— **The Return**. At the end of the called procedure, the RET instruction (with the Operand Size Override prefix) is executed, causing the logical processor to pop the 2-byte return address from the stack into the IP register. The upper 16-bits of the EIP register are cleared to 0.

It should be stressed that, in this case, due to the clearing of the upper 16-bits of the EIP register both the far call and the called procedure must reside in the lower 64KB of the 32-bit code segment.

Call/Ret Operand Size Matching

To ensure proper stack management, the programmer must ensure that the size of the push (2- or 4-bytes) performed by the near call is matched by the size of the pop (2- or 4-bytes) performed by the RET at the end of the called procedure. In other words, make sure that the effective operand size for both instructions match.

Near Call/Return Forms

Table 14-8 on page 445 describes the two forms of the near Call instruction as well as the two forms of the near Return instruction:

- Near Call using instruction pointer-relative addressing.
- Near Call that directly specifies the branch target address within the current code segment.
- Near Return.
- Near Return with parameter deallocation.

Table 14-8: Near Call/Return Forms

Instruction Type	Opcode	Effective Operand Size	Description
Call *relative*	E8	16-bits	• Branch target address = IP ± the 16-bit signed displacement specified as part of the instruction. The upper 16-bits of the EIP register are cleared to zero. • Return address pushed onto the stack consists of the 16-bit (2-byte) content of the IP register.
		32-bits	• Branch target address = EIP ± the 32-bit signed displacement specified as part of the instruction. • Return address pushed onto the stack consists of the 32-bit (4-byte) content of the EIP register.

Table 14-8: Near Call/Return Forms (Continued)

Instruction Type	Opcode	Effective Operand Size	Description
Call *reg/mem*	FF /2	16-bits	• Branch target address is identified in the specified 16-bit register or 16-bit memory location. The upper 16-bits of the EIP register are cleared to zero. • Return address pushed onto the stack consists of the 16-bit (2-byte) content of the IP register.
		32-bits	• Branch target address is identified in the specified 32-bit register or 32-bit memory location. • Return address pushed onto the stack consists of the 32-bit (4-byte) content of the EIP register. *Note: this form is not supported in 64-bit Mode.*
Ret	C3	16-bits	Near Return. Pops 2-bytes from stack into IP and clears upper 16-bits of EIP to zero.
		32-bits	Near Return. Pops 4-bytes from stack into EIP.
Ret *imm16*	C2	16-bits	Near Return. • Pops 2-bytes from stack into IP and clears upper 16-bits of EIP to zero. • Adjusts stack upward *n* bytes (*n* is specified by 16-bit immediate value in instruction) to release space used by caller to pass parameters to called procedure.
		32-bits	Near Return. • Pops 4-bytes from stack into EIP. • Adjusts stack upward *n* bytes (*n* is specified by 16-bit immediate value in instruction) to release space used by caller to pass parameters to called procedure.

Table 14-8: Near Call/Return Forms (Continued)

Instruction Type	Opcode	Effective Operand Size	Description
Note: FF /2 represents the 1-byte opcode FF wherein the ModRM byte's Operand 2 field (i.e., the REG field) = 2 (010b) and acts as a 3-bit extension of the opcode to select the near Call instruction. Refer to Figure 7-10 on page 182.			

Far Calls

General

A far Call instruction calls a procedure in a different code segment and, as such, must specify the branch target address in the form of:

- A new 16- or 32-bit offset address, and
- A new 16-bit CS selector.

Far Call Forms

Table 14-9 on page 448 describes the two forms of the far Call instruction as well as the two forms of the far Return instruction (far Return with and without parameter deallocation). There are five possible scenarios when executing a far Call:

1. Calling a procedure that resides in a different code segment with the same privilege level. See "Far Call, Same Privilege Level" on page 451.
2. Calling a procedure that resides in a different code segment that is more privileged. See "Far Call to a More-Privileged Procedure" on page 451.
3. Calling a procedure in a 16-bit code segment from a 32-bit code segment. See "Far Call From 32-bit CS to 16-bit CS" on page 466.
4. Calling a procedure in a 32-bit code segment from a 16-bit code segment. See "Far Call From 16-bit CS to 32-bit CS" on page 471.
5. Calling a procedure that resides in a different task. See "Far Call to a Procedure in a Different Task" on page 452.

Table 14-9: Far Call/Return Forms

Call Type	Opcode	Effective Operand Size	Description
Call Far *ptr*	9A	16-bits	• Far call direct. • Branch target address is specified as a 4-byte value (CS:IP) contained within the instruction. *Note: this form is not supported in 64-bit Mode.*
		32-bits	• Far call direct. • Branch target address is specified as a 6-byte value (CS:EIP) contained within the instruction. *Note: this form is not supported in 64-bit Mode.*
Call Far *mem*	FF /3	16-bits	• Far call indirect. • Branch target address is specified as a 4-byte value (CS:IP) contained in the specified memory location.
		32-bits	• Far call indirect. • Branch target address is specified as a 6-byte value (CS:EIP) contained in the specified memory location.

Table 14-9: Far Call/Return Forms (Continued)

Call Type	Opcode	Effective Operand Size	Description
Ret Far	CB	16-bits	Return to caller: **If caller at same privilege level**: • Restore CS:IP from stack and resume execution of caller's code. **If caller less-privileged**: • Restore CS:IP from called procedure's stack. • Restore caller's stack (SS:SP) from called procedure's stack. • Resume execution of caller's code.
		32-bits	Return to caller: **If caller at same privilege level**: • Restore CS:EIP from stack and resume execution of caller's code. **If caller less-privileged**: • Restore CS:EIP from called procedure's stack. • Restore caller's stack (SS:ESP) from called procedure's stack. • Resume execution of caller's code.

Table 14-9: Far Call/Return Forms (Continued)

Call Type	Opcode	Effective Operand Size	Description
Ret Far *imm16*	CA	16-bits	Return to caller: **If caller at same privilege level**: • Restore CS:IP from stack. • Deallocate *n* bytes (space allocated for passed parameters) from stack (n = specified 16-bit value). • Resume caller's code. **If caller less-privileged**: • Restore CS:IP from called procedure's stack. • Restore caller's stack (SS:SP) from called procedure's stack. • Deallocate *n* bytes (space allocated for passed parameters) from stack (n = specified 16-bit value). • Resume caller's code.
		32-bits	Return to caller: **If caller at same privilege level**: • Restore CS:EIP from stack. • Deallocate *n* bytes (space allocated for passed parameters) from stack (n = specified 16-bit value). • Resume caller's code. **If caller less-privileged**: • Restore CS:EIP from called procedure's stack. • Restore caller's stack (SS:ESP) from called procedure's stack. • Deallocate *n* bytes (space allocated for passed parameters) from stack (n = specified 16-bit value). • Resume caller's code.

Note: FF /3 represents the 1-byte opcode FF wherein the ModRM byte's Operand 2 field (i.e., the REG field) = 3 (011b) and acts as a 3-bit extension of the opcode to select the far Call instruction. Refer to Figure 7-10 on page 182.

Far Call, Same Privilege Level

A far Call to a procedure that resides in a different code segment but at the same privilege level as the caller can be accomplished in one of two ways:

- **Direct branch**. The 16-bit CS selector portion of the specified branch target address selects the CS descriptor (in the GDT or LDT) that describes the target code segment. In this case, the target CS descriptor's DPL is the same as the CPL (i.e., the privilege level) of the calling program. The 16- or 32-bit offset portion of the branch target address specifies the offset of the target procedure within the target code segment. The operand size in effect when the Call is executed determines the size of the offset (16- or 32-bits) portion of the branch target address:
  1. The logical processor pushes the current contents of the CS:IP or CS:EIP register pair to the stack to save the caller's return address.
  2. The CS selector portion of the called procedure's branch target address is loaded into the CS register.
  3. The logical processor reads the selected descriptor from the GDT or LDT and performs the segment type, privilege, and attribute checks.
  4. The logical processor loads the 16- or 32-bit offset portion of the called procedure's branch target address specified by the instruction into the IP or EIP register.
  5. The logical processor begins execution of the called procedure.
- **Indirect through a Call Gate**. Alternatively, the CS selector portion of the called procedure's branch target address could select a Call Gate descriptor (in the GDT or LDT) that contains the address of the called procedure in segment:offset format. In this case, the DPL of the Call Gate would be the same as the CPL (i.e., the privilege level) of the calling program. An indirect call through a Call Gate is described in "Indirect Procedure Far Call Through a Call Gate" on page 452.

Far Call to a More-Privileged Procedure

There are two possible cases:

1. **Target resides in a Conforming code segment**. The called procedure resides in a more-privileged but Conforming code segment. This case is very similar to a far call wherein the called procedure resides in a different code segment but at the same privilege level as the caller. In this case, although the DPL of the target code segment is the same as or more-privileged than the caller's CPL, the logical processor *permits the call but doesn't change its CPL (it retains the caller's CPL)*. It executes the called procedure at the same privilege level as that of the caller.

2. **Target resides in a Non-Conforming code segment**. The called procedure resides in a more-privileged Non-Conforming code segment:

   — **Direct call won't work**. If this is attempted using a far call wherein the CS selector portion of the branch target address selects a CS descriptor with a DPL that is more privileged than the CPL of the caller, it will result in the generation of a GP exception.

   — **Must use a Call Gate**. In this case, the CS selector portion of the branch target address must select a Call Gate descriptor rather than a CS descriptor. The full branch target address of the called procedure (in segment:offset form) is contained in the Call Gate and the offset portion of the branch target address specified by the Call instruction is discarded. A full description of Call Gate operation may be found in "Indirect Procedure Far Call Through a Call Gate" on page 452.

Far Call to a Procedure in a Different Task

A far Call can trigger an automatic suspension of the current task and a switch to another task. When the called task completes and the IRET instruction is executed, this will cause another automatic task switch back to the calling task at the instruction immediately following the far Call. This topic is covered in detail in "Calling Another Task" on page 670.

In Protected Mode, the logical processor always uses the segment selector portion of the far address to access the corresponding descriptor in the GDT or LDT. The descriptor type (code segment, Call Gate, Task Gate, or TSS) and access rights determine the type of call operation to be performed.

Indirect Procedure Far Call Through a Call Gate

Example Scenario Defines the Problem

The Scenario

Refer to Figure 14-7 on page 453.

- Assume that the OS kernel includes a privilege level 0 CS containing procedures designed to handle requests from other programs.
- Some of the procedures within this code segment should only be accessible by programs executing at privilege levels 1 and 2. Any attempt to call one of these procedures by a privilege level 3 program (an application program) should be rejected (i.e., result in a GP exception).

- Other procedures within the same OS code segment are designed to handle requests from application programs (i.e., programs executing at privilege level = 3).
- The remaining procedures should only be accessible to privilege level 0 code within the OS itself.

The Problem

The problem is a code segment has one assigned privilege level (in this example, 0), which means that all procedures within this code segment execute at privilege level 0:

- If it were a **Non-Conforming CS**, any attempt to call or jump to one of these procedures by a program executing at another, less-privileged level would result in a GP exception.
- Making it a **Conforming CS** isn't the answer because then any and all procedures within this code segment could then be successfully called by programs with lower privilege levels.

Figure 14-7: Example Scenario

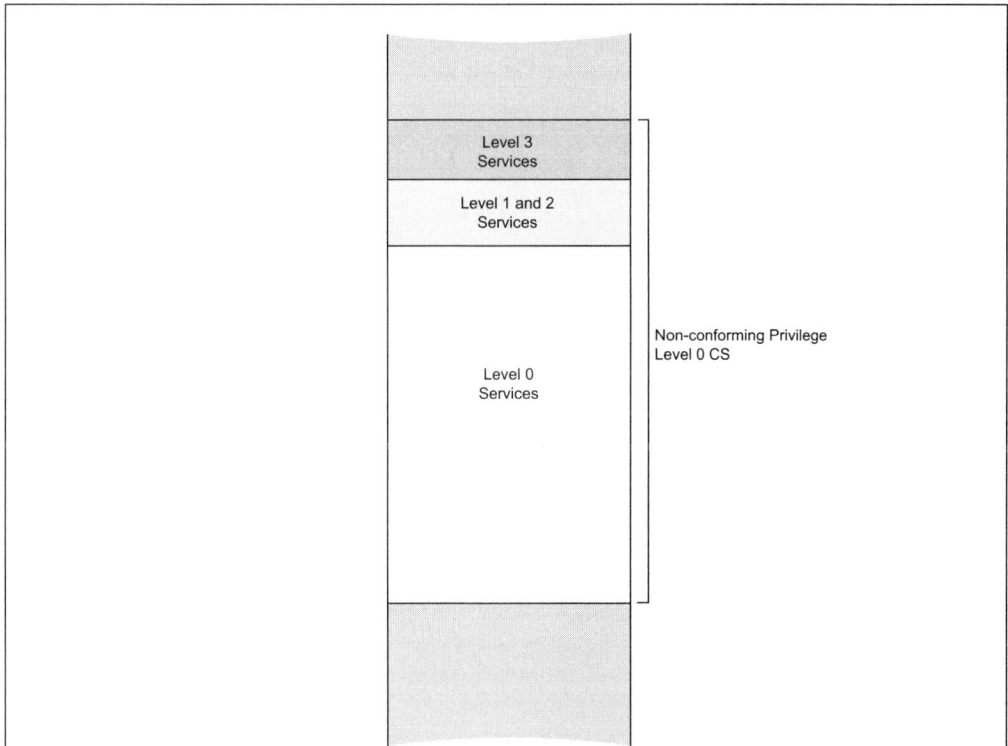

The Solution—Different Gateways

The solution is to define separate portals to control access to each procedure within the code segment. Each portal would contain the entry point of its associated procedure and would limit access to the procedure based on the privilege level of the caller. It would reject access attempts by programs executing at some privilege levels while permitting access attempts by programs executing at others. Such portals are referred to as *Call Gates*.

A Call Gate is a special form of OS descriptor which may reside in either the GDT or LDT. It may not reside within the Interrupt Descriptor Table (IDT). A Call Gate is used to transfer control to a procedure whose privilege level is the same as or more privileged than that of the calling program.

- **Far Call instructions** can use Call Gates to transfer control to procedures that execute at the same or a higher privilege level than that of the caller.
- **Far Jump instructions** can use Call Gates to transfer control:
  — To a procedure in a Non-Conforming code segment with the same privilege level as that of the far jump.
  — To code residing in a Conforming code segment that is assigned the same or a more privileged level.

A Call Gate descriptor contains an indirect pointer to the called procedure in the form of a CS:EIP (or CS:IP) pointer that identifies the target code segment and the offset of the target procedure within it.

To select a Call Gate, the programmer executes a far Call or a far Jump to load the 16-bit selector of a Call Gate descriptor into the CS register. The CS selector identifies the GDT or LDT entry containing the Call Gate descriptor, while *the offset portion of the branch target address is discarded*.

The Call Gate Descriptor

The format of a 32-bit Call Gate descriptor is illustrated in Figure 14-8 on page 456 (although there are also 286 Call Gates, it is not illustrated here). It consists of the elements described in Table 14-10 on page 455.

Table 14-10: 32-bit Call Gate Descriptor Elements

Field	Description
P	**Segment Present** bit. • 0 = descriptor contents not valid. • 1 = contents valid.
DPL	**Descriptor Privilege Level** of the Call Gate.
S	**System** descriptor bit must be 0 in a Call Gate.

X	**Call Gate Type:**
	• 0 = **16-bit Call Gate** (formatted for the 286 processor; see Figure 14-19 on page 471). A 16-bit Call Gate descriptor exhibits the following differences from a 32-bit Call Gate descriptor:
	  - The Count field indicates the number of words rather than dwords to be copied to the called procedure's stack.
	  - Bytes 6 and 7 are reserved (because 286 segments had a maximum size of 64KBs, the offset is a 16- rather than a 32-bit value).
	• 1 = **32-bit Call Gate** (formatted for processors introduced after the 286).

Byte 5, [2:0]	System descriptor **Type** field = 100b. Combined with S = 0, identifies this as a Call Gate descriptor. The X bit (bit [3] of byte 5) defines whether it is a 16- or a 32-bit Call Gate.
Dword Count	In a 32-bit Call Gate descriptor, tells the logical processor how many dword parameters to copy from the caller's stack to the stack of the called procedure (see section entitled "Automatic Stack Switch" on page 462). Please note that most OSs do not use this feature.
Selector	Identifies the CS descriptor in the GDT or LDT that contains the base address of the target code segment within which the called procedure resides.
Offset	Identifies the offset of the called procedure's entry point within the target code segment (see the previous row).

Figure 14-8: 32-bit Call Gate Descriptor Format

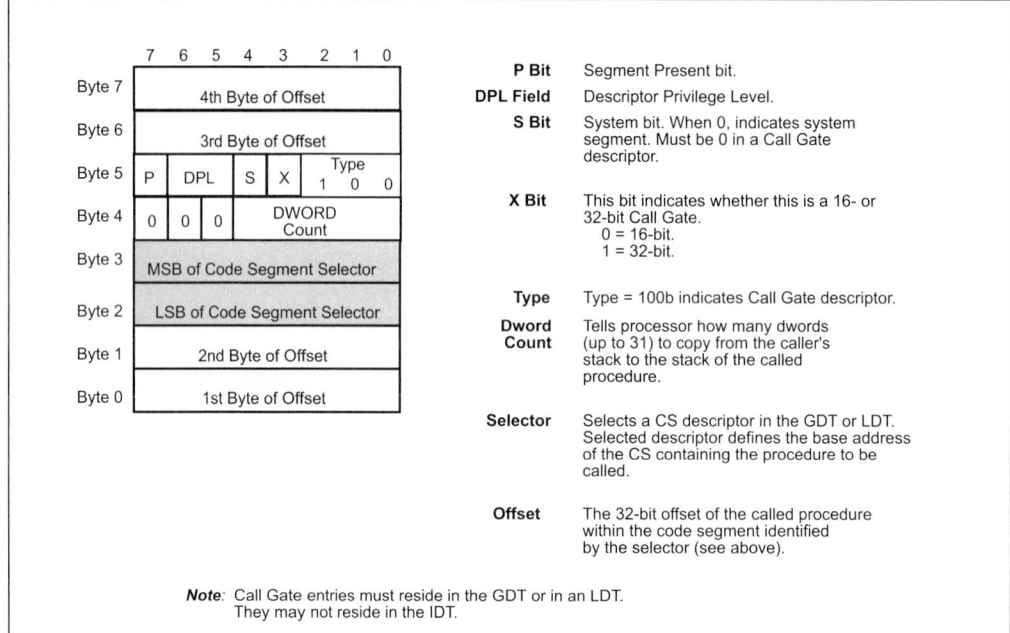

Note: Call Gate entries must reside in the GDT or in an LDT. They may not reside in the IDT.

Call Gate Example

Execution Begins

Assume that the following instruction is executed by an application program (i.e., a program executing at privilege level 3):

```
call 0067:00000000;call a privilege level 0 procedure
                   ;through the Call Gate in entry 12d
                   ;of the currently executing program's
                   ;LDT
```

Before permitting the call to take place, the logical processor must determine if this is a far call directly to a target location in a CS or a far call that selects a Call Gate descriptor in the LDT or GDT. To do this, the logical processor reads the segment descriptor identified by the segment portion (0067h) of the target address placed into the CS register. Figure 14-9 on page 457 illustrates the contents of the CS register which selects entry 12d (the index field contains Ch, or 12d) in the LDT (TI = 1). The RPL field indicates that the branch target address was originated (i.e., created) by a privilege level 3 program.

Figure 14-9: 16-bit Segment Selector in Far Call Selects LDT Entry 12

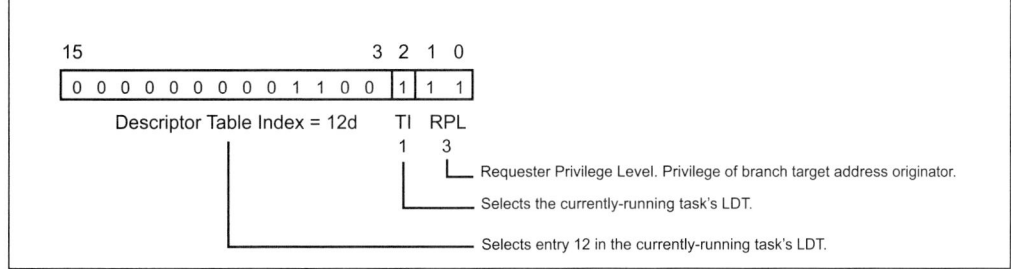

Call Gate Descriptor Read

The descriptor read from entry 12d in the LDT is pictured in Figure 14-10 on page 458. The logical processor examines the S bit plus the Type field to determine the descriptor type:

- S = 0, indicating that it is a special system segment descriptor.
- Type = 1100b, indicating it is a 32-bit Call Gate descriptor.

Table 14-11 on page 457 provides a breakdown of the selected Call Gate descriptor's contents.

Table 14-11: Example Call Gate Descriptor Elements (see Figure 14-10)

Field	Location	Description
P	Byte 5, bit 7	P = 1, indicating that the descriptor is valid.
DPL	Byte 5, bits [6:5]	DPL = 11b (3). Defines the minimum privilege level the caller must have to use the gate. In this case, programs with any privilege level (0, 1, 2, or 3) can use the gate without causing an exception. Read the section entitled "The Call Gate Privilege Check" on page 461 for more information.
S	Byte 5, bit 4	S = 0, indicating that this is a special system segment descriptor (see the next row).

Table 14-11: Example Call Gate Descriptor Elements (see Figure 14-10) (Continued)

Field	Location	Description
Type	Byte 5, bits [3:0]	S = 0 indicates that this is a special, system segment descriptor; and Type = 1100b indicates that it is a 32-bit Call Gate.
Dword Count	Byte 4, bits [4:0]	Dword Count = 00010b, indicating that 2 dword parameters are to be copied from the caller's stack to the called procedure's stack. These represent parameters to be passed to the called procedure.
Selector	Bytes 2 and 3	Selector = 0150h, indicating that the target code segment's descriptor is entry 42d of the GDT (see Figure 14-11 on page 459). The RPL portion has no significance.
Offset	Bytes 0, 1, 6, 7	The offset = 00003400h, indicating that the called procedure starts at offset 00003400h in the target code segment.

Figure 14-10: Example Call Gate Descriptor

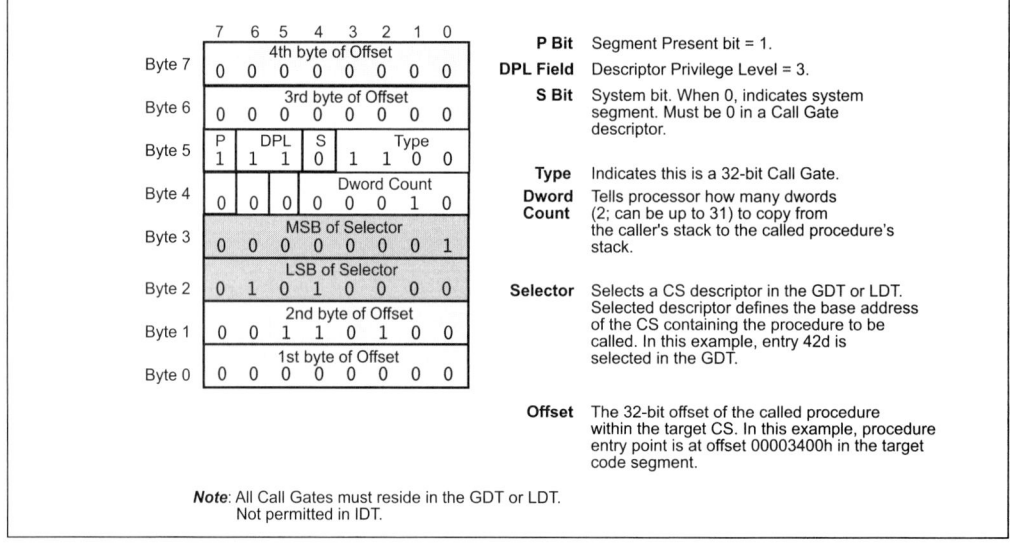

Call Gate Contains Target Code Segment Selector

Table 14-11 on page 457 and Figure 14-10 on page 458 describe the code segment selector (0150h) specified in the Call Gate descriptor. Figure 14-11 on page 459 shows the selector divided into its component fields. The descriptor for the target code segment is in entry 42d of the GDT.

Figure 14-11: Call Gate in LDT Entry 12 Contains This CS Selector

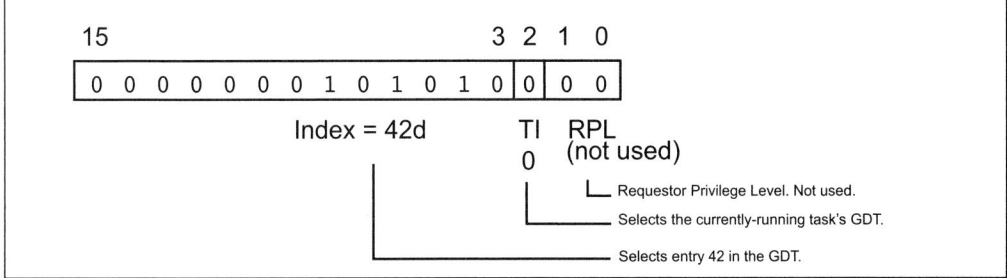

Target Code Segment Descriptor Read

The logical processor reads the CS descriptor pictured in Figure 14-12 on page 460 from entry 42d in the GDT. The descriptor's elements are described in Table 14-12 on page 459.

Table 14-12: Example Code Segment Descriptor

Field	Location	Description
G	Byte 6, bit 7	G = 0, indicating that the 20-bit limit (i.e., CS size) is expressed in bytes rather than in 4KB pages.
Limit	Byte 0, 1, and bits [3:0] of byte 6	20-bit segment limit (i.e., length) = 1EE3Dh (126,525d bytes).
D	Byte 6, bit 6	D = 1, indicating that this is a 32-bit code segment.
Avl	Byte 6, bit 5	Avl = 0. This is an OS-specific bit and is ignored by the hardware.
P	Byte 5, bit 7	P = 1, indicating that the descriptor is valid and the code segment is present in memory.
DPL	Byte 5, bits [6:5]	DPL of the code segment = 3 (the least privileged level). See the section entitled "The Call Gate Privilege Check" on page 461 for more information.

Table 14-12: Example Code Segment Descriptor (Continued)

Field	Location	Description
S	Byte 5, bit 4	S = 1, indicating that this is not a special, system segment (rather, is a code or data segment; see the next row).
C/D	Byte 5, bit 3	C/D = 1, indicating that this is a code rather than a data/stack segment.
C	Byte 5, bit 2	C = 0, indicating that this is a Non-Conforming code segment. See the section entitled "Conforming and Non-Conforming Code Segments" on page 438 for more information.
R	Byte 5, bit 1	R = 0, indicating that this is an execute-only code segment (neither data reads nor writes are allowed).
A	Byte 5, bit 0	A = 1, indicating that the code segment has been accessed at least once since it was established in memory.
Base	Bytes 2, 3, 4, 7	32-bit base address of code segment = 00131BCCh.

Figure 14-12: Descriptor for 32-bit CS Containing Called Procedure

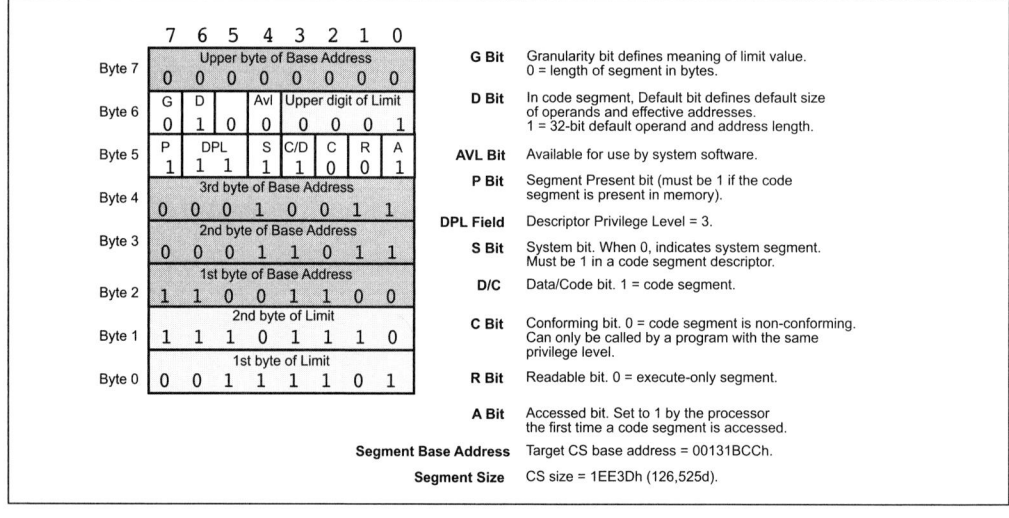

The Big Picture

Figure 14-13 on page 461 illustrates the overall relationship of the instruction, the Call Gate, the code segment descriptor, and the called procedure.

Figure 14-13: Bird's Eye View of Example Far Call through a Call Gate

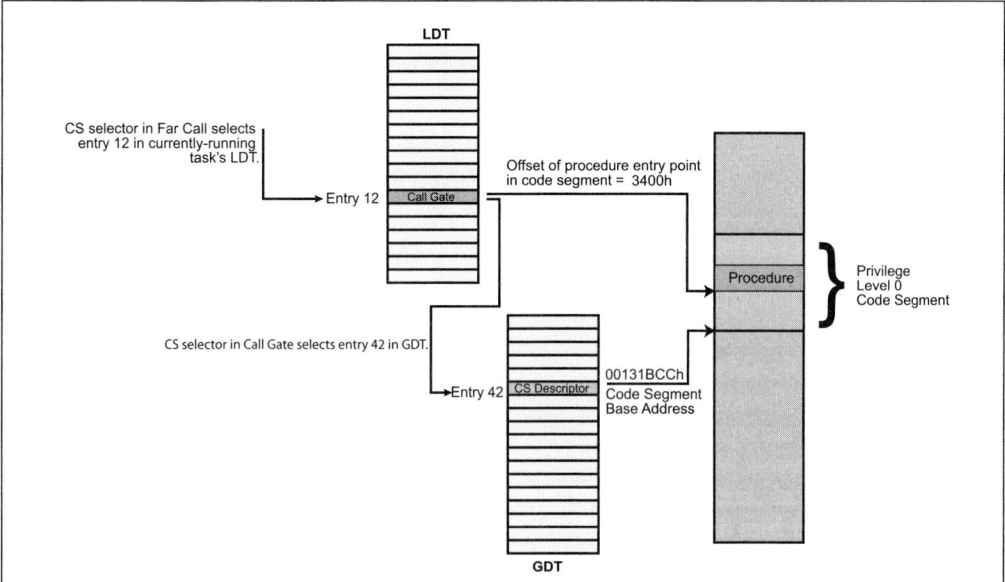

The Call Gate Privilege Check

Refer to Figure 14-15 on page 465. When the CS portion of a far call's or far jump's branch target address selects a Call Gate in the GDT or LDT, three privilege level checks are performed before the call or jmp is permitted to proceed. If a far call selects a Call Gate which points to a more privileged procedure in a Non-Conforming code segment, the logical processor automatically switches to a clean stack preallocated by the OS before it proceeds with the procedure call. This topic is covered in the next section.

Automatic Stack Switch

Background

When a call instruction is executed, the logical processor automatically pushes the return address onto the stack (EIP for a 32-bit near call; CS:EIP for a 32-bit far call). The address pushed onto the stack points to the instruction immediately following the call. Having done so, the logical processor places the branch target address into the CS:EIP register pair and resumes instruction fetching from that address (i.e., from the entry point of the called procedure).

When the RET instruction at the end of the called procedure is executed, the logical processor pops the return address from the stack back into:

- The EIP register for a 32-bit near RET;
- The CS:EIP register pair for a 32-bit far RET.

It then resumes instruction fetching from that address (i.e., at the instruction immediately following the Call instruction). Execution of the caller's program resumes at this point.

A Potential Problem

When calling a procedure that executes at a higher privilege level through a Call Gate, some additional steps are necessary due to a potential, stack-related problem. If the called procedure uses the same stack (pointed to by SS:ESP, or SS:SP) as the caller, the stack allocated for the calling program's use may prove too small to hold any additional values that the called procedure may push onto the stack. This would result in a Stack Overflow Exception.

The Solution: Pre-Allocated Stacks

The logical processor addresses this problem by automatically switching to a new stack of sufficient size to hold CS:EIP (the address to return to in the calling program), SS:ESP (the pointer to the calling program's stack area) and any parameters that are passed by the caller (on the caller's stack), as well as any local variables that the called procedure may subsequently need to push onto the stack.

When a procedure call (to a more privileged procedure) is made through a Call Gate, the logical processor automatically switches to the stack that was pre-allocated (by the OS) to accommodate the CS:EIP, SS:ESP and parameters from the caller's stack as well as any local variables that the called procedure may subsequently need to push onto the stack. The logical processor obtains the start address of the pre-allocated stack (in the form of a new SS:ESP value) from the

TSS associated with the currently-running task (Figure 14-14 on page 464). If, for example, the call is to a level 0 procedure:

1. The logical processor saves the current contents of the SS:ESP register pair (i.e., the pointer to the caller's stack) in temporary holding registers.
2. It then loads the SS:ESP register pair with the pre-allocated stack pointer obtained from the TSS's SS0:ESP0 fields.
3. The logical processor then pushes the following items onto the fresh stack:
   — Caller's SS, 0-padded to 32-bits.
   — Caller's ESP.
   — Number of dword parameters specified in Call Gate are copied from old stack to new stack.
   — CS of caller's return address, 0-padded to 32-bits.
   — EIP of caller's return address

When calling a procedure through a Call Gate, the actions in Figure 14-15 on page 465 are performed.

Figure 14-14: Task State Segment (TSS) Format

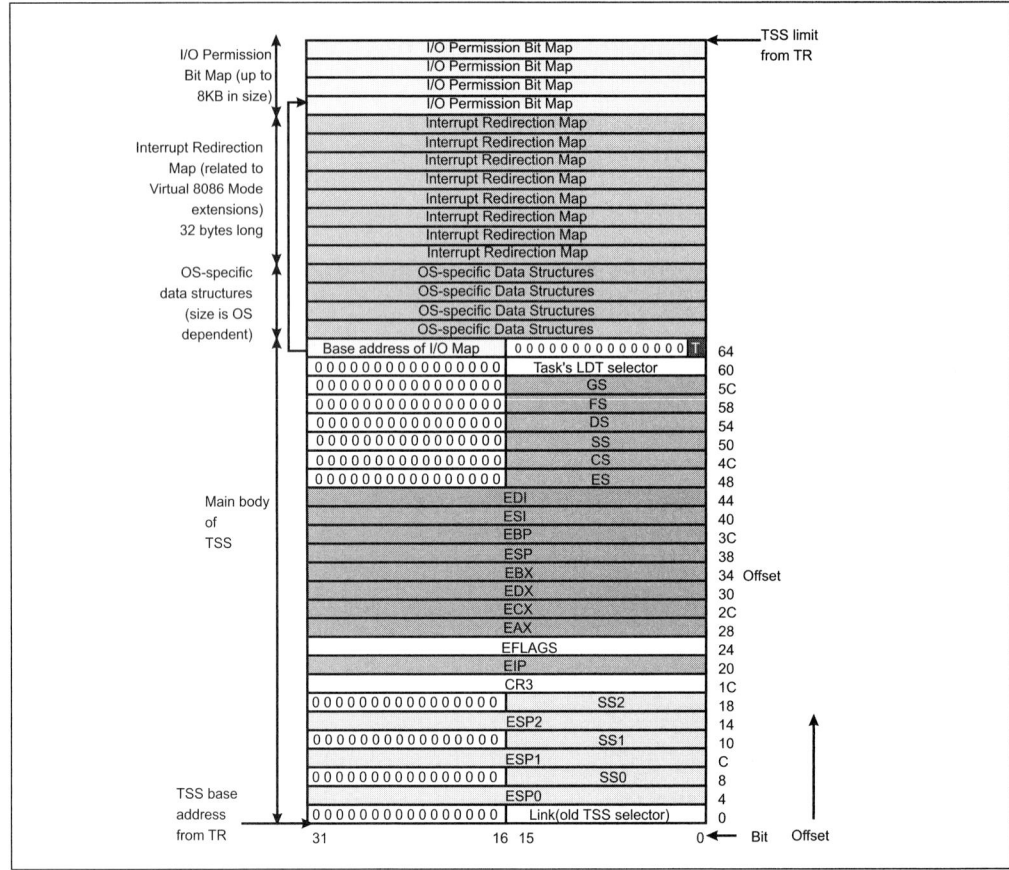

Figure 14-15: Automatic Privilege Check and Stack Build (assumes called procedure resides in a 32-bit code segment)

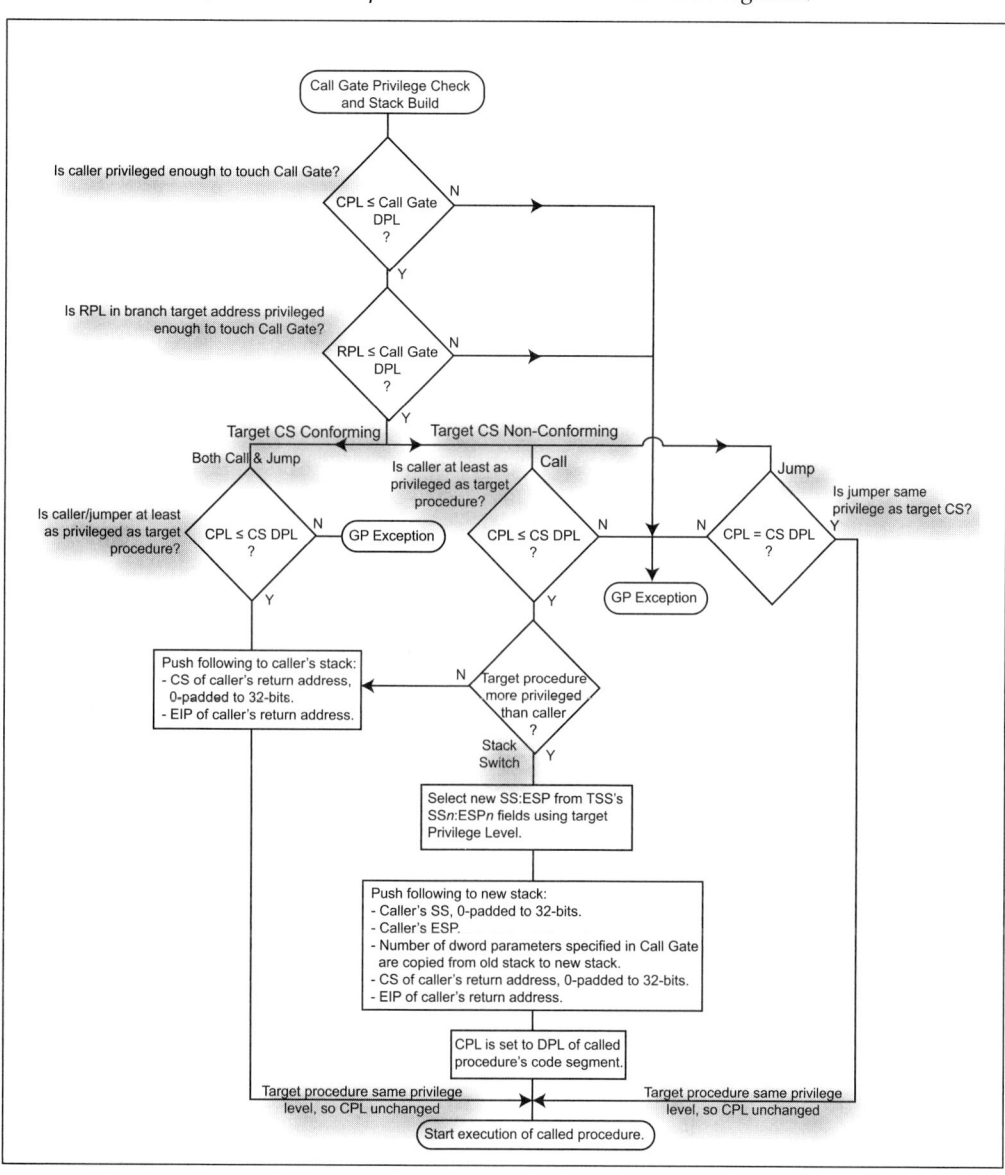

Far Call From 32-bit CS to 16-bit CS

General

Any of three methods can be used to call a procedure in a 16-bit CS from a procedure in a 32-bit CS:

- **Method 1: Place an Operand Size Override prefix before the far call instruction.** A detailed description can be found in "Method 1: Far Call with Operand Size Override Prefix" on page 466.
- **Method 2: Execute a far call wherein the CS portion of the branch target address selects a 16-bit Call Gate** in the GDT or LDT. A detailed description can be found in "Method 2: Far Call Via 16-bit Call Gate" on page 467.
- **Method 3**: Call a 32-bit procedure that will perform the far call to the 16-bit procedure on behalf of the caller. This 32-bit/16-bit interface procedure will shield the caller from problems incurred when calling the 16-bit procedure. A detailed description of this method can be found in "Method 3: Call 32-bit/16-bit Interface Procedure" on page 470.

Method 1: Far Call with Operand Size Override Prefix

Modify the 32-bit code by prefacing the far call with the Operand Size Override prefix. The far call will then behave as if it were executed in a 16-bit code segment (see Figure 14-16 on page 467). It's important to note that this method involves *two serious constraints*:

1. If the call is to a Non-Conforming 16-bit code segment, the caller's privilege level must be the same as the target CS's DPL (or it will result in a GP exception).
2. The far call instruction in the 32-bit code segment must reside in the first 64KB of the caller's code segment.

Both of these problems can be avoided by using method 3 (see "Method 3: Call 32-bit/16-bit Interface Procedure" on page 470).

Figure 14-16: Calling 16-bit Procedure From 32-bit Code Using Far Call With Operand Size Override Prefix

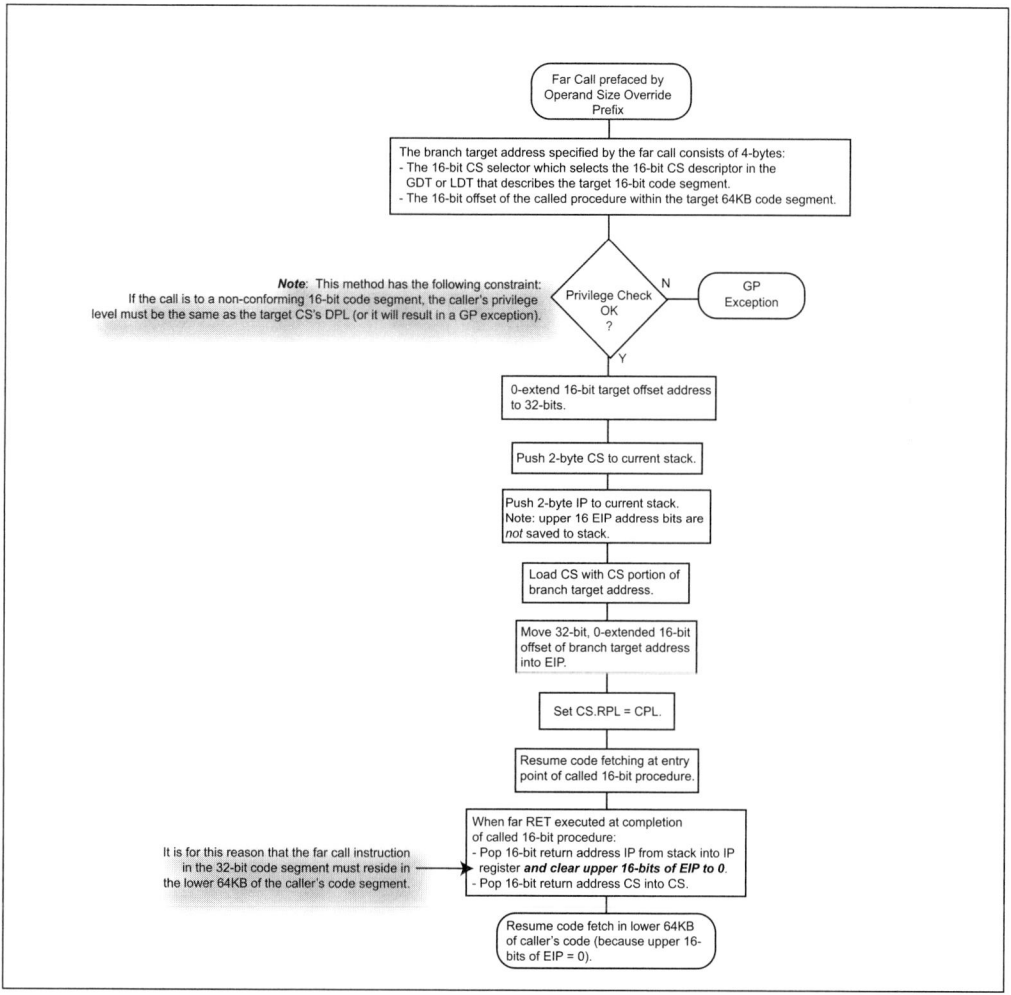

Method 2: Far Call Via 16-bit Call Gate

Using this method, the CS portion of the branch target address selects a 16-bit Call Gate (see Figure 14-19 on page 471) in the GDT or LDT. The far call is not preceded by an Operand Size Override prefix and behaves as detailed in Figure

14-17 on page 469. Figure 14-18 on page 470 details the behavior of the subsequent far return instruction executed at the end of the 16-bit procedure and highlights two problems:

Problem 1. The offset portion of the return address has been truncated from 32- to 16-bits and the upper 16-bits of the EIP register are 0. For this reason, the far Call instruction that called the 16-bit procedure via the 16-bit Call Gate *must* be located in the first 64KB of the 32-bit code segment.

Problem 2. On return to the 32-bit caller's code, the upper 16-bits of the 32-bit ESP register have been corrupted rendering the caller's stack unusable.

Both of these problems can be avoided by using method 3 (see "Method 3: Call 32-bit/16-bit Interface Procedure" on page 470).

Figure 14-17: Calling 16-bit Procedure From 32-bit Code Using a 16-bit Call Gate

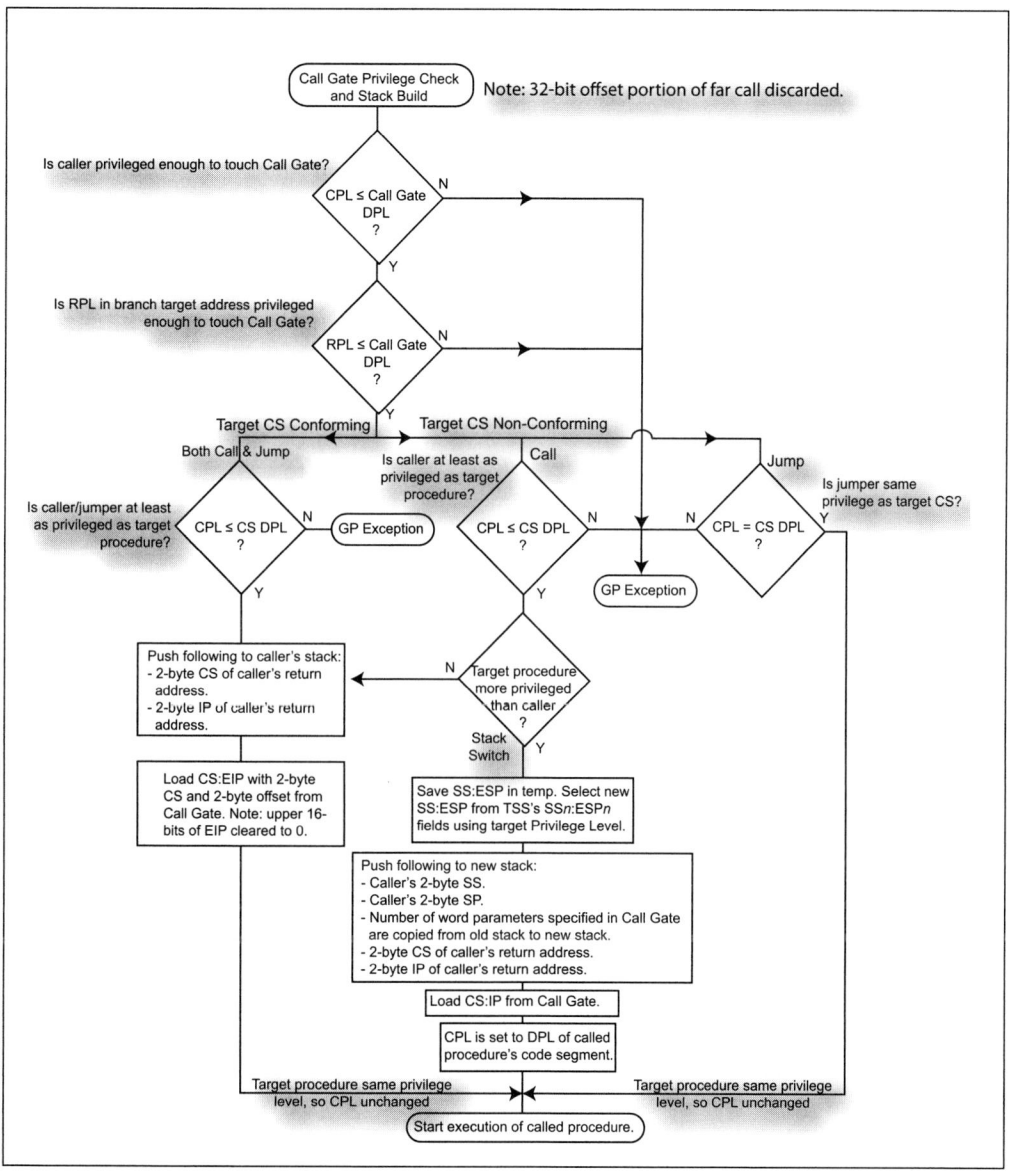

Figure 14-18: Far Return From 16-bit Procedure to 32-bit Caller

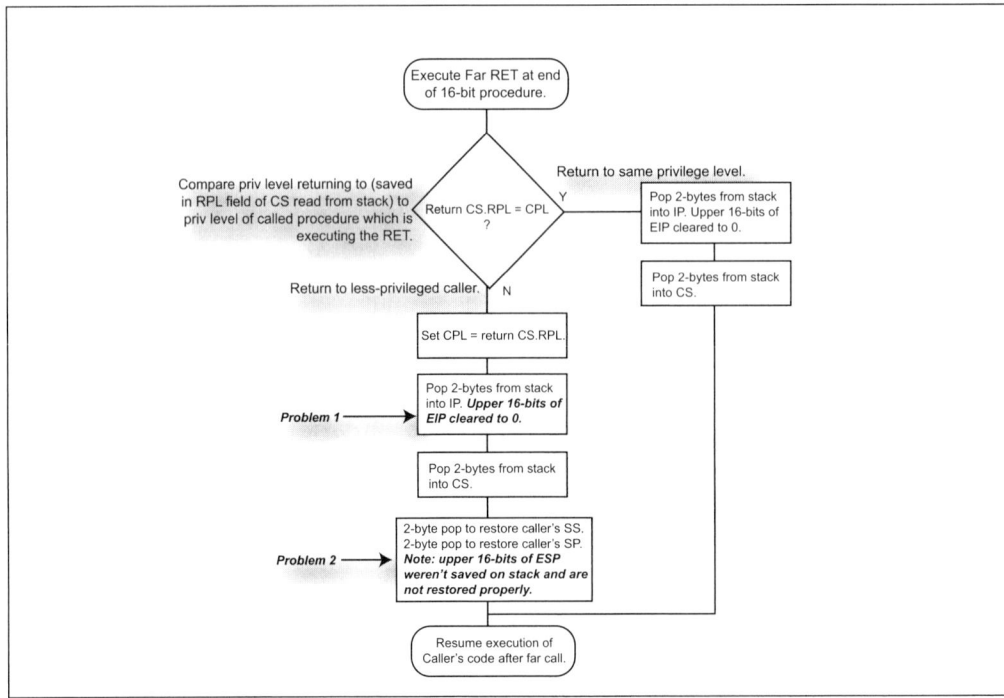

Method 3: Call 32-bit/16-bit Interface Procedure

As already demonstrated, both method 1 and method 2 introduce problems/constraints when a 16-bit procedure is called by 32-bit code. These complications can be avoided by implementing a 32-bit/16-bit interface procedure that will act as the intermediary when 32-bit code needs to call a 16-bit procedure. The interface module would have the following characteristics:

- It is implemented as 32-bit code.
- When a request is passed to it by another 32-bit entity, it saves the following items before calling the 16-bit procedure:
  — The full 32-bit EIP value pushed to the stack (this is the offset portion of the address to return to in the caller's 32-bit code segment).
  — The full 32-bit stack pointer used by the caller.

- It then calls the 16-bit procedure using a 16-bit Call Gate. As demonstrated earlier, this will result in the truncation of the 32-bit EIP address as well as the corruption of the upper 16-bits of ESP.
- On return from the 16-bit procedure, it restores the original contents of EIP and ESP before returning to the originator of the request.

Figure 14-19: 16-bit, 286-Compliant Call Gate Descriptor

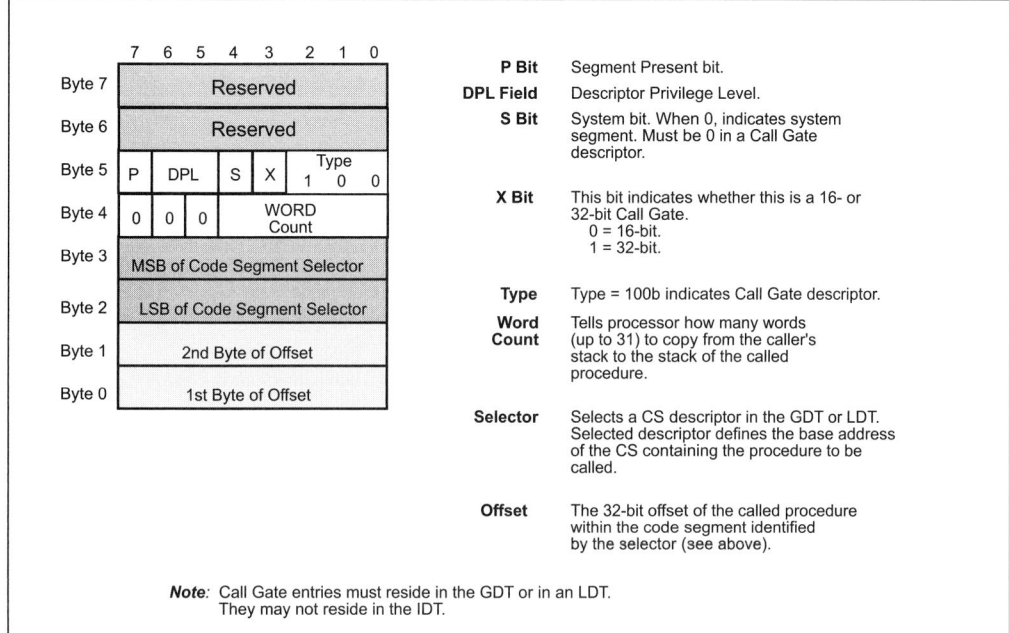

Far Call From 16-bit CS to 32-bit CS

Either of two methods can be used to call a procedure in a 32-bit CS from a 16-bit CS:

- **Method 1: Place an Operand Size Override prefix before the far call instruction.** A detailed description can be found in "Method 1: Far Call With an Operand Size Prefix" on page 472.
- **Method 2: Execute a far call wherein the CS portion of the branch target address selects a 32-bit Call Gate** in the GDT or LDT. A detailed description can be found in "Method 2: Far Call Via a 32-bit Call Gate" on page 473.

Method 1: Far Call With an Operand Size Prefix

Modify the 16-bit code by prefacing the far call with the Operand Size Override prefix. The far call will then behave as if it were executed in a 32-bit code segment (see Figure 14-20 on page 472). It's important to note that this method involves *one serious constraint*:

- If the call is to a Non-Conforming 32-bit code segment, the caller's privilege level must be the same as the target CS's DPL (or it will result in a GP exception). This constraint can be overcome using method 2.

*Figure 14-20: Calling 32-bit Procedure From 16-bit Code Using Far Call
With Operand Size Override Prefix*

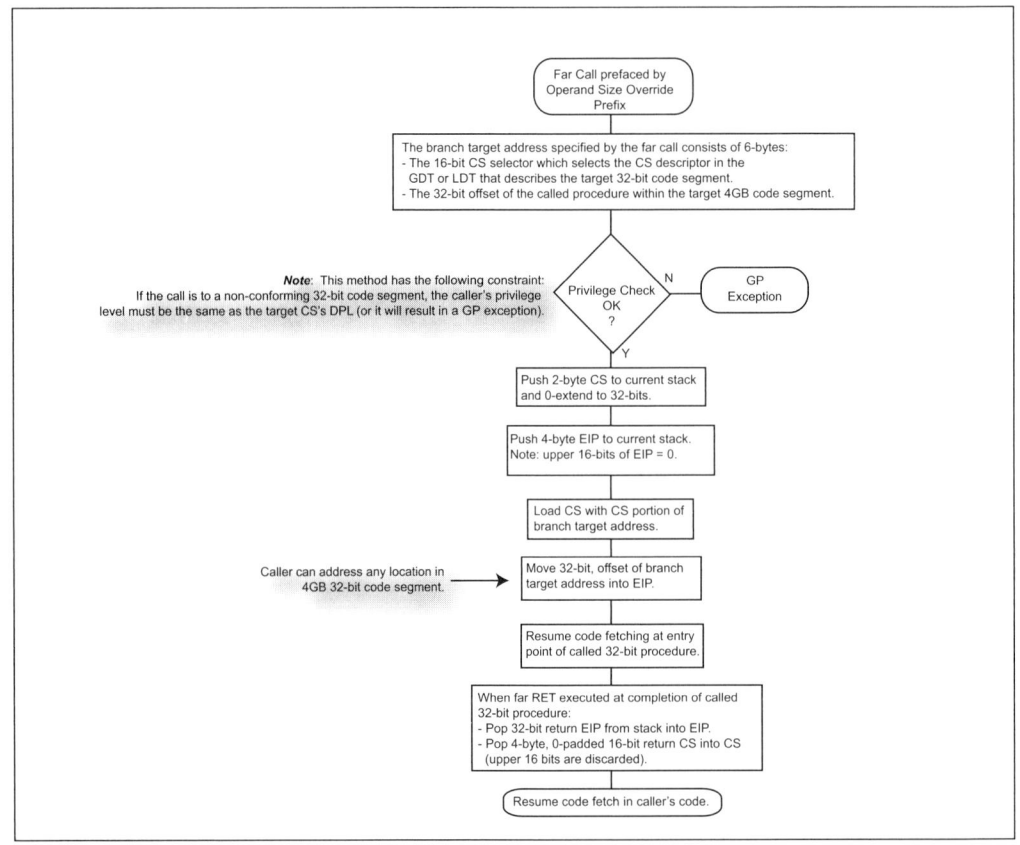

Method 2: Far Call Via a 32-bit Call Gate

Using this method, the CS portion of the branch target address selects a 32-bit Call Gate (see Figure 14-21 on page 473) in the GDT or LDT. The far call is not preceded by an Operand Size Override Prefix and behaves as detailed in Figure 14-22 on page 474. Figure 14-23 on page 475 details the behavior of the subsequent far return instruction executed at the end of the 32-bit procedure.

Figure 14-21: 32-bit Call Gate Descriptor Format

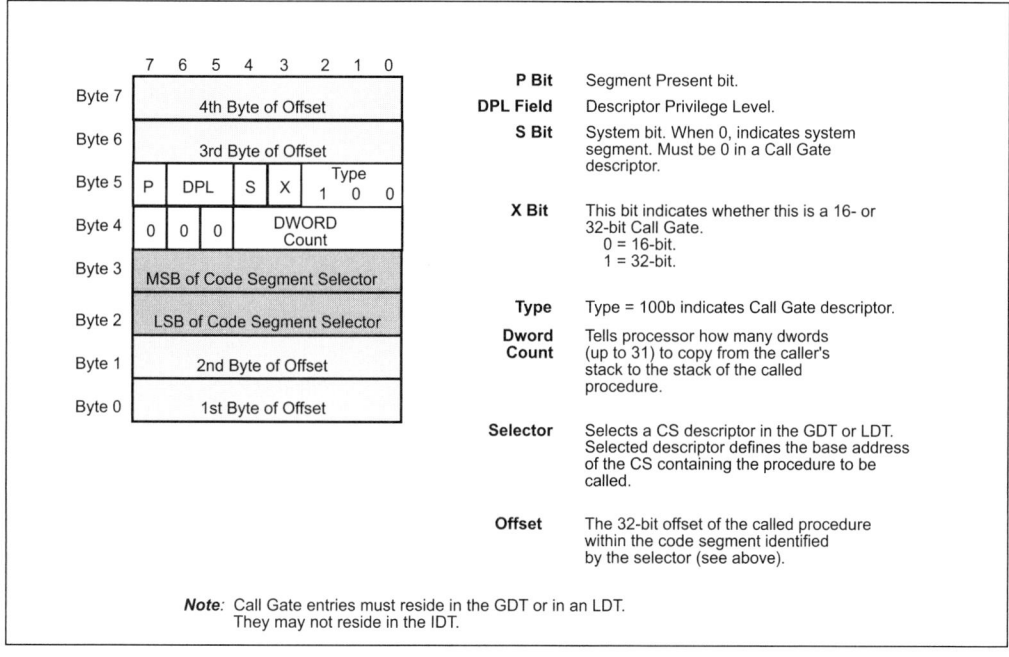

P Bit	Segment Present bit.
DPL Field	Descriptor Privilege Level.
S Bit	System bit. When 0, indicates system segment. Must be 0 in a Call Gate descriptor.
X Bit	This bit indicates whether this is a 16- or 32-bit Call Gate. 0 = 16-bit. 1 = 32-bit.
Type	Type = 100b indicates Call Gate descriptor.
Dword Count	Tells processor how many dwords (up to 31) to copy from the caller's stack to the stack of the called procedure.
Selector	Selects a CS descriptor in the GDT or LDT. Selected descriptor defines the base address of the CS containing the procedure to be called.
Offset	The 32-bit offset of the called procedure within the code segment identified by the selector (see above).

Note: Call Gate entries must reside in the GDT or in an LDT. They may not reside in the IDT.

Figure 14-22: Calling 32-bit Procedure From 16-bit Code Using a 32-bit Call Gate

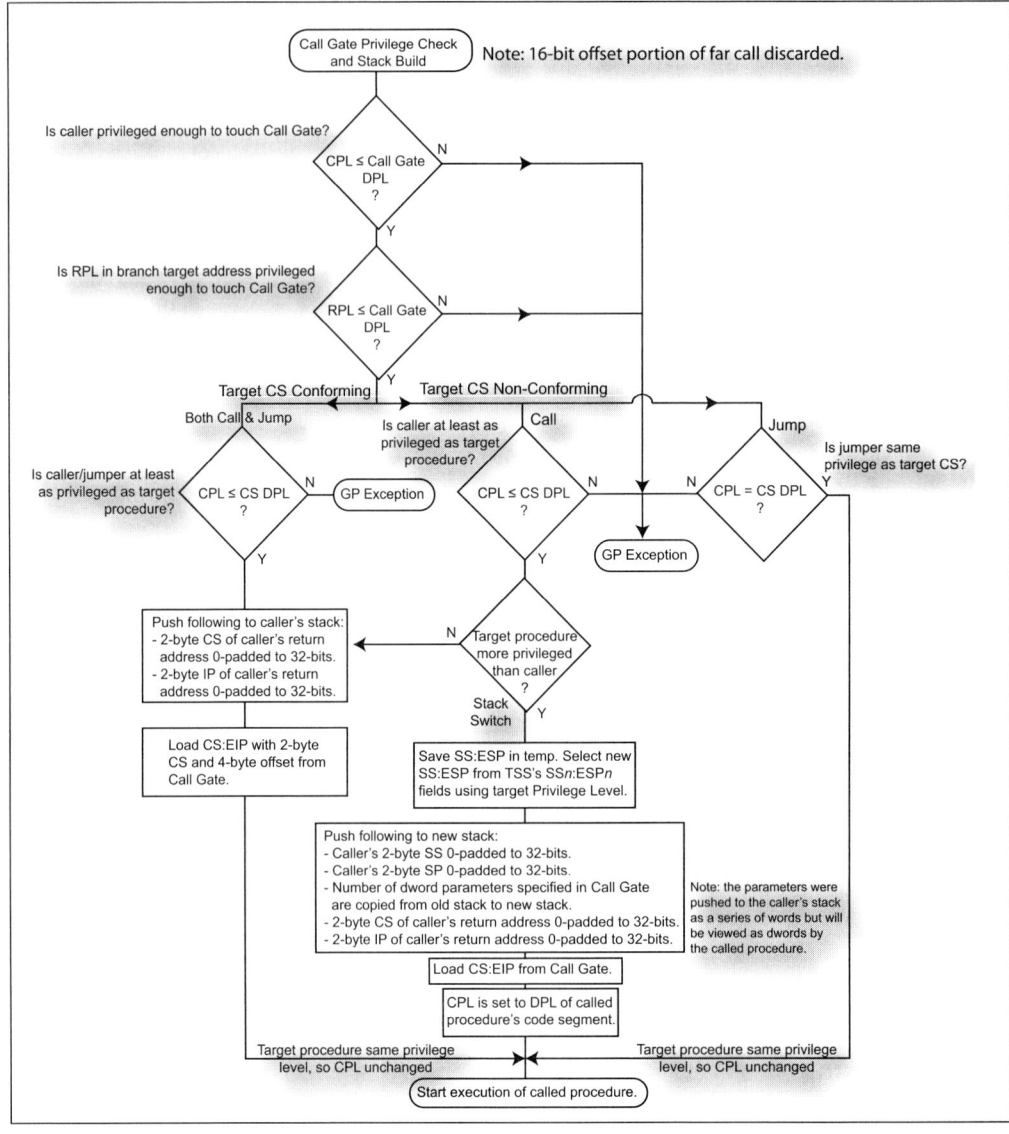

Figure 14-23: Far Return From 32-bit Procedure to 16-bit Caller

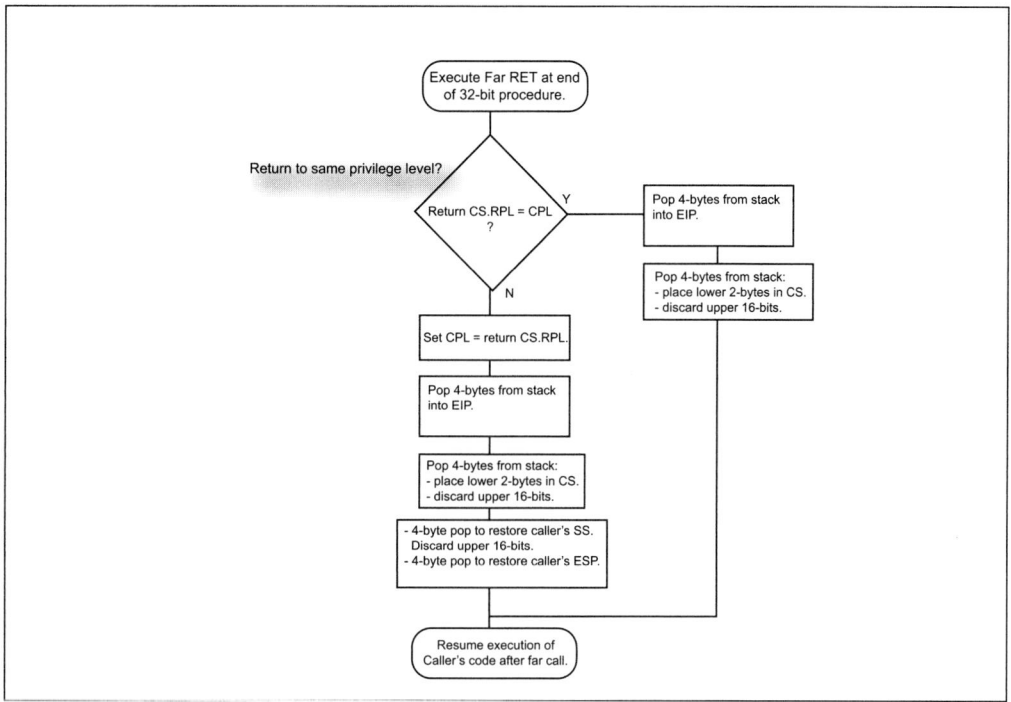

Far Returns

General

A far return instruction is executed at the completion of a called procedure to return control back to the caller (which resides in a different code segment) at the instruction immediately following the far call instruction. There are two basic scenarios:

1. **Return to same privilege level**. The caller and the called procedure each reside in code segments with the same privilege level. In this case, the called procedure used the same stack as the caller and no stack switch was necessary. The far RET instruction causes the logical processor to pop the caller's return address from the stack into the CS:IP or CS:EIP register pair and the

logical processor resumes execution at the instruction immediately following the far call instruction.

2. **Return to lesser privilege level**. The called procedure resides in a more-privileged, Non-Conforming code segment and the caller invoked it via a Call Gate in the GDT or LDT. In this case, rather using the caller's stack and risking a stack overflow, the called procedure used a fresh, preallocated stack. Before jumping to the called procedure the logical processor switched to the new stack and pushed the following items onto it:
   — The SS:SP or SS:ESP which points to the caller's stack.
   — If the Call Gate's parameter count field was non-zero, n parameters are copied from the caller's stack to the called procedure's stack.
   — The contents of the CS:IP or CS:EIP register pair.

The effective operand size at the time of the RET instruction's execution dictates whether the pops are 2-byte or 4-byte operations.

Far Return Forms

Table 14-13 on page 477 describes the two forms of the far RET instruction:

- Far Return.
- Far Return with parameter deallocation.

Table 14-13: Far Return Forms (in Protected Mode)

Call Type	Opcode	Effective Operand Size	Description
RET	CB	16-bits	**Return to same privilege level**: 1. Pop 2-bytes into IP. Clear upper 16-bits of EIP to 0. 2. Pop 2-bytes into CS register. **Return to lesser privilege level**: 1. Restore CPL to caller's privilege level: — Set CPL from RPL field of CS selector on stack. 2. Pop 2-bytes into IP. Clear upper 16-bits of EIP to 0. 3. Pop 2-bytes into CS register. 4. Set CS register RPL = CPL. 5. Restore caller's stack: — Pop 2-bytes from called procedure's stack into SS register. — Pop 2-bytes from called procedure's stack into SP register. Clear upper 16-bits of ESP to 0. 6. For 4 data segment registers: — If segment register selects a segment whose DPL renders it inaccessible at the CPL, set segment register = 0 (i.e., point it to null descriptor in GDT).
		32-bits	**Return to same privilege level**: 1. Pop 4-bytes into EIP. 2. Pop 4-bytes. Place 2 in CS; discard other 2. **Return to lesser privilege level**: 1. Restore CPL to caller's privilege level: — Set CPL from RPL field of CS selector on stack. 2. Pop 4-bytes into EIP. 3. Pop 4-bytes. Place 2 in CS; discard other 2. 4. Set CS register RPL = CPL. 5. Restore caller's stack: — Pop 4-bytes from called procedure's stack. Place 2 in SS; discard other 2. — Pop 4-bytes from called procedure's stack into ESP register. 6. For 4 data segment registers: — If segment register selects a segment whose DPL renders it inaccessible at the CPL, set segment register = 0 (i.e., point it to null descriptor in GDT).

Table 14-13: Far Return Forms (in Protected Mode) (Continued)

Call Type	Opcode	Effective Operand Size	Description
RET *imm16*	CA	16-bits	With following addition, same as *RET without imm16* (operand size 16-bits) in this table: • Adjusts stack upward *n* bytes (*n* is specified by 16-bit immediate value in instruction) to release space in which caller passed parameters to called procedure.
		32-bits	With following addition, same as *RET without imm16* (operand size 32-bits) in this table: • Adjusts stack upward *n* bytes (*n* is specified by 16-bit immediate value in instruction) to release space in which caller passed parameters to called procedure.

15 *Data and Stack Segments*

The Previous Chapter

The previous chapter provided a detailed description of code segments (both Conforming and Non-Conforming), privilege checking, and Call Gates. The following topics were covered:

- Selecting the Active Code Segment.
- CS Descriptor.
- Accessing the Code Segment.
- Short/Near Jumps.
- Unconditional Far Jumps.
- Privilege Checking.
- Jumping from a Higher-to-Lesser Privileged Program.
- Direct Procedure Calls.
- Indirect Procedure Far Call Though a Call Gate.
- Automatic Stack Switch.
- Far Call From 32-bit CS to 16-bit CS.
- Far Call From 16-bit CS to 32-bit CS.
- Far Returns.

This Chapter

This chapter provides a detailed description of Data and Stack segments (including Expand-Up and Expand-Down Stacks) and privilege checking when accessing data or stack segments. The following topics are covered:

- The Data Segments.
  — General.
  — Two-Step Permission Check.

- — An Example.
- Selecting and Accessing a Stack Segment.
  - — Introduction.
  - — Expand-Up Stack.
  - — Expand-Down Stack.
    - – The Problem.
    - – Expand-Down Stack Description.
    - – An Example.
    - – Another Example.

The Next Chapter

The next chapter covers the following topics:

- Summarizes the evolution of the virtual-to-physical address translation facilities on the x86 processors and provides a backgrounder on memory and disk management.
- The concept of virtual memory is introduced as well as the advantages of address translation.
- The first and second generation virtual-to-physical address translation mechanisms are described in detail.
- The role of the Translation Lookaside Buffer (TLB) is described, as well as the Global Page feature and TLB maintenance.
- Page Directory Entries (PDEs) and Page Table Entries (PTEs) are described in detail.
- Page access permission.
- Missing page or Page Table.
- Page access history.
- 4MB pages.
- PSE-36 Mode.
- Execute Disable feature.
- Page caching rules.
- Page write protection.

A Note Regarding Stack Segments

While the stack segment is, in reality, nothing more than a read/writable data segment, it is treated separately in this chapter because it is used differently than the typical data segment.

Chapter 15: Data and Stack Segments

Data Segments

General

x86 processors introduced after the 286 implement four data segment registers (as opposed to just one, DS, in the 286): DS, ES, FS and GS. They permit software to identify up to four separate data segments (in memory) that can be accessed by the currently executing program.

To access data within any of the four data segments, the programmer must first load a 16-bit descriptor selector into the respective data segment register. In Real Mode, the value in a data segment register specifies the upper 16-bits of the 20-bit zero-extended memory start address of the data segment. In Protected Mode, the value selects a data segment descriptor in either the GDT or LDT. Figure 15-3 on page 484 illustrates the format of a 32-bit data segment descriptor (in a 286-style 16-bit data segment descriptor, bytes 6 and 7 are reserved).

Two-Step Permission Check

In order to successfully access one or more locations in a data segment, two permission checks must be passed:

1. **Descriptor pre-load privilege check.** Refer to Figure 15-1 on page 482. The currently running program must have sufficient privilege to select the target data segment descriptor in the GDT or LDT. Assuming it does, the selected data segment descriptor is loaded into the invisible portion of the respective data segment register.
2. **Access type/limit checks.** Before any subsequent access is permitted within a data segment, the logical processor must verify that the access type is permitted (e.g., that a write is permitted) and must also verify that the specified location (i.e., offset) falls within the bounds of the targeted data segment.

Figure 15-1: Data Segment Descriptor Pre-Load Privilege Check

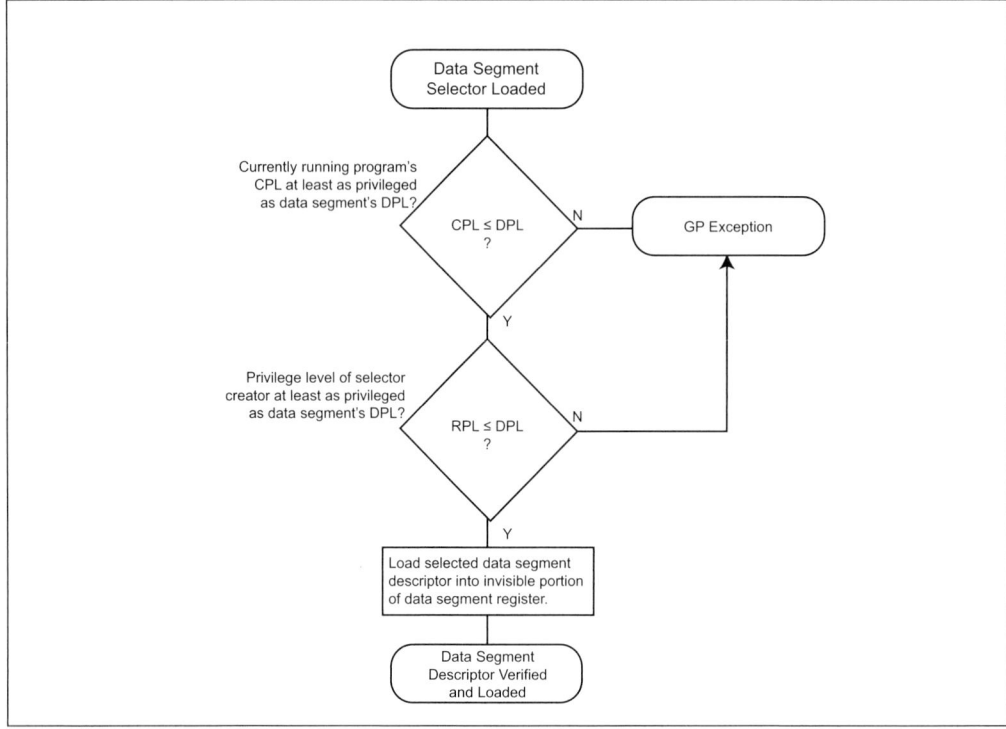

An Example

Consider this example (assumes code is fetched from a Non-Conforming CS with a DPL of 2):

```
mov ax, 4f36    ;load ds register
mov ds, ax      ;
mov al, [0100]  ;read 1 byte from data segment into al
mov [2100], al  ;write 1 byte to data segment from al
```

The value 4F36h in the DS register is interpreted by the logical processor as indicated in Figure 15-2 on page 484. The logical processor accesses LDT entry 2534 to obtain the data segment descriptor. The selector's RPL = 2 indicating that a privilege level 2 program created the selector value. Figure 15-3 on page 484 illustrates the example data segment descriptor fetched from the LDT. The segment is:

- A data segment (C/D = 0).
- 31,550 bytes in length.
- Starting at memory location 00083EA0h.
- DPL = 2.
- Read/Writable.

Assuming that the descriptor pre-load privilege check is successful (in this case, it is: CPL, DPL, RPL all = 2), the 8-byte segment descriptor is loaded into the invisible portion of the DS register by the second instruction.

When the third instruction (MOV AL,[0100]) is executed, the logical processor compares the CPL of the currently running program (2) to the DS segment's DPL (2) and permits the access (RPL was verified earlier). It also performs a limit check to ensure that the specified offset, 0100h, doesn't exceed the length of the DS data segment. 0100h is compared to the segment size in the DS cache register. Since 0100h is less than 07B3Eh, the access is within the segment's bounds. The logical processor therefore permits the access. The offset, 0100h, is added to the segment base address, 00083EA0h, yielding virtual memory address 00083FA0h. One byte is read from this location and placed in the AL register. The next MOV instruction (MOV [2100], AL) involves a memory write into the DS data segment. Before permitting this, the logical processor checks the descriptor's W bit to ensure that the target segment is writable (it is). Another limit check is performed to ensure that offset 2100h doesn't exceed the segment length. The offset, 2100h, is then added to the segment's base address, 00083EA0h, yielding virtual memory address 00085FA0h. The byte in the AL register is written into this memory location.

The following code fragment is the same as the previous one except for the fact that it accesses the GS data segment instead of the DS data segment (the last two instructions are prefaced by the GS Segment Override prefix).

```
mov ax, 4f36      ;load gs register
mov gs, ax        ;
mov al, gs:[0100] ;read from gs data segment
mov gs:[2100], al ;write to gs data segment
```

Figure 15-2: Example Value in DS Register

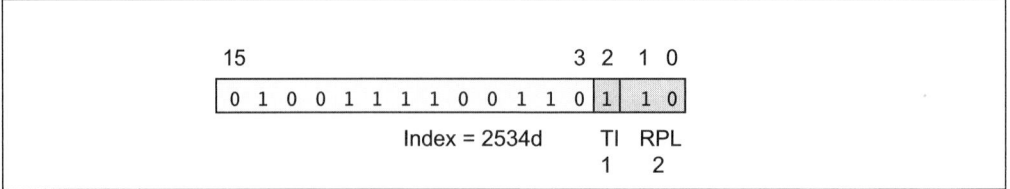

Figure 15-3: Example Data Segment Descriptor

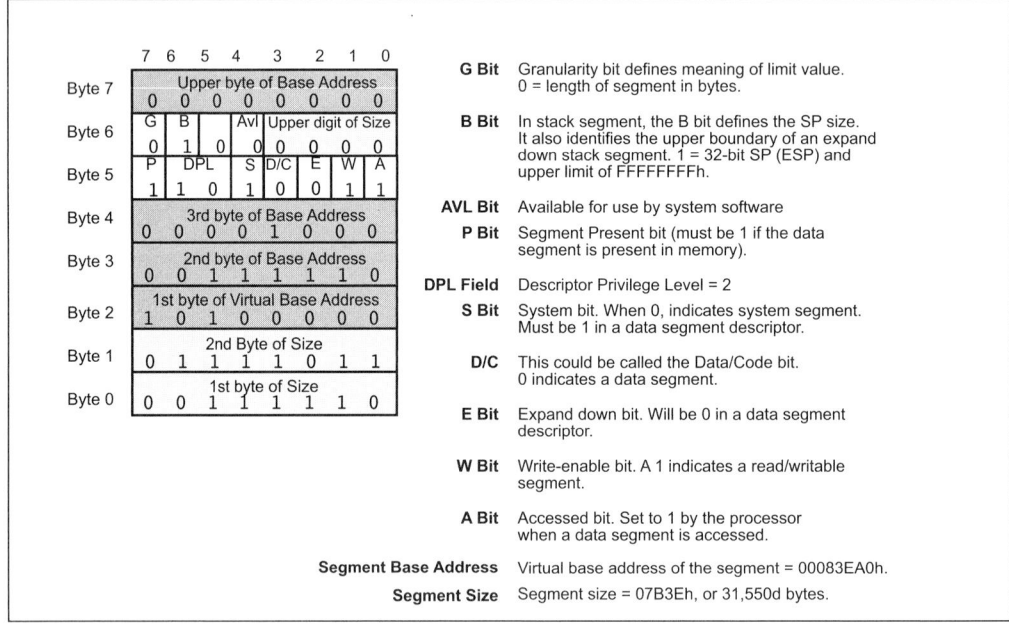

Selecting and Accessing a Stack Segment

Introduction

A stack segment is a form of data segment. Its descriptor must identify it as a read/writable segment so that the logical processor may perform both pushes (i.e., writes to the stack) and pops (i.e., reads from the stack). The descriptor also describes the stack type. A stack may be designated as either:

- **Expand-up stack** (the most common type). Previously described in "Accessing the Stack Segment" on page 297 and also in "Expand-Up Stack" on page 485.
- **Expand-down stack**. A description of the expand-down stack can be found in the section entitled "Expand-Down Stack" on page 487.

It should be noted that most OSs implement expand-up stacks.

Expand-Up Stack

The discussion that follows describes the operation of an expand-up stack (see Figure 15-4 on page 486). Assume that the logical processor is in Protected Mode and the following series of instructions is executed:

```
mov    ax, 02ff           ;put 02ffh in ss
mov    ss, ax             ;
mov    esp, 00005ffe      ;set stack pointer initial value
push   ebx                ;save ebx in stack
mov    bx, [0100]         ;read value from memory to bx
add    cx, bx             ;add bx to cx, result in cx
pop    ebx               ;restore original value in ebx
```

The first two instructions load the SS register with the selector value 02FFh (see Figure 15-5 on page 487). The logical processor reads the segment descriptor from entry 95d in the LDT (TI bit = 1, indicating LDT, and the index field contains 95d), performs privilege checking (see Figure 15-1 on page 482) and ensures that the descriptor defines a read/write data segment (W = 1). The example stack segment descriptor is illustrated in Figure 15-6 on page 487 and has the following characteristics:

- The segment is a data/stack segment (System bit = 1 and C/D = 0).
- It can be read and written (W bit = 1) and is therefore eligible to be used as a stack.
- The B (Big) bit = 1 indicating that the 32-bit ESP register (rather than the 16-bit SP register) is used to access it.
- It can be accessed by a program with any privilege level (DPL = 3).
- The TOS (Top of Stack) = 89E9Eh (base 83EA0h + ESP of 5FFEh).
- It is an expand-up stack (E bit = 0). As items are pushed onto the stack, it grows downward from the (base + limit) towards its base address.
- Its virtual base address is 00083EA0h.

This example assumes that the currently-active code segment's default operand size is 32-bits (in other words, the code segment descriptor's D bit = 1, indicating that this is 32-bit code). When this is the case, the 32-bit ESP register is decremented by four during the execution of a push. When executing 16-bit code (D = 0), the 16-bit SP register would be decremented by two.

When the Push instruction in the example code fragment is executed:

1. The logical processor decrements ESP by four.
2. It performs a limit check to ensure that the new ESP value (0005FFEh - 4 = 0005FFAh) doesn't exceed the size of the stack specified in the descriptor (5FFAh is < 7B3Eh).
3. It also checks to ensure that decrementing ESP by four doesn't decrement ESP below offset 00000000h in the stack. If this were the case, a Stack Exception would be generated.
4. The memory address is formed by adding the current contents of the ESP register (0005FFAh) to the segment's base address (00083EA0h), yielding memory address 00089E9Ah.
5. The four bytes from EBX are written into memory locations 00089E9Ah - 00089E9Dh.

When the Pop instruction in the code fragment is executed:

1. The logical processor performs a four byte read from memory starting at the location currently pointed to by ESP + the stack segment's base address.
2. The four bytes from memory locations 00089E9Ah - 00089E9Dh are read, with the byte from location 00089E9Ah (the lower location) placed in the LSB of EBX (BL) and the byte from location 00089E9Dh placed in its MSB.
3. The logical processor then increments ESP by four (to 5FFEh). If this resulted in an ESP value that exceeds the stack limit, a Stack exception would be generated.

Figure 15-4: Expand Up Stack Approaching a Full Condition

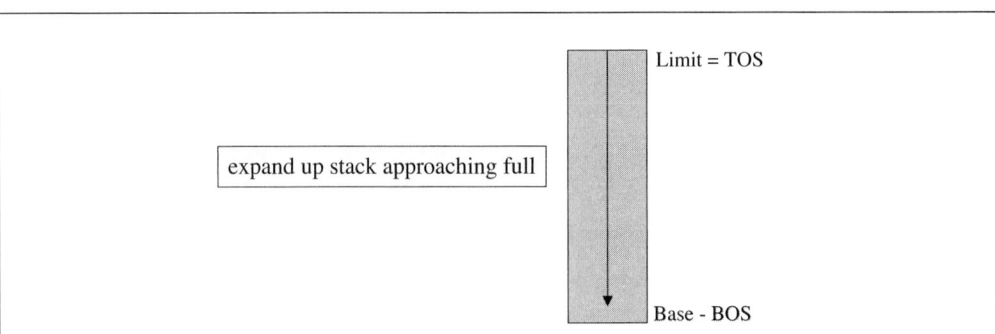

Figure 15-5: Example Value in SS Register

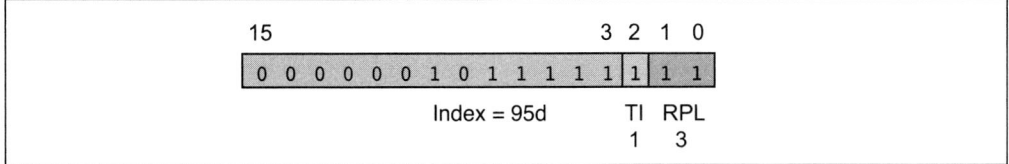

Figure 15-6: Example Stack Segment Descriptor

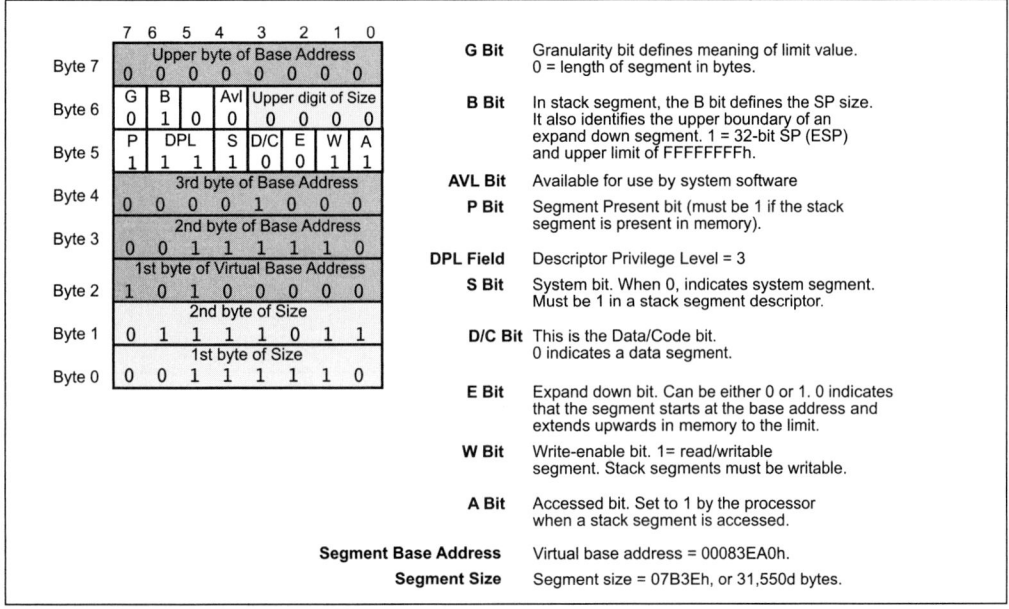

		Description
G Bit		Granularity bit defines meaning of limit value. 0 = length of segment in bytes.
B Bit		In stack segment, the B bit defines the SP size. It also identifies the upper boundary of an expand down segment. 1 = 32-bit SP (ESP) and upper limit of FFFFFFFFh.
AVL Bit		Available for use by system software
P Bit		Segment Present bit (must be 1 if the stack segment is present in memory).
DPL Field		Descriptor Privilege Level = 3
S Bit		System bit. When 0, indicates system segment. Must be 1 in a stack segment descriptor.
D/C Bit		This is the Data/Code bit. 0 indicates a data segment.
E Bit		Expand down bit. Can be either 0 or 1. 0 indicates that the segment starts at the base address and extends upwards in memory to the limit.
W Bit		Write-enable bit. 1= read/writable segment. Stack segments must be writable.
A Bit		Accessed bit. Set to 1 by the processor when a stack segment is accessed.
Segment Base Address		Virtual base address = 00083EA0h.
Segment Size		Segment size = 07B3Eh, or 31,550d bytes.

Expand-Down Stack

The Problem

Assume that the programmer pushes a number of parameters onto the stack and that some of these values are pointers to other values that were pushed onto the stack earlier. These pointers take the form of an offset from the BOS (bottom of stack).

For example, assume that the value 1234h is pushed into the stack at position (i.e., offset) 00003000h (ESP = 00003000h) and that the programmer later pushes a pointer to that value into stack position 00002FF0h. The value 1234h is stored in the stack at offset 00003000h, while stack location (offset) 00002FF0h contains the value 00003000h, the pointer to the stack location where the value 1234h is actually stored.

Now assume that the stack is approaching a full condition (it has almost been decremented down to its base address; see Figure 15-4 on page 486). To make the stack larger (and thereby prevent a Stack Overflow condition), the programmer copies the current stack onto the top of a larger stack segment (see Figure 15-7 on page 488). Any pointers stored in the stack (such as the one at offset 00002FF0h in the older, smaller stack) are now wrong (because the base address has been changed relative to where the pointer and the location it points to now reside). The value 1234h now resides at an offset other than 00003000h within the new, larger stack segment.

- Enlarging the stack by lowering the base address renders stored pointers incorrect. See Figure 15-8 on page 489.
- Enlarging the stack by increasing the stack limit will not head off a stack overflow. See Figure 15-9 on page 489.

The expand-down stack (see the next section) solves the problem.

Figure 15-7: Copying to a Larger Stack Renders Stored Pointers Incorrect

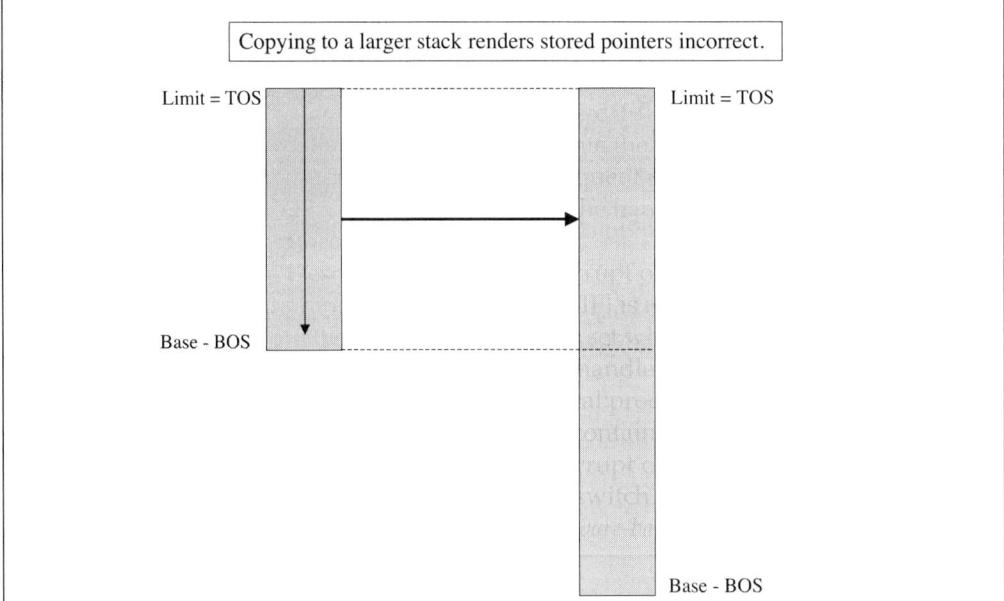

Figure 15-8: Enlarging the Stack by Lowering Stack Base Renders Stored Pointers Incorrect

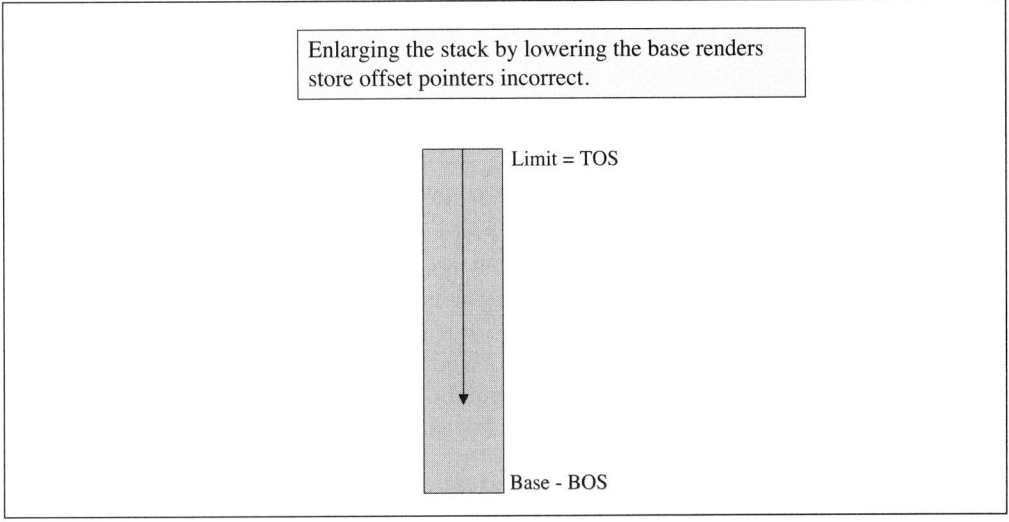

Figure 15-9: Enlarging Stack by Increasing Limit Won't Head Off a Stack Overflow

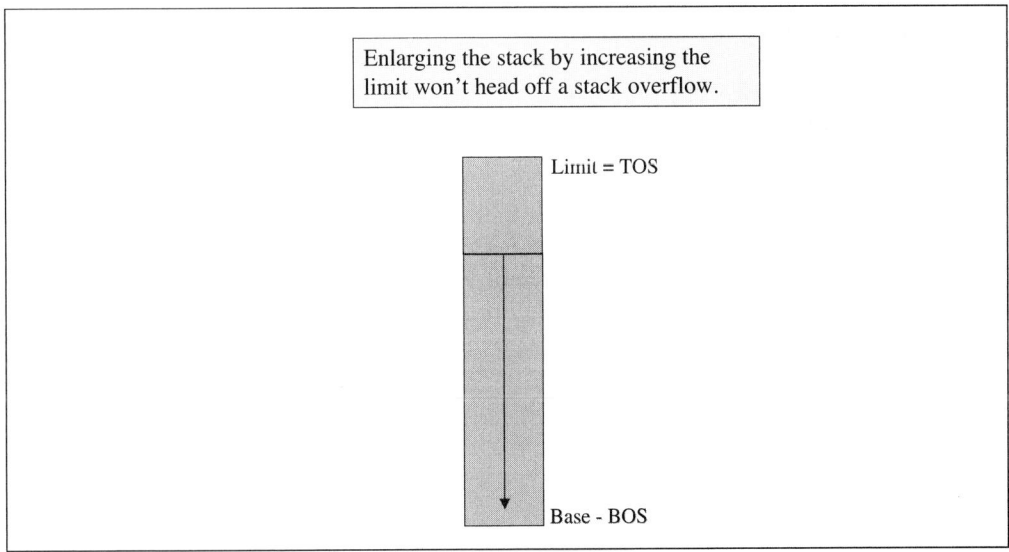

Expand-Down Stack Description

Most OSs implement expand-up stacks (see "Expand-Up Stack" on page 485). However, a stack segment with E = 1 in its descriptor is defined as an expand-down stack. The author has always found this name to be misleading. As with an expand up stack, the stack still grows downward towards its floor as items are pushed into the stack. The only real difference is that the stack now has an artificial floor.

Refer to Figure 15-10 on page 491. An expand down stack is different from an expand up stack in the following ways:

- The stack segment's base address specifies the real, ultimate floor of the stack (see the next bullet item).
- Refer to Figure 15-11 on page 492. The limit specified in the stack segment descriptor no longer specifies the stack size. Rather, it specifies an artificial stack floor. The artificial floor = the actual stack segment base address + the limit + 1.
- The offset of the Top of Stack (TOS) from the stack segment's actual base address is either FFFFh (if the B, or Big, bit in the stack segment descriptor = 0), or FFFFFFFFh (if the B, or Big, bit in the stack segment descriptor = 1).

An Example

As an example, assume that the stack segment is an expand-down stack, the segment's base address is 00000000h, its limit is FFFh, and that the B bit = 1 in its descriptor. This means that:

- The stack segment's ultimate base address is virtual address 00000000h.
- Its artificial floor is currently set to 00000000h + FFFh + 1 = 00001000h.
- The offset of the TOS is FFFFFFFFh before anything is pushed onto the stack. The TOS therefore = 00000000h + FFFFFFFF = FFFFFFFFh.
- The first 32-bit object pushed into the stack is stored in locations FFFFFFFBh (FFFFFFFFh - 4) through FFFFFFFEh.
- As additional items are pushed onto the stack, the stack grows downward towards its artificial floor (at location 00001000h).
- If the stack is full and an attempt is made to push another item onto the stack (causing it to fall through its artificial floor), a stack exception is generated.
- The OS's stack exception handler can then adjust the artificial floor downwards towards it actual base address by decreasing the segment descriptor's limit value.
- After doing so, the handler can return to and re-execute the Push instruction that caused the stack overflow exception. It will now re-execute successfully because the artificial floor has been lowered.

Another Example

As another example, assume that the stack segment is an expand-down stack, the segment's base address is 02000000h, its limit is FFFh, and that the B bit = 1 in its descriptor. This means that:

- The stack segment's ultimate virtual base address is 02000000h.
- Its BOS (i.e., its artificial floor) is currently set to 02000000h + FFFh + 1 = 02001000h.
- The offset of the TOS is FFFFFFFFh before anything is pushed onto the stack. The TOS therefore = 02000000h + FFFFFFFFh = 01FFFFFFh.
- The first 32-bit object pushed into the stack is stored in locations 01FFFFFBh - 01FFFFFEh.
- As additional items are pushed onto the stack, the stack grows downward towards its artificial floor (at location 02001000h).
- If the stack is full and an attempt is made to push another item onto the stack, a stack exception is generated.
- The OS's stack exception handler can then adjust the artificial floor downwards towards it actual base address by decreasing the segment descriptor's limit value.
- After doing so, the handler can then return to and re-execute the Push instruction that caused the stack overflow exception. It will now re-execute successfully because the artificial floor has been lowered.

Figure 15-10: Expand-Down Stack Approaching Full

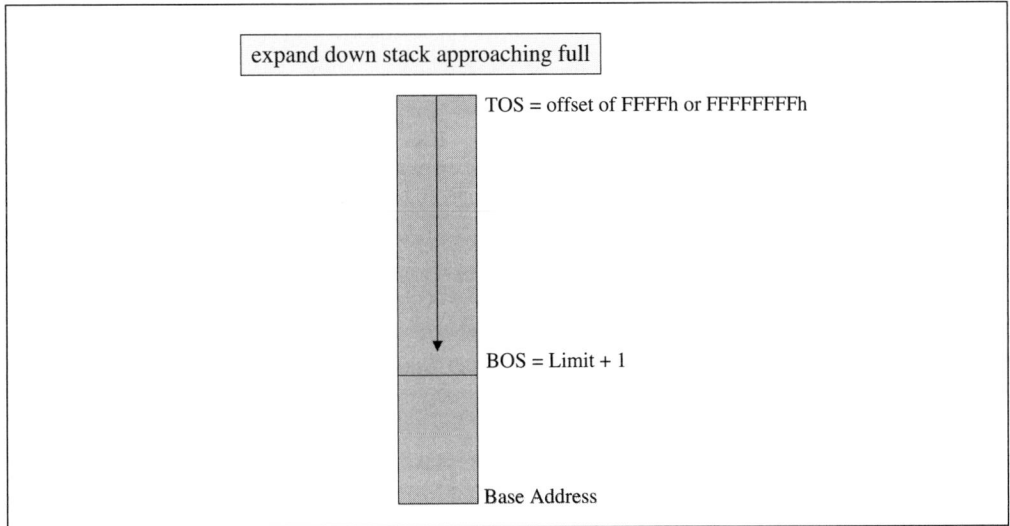

Figure 15-11: Decreasing Limit Lowers the Stack's Artificial Floor

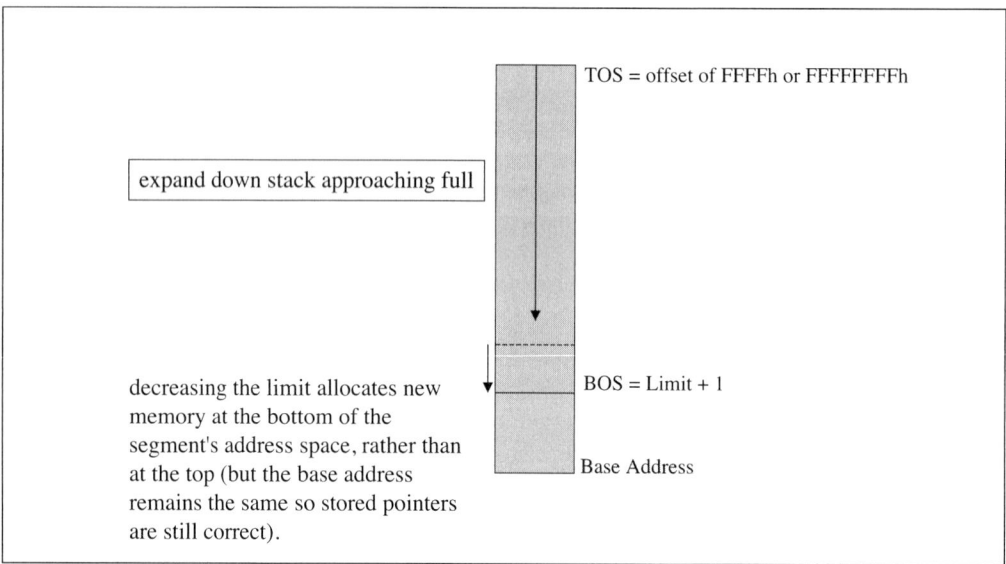

expand down stack approaching full

TOS = offset of FFFFh or FFFFFFFFh

BOS = Limit + 1

Base Address

decreasing the limit allocates new memory at the bottom of the segment's address space, rather than at the top (but the base address remains the same so stored pointers are still correct).

16 *IA-32 Address Translation Mechanisms*

The Previous Chapter

The previous chapter provided a detailed description of Data and Stack segments (including Expand-Up and Expand-Down Stacks) and privilege checking. The following topics were covered:

- The Data Segments.
  - General.
  - Two-Step Permission Check.
  - An Example.
- Selecting and Accessing a Stack Segment.
  - Introduction.
  - Expand-Up Stack.
  - Expand-Down Stack.
    - The Problem.
    - Expand-Down Stack Description.
    - An Example.
    - Another Example.

This Chapter

This chapter covers the following topics:

- Summarizes the evolution of the virtual-to-physical address translation facilities on the x86 processors and provides a backgrounder on memory and disk management.

- The concept of virtual memory is introduced as well as the advantages of address translation.
- The first and second generation virtual-to-physical address translation mechanisms are described in detail.
- The role of the Translation Lookaside Buffer (TLB) is described, as well as the Global Page feature and TLB maintenance.
- Page Directory Entries (PDEs) and Page Table Entries (PTEs) are described in detail.
- Page access permission.
- Missing page or Page Table.
- Page access history.
- 4MB pages.
- PSE-36 Mode.
- Execute Disable feature.
- Page caching rules.
- Page write protection.

The Next Chapter

The next chapter describes the operational characteristics of various types of memory targets (UC, WC, WP, WT, and WB) and the role of the Memory Type and Range Registers (MTRRs). It defines the concept of speculatively executed loads and describes issues related to the logical processor's Posted Memory Write Buffer (PMWB) and Write-Combining Buffers (WCBs).

Three Generations

Over the years, the x86 address translation mechanism has experienced three major evolutionary changes (as well as a number of smaller, incremental changes). Consequently, the author has divided the discussion into three major sections:

- **1st-generation paging**. The address translation mechanism was first introduced in the x86 product line with the advent of the 386 processor. This mechanism (including some minor enhancements added in the 486 and Pentium) is what the author refers to as the *first-generation paging* mechanism. It should be noted, however, that page address translation was actually first introduced in mainframe computers many years earlier.
- **2nd-generation paging**. The next major evolutionary jump, PAE-36 Mode, was first implemented in the Pentium Pro processor.
- **3rd-generation paging**. Part of the Intel 64 architecture.

The first and second generations are covered in this chapter. The third generation is covered in "IA-32e Address Translation" on page 983.

Demand Mode Paging Evolution

Since the advent of the 386 processor, a number of enhancements have been made to the Paging mechanism. Table 16-1 on page 495 tracks the evolutionary changes that appeared in successive generations of the x86 processor family.

Table 16-1: Paging Evolution

Processor	Enhancement	Described in
386	-	**First-generation address translation**. Virtual-to-physical address translation was first introduced to the x86 product family with the advent of the 386 processor. Using this mechanism, a 2-level lookup is used to translate a 32-bit virtual address into a 32-bit physical memory address.
486	Write Protect feature	A complete description of this minor enhancement can be found in "Example Usage: Unix Copy-on-Write Strategy" on page 569.
486	Caching Rules	Minor enhancements: • CR3[PCD] and CR3[PWT] were added. A complete description can be found in "Translation Table Caching Rules" on page 585. • PCD and PWT bits were added to each Page Directory Entry (PDE). Refer to "Defining a Page's Caching Rules" on page 585. • PCD and PWT bits were added to each Page Table Entry (PTE). Refer to "Defining a Page's Caching Rules" on page 585.
Pentium	4MB Pages	The Page Size Extension (PSE) feature was added. This minor enhancement was first implemented in the Pentium and was migrated into the later versions of the 486. A complete description can be found in "4MB Pages" on page 550.
Pentium	Global pages	A minor enhancement. A complete description can be found in "Global Pages" on page 526.

Table 16-1: Paging Evolution (Continued)

Processor	Enhancement	Described in
Pentium Pro	PAE-36 Mode (2nd generation paging)	**Second-generation address translation**. Using this mechanism, a 3-level lookup is used to translate a 32-bit virtual address into a 36-bit physical memory address. A complete description can be found in "Second-Generation Paging" on page 553.
Pentium II	PSE-36 Mode	This was a minor enhancement added in the Pentium II Xeon (the very first Xeon processor). A complete description can be found in "PSE-36 Mode Background" on page 575.
	PAT feature	Page Attribute Table feature (a minor enhancement). A complete description can be found in "PAT Feature (Page Attribute Table)" on page 587.
Pentium 4	Intel 64	**Third-generation address translation**. The Intel 64 architecture introduced the third-generation address translation mechanism. Using this mechanism, a 4-level lookup can translate a 48-bit virtual address into a physical memory address up to 48-bits in width (*note*: current implementations translate a 48-bit virtual address into a 40-, 41-, or 48-bit physical address).

Background

Memory and Disk: Block-Oriented Devices

Mass storage devices are block-oriented devices. Information is stored on a disk as a series of fixed-length blocks of information and the OS manages disks in that manner. From the perspective of the OS kernel, memory is also managed as a series of fixed-length blocks—referred to as pages—of storage.

Definition of a Page

The OS kernel's memory manager (frequently referred to as the *malloc*, or memory allocation, facility) manages memory as a series of pages of information, each of a uniform size, each starting on an address boundary divisible by its size. The most common page size used by many computer architectures is the 4KB page with each page starting on an address boundary divisible by 4KB. As an example:

- The first page of physical memory occupies locations 00000000h-00000FFFh.
- The second occupies locations 00001000h-00001FFFh.
- The third occupies locations 00002000h-00002FFFh.
- etc.

It should also be mentioned that in the x86 architecture, while the majority (perhaps all of) memory is managed as 4KB pages, an OS may also support treating some (few) areas of memory as large pages (2MB or 4MB in size). This topic is covered later in this chapter.

Example Scenario: Block Transfer from Disk to Memory

The following example scenario is intended as a high-level demonstration of the similarity between the OS's treatment of memory allocation requests and its management of disk-based information. The example assumes that an application has issued a request to the OS to fetch a block of information from a mass storage device into physical memory. In response:

1. The OS passes the request to the disk device driver.
2. The device driver issues a request to the OS to locate and reserve the requisite number of free memory pages to receive the data. In response, the OS returns the start address of the memory buffer to the driver.
3. The driver issues a command to the disk controller instructing it to read the requested number of pages of information from the disk and to write the information into memory starting at the beginning of the memory-based buffer.
4. Rather than wasting time while the disk controller completes the operation, the OS:
   — Makes an entry in the scheduler's event queue associating the subsequent completion of the disk operation with the current task.
   — Suspends the currently-running task and starts or resumes another one.
5. In the meantime, the disk controller seeks the read/write head mechanism to the proper cylinder, waits for the start sector to arrive under the read head, and then reads the requested number of pages (blocks) of information into a controller buffer.

6. The controller then performs a burst memory write transaction to write the requested information into the pre-allocated buffer in system memory.
7. Upon completion of the write, the controller generates a device-specific interrupt request to the logical processor.
8. The currently-running task is interrupted and the logical processor executes the interrupt handler within the disk driver. The handler interrogates the disk controller and discovers that the reason for the interrupt was the conclusion of the disk transfer.
9. Checking its event queue, the OS scheduler determines that the previously-suspended task can now be resumed. Consequently, it suspends the currently-running task and resumes execution of the previously-suspended task.
10. The task can now access the requested pages of information in memory.

A Poor Memory Allocation Strategy

The following example highlights a highly-inefficient approach to memory management:

1. **Assumption**: the machine has been up and running for awhile. As a result, many memory pages are currently in use by various tasks. The pages that are currently free (i.e., not in use) are scattered throughout physical memory. If an application were to issue a request for a memory buffer multiple pages in length, the OS may or may not be able to find a contiguous block of free pages large enough to fulfill the request.
2. An application calls the OS memory allocation facility (malloc) and requests a buffer 32KB in size (e.g., for a text document).
3. Malloc manages memory in 4KB increments with each page starting on an address divisible by 4K.
4. Malloc looks for eight available free pages in memory (8 x 4K = 32K).
5. Assume it finds eight pages starting at the following physical (i.e., actual) memory addresses:
    — 1F097000h
    — 01AF2000h
    — 78C14000h
    — 9FD1A000h
    — 3301A000h
    — FC0A7000h
    — 3BE1E000h
    — 00020000h

Although, malloc could be designed in such a manner that it returns a list containing the start addresses of the eight physical pages to the application, this would obviously be a terrible solution.

Applications Are Presented With a Simplified World-View

Introduction

The previous chapters described the manner in which instructions (and the code fetch logic) address memory:

* 32-bit offset + 32-bit segment base address = 32-bit virtual (also referred to as linear) address.

If the address translation mechanism isn't enabled (i.e., if paging were not used by the OS kernel), the resultant address is *not* a virtual but rather the actual physical memory address. Since virtually all modern OSs do use paging, however, the remainder of this chapter assumes that the virtual address is submitted to the paging logic for translation into the actual physical address of the target object in memory.

Life Without Paging Would Be Chaotic

Refer to Figure 16-1 on page 500. As highlighted in "A Poor Memory Allocation Strategy" on page 498, it is highly possible that the pages of memory allocated to hold an application's code and data are, in reality, scattered throughout physical memory. Dealing with such a reality, however, would make the programmer's life a nightmare.

Figure 16-1: Life Without Address Translation

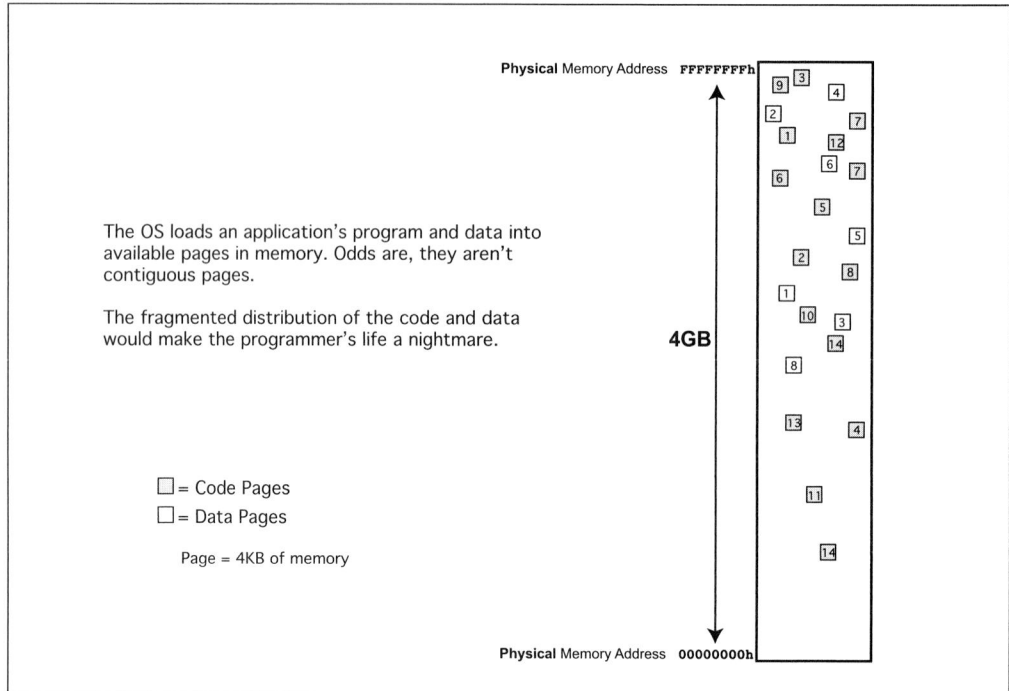

The Virtual World Is a Simple One

Refer to Figure 16-2 on page 501. The address translation mechanism creates the illusion that the application's code and data space consists of contiguous ranges. Figure 16-3 on page 502 through Figure 16-7 on page 506 illustrate how the address translation logic redirects the virtual addresses generated by the application to the correct locations in physical memory.

Figure 16-2: Life With Address Translation

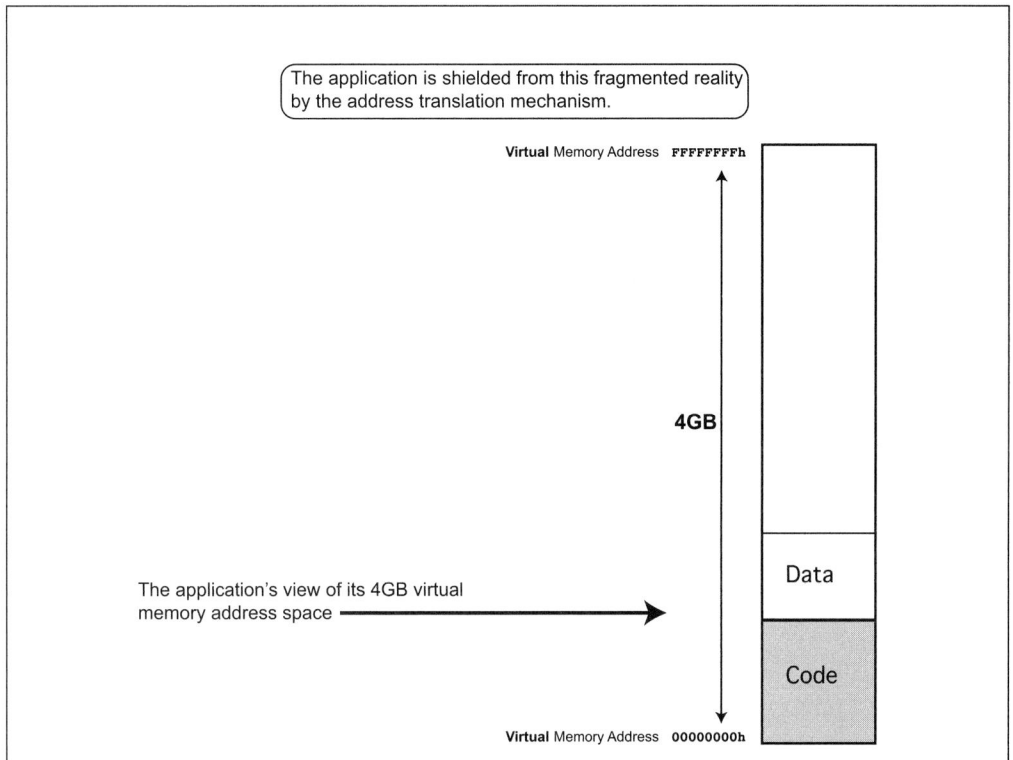

In Figure 16-3 through Figure 16-5, the application is shown addressing locations in the first three contiguous pages of its virtual code address space. Invisible to the application, the address translation logic translates those addresses into the corresponding addresses in the perhaps widely-scattered pages of physical memory assigned to hold the application's code.

Figure 16-3: Address Translation Redirects Access 1

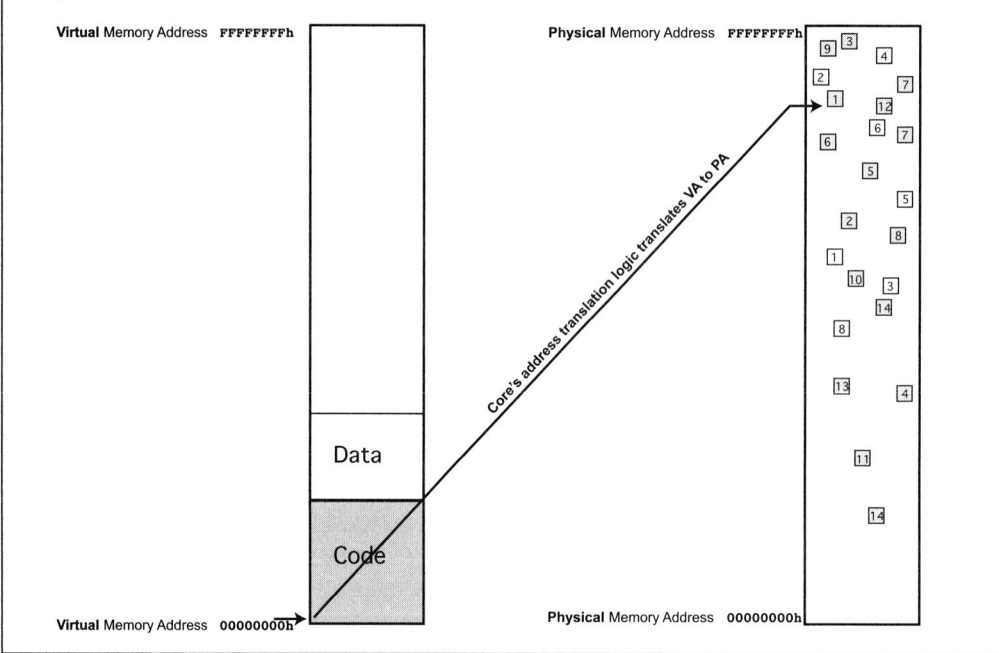

Figure 16-4: Address Translation Redirects Access 2

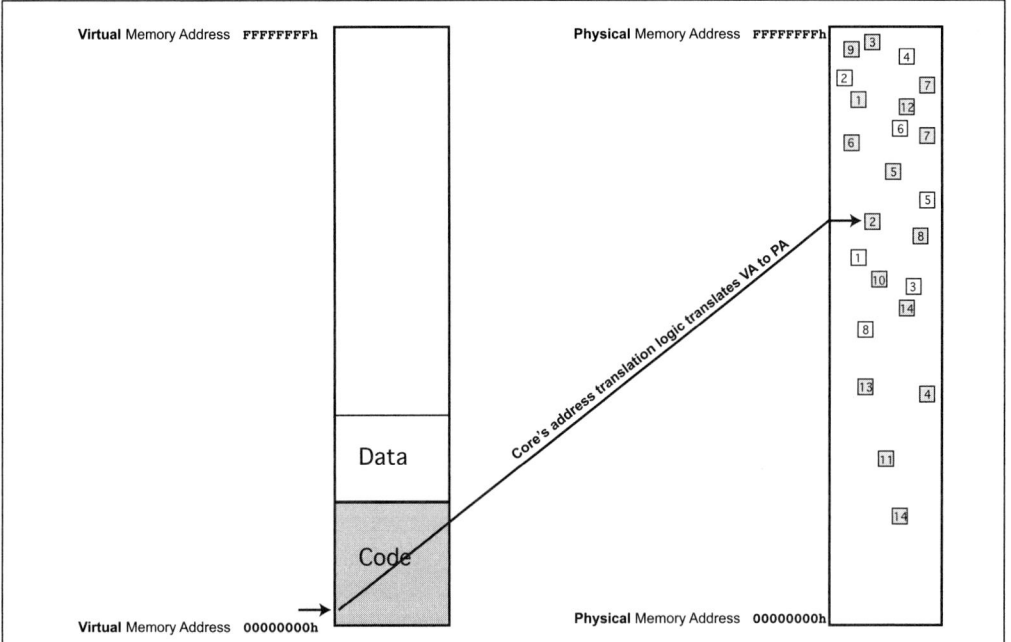

Figure 16-5: Address Translation Redirects Access 3

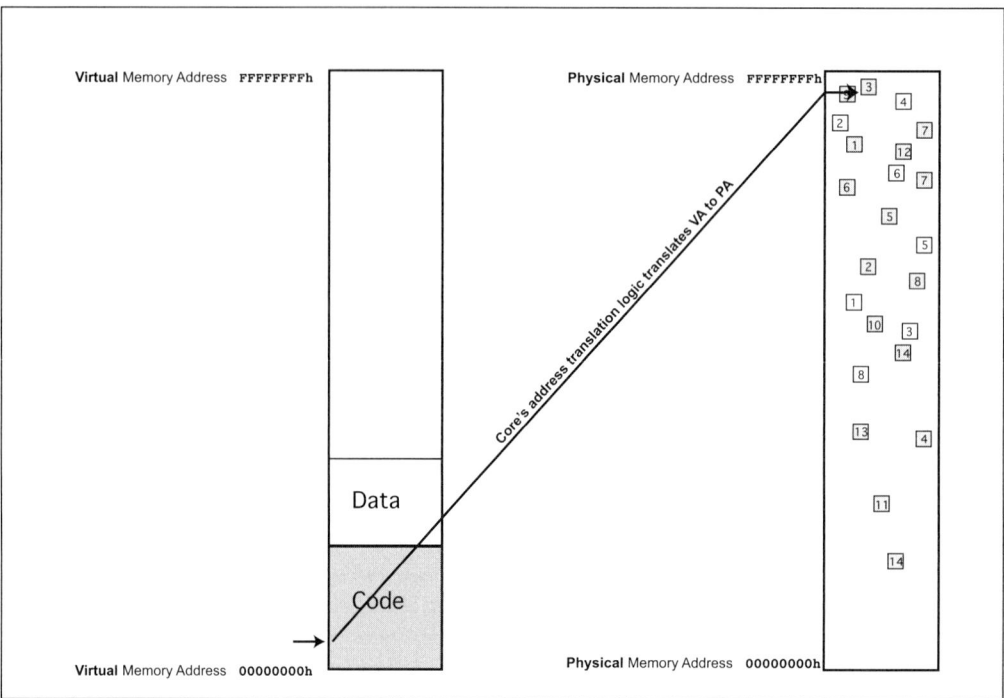

In Figure 16-6 and Figure 16-7, the application is shown addressing locations in the first two contiguous pages of its virtual data address space. Invisible to the application, the address translation logic translates those addresses into the corresponding addresses in the perhaps widely-scattered pages of physical memory assigned to hold the application's data.

Figure 16-6: Address Translation Redirects Access 4

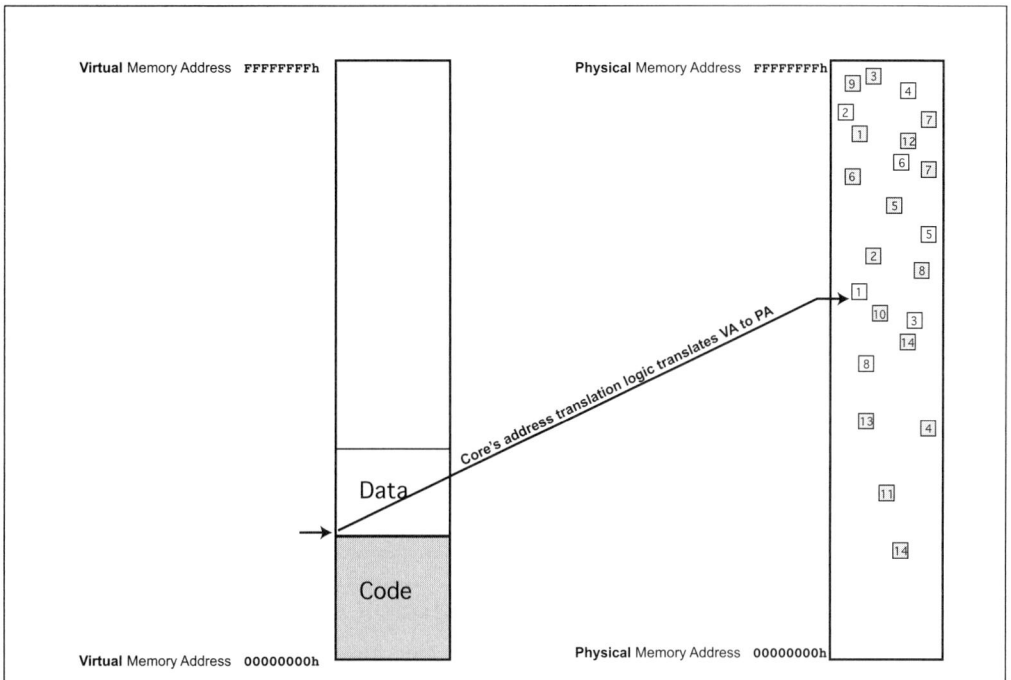

Figure 16-7: Address Translation Redirects Access 5

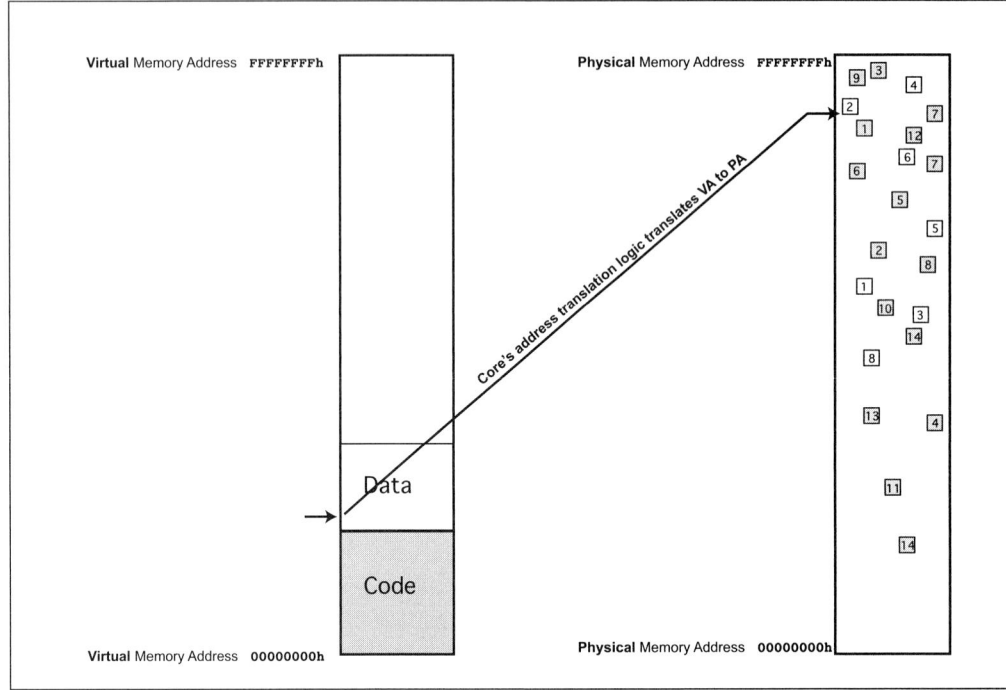

Virtual Address Space Partitioning

Refer to Figure 16-8 on page 507. From the viewpoint of the x86 processor's first generation paging mechanism, the 4GB virtual address space is subdivided into 1024 regions each of which is 4MB in size. Each 4MB region is further subdivided into 1024, 4KB pages:

- The upper 10 virtual address bits [31:22] identify the target 4MB region (1-of-1024 regions) and selects the entry in the Page Directory associated with the addressed 4MB virtual address region (region 4 in the illustration). Page Directory Entry 4 contains the physical base address of the Page Table that catalogs the location of the 1024 pages that comprise region 4.
- The next 10 virtual address bits [21:12] identify the target 4KB page (1-of-1024) within the target 4MB region. In the illustration, this portion of the virtual address selects the entry (Page Table Entry 34) in the region 4 Page Table associated with the addressed virtual page (page 34 in region 4). Page

Table Entry (PTE) 34 contains the physical start address of the target 4KB page in memory. It also contains a series of attribute bits associated with the target page.
*   The lower 12 virtual address bits [11:0] identify the exact start address (1-of-4096 locations) within the target page.

Figure 16-8: First Generation 4GB Virtual Address Space Partitioning

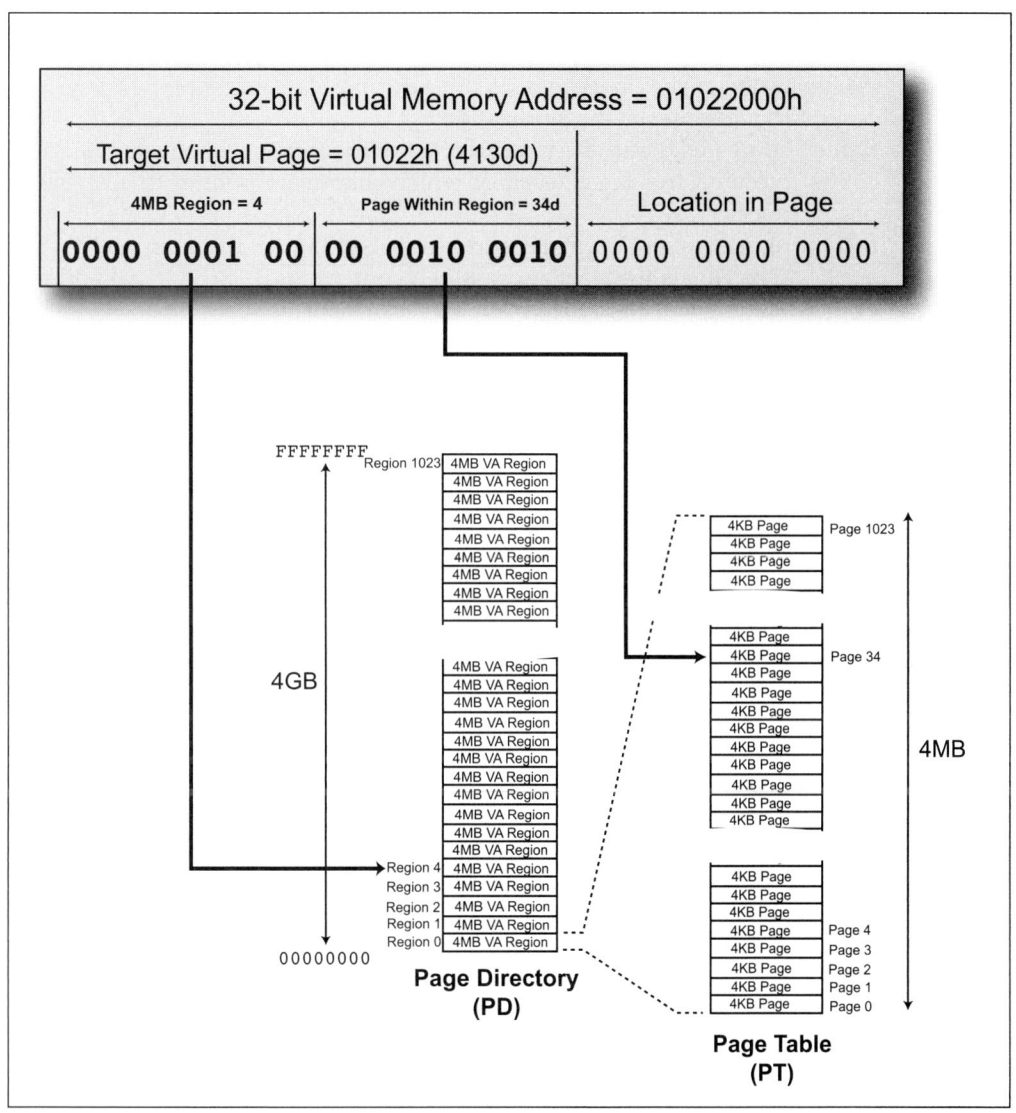

Example Virtual Buffer Allocation

Refer to Figure 16-9 on page 509. In this example, an application makes a call to malloc requesting the allocation of a 3.6MB memory buffer for its use. In order to fulfill this request, the OS takes the following actions:

1. Locates 900 memory pages (900 x 4KB = 3.6MB) that are currently free (i.e., not allocated to any task). These pages are scattered throughout physical memory.
2. As illustrated earlier, malloc does not return a list containing 900 physical page start addresses to the application.
3. Rather, it creates a series of contiguous entries in the application's Page Tables (more on this later), each of which contains a pointer to a physical page in memory.
4. It then returns a single virtual address (01800000h in the example) to the application. This is the start address of a contiguous 3.6MB virtual address range spanning 900 contiguous 4KB pages of *virtual* address space.
5. When the application subsequently addresses any location within this virtual address range, the paging logic must somehow translate the virtual page address into the appropriate physical page address and then use *that* address to address memory on behalf of the application.

Figure 16-9: Example Virtual Buffer

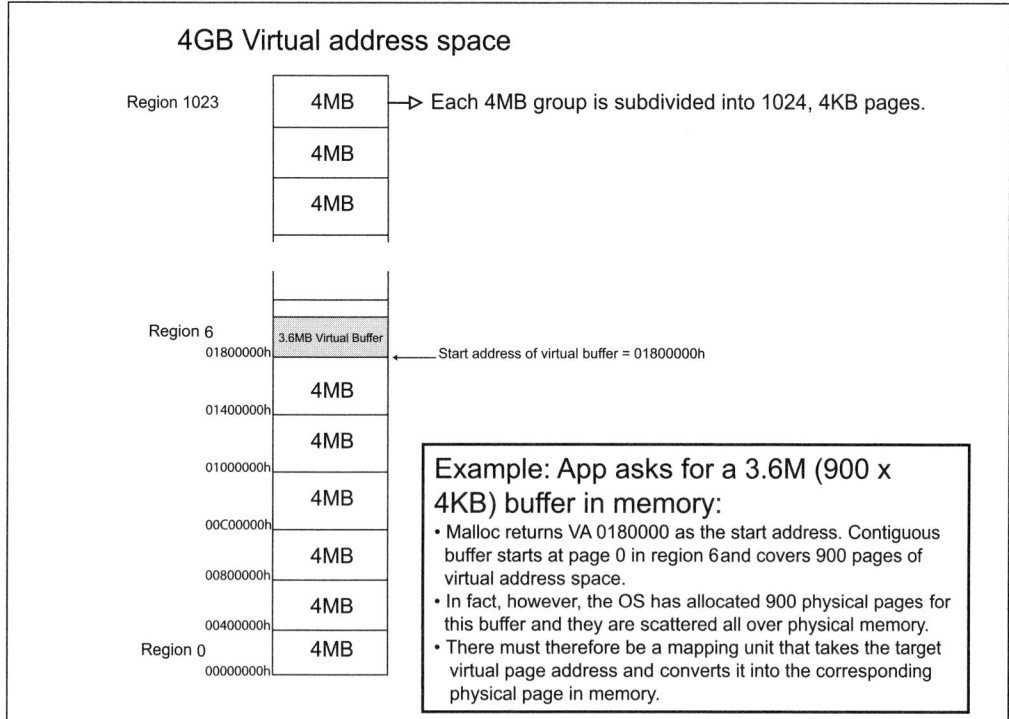

Address Translation Advantages

Introduction

There a number of reasons why most OSs treat the memory address generated by program execution as a virtual rather than a physical memory address. The following sections provide a brief summary of the various advantages associated with the address translation mechanism.

Simplifies Memory Management

As already illustrated, the application programmer is provided with a greatly-simplified view of the world: even though the areas of memory allocated for its code and data may in reality be scattered all over physical memory, the application is shielded from such complexity. Unknown to the application, when it addresses an item in virtual memory space, the logical processor's paging unit remaps the virtual memory address to the correct location in physical memory.

Efficient Memory Usage

A Wasteful Approach

Consider the following scenario:

1. A machine has 256MB of RAM memory (a ridiculously small amount by today's measure, but this is just an example, after all).
2. The ROM-based Power-On Self-Test (POST) completes execution and the boot program reads (i.e., boots) the OS loader program into memory.
3. The OS loader reads the entire OS into memory, consuming 250MB of memory (this is just an example; in this day and age, it would be a rare OS indeed that were this small). The OS is a multitasking OS, permitting the end user to start multiple programs. Under the control of its task scheduler, the OS rapidly timeslices between them, giving the appearance that all of the programs run simultaneously.
4. The user tells the OS to start a word processing application. In response, the OS loads the entire application into memory, consuming 3MB (once again, a ridiculously small amount) of memory and leaving only 3MB of available memory.
5. The user starts another application which is loaded in its entirety into memory, consuming an additional 2.5MB of memory.
6. 255.5MB of memory is now in use and only .5MB remains free. The user attempts to start another application, causing the OS to respond that there is insufficient memory.

In this scenario, both the OS loader and the OS task manager manage the pool of free memory in a very inefficient fashion. The entire OS is loaded into memory even though large portions of the OS code may never be required during the current work session. Furthermore, each time the user starts a program, the OS loads the entire program into memory. Once again, large portions of the application's code may never be required during the current work session. As an example, Microsoft Word implements hundreds of features, most of which are never called upon during a typical work session.

A Better Approach: Load On Demand

The OS loader should be designed to load only the portions of the OS:

- That are necessary to load and run application programs.
- That are used very frequently and should therefore remain in memory in order to yield good performance.

The remainder of the OS should be kept on disk until it is required.

Likewise, the OS application program loader should be designed to load only enough of an application program into memory to get it started. Additional portions of the application program should only be read into memory upon demand. Paging (often referred to as demand-mode paging) provides a great solution to this problem.

Attribute Assignment

As previously described in "IA-32 Flat Memory Model" on page 409 and "No Protection? Paging Takes Care of It" on page 412, while the implementation of the flat memory model by an OS kernel effectively eliminates segmentation, it also creates a major problem: many of the protections afforded by segmentation are also eliminated. The paging unit comes to the rescue.

When a virtual memory address is submitted to the paging unit for translation, it selects a Page Table Entry (PTE) that contains the start address of the physical memory page to which this virtual address is mapped. In addition, the PTE also contains a series of attributes that describe the currently-running program's access rights within that page:

- The minimum privilege level the program must have to access any location within the page.
- The read/writability of the page.
- The memory type assigned to the page (e.g., whether its cacheable or not and, if it is, how the logical processor should handle reads and writes—i.e., loads and stores—within the page).
- Whether the page is globally shared among multiple tasks.

All of these topics are described in detail later in this chapter.

Track Access History

Each PTE also contains two bits—the *D*irty and *A*ccessed bits—that the logical processor hardware uses to track access history within the page.

Allows DOS Applications to Co-Exist

Problem: Running Multiple DOS Programs

Application programs designed for the DOS environment were written using 8088 code and only access information in the first 1MB of memory space (00000000h - 000FFFFFh). Furthermore, each DOS application believes itself to be the only program executing and, as long as it doesn't corrupt the OS (which also resides in the first 1MB area), it can access any location within the first 1MB of memory space.

If a multitasking OS were to load two or more DOS application programs into the first 1MB of memory, the second one would almost certainly overwrite a portion of the first one (thereby rendering it useless). Even if they occupied mutually-exclusive areas of the first 1MB (highly unlikely), each of the programs would feel free to write into the memory areas occupied by the other program(s). In a word, anarchy!

Solution: Address Redirection

The OS can multitask multiple DOS applications by taking the following precautions:

- Load each DOS application program into a separate 1MB area of memory (other than the first MB).
- When a DOS program is executing, it only generates virtual memory addresses within the first 1MB of memory (i.e., addresses 00000h - FFFFFh). Since it actually resides in a 1MB area other than the first MB, the logical processor must in some manner automatically redirect each of its memory accesses to the same relative location within the MB of memory it really resides in. Figure 16-10 on page 513 illustrates a scenario wherein two DOS application programs have been loaded into different 1MB memory areas along with a complete copy of what each expects to find in the 1st MB of memory space.

Once again, the paging logic comes to the rescue. Each DOS application has its own, private set of Page Tables that have been set up to redirect their accesses within the first MB of virtual address space to the same relative location within the 1MB memory area in which it actually resides.

Figure 16-10: Paging Redirects DOS Accesses to a Discrete 1MB Area

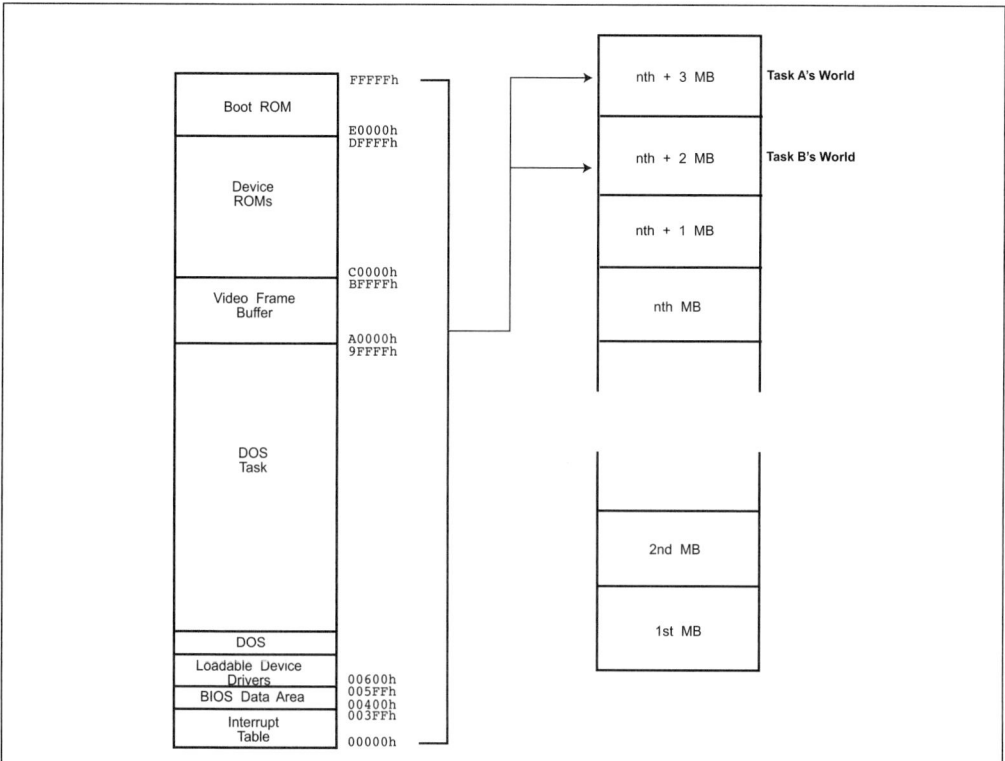

First-Generation Paging

Definition of First Generation Paging

The page address translation mechanism was first introduced in the x86 product line with the advent of the 386 processor. This mechanism (including some minor enhancements added in the 486 and Pentium) is what the author refers to as the first generation paging mechanism. It should be stressed that the terms first-, second-, and third-generation paging are the author's (not Intel's and not AMD's).

First-generation paging is in use by the OS kernel when all of the following are true:

- 1st generation paging is enabled (CR0[PG] = 1).
- PAE-36 mode (2nd generation) paging is disabled (CR4[PAE] = 0).
- PSE-36 mode paging is disabled (CR4[PSE] = 0).
- IA-32e (3rd generation) paging is disabled (EFER[LME] = 0).

PAE-36 and PSE-36 paging modes are described later in this chapter and IA-32e paging is described in "IA-32e Address Translation" on page 983.

Paging Logic's Interpretation of a Virtual Address

Figure 16-11 on page 514 illustrates how the logical processor's paging unit interprets the 32-bit virtual address produced by the segmentation logic. Each of the three fields contains a binary-weighted value:

- The upper 10-bits identifies the target 4MB virtual address region (1-of-1024). In the example, 4MB virtual region 4 is being addressed.
- The middle 10-bits identifies the target virtual 4KB page (1-of-1024) within the selected region. In the example, virtual page 34d in region 4 is being addressed.
- The lower 12-bits of the virtual address identifies the exact target location (1-of-4096) within the selected page. In the example, location 000h is being addressed.

Figure 16-11: Example Virtual Address

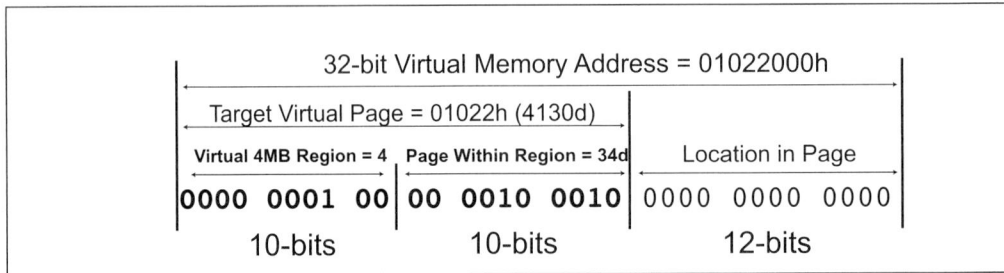

First-Generation Paging Overview

The Set-Up

The example used in "A Poor Memory Allocation Strategy" on page 498 described a scenario wherein an application issued a request to malloc for a 32KB memory buffer in response to which malloc returned a list containing the start physical addresses of eight widely-scattered 4KB memory pages (8 x 4KB = 32KB).

In reality, a well-designed malloc facility would simply return the start address of a contiguous 32KB buffer in virtual memory address space. Before doing so, however, it would initialize eight contiguous Page Table Entries (PTEs) entries in the application's Page Tables as shown in Figure 16-12 on page 518.

1. Before starting the application:
   — The OS kernel allocated memory for the application's initial code and data areas.
   — It created the application's address translation tables in memory and initialized CR3 with the physical base address of the top-level address translation directory.
     – It created the application's top-level Page Directory (PD) in memory and loaded CR3 with the 4KB-aligned physical base address of the PD. This directory can have up to 1024 PD entries (PDEs) each of which corresponds to a 4MB virtual address region (see Figure 16-8 on page 507) consisting of 1024, 4KB pages. Each PDE contains the start physical memory address of a second-level Page Table (PT).
     – The OS kernel uses the 1024 entries (PTEs) in a memory-based Page Table to record the presence or absence of a physical page in memory. If the corresponding page is currently present in memory, the respective PTE contains the 4KB-aligned start physical address of the page in memory.
2. In this example, once started the application calls malloc and requests a buffer 32KB in size (e.g., for a text document).
   — Malloc manages memory in 4KB increments with each page starting on an address divisible by 4KB.
3. Malloc looks for eight available free pages in memory (8 x 4K = 32K).
4. Refer to Figure 16-12 on page 518 and assume malloc locates eight available pages starting at the following physical (i.e., actual) memory addresses:
   — 1F097000h

- 01AF2000h
- 78C14000h
- 9FD1A000h
- 3301A000h
- FC0A7000h
- 3BE1E000h
- 00020000h

5. Malloc returns the 4KB-aligned start address of a contiguous virtual 32KB memory area to the application. In the example scenario, the virtual start address returned = 01022000h and the 32KB buffer spans the contiguous virtual memory address range 01022000h - 01029FFFh. The application is shielded from the reality that the eight physical pages are strewn throughout memory.

6. The virtual address range assigned to the buffer encompasses eight contiguous virtual pages—34 through 41—in 4MB virtual region number 4. Consequently:
   - If Page Table 4 hadn't already been created, it is created in memory and its 4KB-aligned physical start address is recorded in PDE 4.
   - The 4KB-aligned physical start addresses of the eight physical pages allocated to the buffer are recorded in PTEs 34 - 41 which correspond to virtual pages 34 - 41 in 4MB region number 4.

Virtual-to-Physical Address Translation

The Goal. When a virtual memory address is submitted to the paging unit for translation (see Figure 16-11 on page 514), the goal is to replace the upper 20-bits (the virtual page address) of the virtual address with the upper 20-bits of the corresponding physical page address in memory. The logical processor's paging unit accomplishes this using the virtual page address to perform a lookup in the address translation tables set up for the application by the OS.

The Translation. Figure 16-12 through Figure 16-15 and their accompanying descriptions define the actions taken as the currently-running program performs accesses within the first four of the eight virtual pages comprising the 32KB buffer. The logical processor knows the location of the current application's top-level translation directory (i.e., the Page Directory) because CR3 contains its 4KB-aligned physical base address.

Definitions:

- PD stands for the top-level Page Directory.
- PDE stands for Page Directory Entry (e.g., PDE 4 stands for PDE number 4).

— PT stands for a second-level Page Table.
— PTE stands for Page Table Entry (e.g., PTE 34 stands for PTE number 34).
— In the illustrations, VA and PA correspond to virtual address and physical address.

1. Refer to Figure 16-12 on page 518. When any location within the first page of the virtual buffer (i.e., locations 01022000h - 01022FFFh) is accessed, the logical processor is addressing page 34 in virtual 4MB region number 4.

2. The paging unit uses the upper 10 bits of the virtual address to select the entry in the PD corresponding to the currently-addressed virtual 4MB region (in this case, region 4). The paging unit calculates the start address of PDE 4 as follows:
    — PD physical base address from CR3 + (PDE group number x 4 bytes per entry).

3. Reading PDE 4 from memory, it now knows the base physical address of Page Table 4 which catalogs the location of the 1024 pages that comprise virtual 4MB region number 4.

4. The paging unit uses the middle 10-bits of the virtual address to select PTE 34 which tracks the location of virtual 4MB region number 4, page 34. It calculates the start address of PTE 34 as follows:
    — PT 4's physical base address (obtained from PDE 4) + (page number x 4 bytes per entry).

5. PTE 34 indicates that the target page is present in memory starting at physical address 00020000h (in actuality, the PTE only contains the upper 20 bits of the physical page address; since it is a rule that pages start on address boundaries divisible by 4KB, the lower 12 bits are assumed to be 0).

6. The paging unit replaces the virtual page address (i.e., the upper 20-bits of the virtual address) with the upper 20-bits of the physical page address obtained from PTE 34. The lower 12-bits of the virtual address identify the exact target location in the page and are never translated.

Figure 16-12: Accesses to Virtual Page 34 in Virtual 4MB Region Number 4

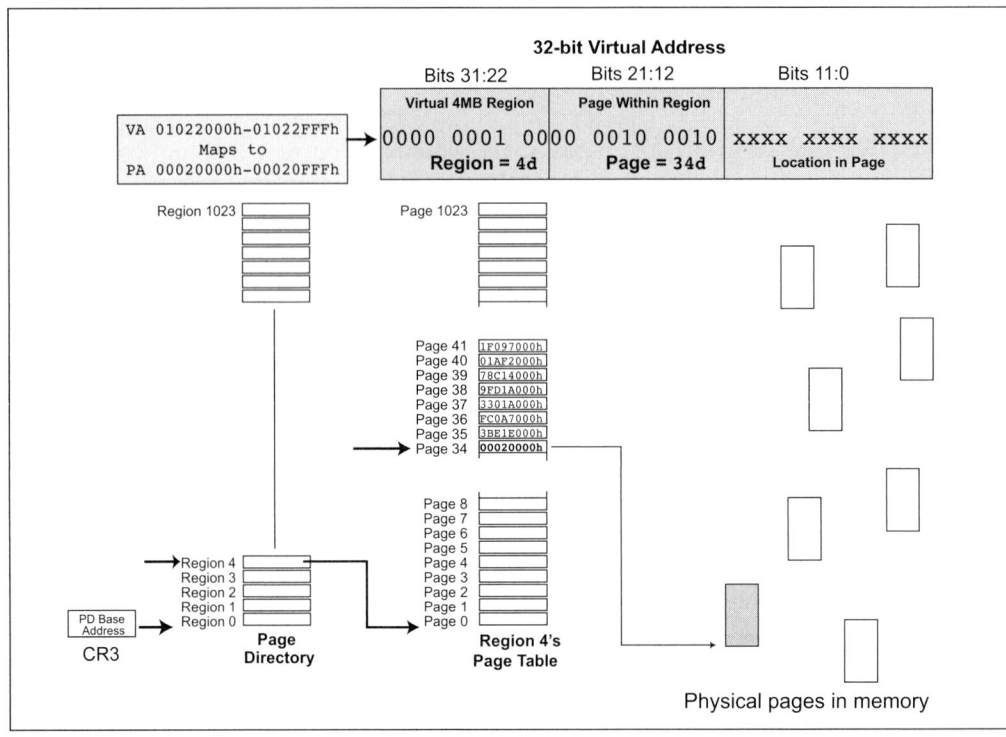

1. Refer to Figure 16-13 on page 519. When any location within the second page of the virtual buffer (i.e., locations 01023000h - 01023FFFh) is accessed, the logical processor is addressing page 35 in virtual 4MB region number 4.

2. The paging unit uses the upper 10 bits of the virtual address to select the entry in the PD corresponding to the currently-addressed virtual 4MB region number (in this case, region 4). The paging unit calculates the start address of PDE 4 as follows:

    — PD physical base address from CR3 + (PDE region number x 4 bytes per entry).

3. Reading PDE 4 from memory, it now knows the base physical address of Page Table 4 which catalogs the locations of the 1024 pages that comprise virtual 4MB region number 4.

4. The paging unit uses the middle 10-bits of the virtual address to select PTE 35 which tracks the location of region 4, page 35. It calculates the start address of PTE 35 as follows:

    — PT 4's physical base address (obtained from PDE 4) + (page number x 4 bytes per entry).

5. PTE 35 indicates that the target page is present in memory starting at physical address 3BE1E000h (in actuality, the PTE only contains the upper 20 bits of the physical page address; since it is a rule that pages start on address boundaries divisible by 4KB, the lower 12 bits are assumed to be 0).

6. The paging unit replaces the virtual page address (i.e., the upper 20-bits of the virtual address) with the upper 20-bits of the physical page address obtained from PTE 35. The lower 12-bits of the virtual address identify the exact target location in the page and are never translated.

Figure 16-13: Accesses to Virtual Page 35 in Virtual 4MB Region Number 4

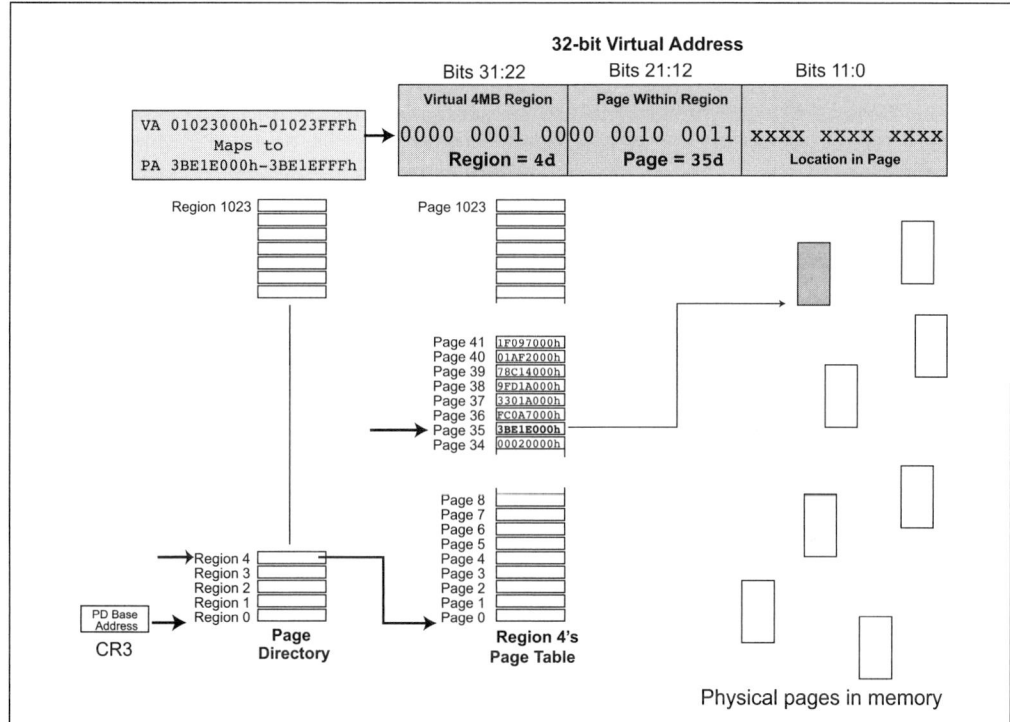

1. Refer to Figure 16-14 on page 520. Whenever any location within the third page of the virtual buffer (i.e., locations 01024000h - 01024FFFh) is accessed, the logical processor is addressing page 36 in virtual 4MB region number 4.

2. The paging unit uses the upper 10 bits of the virtual address to select the entry in the PD corresponding to the currently-addressed virtual 4MB region number (in this case, region 4). The paging unit calculates the start address of PDE 4 as follows:

   — PD physical base address from CR3 + (PDE virtual 4MB region number x 4 bytes per entry).

3. Reading PDE 4 from memory, it now knows the base physical address of Page Table 4 which catalogs the locations of the 1024 pages that comprise virtual 4MB region number 4.

4. The paging unit uses the middle 10-bits of the virtual address to select PTE 36 which tracks the location of region 4, page 36. It calculates the start address of PTE 36 as follows:
   — PT 4's physical base address (obtained from PDE 4) + (page number x 4 bytes per entry).

5. PTE 36 indicates that the target page is present in memory starting at physical address FC0A7000h (in actuality, the PTE only contains the upper 20 bits of the physical page address; since it is a rule that pages start on address boundaries divisible by 4KB, the lower 12 bits are assumed to be 0).

6. The paging unit replaces the virtual page address (i.e., the upper 20-bits of the virtual address) with the upper 20-bits of the physical page address obtained from PTE 36. The lower 12-bits of the virtual address identify the exact target location in the page and are never translated.

Figure 16-14: Accesses to Virtual Page 36 in Virtual 4MB Region Number 4

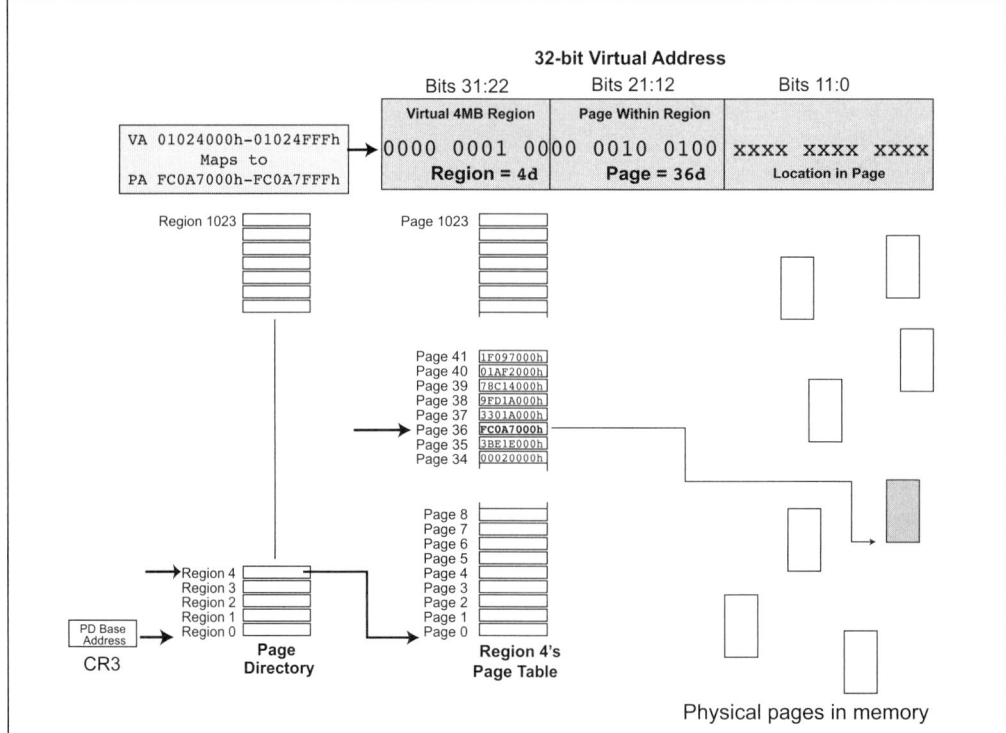

1. Refer to Figure 16-15 on page 522. Whenever any location within the fourth page of the virtual buffer (i.e., locations 01025000h - 01025FFFh) is accessed, the logical processor is addressing page 37 in virtual 4MB region number 4.

2. The paging unit uses the upper 10 bits of the virtual address to select the entry in the PD corresponding to the currently-addressed virtual 4MB region number (in this case, region 4). The paging unit calculates the start address of PDE 4 as follows:
   — PD physical base address from CR3 + (PDE virtual 4MB region number x 4 bytes per entry).

3. Reading PDE 4 from memory, it now knows the base physical address of Page Table 4 which catalogs the locations of the 1024 pages that comprise virtual 4MB region number 4.

4. The paging unit uses the middle 10-bits of the virtual address to select PTE 37 which tracks the location of region 4, page 37. It calculates the start address of PTE 37 as follows:
   — PT 4's physical base address (obtained from PDE 4) + (page number x 4 bytes per entry).

5. PTE 37 indicates that the target page is present in memory starting at physical address 3301A000h (in actuality, the PTE only contains the upper 20 bits of the physical page address; since it is a rule that pages start on address boundaries divisible by 4KB, the lower 12 bits are assumed to be 0).

6. The paging unit replaces the virtual page address (i.e., the upper 20-bits of the virtual address) with the upper 20-bits of the physical page address obtained from PTE 37. The lower 12-bits of the virtual address identify the exact target location in the page and are never translated.

Figure 16-15: Accesses to Virtual Page 37 in Virtual 4MB Region Number 4

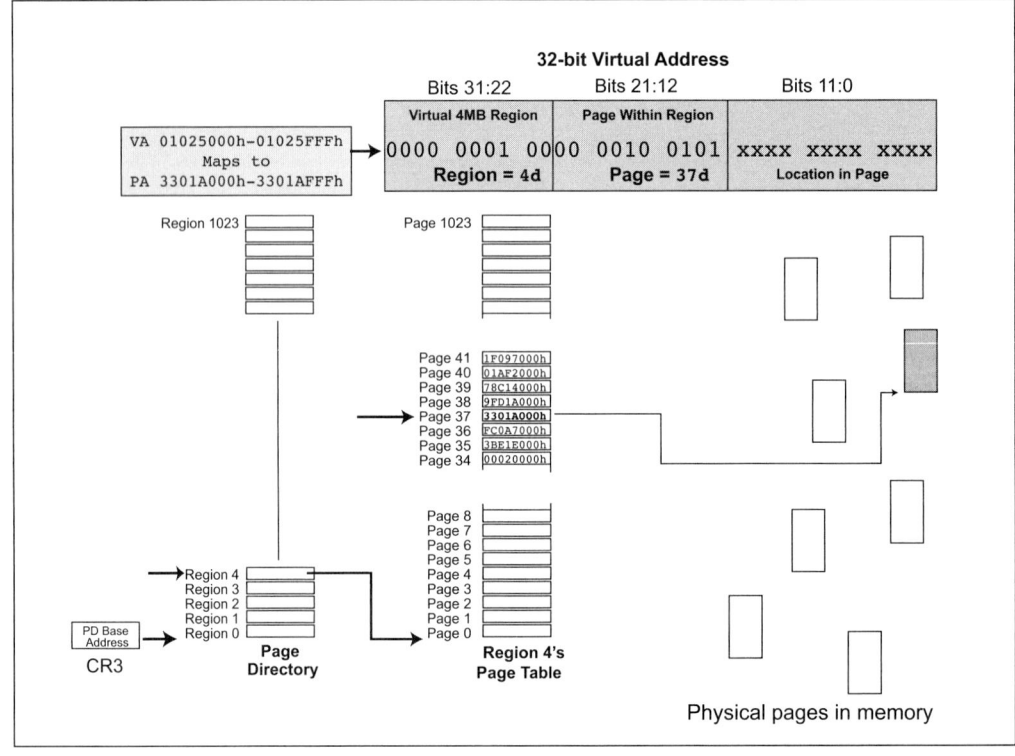

Two Overhead Memory Reads Take a Toll

Before the logical processor can access a memory location, the paging unit must perform two overhead memory reads to access the PDE and a PTE. This can have a severe effect on performance.

When a page is first accessed, the logical processor performs these two memory reads to obtain the selected PDE and PTE. To eliminate the need to access this same PTE for future accesses within the same page, however, x86 processors incorporate a relatively small, special-purpose cache—referred to as the **Translation Lookaside Buffer, or TLB**—that retains copies of the most-recently accessed PTEs. The presence, size, and organization of the TLB can vary from processor to processor and is outside the scope of the ISA specification. While the earlier processors incorporated a single TLB to keep copies of the PTEs for

the most-recently accessed pages, today's processors implement split TLBs:
- The code or instruction TLB (ITLB) caches the PTEs for code pages.
- The data TLB (DTLB) caches the PTEs for data pages.

The TLBs

Figure 16-16 on page 524 illustrates the relationship of the TLBs to the segmentation logic, the paging unit, and the logical processor's code and data caches.

The 32-bit virtual (linear) address created by the segmentation logic is submitted to the paging unit for a lookup. The TLBs are very fast lookaside caches that sit off to the side (hence the term *lookaside*). As the virtual address is submitted to the Paging logic for a lookup in the memory-based address translation tables, it compares the upper 20 bits of the virtual address (i.e., the target virtual page address) to the PTEs stored in its cache.

TLB Miss

If the TLB lookup results in a miss, the paging unit (which, because it has to perform accesses to the PD and PT, is much slower than the TLB) is permitted to proceed with the two overhead memory reads to obtain the PDE and PTE. When the PTE is obtained, two actions are taken:

1. The 32-bit physical memory address is created from the upper 20 bits of the physical page address (obtained from the PTE) and the lower 12 bits of the virtual address. The resultant 32-bit physical memory address is the one that is submitted to the code or data cache for a lookup.
2. The paging unit also creates an entry in the TLB consisting of approximately 45 bits. While neither Intel nor AMD defines the content of a TLB entry, it makes sense that it would contain the elements listed below:
   — A bit that indicates whether this TLB entry contains valid page mapping information (i.e., a valid PTE).
   — The upper 20 bits of the virtual address (i.e., the virtual page number).
   — The upper 20 bits of the physical page address (i.e., the physical page number) that the virtual page address is mapped to.
   — The page attributes obtained from the PTE.

Any subsequent accesses within the same virtual page have identical settings in the upper 20 bits and will therefore result in a TLB hit.

TLB Hit

In the case of a TLB hit, the TLB inhibits the paging unit from generating the two overhead memory reads to obtain the PDE and PTE. Instead, the TLB supplies the upper 20 bits of the physical page address, while the lower 12 bits are supplied directly by the lower 12 bits of the virtual address. The resultant 32-bit physical memory address is the one used to access the code or data cache.

Figure 16-16: Code and Data TLBs

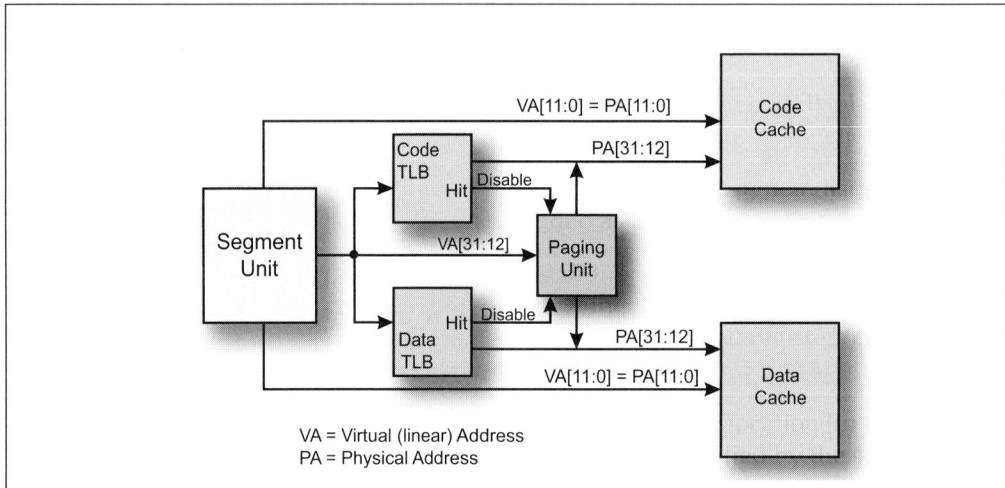

TLB Maintenance

Once a PTE has been copied into the TLB, the paging unit no longer needs to access the original entry in the Page Table in memory in order to translate any address within the associated virtual page. Any access within a page with a cached PTE uses the mapping and protection information in the TLB rather than the PTE in memory.

On the surface, it would seem that any change (i.e., memory write) that the OS makes to a PTE in memory can be detected by the TLB and that it can *snarf* a copy of the change to keep its TLB entry current. However, this is typically not the case. The TLB is not aware of writes performed to PTEs in the Page Tables in memory. As a result, the OS must take care to ensure that the TLBs always contain up-to-date PTEs. If this were not done, subsequent accesses within a page with a stale cached entry would use the stale mapping and protection information rather than the fresh copy of the PTE in memory. The sections that follow discuss the methods utilized by the OS and the logical processor to ensure that the TLB doesn't use stale entries to perform address mapping and protection checks.

TLBs Are Cleared on Task Switch or Page Directory Change

CR3 contains the base physical address of the top-level Page Directory in memory. Assume that the logical processor's TLB has been caching PTEs from the Page Tables associated with the currently-running task. When a new task is started or resumed, the new value loaded into CR3 identifies an entirely new set of Page Tables with different virtual-to-physical address mappings and protection definitions. By definition, this makes every PTE currently residing in the TLB stale. Any time a new value is loaded into CR3, the logical processor therefore automatically clears all PTEs from the TLB. A new value is loaded into CR3 under the following circumstances:

- **Task switch**. When a task switch occurs, the logical processor's register set is saved in order to snapshot the state of the task being suspended and then reloaded with the context of the new task being started or resumed. As a result, CR3 is loaded with a new Page Directory base address and all TLB entries are invalidated (eliminating all PTEs cached from the set of Page Tables associated with the suspended task).
- **OS programmer loads a new value into CR3**. When a privilege level 0 program is executing, the programmer may choose to switch to a new set of mappings. This is accomplished by creating a new Page Directory and set of Page Tables and then loading CR3 with the base address of the new Page Directory. All TLB entries are invalidated (eliminating all PTEs cached from the old set of Page Tables).

Updating a Single Page Table Entry

When a PTE must be updated, the OS performs a memory write to the appropriate location in the target Page Table. Whenever the contents of a PTE is altered, the programmer must explicitly instruct the TLB to discard the now stale copy of the affected PTE (referred to as a TLB shootdown). This is accomplished by execution of the INVLPG (Invalidate Page Table Entry) instruction. The 32-bit virtual page address supplied as the instruction operand is used to perform the TLB lookup and the TLB invalidates the targeted cache entry.

The 386 did not implement the INVLPG instruction. When a change was made to a PTE, the programmer would load CR3 with the start physical address of the PD again, thereby forcing the logical processor to invalidate all entries in the TLB. Obviously this heavy-handed approach took quite a toll on performance.

Global Pages

Problem

When a task switch occurs, CR3 is loaded with the 4KB-aligned base address of the new task's PD, thereby selecting the set of page address translation tables associated with the new task. As a result, the logical processor automatically deletes all PTEs currently cached in the TLB (because they were cached from the address translation tables associated with the previous task). The resultant TLB misses that occur negatively affects performance at the start of the new task. There are, however, some virtual-to-physical mappings that are common across all tasks (e.g. interrupt handlers, some OS services, etc.). These entries do not need to be flushed when changing CR3. It would be nice to have a way to indicate pages that are common across multiple tasks versus those that are not: in other words, a way of defining global pages versus non-global (local) pages.

Global Page Feature

The Pentium Pro introduced the Global Page feature (and it is supported in all subsequent x86 processors). A processor's support for this feature may be determined by executing a CPUID request type 1 and checking that EDX[PGE] = 1. It is enabled by setting CR4[PGE] = 1 (see Figure 16-17 on page 527).

The OS can designate one or more pages as being global to multiple tasks by setting:

- (with PAE disabled and a 4KB page) the 4KB page's PTE[G] bit = 1 (see Figure 16-18 on page 527).
- (with PAE disabled and a 4MB page) the 4MB pages's PDE[G] bit = 1 (see Figure 16-34 on page 551).
- (with PAE enabled and a 4KB page) the 4KB page's PTE[G] bit = 1 (see Figure 16-49 on page 566).
- (with PAE enabled and a 2MB page) the PDE[G] bit = 1 (see Figure 16-46 on page 564).

Whenever a task switch occurs and CR3 is loaded with the address of the top level directory for the new task, the logical processor purges all PTEs from the TLB *with the exception of those marked as global pages*. The PTEs and PDEs for global pages are retained. Intel documentation says the global PTEs are retained in the TLB for an indeterminate period of time. In fact, they are retained until the TLB's LRU (Least-Recently Used) algorithm causes a global PTE that hasn't been selected in a long time to be cast out to make room for a new PTE.

Figure 16-17: CR4[PGE] Enables/Disables the Global Page Feature

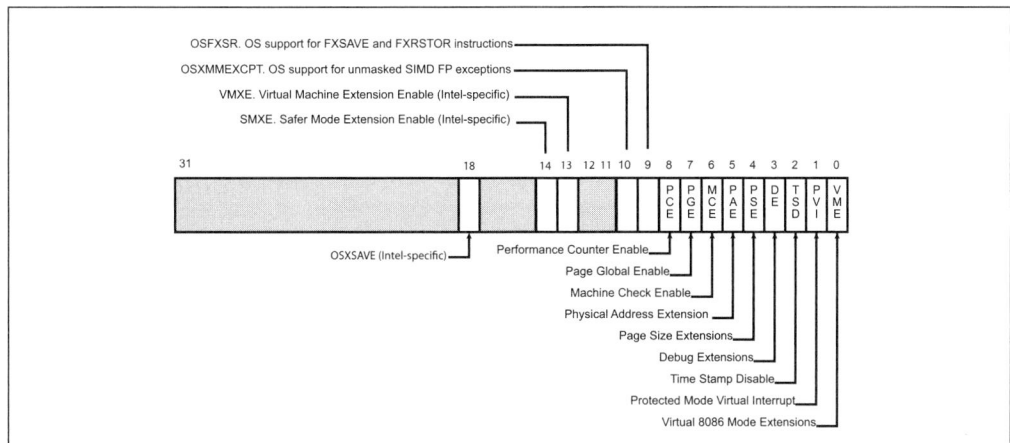

Figure 16-18: 32-bit Page Table Entry (PTE)

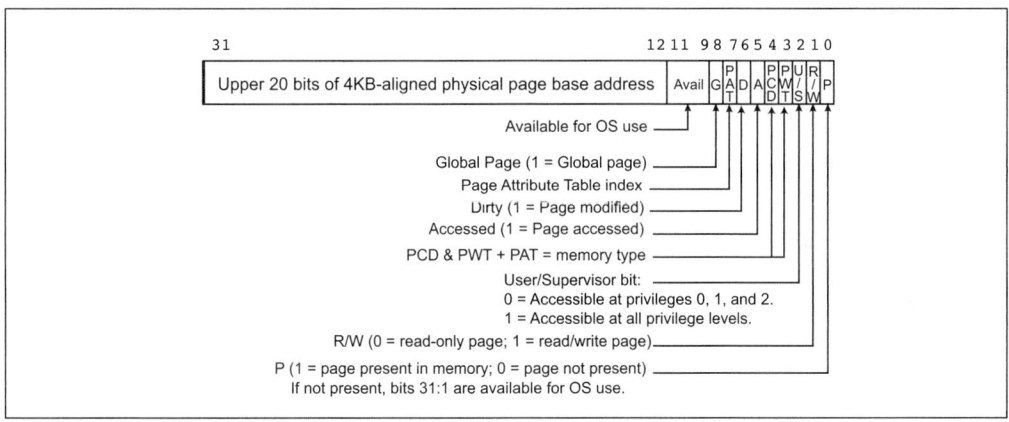

Enabling Paging

Before enabling the paging unit, the OS programmer must create a minimum of two tables in memory:

- The top-level Page Directory. Each PDE is initialized to point to a second-level Page Table in memory.
- A minimum of one Page Table. Each PTE points to a physical page in memory.

The 1024 PTEs in a Page Table identify the physical location of the 1024 pages that comprise the related 4MB virtual address region.

See Figure 16-19 on page 528. After creating the tables in memory, the OS loads the 4KB-aligned physical base address of the Page Directory into CR3. The upper 20 bits of the 32-bit physical base address are stored in CR3[31:12] and the lower 12 bits of the directory base address are assumed to be zero (the Page Directory must start on a 4KB address boundary). The PCD and PWT bits in CR3 tell the logical processor what policy to use regarding caching PDEs that are from read from the Page Directory (see Table 16-2 on page 528).

The OS then enables paging by setting CR0[PG] = 1 (see Figure 16-20 on page 529). From that point forward, the paging unit intercepts all 32-bit virtual memory addresses generated by the segmentation unit and performs address translation.

Figure 16-19: Control Register 3 (CR3)

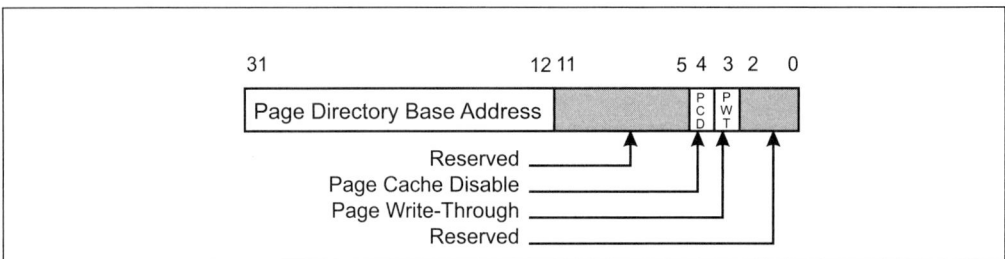

Table 16-2: Page Directory Caching Policy

PCD	PWT	Policy
0	0	The area of memory containing the PD is to be treated as cacheable, WB (Write-Back) memory. For more information, refer to "Cacheable Write-Back (WB) Memory" on page 614.
0	1	The area of memory containing the PD is to be treated as cacheable, WT (Write-Through) memory. For more information, refer to "Cacheable Write-Through (WT) Memory" on page 613.
1	x	The area of memory containing the PD is to be treated as uncacheable (UC) memory. For more information, refer to "Uncacheable (UC) Memory" on page 610.

Figure 16-20: Control Register 0 (CR0)

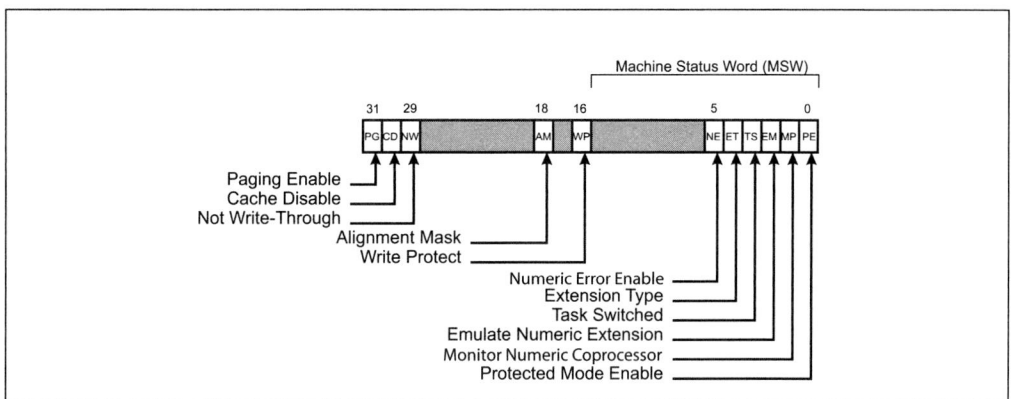

Detailed Description of PDE and PTE

PDE Layout

PDE layout comes in two flavors:

- A PDE that points to a second-level Page Table (see Figure 16-21 on page 530) that catalogs the location of the 1024, 4KB pages that comprise a 4MB virtual address region.
- A PDE that points to a single 4MB page. This is the case if the Page Size Extension (PSE) feature has been enabled by the OS (by setting CR4[PSE] = 1), and a PDE's PS bit = 1. *A description of the PSE feature can be found in "PSE-36 Mode (PAE-36 Mode's Poor Cousin)" on page 574.*

Figure 16-21 on page 530 illustrates the layout of a 32-bit PDE that points to a second-level Page Table. Table 16-3 on page 530 defines the meaning of each bit field.

Figure 16-21: 32-bit Page Directory Entry (PDE) Pointing to a Page Table

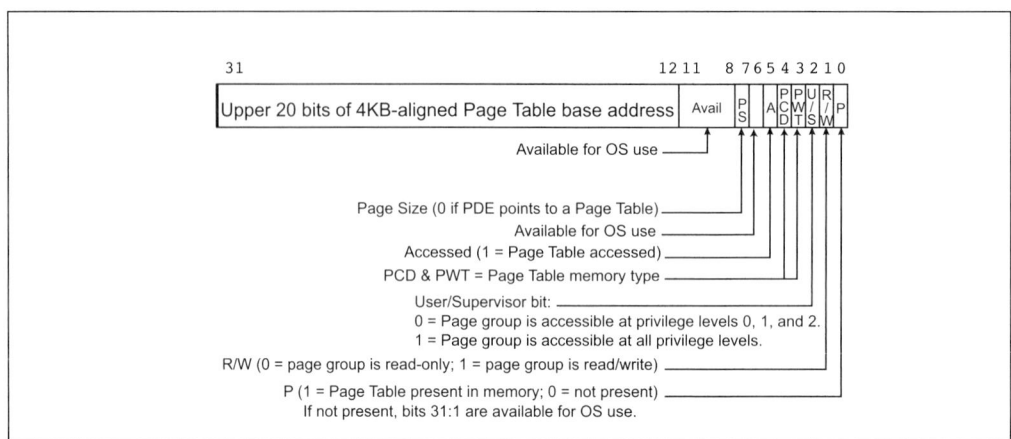

Table 16-3: Layout of PDE Pointing to a Second-Level Page Table

Field	Description
P	• P = 1 if the **Page Table** is **present** in memory. • If P = 0, the Page Table is not currently in memory. It may be on a mass storage device and bits [31:1] of the entry can be used by the OS to indicate the mass storage address.
R/W	See Figure 16-23 on page 534. • 0 = The 1024, 4KB pages in the 4MB virtual address region are read-only. • 1 = The 1024, 4KB pages in the 4MB virtual address region are read/writable. Also refer to the description of CR0[WP] in "Example Usage: Unix Copy-on-Write Strategy" on page 569.
U/S	See Figure 16-24 on page 535. • 0 = The 1024, 4KB pages in the 4MB virtual address region are accessible at privileges 0, 1 and 2 (i.e., by Supervisor privilege level programs). • 1 = The 1024, 4KB pages in the 4MB virtual address region are accessible at all privilege levels.

Table 16-3: Layout of PDE Pointing to a Second-Level Page Table (Continued)

Field	Description
PWT PCD	These 2 bits instruct the logical processor regarding the cacheability of the Page Table pointed to by this PDE: PCD PWT 0 0 Page Table is cacheable, WB (Write-Back) memory. 0 1 Page Table is cacheable, WT (Write-Through) memory. 1 0 Page Table is uncacheable (UC) memory. 1 1 Page Table is uncacheable (UC) memory.
A	Automatically set to one by the logical processor the first time the second-level Page Table is accessed.
PS	• **0** = PDE points to a **second-level Page Table** (see Figure 16-21 on page 530) that catalogs the location of the 1024, 4KB pages that comprise a 4MB virtual address region. • **1** = PDE points to a **single 4MB page**. This is the case if the Page Size Extension (PSE) feature has been enabled by the OS (by setting CR4[PSE] = 1), and a PDE's PS bit = 1. A description of the PSE feature can be found in "PSE-36 Mode (PAE-36 Mode's Poor Cousin)" on page 574.
Avail	This 4-bit field is ignored by hardware and is available to the OS for usage. It can be used to define additional, OS-specific Page Table attributes.
PT Base	The upper 20-bits of the physical base address of the second-level Page Table that catalogs the location of the 1024, 4KB pages in this 4MB virtual address region. This field contains the upper 20 bits and the lower 12 bits are assumed to be 0 (because Page Tables are aligned on a 4KB address boundary).

PTE Layout

Figure 16-22 on page 532 illustrates the layout of a 32-bit PTE. Table 16-4 on page 532 defines the meaning of each bit field.

Figure 16-22: 32-bit Page Table Entry (PTE)

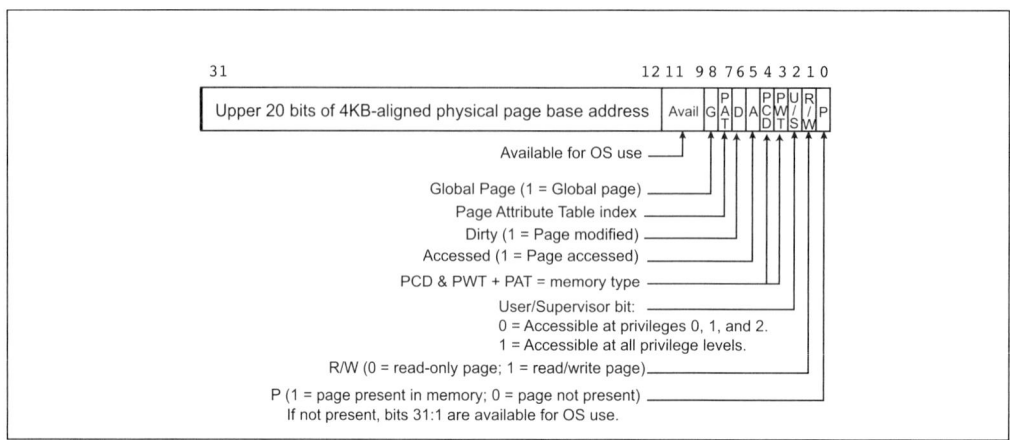

Table 16-4: Layout of PTE

Field	Description
P	• 1 = **Page** is **present** in memory. • 0 = **Page** is **not currently in memory**. It may be on a mass storage device and bits [31:1] of the entry can be used by the OS to indicate the mass storage address.
R/W	See Figure 16-23 on page 534. • 0 = The 4KB page is read-only. • 1 = The 4KB page is read/writable. Also refer to the description of CR0[WP] in "Example Usage: Unix Copy-on-Write Strategy" on page 569 and to "The Read/Write Check" on page 537.
U/S	See Figure 16-24 on page 535. • 0 = The 4KB page is accessible at privileges 0, 1 and 2. • 1 = The 4KB page is accessible at all privilege levels.

Table 16-4: Layout of PTE (Continued)

Field	Description
PWT PCD PAT	These 3 bits instruct the logical processor regarding the cacheability of the Page pointed to by this PTE. See "Defining a Page's Caching Rules" on page 585 for more information.
A	Automatically set to one by the logical processor the first time the 4KB page is accessed.
D	**Dirty** (i.e., modified) bit. Automatically set to one by the logical processor the first time a modification is made within the page pointed to by this PTE. • **0** = No modifications have been made within the page pointed to by this PTE. • **1** = One or more modifications have been made within the page pointed to by this PTE.
G	**Global** page. • 0 = The virtual-to-physical mapping of this page applies only to this application. • 1 = The virtual-to-physical mapping of this page applies to multiple applications. This bit only has meaning if the OS has enabled the Global Page feature by setting CR4[PGE] = 1. Otherwise it is ignored by hardware and is available for an OS-specific use. See "Global Pages" on page 526 for more information.
Avail	This 3-bit field is ignored by hardware and is available to the OS for usage. It can be used to define additional, OS-specific page attributes.
Page Base	The upper 20-bits of the physical base address of the target 4KB page. This field contains the upper 20 bits; the lower 12 bits are assumed to be 0 (because 4KB pages are aligned on a 4KB address boundary).

Figure 16-23: Effective Read/Write Permission Determination

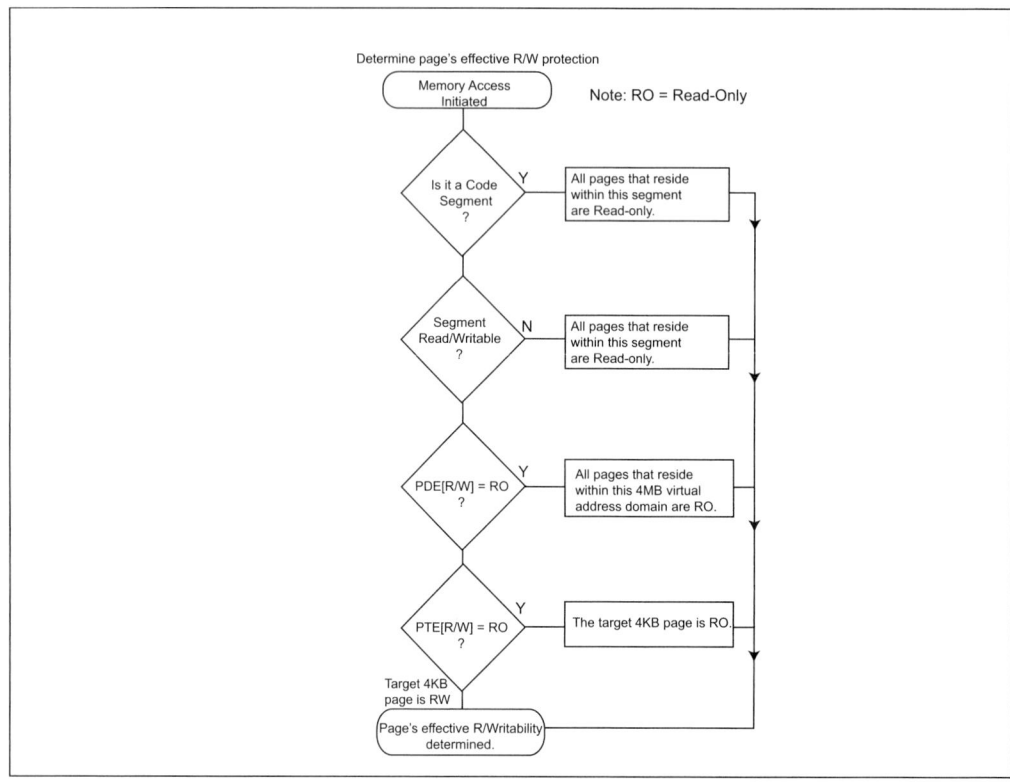

Figure 16-24: User/Supervisor Permission Determination

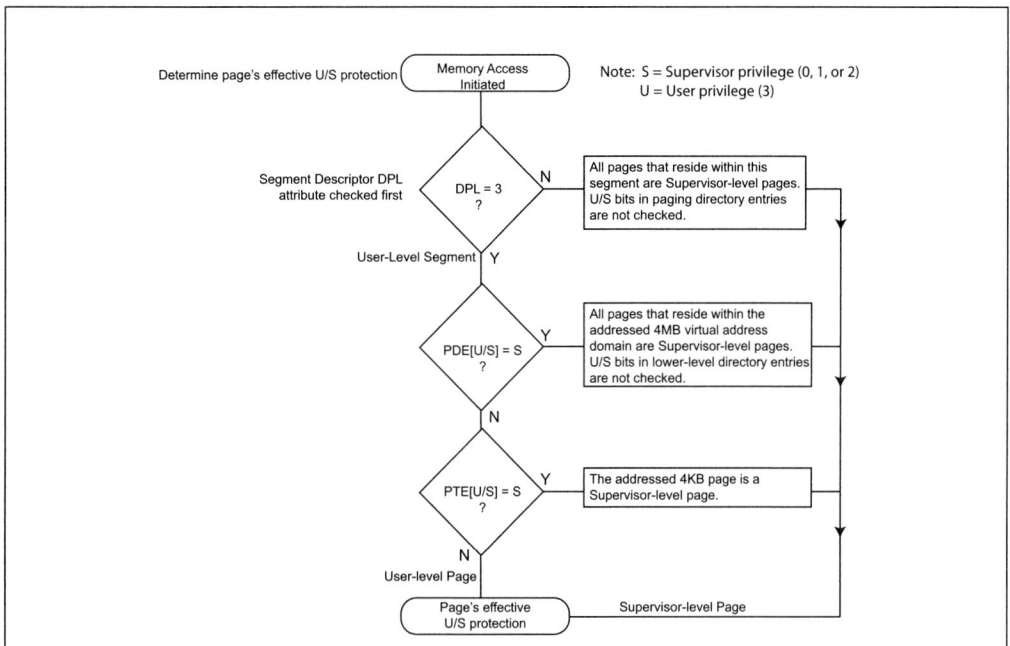

Checking Page Access Permission

No performance penalty is incurred in order to perform the page privilege and access rights checks. The paging unit performs these checks in parallel with address translation. The two sections that follow describe the privilege level and access rights checks.

The Privilege Check

Segment Privilege Check Takes Precedence Over Page Check

Refer to Figure 16-24 on page 535. The logical processor always evaluates segment-level protection before performing the page-level protection check. As an example, assume that a segment (code or data) has been defined as 64KB in length and starts on a page boundary (i.e., an address divisible by 4KB). Also assume that the DPL of the segment descriptor is set to 3. This means that the segment may be accessed by a program with a CPL (current privilege level) of 0, 1, 2, or 3 (in other words, it can be accessed by any program).

The segment encompasses 16 pages (16 * 4KB = 64KB). There is a separate PTE for each page within the segment, each with a U/S bit (see Figure 16-22 on page 532) defining the privilege level necessary to access the page. In this example, some of the PTEs have U/S = 0, while other have U/S = 1. The CPL of the current program must have a privilege level of 0, 1, or 2 to access a supervisor page (U/S = 0), while any program can access a page with U/S = 1 (user access permitted).

When a code or data memory access is attempted, the logical processor first checks for sufficient privilege at the segment level before checking for sufficient privilege to access the target page within the segment. *If the currently executing program doesn't have sufficient segment-level privilege, the page-level privilege check isn't performed* and the access isn't permitted to proceed (i.e., it causes a GP exception). If, on the other hand, the segment privilege check passes, the page-level check is then performed. If it passes, the access is permitted; otherwise, it results in a Page Fault exception.

U/S Bit in PDE and PTE Are Checked

Both the PDE and the PTE have a U/S bit. The *page level protection check is based on the more restrictive of the two U/S bit settings.* The U/S bit in the PDE defines the privilege level necessary to access any page within the 4MB virtual address region, while a PTE's U/S bit defines the privilege level necessary to access any location within a specific page in the region. Table 16-5 on page 536 illustrates the effect of the four possible U/S bit combinations.

Table 16-5: Effect of PDE/PTE U/S Bit Settings

PDE's U/S bit	PTE's U/S bit	Page can be accessed by
0	x	Supervisor program (i.e., one running at privilege level 0, 1, or 2).
1	0	
1	1	Any program (supervisor or user; user is privilege level 3).

Accesses with Special Privilege

Regardless of the currently executing program's CPL, the following accesses have an implied privilege level of 0 (i.e., they have supervisor privilege):

- Accesses to segment descriptors in the GDT, LDT, and IDT descriptor tables.
- Accesses to the privilege level 0, 1, or 2 stacks caused by execution of a Call instruction, or an interrupt or exception. This occurs when the called program or interrupt/exception handler resides within a code segment with a DPL of 0, 1, or 2.

The Read/Write Check

Refer to Figure 16-23 on page 534. Whether a page is restricted to read accesses or permits both reads and writes is defined by the state of the R/W bit in both the PDE and PTE. As with the U/S privilege check, the read/write check is performed *based on the more restrictive of the two W bit settings*. An attempt to write to a page with read-only access results in a Page Fault exception (see "Page Faults" on page 545 in this chapter).

Note: The 486 and subsequent x86 processors implement CR0[WP]. If the OS sets CR0[WP] = 1 and a program with supervisor privilege (0, 1, or 2) attempts a write to a read-only page, a GP exception is generated. Otherwise, it is permitted. Table 16-6 on page 537 assumes that CR0[WP] = 0. See "Example Usage: Unix Copy-on-Write Strategy" on page 569.

Table 16-6: Effect of R/W Bit Settings

PDE's R/W Bit	PTE's R/W Bit	Page Accesses Rule
0	x	Read-only by user programs. Read/write by supervisor programs.
1	0	
1	1	Read/write by all programs.

Missing Page or Page Table

Introduction

The translation of a virtual address to a physical address is a 2-step process:

1. The upper 10-bits of the virtual address (i.e., the 4MB virtual address range selector) is used to select a PDE in the Page Directory. If bit 0, the Present bit, is set to one, then the PDE is valid and the second-level page table is present in memory. If the Present bit is cleared to zero, the second-level Page Table is not present in memory and it results in a Page Fault exception.
2. The middle 10-bits of the virtual address (i.e., the page selector) is then used to select a PTE in the Page Table within the selected 4MB virtual address range. If bit 0, the Present bit, is set to one, then the PTE is valid and the target physical page is present in memory. If the Present bit is cleared to zero, the target page is not present in memory and it results in a Page Fault exception.

The following sections provide a detailed description of the *page table not present* and *page not present* conditions, as well as a detailed description of the conditions that can cause a Page Fault exception.

Page Table Not Present

If P = 0 in the selected PDE, the target Page Table isn't currently in memory. This results in a Page Fault exception. The return address pushed onto the stack points to the instruction that submitted the 32-bit virtual address to the paging unit. The logical processor latches the virtual address into CR2, the Page Fault Address register (see Figure 16-28 on page 541), so that it may be examined by the OS's Page Fault exception handler. The actions taken are illustrated in Figure 16-25 through Figure 16-27.

Once the proper Page Table has been loaded into memory and the respective PDE has been updated to point to it, the paging unit may proceed with the address translation.

Figure 16-25: Page Table Not in Memory (1-of-3)

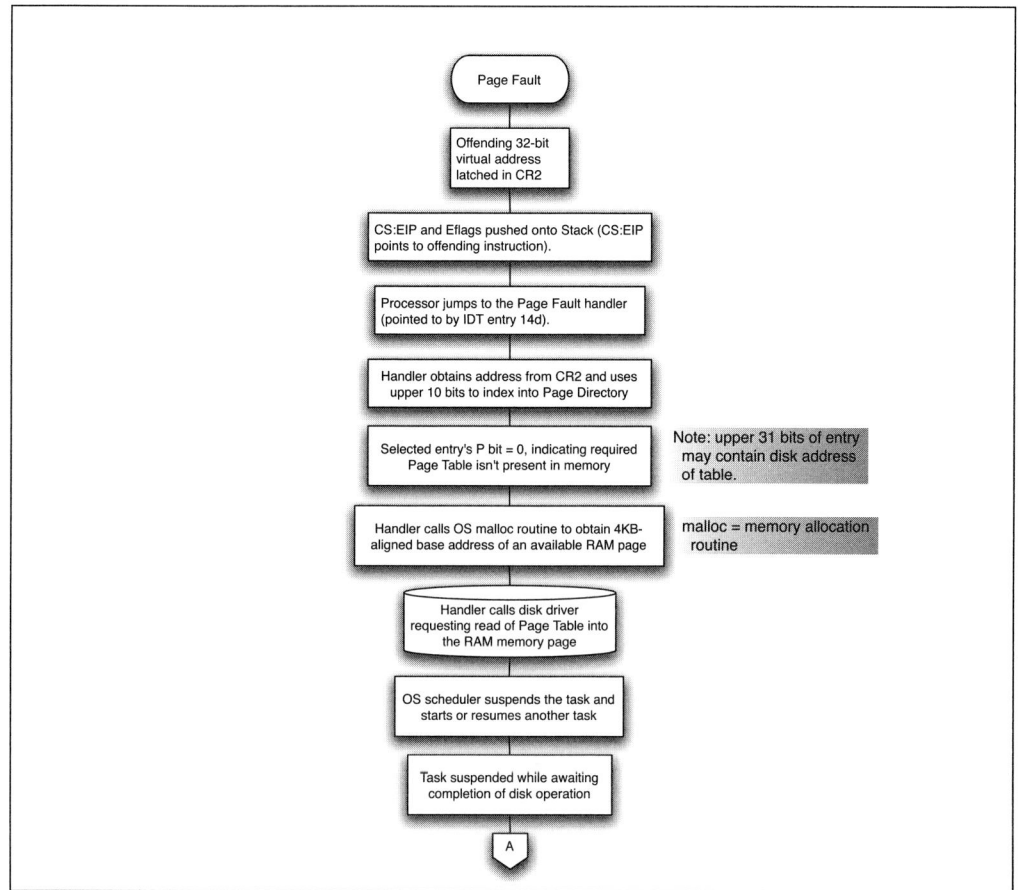

Figure 16-26: Page Table Not in Memory (2-of-3)

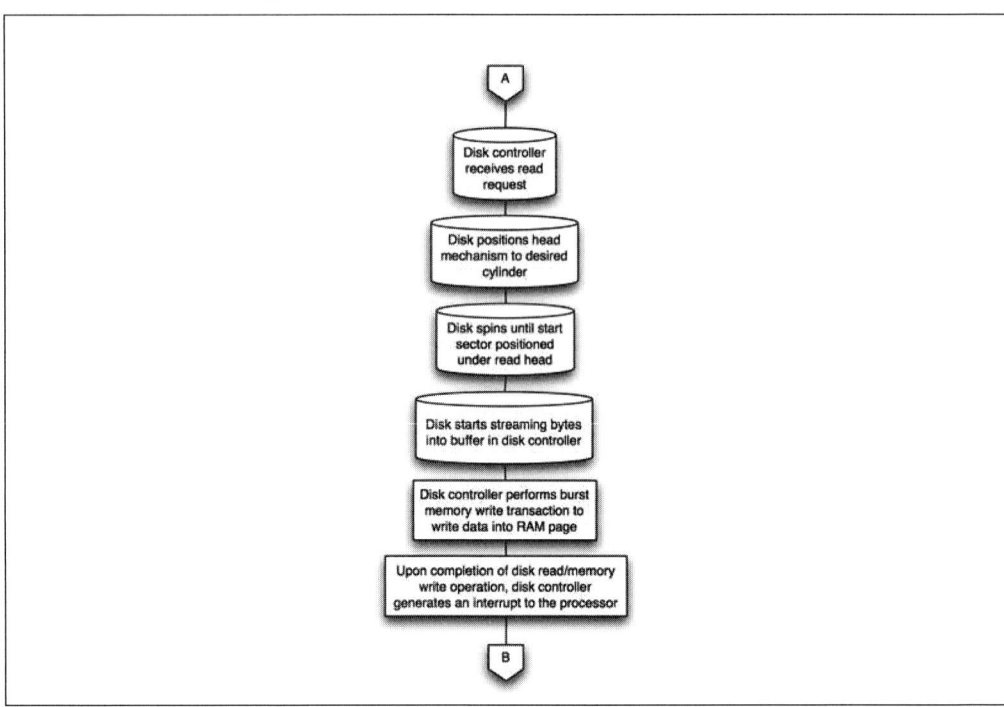

Figure 16-27: Page Table Not in Memory (3-of-3)

B — Disk controller interrupts the processor

Processor suspends current task and jumps to the disk driver's interrupt handler

Handler interrogates disk controller and ascertains that requested disk page is in memory

Disk driver passes completion notice to the OS scheduler

Scheduler passes control to Page Fault handler

In the Page Directory entry, handler sets the Present bit = 1 and inserts the 4KB aligned start address of the Page Table. Also:
- W bit = 0 to protect the table from write attempts.
- U/S = 0 to protect the table from accesses by application programs.

The last instruction executed in the Page Fault handler is the iret instruction. When executed, it causes the processor to pop the return address into CS:EIP from the stack and to resume execution at the same instruction that caused the Page Fault.

The offending instruction is re-executed and the same 32-bit virtual address is submitted to the Paging Unit for a lookup in the page directory. The same PDE is selected, but this time P = 1, indicating that the Page Table is in memory and its base address is contained in bits [31:12] of the PDE

End

Figure 16-28: Page Fault Register (CR2)

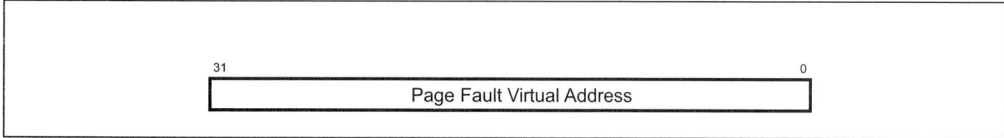

31	0
Page Fault Virtual Address	

Figure 16-29: PDE or PTE when Page Table (or page) not Present in Memory

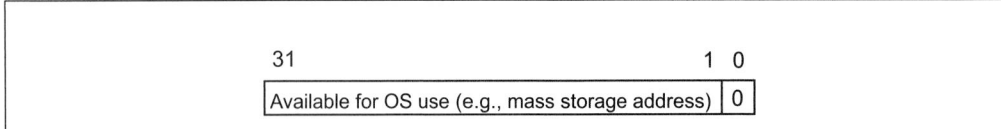

Page Not Present

If P = 0 in the selected PTE (see Figure 16-22 on page 532), although the Page Table is in memory, the target page isn't, resulting in a Page Fault exception. The return address pushed onto the stack points to the instruction that submitted the 32-bit virtual address to the paging unit. The logical processor latches the virtual address into CR2, the Page Fault Address register (see Figure 16-28 on page 541), so that it may be examined by the OS's Page Fault exception handler. The actions taken are illustrated in Figure 16-30 through Figure 16-32.

Please note: In Figure 16-32 on page 545, prior to the execution of the IRET instruction the INVLPG instruction should be executed to invalidate the stale PTE in the TLB.

Once the page has been loaded into memory and the respective PTE has been updated to point to it, the paging unit may proceed with the address translation.

Figure 16-30: Page Not in Memory (1-of-3)

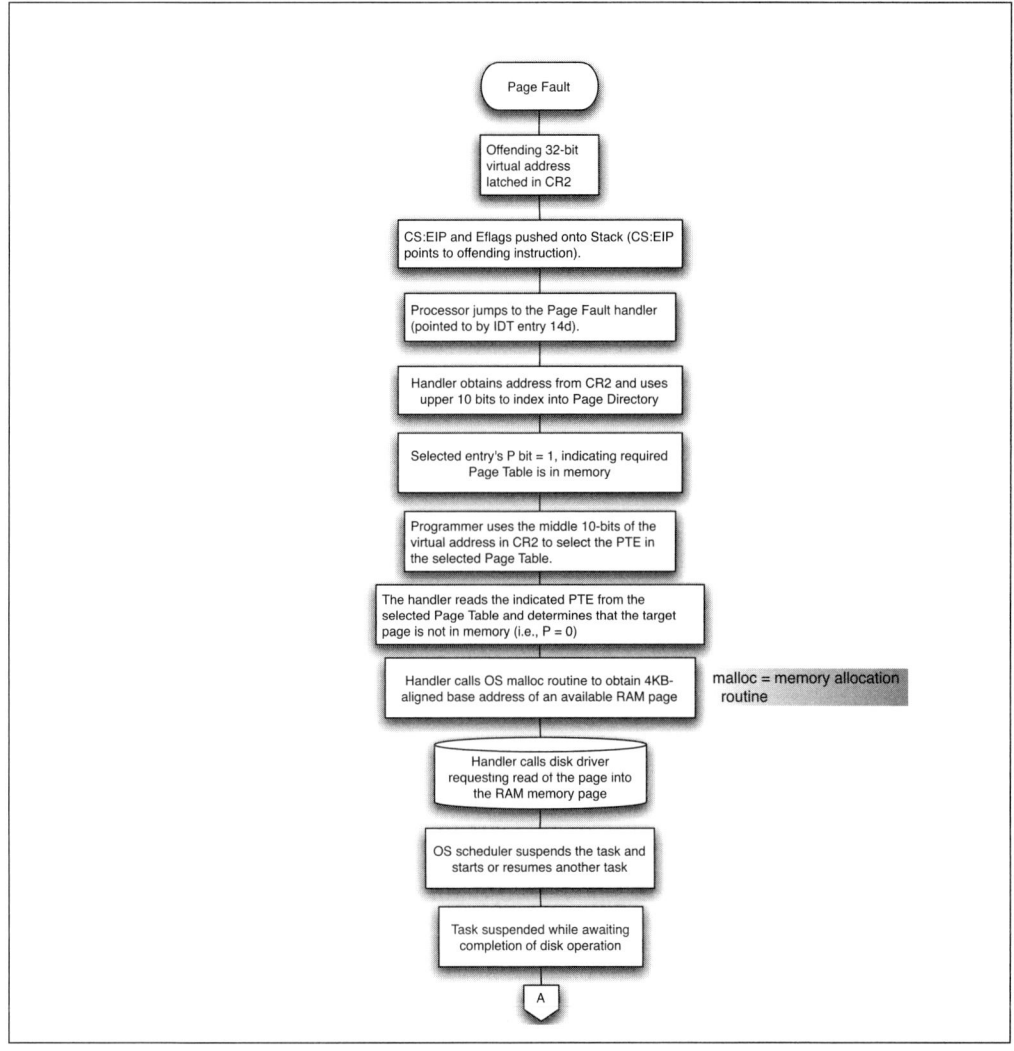

Figure 16-31: Page Not in Memory (2-of-3)

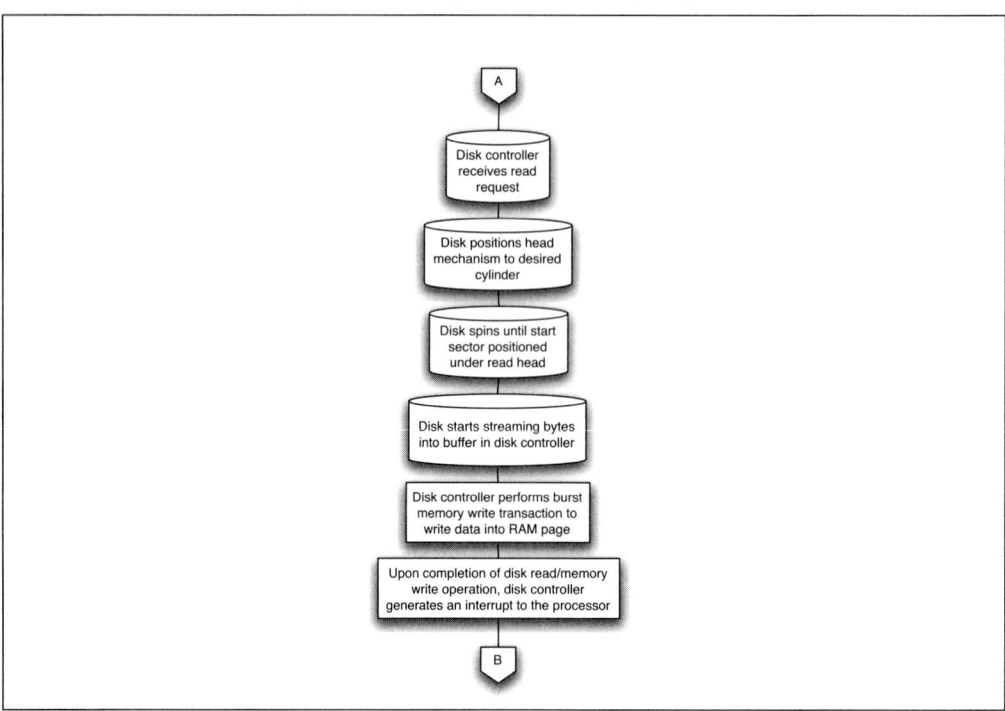

Figure 16-32: Page Not in Memory (3-of-3)

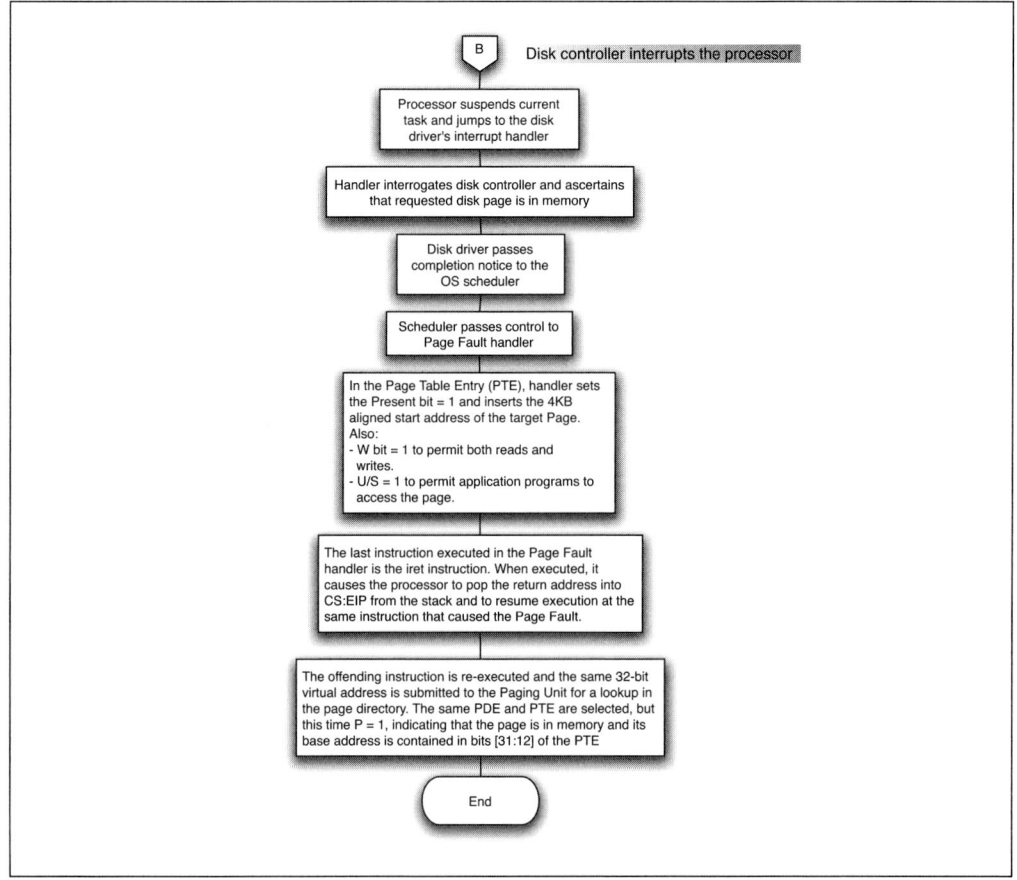

Page Faults

Page Fault Causes

Any one of the following events results in the generation of a Page Fault exception:

1. The selected PDE's P bit = 0, indicating that the selected Page Table is not present in memory.
2. The selected PTE's P bit = 0, indicating that the target page is not present in memory.

3. An attempt to write to a read-only page.
4. Code running in user mode attempts to write to a read-only page.
5. If CR0[WP] = 1, a Page Fault also occurs on an attempt by code with super-visor privilege (0, 1, or 2) to write to a read-only page.
6. Insufficient page-level privilege to access the Page Table or the page.
7. A reserved bit set to one in the PDE or PTE.
8. The Execute Disable feature is enabled and an instruction fetch was attempted from a data page with the Execute Disable bit set to one in its respective PTE.

If the Page Fault occurs due to a page not present or a page privilege access violation (insufficient privilege or writes not permitted), the A bit is affected in the PDE, but not in the PTE. The PTE's A and D bits are only affected if the page access succeeds.

Page Fault During a Task Switch

This description assumes that the OS is using the x86 processor's hardware-based task switching mechanism (most main-steam OSs do not use it). During a task switch, the logical processor must access memory for the following reasons:

1. To read the GDT to obtain the TSS descriptor for the new task.
2. To read the values stored in the new task's TSS to check them for correctness.
3. Before switching to the new task, to *snapshot* the logical processor register set in the current task's TSS.
4. To reload the logical processor's register set with the values from the new task's TSS.
5. To resume execution using the new values.

A Page Fault may occur during any of these accesses. If a Page Fault occurs during 1 or 2, the exception occurs in the context of the old task. In other words, the old task's stack is used and the CS:EIP values pushed onto the stack point to the next instruction of the old task.

If the Page Fault occurs during 3 or 4, the exception occurs in the context of the new task. In other words, the new task's stack is used and the CS:EIP values pushed onto the stack point to the next instruction of the new task. If the OS permits Page Faults to occur during a task switch (i.e., the OS doesn't guarantee that the GDT and both the old and new TSSs are resident in memory), the Page Fault handler should be called through a Task Gate in the Page Fault's IDT entry (note that, because the x86 processor's hardware-based task switching mechanism is not supported in IA-32e Mode, this is not supported in IA-32e Mode).

Page Fault while Changing to a Different Stack

The following instruction sequence was frequently used in pre-386 code to change to a new stack:

```
mov ss,ax          ;move stack segment pointer to ss
mov sp, stacktop   ;move TOS offset to sp from memory
```

The second instruction fetches the top-of-stack (TOS) value from memory and places into the SP register. There is no danger of a Page Fault when the second instruction is executed on a pre-386 processor because paging wasn't supported. However, a Page Fault could result when the same code is executed on a post-286 processor with paging enabled.

If a Page Fault were to occur at this point, the stack segment base address has already been changed, but the stack pointer register still points to the top of the old stack. When the logical processor begins its automatic sequence to jump to the Page Fault exception handler, it pushes CS:EIP, and Eflags to the stack. If the Page Fault handler is at the same privilege level and in the same task, the register values are therefore pushed into spurious memory locations. This can be prevented by using the LSS (Load SS) instruction instead of the two-instruction sequence shown.

On the other hand, they are correctly pushed to a new stack (not the spurious one) if the Page Fault exception entry in the IDT contains a Task Gate (not permitted in IA-32e Mode), or if the exception handler is in the same task but at a higher privilege level.

Page Fault Error Code

In addition to latching the 32-bit virtual address in CR2, a 32-bit error code is pushed onto the stack when a Page Fault exception occurs. Its format differs from that of error codes associated with other exceptions, however. The normal error code format is shown in Figure 19-25 on page 739, while that for a Page Fault is shown in Figure 16-33 on page 548. Table 16-7 on page 548 details the interpretation of the Page Fault error code pushed onto the stack.

Additional Page Fault Information

Additional information on the Page Fault exception can be found in "Page Fault Exception (14)" on page 766.

Table 16-7: Page Fault Exception Error Code Status Bit Interpretation

Bit	Description
P	• 0 = page not present. • 1 = page protection violation.
R/W	• 0 = Access attempt was a memory read. • 1 = Access attempt was a memory write. Note: The cause of the fault was not necessarily the fact that a read or write was attempted.
U/S	• 0 = Access attempted by a program with supervisor access (0, 1, or 2). • 1 = Access attempted by a program with user access (privilege level 3). Note: The cause of the fault was not necessarily a privilege violation.
RSVD	• 0 = Fault not caused by reading a 1 from a reserved bit. • 1 = Fault was caused by reading a 1 from a reserved bit. This can only occur when CR4[PSE] = 1, or CR4[PAE] = 1.
I/D	• 0 = Fault not caused by an instruction fetch. • 1 = Fault caused by an instruction fetch. This bit only has meaning if the Execute Disable feature is enabled (both EFER[NXE] = 1 and CR4[PAE] = 1). Additional information can be found in "Execute Disable Feature" on page 579.

Figure 16-33: Page Fault Error Code Format

Access History

A page of information in memory typically (but not always) originates on mass storage and is copied into memory by the OS's Page Fault handler when a program requires access to one or more locations within the page. When the logical processor first accesses a page, it automatically sets the A (*Accessed*) bit in the corresponding PTE = 1. On the first write to any location within a page, the logical processor also automatically sets the D (*Dirty*; Modified would be a better name for this bit) bit = 1. Once set, it's the programmer's responsibility to clear the bits (the logical processor will not clear them). When the Dirty bit is set to one, it indicates that the copy of the page in memory is no longer the same as the original page on mass storage. Of the two, the page in memory is fresh while the one on disk is stale. These bits can serve a number of purposes. Uses include:

- **Periodic flush-to-disk**. The OS can schedule a task to be executed on a periodic basis that scans the PTEs looking for any pages that have been modified. The page is copied to disk (to freshen the permanent copy) and the **A** and **D** bits are cleared by the task. This ensures that in the event of a power failure, the information on disk has been updated to reflect all changes performed up until the most recent refresh.

- **Returning unpopular pages to the free pool**. The OS can schedule a task to be executed on a periodic basis that scans the Page Tables (and the Page Directory) looking for pages (or Page Tables) that have not been accessed in a while (the algorithm implemented by the OS to track the *age* of a page is OS-specific). These pages could then be eliminated from physical memory to increase the pool of free memory. The P bit is cleared to zero in the respective PTE or PDE.

- **Loading a new page over an unpopular one**. When a Page Fault occurs because a Page Table or a page isn't in memory (P = 0), the Page Fault exception handler program must load the required Page Table or page into memory. In order to do this, the handler must locate an unused 4KB page of physical memory to load the new Page Table or page into. If the free memory pool is running low, the OS may have to swap a page currently in memory back to disk to make room for the new Page Table or page. The Page Directory and Page Tables can be scanned and the D and A bits checked to locate a page to swap out to disk. If the selected page is *clean*, the programmer can clear its respective PTE's P bit to mark it as not present. The new page can then be loaded into that page in memory and its respective PTE updated (P = 1 and set the page's base address to that of the physical page) to reflect the presence and location of the page.

- **Flush-to-disk on system shutdown**. When the user commands the OS to shutdown, the OS scans the Page Tables and Page Directory and writes all modified Page Tables and pages to disk. Only when all modified Page Tables and pages have been written to disk would the user be given permission to power down the system (or the system could do a power down under program control).

4MB Pages

Basic Concept

Memory is generally managed as a series of 4KB pages, but an OS that supports 4MB page capability can also set up one or more 4MB pages (the intent really is that only a relative few 4MB pages might be allocated) in addition to the 4KB pages of which most of memory is comprised. The concept is simple.

As covered earlier, the 4GB virtual memory space is subdivided into 1024, 4MB virtual address regions each of which is, in turn, subdivided into 1024, 4KB pages. Normally, the PDE corresponding to a 4MB virtual address region points to the second-level Page Table that catalogs the location of the 1024, 4KB pages that populate the region. Using the Page Size Extension (PSE) feature, the OS memory manager can choose to set up a PDE that points directly to a 4MB page in physical memory rather than to a second-level Page table.

The PSE feature was first implemented in the Pentium, was migrated into the later versions of the 486 and is present in all x86 processors introduced subsequent to the Pentium.

Enabling the PSE Feature

Enabling 4MB page capability is accomplished by setting CR4[PSE] = 1 (PSE = Page Size Extension). 4MB page capability is detected by executing a CPUID request type 1. EDX[PSE] = 1 indicates that it is supported.

Simplifies Housekeeping

Assume that a task must access a large buffer in memory and that the same memory type (i.e., cacheability rules) and access rules must be assigned throughout the buffer's memory range. As an example, assume it is a 4MB video frame buffer in memory. Using the 4KB paging mechanism already described, the OS would have to set up 1024 PTEs, each associated with a 4KB page within the buffer and each with identical attribute bit settings (i.e., the attribute bits that define the logical processor rules of conduct within the page). Setting up and maintaining 1024 PTEs represents a lot of housekeeping.

How To Set Up a 4MB Page

Assuming that the OS has set CR4[PSE] = 1, it can set up a 4MB page by creating a PDE as shown in Figure 16-34 on page 551:

- PDE[7] is the PS (Page Size) bit. It must be set to 1.
- PDE[31:22] contains the upper 10 bits of a 4MB page in physical memory. The logical processor assumes that the lower 22 bits are all zero.

Theoretically, the OS can set up any number of PDEs (up to the 1024 entry maximum size of the Page Directory) as 4MB page entries. In reality, however, the intent of the system architects is that not very many will exist at a given moment in time. This is highlighted by issuing a CPUID request to obtain the information about a processor's caches. The information returned regarding the TLB implementation includes the number of TLB entries reserved for PDEs that point to 4MB pages. The number of entries allocated to storing translations for large pages (4MB) is typically much smaller the number of entries allocated for storing small page (4KB) PTEs.

The 3-bits consisting of PAT, PCD and PWT define the 4MB page's memory type (see "Page Caching Rules" on page 587).

Figure 16-34: PDE Pointing to 4MB Page

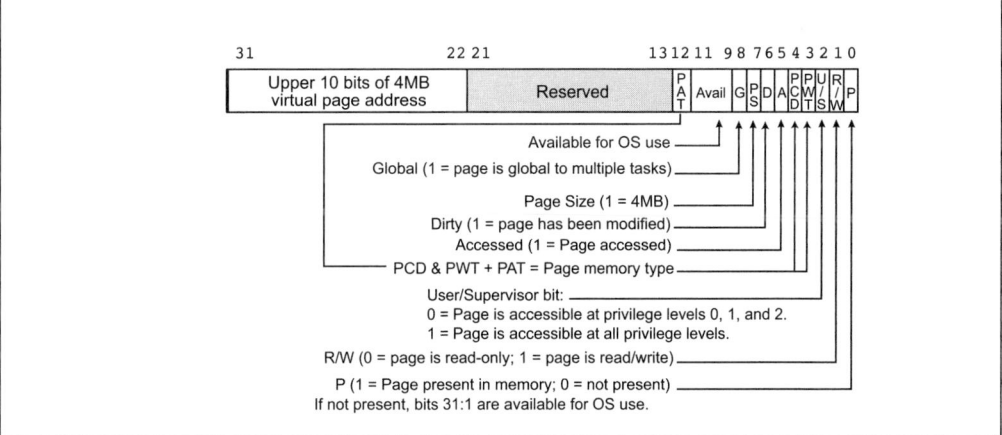

The Address Translation

See Figure 16-35 on page 552. When a 32-bit virtual memory address is submitted to the paging unit for translation, the upper 10 bits selects one of the PDEs in the Page Directory. If PDE[PS] = 1, this PDE contains the 4MB-aligned physical base address of a 4MB page in memory and the PDE attribute bits define the logical processor's rules of conduct when performing a read or write access anywhere within the 4MB region of memory.

Figure 16-35: 4MB Page Address Translation

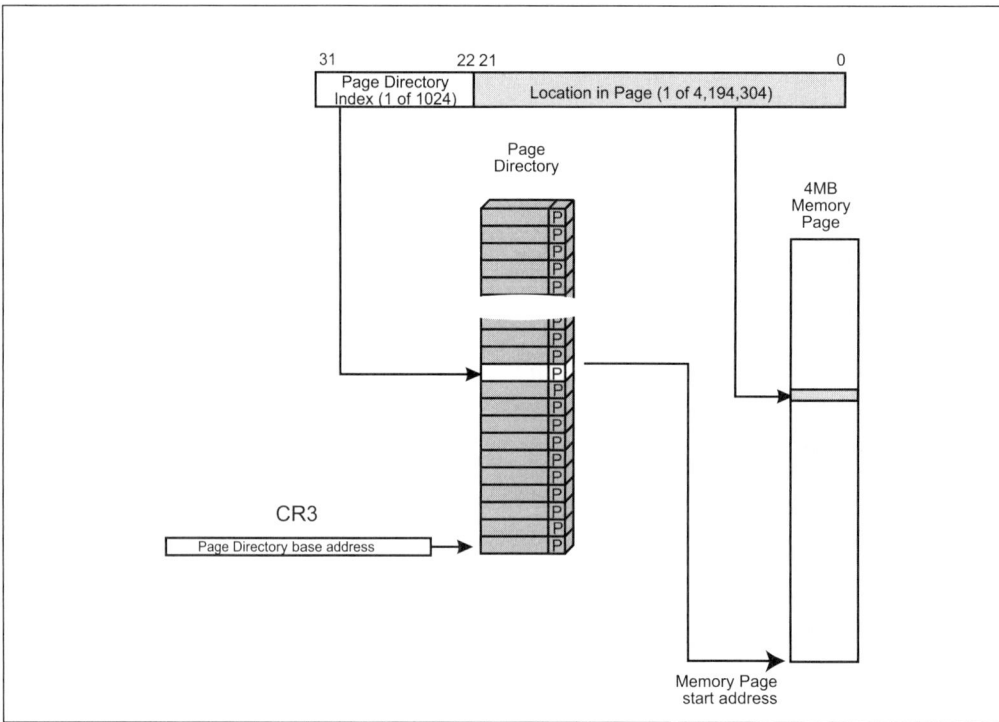

Second-Generation Paging

First-Gen Problem: 4GB Physical Memory

When an OS uses the first-generation paging mechanism, the 32-bit virtual address produced by adding a 32-bit offset to 32-bit segment base address is translated into a 32-bit physical memory address. This is acceptable if the machine has no more than 4GB of physical memory installed. In a machine with more than 4GB of physical memory installed, however, memory above the 4GB address boundary remains inaccessible. Prior to the advent of the Pentium Pro (P6), however, this was a moot point because the earlier processors only implemented a 32-bit address bus.

Beginning with the Pentium Pro, the majority of processors intended for the desktop or server market have had the ability to physically address more than 4GB of memory. This would have been a moot point, though, if the same paging mechanism was used (i.e., one that translated a 32-bit virtual address into a 32-bits physical address). Starting with the Pentium Pro (but excluding all or most laptop models), IA-32 processors have implemented a 36-bit (or wider) address bus, thereby permitting them to address up to 64GB (or more) of physical memory.

The Solution: PAE-36 Mode

Introduced in the Pentium Pro, PAE-36 Mode (36-bit Physical Address Extension) permits a 32-bit virtual memory address to be translated to a 36-bit physical memory address (see "Enlarged Physical Address Space" on page 559 regarding subsequent enhancement) located anywhere within a 64GB addressable address space. The remainder of this section provides a detailed description of PAE-36 Mode. A logical processor's support for this feature may be determined by executing a CPUID request type 1 and checking EDX[PAE] (a one indicates it is supported).

Enabling PAE-36 Mode

PAE-36 Mode is enabled by setting CR4[PAE] = 1 (see Figure 16-36 on page 554). Note that the logical processor must also be operating in Protected Mode (CR0[PE] = 1) with Paging enabled (CR0[PG] = 1).

CR4[PSE] Is "Don't Care"

When PAE Mode is enabled (CR4[PAE] = 1), the ability to designate a page as a *large* page is automatically enabled (and CR4[PSE] is a *don't care* bit). It should be noted that when in PAE Mode, however, a large page is 2MB rather than 4MB in size. More on this can be found in "Step 2b: PDE Points to a 2MB Physical Page" on page 563.

Figure 16-36: CR4[PAE] Enables/Disables PAE-36 Mode Feature

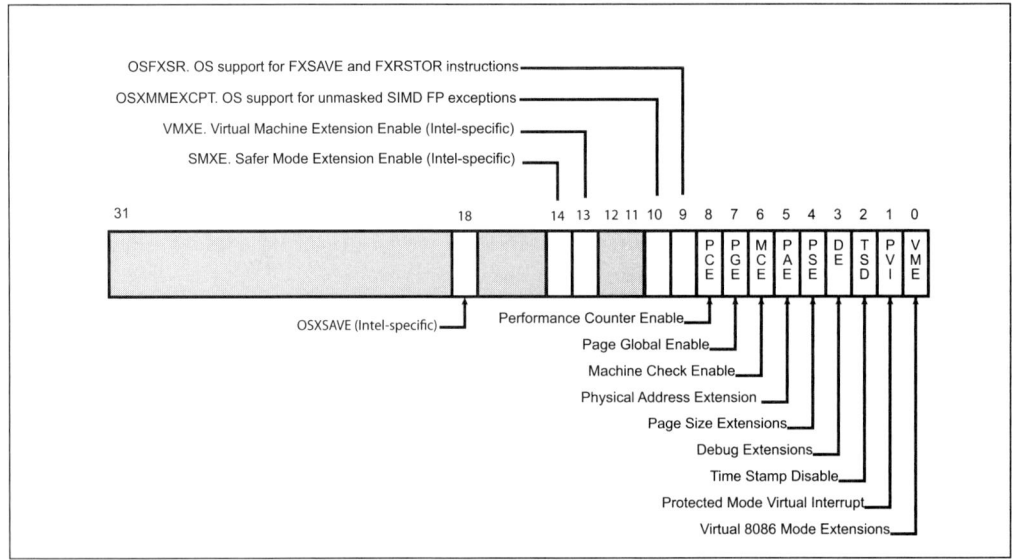

Application Still Limited to a 4GB Virtual Address Space

With 2nd generation paging enabled, the currently executing program is still limited to a 32-bit (i.e., 4GB) virtual address space consisting of a total of 1M (2^{20}) 4KB pages, but the paging unit can now map (i.e., translate) the specified 32-bit virtual address to a destination physical page anywhere in a 64GB (rather than 4GB) physical address space. The translation is performed using a 3-level, rather than a 2-level, directory lookup.

Virtual Address Space Partitioning

First Generation Partitioning

Refer to Figure 16-37 on page 555. When first-generation paging is enabled, the paging unit views the 4GB virtual address space partitioning as follows:

- The upper 10-bits of the virtual address (31:22) selects 1-of-1024 4MB virtual address regions.
- The middle 10-bits (21:12) selects the target 4KB page (1-of-1024) within that 4MB virtual address region.
- The lower 12-bits (11:0) identifies the target location within the page.

Figure 16-37: First-Generation Virtual Address Space Partitioning

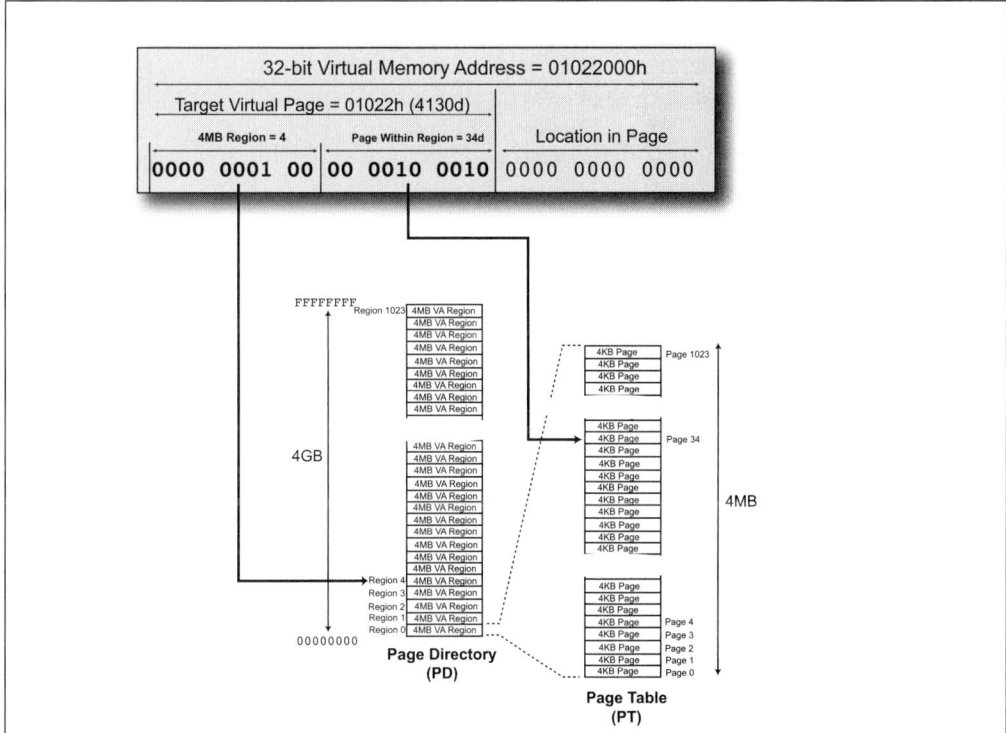

Second Generation Partitioning

Refer to Figure 16-36 on page 554. When PAE-36 Mode (i.e., second generation paging) is enabled (by setting CR4[PAE] = 1), the paging unit views the 4GB virtual address space partitioning as follows:

1. The most-significant 2-bits (31:30) identify the target 1GB virtual address range (1 of 4) and selects the entry (PDPTE) in the Page Directory Pointer Table (PDTP) associated with the addressed 1GB virtual address block (1GB block 0 in the illustration). PDPTE 0 contains the physical base address of Page Directory 0 which catalogs the 512 2MB virtual address regions (512 x 2MB = 1GB) that comprise virtual address block 0.
2. The next nine bits (29:21) identify 1 of 512 2MB virtual address regions within the target 1GB virtual address block. It also selects a PDE (PDE 8 in this example) in the selected Page Directory (PD 0). The selected PDE points to the 3rd level Page Table that catalogs the location of the 512 4KB pages that comprise the targeted 2MB virtual address region (region 8 in the example).
3. The next nine bits (20:12) identify the target 4KB page (1-of-512) within the target 2MB virtual address region. It also selects the PTE (PTE 34 in this example) containing the base physical address of the target 4KB page.

The lower 12-bits (11:0) identifies the target location within the page.

Figure 16-38: Second-Generation (PAE-36) Virtual Address Space Partitioning

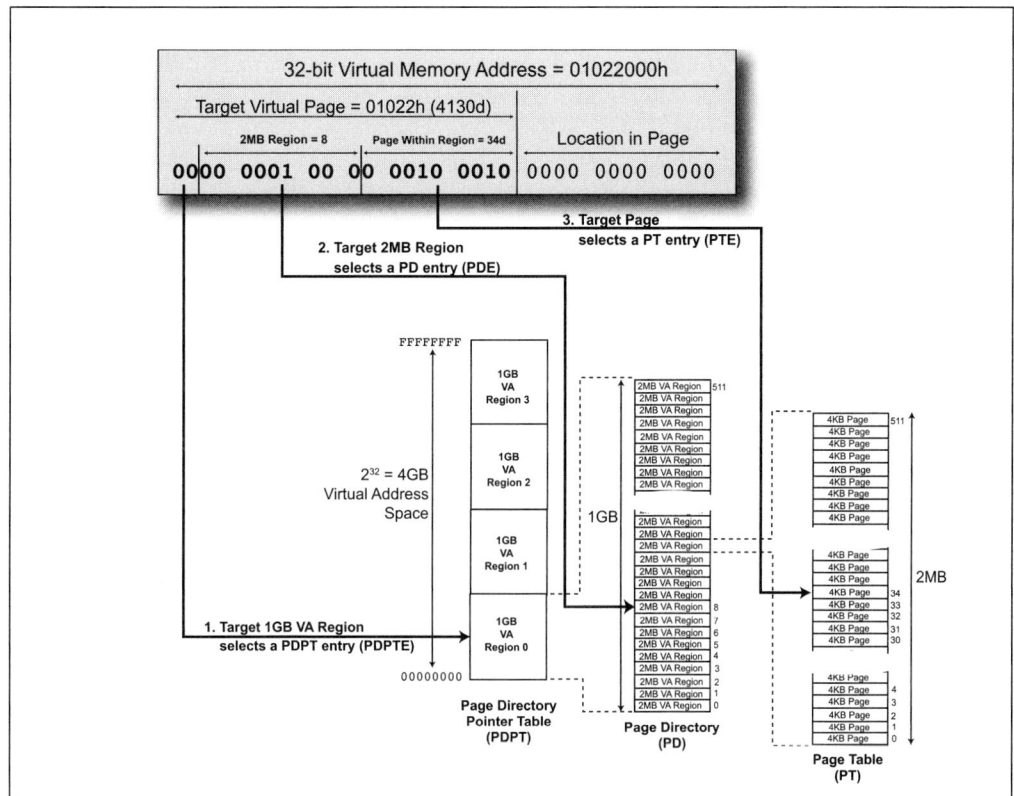

Second Generation Uses 3-Level Lookup Mechanism

As already demonstrated, while the first-generation paging mechanism utilized a 2-level lookup, the second-generation mechanism (i.e., PAE-36 Mode) uses a 3-level lookup (see Figure 16-39 on page 558). There are now three levels of directories:

1. The top-level Page Directory Pointer Table (PDPT) has 4 entries (PDPTEs) corresponding to the four 1GB virtual address blocks the overall 4GBs of virtual address space is divided into. Each PDPTE points to a second-level Page Directory.
2. There are now four Page Directories, each with 512 PDEs, and each PDE points to either:

 — If the PDE's PS bit = 0, a Page Table that catalogs the location of the 512 4KB pages within the targeted 2MB virtual address region.
 — If the PDE's PS bit = 1, a 2MB page (PAE-36 Mode does not support 4MB pages.)
3. The 512 PTEs in a Page Table catalog the location of the 512 4KB pages that populate a 2MB virtual address region.

Figure 16-39: PAE-36 Mode Uses 3-Level Lookup

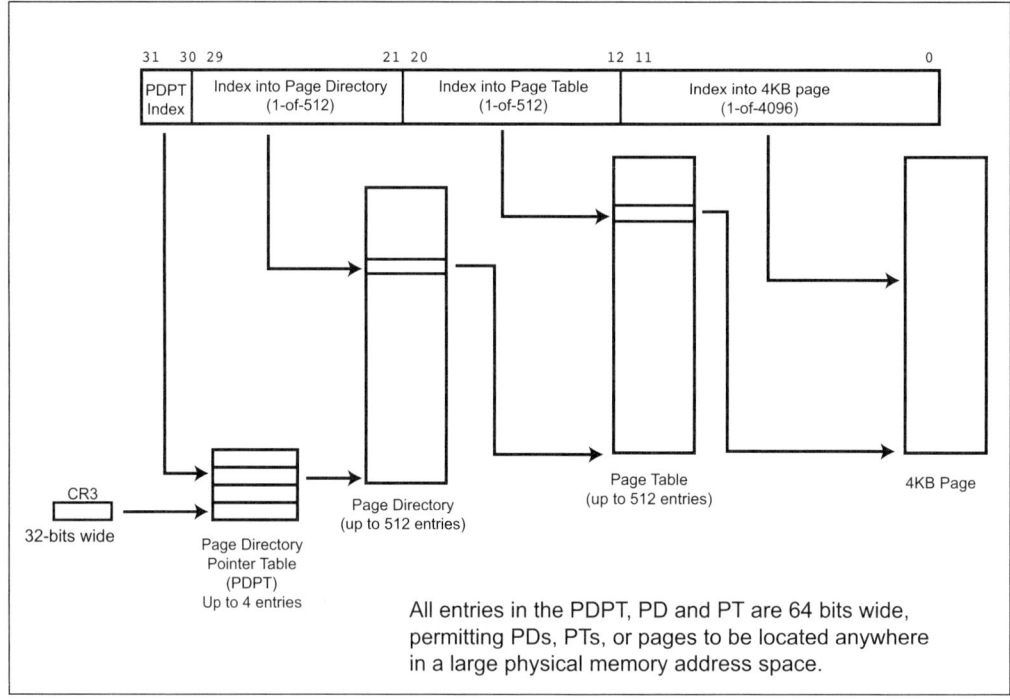

CR3 Points to PDPT in Lower 4GB

Whenever a task switch occurs, the OS kernel loads CR3 (see Figure 16-40 on page 559) with the pointer to the top-level address translation table (the PDPT) associated with the current task. Since CR3 is only 32-bits wide in Protected Mode, the PDPT must reside in the lower 4GB of physical memory. CR3[31:5] specifies the upper 27 bits of the PDPT's 32-byte aligned physical base address (the logical processor assumes the lower five address bits are zero).

See Table 16-8 on page 559. CR3[PWT] and CR3[PCD] tell the logical processor whether or not the PDPT entries can be cached and, if so, whether to treat the area of memory containing the table as cacheable Write Through or cacheable Write Back memory.

Table 16-8: PCD and PWT Bit Settings

PCD	PWT	Memory Type
0	0	The logical processor is permitted to cache entries from the PDPT and treats the area of memory containing the table as cacheable Write Back (WB) memory wherein cached table entries can be in the M, E, S or I state. See "Cacheable Write-Back (WB) Memory" on page 614 for more information.
0	1	The processor is permitted to cache entries from the PDPT and treats the area of memory containing the table as cacheable Write Through (WT) memory wherein cached table entries can be in the S or I state. See "Cacheable Write-Through (WT) Memory" on page 613 for more information.
1	x	The logical processor is not permitted to cache entries from the PDPT (it is treated as UC memory). See "Uncacheable (UC) Memory" on page 610 for more information.

Figure 16-40: CR3 Format With PAE-36 Mode Enabled

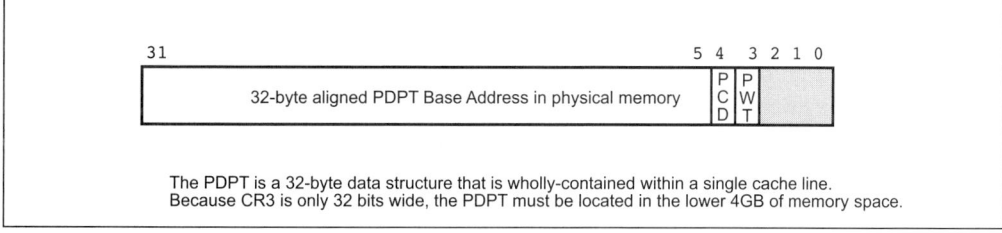

Enlarged Physical Address Space

While CR3 is only 32-bits wide restricting placement of the PDPT to the lower 4GB of physical memory, PDPT entries (PDPTEs), Page Directory entries (PDEs), and Page Table entries (PTEs) are all 64-bits wide. Theoretically, this would seem to permit the PDs, PTs and pages to be located anywhere in a 2^{64} physical address space. Early implementations of PAE-36 Mode translated the 32-bit virtual address into a 36-bit physical memory address (hence the name). Now, however, the specification has been enhanced to allow support for translating the 32-bit virtual address into a physical memory address up to 52-bits in size (large enough for just about anyone's needs).

- The actual size supported by a specific processor may be discovered by executing a CPUID request type 80000008h and checking the value returned in EAX[7:0] (Intel refers to this value as *maxphyaddr*).
- At the time of this writing, current-day implementations typically support a 2^{40} physical address space (one terabyte).
- If a specific processor does not support the type 80000008h CPUID request, then it only supports a 2^{36} (64GB) physical address space.

The Translation

Step 1: PDPT Lookup

Refer to Figure 16-41 on page 561 and Figure 16-42 on page 561. The upper two virtual address bits ([31:30]) identify the targeted 1GB virtual address range and select the corresponding entry in the PDPT. The selected PDPT entry (PDPTE) is 64-bits wide and, if valid (PDPTE[P] = 1), points to the Page Directory that catalogs the location of the 512 Page Tables associated with the targeted 1GB virtual address range. PDPTE[P] is the Present bit:

- **PDPTE[P] = 0**: The Page Directory (the second-level directory) **is not present** in memory. Selection of this PDPTE causes the logical processor to experience a Page Fault exception. The other bits in the selected PDPTE are ignored by the hardware and are available for use by the OS.
- **PDPTE[P] = 1**: The Page Directory (the second-level directory) **is present** in memory. PDPTE[35:12] contains the upper 24 bits of the Page Directory's 4KB-aligned 36-bit physical base address (see the note in Figure 16-42 on page 561) and PDPTE[PCD] and PDPTE[PWT] specify what caching policy the logical processor must use when accessing the Page Directory (see Table 16-8 on page 559). The Page Directory base address can be anywhere in a 64GB physical memory address space.

Figure 16-41: Step 1: IA-32 PAE Mode: PDPTE Selection

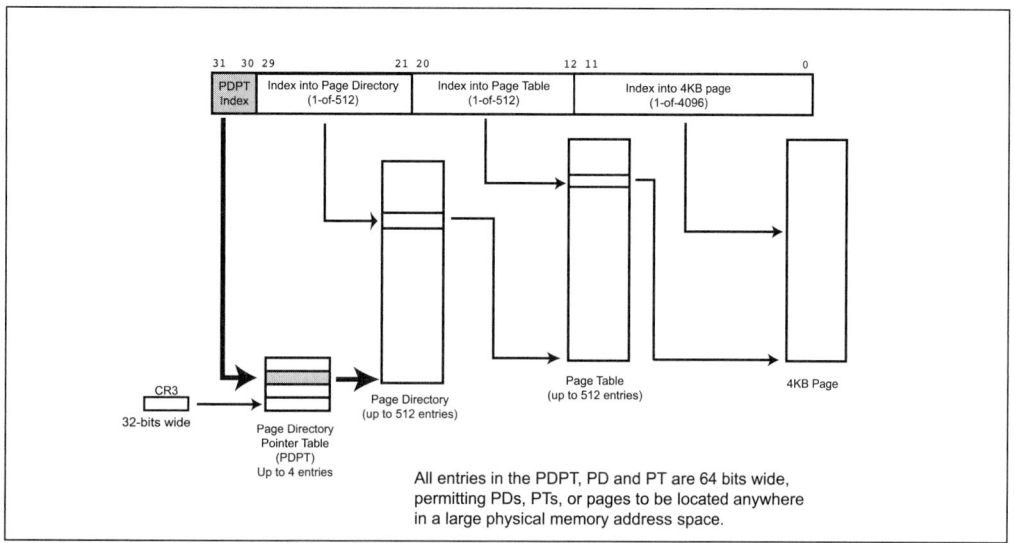

Figure 16-42: IA-32 PAE Mode: PDPT Entry (PDPTE) Format

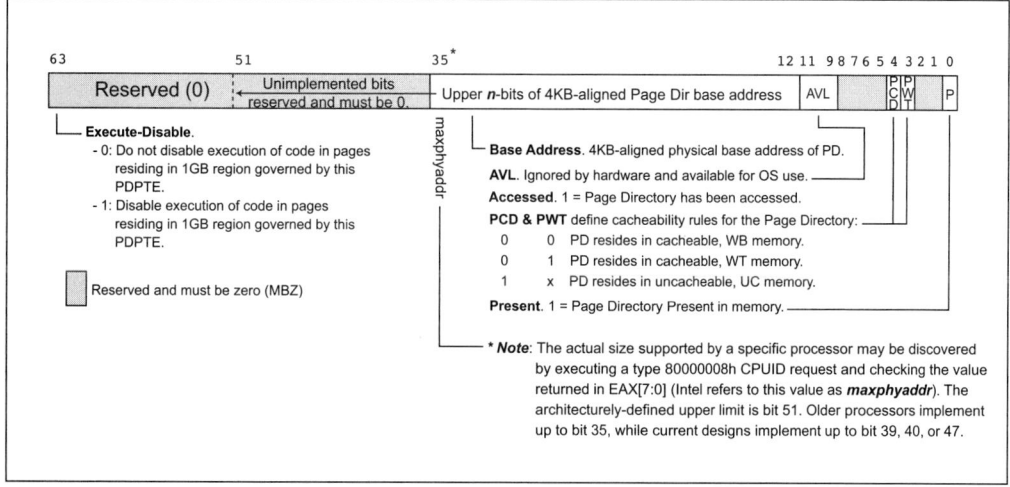

Step 2: Page Directory Lookup

Refer to Figure 16-43 on page 562. Virtual address bits [29:21] select 1-of-512 entries (PDEs) in the selected Page Directory. The selected PDE is associated with the targeted 2MB virtual address range:

- If the Present bit in the PDE = 0, the PDE is not valid and the PT is not currently in memory. This causes the logical processor to experience a Page Fault exception.
- If the Present bit in the selected PDE = 1, then the entry is valid and contains either:
  — The 4KB-aligned physical base address of the Page Table (PT) that catalogs the location of the 512 4KB pages in the targeted 2MB virtual address range
  — The physical base address of the targeted 2MB page in memory.

Assuming the selected PDE is valid (i.e., PDE[P] = 1), it has one of the formats described in the next two sections.

Figure 16-43: Step 2: IA-32 PAE Mode: PDE Selection

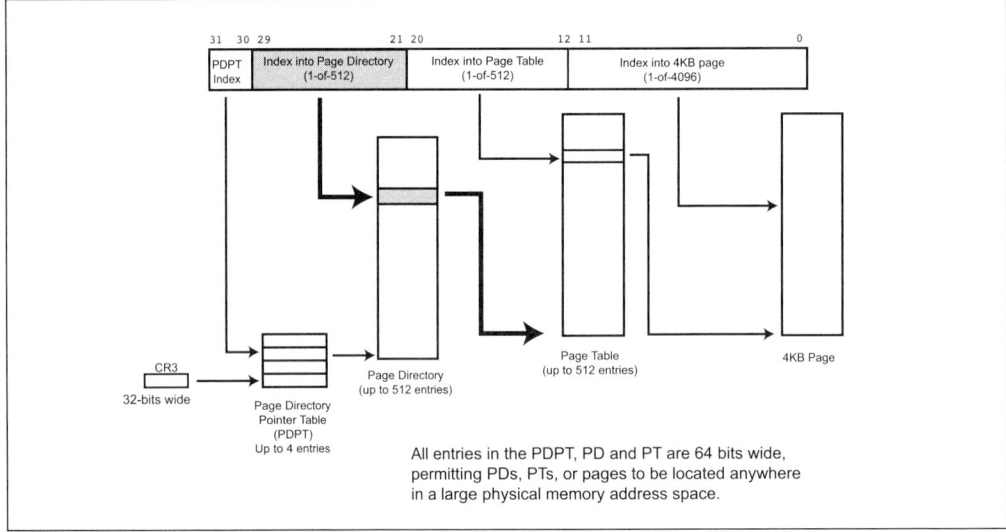

Step 2a: PDE Points to a Page Table. When PDE[PS] = 0, the PDE contains the upper 24 bits (or more; implementation-specific) of the 4KB-aligned physical base address of the Page Table (PT) that catalogs the location of the 512 4KB pages in the selected 2MB virtual address range. The PDE format is the one illustrated in Figure 16-44 on page 563.

The final step in the address translation is described in "Step 3: Page Table Lookup" on page 565.

Figure 16-44: IA-32 PAE Mode: PDE Pointing to a 4KB Page Table

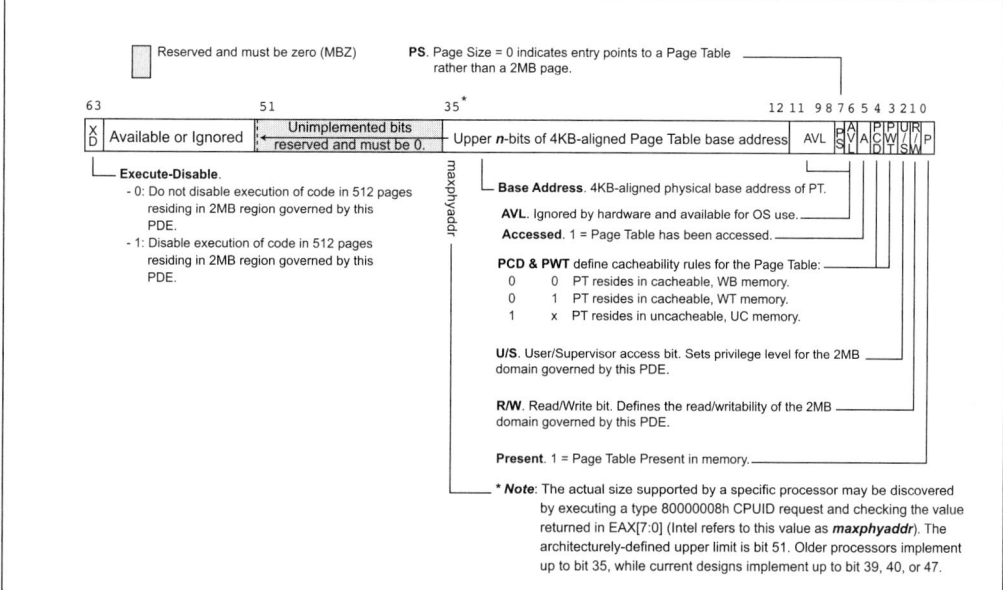

Step 2b: PDE Points to a 2MB Physical Page. When PDE[PS] − 1, the PDE contains the 2MB-aligned physical base address of the targeted 2MB page (see Figure 16-45 on page 564). In this case, no third-level lookup is performed and the address translation is complete. The final physical memory address is constructed as follows:

— The upper 15 bits (or more if maxphyaddr is > 35) of the physical memory address is supplied by PDE[BaseAddress] and
— The lower 21 bits is supplied by virtual address bits [20:0].

The PDE format for a 2MB page is illustrated in Figure 16-46 on page 564. The 3-bits consisting of PAT, PCD and PWT define the page's memory type (see "Page Caching Rules" on page 587).

Figure 16-45: IA-32 PAE Mode: 2MB Physical Page Selected

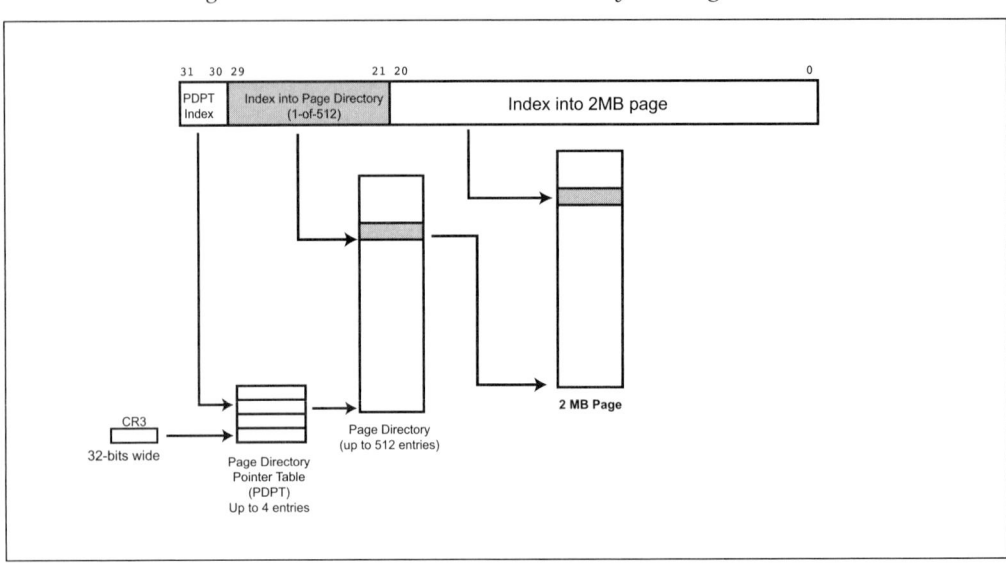

Figure 16-46: IA-32 PAE Mode: PDE Pointing to a 2MB Physical Page

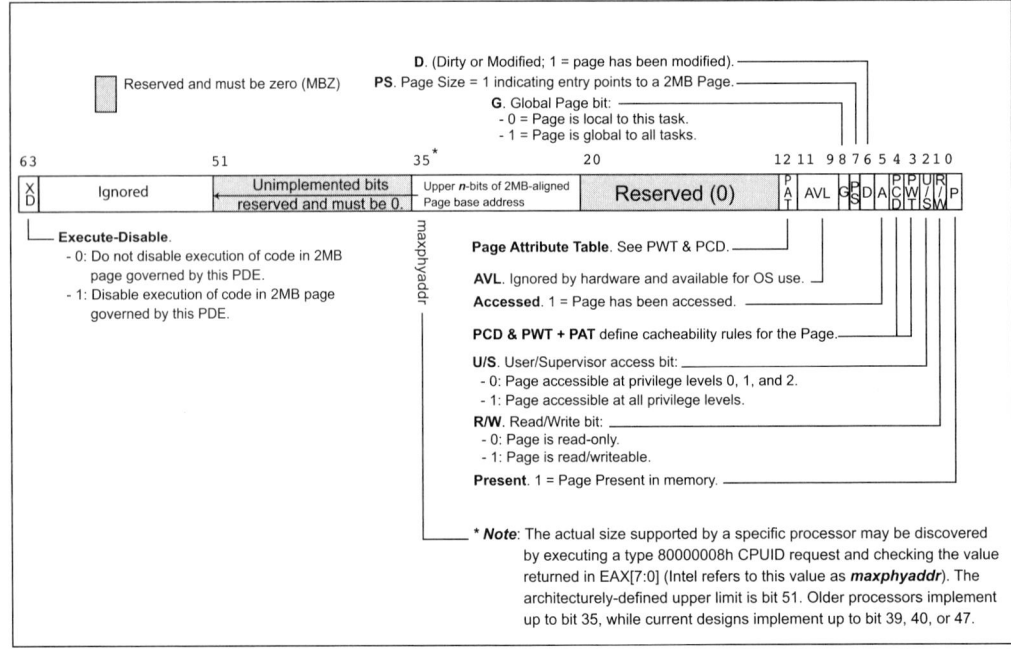

Step 3: Page Table Lookup

If the selected PDE is valid (i.e., PDE[P] = 1) and PDE[PS] = 0, then the PDE (see Figure 16-44 on page 563) points to the third and final lookup table, the Page Table. As illustrated in Figure 16-47 on page 565, the paging unit uses virtual address bits [20:12] to index into the selected Page Table. The selected PTE has the format shown in Figure 16-49 on page 566. Finally, address bits [11:0] (which are never translated) are used to select the target location within the 4KB physical page.

The final, physical memory address is constructed as follows (see Figure 16-48 on page 566):

- The upper 24 bits (or more if maxphyaddr is > 35) of the physical memory address is supplied by PTE[BaseAddress].
- The lower 12 bits are supplied by virtual address bits [11:0].

The 3-bits consisting of PAT, PCD and PWT define the page's memory type (see "Page Caching Rules" on page 587).

Figure 16-47: IA-32 PAE Mode: PTE Selection

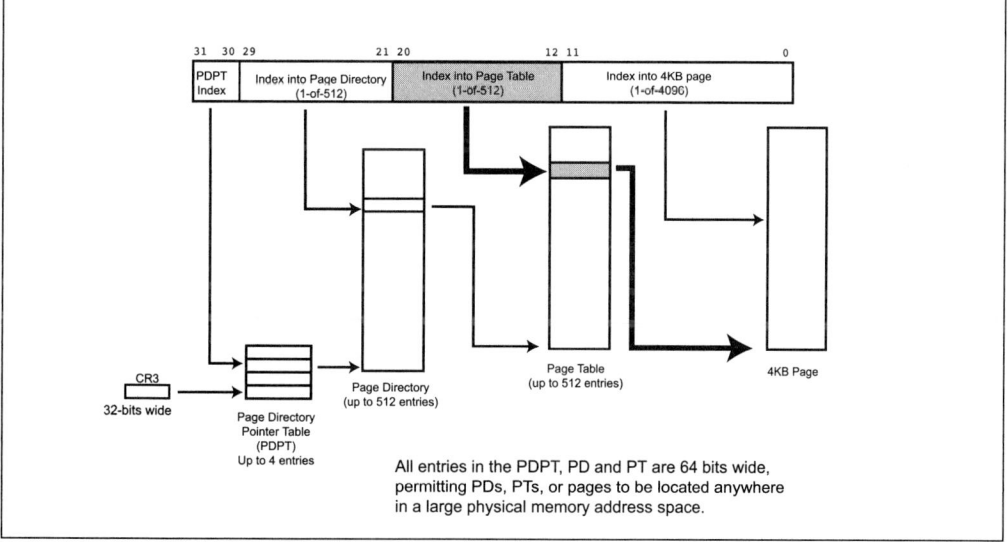

Figure 16-48: IA-32 PAE Mode: 4KB Page Location Selection

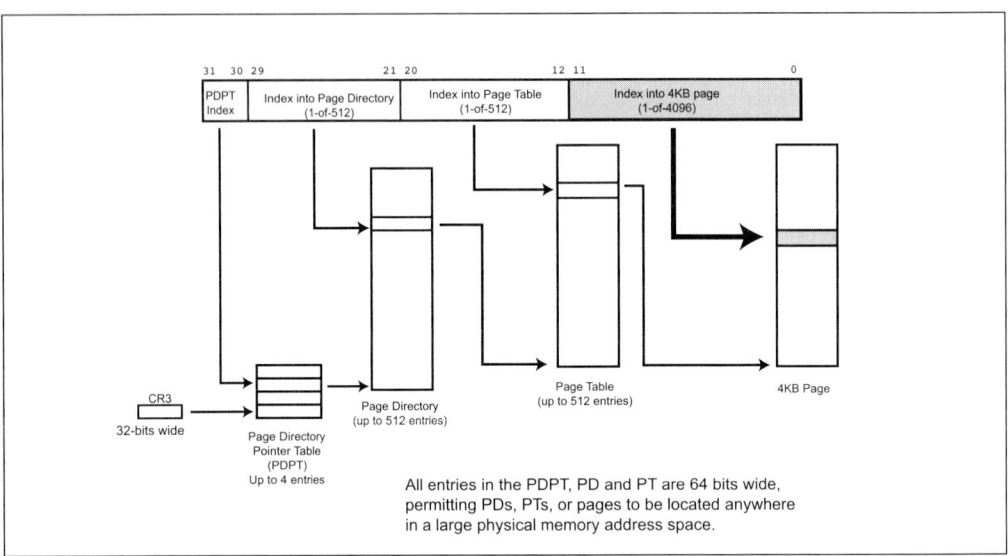

Figure 16-49: IA-32 PAE Mode: PTE Pointing to a 4KB Physical Page

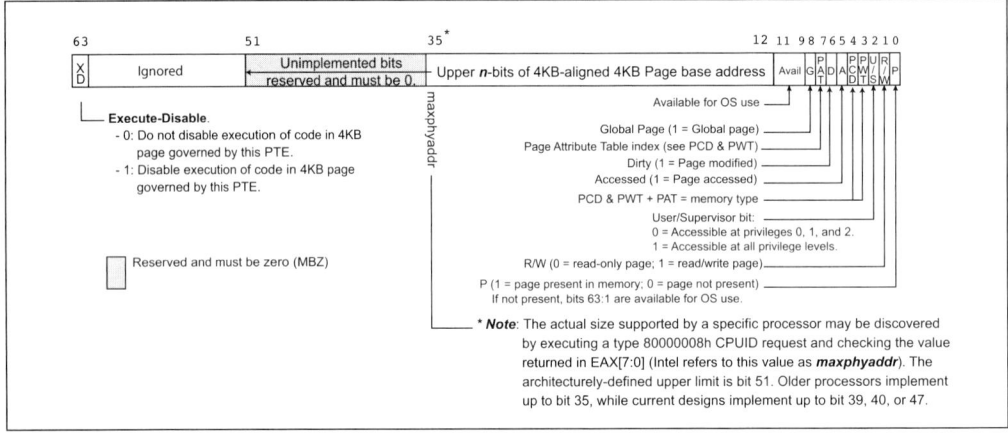

Page Protection Mechanisms

General

Figure 16-50 on page 567 and Figure 16-51 on page 568 illustrate the logic used to determine a page's effective R/W and U/S permissions.

Figure 16-50: Read/Write Permission Determination

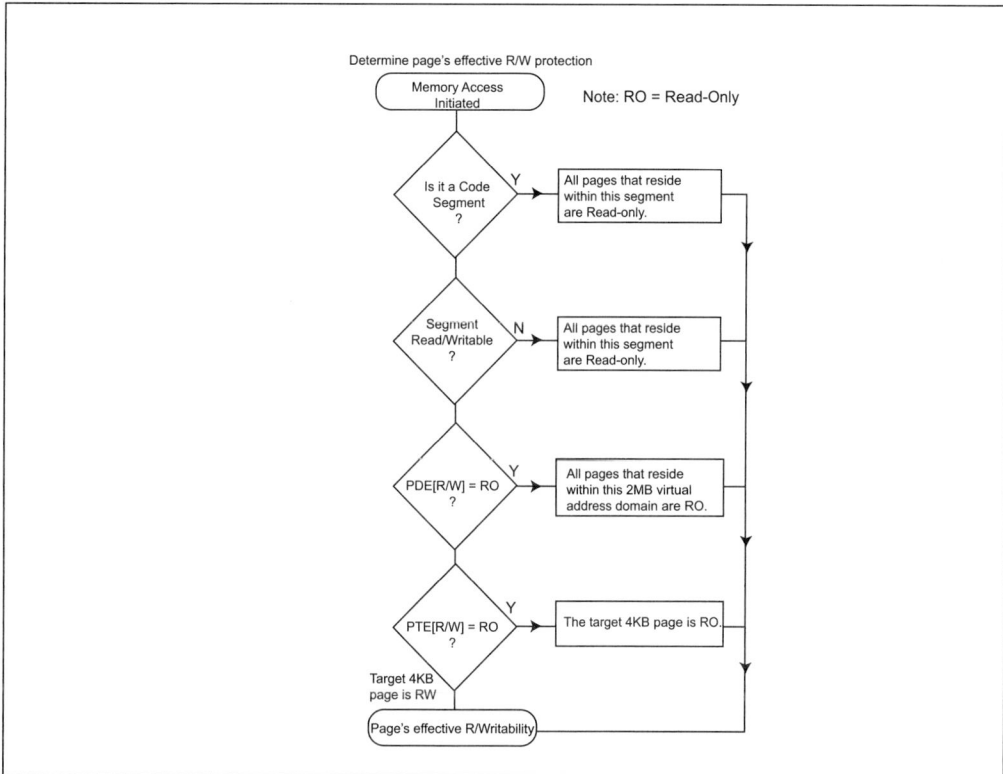

Figure 16-51: User/Supervisor Permission Determination

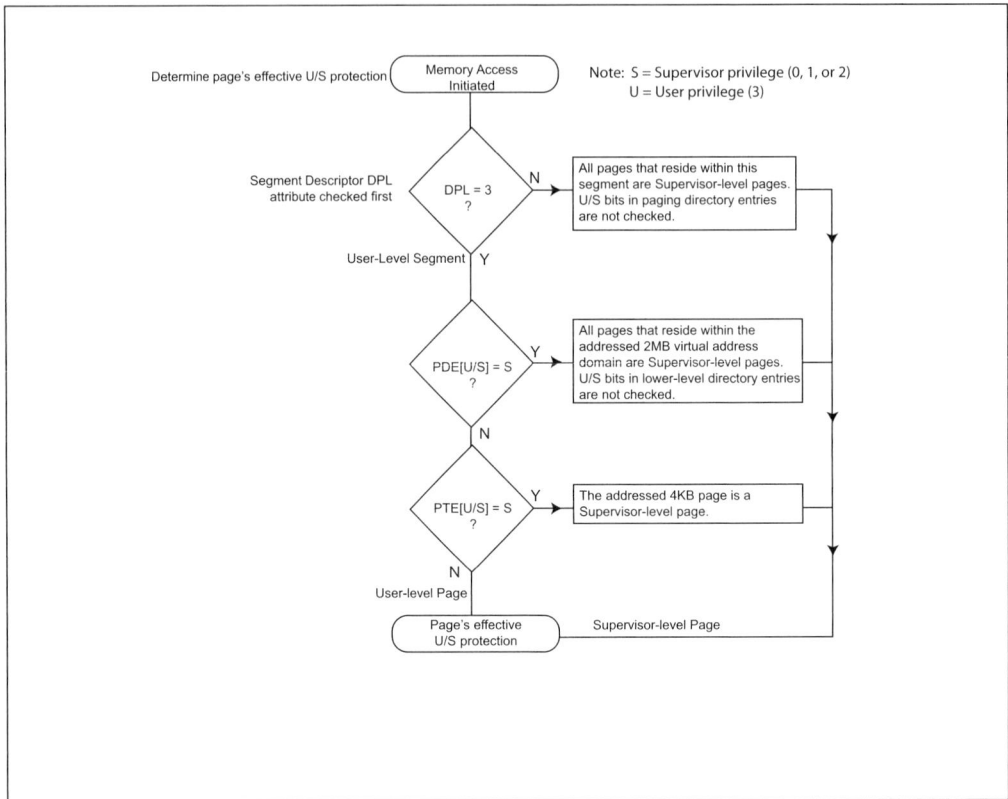

Write-Protection

The logic used to determine whether a write to a page will be allowed to proceed or will result in an exception varies slightly in the Intel and AMD implementations and is controlled by the current state of CR0[WP] (see Figure 16-52 on page 569):

- Figure 16-53 on page 570 illustrates the logic used by Intel.
- Figure 16-54 on page 571 illustrates the logic used by AMD.

Figure 16-52: CR0

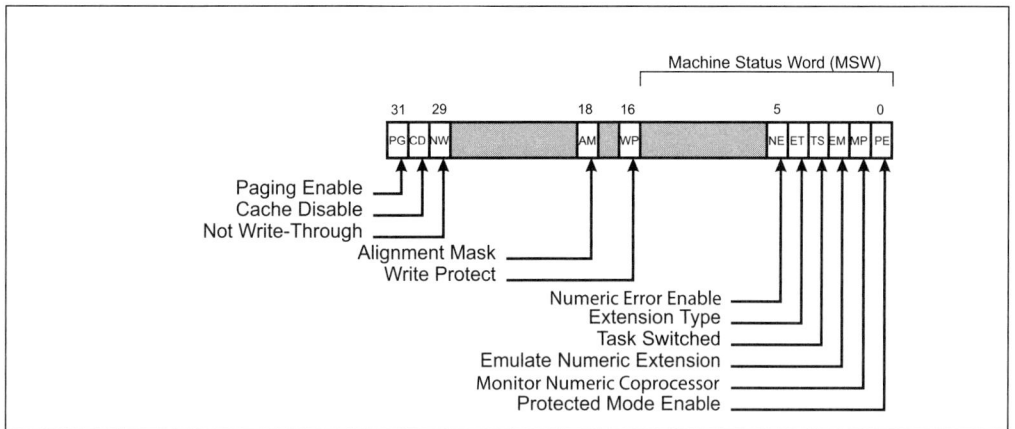

Example Usage: Unix Copy-on-Write Strategy

An OS (e.g., Unix) can handle the creation of a duplicate task (referred to as spawning or forking) in one of two ways:

- **Multiple task copies**. When a new task is created, the OS can make a complete copy of the parent task in memory. This method is obviously memory intensive.
- **One copy of task**. Alternatively, the copy-on-write strategy saves memory space and time by mapping the child task's (i.e., the new task's) segments and pages to the same segments and pages used by the parent task. As long as the two tasks only perform read accesses to a page, they are accessing the same physical page in memory. The OS only creates a copy of a page that is private to a task when one of the tasks attempts to write to the page. By setting CR0[WP] and marking the shared pages as read-only, a Page Fault exception is generated when the currently executing program (no matter its privilege level) attempts to write to the page. The OS can make a private copy of that page (for the use of the cloned copy of the task) upon detection of the Page Fault exception, and may then permit the write to the private page.

Figure 16-53: Write-Protection (Intel approach)

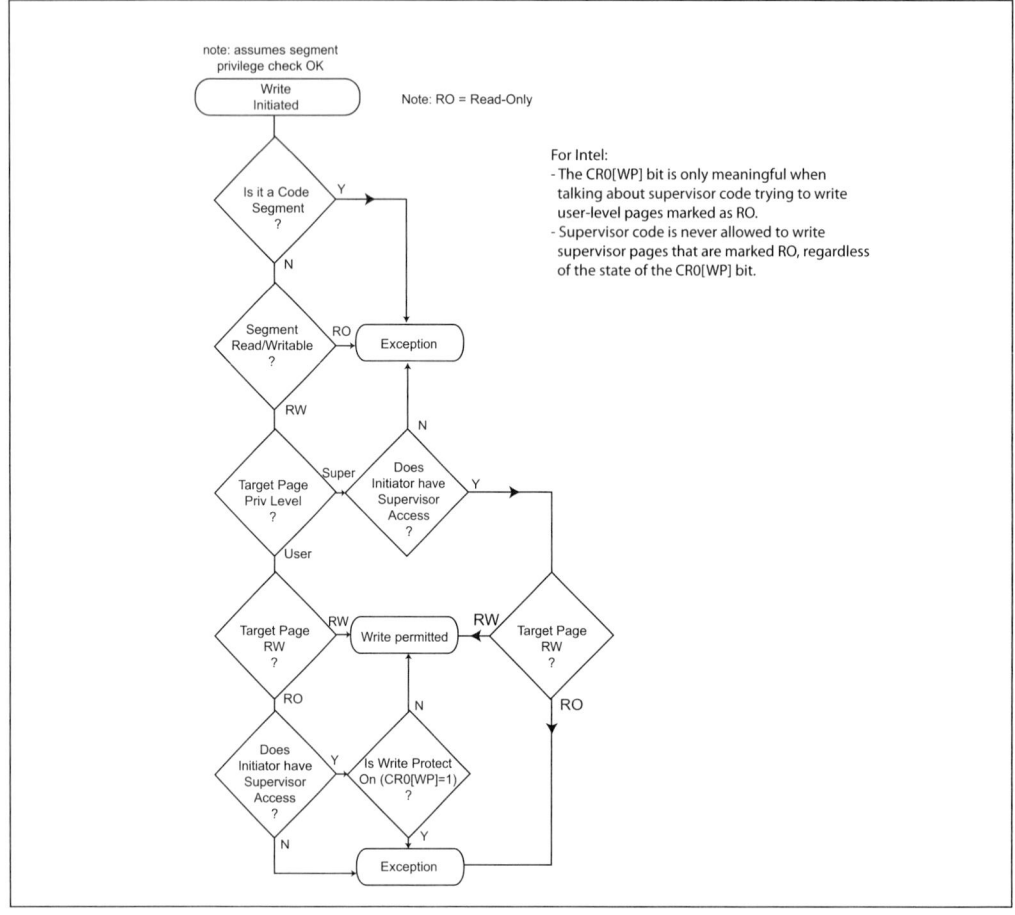

Figure 16-54: Write-Protection (AMD approach)

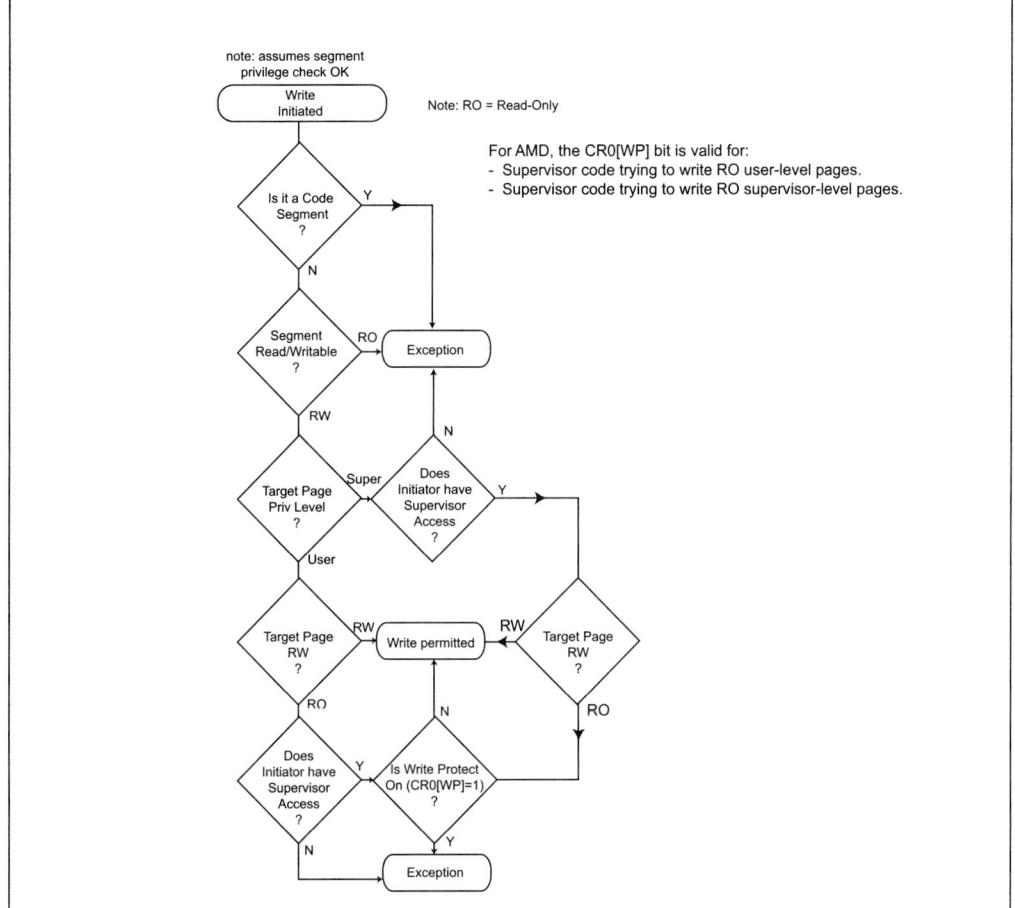

3-Level Lookup—Increased TLB Size

Earlier in the discussion of first-generation paging, it became obvious that performing the 2-level lookup to translate the address would impact performance. The solution was the TLB (see "Two Overhead Memory Reads Take a Toll" on page 522). It should now be obvious that, with the 3-level lookup involved in second-generation paging, the importance of the TLBs cannot be overstated. In the event of a TLB miss, performance will take a real hit as the three overhead memory reads are performed in order to translate the address. Once those reads are done, however, the target PTE (or, in the case of a 2MB page, the target PDE) is then cached in the TLB and any subsequent accesses within the same 4KB page will complete much faster because the TLB hit cancels the three overhead memory reads.

The TLBs in logical processors that implement second-generation paging are larger than those found in earlier processors that only implemented the first-generation paging mechanism.

The earliest IA-32 processors implemented a single TLB that cached PTEs for both code and data pages. Later processors implement both code and data TLBs (i.e., split TLBs). In many designs, separate TLBs may be used to cache PDEs for 4MB and 2MB pages. In addition, modern processors not only have separate TLBs for code and data accesses, but in many cases also include second-level TLBs that cache entries evicted from the first-level TLBs.

Microsoft PAE Support

Table 16-9 on page 572 defines the amount of physical memory supported by various versions of Windows. For additional, up-to-date information, go to:

* http://msdn.microsoft.com/en-us/library/aa366778(VS.85).aspx

Table 16-9: 32-bit Windows PAE Support

Windows OS Version	PAE Supported ?	Comments
Windows 2000 Advanced Server	Y	8GB. Artificially limited to 8GB.
Windows 2000 Datacenter Server	Y	32GB. Artificially limited to 32GB.

Table 16-9: 32-bit Windows PAE Support (Continued)

Windows OS Version	PAE Supported ?	Comments
Windows XP	N	4GB. The 32-bit version of Windows XP did support PAE starting with Service Pack 2. The reason they supported it was not because they wanted a larger address space (because they didn't, they were still limited to 4GB as indicated in this table), but they wanted the No Execute bit. This is what they call DEP (Data Execution Protection). They could only get access to the NX bit with PAE enabled.
Windows Server 2003 Enterprise Edition	Y	32GB. Artificially limited to 32GB.
Windows Server 2003 R2 (or SP1) Enterprise Edition	Y	64GB. Artificially limited to 64GB.
Windows Server 2003 Datacenter Edition	Y	128GB. Supports more than the 64GB limit of the original 36-bit PAE Mode, so the OS can only make full use of the 128GB limit if executed on a processor that can address more than 64GB of physical memory.
Windows Server 2003 Standard Edition	N	4GB. The 32-bit version of Windows XP did support PAE starting with Service Pack 2. The reason they supported it was not because they wanted a larger address space (because they didn't, they were still limited to 4GB as indicated in this table), but they wanted the No Execute bit. This is what they call DEP (Data Execution Protection). They could only get access to the NX bit with PAE enabled.

Table 16-9: 32-bit Windows PAE Support (Continued)

Windows OS Version	PAE Supported ?	Comments
Windows Vista	N	4GB. The 32-bit version of Windows XP did support PAE starting with Service Pack 2. The reason they supported it was not because they wanted a larger address space (because they didn't, they were still limited to 4GB as indicated in this table), but they wanted the No Execute bit. This is what they call DEP (Data Execution Protection). They could only get access to the NX bit with PAE enabled.
Windows Server 2008 Enterprise or Datacenter Edition	Y	64GB. Supports up to the 64GB limit of the original 36-bit PAE Mode.
Windows Server 2008 other editions	N	4GB. The 32-bit version of Windows XP did support PAE starting with Service Pack 2. The reason they supported it was not because they wanted a larger address space (because they didn't, they were still limited to 4GB as indicated in this table), but they wanted the No Execute bit. This is what they call DEP (Data Execution Protection). They could only get access to the NX bit with PAE enabled.

Linux PAE Support

The Linux 2.6 kernel was the first Linux kernel to support PAE-36 Mode. The OS permits up to 3GB of memory to be allocated for each task and reserves 1GB of memory space for the OS kernel.

PSE-36 Mode (PAE-36 Mode's Poor Cousin)

One new software feature, the PSE-36 feature, was introduced in the Pentium II Xeon (and is present in all subsequent processors). It is described in the sections that follow.

PSE-36 Mode Background

Prior to the introduction of PAE-36 Mode (see "Second-Generation Paging" on page 553) in the Pentium Pro, the paging mechanism (see "First-Generation Paging" on page 513) translated the 32-bit virtual address into a 32-bit physical memory address. This constrained the OS to the lower 4GB of address space.

The second-generation paging mechanism (see "Second-Generation Paging" on page 553), using a 3-level lookup (rather than the first-generation's 2-level lookup), permitted the OS to translate a 32-bit virtual memory address to any address within a significantly larger physical memory address space. However, implementing PAE-36 Mode necessitated a rewrite of the paging portion of the OS kernel to use the 3-level directory structure. In addition, entries in each of the three directory structures (i.e., the PDPT, the Page Directories, and the Page Tables) had to be expanded from 32- to 64-bits in width.

The Pentium II Xeon introduced an alternative feature referred to as PSE-36 Mode, one that, while permitting a 32-bit virtual address to be translated into a 36-bit physical memory address, did not require a major rewrite of the paging portion of the OS kernel. It uses the same 2-level directory structure as the first-generation paging mechanism and each entry in the Page Directory and the Page Tables is still 32-bits in width. However, as described in the following sections, PSE-36 Mode is neither as elegant, nor as flexible as PAE-36 Mode.

Intel collectively referred to the PSE-36 and PAE-36 features as ESMA (Extended Server Memory Architecture).

Detecting PSE-36 Mode Capability

The programmer can determine whether or not a processor supports PSE-36 Mode by executing a CPUID request type 1 and checking EDX[17] to see if it is set to one.

Enabling PSE-36 Mode

PAE-36 and PSE-36 Modes are mutually exclusive. Assuming that a processor supports PSE-36 Mode, the OS can enable it by turning off PAE-36 Mode and turning on PSE Mode (i.e., 4MB Page capability). In other words, it is enabled by clearing CR4[PAE] to zero and setting CR4[PSE] = 1 (see Figure 16-55 on page 576). Turning on PSE-36 Mode simultaneously enables 4MB page capability (see "4MB Pages" on page 550) and PSE-36 Mode.

Figure 16-55: CR4

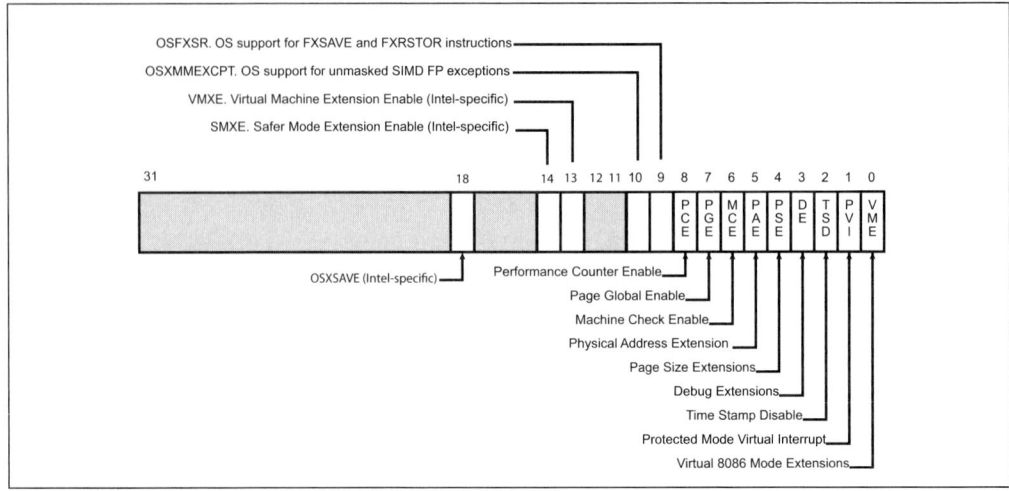

Per Application Virtual Memory Space = 4GB

Turning on PAE-36 or PSE-36 Mode does not change the fact that the currently executing program can only specify 32-bit virtual memory addresses for memory accesses. In other words, the program is still limited to a 4GB virtual memory address space. However, using either PAE-36 or PSE-36 Mode, a 32-bit virtual address can be translated into a 36-bit physical memory address that is either below or above the 4GB address boundary.

First-Generation Lookup Mechanism

Unlike the second-generation address translation mechanism (PAE-36 Mode) which uses a 3-level lookup, PSE-36 Mode uses a 2-level lookup just like the first-generation paging mechanism ("First-Generation Paging" on page 513) to convert a 32-bit virtual memory address into a 36-bit physical memory address.

Selected PDE Can Point to 4KB Page Table or a 4MB Page

The upper 10 bits of the 32-bit virtual address are used as an index into the Page Directory, selecting a 32-bit PDE. With PSE-36 Mode enabled, however, the PDE can assume one of two possible formats:

- The PDE may point to a Page Table that defines the location of the 1024, 4KB pages that populate the 4MB virtual address range selected by the upper 10-bits of the virtual address. In other words, the lookup converts the 32-bit virtual address into a 32-bit physical base address in the lower 4GB of physical memory space (it is 100% compatible with the first-generation paging mechanism).
- The PDE may contain the base address of a 4MB page that lies either below or above the 4GB address boundary (see Figure 16-56 on page 578).

Virtual Address Maps to a 4MB Page in 64GB Space

If the PDE[PS] = 1 in the selected PDE, then the PDE has the format illustrated in Figure 16-56 on page 578. The 3-bits consisting of PAT, PCD and PWT define the page's memory type (see "Page Caching Rules" on page 587). Taken together, the two bit fields labeled PA-1 and PA-2 (Physical Address fields) define the upper 14 bits of the 36-bit, 4MB-aligned base address of a 4MB physical page in memory. The paging unit appends the lower 22 bits of the virtual address to the 14 physical address bits from the PDE to create the 36-bit 4MB-aligned target physical memory address.

Of course, if the PDE[P] bit = 0, the logical processor experiences a Page Fault exception (see "Missing Page or Page Table" on page 538). This can happen for one of two reasons:

- The Page Table the entry should point to is currently not in memory.
- The 4MB page of information is currently not in memory.

The OS Page Fault exception handler must make the determination which of these two conditions is the case and take the appropriate action (i.e., either load the 4KB Page Table or the 4MB page into memory).

Figure 16-56: PDE Points to a 4MB Page Below or Above the 4GB Address Boundary

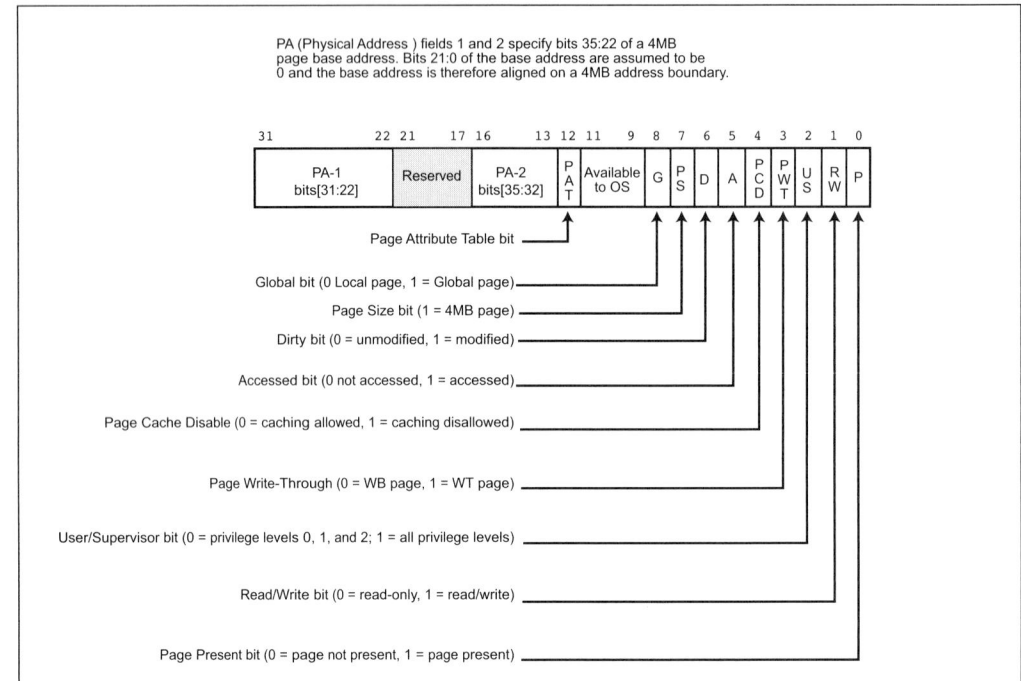

Windows and PSE-36

For a period of time while Microsoft was re-designing the OS kernel to take advantage of PAE-36 Mode, Windows implemented PSE-36 Mode as a simpler stop-gap measure that would—albeit in a very clunky manner—allow access to physical memory above the 4GB address boundary. It was implemented as a a RAM disk driver. The following sequence illustrates how it worked:

- The OS kernel itself did not enable or use PSE-36 Mode.
- The application had to be rewritten so as to call the PSE-36 driver when it required access to memory above the 4GB address boundary.
- When called, the driver temporarily turned on PSE-36 Mode to accomplish the access above the 4GB address boundary for the calling application.

As an example, to write to memory above the 4GB boundary, the following steps were taken:

1. The application wrote the data to be transferred into a buffer somewhere in the lower 4GB of memory.
2. The application then called the PSE-36 Mode driver with a request to transfer the data from the buffer in memory below the 4GB address boundary into a 4MB page in memory above the 4GB address boundary.
3. The driver temporarily switched the logical processor into PSE-36 mode.
4. The driver copied the data from the buffer in the lower 4GB of memory to the 4MB memory buffer above the 4GB boundary.
5. The driver turned off PSE-36 mode and returned control to the caller.

A read would require the reverse of the actions listed. It should be obvious that performance was poor due to need for the buffer copy operation. It should also be stressed that all applications still shared the lower 4GB of memory.

AMD Enhanced PSE-36 to PSE-40

AMD enhanced PSE-36 Mode in AMD-64 processors and Intel followed suit. By expanding the upper-end of a 4MB PDE's PA-2 field (see Figure 16-56 on page 578) by four bits, a 32-bit virtual address can be translated into a 40-bit physical memory address. This would allow 4MB pages to be defined anywhere in a 1TB (terabyte) physical memory address space.

Execute Disable Feature

The Execute Disable feature is only available when the 2nd-generation address translation mechanism (PAE-36 Mode) is in use.

Problem: Malicious Code

The Overflow

Consider the simple C program that immediately precedes Figure 16-57 on page 581:

1. Assume that the stack is empty to begin with (and ESP is pointing to the location just above *arg1* in Figure 16-57 on page 581).
2. *Main* executes. Before calling the *GetInput* procedure, it first pushes two 32-bit integer arguments onto the stack (**A**).
    — ESP then points to start address of *arg2* on the stack.

3. EBP contains the base address of Main's Stack Frame (i.e., the Main procedure' area of the stack).

4. It then calls the GetInput procedure using a near call instruction. The execution of the Call causes the logical processor to push the 4-byte contents of EIP to the stack (**B**).

— ESP now points to the start address of the saved copy of EIP (which points to the instruction immediately following the GetInput procedure call in *Main*).

5. Immediately upon entry to the called procedure, the program saves the pointer to the caller's stack frame by pushing EBP onto the stack (**C**).

— ESP then points to the start address of the caller's EBP on the stack.

— The program then copies the current stack frame pointer from ESP to EBP.

6. The called procedure then subtracts 8 from ESP to allocate 2 dwords of memory for its local variables (integers *a* and *b)*:

— ESP has been decremented to point to the start address of the area of memory in which the two 32-bit integers will be stored.

7. The called procedure then subtracts 16 from ESP to allocate 4 dwords of memory for the buffer (*buff*) that has been declared:

— ESP has been decremented to point to the start address of the memory set aside as the input buffer.

8. Having allocated memory for the three local variables (2 integers plus the buffer), the *gets* function is called. ***Here's the key: as the user inputs data to buff in the gets function, the gets function (a crudely-designed procedure) does not check to determine when a buffer full condition has been reached; it just keep accepting data until the user presses return.***

If the user enters no more than 16 bytes of data, everything is cool. If, however, the user enters:

- 16 bytes (fills the buffer),
- + 4 more bytes (overwrites the first local integer variable),
- + 4 more bytes (overwrites the second local integer variable),
- + 4 more bytes (overwrites the caller's stack frame pointer),
- + 4 more bytes (*overwrites the address to return to upon completion of the GetInput procedure*)

then something ***bad*** will happen when the GetInput procedure executes the return instruction to return to *main*. Exactly what happens depends on what data overwrote the return address (because that's the address the logical processor will return to). One thing's for sure: something bad will happen!

```
GetInput (int a, int b)
{
        /* ints a & b are't used in this example*/
        char  buff[16];  /* 16-byte-buffer */

        gets(buff);        /* operator inputs to buffer */
        puts (buff);       /* buffer content to screen */
}

main ()
{
        int x;
        int y;

        x = 19;
        y = 237;
        GetInput (x,y);
        Return 0;
}
```

Figure 16-57: Stack Usage in C Function Call

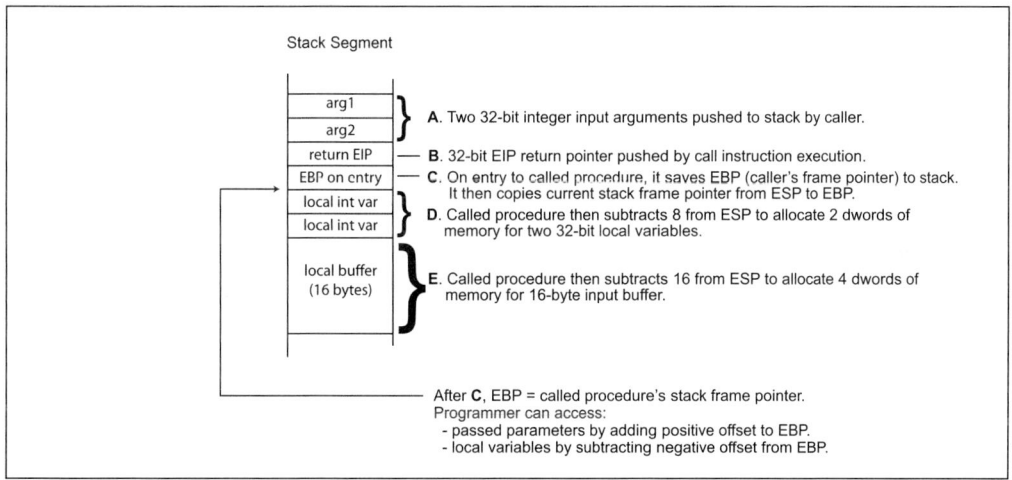

The Exploit

See Figure 16-58 on page 582. Carrying the example a little bit further, assume that the data entered by the user consists of:

1. Enough data to overwrite everything up to the return address.
2. A return address that points to a location higher up in stack memory.

3. And then a series of machine language instructions that comprise a program with evil intentions.

The user enters all of this, overflowing the buffer, trashing the local variables, the old EBP, the correct return address, and then it loads the evil program (referred to as *shellcode*) above the trashed return address. When the GetInput procedure completes and executes the return instruction, the logical processor will jump to the altered return address (i.e., the entry point in the shellcode). Very bad, exploit-specific things will then happen.

Figure 16-58: The Exploit

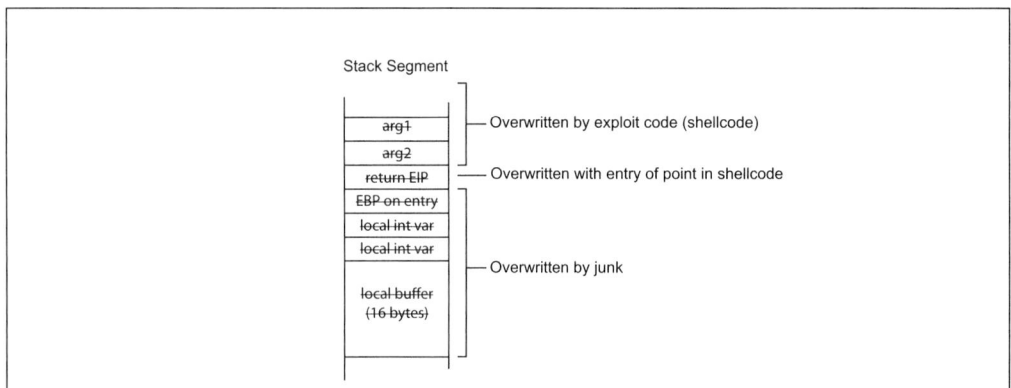

The Fix: Intercept Code Fetches from Data Pages

The logical processor's ability to fetch and execute the exploit code from the stack (which is a read/write data segment) could have been prevented if there were some way of designating the stack as no-execute memory (i.e., from which no code fetches are permitted). An OS can implement that capability by enabling and using the Execute-Disable feature.

Enabling the Execute-Disable Feature

Whether or not a processor implements the Execute Disable feature can be determined by executing a CPUID request type 80000001h and checking for a one in EDX[20]. Assuming it is supported, the feature is enabled by setting EFER[NXE] = 1 (although No Execute Enable is an AMD name, Intel does use it for this bit; see Figure 16-59 on page 583). Attempting to set this bit to one in a processor that doesn't support the Execute Disable feature results in a GP exception.

Figure 16-59: Execute Disable Feature Enable Is in the EFER Register

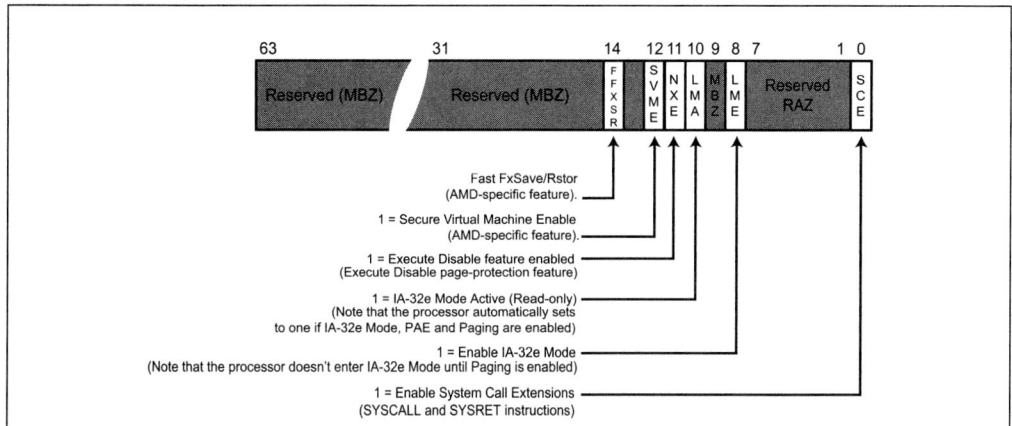

Available in both IA-32 and IA-32e Mode

Although many people think that the Execute Disable feature is only a 64-bit feature, it can be used in both 32-bit and 64-bit modes.

How It Works

Refer to the following figures:

- Note the XD bit is not implemented in PDPT entries.
- Figure 16-60 on page 584.
- Figure 16-61 on page 584.
- Figure 16-62 on page 585.

Notice that in each of these entries, bit 63 is designated as the XD (Execute Disable) bit. Assuming that the Execute Disable feature is enabled (EFER[NXE] = 1), if the currently-running program should attempt to perform a code fetch from a page with XD = 1, the logical processor generates a Page Fault exception (see "Page Faults" on page 545) and the I/D status bit is set to one in the error code pushed onto the stack (see "Page Fault Error Code" on page 547). When the Execute Disable feature is disabled, the XD bit in the PDE and PTE is reserved.

Figure 16-60: PDE Pointing to a 4KB Page Table

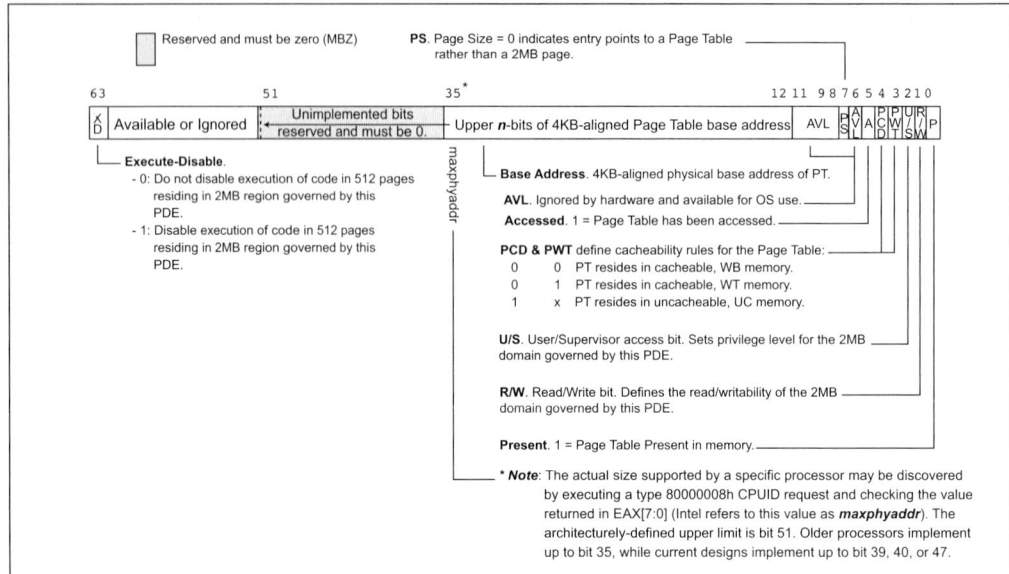

Figure 16-61: PDE Pointing to a 2MB Physical Page

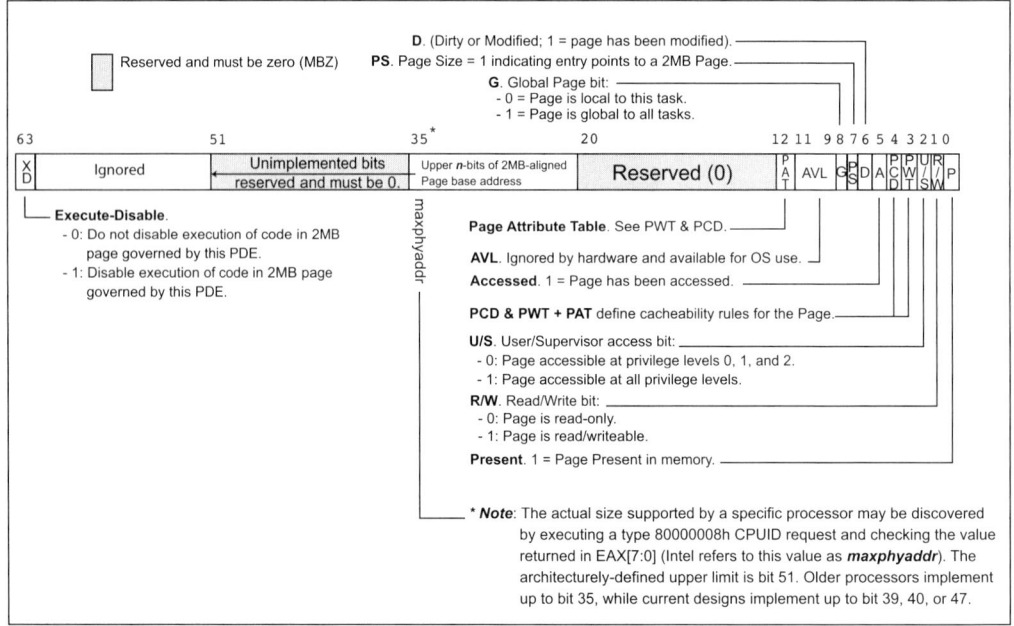

Figure 16-62: PTE Pointing to a 4KB Physical Page

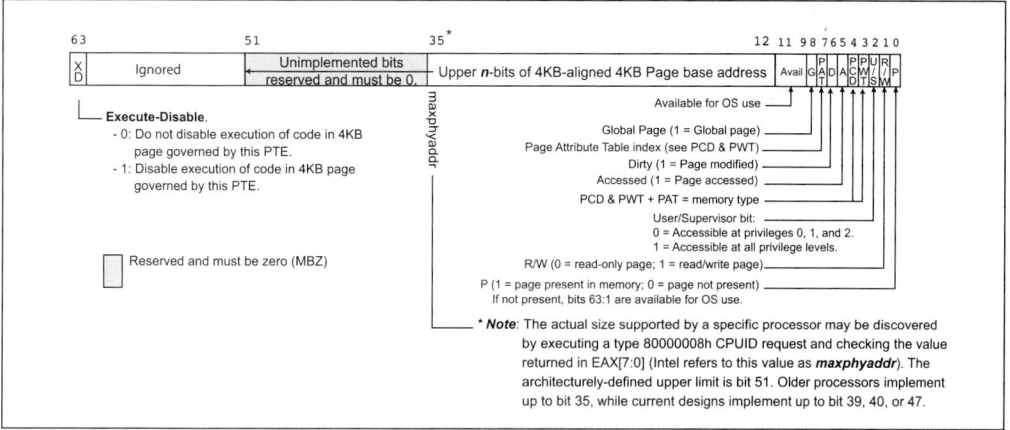

Defining a Page's Caching Rules

Introduction

In order to ensure proper operation (both programmatically as well as proper operation of memory-mapped IO devices), the logical processor must know the rules of conduct to adhere to when performing a memory read or write in a specific area of memory. A detailed description of the memory types can be found in "Memory Type Configuration" on page 599.

When virtual-to-physical address translation is enabled, the logical processor is instructed regarding the rules of behavior it must follow when performing accesses in both the lookup tables as well as the ultimate target physical page.

Translation Table Caching Rules

General

As indicated in the subsections that follow, the logical processor uses two bits—PCD (Page Caching Disable) and PWT (Page Write Through)—to determine the memory type (and therefore the rules of conduct) it must follow when performing reads and writes within an address translation lookup table. Table 16-10 on page 586 defines the possible settings of the PCD and PWT bits.

Table 16-10: Address Translation Table Caching Policy

PCD	PWT	Policy
0	0	The area of memory containing the table is to be treated as cacheable, WB (Write Back) memory (see "Cacheable Write-Back (WB) Memory" on page 614).
0	1	The area of memory containing the table is to be treated as cacheable, WT (Write Through) memory (see "Cacheable Write-Through (WT) Memory" on page 613).
1	x	The area of memory containing the table is to be treated as uncacheable (UC) memory (see "Uncacheable (UC) Memory" on page 610).

First-Generation Paging Tables

First-generation paging uses a 2-level lookup involving two tables:

- **Page Directory**. Refer to Figure 16-19 on page 528. CR3 contains the 4KB-aligned physical base address of the Page Directory as well as two bits, PCD and PWT, that designate the logical processor's rules of conduct when performing reads and writes in the Page Directory.
- **Page Table**. Refer to Figure 16-21 on page 530. The PDE that points to a Page Table contains two bits, PCD and PWT, that designate the logical processor's rules of conduct when performing reads and writes in the respective Page Table.

Second-Generation Paging Tables

Second-generation paging uses a 3-level lookup involving three tables:

- **Page Directory Pointer Table.** Refer to Figure 16-40 on page 559. CR3 contains the 32 byte-aligned physical base address of the PDPT as well as two bits, PCD and PWT, that designate the logical processor's rules of conduct when performing reads and writes in the respective PDPT.
- **Page Directory**. Refer to Figure 16-42 on page 561. Each valid PDPTE contains the 4KB-aligned physical base address of a Page Directory as well as two bits, PCD and PWT, that designate the logical processor's rules of conduct when performing reads and writes in the respective Page Directory.
- **Page Table**. Refer to Figure 16-44 on page 563. The PDE that points to a Page Table contains two bits, PCD and PWT, that designate the logical pro-

cessor's rules of conduct when performing reads and writes in the respective Page Table.

Page Caching Rules

Three bits—PAT (Page Attribute Table), PCD and PWT—designate the logical processor's rules of conduct when performing reads and writes within a 4KB, 2MB, or 4MB page. For a detailed explanation regarding how this 3-bit field designates the rules of conduct for a page, refer to:

- Figure 16-22 on page 532 illustrates a 1st-generation PTE pointing to a 4KB page.
- Figure 16-34 on page 551 illustrates a 1st-generation PDE pointing to a 4MB page.
- Figure 16-46 on page 564 illustrates a 2nd-generation PDE pointing to a 2MB page.
- Figure 16-49 on page 566 illustrates a 2nd-generation PTE pointing to a 4KB page. The same format is used by a PTE pointing to a 4KB page when PSE-36 Mode is active rather than PAE-36 Mode.
- When PSE-36 Mode is active rather than PAE-36 Mode, Figure 16-56 on page 578 illustrates a PDE pointing to a 4MB page.

PAT Feature (Page Attribute Table)

What's the Problem?

In order to ensure proper operation of the software environment as well as that of memory-mapped IO devices, it is imperative that the logical processor know the proper way to behave when performing a memory access within any given region of memory space.

The BIOS programs the memory type for each memory range into the MTRRs (Memory Type and Range Registers; see "Memory Type Configuration" on page 599) at startup time. When the OS is subsequently booted and sets up the address translation tables associated with each task, it must initialize the memory type for both the address translation tables as well as the physical memory pages belonging to the task. In earlier processors, there were only two bits available for this purpose: PCD and PWT. Using a 2-bit field to define a page's memory type imposes an obvious limit of no more than four possible memory types to choose from (in reality, PCD and PWT only permit three memory types—WB, WT and UC; see Table 16-10 on page 586). The PAT feature addresses this issue.

Detecting PAT Support

The programmer can determine whether or not a processor supports the PAT feature by performing a CPUID request type 1 and verifying that EDX[PAT] = 1. *If a processor supports PAT, the PAT feature is always enabled.*

PAT Allows More Memory Types

In a processor that supports the PAT feature, each PTE that points to a 4KB page and each PDE that points to a 2MB or 4MB page (see "Page Caching Rules" on page 587) not only contains the PCD and PWT bits, but a third bit (formally reserved) referred to as the PAT*i* (PAT Index) bit:

At first glance, it might seem that expanding the memory type field from 2 to 3 bits would permit 1 of 8 memory types to be selected rather 1 of 3 (when using just PCD and PWT). However, this 3-bit field does not specify the memory type directly. Rather, these three bits select one of eight possible fields in the IA32_CR_PAT MSR (see Figure 16-63 on page 588 and Table 16-11 on page 588). This MSR resides at MSR address 277_{10} (and is guaranteed to remain at this address). The value (see Table 16-12 on page 589) in the selected field of the MSR defines the memory type (1 of 5 currently-defined types; note: UC- is not a separate memory type) assigned to the page. *It should be noted that the Intel Architecture Software Developer's Manual Volume 3a: System Programming Guide indicates that each entry (i.e., field) in the IA32_CR_PAT MSR contains an 8-bit value. This is incorrect. Each entry contains a 3-bit value.*

Figure 16-63: IA32_CR_PAT MSR

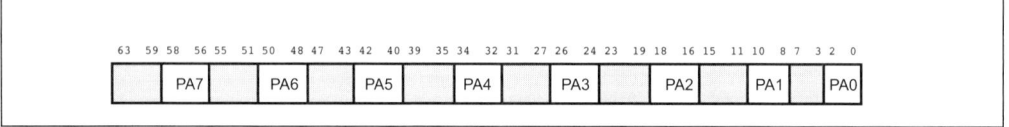

Table 16-11: Bit Field Selection in the IA32_CR_PAT MSR

PATi	PCD	PWT	Selected Entry in IA32_CR_PAT MSR
0	0	0	PA0
0	0	1	PA1

Table 16-11: Bit Field Selection in the IA32_CR_PAT MSR (Continued)

PATi	PCD	PWT	Selected Entry in IA32_CR_PAT MSR
0	1	0	PA2
0	1	1	PA3
1	0	0	PA4
1	0	1	PA5
1	1	0	PA6
1	1	1	PA7

Table 16-12: Memory Types That Can Be Encoded in a IA32_CR_PAT MSR Entry

PA Field Value	Memory Type
0	Uncacheable (UC).
1	Write Combining (WC).
2	Reserved. Using this value results in a GP exception being generated.
3	
4	Write Through (WT).
5	Write Protected (WP).
6	Write Back (WB).
7	Uncacheable (UC-). See "The UC- Memory Type" on page 590.

Default Contents of IA32_CR_PAT MSR

Table 16-13 on page 590 shows the default setting for each IA32_CR_PAT MSR field following a power up or a processor reset. Delivering a soft reset (an INIT) to the logical processor does not alter this MSR's contents.

Table 16-13: Default Memory Types in the IA32_CR_PAT MSR *Entries*

Entry	Memory Type
PA0	WB
PA1	WT
PA2	UC-
PA3	UC
PA4	WB
PA5	WT
PA6	UC-
PA7	UC

Memory Type When Page Definition and MTRR Disagree

General. When it has to perform a memory access, the logical processor consults both the MTRRs *and* the selected PTE or PDE to determine the memory type (and the rules of conduct it is to follow). Since it is typically the BIOS that sets up the MTRRs and the OS that sets up the address translation tables, the memory type assigned to a particular memory area may not agree. Table 16-14 on page 591 defines the effective memory type based on the MTRR versus the PDE or PTE memory type assignments. When there is a disagreement, the general rule-of-thumb is that the logical processor will select the more conservative memory type of the two. As with any rule-of-thumb, however, there are always a few exceptions, but with most combinations the more conservative memory type generally wins.

The UC- Memory Type. It should be noted that the UC- (UC Minus) memory type assignment is only available via a PTE or PDE and is not available in the MTRRs. It is actually not a memory type, however. Just like the UC memory type, UC- defines the memory area as uncacheable. However, a WC (Write-Combining) setting in the MTRRs overrides UC- in the PTE or PDE. If the MTRRs define an area as WC and the PTE or PDE defines it as UC, then the effective type is UC.

Table 16-14: Effective Memory Type Determination

MTRR Type	IA32_CR_PAT Type	Effective Memory Type
UC	UC	UC
	UC-	
	WC	WC
	WT	UC
	WB	
	WP	
WC	UC	
	UC-	WC. Although the UC type is more conservative than WC, WC in the MTRRs overrides UC- in the PTE or PDE.
	WC	WC
	WT	UC
	WB	WC
	WP	UC

Table 16-14: Effective Memory Type Determination (Continued)

MTRR Type	IA32_CR_PAT Type	Effective Memory Type
WT	UC	UC. The MTRRs say that this physical memory area is cacheable, while this particular PTE or PDE says it's not. One or more other PTEs or PDEs may map to the same physical memory area covered by this MTRR setting and one or more of them may say it's cacheable (in which case, the logical processor may have already cached information from this physical memory area). For this reason, the logical processor is required to check its caches. This situation is referred to as page aliasing and it is not recommended.
	UC-	
	WC	WC
	WT	WT
	WB	
	WP	WP
WB	UC	UC. The MTRRs say that this physical memory area is cacheable, while this particular PTE or PDE says it's not. One or more other PTEs or PDEs may map to the same physical memory area covered by this MTRR setting and one or more of them may say it's cacheable (in which case, the logical processor may have already cached information from this physical memory area). For this reason, the logical processor is required to check its caches. This situation is referred to as page aliasing and it is not recommended.
	UC-	
	WC	WC
	WT	WT
	WB	WB
	WP	WP

Table 16-14: Effective Memory Type Determination (Continued)

MTRR Type	IA32_CR_PAT Type	Effective Memory Type
WP	UC	UC. The MTRRs say that this physical memory area is cacheable, while this particular PTE or PDE says it's not. One or more other PTEs or PDEs may map to the same physical memory area covered by this MTRR setting and one or more of them may say it's cacheable (in which case, the logical processor may have already cached information from this physical memory area). For this reason, the logical processor is required to check its caches. This situation is referred to as page aliasing and it is not recommended.
	UC-	WC
	WC	
	WT	WT
	WB	WP
	WP	

Altering IA32_CR_PAT MSR

The MSR is read/writable and is accessed using the RDMSR and WRMSR instructions. The contents of the MSR's eight fields can be changed by writing to the IA32_CR_PAT MSR using the WRMSR instruction. Table 16-12 on page 589 defines the values that can be written to a field. Any attempt to write an undefined memory type results in the generation of a GP exception.

Ensuring IA32_CR_PAT and MTRR Consistency

The OS can redefine the memory type assigned to a memory area in any of three ways:

- By changing the MTRR settings.
- By changing the PATi, PCD, PWT settings for the page.
- By changing the contents of the IA32_CR_PAT MSR.

Changing the memory type has ramifications regarding information that may be currently cached within the logical processor (in its caches and/or TLBs).

The following discussion applies to changing the MTRR and/or IA32_CR_PAT MSR settings.

In a multiprocessor system, the OS must maintain MTRR and IA32_CR_PAT MSR consistency between all of the logical processors in the system (i.e., all logical processors must have the same MTRR and IA32_CR_PAT MSR settings). Logical processors do not automatically maintain this consistency.

When the OS sets up the logical processors, it must load the MTRRs of the boot processor while the E bit (the Enable bit) in its MTRRdefType register = 0. This disables the MTRRs. The OS then directs other logical processors to load their MTRRs with the same memory map/type definitions and their IA32_CR_PAT MSRs with the same settings as its own. After all of the logical processors have loaded their MTRRs and IA32_CR_PAT MSRs, the OS signals them to enable their MTRRs. Barrier synchronization is used to prevent further memory accesses until all logical processors indicate that their MTRRs have been enabled. This synchronization is likely to be a shoot-down style algorithm, with shared variables and inter-processor interrupts.

When any change is made to the MTRR or IA32_CR_PAT MSR settings in an MP system, the OS must once again force all of the other logical processors to also load the revised settings into their MTRRs and IA32_CR_PAT MSRs. To do so, the OS places a program in memory that, when executed by a logical processor, causes it to set its MTRRs and IA32_CR_PAT MSR to the same settings. The OS then causes the Local APIC on the logical processor running the OS kernel to transmit an Inter-Processor Interrupt (IPI) message to the Local APICs associated with all of the other logical processors. This message contains the start address of the program to be run and instructs each of the other logical processors to execute the program. Refer to the description of the SIPI in "How the APs are Discovered and Configured" on page 1381 for a description of this process.

When executed by each of the logical processors, the program causes a logical processor to perform the following steps:

1. Disable recognition of external hardware interrupts (by executing the CLI instruction).
2. Wait for all of the logical processors to reach this point (this could be signaled through a memory semaphore).
3. Disable all caching by setting CR0[CD] = 1 and CR0[NW] = 0.
4. Cause the logical processor to flush its caches by executing the WBINVD instruction. Note that on a logical processor that supports self-snooping (as indicated by EDX[SS] =1 on a CPUID request type 1), this step is unneces-

sary. For a description of self-snooping, refer to the discussion of Self-Modifying Code that can be found in the MindShare book entitled, *The Unabridged Pentium 4*.

5. Set CR4[PGE] = 0 to disable the global page feature.

6. Cause the logical processor to flush all PTEs and PDEs from its TLBs. This is accomplished by setting CR3 to the same value that it already contains (execute a MOV from CR3 to another register and then a MOV from that register back to CR3.)

7. Disable the logical processor's MTRR registers (by clearing the E bit in the MTRRdefType register). If only the contents of one or more variable-range MTRR register pairs are being modified, software may clear the valid bit for each of the affected register pairs instead.

8. Change the contents of the MTRRs that need to be modified.

9. Enable all of the MTRR registers (by setting the E bit in the MTRRdefType register). If only the contents of one or more variable-range MTRR register pairs were modified and their individual valid bits were cleared, then set the valid bits for those register pairs instead.

10. Flush all caches and all TLBs a second time (see steps 4 and 6). The TLB flush is required for Pentium 4 and P6 family processors. Executing the WBINVD instruction is not needed on the Pentium 4 and P6 family processors, but it may be needed in future systems.

11. Re-enable caching by setting CR0[CD] = 0 and CR0[NW] = 0.

12. If CR4[PGE] was cleared to zero earlier in the process, set CR4[PGE] = 1.

13. Wait for all of the logical processors to reach this point (this could be signaled through a memory semaphore).

14. Reenable recognition of external hardware interrupts (by executing the STI instruction).

Assigning Multiple Memory Types to a Single Physical Page

Consider the following:

- Any of the five possible memory types (six, if you count UC-) can be specified in a PTE or a PDE.
- More than one virtual memory address range can be mapped to the same physical memory address range.
- Each of the PTEs or PDEs that map to the same physical address range could define its memory type differently.

Intel does not support this practice because it may lead to undefined operations that can result in a system failure. Special care must be taken that a WC page must never be aliased to a cacheable page because, on a specific processor implementation, writes to WC memory (which is not cacheable) may not cause a cache lookup and invalidation to ensure that cache consistency is maintained.

When remapping a page previously mapped as a cacheable memory type to a the WC memory type, the OS can avoid the aliasing issue as follows:

1. Remove the PTE or PDE that had mapped the page to a cacheable memory type (i.e., clear the Present bit to 0 in the PTE or PDE).
2. Flush the TLBs (see step 6 in "Ensuring IA32_CR_PAT and MTRR Consistency" on page 593) of all logical processors that may have used the mapping, even speculatively.
3. Create a PTE or PDE that maps to the same physical address, but with the new memory type.
4. Flush the caches on all logical processors that may have used the mapping previously (see steps 3 and 4 in "Ensuring IA32_CR_PAT and MTRR Consistency" on page 593). On logical processors that support self-snooping (as indicated by EDX[SS] =1 on a CPUID request type 1), this step is unnecessary.

Compatibility with Earlier IA-32 Processors

If an x86 processor implements the IA32_CR_PAT MSR, the PAT feature is always active and the PDE's or a PTE's 3-bit PATi, PCD and PWT value selects the entry in the IA32_CR_PAT MSR that defines the page's memory type.

If the system is running an OS that does not support the PAT feature, the following are true:

*   The OS treats the PATi bit in PDEs (bit 12) and PTEs (bit 7) as a reserved bit. This being the case, the OS ensures that the PATi bit is cleared to 0.
*   The OS sets up the PDE's or PTE's PCD and PWT bits in the manner defined for earlier processors that did not implement the PAT feature. Table 16-15 on page 597 defines these settings.

When an OS that doesn't support the PAT feature is being used, the fact that the PDE and PTE PATi bit is reserved and always cleared to 0 causes the 3-bit PATi, PCD, PWT value to select fields 0, 1, 2 or 3 in the IA32_CR_PAT MSR. As can be seen in Table 16-13 on page 590, the default values present in fields 0 - 3 of the PAT Table MSR are backward-compatible with the memory types assigned by older processors based on the PCD/PWT setting.

Table 16-15: Pre-PAT Interpretation of the PCD and PWT Bits

PCD	PWT	Memory Type
0	0	Caching is enabled within the Page Table or the page and the memory type is WB.
0	1	Caching is enabled within the Page Table or the page and the memory type is WT.
1	x	Caching is disabled within the Page Table or the page and the memory type is UC.

Third Generation Paging

This chapter focused on the 1st- and 2nd-generation paging mechanisms supported in IA-32 Mode. The 3rd-generation paging mechanism introduced with the advent of IA-32e Mode is covered in "IA-32e Address Translation" on page 983.

17 *Memory Type Configuration*

The Previous Chapter

The previous chapter covered the following topics:

- Evolution of demand mode paging on the x86 processors. Backgrounder on memory and disk management.
- Virtual memory concept and advantages of address translation.
- First and second generation virtual-to-physical address translation mechanisms.
- Role of the Translation Lookaside Buffer (TLB). Global Page feature and TLB maintenance.
- Page Directory Entries (PDEs) and Page Table Entries (PTEs).
- Page access permission.
- Missing page or Page Table.
- Page access history.
- 4MB pages.
- PSE-36 Mode.
- Execute Disable feature.
- Page caching rules.
- Page write protection.

This Chapter

This chapter describes the operational characteristics of various types of memory targets (UC, WC, WP, WT, and WB) and the role of the Memory Type and Range Registers (MTRRs). It defines the concept of speculatively executed loads and describes issues related to the logical processor's Posted Memory Write Buffer (PMWB) and Write-Combining Buffers (WCBs).

The Next Chapter

The next chapter contrasts hardware- versus software-based tasking switching and provides a conceptual overview of task switching as well as a detailed description of the hardware-based task switching mechanism. The following topics are covered:

- Hardware- vs. Software-Based Task Switching
- A Condensed Conceptual Overview
- A More Comprehensive Overview
- Hardware-Based Task Switching
  — It's Slow
  — Why Didn't OSs Use It?
  — Why Wasn't It Improved?
  — Why Does It Still Exist?
  — Introduction to the Key Elements
  — The Trigger Events
  — The Descriptors
  — The Task Register
  — TSS Data Structure Format
  — Comprehensive Task Switch Description
  — Calling Another Task
  — Task Switching and Address Translation
  — Switch from Higher-Privilege Code to Lower

Characteristics of Memory Targets

Introduction

When the logical processor must perform a memory access, it is important that it understand the operational characteristics of the target device in order to ensure proper operation. If it does not, the manner in which the memory access is accomplished may result in improper operation of the device or of the program.

Example Problem: Caching from MMIO

As an example, assume that an area of memory is populated with a series of memory-mapped IO (MMIO) registers associated with one or more devices.

Now assume that the program performs a 4-byte memory read to obtain the status of a device from its 32-bit, device-specific status register. If the logical processor were to assume that the region of memory being accessed is cacheable, it would perform a lookup in its caches and, in the event of a cache miss, would initiate a memory read to obtain not only the four requested locations, but would in fact read from all locations that encompass the line within which the desired four locations reside. This could result in a serious problem. The contents of *all* of the memory-mapped IO ports within that line of memory space would be read and cached in the processor. If the program subsequently issued a request to access any of those locations, it would result in a cache hit and:

- **If it's a read**: the requested data is supplied from the cache, *not* from the actual IO device that implements that memory-mapped IO port. This means that the data or status obtained would not represent the current, up-to-date contents of the location read. This desynchronization between a device driver and its related device can result in erroneous operation.
- **If it's a write**: the line in the cache is updated but, if the memory area is designated as WB (cacheable Write-Back) memory, the data is not written to memory. The actual memory-mapped IO device therefore does not receive the write.

Early Processors Implemented Primitive Mechanism

The example just described is but one case wherein the logical processor's lack of knowledge regarding the rules of conduct it must follow within a given memory area can result in spurious operation. In a very limited sense, the 486 and Pentium processors possessed a mechanism that permitted the OS kernel to define the characteristics of a region of memory. Each PTE (Page Table Entry) contained two bits, PCD and PWT, that permitted the OS to define a 4KB memory page as cacheable Write Through (WT), cacheable Write Back (WB), or uncacheable (UC) memory. This solution was insufficient for two reasons:

- The OS typically is not platform-specific and therefore doesn't necessarily know the characteristics of the various devices that populate memory space. The BIOS, on the other hand, *is* platform-specific but it is the OS and not the BIOS that sets up and maintains the Page Tables in memory.
- There are many different types of devices and some require different processor operation than that defined using the PTE's PCD and PWT bits (the WB, WT and UC memory types). Be advised that the later addition of the PAT feature [see "PAT Feature (Page Attribute Table)" on page 587] permitted the OS to assign any memory type to a page).

Solution/Problem: Chipset Memory Type Registers

When a program executing on the 486 or the Pentium had to initiate a memory access, the processor's internal hardware consulted the PTE[PCD] and PTE[PWT] bits to determine the rules of conduct to follow within the addressed memory page. If the memory access necessitated the performance of a transaction on the FSB (Front-Side Bus), during the memory transaction the processor transmitted the state of the PCD and PWT bits on its PCD and PWT output pins. Using the memory address output by the processor, the chipset would consult a chipset design-specific register set to determine the rules of conduct to be followed within the addressed memory area. If there was a disagreement between the OS-defined rules (as output on PCD and PWT) and the chipset's rules (as defined by the contents of its register set), the chipset would defer to the more conservative memory type (i.e., the less aggressive of the two memory types). As an example, if the processor initiated a cache line read on the FSB and the chipset said it was UC (uncacheable) memory while the processor said it was WB (cacheable Write Back) memory, the chipset would inform the processor that the entire line would *not* be returned (as the processor requested), but rather just the requested data item that caused a cache miss would be returned.

The chipset's register set was programmed by the BIOS at startup time. The problem with this approach is that the chipset's register set was implemented in a chipset-specific manner outside the scope of any industry standard specification. There would therefore have to be a separate version of the BIOS to cover all of the possible chipset types that would be used on system boards incorporating the BIOS.

Solution: Memory Type Register Set

With the advent of the Pentium Pro, Intel migrated the memory type configuration register set that had historically resided in the chipset into the processor itself. This register set is referred to as the Memory Type and Range Registers (MTRRs). While the MTRRs were, in fact, implemented identically in all members of the P6 and Pentium 4 processor families, they were *not* part of the x86 ISA specification and therefore not guaranteed to be implemented identically (or, for that matter, at all) in any given processor model. With the advent of the Pentium 4, however, the MTRRs were officially defined as part of the x86 ISA (and the register names are preceded by *IA32*). They are implemented as MSRs and are accessed using the RDMSR and WRMSR instructions.

MTRR Feature Determination

To determine if a processor supports the MTRR registers, execute a CPUID request type 1. EDX[15] = 1 indicates that the MTRRs are supported. Additional information regarding the MTRR registers can be obtained by reading from the read-only MTRRCAP register (MTRR Capabilities register; see Figure 17-1 on page 603):

- WC = 0 indicates that the WC (Write-Combining) memory type is not supported, while WC = 1 indicates it is. See "Uncacheable Write-Combining (WC) Memory" on page 611 for a detailed explanation of the WC memory type.
- FIX = 0 indicates that the optional Fixed-Range MTRRs aren't supported, while FIX = 1 indicates they are. A detailed description of the Fixed-Range MTRRs can be found in "Fixed-Range MTRRs" on page 605.
- VCNT = the number of Variable-Range MTRR register pairs that are implemented. A detailed description of the Variable-Range MTRRs can be found in "Variable-Range MTRRs" on page 607.
- SMRR = 1 indicates the SM Range register pair is supported (see "Protecting Access to SM Memory" on page 1182).

Figure 17-1: MTRRCAP Register

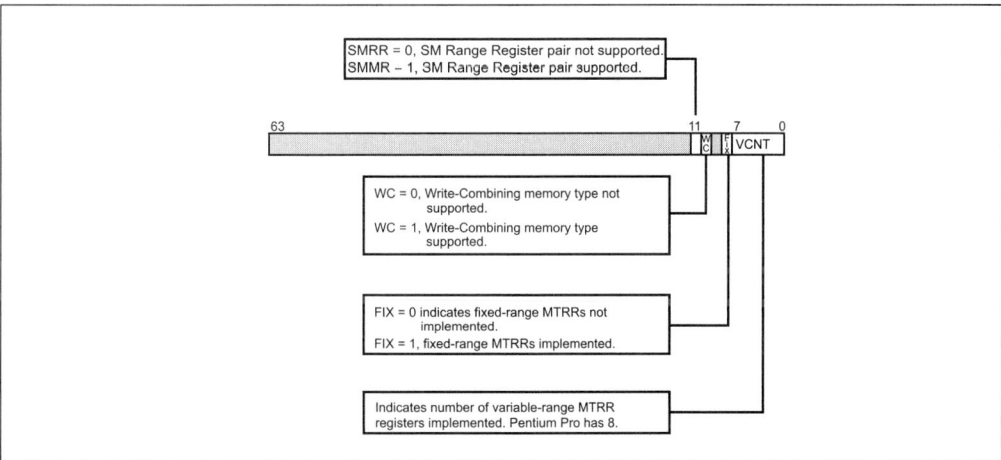

MTRRs Are Divided Into Four Categories

The MTRRs are divided into four categories:

- A read-only capabilities register (see Figure 17-1 on page 603).
- A control register (see Figure 17-2 on page 604) used to enable or disable the two types of MTRRs and to define the default memory type (which is applied to memory ranges not covered by the fixed or variable-range registers).
- An optional set of Fixed-Range MTRRs used to designate the type of memory devices that populate the first megabyte of memory space.
- One or more Variable-Range MTRR register pairs that permit the programmer to specify the start and end address of a memory range and the memory type assigned to the range.

MTRRDefType Register

The MTRRDefType register (MTRR Default Memory Type register; see Figure 17-2 on page 604) defines the memory type for regions of memory not covered by the currently-enabled MTRRs (or for all of memory if the MTRRs are disabled). Reset clears the MTRRDefType register, disabling all MTRRs and defining all of memory as the UC (UnCacheable) type.

Figure 17-2: MTRRDefType Register

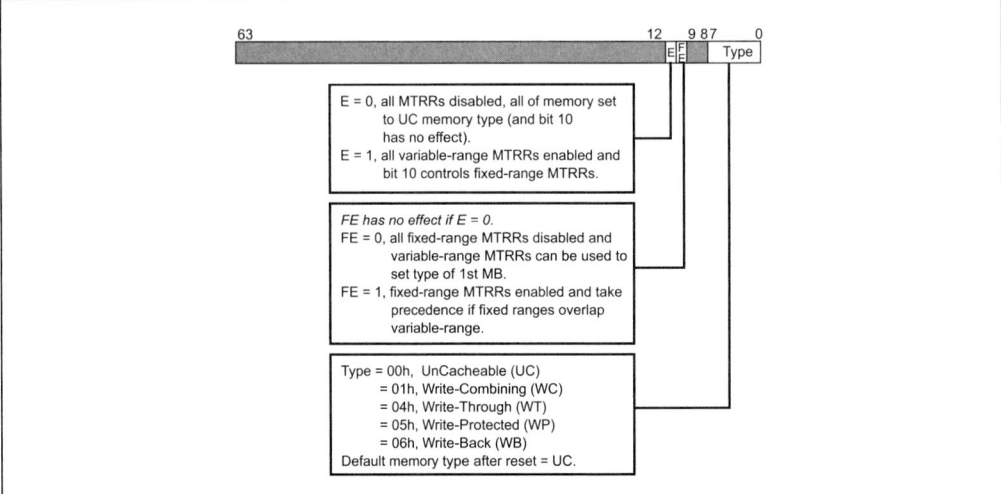

Chapter 17: Memory Type Configuration

State of the MTRRs after Reset

Reset disables all of the MTRRs by clearing the MTRRdefType register. All of memory space is assigned the uncacheable (UC) memory type. After the logical processor starts executing the POST (Power-On Self-Test in firmware), the programmer can change the default rules of conduct by changing the value in the register's TYPE field. The MTRRdefType register is implemented as a Model-Specific Register, or MSR, and is accessed using the RDMSR and WRMSR instructions. Once the MTRRs are enabled, the rules of conduct (i.e., the memory type) specified in the TYPE field is used for any accesses within ranges not covered by the MTRRs.

Fixed-Range MTRRs

The Problem: Legacy Issues

Historically speaking, the first megabyte of memory space (00000000h - 000FFFFFh) in PC-compatible machines was typically populated with a number of special-purpose memory (or memory-mapped IO) devices. Such devices might require the logical processor to observe special rules of conduct when reading from or writing to them.

For this reason, Intel included a set of MTRRs that the BIOS and/or OS uses to define the memory types within the first megabyte of memory space. Over time, it was thought that machine design might eventually evolve to the point where the likelihood of this memory area being populated by special-purpose memory devices would decrease and eventually be eliminated. For this reason, it is optional whether or not a processor actually implements the Fixed-Range MTRRs. As mentioned earlier, a read-only bit in the MTRRCAP MSR (see Figure 17-1 on page 603) indicates whether or not the processor supports this set of registers.

Enabling the Fixed-Range MTRRs

If they are implemented, the Fixed-Range MTRRs are enabled by setting the E bit (MTRR master enable bit) and the FE bit (Fixed-Range register enable bit) = 1 in the MTRRDefType register (see Figure 17-2 on page 604).

Defining Memory Types in Lower 1MB

When present and enabled, the manner in which the Fixed-Range MTRRs have been programmed defines the logical processor's rules of conduct when performing memory accesses within the first MB of memory space (see Figure 17-3 on page 607). This region is subdivided into 88 subregions by the 11 Fixed-Range MTRRs (see Table 17-1 on page 606). Note that each of the Fixed-Range MTRR registers is 64-bits wide and is subdivided into eight fields of eight bits each. The 8-bit value placed in each field defines the memory type (the same values as those indicated in the TYPE field in Figure 17-2 on page 604) for the area associated with the respective bit field.

Table 17-1: The Fixed Range MTRRs

63 56	55 48	47 40	39 32	31 24	23 16	15 8	7 0	Register
70000-7FFFF	60000-6FFFF	50000-5FFFF	40000-4FFFF	30000-3FFFF	20000-2FFFF	10000-1FFFF	00000-0FFFF	MTRRfix64K_00000 8, 64KB regions
9C000-9FFFF	98000-98FFF	94000-97FFF	90000-93FFF	8C000-8FFFF	88000-8BFFF	84000-87FFF	80000-83FFF	MTRRfix16K_80000 8, 16KB regions
BC000-BFFFF	B8000-BBFFF	B4000-B7FFF	B0000-B3FFF	AC000-AFFFF	A8000-ABFFF	A4000-A7FFF	A0000-A3FFF	MTRRfix16K_A0000 8, 16KB regions
C7000-C7FFF	C6000-C6FFF	C5000-C5FFF	C4000-C4FFF	C3000-C3FFF	C2000-C2FFF	C1000-C1FFF	C0000-C0FFF	MTRRfix4K_C0000 8, 4KB regions
CF000-CFFFF	CE000-CEFFF	CD000-CDFFF	CC000-CCFFF	CB000-CBFFF	CA000-CAFFF	C9000-C9FFF	C8000-C8FFF	MTRRfix4K_C8000 8, 4KB regions
D7000-D7FFF	D6000-D6FFF	D5000-D5FFF	D4000-D4FFF	D3000-D3FFF	D2000-D2FFF	D1000-D1FFF	D0000-D0FFF	MTRRfix4K_D0000 8, 4KB regions
DF000-DFFFF	DE000-DEFFF	DD000-DDFFF	DC000-DCFFF	DB000-DBFFF	DA000-DAFFF	D9000-D9FFF	D8000-D8FFF	MTRRfix4K_D8000 8, 4KB regions
E7000-E7FFF	E6000-E6FFF	E5000-E5FFF	E4000-E4FFF	E3000-E3FFF	E2000-E2FFF	E1000-E1FFF	E0000-E0FFF	MTRRfix4K_E0000 8, 4KB regions
EF000-EFFFF	EE000-EEFFF	ED000-EDFFF	EC000-ECFFF	EB000-EBFFF	EA000-EAFFF	E9000-E9FFF	E8000-E8FFF	MTRRfix4K_E8000 8, 4KB regions
F7000-F7FFF	F6000-F6FFF	F5000-F5FFF	F4000-F4FFF	F3000-F3FFF	F2000-F2FFF	F1000-F1FFF	F0000-F0FFF	MTRRfix4K_F0000 8, 4KB regions
FF000-FFFFF	FE000-FEFFF	FD000-FDFFF	FC000-FCFFF	FB000-FBFFF	FA000-FAFFF	F9000-F9FFF	F8000-F8FFF	MTRRfix4K_F8000 8, 4KB regions

Figure 17-3: First MB of Memory Space

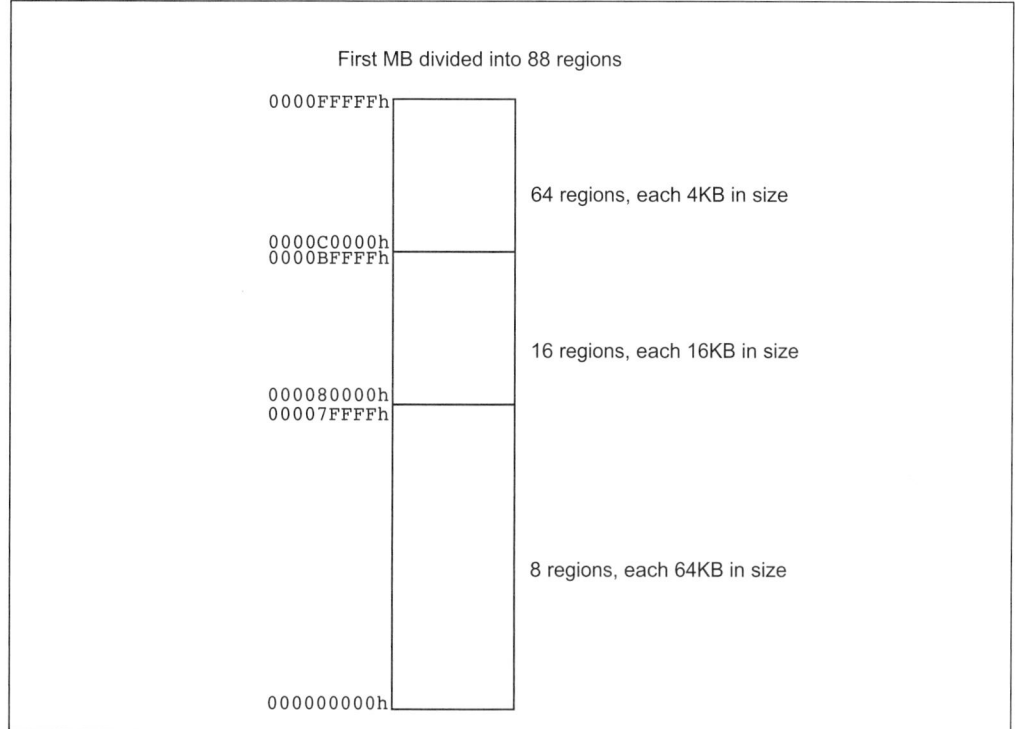

Variable-Range MTRRs

How Many Variable-Range Register Pairs?

The number of Variable-Range register pairs supported by a processor is design-specific and can be read from the read-only MTRRCAP register (see Figure 17-1 on page 603).

Variable-Range Register Pair Format

Each Variable-Range register pair consists of a base and a mask register. The format of a register pair is illustrated in Figure 17-4 on page 608. Note that the letter *n* indicates the number of the register pair (e.g., 0 - 7 for the P6 processors).

Figure 17-4: Format of Variable-Range MTRRPhys Register Pair

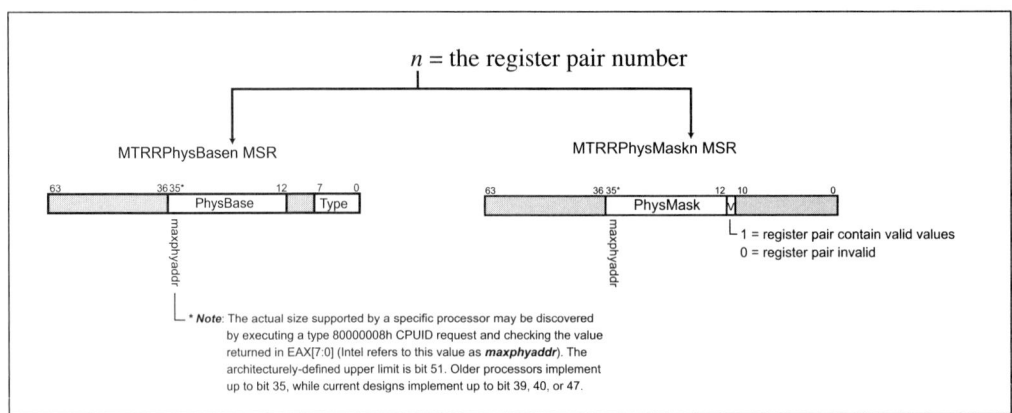

MTRRPhysBase*n* Register

The Base register (Figure 17-4 on page 608) is used to assign the physical base address of the memory region whose memory type is defined by the lower eight bits of the Base register. The programmer does not specify the lower 12 bits of the base address. The base address assigned must be aligned on an address divisible by the range size defined in the MTRRPhysMask register's PhysMask field (see Figure 17-4 on page 608 and the next section).

MTRRPhysMask*n* Register

The Mask register (Figure 17-4 on page 608) is used to define the size of the memory range (using the register's PhysMask field). V (Valid) = 0 indicates that the register pair hasn't been initialized, while V = 1 indicates that the pair contains valid information.

When 000h is appended beneath the 6-digit (hex) value specified in the PhysMask field, the binary-weighted value of the least-significant 1-bit in the mask indicates the size of the memory region defined by the register pair. Note that the PhysMask field must contain all 1-bits starting with the least-significant 1-bit and extending through the upper-most implemented bit (referred to as maxphyaddr by Intel).

Programming Variable-Range Register Pairs

Here are two example configurations of the Variable-Range MTRRs:

1. Base = 0000000A20000006h, Mask = 0000000FFF000800h. This specifies that the base address = A20000000h, the memory type = write back (6 = WB), and the size = 16MB.
2. Base = 0000000549200004h, Mask = 0000000FFFFE0800h. This specifies that the base address = 549200000h, the memory type = write through (4 = WT), and the size is 128KB.

Note: These examples assume a maxphyaddr (see Figure 17-4 on page 608) of 36-bits.

Enabling Variable-Range Register Pairs

The Variable-Range MTRR register pairs are mass-enabled by setting the E bit in the MTRRDefType register = 1 (see Figure 17-2 on page 604).

Memory Types

Memory Type Defines Processor Aggressiveness

Assigning the UC (uncacheable) memory type to a range of memory addresses basically instructs the logical processor to do exactly what it's told by the programmer and no more. In other words, it is constrained from accomplishing the memory access in a manner that, while it would increase processor performance, might result in improper operation.

At the other end of the spectrum, assigning the WB (cacheable Write-Back) memory type to a range of memory addresses permits the logical processor to engage in actions that would accomplish the desired memory access in a manner that would very likely result in higher performance.

Five Memory Types

Using the MTRRdefType register or the individual fixed-length and/or variable-range MTRRs, the programmer can define each memory range as one of five types (note that they are listed in order of aggressiveness: UC yields good behavior but very low performance while WB yields the best overall performance):

- Uncacheable, or UC.
- Uncacheable Write-Combining, or WC.
- Cacheable Write-Protect, or WP.
- Cacheable Write-Through, or WT.
- Cacheable Write-Back, or WB.

The rules of conduct within the five types of memory areas are defined in the sections that follow. *x86 processors never perform speculative writes (because there is no way to "undo" the write if it is later discovered that the write should not have been performed).*

Uncacheable (UC) Memory

The rules that the logical processor follows when performing memory reads and writes in a memory range designated as UC are as follows:

- Cache lookups are performed and, in the event of a cache hit, the line is evicted from the cache. This scenario would arise if the memory area had previously been designated as one of the cacheable memory types but is now designated as UC memory.
- In the event of a cache miss, read requests are not turned into line reads from memory. They are performed as is (e.g., a 1, 2, 4 or 8-byte access). The data returned is routed directly to the requester (e.g., for placement in a register) and is not placed in any cache.
- Memory writes are first posted in the logical processor's posted memory write buffer and are later performed to memory in original program order (see "Posted-Write Related Issues" on page 618 for more information). When the posted writes are ultimately dumped to external memory, they are always performed in strict program order.
- Speculative reads are not performed (see "The Definition of a Speculatively Executed Load" on page 615).

In other words, the logical processor is very well-behaved within a UC memory area. For this reason, the UC type is well-suited to memory regions populated by memory-mapped IO devices. On the negative side, accesses within UC memory yield low performance due to lack of caching and speculative read constraining.

Uncacheable Write-Combining (WC) Memory

Description

The WC memory type is useful for linear video frame buffers. See "WCB Usage" on page 620 for an example of WCB usage.

Note that the programmer must check the WC bit in the MTRRcap register (see Figure 17-1 on page 603) to determine if the WC memory type is supported. Like the UC memory type, WC memory is not cacheable. Writes to uncacheable WC memory are first accumulated in internal WCBs (Write-Combining Buffers) and are later flushed to physical memory (see "Posted-Write Related Issues" on page 618 and "WCB Usage" on page 620). The number of WCBs is design-specific.

The rules that the logical processor follows when performing memory reads and writes in a memory range designated as uncacheable WC are as follows:

- Cache lookups are performed and, in the event of a cache hit, the line is evicted from the cache. This scenario would arise if the memory area had previously been designated as one of the cacheable memory types but is now designated as WC memory.
- In the event of a cache miss, read requests are not turned into line reads from memory. They are performed as is (e.g., a 1, 2, 4 or 8-byte access). The data returned is routed directly to the requester (e.g., for placement in a register) and is not placed in any cache.
- Speculative execution of loads is permitted (see "The Definition of a Speculatively Executed Load" on page 615).
- When one or more bytes are to be written to memory, a Write Combining Buffer (WCB) memorizes the start address of the block (i.e., the line; each WCB can hold one line of information; the cache line size—and therefore the WCB size—is processor design-specific) that the bytes are to be written to as well as the bytes to be written within the block.
- In a P6 family processor, the contents of the WCB are written to memory under the following conditions:

- — If any additional writes within WC memory are performed to a different line of memory space when all of the WCBs are currently in use, the logical processor will flush one of the WCBs to memory. The empty WCB will then be available to record the new line start address and the bytes to be written to that line.
- — Execution of a serializing instruction (e.g., CPUID, IRET, RSM), an IO instruction, or a locked read/modify/write operation causes the logical processor to flush all write buffers to memory before proceeding to the next instruction.
- In later processors, a WCB is automatically dumped to memory when it becomes full (thereby freeing up the buffer to absorb additional writes to WC memory).

When flushing a WCB to memory, the logical processor will take one of two courses of action:

- If the WCB is full (i.e., bytes have been posted to be written to every location in the line), the logical processor will perform a full line write transaction to write the entire line to memory.
- If all bytes a the WCB are not valid, the logical processor will perform the appropriate number of qword or partial-qword write transactions to write the updates to memory. As an example, if there are five bytes to be written to the first qword and three to be written to the third qword of the line, the logical processor may perform two separate write transactions:
  - — One specifying the start address of the first qword and writing to five, possibly non-contiguous, locations within it.
  - — One specifying the start address of the first qword and writing to three, possibly non-contiguous, locations within it.

Weakly-Ordered Writes

The WC memory type differs from all four of the other memory types in one important regard: *while memory writes to UC, WP, WT, and WB memory are always performed in strict program order, writes to WC memory oftentimes are not.* Instead, they are cued up in the WCBs and, when those buffers are ultimately dumped to external memory, are performed in a manner dictated by the WCB contents and by processor design.

Cacheable Write-Protect (WP) Memory

The cacheable WP memory type is useful for shadow RAM. ROM code is copied to shadow RAM by the BIOS after which the ROM is disabled and the shadow RAM is mapped to the ROM's address range. Information fetched from shadow RAM may be cached for good performance, but cannot be changed in the cache (thereby simulating ROM memory). It should be noted that writes, although not performed in the cache, are performed to system memory. It is the memory controller's responsibility to ignore memory writes to WP memory.

The rules that the logical processor follows when performing memory reads and writes in a memory range designated as cacheable WP memory are as follows:

- Cache lookups are performed:
    - **Read miss**. On a cache read miss, the entire line is fetched from memory and placed in the cache (in the Shared state).
    - **Read hit**. On a cache read hit, the requested data is supplied by the cache and a memory access does not take place.
    - **Write miss**. On a cache write miss, the data is posted in the logical processor's posted memory write buffer to be written to memory later (see "Posted-Write Related Issues" on page 618). When the posted writes are ultimately dumped to external memory, they are always performed in strict program order.
    - **Write hit**. On a cache write hit, the cache line is invalidated and the data is posted in the logical processor's posted memory write buffer to be written to memory later (see "Posted-Write Related Issues" on page 618). When other processors snoop the write to external memory, they also invalidate any copy of the line that is resident in their caches.
- Speculative reads (i.e., loads) are allowed (see "The Definition of a Speculatively Executed Load" on page 615).
- Lines are never marked Modified. They may only be in the Shared or Invalid states.

Cacheable Write-Through (WT) Memory

The rules that the logical processor follows when performing memory reads and writes in a memory range designated as cacheable WT memory are as follows:

- Cache lookups are performed:
    - **Read miss**. On a cache read miss, the entire line is fetched from memory and placed in the cache in the **S** state (Shared).
    - **Read hit**. On a cache read hit, the requested data is supplied by the cache and a memory access does not take place.

- **Write miss**. On a cache write miss, the data is posted in the logical processor's posted memory write buffer to be written to memory later (see "Posted-Write Related Issues" on page 618). When the posted writes are ultimately dumped to external memory, they are always performed in strict program order.
    - **Write hit**. On a cache write hit, the cache line is updated (but the line is *not* marked *M*odified; it remains in the **S** state) and the data is posted in the logical processor's posted memory write buffer to be written to memory later (see "Posted-Write Related Issues" on page 618). When the posted writes are ultimately dumped to external memory, they are always performed in strict program order.
- Lines are never marked *M*odified. They may only be in the *S*hared or *In*valid states.
- Speculative reads are allowed (see "The Definition of a Speculatively Executed Load" on page 615).
- A write updates the L1 Data Cache, but invalidates the L2 and L1 Code Caches on a triple hit (see the description of self-modifying code in the MindShare book entitled *The Unabridged Pentium 4*).

Cacheable Write-Back (WB) Memory

The cacheable WB memory type yields the best overall performance. Reads and writes can be serviced solely in the cache without performing memory accesses, so memory traffic is greatly diminished. Ideally, most of system memory should be designated as the WB memory type.

The rules that the logical processor follows when performing memory reads and writes in a memory range designated as cacheable WB memory are as follows:

- Cache lookups are performed:
    - **Read miss**. On a cache read miss, the entire line is fetched from memory and placed in the cache (in the *E*xclusive or *S*hared state based on the snoop result; i.e., whether or not another logical processor indicated that it also has a copy of the line).
    - **Read hit**. On a cache read hit, the requested data is supplied by the cache and a memory access does not take place.
    - **Write miss**. On a cache write miss, the entire line is read from memory using the Memory Read and Invalidate transaction type. This is referred to as an *allocate-on-write miss policy*. When the memory transaction is performed on the external interface, it is latched and snooped in the caches of all other processors:

- Any other cache that has a snoop hit on a line in the *E*xclusive or *S*hared state must invalidate its copy (i.e., E -> I, or S -> I).
- Any other cache with a snoop hit on a line in the *M*odified state must source the modified line to the requesting logical processor and to memory and invalidate its copy (i.e., M -> I). When the requesting logical processor receives the line, it places it into the cache, writes into it and marks it as M.
— **Write hit**. On a cache write hit, the cache line is updated:
  - If the line was in the E state, it is changed to the M state (E -> M).
  - If it was already in the M state, it stays in the M state (M -> M).
  In either case, no memory access takes place and system memory is not updated. If the line was in the S state, the processor performs a 0-byte Memory Read and Invalidate memory transaction on the external interface to kill copies of the line in the caches of other logical processors. When the transaction has been completed, the line accepts the write data and transitions from the S to the M state.
- Speculative reads are permitted (see "The Definition of a Speculatively Executed Load" on page 615).

The Definition of a Speculatively Executed Load

Consider the following code fragment:

```
sub  eax,ebx
je   bypass          ;jump to bypass if result was zero
mov  eax,mem1        ;read memory variable into eax
mov  ebx,mem2        ;and another variable into ebx
bypass:
```

Starting with the advent of the Pentium Pro, x86 processors perform out-of-order program execution in order to achieve the best possible performance. If the memory type of the example data variables is WC, WP, WT, or WB, the logical processor is permitted to speculatively execute the two load instructions before the conditional branch instruction is executed and resolved. The data that is returned is placed in the two Load Buffers that were reserved for the two read requests. If the conditional branch instruction jumps around the two loads when it is executed, the loads should not have been executed. In that case, the logical processor invalidates the two Load Buffers and the EAX and EBX registers are not loaded with the two memory variables.

If the attempted speculative execution of a load would result in a Page Fault exception (i.e., the Present bit in the selected PTE or PDE is cleared to zero), the logical processor will not complete the load. Rather, it will wait until the upstream conditional branch has executed and it has been established that the load should be executed.

Rules as Defined by MTRRs

Assuming that the MTRRs are enabled and have been set up by the programmer, the logical processor interrogates the MTRRs for any memory access to determine its rules of conduct. The determination is made as indicated in Table 17-2 on page 616.

Table 17-2: Memory Type Determination Using MTRRs

Scenario	Resulting Memory Type
Memory address within first MB, fixed-range MTRRs present and enabled, and address not within range defined by any of the variable-length MTRR register pairs.	Type defined by the fixed-length MTRR for the range.
Address within first MB, fixed-length MTRRs disabled (or not present), and address not within a range defined by any of the variable-length MTRR register pairs.	Type defined by TYPE field in the MTRRdefType register.
Address within first MB, fixed-length MTRRs disabled (or not present), and address within a range defined by one of the variable-length MTRR register pairs.	Type defined by the variable-length register pair for the range.

Table 17-2: Memory Type Determination Using MTRRs (Continued)

Scenario	Resulting Memory Type
Fixed-length MTRRs disabled (or not present), and address within a range defined by more than one variable-length MTRR register pair.	• If all of the respective variable-length register pairs define the range identically, then the type is the one defined by them. • If the respective variable-length register pairs define the range as UC and any other memory type, then the type is UC. • If the respective variable-length register pairs define the range as WT and WB, then the type is WT. • If the respective variable-length register pairs are different and define combinations other than those defined above, then the behavior of the logical processor is undefined.
Address not within first MB, but not within a range defined by any of the variable-length MTRR register pairs.	Type defined by TYPE field in the MTRRdefType register.
Address not within first MB and within a range defined by one of the variable-length MTRR register pairs.	Type defined by TYPE field in a variable-range register pairs.

Memory Type Provided in Memory Transaction

Whenever the logical processor performs a memory read or write transaction on the external interface, it outputs the memory type as part of the transaction request. In this manner, the memory controller and an external cache (if present) are also informed of the rules of conduct within the addressed memory area.

Paging Also Defines Memory Type

It is the BIOS that typically sets up the MTRRs at startup time to define the logical processor's rules of conduct in various memory regions. When the OS is booted and is given control, it sets up the address translation tables to define the logical processor's rules of conduct within various memory pages. So to whom does the logical processor pay attention: the MTRR settings or the settings in PDEs and PTEs? The answer can be found in "Memory Type When Page Definition and MTRR Disagree" on page 590. Generally, in the event of a conflict it goes with the less aggressive memory type.

In an MP System, MTRRs Must Be Synchronized

Intel considers it critical that the MTRR settings in each logical processor in a multicore/multiprocessor system must be configured identically. This subject is discussed in "Ensuring IA32_CR_PAT and MTRR Consistency" on page 593.

Posted-Write Related Issues

General

Refer to Figure 17-5 on page 620. The following memory writes are posted in special logical processor buffers and written to memory at a later time:

- Writes to UC, WP, and WT memory are recorded in the logical processor's Posted Memory Write Buffer (PMWB).
- Writes to uncacheable WC memory are recorded in the logical processor's Write-Combining Buffers (WCBs).

Note that writes to WB memory are recorded in the logical processor's caches but are not written to memory unless a modified line is flushed from the caches to memory.

The logical processor dumps its PMWB and WCBs to memory when a *synchronizing event* occurs (see the next section). Although memory writes in the PMWB are flushed to memory in strict program order (i.e., in the order in which they were posted), writes to WC memory are weakly-ordered (i.e., when the WCBs are flushed to memory, the order in which the data is written is processor-design specific).

Synchronizing Events

The following is a list of the events that will cause a logical processor to flush its Posted Memory Write Buffer (PMWB) and Write-Combining Buffers (WCBs) to memory (in other words, force the logical processor to synchronize memory):

- The execution of the IN or OUT IO instructions.
- A read from UC memory.
- When a SFENCE instruction is executed.
- When an MFENCE instruction is executed.
- When the logical processor sends an Interrupt Acknowledge to the 8259A interrupt controller.
- The execution of a locked Read/Modify/Write operation.
- When the BINIT# signal is asserted (on processors that utilize the FSB).
- Serializing instructions (which are also synchronizing) force the logical processor to temporarily cease out-of-order program execution until all of the instructions up to and including the serializing instruction have completed execution and their results have been committed to the logical processor's register set. The following are the synchronizing instructions:
  — The execution of WBINVD, INVD, WRMSR, or a move into CR0 that alters the state of the CD bit (Cache Disable), causes the execution of both threads on both logical processors to be serialized (if Hyper-Threading is supported and enabled).
  — The privileged serializing instructions: MOV to a Control Register, MOV to a Debug Register, WRMSR, INVD, INVLPG, WBINVD, LGDT, LLDT, LIDT, and LTR.
  — The non-privileged serializing instructions: CPUID, IRET, and RSM.
  — The non-privileged memory ordering instructions:
    – SFENCE.
    – MFENCE.
    These two instructions cause the logical processor to drain all of its Store Buffers and WCBs to memory before executing any store instructions beyond the fence. These instructions have a less damaging effect on performance (than, for instance, the CPUID instruction) because the logical processor is permitted to execute non-store instructions (and, in the case of the MFENCE instruction, non-load instructions) beyond the fence before the buffer draining has been completed.

PMWB and WCBs Aren't Snooped

If another logical processor starts a memory access to any memory type other than WB, the logical processor snoops its caches *but not its PMWB or WCBs*. If programs running on different logical processors share access to a memory buffer that is not WB:

- A memory semaphore should be requested from the OS.
- Before accessing the shared buffer, software should perform a locked Read/

Modify/Write of the semaphore (e.g., lock cmpxchg) to determine if the buffer is already in use by another program.

- If it is, go into a spin wait loop waiting for the semaphore location to be cleared. The clearing of the semaphore should be accomplished using a locked Read/Modify/Write because it is one of the synchronizing events (and therefore causes a buffer flush to update memory).

Figure 17-5: Handling of Posted Writes by Memory Type

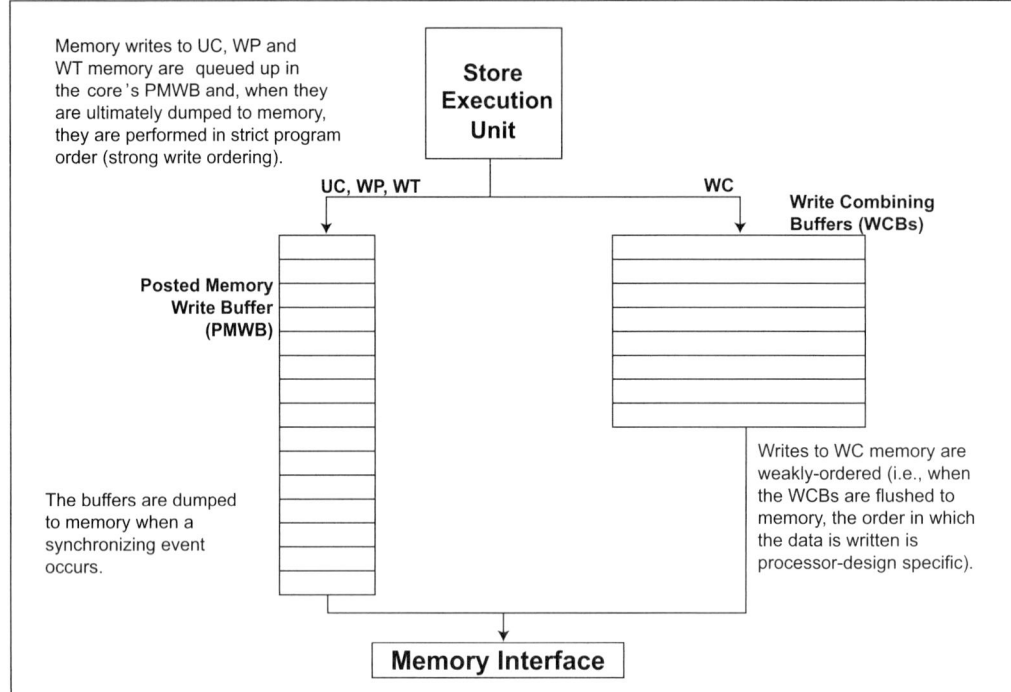

WCB Usage

An Example

Figure 17-6 on page 621 illustrates a logical processor with four WCBs (the number of WCBs implemented is design-specific). Each WCB can record writes within a specific line of WC memory space. The size of a WCB is the same as the logical processor's data cache line size (which is processor design-specific). In the example shown, the data cache line size is 64-bytes. A WCB is comprised of:

- An address field that, on the first write within a line of WC memory space, records the start physical memory address of the line.
- A data field in which any writes to that line of WC memory space are recorded.

Note: The examples shown in Figure 17-7 through Figure 17-13 assume that the virtual addresses translate into the same physical memory addresses.

Figure 17-6: Four Empty WCBs

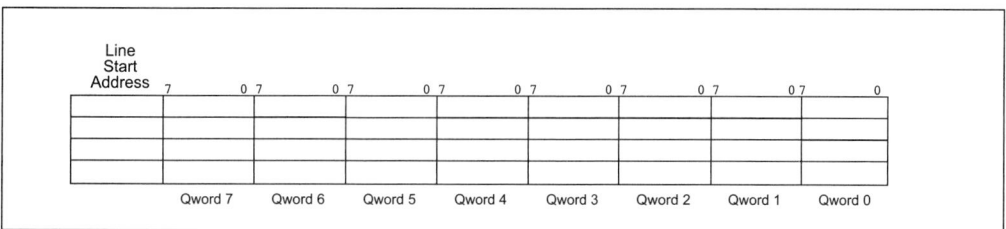

Figure 17-7: 4-byte Write to WC Memory

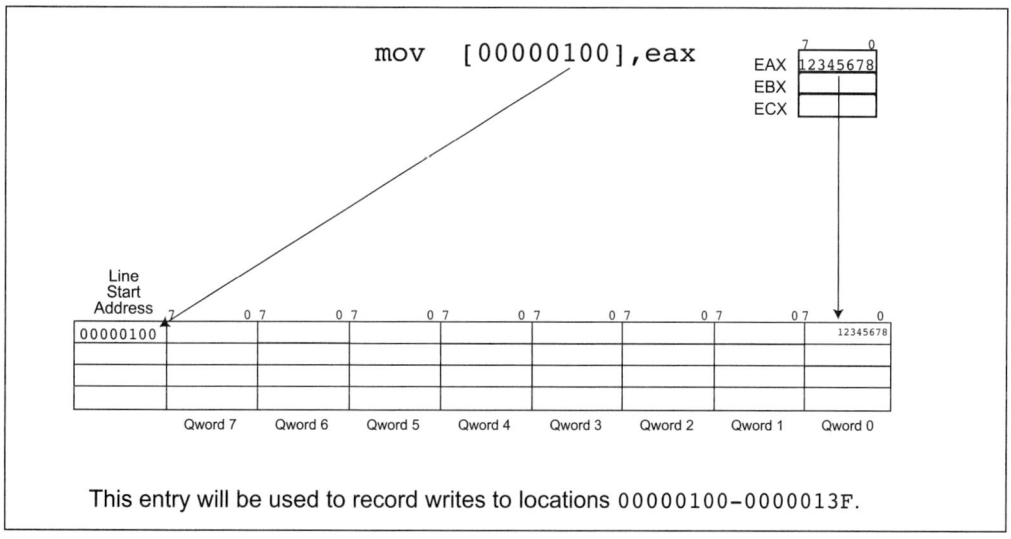

In Figure 17-7, a dword (12345678h) is written to locations 00000100h - 00000103h. The start address of the line being written to (the line comprised of locations 00000100h - 0000013Fh) is recorded in the address field of an unused WCB and the dword is recorded in the appropriate locations within the buffer.

Figure 17-8: 1-byte Write to WC Memory

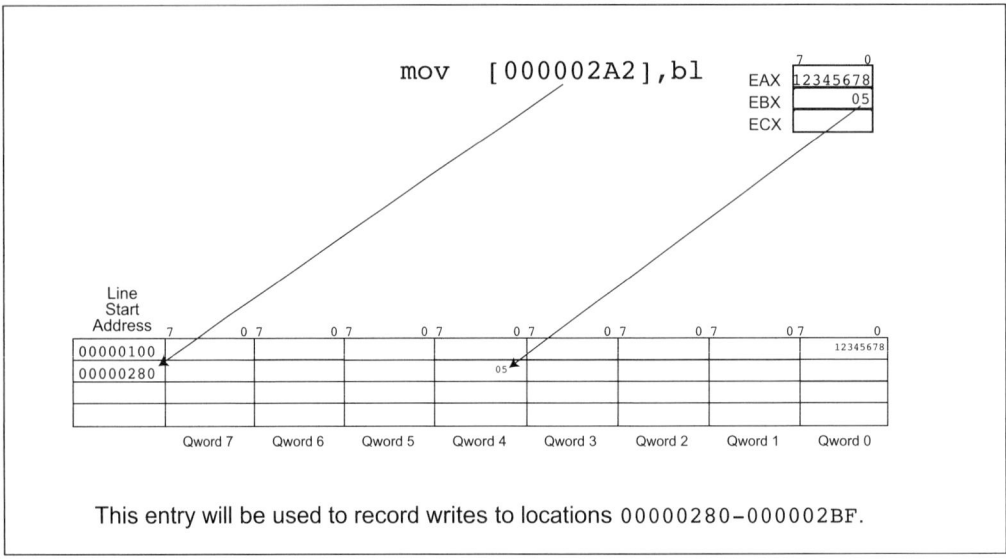

This entry will be used to record writes to locations `00000280-000002BF`.

In Figure 17-8, one byte (05h) is written to location 000002A2h. Since this write is to a different line of WC memory, another WCB must be allocated to record any writes to the new line. The start address of the line being written to (the line comprised of locations 00000280h - 000002BFh) is recorded in the address field of an unused WCB and the byte is recorded in the appropriate location within the buffer.

Figure 17-9: 1-byte Write to WC Memory

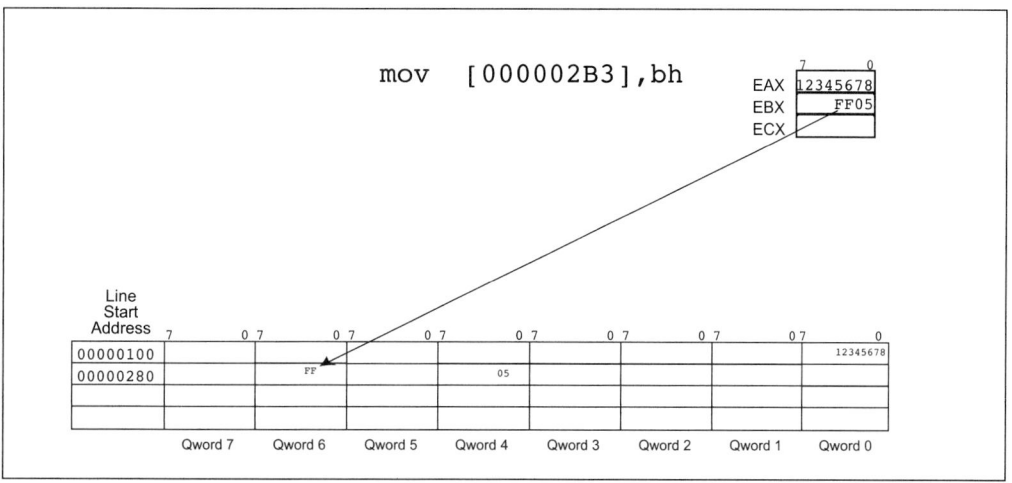

In Figure 17-9, one byte (FFh) is written to location 000002B3h. Since a WCB has already been allocated to record any writes to the line consisting of locations 00000280h - 000002BFh, the byte is recorded in the appropriate location within that buffer.

Figure 17-10: Sixteen 4-byte Writes to WC Memory

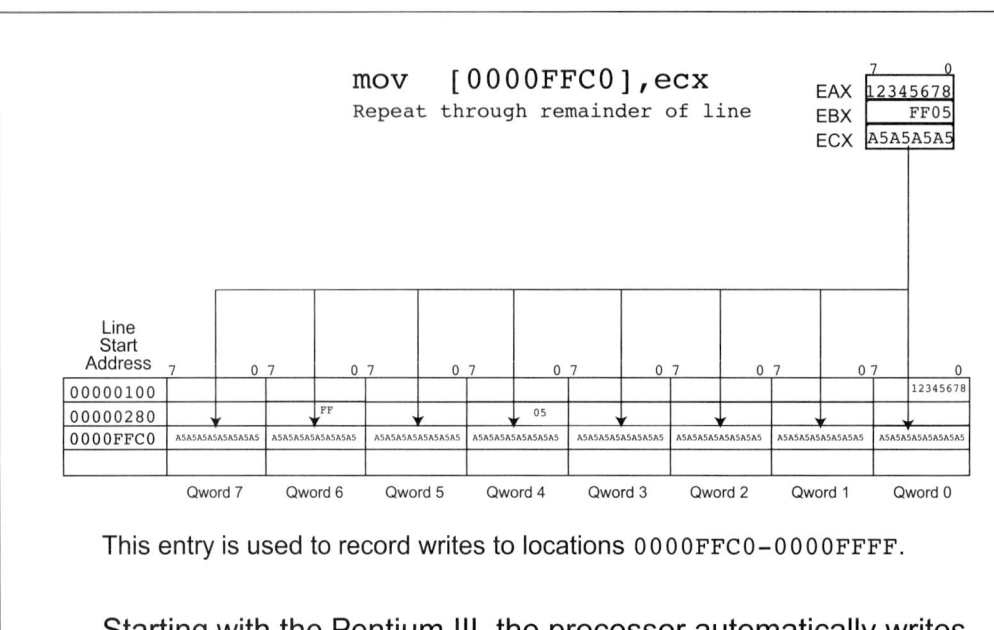

In Figure 17-10, sixteen successive dwords (a total of 64-bytes) are written to memory locations 0000FFC0h - 00000000FFFFh. On the first dword write, another unused WCB is allocated to record writes within the new line, the start address (0000FFC0h) is recorded in the address field, and, as the successive writes are performed, the sixteen dwords are recorded in the appropriate buffer locations.

- Prior to the Pentium III, although this WCB is now full, the logical processor would not automatically dump it to memory in order to free it up.
- Starting with the Pentium III, however, the logical processor will automatically dump a WCB when it has become full.

Figure 17-11: 8-byte Write to WC Memory

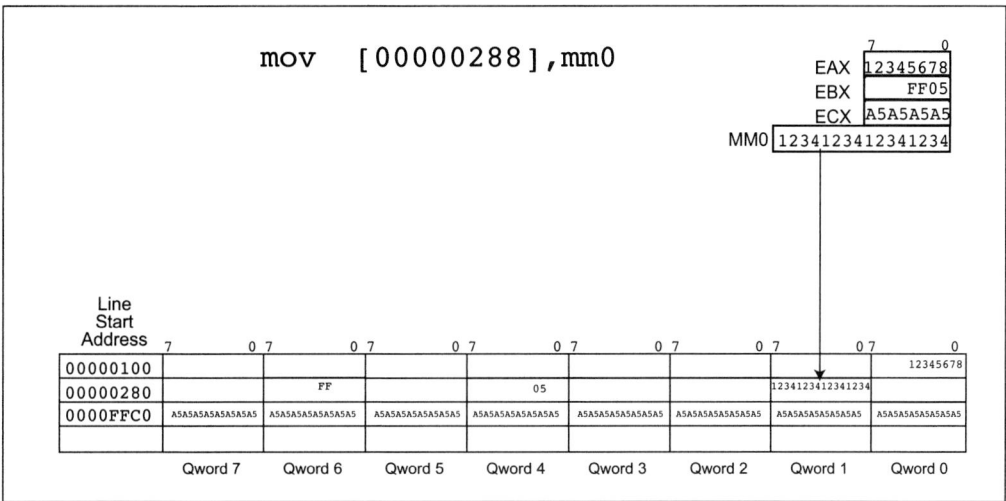

In Figure 17-11, a qword (8-bytes: 1234123412341234h) is written to locations 00000288h - 0000028Fh. Since a WCB has already been allocated to record any writes to the line consisting of locations 00000280h - 000002BFh, the qword is recorded in the appropriate location within that buffer.

Figure 17-12: 1-byte Write to WC Memory

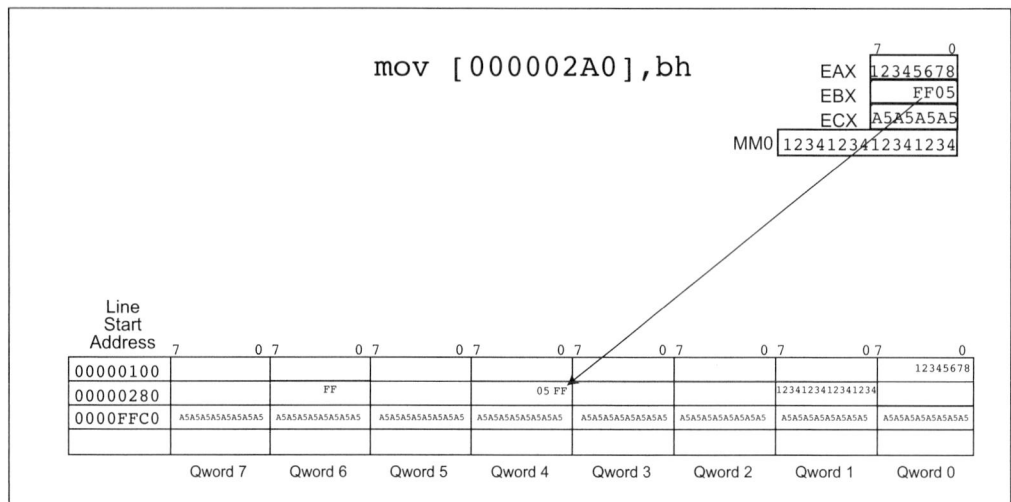

In Figure 17-12, a byte (FFh) is written to location 000002A0h. Since a WCB has already been allocated to record any writes to the line consisting of locations 00000280h - 000002BFh, the byte is recorded in the appropriate location within that buffer.

Figure 17-13: Example of Write Collapsing in WC Memory

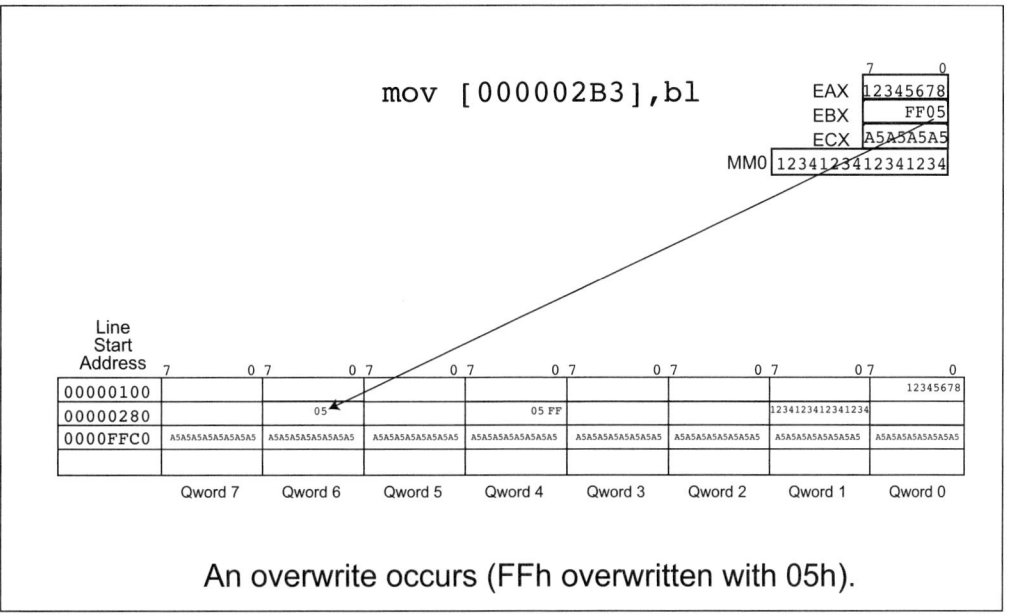

An overwrite occurs (FFh overwritten with 05h).

In Figure 17-13, a byte (05h) is written to location 000002B3h (a location to which a byte had already been written earlier). As a result, the new byte (05h) is recorded over the earlier one (FFh). This characteristic of the WC memory type is referred to as *write-collapsing*. The net result is that when the WCB is ultimately dumped to memory (because the buffer becomes full or because of a synchronizing event) earlier bytes that were overwritten are never actually be written to memory.

All WCBs in Use

If all of the WCBs are in use and the logical processor must perform a store to a different line of WC memory space, the logical processor will stall that store and any subsequent WC stores until it completes the dump of at least one WCB so it can free up a WCB to absorb the write.

Draining the WCBs

The logical processor drains its Posted Memory Write Buffer (PMWB) and its WCBs to memory whenever a synchronizing event occurs (i.e., an event that causes the logical processor to synchronize memory thereby bringing it up to date). Please note that when a synchronizing event occurs, modified lines from the WB memory type are *not* flushed to memory!

- The order in which the logical processor dumps its PMWB is *always* in strict program order.
- However, the order in which it dumps its WCBs is processor design-specific.

18   *Task Switching*

The Previous Chapter

The previous chapter described the operational characteristics of various types of memory targets (UC, WC, WP, WT, and WB) and the role of the Memory Type and Range Registers (MTRRs). It defined the concept of speculatively executed loads and described issues related to the logical processor's Posted Memory Write Buffer (PMWB) and Write-Combining Buffers (WCBs).

This Chapter

This chapter contrasts hardware- versus software-based tasking switching and provides a conceptual overview of task switching before providing a detailed description of the hardware-based task switching mechanism. The following topics are covered:

- Hardware- vs. Software-Based Task Switching
- A Condensed Conceptual Overview
- A More Comprehensive Overview
- Hardware-Based Task Switching
  - It's Slow
  - Why Didn't OSs Use It?
  - Why Wasn't It Improved?
  - Why Does It Still Exist?
  - Introduction to the Key Elements
  - The Trigger Events
  - The Descriptors
  - The Task Register
  - TSS Data Structure Format
  - Comprehensive Task Switch Description
  - Calling Another Task
  - Task Switching and Address Translation
  - Switch from Higher-Privilege Code to Lower

The Next Chapter

The next chapter provides a detailed description of interrupt and exception handling in Protected Mode. This includes detailed coverage of:

- The IDT.
- Interrupt and Trap Gate operation.
- Task Gate operation.
- Interrupt and exception event categories.
- State save (and stack selection).
- The IRET instruction.
- Maskable hardware interrupts.
- Non-Maskable Interrupt (NMI).
- Machine Check exception.
- SM interrupt (SMI).
- Software interrupt instructions.
- Software exceptions.
- Interrupt/exception priority.

Hardware- vs. Software-Based Task Switching

The 386 introduced a number of well-received features, but for many OS vendors, its hardware-based task switching mechanism was not considered one of them. On the one hand, it permits the automation of the OS scheduler's job of switching from one task to another after the current task's timeslice has expired. On the other hand, the hardware mechanism's indulgence in an excessive validity checks renders it ponderously slow.

As a result, major OS vendors chose not to utilize the hardware mechanism and instead implemented task switching solely under the control of software (the exact implementation is OS design-specific). In tacit recognition of this reality, the hardware switching mechanism is disabled in IA-32e Mode (any attempted use of it is, in fact, considered illegal and results in an exception). The hardware mechanism is, however, supported in IA-32 Mode and is, for completeness, described in detail in this chapter. The two sections in this chapter entitled:

- "A Condensed Conceptual Overview" on page 631,
- and "A More Comprehensive Overview" on page 631

provide an introduction to task switching applicable to both the software- and -hardware-based mechanisms. A description of software-based task switching can be found in "Scheduler's Software-Based Task Switching Mechanism" on page 977.

A Condensed Conceptual Overview

The task switching concept is simple:

1. The OS scheduler selects the next task to run.
2. It initializes the logical processor's register set with the appropriate startup values.
3. It triggers a hardware timer (the timeslice timer; typically the Local APIC timer is used) configured to run for the timeslice assigned to that task (e.g., 10ms).
4. The logical processor starts executing the task and continues to do so until either:
   — The timer expires and generates an interrupt.
   — The task requires something that will take a while to complete (e.g., it issues a request to the OS to load some information from disk to memory). In this case, the OS scheduler will suspend the task (more on this later).
5. Assuming the task's timeslice has expired (i.e., the timer generates an interrupt), the event interrupts the execution of the task and returns control back to the OS kernel (specifically, to the task scheduler).
6. The scheduler suspends the task by recording the state of the logical processor's register set in a special data structure the scheduler has associated with that task.
7. It then selects the next task to start or resume and goes back to step 2.

A More Comprehensive Overview

It should be stressed that the details of task switching are OS design-specific. This discussion is conceptual (and general) in nature and applies to both software- and hardware-based task switching.

The Scheduler and the Task Queue

Some of the critical components involved in task switching are:

- **Task Scheduler**. The kernel's task scheduler is responsible for managing the task switching environment.
- **Task Queue**. Maintained by the scheduler, the **task queue** is used to keep track of:

— The currently-running tasks.
— Any pending events associated with those tasks. A task may have been suspended earlier after issuing a request to the OS. As an example, while a task was running, it may have issued a request to the OS for a block of information to be read from disk and placed in memory. Since this would take quite a while to complete, pending completion of the request the OS would suspend the task and start or resume another one. The scheduler would create an entry in the event queue associating the pending disk controller completion interrupt with the resumption of the previously-suspended task.
- **Timer**. The Local APIC's programmable timer is used by the task scheduler to assign the amount of time a task is permitted to execute on the logical processor before it is interrupted and control is returned to the scheduier.

Setting Up a Task

In preparation for running a task, the scheduler must:

- Load the application's startup code and data into memory. The remainder of the application remains on disk and will only be read into memory on demand (i.e., if it's required).
- Set up a series of kernel tables in memory that are necessary to support a task.
- Set up the kernel registers that tell the logical processor the location and size of these tables.

The sections that follow provide additional information about the associated tables and registers.

The Task Data Structure

Refer to Figure 18-1 on page 634. The scheduler must create a register save/restore data structure (let's call it the Task Data Structure, or TDS) in memory for each task that will be run:

- When a task is initially set up, the TDS fields will be initialized with the values to be loaded into the logical processor's register set when the task is first started.
- When starting or resuming the execution of a task, many of the logical processor's registers will be loaded from this data structure.
- When suspending a task, the registers will be saved in the task's data structure.

When the x86 hardware-based task switching mechanism is used, the TSS (Task State Segment) data structure fulfills much of the TDS's role. Note: the format (and name) of the Task Data Structure is OS design-specific.

The LDT

Refer to Figure 18-1 on page 634. The scheduler may optionally set up a Local Descriptor Table (LDT) in memory for each task. The entries in this table describe:

- The areas of memory (i.e., code and data segments) that are private to a task.
- The start address of kernel procedures that may be called by the task.
- One or more Task Gate descriptors. These are only used if the OS uses the x86 hardware-based task switching mechanisms (which modern OSs do not).

The TSS

Refer to Figure 18-1 on page 634. The scheduler sets up a special data structure called a Task State Segment (TSS; this was referred to as the Task Data Structure earlier), in memory for each task. Some of the fields in this x86-specific data structure may be accessed by the logical processor during the execution of a task. Although the TSS is heavily-utilized if the OS uses the x86 hardware-based task switching mechanism (which modern OSs do not), some of the TSS fields are still utilized by the logical processor when running an OS that uses software-based task switching (see "Real World TSS Usage" on page 968).

Figure 18-1: Task A's TDS, LDT and TSS

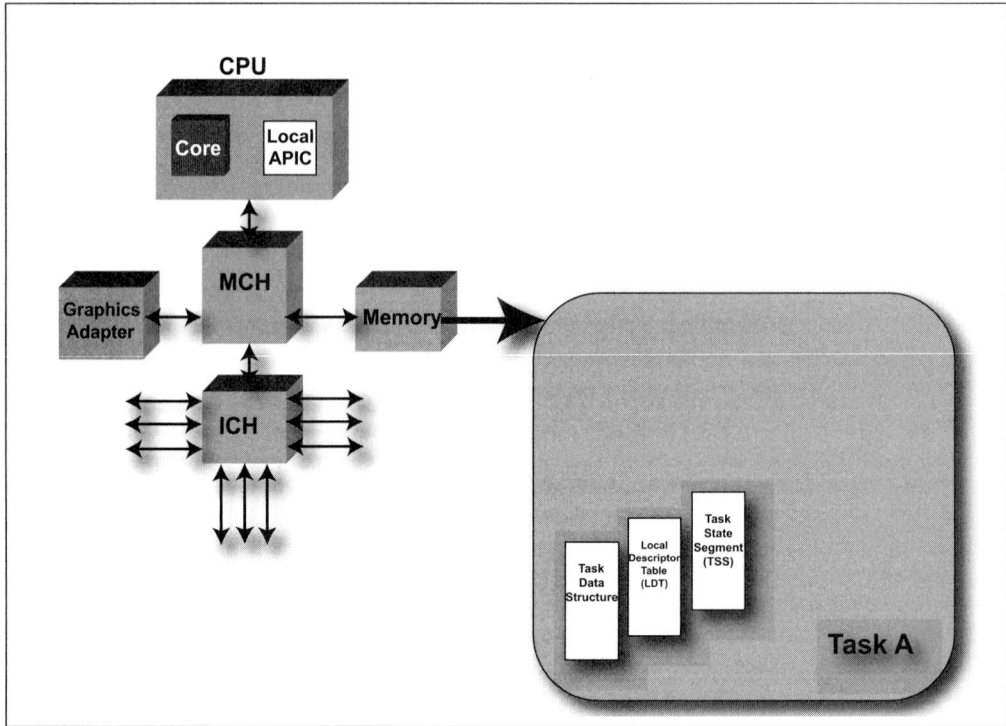

The Address Translation Tables

Refer to Figure 18-2 on page 635. The scheduler sets up the directories and tables (see "IA-32 Address Translation Mechanisms" on page 493) that will be used by the logical processor to translate the virtual addresses generated by the task into the appropriate physical memory addresses. When a switch to this task occurs, the logical processor (if the OS uses the hardware-based task switching mechanism) or the programmer (if software-based task switching is used) will load CR3 with the physical base address of the top-level address translation directory.

Figure 18-2: CR3 Points to Task A's Address Translation Tables

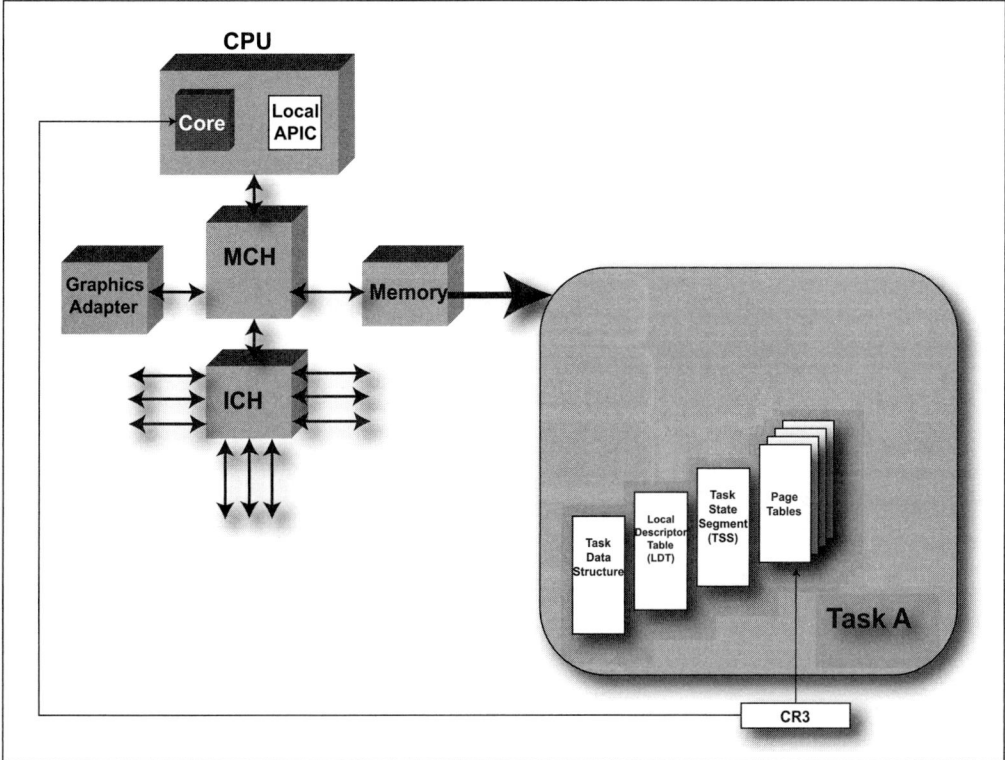

The GDT and GDTR Register

Refer to Figure 18-3 on page 636. Before initiating any tasks, the OS kernel sets up the GDT (Global Descriptor Table) in memory and executes the LGDT instruction to load the GDTR register with the base address and size of the GDT.

The entries in this table define:

- Code and Data segments globally accessible by multiple tasks.
- The base address and length of the LDT associated with each task.
- The start address of kernel procedures that may be called by multiple tasks.
- The base address and length of the TSS associated with each task (also see "Real World TSS Usage" on page 968).
- One or more Task Gate descriptors. These are only used if the OS uses the x86 hardware-based task switching mechanism (modern OSs don't).

Figure 18-3: The GDT and the GDTR Register

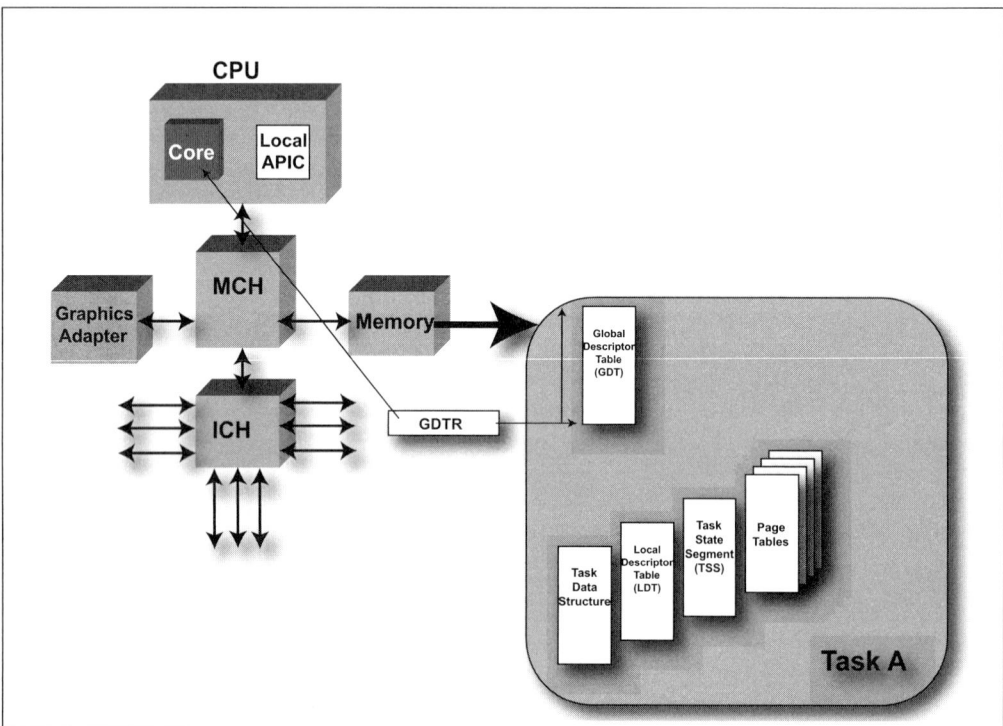

The LDTR Register

Refer to Figure 18-4 on page 637. When a switch to this task occurs, the logical processor (if the OS uses the hardware-based task switching mechanism) or the programmer (using the LLDT instruction if software-based task switching is used) will load the LDTR register with a 16-bit value that selects a GDT entry containing the LDT descriptor associated with the task being started or resumed. In response, the logical processor reads the base address and size of the LDT associated with the task from the descriptor into the invisible part of the LDTR.

Figure 18-4: The LDTR and Task A's LDT Register

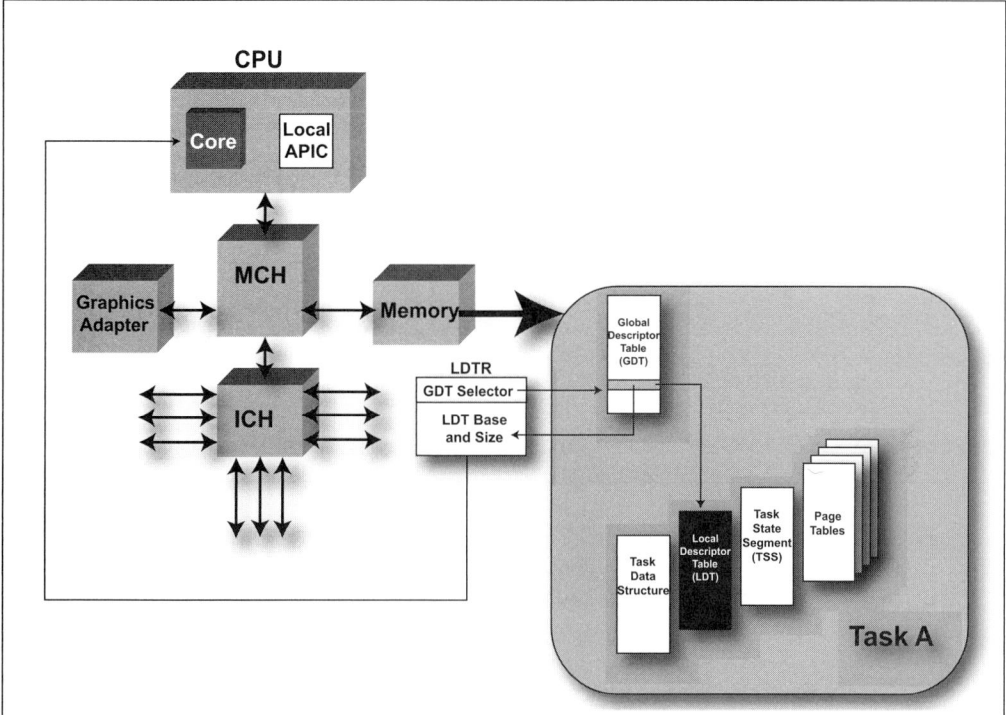

The Task Register (TR)

Refer to Figure 18-5 on page 638. When a switch to this task occurs, the logical processor (if the OS uses the hardware-based task switching mechanism) or the programmer (using the LTR instruction if software-based task switching is used) will load the TR register with a 16-bit value that selects a GDT entry containing the TSS descriptor associated with the task being started or resumed. In response, the logical processor reads the base address and size of the TSS data structure associated with the task from the descriptor into the invisible part of the TR. Also see "Real World TSS Usage" on page 968.

Figure 18-5: The TR Register and Task A's TSS

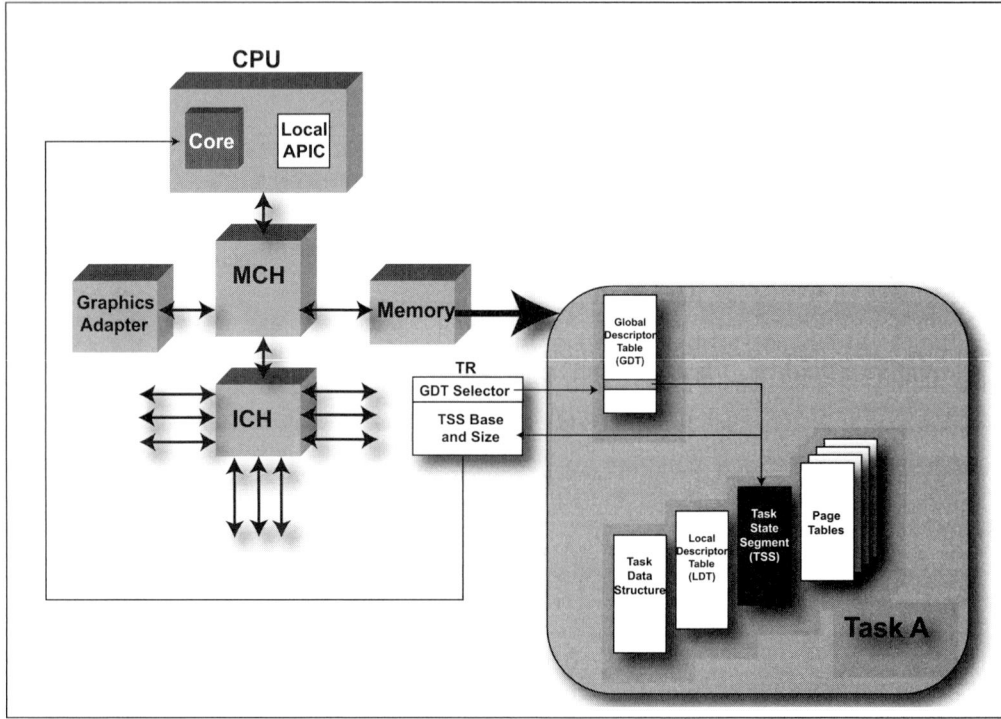

Starting a Task

Once all of the appropriate data structures and tables associated with a new task have been created in memory and the system registers (CR3, GDTR, LDTR and TR) have been initialized with their start addresses and sizes, the groundwork has been laid for a switch to that task. Prior to the actual switch, most of the logical processor's register set (other than the CS:EIP register pair) will be loaded with their initial values from the TDS associated with the task. Just prior to actually starting the task, the scheduler programs the logical processor's Local APIC timer with the timeslice assigned to the task (e.g., 10ms) and then triggers (i.e., starts) the timer. The scheduler then starts the task. Virtually all modern OSs use a software-based task switching mechanism and start (or resume) a task by pushing the initial CS:EIP and SS:ESP values onto the privilege level 0 stack and then executing the IRET (Interrupt Return) instruction. In response, the logical processor pops the task's initial values into the CS:EIP register pair and the initial stack values into the SS:ESP register pair and begins execution of the task.

Suspend Task and Resume Scheduler Execution

When the count loaded into the Local APIC timer (i.e., the logical processor's Local APIC timer) is exhausted, the current task's assigned slice of processor time has expired. The timer completion interrupt causes the logical processor to jump back to the OS scheduler:

- **If the hardware-based task switching mechanism is being used**:
  — The interrupt vector associated with the timeslice timer selects a Task Gate descriptor in the IDT (Interrupt Descriptor Table) and this descriptor, in turn, selects the TSS descriptor associated with the scheduler task.
  — As a result, the logical processor automatically records the contents of many of its registers in the TSS associated with the task being suspended.
  — It then reloads its registers from the TSS associated with the scheduler.
  — Having completed the register reload, it then resumes program execution at the location now pointed to by the CS:EIP register pair, causing it to resume execution of the scheduler task.
- **If a software-based task switching mechanism is being used**:
  — The interrupt vector associated with the timeslice timer causes the logical processor to jump to and resume execution of the scheduler.
  — In response, the scheduler records the contents of many of the logical processor's registers in the TDS associated with the task being suspended (see Figure 18-6 on page 640). It obtains the contents of the CS, EIP and Eflags registers from the values pushed onto the stack as a result of the interrupt.
  — Having recorded the state (i.e., context) of the logical processor at the point of the previous task's suspension, the scheduler then, if necessary, reloads the logical processor's registers from the TDS associated with the scheduler (see Figure 18-7 on page 641) and the scheduler resumes execution in the same state it was in when it was suspended earlier in time.

Figure 18-6: Task A's Suspension

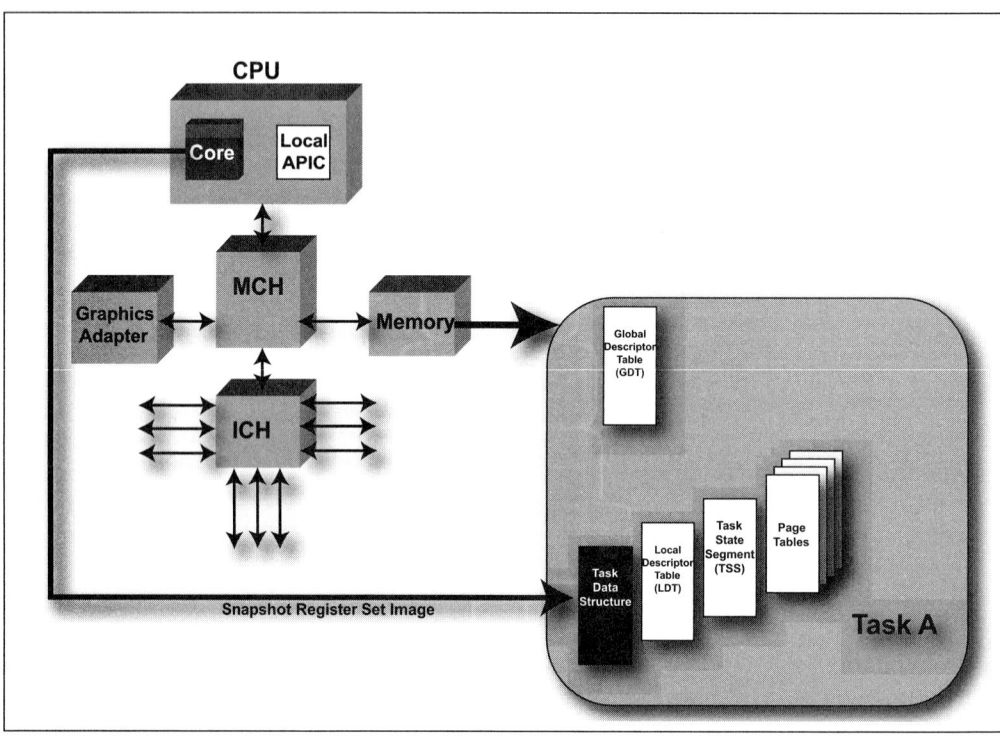

Figure 18-7: Scheduler's Resumption

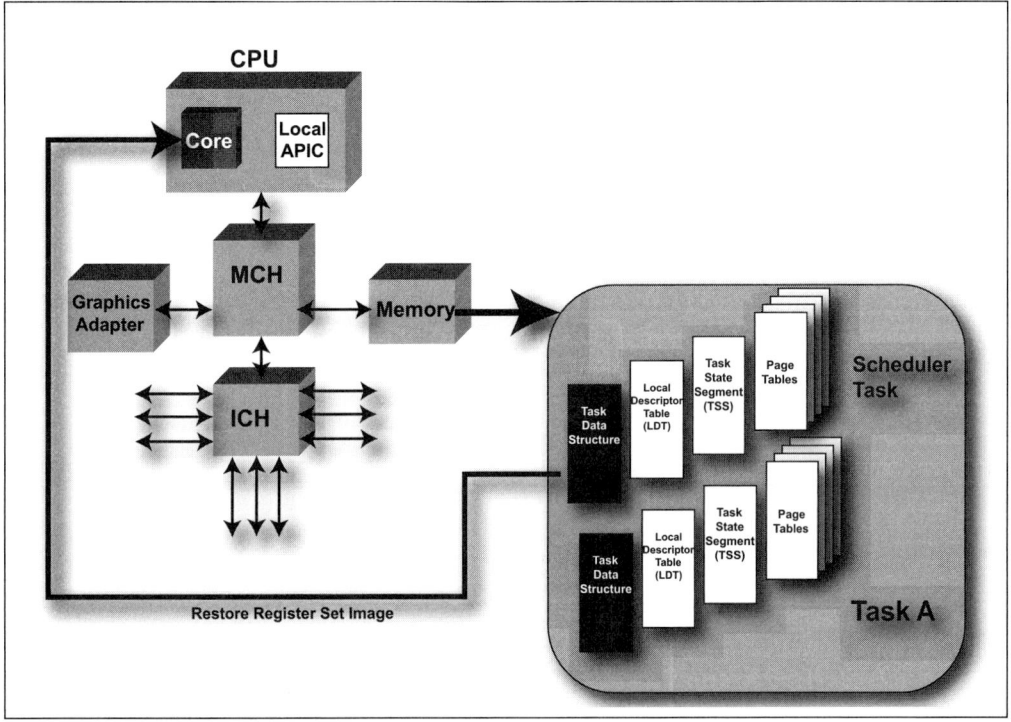

Hardware-Based Task Switching

It's Slow

Before loading the values from the target TSS into the registers, the logical processor performs extensive validity checks on all of them to ensure they are correct (i.e., they won't cause any problems). In other words, the hardware doesn't trust the OS to set up the TSSs correctly. This extensive hardware validation substantially adds to the amount of time it takes to actually start (or resume) execution of a task, so modern OSs do not use the x86 hardware-based automatic task switching mechanism. Rather, the task switch is handled solely by kernel software.

Why Didn't OSs Use It?

At the time of the 386's introduction, Unix was the most prevalent multitasking OS. Since other processor architectures to which Unix had already been ported didn't implement similar hardware-assisted task switching, task switching was handled purely in software. It would have required a kernel rewrite to take advantage of it and—considering its poor performance—would have proven counter-productive.

Why Wasn't It Improved?

The hardware task switching mechanism could have been redesigned to improve performance, but what would have been the point? The software-based task switching mechanism already implemented was already operational and worked well.

Why Does It Still Exist?

- It doesn't use much silicon.
- It's not worth the effort to eliminate it.
- You might break something else in the process of ripping it out.

Introduction to the Key Elements

The key elements associated with the x86 hardware-based task switching mechanism are listed in Table 18-1 on page 643.

Table 18-1: Hardware-based Task Switching's Key Elements

Element	Description	Used in Software-based Switching?
TSS	**Task State Segment data structure**. The scheduler creates one for each task (including itself; the scheduler is a task like any other). The TSS serves the purpose of the Task Data Structure mentioned in the overview (see "A More Comprehensive Overview" on page 631).	Yes
TSS descriptor	The scheduler sets up one TSS descriptor per task in the GDT (these descriptors cannot reside in the LDT or IDT). **Contents**: Besides the descriptor type field, the TSS descriptor contains: • **Base Address**: The virtual base address of a task's TSS data structure in memory. • **Size**: The size of the data structure. • **DPL**: The minimum privilege level (DPL) that the currently-running program must have in order to successfully cause a task switch. Note that if a Task Gate descriptor is used to indirectly select a TSS descriptor, the TSS descriptor's DPL is not used (see the next row). • **Busy bit**: The Busy bit indicates whether the task associated with this descriptor is currently busy (i.e., it is either the currently-active task or one that has been suspended but not yet completed).	Yes

Table 18-1: Hardware-based Task Switching's Key Elements (Continued)

Element	Description	Used in Software-based Switching?
Task Gate descriptor	The Task Gate descriptor provides an indirect method to perform a far jump or a far call to another task. **Contents**: Besides the descriptor type field, this descriptor contains the following fields: • **DPL**: The gate's DPL. • **TSS Selector**: A 16-bit value that selects the TSS descriptor of the target task. Note that when a TSS descriptor is selected indirectly through a Task Gate, its DPL is not used in the privilege check. **Location**: Although the TSS descriptor is restricted to the GDT, the Task Gate descriptor can reside in either the GDT, the currently-running task's LDT, or in the IDT (see the description of the Timer in this table). **Privilege Check**: Before permitting the task switch, the logical processor first verifies that the CPL of the currently-running program and the RPL specified in the branch target address are both at least as privileged as the Task Gate descriptor's DPL.	No

Table 18-1: Hardware-based Task Switching's Key Elements (Continued)

Element	Description	Used in Software-based Switching?
TR	**Task register**. 16-bit value selects the TSS descriptor that points to the TSS associated with the current task. The logical processor loads the TSS's base address and size into invisible part of the TR register. **Initialization**: Before causing a switch to the first task after system initialization, the scheduler executes the **LTR instruction** (a privilege level 0 instruction) which causes the logical processor to: • Load the scheduler's own TSS descriptor into the invisible part of the TR. When the first task switch is subsequently triggered, the logical processor suspends the scheduler by making a snapshot of the logical processor's registers in the scheduler's TSS data structure. • Set the Busy bit in the scheduler's TSS descriptor to mark the task as the currently-active task. After causing a switch to the first task, there is no further need for the scheduler to execute the LTR instruction. The TR will be automatically loaded with the TSS descriptor of each task as each subsequent task switch occurs. Any program running at any privilege level can execute the **STR instruction** to store the 16-bit TSS descriptor selector from the visible portion of the TR to memory.	Yes
Timer	• During system initialization, the scheduler loads the IDT entry associated with the Local APIC timer with a Task Gate descriptor pointing to the scheduler's TSS descriptor. • Prior to causing a switch to a task, the scheduler initializes the Local APIC's programmable timer with the timeslice assigned to the task. • When the timer expires and generates an interrupt, the Task Gate in the IDT is selected and the GDT selector in the Gate, in turn, selects the scheduler's TSS descriptor. This causes the current task to be suspended and the scheduler task to be resumed.	Yes

The Trigger Events

A number of events can cause the logical processor to suspend the current task and start or resume another task. Table 18-2 on page 646 provides a description of each trigger event. The sections that follow detail the sequence of actions taken by the logical processor when suspending the current task and starting or resuming another one.

Table 18-2: Events that Cause a Task Switch

Event	Description
The CS portion of a Far Call/Far jump branch target address selects TSS descriptor in GDT	**Privilege Check**: A privilege check is performed to determine if the currently executing program has sufficient privilege (CPL ≤ DPL) to jump to or call the target task. **The Switch**: • The state of the current task is stored in the TSS pointed to by the TR register (i.e., the TSS of the currently-active task). • The offset portion of the branch target address is discarded. • The logical processor loads the 16-bit segment selector of the branch target address into the visible portion of the TR (this selects the new TSS descriptor). • The logical processor loads the invisible part of the TR with the base address and size of the target task's TSS. • The register values from the target task's TSS are loaded into the logical processor's register set. • The logical processor starts fetching code from the address now pointed to by the CS:EIP register pair (i.e., the entry point in the target task). More detailed information can be found in "Comprehensive Task Switch Description" on page 665.

Table 18-2: Events that Cause a Task Switch (Continued)

Event	Description
The CS portion of a Far Call/Far jump selects Task Gate descriptor in the GDT or LDT	All TSS descriptors must reside in the GDT and the DPL of a TSS descriptor is typically set to zero. This means that a program that resides at a less-privileged level could not switch to the task associated with the target TSS. Task Gate descriptors, on the other hand, can reside in the GDT, LDT or the IDT. If the currently-running program executes a far jump or a far call that selects a Task Gate descriptor in its LDT or in the GDT, and it has sufficient privilege (if the less-privileged of the currently executing program's CPL and RPL is at least as privileged as the Task Gate's DPL; the TSS DPL is ignored), it can cause the logical processor to suspend the current task and switch to the target task associated with the selected TSS. The Task Gate format is illustrated in Figure 18-9 on page 651 and is described in the section entitled "Task Gate Descriptor" on page 649. Also refer to the section entitled "Comprehensive Task Switch Description" on page 665.
INT *nn* where *nn* selects a Task Gate in IDT	When the logical processor executes an INT *nn* instruction, the value *nn* acts as an index into the IDT. If the selected IDT entry contains a Task Gate descriptor and the program executing the INT instruction has sufficient privilege (its CPL is at least as privileged as the gate's DPL), a task switch results. Additional information can be found in the sections entitled "Task Gate Descriptor" on page 649 and "Switch Due to a BOUND/INT/INTO/INT3 Instruction" on page 667.

Table 18-2: Events that Cause a Task Switch (Continued)

Event	Description
Hardware interrupt selects a Task Gate in IDT	When a hardware interrupt request is detected by the logical processor, the interrupt vector obtained from the interrupt controller is used as an index into the IDT. If the selected IDT entry contains a Task Gate descriptor, a task switch results (exceptions, interrupts and execution of the IRET instruction cause a task switch regardless of the Task Gate's DPL). Additional information can be found in the sections entitled "Task Gate Descriptor" on page 649 and "Comprehensive Task Switch Description" on page 665.
Software exception selects a Task Gate in IDT	When a software exception condition is detected by the logical processor, the type of exception condition determines the index into the IDT. If the selected IDT entry contains a Task Gate descriptor, a task switch results (exceptions, interrupts and execution of the IRET instruction cause a task switch regardless of the Task Gate's DPL). Additional information can be found in the sections entitled "Switch Due To an Interrupt or Exception" on page 665 and "Comprehensive Task Switch Description" on page 665.
IRET execution when Eflags[NT] bit set	Refer to the sections entitled "Link Field (to Old TSS Selector)" on page 665 and "Calling Another Task" on page 670 for a detailed description.

The Descriptors

TSS Descriptor

The TSS descriptor (the 16-bit format is not shown; a 32-bit TSS descriptor is pictured in Figure 18-8 on page 649) may only reside in the GDT and describes the following characteristics of a task's TSS:

- The 32-bit virtual base address of the TSS data structure.
- The 20-bit Limit (i.e., the size) of the TSS data structure.

- The DPL of the TSS. A far call or a far jump instruction can cause a task switch if the currently executing program's CPL is at least as privileged as the TSS descriptor's DPL. The segment portion of the branch target address selects the entry in the GDT that contains the TSS descriptor. The offset portion of the branch target address is irrelevant and is discarded.
- Whether the target task is currently busy (i.e., it is the currently-running task or one that is currently suspended but not completed; a detailed discussion of the Busy bit can be found in "LTR Instruction and the Busy Bit" on page 677).

The minimum size of a TSS is 104 bytes (67h; the size of the TSS main body). If the TSS limit is set to less than this value, an invalid TSS exception is generated. An attempt to load a TSS descriptor into a segment register causes a GP exception.

Figure 18-8: The 32-bit TSS Descriptor Format

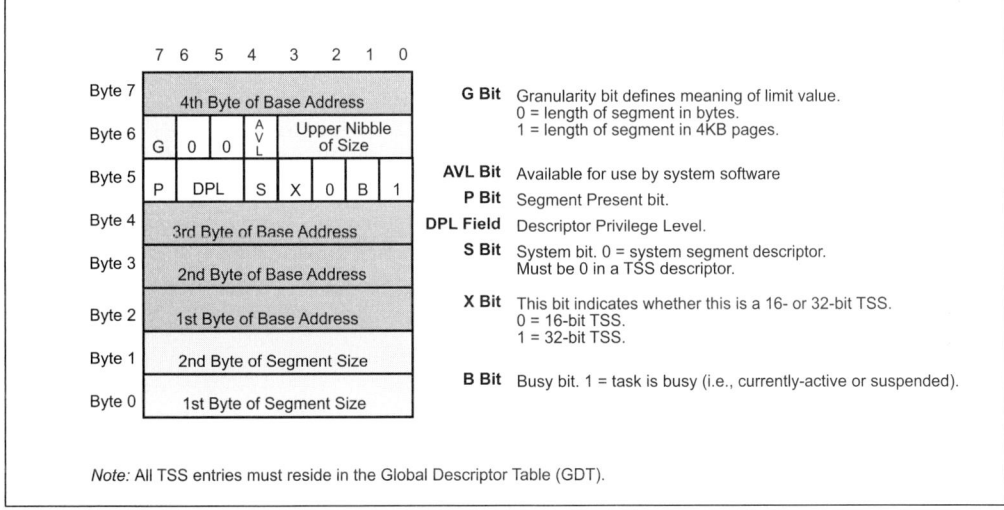

Task Gate Descriptor

While TSS descriptors must reside in the GDT, Task Gate descriptors may reside in the GDT, an LDT, or the IDT. Figure 18-9 on page 651 illustrates the format of a Task Gate descriptor (the format is the same for the 286 and subsequent processors). It contains a 16-bit value that selects an entry in the GDT containing a TSS descriptor.

Task Gate Selected by a Far Call/Jump. When a far call or a far jump selects a Task Gate descriptor in the GDT or LDT, the DPL of the Task Gate, rather than the DPL of the TSS descriptor, is checked during the privilege level check (the DPL of the TSS is ignored). A task switch occurs if the less-privileged of the RPL or CPL is at least as privileged as the Task Gate's DPL value. As examples:

— A Task Gate with DPL = 3 permits any program to jump to or call the task pointed to by the TSS descriptor.
— A Task Gate with DPL = 2 permits programs with privilege levels of 0, 1 or 2 to cause a task switch, while an attempt by a privilege level 3 program would cause a GP exception.

It should be noted that the offset portion of the branch target address is irrelevant and is discarded.

Gate Selected by Hardware Interrupt/Software Exception. See Figure 18-10 on page 651. When a hardware interrupt or software exception selects an IDT entry containing a Task Gate it causes a task switch. Both the Task Gate's and the TSS descriptor's DPL are ignored. In other words, the privilege check isn't performed. More detail can be found in "Comprehensive Task Switch Description" on page 665.

Task Gate Selected by a Software Interrupt Instruction. If an INT *nn*/INTO/INT3 or a BOUND instruction selects an IDT entry containing a Task Gate, the privilege check is performed. The DPL of the Task Gate, rather than that of the TSS descriptor, is checked (and the DPL of the TSS is ignored). A task switch occurs if the CPL is at least as privileged as the Task Gate's DPL value.

Figure 18-9: The Task Gate Format

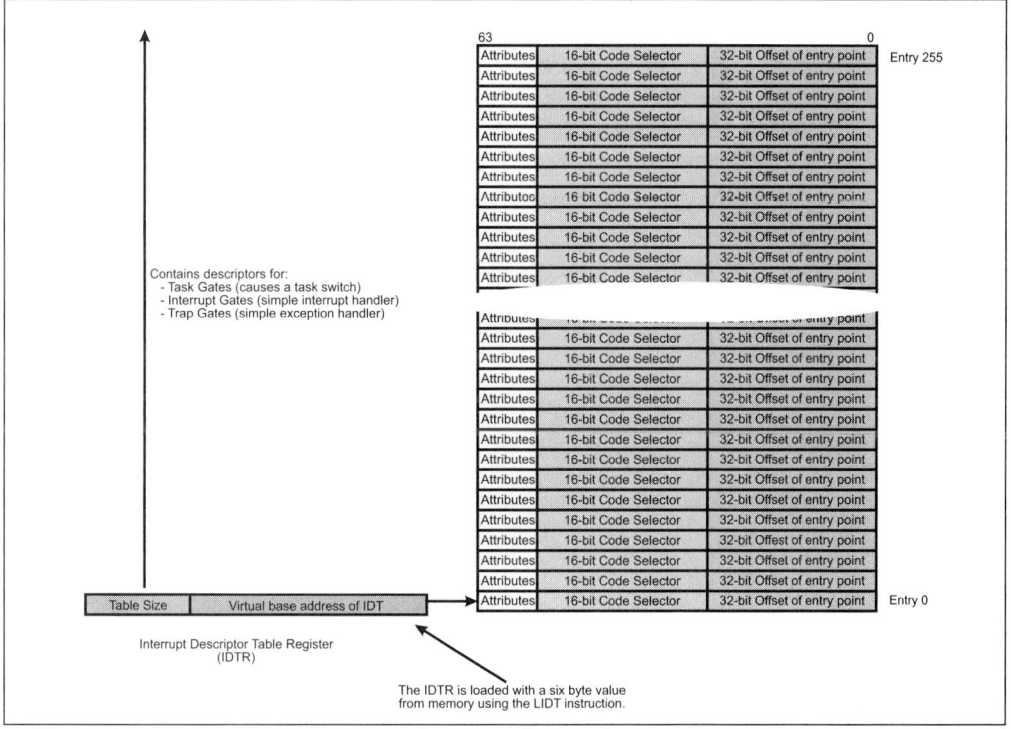

P Bit	Segment Present bit.
DPL Field	Descriptor Privilege Level.
S Bit	System bit. When 0, indicates system segment. Must be 0 in a Task Gate descriptor.
Byte 5[3:0]	With S = 0, 0101b indicates Task Gate descriptor.
TSS Selector	Selects a GDT entry containing the TSS descriptor of the task to be switched to. The selected TSS descriptor contains the base address, limit and attributes of the target task's TSS.

Note: A Task Gate descriptor may reside in the Global, Local or Interrupt Descriptor Tables.

Figure 18-10: The IDT (Interrupt Descriptor Table)

The Task Register

General

The logical processor uses the TR register (see Figure 18-11 on page 654) to locate the TSS data structure associated with the currently-running task. Loading the TR register with a new TSS selector occurs in two ways:

- **Initial TR Load**. Initially, the scheduler executes the LTR instruction to load the TSS selector for the scheduler's own TSS descriptor into the TR register. When the first task switch is subsequently triggered, the logical processor suspends the scheduler by making a snapshot of its registers in the scheduler's TSS data structure.
- **Subsequent TR Loads**. On any subsequent task switch, the TR register is automatically loaded with the TSS descriptor associated with the task being switched to.

Loading a new 16-bit value into the TR causes the logical processor to read the selected TSS descriptor from the GDT into the invisible part of the TR. If the selected GDT entry contains any other type of descriptor, or if the selected TSS descriptor has its Busy bit set to one (indicating the task is the currently-running task or one that is currently suspended but not yet completed), the logical processor generates a GP exception. A GP exception is also generated if the 16-bit value has TI = 1, selecting the LDT rather than the GDT.

TR Instruction Pair

The instruction set provides two instructions the programmer can use to place a new value in the TR or to obtain the current value from it. The LTR (Load Task Register) and STR (Store Task Register) instructions may only be executed when the logical processor is in Protected Mode (CR0[PE] = 1). Attempted execution of either while in Real Mode results in an Invalid Opcode exception. The STR instruction can be executed at any privilege level, while the LTR instruction can only be executed by a program executing at privilege level zero. An attempt to execute the LTR instruction at any other privilege level results in a GP exception.

> **STR Instruction.** At any privilege level, the programmer may use the STR instruction to obtain (from the TR) the selector for the currently-executing task's TSS descriptor in the GDT. The 16-bit value may be placed either into a 16-bit GPR or into memory. Using this value, the programmer can then read the TSS descriptor from the GDT to discover the base address and

limit (i.e., the size of) the current task's TSS data structure (but only if it is permitted to access the area of memory in which the GDT resides).

LTR Instruction. *Intended use of LTR instruction*: The TR contents after reset is undefined. This instruction is typically used at startup time to identify the OS code's startup TSS. If the TR were not initialized in this manner, the first task switch would cause the logical processor to save its register set into the area of memory identified by the junk TSS address and size currently in the invisible part of the TR. In other words, the register set would be stored into some undefined region of memory. This could have catastrophic results.

At privilege level 0, the programmer may execute the LTR instruction to place a new 16-bit value into the TR. *It should be noted that loading a new TSS descriptor selector into the TR does not cause a task switch.* When executed, the logical processor performs the following actions:

— Validates that the current program's CPL is sufficiently-privileged to perform a task switch (since the CPL of the program executing the LTR instruction must be zero, this isn't a problem).
— Generates a GP Exception if the indicated GDT entry does not contain a TSS descriptor or if the descriptor's Busy bit is set to one (indicating the related task is the currently-running task or one that is suspended).
— Generates a Segment Not Present exception if P = 0 in the TSS descriptor.
— Generates a Page Fault exception if the page containing the TSS is not currently in memory.
— Generates a GP exception if the CS selector in the TSS data structure does not select a code segment.
— Generates a GP exception if any of the data segment selectors in the TSS data structure do not select a data segment.
— Generates a Stack exception if the SS selector in the TSS data structure doesn't select a stack segment (i.e., a read/writable data segment).
— The invisible portion of the TR is loaded with the base address and limit of the new TSS.
— The Busy bit in the TSS descriptor is set to one indicating that the task associated with this TSS is currently the focus task (note: focus is the author's term in this context).

As stated earlier, the LTR instruction does not cause a task switch. In other words, although the logical processor verifies the integrity of the new TSS and marks it busy, it does not reload its register set from the new TSS.

Figure 18-11: The Task Register

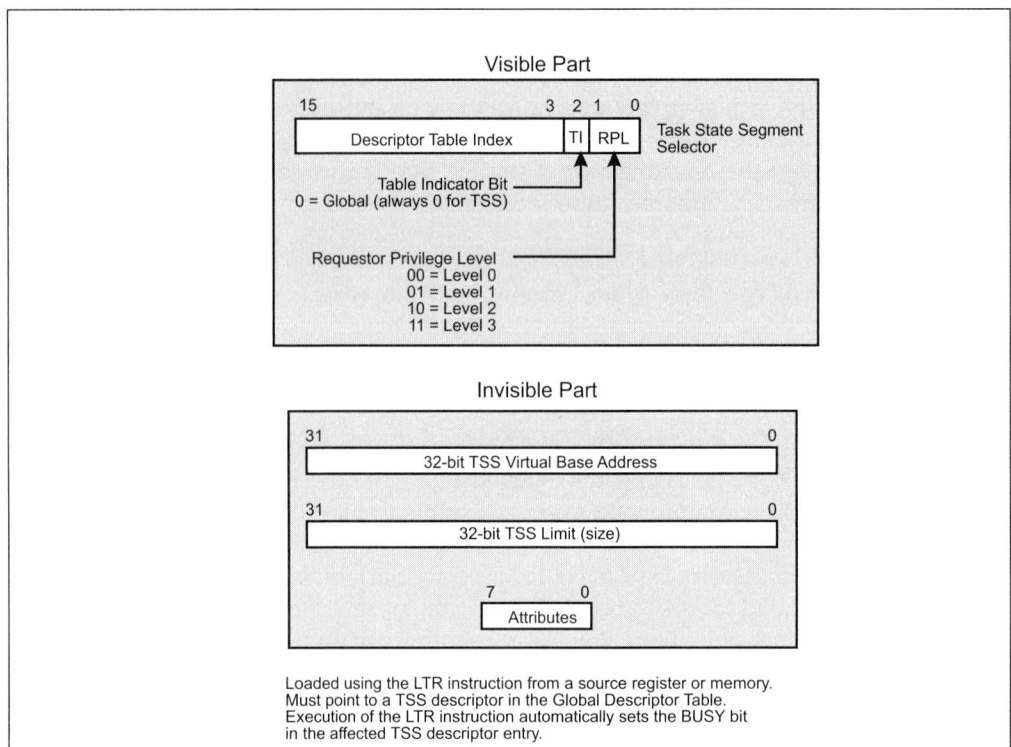

TSS Data Structure Format

General

The 286 implemented a different TSS data structure than that defined for the post-286 processors (it isn't covered in this book). All post-286 processors define the TSS data structure illustrated in Figure 18-12 on page 656 (the 32-bit TSS).

- Note that the 386 and the early 486 processors did not implement the Interrupt Redirection Map. It was first implemented in the Pentium and then migrated to the later versions of the 486 and all subsequent x86 processors. It is described in "Software Interrupt Instruction Handling" on page 825.

Required Fields

At a minimum, the TSS must include locations 00h through 67h (104d locations). This area consists of three types of fields:

- **Reserved fields**. Those locations shown as zeros are **reserved** by Intel and must not be used.
- **Dynamic fields**. The dynamic fields are read by the logical processor whenever the task is started or resumed and are automatically updated by the logical processor whenever the task is suspended (hence the term *dynamic* because these fields change dynamically during system operation).
- **Static fields**. The static fields, initialized by the OS, are read by the logical processor but are not written to (in other words, they remain static).

Optional Fields

The portion of the TSS above location 67h consists of three areas:

- **OS-specific**. The OS may utilize the optional area starting at location 68h for OS-specific data related to the task. The size and interpretation of this area is OS-specific. As an example, the OS could use the FSAVE instruction to save the contents of the FPU's registers in this area after a task has been suspended due to a task switch.
- **Interrupt Redirection Bitmap**. The Interrupt Redirection Bit Map (first implemented in the Pentium) consists of 32-bytes (8-dwords) and is only present when both of the following are true:
  — The TSS is associated with a DOS task.
  — The OS supports the VM86 Mode extensions enabled by setting CR4[VME] = 1 (note: not implemented until the Pentium).
- **IO Permission Bitmap**. The IO Permission Bit Map can be up to 8KB in size and is necessary if the OS supports IO protection (see "IO Port Access Protection" on page 659). Also see "Real World TSS Usage" on page 968.

The sections that follow describe each field in the TSS.

Figure 18-12: 32-bit Task State Segment (TSS) Format

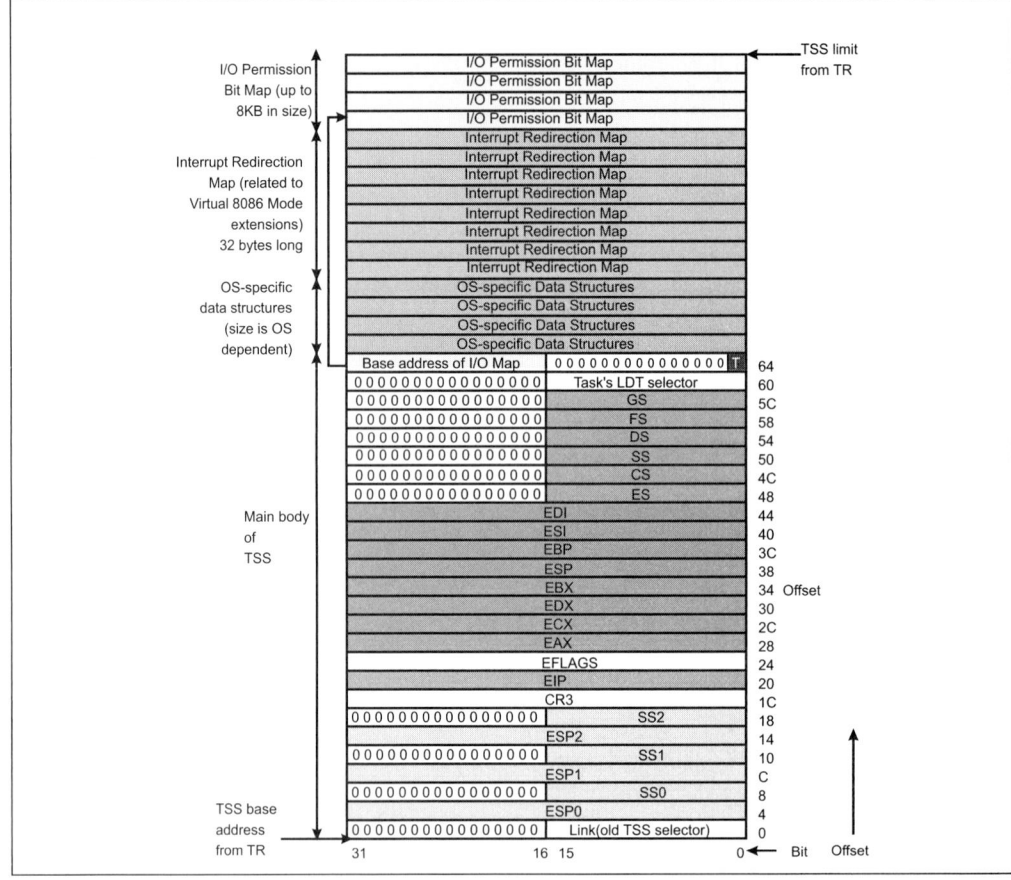

Register Snapshot Area

When a task switch occurs, the contents of the logical processor registers are stored in the respective fields of the current task's TSS. Once the snapshot of logical processor state at the point of suspension is complete:

- The logical processor loads the target task's TSS descriptor into the TR register.
- It then reloads the registers associated with these fields from the respective fields of the target task's TSS.

LDT Selector Field. The 16-bit value loaded into the LDTR (LDT register) selects an LDT descriptor in the GDT which is then loaded into the invisible portion of the LDTR. This field permits the OS to define a separate LDT for each task defining the memory segments that are *local* to the task, the OS services it is permitted to call, and, if hardware-based task switching is used, Task Gates pointing to other tasks it is permitted to switch call.

Segment Register Fields. The OS stores the initial values to be loaded into the data segment registers (DS, ES, FS and GS), stack segment register (SS), and code segment register (CS) in these TSS locations. When the task is started or resumed, these values are automatically read into the respective registers, thereby automatically selecting the code, stack and data segments to be used at task initiation or resumption. When the task is suspended, the contents of the segment registers are stored here.

General Purpose Register Fields. The OS stores the initial values for the EDI, ESI, EAX, EBX, ECX, EDX and EBP registers in these TSS locations. When the task is started or resumed, these values are automatically read into the respective logical processor registers. When the task is suspended, the contents of the logical processor's general registers are stored here.

SS:ESP Register Pair Fields. The OS stores the initial value for the SS:ESP register pair in these two TSS fields. When the task is started or resumed, these values are automatically read into the SS:ESP register pair. The SS:ESP fields tell the logical processor the base address of the stack and the top-of-stack. When the task is suspended, the contents of the SS:ESP register pair are stored in these two fields.

Extended Flags (Eflags) Register Field. The OS stores the initial value for the Eflags register in this TSS location. When the task is started or resumed, this value is automatically read into the logical processor's Eflags register. The Eflags register's initial settings tells the logical processor:

— If interrupt recognition is enabled or disabled.
— If debug single-step capability is enabled or disabled.
— The direction to be used during string operations.
— The minimum privilege level at which to permit IO operations.
— If VM86 mode is enabled or disabled.

When the task is suspended, the contents of the Eflags register is stored here.

CS:EIP Register Pair Fields. The OS stores the initial value for the CS:EIP register pair in these two TSS fields. When the task is started or resumed, these values are automatically read into the CS:EIP register pair to identify where the next instruction is to be fetched from. When the task is suspended, the contents of the CS:EIP register pair are stored in these two fields.

Control Register 3 (CR3) Field. The OS stores the initial value for CR3 in this TSS location and, when the task is started, this value is automatically read into CR3 register (Figure 18-13 on page 658 and Figure 18-14 on page 659). It points to the root directory used to translate the task's virtual addresses into physical addresses:

— Page Directory when using first-generation address translation;
— Page Directory Pointer Table when using second-generation address translation.

This permits the OS to specify a different set of address translation tables for each task. In this way, two tasks that both attempt to use the same virtual address range can have their memory accesses mapped to mutually-exclusive physical memory areas by the address translation mechanism, thereby isolating them from each other in a manner that is transparent to the tasks themselves. The chapter entitled "IA-32 Address Translation Mechanisms" on page 493 provides a detailed discussion of the address translation mechanism. When the task is suspended, the contents of CR3 is stored in this TSS field.

Figure 18-13: CR3 Format When Using First-Generation Address Translation

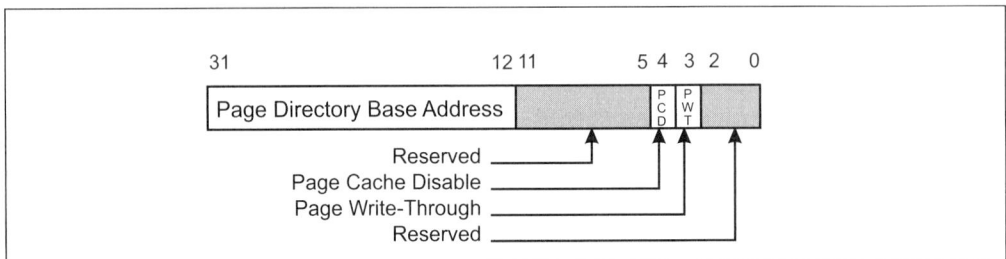

Figure 18-14: CR3 Format When Using Second-Generation Address Translation

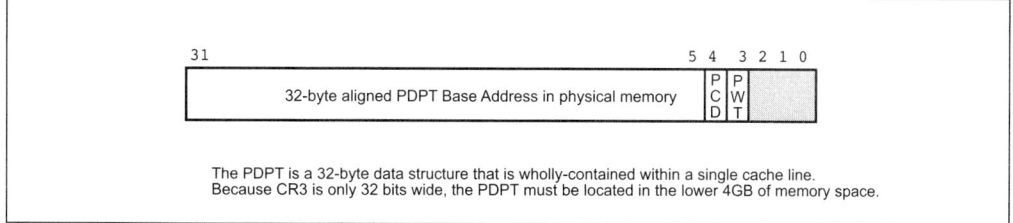

Debug Trap Bit (T)

The debug Trap bit (T) resides in bit zero of TSS location 64h. A debug exception occurs whenever a task switch occurs to a task with the Trap bit = 1 in its TSS. In other words, this provides a breakpoint on task switch capability.

IO Port Access Protection

Also see "Real World TSS Usage" on page 968.

IO Protection in Real Mode. When the logical processor is operating in Real Mode, there isn't any IO protection. In other words, any program may execute IO instructions (IN, OUT, INS, OUTS) at any time. As stated earlier in "IO Port Anarchy" on page 374, the inability of the OS to restrict application programs from communicating directly with IO ports can result in problems when multitasking. When operating in Protected Mode, the OS can place restraints on the ability of application programs to communicate directly with some or all IO ports. The manner in which this is done is discussed in the sections that follow.

Definition of IO Privilege Level (IOPL). When the OS initially sets up the TSS for a task, it sets up the desired initial Eflags register image in the task's TSS. A subset of this image is the Eflags[IOPL] field (see Figure 18-15 on page 660). Whenever a task is started (or resumed), the logical processor copies the register images from the task's TSS into its register set. Thus, the logical processor's IOPL is automatically set to the value from the TSS whenever the task is started or resumed.

If the CPL of the currently-executing program is numerically <= IOPL (i.e., the program's privilege level is the same as or more privileged than the IOPL threshold value), the logical processor permits the program to execute IOPL-sensitive instructions. The sensitive instructions are:

— **IN**. IO read instruction.
— **INS**. IO string read instruction.
— **OUT**. IO write instruction.
— **OUTS**. IO write string instruction.
— **CLI**. Clear Interrupt Enable instruction.
— **STI**. Set Interrupt Enable instruction.

If the CPL > IOPL and the instruction being executed is a CLI or STI, a GP (General Protection) exception is generated. If the instruction is one of the IO instructions, the manner in which the privilege check is performed differs based on whether the logical processor is in VM86 Mode (Virtual 8086 Mode) or not. The differences are described in the next two sections.

Figure 18-15: Eflags Register

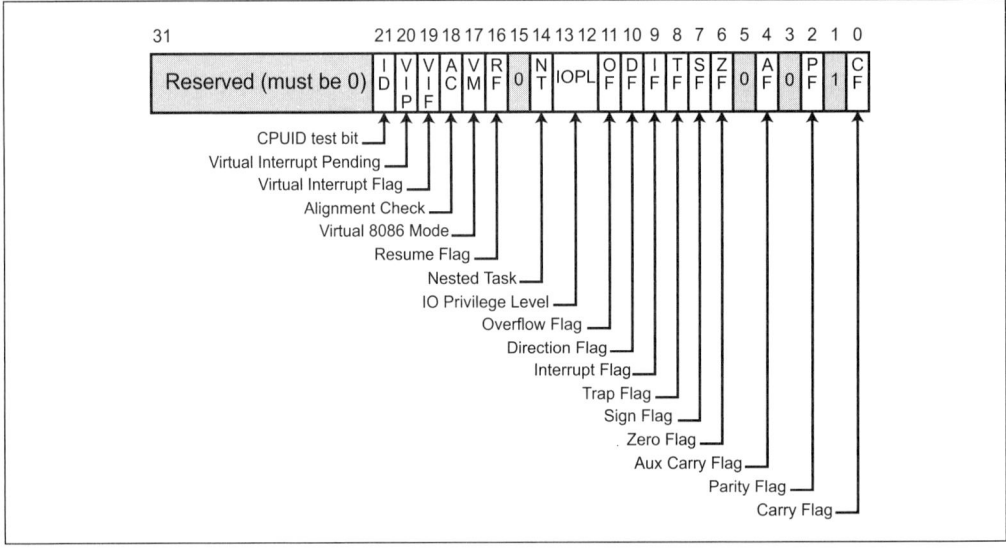

IO Permission Check in Protected Mode. When the logical processor is in Protected Mode but not VM86 Mode (i.e., Eflags[VM] = 0; the logical processor is executing a Protected Mode task rather than a DOS task) and the task attempts to execute an IOPL-sensitive instruction, the privilege check is performed in the following manner:

— **CPL <= IOPL**. If the CPL of the currently executing program is numerically <= the IOPL (i.e., program's privilege level is the same as or better than the IOPL), no exception is generated and the instruction is executed.

— **CPL > IOPL and IO instruction**. If the CPL is numerically > the IOPL (i.e., the program's privilege level is not as privileged as the threshold value specified in the IOPL field) and the instruction is one of the IO instructions (IN, OUT, INS, or OUTS), then the logical processor uses the target port address to index into the current task's IO Permission Bit Map (in its TSS) to determine if the current application is permitted to access the addressed IO port(s). If the bit(s) selected by the IO port address (see "IO Permission Bit Map" on page 661) indicates that the task is permitted to access the indicated IO port(s), no exception is generated and the IO instruction is executed. Otherwise, a GP exception is generated.

— **CPL > IOPL and CLI/STI**. If the CPL is numerically > the IOPL (i.e., the program's privilege level is not as good as the IOPL) and the instruction is either CLI or STI, then the logical processor generates a GP exception.

The IO Permission Bit Map is described in "IO Permission Bit Map" on page 661. For a discussion of memory-mapped IO protection, refer to "Memory-Mapped IO" on page 802.

IO Permission Check in VM86 Mode. When the logical processor is operating in the VM86 SubMode of Protected Mode (i.e., Eflags[VM] = 1) and it attempts to execute an IO instruction (IN, INS, OUT, or OUTS), the privilege check is performed as follows:

— The IOPL is not checked at all (VM86 tasks by definition operate at privilege level 3).

— The logical processor checks the current task's IO Permission Bit Map (in its TSS) to determine if the current application is permitted to access the addressed IO port(s). If the bit map indicates that the task is permitted to access the indicated IO port(s), no exception is generated and the IO instruction is executed. Otherwise, a GP exception is generated.

The IO Permission Bit Map is described in the next section. A detailed description of VM86 mode can be found in the chapter entitled "Virtual 8086 Mode" on page 783.

IO Permission Bit Map

Also see "Real World TSS Usage" on page 968.

Required or Optional? The two sections entitled "IO Permission Check in Protected Mode" on page 660 and "IO Permission Check in VM86 Mode" on page 661 referred to the IO Permission Bit Map in the TSS (pictured in Figure 18-12 on page 656). Implementation of the IO Permission Bit Map is mandatory under the following circumstances:

— The bit map is mandatory for any VM86 task (i.e., DOS task) that accesses IO-mapped IO ports.
— The bit map is mandatory for any non-VM86 Protected Mode task where the CPL of any part of the task that attempts IO is not as privileged as the Eflags[IOPL] threshold value.

In both cases, the logical processor interrogates the bit map in the TSS to determine whether or not to grant access to the addressed IO port(s).

The bit map is optional under the following circumstances:

— The bit map is optional if no code in the task ever attempts to execute an IO instruction (IN, OUT, INS, or OUTS). In other words, the program doesn't access any IO ports, or it does but all IO devices are memory- rather than IO-mapped. This is true both in the case of a VM86 task or a non-VM86, Protected Mode task.
— The bit map is optional if no code (within the task) attempts to execute an IO instruction while executing with a CPL less-privileged than that specified in the Eflags[IOPL] field.

The Bitmap Offset Field. Locations 66h and 67h of the TSS contain the 16-bit, byte-specific offset of the bit map start address from the TSS base address. Since the bit map resides at the end of the TSS, the end of the bit map is delineated by the size of the TSS itself (specified in the TSS descriptor in the GDT).

The Permission Check. To determine if the current task has permission to access the IO port(s) addressed by the currently executing IO instruction, the logical processor uses the IO port address to index into the IO permission bit map in the TSS. It checks the respective permission bit (or bits, if the IO instruction will access more than one IO port) to determine whether or not to permit the access.

— If the respective bit = 0, the access is permitted.
— If the bit = 1, a GP exception is generated.
— If the IO instruction will access multiple locations, the permission bits corresponding to each port are tested.

In order to designate the permission state for every possible IO port, 64K bits would be required (one bit for each of the possible 64K IO ports, 0000h - FFFFh). This would mean that the map would have to be 8KB in length

(8KB * 8 bits/byte = 64K bits). In practice, however, the OS programmer only has to define the permission state for IO port 0000h through the highest IO port address the task may attempt to access. As an example, if the task only attempts to access the first 80 IO ports (0000h - 004Fh), the map would be 10 bytes in length (10 bytes * 8 bits/byte = 80-bits).

IO ports are addressed at byte-specific addresses. In addition, an x86 processor may address a set of contiguous IO locations when executing an IO instruction.

```
in al,00h  ;reads from io port 0000h
in ax,00h  ;reads from io ports 0000h and 0001h
in eax,00h  ;reads from io ports 0000h through 0003h
```

In this example, each of the four addressed IO ports fall within the first eight IO port addresses. The permission bits for all of them are therefore found within the first location (consisting of eight bits) in the bit map. The logical processor would only have to read the bit map's first location to check the respective permission bits. This example

```
in ax,07h  ;reads contents of io ports 0007h and 0008h
```

reads the 8th and 9th IO locations (IO ports 0007h and 0008h). The permission bit for port 0007h is the last bit of the bit map's first location, while the permission bit for port 0008h is the first bit of the bit map's second location. Before permitting this IO instruction to execute, therefore, the logical processor would have to read the first two locations from the bit map to check the permission bits related to the addressed ports.

In reality, x86 processors are designed to always read two locations at a time when checking permission. This presents an interesting situation. Say that the highest IO port that a task is permitted to access is 004Fh. This is the 80th IO port. The bit map would have to be 10 locations long—a total of 80 bits. Now assume that the following instruction is attempted:

```
in al, 4fh  ;read contents of io port 004f
```

The logical processor would read the 10th and 11th bit map locations (remember that it always reads two bit map locations at a time). In other words, its reading one location beyond the end of the bit map. For this reason, the following must be true:

- The location immediately following the end of the actual bit map must be present and its contents must be FFh (i.e., all bits = 1, forbidding access to all eight ports).
- The TSS descriptor's limit must be set to include this last location.

Interrupt Redirection Bit Map

This VM86 Mode feature, an optimization designed to enhance support for running DOS applications in Protected Mode, was not implemented until the advent of the Pentium. The base address of the IO Permission Bitmap also tells the logical processor where the Interrupt Redirection Bitmap is located (i.e., it's located directly beneath the IO Permission Bitmap. A detailed description can be found in "Software Interrupt Instruction Handling" on page 825.

OS-Specific Data Structures

The OS may use the TSS area between the IO base address field and the start address of the IO Permission Bit Map to store OS-specific data structures. As an example, assume that an application is using the x87 FPU to perform floating-point math operations and that its assigned timeslice expires causing a task switch back to the task scheduler. Although many of the logical processor's registers are automatically stored in the application's TSS, you'll notice (looking at Figure 18-12 on page 656) that there are no TSS fields allocated to store the contents of the x87 FPU's register set. Before switching to another task, the scheduler could execute the FSAVE instruction to save the contents of the FPU's registers in the OS-specific area of the suspended task's TSS.

Privilege Level 0 - 2 Stack Definition Fields

Also see "Real World TSS Usage" on page 968.

When a program within the current task calls a more privileged program (within the same task), the logical processor automatically switches to a new stack and copies the following items to the newly-created stack:

- The pointer (SS:ESP) to the caller's stack.
- The return address (CS:EIP).
- Any parameters pushed onto the caller's stack to be passed to the called procedure.

The following fields in the TSS define where the new stack is located and how large it is:

- The SS2:ESP2 fields define the base address and top-of-stack for an empty stack pre-allocated by the OS kernel for the use of privilege level 2 procedures.
- The SS1:ESP1 fields define the base address and top-of-stack for an empty stack pre-allocated by the OS kernel for the use of privilege level 1 procedures.

- The SS0:ESP0 fields define the base address and top-of-stack for an empty stack pre-allocated by the OS kernel for the use of privilege level 0 procedures.

A more detailed description can be found in the section entitled "Automatic Stack Switch" on page 462.

Link Field (to Old TSS Selector)

A detailed description can be found in "Calling Another Task" on page 670.

Comprehensive Task Switch Description

Figure 18-16 on page 668 through Figure 18-18 on page 670 provide a detailed description of the steps taken by the logical processor when performing a switch from one task to another. Table 18-3 on page 665 provides additional information related to some of the task switch trigger conditions.

Table 18-3: Additional Information Related to Task Switch Triggers

Trigger Condition	Additional Information
Switch Due To an Interrupt or Exception	A task switch results when a hardware interrupt or a software exception selects an entry in the IDT (Interrupt Descriptor Table, pictured in Figure 18-10 on page 651) that contains a valid Task Gate. A privilege check is not performed.

Table 18-3: Additional Information Related to Task Switch Triggers (Continued)

Trigger Condition	Additional Information
Switch Due to a Far Call or a Far Jump	A far call or jump instruction causes a task switch under the following circumstances (note: the offset portion of the branch target address is irrelevant and is discarded): • **TSS selected**. When a far call or jump selects a TSS descriptor in the GDT. In this case, the lesser privileged of the selector RPL (in the branch target address) and the currently executing program's CPL must meet or exceed the privilege level indicated by the TSS descriptor's DPL. This is typically zero, restricting direct access to TSS descriptors to privilege level 0 programs. • **Task Gate selected**. When a far call or jump selects a Task Gate descriptor in either the GDT or LDT. In this case, the lesser privileged of the selector RPL (in the branch target address) and the currently executing program's CPL must meet or exceed the privilege level of the Task Gate descriptor's DPL (which can be different than the DPL of the TSS descriptor it points to in the GDT). The difference between the two is in how the privilege check is performed.

Table 18-3: Additional Information Related to Task Switch Triggers (Continued)

Trigger Condition	Additional Information
Switch Due to a BOUND/INT/INTO/INT3 Instruction	A task switch occurs if any of the following instructions select a Task Gate in the IDT: • The BOUND instruction generates a Bound Range Exceeded exception if the supplied array index is not within the bounds of the indicated memory array. This selects IDT entry 5. If this entry contains a Task Gate descriptor, a task switch occurs. No privilege check is performed. The resultant task switch and return is handled in the same manner as an exception (because it is one). The actions taken are detailed in Figure 18-16 on page 668. • The INT3 (Breakpoint) instruction selects IDT entry 3. If this entry contains a Task Gate descriptor, a task switch occurs. No privilege check is performed. • The INT *nn* instruction selects entry *nn* in the IDT. If entry *nn* contains a Task Gate descriptor and the CPL of the currently-executing program meets or exceeds the DPL of the Task Gate descriptor, a task switch occurs. • When the INTO (Interrupt On Overflow) instruction detects that Eflags[OF] = 1, the logical processor selects IDT entry 4. If this entry contains a Task Gate descriptor, a task switch occurs. No privilege check is performed. If the instruction is INT *nn* or INTO, the resultant task switch and return is handled in the same manner as a far call. The actions taken are detailed in the section entitled "Calling Another Task" on page 670.
Switch Due to Execution of an IRET	A task may be *called* due to any of the following: • Interrupt. • Exception. • Execution of the INT *nn*, INTO, INT3, or BOUND instruction. • Execution of a Call instruction. Prior to entering the called task, the logical processor sets Eflags[NT]. The last instruction executed in the called task is the IRET instruction. When the IRET instruction is executed with Eflags[NT] = 1, this triggers a task switch which causes the logical processor to switch back to the calling task. See "Calling Another Task" on page 670.

Figure 18-16: Task Switch Flowchart (1-of-3)

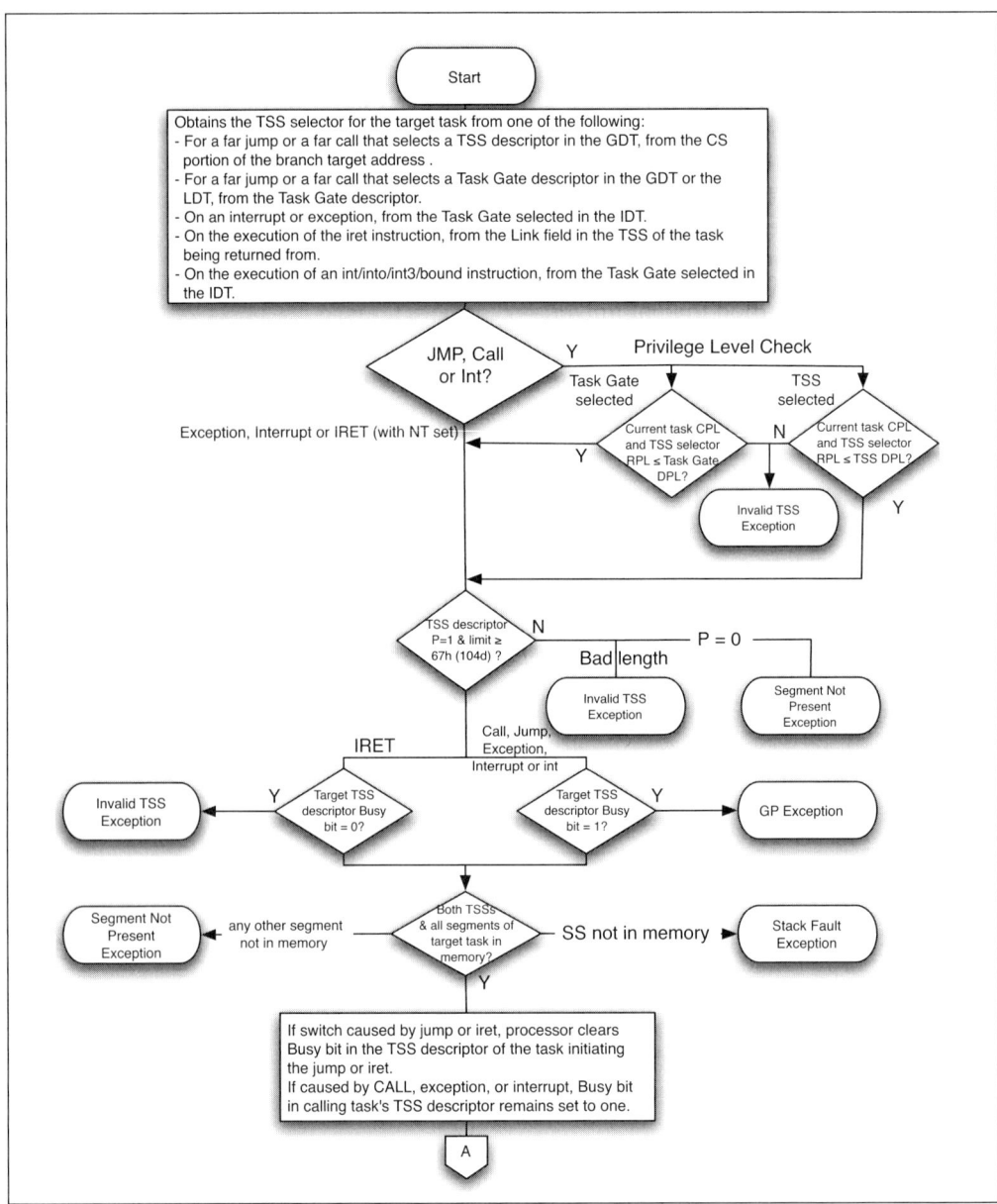

Figure 18-17: Task Switch Flowchart (2-of-3)

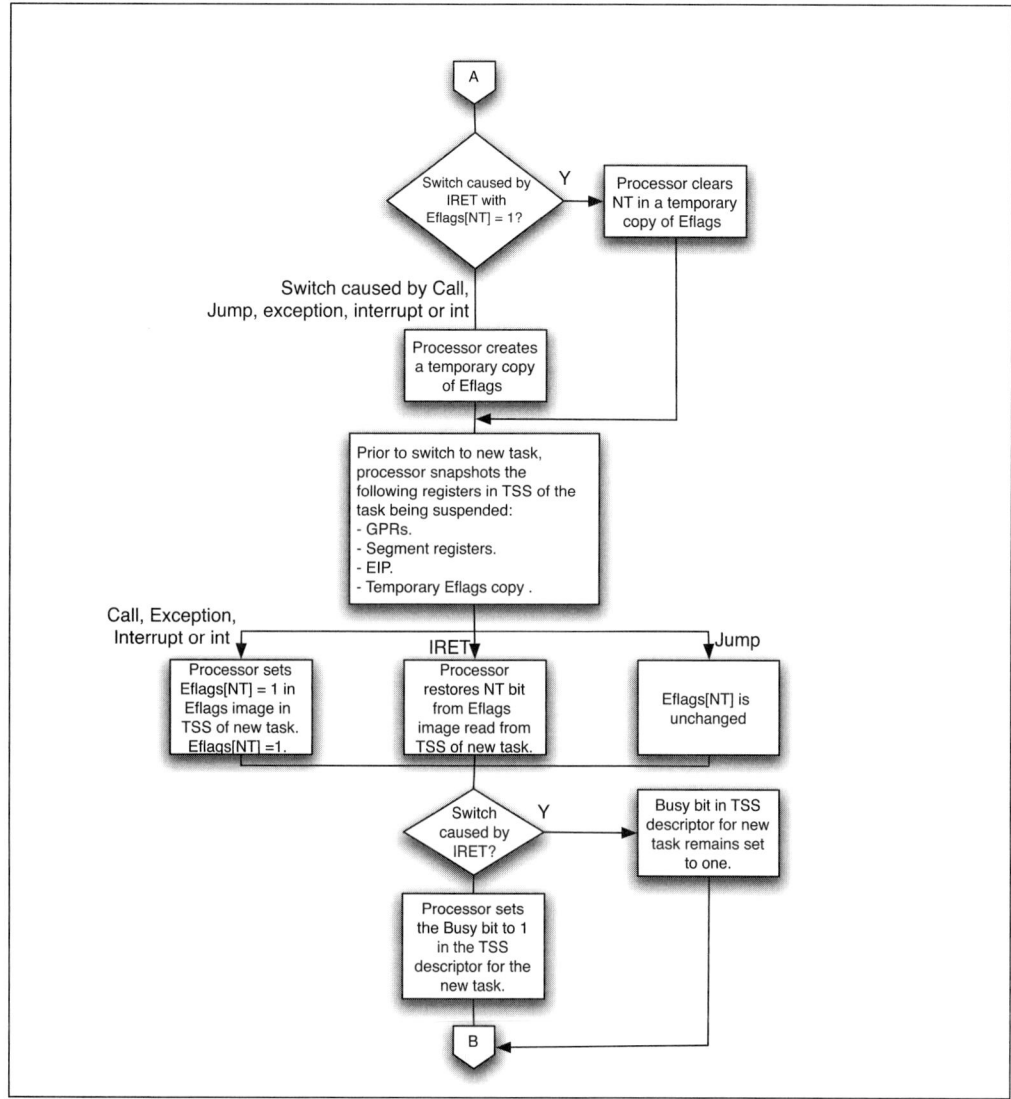

Figure 18-18: Task Switch Flowchart (3-of-3)

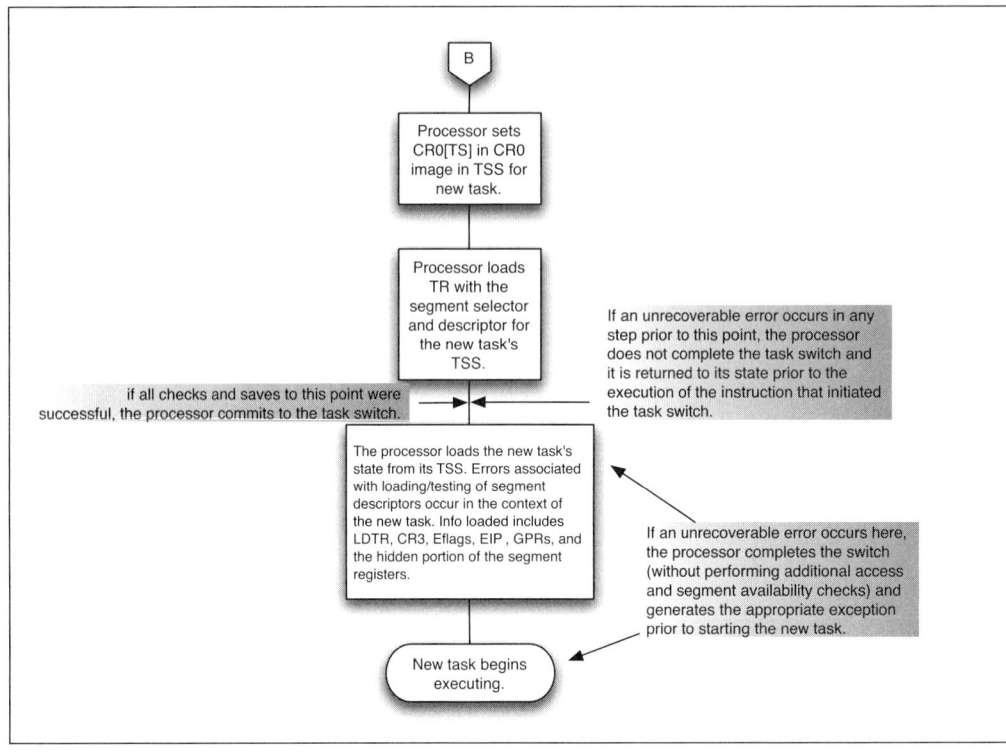

Calling Another Task

An Overview

Assume that task A is executing and one of the following three scenarios occurs:

Scenario 1. **Call selects TSS or Task Gate**. In task A, a far call is executed and the selector portion of the branch target address selects task B's TSS descriptor in the GDT, or a Task Gate descriptor in the GDT or LDT which points to task B's TSS descriptor. In other words, task A is calling task B as if it were a procedure.

Scenario 2. **Interrupt selects Task Gate**. An interrupt (i.e., a hardware interrupt or a software interrupt instruction) is detected while task A is executing and the interrupt vector selects an IDT entry containing a Task Gate descriptor that points to task B's TSS descriptor in the GDT.

Scenario 3. **Exception selects Task Gate**. A software exception condition is detected while task A is executing and the exception type selects an IDT entry containing a Task Gate descriptor that points to task B's TSS descriptor in the GDT.

In all three cases, task B is being called as if it were a procedure. In response, the logical processor will have to:

- Suspend task A.
- Save a task pointer so it can return task A it after the called task completes.
- Switch to task B.
- Set a flag indicating that upon completion of task B, it should switch back to task A and resume execution where it left off.

A Comprehensive Example

Figure 18-19 through Figure 18-23 provide a detailed example wherein:

0. Initial state: Task A is running (see Figure 18-19 on page 672).
1. Task A calls task B (see Figure 18-20 on page 673).
2. Task B calls task C (see Figure 18-21 on page 674).
3. Task C completes and returns to task B (Figure 18-22 on page 675).
4. Task B completes and returns to task A (Figure 18-23 on page 676).

Figure 18-19: Task A Running

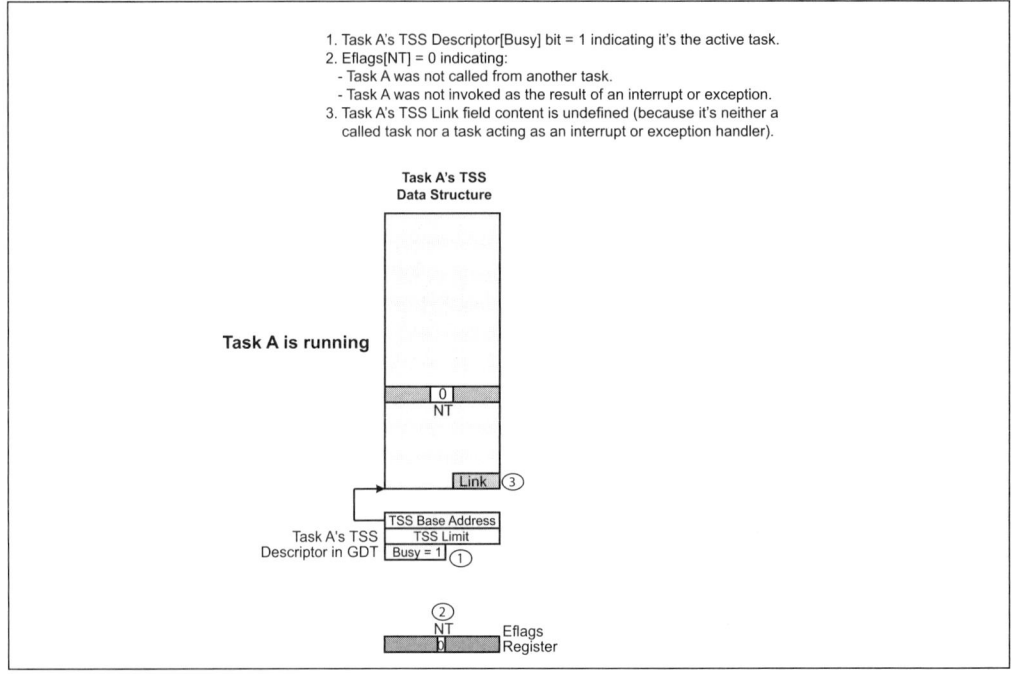

Figure 18-20: Task A Calls Task B

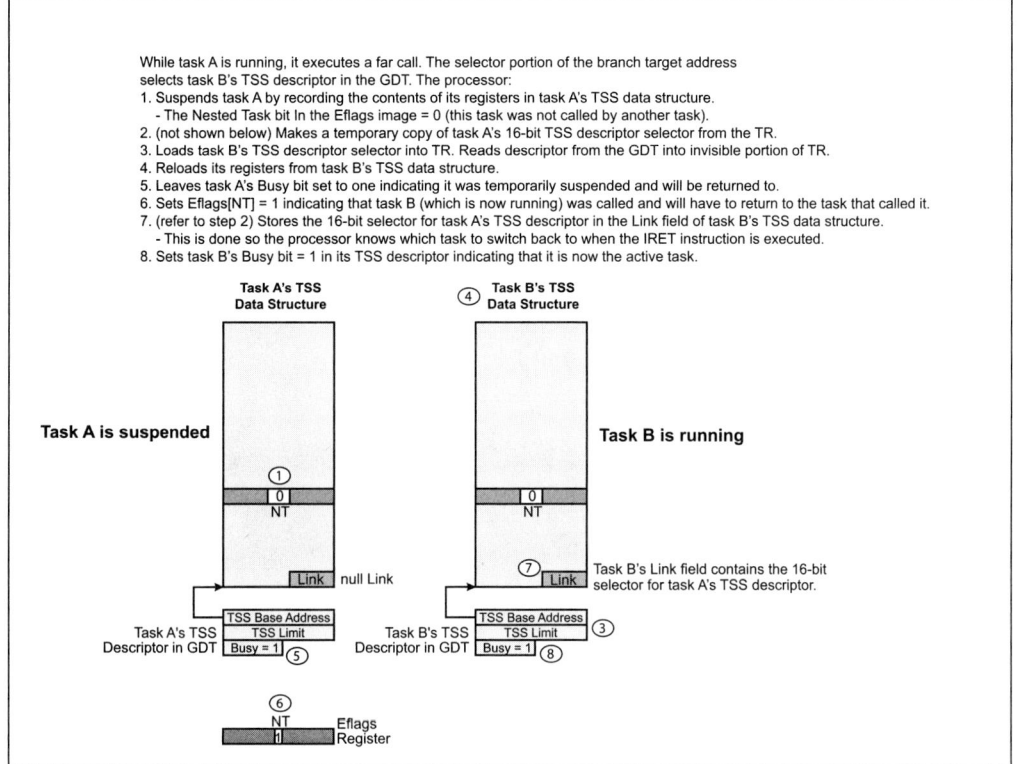

While task A is running, it executes a far call. The selector portion of the branch target address selects task B's TSS descriptor in the GDT. The processor:
1. Suspends task A by recording the contents of its registers in task A's TSS data structure.
   - The Nested Task bit In the Eflags image = 0 (this task was not called by another task).
2. (not shown below) Makes a temporary copy of task A's 16-bit TSS descriptor selector from the TR.
3. Loads task B's TSS descriptor selector into TR. Reads descriptor from the GDT into invisible portion of TR.
4. Reloads its registers from task B's TSS data structure.
5. Leaves task A's Busy bit set to one indicating it was temporarily suspended and will be returned to.
6. Sets Eflags[NT] = 1 indicating that task B (which is now running) was called and will have to return to the task that called it.
7. (refer to step 2) Stores the 16-bit selector for task A's TSS descriptor in the Link field of task B's TSS data structure.
   - This is done so the processor knows which task to switch back to when the IRET instruction is executed.
8. Sets task B's Busy bit = 1 in its TSS descriptor indicating that it is now the active task.

Figure 18-21: Task B Calls Task C

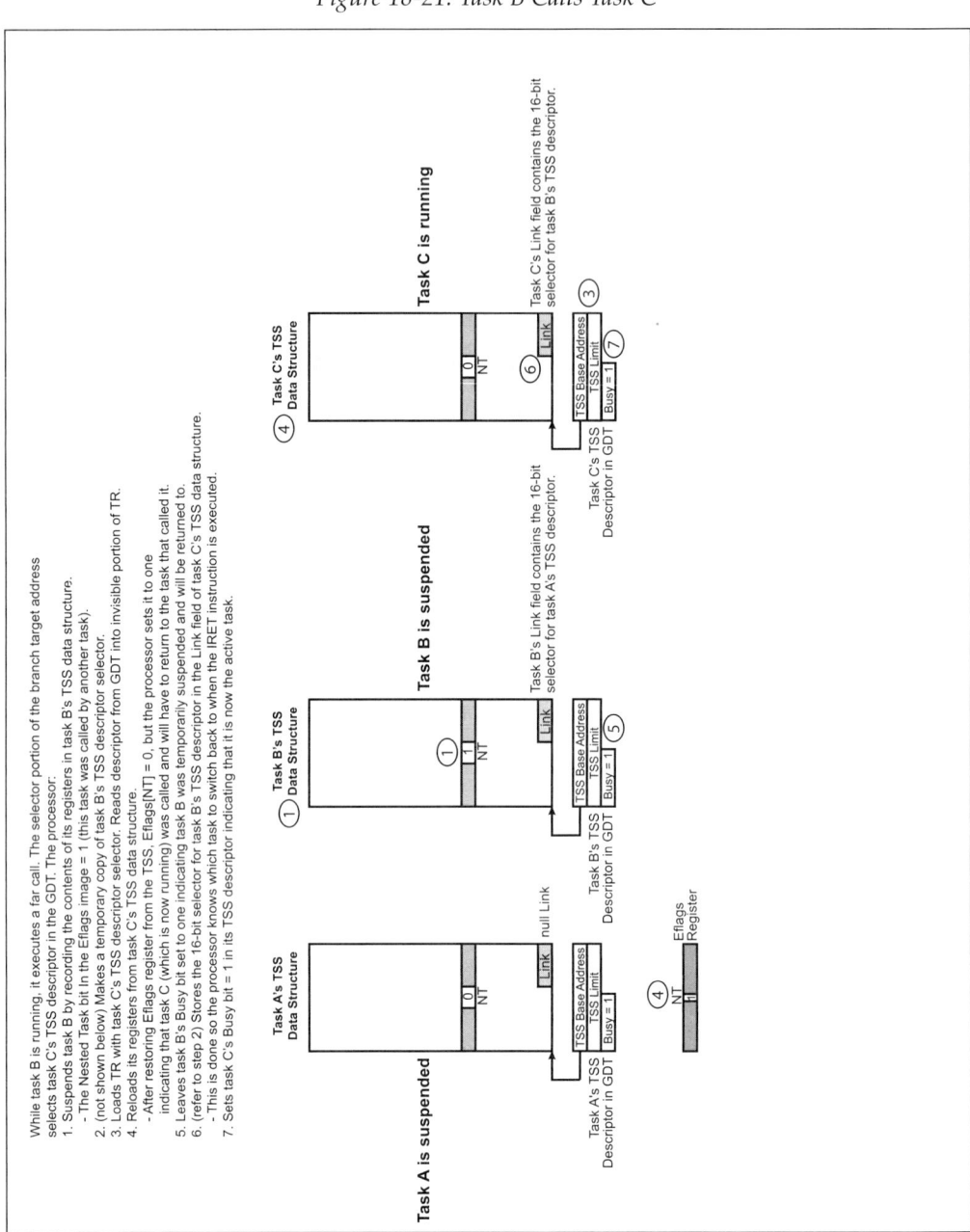

Figure 18-22: Task C Executes IRET

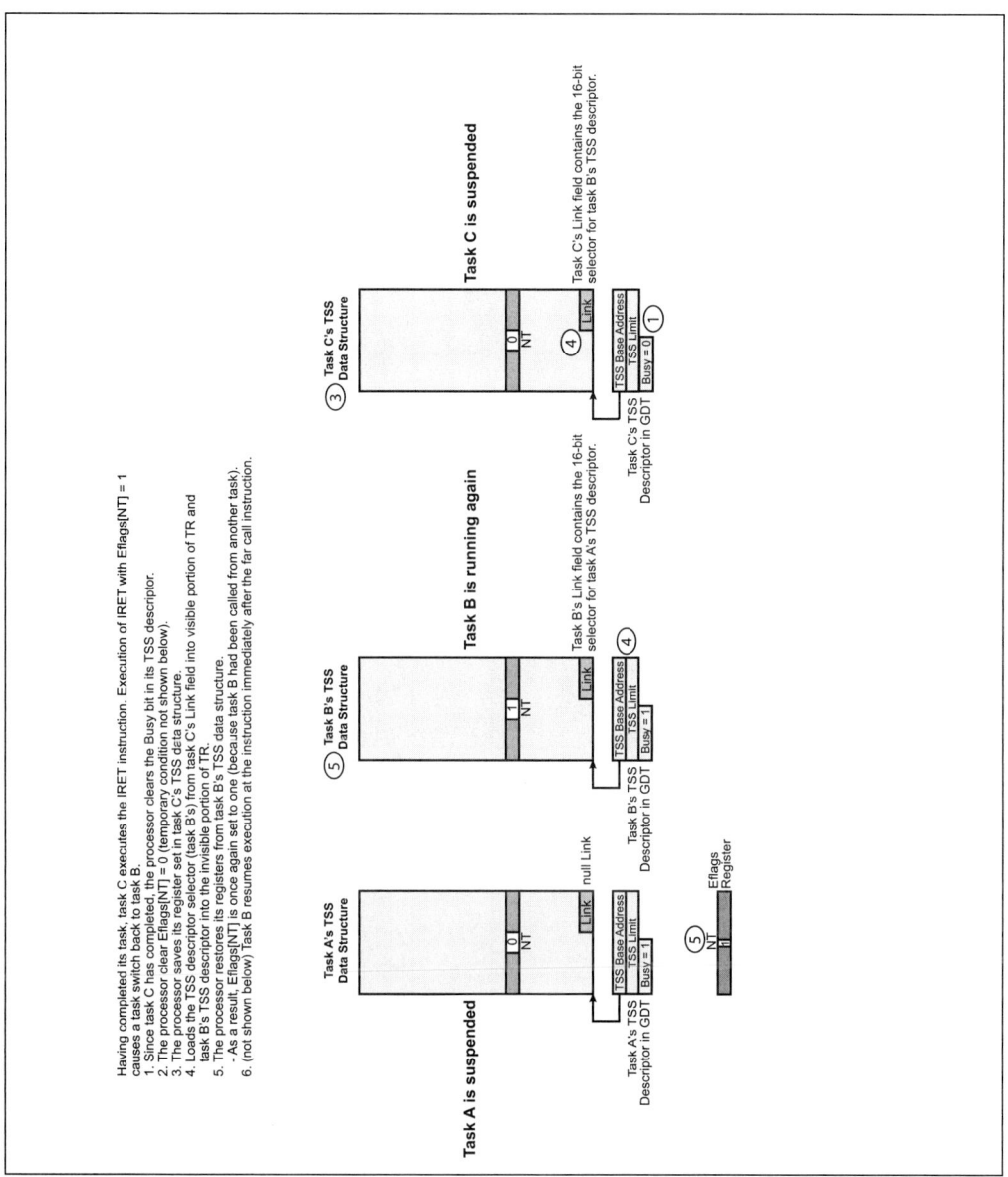

Figure 18-23: Task B Executes IRET

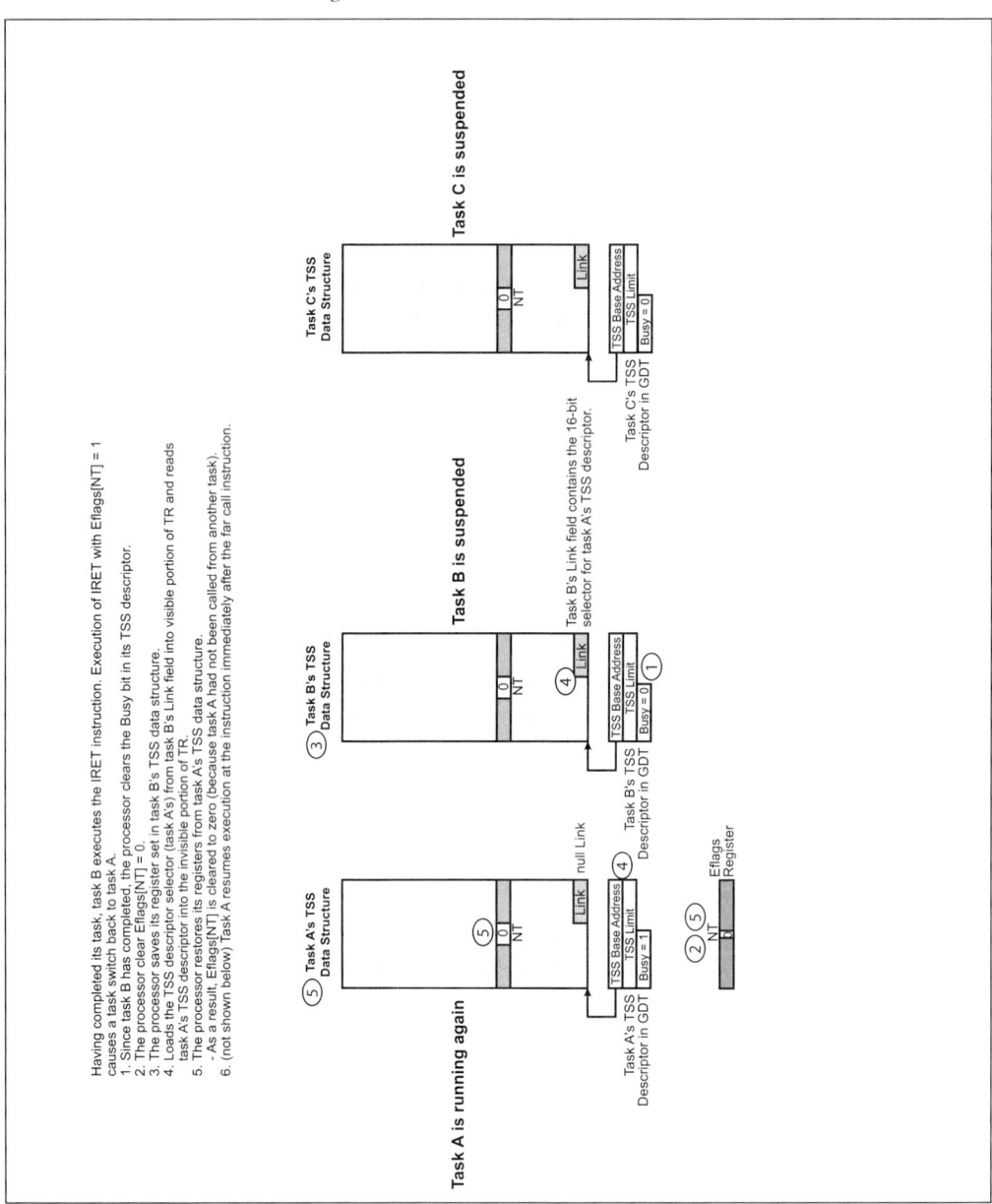

LTR Instruction and the Busy Bit

The Busy bit in a TSS descriptor is set to one under two circumstances:

Initially (immediately after power-up), the TR register contents is undefined. Before causing a switch to the first task after system initialization, the scheduler executes the **LTR instruction** (a privilege level 0 instruction) which causes the logical processor to:

- Load the scheduler's own TSS descriptor into the invisible part of the TR. When the first task switch is subsequently triggered, the logical processor suspends the scheduler task by making a snapshot of its registers in the scheduler's TSS data structure (pointed to by the base address stored in the invisible portion of the TR register).
- Set the Busy bit in the scheduler's TSS descriptor to mark the task as the currently-active task.

When Is Busy Cleared?

The logical processor automatically clears a task's Busy bit under three circumstances:

1. When a task is terminated by a far jump to another task (performing an unconditional jump to another task implies that the current task has completed and is therefore not busy anymore).
2. If the current task was invoked by an interrupt or an exception (the task is being used as an interrupt or exception handler), at the conclusion of the task the execution of the IRET instruction causes the task's Busy bit to be cleared and a switch back to the interrupted task.
3. When the timeslice timer expires it selects a Task Gate descriptor in the IDT. During the resulting switch back to the scheduler task, the logical processor clears the Busy bit of the task just suspended and sets the scheduler's Busy bit.

Critical Error: Switching to a Busy Task

The logical processor generates a GP exception if the target task for a switch is already busy. This is considered a serious error because busy implies that the target task saved a link back to another task in its TSS when it was entered earlier. The fact that its Busy bit is still set indicates it was originally entered via a Call, or an interrupt/exception and has not yet returned to the task that originally passed control to it. If the logical processor permits another task to enter it, the link will be overwritten with a new one, thereby rendering it incapable of find its way back to the task that originally switched to it.

Busy Toggle Is a Locked Operation

The logical processor automatically asserts its LOCK# output whenever it accesses the Busy bit in a TSS descriptor to read and update it (a read/modify/write—RMW—operation). In a multiprocessor system, this ensures that two (or more) logical processors will not access a TSS descriptor's Busy bit *simultaneously* and erroneously switch to the same task.

Linkage Modification

Refer to Figure 18-22 on page 675. Task A called task B which, in turn, called task C. When an IRET instruction is executed at the end of task C, a task switch back to task B will result (using the TSS selector stored in task C's Link field). Now assume that the programmer wants the IRET instruction at the end of task C to cause a task switch to A, rather than B. This is accomplished in the following manner:

1. Disable interrupts by executing a CLI instruction.
2. To remove task B from the return path, replace the contents of task C's Link field (which currently contains the GDT selector for task B's TSS descriptor) with the selector for task A's TSS descriptor.
3. Clear the Busy bit in task B's TSS descriptor.
4. Reenable interrupt recognition with an STI instruction.
5. Execute the IRET instruction.

Task Switching and Address Translation

One GDT to Serve Them All

The OS kernel creates the GDT in memory and programs the GDTR (GDT register) with its virtual base address (and size). The GDT entries define code and data segments common to multiple applications as well as special segments (i.e., descriptors such as TSS descriptors, Task Gates, Call Gates, etc.) used by the OS kernel.

It's important to note that the contents of the GDTR does not change when a task switch occurs. This means that all tasks use the same GDT to access the pool of common segments.

CR3 contains the base physical memory address of the address translation mechanism's top-level directory:

- When using the first-generation address translation mechanism: the Page Directory.
- When using the second-generation address translation mechanism (PAE Mode): the Page Directory Pointer Table (PDPT).
- When using the third-generation address translation mechanism (IA-32e Mode): the Page Map Level 4 Table (PML4T).

When a task switch occurs, CR3 is changed to point to the top-level translation table for the new task (by updating it from the CR3 field in the new task's TSS). It is important that the address translation tables for every task be set up to map accesses to the GDT's virtual address range to the same range of locations in physical memory. The goal of a shared GDT would be defeated if each task mapped the GDT's virtual address range to different physical memory ranges. They would be using different GDTs.

Each Task Can Have Different Virtual-to-Physical Mapping

Each time that a task switch occurs, the logical processor updates CR3 with the physical start memory address of the new task's top-level address translation table. In other words, by placing different addresses in the CR3 field of each TSS, each task can use a different set of tables to perform the virtual-to-physical address conversion.

TSS Mapping Must Remain the Same for All Tasks

The virtual-to-physical mapping for the range of addresses associated with all TSS segments must remain constant for all tasks. In other words, these virtual address ranges must be translated identically by all tasks. When a task switch occurs from task A to task B:

- The register set's current contents is saved in task A's TSS (using task A's translation tables to perform the translation of the TSS's virtual range to its physical range).
- The task switch then occurs and the register set is reloaded from task B's TSS segment.
- The Link field of task B's TSS is set to the GDT selector for task A's TSS descriptor.
- CR3 is loaded with the base address of task B's top-level translation table.
- When task B has completed and it's time to resume task A, the logical processor must restore its register set from task A's TSS. It uses task B's translation tables to perform the translation of task A's TSS virtual range to its physical range.

If task B's translation tables translate task A's TSS virtual range to a different physical range than task A's translation tables when it stored the register image, the logical processor would restore the wrong information to its register set.

Placement of a TSS Within a Page(s)

An unrecoverable error results if a GP exception or a Page Fault (due to the target physical page not being in memory) occurs after the logical processor has started to read the TSS for the new task when performing a task switch. To prevent this, the following rules must be adhered to:

- If possible, place the entire first 104 bytes of the TSS (i.e., the part accessed during a task switch) within a single page. If necessary, the TSS can straddle a page boundary (i.e., an address divisible by 4KB), but both pages must be present in memory (P = 1 in both of their Page Table Entries).
- The page or pages that contain the old and new TSSs must be present in memory and must be marked read/write (in the Page Table Entry).

Switch from More-Privileged Code to Lower

As covered earlier in "Jumping from a Higher-to-Lesser Privileged Program" on page 441, jumping from a more-privileged code segment (i.e., the OS kernel; specifically, the scheduler) to a lower-privilege one (a privilege level 3 application) is not allowed in the x86 architecture. However, since the hardware-based task switching mechanism doesn't use jumps to transfer control from one task to another, this is not an issue.

Software-Based Task Switching

A description of software-based task switching may be found in "Scheduler's Software-Based Task Switching Mechanism" on page 977.

19 *Protected Mode Interrupts and Exceptions*

The Previous Chapter

The previous chapter contrasted hardware- versus software-based tasking switching and provided a conceptual overview of task switching. It then provided a detailed description of the hardware-based task switching mechanism. The following topics were covered:

- Hardware- vs. Software-Based Task Switching
- A Condensed Conceptual Overview
- A More Comprehensive Overview
- Hardware-Based Task Switching
  — It's Slow
  — Why Didn't OSs Use It?
  — Why Wasn't It Improved?
  — Why Does It Still Exist?
  — Introduction to the Key Elements
  — The Trigger Events
  — The Descriptors
  — The Task Register
  — TSS Data Structure Format
  — Comprehensive Task Switch Description
  — Calling Another Task
  — Task Switching and Address Translation
  — Switch from Higher-Privilege Code to Lower

This Chapter

This chapter provides a detailed description of interrupt and exception handling in Protected Mode. This includes detailed coverage of:

- The IDT.
- Interrupt and Trap Gate operation.

- Task Gate operation.
- Interrupt and exception event categories.
- State save (and stack selection).
- The IRET instruction.
- Maskable hardware interrupts.
- Non-Maskable Interrupt (NMI).
- Machine Check exception.
- SM interrupt (SMI).
- Software interrupt instructions.
- Software exceptions.
- Interrupt/exception priority.

A detailed description of the Local and IO APICs can be found in "The Local and IO APICs" on page 1239.

The Next Chapter

The next chapter provides a detailed description of VM86 Mode (also known as Virtual 8086 Mode). This includes the following topics:

- Switching Between Protected Mode and VM86 Mode.
- Real Mode Application's World View.
- Sensitive Instructions.
- Handling Direct IO.
- Handling Exceptions.
- Hardware Interrupt Handling in VM86 Mode
- Software Interrupt Instruction Handling
- Halt Instruction in VM86 Mode
- Protected Mode Virtual Interrupt Feature
- Registers Accessible in Real/VM86 Mode
- Instructions Usable in Real/VM86 Mode

Handler vs. ISR

The program executed to service a hardware interrupt or a software exception is commonly referred to as either a handler or an Interrupt Service Routine (ISR). For consistency and brevity's sake, the author has elected to use the term *handler*.

Real Mode Interrupt/Exception Handling

Real Mode handling of hardware and software interrupts as well as software exceptions was covered earlier in "Real Mode Interrupt/Exception Handling" on page 316. The following figures provide an overview of Real Mode event handling:

- Refer to Figure 19-1 on page 683.
- Refer to Figure 19-2 on page 684.

The remainder of this chapter focuses on interrupt and exception handling in Protected Mode.

Figure 19-1: Real Mode Interrupt Handling

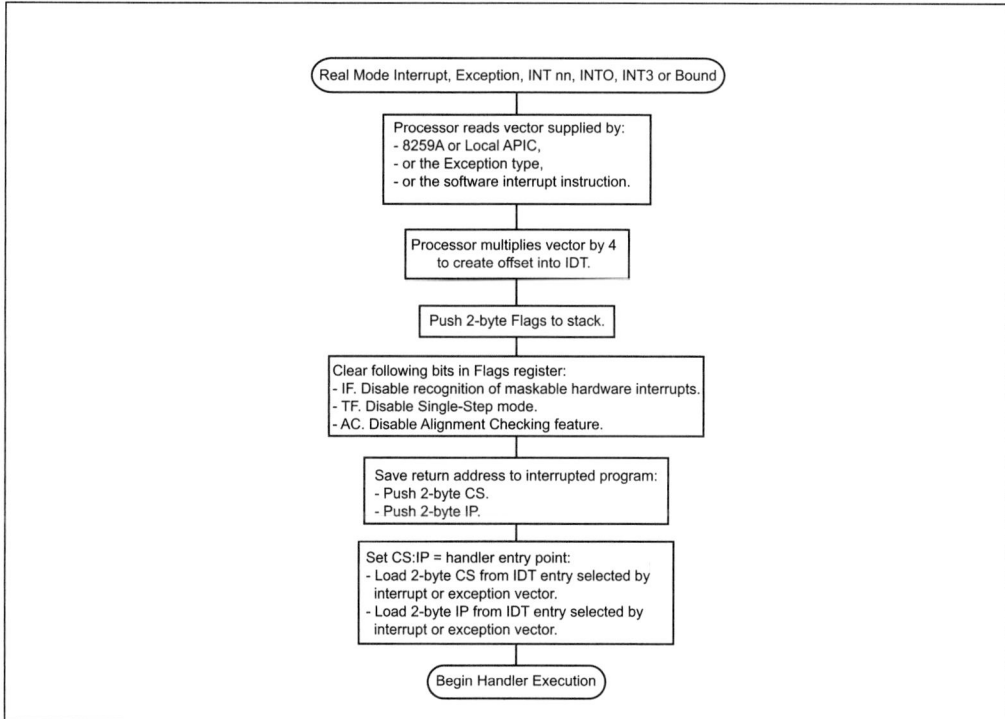

Figure 19-2: Return From Real Mode Handler To Interrupted Real Mode Application

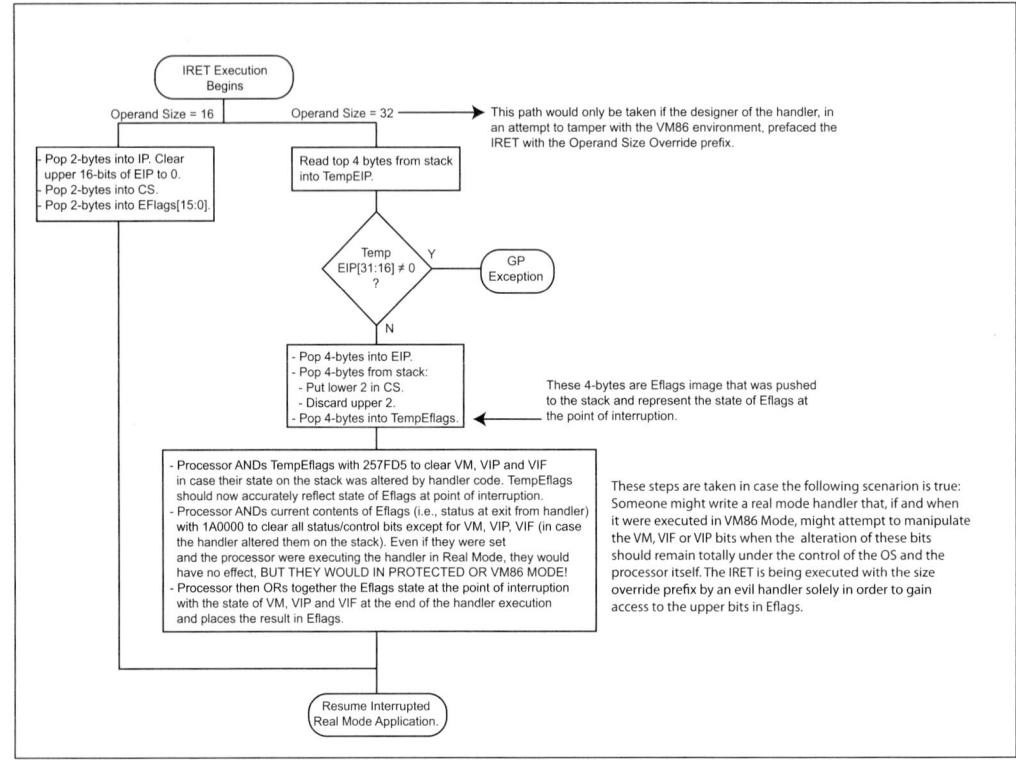

The IDT

General

In Real Mode, the OS permits the logical processor to execute a single program at a time (i.e., multitasking is not supported). The BIOS, OS services, interrupt and exception handlers exist solely to support the program that is executing. This being the case, there is no need to restrict access to these services when the program executes a software interrupt instruction. The Protected Mode environment, on the other hand, was specifically designed to support a multitasking OS and must therefore provide protection from code being called by an entity with insufficient privilege. If the currently-executing program attempts to access an interrupt or exception handler using a software interrupt instruction (INT nn, INTO, INT3, or BOUND), the logical processor must check to ensure that the program is permitted to access the target handler. If the program has insufficient privilege, a GP exception is generated.

In order to locate the appropriate handler to service an event, the logical processor must know the start address of the Interrupt Descriptor Table (IDT) in memory as well as the entry point of each event handler, and must also know the access rules associated with entry to each of the respective handlers. Each entry in the IDT must contain a descriptor defining:

- The start virtual address of the code segment containing the handler.
- The start address, or offset, of the respective handler's entry point within the target code segment.
- The DPL (Descriptor Privilege Level) that must be matched or exceeded by the currently-running program's CPL (Current Privilege Level) in order to successfully access the handler using one of the software interrupt instructions.

Protected Mode IDT and the IDTR

Figure 19-3 on page 687 illustrates the Protected Mode IDT. The OS creates the table in memory and places its virtual base address and size in the IDTR (IDT register) using the LIDT instruction:

- In a 16-bit, 286-compliant OS environment, LIDT loads a 24-bit base address and 16-bit size into the IDTR.
- In a 32-bit OS environment, LIDT loads a 32-bit base address and 16-bit size into the IDTR. Figure 19-4 on page 688 illustrates the IDTR in 32-bit mode.

LIDT can only be executed at privilege level zero when in Protected Mode, but can also be executed in Real Mode when initially setting up the Real or Protected Mode IDT. The current contents of the IDTR may also be saved in memory using the SIDT (Store IDT) instruction.

Though the IDT may contain up to 256d entries (one 8-byte descriptor for each type of interrupt and exception), the entire table need not be populated if the system doesn't use all of the entries. The limit field in the IDTR must reflect the actual length of the IDT in bytes (e.g., if the OS only uses entries 0 - 149, the table length should be set to 150 x 8). When an interrupt or exception occurs, the logical processor calculates the offset into the table by multiplying the interrupt vector (i.e., table entry number) by eight. The resulting offset is then added to the table's virtual base address (supplied by the IDTR) to form the start address of the selected 8-byte descriptor. If the calculated offset (+ 7 to cover the full range of eight locations that contain the selected 8-byte descriptor) exceeds the table's size (specified in the IDTR), the logical processor ceases to fetch instructions, executes a Shutdown transaction on the external interface, and stops (for more information, refer to the Shutdown description found in "Shutdown Mode" on page 755). If the address is within the table's limits, the logical processor reads the 8-byte descriptor from memory. Three types of descriptors may be found in the IDT:

- **Interrupt Gate Descriptor**. When an interrupt or exception selects an IDT entry containing an Interrupt Gate, Eflags[IF] is cleared after Eflags is pushed onto the stack. This prevents the interrupt/exception handler from being interrupted by a maskable hardware interrupt.
- **Trap Gate Descriptor**. When an interrupt or exception selects an IDT entry containing a Trap Gate, Eflags[IF] is not cleared after Eflags is pushed onto the stack. If Eflags[IF] was already set when the interrupt or exception was detected, the interrupt/exception handler will continue to recognize maskable interrupts.
- **Task Gate Descriptor**. When an interrupt or exception selects an IDT entry containing an Task Gate, a task switch occurs, the logical processor sets Eflags[NT] = 1, and the target task acts as the event handler. When the IRET is executed at the completion of the handler task and Eflags[NT] = 1, the logical processor switches back to and resumes the suspended (interrupted) task.

Figure 19-3: Protected Mode Interrupt Descriptor Table (IDT)

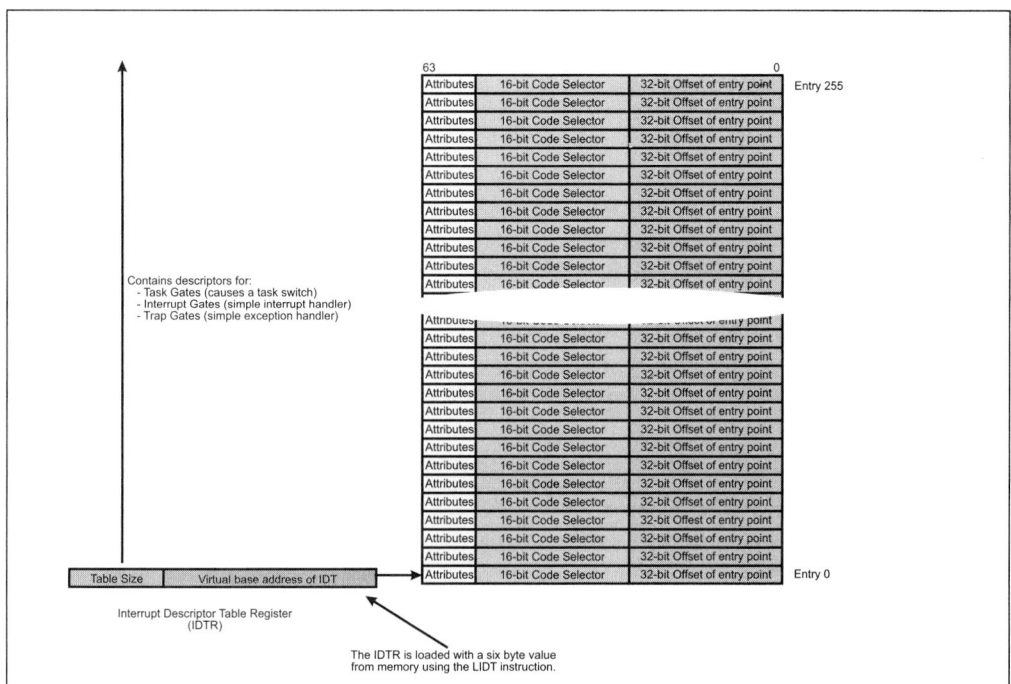

Figure 19-4: Interrupt Descriptor Table Register (IDTR)

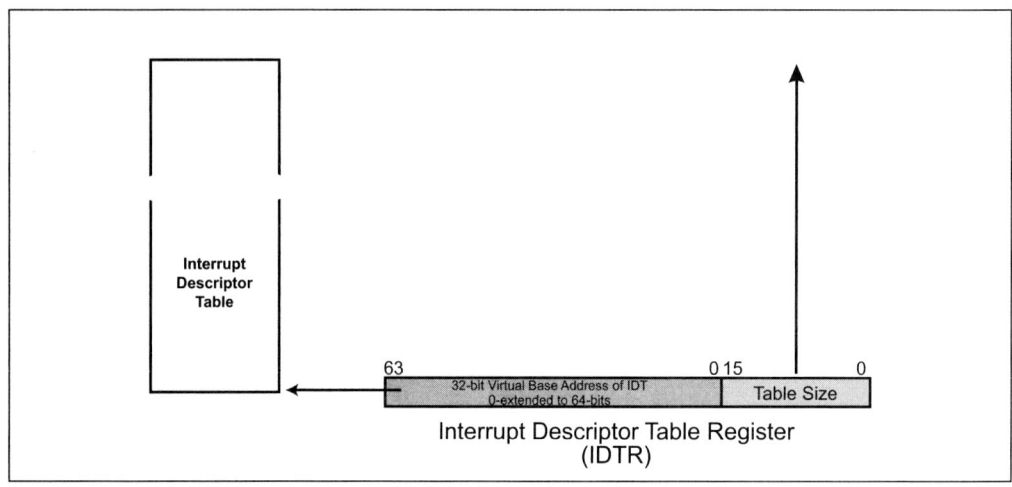

The Gates

Introduction

Refer to Table 19-1 on page 689. Although it is not a rule, an IDT entry selected by a maskable hardware interrupt typically contains an Interrupt Gate descriptor, while one selected by a software exception or a software interrupt instruction typically contains a Trap Gate descriptor. Alternatively, either could contain a Task Gate descriptor (if a separate task is used as the interrupt or exception handler).

The only difference between the Interrupt and Trap gates is this: after pushing the CS:EIP register pair and the Eflags register onto the stack, an Interrupt Gate causes the logical processor to disable recognition of additional maskable hardware interrupts (by setting Eflags[IF] = 0), while the Trap Gate doesn't. The following sections provide a detailed description of the IDT gate types.

Table 19-1: Introduction to the IDT Gate Types

IDT Gate Type	Processor Actions
Interrupt Gate	Figure 19-5 on page 693 illustrates a 32-bit Interrupt Gate. In a 16-bit Interrupt Gate, the X bit = 0 and the fourth byte of the offset is reserved. Hardware interrupts typically select an IDT entry containing an Interrupt Gate descriptor. In response, the logical processor: 1. Pushes the contents of the CS:EIP register pair and the Eflags register onto the stack. Note that CS:EIP points to the next instruction in the interrupted program. 2. If it is set, clears Eflags[IF] to mask out recognition of external hardware interrupts while the handler executes. 3. Places the new CS:EIP value obtained from the gate into the CS:EIP register pair. 4. Executes the body of the event handler. 5. The last instruction in the handler, an IRET, causes the logical processor to pop the old values back into the CS:EIP register pair and the Eflags register. If Eflags[IF] was set at the time of event detection, this re-enables recognition of maskable hardware interrupts.

Table 19-1: Introduction to the IDT Gate Types (Continued)

IDT Gate Type	Processor Actions
Trap Gate	Figure 19-6 on page 694 pictures a 32-bit Trap Gate. In a 16-bit Trap Gate, the X bit = 0 and the fourth byte of the offset is reserved. A software exception or the execution of a software interrupt instruction typically selects an IDT entry containing an Trap Gate descriptor. In response, the logical processor: 1. Pushes the contents of the CS:EIP register pair and the Eflags register onto the stack. – **Note**: It does *not* clear Eflags[IF] to disable recognition of external hardware interrupts. This is what differentiates a Trap Gate from an Interrupt Gate. – **Note**: Depending on the type of event that caused the interruption, the return address pushed onto the stack is either the address of the instruction that caused a software exception or the address of the next instruction. 2. Places the new CS:EIP value obtained from the gate into the CS:EIP register pair. 3. Executes the body of the event handler. 4. The last instruction in the handler, an IRET, causes the logical processor to pop the old values back into the CS:EIP register pair and the Eflags register.

Table 19-1: Introduction to the IDT Gate Types (Continued)

IDT Gate Type	Processor Actions
Task Gate	See Figure 19-9 on page 697. Any type of event (hardware or software) might select an IDT entry containing a Task Gate descriptor. The gate contains a 16-bit selector that identifies a TSS descriptor in the GDT. This triggers the logical processor to suspend the current task and switch to the task associated with the target TSS descriptor. In response, the logical processor: 1. Suspends the interrupted task by recording the contents of many of the logical processor's registers in the TSS associated with the interrupted task. 2. Copies the TSS descriptor selector in the TR (which identifies the TSS associated with the interrupted task) to the Link field in the TSS associated with the task that will act as the event handler. 3. Reloads its register set from the TSS associated with the handler. 4. Sets the Nested Task bit (Eflags[NT]) to indicate that, at the conclusion of the task acting as the handler, the logical processor should switch back to the interrupted task. 5. Loads the TR with the TSS descriptor selector and the TSS descriptor associated with the task that will act as the event handler. 6. Executes the task to handle the event. 7. When executed with Eflags[NT] = 1, the last instruction in the handler (the IRET) causes the logical processor to clear Eflags[NT], suspend the current task (i.e., the handler), and switch back to the interrupted task (using the TSS descriptor selector stored in the Link field of the handler task's TSS). Note: Since modern OSs do not use the automatic task switch mechanism, Trap Gates are not found in their IDTs.

Interrupt Gate

As mentioned earlier, selection of an IDT entry containing an Interrupt Gate causes the logical processor to disable recognition of maskable hardware interrupts before jumping to the handler pointed to by the gate. Figure 19-5 on page 693 illustrates the format of an 32-bit Interrupt Gate Descriptor and Table 19-2 on page 692 describes each field.

Table 19-2: Elements of Interrupt Gate Descriptor

Element	Description
Offset	The 32-bit **offset** of the handler's entry point within the target code segment.
Code segment selector	The 16-bit **segment selector** identifies the code segment descriptor (in the GDT or LDT) that describes the code segment containing the handler.
X bit	The **X bit** defines this as either a 16- (X = 0) or 32-bit (X = 1) Interrupt Gate descriptor.
S bit	The **System bit** must be set to zero indicating that this descriptor defines a special system segment (rather than a code or data segment).
Byte 5[2:0]	**Descriptor Type** field. In combination with S = 0, a Type value of 110b indicates that this is an Interrupt Gate descriptor. The X bit further defines it as either a 16- or 32-bit Interrupt Gate descriptor. The format shown in Figure 19-5 on page 693 is that of a 32-bit descriptor. Byte 7 is reserved in a 16-bit (i.e., a 286) Interrupt Gate descriptor.
DPL	Descriptor Privilege Level: • Not checked if the gate is selected by a maskable hardware interrupt or the detection of a software exception condition. • If the gate is selected due to the execution of a software interrupt instruction, the CPL of the calling program must be at least as privileged as the gate's DPL. If it isn't, a GP exception is generated.
P bit	The **Segment Present bit** must be set to one or a Segment Not Present exception is generated.

Figure 19-5: 32-bit Interrupt Gate Descriptor Format

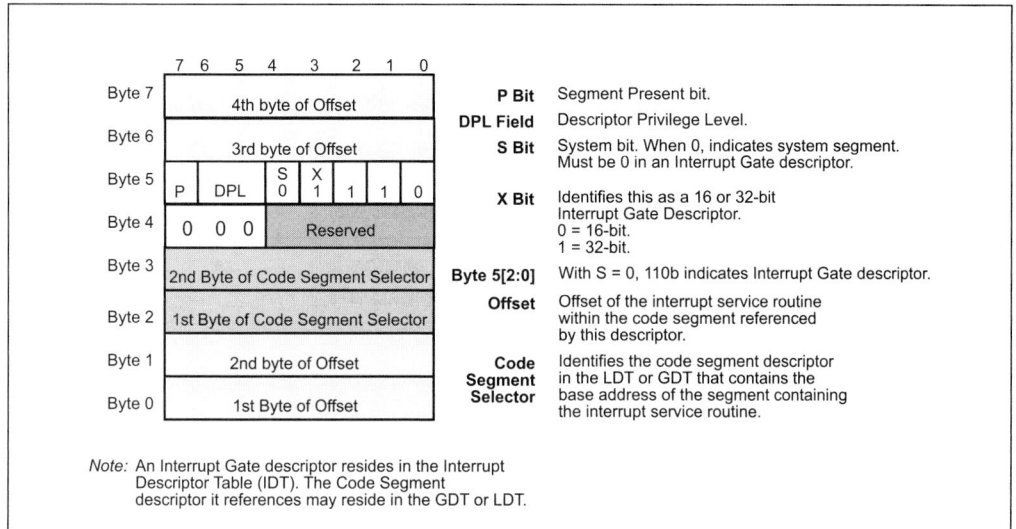

Trap Gate

The difference between an Interrupt Gate and a Trap Gate is the treatment of Eflags[IF]:

- When an interrupt or exception selects an IDT entry containing an Interrupt Gate, Eflags[IF] is cleared after Eflags is pushed onto the stack. This prevents the interrupt/exception handler from being interrupted by a subsequent maskable interrupt.
- When an interrupt or exception selects an IDT entry containing a Trap Gate, Eflags[IF] is *not* cleared after Eflags is pushed onto the stack. If Eflags[IF] was already set when the interrupt or exception was detected, the logical processor will continue to recognize maskable interrupts.

The format of a 32-bit Trap Gate is illustrated in Figure 19-6 on page 694.

Figure 19-6: 32-bit Trap Gate Format

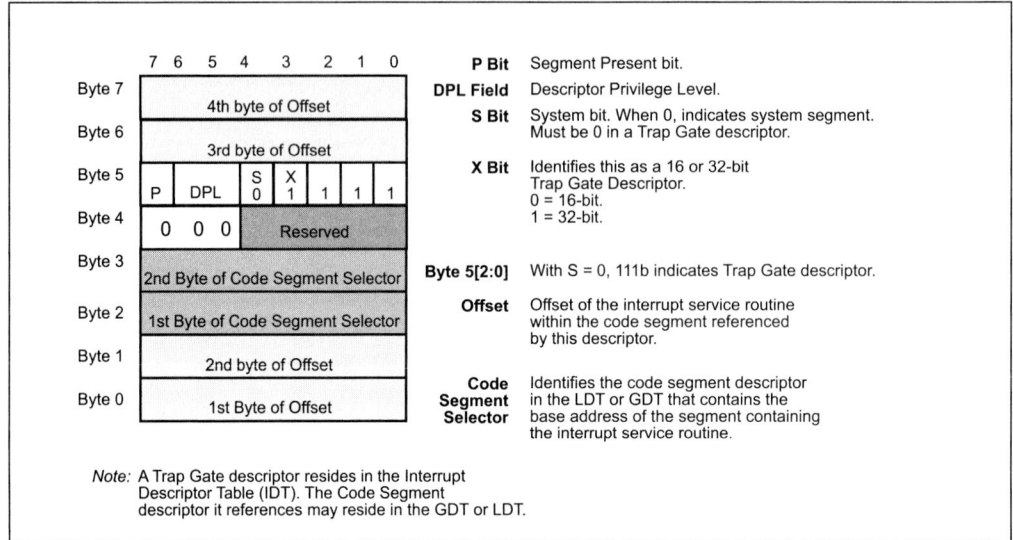

Actions Taken When Interrupt or Trap Gate Selected

When an IDT entry containing an Interrupt or Trap Gate is selected by a maskable hardware interrupt, a software exception, or the attempted execution of a software interrupt instruction, the sequence of events taken are described in Figure 19-7 on page 695 and Figure 19-8 on page 696. It should be noted that the logical processor performs a number of additional validity checks in addition to those shown in the flowchart.

Figure 19-7: Interrupt/Trap Gate Operation (1-of-2)

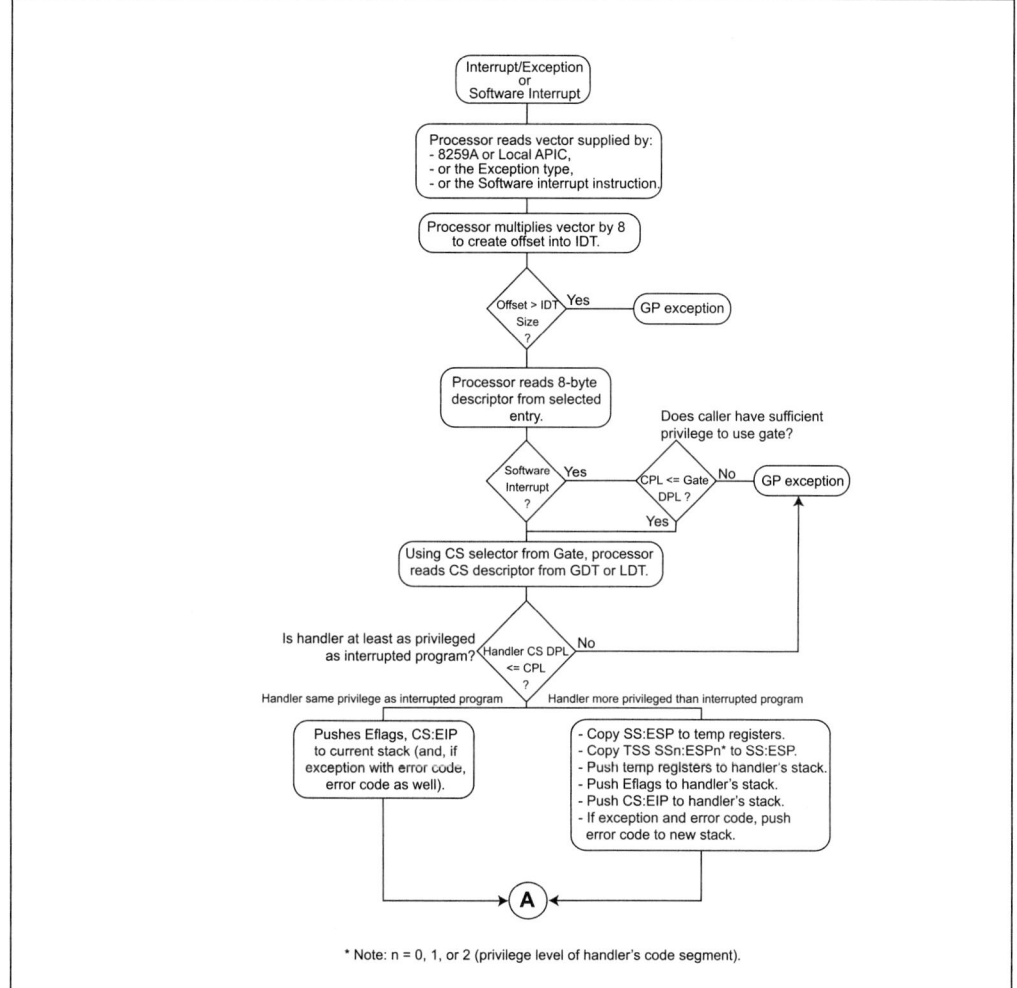

Figure 19-8: Interrupt/Trap Gate Operation (2-of-2)

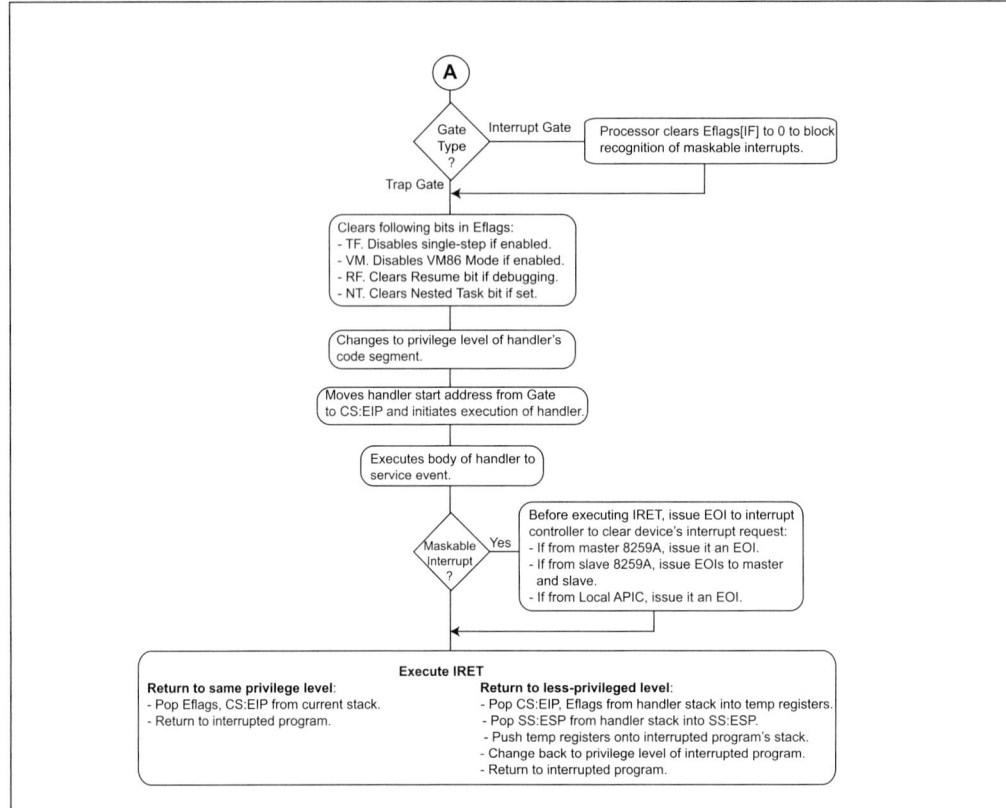

Actions Taken When Task Gate Selected

At the risk of becoming tedious (probably too late for that), the author must once again point out the x86 hardware-based task switching mechanism is not used by any mainstream OSs.

The OS programmer may wish to use a separate task (rather than a handler within the same task) to service an interrupt or exception. This is accomplished by creating a Task Gate in the IDT entry corresponding to the interrupt or exception. The Task Gate format is illustrated in Figure 19-9 on page 697.

When the interrupt or exception event occurs (or a software interrupt instruction is executed), the logical processor indexes into the IDT and reads the selected descriptor. If it is a Task Gate descriptor, the logical processor executes a task switch (refer to "Comprehensive Task Switch Description" on page 665 and "Calling Another Task" on page 670 for a full description of the switch and the return to the interrupted task).

When an interrupt, exception or a software interrupt instruction causes a task switch, the logical processor saves its context (i.e., the contents of many of its registers) in the interrupted task's TSS and then switches to the interrupt (or exception) handler task by reloading the register set from the handler task's TSS. The Eflags[NT] (Nested Task) bit is set to one. In performing the task switch, the logical processor also stores the 16-bit selector for the interrupted task's TSS in the Link entry of the handler's TSS. At the conclusion of handler execution, the last instruction is an IRET. When the IRET is executed with Eflags[NT] = 1, the logical processor reloads the TR (Task Register) with the TSS selector (obtained from the handler's TSS Link field) for the task that was interrupted. This causes a task switch back to the interrupted task and the reloading of Eflags with its original value clears the NT bit.

Figure 19-9: Task Gate Format

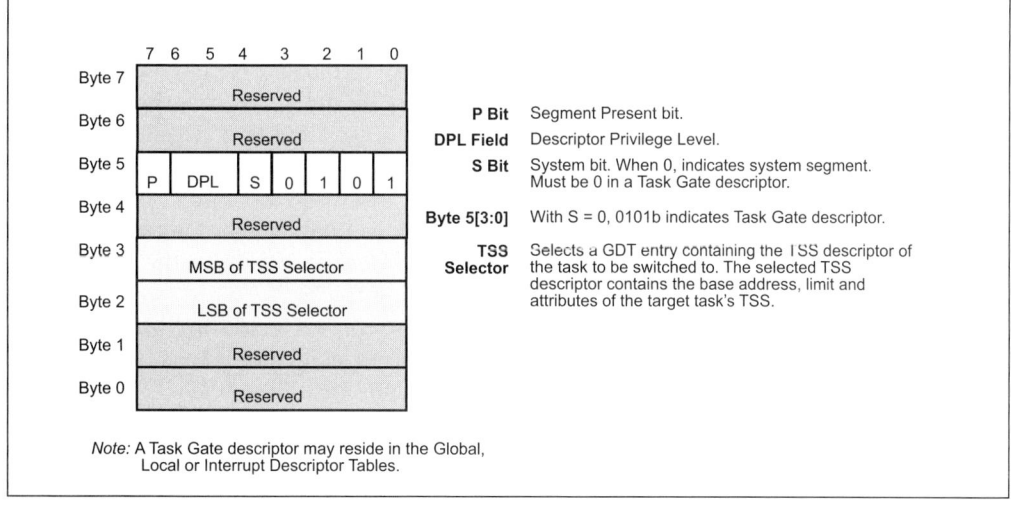

Note: A Task Gate descriptor may reside in the Global, Local or Interrupt Descriptor Tables.

Interrupt/Exception Event Categories

Six types of events can cause the currently executing program to be interrupted:

1. **Maskable hardware interrupts** (see "Maskable Hardware Interrupts" on page 713). An interrupt request from a hardware device is recognized if recognition of external interrupts is enabled (Eflags[IF] = 1). Referred to as a

maskable interrupt request, it is delivered to the logical processor by one of the following:

— The logical processor's Local APIC. This could be due to any of the following events:

- Assertion of the processor's LINT0 input (Local Interrupt pin 0).
- Assertion of the processor's LINT1 input (Local Interrupt pin 1).
- A timeout of the Local APIC's programmer timer.
- A Performance Counter overflow condition.
- A thermal interrupt originating on the processor die.
- Receipt of an interrupt originated by a device adapter and delivered to the IO APIC which, in turn, formulated and transmitted an IPI (Inter-Processor Interrupt) message packet to the logical processor's Local APIC over the processor's external interface.
- Receipt of an IPI (Inter-Processor Interrupt) message packet originated by the Local APIC associated with another logical processor and forwarded over the processor's external interface.

— If the logical processor's Local APIC is disabled, maskable interrupt requests from external hardware devices are first delivered to an external interrupt controller (e.g., an 8259A) which then, in turn, asserts the processor's INTR input.

2. **NMI** [see "Non-Maskable Interrupt (NMI) Requests" on page 723]. Receipt of an NMI from the chipset. An NMI can be delivered in either of the following ways:

— If the logical processor's Local APIC is disabled, the chipset asserts the processor's NMI input.

— If the logical processor's Local APIC is enabled, the chipset sends an NMI IPI (Inter-Processor Interrupt) message packet to the logical processor over the processor's external interface.

3. **SMI** (System Management Interrupt). The chipset sends an SMI to a logical processor to inform software of a platform-specific event (e.g., a thermal or power management event). It can be sent in one of two ways:

— If the Local APIC is enabled, the SMI is delivered to the logical processor over the processor's external interface in an IPI (Inter-Processor Interrupt) message packet.

— If the logical processor's Local APIC is disabled, the SMI is delivered to the processor by asserting its SMI# input.

A complete description of SMM (System Management Mode) can be found in "System Management Mode (SMM)" on page 1167.

4. **Software interrupt** (see "Software Interrupts" on page 725**)**. Execution of a software interrupt instruction (BOUND, INT, INTO, or INT3 instruction).

5. **Software exception** (see "Software Exceptions" on page 728). Detection of a software exception while attempting to execute an instruction.

6. **Machine Check hardware exception** (see "Machine Check Exception" on page 724). Although categorized as an exception, the Machine Check exception is not caused by a software condition. Rather, it is caused by:
   — Hardware errors internal to the logical processor (e.g., a Microcode ROM checksum error, or a uncorrectable ECC error when accessing a processor cache).
   — Or problems related to transfers over the processor's external interface.

General Event Handling

This section contains a series of flowcharts that detail the automatic actions taken by the logical processor when any of the following event types are detected while the logical processor is in Protected Mode:

- **Maskable hardware interrupt** from an external hardware device. Upon detecting a maskable hardware interrupt, the logical processor issues a request for the interrupt vector (i.e., the IDT entry) to the interrupt controller (either the legacy 8259a or the logical processor's Local APIC).
- **Software exception** resulting from an error detected upon the attempted execution of an instruction. Each type of software exception condition is associated with a specific IDT entry.
- **Software interrupt** instruction. This would include the INT *nn*, INTO, INT3 and BOUND instructions.
  — The INT instruction's *nn* operand selects the respective IDT entry.
  — IDT entry 04h is associated with the Interrupt on Overflow (INTO) instruction.
  — IDT entry 03h is associated with the INT3 (Breakpoint) instruction.
  — IDT entry 05h is associated with the BOUND instruction.
- **NMI**. The chipset generated an NMI to a logical processor after detecting a catastrophic hardware error external to the processor. Upon detecting an NMI, the logical processor automatically selects IDT entry 2 (the entry dedicated to the NMI interrupt).
- **Machine Check exception**. The logical processor detected a serious hardware error either internally or on its external interface. Upon detecting a Machine Check exception, the logical processor automatically selects IDT entry 18 (the entry dedicated to the Machine Check exception).

It should be noted that, in the interest of flowchart simplicity, the author has included many but not all of the validity checks performed by the logical processor.

When an event is detected, the logical processor initiates the actions shown in Figure 19-10 on page 700. Note that there are four possible (shaded) exit paths from this flowchart:

- If the event selects an IDT entry containing a Task Gate, the flow continues in Figure 19-14 on page 704.
- If the interrupted program is a VM86 program (i.e., a DOS task), the flow continues in Figure 19-13 on page 703.
- If the interrupted program is a Protected Mode program and the handler is more privileged than the interrupted program, the flow continues in Figure 19-12 on page 702.
- If the interrupted program is a Protected Mode program and the handler has the same privilege level as the interrupted program, the flow continues in Figure 19-11 on page 701.

Figure 19-10: Event Detected

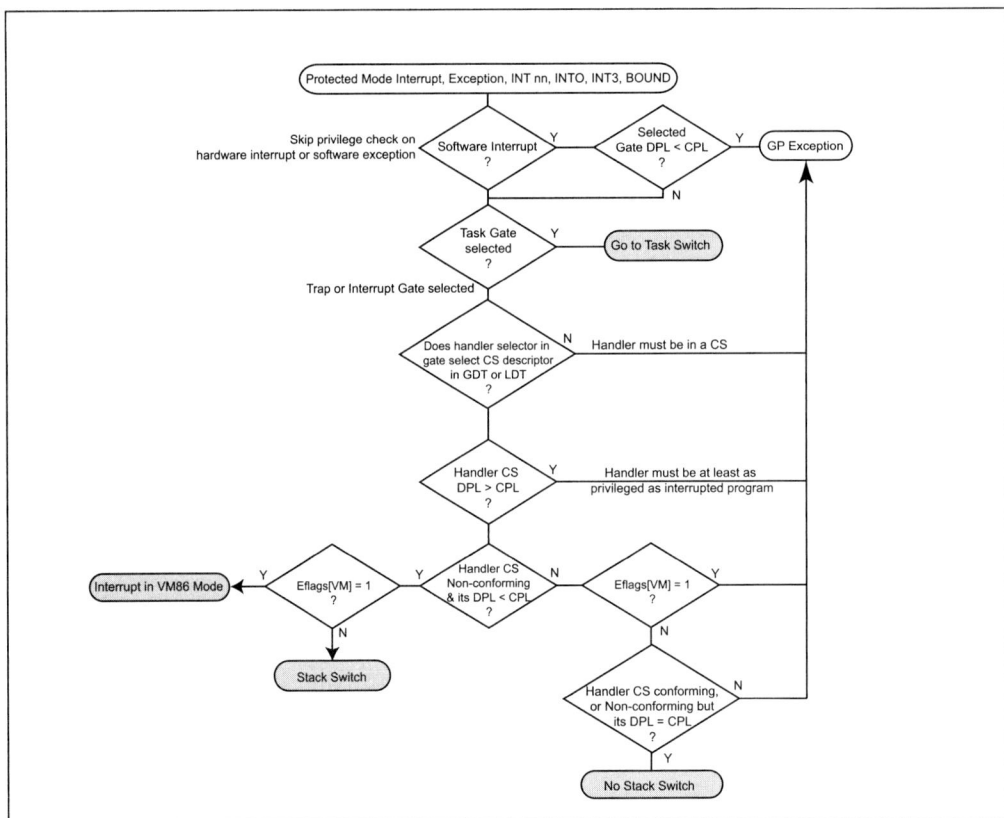

Figure 19-11: Interrupted Program and Handler at Same Privilege Level

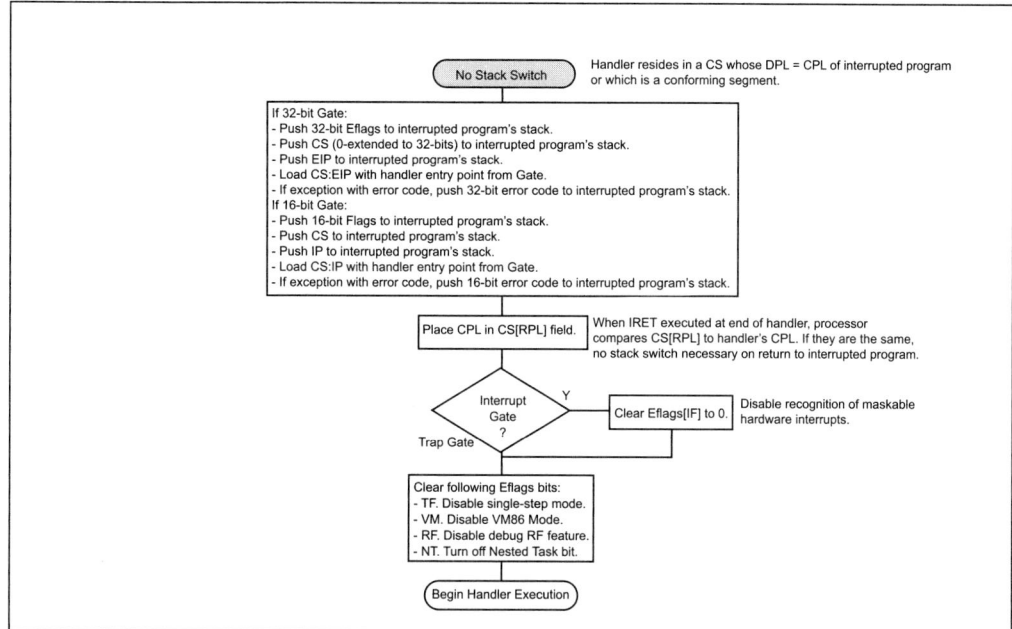

Figure 19-12: Handler More-Privileged than Interrupted Program

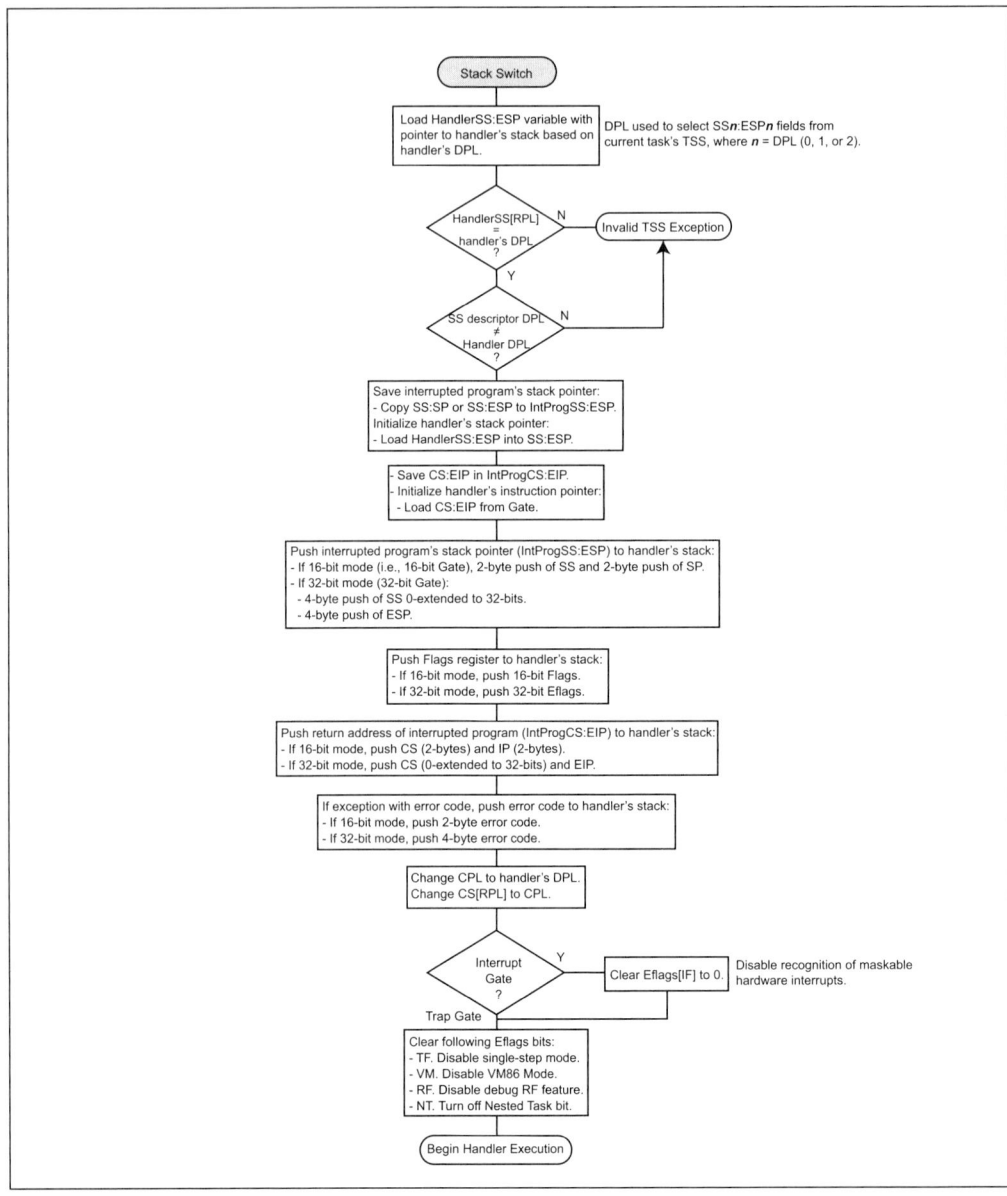

Figure 19-13: VM86 Mode Program Interrupted

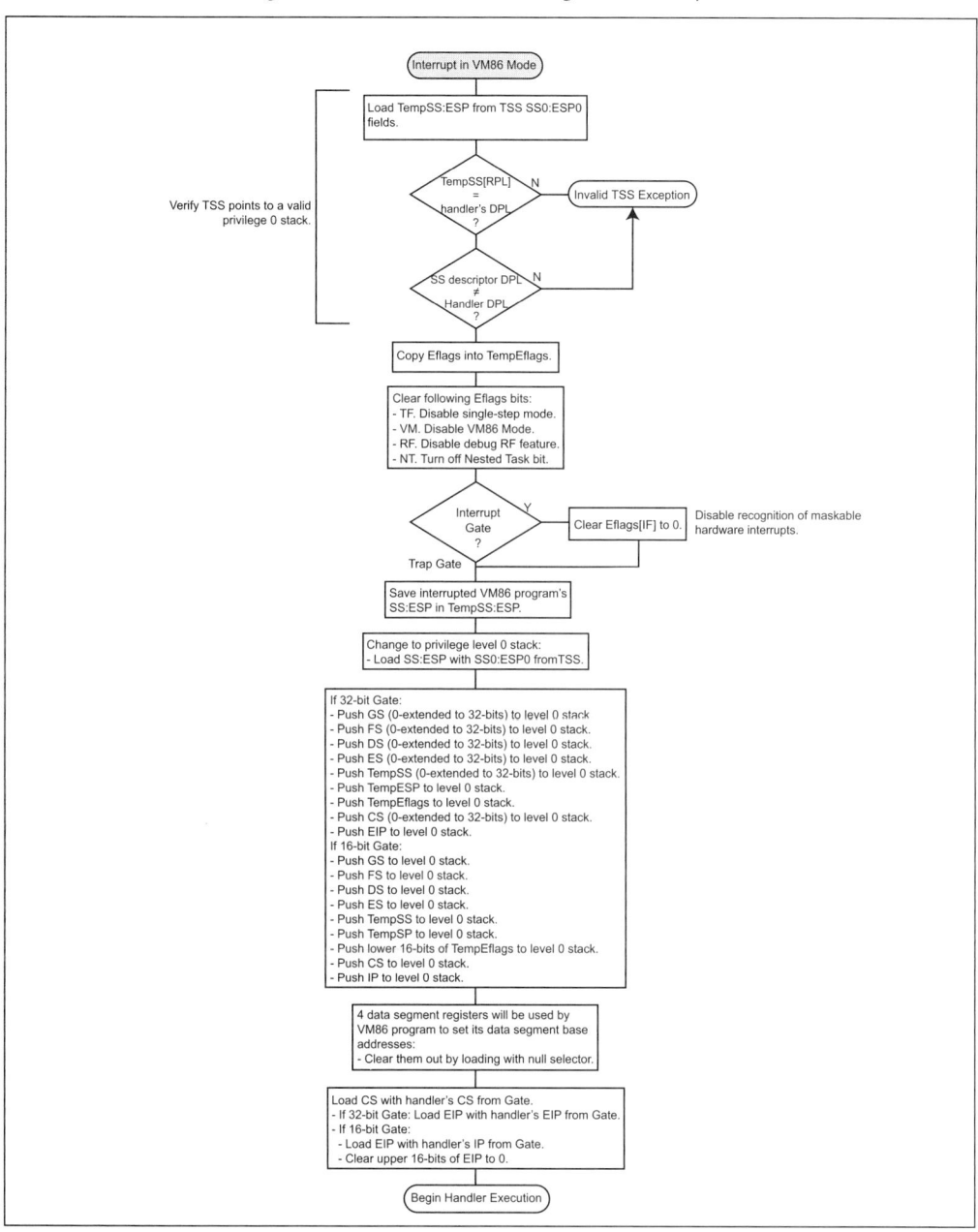

Figure 19-14: Interrupt Causes Task Switch

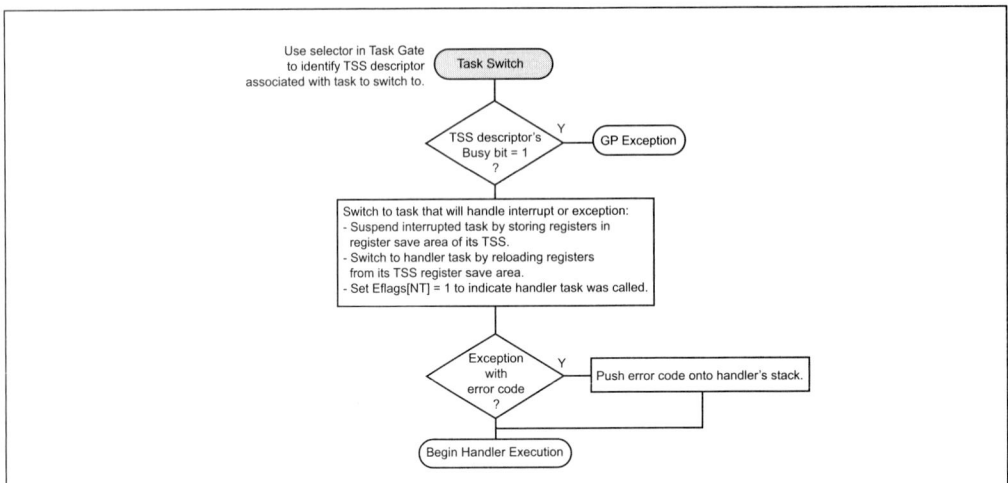

State Saved on Stack (but which stack?)

Before jumping to the interrupt/exception handler, the logical processor saves state information on the stack. At a minimum, this state information consists of the return address (in the form of the current CS:EIP contents) and the logical processor's basic operational status (represented by the current contents of the Eflags register).

Whether or not additional items are automatically saved on the stack depends on whether the handler resides at the same or a more privileged level than the interrupted program and, if it is an exception event, whether or not the exception pushes an error code (see "Exception Error Codes" on page 735) onto the stack. The four possible cases are listed in Table 19-3 on page 705. Please note that the table assumes that the selected IDT entry contains a 32- rather than a 16-bit Interrupt or Trap Gate.

Table 19-3: Interrupt/Exception Handler State Save Cases

Case	Description
- Handler at same privilege level. - No error code.	The only items pushed onto the stack are the Eflags, CS and EIP register contents (see Figure 19-15 on page 706). In this example, the event does not supply an error code to the handler. The target handler resides at the same privilege level as the interrupted program, so there is no need to switch to a fresh stack for the handler's use (i.e., the stack associated with the interrupted program is used).
- Handler at same privilege level. - Exception with error code.	The items pushed onto the stack are the Eflags, CS and EIP register contents (see Figure 19-16 on page 707). In addition, a 32-bit, exception-specific error code is pushed onto the stack. The target handler resides at the same privilege level as the interrupted program, so there is no need to switch to a fresh stack for the handler's use (i.e., the stack associated with the interrupted program is used).
- Handler at higher privilege level. - No error code.	The items pushed onto the stack are SS, ESP, Eflags, CS and EIP. The handler resides at a more-privileged level than the interrupted program (DPL < CPL), so the logical processor uses the stack that was preallocated for the handler's privilege level (rather than the interrupted program's stack) to save: • the pointer to the interrupted program's stack (SS:ESP), • Eflags, • and CS and EIP. The pointer to the new stack is obtained from the current TSS (see Figure 19-19 on page 708). Depending on the privilege level of the handler (0, 1, or 2), it consists of either SS0:ESP0, SS1:ESP1, or SS2:ESP2. The stack switch process is described in Figure 19-12 on page 702. Figure 19-17 on page 707 illustrates the contents of the handler's stack upon entry to the handler.

Table 19-3: Interrupt/Exception Handler State Save Cases (Continued)

Case	Description
- Handler at higher privilege level. - Exception with error code.	The items pushed onto the stack are SS, ESP, Eflags, CS and EIP. In addition, a 32-bit, exception-specific error code is pushed onto the stack. The exception handler resides at a higher privilege level than the interrupted program (DPL < CPL), so the logical processor must use the stack for the handler's privilege level (rather than the interrupted program's stack) to save: • the pointer to the interrupted program's stack (SS:ESP), • Eflags, • CS:EIP, • and the error code. The pointer to the new stack is obtained from the current TSS (see Figure 19-19 on page 708). Depending on the privilege level of the handler, it consists of either SS0:ESP0, SS1:ESP1, or SS2:ESP2. The stack switch process is described in Figure 19-12 on page 702. Figure 19-18 on page 707 illustrates the contents of the handler's stack upon entry to the handler.

Figure 19-15: Same Privilege Level and No Error Code

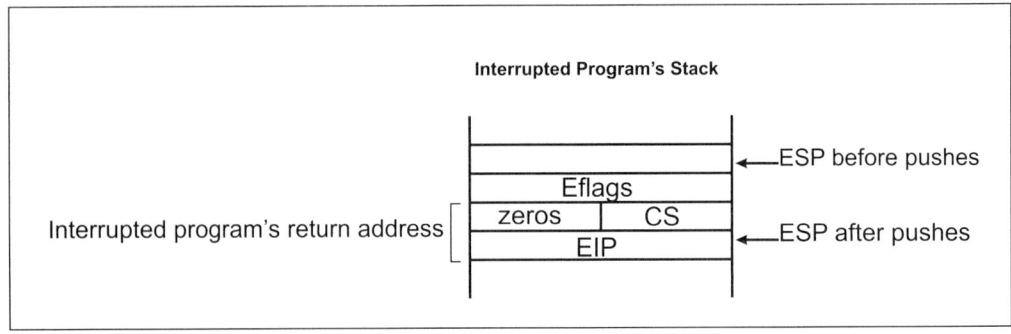

Figure 19-16: Same Privilege Level with Error Code

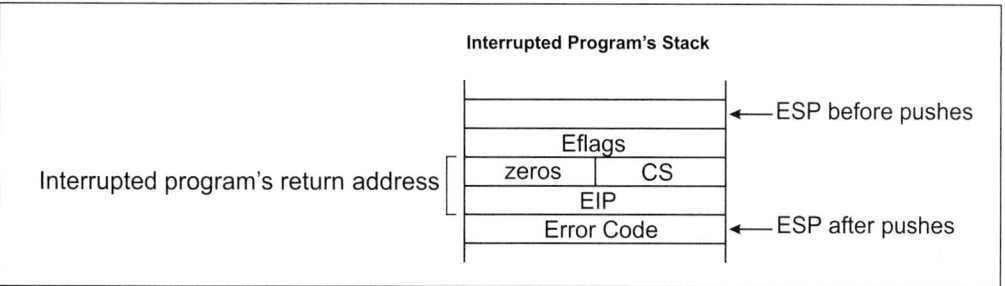

Figure 19-17: Privilege Level Switch without Error Code

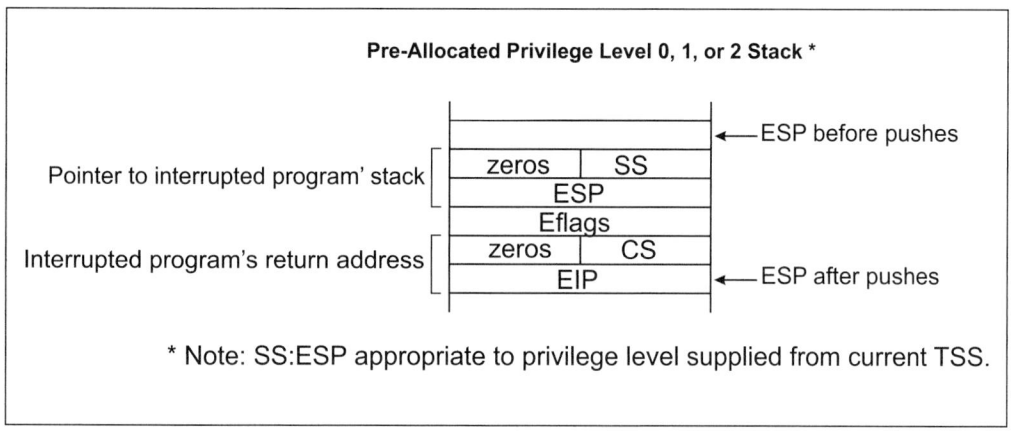

Figure 19-18: Privilege Level Switch with Error Code

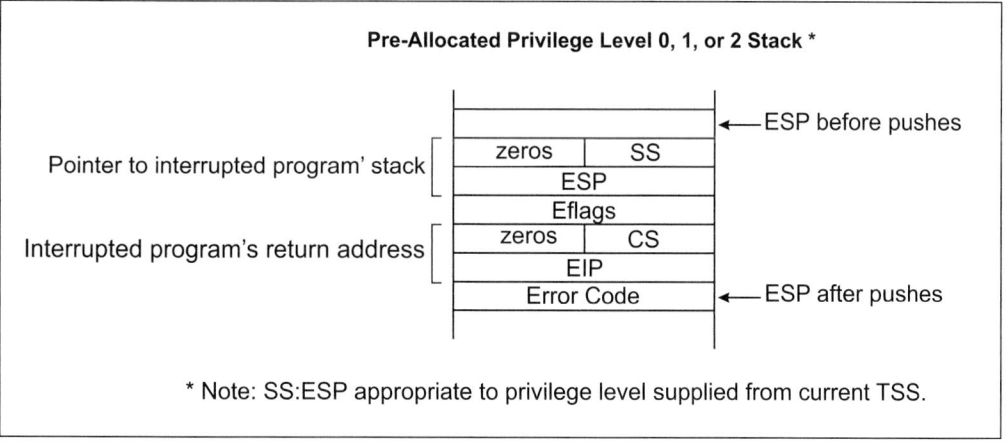

Figure 19-19: 32-bit Task State Segment (TSS) Format

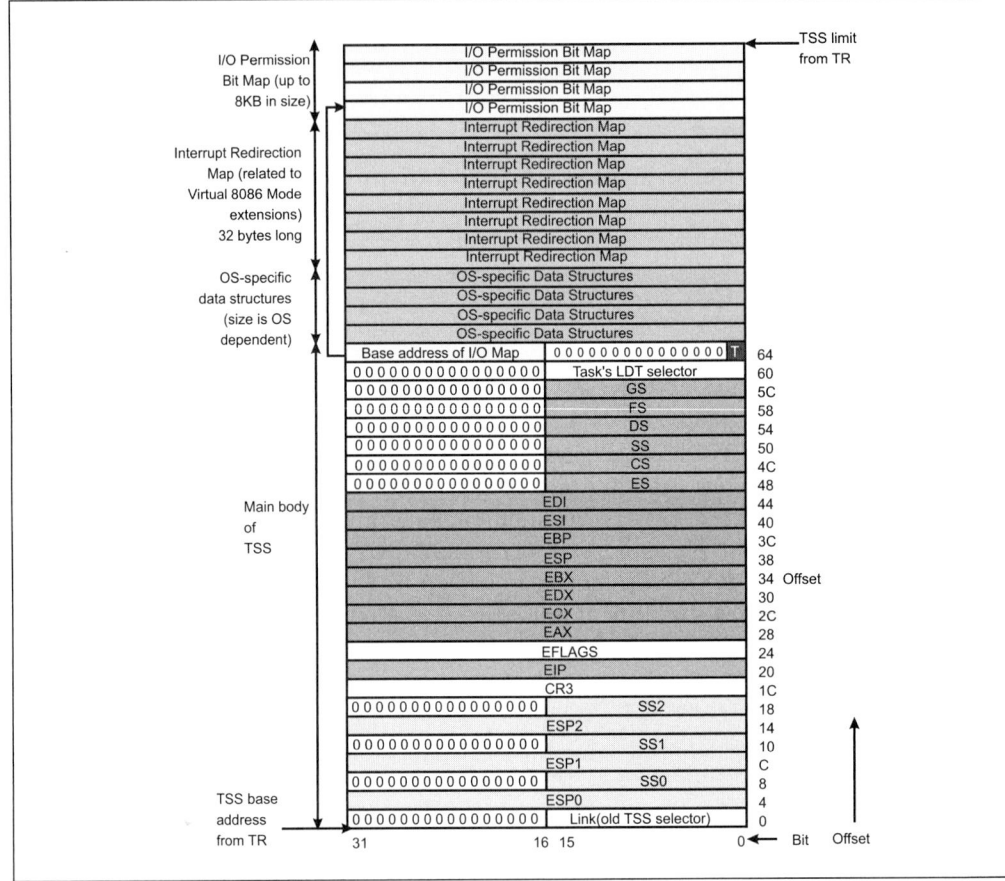

Return to the Interrupted Program

General

At the conclusion of the handler, the last instruction executed is the IRET (Interrupt Return). When executed, it returns program execution to the interrupted program at the point of interruption:

- In the case of a hardware interrupt, execution resumes at the instruction that would have been executed next if the interrupt had not occurred.
- In the case of a software interrupt instruction, execution resumes at the instruction immediately following the software interrupt instruction.

- If the interruption was caused by a software exception, depending on whether the exception was a fault or a trap, execution of the interrupted program resumes:
  — On a **Fault**, by re-executing the instruction that caused the exception.
  — On a **Trap**, by executing the next instruction.

The IRET Instruction

Table 19-4 on page 709 defines the IRET opcode and the flowcharts that follow detail the logical processor's actions when executing IRET under various circumstances:

1. Return from Real Mode handler to interrupted Real Mode application. Refer to Figure 19-2 on page 684.
2. Return from a Protected Mode handler to interrupted Protected Mode program. Refer to Figure 19-20 on page 710 (the figure details the logical processor actions taken when IRET is executed with an operand size of 32-bits; 16-bit operation is not shown).
3. Interrupt/exception caused a task switch. When IRET is executed at the completion of the task acting as the handler, the logical processor is sensitive to the state of the Eflags[NT] bit. IRET execution when NT = 1 causes a return to the interrupted task. Refer to Figure 19-21 on page 711 (the figure details actions taken when IRET is executed with an operand size of 32-bits; 16-bit operation is not shown).
4. Return from a VM86 Mode handler (i.e., a Real Mode handler) to an interrupted VM86 Mode application. Refer to Figure 19-22 on page 711.
5. Return from a Protected Mode handler to an interrupted VM86 Mode application. Refer to Figure 19-23 on page 712 (the figure details actions taken when IRET is executed with an operand size of 32-bits; 16-bit operation is not shown).

Table 19-4: The Interrupt Return (IRET) Instruction

Mnemonic	Opcode	Effective Operand Size	Description
IRET	CF	16-bits	Pops to restore interrupted program's registers are 2-bytes each.
		32-bits	Pops to restore interrupted program's registers are 4-bytes each.

Figure 19-20: Return From Protected Mode Handler To Interrupted Protected Mode Program

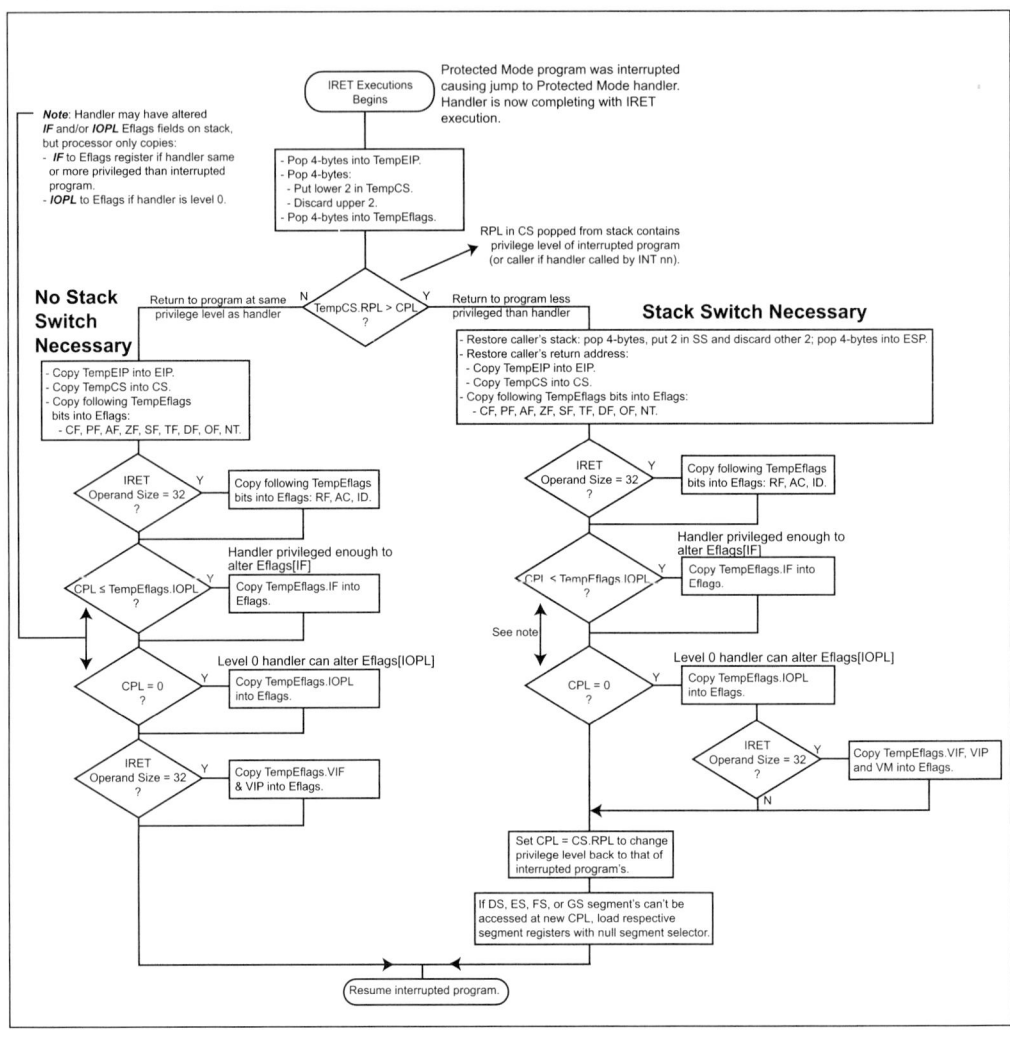

Figure 19-21: Return to Interrupted Task (Interrupt/Exception Caused a Task Switch)

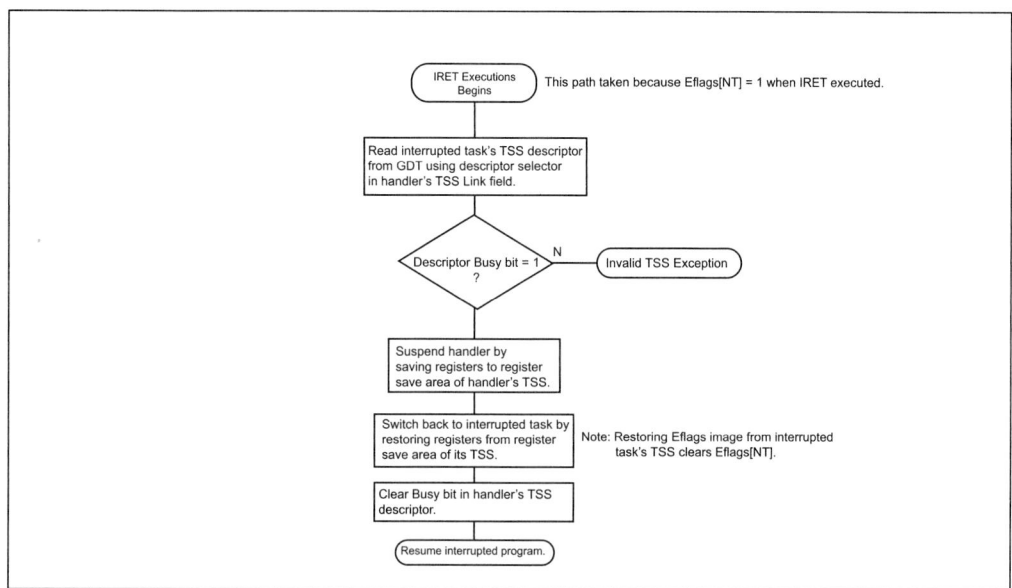

Figure 19-22: Return From a VM86 Mode Handler (i.e., a Real Mode Handler) to an Interrupted VM86 Mode Program

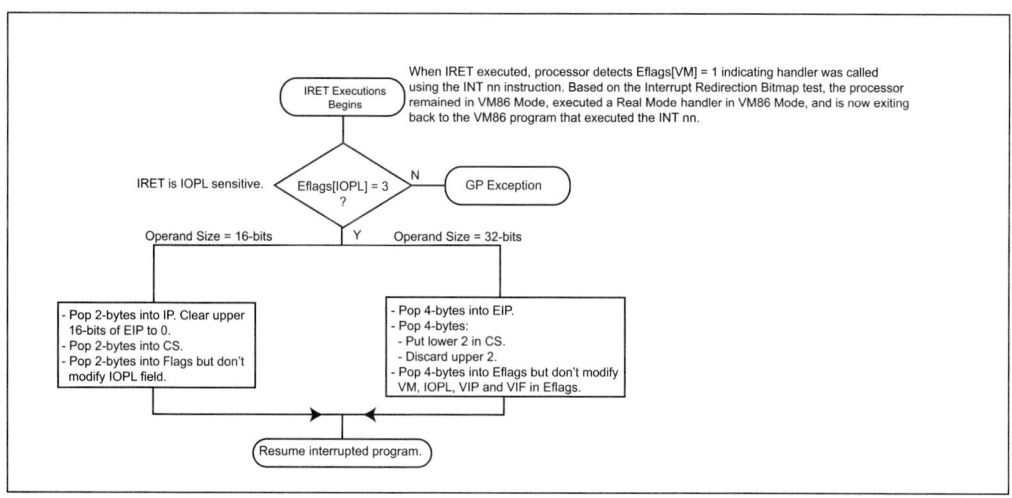

Figure 19-23: Return From Protected Mode Handler to Interrupted VM86 Mode Program

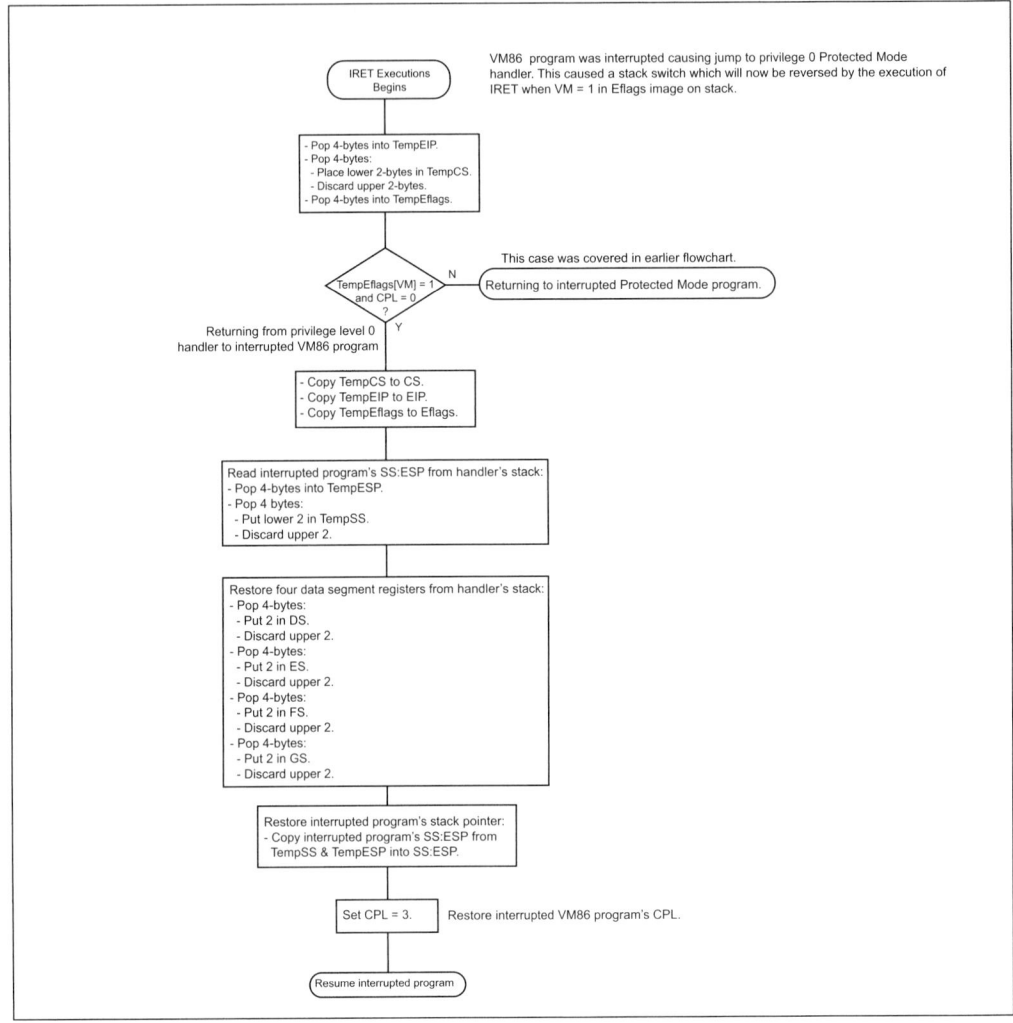

Maskable Hardware Interrupts

General

IO devices typically generate an interrupt request to signal conditions such as:

- An action required on the part of the device driver in order to continue operation.
- A previously-initiated operation has been completed with no errors encountered.
- A previously-initiated operation has encountered an error condition and cannot continue.

In any of these cases, the device adapter generates a device-specific interrupt to one of the following:

- The IO APIC.
- The legacy 8259A PIC.

In turn, the interrupt controller delivers the request to the logical processor. These are referred to as maskable interrupts because the programmer may disable the logical processor's ability to recognize any of them and may also program the external interrupt controller to selectively disable recognition of interrupt requests from specific devices.

All maskable interrupt requests are temporarily ignored by the logical processor if the programmer has disabled recognition by successfully executing a Clear Interrupt Enable (CLI) instruction. This clears the Eflags[IF] bit to zero, causing the logical processor to ignore maskable hardware interrupts until a Set Interrupt Enable (STI) instruction is executed.

This feature must be used cautiously as it delays the logical processor's servicing of interrupt requests generated by hardware devices. Many IO devices are sensitive to lengthy delays while awaiting service and may suffer data overrun or underrun conditions if their interrupt requests are not serviced on a timely basis.

Maskable Interrupt Vector Delivery

If maskable hardware interrupt recognition is enabled and a maskable interrupt is detected, the logical processor initiates servicing of the hardware request upon completion of the currently executing x86 instruction. This portion of the discussion assumes that the system interrupt controller consists of one or two 8259A Programmable Interrupt Controllers (PIC; the APIC did not make its appearance until the Pentium P54C). A detailed description of Local and IO APIC operation can be found in "The Local and IO APICs" on page 1239. In response to the detection of a maskable hardware interrupt, the following actions are performed by the logical processor:

1. On x86 processors prior to the advent of the Pentium Pro, two back-to-back Interrupt Acknowledge transactions were generated on the processor's external interface. Starting with the advent of the Pentium Pro, this was reduced to a single Interrupt Acknowledge transaction. This instructs the 8259A interrupt controller to prioritize the currently-pending interrupt requests from IO devices and to return the interrupt vector number associated with the highest-priority pending request (the 8-bit vector is used as an index into the IDT in memory).

2. Using the vector to select an IDT entry, the logical processor reads the contents of the indicated IDT descriptor from memory.

PC-Compatible Vector Assignment

Table 19-5 on page 715 and Figure 19-24 on page 719 define the legacy hardware interrupt request line assignment in a PC-compatible machine and identifies the IDT entry number associated with each.

The table also highlights a particularly peculiar characteristic of the PC-compatible architecture. The original IBM PC was based on the 8088 and Intel reserved IDT entries 0 - 7 for the software exception conditions that might be encountered by the processor. Avoiding these first eight IDT entries when assigning interrupt vectors to platform hardware devices, the IBM PC BIOS programmed the 8259A interrupt controller (there was only one in the original PC) to associate IDT entries 8 - 15 with hardware interrupt request lines IRQ0 - IRQ7. In order to remain backward-compatible, the 286-based IBM PC-AT's interrupt controller was also programmed to use IDT entries 8 - 15 for these hardware interrupts. However, the 286 generated additional types of software exceptions (above and beyond those generated by the 8086/8088) and these new exceptions also used IDT entries 8 - 13 (thereby overlapping with many of the IDT entries used by IBM for interrupts generated by hardware devices). Later machines based on the 386 added additional exceptions which used IDT entries 14 and 15. In other words, IDT entries 8 - 15 could be selected for either of two possible events:

- A hardware interrupt.
- A software exception.

Table 19-5 on page 715 explains the software actions taken to ensure that all hardware and software events were serviced correctly.

Table 19-5: PC-Compatible IRQ Assignment

IRQ Line	IDT Entry	Typically Used By
0	08h	**System timer**. The same vector is used by the **Double-Fault exception**. This means that the occurrence of either a system timer tick (IRQ0) or a Double-Fault exception vectors to IDT entry 08. In a PC, the system timer interrupt handler hooks this entry prior to the OS boot. During OS initialization, the OS reads and saves the pointer to the timer handler and installs the pointer to its Double-Fault exception handler in IDT entry 08. If either event occurs during run-time, the logical processor jumps to the OS Double-Fault exception handler. The Double-Fault exception handler determines if external interrupts are enabled by testing for Eflags[IF] = 1 on the stack. If recognition is not enabled, it executes the body of the exception handler to service the Double-Fault condition. If recognition is enabled, it polls bit 0 in the master 8259A interrupt controller's IRR (Interrupt Request Register) to determine if the system timer has ticked (IRQ0 was asserted). If it has, it jumps to and executes the system timer interrupt handler. If it hasn't, it executes the exception handler to service the Double-Fault.

x86 Instruction Set Architecture

Table 19-5: PC-Compatible IRQ Assignment (Continued)

IRQ Line	IDT Entry	Typically Used By
1	09h	**Keyboard interface**. The same vector is used by a **Coprocessor Segment Overrun abort exception** (note: this exception was eliminated in the 386 but the description is included for historical purposes). Occurrence of either a keyboard request (IRQ1) or an Overrun exception vectored to IDT entry 09. In a PC, the keyboard handler hooks this entry prior to OS boot. During OS initialization, the OS reads and saves the pointer to the keyboard handler and installs the pointer to its Segment Overrun exception handler in IDT entry 09. If either event occurs during run-time, the logical processor jumped to the OS's Overrun exception handler. The exception handler determined if external interrupts recognition was enabled by testing for Eflags[IF] = 1 on the stack. If recognition wasn't enabled, it executed the body of the exception handler. If recognition was enabled, it polled bit 1 in the master 8259A interrupt controller's IRR (Interrupt Request Register) to determine if the keyboard had generated a request (on IRQ1). If it had, it jumped to and executed the keyboard handler.
2	0Ah (10)	Requests from slave interrupt controller.
3	0Bh (11)	**Serial port two**. The same vector is used by a **Segment Not Present exception**. Occurrence of either a serial port 2 interrupt or a Segment Not Present exception vectors to IDT entry 11. In a PC, the serial port handler hooks this entry prior to OS boot. During OS initialization, the OS reads and saves the pointer to the serial port handler and installs the pointer to its Segment Not Present exception handler in IDT entry 11. If either event occurs during run-time, the logical processor jumps to the OS Segment Not Present exception handler. The exception handler determines if external interrupts are enabled by testing for Eflags[IF] = 1 on the stack. If recognition is not enabled, it executes the body of the exception handler. If recognition is enabled, it polls bit 3 in the master 8259A interrupt controller's IRR (Interrupt Request Register) to determine if a serial port interrupt (IRQ3) is pending. If it is, it jumps to and executes the body of the serial port handler.

716   **Visit MindShare Training at www.mindshare.com**

Table 19-5: PC-Compatible IRQ Assignment (Continued)

IRQ Line	IDT Entry	Typically Used By
4	0Ch (12)	**Serial port one**. The same vector is used by a **Stack Fault exception**. Occurrence of either a serial port one request (IRQ4) or a Stack exception vectors to IDT entry 12. In a PC, the serial port one interrupt handler hooks this entry prior to OS boot. During OS initialization, the OS reads and saves the pointer to the serial port handler and installs the pointer to its Stack exception handler in IDT entry 12. If either event occurs during run-time, the logical processor jumps to the OS stack exception handler. The exception handler determines if external interrupts are enabled by testing for Eflags[IF] = 1 on the stack. If recognition is not enabled, the body of the exception handler is executed. If recognition is enabled, it polls bit 4 in the master 8259A interrupt controller's IRR (Interrupt Request Register) to determine if serial port one is generating a request (on IRQ4). If it is, it jumps to and executes the serial port handler.
5	0Dh (13)	**Parallel port two**. The same vector is used by a **GP exception**. Occurrence of either a parallel port 2 interrupt or a GP exception vectors to IDT entry 13. In a PC, the parallel port handler hooks this entry prior to OS boot. During OS initialization, the OS reads and saves the pointer to the parallel port handler and installs the pointer to its GP exception handler in IDT entry 13. If either event occurs during run-time, the logical processor jumps to the OS GP exception handler. The exception handler determines if external interrupts are enabled by testing for Eflags[IF] = 1 on the stack. If recognition is not enabled, it executes the body of the exception handler. If recognition is enabled, it polls bit 5 in the master 8259A interrupt controller's IRR (Interrupt Request Register) to determine if parallel port 2 is generating an interrupt (IRQ5). If it is, it jumps to and executes the body of the parallel port handler.

Table 19-5: PC-Compatible IRQ Assignment (Continued)

IRQ Line	IDT Entry	Typically Used By
6	0Eh (14)	**Floppy interface**. The same vector is used by a **Page Fault exception**. Occurrence of either a floppy interrupt or a Page Fault exception vectors to IDT entry 14. In a PC, the floppy interrupt handler hooks this entry prior to OS boot. During OS initialization, the OS reads and saves the pointer to the floppy handler and installs the pointer to its Page Fault exception handler in IDT entry 14. If either event occurs during run-time, the logical processor jumps to the OS Page Fault exception handler. The exception handler determines if external interrupts are enabled by testing for Eflags[IF] = 1 on the stack. If recognition is not enabled, it executes the body of the exception handler. If recognition is enabled, it polls bit 6 in the master 8259A interrupt controller's IRR (Interrupt Request Register) to determine if the floppy is generating a request (IRQ6). If it is, it jumps to and executes the body of the floppy handler.
7	0Fh (15)	**Parallel port one**.
The IBM PC-AT added a second 8259a interrupt controller and the following eight IRQ lines:		
8	70h (112)	Alarm output of the real-time clock (RTC) chip.
9	71h (113)	VGA vertical retrace interrupt.
10	72h (114)	Available for use by expansion cards.
11	73h (115)	Available for use by expansion cards.
12	74h (116)	Mouse interface interrupt.
13	75h (117)	Error output of the FPU.
14	76h (118)	Hard drive interface interrupt.
15	77h (119)	Available for use by expansion cards.

Figure 19-24: Hardware Device Interrupt Assignments in a PC-Compatible Platform

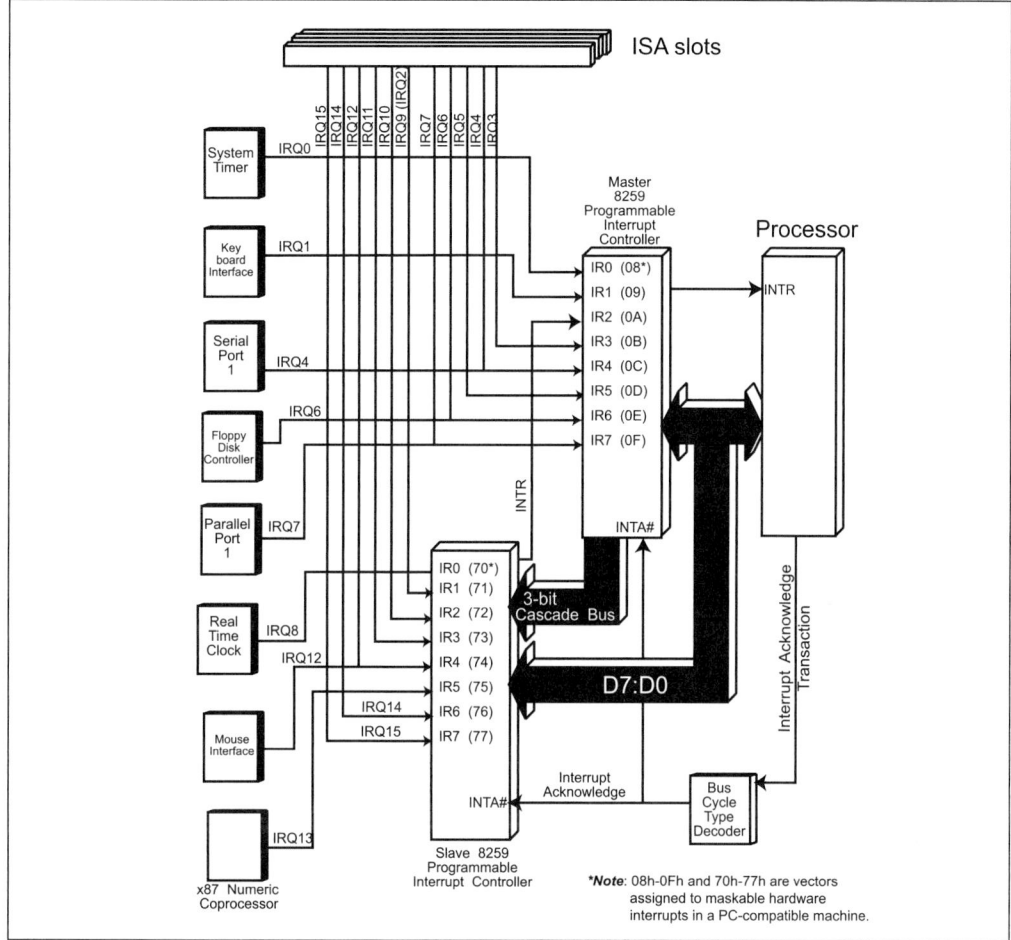

Actions Performed by the Handler

After entering the device-specific interrupt handler (part of the device driver), the handler performs the following actions:

1. Save (in stack memory) the contents of any registers that will be altered within the handler. In order to ensure proper operation upon returning to the interrupted program, all logical processor registers must contain their original contents.

2. Check the device's status and perform any device-specific servicing requested by the device.

3. Issue an End-of-Interrupt (EOI) command to the 8259A interrupt controller to clear the request.

4. Execute an Interrupt Return (IRET) instruction. This causes the logical processor to pop the original CS, EIP and Eflags values from the stack and load them into their respective registers (thereby automatically reenabling recognition of external, hardware interrupts if the IF bit = 1 in the Eflags stack image).

5. The logical processor resumes execution of the interrupted program.

Effect of CLI/STI Execution

General

The ability of the currently-running program to successfully execute the CLI and STI instructions is governed by a number of factors:

- Whether or not the logical processor is in Protected or Real Mode.
- If it is in Protected Mode:
  — **VM86 Mode?** Whether or not the currently-running program is a DOS task running in VM86 Mode (as governed by the Eflags[VM] bit). A detailed description of VM86 Mode can be found in "Virtual 8086 Mode" on page 783.
    – **VME = 1?** If the currently-running program is a DOS task running in VM86 Mode, whether or not the OS has enabled the VM86 Mode Extensions (using CR4[VME]). Additional information on the VME feature may be found in "VM86 Extensions" on page 818.
  — **Protected Mode task. PVI on?** If the currently-running task is not a VM86 task, whether or not the Protected Mode Virtual Interrupt feature has been enabled by the OS (using CR4[PVI]). Additional information on the PVI feature may be found in "Protected Mode Virtual Interrupt Feature" on page 832.
  — **CPL** of the currently-running program.
  — **IOPL value**. The privilege level threshold value specified in the Eflags[IOPL] field.

Based on these factors, Table 19-6 on page 721 provides an overview of the effect when a program attempts to execute the CLI/STI instructions. The following key applies to the table column headings:

- **PE**. The state of the Protected Mode Enable bit in CR0.
- **VM**. The state of the Virtual Machine bit (VM86 Mode) in the Eflags register.

- **IOPL**. The threshold value programmed into the Eflags[IOPL] field.
- **CPL**. The privilege level of the currently running program.
- **PVI**. The state of the Protected Mode Virtual Interrupt (PVI) bit in CR4.
- **VME**. The state of the Virtual Machine Extensions bit in CR4.

Table 19-6: Results of CLI/STI Execution

PE	VM	IOPL is numeri cally	CPL	PVI	VME	Result of CLI/STI Execution
Real Mode · CR0[PE] = 0						
0	x	x	x	x	x	Real Mode application can successfully mask and unmask the recognition of maskable hardware interrupts (i.e., CLI/STI do affect the state of the Eflags[IF] bit).
Protected Mode task, but not a VM86 (DOS) task · CR0[PE] = 1. · Eflags[VM] = 0].						
1	0	>= CPL	x	x	x	Irrespective of VME and PVI state, CPL passes IOPL test. CLI/STI affect the state of the Eflags[IF] bit.
1	0	< CPL	3	1	x	Protected Mode Virtual Interrupt feature enables level 3 Protected Mode application to change VIF instead of IF with CLI/STI. Execution of STI while Eflags[VIP] = 1 results in GP exception.
1	0	< CPL	< 3	x	x	Program with CPL = 1 or 2 fails IOPL test (IOPL = 0). CLI/STI cause GP exception.
1	0	< CPL	x	0	x	PVI off and CPL fails IOPL test, so CLI/STI results in GP exception.

Table 19-6: Results of CLI/STI Execution (Continued)

PE	VM	IOPL is numerically	CPL	PVI	VME	Result of CLI/STI Execution

VM86 (DOS) task running under Protected Mode
- Eflags[VM] = 1.
- CR0[PE] = 1.
- DOS task is privilege level 3 by definition.

PE	VM	IOPL is numerically	CPL	PVI	VME	Result of CLI/STI Execution
1	1	3	3	x	x	DOS task passes IOPL test, so executing CLI/STI changes IF bit.
1	1	< 3	3	x	1	VM86 Mode Extension (VME) feature enables DOS task to change VIF instead of IF with CLI/STI. Execution of STI while Eflags[VIP] = 1 results in GP exception.
1	1	< 3	3	x	0	VME off and IOPL < 3, so DOS task cannot execute CLI/STI without causing GP exception.

Other Events That Affect Interrupt Flag Bit

Other operations that can alter the state of Eflags[IF] are:

- Reset clears Eflags[IF], inhibiting recognition of maskable interrupts.
- With the exception of the VM and RF bits, the PUSHF (Push Flags) instruction copies the contents of the Eflags register to the stack (the register image on the stack has VM and RF cleared to zero). The Eflags image, including IF, can then be examined, modified in stack memory, and, when the image is popped back into the Eflags register, IF assumes the new state.
- The POPF instruction copies the Eflags image on the stack back into the Eflags register.
- A task switch modifies the Eflags register when it copies the Eflags field from the new TSS into Eflags. Hardware-based task switching is covered in the chapter entitled "Task Switching" on page 629.
- The IRET instruction copies the Eflags image from the stack back into the Eflags register.
- An interrupt that selects an IDT entry containing an Interrupt Gate descriptor clears Eflags[IF] after Eflags has been copied to stack memory.

Protected Mode Virtual Interrupt Feature

See "Protected Mode Virtual Interrupt Feature" on page 832 for a detailed description of the PVI feature.

Non-Maskable Interrupt (NMI) Requests

NMI requests are issued by the chipset to signal that a serious hardware condition has been detected on the system board. The programmer cannot disable the logical processor's ability to recognize and respond to an NMI.

An NMI can be received in two ways:

- If the logical processor's Local APIC is disabled, NMIs are delivered to it on the processor's LINT0 or LINT1 input pin.
- If the logical processor's Local APIC is enabled, NMIs are delivered to it in an IPI message packet over the processor's external interface.

PC-Compatible NMI Logic

In the PC-compatible world, NMI is used to report catastrophic hardware failures (such as a system board DRAM parity check or an uncorrectable ECC error) to the OS. The programmer may mask out the external hardware's ability to generate NMI by writing a one to bit seven of IO port 70h (note this is the default state of the NMI Mask bit). Caution should be exercised, however, because bits [6:0] of this same IO port are assigned to the Real-Time Clock (RTC) chip's address port. Although bit seven of IO port 70h can be used to block the assertion of NMI, the programmer has no way of commanding the logical processor not to service an NMI request should it detect it. Care should be taken to initialize IDT entry 2 with the pointer to the NMI handler before software writes to IO port 70h to unmask the NMI generation logic.

NMI Description

When an NMI request is detected, the logical processor saves its place (CS:EIP) on the stack and jumps to the NMI handler pointed to by IDT entry 2. The logical processor automatically disables recognition of any additional NMI interrupts until the IRET instruction is executed at the end of the NMI handler. In Protected Mode, it is recommended that an Interrupt Gate descriptor (rather than a Trap Gate) be placed in IDT entry 2 so recognition of maskable hardware interrupts will also be disabled before the logical processor enters the NMI handler.

In the handler, the programmer polls the various external hardware devices (typically, the chipset) capable of generating an NMI in order to discover the source and type of failure. Upon discovering the source of the failure, a failure-specific message is typically output to the display, maskable interrupt recognition is disabled, and a HLT instruction is executed. In response to the HLT instruction, the logical processor broadcasts a halt message on its external interface (to inform external logic—the chipset—of its intention to stop fetching and executing instructions) and ceases to fetch and execute instructions.

More Detailed Coverage of Hardware Interrupt Handling

For more detailed coverage of hardware interrupt generation and servicing in both the PC-compatible environment as well as other environments, refer to "The Local and IO APICs" on page 1239. *It should be stressed that the current chapter typically describes externally-generated hardware handling when a logical processor's Local APIC is disabled and the external 8259a controller is being used instead.*

Machine Check Exception

Although the term exception is used (implying that a Machine Check is generated as the result of an error incurred when an instruction is executed), a Machine Check exception is generated in response to hardware-related errors. If the logical processor is enabled to do so, this exception is generated when the logical processor detects hardware errors that generally fall within the following categories:

- Processor external interface transaction errors.
- Uncorrectable ECC errors detected on internal caches.
- Parity errors detected on the processor's external interface or on internal ROM devices (such as the processor's Microcode ROM).
- Storage errors in the processor's internal caches or TLBs.

A detailed description of this exception can be found in "Machine Check Exception (18)" on page 778. Also see "Machine Check Architecture (MCA)" on page 1207.

SMI (System Management Interrupt)

The types of operations that typically fall under the heading of System Management are power management and management of the system's thermal environment (e.g., temperature monitoring in the platform's various thermal zones and fan control). It should be stressed, however, that system management is not necessarily limited to these specific areas.

The following are some example situations that would require action by the SM handler program:

- A laptop chipset implements a timer that tracks how long it's been since the hard drive was last accessed. If this timer should elapse, the chipset generates an SMI to the logical processor to invoke the SM handler. In the handler, software checks a chipset-specific status register to determine the cause of the SMI (in this case, a prolonged cessation of accesses to the hard drive). In response, the SM handler issues a command to the hard disk controller to spin down the spindle motor (to save on energy consumption).
- A laptop chipset implements a timer that tracks how long it's been since the keyboard and/or mouse was used. If this timer should elapse, the chipset generates an SMI to the logical processor to invoke the SM handler. In the handler, software checks a chipset-specific status register to determine the cause of the SMI (in this case, a prolonged cessation of user interaction). In response, the SM handler issues a command to the display controller to dim or turn off the display's backlighting (to save on energy consumption).
- In a server platform, the chipset or system board logic detects that a thermal sensor in a specific zone of the platform is experiencing a rise in temperature. It generates an SMI to the logical processor to invoke the SM handler. In the handler, software checks a chipset-specific status register to determine the cause of the SMI (in this case, a potential overheat condition). In response, the SM handler issues a command to the system board's fan control logic to turn on an exhaust fan in that zone.

A complete description of SM Mode can be found in "System Management Mode (SMM)" on page 1167.

Software Interrupts

Figure 19-7 on page 695 and Figure 19-8 on page 696 illustrate the actions taken by the logical processor when a software interrupt instruction is executed. Additional detail may be found in Figure 19-10 on page 700 through Figure 19-14 on page 704.

INT *nn* Instruction

The software interrupt instruction (INT *nn*) emulates the hardware interrupt mechanism. The 8-bit interrupt vector (i.e., the index—*nn*—into the IDT) is supplied as the instruction operand rather than by the interrupt controller. Consider the following example instruction (assume that the system is a PC running DOS):

```
INT 13h ;call disk bios routine
```

When this instruction is executed by the logical processor, the following events take place:

1. The logical processor uses the immediate operand, 13h, as an index into the IDT and reads the contents of IDT entry 13h (19).
2. Pushes the contents of its CS, EIP and Eflags registers onto the stack. This is necessary to save its place in the interrupted program, as well as saving the state of the interrupt enable bit (Eflags[IF]).
3. The logical processor's handling of the Eflags[IF] bit depends on the type of gate that occupies the selected IDT entry:
   — If it's a Trap Gate, Eflags[IF] is unaffected.
   — If it's an Interrupt Gate, Eflags[IF] is cleared to zero disabling recognition of maskable hardware interrupts.
4. Jumps to the device-specific handler pointed to by the selected IDT entry.
5. At the end of the handler, an interrupt return (IRET) instruction is executed, causing the logical processor to pop the original CS, EIP and Eflags values from the stack into their respective registers.
6. The logical processor resumes execution of the interrupted program.

INTO Instruction

Interrupt on Overflow. Useful because the signed and unsigned arithmetic instructions cannot detect an overflow of the result. A detailed description of this exception can be found in "Overflow Exception (4)" on page 748. When executed, the logical processor tests the state of Eflags[OF]:

- If the overflow flag is clear, the logical processor takes no action and falls through to the next instruction.
- If the overflow flag is set, the logical processor reads the Interrupt or Trap Gate descriptor from IDT entry 4 and executes the overflow handler it points to.

BOUND Instruction

Generated by the BOUND instruction if the specified array index is not within the bounds of the specified memory array. A detailed description of this exception can be found in "Array Bounds Check Exception (5)" on page 748.

- If the array index is within the bounds of the memory array, the logical processor takes no action and falls through to the next instruction.
- If the array index is not within the bounds of the memory array, the logical processor reads the Interrupt or Trap Gate descriptor from IDT entry 5 and executes the Bound handler it points to.

INT3 (Breakpoint) Instruction

Also referred to as the Breakpoint instruction. When executed, it causes the logical processor to unconditionally read the Interrupt or Trap Gate descriptor from IDT entry 3 and execute the debug exception handler it points to. A detailed description of this exception can be found in "Breakpoint Exception (3)" on page 746. Unlike the 2-byte INT 03 instruction, this 1-byte instruction (opcode = CCh) can be used to replace the first byte of any instruction—including a single byte instruction—with a breakpoint without over-writing other code. This software interrupt instruction differs from the other software interrupt instructions in the following ways when it is executed while the logical processor is in VM86 Mode (see "Software Interrupt Handling in VM86 Mode" on page 826):

- When executed with CR4[VME] = 1, the logical processor does not consult the Interrupt Redirection bitmap in the TSS to determine whether it should execute the Real Mode handler or Protected Mode handler. Rather, it unconditionally executes the Protected Mode handler.
- The logical processor does not check the CPL of the VM86 program (3) against the threshold level specified in Eflags[IOPL]. Rather, it unconditionally executes the Protected Mode handler.

Software Exceptions

General

Software-generated exceptions fall into two categories:

- Software exceptions generated as a result of an error condition detected while attempting execution of an instruction. The type of error condition defines the IDT entry that is vectored to.
- Software exceptions deliberately generated by execution of software interrupt instructions: BOUND, INT *nn*, INTO, and INT3 instructions:
  — Execution of an INT *nn* instruction vectors to entry *nn* in the IDT.
  — Execution of an INTO instruction vectors to IDT entry 4 if Eflags[OF] = 1.
  — Execution of the INT3 instruction (the breakpoint instruction) vectors to IDT entry 3.
  — Conditionally generated by the BOUND instruction if the indicated array index is not within the bounds of the indicated memory array (this causes the logical processor to vector to IDT entry 5).

Faults, Traps, and Aborts

Due to a problem associated with an instruction or with its operand, the attempted execution of the instruction may result in an error condition. Problems of this nature are referred to as software exception conditions. When such a problem is detected, the logical processor invokes a special exception handler designed to attempt (if possible) a graceful recovery from the respective exception condition.

Software initializes the respective IDT entries with the pointers to the various exception handlers. Software exceptions are categorized as faults, traps, or aborts. These terms are defined in Table 19-7 on page 729. Table 19-8 on page 729 defines each software exception and identifies whether it is a fault, trap, or abort.

Table 19-7: Software Exception Types

Type	Definition
Fault	**CS:EIP is rewound to point to the instruction that caused the error event.** The CS:EIP pointer pushed onto the stack points to the offending instruction rather than the one after it. The fault is reported with the logical processor restored to a state that permits the instruction to be restarted (i.e., all registers are restored to their original state prior to the attempted execution of the instruction).
Trap	**CS:EIP points to the instruction following the one that caused the error event.** The CS:EIP pointer pushed onto the stack points to the instruction immediately following the offending instruction. If the trap occurs during execution of an instruction that alters program flow (e.g., a jump), the return address on the stack points to the branch target address (i.e., the address being jumped to). If the instruction is a string instruction and has a repeat prefix and the count has not yet been exhausted, the return address points to the same instruction and the values in the other registers related to the instruction contain the values for the next iteration.
Abort	**CS:EIP may not be reliable**. An abort does not always push a reliable return address onto the stack. This makes it impossible for the exception handler to reliably resume program execution assuming it was able to fix the problem that caused the exception.

Table 19-8: Exception Categories

Vector	Description	Type
0	A Divide-By-Zero exception can be generated during execution of the DIV or IDIV instruction. A detailed description of this exception can be found in "Divide-by-Zero Exception (0)" on page 743.	fault

Table 19-8: Exception Categories (Continued)

Vector	Description	Type
1	**A debug exception** caused by the detection of an instruction address breakpoint. A detailed description of this exception can be found in "Debug Exception (1)" on page 744.	fault
	A debug exception caused by the detection of a data address breakpoint.	trap
	A Debug exception caused by a General Detect condition. This occurs when an attempt is made to use the logical processor's debug registers when they are already in use by an In-Circuit Emulator (ICE).	fault
	A Debug exception caused by the single-step interrupt.	trap
	A Debug exception caused by a task-switch breakpoint (i.e., a task switch occurs to a task that has the Trap bit set to one in its TSS).	trap
2	**NMI** is a form of hardware interrupt, not a software exception.	trap
3	The INT3 instruction is also referred to as the **Breakpoint** instruction. Unlike the 2-byte INT *nn* instruction, it is 1-byte long. A detailed description of this exception can be found in "Breakpoint Exception (3)" on page 746.	trap
4	Generated by the execution of the **INTO** instruction if Eflags[OF] = 1. Useful because the signed and unsigned arithmetic instructions cannot detect an overflow of the result. A detailed description of this exception can be found in "Overflow Exception (4)" on page 748.	trap
5	Generated by the **BOUND** instruction if the specified array index is not within the bounds of the specified memory array. A detailed description of this exception can be found in "Array Bounds Check Exception (5)" on page 748.	fault

Table 19-8: Exception Categories (Continued)

Vector	Description	Type
6	• Generated when an **invalid opcode** is detected upon the attempted execution of an instruction (instruction prefetch cannot cause this exception). • Also generated when an invalid operand is used with an instruction (e.g., specifying a register as the target of a jump). • Use of the LOCK prefix with instructions for which locking is not supported also causes this exception. A detailed description of this exception can be found in "Invalid OpCode Exception (6)" on page 749.	fault
7	The **Device Not Available** (DNA) exception is generated under two circumstances: • CR0[EM] = 1 (indicating that FPU is not present) and a FP instruction is encountered. This exception handler can be used to emulate the execution of FP instructions. • CR0[TS] = 1, CR0[MP] = 1, and a WAIT or ESC instruction is encountered. The FPU is about to execute a FP instruction associated with a new task after a task switch has occurred (but the FPU registers were not automatically saved on a task switch). A detailed description of this exception can be found in "Device Not Available (DNA) Exception (7)" on page 751.	fault
8	**Double-Fault encountered.** The logical processor encountered a fault while attempting to call an exception handler for a previously-encountered fault. Most of the time this can be handled by servicing the two exceptions serially, but some combinations are unrecoverable. Such combinations result in a Double-Fault exception. If a third exception occurs while the logical processor is attempting to call the Double-Fault handler, the logical processor broadcast a Shutdown message to the chipset and then enters the Shutdown state. A detailed description of this exception can be found in "Double Fault Exception (8)" on page 752.	abort

Table 19-8: Exception Categories (Continued)

Vector	Description	Type
9	The **Coprocessor Segment Overrun abort** is reserved in the post-286 processors. It was only generated by the 286 when a page or segment violation was detected during the transfer of a FP operand to or from memory. The later processors generate exception 13h instead (General Protection). A detailed description of this exception can be found in "Coprocessor Segment Overrun Exception (9)" on page 756.	abort
10 *	**Invalid TSS fault**. Generated if a task switch is attempted to a task with an invalid TSS data structure. A detailed description of this exception can be found in "Invalid TSS Exception (10)" on page 757.	fault
11 *	**Segment Not Present**. Generated when the selected segment descriptor (CS, DS, ES, FS, GS) is not present in memory (its P bit = 0). An SS descriptor with P = 0 results in a Stack exception (number 12). A detailed description of this exception can be found in "Segment Not Present Exception (11)" on page 759.	fault
12	**Stack exception** occurs for one of three reasons: • A Stack Underflow or Overflow error (in other words, too many pops or pushes). • An attempt to load the SS register with a selector for a descriptor marked not present (P = 0). • An attempt to load the SS register with a selector for a descriptor that doesn't describe a read/writable data segment. A detailed description of this exception can be found in "Stack Exception (12)" on page 761.	fault
13	**General Protection (GP)** exception. All protection violations that don't cause another exception cause a GP exception. A detailed description of this exception can be found in "General Protection (GP) Exception (13)" on page 763.	fault or trap

Table 19-8: Exception Categories (Continued)

Vector	Description	Type
14 *	**Page Fault** exception. Occurs for one the following reasons: • The selected PDE's P bit = 0, indicating that the selected Page Table (or 4MB or 2MB page) is not present in memory. • The selected PTE's P bit = 0, indicating that the target 4KB page is not present in memory. • Code running in user mode attempts to write to a read-only page. • If CR0[WP] = 1, a Page Fault occurs on an attempt by code with supervisor privilege (0, 1, or 2) to write to a write-protected user page (i.e., PTE[U/S] = 1 and R/W = 0). • Insufficient privilege to access the Page Table or the page. • A reserved bit set to one in the selected PDE or PTE. If the Page Fault occurs due to a page not present or a page privilege access violation (insufficient privilege or writes not permitted), the A bit is affected in the PDE, but not in the PTE. The PTE's A and D bits are only affected if the page access succeeds. A detailed description of this exception can be found in "Page Fault Exception (14)" on page 766. Also see "1A-32e Address Translation" on page 983.	fault
15	Reserved.	n/a
16	**FP error** exception. Error generated by the attempted execution of a FP math instruction. It can only occur when CR0[NE] = 1. A detailed description of this exception can be found in "FPU Exception (16)" on page 770.	fault

Table 19-8: Exception Categories (Continued)

Vector	Description	Type
17	**Alignment Check** exception. The occurrence of this exception indicates that the logical processor detected an unaligned multi-byte memory operand when alignment checking was enabled. Alignment checks are only carried out in data (or stack) segments (not in code or system segments). An example of an alignment-check violation is a word (a 2-byte data object) stored in memory starting at an odd byte address, or a dword stored in memory starting at an address that is not divisible by four. A detailed description of this exception can be found in "Alignment Check Exception (17)" on page 774.	fault
18	**Machine Check** exception. If enabled, this exception is generated when the logical processor detects hardware errors that generally fall within the following categories: • Processor external interface transaction errors. • Uncorrectable ECC errors detected on internal caches. • Parity errors detected on the processor's external interface or on internal ROM devices (such as the processor's Microcode ROM). • Storage errors in the processor's internal caches or TLBs. A detailed description of this exception can be found in "Machine Check Exception (18)" on page 778. Also see "Machine Check Architecture (MCA)" on page 1207.	abort
19	The **SIMD FP exception** (exception 19). Added with the advent of the Pentium III processor. SIMD FP exceptions are generated independently from the x87 FP exceptions. Generation of an SSE SIMD FP exception does not result in the assertion of the processor's FERR# output pin (regardless of the CR0[NE] setting), and the state of the processor's IGNNE# input pin has no effect on the SSE SIMD FP logic. A detailed description of this exception can be found in "SIMD Floating-Point Exception (19)" on page 779.	fault
20-31	**Intel reserved**. Do not use. These IDT entries are reserved for future use.	n/a

Table 19-8: Exception Categories (Continued)

Vector	Description	Type
32-255	Available for use by maskable hardware interrupts and with the INT *nn* instruction.	traps
* Note: These exceptions do not occur in Real Mode, but may occur in VM86 mode.		

Instruction Restart After a Fault

When the logical processor generates any of the fault exceptions, it restores all of its registers to the state that they were in prior to the attempted execution of the offending instruction. The return address pushed onto the stack by the exception therefore points to the instruction that caused the fault. This permits the fault handler to examine the instruction in question and determine whether or not it can correct the problem and, if so, then re-execute the instruction successfully (by executing an IRET instruction).

A classic example would be a Page Fault exception. Among other reasons, it can occur because the target page of information is not currently present in memory. In the exception handler, the programmer could take the following actions:

1. Read the page from mass storage into an available physical page in memory.
2. Create a Page Table Entry (PTE) mapping the 4KB virtual page address to the respective physical page address.
3. Resume execution of the interrupted program at the instruction that caused the Page Fault exception (by executing an IRET instruction).

When the instruction is re-executed, the access takes place successfully because the target page is now present in memory, resulting in a successful Page Table lookup and therefore a successful address translation.

Exception Error Codes

The logical processor pushes a 32-bit error code (if the current code segment's default operand size is 16-bits, it's a 16-bit error code) onto the stack for certain types of software exception conditions. Table 19-9 on page 736 lists the exceptions that return error codes. The standard format of an error code is shown in Figure 19-25 on page 739. The error code indicates the following:

- **EXT**. The EXT bit = 1 if an event external to the program caused the error. As an example, EXT = 1 if a hardware interrupt selected a Task Gate pointing to an invalid TSS selector in the IDT.
- **IDT = 1**. The IDT bit = 1 if the error is associated with an entry in the IDT. In this case, the Selector Index field indicates the IDT entry in question.
- **IDT = 0**. A zero in the IDT bit indicates that the error is associated with an entry in the LDT or GDT.
- **TI bit**. If IDT = 0, the state of the TI (Table Indicator) bit indicates whether the entry in question resides in the GDT (TI = 0), or LDT (TI = 1). The Selector Index field indicates the table entry in question.

Table 19-9: Exceptions that Return Error Codes

Exception Type	Vector	Does the error code have the standard format shown in Figure 19-25 on page 739?
Double-Fault exception	8	No. Always pushes an error code value of 00000000h.
Invalid TSS exception	10	Yes. The error code identifies the segment selector index for the segment descriptor that caused the violation. • If EXT = 1, it indicates that the exception was caused by an event asynchronous to the currently-running program (e.g., if a hardware interrupt handler using a Task Gate attempted a task switch to an invalid TSS).
Segment Not Present exception	11	Yes. The error code identifies the segment selector index for the segment descriptor that caused the violation. • If EXT = 1, it indicates that the exception resulted from an asynchronous event (NMI or INTR) that caused an interrupt which subsequently referenced a segment that isn't present in memory. • IDT = 1 if the error code refers to an IDT entry containing a descriptor with the Present bit = 0.

Table 19-9: Exceptions that Return Error Codes (Continued)

Exception Type	Vector	Does the error code have the standard format shown in Figure 19-25 on page 739?
Stack Fault exception	12	Yes. • If the exception occurred because the stack segment isn't present in memory or due to a stack overflow of the fresh stack during an inter-privilege-level call, the error code contains a segment selector for the segment that caused the exception. The exception handler can test the Present bit in the segment descriptor pointed to by the segment selector to determine the cause of the exception. • For a normal limit violation (on a stack segment already in use) the error code is set to 0.
GP exception	13	Yes. If the fault was detected while loading a segment descriptor from memory, the error code contains either a segment selector or the IDT vector number for the descriptor; otherwise, the error code is 0. The source of the selector in an error code may be any of the following: • An instruction operand. • A selector from a gate which is the operand of the instruction. • A selector from a TSS involved in a task switch. • IDT vector number.

Table 19-9: Exceptions that Return Error Codes (Continued)

Exception Type	Vector	Does the error code have the standard format shown in Figure 19-25 on page 739?

Page Fault exception	14	Error code has a special format (see Figure 19-26 on page 739). CR2 contains the 32-bit virtual address that caused the fault. The error code tells the exception handler five things:
		1. **P** indicates whether the exception was due to a page not present, or either an access rights violation or a set reserved bit.
		2. **R/W** indicates whether the memory access that caused the exception was a read (0) or write (1).
		3. **U/S** indicates whether the logical processor was executing at User (1) or Supervisor privilege (0) level at the time of the exception. Note: Supervisor privilege levels are 0, 1, and 2.
		4. **RSVD**. The RSVD bit indicates that the logical processor detected a 1 in one or more reserved bits of the selected PDE (when CR4[PSE] or CR4[PAE] = 1). For more information on PSE, refer to "4MB Pages" on page 550. For more information on PAE, refer to "Second-Generation Paging" on page 553.
		5. **I/D**. An instruction fetch was attempted from a data page:
		  – 0 = Fault not caused by an instruction fetch.
		  – 1 = Fault caused by an instruction fetch. Additional information can be found in "Execute Disable Feature" on page 579.
		If a Page Fault is caused by a page-level protection violation, the Accessed bit in the PDE is set when the fault occurs. The behavior of x86 processors regarding the Accessed flag in the corresponding PTE is model-specific and not architecturally defined.

Alignment Check exception	17	No. Always pushes an error code value of 00000000h.

Figure 19-25: Standard Error Code Format

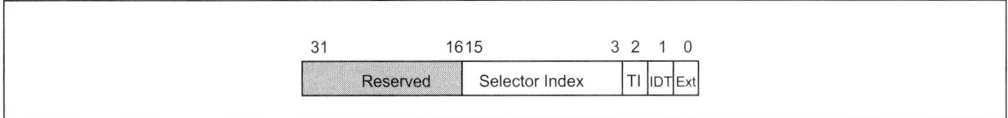

Figure 19-26: Page Fault Error Code Format

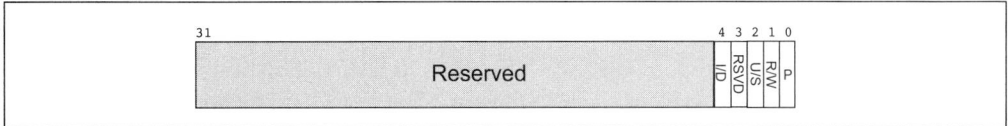

Interrupt/Exception Priority

The logical processor can only execute one program at a time. This being the case, if multiple interrupts and/or exception conditions occurred simultaneously, the logical processor must decide which one to service.

The x86 processor family divides the possible types of interrupts and exceptions into ten classes (listed in Table 19-10 on page 739). Class one is the highest priority group, while class ten is the lowest. *Please note that the table reflects the classes defined as of this writing.* The logical processor services the exception or interrupt from the highest class. Lower priority exceptions are discarded, while lower priority interrupts are held in the pending state. Discarded exception conditions will be generated again when the current handler returns execution to the point of interruption and reexecutes the offending instruction.

Table 19-10: Interrupt/Exception Priority

Class	Class Description	Ranking Within Class (highest shown first)
1 Highest Priority	Hardware Reset and Machine Checks.	Reset. The platform (i.e., the chipset) asserts the Reset signal to the processor.
		Machine Check exception due to the detection of a serious hardware-related problem either within the processor on its external interface.

Table 19-10: Interrupt/Exception Priority (Continued)

Class	Class Description	Ranking Within Class (highest shown first)
2	Trap on a task switch.	When a switch to a new task occurs, the T bit (Trap bit) is set to one in the TSS of the new task.
3	Special external hardware interrupts	**Flush**. The chipset asserts the FLUSH# signal to the processor to force a cache flush (e.g., on a switch to SMM). Starting with the Pentium 4 processor, the FLUSH# signal is no longer implemented.
		Stop Clock. The chipset asserts the STPCLK# signal to the processor, commanding the processor to turn off its internal clock (as a power conservation measure).
		SMI. The chipset sends an SMI to the logical processor to switch it into SMM.
		INIT. The chipset sends an INIT to the logical processor. This is a soft reset (see "Hot Reset and 286 DOS Extender Programs" on page 311 for more information).
4	A Trap on the previous instruction.	Breakpoint caused by the execution of the INT3 breakpoint instruction.
		Debug trap exceptions due to: • A Single-step exception (Eflags[TF] = 1). • An IO or a memory data access breakpoint address match was detected by the Debug breakpoint register logic.
5	NMI.	NMI. The chipset sends a Non-Maskable Interrupt to the logical processor, typically to report that a serious hardware-related problem was detected in the platform.
6	Maskable hardware interrupts	A device-related interrupt has been sent to the logical processor.

Table 19-10: Interrupt/Exception Priority (Continued)

Class	Class Description	Ranking Within Class (highest shown first)
7	Code breakpoint fault.	A memory instruction fetch breakpoint address match was detected by the Debug breakpoint register logic.
8	A Fault caused by the fetch of the next instruction.	Code segment limit violation. When the EIP value was added to the code segment's base address, the resultant 32-bit virtual address exceeded the length of the code segment.
		A Page Fault occurred on an instruction prefetch.
9	A Fault was generated during the decode of the next instruction.	The instruction length is > 15 bytes (includes prefixes).
		The instruction has an illegal opcode.
		The FPU is not available. This is also referred to as the DNA (Device Not Available) exception.

Table 19-10: Interrupt/Exception Priority (Continued)

Class	Class Description	Ranking Within Class (highest shown first)
10 Lowest Priority	A Fault was detected during the execution of an instruction.	**Overflow**. An INTO instruction was executed with Eflags[OF] = 1.
		An error was detected when the BOUND instruction was executed.
		Invalid TSS. The instruction caused the logical processor to select a TSS descriptor and the TSS it points to contains invalid information.
		Segment Not Present. An instruction loaded a new value into one of the segment registers. The Segment Present bit in the selected GDT or LDT descriptor = 0, indicating that the segment is not currently present in memory.
		Stack exception. See "Stack Exception (12)" on page 761.
		General Protection. See "General Protection (GP) Exception (13)" on page 763.
		Data Page Fault. The target page on a data access is not currently present in memory.
		Alignment Check. See "Alignment Check Exception (17)" on page 774.
		x87 FPU exception. An error occurred while the x87 FPU was performing a FP operation.
		SIMD FP exception. An error occurred while the logical processor was executing an SSE or SSE FP operation.

Detailed Description of Software Exceptions

This section provides a detailed description of each of the currently-defined software exceptions.

Divide-by-Zero Exception (0)

Processor Introduced In

This exception was first introduced in the 8088 processor and is implemented in all subsequent x86 processors.

Exception Class

This is an instruction Fault.

Description

The occurrence of this exception indicates that the divisor operand for a DIV or IDIV instruction is 0 or that the result cannot be represented in the number of bits specified for the destination operand.

Error Code

No error code is pushed onto the stack.

Saved Instruction Pointer

The contents of the CS:EIP register pair saved on the stack points to the instruction that generated the exception.

Processor State

A program state change does not accompany this error. The exception occurs before the faulting instruction is executed.

Debug Exception (1)

Processor Introduced In

This exception was first introduced in the 8088 processor and is implemented in all subsequent x86 processors.

Exception Class

This can be either a Trap or a Fault. The exception handler can distinguish between a trap and fault by examining the contents of DR6 (the Debug Breakpoint Status register) and the other debug registers.

Description

The occurrence of this exception indicates that one or more debug exception conditions has been detected. Whether the exception is a fault or a trap depends on the condition.

Table 19-11: Debug Exception Conditions and Exception Class

Condition	Exception Class
Instruction fetch breakpoint detected by the Debug register logic.	Fault
Data read or write breakpoint detected by the Debug register logic.	Trap
IO read or write breakpoint detected by the Debug register logic. Note this capability was introduced in the Pentium and is enabled by setting CR4[DE] = 1.	Trap
General Detect condition (attempt to access debug register while they are in use by an ICE tool).	Fault
Single-step exception due to Eflags[TF] = 1.	Trap
Task switch to a task with the Trap bit set in its TSS.	Trap
Execution of INT 01 instruction.	Trap

Error Code

No error code is pushed onto the stack. The handler can examine the Debug registers to determine which condition caused the exception.

Saved Instruction Pointer

In the event of a Fault, the CS:EIP value pushed onto the stack points to the instruction that generated the exception.

In the event of a Trap, the CS:EIP value pushed onto the stack points to the instruction following the one that generated the exception.

Processor State

In the event of a Fault, a program state change does not accompany the exception. The exception occurred before the faulting instruction was executed. The logical processor can resume normal execution upon returning from the debug exception handler.

In the event of a Trap, a program state change does accompany the exception. The instruction or task switch being executed is allowed to complete before the exception is generated. The new state of the program is not corrupted and execution of the program can continue reliably.

The Resume Flag Prevents Multiple Debug Exceptions

When a debug instruction breakpoint exception occurs, the logical processor jumps to the debugger's exception handler. Because this exception is a fault, the CS:EIP return address value on the stack points to the instruction that caused the exception, rather than to the instruction that follows it. In the handler, the breakpoint is reported to the programmer. If the programmer chooses to resume the interrupted program and executes an IRET rather than an IRETD (Interrupt Return from Debugger), execution of the interrupted program resumes at the same instruction and the same exception is generated again.

To prevent this, the exception handler should set the Eflags[RF] (Resume Flag) bit in the Eflags image on the stack. In addition, an IRETD rather than an IRET should be executed at the end of the exception handler. When the IRETD is executed, the logical processor loads the Eflags register from the stack, thus setting the Eflags[RF] bit. Execution of IRETD with RF = 1 causes the logical processor to resume execution of the interrupted program at the instruction that caused the exception, but it does not generate the instruction address breakpoint exception again.

NMI (2)

Processor Introduced In

This hardware interrupt (it is not an exception) was first introduced in the 8088 processor and is implemented in all subsequent x86 processors.

Exception Class

This is not an exception. Rather, it is a hardware interrupt generated by asserting the processor's NMI pin or by the receipt of an NMI interrupt message sent by the IO APIC to the processor's Local APIC (note: the APIC was not added until the advent of the P54C version of the Pentium processor). This interrupt causes the NMI interrupt handler to be called.

Error Code

No error code is pushed onto the stack.

Saved Instruction Pointer

The logical processor always recognizes an NMI interrupt on an instruction boundary. The contents of CS:EIP saved on the stack points to the instruction that would have been executed next if the NMI had not occurred.

Processor State

A program or task can be safely resumed upon returning from the NMI interrupt handler, provided the interrupt handler saves the state of the logical processor before handling the interrupt and restores the logical processor's state prior to a return.

Breakpoint Exception (3)

Processor Introduced In

This exception was first introduced in the 8088 processor and is implemented in all subsequent x86 processors.

Exception Class

This is an instruction Trap.

Description

The occurrence of this exception indicates that a breakpoint instruction (INT 3) was executed. Typically, a debugger sets a breakpoint by replacing the first opcode byte of an instruction with the opcode for the INT 3 instruction. Unlike the two byte INT *nn* instruction, this instruction is one byte long, so it can even be used to replace the opcode of a single byte instruction (using the INT *nn* instruction to do so would entail overwriting the first byte of the next instruction as well).

Starting with the 386, x86 processors implement the Debug registers, permitting software to activate up to four breakpoint access comparators. If more than four breakpoints are needed, the INT 3 instruction can be used.

This exception can also be generated by executing the INT *nn* instruction with an operand of 03.

Error Code

No error code is pushed onto the stack.

Saved Instruction Pointer

The contents of CS:EIP saved on the stack points to the instruction following the INT 3 instruction.

Processor State

The state of the program is unchanged because the INT 3 instruction does not affect any register or memory locations. The debugger can resume the suspended program after replacing the INT 3 instruction that caused the breakpoint with the original opcode and decrementing the EIP value stored on the stack. On returning from the debugger, program execution resumes with the replaced instruction.

Overflow Exception (4)

Processor Introduced In

This exception was first introduced in the 8088 processor and is implemented in all subsequent x86 processors.

Exception Class

This is an instruction Trap.

Description

This exception is generated when the INTO (Interrupt on Overflow) instruction is executed while Eflags[OF] = 1.

Some arithmetic instructions (e.g., ADD and SUB) perform signed and unsigned arithmetic and set either Eflags[OF] or Eflags[CF] to indicate either signed overflow or unsigned overflow condition, respectively.

Error Code

No error code is pushed onto the stack.

Saved Instruction Pointer

The CS:EIP value saved on the stack points to the instruction following the INTO instruction.

Processor State

The state of the logical processor is unchanged. The INTO instruction does not affect any register or any memory locations. The logical processor resumes normal execution upon returning from the overflow exception handler.

Array Bounds Check Exception (5)

Processor Introduced In

This exception was first introduced in the 286 and is implemented in all subsequent x86 processors.

Exception Class

This is an instruction Fault.

Description

The occurrence of this exception indicates that a "bound range exceeded" fault was detected when the BOUND instruction was executed. When executed, the BOUND instruction verifies that a signed index value falls within the upper and lower bounds of an array located in memory.

Error Code

No error code is pushed onto the stack.

Saved Instruction Pointer

The CS:EIP value saved on the stack points to the BOUND instruction that generated the exception.

Processor State

A program-state change does not accompany the bounds-check fault, because the operands for the BOUND instruction are not modified. Returning from the BOUND-range-exceeded exception handler causes the BOUND instruction to be restarted.

Invalid OpCode Exception (6)

Processor Introduced In

This exception was first introduced in the 286 and is implemented in all subsequent x86 processors.

Exception Class

This is an instruction Fault.

Description

The occurrence of this exception indicates that the logical processor:

- Attempted to execute an invalid or reserved opcode.
- Attempted to execute an instruction with an operand type that is invalid for

its accompanying opcode; for example, when the source operand specified for the LES instruction is not a memory location.

- Attempted to execute an MMX or SSE instruction on a logical processor that does not support MMX or SSE.
- Attempted to execute an MMX or SSE instruction (with the exception of MOVNTI, PAUSE, PREFETCHH, SFENCE, LFENCE, MFENCE, or CLFLUSH) when CR0[EM] = 1.
- Attempted to execute an SSE instruction when CR4[OSFXSR] = 0 (other than MASKMOVQ, MOVNTQ, MOVNTI, PREFETCHH, SFENCE, LFENCE, MFENCE, and CLFLUSH, or the 64-bit versions of PAVGB, PAVGW, PEXTRW, PINSRW, PMAXSW, PMAXUB, PMINSW, PMINUB, PMOVMSKB, PMULHUW, PSADBW, PSHUFW, PADDQ, and PSUBQ).
- Attempted to execute an SSE instruction on a logical processor that causes a SIMD FP exception when CR4[OSXMMEXCPT] = 0.
- Executed the UD2 instruction (the CS:EIP value stored on the stack points at the UD2 instruction). The UD2 instruction is guaranteed to generate an invalid opcode exception.
- Detected a LOCK prefix preceding an instruction that can not be locked or one that can be locked but the destination operand is not a memory location.
- Attempted to execute an LLDT, SLDT, LTR, STR, LSL, LAR, VERR, VERW, or ARPL instruction while in Real Mode or VM86 Mode.
- Attempted to execute the RSM instruction while not in SMM mode.

In the x86 processors that perform out-of-order speculative instruction execution (i.e., all x86 processors starting with the Pentium Pro), this exception is not generated until the attempted retirement of a speculatively-executed invalid instruction. Decoding and speculatively executing an invalid opcode does not generate this exception. In processors earlier than the Pentium Pro, this exception was not generated due to the prefetching and preliminary decoding of an invalid instruction.

Opcodes D6h and F1h are reserved undefined opcodes, but they do not generate an invalid opcode exception when executed.

Error Code

No error code is pushed onto the stack.

Saved Instruction Pointer

The CS:EIP value saved on the stack points to the instruction that generated the exception.

Processor State

The processor state does not change because the invalid instruction is not executed.

Device Not Available (DNA) Exception (7)

Processor Introduced In

This exception was first introduced in the 286 and is implemented in all subsequent x86 processors.

Exception Class

This is an instruction Fault.

Description

General. The DNA exception is generated when one the following conditions is detected:

— The logical processor executed an x87 FP instruction while CR0[EM] = 1.
— The logical processor executed an WAIT or FWAIT instruction when both CR0[MP] and CR0[TS] = 1, regardless of the setting of CR0[EM].
— The logical processor executed an x87, MMX or SSE instruction (with the exception of MOVNTI, PAUSE, PREFETCHH, SFENCE, LFENCE, MFENCE, and CLFLUSH instructions) while the CR0[TS] = 1 and CR0[EM] = 0.

X87 FPU Emulation. Software sets CR0[EM] = 1 if the processor does not include an integrated x87 FPU and a 287 or 387 numeric coprocessor is not present on the system board. A DNA exception is then generated whenever an x87 instruction is encountered, and the exception handler acted as a FP instruction emulation routine. The exception handler reads the FP instruction pointed to by the CS:EIP value on the stack and then calls the appropriate emulation routine.

CR0[TS]: Task Switch, But FP/SSE Registers Not Saved. CR0[TS] = 1 indicates that a task switch has occurred since the last time an x87, MMX, or SSE instruction was executed, but the contents of the x87 FPU's registers and the SSE register set (the XMM registers and the MXCSR register) were not saved when the task switch occurred. When CR0[TS] = 1 and CR0[EM] = 0, the logical processor generates a DNA exception when an x87, MMX, or SSE instruction is encountered (with the exception of the instructions listed earlier). The DNA exception handler saves the x87 FPU registers, the XMM registers, and the MXCSR register in the TSS associated with the task that last performed x87, MMX or SSE operations. The exception handler then sets CR0[TS] = 0 and returns to the instruction in the current task that caused the DNA exception. The x87, MMX, or SSE instruction encountered in the current task then executes without causing a DNA exception (because CR0[TS] = 0).

CR0[MP]. CR0[MP] is used with CR0[TS] to determine if WAIT or FWAIT instructions should generate a DNA exception. CR0[MP] extends the function of CR0[TS] to the WAIT and FWAIT instructions, thereby permitting the DNA handler to save the x87 FPU's register set before the WAIT or FWAIT instruction is executed. Software (i.e., the OS) should always set CR0[MP] = 1 on all x86 processors from the 486DX on forward (because all of those processors have an integrated x87 FPU).

Error Code

No error code is pushed onto the stack.

Saved Instruction Pointer

The CS:EIP value saved on the stack points to the FP instruction or the WAIT or FWAIT instruction that generated the exception.

Processor State

The processor state does not change because the instruction that generated the exception is not executed.

Double Fault Exception (8)

Processor Introduced In

This exception was first introduced in the 286 and is implemented in all subsequent x86 processors.

Exception Class

This is an instruction Abort.

Description

The occurrence of this exception indicates that the logical processor detected a second exception while calling an exception handler for a prior exception. In most cases, when the logical processor detects another exception while trying to call an exception handler, the two exceptions can be handled serially (i.e., service the first, higher-priority condition, return to and reexecute the offending instruction, and then handle the second condition). In some cases, however, the logical processor cannot handle them serially. In that case, it generates the Double Fault exception.

Exceptions are divided into three classes: benign exceptions, contributory exceptions, and page faults (see Table 19-12 on page 754). Table 19-13 on page 755 shows the various combinations of exception classes that result in the generation of a Double Fault exception.

Since the Double Fault exception is an abort type exception, the interrupted program or task cannot be safely restarted or resumed. The Double Fault handler collects diagnostic information about the state of the machine and, when possible, shuts the application and/or system down gracefully or restarts the system.

Table 19-12: Interrupt and Exception Classes

Class	Vector	Description
Benign Exceptions and Interrupts	1	Debug exception.
	2	Assertion of the processor's NMI hardware interrupt input.
	3	Breakpoint exception.
	4	Overflow exception.
	5	BOUND Range Exceeded exception.
	6	Invalid Opcode exception.
	7	Device Not Available exception.
	9	Coprocessor Segment Overrun exception.
	16	x87 FP Error exception.
	17	Alignment Check exception. Note that this exception was first introduced on the 486.
	18	Machine Check exception. Note that this exception was first introduced on the Pentium.
	19	SIMD FP exception. Note that this exception was first introduced on the Pentium III.
	All	INT nn (where nn = the programmer-supplied vector).
	All	Assertion of the processor's INTR hardware interrupt input (the vector is supplied to the logical processor by the external interrupt controller).
Contributory Exceptions	0	Divide by zero exception.
	10	Invalid TSS exception.
	11	Segment Not Present exception.
	12	Stack Fault exception.
	13	General Protection (GP) exception.
Page Faults	14	Page Fault exception.

Table 19-13: Exception Combinations Resulting in a Double Fault Exception

1st Exception	Second Exception		
	Benign	**Contributory**	**Page Fault**
Benign	Handle exceptions serially	Handle exceptions serially	Handle exceptions serially
Contributory	Handle exceptions serially	Generate a Double Fault	Handle exceptions serially
Page Fault	Handle exceptions serially	Generate a Double Fault	Generate a Double Fault

If the logical processor encounters another exception while attempting to call the Double Fault handler, it enters Shutdown Mode (see the next section). This is sometimes unofficially referred to as a Triple Fault condition.

Shutdown Mode

In Shutdown Mode, the logical processor stops executing instructions until one of the following is detected:

- An NMI interrupt.
- An SMI interrupt.
- A hardware reset.
- The assertion of the processor's INIT# input or the receipt of an INIT IPI message.

Upon entering Shutdown Mode, the processor outputs the Shutdown message on its external interface. This informs the platform logic external to the processor (i.e., the chipset) that the logical processor has entered the Shutdown state. In response, the platform logic may take an action such as:

- Turn on an indicator light on the front panel.
- Generate an NMI interrupt. In the NMI handler, the programmer obtains status information from the chipset, determines that the logical processor has shutdown, records diagnostic information, and takes one of the following actions:
  — Commands the chipset to assert RESET# to the processor.
  — Commands the chipset to assert INIT# to the processor.
  — Commands the chipset to assert SMI# to the processor.

If the shutdown occurs while the logical processor is executing the NMI interrupt handler, the logical processor can only be restarted by asserting RESET# to the processor.

Error Code

The logical processor always pushes an error code of 0 onto the stack of the Double Fault handler.

Saved Instruction Pointer

The CS:EIP value saved on the stack is undefined.

Processor State

The logical processor state following a Double Fault exception is undefined. The interrupted program or task therefore cannot be safely resumed or restarted.

Coprocessor Segment Overrun Exception (9)

Processor Introduced In

This exception was first introduced in the 286 and was implemented in the 386 and early versions of the 486 processor (prior to the integration of the FPU onto the processor die in the 486DX). Since then, no subsequent x86 processors implement it and it is now reserved.

Exception Class

This is an instruction Abort.

Description

Reserved starting with the advent of the 486DX. The occurrence of this exception indicates that the 386 detected a Page Fault or Segment Not Present exception while transferring the middle portion of an operand to the 387 math coprocessor. Starting with the 486DX processor, this condition is reported as a General Protection exception.

Error Code

No error code is pushed onto the stack.

Saved Instruction Pointer

The CS:EIP value saved on the stack points to the instruction that generated the exception.

Processor State

The processor state after a Coprocessor Segment Overrun exception is undefined. The interrupted program or task therefore cannot be safely resumed or restarted. The only action that the exception handler can take is to save CS:EIP and reinitialize the x87 FPU using the FNINIT instruction.

Invalid TSS Exception (10)

Processor Introduced In

This exception was first introduced in the 286 and is implemented in all subsequent x86 processors.

Exception Class

This is an instruction Fault.

Description

Indicates that a task switch was attempted but invalid information was detected in the TSS for the target task. Table 19-14 on page 757 shows the conditions that will cause an invalid-TSS exception to be generated. In general, these invalid conditions result from protection violations for:

- The TSS descriptor.
- The LDT pointed to by the TSS.
- Any of the segments referenced by the TSS.

Table 19-14: Invalid TSS Conditions

Error Code Index Field Contains	Invalid Condition
TSS segment selector index	TSS segment limit less than 67h for 32-bit TSS or less than 2Ch for 16-bit TSS.
LDT segment selector index	Invalid LDT or LDT not present.
Stack-segment selector index	Stack-segment selector exceeds descriptor table limit.
Stack-segment selector index	Stack segment is not writable.
Stack-segment selector index	Stack segment DPL/CPL.
Stack-segment selector index	Stack-segment selector RPL/CPL.

Table 19-14: Invalid TSS Conditions (Continued)

Error Code Index Field Contains	Invalid Condition
Code-segment selector index	Code-segment selector exceeds descriptor table limit.
Code-segment selector index	Code segment is not executable.
Code-segment selector index	Non-Conforming code segment DPL/CPL.
Code-segment selector index	Conforming code segment DPL greater than CPL.
Data-segment selector index	Data-segment selector exceeds descriptor table limit.
Data-segment selector index	Data segment not readable.

This exception can be generated either in the context of the original task or in that of the target task. Until the logical processor has completely verified the presence of the target task's TSS, the exception is generated in the context of the original task. Once the existence of the target task's TSS is verified, the task switch is considered complete. Any invalid-TSS conditions detected after this point are handled in the context of the new task. A task switch is considered complete when the Task Register (TR) is loaded with the segment selector for the target task's TSS and, if the switch is due to a call, an interrupt or an exception, the Link field of the new TSS has been updated with the TSS selector for the calling or interrupted task. For more information, refer to "Comprehensive Task Switch Description" on page 665.

Entry 10 in the IDT must contain a Task Gate pointing to a task that will act as the Invalid TSS handler. Handling this exception inside the faulting TSS context is not recommended because the logical processor state may not be consistent.

Error Code

An error code containing the segment selector index for the segment descriptor that caused the violation is pushed onto the stack of the exception handler. If the error code's EXT flag is set (see Figure 19-25 on page 739 and Table 19-9 on page 736), it indicates that the exception was caused by an event external to the currently-running program (e.g., if an external hardware interrupt handler called using a Task Gate attempted a task switch using an invalid target TSS).

Saved Instruction Pointer

If the exception was detected before the task switch was carried out, the CS:EIP value saved on the stack points to the instruction that invoked the task switch. If the exception was detected after the task switch, the CS:EIP value saved on the stack points to the first instruction of the new task.

Processor State

Whether or not the Invalid TSS handler can recover from the fault depends on the error condition than causes the fault.

If an invalid TSS exception occurs during a task switch, it can occur before or after the commit-to-new-task point (see Figure 18-16 on page 668). If it occurs before the commit point, no logical processor state change occurs. If it occurs after the commit point (after the segment descriptor information for the new segment selectors have been loaded into the segment registers), the logical processor will load all the state information from the new TSS into its register set before it generates the exception. The logical processor first loads all of the segment registers with the segment selectors from the TSS, loads the respective segment descriptors from the GDT and/or LDT, and then checks the descriptors for validity. If an Invalid TSS exception is detected, the remaining segment registers are loaded but not checked for validity and therefore may not be usable for referencing memory.

The Invalid TSS handler should assume that using the segment selectors found in the CS, SS, DS, ES, FS, and GS registers may result in the generation of another exception. For this reason, the exception handler should load all segment registers with new values before trying to resume the new task; otherwise, GP exceptions may result later under conditions that make diagnosis more difficult.

Segment Not Present Exception (11)

Processor Introduced In

This exception was first introduced in the 286 and is implemented in all subsequent x86 processors.

Exception Class

This is an instruction Fault.

Description

The occurrence of this exception indicates that the Present bit of a segment descriptor or gate descriptor = 0, indicating that the descriptor is not valid. This exception can occur during any of the following operations:

- While attempting to load the CS, DS, ES, FS, or GS registers (note that detection of a Segment Not Present condition while loading the SS register results in the generation of a Stack Fault exception).
- While attempting to load the LDTR using an LLDT instruction. Detection of a not-present LDT while loading the LDTR during a task switch operation causes an Invalid TSS exception to be generated.
- When executing the LTR instruction and the TSS is marked not present.
- While attempting to use a gate descriptor or a TSS descriptor that is marked as not present, but is otherwise valid.

Much like Paging, an OS could use the Segment Not Present exception in the same manner as a Page Fault exception to implement on-demand loading of segments of information into memory from a mass storage device.

Error Code

An error code containing the segment selector index for the segment descriptor that caused the violation is pushed onto the stack of the exception handler. If the error code's EXT flag is set (see Figure 19-25 on page 739 and Table 19-9 on page 736), it indicates that the exception was caused by NMI or INTR wherein the interrupt vector selected an IDT entry that contained a descriptor with the Present bit = 0. The IDT bit in the error code = 1 if the error code refers to an IDT entry.

Saved Instruction Pointer

The CS:EIP value saved on the stack normally points to the instruction that generated the exception. However, if the exception occurred while the logical processor was loading the segment descriptors using the segment selectors in a new TSS, the CS:EIP value on the stack points to the first instruction in the new task. If the exception occurred while accessing a gate descriptor, the CS:EIP value saved on the stack points to the instruction that resulted in the descriptor being accessed (e.g., a call instruction that selects a Call Gate).

Processor State

If this exception occurs as the result of loading a register (CS, DS, SS, ES, FS, GS, or LDTR), a logical processor state change does occur (the register is not loaded). Recovery from this exception is accomplished by loading the missing segment into memory, updating the segment descriptor and marking it as present.

If the exception occurs while accessing a gate descriptor, a logical processor state change does not occur. Recovery from this exception is accomplished by creating a valid gate descriptor and then re-executing the instruction that selected the gate descriptor.

If the exception occurs during a task switch, it can occur before or after the commit-to-new-task point (see Figure 18-16 on page 668). If it occurs before the commit point, no logical processor state change occurs. If it occurs after the commit point, the logical processor loads its registers from the new TSS (without performing any additional limit, present, or type checks) before it generates the exception. The exception handler therefore cannot rely on the validity of the segment selectors in the segment registers.

The handler should assume that using the segment selectors found in the CS, SS, DS, ES, FS, and GS registers may result in the generation of another exception. For this reason, the exception handler should load all of the segment registers with new values before trying to resume the new task; otherwise, GP exceptions may result later under conditions that make diagnosis more difficult.

Stack Exception (12)

Processor Introduced In

This exception was first introduced in the 286 and is implemented in all subsequent x86 processors.

Exception Class

This is an instruction Fault.

Description

The occurrence of this exception indicates that one of the following stack-related conditions was detected:

- When a limit violation is detected during an operation that refers to the SS register. Operations that can cause a limit violation include stack-oriented instructions such as POP, PUSH, CALL, RET, IRET, ENTER, and LEAVE, as well as other memory references which implicitly or explicitly use the SS register (e.g., MOV AX, [BP+6] or MOV AX, SS:[EAX+6]). The ENTER instruction generates this exception when there is not enough stack space for allocating local variables.
- When a stack Segment Not-Present condition is detected while loading the SS register. This can occur during:
  — A task switch.
  — The execution of a call instruction to a procedure at a different privilege level.
  — A return to a procedure at a different privilege level.
  — The execution of the LSS instruction.
  — The execution of a MOV or POP instruction to the SS register.

Recovery from this fault can be accomplished by either:

- Extending the limit of the stack segment (on a limit violation).
- Loading the missing stack segment into memory (on a not present condition).

Error Code

If the exception is caused by a stack Segment Not Present or by an overflow of the new stack during an inter-privilege level call, the error code saved on the stack (see Figure 19-25 on page 739) contains a segment selector for the segment that caused the exception. The exception handler can test the Present bit in the segment descriptor pointed to by the segment selector to determine the cause of the exception.

For a limit violation (on a stack segment already in use) the error code saved on the stack is 0.

Saved Instruction Pointer

The CS:EIP value saved on the stack generally points to the instruction that generated the exception. However, if the exception was caused by an attempt to load a segment selector into the SS register that selects a descriptor with the Present bit = 0 during a task switch, the CS:EIP value saved on the stack points to the first instruction of the new task.

Processor State

A logical processor state change does not generally accompany a Stack Fault exception, because the instruction that caused the fault is not executed. The instruction can therefore be re-executed after the exception handler has corrected the Stack Fault condition.

If a Stack Fault occurs during a task switch, it occurs after the commit-to-new-task point (see Figure 18-16 on page 668). The logical processor loads its registers from the new TSS (without performing any additional limit, present, or type checks) before it generates the exception.

The handler should therefore assume that using the segment selectors found in the CS, SS, DS, ES, FS, and GS registers may result in the generation of another exception. For this reason, the exception handler should load all of the segment registers with new values before trying to resume the new task; otherwise, GP exceptions may result later under conditions that make diagnosis more difficult.

General Protection (GP) Exception (13)

Processor Introduced In

This exception was first introduced in the 286 and is implemented in all subsequent x86 processors.

Exception Class

This is an instruction Fault.

Description

The occurrence of this exception indicates that the logical processor detected a General Protection violation. The conditions that can cause this exception comprise all of the protection violations that do not cause another type of exception to be generated. Any of the following conditions will result in the generation of a General Protection exception:

- Exceeding the segment limit when accessing the CS, DS, ES, FS, or GS segments.
- Exceeding the segment limit when referencing a descriptor table (i.e., the GDT, LDT or IDT; except during a task switch or a stack switch).
- Transferring execution to a segment wherein the attributes define it as not executable.

- An attempt to write to a code segment or to a read-only data segment.
- An attempt to perform a data read from an execute-only code segment.
- Loading SS with a selector for a read-only segment (unless the selector is read from the new TSS during a task switch, in which case an Invalid TSS exception occurs).
- Loading SS, DS, ES, FS, or GS with a selector for a system segment (i.e., the descriptor's S bit = 0).
- Loading DS, ES, FS, or GS with a selector for an execute-only code segment.
- Loading SS with a selector for an executable code segment or with a null segment selector.
- Loading CS with a selector for a data segment or for a null segment selector.
- Accessing memory using DS, ES, FS, or GS when it contains a null segment selector.
- Switching to a busy task during a call or jump that selects a TSS.
- Switching to an available (non-busy) task during the execution of an IRET instruction.
- Using a selector on a task switch that points to a TSS descriptor in the current task's LDT. TSS descriptors can only reside in the GDT.
- Exceeding the maximum instruction length limit of 15 bytes (this only can occur when redundant prefixes are placed before an instruction).
- Loading CR0 so as to enable paging and disable Protected Mode (CR0[PG] = 1 and CR0[PE] = 0).
- Loading CR0 so CR0[NW] = 1 and CR0[CD] = 0 (this is a reserved combination).
- When the vector selects an IDT entry that does not contain an Interrupt Gate, Trap Gate, or a Task Gate.
- An attempt to access an interrupt or exception handler through an Interrupt Gate or a Trap Gate from VM86 mode and the handler's code segment DPL is not 0.
- An attempt to write a 1 into a reserved bit of CR4 (CR4 is only present in processors introduced in later model 486s and subsequent x86 processors).
- An attempt to execute a privileged instruction when the CPL is not equal to 0.
- An attempt to write to a reserved bit in an MSR (MSRs are present in the Pentium and later x86 processors).
- An attempt to access a gate that contains a null segment selector.
- Executing the INT *nn* instruction when the CPL > the DPL of the referenced Interrupt Gate, Trap Gate, or Task Gate.
- The segment selector in a Call Gate, Interrupt Gate, or a Trap Gate does not point to a code segment.
- The segment selector specified as the operand of the LLDT instruction selects an entry in the LDT rather than the GDT, or that selects a descriptor

in the GDT that is not an LDT descriptor.

- The segment selector specified as the operand of the LTR instruction selects an entry in the LDT rather than the GDT, or that selects a TSS descriptor with its Busy bit = 1.
- The target code segment selector for a call, jump, or RET is null.
- If CR4[PAE] and/or CR4[PSE] = 1 and the logical processor detects any reserved bits in a PDPT entry set to 1 (PAE Mode—2nd-generation address translation—was first implemented in the Pentium Pro and PSE Mode was first implemented in the Pentium). These bits are checked during any write to CR0, CR3, or CR4 (CR4 was first implemented in the Pentium, later model 486s and is present in subsequent x86 processors) that causes a reloading of the PDPT entry.
- An attempt to set any of the reserved bits in the MXCSR register = 1.
- Executing an SSE/SSE2/SSE3/SSSE3/SSE4 instruction that attempts to access a 128-bit memory location using an address that is not aligned on a 16-byte boundary when the instruction requires 16-byte alignment (SSE was first implemented on the Pentium III). This condition also applies to the stack segment.
- Violating any of the privilege rules described in the Intel or AMD system programming guides.

A program or task can be restarted following any GP exception. If the exception occurs while attempting to call an interrupt handler, the interrupted program within which the exception occurred can be restarted, but the interrupt may be lost.

Error Code

If the fault condition was detected while loading a segment descriptor, the error code (see Figure 19-25 on page 739 and Table 19-9 on page 736) contains a segment selector index or an IDT vector number for the offending descriptor; otherwise, the error code saved on the stack = 0. The source of the selector in an error code may be any of the following:

- An instruction operand.
- A selector from a gate which was selected by an instruction.
- A selector from a TSS involved in a task switch.
- An IDT vector number.

Saved Instruction Pointer

The CS:EIP value saved on the stack points to the instruction that generated the exception.

Processor State

In general, a logical processor state change does not result from a GP exception (because the invalid instruction or operation is not executed). A GP exception handler can be designed so as to correct any of the conditions that can cause a GP exception and then resume the interrupted program or task.

If a GP exception occurs during a task switch, it can occur before or after the commit-to-new-task point (see Figure 18-16 on page 668). If it occurs before the commit point, no logical processor state change occurs. If it occurs after the commit point, the logical processor loads its registers from the new TSS (without performing any additional limit, present, or type checks) before it generates the exception.

The handler should therefore assume that using the segment selectors found in the CS, SS, DS, ES, FS, and GS registers may result in the generation of another exception. For this reason, the exception handler should load all of the segment registers with new values before trying to resume the new task; otherwise, GP exceptions may result later under conditions that make diagnosis more difficult.

Page Fault Exception (14)

Processor Introduced In

This exception was first introduced in the 386 and is implemented in all subsequent x86 processors.

Exception Class

This is an instruction Fault.

Description

The occurrence of this exception indicates that the logical processor detected one of the following conditions while attempting to translate a virtual memory address into a physical memory address:

- The page Present bit in the selected PDE or the PTE = 0, indicating that the selected Page Table or the selected physical page is not present in memory. In this case, the Page Fault exception handler can obtain the missing Page Table and/or page from mass storage, place it in memory, fill in the selected PDE and/or PTE, and then re-execute the instruction that caused the Page Fault.

- The procedure attempting to access a page does not have sufficient privilege to do so. It's OS- and situation-specific whether or not the Page Fault exception handler fixes this problem (by adjusting the U/S bit in the selected PDE and/or PTE) and then permits the access.
- The currently-executing program has a privilege level other than 0 and attempted to write to a read-only page. It should be noted that, in the 386 a supervisor level program (i.e., with a privilege level of 0, 1 or 2) could write to a read-only page without causing a Page Fault exception. See the next bullet item for information on x86 processors after the 386.
- Starting with the 486, all x86 processors implement CR0[WP]. When CR0[WP] = 1, a Page Fault exception is generated when a supervisor level program (i.e., with a privilege level of 0, 1 or 2) attempts to write to a read-only page wherein the U/S bit = 0.
- The attempted access selected a PDE wherein one or more of the reserved bits are set to one.
- An attempt was made to perform a code fetch from a data page.

If a Page Fault is caused by a page-level protection violation, the Accessed bit in the PDE is set when the fault occurs. The behavior of x86 processors regarding the Accessed bit in the corresponding PTE is model-specific and is not architecturally defined.

Error Code

An error code is pushed onto the stack when a Page Fault exception is detected. The error code has a special format (see Figure 19-27 on page 768) that provides the following information to the exception handler:

- P bit:
  — P = 1. The exception was due to P = 0 in either the selected PDE or PTE.
  — P = 0. The exception was due to either an access rights violation or the detection of one or more reserved bits set to one in the selected PDE.
- The R/W bit indicates whether the memory access that caused the exception was a read (0) or write (1).
- The U/S flag indicates whether the offending program was executing at User mode privilege level (3) or at the Supervisor mode privilege level (0, 1, or 2):
  — 0 = Supervisor privilege level.
  — 1 = User mode privilege level.
- When set to one, the RSVD bit indicates that the logical processor detected one or more reserved bits set to one in the selected PDE. This detection feature is only enabled when CR4[PAE] and/or CR4[PSE] = 1:

— CR4[PSE] was first implemented in the Pentium, was migrated backwards into the later versions of the 486, and is present in all subsequent x86 processors.

— CR4[PAE] was first implemented in the Pentium Pro and is present in all subsequent x86 processors.

- The I/D bit indicates if an attempt was made to perform an instruction fetch from a data page. This bit only has meaning if the Execute Disable feature is enabled (both EFER[NXE] = 1 and CR4[PAE] = 1). Additional information can be found in "Execute Disable Feature" on page 579:

— 0 = Fault not caused by an instruction fetch.

— 1 = Fault caused by an instruction fetch.

Figure 19-27: Page Fault Exception Error Code Format

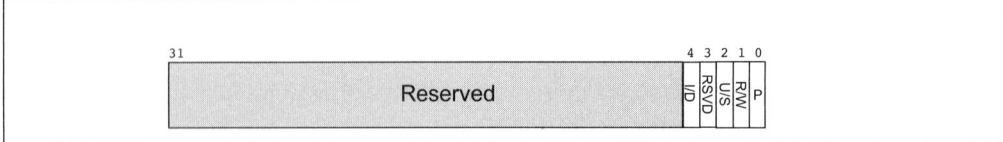

CR2

When a Page Fault exception is detected, the 32-bit virtual address that caused the exception is automatically latched into CR2. The Page Fault handler uses this address to perform a lookup in the address translation tables. If another Page Fault could occur during execution of the Page Fault handler, the handler must push the contents of CR2 onto the stack before the second Page Fault occurs.

Saved Instruction Pointer

The CS:EIP value saved on the stack generally points to the instruction that generated the exception. If the Page Fault exception occurred during a task switch, the CS:EIP value on the stack may point to the first instruction of the new task.

Processor State

The More Common Case. The logical processor state doesn't normally change when a Page Fault exception is generated (because the instruction that caused the exception was not executed). After the Page Fault exception handler has corrected the violation (e.g., by loading the missing page into memory), execution of the program or task can be resumed.

Page Fault During a Task Switch. When a Page Fault exception is generated during a task switch, the logical processor state may change, however. During a task switch, a Page Fault exception can occur during any of following operations:

— While writing the contents of the logical processor's register set into the TSS of the task that is being suspended.
— While reading the GDT to locate the TSS descriptor of the destination task.
— While reading the TSS of the destination task.
— While reading the segment descriptors associated with segment selectors from the destination task.
— While reading the LDT of the destination task to verify the segment register images stored in the new TSS.

In the last two cases the exception occurs in the context of the new task. CS:EIP points to the first instruction of the new task, not to the instruction which caused the task switch (or the last instruction to be executed, in the case of an interrupt). If the OS permits Page Faults to occur during task switches, the Page Fault handler should be called through a Task Gate.

If a Page Fault occurs during a task switch, the logical processor loads its register set from the new TSS (without performing any additional limit, present, or type checks) before it generates the exception. The handler should therefore assume that using the segment selectors found in the CS, SS, DS, ES, FS, and GS registers may result in the generation of another exception. For this reason, the exception handler should load all of the segment registers with new values before trying to resume the new task; otherwise, GP exceptions may result later under conditions that make diagnosis more difficult.

Page Fault During a Stack Switch

Software written for 16-bit x86 processors (i.e., 8088, 8086, 286) often used a pair of instructions to change to a new stack. As an example:

```
MOV SS, AX
MOV SP, StackTop
```

When executing this code on an x86 processor, it is possible to detect a Page Fault, GP exception, or Alignment Check exception after the first instruction completes but before the Stack Pointer register has been loaded. At this point, the new stack segment is being used with the old stack pointer. Very bogus!

If the exception handler is called at the same privilege level and within the same task, the logical processor will use the bogus stack pointer. However, the logical processor will not use the inconsistent stack pointer if the exception handler is implemented as another task or as a more privileged procedure.

In an OS that handles Page Fault, GP, or Alignment Check exceptions within the faulting task (in other words, the handlers are pointed to by Trap Gates or Interrupt Gates, rather than by Task Gates), when software that executes at the same privilege level as the exception handler wishes to change to a new stack it should use the LSS instruction rather than a pair of MOV instructions (as shown in the earlier example). When the exception handler executes at privilege level 0 (as is most often the case), the problem is limited to procedures or tasks that run at privilege level 0 (typically the OS kernel).

Vector (Exception) 15

Vector 15 is reserved in all x86 processors.

FPU Exception (16)

Processor Introduced In

This exception was first introduced in the 486DX and is implemented in all subsequent x86 processors.

Exception Class

This is an instruction Fault.

Description

The occurrence of this exception indicates that the x87 FPU has detected a FP error. CR[NE] =1 enables the generation of this exception (see "CR0[NE]" on page 358 for more information).

The x87 FPU can detect and report six types of FP error conditions:

- Invalid operation:
  — Stack overflow or underflow.
  — Invalid arithmetic operation.
- Divide-by-zero.

- Denormalized operand.
- Numeric overflow.
- Numeric underflow.
- Inexact result (precision).

There are two register bits associated with each of these error types:

- A corresponding Mask bit in the FPU Control register (see Figure 9-6 on page 352).
- A corresponding status bit in the FPU Status register (see Figure 9-7 on page 354).

In addition, the Summary Error (SE) bit in the FPU Status register is set to one whenever any of the unmasked error conditions are detected.

Handling of Masked Errors

When the FPU detects an error type that is currently masked, it sets the respective error status bit in the FPU Status register, but it does not set the Summary Error (SE) status bit in the Status register, nor does it generate a a FPU exception. Rather, the processor takes a default set of actions based on the error type detected and continues with program execution. Table 19-15 on page 771 defines the default set of actions taken when a masked error type is detected.

Table 19-15: FPU Handling of Masked Errors

Error Type	Default Actions Taken
Invalid operation	The logical processor sets the IE bit in the FPU Status register (FSW) and returns an indefinite value or a QNaN. This value overwrites the destination register specified by the instruction.
Divide-by-zero	The logical processor sets the ZE bit in the FPU Status register (FSW) and returns an infinity signed with the exclusive OR of the sign of the operands.

Table 19-15: FPU Handling of Masked Errors (Continued)

Error Type	Default Actions Taken
Denormalized operand	The logical processor sets the DE bit in the FPU Status register (FSW) and executes the instruction. Operating on denormal numbers produces results at least as good as and often better than what can be obtained when denormal numbers are flushed to zero. The programmer can mask this exception so that a computation may proceed, then analyze any loss of accuracy when the final result is delivered.
Numeric overflow	The logical processor sets the OE bit in the FPU Status register (FSW) and returns one of a set of predefined values (based on the currently-selected rounding mode).
Numeric underflow	The logical processor sets the UE bit in the FPU Status register (FSW) when the result is both tiny and inexact. The logical processor returns a denormalized result to the destination operand, regardless of inexactness.
Inexact result (precision)	If a numeric overflow or underflow condition has not occurred, the logical processor sets the PE bit in the FPU Status register (FSW) and stores the rounded result in the destination operand. The currently-selected rounding mode determines the method used to round the result.

Handling of Unmasked Errors

This description assumes that CR0[NE] = 1. When the FPU detects an error type that is currently unmasked (in the FCW register), it sets the respective error status bit in the FPU Status register (FSW). However, it does not immediately set the Summary Error (SE) status bit in the Status register (FSW), nor does it immediately generate a FPU exception.

Rather, it waits until it fetches and decodes the next "waiting" x87 FPU instruction or WAIT/FWAIT instruction in the program's instruction stream. At that time, before actually executing the current instruction, if any of the unmasked error type status bits are set to one in the Status register (FSW), it sets the Summary Error (SE) status bit in the Status register and generates a FPU exception.

x87 FPU errors incurred by a previously-executed computational FPU instruction are not reported via the SE bit or the exception if the logical processor subsequently executes any of the "non-waiting" x87 FPU instructions, which include the FNINIT, FNCLEX, FNSTSW, FNSTSW AX, FNSTCW, FNSTENV, and FNSAVE instructions. They also are not reported on execution of either of the state management instructions, FXSAVE or FXRSTOR.

The FPU exception handler can be designed to permit recovery from any of the error types.

Error Code

No error code is pushed onto the stack.

Saved Instruction Pointer

The CS:EIP value saved on the stack points to the FP or WAIT/FWAIT instruction that was about to be executed when the exception was generated. This is *not* the instruction that generated the error. The address of the offending instruction is automatically latched into the FPU's 48-bit Instruction Pointer register (in CS:EIP format). In addition, if a memory-based data operand is associated with the instruction, its address is automatically latched into the FPU's 48-bit Data Pointer register (in xS:offset format, where xS = DS, ES, FS, or GS and the offset is a 32-bit pointer).

Processor State

Generally, a logical processor state change results from a FPU exception (because the handling of the exception is delayed until the next waiting x87 FP or WAIT/FWAIT instruction following the offending instruction. The x87 FPU saves sufficient information about the error condition in its register set to allow recovery from the error and re-execution of the faulting instruction.

In a situation wherein an instruction is dependent on the results of a previously-executed FP instruction, a WAIT or FWAIT instruction can be inserted in front of the dependent instruction. This will force a yet-to-be-reported x87 FPU error to generate an exception and be handled before the dependent instruction is executed.

Alignment Check Exception (17)

Processor Introduced In

This exception was first introduced in the 486 and is implemented in all subsequent x86 processors.

Background: Misaligned Transfers Affect Performance

In a single transaction on its external interface, the 386 and 486 (which had a dword-aligned address bus and could therefore only address a single dword at a time) could only address a single dword within which to perform a read or write. Consider the following example:

```
mov eax,[0101]
```

When executed, this instruction causes the logical processor to load the 32-bit EAX register with the four bytes from memory locations 00000101h through 00000104h. These are the last three locations in the dword that starts at 00000100h and the first location in the dword that starts at location 00000104h. In order to read these four locations, the logical processor had to:

- Perform a memory data read transaction from the dword starting at location 00000100h indicating a read from locations 00000101h through 00000103h.
- Perform a memory data read transaction from the dword starting at location 00000104h indicating a read from location 00000104h.

This scenario came about because the programmer (or the compiler) did not pay attention to alignment when this 32-bit data object was created in memory. Because it straddles two dwords, the logical processor had to perform two transactions on its external interface whenever it had to read or update this data object. Naturally, this negatively affected performance. The 386 did not provide the ability to flag this condition to the programmer as something that should be fixed in order to optimize execution speed. Starting with the 486, all x86 processors implement a mechanism to flag this condition.

Alignment Is Important!

As indicated in the previous section, misalignment of multi-byte data objects in memory can negatively affect performance. This is true in all x86 processor implementations. If a multi-byte data object straddles a dword address boundary, it may also:

- **Straddle a cache line boundary**. In a post-386 processor, this may result in a double cache miss causing the logical processor to perform two full cache line reads from memory. Not only is this time consuming for the logical processor that experienced the double miss, but it consumes memory bus bandwidth making the bus less available to other entities.
- **Straddle a page address boundary**. This could result in a double Page Fault. In order to obtain the multi-byte data object from memory, the OS Page Fault exception handler would have to read two full pages (4KB each) from disk into memory. Only then could the multi-byte data object be read from memory. See "IA-32 Address Translation Mechanisms" on page 493 for a detailed description of Paging.

Exception Class

This is an instruction Fault.

Description

The occurrence of this exception indicates that the logical processor detected an unaligned access attempt to a multi-byte memory operand when alignment checking is enabled. Alignment checking is only performed for data accesses within data or stack segments (not for accesses in code or system segments). Table 19-16 lists the alignment requirements of various data types recognized by the logical processor.

Table 19-16: Alignment Requirements by Data Type

Data Type	Address Must Be Divisible By
Word (16 bits)	2
Dword (32 bits)	4
32-bit Single Precision FP number	4
64-bit Double Precision FP number	8
80-bit Double Extended Precision FP number	8
Qword (64-bits)	8
Double qword (128 bits)	16
Segment Selector (16 bits)	2

Table 19-16: Alignment Requirements by Data Type (Continued)

Data Type	Address Must Be Divisible By
32-bit Far Pointer	2
48-bit Far Pointer	4
32-bit Pointer	4
GDTR, IDTR, LDTR, or Task Register Contents	4
FSTENV/FLDENV Save Area	4 or 2, depending on the operand size.
FSAVE/FRSTOR Save Area	4 or 2, depending on the operand size.
Bit String	2 or 4 depending on the operand-size attribute.

The Alignment Check exception is only generated on a misaligned access attempted on a data type that should be aligned on word, dword, and qword address boundaries. A GP exception is generated when an access is attempted on a 128-bit data type that is not aligned on an address divisible by 16.

Alignment Checking is enabled when all of the following are true:

- The OS (or some other software entity) has set CR0[AM] = 1.
- Eflags[AC] = 1 while the current task is executing.
- The privilege level of the currently executing program (i.e., its CPL) = 3 and the current task is running in either Protected Mode or VM86 mode.

Implicit Privilege Level 0 Accesses

Memory accesses that are always performed at privilege level 0 (e.g., segment descriptor loads), never result in an Alignment Check exception, even when generated by an access initiated by a program executing at privilege level 3.

Storing GDTR, LDTR, IDTR or TR

An attempt to store the contents of the GDTR, IDTR, LDTR, or the TR in memory while at privilege level 3 can result in an Alignment Check exception. The fault can be avoided by storing the register's contents into memory starting at an address that is divisible by two.

FP/MMX/SSE Save and Restore Accesses

The FXSAVE and FXRSTOR instructions save and restore the contents of the x87 FPU register set and the SSE register set in a 512-byte data structure in memory. The start address specified must be divisible by 16. If the Alignment Check exception is enabled and the CPL of the currently executing program = 3, a misaligned memory operand can cause either:

- An **Alignment Check** exception. If the AC exception is enabled and the CPL = 3, generation of the AC exception is not guaranteed and can be model-specific. In implementations where the AC exception is not generated, a GP exception is generated instead. In addition, the alignment granularity may also vary with implementation. As an example, in a given implementation, an AC exception might be generated when the start address is not aligned on an address divisible by two, whereas a GP exception might result for other misalignments types (4-, 8-, or 16-byte misalignments).
- A **GP exception** is generated for an illegal memory operand effective address in the CS, DS, ES, FS or GS segments. If the AC exception is disabled, a GP exception is generated if the start memory address specified is not aligned on a 16-byte boundary.

MOVUPS and MOVUPD Accesses

The MOVUPS (Move Unaligned Packed SP FP value) and MOVUPD (Move Unaligned Packed DP FP value) instructions perform a 128-bit unaligned load or store. They do not generate GP exceptions when an operand is not aligned on a 16-byte boundary. If alignment checking is enabled, 2-, 4-, and 8-byte misalignments are detected and result in the generation of an Alignment Check exception.

FSAVE and FRSTOR Accesses

The start memory address specified as the operand of the FSAVE and FRSTOR instructions can result in the generation of an alignment check exception. These instructions are rarely used by application programs.

Error Code

An error code of 0 is pushed onto the stack.

Saved Instruction Pointer

The CS:EIP value stored on the stack points to the instruction that generated the exception.

Processor State

A logical processor state change does not result from an AC exception (because the instruction is not executed).

Machine Check Exception (18)

Processor Introduced In

This exception was first introduced in the Pentium and is implemented in all subsequent x86 processors.

Exception Class

This is an instruction Abort.

Description

The logical processor's ability to generate a Machine Check exception is enabled by setting CR4[MCE] = 1.

The occurrence of this exception indicates that the logical processor detected a serious internal hardware error (e.g., an unrecoverable ECC error when accessing an internal cache or TLB) or a serious error on the external interface, or that another entity on the external interface (e.g., the chipset) asserted a signal indicating a serious problem:

- The MCERR# or BINIT# signal.
- On the P6 processor family, the BINIT# signal.
- On the Pentium, the BUSCHK# signal.

The circumstances under which the Machine Check (MC) exception is generated and how the MCA register set is implemented was originally processor design-specific, but is now architecturally-defined [see "Machine Check Architecture (MCA)" on page 1207 for more information]. The CPUID instruction is used to determine whether this feature is present.

Error Code

No error code is pushed onto the stack. The related error information is latched into the MCA (Machine Check Architecture) error logging MSRs.

Saved Instruction Pointer

On later processors, the information saved in the Extended Machine Check State registers is directly associated with the error that caused the Machine Check exception to be generated.

On the P6 and later processor families, if the MCG_STATUS[EIPV] (EIP Valid) bit = 1, the CS:EIP value saved on the stack is directly associated with the error that caused the exception to be generated. If the bit = 0, the CS:EIP value on the stack may or may not be associated with the error.

On the Pentium, the CS:EIP value saved on the stack may or may not have been associated with the error.

Processor State

A logical processor state change always results from a Machine Check exception. Information about the exception can be collected from the Machine Check MSRs, but, generally speaking, the interrupted program cannot be restarted.

If the Machine Check exception is not enabled (CR4[MCE] = 0), a Machine Check condition causes the logical processor to enter the Shutdown state (for more information refer to "Shutdown Mode" on page 755).

SIMD Floating-Point Exception (19)

Processor Introduced In

This exception was first introduced in the Pentium III and is implemented in all subsequent x86 processors.

Exception Class

This is an instruction Fault.

Description

The occurrence of this exception indicates that the logical processor has detected an SSE SIMD FP exception. For this exception to be generated when a specific error type occurs, the respective mask bit (i.e., the bit associated with the error type) in the MXCSR register (Figure 22-3 on page 860) must = 0 (i.e., unmasked).

There are six classes of numeric error conditions that can be detected while executing an SSE SIMD FP instruction:

- Invalid operation.
- Divide-by-zero.
- Denormal operand.
- Numeric overflow.
- Numeric underflow.
- Inexact result (Precision).

The invalid operation, divide-by-zero, and denormal-operand exceptions are pre-computation exceptions; that is, they are detected before any arithmetic operation occurs. The numeric underflow, numeric overflow, and inexact result exceptions are post-computational exceptions.

When a SIMD (Single Instruction operating upon Multiple Data items; see "The SSE Facilities" on page 851 for more information) FP exception occurs, the logical processor does one of the following:

- It handles the exception automatically by producing the most reasonable result and allowing program execution to continue undisturbed. This is the response to masked error types.
- It generates a SIMD FP exception, invoking the exception handler. This is the response to unmasked error types.

Each of the six SIMD FP error conditions has two associated bits in the MXCSR register:

- A mask bit which, when set to one, prevents the associated error type from generating an exception.
- A status bit which, when set to one, indicates that the respective error type was detected.

If an error type is masked, the logical processor takes an appropriate automatic default action and continues with the computation. If the exception is unmasked and the OS implements a SIMD FP exception handler (as indicated by the OS having set CR4[OSXMMEXCPT] = 1), and the respective error type is detected, then the exception handler is invoked through a SIMD FP exception. If the error type is unmasked and CR4[OSXMMEXCPT] = 0 (indicating that the OS does not implement a SIMD FP exception handler), an Invalid Opcode exception is generated rather than a SIMD FP exception.

Unlike x87 FPU exceptions, SIMD FP exceptions are precise and occur immediately (see "FP Error Reporting" on page 357 for more information).

Chapter 19: Protected Mode Interrupts and Exceptions

If a SIMD FP error of a specific type occurs while recognition of that error type is masked and recognition of that error type is subsequently unmasked, then no exception is generated when the error type is unmasked.

When SSE SIMD FP instructions operate on two or four data operands packed into an XMM register, multiple SIMD FP error conditions may be detected. If the operation performed on each of the packed data operands results in no more than one error per operand, the error status bits associated with each of those errors are set in the MXCSR register.

However, if the operation performed on any of the packed data operands results in the detection of two or more error conditions, only one exception condition is reported (and the precedences are shown in Table 19-17 on page 781). This sometimes results in a higher priority error being reported and a lower priority error being ignored.

Table 19-17: SIMD FP Error Priorities

Priority	Description
1 (highest)	Invalid operation error due to SNaN operand (or any NaN operand for maximum, minimum, or certain compare and convert operations).
2	QNaN operand. Though a QNaN is not an error, the handling of a QNaN operand has precedence over lower priority errors. For example, a QNaN divided by zero results in a QNaN, not a divide-by-zero error.
3	Any other invalid operation error not mentioned above or a divide-by-zero error. If masked, then instruction execution continues, and a lower priority error can occur as well.
4	Denormal operand error. If masked, then instruction execution continues, and a lower priority error can occur as well.
5	Numeric overflow and underflow errors, possibly in conjunction with the inexact result error. If masked, then instruction execution continues, and a lower priority error can occur as well.
6 (lowest)	Inexact result error.

Exception Error Code

No error code is pushed onto the stack.

Saved Instruction Pointer

The CS:EIP value saved on the stack points to the SSE instruction that caused the SIMD FP exception.

Processor State

The logical processor state does not change as the result of a SIMD FP exception. The handling of the exception is immediate (i.e., precise) unless the detected error is masked. The state information available in the register set and on the stack is often sufficient to allow recovery from the error and re-execution of the offending instruction.

Legacy Problem: 2-Step SS:ESP Update

Problem Description

Assume that the programmer executes the following code to switch to a different stack:

```
mov ss,ax          ;move new value into ss
mov esp, stacktop  ;move new top-of-stack offset into esp
```

Now assume that the logical processor is interrupted after execution of the first move but before the second begins execution. When the logical processor pushes the CS, EIP and Eflags values onto the stack, it will be using the new stack segment descriptor to obtain the stack base address and the old ESP value—in other words, you've got a mess on your hands.

The Solution

To prevent this problem, x86 processors automatically inhibit recognition of interrupts and debug exceptions after either a move to SS or a pop to SS instruction until the instruction boundary following the next instruction is reached. If the LSS (load full pointer into SS) instruction is used (instead of two moves), this problem does not occur. The double-move method is often used, however.

20 *Virtual 8086 Mode*

The Previous Chapter

The previous chapter provided a detailed description of interrupt and exception handling in Protected Mode. This included detailed coverage of:

- The IDT.
- Interrupt and Trap Gate operation.
- Task Gate operation.
- Interrupt and exception event categories.
- State save (and stack selection).
- The IRET instruction.
- Maskable hardware interrupts.
- Non-Maskable Interrupt (NMI).
- Machine Check exception.
- SM interrupt (SMI).
- Software interrupt instructions.
- Software exceptions.
- Interrupt/exception priority.

This Chapter

This chapter provides a detailed description of VM86 Mode (also known as Virtual 8086 Mode). This includes the following topics:

- Switching Between Protected Mode and VM86 Mode.
- Real Mode Application's World View.
- Sensitive Instructions.
- Handling Direct IO.
- Handling Exceptions.
- Hardware Interrupt Handling in VM86 Mode
- Software Interrupt Instruction Handling
- Halt Instruction in VM86 Mode

- Protected Mode Virtual Interrupt Feature
- Registers Accessible in Real/VM86 Mode
- Instructions Usable in Real/VM86 Mode

The Next Chapter

The next chapter introduces the MMX register set and the original MMX instruction set. The SIMD programming model is introduced, how to deal with unpacked data as well as math underflows and overflows, and the elimination of conditional branches. Handling a task switch is described and the instruction set syntax is introduced.

A Special Note

The terms DOS task, VM86 task, and Real Mode task may be used interchangeably in this chapter (the vast majority of VM86 tasks are DOS tasks and, as such, intended to run in Real Mode). It should not be construed, however, that only DOS tasks are VM86 candidates. Any Real Mode application executed by a multitasking OS must be run under VM86 Mode.

Real Mode Applications Are Dangerous

The chapter entitled "Multitasking-Related Issues" on page 367 introduced some of the ways in which a Real Mode application might prove disruptive in a multitasking environment:

- Access memory belonging to currently-suspended programs.
- Communicate directly with IO ports (and thereby alter the state of device adapters).
- Call OS kernel code (including procedures it may not be allowed to access).
- Execute the CLI or STI instruction to disable or enable recognition of maskable hardware interrupts. The PUSHF and POPF instructions can also be used to change the state of the Eflags[IF] bit).
- Utilize a software interrupt instruction to call the BIOS or the Real Mode OS. A Real Mode application assumes it's running under a Real Mode OS rather than a multitasking, Protected Mode OS. Consequently, all OS calls initiated by the application should be intercepted and passed to the host OS (or another program that substitutes for the DOS OS).

Solution: a Watchdog

When the scheduler switches to a Real Mode application, it sets the Eflags[VM] bit to one (see Figure 20-2 on page 787). This activates a logical processor mechanism (the VM86 logic) that monitors the behavior of the application on an instruction-by-instruction basis. Any operation that might prove destabilizing to the overall multitasking environment (referred to as a *sensitive* operation) is intercepted and an exception is generated to inform Virtual Machine Monitor (VMM) handler. There are a number of elements associated with this mechanism:

1. **Monitor logic**. The VM86 hardware detects the attempted execution of the sensitive instructions. First introduced in the 386, this mechanism was improved with the Pentium's addition of the VM86 Extensions (VME) feature.
2. **GP exception**. A GP exception is generated when a sensitive operation is detected.
3. **Monitor program**. If the GP exception handler determines it was invoked by the VM86 logic, it calls a special privilege level 0 procedure referred to as the VMM (Virtual Machine Monitor) to handle the event.
4. **TSS**. The scheduler creates a TSS data structure (see Figure 20-1 on page 786) for each Real Mode application. Several TSS elements are specifically-associated with VM86 Mode:
   — IO permission bitmap.
   — Interrupt redirection bitmap.
   — The VM bit in the Eflags register field.
   — The IOPL field in the Eflags register field.
5. **VM86 Extensions**. An OS may or may not activate the VM86 Mode Extensions by setting CR4[VME] = 1. If it is enabled, the following elements come into play:
   — Eflags[VIF] and Eflags[VIP] bits.
   — Interrupt redirection bitmap consultation.
6. **IOPL threshold**. The threshold value in Eflags[IOPL].

Figure 20-1: Task State Segment (TSS)

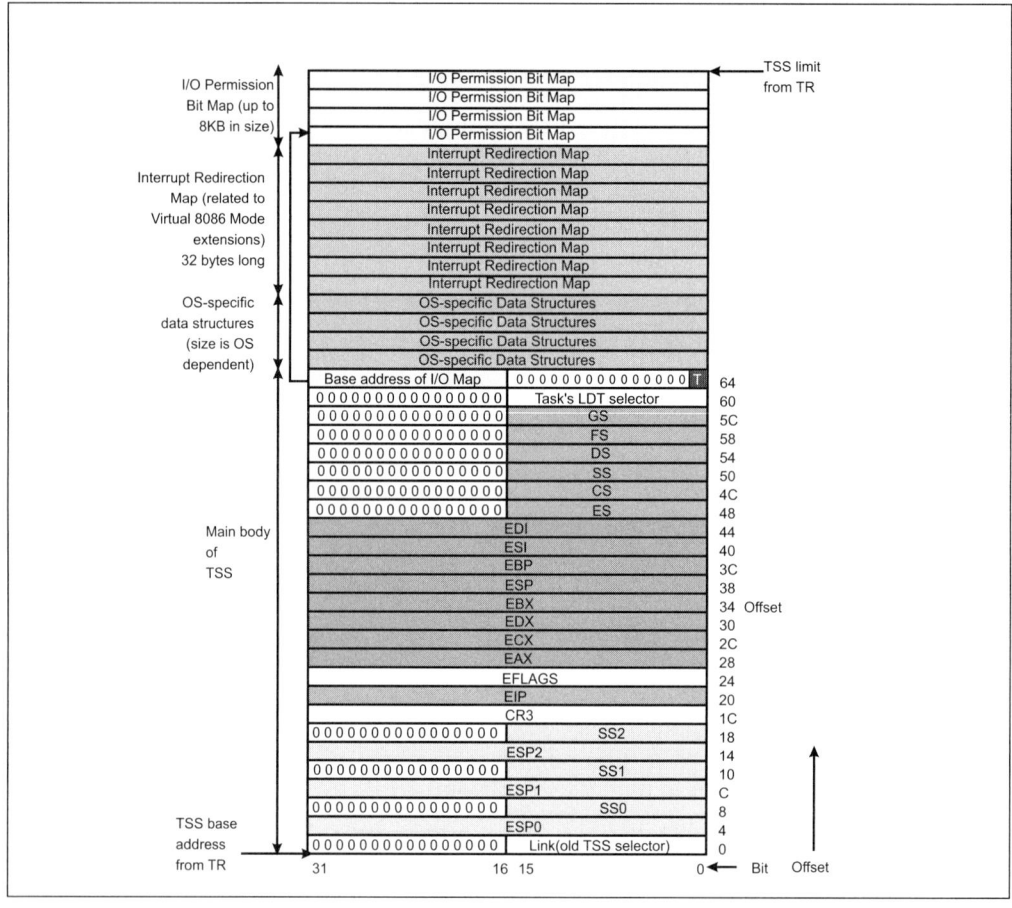

Figure 20-2: Eflags Register

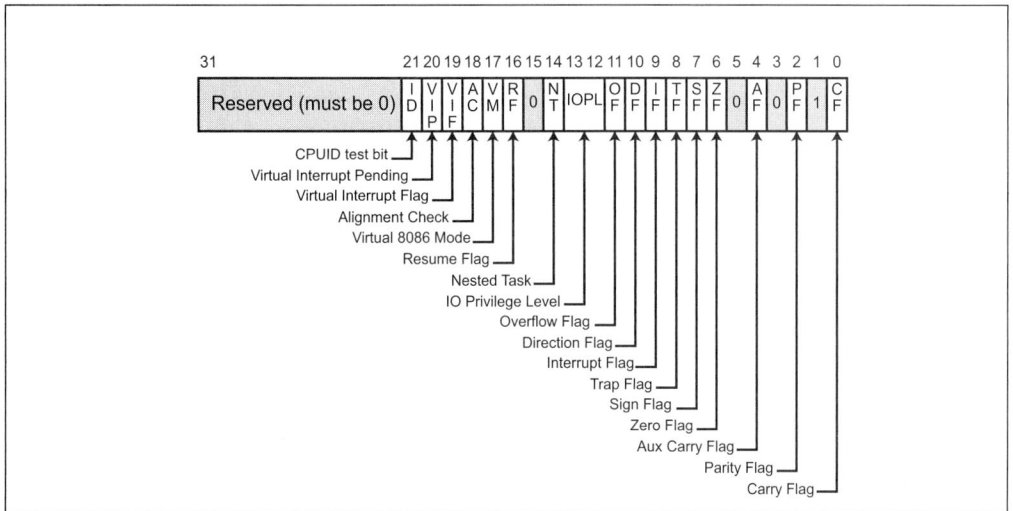

Real Mode Applications Run at Privilege Level 3

By definition, when run in VM86 Mode under Protected Mode, Real Mode applications run at the lowest privilege level, 3.

Switching Between Protected Mode and VM86 Mode

Eflags[VM] = 1 Switches Processor into VM86 Mode

When the logical processor is operating in Protected Mode (CR0[PE] = 1) but Eflags[VM] = 0, it is executing a standard Protected Mode task rather than a Real Mode task. If Eflags[VM] is set to one, though, it is running a Real Mode task in VM86 Mode (and the VM86 monitor logic remains activated as long as Eflags[VM] = 1).

The setting of the Eflags[VM] bit also modifies how the logical processor interprets the contents of the segment registers:

- **VM = 0**. The 16-bit value in a segment register is interpreted as a segment selector that selects a segment descriptor in either the GDT or LDT.
- **VM = 1**. Just as in Real Mode, the value in each segment register is interpreted as the upper 16-bits of the respective segment's 20-bit base address.

But Software Cannot Directly Access Eflags[VM]

Software—even level 0 software—does not have the ability to directly read or alter the state of Eflags[VM]. This raises four important questions:

1. How does the task scheduler activate VM86 Mode when it is starting or resuming the execution of a Real Mode task?
2. What causes the logical processor to exit VM86 Mode and return to Protected Mode?
3. When an interrupt or exception occurs, how does the selected Protected Mode handler know that the interrupted task was a Real Mode task and the VMM should therefore be called to handle the event?
4. After the VMM (which is a level 0 Protected Mode procedure) handles an event that occurred during the execution of a Real Mode task, how does it switch the logical processor back into VM86 Mode?

The answers to these four questions are addressed in the next four sections.

Scheduler Activates VM86 Mode

There are only two ways in which the OS task scheduler can activate VM86 Mode when it is starting or resuming a task:

- **Hardware task switch**. If the x86 hardware-based task switching mechanism is used (note: most modern OSs do *not* use it), there are two ways to set Eflags[VM] = 1:
  — Execution of a far jump or a far call wherein the selector portion of the branch target address selects either a TSS descriptor in the GDT or a Task Gate descriptor in the GDT or LDT *and the VM bit is set to one in the Eflags register image in the target task's TSS*.
  — The execution of an IRET instruction at the conclusion of a task called from another task. In this case, the logical processor detects Eflags[NT] = 1 when it executes the IRET. It then uses the Link field in the current task's TSS to select the TSS of the calling task and reloads its registers (including Eflags) from the images stored in the calling task's TSS. If VM = 1 in the Eflags register image, the logical processor returns to VM86 Mode.

- **IRET at level 0**. In an OS that uses a software-based task switching mechanism, the scheduler can cause VM86 Mode to be activated by placing the following items on the level 0 stack and then executing the IRET instruction:
  — CS:EIP pointing to the first instruction to be executed in the Real Mode task.
  — The desired contents to be loaded into the Eflags register (with VM = 1).
  — SS:ESP pointing to the level 3 stack to be used by the Real Mode task.
  — The desired contents to be loaded into the four data segment registers (DS, ES, FS, GS).
  Note: The logical processor only copies a one into Eflags[VM] if the IRET is executed from a level 0 code segment.

Exiting VM86 Mode

There are only two ways to exit VM86 Mode and return to Protected Mode:

- **Hardware task switch**. Through an automatic task switch to a task wherein the VM bit in the task's TSS Eflags image field = 0. For example, when the Real Mode task's timeslice expires, the Local APIC timer generates an interrupt that selects an IDT entry containing a Task Gate that points to the scheduler's TSS.
- **Interrupt or Exception**. When an interrupt or exception selects a Trap or Interrupt Gate in the IDT. In this case, before initiating the execution of the selected Protected Mode handler:
  — The logical processor stores the following items in the level 0 stack (CS:EIP, Eflags, SS:ESP, and the contents of the four data segment registers (DS, ES, FS, GS).
  — It then clears Eflags[VM] (along with NT, RF and TF) to zero, thereby exiting VM86 Mode and entering Protected Mode.
  — It also clears the four data segment registers to 0.
  It then begins execution of the Protected Mode interrupt or exception handler. Note: when the logical processor is in VM86 Mode and an interrupt or exception is recognized, the handler pointed to by the selected Interrupt or Trap Gate must reside in level 0, Non-Conforming code segment. If it does not, it results in a GP exception.

Determining Interrupted Task Is a Real Mode Task

On entry to a Protected Mode interrupt or exception handler, the handler may determine that the event occurred while running a Real Mode task by examining the Eflags image saved on the level 0 stack. If VM = 1 in the image, the handler then calls the VMM to handle the event.

Returning to VM86 Mode from VMM

When the VMM concludes handling an event associated with a Real Mode task, it executes a RET instruction to return control to the Protected Mode handler that called it. The handler, in turn, executes an IRET instruction which causes the logical processor to reload CS:EIP, Eflags, SS:ESP and the four data segment registers (DS, ES, FS, GS) from the level 0 stack. This switches the logical processor back into VM86 Mode before it resumes execution of the interrupted Real Mode task.

VMM Passes Control to Real Mode Interrupt/Exception Handler

For a detailed description of this issue, refer to "VMM Passes Control To Real Mode Handler" on page 829.

Real Mode Application's World View

The DOS World

Most (but not all) Real Mode applications were written to run under the single-task DOS OS. Each DOS task believes that it resides within and interacts with other programs residing within the first megabyte of memory space (the virtual address range from 00000000h - 000FFFFFh). In the DOS environment, memory is utilized as shown in Figure 20-4 on page 793:

- The Real Mode IDT (see Figure 20-3 on page 791) occupies the first KB of space (00000h - 003FFh) and contains pointers to:
  — BIOS routines in the boot ROM.
  — DOS OS services.
  — NMI handler in the boot ROM.
  — 8088 exception handlers in the boot ROM.
  — Device adapter interrupt handlers.
  — Other miscellaneous services.

- The BIOS Data Area is the area of RAM memory reserved for the use of the BIOS.
- During the OS boot process, loadable device drivers are loaded from disk into the area of RAM memory directly above the BIOS Data Area.
- The DOS OS is loaded immediately after that.
- The DOS application is loaded immediately after DOS.
- The video RAM (i.e., video frame buffer) on the display adapter occupies the 128KB area from A0000h - BFFFFh.
- Device ROMs on add-in cards occupy the 128KB area from C0000h - DFFFFh.
- Initially, the boot ROM occupied the 64KB area from F0000h - FFFFFh; E0000h - EFFFFh was reserved for an expansion ROM, but the boot ROM eventually grew until it now occupies the entire 128KB range.

Figure 20-3: Real Mode IDT

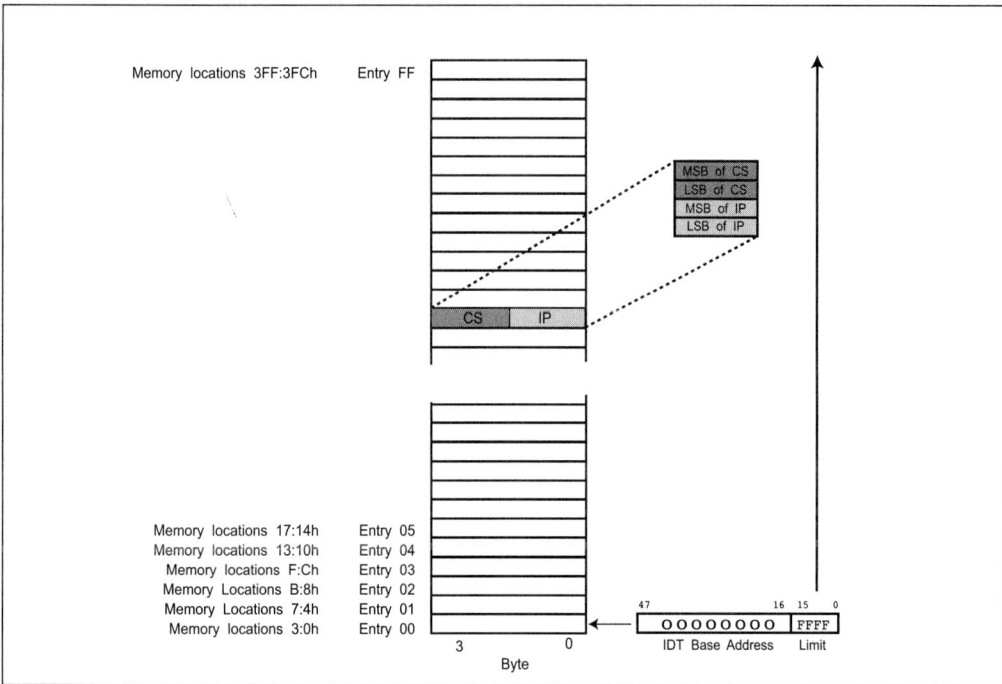

Memory Address Formation in VM86 Mode

When the logical processor is operating in VM86 Mode, memory addresses are formed just as they are in Real Mode:

16-bit base from segment register zero-extended to 20-bits

+

16-bit offset specified in IP, SP or as an instruction operand

=

20-bit address in the first MB of virtual memory space.

When a new value is moved into a segment register and the logical processor is in Protected Mode (CR0[PE] = 1), the logical processor checks the state of Eflags[VM] (see Figure 20-2 on page 787) to determine how to use the new value:

- **Eflags[VM] = 0**. The logical processor is not in VM86 mode. It therefore treats the segment register value as a selector to select a descriptor from either the GDT or LDT. The selected descriptor defines the base address, size, and attributes of the segment.
- **Eflags[VM] = 1**. The logical processor is in VM86 mode. It therefore interprets the segment register value (plus a least-significant hex digit of 0h) as the segment's 20-bit base address and the segment has an implicit length of 64KB.

Figure 20-4: DOS Task's Perception of the 1st MB of Memory Space

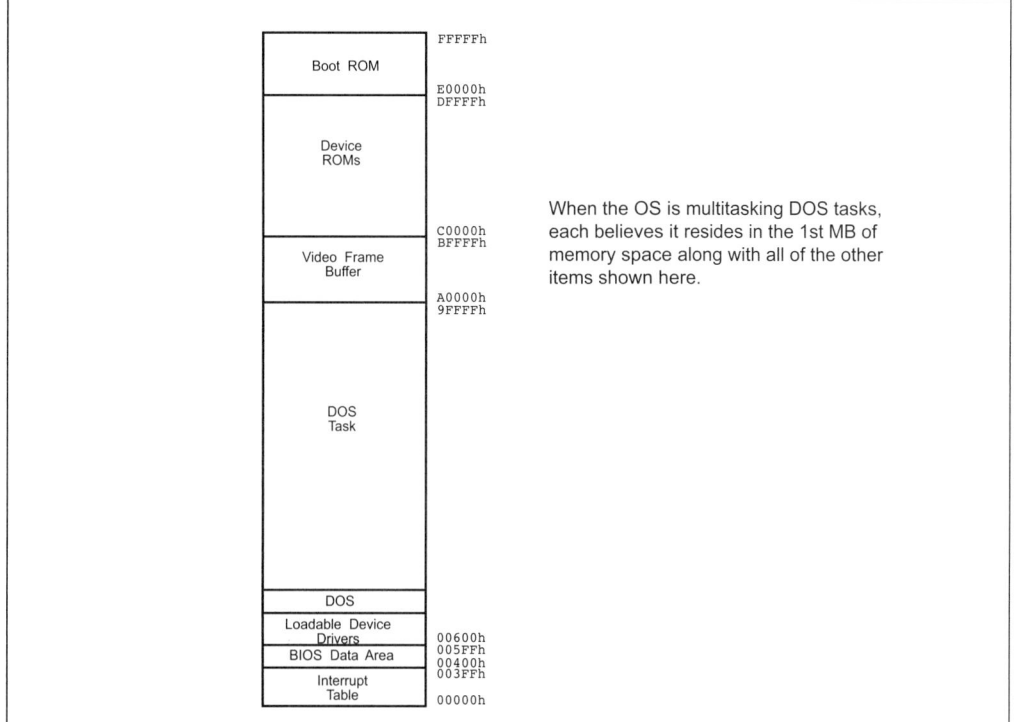

Multiple DOS Domains in Separate 1MB Areas

If multiple DOS tasks are being run under a multitasking OS, each, when active, performs memory reads and writes within the first MB of virtual memory space. Unless something is done to prevent it, the currently-executing DOS task could easily alter the contents of memory locations in use by other DOS tasks that are currently suspended. This would obviously cause severe problems.

The problem is avoided using the virtual-to-physical address translation mechanism. As it does for any task, the OS task scheduler sets up a set of address translation tables to direct the application's memory accesses to the appropriate physical areas of memory. Before starting or resuming the task, the scheduler ensures that the CR3 register is loaded with the base physical address of the application's top-level address translation table. Figure 20-5 on page 795 illustrates an example wherein the user wishes to run two DOS applications.

- The OS scheduler creates two, separate alternate realities for the two tasks. For each task, it allocates a contiguous 1MB block of physical memory starting on an address boundary divisible by 1MB. It populates each 1MB area with:
  — A copy of the Real Mode IDT and event handlers.
  — A copy of the BIOS Data Area.
  — Copies of the Real Mode loadable device drivers.
  — A copy of the DOS OS.
  — A copy of the application itself.
  — A video frame buffer for its use.
  — Copies of any device ROMs.
  — A copy of the boot ROM code.
- When DOS task A is started or resumed, CR3 is loaded with the base physical address of task A's top-level address translation table. Task A's address translation tables translate any 20-bit virtual address it generates into the same relative physical address within the MB of physical memory in which it and its related entities (e.g., a copy of the Real Mode interrupt table, a copy of DOS, etc.) reside.
- Likewise, when DOS task B is started or resumed, CR3 is loaded with the base physical address of task B's top-level address translation directory. Task B's address translation tables translate any 20-bit virtual address it generates into the same relative physical address within the MB of physical memory in which it and its related entities (e.g., a copy of the Real Mode interrupt table, a copy of DOS, etc.) reside.

Figure 20-5: Paging Mechanism Used to Redirect DOS Task Memory Accesses

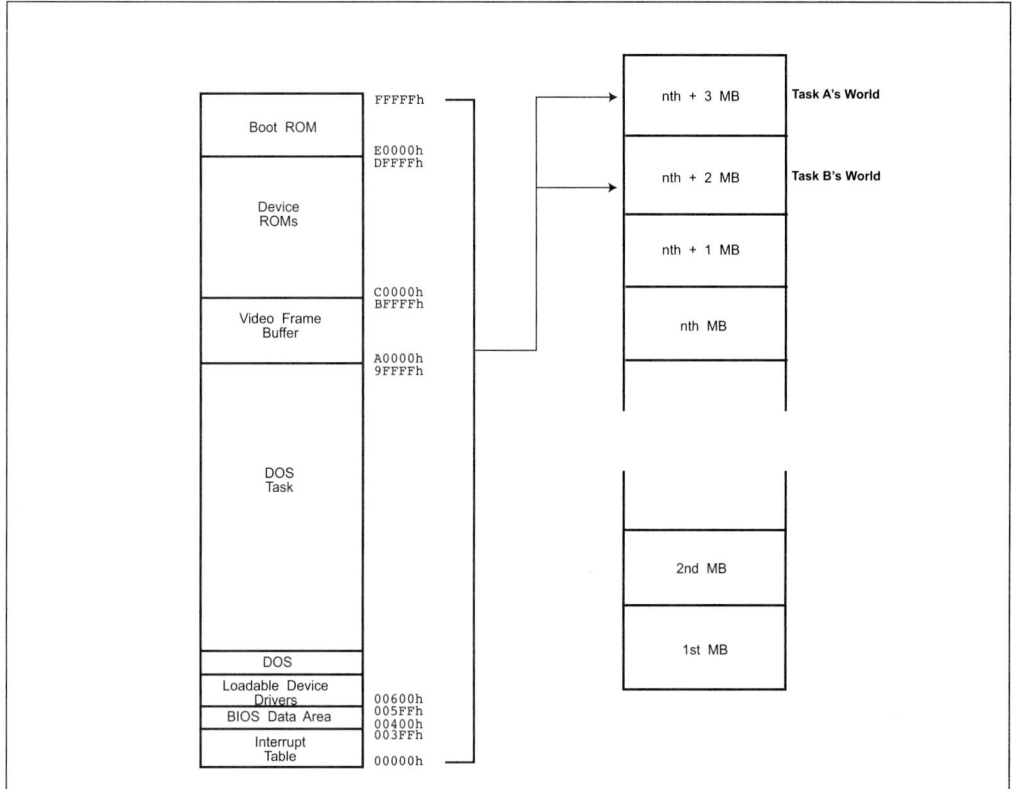

VMM Should Not Reside in the HMA

A DOS task is capable of performing memory accesses within the first MB of its virtual memory address space. Some DOS tasks written to run on the post-8086 processors (i.e., 286 and later) can also generate memory accesses within the virtual memory address range from 0000000h - 0010FFEFh (for additional information, refer to "Dealing with Segment Wraparound" on page 796).

In order to ensure that the DOS task does not read or write the memory area occupied by the VMM, the VMM should be located somewhere above virtual memory address 0010FFEFh. The memory range from 00100000h through 0010FFEFh is sometimes referred to as the High Memory Area (HMA; see "Accessing Extended Memory in Real Mode" on page 307).

x86 Instruction Set Architecture

Dealing with Segment Wraparound

8088/8086 Processor

The 8088/8086 processors implemented 20 address signal lines on their external interfaces. Memory addresses were formed by adding the 16-bit programmer-specified offset to a 20-bit segment start address. Consider the following Real Mode code fragment:

```
mov  ax, ffff     ;set ds base address = ffff0h
mov  ds, ax       ;
mov  al, [0010h]  ;read one byte into al register
```

When the third instruction is executed, the processor extends the 16-bit DS value by adding a hex digit of 0 on its lower end, yielding a 20-bit data segment base address of FFFF0h. The offset 0010h is added to the base address, resulting in the 21-bit memory address 100000h. This is the first location of the second MB of memory space (i.e., the first location in extended memory). When the 8086/8088 drove the address onto its external interface to perform the memory read, the upper bit was stripped off (because the processor only implemented address lines A[19:0]). This resulted in a read from memory address 00000h, rather than 100000h. In other words, the processor wrapped around to the bottom of the first MB of memory. With a segment base address of FFFF0h, any offset from 0010h - FFFFh causes a wraparound to locations at the bottom of memory.

286 and Later Processors

Starting with the 286, all x86 processors implement more than 20 address signal lines on the external interface. When the code fragment illustrated earlier is executed on one of the later processors, the logical processor generates address 00100000h and, because address signal line A20 *is* implemented on the processor's external interface, it can access extended memory. If the offset specified by the programmer were FFFFh, the location accessed would be 0010FFEFh.

Solutions

Some DOS programs depend on segment wraparound occurring (because they were written to run on the 8088/8086) while others (written to run on later processors) expect to be able to access the extended memory directly above the first MB (known as the HMA, or High Memory Area):

- **When a Task expects segment wraparound**. The currently-executing DOS task may require that accesses to virtual locations 00100000h - 0010FFEF be translated to locations 00000000h - 0000FFEFh in the task's assigned 1MB block of physical memory. In this case, the task's address translation tables must be set up to map accesses within both ranges (00100000h - 0010FFEF and 00000000h - 0000FFEFh) to locations 00000000h - 0000FFEFh in the task's assigned 1MB block of physical memory.

- **When a task does not expect segment wraparound**. The currently-executing DOS task may want accesses to virtual addresses 00100000h - 0010FFEFh to access an area of physical memory other than locations 00000000h - 0000FFEFh in the task's assigned 1MB block of physical memory. In this case, the task's address translation tables must be set up to map accesses within the two ranges range to different areas of physical memory.

Using the Address Size Override Prefix

Although it is legal to use an address size override prefix to force an instruction to generate a 32-bit address, an exception results if the specified offset is greater than 64KB (i.e., > 0000FFFFh):

- A GP exception is generated if the logical processor is addressing a segment other than the stack.
- A Stack exception results if the logical processor is addressing the stack.

Sensitive Instructions

Problematic Instructions

In addition to IO instructions (see "Handling Direct IO" on page 800), a Real Mode task may attempt to execute other instructions that may interfere with the multitasking OS or other tasks that are currently suspended, or that may attempt to call services provided by another OS (e.g., DOS) or by the BIOS. The problematic instructions are:

- CLI.
- STI.
- PUSHF.
- POPF.
- INT nn.
- IRET.

These problematic instructions are described in the following subsections.

CLI (Clear Interrupt Enable) Instruction

Refer to Figure 20-6 on page 798. If a Real Mode task is permitted to execute the CLI instruction, the interrupt enable bit (Eflags[IF]) is cleared to 0 and the logical processor will not recognize subsequent external hardware interrupts received on its INTR input (or via the logical processor's Local APIC). Although the currently-executing Real Mode program may not care to be interrupted by IO devices at this point, an IO device that had been stimulated by another (currently-suspended) program at an earlier time may signal for service. The currently-executing program, unaware that this device was previously stimulated by another program, therefore thinks it can disable interrupt recognition without any ill consequences. This is obviously not the case in a multitasking OS.

STI (Set Interrupt Enable) Instruction

Refer to Figure 20-6 on page 798. If the DOS task is permitted to execute the STI instruction, the interrupt enable bit (Eflags[IF]) is set to one and the logical processor will recognize subsequent external hardware interrupts received on its INTR input (or via the logical processor's Local APIC). Although the currently-executing DOS program may not mind being interrupted by IO devices at this point, the OS (without the knowledge of the currently-executing program) may have disabled interrupt recognition for some reason. Unaware of this, the currently-executing program therefore thinks it can enable interrupt recognition without any ill consequences. Once again, this is not necessarily the case in a multitasking OS.

Figure 20-6: Using CLI/STI Instructions to Disable/Enable Interrupt Recognition

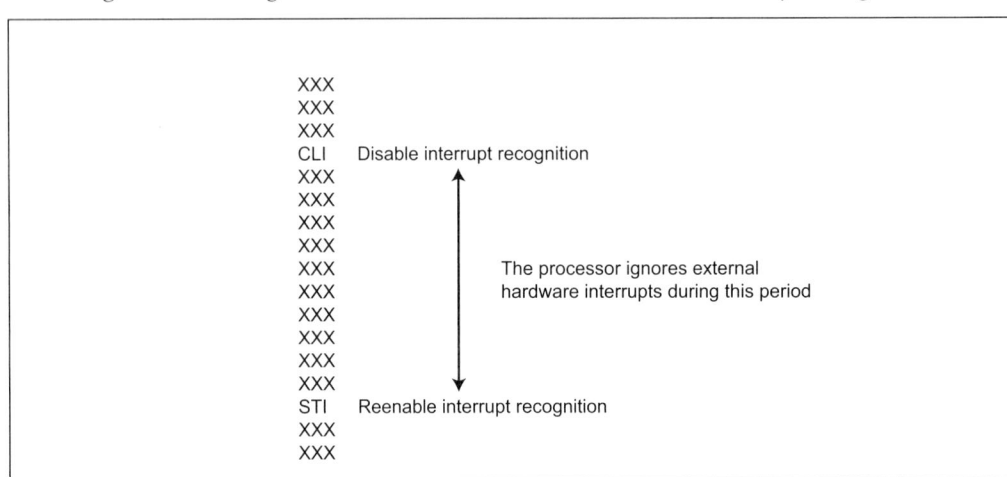

PUSHF (Push Flags) Instruction

If the Real Mode task is permitted to execute the PUSHF instruction, the Eflags register is copied to the stack and the Eflag[VM] and Eflag[RF] bits are then cleared. This would disable VM86 Mode, preventing the logical processor from continued monitoring of the VM86 task's behavior.

POPF (Pop Flags) Instruction

When executed, the POPF instruction copies the Eflags image from the stack into the Eflags register. If the programmer had altered this image on the stack, a number of problems could result:

- The VM bit could be cleared, disabling VM86 mode and preventing the logical processor from continued monitoring of the VM86 task's behavior.
- The IF bit could be cleared and the logical processor would no longer recognize external hardware interrupts.
- The IF bit could be set and the logical processor would recognize external hardware interrupts.

INT *nn* (Software Interrupt) Instruction

Refer to Figure 20-7 on page 800. DOS applications frequently call DOS or BIOS routines using the software interrupt instruction. It may be that the multitasking OS would prefer that all or some of the software interrupt calls be handled differently. For this reason, VM86 Mode is sensitive to the software interrupt instruction.

IRET (Interrupt Return) Instruction

Like the POPF instruction, the IRET instruction copies the Eflags image from the stack into the Eflags register. If the programmer had altered this image in memory, the same types of problems could result:

- The VM bit could be cleared, disabling VM86 mode and preventing the logical processor from continued monitoring of the VM86 task's behavior.
- The IF bit could be cleared and the logical processor would no longer recognize external hardware interrupts.
- The IF bit could be set and the logical processor would recognize external hardware interrupts.

Figure 20-7: DOS Tasks Use INT Instructions

```
XXX
XXX
XXX
INT  21    Calls DOS using the pointer from entry 21 in the Interrupt Table
XXX
XXX
XXX
INT  13    Calls the disk BIOS routine using the pointer from entry 13 in the Interrupt Table
XXX
XXX
```

Solution: IOPL Sensitive Instructions

For the reasons stated in the previous sections, while in VM86 Mode x86 processors sense the attempted execution of any of these instructions so they can be handled in a manner that will prevent destabilization of the multitasking OS environment.

Before starting or resuming the execution of a Real Mode task, the scheduler ensures that the sensitivity threshold value in the 2-bit Eflags[IOPL] field (see Figure 20-2 on page 787) is set to a value < 3 (VM86 tasks—i.e., Real Mode applications—run at privilege level 3). As a result, the attempted execution of any of the sensitive instructions will be detected so they can be handled. This subject is covered in detail in subsequent sections of this chapter.

Handling Direct IO

The Problem

The problem was described earlier in "IO Port Anarchy" on page 374. The sections that follow describe the methods used to monitor task IO accesses in both IO and memory-mapped IO space.

IO-Mapped IO

IO Permission in Protected Mode

When the logical processor is in Protected Mode (CR0[PE] = 1) but not in VM86 mode (Eflags[VM] = 0) and it attempts to execute an IOPL-sensitive instruction (note: in Protected Mode, the IO instructions—IN, OUT, INS, OUTS—are sensitive to the threshold value programmed into the Eflags[IOPL] field by the OS), the privilege check is performed in the following manner:

- If the CPL is numerically ≤ the IOPL (i.e., the program's privilege level is the same as or more privileged than the IOPL; see Figure 20-2 on page 787), no exception is generated and the IO instruction is permitted to execute.
- If the CPL fails the IOPL test and the instruction is one of the IO instructions (IN, OUT, INS, or OUTS), the logical processor checks the task's IO Permission Bit Map in its TSS (see Figure 20-8 on page 802) to determine if the current application is permitted access to the addressed IO port(s). The addressed IO port addresses are used to index into the bitmap, the appropriate byte(s) is read and the respective bits checked. If the bit map indicates that the task is permitted to access the indicated IO port(s), no exception is generated and the IO instruction is executed. Otherwise, a GP exception is generated:
  — If all of the selected bits are zero, the IO access is permitted.
  — If any of the selected bits are set to one, a GP exception is generated.

IO Permission in VM86 Mode

When the logical processor is in VM86 mode (i.e., Eflags[VM] = 1) and it attempts to execute an IO instruction (IN, INS, OUT, or OUTS), the permission check is performed as follows:

- The CPL (which is 3 by definition for a VM86 task) is not checked against the IOPL threshold value at all (it *is* checked in Protected Mode).
- The logical processor unconditionally checks the task's IO Permission Bit Map in its TSS (see Figure 20-8 on page 802) to determine if the current application is permitted access to the addressed IO port(s). If the bit map indicates that the task is permitted to access the indicated IO port(s), no exception is generated and the IO instruction is executed. Otherwise, a GP exception is generated:
  — If all of the selected bits are zero, the IO access is permitted.
  — If any of the selected bits are set to one, a GP exception is generated.

Figure 20-8: Solving the IO Problem: When VM = 1, IOPL is don't care

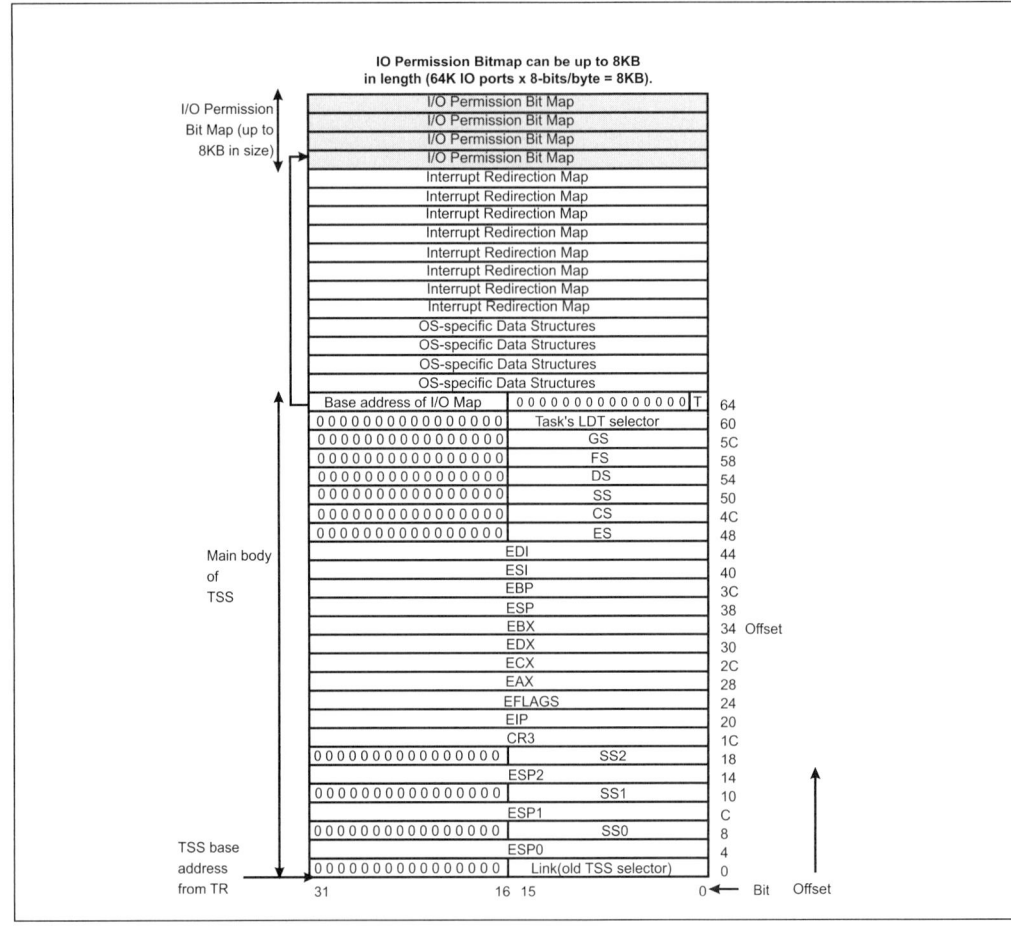

Memory-Mapped IO

The system may implement memory-mapped IO ports that are used to communicate with IO devices. Just as with IO-mapped IO ports, the OS should provide a mechanism that permits the current task to communicate directly with some memory-mapped IO ports while denying direct access to others. This can be implemented using the address translation mechanism.

In assigning memory ranges to memory-mapped IO (MMIO) ports implemented within various device adapters, the system configuration software should group the memory-mapped IO ports into one or more 4KB pages of physical memory address space.

To Permit an Access

Each task has its own, dedicated set of address translation tables. When a task attempts to access a memory-mapped IO port that it is permitted to access, the port's virtual address selects a PTE that indicates the page is currently-present in memory. There are two possibilities:

- The virtual MMIO address used by the task (obtained from the OS services) *is* the actual physical address assigned to the port. In this case, the selected PTE translates the virtual address into the same physical address and the logical processor permits the access.
- The virtual MMIO address used by the task (obtained from the OS services) is *not* the same as the actual physical address actually assigned to the port. In this case, the selected PTE translates the virtual address into the correct physical address and permits the access.

To Deny an Access

When the task attempts to access a memory-mapped IO port that it is not permitted to access, the port's virtual address selects a PTE that indicates the page is not currently-present in memory. This results in the generation of a *Page Fault* exception. The OS kernel can then decide whether to permit the access or not. If it chooses not to permit it, it could either emulate the access in an OS-friendly manner, or, if not other course of action is feasible, could terminate the task.

For Finer Control

To achieve a finer level of control over a task's ability to access MMIO ports, the PTE associated with a page occupied by MMIO ports could be marked as:

- Supervisor-only access,
- and/or read-only access.

Handling Video Frame Buffer Updates

As discussed earlier, each DOS program owns a 1MB block of virtual memory space that it *thinks* is the first megabyte of physical memory space. Many DOS programs update the video frame buffer in memory directly (rather than making a BIOS or DOS function call to do so) by performing memory writes to the display frame buffer area (memory addresses 000A0000h - 000BFFFFh). The OS sets up the address translation for each VM86 task to direct all accesses within the virtual address range 000A0000h - 000BFFFFh to a separate physical memory buffer (a *virtual* video frame buffer) for each task.

Whenever a DOS task is resumed, the VMM can then copy the DOS program's *virtual frame buffer* into the actual video frame buffer residing in physical memory locations 000A0000h - 000BFFFFh. At some point (due to timeslice exhaustion or some other event), the OS suspends the VM86 task and transfers control to another task. If the next task is another VM86 task, the OS first copies that task's virtual frame buffer into the real frame buffer and then resumes the task. This ensures that the screen looks just as it did at the point when the task was suspended earlier.

Handling Exceptions in VM86 Mode

Processor Actions

When a software exception condition is detected, the vector selects the associated IDT entry in the Protected Mode IDT (see Figure 20-9 on page 808). The OS may have placed one of three types of descriptors in the selected IDT entry:

- An **Interrupt Gate** descriptor (see Figure 19-5 on page 693). This is the most likely choice for a hardware interrupt because it causes the logical processor to automatically disable recognition of additional maskable hardware interrupts.
- A **Trap Gate** descriptor (see Figure 19-6 on page 694). Unlike the Interrupt Gate, the selection of a Trap Gate will not cause the logical processor to disable recognition of subsequent maskable hardware interrupts. *This choice is more likely to be placed in an IDT entry associated with a software exception condition.* It can be used in an entry associated with a maskable hardware interrupt, though, if the designer of the handler doesn't mind the handler itself being interrupted.
- A **Task Gate** descriptor (see Figure 19-9 on page 697). In this case, the detection of the Task Gate causes the logical processor to perform an automatic task switch to another task that will act as the exception handler. This is described in "Option 3: Exception Handled by Another Task" on page 808.

The following discussion assumes that the selected IDT entry contains an Interrupt Gate or a Trap Gate. The logical processor takes the following actions:

1. Copies SS:ESP to temp registers. Loads SS:ESP from the current task's TSS SS0:ESP0 fields to select the privilege level 0 stack preallocated by the OS kernel. It then pushes the following onto the new stack:

— CS:EIP which points to the next instruction that would have been executed in the Real Mode task if it hadn't incurred an exception.

— SS:ESP copy from temp registers. This is the pointer to Real Mode application's stack.

— Eflags register. After pushing it to the stack, the logical processor clears the following Eflags bits: VM, NT, RF and TF:

– If the selected IDT entry contains an Interrupt Gate (rather than a Trap Gate), it also clears IF to disable recognition of subsequent maskable interrupts.

– Clearing VM causes the logical processor to exit VM86 Mode and enter Protected Mode.

— ES, DS, FS and GS are pushed onto the stack. *Note: this only occurs when calling an event handler from VM86 Mode.*

2. Loads the four data segment registers with 0 (this would select entry 0, the null entry, in the GDT). *Note: this only occurs when calling an event handler from VM86 Mode.* This is done so that the Real Mode segment base addresses contained in the segment registers won't erroneously select descriptors in the GDT or LDT. A selector of 0 selects GDT entry 0, a null entry whose selection never causes an exception.

3. CS:EIP are loaded with the entry point of the Protected Mode exception handler from the IDT entry selected by the exception vector.

4. Begins execution of the Protected Mode exception handler. *Note that Protected Mode handlers called from VM86 Mode must reside in Non-Conforming privilege level 0 code segments.* If they do not, a GP exception is generated. The error code pushed on the stack contains the selector of the code segment to which a call was attempted.

The designer of the Protected Mode exception handler has three options available:

Option 1. Service the exception by executing the body of the selected Protected Mode handler. This option is described in "Option 1: Protected Mode Handler Services Exception" on page 806.

Option 2. Determining that the exception occurred while a Real Mode application was running, it can pass the event to the VMM program for handling. This can be determined by looking at the VM bit in the Eflags image that was pushed onto the stack. This option is described in "Option 2: Handler Passes Exception to VMM for Servicing" on page 806.

Option 3. Service the exception by switching to another task which will act as the handler. This option is described in "Option 3: Exception Handled by Another Task" on page 808.

Option 1: Protected Mode Handler Services Exception

In this case, the exception is serviced by executing the body of the Protected Mode exception handler that has just been entered. After the handler has serviced the event, it executes the IRET instruction causing the logical processor to take the following actions:

1. Determines that the interrupted task was a VM86 task by validating that:
   - The logical processor is currently operating in Protected Mode (CR0[PE] = 1),
   - It is executing at privilege level 0 (DPL of currently-active code segment = 0),
   - And that VM = 1 in the Eflags image on the privilege level 0 stack.
2. Loads CS:EIP from the current stack. This points to the next instruction to be executed in the interrupted VM86 task.
3. Loads Eflags from the current stack. This sets Eflags[VM] = 1, re-activating VM86 Mode.
4. Pops SS:ESP from the current stack into temp registers (this is the pointer to the interrupted VM86 task's stack, but we don't want to switch back to it until the four data segment registers have been restored from the stack).
5. Reloads the four data segment registers (DS, ES, FS, GS) from the current stack.
6. Move the temp registers into SS:ESP, thereby restoring the pointer to the interrupted VM86 task's stack.
7. Sets CPL = 3 (because all VM86 tasks run at privilege level 3).
8. Resume instruction fetching from the interrupted VM86 task.

Note: If the CPL of the handler executing the IRET is not 0, the logical processor can not set Eflags[VM] = 1 when it pops the Eflags image from the handler's stack.

Option 2: Handler Passes Exception to VMM for Servicing

In this case, having determined that the exception occurred during the execution of a Real Mode application (the VM bit was set in the Eflags register image on the privilege level 0 stack), the Protected Mode exception handler calls the VMM and passes its vector number to it. The VMM has two options:

- It can service the event itself and then execute a RET instruction to return control to the Protected Mode exception handler that called it. The handler, in turn, will then execute an IRET instruction to switch the logical processor back into VM86 Mode and return control back to the interrupted Real Mode application.
- It can pass the event to the corresponding Real Mode exception handler for handling. In this case, the following actions are taken.

1. In preparation for passing control to the respective Real Mode exception handler, the VMM obtains the following items from the privilege level 0 stack and pushes them onto the privilege level 3 stack being used by the Real Mode application (it obtains the privilege level 3 stack pointer from the privilege level 0 stack; see step 1 under the heading "Processor Actions" on page 804):
   — Real Mode only supports a 16-bit Flag register, so the lower 16-bits of the 32-bit Eflags image from the privilege level 0 stack are pushed onto the Real Mode application's stack.
   — Real Mode only supports a 16-bit IP register, so CS and the lower 16-bits of the 32-bit EIP pointer image from the privilege level 0 stack are pushed onto the Real Mode application's stack.
2. Using the vector passed to it from the Protected Mode exception handler, the VMM indexes into the Real Mode application's IDT and obtains the pointer to the corresponding Real Mode exception handler.
3. It then replaces the CS:EIP pointer stored in the privilege level 0 stack with the address of the Real Mode exception handler. Before doing so, however, the VMM makes a copy of the original CS:EIP pointer for later use (it is the address to return to in the Real Mode program after the exception is handled; see step 6).
4. The VMM executes an IRET instruction which switches the logical processor back into VM86 Mode and transfers control to the Real Mode exception handler. The handler services the event and then executes an IRET instruction.
5. Since IRET is a sensitive instruction in VM86 Mode, the attempt to execute it causes a GP exception. Determining that the event occurred in a Real Mode application, the Protected Mode GP handler calls the VMM.
6. The VMM then restores the return address (CS:EIP) on the privilege level 0 stack so it points to the location in the Real Mode application to return to after the exception was handled (saved in step 3).
7. The VMM executes an IRET instruction which switches the logical processor back into VM86 Mode where it resumes execution of the Real Mode application again.

Option 3: Exception Handled by Another Task

In this case, the exception selected a Protected Mode IDT entry containing a Task Gate. The Task Gate descriptor, in turn, contains the selector for a TSS descriptor in the GDT. This TSS descriptor contains the virtual base address and size of the TSS associated with the task that will act as the exception handler. As a result, a task switch occurs and, since this is effectively a call to the exception handler task, the Eflags[NT] bit is set to 1. A complete description of this type of task switch can be found in "Calling Another Task" on page 670.

Figure 20-9: Protected Mode IDT

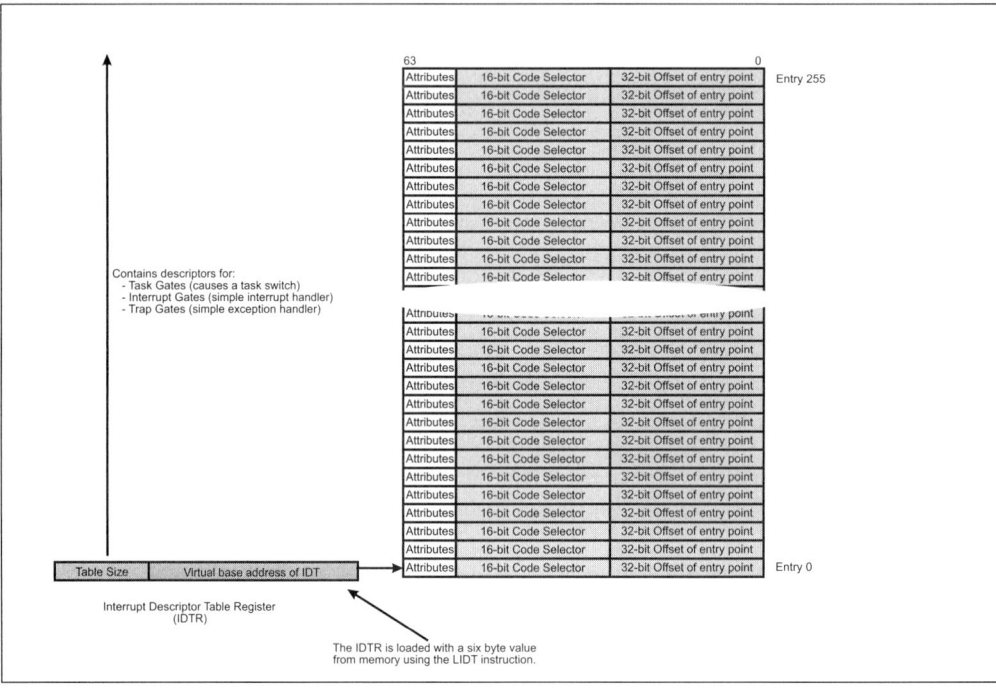

Hardware Interrupt Handling in VM86 Mode

NMI, SMI, and Maskable Interrupts

Interrupts originated by hardware devices fall into the four categories described in Table 20-1 on page 809. While handling of NMI and SMI are described in the table, handling of maskable hardware interrupts while in VM86 Mode requires more attention and is described in more detail in the sections that follow.

Table 20-1: Hardware Interrupt Types

Interrupt Type	Description

NMI	Non-Maskable Interrupts initiated by the chipset to signal serious, hardware-related failures:
	• An NMI can be received in two ways:
	  – If the logical processor's Local APIC is disabled, NMIs are delivered to the processor on its LINT0 or LINT1 input pin.
	  – If the logical processor's Local APIC is enabled, NMIs are delivered to the logical processor in an IPI message packet over the processor's external interface.
	• An NMI interrupt received during VM86 Mode operation is handled in the same manner as it would in any other mode:
	  – The logical processor selects entry 2 in the Protected Mode IDT and takes the actions described in "Processor Actions" on page 804.
	  – It is recommended that entry 2 contain an Interrupt Gate descriptor so that recognition of external hardware interrupts are masked before the logical processor transfers control to the Protected Mode NMI handler.
	• On completion of the NMI handler, execution of the IRET instruction causes the logical processor to reenter VM86 Mode and resume execution of the Real Mode application.
	A detailed description of NMI may be found in "NMI Description" on page 723.

Table 20-1: Hardware Interrupt Types (Continued)

Interrupt Type	Description

Maskable hard-ware interrupts	**Maskable hardware interrupts** initiated by external device adapters and also by logic local to a processor (e.g., internal thermal events, performance monitoring logic, local timer, etc.). Whether or not the logical processor recognizes the receipt of a maskable hardware interrupt depends on the current state of Eflags[IF] (0 = recognition disabled; 1 = enabled).
	• The state of the IF bit is controlled using the CLI (Clear Interrupt) and STI (Set Interrupt) instructions. It can also be altered using the PUSHF and POPF instructions.
	• The logical processor's handling of the CLI/STI/PUSHF/POPF instructions while in VM86 Mode is described in:
	  – "VM86 Task Executes CLI When VME = 0" on page 812.
	  – "STI/POPF/PUSHF/IRET Handling When VME = 0" on page 816.
	  – "CLI/STI/POPF/PUSHF Handling When VME = 1" on page 818.
	Assuming recognition is enabled and a maskable interrupt is detected, the logical processor takes the actions described in "Maskable Hardware Interrupts" on page 713.

SMI	System Management Interrupts initiated by the chipset in response to platform-specific events (e.g., external thermal and power management events). In VM86 Mode, the logical processor responds to the receipt of an SMI just as it would in any other mode. A detailed description of SMM may be found in "System Management Mode (SMM)" on page 1167.
IPIs	IPIs (Inter-Processor Interrupts). IPI messages sent from one logical processor to another via the processor's external interface or by the IO APIC in the chipset. An IPI message may contain an NMI, SMI, or a maskable hardware interrupt, in which case they would be handled as described in this table. A detailed description of IPI messaging may be found in "SW-Initiated Interrupt Message Transmission" on page 1351.

Real Mode Application's Unreal Reality

The first question is whether or not the logical processor will recognize a maskable hardware interrupt should one be delivered to it. This is governed by the state of Eflags[IF] (0 = recognition disabled; 1 = enabled) and the state of the IF bit is controlled using the CLI (Clear Interrupt) and STI (Set Interrupt) instructions. It can also be affected using the PUSHF and POPF instructions.

At a given moment in time, only the Protected Mode OS kernel knows the complete state of the machine. As an example, the kernel is likely to know whether or not any high-priority hardware interrupts are expected during a given period of time and, based on this knowledge, can make an intelligent decision as to whether or not it is safe to disable recognition of maskable interrupts. A Real Mode application running under VM86 Mode, on the other hand, has a delusional view of the machine's current state: it believes that it is the only program running and that it can therefore safely make decisions regarding when to disable or enable interrupt recognition. This is why the logical processor is sensitive to the attempted execution of the CLI and STI instructions (along with the PUSHF and POPF instructions) when it is operating in VM86 Mode. To be more precise, if:

1. The logical processor is currently executing a Real Mode application under VM86 Mode (Eflags[VM] = 1),
2. And the VM86 Extensions are not enabled (i.e., CR4[VME] = 0),
3. And the Real Mode application's IOPL threshold value (specified in the Eflags[IOPL] field while it's running) is set to a value < 3,

then a GP exception is generated when the logical processor attempts to execute any of the following instructions:

- CLI
- STI
- POPF
- PUSHF
- INT nn
- IRET

Determining that the exception occurred while a Real Mode task was running (by examining the state of VM in the Eflags image on the level 0 stack) the GP handler calls the VMM so it can decide how to safely emulate the Real Mode task's attempt to change the state of the Eflags[IF] bit.

The next section assumes that conditions 1, 2, and 3 (above) are true when a Real Mode application attempts to disable recognition of maskable hardware interrupts by executing the CLI instruction.

VM86 Task Executes CLI When VME = 0

This section assumes that conditions 1, 2, and 3 (in "Real Mode Application's Unreal Reality" on page 811) are true when a Real Mode application attempts to disable recognition of maskable hardware interrupts by executing the CLI instruction.

Refer to Figure 20-10 on page 814, Figure 20-11 on page 815 and Figure 20-12 on page 815. The VM86 task has attempted to disable recognition of maskable hardware interrupts (because it doesn't want to be disturbed by interrupts during the execution of a critical code section). The logical processor did not successfully execute the instruction, so interrupt recognition is still enabled upon entry to the VMM. There are **three possible cases**:

Case 1. **IF already 0**. The VMM checks the state of the IF bit in the Eflags image on the privilege level 0 stack and determines that interrupt recognition had already been disabled (by the VMM or OS) at some earlier point in time. In this case, the VMM adjusts the return pointer on the privilege level 0 stack to point to the instruction following the CLI that caused the exception, and then executes an IRET to resume execution of the interrupted Real Mode task at the instruction that follows the CLI.

Case 2. **Allow CLI**. The VMM may know that this is a safe time to disable interrupt recognition (because no high-priority interrupts are expected). In this case, the VMM could choose to execute a CLI instruction on behalf of the VM86 task, adjust the return pointer on the privilege level 0 stack to point to the instruction following the CLI that caused the exception, and then execute an IRET to resume execution of the interrupted Real Mode task at the instruction that follows the CLI.

Case 3. **Disallow CLI**. The VMM may know that this not a safe time to disable recognition of hardware interrupts. *The text that follows provides a detailed description of this case.*

CLI Handling

The multitasking OS cannot permit the Real Mode task (which is unaware of the existence of the multitasking OS or other, currently-suspended tasks) to summarily disable interrupt recognition. At an earlier point in time, another task may have stimulated an IO device (e.g., a disk interface) to perform an operation and generate an interrupt upon its completion. The device may complete the requested operation and generate the interrupt while the Real Mode task is executing. Furthermore, some devices are quite sensitive to being serviced on a timely basis. The Real Mode task is unaware of any of this.

Refer to Figure 20-10 on page 814. Based on the attempted execution of the CLI instruction, the VMM will note (in a memory location) that the currently-executing task prefers not to be interrupted. In other words, the VMM maintains a virtual copy of the Eflags[IF] bit in software. It alters the return address on the privilege level 0 stack to point to the instruction that follows the CLI and then executes the IRET to resume execution of the interrupted Real Mode task at the instruction that follows the CLI.

Subsequent High-Priority Interrupt Detected

Refer to Figure 20-11 on page 815. If a hardware interrupt should subsequently occur, the Real Mode task *is* interrupted and the hardware interrupt's Protected Mode handler then passes control to the VMM. If the VMM knows that the interrupting device requires fast servicing, it immediately executes either the Protected Mode or Real Mode handler to service the device. In other words, it ignores the preference of the Real Mode task that it not be interrupted. In this case, the Real Mode task was interrupted even though it preferred not to be. The VMM designer should make every attempt to accomplish the check just described as expeditiously as possible and return control to the interrupted task. Otherwise, the interrupted Real Mode task may not function correctly (because of the lengthy delay imposed by VMM software overhead necessary to determine whether to service the hardware interrupt right away or to defer servicing it until either an STI instruction is executed or the task's timeslice has expired).

Servicing of Lower-Priority Interrupt Deferred

On the other hand, the VMM may determine that:

- Since the virtual copy of the Eflags[IF] bit indicates that the VM86 task prefers not to be interrupted, and
- The interrupting device is one that can tolerate some delay in being serviced,
- It will defer execution of the device's interrupt handler until either an STI instruction is executed or the task's timeslice has expired

In this case, the VMM sets a bit in a VMM-specific data structure (let's call it the Deferred Interrupt Table) indicating that the specified interrupt handler should be executed when either an STI instruction is executed or the task's timeslice has expired. The VMM then executes the IRET instruction to resume execution of the interrupted Real Mode task. Refer to Figure 20-12 on page 815. Later, when the Real Mode task executes an STI or when its timeslice has expired and a task switch occurs back to the OS scheduler, the scheduler checks the Deferred Interrupt table (mentioned earlier) to determine if the servicing of any hardware interrupt(s) was deferred. If one or more were deferred, the OS calls the respective interrupt handler(s) to service the hardware device(s). As the note in the illustration states, the VMM may choose to call either the Real Mode or Protected Mode interrupt handlers to handle the deferred events.

Figure 20-10: VMM Handling of CLI Instruction

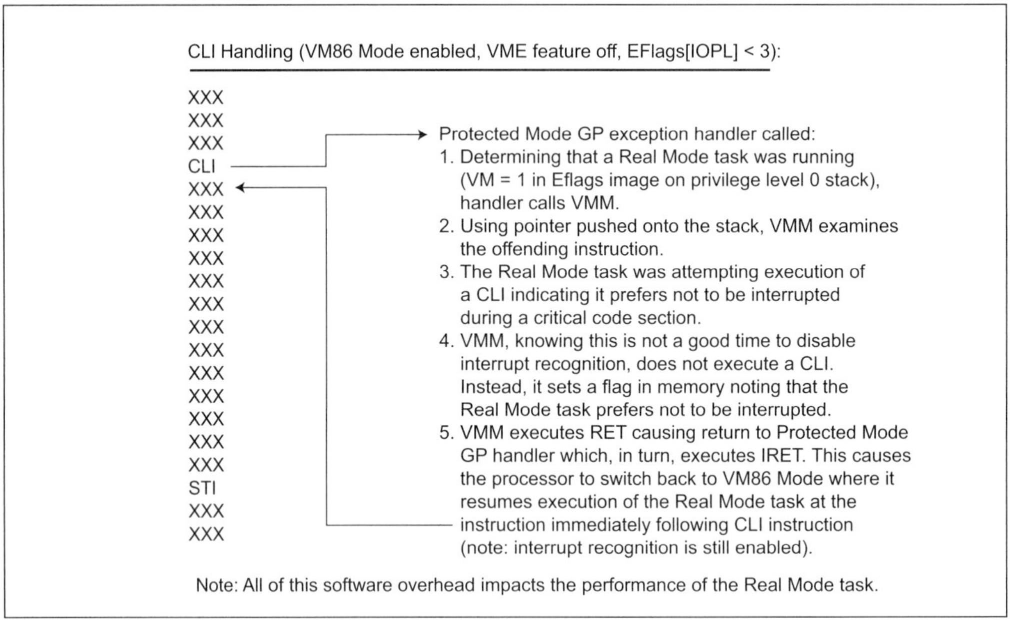

CLI Handling (VM86 Mode enabled, VME feature off, EFlags[IOPL] < 3):

XXX
XXX
XXX
CLI
XXX
XXX
XXX
XXX
XXX
XXX
XXX
XXX
XXX
XXX
XXX
XXX
STI
XXX
XXX

Protected Mode GP exception handler called:
1. Determining that a Real Mode task was running (VM = 1 in Eflags image on privilege level 0 stack), handler calls VMM.
2. Using pointer pushed onto the stack, VMM examines the offending instruction.
3. The Real Mode task was attempting execution of a CLI indicating it prefers not to be interrupted during a critical code section.
4. VMM, knowing this is not a good time to disable interrupt recognition, does not execute a CLI. Instead, it sets a flag in memory noting that the Real Mode task prefers not to be interrupted.
5. VMM executes RET causing return to Protected Mode GP handler which, in turn, executes IRET. This causes the processor to switch back to VM86 Mode where it resumes execution of the Real Mode task at the instruction immediately following CLI instruction (note: interrupt recognition is still enabled).

Note: All of this software overhead impacts the performance of the Real Mode task.

Figure 20-11: Real Mode Task Is Interrupted

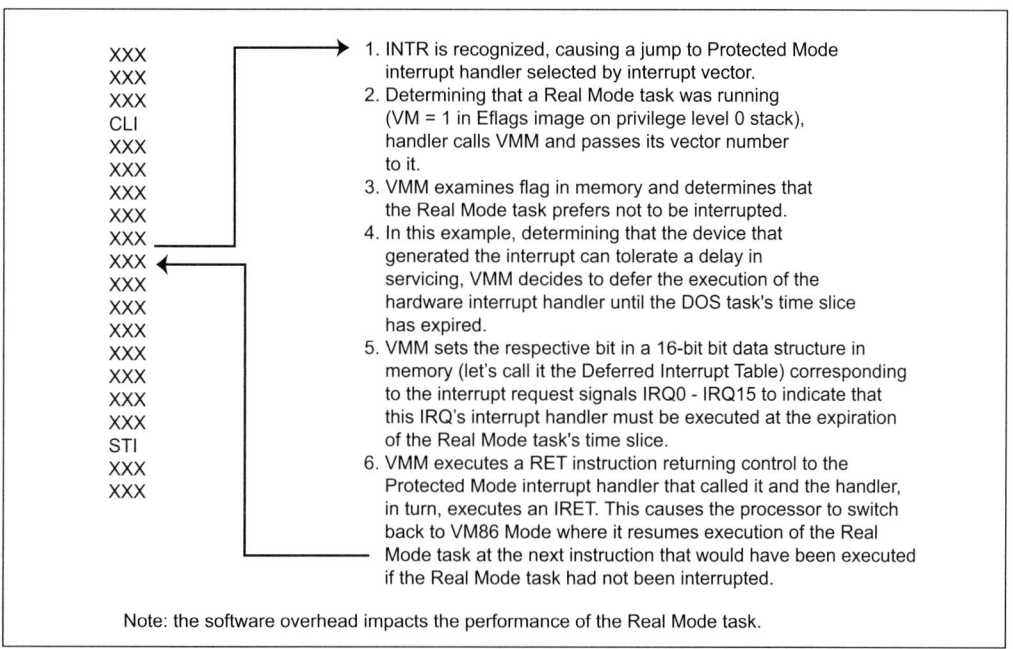

```
XXX          1. INTR is recognized, causing a jump to Protected Mode
XXX             interrupt handler selected by interrupt vector.
XXX          2. Determining that a Real Mode task was running
CLI             (VM = 1 in Eflags image on privilege level 0 stack),
XXX             handler calls VMM and passes its vector number
XXX             to it.
XXX          3. VMM examines flag in memory and determines that
XXX             the Real Mode task prefers not to be interrupted.
XXX          4. In this example, determining that the device that
XXX             generated the interrupt can tolerate a delay in
XXX             servicing, VMM decides to defer the execution of the
XXX             hardware interrupt handler until the DOS task's time slice
XXX             has expired.
XXX          5. VMM sets the respective bit in a 16-bit bit data structure in
XXX             memory (let's call it the Deferred Interrupt Table) corresponding
XXX             to the interrupt request signals IRQ0 - IRQ15 to indicate that
XXX             this IRQ's interrupt handler must be executed at the expiration
STI             of the Real Mode task's time slice.
XXX          6. VMM executes a RET instruction returning control to the
XXX             Protected Mode interrupt handler that called it and the handler,
                in turn, executes an IRET. This causes the processor to switch
                back to VM86 Mode where it resumes execution of the Real
                Mode task at the next instruction that would have been executed
                if the Real Mode task had not been interrupted.

   Note: the software overhead impacts the performance of the Real Mode task.
```

Figure 20-12: When the Real Mode Task's Timeslice Expires

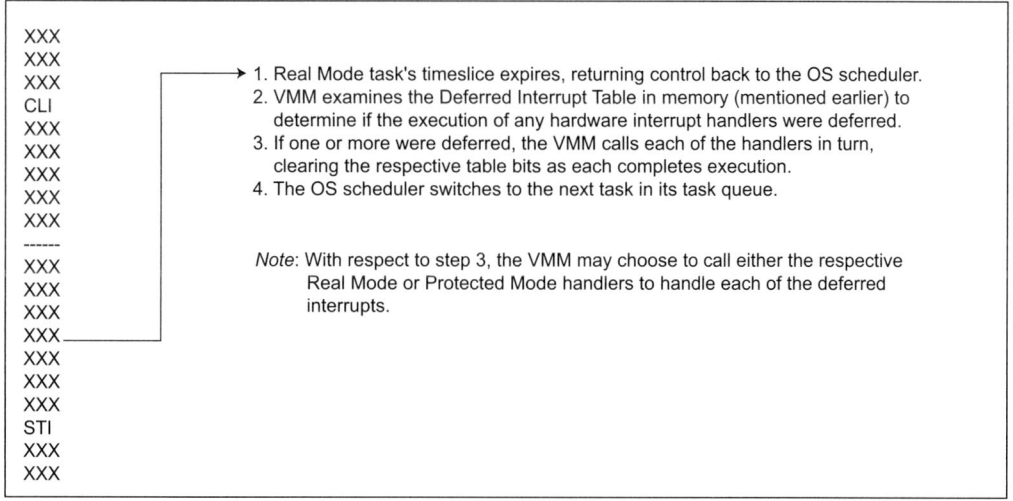

```
XXX
XXX
XXX          1. Real Mode task's timeslice expires, returning control back to the OS scheduler.
CLI          2. VMM examines the Deferred Interrupt Table in memory (mentioned earlier) to
XXX             determine if the execution of any hardware interrupt handlers were deferred.
XXX          3. If one or more were deferred, the VMM calls each of the handlers in turn,
XXX             clearing the respective table bits as each completes execution.
XXX          4. The OS scheduler switches to the next task in its task queue.
XXX

------
XXX          Note: With respect to step 3, the VMM may choose to call either the respective
XXX             Real Mode or Protected Mode handlers to handle each of the deferred
XXX             interrupts.
XXX
XXX
XXX
XXX
STI
XXX
XXX
```

STI/POPF/PUSHF/IRET Handling When VME = 0

The logical processor's handling of the CLI instruction when operating in VM86 Mode with the VME feature off was described in the previous section. The sections that follow describe the handling of the other IOPL sensitive instructions.

Attempted Execution of STI Instruction (VME = 0)

If a Real Mode task running in VM86 Mode attempts to execute the STI (Set Interrupt) instruction while the VM86 VME feature is off (CR4[VME] = 0), it results in a GP exception. Determining that the problem occurred in a Real Mode task (by looking at the VM bit in the Eflags register image on the privilege level 0 stack), the GP handler calls the VMM. There are three possibilities:

Case 1. **IF already 1**. The VMM checks the state of the IF bit in the Eflags image on the privilege level 0 stack and determines that interrupt recognition is already enabled. In this case, the VMM adjusts the return pointer on the privilege level 0 stack to point to the instruction following the STI that caused the exception, and then executes an IRET to resume execution of the interrupted Real Mode task at the instruction that follows the STI.

Case 2. **Allow STI**. The VMM may know that this is a safe time to enable interrupt recognition. In this case, the VMM could choose to execute an STI instruction on behalf of the VM86 task, adjust the return pointer on the privilege level 0 stack to point to the instruction following the STI that caused the exception, and then execute an IRET to resume execution of the interrupted Real Mode task at the instruction that follows the STI.

Case 3. **Disallow STI**. The VMM knows that this is not a safe time to reenable recognition of hardware interrupts. In this case, the VMM adjusts the return pointer on the privilege level 0 stack to point to the instruction following the STI that caused the exception, and then executes an IRET to resume execution of the interrupted Real Mode task at the instruction that follows the STI.

Attempted Execution of PUSHF Instruction (VME = 0)

If a Real Mode task running in VM86 Mode attempts to execute the PUSHF (Push Flags) instruction while the VM86 VME feature is off (CR4[VME] = 0), it results in a GP exception. Determining that the problem occurred in a Real Mode task (by looking at the VM bit in the Eflags register image on the privilege level 0 stack), the GP handler calls the VMM.

If the Real Mode task were permitted to execute the PUSHF, the Eflags register would be copied to the stack and the Eflag[VM] and Eflag[RF] bits would be automatically cleared. This would disable VM86 mode, preventing the logical processor from continued monitoring of the Real Mode task's behavior. The VMM could emulate this in a benign fashion, copying the Eflags contents to the Real Mode task's stack (SS:ESP are on the privilege level 0 stack) without clearing Eflags[VM]. The VMM adjusts the return pointer on the privilege level 0 stack to point to the instruction following the PUSHF that caused the exception, and then executes an IRET to resume execution of the interrupted Real Mode task at the instruction that follows the PUSHF.

Attempted Execution of POPF Instruction (VME = 0)

If a Real Mode task running in VM86 Mode attempts to execute the POPF (Pop Flags) instruction while the VM86 VME feature is off (CR4[VME] = 0), it results in a GP exception. Determining that the problem occurred in a Real Mode task (by looking at the VM bit in the Eflags register image on the privilege level 0 stack), the GP handler calls the VMM.

When executed, the POPF instruction copies the Eflags image on the stack into the Eflags register. If the programmer had altered this image, a number of problems could result:

- The VM bit could be cleared, disabling VM86 mode and preventing the logical processor from continued monitoring of the Real Mode task's behavior. The VMM must copy the Eflags image from the Real Mode task's stack into the Eflags register, but ensure that the VM bit remains set to one.
- The IF bit could be cleared, disabling the logical processor's ability to recognize external hardware interrupts. The VMM could treat this attempt to disable interrupt recognition in the same manner as an attempt to execute a CLI instruction (see "VM86 Task Executes CLI When VME = 0" on page 812).
- The IF bit could be set, re-enabling the logical processor's ability to recognize external hardware interrupts. The VMM could treat this attempt to enable interrupt recognition in the same manner as an attempt to execute a STI instruction (see "Attempted Execution of STI Instruction (VME = 0)" on page 816).

Attempted Execution of IRET Instruction (VME = 0)

In some cases the VMM may pass control to a Real Mode handler to service an interrupt or exception. This is accomplished by adjusting the return address on the privilege level 0 stack to point to the target Real Mode handler and then executing the IRET instruction. This switches the logical processor back into VM86 Mode and passes control to the Real Mode handler. At the conclusion of the Real Mode handler, the attempted execution of the IRET instruction in VM86 Mode results in a GP exception. The Protected Mode GP handler calls the VMM, which replaces the original return address on the privilege level 0 stack and then executes IRET again. This switches the logical processor back into VM86 Mode and passes control back to the interrupted Real Mode task. See "VMM Passes Control To Real Mode Handler" on page 829 for a more detailed description of this process.

CLI/STI/POPF/PUSHF Handling When VME = 1

VM86 Extensions

The VME (VM86 Extensions) feature provides two improvements to VM86 Mode and was first implemented in the Pentium, migrated into the later versions of the 486, and is present in all subsequent x86 processors. Whether or not these improvements are activated is controlled by CR4[VME] (see Figure 20-13 on page 819). When CR4[VME] = 1, the following features are enabled:

- Improved handling of the INT *nn* instruction using the Interrupt Redirection Bitmap in the Real Mode task's TSS. For a complete description, refer to "Software Interrupt Instruction Handling" on page 825.
- Improved handling of CLI/STI/POPF/PUSHF instructions using the VIF and VIP bits in the Eflags register.

Executing a CPUID request type 1 returns the logical processor's capabilities (EDX bit 1 indicates whether or not a logical processor supports the VME feature).

Figure 20-13: CR4

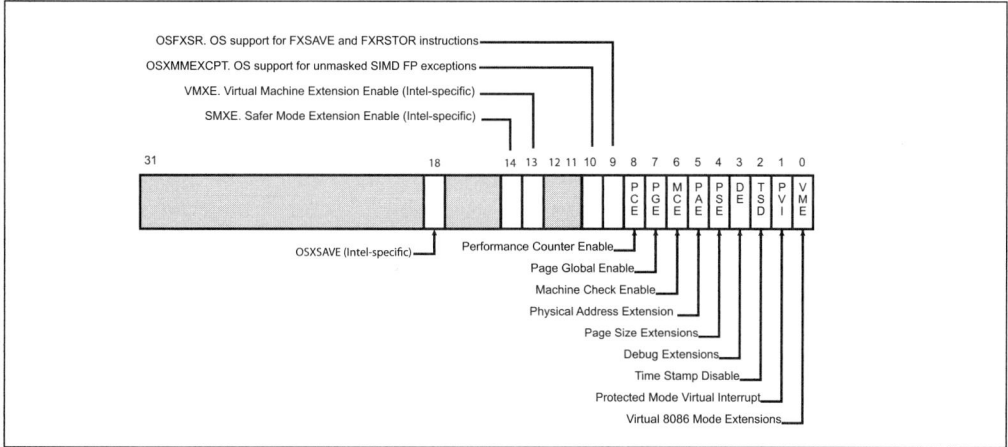

Background

As described earlier, a Real Mode task that attempts the execution of the CLI/STI/POPF/PUSHF instructions when the logical processor

- is in VM86 Mode,
- with the VME feature turned off (CR4[VME] = 0),
- and the IOPL threshold value in Eflags set to a value less than 3

suffers a substantial amount of software overhead. This can result in poor performance or perhaps cause the Real Mode task to malfunction. The attempted execution of one of these instructions results in a GP exception and the VMM is called to determine how to handle it. As described in the next section, turning on the VME feature can eliminate virtually all of this software overhead:

- The logical processor successfully executes the instruction without generating a GP exception, the VMM is not called and the logical processor falls through to the next instruction and continues program execution.

When VME = 1 and IOPL = 3, Task Can Control Eflags[IF]

By definition, a Real Mode task has a CPL of 3. This being the case, if the Eflags[IOPL] is set to 3 when a Real Mode task attempts to execute a CLI, STI, POPF or PUSHF instruction, the instruction executes normally without causing an exception. In other words, the Real Mode task is permitted to enable and disable recognition of maskable hardware interrupts at will.

When VME = 1 and IOPL < 3, Task Controls VIF, Not IF

If the IOPL for a Real Mode task is set to a value < 3, any attempt to execute the CLI, STI, POPF or PUSHF instructions has no effect on the Eflags[IF] bit. Instead, the change (if any) is made to Eflags[VIF]:

- As always, the state of Eflags[IF] is what controls the logical processor's ability to recognize a maskable hardware interrupt.
- The state of Eflags[VIF], on the other hand, merely notes the preference of the Real Mode task to be disturbed (VIF = 1) or not (VIF = 0) by maskable interrupts during a given period of time.

Eflags[VIP] Is Controlled by the VMM

The Virtual Interrupt Pending bit is never set or cleared automatically by the logical processor. Rather, the VMM software controls it:

- The VMM clears Eflags[VIP] to 0 if it has not deferred the servicing of any maskable hardware interrupts during a period when:
  — IF = 1 (interrupt recognition is enabled),
  — and VIF = 0 (the Real Mode task has indicated that it prefers not to be interrupted).
- The VMM sets Eflags[VIP] = 1 if it has deferred the servicing of one or more maskable hardware interrupts during a period when:
  — IF = 1 (interrupt recognition is enabled),
  — and VIF = 0 (the Real Mode task has indicated that it prefers not to be interrupted).

Software Cannot Directly Access Eflags[VIP]

Something important to keep in mind relative to the preceding topic: although level 0 software can directly manipulate some bits in the Eflags register, it cannot directly read or alter the state of Eflags[VIP]. In order to read its current state, the VMM must read the Eflags image from the level 0 stack. If it must change the state of the bit, it must change its state in the stack image and then execute a RET or an IRET which causes the logical processor to reload the Eflags register from the stack image.

CLI Followed by a Maskable Interrupt

Refer to Figure 20-14 on page 823. When a Real Mode task with an IOPL < 3 attempts execution of the CLI instruction with CR4[VME] = 1, the state of the Eflags[IF] bit is not affected. Rather, the logical processor clears Eflags[VIF] to 0

(VIF is a virtual copy of the IF bit). Its state has absolutely no effect on the logical processor's operation and merely records whether or not the Real Mode task prefers not to be disturbed by maskable interrupts. Assuming that Eflags[IF] = 1, it remains so and the logical processor's ability to recognize an externally-generated maskable hardware interrupt remains enabled.

Figure 20-15 on page 824 assumes that Eflags[IF] = 1 on entry to this code fragment. Although a CLI is executed, Eflags[IF] remains set to one and, if an external hardware interrupt is subsequently detected on the processor's INTR input (or is delivered to the logical processor by its Local APIC), it is recognized on the next instruction boundary. The CLI clears Eflags[VIF] to 0 to indicate it prefers not to be disturbed by maskable hardware interrupts. When a maskable interrupt is subsequently detected, the following actions are taken:

1. The logical processor ceases executing the interrupted program.
2. The logical processor obtains the 8-bit interrupt vector from either the external 8259A interrupt controller or from the Local APIC.
3. It uses the vector to index into the Protected Mode IDT and reads the 8-byte descriptor. Assuming it's an Interrupt Gate or a Trap Gate (not a Task Gate), the logical processor automatically switches to the level 0 stack that was preallocated by the OS by moving the level 3 stack pointer from SS:ESP into temp registers and then loading the contents of the Real Mode task's TSS SS0:ESP0 fields into SS:ESP. Having done so, it then pushes the contents of the following registers onto the level 0 stack (see Figure 20-16 on page 824):
   — **CS:EIP**. Address to return to in the Real Mode task after the interrupt has been handled.
   — **Eflags**. State of the Eflags register at the point of interruption in the Real Mode task.
   — Temp register pair containing the **Privilege level 3 stack pointer** used by the Real Mode task.
   — **ES, DS, FS, GS**. Real Mode data segment base addresses.
4. It then loads CS:EIP with the Protected Mode handler entry point obtained from the Gate descriptor in the IDT and begins execution of the handler.
5. The Protected Mode interrupt handler examines the VM bit in the Eflags image saved on the level 0 stack and determines that the interrupted program was a Real Mode task. As a result, the handler calls the VMM and passes it the vector associated with the interrupt.
6. The VMM determines that Eflags[VIF] = 0 indicating that the interrupted Real Mode task prefers not to bear the burden of servicing hardware devices right now. The VMM then evaluates the vector number delivered to it by the Protected Mode handler and makes one of two determinations:

A. **Handler execution deferred**. If, in the VMM's estimation, the interrupting device can tolerate some delay in being serviced, it takes the following actions:

1. The VMM sets a bit in the Deferred Interrupt Table in memory (an OS-specific data structure) indicating the IRQ number of the handler whose execution is being deferred until the Real Mode task indicates it doesn't mind being interrupted (by its subsequent execution of an STI instruction).

2. The VMM sets Eflags[VIP] (Virtual Interrupt Pending) = 1 in the Eflags image on the level 0 stack to indicate that the execution of one or more hardware interrupt handlers have been deferred until the Real Mode task indicates it doesn't mind being interrupted (by its subsequent execution of an STI instruction).

3. The VMM executes a RET to return control to the Protected Mode interrupt handler which, in turn, executes an IRET which switches the logical processor back into VM86 Mode and resumes execution of the interrupted Real Mode task.

B. **Handler executed now**. If, in the VMM's estimation, the interrupting device requires rather more timely servicing, it executes a RET to return control to the Protected Mode interrupt handler and instructs it to service the device now. The body of the handler is executed, thereby satisfying the device's request for servicing. The handler then executes an IRET which switches the logical processor back into VM86 Mode and resumes execution of the interrupted Real Mode task. If the additional software overhead incurred as a result of servicing a hardware device adversely affects the Real Mode task, so be it. The VMM must give precedence to the health of the overall machine rather than to the Real Mode task.

Subsequent STI Effect Depends on Eflags[VIP]

If the Real Mode task executes the STI instruction to reenable recognition of maskable hardware interrupts, the action's taken by the logical processor depend on the current state of Eflags[VIP]:

- **VIP = 0** indicates that the VMM did not defer the servicing of any hardware devices due to the Real Mode task's preference not to be interrupted (as indicated by VIF = 0). In this case, the STI instruction completes execution, setting Eflags[VIF] = 1 to indicate that the Real Mode task does not mind being interrupted now.

- **VIP = 1** indicates that the VMM did defer the servicing of one or more hardware devices due to the Real Mode task's preference not to be interrupted (as indicated by VIF = 0). In this case, execution of the STI instruction causes the following actions to be taken:

1. A GP exception is generated.
2. Determining that the exception happened in a Real Mode task, the GP handler calls the VMM.
3. Determining that the offending instruction is an STI, the VMM calls the respective hardware interrupt handler (pointed to by the respective entry in the Real Mode or Protected Mode IDT) to execute the deferred handler.
4. Once all of the deferred handlers have been run, the VMM clears the respective bits in the OS-specific Deferred Interrupt Table.
5. The VMM clears the VIP bit in the Eflags image on the level 0 stack.
6. The VMM executes a RET to the GP handler which, in turn, executes an IRET. This switches the logical processor back into VM86 Mode and it reexecutes the STI, this time successfully, and sets Eflags[VIF] = 1.

Figure 20-14: Efficient Handling of the CLI/STI Instructions

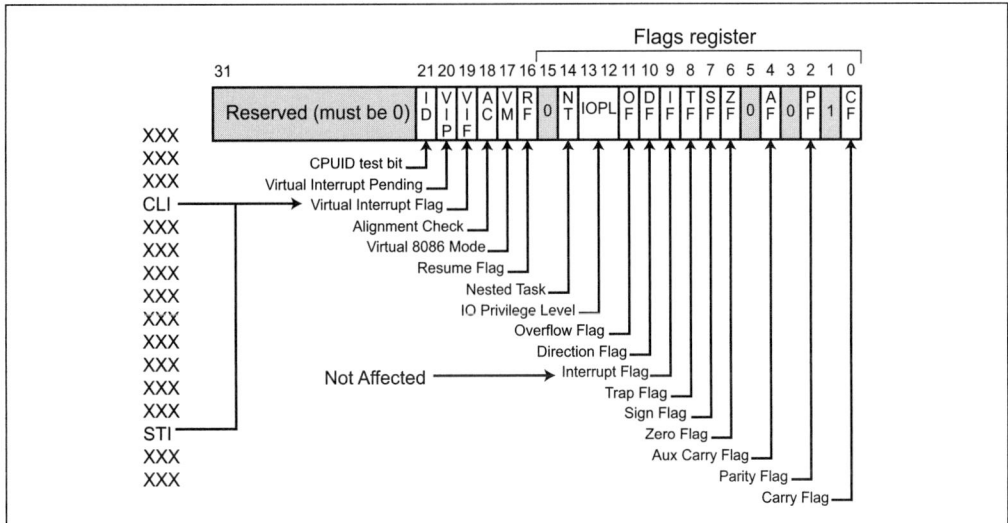

Figure 20-15: Interrupt Received After CLI Execution

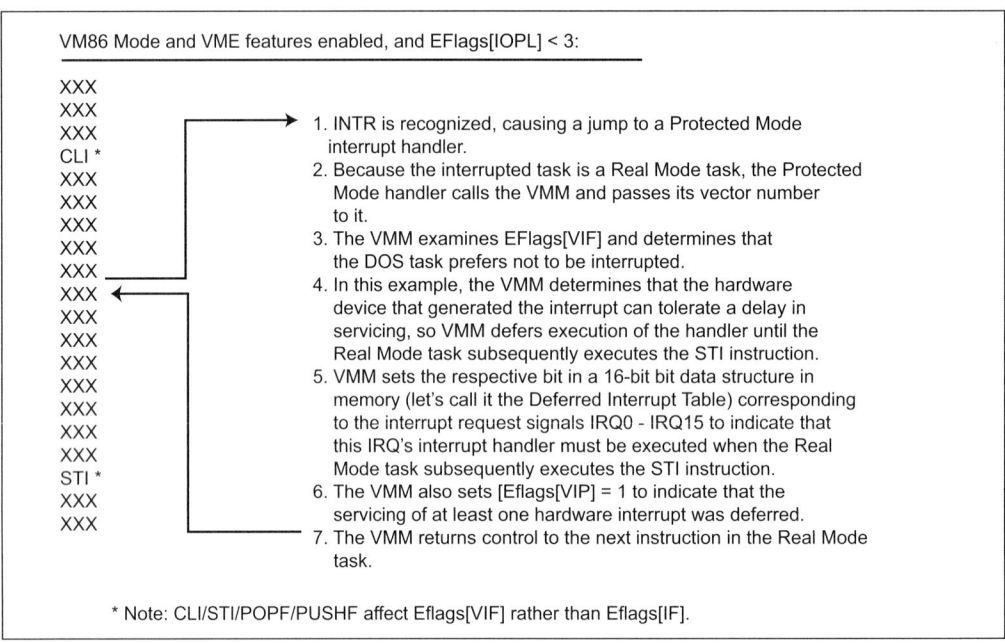

VM86 Mode and VME features enabled, and EFlags[IOPL] < 3:

XXX
XXX
XXX
CLI *
XXX
XXX
XXX
XXX
XXX
XXX
XXX
XXX
XXX
XXX
XXX
XXX
STI *
XXX
XXX

1. INTR is recognized, causing a jump to a Protected Mode interrupt handler.
2. Because the interrupted task is a Real Mode task, the Protected Mode handler calls the VMM and passes its vector number to it.
3. The VMM examines EFlags[VIF] and determines that the DOS task prefers not to be interrupted.
4. In this example, the VMM determines that the hardware device that generated the interrupt can tolerate a delay in servicing, so VMM defers execution of the handler until the Real Mode task subsequently executes the STI instruction.
5. VMM sets the respective bit in a 16-bit bit data structure in memory (let's call it the Deferred Interrupt Table) corresponding to the interrupt request signals IRQ0 - IRQ15 to indicate that this IRQ's interrupt handler must be executed when the Real Mode task subsequently executes the STI instruction.
6. The VMM also sets [Eflags[VIP] = 1 to indicate that the servicing of at least one hardware interrupt was deferred.
7. The VMM returns control to the next instruction in the Real Mode task.

* Note: CLI/STI/POPF/PUSHF affect Eflags[VIF] rather than Eflags[IF].

Figure 20-16: Privilege Level 0 Stack After Interrupt/Exception in VM86 Mode

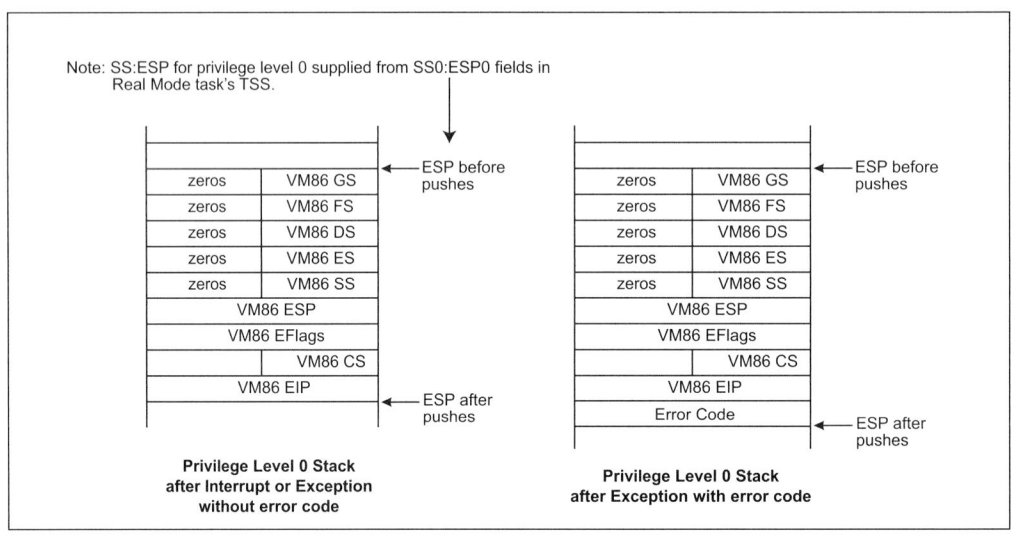

Note: SS:ESP for privilege level 0 supplied from SS0:ESP0 fields in Real Mode task's TSS.

zeros	VM86 GS
zeros	VM86 FS
zeros	VM86 DS
zeros	VM86 ES
zeros	VM86 SS
VM86 ESP	
VM86 EFlags	
	VM86 CS
VM86 EIP	

ESP before pushes
ESP after pushes

**Privilege Level 0 Stack
after Interrupt or Exception
without error code**

zeros	VM86 GS
zeros	VM86 FS
zeros	VM86 DS
zeros	VM86 ES
zeros	VM86 SS
VM86 ESP	
VM86 EFlags	
	VM86 CS
VM86 EIP	
Error Code	

ESP before pushes
ESP after pushes

**Privilege Level 0 Stack
after Exception with error code**

A Special Case

If, immediately after the execution of a POPF or IRET instruction, or a task switch, the logical processor detects both Eflags[VIF] and [VIP] = 1, a GP exception is generated. If the exception occurred in a Real Mode task, the GP handler calls the VMM which:

- Services the previously-deferred maskable hardware interrupts,
- Clears the respective bits in the OS-specific Deferred Interrupt Table,
- Clears the VIP bit in the Eflags image on the level 0 stack,
- and executes a RET to return to the GP handler.

The GP handler then executes an IRET to return control back to the Real Mode task.

POPF/PUSHF Handling

As with the CLI and STI instructions, the execution of the POPF or PUSHF instruction by a Real Mode task does not cause a GP exception when the VME feature is enabled and the IOPL < 3. Any change that the instruction would normally make to Eflags[IF] is made to Eflags[VIF] instead and no exception is generated.

Software Interrupt Instruction Handling

When an application executes a software interrupt instruction (INT *nn*, INTO, INT3, or BOUND; see "Software Interrupts" on page 725), the logical processor selects an IDT entry (entry *nn*, 04, 03, or 05, respectively) and calls the handler pointed to by the selected Interrupt or Trap Gate descriptor. Various protection mechanisms exist to prevent an application from calling a procedure it is not privileged enough to access.

Software Interrupt Handling in Protected Mode

If the OS wishes to prevent a level 3 Protected Mode application from calling procedures residing in a more-privileged code segment using software interrupt instructions, it sets the DPL in the IDT entry's DPL field to a value that is less than 3. Any attempt on the part of a program with a CPL of 3 to execute the INT *nn*, INTO, BOUND, or INT3 instruction will then result in the generation of a GP exception. It is OS design-specific as to how the intercepted call will be handled.

Software Interrupt Handling in VM86 Mode

When the logical processor is operating in VM86 Mode, the manner in which it handles the attempted execution of the INT *nn* instruction depends on three factors:

- Whether or not the VM86 Extensions are enabled via CR4[VME].
- The threshold value in the Eflags[IOPL] field.
- If the VM86 Extensions are enabled (CR4[VME] = 1), the value (0 or 1) of the bit that is selected (by *nn*) in the Real Mode task's TSS Interrupt Redirection Bitmap (see Figure 20-1 on page 786).

Table 20-2 on page 826 defines the actions taken by the logical processor based on the state of these three elements. Please note that the CPL of a Real Mode task running under VM86 Mode is always 3:

- Methods 1 and 2 are used when the VM86 Mode Extensions are disabled (CR4[VME] = 0).
- Methods 3 - 6 are used when the VM86 Mode Extensions are enabled (CR4[VME] = 1).

INT3 Is Special

The handling of INT3, the debug breakpoint instruction, is special in VM86 Mode. Refer to "INT3 (Breakpoint) Instruction" on page 727.

Table 20-2: INT nn Handling Methods in VM86 Mode

Method	VME	IOPL	Selected Bit in Map	INT *nn* execution attempted. Processor response:
The two rows that follow describe conditions when the Virtual 8086 Mode Extensions are disabled (CR4[VME] = 0).				

Table 20-2: INT nn Handling Methods in VM86 Mode (Continued)

Method	VME	IOPL	Selected Bit in Map	INT *nn* execution attempted. Processor response:
1	0	3	VME off, so bit map not used	**Protected Mode handler selected.** Although INT *nn* is a sensitive instruction, execution is permitted because task's CPL (3) matches Eflags[IOPL] threshold setting (3). 1. Vector *nn* selects IDT entry *nn*. The Interrupt or Trap Gate descriptor contains respective Protected Mode handler's entry point. 2. SS:ESP moved into temp registers and SS0:ESP0 fields copied into SS:ESP register pair from task's TSS (switch to privilege 0 stack). 3. Pushes GS, FS, DS, ES onto privilege level 0 stack. 4. Pushes caller's stack pointer (SS:ESP from temp registers), Eflags, CS:EIP onto privilege level 0 stack. 5. Clears Eflags VM, RF, NT, TF bits and, if selected IDT gate is Interrupt Gate, IF bit as well. Trap Gate leaves TF bit untouched. 6. Clears four data segment registers to 0. 7. Loads CS:EIP from gate. 8. Starts execution of handler.
2	0	< 3	VME off, so bit map not used	**GP exception.** Attempted execution of sensitive instruction causes a GP exception (privilege 3 task failed IOPL threshold test). The Protected Mode GP handler calls the VMM who must decide how to handle the INT *nn* attempt (fetches offending instruction using task's CS:EIP on stack). Basically, it has four choices: 1. It can forbid the action and abort the task. 2. It can handle the request itself. 3. It can call the respective Protected Mode handler to handle the request. 4. It can call the respective Real Mode handler to handle the request. For a detailed description of how this handled, see "VMM Passes Control To Real Mode Handler" on page 829.

Table 20-2: INT nn Handling Methods in VM86 Mode (Continued)

Method	VME	IOPL	Selected Bit in Map	INT *nn* execution attempted. Processor response:
The four rows that follow describe conditions when the Virtual 8086 Mode Extensions are disabled (CR4[VME] = 1).				
3	1	< 3	1	**GP exception.** CR4[VME] = 1, so software interrupt redirection bitmap consulted. Bit selected by *nn* = 1. Combination of IOPL threshold test failure and selected bit = 1 results in a GP exception. Protected Mode GP handler calls the VMM who must decide how to handle the INT *nn* attempt (fetches offending instruction using task's CS:EIP on stack). Basically, it has four choices (refer to the four choices listed in method 2 in this table).
4	1	3	1	**Protected Mode handler selected.** Sensitive instruction allowed because IOPL = 3. CR4[VME] = 1, so software interrupt redirection bitmap consulted. Bit selected by *nn* = 1, so the logical processor jumps to the Protected Mode handler pointed to by IDT entry *nn*. See steps 1 - 8 in method 1.
5	1	3	0	**Real Mode handler selected.** Sensitive instruction allowed because IOPL = 3. CR4[VME] = 1, so software interrupt redirection bitmap is consulted. Bit selected by *nn* = 0, so the logical processor jumps to the Real Mode handler pointed to by Real Mode IDT entry *nn* (Real Mode IDT starts at virtual address 0). 1. Pushes Eflags to stack. 2. Clears Eflags IF and TF bits, disabling recognition of maskable interrupts and of single-step mode (if it was enabled). 3. Pushes CS:IP to stack. 4. Jumps to Real Mode handler pointed to by Real Mode IDT entry *nn*. *It's important to note that in this scenario, the logical processor does not exit VM86 Mode to service the interrupt.*

Table 20-2: INT nn Handling Methods in VM86 Mode (Continued)

Method	VME	IOPL	Selected Bit in Map	INT *nn* execution attempted. Processor response:
6	1	< 3	0	**Real Mode handler selected.** Although the IOPL threshold is set to a value less than 3 (the task's privilege level = 3), because CR4[VME] = 1 the software interrupt redirection bitmap is nonetheless consulted and the bit selected by *nn* = 0, so the logical processor jumps to the Real Mode handler pointed to by Real Mode IDT entry *nn* (Real Mode IDT starts at virtual address 0). In other words, method 6 handling of a software interrupt instruction appears to be identical to method 5. There are differences, however: 1. The contents of the Eflags register is pushed to the stack, but: – The IOPL value in the stack image is adjusted to 3. – In the stack image, the value of the Eflags[VIF] bit is copied into the IF bit. 2. Clears Eflags VIF (rather than IF as in method 5) and TF bits. This does not disable recognition of maskable interrupts, but it does disable single-step mode (if it was enabled). 3. Pushes CS:IP to stack. 4. Jumps to Real Mode handler pointed to by Real Mode IDT entry *nn*. *It's important to note that in this scenario, the logical processor does not exit VM86 Mode to service the interrupt.*

VMM Passes Control To Real Mode Handler

When the VME feature is not enabled and the attempted execution of an INT *nn* instruction results in a GP exception (see methods 2 and 3 in Table 20-2 on page 826), the GP exception handler calls the VMM which must decide how to handle the event (it fetches the offending instruction from memory using the Real Mode task's CS:EIP on the privilege level 0 stack). Basically, it has four choices:

1. It can forbid the action and abort the task.
2. It can handle the request itself.
3. It can call the respective Protected Mode handler to handle the request.
4. It can call the respective Real Mode handler to handle the request. To pass control to the corresponding Real Mode handler, the VMM takes the actions illustrated in Figure 20-17 on page 830 and Figure 20-18 on page 831.

Figure 20-17: VMM Passes Control to a Real Mode Handler (1-of-2)

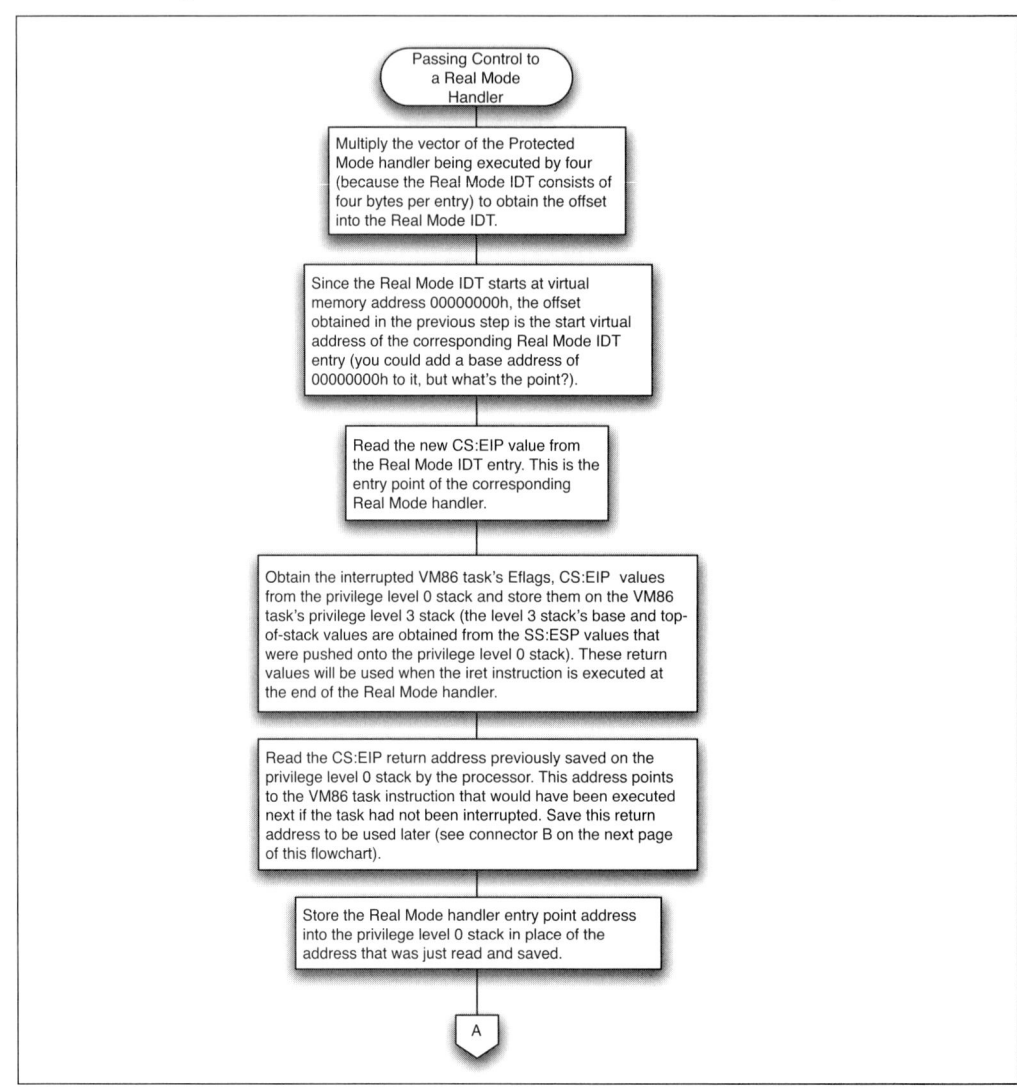

Figure 20-18: VMM Passes Control to a Real Mode Handler (2-of-2)

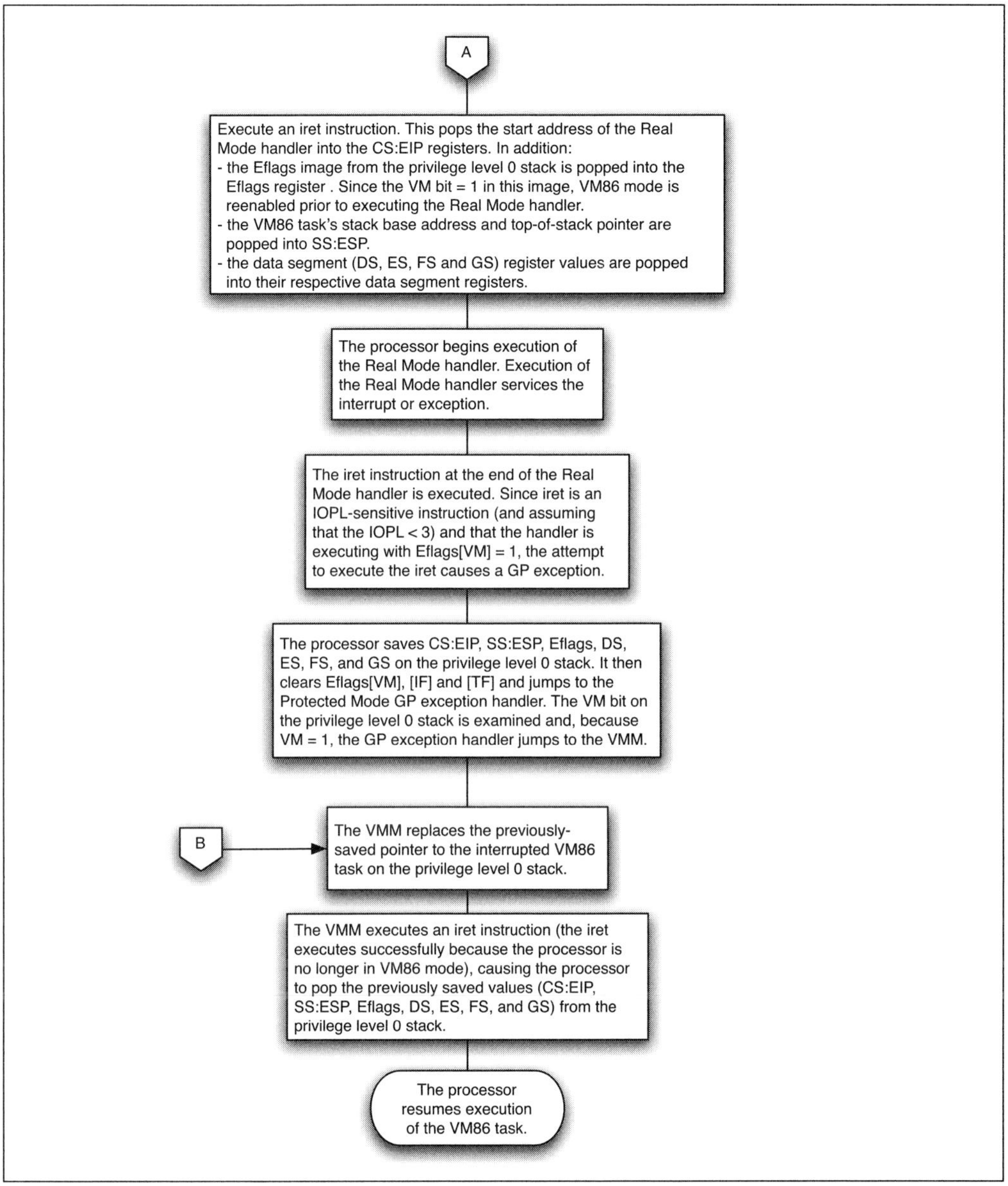

A

Execute an iret instruction. This pops the start address of the Real Mode handler into the CS:EIP registers. In addition:
- the Eflags image from the privilege level 0 stack is popped into the Eflags register. Since the VM bit = 1 in this image, VM86 mode is reenabled prior to executing the Real Mode handler.
- the VM86 task's stack base address and top-of-stack pointer are popped into SS:ESP.
- the data segment (DS, ES, FS and GS) register values are popped into their respective data segment registers.

The processor begins execution of the Real Mode handler. Execution of the Real Mode handler services the interrupt or exception.

The iret instruction at the end of the Real Mode handler is executed. Since iret is an IOPL-sensitive instruction (and assuming that the IOPL < 3) and that the handler is executing with Eflags[VM] = 1, the attempt to execute the iret causes a GP exception.

The processor saves CS:EIP, SS:ESP, Eflags, DS, ES, FS, and GS on the privilege level 0 stack. It then clears Eflags[VM], [IF] and [TF] and jumps to the Protected Mode GP exception handler. The VM bit on the privilege level 0 stack is examined and, because VM = 1, the GP exception handler jumps to the VMM.

B

The VMM replaces the previously-saved pointer to the interrupted VM86 task on the privilege level 0 stack.

The VMM executes an iret instruction (the iret executes successfully because the processor is no longer in VM86 mode), causing the processor to pop the previously saved values (CS:EIP, SS:ESP, Eflags, DS, ES, FS, and GS) from the privilege level 0 stack.

The processor resumes execution of the VM86 task.

Halt Instruction in VM86 Mode

If the Real Mode application attempts to execute the Halt (HLT) instruction while the logical processor is operating in VM86 Mode, a GP exception is generated. Determining that the interrupted task was a VM86 task, the GP handler calls the VMM. Examining the offending instruction, the VMM must decide how to handle the task's attempt to halt the logical processor. Since a halted logical processor is an unproductive one, the VMM will almost certainly instruct the scheduler to suspend the task and resume the execution of another one.

Protected Mode Virtual Interrupt Feature

General

The PVI feature is available in Protected Mode, not in VM86 Mode. It is only included here because it, like VM86 Mode's VME feature, makes use of the Eflags VIF and VIP bits. It is activated if the OS kernel sets CR4[PVI] = 1 and is described below.

Assume that the following conditions are true:

- CR0[PE] = 1. The logical processor is currently in Protected Mode.
- CR4[PVI] = 1. The Protected Mode Virtual Interrupt feature is enabled.
- CPL = 3. The currently-executing Protected Mode task is running at level 3.
- Eflags[IOPL] < 3. The IOPL threshold value for the current task = 3.

Under these conditions, if the Protected Mode task attempts to enable or disable recognition of maskable interrupts (by executing STI or CLI), it does not have direct control over Eflags[IF]. Rather, the attempted execution of STI or CLI—POPF, PUSHF, IRET and INT *nn* are not affected by the PVI feature—affects Eflags[VIF] instead.

The following sections describe PVI operation and assume that the following conditions are currently true:

- Eflags[IF] = 1 and recognition of maskable interrupts is therefore enabled.
- Eflags[VIF] = 1 indicating that the current running application doesn't mind being interrupted.
- Eflags[VIP] = 0 indicating that software has not deferred the execution of any maskable interrupt handlers.

1. Task executes CLI, Clears VIF

Reaching a critical point in application code, the application executes a CLI to disable recognition of maskable interrupts during a critical code section. The Eflags[IF] bit is not affected but Eflags[VIF] is cleared to 0 indicating that the application prefers not to be disturbed by maskable interrupts.

2. Maskable Interrupt Occurs and Is deferred

A maskable interrupt is detected by the logical processor and is recognized (because Eflags[IF] = 1). As a result:

1. The logical processor jumps to the respective Protected Mode handler.
2. The handler checks the state of the VIF bit in the Eflags image on the stack and determines that the application prefers not to be impacted by the execution of the event handler at this time.
3. The handler records the deferral of the handler body in an OS-specific data structure.
4. The handler sets the VIP bit to one in the Eflags image on the stack (indicating that the execution of the handler has been deferred) and executes the IRET instruction to return to the interrupted application.

3. Task Executes STI

Having completed execution of the critical code section, the application now executes the STI instruction to reenable recognition of maskable interrupts:

1. The attempted execution of STI while Eflags[VIP] = 1 results in the generation of a GP exception.
2. Consulting the OS-specific data structure in which interrupt handler deferrals are recorded, the GP handler calls the indicated handler which services the device.
3. The GP handler then clears the VIP bit in the Eflags image on the stack and executes the IRET instruction.
4. The logical processor reexecutes the STI, this time successfully, and the VIF bit is set to one to indicate that the application no longer minds being interrupted by maskable interrupts.

Registers Accessible in Real/VM86 Mode

A program operating in Real Mode or VM86 Mode has access to:

- All of the registers originally present in the 8086.
- The two additional data segment registers—FS and GS.
- Using the Operand Size Override prefix, the 386-compatible 32-bit GPR registers (e.g., EAX, EBX, etc.).
- The x87 FPU register set.
- The MMX registers: MM0 - MM7.
- The SSE register set: XMM0 - XMM7 and the MXCSR register.

All of the Segment Override prefixes including the FS and GS segment override prefixes may be used. As an example:

```
mov  ah, fs:[0100] ;read byte from location 0100h in fs
                   ;data segment into ah register
```

Instructions Usable in Real/VM86 Mode

Refer to the Intel or AMD documentation for a complete list of instructions that may be successfully executed in Real Mode or VM86 Mode. Attempted execution of any unsupported instruction results in the generation of an Invalid-Opcode exception.

21 *The MMX Facilities*

The Previous Chapter

The previous chapter provided a detailed description of VM86 Mode (also known as Virtual 8086 Mode). This included the following topics:

- Switching Between Protected Mode and VM86 Mode.
- Real Mode Application's World View.
- Sensitive Instructions.
- Handling Direct IO.
- Handling Exceptions.
- Hardware Interrupt Handling in VM86 Mode
- Software Interrupt Instruction Handling
- Halt Instruction in VM86 Mode
- Protected Mode Virtual Interrupt Feature
- Registers Accessible in Real/VM86 Mode
- Instructions Usable in Real/VM86 Mode

This Chapter

This chapter introduces the MMX register set and the original MMX instruction set. The SIMD programming model is introduced, how to deal with unpacked data as well as math underflows and overflows, and the elimination of conditional branches. Handling a task switch is described and the instruction set syntax is introduced.

The Next Chapter

The next chapter describes the SSE, SSE2 and SSE 3 instruction sets and summarizes the SSSE3, SSE4.1 and SSE4.2 instruction sets.

Introduction

The MMX instruction set was first introduced in the P55C version of the Pentium and consisted of 47 new instructions. In addition, there are eight MMX data registers (MM0 - MM7; see Figure 21-1 on page 836). As shown in the illustration, the lower 64-bits of the x87 FPU data registers perform double-duty:

- They are used as MMX data registers when MMX code is executed.
- They are used as x87 FPU data registers when x87 FPU code is executed.

Over the years, the core concept introduced with the advent of MMX—instructions capable of simultaneously operating on multiple data items packed into wide registers—has continued to expand as Intel introduced the SSE (Streaming SIMD Extensions, where SIMD stands for *S*ingle *I*nstruction operating on *M*ultiple *D*ata items), SSE2, SSE3, SSSE3 (Supplemental SSE3), SSE4.1 and SSE4.2 instruction sets.

This chapter is not intended as an in-depth look at the initial MMX instruction set. Rather, it provides an overview of the basic concepts introduced with the advent of the MMX instruction set.

Figure 21-1: MMX Register Set

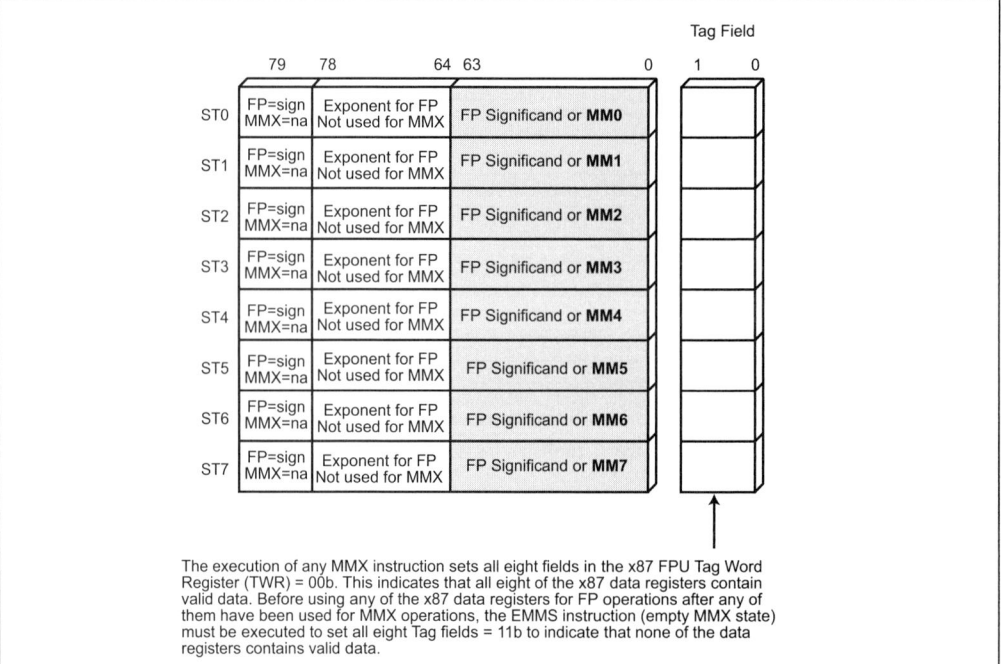

The execution of any MMX instruction sets all eight fields in the x87 FPU Tag Word Register (TWR) = 00b. This indicates that all eight of the x87 data registers contain valid data. Before using any of the x87 data registers for FP operations after any of them have been used for MMX operations, the EMMS instruction (empty MMX state) must be executed to set all eight Tag fields = 11b to indicate that none of the data registers contains valid data.

Detecting MMX Capability

Whether or not a processor supports MMX is detected by executing a CPUID request type 1 in response to which the processor capabilities bit mask is returned in the EDX register (bit 23 = 1 indicates the processor supports MMX).

The Basic Problem

Assumptions

Refer to Figure 21-2 on page 840. As an example, assume that there are two video frame buffers in memory (it should not be assumed, however, that MMX is only intended for processing video data) and that the current video mode has the following characteristics:

- Each location in the two buffers represents the color of one pixel. The first buffer location corresponds to the first pixel on the left end of the first line of pixels on the screen, the second buffer location corresponds to the second pixel on the left end of the first line of pixels on the screen, etc.
- A single location contains 8-bits (one byte), so a pixel can be any one of 256 possible colors (as represented by the values 00h - FFh).
- The video controller is currently operating at a resolution of 1024 x 786, so cach of the two video frame buffers consists of 786,432 locations.

The Operation

Now assume that the programmer wants to:

1. Read the byte from the first location of one buffer,
2. Read the first location of the other buffer,
3. Add the two bytes together, and
4. Store the result back into the first location of the second buffer.

Repeat the operation for every pixel in the two frame buffers.

Example: Processing One Pixel Per Iteration

This could be accomplished in the following manner:

1. Read a byte (a pixel) from buffer one into a 1-byte register (e.g., AL).
2. Read the corresponding byte from buffer two into another 1-byte register (e.g., BL).
3. Add AL and BL together and store the result in the respective location in buffer two.
4. Since the add may result in the generation of a carry, the programmer has to decide whether to discard the carry or to factor it into the result. If the possibility of a carry must be dealt with, the programmer must include a conditional branch after the add that will either:

   — jump to the code that handles the carry,
   — or loop back to process the next pixel from the two buffers.

As indicated in the illustration, this would result in 786,432 x 2 memory reads and 786,432 memory writes. This code would generate a tremendous number of memory accesses which may or may not hit on the logical processor's internal caches. Any misses would result in memory transactions being performed on the processor's external interface. This would degrade performance in two ways:

- In a multiprocessor system wherein the processors share the same external interface, the interface bandwidth available to the other processor(s) could be substantially impacted.
- Since the external interface typically operates at a substantially slower rate of speed than the logical processor, the memory accesses would be time consuming.

Example: Processing Four Pixels Per Iteration

The number of memory accesses could be reduced by reading four bytes at a time from each buffer:

1. Read four bytes from one buffer into a 32-bit GPR register (e.g., EAX).
2. Read the corresponding four bytes from the other buffer into another 32-bit GPR register (e.g., EBX).
3. Add EAX and EBX together and store the result in one of the buffers.

There is a problem inherent in such a simplistic approach. The four bytes read into EAX from the first buffer represent four independent pixel values. Like-wise, the four bytes read into EBX from the second buffer represent four inde-pendent pixel values. If the programmer were to add EAX and EBX together, the logical processor would treat the contents of each register as a 32-bit integer value. The result is therefore completely erroneous. To fix this, the programmer would have to do something like the following (yes, the author acknowledges this is a simplistic and incomplete approach; the intention here is to highlight that a lot of work is involved):

```
  mov   i,0
Loop:
  mov   eax,x[i]    ;read four pixels into eax starting at
                    ;the ith location in frame buffer x
  mov   ebx,y[i]    ;read four pixels into ebx starting at
                    ;the ith location in frame buffer y
  call  ShiftIsolateAdd;isolate LSBs in both registers and add
  jnc   Byte2       ;check for carry
  call  CarryHandler;call handler if carry set
Byte2:
  call  ShiftIsolateAdd;isolate next byte in both registers & add
  jnc   Byte3       ;check for carry
  call  CarryHandler    ;call handler if carry set
Byte3:
  call  ShiftIsolateAdd  ;isolate 3rd byte in both registers & add
  jnc   Byte4            ;check for carry
  call  CarryHandler     ;call handler if carry set
Byte4:
  call  ShiftIsolateAdd  ;isolate MSB in both registers & add
  jnc   StoreResult      ;check for carry
  call  CarryHandler     ;call handler if carry set

StoreResult:
  mov   y[i],ebx         ;store 4 pixel result in buffer y
  add   i,4              ;point to next dword
  cmp   i,BufferEnd      ;check for end of buffer
  jnz   Loop             ;continue if not done
Done:
```

Although reading four pixels at a time from each buffer and writing four pixels at a time decreases the number of memory accesses, the programmer has to engage in a fair amount of bit-slinging in order to accomplish the goal. In addition, a conditional branch is performed after each add to see if a carry resulted and has to be dealt with. Starting with the Pentium Pro (it and subsequent processors have deep instruction pipelines which must be flushed and refilled on a branch misprediction), mispredicted branches result in a very serious performance penalty. In this case, the conditional branches are dependent on completely unpredictable pixel data being received from a video source, so the misprediction rate will almost certainly be quite high.

Figure 21-2: Example Operation on Dual Frame Buffers

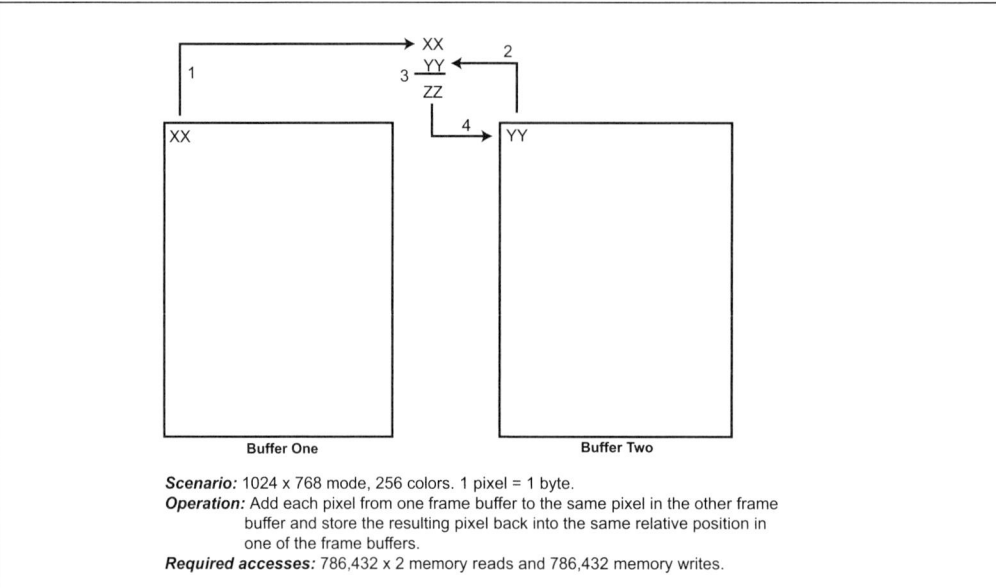

Scenario: 1024 x 768 mode, 256 colors. 1 pixel = 1 byte.
Operation: Add each pixel from one frame buffer to the same pixel in the other frame buffer and store the resulting pixel back into the same relative position in one of the frame buffers.
Required accesses: 786,432 x 2 memory reads and 786,432 memory writes.

MMX SIMD Solution

Refer to Figure 21-3 on page 841. MMX instructions can perform a simultaneous operation on bytes, words or dwords that are packed into 64-bit MMX registers. This is referred to as a **S**ingle **I**nstruction operating on **M**ultiple **D**ata items (SIMD). The programmer can read 64-bits (8-bytes, 4-words, or 2-dwords) from memory into an MMX register using one instruction. In the example illustrated, the programmer has loaded eight bytes packed into MMX register MM0, another eight bytes packed into MM1, and then executed a PADDB instruction (an add on packed bytes). Loading 8- rather than 4-bytes into a register at a time substantiality reduces the number of memory accesses that have to be performed. Furthermore, the MMX execution unit has eight independent adders that operate simultaneously on the 8 bytes in each of the registers. This results in a dramatic reduction in compute time.

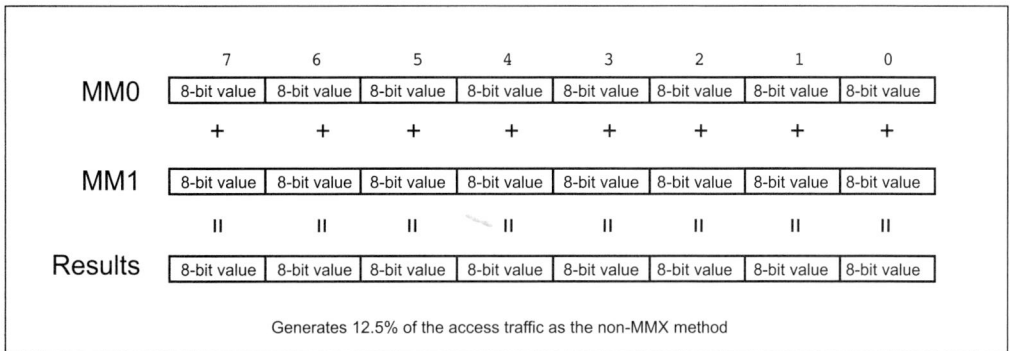

Figure 21-3: MMX SIMD Solution Increase Throughput

Dealing with Unpacked Data

Refer to Figure 21-4 on page 842. Sometimes, the data the programmer wishes to perform a SIMD operation on is stored in memory in unpacked form. As an example, there is a video text mode wherein each text character in the video frame buffer is immediately followed by an attribute byte defining its attributes (e.g., underscore, blink, etc.). The programmer may wish to perform a SIMD operation on just the text characters or just the attributes (in other words, on every other byte).

The MMX instruction set includes instructions that can read unpacked data from memory and pack it into an MMX register. Conversely, instructions are included that take data packed in an MMX register and stores it to memory in unpacked form.

Figure 21-4: Dealing with Unpacked Data

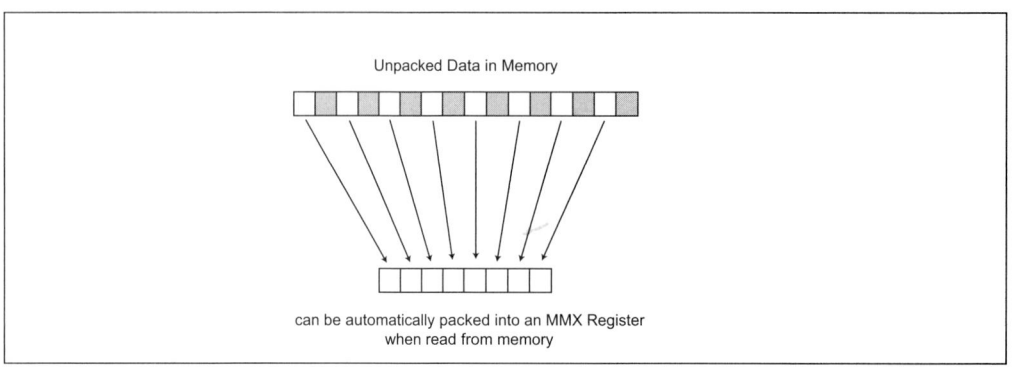

Dealing with Math Underflows and Overflows

MMX technology provides three ways to handle out-of-range conditions:

- **Wraparound math**. Using wraparound math, a true out-of-range result is truncated: the carry or overflow is ignored and only the lsbs of the result are stored in the destination. Wraparound math can be used in applications that control the range of operands to prevent out-of-range results. Care should be taken, however; if the range of operands is not controlled, wraparound math can result in large errors (e.g., adding two large, signed numbers can result in positive overflow and produce a negative result).
- **Signed, saturated math**. Using signed, saturated math, out-of-range results are automatically clamped to the representable range of signed integers for the integer size being operated on (see Table 21-1 on page 843). Two examples:
  — If an operation on signed word integers results in a positive overflow, the result is clamped (i.e., *saturated*) to 7FFFh, the largest positive integer that can be represented in 16-bits.
  — If in the same scenario a negative overflow occurs, the result is saturated to 8000h.
- **Unsigned, saturated math**. Using unsigned, saturated math, out-of-range results are automatically clamped to the representable range of unsigned integers for the integer size being operated on. Positive overflow when operating on unsigned byte integers results in FFh being returned and negative overflow results in 00h being returned.

Saturated math lends itself well to many overflow scenarios. As an example, when performing color calculations, saturation causes a color to remain pure black or pure white and does not result in color inversion. It also prevents wrap-around artifacts from affecting a computation (when operand range checking is not used).

It should be noted that MMX instructions do not indicate overflow or under-flow by generating exceptions or setting flags in the Eflags register.

Table 21-1: Data Range Limits for Saturation

Data Type	Lower Limit		Upper Limit	
	Hex	Decimal	Hex	Decimal
Signed Byte	80h	-128	7Fh	127
Signed Word	8000h	32,768	7FFFh	32,767
Unsigned Byte	00h	0	FFh	255
Unsigned Word	0000h	0	FFFFh	65,535

Elimination of Conditional Branches

Introduction

As mentioned earlier (see "Example: Processing Four Pixels Per Iteration" on page 838), later x86 processors (starting with the Pentium Pro) experience a deep performance dip if the logical processor mispredicts a conditional branch and fetches the wrong instructions into the processor pipeline to be executed after the branch instruction. Conditional branches are especially troublesome if the condition being tested is based on the state of unpredictable data (e.g., video data).

Non-MMX Chroma-Key/Blue Screen Compositing Example

When the weather person is shown on TV in front of the weather map, this is really the result of the real-time merging of two video frame buffers: one contains the data received from a camera pointing at the map, while the other contains the data received from a camera pointing at the person walking around in front of a blue background. The program is constantly studying the buffer containing the person pixels and, wherever a blue pixel is detected, it is replaced with the same pixel from the map video buffer.

The code fragment shown in Figure 21-5 on page 844 compares the value representing the color blue against the ith location in the weather person's video frame buffer. The compare is followed by a conditional branch and one of two actions is taken based on the results of the comparison:

- **Pixel not blue**. If the pixel in the weather person's buffer isn't blue, the program jumps to next_pixel (not shown). In next_pixel, the pointer value (i) is incremented and a compare for the end of buffer is performed. If the end of buffer has not been reached, the code fragment shown is repeated again for the next pixel. When the end of buffer is reached, the process starts over again.
- **Pixel blue**. If the pixel currently being processed in the weather person's buffer *is* blue, it is replaced with the same pixel from buffer y (i.e., the map buffer). The program would then execute next_pixel again and continue to do so until the entire buffer has been processed (after which it would start over again at the beginning of the frame buffer).

As shown, this process is slow because it doesn't use the wider MMX registers to store the pixel information or to perform the comparison. It will also result in abysmal performance due to the almost certainly high incidence of mispredicted branches based on the comparisons of random video data.

Figure 21-5: Conditional Branches Can Severely Decrease Performance

---

Scenario: Merge weather person with weather map.

Assumptions: 16-bit color mode, packed pixels.

Traditional Solution (must be repeated for each pixel):

```
cmp   x[i], BLUE    ;check if pixel is blue
jne   next_pixel    ;if, not process next pixel
mov   x[i], y[i]    ;pixel = blue, so replace with respective map pixel
```

MMX Chroma-Keying/Blue Screen Compositing Example

Figure 21-6 on page 846 shows an example MMX code fragment that can be used to accomplish the chroma-keying effect. Some things to note:

- In the example, the current video mode represents a pixel using 16-bits.
- Throughput is considerably enhanced by using MMX's SIMD capability to process four pixels at a time (4 x 16 = 64-bits, the width of an MMX register).
- There are no conditional branches, thereby eliminating the potential performance degradation that accompanies mispredicted branches.

The code fragment consists of the following instructions:

1. **mov mm0, x[i].** This instruction moves four packed words (i.e., pixels) from memory starting at the *i*th location in frame buffer x (i.e., the weather person's buffer) into MMX register MM0.

2. **pcmpeqw mm0, BLUE.** Refer to Figure 21-6 on page 846. The prefix *p* stands for *packed*, while the suffix *w* stands for *words*. This instruction compares the four word values in the memory location labeled BLUE to the four pixels in register MM0. The value BLUE in memory consists of four pixel values (packed into four contiguous memory locations) that represent the color blue. As shown at the bottom of Figure 21-6 on page 846, the instruction produces an array of four, 16-bit true/false indicators in MMX register MM0.

3. **pandn x[i], mm0.** Refer to Figure 21-7 on page 846. Each bit of the resulting four, 16-bit pixels in the weather person buffer (starting at the *i*th location) is set to 1 if the corresponding bit in the first operand (the four pixels from the weather person buffer) is 0 and the corresponding bit in the second operand (the true/false mask in MMX register 0) is 1; otherwise, it is set to 0. This has the net effect of zeroing the blue pixels in the next four pixel locations in the weather person buffer.

4. **pand mm0, y[i].** As shown in Figure 21-8 on page 847, this instruction zeros pixels in the next four locations of the map image that must be replaced by the respective pixels from the weather person image.

5. **por x[i], mm0.** As shown in Figure 21-9 on page 847, this instruction combines the non-zero pixels within the next four pixels from the map image with the non-zero pixels (of the person) from the weather person image and stores the resulting four composite pixels in the weather person buffer.

Figure 21-6: Example MMX Operation (1-of-4)

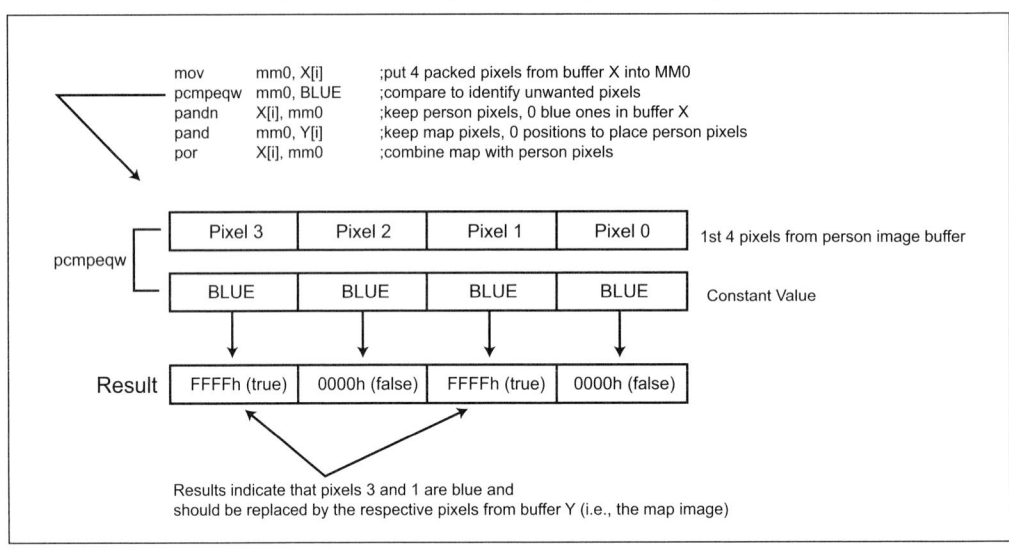

Figure 21-7: Example MMX Operation (2-of-4)

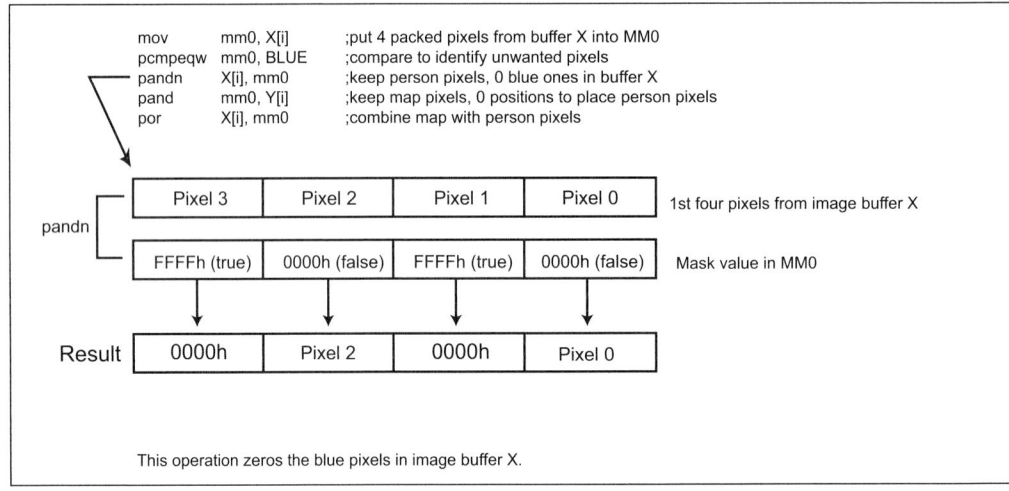

Figure 21-8: Example MMX Operation (3-of-4)

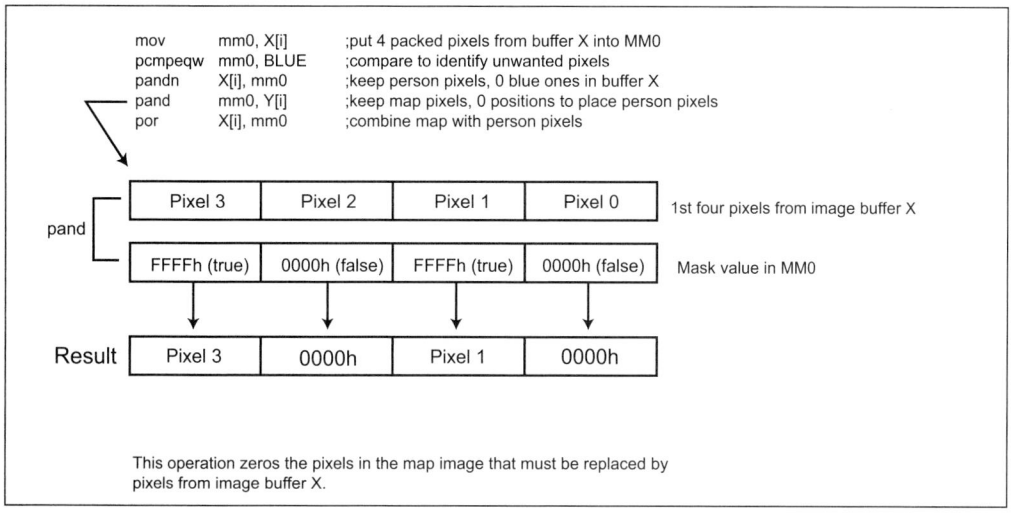

Figure 21-9: Example MMX Operation (4-of-4)

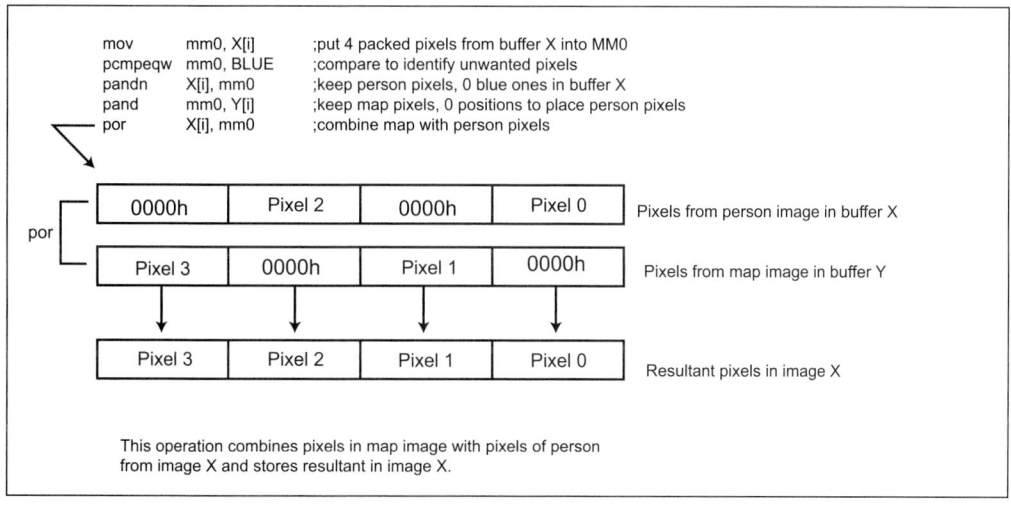

Changes To the Programming Environment

Refer to Figure 21-1 on page 836. As mentioned earlier, the logical processor doesn't actually implement a separate MMX register set. Rather, the eight 64-bit MMX registers, MM[7:0], are aliased over the lower 64-bits of the eight x87 FPU data registers. When the logical processor is executing x87 FP instructions, the data registers are treated as a stack of eight, 80-bit FP data registers. When it executes an MMX instruction, however, the lower 64-bits of the eight data registers are treated as the MMX registers, each of which is 64 bits wide mapped into the lower 64-bits of the FP data registers. Also, as indicated in the note at the bottom of the figure, the execution of any MMX instruction sets all eight fields in the x87 FPU Tag Word Register (TWR) = 00b. This erroneously indicates that all eight of the x87 data registers contain valid data. Before using any of the x87 data registers for FP operations after any have been used for MMX operations, the EMMS instruction (Empty MMX state) must be executed to set all eight Tag fields = 11b to indicate that none of the data registers contains valid FP data.

Handling a Task Switch

Refer to "CR0[TS]: Task Switch, But FP/SSE Registers Not Saved" on page 751.

MMX Instruction Set Syntax

The original MMX instruction set is summarized in Table 21-2 on page 848 and Table 21-3 on page 849. Note that some of the instructions include the *B*, *W*, or *D* suffix at end. This indicates that the instruction operates upon packed bytes, words, or dwords. A conversion instruction converts one data type to another, so it has two suffix characters at the end to indicate the *from* and *to* data types. As an example, the PACKUSWB instruction converts eight signed word integers from the two specified 64-bit sources into eight unsigned byte integers using unsigned saturation.

Table 21-2: MMX Instruction Set Summary, Part 1

Category	Instruction Type	Wraparound Version	Signed Saturated Version	Unsigned Saturated Version
Arithmetic	Addition	PADDB, PADDW, PADDD	PADDSB, PADDSW	PADDUSB, PADDUSW
	Subtraction	PSUBB, PSUBW, PSUBD	PSUBSB, PSUBSW	PSUBUSB, PSUBUSW
	Multiplication	PMULL, PMULH		
	Multiply and Add	PMADD		

Table 21-2: MMX Instruction Set Summary, Part 1 (Continued)

Category	Instruction Type	Wraparound Version	Signed Saturated Version	Unsigned Saturated Version
Comparison	Compare for =	PCMPEQB, PCMPEQW, PCMPEQD		
	Compare for >	PCMPGTPB, PCMPGTPW, PCMPGTPD		
Conversion	Pack		PACKSSWB, PACKSSDW	PACKUSWB
Unpack	Unpack High	PUNPCKHBW, PUNPCKHWD, PUNPCKHDQ		
	Unpack Low	PUNPCKLBW, PUNPCKLWD, PUNPCKLDQ		

Table 21-3: MMX Instruction Set Summary, Part 2

Category	Instruction Type	Data Operand Size	
		Packed	Full Qword
Logical	And		PAND
	And Not		PANDN
	Or		POR
	Exclusive OR		PXOR
Shift	Shift Left Logical	PSLLW, PSLLD	PSLLQ
	Shift Right Logical	PSRLW, PSRLD	PSRLQ

Table 21-3: MMX Instruction Set Summary, Part 2 (Continued)

Category	Instruction Type	Data Operand Size	
	Shift Right Arithmetic	PSRAW, PSRAD	
		Dword Transfers	Qword Transfers
Data Transfer	Register to Register	MOVD	MOVQ
	Load from Memory	MOVD	MOVQ
	Store to Memory	MOVD	MOVQ
Empty MMX State	EMMS	na	

22 *The SSE Facilities*

The Previous Chapter

The previous chapter introduced the MMX register set and the original MMX instruction set. The SIMD programming model was introduced, how to deal with unpacked data as well as math underflows and overflows, and the elimination of conditional branches. Handling a task switch was described and the instruction set syntax was introduced.

This Chapter

This chapter describes the SSE, SSE2 and SSE 3 instruction sets and summarizes the SSSE3, SSE4.1 and SSE4.2 instruction sets. It also completes the discussion of the IA-32 programming environment.

The Next Chapter

The next chapter provides a detailed description of the IA-32e OS environment. The following topics are covered:

- Mode Switching Overview.
- Virtual Memory Addressing in IA-32e Mode.
- In 64-bit Mode, Hardware-Enforced Flat Model.
- 64-bit Instruction Pointer.
- Instruction Fetching.
- RIP-Relative Data Accesses.
- Changes To Kernel-Related Registers and Structures.
- Address Translation Mechanism.
- GDT/LDT Descriptor Changes.
- GDT and GDTR Changes.
- LDT and LDTR Changes.
- IDT/IDTR and Interrupt/Exception Changes.
- Interrupt/Trap Gate Operational Changes.

- IRET Behavior.
- IA-32e Call Gate Operation.
- TR and TSS Changes.
- Register Set Expansion (in 64-bit Mode).
- Scheduler's Software-Based Task Switching Mechanism.

Chapter Objectives

This chapter is not intended to provide a detailed description of each instruction in the SSE instruction sets. That role is already more than adequately fulfilled by the Intel and AMD instruction set reference manuals. Rather, the intention here is two-fold:

- To provide a fundamental understanding of the SSE architecture and how it works.
- To provide additional descriptions of some of the more odd or interesting instructions in the SSE instruction sets.

The SSE facilities are described in the same order in which they were introduced: SSE, SSE2, SSE3, SSSE3, SSE4.1, and SSE 4.2.

SSE: MMX on Steroids

As shown in Table 22-1 on page 852, application performance enhancement has been steadily addressed over the years by the expanding role of the SIMD programming model. It would be incorrect, however, to describe the SSE facilities solely as an expansion of MMX's SIMD programming model. As will be demonstrated in this chapter, while many of the SSE instructions do, in fact, expand on the SIMD programming model, many other non-SIMD instructions were added to address application-specific performance issues.

Table 22-1: Evolution of SIMD Model

Instruction Set	Introduced in	Description
MMX	Pentium P55C	47 new instructions. As described in "The MMX Facilities" on page 835, the SIMD concept was first introduced with the advent of MMX: • Introduction of the SIMD model. • Eight 64-bit registers (MM0:MM7) available for SIMD operations on packed data.

Table 22-1: Evolution of SIMD Model (Continued)

Instruction Set	Introduced in	Description

SSE	Pentium III	70 new instructions. The SIMD model was expanded with the introduction of the SSE (Streaming SIMD Extensions) instruction set and register set:
		• Eight dedicated 128-bit data registers (XMM0 - XMM7) available for SIMD operations on packed data.
		• The ability to perform SIMD packed and scalar FP operations on 32-bit DP FP numerical values.
		• MXCSR Control/Status register added to control SSE FP operations:
		  – SSE FP exception masking and status.
		  – Enable/disable DAZ (Denormals-As-Zero) performance enhancement mode.
		  – Enable/disable FTZ (Flush-to-Zero) performance enhancement mode.
		When SSE was originally introduced, it was under the name Internet SSE (the word *Internet* was appended to just about everything during those crazy 1990s).

SSE2	130nm Pentium 4	144 new instructions. • Added the ability to perform both scalar and packed FP operations on 64-bit DP FP numbers. • The programmer can pack two, 64-bit DP FP numbers in each of two 128-bit XMM registers and then perform a packed FP operation on them (or between two numbers packed in an XMM register and two in memory). • MMX instructions enhanced to perform operations on data items packed in the XMM registers (prior to this, MMX instruction could only operate on data in MMX registers). • The CLFLUSH, MFENCE, LFENCE and new streaming store (commonly referred to as non-temporal store) instructions were added. • The PAUSE instruction was added to enhance performance when Hyper-Threading is enabled.

Table 22-1: Evolution of SIMD Model (Continued)

Instruction Set	Introduced in	Description

SSE3	90nm Pentium 4	13 new instructions.
		• One x87 FPU instruction (FISTTP) that improves x87 FP-to-integer conversion.
		• One SIMD integer instruction providing a specialized 128-bit unaligned data load.
		• Nine new SIMD FP instructions:
		  – 3 instructions that enhance performance of Load/Move/Duplicate operations.
		  – 2 instructions that perform simultaneous add/subtract operations on SP FP numbers packed into a pair of XMM registers.
		  – 4 instructions that perform horizontal rather than vertical add and subtract operations on packed FP numbers.
		• Two thread-synchronization instructions (MONITOR and MWAIT) that provide a more elegant solution than the PAUSE instruction (added in SSE2) in applications employing Hyper-Threading.
		• They can use GPRs rather than MMX or SSE registers.

Table 22-1: Evolution of SIMD Model (Continued)

Instruction Set	Introduced in	Description
SSSE3	Core 2 Duo	32 new instructions. The SSSE3 (Supplemental SSE3) instructions were added to accelerate multimedia and signal-processing applications using SIMD integer techniques. They operate on bytes, words, and dwords packed into MMX registers, XMM registers, or memory: • Twelve horizontal add/subtract instructions. • Six instructions that compute the absolute values of packed bytes, words and dwords. • Two multiply and add instructions. • Two Multiply and Add Packed Signed and Unsigned Bytes instructions that accelerate packed-integer multiply operations and produce integer values with scaling. • Two instructions that perform the byte-wise, in-place shuffle defined by a second shuffle control operand. • Six instructions that negate packed integers in the destination operand if the sign of the corresponding element in the source operand is less than zero. • Two instructions that align data from the composite of two operands.

Table 22-1: Evolution of SIMD Model (Continued)

Instruction Set	Introduced in	Description
SSE4 comprises of two sets of extensions: • SSE4.1 • SSE4.2		
SSE4.1	45nm Core 2 Duo (Penryn)	47 new instructions. Designed to improve performance of media, imaging, and 3D workloads, these instructions improve compiler vectorization and significantly increase support for packed dword computation. Provides a hint that can improve memory throughput when reading from WC memory. SSE4.1 instructions operate on XMM registers: • Two instructions perform packed dword multiplication. • Two instructions calculate FP dot products with input/output selects. • One instruction performs a load with a streaming hint. • Six instructions simplify packed blending. • Eight instructions expand support for packed integer Min/Max functions. • Four instructions support FP rounding with selectable rounding mode and precision exception override. • Seven instructions improve data insertion and extraction from XMM registers • Twelve instructions improve packed integer format conversions (sign and zero extensions). • One instruction improves SAD (Sum Absolute Difference) generation for small block sizes. • One instruction aids horizontal searching operations. • One instruction improves masked comparisons. • One instruction adds qword packed equality comparisons. • One instruction adds dword packing with unsigned saturation.

Table 22-1: Evolution of SIMD Model (Continued)

Instruction Set	Introduced in	Description
SSE4.2	Core i7 (Nehalem)	7 new instructions. The seven SSE4.2 instructions improve performance in the following areas: • SIMD-based string and text processing. • Application-Targeted Accelerator (ATA) instructions. • A SIMD integer instruction that enhances 128-bit integer SIMD capability. Two of the SSE4.2 instructions operate on GPRs while the remaining five operate on XMM registers.

Streaming SIMD Extensions (SSE)

In the context of this discussion, the term SSE refers to the SSE1 instruction set and register set introduced with the advent of the Pentium III.

The Motivation Behind SSE

The single most important motivation behind the implementation of both MMX and SSE was the improved performance of multimedia applications:

- While MMX's SIMD capability supported the acceleration of integer-based applications, MMX did not extend the SIMD programming model into the realm of FP-intensive applications.
- SSE extended the SIMD model to include support for 32-bit SP FP math operations.
- SSE provided new instructions specifically tailored to boost the performance of multimedia applications.
- SSE enhanced certain types of memory write operations (i.e., stores) to make more efficient use of external interface bandwidth. This is a reference to streaming stores (also referred to as non-temporal stores).

It should be noted that many applications outside the realm of multimedia applications can also realize significant benefit from utilization of the SSE feature set.

Detecting SSE Support

The programmer can determine if a processor supports the SSE instruction and register sets by performing a CPUID request type 1 and verifying that the SSE bit returned in the EDX capability bit mask = 1.

The SSE Elements

The implementation of SSE was accomplished by adding the following elements to the logical processor architecture:

- **Instructions.** 70 new instructions (the SSE1 instruction set) were added to the instruction set.
- **Data registers.** Eight, 128-bit data registers (XMM - XMM7) were added to the architecture (see Figure 22-1 on page 859). Unlike the MMX registers which are aliased over the lower 64-bits of each of the x87 FPU's data registers, the XMM registers are implemented as separate registers.
- **Control/status register.** A Control/Status register (MXCSR; Figure 22-1 on page 859) which:
  — Controls the generation of SSE FP exceptions (via six FP exception masking bits).
  — Records the status of SSE FP operations (via six FP exception error status bits).
  — Enables/disables two SSE FP performance enhancement modes (FTZ and DAZ modes).
- **Exception.** A new SIMD FP exception (exception 19) was added to report SSE SIMD FP errors to the OS.

The SSE instructions can be divided into the following categories:

- SIMD FP instructions that simultaneously operate on four, 32-bit, Single Precision (SP) FP numbers.
- Scalar FP instructions. First, a definition of scalar: a single number, as opposed to a matrix of numbers. As an example, scalar multiplication refers to the operation of multiplying one number (one scalar value) by another and the term scalar is used to differentiate this from matrix (i.e., SIMD) math operations.
- Cacheability instructions including prefetches into different levels of the cache hierarchy.
- Control instructions.
- Data conversion instructions (from one data type to another).

- New media extension instructions such as the PSAD and the PAVG that accelerate encoding and decoding, respectively.

Figure 22-1: The SSE Register Set

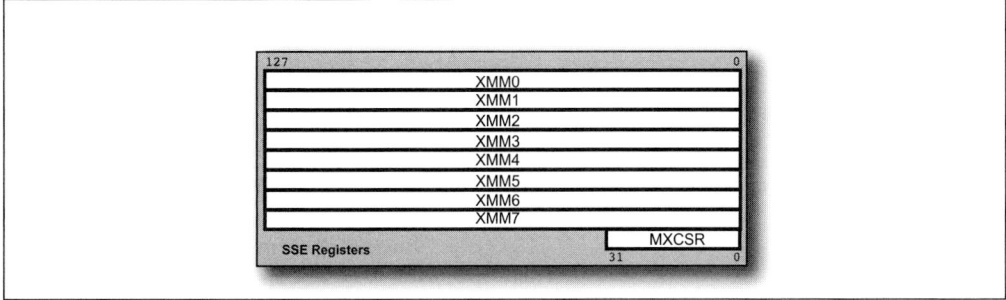

SSE Data Types

Refer to Figure 22-2 on page 859. The SSE data types may be categorized as follows:

- 16 bytes packed into an XMM register or into a memory variable.
- 8 words packed into an XMM register or into a memory variable.
- Four 32-bit integers packed into an XMM register or into a memory variable.
- *Four 32-bit single-precision (SP) FP numbers packed into a single XMM register or into a memory variable. At the introduction of SSE, this was a newly-introduced data type. A tutorial on SP FP numbers can be found in "32-bit SP FP Numeric Format" on page 346.*
- 2 qwords packed into an XMM register or into a memory variable.

Figure 22-2: SSE Data Types

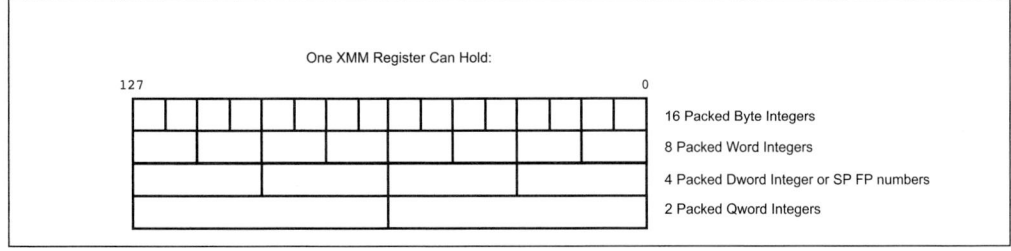

The MXCSR

MXCSR Description

The MXCSR (the SSE Control/Status register) is pictured in Figure 22-3 on page 860 and its bit fields are described in Table 22-2 on page 861.

Figure 22-3: The MXCSR Register

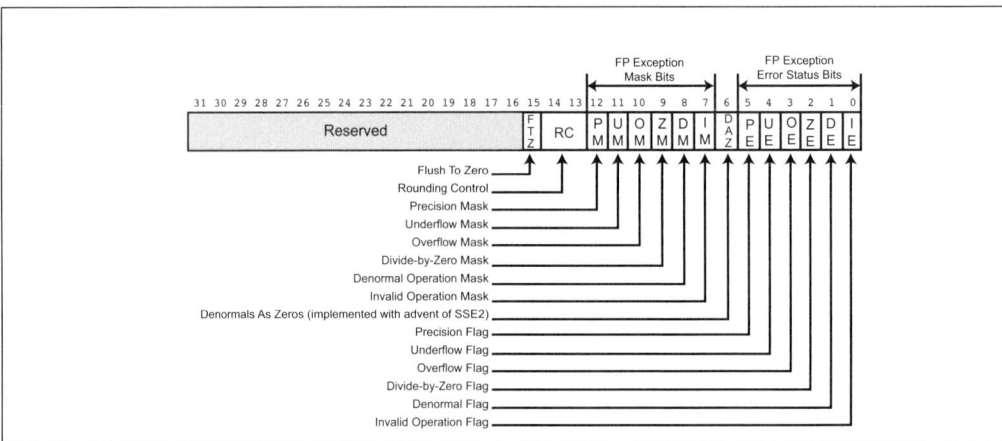

Table 22-2: The MXCSR Register Bit Field Definitions

Field Name	Width (in bits)	Description
FP Exception Error Status Bits	6 bits	When performing a SIMD FP operation, the logical processor may experience any of six different types of error conditions each with a corresponding error bit in MXCSR: • IE. Invalid operation error. • DE. Denormal operand error. • ZE. Divide-by-zero. • OE. Overflow error. • UE. Underflow error. • PE. Precision error. They are *sticky* bits; after a bit is set, it remains set until explicitly cleared by software using the LDMXCSR or FXRSTOR instruction. All six error types (except the Denormal Operand error) are defined in the IEEE 754 Standard, and are the same exceptions generated by the x87 FPU. Unlike x87 exceptions, however, all of the SIMD FP exceptions are precise (i.e., they are generated as soon as the instruction is executed). Each of the six exception conditions also has a corresponding mask bit. The mask bits can be set using either the LDMXCSR or FXRSTOR instruction and the mask and error bits can be read using either the STMXCSR or FXSAVE instruction. If an unmasked SIMD FP exception is generated and CR4[OSXMMEXCEPT] = 1 (see "Enable the SSE SIMD FP Exception" on page 884), the logical processor generates the SIMD FP exception. If CR4[OSXMMEXCEPT] = 0, the logical processor generates an Invalid Opcode exception on the first SSE instruction that results in a SIMD FP exception condition.

Table 22-2: The MXCSR Register Bit Field Definitions (Continued)

Field Name	Width (in bits)	Description
FP Exception Mask Bits	6 bits	Bits [12:7] provide individual mask bits for the SIMD FP exceptions: • 1 = The exception is masked (i.e., disabled). • 0 = the exception is unmasked (i.e., enabled). The mask bits are set to one on a power-up or reset, causing all SIMD FP exceptions to be initially masked. They can be changed using either the LDMXCSR or FXRSTOR instruction, and the mask and error bits can be read using either the STMXCSR or FXSAVE instruction.
FP Rounding Control	2 bits	• 00B. Round to nearest (even). Rounded result is the closest to the infinitely precise result. If two values are equally close, the result is the even value (i.e., the one with the lsb = 0). This the Default setting after power-up or reset. • 01B. Round down (toward -∞). Rounded result is closest to but no greater than the infinitely precise result. • 10B. Round up (toward +∞). Rounded result is closest to but no less than the infinitely precise result. • 11B. Round toward zero (Truncate). Rounded result is closest to but no greater in absolute value than the infinitely precise result.

Table 22-2: The MXCSR Register Bit Field Definitions (Continued)

Field Name	Width (in bits)	Description
FTZ	1	Enables Flush to Zero mode [refer to "Accuracy vs. Fast Real-Time 3D Processing (FTZ)" on page 880]. Controls the masked response to a SIMD FP underflow condition. When the underflow exception is masked and FTZ Mode is enabled, the logical processor acts as follows when it detects a FP underflow condition: • Returns a zero result with the sign of the true result. • Sets the Precision (PE) and Underflow (UE) exception error bits in MXCSR. If the Underflow exception is unmasked, the FTZ bit is ignored. FTZ mode is not compatible with the IEEE 754 Standard. The IEEE-mandated masked response to an Underflow is to deliver the denormalized result. This mode is provided primarily for performance reasons. At the cost of a slight precision loss, faster execution can be achieved for applications where underflows are common and rounding the underflow result to zero can be tolerated. The FTZ bit is cleared on a power-up or reset, disabling FTZ mode.
DAZ	1	The Denormals As Zeros bit was first implemented with the advent of SSE2. See "Your Choice: Accuracy or Speed (DAZ)" on page 889 for more information.

Loading and Storing the MXCSR

The LDMXCSR and STMXCSR instructions are used to load the MXCSR register from memory, or to store its contents to memory.

SIMD (Packed) Operations

Much like the vertical integer operations performed by MMX (see "MMX SIMD Solution" on page 840), four SP FP operations can be executed simultaneously using the SSE SIMD FP capability. Figure 22-4 on page 864 illustrates a SIMD add operation on four, 32-bit SP FP numbers packed in XMM0 and another four packed in XMM1. In the example, the results of the four separate add operations are deposited in XMM0.

All instruction mnemonics for packed SP FP operations have the **ps** (packed SP FP) suffix appended after the operation type (e.g., ADDPS = add packed SP FP numbers).

Figure 22-4: Example SSE SIMD FP Operation on Packed 32-bit SP FP Numbers

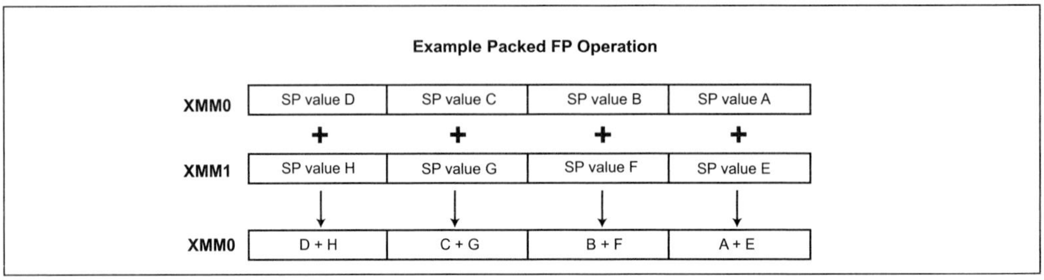

Example Packed FP Operation

XMM0	SP value D	SP value C	SP value B	SP value A
	+	**+**	**+**	**+**
XMM1	SP value H	SP value G	SP value F	SP value E
	↓	↓	↓	↓
XMM0	D + H	C + G	B + F	A + E

Scalar Operations

Unlike a packed operation, a scalar operation only operates on the least-significant SP FP numeric value in an XMM register. As an example, Figure 22-5 on page 864 illustrates a SIMD scalar operation wherein the least-significant SP FP numeric value in each of the two XMM registers are added and the result is deposited in the least-significant part of the destination XMM register. The upper three 32-bit SP FP numbers in each of the two registers are unaffected.

Figure 22-5: Example SSE SIMD Scalar Operation

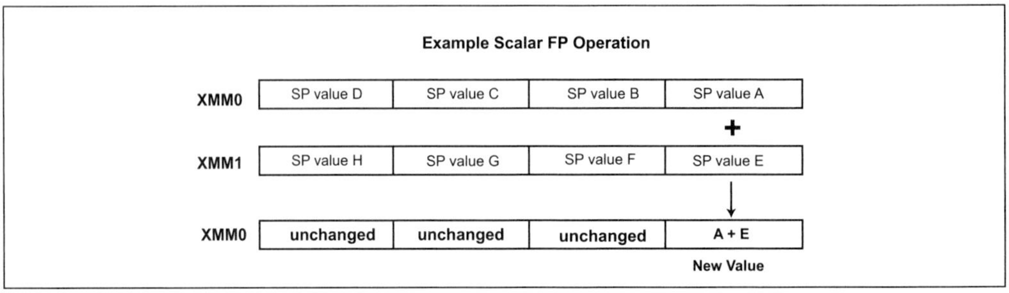

Example Scalar FP Operation

XMM0	SP value D	SP value C	SP value B	SP value A
				+
XMM1	SP value H	SP value G	SP value F	SP value E
				↓
XMM0	unchanged	unchanged	unchanged	A + E
				New Value

Cache-Related Instructions

The SSE instruction set includes the PREFETCHh instruction (described in the next section) that can be used to prefetch a line into a specified cache level in anticipation of a subsequent access within the line. In addition, specialized streaming store (i.e., non-temporal memory write) instructions are also included (a description can be found in "Streaming Store Instructions" on page 868).

Overlapping Data Prefetch with Program Execution

When the logical processor executes a load (i.e., a memory data read) within an area of memory designated as cacheable, it performs a lookup in the L1 data cache. If the line is not in the cache, the request is forwarded to the L2 cache for fulfillment. If the requested line is not present in the L2 cache (and assuming the processor does not include an L3 cache), the logical processor must forward the request to system memory over the external interface for fulfillment. The external interface runs at a fraction of program execution speed, so the line fetch from system memory takes a considerable amount of time. Meanwhile, the load is stalled until the data is fetched from memory. If program execution results in a considerable number of load misses, the logical processor begins to stall. Obviously, if the execution of a load results in a cache hit, the load completes very quickly and program execution speed benefits.

The Pentium III added a new instruction, PREFETCHh, to increase the likelihood of a cache hit when the load is executed. Consider the following code fragment:

```
prefetchh
xxx
xxx
xxx
xxx
    .
    .
    .
load DataVariable
```

The logical processor treats the PREFETCHh instruction as a hint that the line specified by the instruction will probably be needed by the program in the not-too-distant future. Normally, when a load is executed, the logical processor cannot retire it until the load completes (i.e., until the line containing the requested data has been fetched into the cache and the requested data that caused the miss has been placed in the target register). When the line fetch request caused by the execution of a PREFETCHh instruction is dispatched to the cache hierarchy for a lookup, however, it is considered completed and, consequently, is retired immediately. Program execution continues. Meanwhile, the cache lookup(s) is performed and, in the event of a miss on all cache levels, the processor dispatches the line read request to system memory over the external interface for fulfillment. The line is returned from memory and placed in the level of cache specified by the PREFETCHh instruction.

There are actually two benefits involved:

- **Primary Benefit**. When the currently-running program gets to the point where it must access any data item within the line that was prefetched, it may already be in the cache and the load or store can complete very quickly.
- **Secondary Benefit**. The program can specify into which cache level the line will be fetched. As an example, the programmer may specify that the line be prefetched into the L2 cache and not into the L1 data cache. As a result, the line is placed in the L2 cache so the logical processor has relatively quick access to it, but it is not placed in the L1 data cache. The L1 data cache therefore does not have to evict another line that may already reside in the cache in order to make room for the prefetched line. The PREFETCHh instruction helps prevent the unnecessary eviction of lines from the cache.

Currently, there are four forms of the PREFETCHh instruction as specified in Table 22-3 on page 867. The form is encoded into the machine-level instruction using bits [5:3] of the instruction's ModRM byte (i.e., the Operand 2 field). A 3-bit field has eight possible values, so there is room for the future addition of up to four additional forms. The table makes reference to the terms *temporal* and *non-temporal* data:

- **Temporal data** is data that the currently-executing program will probably require access to in the near-term.
- **Non-temporal data** is data that the currently-executing program will probably not require access to in the near-term.

As noted in the table, it is actually processor design-specific into which cache level(s) the target line will actually be placed. In a case where the programmer must know into which cache level(s) the target line will be prefetched, the programmer must check the processor type (using the CPUID instruction) to determine the processor-specific behavior exhibited by this instruction.

The following are additional characteristics of the PREFETCHh instruction:

- The specification frequently refers to the PREFETCH*h* instruction. The *h* stands for the type of *hint*.
- A specific processor implementation may ignore specific hint type(s).
- If the virtual-to-physical address translation selects a page that is not currently present in memory, the logical processor does *not* generate a Page

Fault exception. Rather, it just treats the prefetch as a NOP.

- If the data is already present in a cache level closer to the logical processor than the level specified by the instruction, the instruction acts as a NOP.
- Other than improved performance, the instruction does not affect the behavior of the program.
- A prefetch from UC (Uncacheable) or WC (Write Combining) memory is ignored (because both are uncacheable).
- The amount of data prefetched is design-dependent (i.e., it is the cache line size for the specified processor cache), but is always a minimum of 32-bytes.
- Only placing data in the L1 preserves data currently resident in the L2 (and vice versa). If an L2 data line is cast out, obviously it is no longer available for fast access by the logical processor. In addition, if the line being cast out is a modified line, it causes a writeback of the line on the external interface (consuming bus bandwidth).
- It should be noted that the logical processor can speculatively fetch and cache data from system memory regions that are assigned a memory type that permits speculative reads (i.e., WB, WT, WP and WC memory; see "The Definition of a Speculatively Executed Load" on page 615; refer to "Memory Type Configuration" on page 599 for a detailed description of the memory types). The PREFETCH*h* instruction is considered a hint to this speculative behavior. Because speculative fetching can occur at any time and is not necessarily tied to instruction execution, a PREFETCHh instruction is not ordered with respect to the fence instructions (MFENCE, SFENCE, and LFENCE) or to locked memory accesses. A PREFETCHh instruction is also unordered with respect to the CLFLUSH instruction, other PREFETCH*h* instructions, or any other general instruction. However, it is ordered with respect to serializing instructions (see "Synchronizing Events" on page 618) such as CPUID, WRMSR, OUT, and MOV to a CR.

Table 22-3: Prefetch Instruction Behavior

Instruction Form	Description	Pentium III Behavior	Pentium 4 Behavior *
PREFETCH*T0*	Temporal data. Prefetch data into all levels of the cache hierarchy.	Model-specific whether it's placed in the L1 or L2 cache.	The line is placed in the L2 cache.

Table 22-3: Prefetch Instruction Behavior (Continued)

Instruction Form	Description	Pentium III Behavior	Pentium 4 Behavior *
PREFETCHT1	Temporal data with respect to L1 cache. Prefetch data into L2 and higher.	The line is placed in the L2 cache.	The line is placed in the L2 cache.
PREFETCHT2	Temporal data with respect to L2. Prefetch data into L2 and higher.	The line is placed in the L2 cache.	The line is placed in the L2 cache.
PREFETCHNTA	Non-temporal data with respect to all cache levels. Prefetch data into non-temporal cache structure and into a location close to the logical processor, minimizing cache pollution. NTA stands for Non-Temporal Access.	The line is placed in the L1 cache.	The line is placed in the L2 cache.

* Note: As of this writing, Intel manuals do not describe the instruction's behavior when executed on processors introduced after the Pentium 4.

Streaming Store Instructions

Introduction. When a store is performed to an area of memory designated as cacheable (i.e., WB, WT, or WP memory), the logical processor performs a lookup in its internal caches. The logical processor's handling of the memory write is defined by the type of memory as well as whether or not the cache lookup results in a hit or a miss. Table 22-4 on page 869 defines the logical processor's actions by memory type.

The currently-executing program may perform a store to an area of memory designated as WB memory, but may *know* that it will not be accessing any data within that line for quite a while. As can be seen in the table, this can have a number of negative consequences. One solution would be to designate the area of memory as some type other than WB. This, however, is a draconian solution in that, at some other point in time, the program may need the performance benefits yielded by designating the region as WB memory. Prior to the advent of the Pentium III (and SSE), this was the only solution.

A better approach would be to utilize a special type of store instruction to perform the memory write. The Pentium III's SSE instruction set included three such instructions: MOVNTPS, MOVNTQ and MASKMOVQ. They are frequently referred to by the following interchangeable terms:

— Streaming stores.
— Non-temporal stores.

and are described in the sections that follow.

Table 22-4: Processors Actions on a Store to Cacheable Memory

Memory Type	Actions on a Cache Miss	Actions on a Cache Hit
WP	The write's start address and the bytes to be written are posted in the logical processor's Posted Memory Write Buffer (PMWB) and are written to memory later. The line is not fetched from memory and placed in the cache.	The target byte(s) within the cache line are *not* updated and the line is invalidated in the cache. The write's start address and the bytes to be written are posted in the logical processor's Posted Memory Write Buffer (PMWB) and are written to memory later.
WT	The write's start address and the bytes to be written are posted in the logical processor's PMWB and are written to memory later. The line is not fetched from memory and placed in the cache.	The target byte(s) within the cache line are updated. The write's start address and the bytes to be written are posted in the logical processor's PMWB and are written through to memory later.

Table 22-4: Processors Actions on a Store to Cacheable Memory (Continued)

Memory Type	Actions on a Cache Miss	Actions on a Cache Hit
WB	The processor arbitrates for ownership of the external interface and performs a Memory Read and Invalidate transaction to fetch the most up-to-date copy of the line. This transaction type is sometimes referred to as a RWITM (Read With Intent To Modify) because the logical processor is fetching the line with the intent to modify it. It is also referred to as an RFO (Read For Ownership) because it is guaranteed to have the *only* copy of the line (see below). When it receives the line, it places it in its cache, immediately stores into it and marks it Modified (M). If any other processor observing the RWITM transaction has a copy of the line: • In the E or the S state, it must delete it. • In the M state, it must source the line to the logical processor that initiated the RWITM and must also delete it from its own cache (hence the term RFO). *Disadvantages:* • *The RWITM consumes external interface bandwidth.* • *The RWITM kills any copies of the line that may be in the caches of other logical processors. This results in cache misses if a program on another logical processor subsequently attempts to access the line.* • *When the line is placed in the logical processor's L1 data and L2 caches, it may very well cause the castout of a line that is already in the cache.*	If the logical processor has a copy of the line, the line's current state dictates the handling of the write: • If the line is in the E state, the data is written into the cache line and the line changes to the M state. • If the line is in the S state, the processor arbitrates for ownership of the external interface and performs a *kill* transaction (actually, it's a Memory Read and Invalidate for 0 bytes). Any other logical processor that has a copy of the line (by definition it would be in the S state) must delete its copy. Upon completion of the kill, the logical processor accepts the write data into the cache line and changes its state from S to M. • If the line is in the M state, the logical processor accepts the write data into the cache line and leaves it in the M state. *Disadvantages:* • *The Kill takes time to complete (the external interface is slow) and the logical processor cannot complete the store until the Kill is completed.* • *The Kill consumes some external interface bandwidth.* • *The Kill deletes any copies of the line that may be in the caches of other logical processors. This results in cache misses if a program on another logical processor subsequently attempts to access the line.* • *When the line is placed in the logical processor's L1 data and L2 caches, it may very well cause the castout of a line that is already in the cache.*

The MOVNTPS Instruction. Refer to Figure 22-6 on page 871. The instruction name stands for *move packed SP FP values into memory using a Non-Temporal hint*. When executed, it stores the four 32-bit, SP FP values packed in the specified XMM register to memory. The start memory address specified must be aligned on a 16-byte (128-bit) boundary.

When this instruction is executed, the logical processor treats the line of memory space being written to as if it were the WC memory type (even though the MTRRs and the PTE or PDE selected by the virtual address may designate it as WB memory). Executing this instruction has the following effects:

— The four, 32-bit SP FP numbers supplied from the specified XMM register are placed into the appropriate locations in one of the logical processor's WC buffers [WCBs; see "Uncacheable Write-Combining (WC) Memory" on page 611 for more information] and the start address of the line is also latched into that WCB. The data will be written to memory at a later time when the WCB is written to memory over the external interface.

— Assuming that the memory type is WB, the line is not fetched from memory, so none of the disadvantages cited in Table 22-4 on page 869 are experienced.

— The logical processor performs a lookup in its internal caches and, if the line is present in the cache, it is evicted from the cache.

Figure 22-6: The MOVNTPS Instruction

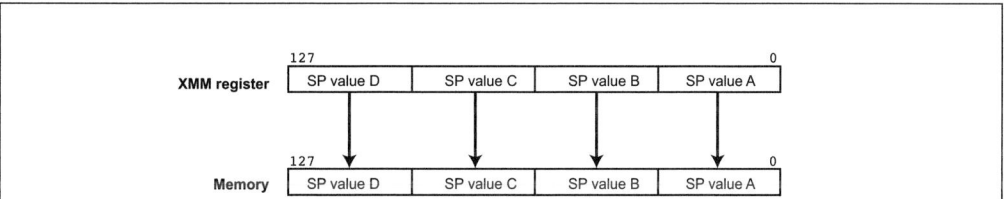

MOVNTQ Instruction. Refer to Figure 22-7 on page 872. This instruction is a Store Qword Using a Non-Temporal Hint. When executed, it moves eight bytes of data from the specified MMX register into memory. When this instruction is executed, the logical processor treats the line of memory space being written to as if it were the WC memory type (even though the MTRRs and the PTE or PDE selected by the virtual address may designate it as WB memory). Executing this instruction has the following effects:

— The eight bytes from the specified MMX register are posted in the appropriate locations in one of the logical processor's WC buffers [WCBs; see "Uncacheable Write-Combining (WC) Memory" on page 611 for more information] and the start address of the line is also latched into that WCB. The data will be written to memory at a later time when the WCB is written to memory using the external interface.

— Assuming that the memory type is WB, the line is not fetched from memory, so none of the disadvantages cited in Table 22-4 on page 869 are experienced.

— The logical processor performs a lookup in its internal caches and, if the line is present in the cache, it is evicted from the cache.

Figure 22-7: The MOVNTQ Instruction

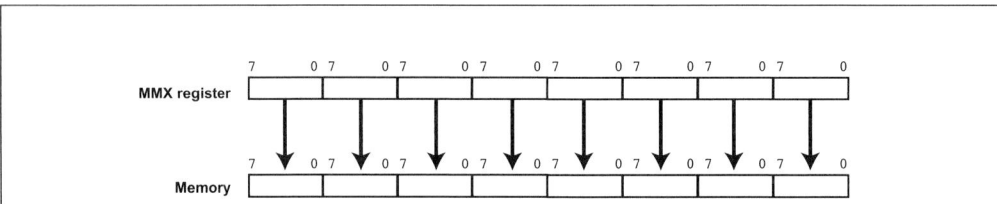

MASKMOVQ Instruction. Refer to Figure 22-8 on page 873. When executed, this instruction uses the bit mask specified in one MMX register to determine which of the eight bytes in another MMX register are to be written to memory. Bit 7 in each byte of the specified MMX mask register indicates whether the corresponding data byte from the other MMX register will be written to memory (1 = write the byte to memory; 0 = do not write it to memory). The memory address is specified in the DS:DI (if executing in 16-bit mode) or the DS:EDI register pair (if executing in 32-bit mode).

Although this instruction does not include the NT designation in its mnemonic, it is, in fact, a non-temporal store.

— The specified bytes from the source MMX register are posted in the appropriate locations in one of the logical processor's WC buffers [WCBs; see "Uncacheable Write-Combining (WC) Memory" on page 611 for more information] and the start address of the line is also latched into that WCB. The data will be written to memory at a later time when the WCB is written to memory over the external interface.

— Assuming that the memory type is WB, the line is not fetched from memory, so none of the disadvantages cited in Table 22-4 on page 869 are experienced.

— The logical processor performs a lookup in its internal caches and, if the line is present in the cache, it is evicted from the cache.

Also refer to "The Masked Move Operation" on page 878.

Figure 22-8: The MASKMOVQ Instruction

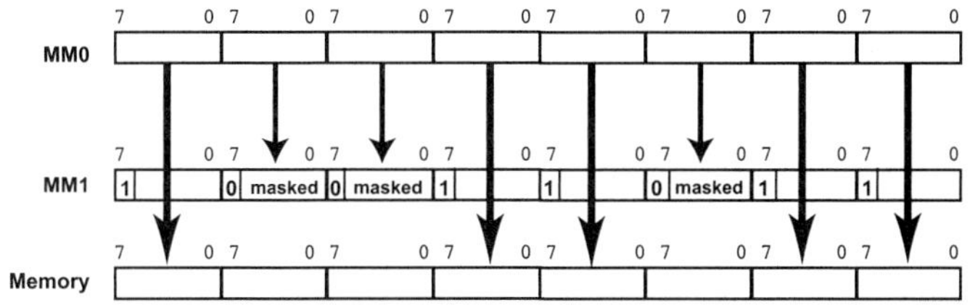

Ensuring Delivery of Writes Before Proceeding

An Example Scenario

Consider a scenario with the following assumptions:

1. The ports used to control and check the status of a graphics adapter have been implemented as memory-mapped IO ports:
   — The status of the adapter is checked by performing a memory read from its status register.
   — Parameters are supplied to the adapter by performing memory writes to its parameter registers.
   — Commands are issued to the adapter by performing memory writes to its command port.
2. Data to be displayed by the adapter is written into its display frame buffer by performing memory writes to locations within the buffer.
3. The memory area within which the memory-mapped IO ports are located is defined as the UC or WC memory type (both of which are uncacheable).
4. The device driver performs a series of memory writes to write a number of parameters into the adapter's parameter registers.
5. A memory write is then performed to the adapter's command register to change the adapter's screen resolution.

Since the memory type assigned to the adapter's memory-mapped IO register set is either UC or WC, the memory writes that were just performed to the parameter and command registers have not yet been performed on the external interface. Rather, they are buffered up either in the logical processor's internal PMWB (if the memory range is defined as the UC memory type), or WCBs (if the memory range is defined as the WC memory type). The parameters and the command have therefore not yet been received by the graphics adapter.

Now assume that in order to ensure proper operation of the driver, it is imperative that the adapter receive the parameters and the command before subsequent memory writes in the program are performed.

SFENCE Instruction

When the SFENCE instruction is placed in a program's flow (see Figure 22-9 on page 875), the logical processor treats it as a fence (i.e., a barrier) in the program flow. It is not permitted to execute any stores that lie beneath the fence until the write data associated with all stores above the fence have been flushed from the logical processor's WCBs (for writes to WC memory) and PMWB (for writes to UC, WP, or WT memory) to external memory over the processor's external interface—in other words, until memory has been brought up-to-date (i.e., until it's been synchronized) with respect to these buffered memory updates.

The logical processor may, however, execute any non-store micro-ops (the logical processor's native, fixed-length instructions rather than legacy IA-32 instructions) that lie beneath the SFENCE instruction before all of the previously-posted writes are dumped to memory.

As shown in Figure 22-9 on page 875, when a store to WC memory is executed, the logical processor posts the write data in one of its WCBs. The data is not written to memory until sometime later when the WCBs and PMWB are flushed to external memory over the external interface.

As shown in Figure 22-10 on page 876, when a store to WB memory is executed and the target line is already in the cache, the logical processor writes the data into the cache line and marks the line as Modified (if it wasn't marked so already). If the line was not already in the cache, the logical processor performs a Memory Read and Invalidate transaction on the external interface to obtain it, places it in the cache, writes to it and marks it Modified. It should be noted that the memory write data is not written to memory.

As shown in Figure 22-11 on page 876, although the logical processor can execute non-store micro-ops that reside beneath the fence, it cannot execute any stores beneath the fence until it has dumped all of the memory writes queued up in its PMWB and WCBs to the external interface (i.e., to memory). Then and only then is the logical processor permitted to execute any stores beneath the fence.

See Figure 22-12 on page 877. If, after the SFENCE has caused the buffer flush, another entity in the system (e.g., another logical processor) attempts to read data from any of the WC or UC memory locations that were written to, the data is sourced from memory (which has received the updates). If another entity in the system attempts to read data from any of the WB memory locations that were written to, it is snooped in this logical processor's caches and results in a hit on a modified line. In the snoop result supplied to the other entity in response to its memory access the processor indicates a hit on a modified line (on the external interface) and supplies the modified line to the other entity.

Figure 22-9: Stores to WC Memory Are Posted in the WCBs

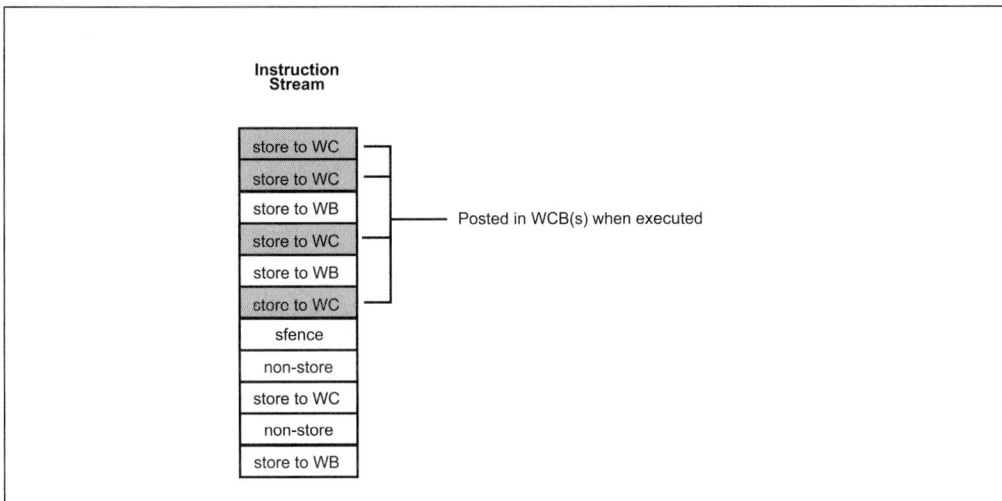

Figure 22-10: Stores to WB Memory Create Modified Cache Lines

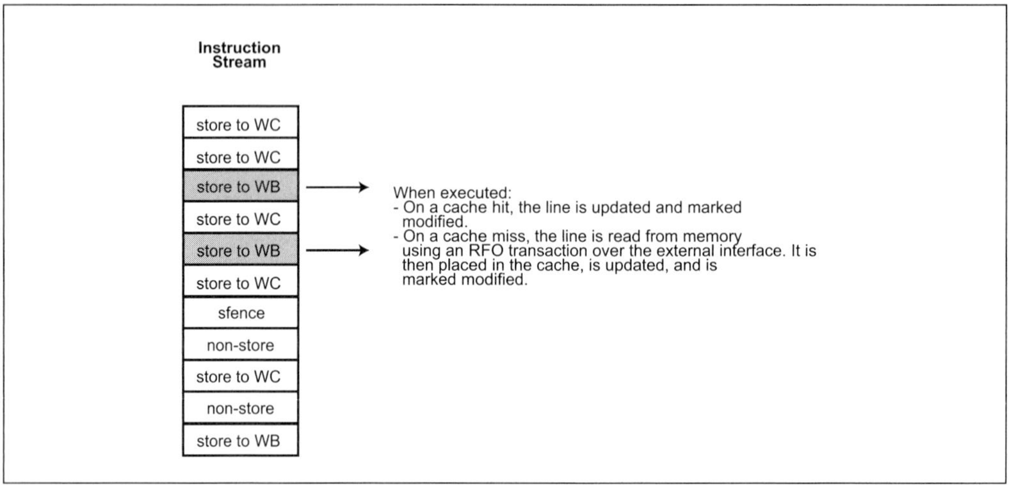

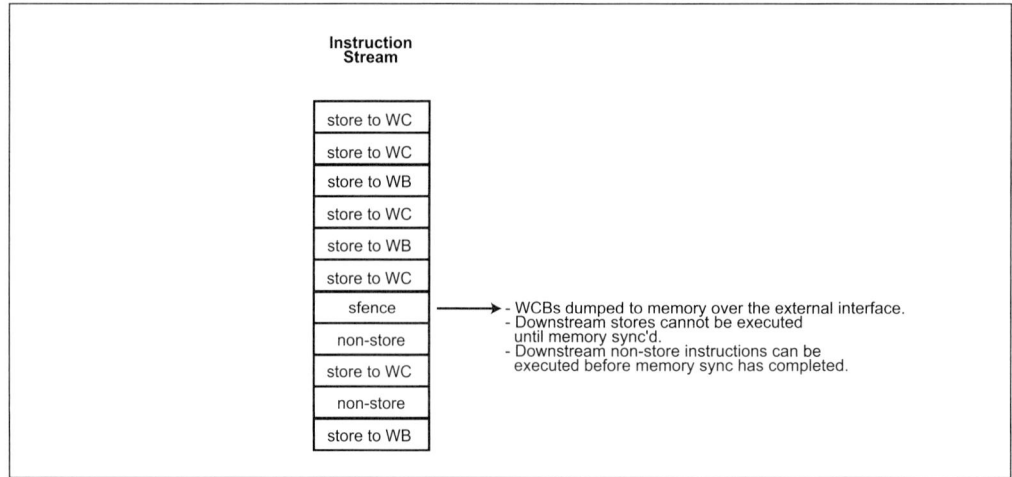

Figure 22-11: SFENCE Blocks the Logical Processor from Executing Downstream Stores

Figure 22-12: Logical Processor Can Execute Downstream Stores After Buffers Are Flushed

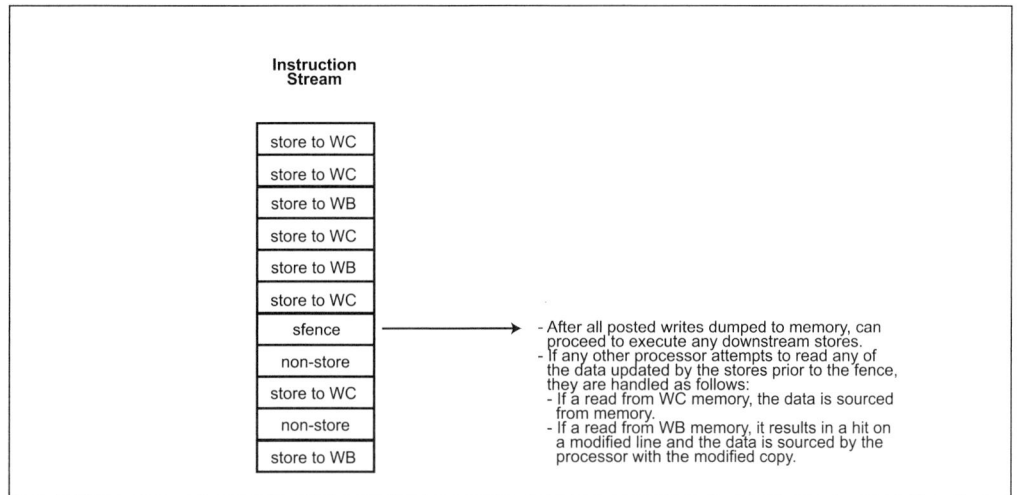

Elimination of Mispredicted Branches

Background

Misprediction of conditional branch instructions causes a deep performance dip (because the entire instruction pipeline must be flushed and refilled from the correct path). Of special concern are conditional branch instructions wherein the branch decision is based on unpredictable data (e.g., based on the state of visual data being received from a video source). MMX and SSE include instructions that were specifically designed to eliminate (wherever possible) conditional branches that are based on unpredictable, random data comparisons.

SSE Misprediction Enhancements

Comparisons and Bit Masks. SSE's SP FP comparison instruction (CMP) is similar to pre-existent MMX instructions (i.e., PCMPEQ, PCMPGT) in that it produces a mask value of all 1's (true) or all 0's (false) for each packed FP value, depending upon the result of the comparison. The resultant true/false masks can then be used with subsequent logical operations (e.g., AND, ANDN, OR, XOR) to perform conditional moves (thereby eliminating comparisons followed by conditional branches). Additionally, four mask bits (the msb of each mask) can be moved to an integer register using the MOVMSKPS/PMOVMSKB instructions. These instructions eliminate data-dependent branching, such as the clip extent and front/back-face culling checks in 3D geometry.

Min/Max Determination. Another important conditional usage model involves finding the maximum or minimum of two values (either packed or scalar values). While this can be accomplished as described in the previous paragraph, the MAX/MIN and PMIN/PMAX instructions accomplish it using a single instruction. It is accomplished by using the carry bit produced by the comparison subtraction (performed to determine the MIN or MAX value of the two) to select which source to forward to a destination. In 3D geometry and rasterization applications, color clamping is an example that benefits from the use of MINPS/PMIN. In addition, many speech recognition engines use the evaluation of a Hidden-Markov Model (HMM), and this function comprises upwards of 80% of execution time. The PMIN instruction improves the kernel performance by 33%, yielding a 19% application gain (note: these numbers are from Intel documentation).

The Masked Move Operation. "MASKMOVQ Instruction" on page 872 described the MASKMOVQ instruction. Using this instruction to conditionally move bytes into memory improves performance when compared to using conditional moves or conditional branches (the other methods inject more micro-ops into the instruction pipeline, and using a conditional branch raises the possibility of branch mispredictions and the resultant performance penalty).

Reciprocal and Reciprocal Square Root Operations

Many basic operations in geometry involve division and the computation of square roots:

- Example geometry operations wherein a division must be performed:
  — Transformation frequently requires dividing each radix's x, y, z (height, width and depth) coordinates by the radix's w (perspective) coordinate.
  — The specular lighting procedure includes a power function. This can be emulated using an approximation function that performs a division.
- Normalization is a common geometry operation requiring the following calculation of the reciprocal of the square root of a value: 1 ÷ the square-root of a value.

In order to provide an efficient method for handling these cases, SSE includes the following two approximation instructions:

- RCP (Reciprocal) and
- RSQRT (Reciprocal Square Root).

The logical processor implements these instructions using hardware lookup tables. While they are inherently less precise (only 12 bits of mantissa versus 24 for the full IEEE-compliant DIV and SQRT), they execute much faster than the full precision versions. If greater precision is required, these instructions can be used with a single Newton-Raphson (N-R) iteration to achieve almost the same precision as the IEEE instructions (yielding approximately 22 bits of mantissa). This N-R iteration for the reciprocal operation involves two multiplies and a subtraction, so it still executes more quickly than the IEEE instructions. When used in a basic geometry pipeline, these instructions can improve overall performance on the order of 15% (once again, Intel's numbers).

MPEG-2 Motion Compensation

Motion compensation (sometimes referred to as tweening, for in-between) is the process of reconstructing each image frame in the output picture stream by interpolating between the pixels that comprise two key image frames. The interpolation consists of averaging the pixels from a macroblock in a frame with the pixels from the same respective macroblock in the next frame. A macroblock consists of a 16 x 16 pixel unit within a frame. The MPEG-2 specification requires that the resultant average must be rounded to the nearest integer (and values that fall exactly at the half way value must be rounded away from zero). This requires that the averaging operation have nine bits of precision.

SIMD instructions in the MMX instruction set provide either 8- or 16-bits of precision. Using the MMX SIMD instructions that operate on packed bytes (rather than packed words) increases the throughput. While the SSE PAVG instruction performs a 9-bit accurate averaging operation on packed bytes, the PAVGW instruction operates on packed words and provides higher accuracy for applications that accumulate a result using several computation instructions.

At the time that SSE was introduced (with the advent of the Pentium III), the Motion Compensation element of a DVD player application executed on a Pentium II-based system operating at a core speed of 266MHz spent about as much time accessing memory as it did executing.

Implementing the Motion Compensation function using the SSE PAVG instruction enabled a 25% kernel speedup (by Intel's measurements), and a 4% to 6% speedup at the application level (depending on the video clip chosen). Intel estimated that the application-level gain could increase to 10% for higher-resolution HDTV digital television formats.

Optimizing 3D Rasterization Performance

Intel's investigation into operations that were not optimized in the 3D realm revealed that MMX's lack of an unsigned multiply operation resulted in inefficient 3D rasterization performance. 3D rasterization is accomplished by operating on unsigned pixel data, and the MMX PMULHW instruction operates only on signed data. Providing an unsigned PMULHUW in the SSE instruction set eliminated the fix-up overhead that was required when using the signed MMX operation, yielding an application-level performance gain of 8%-10%.

Optimizing Motion-Estimation Performance

During the video encode process, an estimated 40% - 70% of the execution time is spent in the motion-estimation function. This stage of the encode pipeline compares a sub-block of the current frame with sub-blocks in the same relative position of the previous and next frames in order to find the best match. The compressed output stream only includes a vector representing the position of the two sub-blocks and the residual difference between the two sub-blocks. Two common comparison metrics are used in motion-estimation:

- Sum-of-square-differences (SSD) and
- Sum-of-absolute-differences (SAD).

SSD could be implemented using an unsigned multiply and accumulate operation (byte to word), but the accumulation range requires 24-bits of precision, (which does not map neatly to a general purpose data-type). The SSE PSADBW (Compute Sum of Absolute Differences) instruction performs a SIMD operation on eight bytes simultaneously (but the accumulation does not exceed a 16-bit word). This SSE instruction replaces approximately seven MMX instructions in the motion-estimation's inner loop (because MMX does not support unsigned byte operations; they must be emulated by zero extension to words and the use of word operations). Intel estimated that the use of the PSADBW instruction could increase the performance of the motion-estimation function by a factor of two.

Accuracy vs. Fast Real-Time 3D Processing (FTZ)

SSE includes two FP arithmetic modes:

- One emphasizes IEEE compliance and exact, single-precision results.
- The other emphasizes computational speed at the expense of a slight loss in precision. The mode selection is controlled by the MXCSR[FTZ] bit (FTZ = Flush-to-Zero). Setting this bit to one selects FTZ mode, while clearing it selects the IEEE-compliance mode of operation.

FTZ mode is well-suited for real-time applications. During computation, it returns a zero result in an underflow situation if the reporting of SSE SIMD FP exceptions is masked. Most real-time 3D applications place the emphasis on speed and are not sensitive to a slight loss in precision.

SSE Alignment Checking

Except in the following cases, the address of a 128-bit (16-byte) packed memory operand must be aligned on a 16-byte boundary:

- Scalar instructions that use a 32-bit memory operand are not subject to alignment requirements.
- The MOVUPS (Move Unaligned Packed SP FP) instruction performs the same operations as the MOVAPS instruction, except that 16-byte alignment of a memory address is not required.

The SIMD FP Exception

The SIMD FP exception (exception 19) was added with the advent of the Pentium III and SSE [see "SIMD Floating-Point Exception (19)" on page 779].

SIMD FP exceptions are generated independently from the x87 FP exceptions. Generation of an SSE SIMD FP exception does not result in the assertion of the processor's FERR# output pin (regardless of the CR0[NE] setting), and the state of the processor's IGNNE# input pin has no effect on the SSE SIMD FP logic. See "Ignoring FP Errors" on page 360 for more information.

Saving and Restoring x87/MMX/SSE Registers

General

The FXSAVE instruction is used to save the contents of the x87 FP/MMX/SSE register sets into a data structure in memory. The FXRSTOR instruction is used to restore the x87 FP/MMX/SSE register sets from the data structure in memory.

MXCSR Mask Field

There are some reserved bits in the SSE Control Status register (i.e., MXCSR) that may be used in future x86 processors. Any attempt to set any reserved bits to one results in the generation of a GP exception.

When the FXSAVE instruction is executed, the logical processor deposits a value into the MXCSR_MASK field (see Figure 22-13 on page 883) that indicates which bits of the MXCSR register are reserved. There are two possibilities:

- If the default value 00000000h is stored in this field, it indicates that the logical processor does not support the DAZ bit (Denormals-As-Zero is bit 6 in MXCSR; this bit was not implemented until the advent of the Pentium 4) and the programmer should assume a mask value of 0000FFBFh (bit 6 is cleared). The Pentium III returned the default value of 00000000h because it did not implement the MXCSR[DAZ] bit. The Pentium 4, on the other hand, did implement the MXCSR[DAZ] bit, so it would return the value 0000FFFFh indicating that none of the MXCSR bits are reserved.
- If a non-zero value is stored in this field, then the programmer should use the stored value as the mask value.

The recommended procedure for obtaining the mask value is as follows:

1. Establish a 512-byte FXSAVE area in memory and zero it.
2. Execute the FXSAVE instruction supplying the start address of the data structure as the operand.
3. After the FXSAVE execution, the logical processor has deposited the value in the MXCSR_MASK field in the FXSAVE image (bytes 28 - 31).

If the mask (the default value of 0000FFBFh or the non-zero value deposited in the MXCSR_MASK field) is AND'd with a value to be written into the MXCSR register, the resulting value will have all reserved bits cleared to zero, guaranteeing that a GP exception will not be generated when the value is written to the MXCSR register.

The mask bits that are set to one indicate MXCSR features (i.e., bits) that are supported, so they can be thought of as feature flags for identifying some of the logical processor's SSE capabilities.

Figure 22-13: x87 FP/MMX/SSE Register Save Data Structure

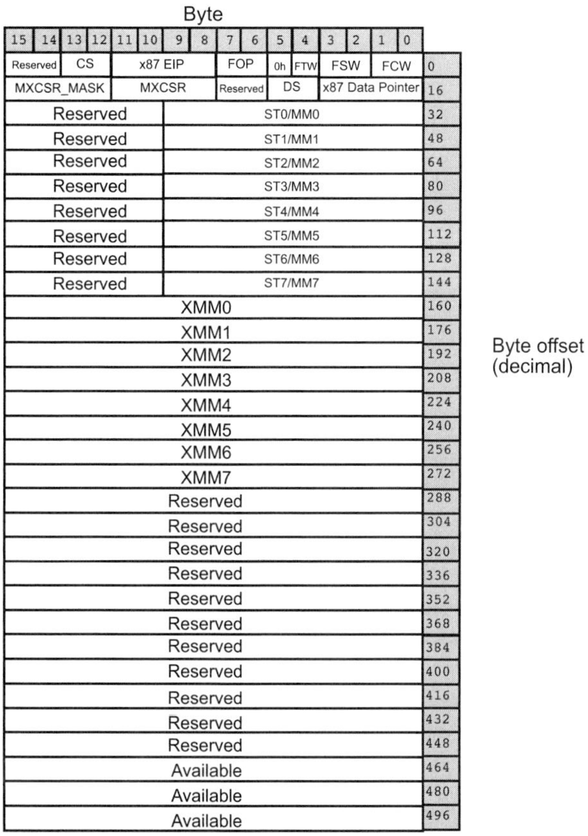

OS Support for SSE

General

An OS may or may not:

- Enable the FXSAVE and FXRSTOR instructions to save the SSE register set in addition to the x87 FPU registers set.
- Support the use of the SSE/SSE2, SSE3, SSSE3, and SSE4 instruction sets.
- Implement an SSE SIMD FP exception handler (i.e., the exception 19 handler).

The OS indicates (to application programs) whether or not it supports these features by appropriately setting or clearing two bits in CR4 (see Figure 22-14 on page 885). The following two subsections describe the effects of these two bits.

Enable SSE Instruction Sets and Register Set Save/Restore

Refer to Figure 22-14 on page 885 and Table 22-5 on page 884. The OS will set CR4[OSFXSR] bit to one if it:

*   Supports the use of the FXSAVE and FXRSTOR instructions to save and restore both the x87 FPU and SSE register sets, and
*   Also supports the use of the SSE, SSE2, SSE3, SSSE3 and SSE4 instruction sets.

Table 22-5: CR4[OSFXSR] Bit

CR4[OSFXSR]	Effect
0	• FXSAVE/FXRSTOR instruction pair only save and restore x87 and MMX registers (not the SSE register set). • The logical processor generates an Invalid Opcode exception if it attempts to execute any SSE, SSE2, SSE3, SSSE3, or SSE4 instruction (with the exception of those noted at the end of this table).
1	• FXSAVE/FXRSTOR instruction pair save and restore the SSE register set as well as x87 and MMX registers. • The logical processor is enabled to execute all of the SSE, SSE2, SSE3, SSSE3, or SSE4 instructions.
The following SSE instructions are always enabled: PAUSE, PREFETCH*h*, SFENCE, LFENCE, MFENCE, MOVNTI, CLFLUSH, CRC32, and POPCNT.	

Enable the SSE SIMD FP Exception

Refer to Figure 22-14 on page 885. The OS will set CR4[OSXMMEXCPT] to one if it implements the SSE FP SIMD exception handler (the exception 19 handler).

SSE SIMD FP exceptions are only generated by SSE SIMD FP instructions. If CR4[OSXMMEXCPT] is cleared to zero, the logical processor generates an Invalid Opcode exception whenever it detects an unmasked SIMD FP exception.

Figure 22-14: OSFXSR and OSXMMEXCPT Bits Added to CR4

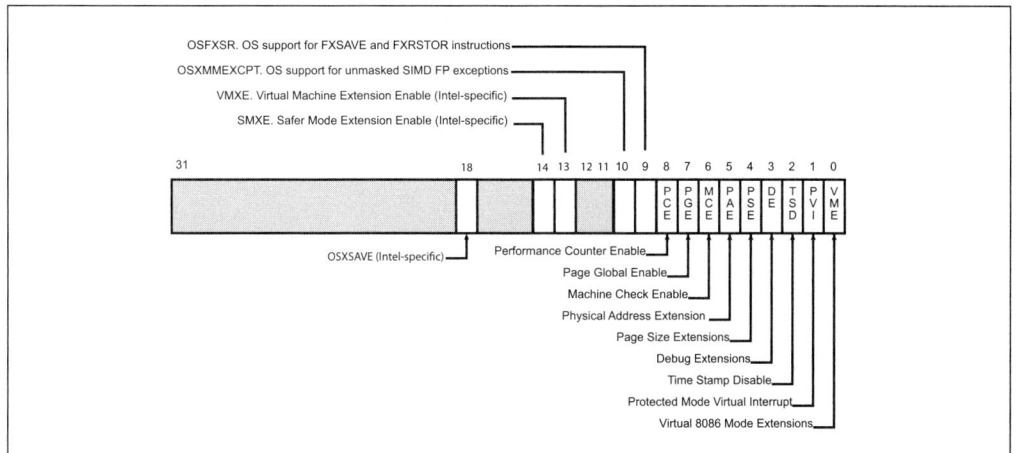

SSE Setup

To set up the SSE, SSE2, SSE3, SSSE3, or SSE4 extensions for use by application programs, the OS must perform the following steps:

1. Set CR4[OSFXSR] = 1 (see "Enable SSE Instruction Sets and Register Set Save/Restore" on page 884).
2. Set CR4[OSXMMEXCPT] = 1 (see "Enable the SSE SIMD FP Exception" on page 884).
3. Clear CR0[EM] to 0. This disables emulation of x87 FPU, MMX/SSE instructions.
4. Clear CR0[MP] to 0. This setting is the required setting for all x86 processors that support the SSE, SSE2, SSE3, SSSE3, or SSE4 extensions.

Summary of the SSE Instruction Set

Table 22-6 on page 886 provides a summary of the instructions introduced in the initial SSE instruction set. The following is a key to the instruction suffixes used in the table:

- ss = scalar SP FP.
- ps = packed SP FP.
- pi = packed dword integers.
- si = signed dword integer.

Table 22-6: SSE Instructions

Data Movement	Arithmetic	Logical	Comparison	Shuffle and Unpack	Conversion	64-bit SIMD Integer	MXCSR State Management	Cacheability and Memory Ordering Related
movaps	addps	andps	cmpps	shufps	cvtpi2ps	pavgb	ldmxcsr	movntq
movups	addss	andnps	cmpss	unpckhps	cvtsi2ss	pavgw	stmxcsr	movntps
movss	mulps	orps	comiss	unpcklps	cvtps2pi	pextrw		maskmovq
movlps	mulss	xorps	ucomiss		cvttps2pi	pinsrw		prefetch
movhps	divps				cvtss2si	pmaxub		SFENCE
movlhps	divss				cvttss2si	pminub		
movhlps	rcpps					pmaxsw		
movmskps	rcpss					pminsw		
	sqrtps					pmovmskb		
	sqrtss					pmulhuw		
	rsqrtps					psadbw		
	rsqrtss					pshufw		
	maxps							
	maxss							
	minps							
	minss							
	subps							
	subss							

The SSE2 Instruction Set

General

The 130nm Pentium 4 added the 144 SSE2 instruction set to the x86 architecture. The programmer may determine whether a processor supports these instructions by executing a CPUID request type 1 and verifying that EDX[26] = 1.

Generally, the SSE2 instructions added the following functionality:

- A new data type, 64-bit DP FP numbers, was added. The programmer can pack two, 64-bit DP FP numbers (see Figure 22-15 on page 887) into each of two XMM registers and then perform packed DP FP operations on them (or between two numbers packed in an XMM register and two in memory).
- New instructions were added to perform scalar operations (see "Scalar Operations" on page 864) on 64-bit DP FP numbers in the XMM registers.
- The MMX and SSE instruction sets were enhanced to perform operations on data items packed in the XMM registers (see Figure 22-15 on page 887).
- The CLFLUSH, MFENCE, LFENCE and new streaming store (i.e., non-temporal store) instructions were added.

Figure 22-15: SSE2 XMM Data types

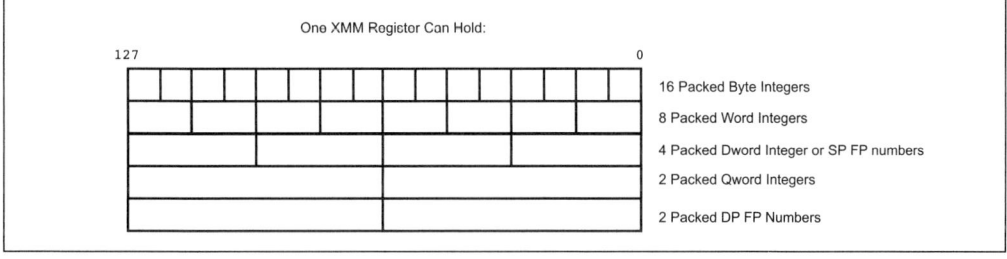

DP FP Number Representation

A primer on the representation of 32-bit SP FP numbers was covered in "32-bit SP FP Numeric Format" on page 346. In the DP FP format, like the 32-bit SP FP format, the digit to the left of the decimal point is assumed to be one. With wider significand (also referred to as the mantissa) and biased-exponent fields, a wider range of values can be represented (2.23×10^{-308} to 1.79×10^{308}, versus 1.18×10^{-38} to 3.40×10^{38} for SP FP numbers).

Figure 22-16: 64-bit DP FP Numeric Format

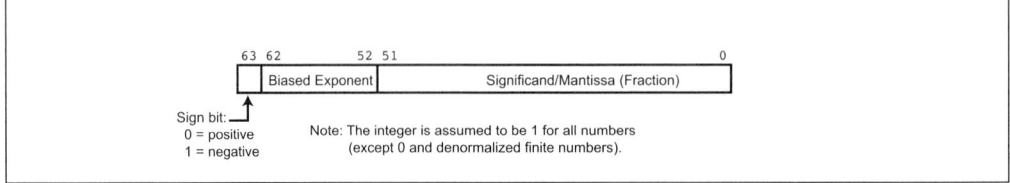

SSE2 Packed and Scalar DP FP Instructions

The SSE2 instructions that can perform operations on packed and scalar DP FP numbers are divided into the following groups:

- The data movement instructions.
- The arithmetic instructions.
- The compare instructions.
- The data type conversion instructions.
- The logical instructions.
- The shuffle instructions.

SSE2 64-Bit and 128-Bit SIMD Integer Instructions

The SSE2 instructions that can perform SIMD operations on packed integers are:

- the MOVDQA (move aligned double qword) instruction.
- the MOVDQU (move unaligned double qword) instruction.
- the PADDQ (packed qword add) instruction.
- the PSUBQ (packed qword subtract) instruction.
- the PMULUDQ (multiply packed unsigned dword integers) instruction.
- the PSHUFLW (shuffle packed low words) instruction.
- the PSHUFHW (shuffle packed high words) instruction.
- the PSHUFD (shuffle packed dword integers) instruction.
- the PSLLDQ (shift double qword left logical) instruction.
- the PSRLDQ (shift double qword right logical) instruction.
- the PUNPCKHQDQ (Unpack high qwords) instruction.
- the PUNPCKLQDQ (Unpack low qwords) instruction.

- the MOVQ2DQ (move qword integer from MMX to XMM registers) instruction.
- the MOVDQ2Q (move qword integer from XMM to MMX registers) instruction.

SSE2 128-Bit SIMD Integer Instruction Extensions

All of the 64-bit MMX and SSE SIMD integer instructions (with the exception of PSHUFW) have been extended to operate on 128-bit packed integer operands in XMM registers. The new 128-bit versions of these instructions follow the same SIMD conventions regarding packed operands as the original 64-bit versions.

As an example, where the 64-bit version of PADDB operates on 8 bytes packed into an MMX register, the 128-bit version has been extended to operate on 16 bytes packed into an XMM register.

Your Choice: Accuracy or Speed (DAZ)

The Pentium III added the SSE instruction set, the XMM registers, and the MXCSR register. As previously described in "Accuracy vs. Fast Real-Time 3D Processing (FTZ)" on page 880, the MXCSR register's FTZ (Flush-To-Zero) bit permits the programmer a choice between a more accurate result or increased processing speed. The Pentium 4 added the DAZ (Denormals As Zero) bit to the MXCSR register (see Figure 22-17 on page 890) for much the same reason.

The IEEE 754 specification defines the range of possible real numbers as falling into the following categories (ranging from most positive to most negative):

- $+ \infty$
- +1.n, where n is > 0 (referred to as positive normal numbers)
- +0.n, where n is > 0 (referred to as positive denormal numbers)
- +0
- -0
- -0.n, where n is > 0 (referred to as negative denormal numbers)
- -1.n, where n is > 0 (referred to as negative normal numbers)
- $- \infty$

When the DAZ bit is set to one, the logical processor converts all denormal source operands to a zero with the sign of the original operand before performing any computations on them. It does not set the Denormal Operand Exception (DE) status bit to one, regardless of the setting of the Denormal Operand mask bit (DM), and does not generate a Denormal Operand exception if the exception is unmasked.

It should be stressed that DAZ mode is not compatible with IEEE Standard 754. In many streaming media applications, rounding a denormal operand to zero does not appreciably affect the quality of the processed data and the performance of the application is increased because exceptions are not generated when a denormal source operand is involved in a FP operation.

- The DAZ bit affects the execution of all SSE (not just SSE1) FP operations.
- The DAZ bit is cleared upon a power-up or reset of the processor, disabling DAZ Mode.
- In all models of the Pentium III and in early models of the Pentium 4, MXCSR[DAZ] was reserved. Setting MXCSR[DAZ] = 1 on a logical processor that doesn't support DAZ mode results in a GP exception. See "MXCSR Mask Field" on page 882 for additional information.

Figure 22-17: The MXCSR Register

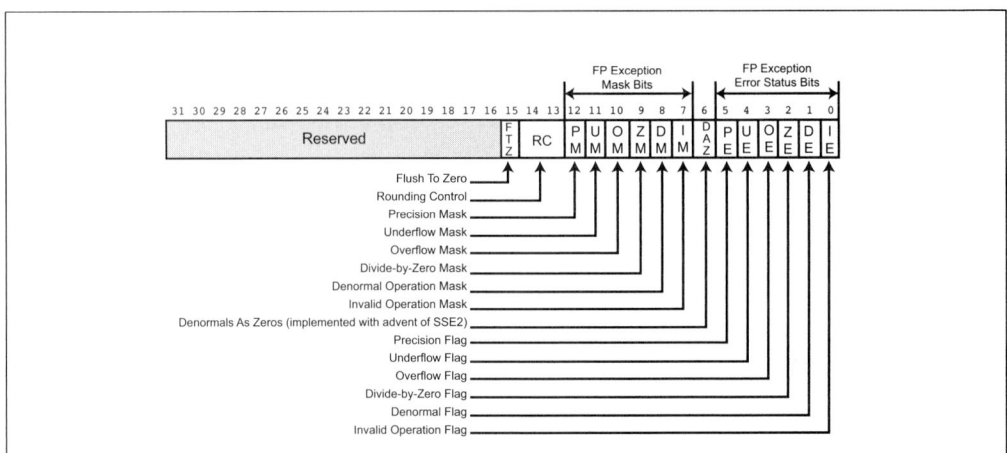

The Cache Line Flush Instruction

The Cache Line Flush instruction has the following characteristics:

- When executed, the logical processor uses the virtual address of the specified one-byte memory operand to perform a lookup in all of its caches. This instruction has no effect if the line is not in any of the caches. The line is invalidated in any cache that contains it. If the line is in the modified state, it is also written back to system memory.
- The memory type (as specified by the MTRRs and the selected PTE or PDE) does not affect this instruction in any way.

- A processor's support for this instruction is determined by executing a CPUID request type 1. The instruction is supported if EDX[19] = 1. In addition, the cache line size (in qwords) is returned in EBX[15:8] (see Figure 22-18 on page 891).
- Although this instruction was first introduced in the Pentium 4 as part of the SSE2 instruction set, a future x86 processor could support SSE2 and CLFLUSH, CLFLUSH but not SSE2, or neither of them (although the author thinks the last option is highly unlikely).
- Because speculative fetching can occur at any time and is not tied to instruction execution, the CLFLUSH instruction is not ordered with respect to the PREFETCH*h* instructions nor any of the speculative fetching mechanisms (i.e., data can be speculatively loaded into a cache just before, during, or after the execution of a CLFLUSH instruction that references the cache line).
- CLFLUSH is only ordered by the MFENCE instruction and is not guaranteed to be ordered by any other fencing or serializing instructions (see "Synchronizing Events" on page 618) or by another CLFLUSH instruction.
- CLFLUSH can be executed at any privilege level and is subject to all permission checking and faults associated with a byte load.
- CLFLUSH can flush a line that was read from an execute-only segment.
- The execution of CLFLUSH sets the Accessed bit but not the Dirty bit in the selected PTE or PTE.

Figure 22-18: The EBX Register After Executing a CPUID Request Type 1

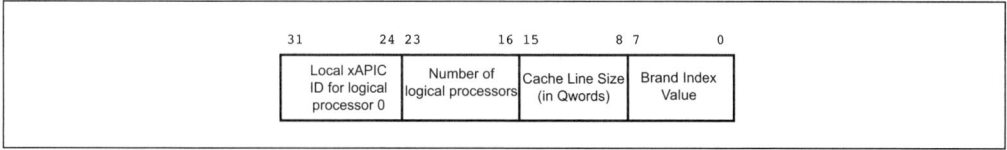

Fence Instructions

MFENCE Instruction

The Memory Fence instruction (first implemented in the Pentium 4) acts as a fence that prevents the logical processor from executing any loads or stores beneath the fence until all loads and stores above the fence have been completed and the logical processor's Store Buffers and WCBs have been drained to memory:

```
mov  eax,10
mov  ebx,memioport1;read from memory mapped IO port 1
mov  edx,memioport2;read from memory mapped IO port 2
mov  memioport3,eax;write to memory mapped IO port 3
mfence              ;cannot perform loads/stores beyond
                    ;fence until all prior loads and
                    ;stores have completed
mov  ecx,memioport4;read from memory mapped IO port 4
```

While the logical processor cannot execute loads or stores beneath the fence until all upstream loads and stores have been completed and its Store Buffers and WCBs have been drained to memory, it can execute non-memory instructions beneath the fence before all of the loads, stores and buffer draining above the fence have been completed. In the following example, the programmer has used the CPUID instruction to accomplish the same goal:

```
mov  eax,10
mov  ebx,memioport1;read from memory mapped IO port 1
mov  edx,memioport2;read from memory mapped IO port 2
mov  memioport3,eax;write to memory mapped IO port 3
mov  eax,1          ;set up for a CPUID request type 1
cpuid               ;acts as a barrier in the code
mov  ecx,memioport4;read from memory mapped IO port 4
```

CPUID is a serializing instruction (see "Synchronizing Events" on page 618). In other words, it acts as a barrier (a fence) in the instruction flow that prevents the logical processor from executing *any* instructions of any type whatsoever until all of the instructions up to and including the fence have completed execution and their results have been committed to the register set. This causes a significant drop in performance due to the constraint placed on out-of-order execution. Using the MFENCE instruction results in better performance.

Although the example assumed that the memory locations read were in UC memory space, the MFENCE instruction can be used to fence loads and stores within any type of memory space.

Using the LFENCE and SFENCE instructions is *not* equivalent to using the MFENCE instruction. The load and store fences are not ordered with respect to each other: the LFENCE can be executed before prior stores, and the SFENCE can be executed before prior loads. The MFENCE instruction should be used whenever the Cache Line Flush instruction (CLFLUSH) is used to ensure that speculative memory references generated by the logical processor do not interfere with the flush.

LFENCE Instruction

General. Consider the following code fragment:

```
mov  ebx,memioport1;read from memory mapped IO port 1
mov  edx,memioport2;read from memory mapped IO port 2
mov  ecx,memioport3;read from memory mapped IO port 3
```

This example performs reads from three memory mapped IO ports in a device adapter and assumes that the ports are in a UC memory range. Proper operation of the example adapter requires that the three memory data read transactions (i.e., loads) be performed in strict program order. Since the logical processor can normally execute loads in any order, this code fragment may result in an improper sequence of the reads on the external interface. The Load Fence instruction (first implemented in the Pentium 4) addresses this situation:

```
mov  ebx,memioport1;read from memory mapped IO port 1
mov  edx,memioport2;read from memory mapped IO port 2
lfence             ;cannot perform loads beyond fence
                   ;until all prior loads have completed
mov  ecx,memioport3;read from memory mapped IO port 3
```

It should be noted that, while the logical processor cannot execute loads beneath the fence until all upstream loads have completed, it can execute non-load instructions beneath the fence before all loads above the fence have completed. In the following example, the programmer has used the CPUID instruction to accomplish the same goal:

```
mov  ebx,memioport1;read from memory mapped IO port 1
mov  edx,memioport2;read from memory mapped IO port 2
mov eax,1          ;set up for a CPUID request type 1
cpuid              ;acts as a barrier in the code
mov  ecx,memioport3;read from memory mapped IO port 3
```

CPUID is a serializing instruction (see "Synchronizing Events" on page 618). In other words, it acts as a barrier (a fence) in the instruction flow that prevents the logical processor from executing *any* instructions of any type whatsoever until all of the instructions up to and including the fence have completed execution and their results have been committed to the register set. This causes a significant drop in performance due to the constraint placed on out-of-order execution. Using the LFENCE instruction results in better performance.

Although the example assumed that the memory locations read were in UC memory space, the LFENCE instruction can be used to fence loads from any type of memory space.

LFENCE Ordering Rules. The LFENCE instruction is executed in order with reference to load instructions, to other instances of the LFENCE instruction, to instances of the MFENCE instruction (see "MFENCE Instruction" on page 891), and to any serializing instructions (e.g., CPUID; see "Synchronizing Events" on page 618). It is not necessarily executed in order with reference to store instructions or to the SFENCE instruction (see "SFENCE Instruction" on page 874).

The LFENCE instruction is not necessarily executed in order with reference to PREFETCH*h* instructions or to any other speculative fetching mechanism (data could be speculative loaded into the cache just before, during, or after the execution of an LFENCE instruction).

SFENCE Instruction

The Store Fence instruction was added as part of the SSE1 instruction set and was described earlier in "SFENCE Instruction" on page 874.

Non-Temporal Store Instructions

Introduction

The category of instructions referred as non-temporal stores (also referred to as streaming stores) was introduced in the Pentium III as part of the SSE instruction set (see "Streaming Store Instructions" on page 868). The addition of the SSE2 instruction set in the Pentium 4 added four additional streaming store instructions:

- The MOVNTDQ Instruction.
- The MOVNTPD Instruction.
- The MOVNTI instruction.
- The MASKMOVDQU instruction.

They are described in the sections that follow.

MOVNTDQ Instruction

Refer to Figure 22-19 on page 895. This instruction is a Store Double Qword to memory using a non-temporal hint. When executed, it moves 16 bytes of data from the specified XMM register into memory. When this instruction is executed, the logical processor treats the line of memory space being written to as if it were the WC memory type (even though the MTRRs and the PTE or PDE selected by the virtual address may designate it as WB memory). Executing this instruction has the following effects:

- The 16 bytes from the specified XMM register are posted in the appropriate locations in one of the logical processor's WC buffers [WCBs; see "Uncacheable Write-Combining (WC) Memory" on page 611 for more information] and the start address of the line is also latched into that WCB. The data will be written to memory at a later time when the WCB is written to memory using the external interface.
- Assuming that the memory type is WB, the line is not fetched from memory, so none of the disadvantages cited in Table 22-4 on page 869 are experienced.
- The logical processor performs a lookup in its internal caches and, if the line is present in the cache, it is evicted from the cache.

The memory type (i.e., if it is UC or WP memory) of the region being written to can override the non-temporal hint (i.e., it will be treated as write to UC or WP memory).

Figure 22-19: The MOVNTDQ Instruction

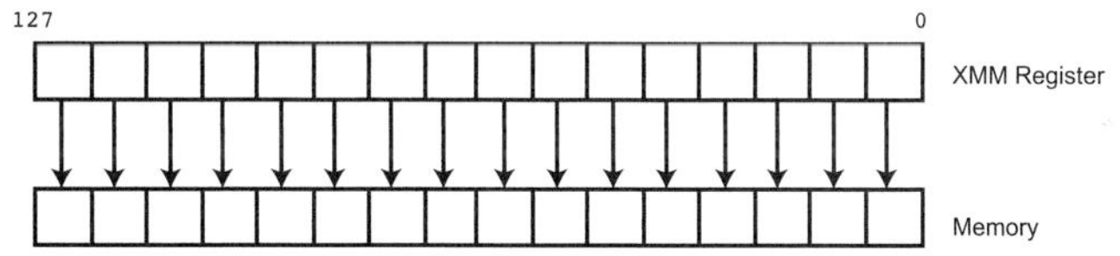

MOVNTPD Instruction

Refer to Figure 22-20 on page 896. The instruction name stands for *move packed DP FP values into memory using a non-temporal hint*. When executed, it stores the two 64-bit DP FP values packed into an XMM register to memory. The start memory address specified must be aligned on a 16-byte (128-bit) boundary.

When this instruction is executed, the logical processor treats the line of memory space being written to as if it were the WC memory type (even though the MTRRs and the PTE or PDE selected by the virtual address may designate it as WB memory). Executing this instruction has the following effects:

- The two 64-bit DP FP numbers supplied from the specified XMM register are posted in the appropriate locations in one of the logical processor's WC buffers [WCBs; see "Uncacheable Write-Combining (WC) Memory" on page 611 for more information] and the start address of the line is also latched into that WCB. The data will be written to memory at a later time when the WCB is written to memory using the external interface.
- Assuming that the memory type is WB, the line is not fetched from memory, so none of the disadvantages cited in Table 22-4 on page 869 are experienced.
- The logical processor performs a lookup in its internal caches and, if the line is present in the cache, it is evicted from the cache.

The memory type (i.e., if it is UC or WP) of the region being written to can override the non-temporal hint (i.e., it will be treated as write to UC or WP memory).

Figure 22-20: The MOVNTPD Instruction

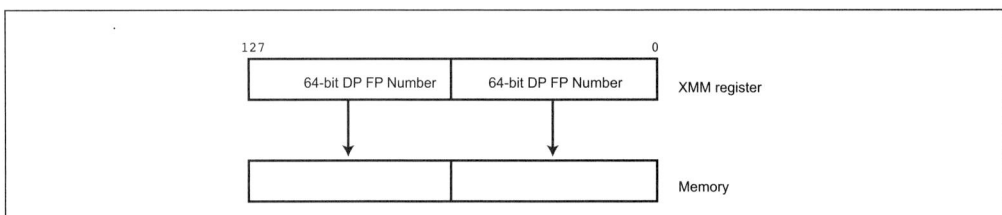

MOVNTI Instruction

Refer to Figure 22-21 on page 897. This instruction stores a 32-bit integer from a GPR to memory using a non-temporal hint. When this instruction is executed, the logical processor treats the line of memory space being written to as if it were the WC memory type (even though the MTRRs and the PTE or PDE selected by the virtual address may designate it as WB memory). Executing this instruction has the following effects:

- The four bytes from the specified GPR are posted in the appropriate locations in one of the logical processor's WC buffers [WCBs; see "Uncacheable Write-Combining (WC) Memory" on page 611 for more information] and the start address of the line is also latched into that WCB. The data will be written to memory at a later time when the WCB is written to memory using the external interface.
- Assuming that the memory type is WB, the line is not fetched from memory, so none of the disadvantages cited in Table 22-4 on page 869 are experienced.

- The logical processor performs a lookup in its internal caches and, if the line is present in the cache, it is evicted from the cache.

The memory type (if it is UC or WP) of the region being written to can override the non-temporal hint (i.e., it will be treated as write to UC or WP memory).

Figure 22-21: The MOVNTI Instruction

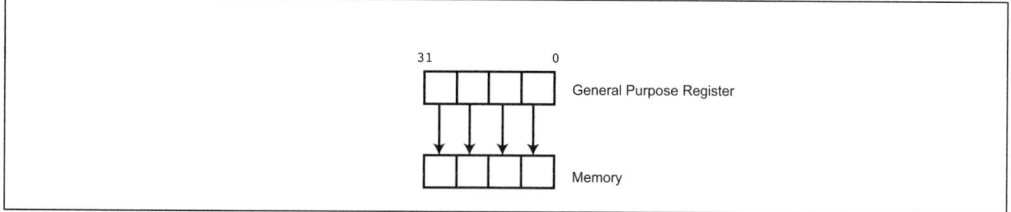

MASKMOVDQU Instruction

General. Refer to Figure 22-22 on page 898. When executed, this instruction uses the bit mask specified in one XMM register to determine which of the 16 bytes in another XMM register are written to memory. Bit 7 in each byte of the specified XMM mask register indicates whether the corresponding data byte from the source XMM register will be written to memory (1 = write the byte to memory; 0 = do not write it to memory). The memory address is specified in the DS:DI (if executing in 16-bit mode) or DS:EDI register pair (if executing in 32-bit mode):

— The specified bytes from the source XMM register are posted in the appropriate locations in one of the logical processor's WC buffers [WCBs; see "Uncacheable Write-Combining (WC) Memory" on page 611 for more information] and the start address of the line is also latched into that WCB. The data will be written to memory at a later time when the WCB is written to memory using the external interface.
— Assuming that the memory type is WB, the line is not fetched from memory, so none of the disadvantages cited in Table 22-4 on page 869 are experienced.
— The logical processor performs a lookup in its internal caches and, if the line is present in the cache, it is evicted from the cache.

The information cited in "MASKMOVQ Instruction" on page 872 also applies to this instruction.

When a Mask of All Zeros Is Used. The logical processor's behavior when a mask of all 0s is specified is as follows:

— No data is written to memory.
— Signaling of a breakpoint (code or data) on this access is not guaranteed; different processor implementations may or may not signal breakpoints.
— Exceptions associated with addressing memory and Page Faults may still be signaled (implementation-dependent).
— If the destination memory is mapped as UC or WP, enforcement of the rules for these memory types is not guaranteed (it is reserved) and is implementation-specific.

Figure 22-22: The MASKMOVDQU Instruction

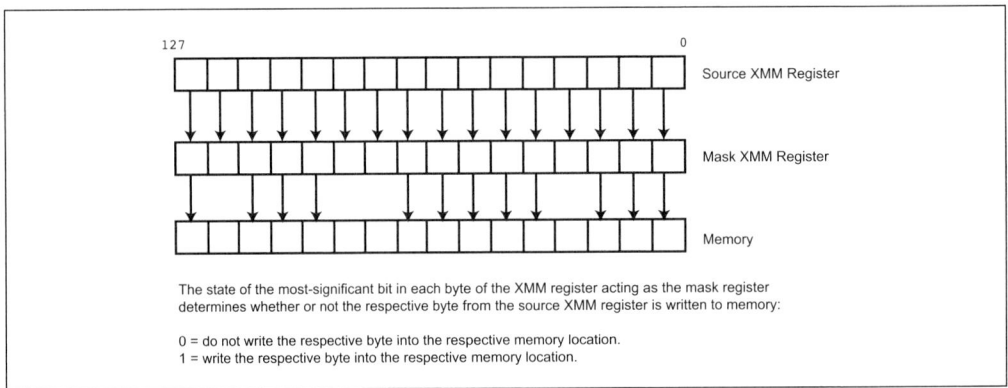

PAUSE Instruction

Hyper-Threading was first introduced on the Pentium 4 processor wherein the instruction streams for two logical processors were both fed into a shared instruction pipeline.

Thread Synchronization

At some point, two threads running side-by-side on two logical processors within a core (in other words, Hyper-Threading has been enabled) may need to sync up with each other. This can be accomplished by having the thread performing the test (Thread A) go into a tight loop repeatedly reading a variable and checking it for a particular value (see the example that follows). When the other thread (Thread B) arrives at the synchronization point, it signals this by writing the expected value into the synchronization variable. The next time the variable is checked by Thread A, it contains the expected value and the tight loop is exited.

The following are two examples of spin-wait loops:

```
do {
} while(sync_var != constant_value)

wait_loop: cmp eax, semaphore
           jne wait_loop
```

The Problem

The thread synchronization method described in the previous section can result in severe performance degradation, however. The following describes the cause of the degradation. In this example:

- Thread A, running on logical processor 0, has arrived at the synchronization point and has entered the spin-wait loop.
- Thread B, running on logical processor 1, has not yet arrived at the synchronization point. When it does, it will signal this by writing to the synchronization variable.

1. When the load to read the synchronization variable is executed by Thread A on logical processor 0, it is placed in one of the core's Load Buffers to await the return of the read data. In the spin-wait loop, each successive read of the variable by Thread A is queued up in a separate Load Buffer while each awaits fulfillment. The loads can be dispatched much faster than the caches can supply the requested data.
2. When Thread B executing on logical processor 1 finally arrives at the synchronization point, it executes the store to the synchronization variable. It is posted in one of the core's Store Buffers allocated to logical processor 1.
3. The core must ensure that the loads issued by Thread A running on logical processor 0 *prior* to Thread B's store receive the pre-store data.
4. It must then ensure that the next load executed in Thread A's spin-wait loop—the one executed immediately after the store by Thread B on logical processor 1—receives the updated data from the Thread B's Store Buffer.
5. Logical processor 1 is not permitted to complete the store until all of the pre-store loads issued by the other logical processor have been fulfilled (with the pre-store data) and retired from the pipeline. Only then is the store permitted to complete.
6. Then, finally, the post-store load is permitted to complete.

The Fix

The Pentium 4 introduced the PAUSE instruction (part of the SSE2 instruction set) to address this issue. When placed in a spin-wait loop, the PAUSE instruction causes a small, hardware-enforced delay between the issuance of each of the loads to read the synchronization variable. The net result is that there will only be one outstanding load that will be serviced by the store when it occurs. This helps the performance of the thread that performs the store because the store can complete more quickly. There are two additional side-benefits:

- The number of micro-ops that the schedulers have to handle for the paused thread is dramatically decreased, thereby allowing the schedulers to provide fast dispatch of the other thread's micro-ops.
- Whenever the number of micro-ops that have to be handled is decreased, the power consumed by the pipeline stages decreases accordingly.

The following is an example use of PAUSE to slow down the rate at which the semaphore is checked:

```
wait_loop: pause
           cmp eax, sync_var
           jne wait_loop
```

Performing a pre-check of the synchronization variable can avoid the delay imposed by the PAUSE (in the event that the other thread had already written to the variable):

```
           cmp eax, sync_var
           je continue
wait_loop: pause
           cmp eax, sync_var
           jne wait_loop
continue:  ...
```

The following is an example showing a locked RMW (read/modify/write; the XCHG instruction performs a locked RMW) being used to check the variable (also referred to as a spin-lock).

```
get_lock:
  mov eax, 1
  xchg eax, mem    ;read current value and set it
  cmp eax, 0       ;was it already set?
  jne spin_loop    ;spin if it was, else fall through
critical_section:
```

```
  <critical section code>
  mov  mem, 0      ;clear the variable
  jmp  continue
spin_loop:
  pause            ;short delay
  cmp  mem, 0      ;
  jne  spin_loop
  jmp  get_lock
continue:
```

When a Thread Is Idle

When a worker thread has run out of work to do, it could enter an idle loop wherein it checks a variable periodically to determine when it is to perform a task. If it might be a relatively long while until it receives a task to perform, the OS scheduler should put that logical processor to sleep by causing it to execute a HLT instruction. In that way, all of the pipeline resources that are partitioned between the two logical processors are recombined and dedicated to the other logical processor.

Spin-Lock Optimization

Spin-locks (see the final example code fragment under "The Fix" on page 900) are typically used when more than one thread may attempt to modify a synchronization variable simultaneously. In this case, a locked RMW should be used to test and change the variable (in case multiple threads are in a race to change the variable).

When the variable is cleared by the thread that had set it, a number of threads on other logical processors may be in a race to set it again. This can result in significant performance degradation. Intel recommends that no more than two threads should have write access to a given synchronization variable. In addition, as shown in the final code fragment in "The Fix" on page 900, the PAUSE instruction could be included in the wait loop. The reader should note, however, that using the PAUSE instruction is not as efficient as using the MONITOR/MWAIT instruction pair which were introduced as part of the SSE3 instruction set (see "MONITOR/MWAIT Instruction Pair" on page 907).

Branch Hints

Two instruction prefixes were added (2Eh and 3Eh) in the SSE2 instruction set (see "Branch Hint Prefix" on page 221). When a conditional branch instruction is prefixed by one of these hints, the first time the branch is seen by a logical processor's branch prediction logic the prefix instructs it as to whether to predict the branch taken or not taken. These prefixes can only be used with conditional branch instructions. There are no mnemonics for them:

- 2Eh—Predict the branch not taken.
- 3Eh—Predict the branch taken.

SSE3 Instruction Set

Introduction

13 new instructions—the SSE3 instruction set—were introduced in the 90nm Pentium 4. No new registers were introduced. The SSE3 instructions fall into five categories:

- One new x87 FP-to-integer conversion instruction:
  — The FISTTP instruction. See "Improved x87 FP-to-Integer Conversion Instruction" on page 902.
- Complex arithmetic instructions:
  — The ADDSUBPS, ADDSUBPD, MOVSLDUP, MOVSHDUP, and MOVDDUP instructions. See "New Complex Arithmetic Instructions" on page 903.
- One new video encoding instruction:
  — The LDDQU instruction. See "Improved Motion Estimation Performance" on page 904.
- Graphics-oriented instructions:
  — The HADDPS, HSUBPS, HADDPD, and HSUBPD instructions. See "Instructions to Improve Processing of a Vertex Database" on page 906.
- Two new thread synchronization instructions:
  — The MONITOR and MWAIT instructions. See "MONITOR/MWAIT Instruction Pair" on page 907.

The sections that follow describe these new instructions.

Improved x87 FP-to-Integer Conversion Instruction

The Problem

When FISTP is executed to convert an x87 FP value into an integer, the logical processor uses the rounding algorithm specified in the x87 FPU's FCW[RC] field (see Figure 9-6 on page 352). The Fortran, C and C++ specifications call for the rounding mode to be set to Chop when converting an x87 FP number to an integer, but the default rounding mode in FCW[RC] is usually set to *even* to minimize rounding errors. Performing the conversion therefore involves the following steps:

```
fstcw [old FCW]        ;store current FCW in memory
movw ax,[old FCW]      ;set ax = current FCW contents
or   ax,c00h           ;change RC setting to Chop
movw [new FCW],ax      ;save new FCW settings in memory
fldcw [new FCW]        ;load new setting into FCW
fistp [INT]            ;convert FP value to an integer
fldcw [old FCW]        ;change FCW back to original
                       ;setting
```

This operation caused the FCW to be changed twice using the FLDCW instruction (and this instruction executes relatively slowly).

The Solution

The new x87 FP-to-integer conversion instruction, FISTTP, ignores FCW[RC] and always uses chop as its rounding mode. Rather than the code fragment shown in the previous section, the same conversion can be accomplished with this code fragment:

```
fisttp [INT]           ;convert FP to integer using
                       ;Chop RC
```

I think that speaks for itself. The FISTTP instruction is available in three precisions: word (16-bit), dword (32-bit), and qword (64-bit).

New Complex Arithmetic Instructions

The following new complex arithmetic instructions were added as part of the SSE3 instruction set:

- ADDSUBPS and ADDSUBPD perform a mix of FP addition and subtraction, removing the need for changing the sign of some operands.
- MOVSLDUP, MOVSHDUP and MOVDDUP (in their memory versions) combine loads with some level of duplication, hence saving the need for a shuffle instruction on the loaded data.

The following code sequence illustrates how to implement a DP complex multiplication using only SSE2 instructions:

```
movapd   xmm0, [mem_X]
movapd   xmm1, [mem_Y]
movapd   xmm2, [mem_Y]
unpcklpd xmm1, xmm1
unpckhpd xmm2, xmm2
mulpd    xmm1, xmm0
mulpd    xmm2, xmm0
xorpd    xmm2, xmm7
shufpd   xmm2, xmm2,0x1
addpd    xmm2, xmm1
movapd   [mem_Z], xmm2
```

The next code sequence accomplishes the same goal using the new SSE3 instructions:

```
movapd   xmm0, [mem_X]
movddup  xmm1, [mem_Y]
movddup  xmm2, [mem_Y+8]
mulpd    xmm1, xmm0
mulpd    xmm2, xmm0
shufpd   xmm2, xmm2,0x1
addsubpd xmm2, xmm1
movapd   [mem_Z], xmm2
```

The real key here is the number of micro-ops that must be executed:

- Seven for the SSE2 example.
- Four for the SSE3 example.

The new complex arithmetic instructions can improve complex multiplication performance by up to 75%.

Improved Motion Estimation Performance

The Problem

A video encoder determines Motion Estimation (ME) by comparing blocks from the current video frame against blocks from the previous frame looking for the closest match. Many of the blocks from the previous frame are unaligned whereas loads of the blocks from the current frame are aligned. Unaligned loads suffer two penalties:

- The performance degradation associated with handling an unaligned access.
- The potential performance degradation associated with accesses that cross cache line boundaries (and may therefore experience a cache miss).

There is not a micro-op capable of loading an unaligned 16-byte data object from memory. As a result, unaligned 16-byte load instructions (e.g., MOVUPS and MOVDQU) are emulated with microcode. Two 8-byte loads are executed and then merged to form the 16-byte result. Naturally, this has a performance cost and, if the access crosses a cache line boundary (a 64-byte L1 data cache line), there can be additional cost incurred.

The Solution

The LDDQU (Load Double Quadword) instruction was added in SSE3 to address the cache line split problem. When executed, this instruction reads 32-bytes from memory starting on a 16-byte aligned address. This is the area that contains the requested, unaligned 16-byte block. Because it loads more bytes than requested, LDDQU should not be used in UC and WC memory areas (because locations will be read that were not requested, possibility changing the state of a MMIO device).

Motion Estimation using SSE/SSE2 instructions:

```
movdqa  xmm0, [current]
movdqu  xmm1, [previous]
psadbw  xmm0, xmm1
paddw   xmm2, xmm0
```

Motion Estimation using SSE3 instructions:

```
movdqa  xmm0, [current]
lddqu   xmm1, [previous]
psadbw  xmm0, xmm1
paddw   xmm2, xmm0
```

Intel estimates that, assuming 25% of the unaligned loads will cross a cache line boundary, the LDDQU instruction can improve the performance of ME by up to 30%. Intel testing indicated that MPEG 4 encoders demonstrated speedups greater than 10%.

The Downside

Use of this instruction may result in reduced performance if the application requires the performance benefit associated with Store Forwarding.

Instructions to Improve Processing of a Vertex Database

Most (graphics) vertex databases are organized as an Array of Structures (AOS), where each vertex structure contains data fields such as the following:

- x, y, z, w. The coordinates of the vertex.
- nx, ny, nz, nw. The coordinates of the normal at the vertex.
- r, g, b, a. The colors at the vertex.
- u0, v0. The first set of 2D texture coordinates.
- u1, v1. The second set of 2D texture coordinates.

SSE is good at handling vertex databases organized as a Structure of Arrays (SOA), where:

- The first array contains the x coordinates of all the vertices;
- The second array contains the y coordinates of all the vertices;
- etc.

Since the AOS approach is the norm for vertex database organization, when using SSE instructions to process database information the data must frequently be loaded from memory and then reorganized using shuffle instructions.

The scalar product operation is the most frequently performed operation in a vertex shader routine. It multiplies three or four pairs of SP FP data elements and the three or four results are then summed. The SSE3 instruction set adds horizontal FP add and subtract instructions (as opposed to the normal vertical SIMD operations) to expedite the evaluation of scalar products. Figure 22-23 on page 907 illustrates an example of a horizontal add or subtract operation.

The code sequences that follow illustrate how a scalar product of four SP pairs of elements can be evaluated with and without the new instructions.

Code using SSE/SSE2 instructions:

```
                ;whole lot of shuffling going on
mulps   xmm0, xmm1
movaps  xmm1, xmm0
shufps  xmm0, xmm1, b1h
addps   xmm0, xmm1
movaps  xmm1, xmm0
shufps  xmm0, xmm0, 0ah
addps   xmm0, xmm1
```

Code using SSE3 instructions:

```
        ;no more shuffling
mulps   xmm0, xmm1
haddps  xmm0, xmm0
haddps  xmm0, xmm0
```

Figure 22-23: Example Horizontal FP Math Operation

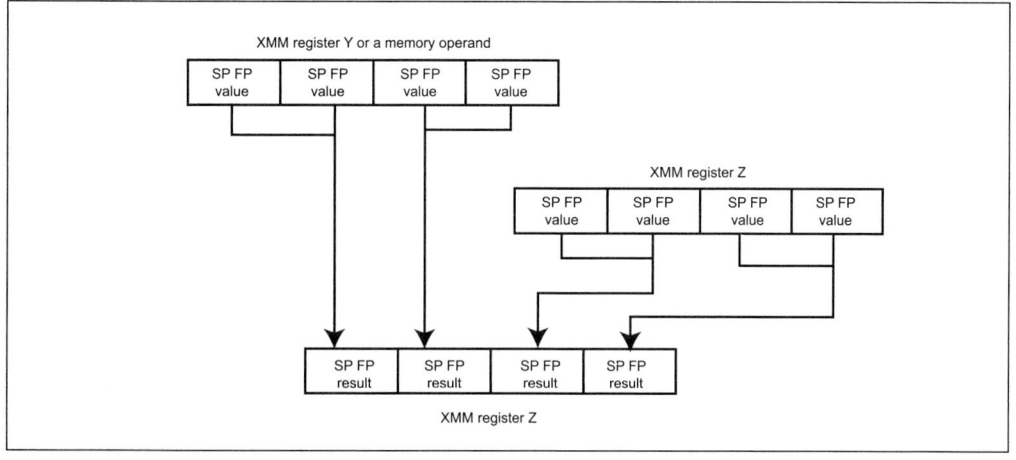

MONITOR/MWAIT Instruction Pair

These two instructions are part of the SSE3 instruction set and were introduced in the 90nm version of the Pentium 4. Together, they provide a much more elegant solution on a processor with Hyper-Threading enabled than the PAUSE instruction (see "PAUSE Instruction" on page 898) introduced as part of the SSE instruction set.

Background

When the OS scheduler has no work to do, it typically enters an idle spin-wait loop until there is something to do. This could also be true of any thread that runs out of work to do. The idle thread is accomplishing no useful work and yet the core's partitioned pipeline resources (resources that are split between the logical processors when Hyper-Threading is enabled; e.g., the micro-op queue, the general micro-op queue, the memory micro-op queue, etc.) remain partitioned. When a thread executing on a logical processor enters the idle state, it makes far better sense to execute a HLT instruction thereby causing the core to recombine the partitioned resources and dedicate all resources to the thread running on the other logical processor that is still performing useful work. If both threads executing on a core should become idle, it would make sense to place the core in a low-power state similar to the AutoHalt Powerdown state.

When one or both of the logical processors are idle, there must be a way to *wake* a logical processor and have it exit the idle state when there is once again useful work (i.e., a thread) for that logical processor to perform.

Monitor Instruction

Three input parameters are supplied with the MONITOR instruction:

- EAX = the offset portion of a virtual memory address defined by DS:Offset (where the offset portion of the address is specified in the EAX register). This must be an address in WB memory. When a special, hardware-based monitoring facility is subsequently activated, the facility monitors for a memory write within a virtual address range starting at this address. The range of addresses covered can be determined by a executing a CPUID request type 5 (introduced in the 90nm Pentium 4) and checking the byte count specified in EAX[15:0].
- ECX = optional extensions to the MONITOR instruction (none of which are currently implemented). This register must contain zero.
- EDX = optional hints to the MONITOR instruction (none of which are currently implemented). This register must contain zero.

When executed, the MONITOR instruction accomplishes the following:

- The logical processor uses the three input parameters to set up a hardware-based monitoring facility that, when subsequently activated, will monitor for a memory write (i.e., a store) to any location(s) within the specified memory area.
- The logical processor sets its Monitor Event Pending Flag (see "Example Code Usage" on page 909 and "The Wake Up Call" on page 909).

Mwait Instruction

Two input parameters are supplied with the MWAIT instruction:

- EAX = optional hints for the MWAIT instruction (none of which are currently implemented). This register must contain zero.
- ECX = optional extensions for the MWAIT instruction (none of which are currently implemented). This register must contain zero.

When executed, the MWAIT instruction accomplishes the following:

- The logical processor that executed the MWAIT instruction ceases program execution and awaits a wake up call (see "The Wake Up Call" on page 909).
- It places the logical processor in a processor design-specific mode. As an example:
  — If the core's other logical processor is still actively executing a thread, the core's partitioned resources are recombined and dedicated to the still active logical processor.
  — If the core's other logical processor is also in the MWAIT state, the core enters a low-power state similar to the AutoHalt Powerdown state.

Example Code Usage

The MONITOR/MWAIT instruction pair is typically used as illustrated in the following code fragment:

```
mov   eax,Trigger          ;eax = offset portion of DS:offset
                           ;store trigger address in WB memory
mov   ecx,Extensions       ;ecx = optional monitor instruction
                           ;extensions
mov   edx,hints            ;edx = hints for monitor instruction
While (!trigger_store_happened) {
     monitor eax,ecx,edx ;trigger monitoring activated and
                           ;Monitor Event Pending Flag is set
     If (!trigger_store_happened) {
          mwait eax,ecx  ;enter optimized state & await trigger
     }
}
```

The Wake Up Call

Any of the following events will cause the logical processor to resume program execution:

- A store to the WB memory address range being monitored causes the logical processor to fall through to the instruction that immediately follows the MWAIT instruction.
- Any maskable interrupt to the logical processor causes it to jump to the appropriate interrupt handler. On return from the handler, execution continues at the instruction immediately following the MWAIT.
- An NMI delivered to the logical processor causes it to jump to the NMI handler. On return from the handler, execution continues at the instruction immediately following the MWAIT.

- An SMI delivered to the logical processor causes it to jump to the SMI handler. On return from the handler, execution continues at the instruction immediately following the MWAIT.
- A Debug exception causes the logical processor to jump to the Debug exception handler. On return from the handler, execution continues at the instruction immediately following the MWAIT.
- A Machine Check exception causes the logical processor to jump to the MC handler.
- The assertion of the processor's BINIT# signal.
- The assertion of the processor's INIT# signal or the delivery of an INIT (Soft Reset) interrupt to the logical processor causes it to jump to the power-on restart address.
- The assertion of the processor's RESET# input causes the logical processor to jump to the power-on restart address.

SSSE3, SSE 4.1, and 4.2

The precursor to SSE, MMX, was described in "The MMX Facilities" on page 835 and the subsequent SSE1, SSE2, and SSE3 additions to the instruction set were described in:

- "Streaming SIMD Extensions (SSE)" on page 857.
- "The SSE2 Instruction Set" on page 887.
- "SSE3 Instruction Set" on page 902.

It should be obvious by now that each extension to the SSE instruction set is comprised of a series of additional instructions designed to address various performance and application-related issues. Rather than detailing the instructions added in SSSE3 and SSE 4.1 and SSE 4.2, the reader may find a summary of these additions listed in Table 22-1 on page 852 and a detailed description of each instruction may be found in the appropriate Intel and AMD documents.

Part 3:
IA-32e OS
Kernel Environment

The Previous Part

Part 2 provided a detailed description of two IA-32 Mode submodes—Real Mode and Protected Mode.

This Part

Part 3 provides a detailed description of the IA-32e OS kernel environment and consists of the following chapters:

- Chapter 23, "IA-32e OS Environment," on page 913.
- Chapter 24, "IA-32e Address Translation," on page 983.

The Next Part

Part 4 provides a detailed description of the Compatibility submode of IA-32e Mode.

23 *IA-32e OS Environment*

The Previous Chapter

The previous chapter described the SSE, SSE2 and SSE 3 instruction sets and summarized the SSSE3, SSE4.1 and SSE4.2 instruction sets.

This Chapter

This chapter provides a detailed description of the IA-32e OS environment. The following topics are covered:

- Mode Switching Overview.
- Virtual Memory Addressing in IA-32e Mode.
- In 64-bit Mode, Hardware-Enforced Flat Model.
- 64-bit Instruction Pointer.
- Instruction Fetching.
- RIP-Relative Data Accesses.
- Changes To Kernel-Related Registers and Structures.
- Address Translation Mechanism.
- GDT/LDT Descriptor Changes.
- GDT and GDTR Changes.
- LDT and LDTR Changes.
- IDT/IDTR and Interrupt/Exception Changes.
- Interrupt/Trap Gate Operational Changes.
- IRET Behavior.
- IA-32e Call Gate Operation.
- TR and TSS Changes.
- Register Set Expansion (in 64-bit Mode).
- Scheduler's Software-Based Task Switching Mechanism.

The Next Chapter

The next chapter provides a detailed description of the third generation address translation mechanism utilized in IA-32e Mode.

The Big Picture

Refer to Figure 23-1 on page 916. Ideally, all of the OS components are implemented as 64-bit code (i.e., they reside in 64-bit code segments and have full access to all of the logical processor's privileged, 64-bit facilities). Among other components, this would include:

- The **task scheduler**:
  1. Before starting or resuming a task, the scheduler would trigger the Local APIC timer.
  2. It then causes the logical processor to jump to the task:
     - If the task resides in a 64-bit code segment (i.e., the L bit in the CS descriptor = 1), the logical processor remains in 64-bit Mode.
     - If the task resides in a 16-bit legacy code segment (i.e., the CS descriptor's L and D bits both = 0), this causes the logical processor to automatically switch into 16-bit Compatibility Mode.
     - If the task resides in a 32-bit legacy code segment (the CS descriptor's L bit = 0 and D bit = 1), this causes the logical processor to automatically switch into 32-bit Compatibility Mode.
  3. In the background, while the logical processor executes the task, the timer continues to decrement.
  4. On timer expiration, the timer interrupt causes the logical processor to perform a far jump back to the scheduler. Since the CS descriptor selected by the far jump selects a CS descriptor wherein the L bit = 1, the logical processor switches back to 64-bit Mode (if it was in Compatibility Mode because the interrupted task was a legacy task).
- All **device drivers (including all hardware interrupt handlers)**. In IA-32e Mode, it is a rule that all interrupt handlers must reside in 64-bit code segments:
  — Upon detection of any hardware interrupt, software exception, or the attempted execution of a software interrupt instruction (INT nn, BOUND, INT3, or INTO), the logical processor would therefore reenter 64-bit Mode (if it was in Compatibility Mode because the interrupted task was a legacy task). Note: the INTO and BOUND instructions are illegal in 64-bit Mode.

- **OS services**. OS services are typically called in one of the following ways:
  - — **Far Call through a Call Gate**. The execution of a far call instruction wherein the segment selector portion of the branch target address selects a Call Gate descriptor in the GDT or LDT. Since in IA-32e Mode it is a rule that the procedure pointed to by a Call Gate must reside in a 64-bit code segment, the far call (or a far jump for that matter) causes a switch to 64-bit Mode.
  - — **Software Interrupt**. The execution of a software interrupt instruction will select either an Interrupt Gate or a Trap Gate descriptor in the IDT and, since it is a rule in IA-32e Mode that all IDT descriptors must point to handlers in 64-bit code segments, the interrupt causes a switch to 64-bit Mode.
  - — **SYSCALL instruction**. Used to make a call to the OS services:
    - – In Intel processors, the SYSCALL instruction can only be executed successfully by 64-bit applications. Otherwise it results in an Undefined Opcode exception.
    - – In AMD processors, the SYSCALL instruction can be executed in any mode.
  - — **SYSENTER instruction**. Used to make a call to the OS services:
    - – In Intel processors, the SYSENTER instruction can be executed in any mode.
    - – In AMD processors, the SYSENTER instruction can only be executed successfully in legacy Protected Mode. Otherwise it results in an Undefined Opcode exception.
- **Software exception handlers**. In IA-32e Mode, it is a rule that all software exception handlers must reside in 64-bit code segments. Upon detection of any software exception, the logical processor would therefore reenter 64-bit Mode (if it was in Compatibility Mode because the interrupted task was a legacy task).

Figure 23-1: 64-bit OS Environment

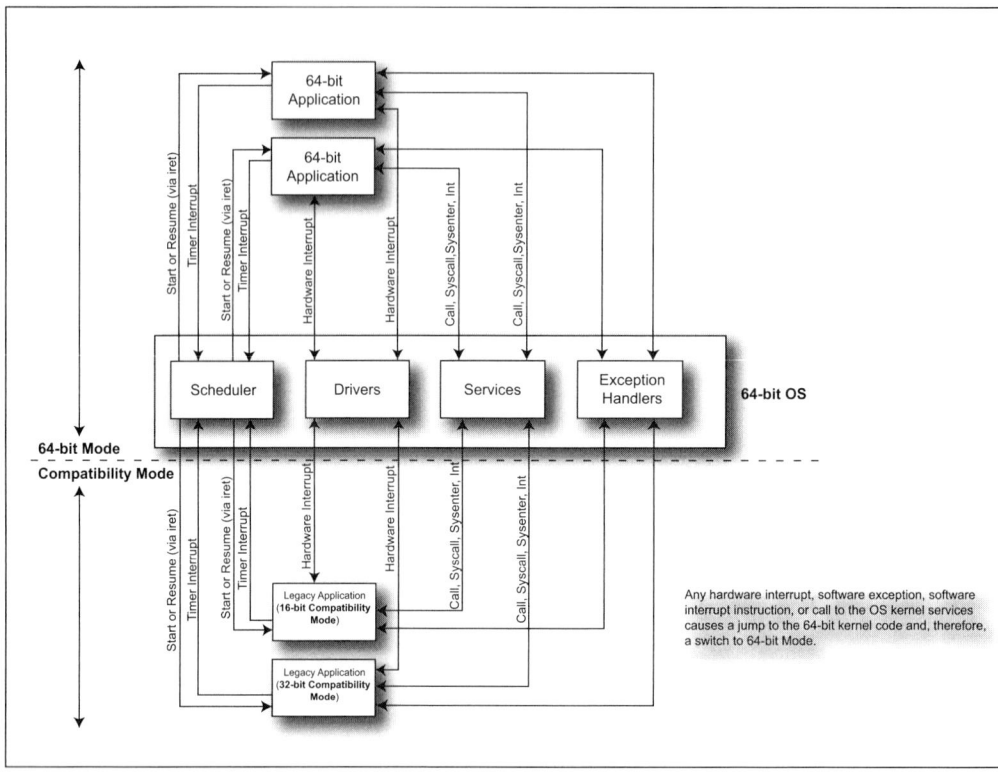

Mode Switching Overview

Booting Into Protected Mode

The basic boot sequence is as follows:

1. Immediately after system power-up, the reset signal remains asserted until the power supply voltages have achieved their required levels and stabilized.
2. The reset signal is deasserted to the processor. One of the logical processors is selected as the Bootstrap processor, begins operation in Real Mode and initiates code fetching from the boot ROM.

3. After completion of the POST (Power-On Self-Test) code, the ROM-based OS boot program is executed, reading the bootstrap loader from the mass storage device's boot sector into RAM and then executing it.

4. The bootstrap loader reads the OS loader program into RAM, jumps to its entry point and executes it.

5. Software sets up the necessary OS structures in memory (GDT, IDT, Page Directory and Page Tables, etc.) in preparation for entering legacy Protected Mode. It then switches the logical processor into Protected Mode.

6. The OS loader reads the OS kernel into memory and then jumps to and executes the OS initialization code.

A more detailed description can be found in "Transitioning to Protected Mode" on page 1113.

Initial Switch from IA-32 to IA-32e Mode

IA-32e Mode is entered by transitioning from legacy Protected Mode to Compatibility Mode. This transition is accomplished as follows (refer to Figure 23-2 on page 919; the numbered list that follows does *not* correlate to the numbered steps shown in the illustration):

1. Switch from Real Mode to legacy Protected Mode (either 16- or 32-bit Protected Mode). This topic is covered in "Transitioning to Protected Mode" on page 1113.
   — Note that there is no requirement that the 1st or 2nd generation address translation mechanism must be activated upon entering Protected Mode. Rather, upon entry to Protected Mode the programmer may choose to immediately set up the 3rd generation address translation tables in preparation for the switch to the Compatibility SubMode of IA-32e Mode.

2. Set up the 3rd generation address translation tables.

3. Point CR3 to the top-level address translation table (i.e., the PML4 directory). Since CR3 is only 32-bits wide in Protected Mode, the initial PML4 directory's physical base address must be in the lower 4GB.

4. Enable 2nd generation address translation by setting CR4[PAE] to 1. Note that although the PAE feature is now enabled, address translation itself has not yet been activated (CR0[PG] is still 0).

5. Set EFER[LME] = 1 as a prerequisite to enabling IA-32e Mode. Since the EFER register is an MSR, this is accomplished by executing the WRMSR instruction.

6. Set CR0[PG] = 1 to activate paging. Since the three prerequisites for IA-32e Mode activation have now been met, IA-32e Mode is also activated (and the

LMA—Long Mode Active—bit in the EFER register is set to one). The three prerequisites are:
— CR4[PAE] = 1. 2nd generation address translation enabled.
— EFER[LME] = 1. Long Mode (i.e., IA-32e Mode) enabled.
— CR0[PG] = 1. Paging enabled.
7. The L bit in the currently-active CS descriptor = 0, so the logical processor is not in 64-bit Mode. Rather, based on the state of the D bit in the currently active CS descriptor, the logical processor is now in either the 16- or 32-bit Compatibility SubMode of IA-32e Mode.
— D = 0. The logical processor is in 16-bit Compatibility Mode.
— D = 1. The logical processor is in 32-bit Compatibility Mode.

Up until this moment, address translation was disabled. The memory address that the MOV CR0 instruction was fetched from was therefore treated as a physical rather than a virtual address. Address translation is now enabled, however, so the memory code read to fetch the next instruction (i.e., the one immediately following the MOV CR0 instruction which enabled address translation) is treated as a virtual address and will be translated into a physical address. In order to fetch the instruction that immediately follows the MOV CR0 in physical memory, the address translation tables must therefore translate this virtual address into the identical physical memory address (a 1-for-1 translation; referred to as identity mapping).

A more detailed description may be found in "Transitioning to IA-32e Mode" on page 1139.

Figure 23-2: Switching to IA-32e Mode

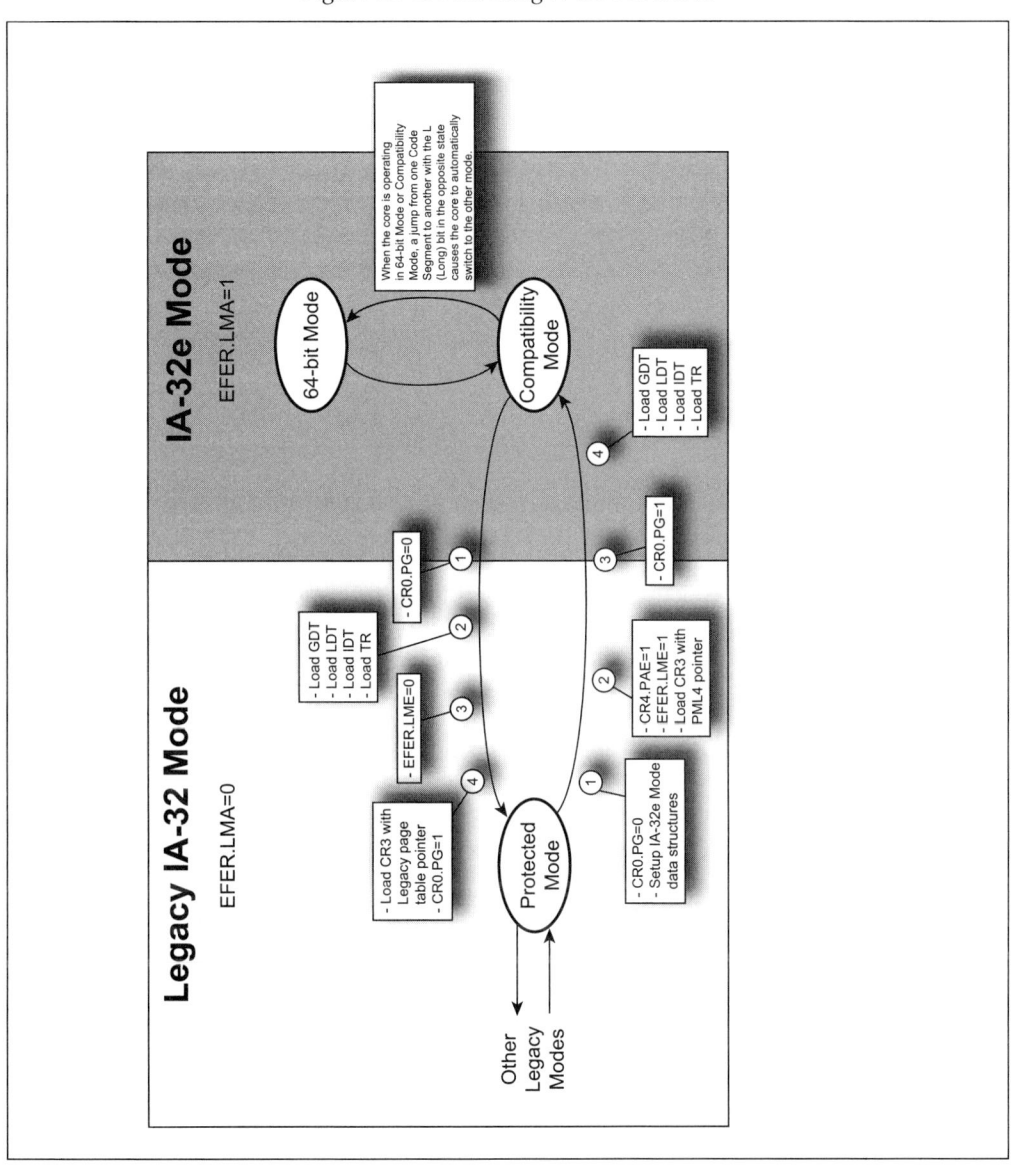

CS D and L Bits Control IA-32e SubMode Selection

As stated in the previous section, when the logical processor first enters IA-32e Mode, it is in either of two Compatibility SubModes:

- **16-bit Compatibility Mode**. If the code that handled the transition into IA-32e Mode is resident in a 16-bit code segment, then the logical processor is in 16-bit Compatibility Mode.
- **32-bit Compatibility Mode**. If the code that handled the transition into IA-32e Mode is resident in a 32-bit code segment, then the logical processor is in 32-bit Compatibility Mode.

The logical processor operates in 64-bit Mode whenever it is fetching code from a 64-bit code segment (as indicated by the L bit in the CS descriptor; see Figure 23-3 on page 922). When the logical processor is operating in Compatibility Mode the 64-bit features (including the 64-bit extended registers) are *not* accessible.

The logical processor automatically switches into 64-bit Mode when any of the following occurs:

- A far jump is executed to a location in a 64-bit code segment.
- An interrupt or an exception occurs. In IA-32e Mode, it is a rule that *all* interrupt and exception handlers must be implemented as 64-bit code.
- A far call is made to a location in a 64-bit code segment.
- A far jump or a far call selects a Call Gate descriptor in the GDT or an LDT.

In each of these cases, a new value is loaded into the CS register and the selected entry in the GDT or LDT contains a code segment descriptor wherein the L bit is set to one indicating that the target segment is a 64-bit code segment (see Figure 23-3 on page 922). This causes the logical processor to automatically switch into 64-bit Mode. Note that when a 64-bit code segment descriptor is selected, the logical processor ignores most of the information in the segment descriptors currently selected by the six segment registers. This is because in 64-bit Mode:

- By definition all segments start at virtual address 0 (except for the FS and GS segments; they can start at a non-zero virtual address).
- By definition all segments are 2^{64} locations in length.
- The code segment descriptor's AVL, R and A bit fields aren't used. Instead, that functionality is now supplied by the corresponding bits in the Page Directory Entry or Page Table Entry (PDE or PTE) selected by the virtual address during virtual-to-physical address translation (a detailed description can be found in "IA-32e Address Translation" on page 983).

- The logical processor will automatically switch back into Compatibility Mode whenever:
  - A far jump or a far call is made to a location in a code segment where the segment descriptor's L bit = 0.
  - The task scheduler executes an IRET to start or resume the execution of a 16- or 32-bit legacy Protected Mode task (see "Scheduler's Software-Based Task Switching Mechanism" on page 977 for more information).

The logical processor's operating mode is selected based on the state of the L and D bits in the current CS descriptor (Table 23-1 on page 921).

*Table 23-1: Target CS's **D** and **L** Bits Control Mode Selection*

L	D	Resulting Mode
0	0	**16-bit Compatibility Mode**. The default operand and address sizes are 16-bits and may be individually changed to 32-bits on an instruction basis by using the Operand Size and/or Address Size Override prefixes.
0	1	**32-bit Compatibility Mode**. The default operand and address sizes are 32-bits and may be individually changed to 16-bits on an instruction basis by using the Operand Size and/or Address Size Override prefixes.
1	0	**64-bit Mode**. The default operand size is 32-bits. The default address size is 64-bits: • Prefacing an instruction with the Operand Size Override prefix specifies an operand size of 16-bits. • When an instruction isn't prefaced with the Operand Size Override prefix and either doesn't include the REX prefix or does but the REX[W] bit = 0, then the operand size is 32-bits. • When an instruction is prefaced with the REX prefix and the REX[W] bit = 1, then the operand size is 64-bits. • Some instructions default to the 64-bit operand size. The default address size of 64-bits may be forced to 32-bits by prefacing an instruction with the Address Size Override prefix. 16-bit addresses are not supported in 64-bit Mode.
1	1	Reserved.

Figure 23-3: CS Descriptor Interpretation in 64-bit Mode

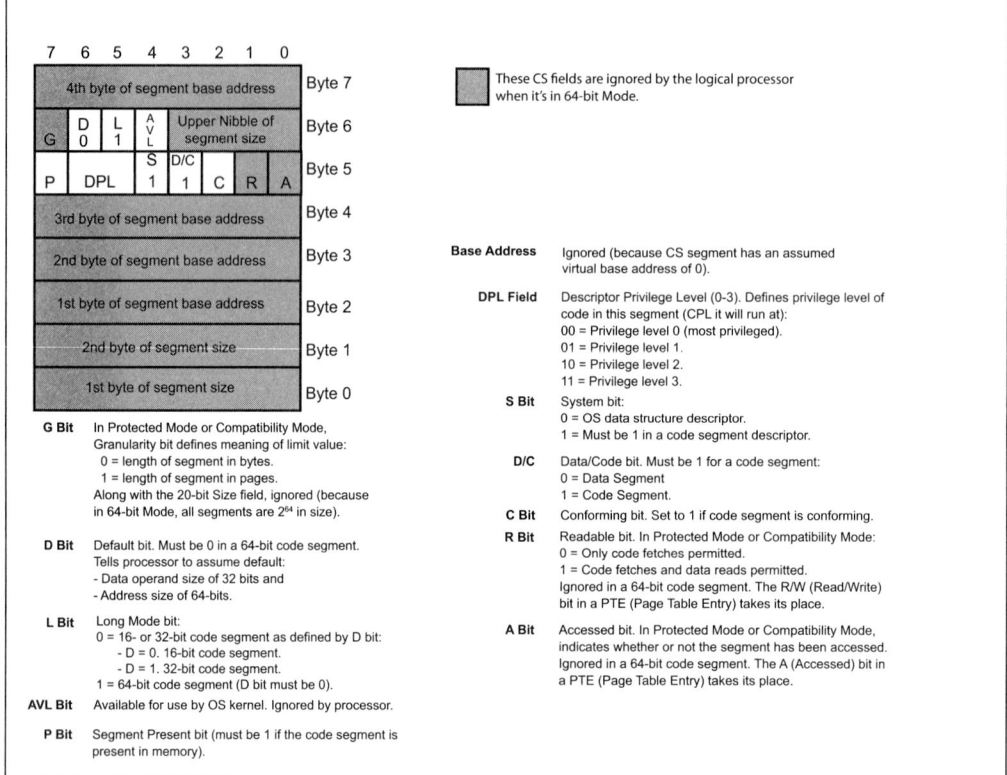

Old and New Applications Running Under a 64-bit OS

Once the logical processor has entered Compatibility Mode, the OS initialization code causes it to transition to 64-bit Mode by performing a far jump (i.e., a jump to a different code segment) to a code segment containing the 64-bit OS kernel code. When the logical processor detects the L bit set to one in the target code segment's descriptor, it switches into 64-bit Mode.

The IA-32e model supports 64-bit applications as well as 16- and 32-bit legacy applications running under the control of a 64-bit OS kernel.

Things You Lose In IA-32e Mode (hint: not much)

While many new features become available when the logical processor is operating in IA-32e Mode (especially the 64-bit SubMode), the following capabilities are no longer available:

- **Real Mode.**
- **VM86 Mode**.
- **Hardware-based task switching** is disabled.
- If executing on an AMD processor, the **SYSENTER and SYSEXIT** instructions are no longer available.
- If executing on an Intel processor, the **SYSCALL and SYSRET** instructions are only available in the 64-bit SubMode of IA-32e Mode and not in the Compatibility SubMode.
- **16- and 32-bit Call Gates** are not supported. All Call Gates in the GDT and LDTs must be implemented as 64-bit Call Gates that point to OS services in a 64-bit code segment.
- 3rd generation address translation is in effect (neither the 1st nor 2nd generation mechanisms are supported). Under this address translation model, pages can be either 4KB or 2MB in size. The **4MB page size is not available**.
- A number of instructions are not available when the logical processor is operating 64-bit Mode (e.g., BOUND, INTO, PUSHA, and POPA).
- The automatic parameter passing feature when using a Call Gate has been eliminated.
- Regarding segmentation while the logical processor is operating in Compatibility Mode, it is 100% compatible with Protected Mode operation. It is, however, disabled when the logical processor is in 64-bit Mode (for more information, see "Virtual Address in 64-bit Mode" on page 926).

Old Applications Live in an Expanded Universe

Old Legacy Universe = 4GB or 64GB

In a legacy 32-bit Protected Mode environment with Paging enabled, the 24- or 32-bit virtual memory address is submitted to the logical processor's virtual-to-physical address translation facility (i.e., the paging logic) and is translated into one of the following:

- Using the 1st generation, 386-style address translation facility (PAE Mode disabled), the 24- or 32-bit virtual address is translated into a 32-bit physical memory address directing the memory access to a location in the first 4GB of physical memory space.

- Using the 2nd generation address translation facility (PAE Mode enabled) introduced in the Pentium II Xeon processor, the 24- or 32-bit virtual address is translated into a 36-bit physical memory address directing the memory access to a location in the first 64GB of physical memory space.

From the perspective of legacy 16- and 32-bit applications running in the Compatibility SubMode of IA-32e Mode, the world looks unchanged from that of legacy Protected Mode. The virtual memory addresses generated by instructions are still either:

- **24-bits in size**. When a virtual memory address is generated by 286-compatible code, the 16-bit operand offset is added to the 24-bit segment virtual base address supplied from the 286-compatible segment descriptor yielding a 24-bit virtual memory address (16MB) which is expanded to a 64-bit virtual address by zero-filling bits 63:24).
- **32-bits in size** (32-bit segment base address + 32-bit offset) for a 32-bit application written to run on the 386 (or a later processor), yielding a 32-bit virtual address space (4GB).

IA-32e Universe Is At Least 16 Times Larger

In Compatibility Mode, however, the world is a far bigger place than the old application realizes.

- The 24- or 32-bit virtual address generated by an instruction or by the instruction fetch logic is expanded into a 64-bit virtual address (by zero-filling the upper 40-bits or 32-bits).
- Using the 3rd generation address translation facility introduced in IA-32e Mode, theoretically a 48-bit virtual address could be translated into a 48-bit physical memory address.
  - Note, however, that not all current-day implementations of the IA-32e address translation facility are capable of translating the lower 48-bits of the 64-bit virtual address into a 48-bit physical memory address. Some are limited to translating the 48-bit virtual address into a 40- or 41-bit physical memory address.

Today's reality is that a legacy 16- or 32-bit application's memory accesses can be redirected (by the address translation facility) to locations anywhere in a 1TB physical memory space, *a space **sixteen times bigger** than that available in legacy Protected Mode*.

In addition, the 64-bit OS kernel and any 64-bit applications receive the full benefit of the new features that are only available when the logical processor is operating in 64-bit Mode. For a complete description of the expanded facilities, see:

- "64-bit Register Overview" on page 1023.
- "64-bit Operands and Addressing" on page 1041.
- "64-bit Odds and Ends" on page 1075.

Virtual Memory Addressing in IA-32e Mode

Virtual Address in Compatibility Mode

Segmentation is active in Compatibility Mode, so the virtual address is formed by adding the operand offset to the segment base address. There are two possible cases (see Table 23-2 on page 925).

Table 23-2: Virtual Address Calculation in Compatibility Mode

SubMode	Virtual Address Calculation
16-bit Compatibility Mode	The 16-bit offset is added to the 24-bit segment base address to form a 24-bit virtual memory address (in a 16MB virtual address space). The address is extended to a 64-bit virtual address in canonical form (see "Canonical Address" on page 1063): • Address bits 24 through the most-significant implemented bit (processor-design specific) are zero-filled. • The state of the most-significant implemented address bit (0 in this case) is duplicated through bit 63.
32-bit Compatibility Mode	The 32-bit offset is added to the 32-bit segment base address to form a 32-bit virtual memory address (in a 4GB virtual address space). The address is extended to a 64 bit virtual address in canonical form: • Address bits 32 through the most-significant implemented bit (processor-design specific) are zero-filled. • The state of the most-significant implemented address bit (0 in this case) is duplicated through bit 63.

Virtual Address in 64-bit Mode

Segmentation is disabled when the logical processor is operating in 64-bit Mode. Since segments by definition start at virtual address 0, the segment base address field in the respective segment descriptor is ignored and the 64-bit operand offset therefore represents the 64-bit virtual address (in canonical form). As shown in Table 23-3 on page 926, accesses within the FS or GS data segments are an exception.

Table 23-3: Virtual Address Calculation in 64-bit Mode

Operation	Virtual Address Calculation
Code fetch	The base address of the code segment is zero and the 64-bit virtual address (in canonical form) consists of the contents of the 64-bit RIP register.
DS/ES access	The base address of the data segment is zero and the 64-bit virtual address (in canonical form) consists of the contents of the 64-bit operand offset.
Stack access	The base address of the stack segment is zero and the 64-bit virtual address (in canonical form) consists of the contents of the 64-bit RSP register.
FS/GS access	If an instruction is prefaced by the FS or GS Segment Override prefix, the specified 64-bit operand offset is added to the 64-bit segment base address to form the 64-bit virtual address (in canonical form). The programmer may set the FS and/or GS data segment base address to a non-zero, 64-bit value by executing a WRMSR to the FS_Base or GS_Base MSR registers.

In Compatibility Mode, Segmentation Is Operative

To ensure backward-compatibility, the logical processor's segmentation logic remains fully-operational (and backward-compatible with Protected Mode) when the logical processor is in Compatibility Mode.

In 64-bit Mode, Hardware-Enforced Flat Model

General

Because virtually no modern OSs make use of the segmented memory model, switching a logical processor into 64-bit Mode causes it to enforce the Flat Memory Model by largely disabling the segmented memory logic (in a very limited sense, CS, FS, and GS segments are an exception). It should be noted, however, that anytime the 64-bit OS kernel causes the logical processor to jump to a 16- or 32-bit legacy code segment (one in which the L bit = 0), the segmentation logic is immediately reenabled in order to maintain backward-compatibility.

New Segment Selector Causes Descriptor Read

The only segment registers actively used in 64-bit Mode are:

- The CS register (and only a subset of the CS descriptor information is actually used).
- The FS and GS registers. See Table 23-3 on page 926.

Even so, loading a new selector value into *any* segment register while the logical processor is in 64-bit Mode still causes it to load all of the selected segment descriptor's elements into the invisible part of the respective segment register. This is necessary because the 64-bit OS may be initializing the segment registers in preparation for the initiation or resumption of a legacy 16- or 32-bit application.

Segment Register Usage in 64-bit Mode

Generally speaking, the logical processor exhibits the following behavior when it is in 64-bit Mode:

- **DS, ES and SS segments** (see Figure 23-4 on page 933). Descriptor contents are ignored and the segment is assumed to have the following characteristics:
  — Its virtual base address is 0.
  — Its virtual length = 2^{64} locations.
- **FS and GS segments** (see Figure 23-5 on page 934). When the FS or GS register is loaded with a 16-bit selector, the logical processor loads the selected

descriptor into the invisible portion of the respective segment register. With the exception of the 32-bit segment base address, however, the remainder of the descriptor is ignored. Privilege level 0 code may write a full 64-bit virtual base address into the base address field in the invisible portion of the register by executing the WRMSR instruction to the FS_Base or GS_Base MSR.

- **CS segment** (see Figure 23-3 on page 922). Most of the descriptor contents are ignored and the segment is assumed to have the following characteristics:
  - Its virtual base address is 0.
  - Its virtual length = 2^{64} locations.
  - It is read-only.
  - The logical processor uses the unshaded bit fields in Figure 23-3 on page 922.

Table 23-4 on page 929 summarizes the operation of the six segment registers when the logical processor is operating in 64-bit Mode.

Table 23-4: Segment Register Operation in 64-bit Mode

Segment	Description

CS	Refer to Figure 23-3 on page 922. When a new 16-bit descriptor selector value is loaded into the CS register in 64-bit Mode, the logical processor treats the attributes obtained from the selected descriptor as follows:
	• **Ignored Fields**:
	  – The code **segment base address** is ignored and a hardware-enforced base address of 0 is assumed.
	  – The code **segment size** (i.e., the size field and the Granularity bit) is ignored (because all segments are assumed to be 2^{64} bytes in size). On a code fetch, the Paging logic validates that a 64-bit virtual address is within the bounds of the current code segment when it translates the virtual address into a physical memory address.
	  – The **Readable (R) and Accessed (A) bits** are ignored. Their functionality is, instead, defined by the corresponding attribute bits in Page Directory and Page Table Entries (PDEs and PTEs).
	• **Effective Fields**:
	  – The segment Present bit (P) must be a one.
	  – The System (S) bit must = 1 and the D/C (Data or Code) bit must = 1 indicating that this is, in fact, a code segment descriptor.
	  – The Conforming bit (C) indicates whether this a Conforming or Non-Conforming code segment (refer to "Conforming and Non-Conforming Code Segments" on page 438).
	  – The L bit = 1 (indicating this is a 64-bit code segment, rather than a 16- or 32-bit code segment).
	  – The D bit must = 0, selecting default operand and address sizes of 32- and 64-bits, respectively.
	  – The DPL (Descriptor Privilege Level) field indicates the privilege level of the code within the current code segment program.
	When performing a code memory access using the virtual address in the 64-bit RIP register, the logical processor validates that the address is in canonical form (see "Canonical Address" on page 1063).

Table 23-4: Segment Register Operation in 64-bit Mode (Continued)

Segment	Description
DS ES SS	Figure 23-4 on page 933 illustrates the format of a data segment descriptor and its interpretation when the logical processor is in 64-bit Mode. Since a Stack segment is nothing more than a read/writable data segment, there is no such thing as a stack segment descriptor per se. • **Only one attribute field is validated**: – Although loading a new selector value into any of these segment registers causes the logical processor to load the selected segment descriptor's attributes into the invisible part of the respective segment register, the only one validated is the **segment P bit** (it must be a one, indicating that a valid segment descriptor was selected). • **Ignored Fields**: – The data **segment base address** is ignored and a hardware-enforced base address of 0 is assumed. – The data **segment size** (i.e., the size field and the Granularity bit) is ignored (because all segments are assumed to be 2^{64} bytes in size). The Paging logic validates that a 64-bit virtual address is within the domain of the currently-running program when it translates the virtual address into a physical memory address. – The **Big (Big stack) bit** is ignored (because the stack is assumed to start at virtual address 0 and the 64-bit RSP stack pointer is used to address stack locations). – The **DPL** (Descriptor Privilege Level) field is ignored (and the User/Supervisor bit in the Page Directory Entry or Page Table Entry selected by the virtual address is checked instead). – The **S** (System segment), **C/D** (Code or Data), and **W** (Writable) bits are ignored (and the R/W bit in the Page Directory Entry or Page Table Entry selected by the virtual address is checked instead). – The **E** (Expand down stack) bit is ignored (because Expand Down stacks [see "Expand-Down Stack" on page 487] are not supported in 64-bit Mode). – The **A** (Accessed) bit is ignored (and the Dirty and Accessed bits in the Page Directory or Page Table Entry selected by the virtual address are used instead). When performing a memory data access using the virtual address generated by instruction execution, the logical processor validates that the address is in canonical form (see "Canonical Address" on page 1063) and generates a GP exception if it isn't.

Table 23-4: Segment Register Operation in 64-bit Mode (Continued)

Segment	Description
FS GS	**Like the DS, ES, or SS segment registers**, when a new selector value is loaded into either of these segment registers in 64-bit Mode, the logical processor loads the selected segment descriptor's attributes into the invisible part of the respective segment register. The only one it validates, however, is the segment Present (P) bit. **Unlike the DS, ES, and SS registers** (where hardware assumes a segment base address of 0), however, the logical processor's segmentation logic *does* use the segment's base address field in computing a virtual memory address (i.e., segment base + offset = virtual address). It should be noted, though, that when a new selector value is loaded into either of these registers, only a 32-bit segment base address is loaded into the segment register's invisible part (because a data segment descriptor only contains a 32-bit base address field; see Figure 23-5 on page 934). 　– In this case, the upper 32-bits of the 64-bit base address field in the invisible portion of the segment register are cleared to 0. Software running at privilege level 0 can write a 64-bit base address (which must be in Canonical form; see "Canonical Address" on page 1063) directly into the base address field of the invisible portion of the FS or GS segment register by executing a WRMSR (Write MSR) instruction to one of the following two MSR (Model-Specific) registers: • The FS_Base MSR address is C000_0100h. • The GS_Base MSR address is C000_0101h. In 64-bit Mode, when the new SWAPGS instruction (see "SwapGS Instruction" on page 1076) is executed it causes the logical processor to swap the 64-bit base address currently residing in the invisible part of the GS register with the 64-bit base address currently in the KernelGSbase MSR (which acts as a temporary save register to save the GS base address while kernel code is executing). The kernel code can then access information stored in the GS data segment and, when it's done, can execute the SWAPGS instruction once again to restore the original GS base address.

Table 23-4: Segment Register Operation in 64-bit Mode (Continued)

Segment	Description
	Segment Overrides in 64-bit Mode: The topic of segment overrides is covered in "Segment Override Prefix" on page 220. Segment override prefix usage has the following characteristics in 64-bit Mode: • In 64-bit Mode, the CS, DS, ES, SS segment overrides are ignored (because they all start at 0). • The FS and GS prefixes are valid in 64-bit Mode. As an example: – mov rax, gs:[offset] loads the qword from the address formed by GS base + the specified 64-bit offset into the RAX register. • In 64-bit Mode, memory accesses using the FS or GS Segment Overrides are not checked for a runtime limit nor are they subjected to attribute-checking. Instead, these checks are performed by the address translation logic.

Figure 23-4: DS/ES/SS Segment Descriptor Interpretation in 64-bit Mode

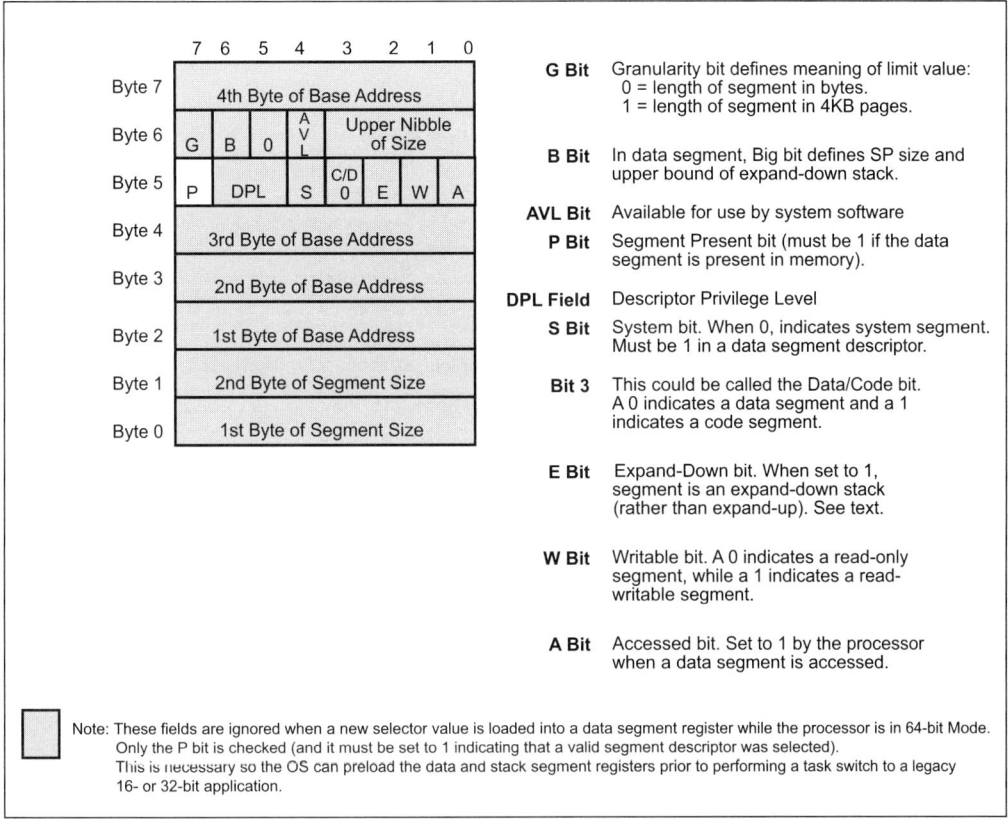

G Bit   Granularity bit defines meaning of limit value:
0 = length of segment in bytes.
1 = length of segment in 4KB pages.

B Bit   In data segment, Big bit defines SP size and upper bound of expand-down stack.

AVL Bit   Available for use by system software

P Bit   Segment Present bit (must be 1 if the data segment is present in memory).

DPL Field   Descriptor Privilege Level

S Bit   System bit. When 0, indicates system segment. Must be 1 in a data segment descriptor.

Bit 3   This could be called the Data/Code bit. A 0 indicates a data segment and a 1 indicates a code segment.

E Bit   Expand-Down bit. When set to 1, segment is an expand-down stack (rather than expand-up). See text.

W Bit   Writable bit. A 0 indicates a read-only segment, while a 1 indicates a read-writable segment.

A Bit   Accessed bit. Set to 1 by the processor when a data segment is accessed.

Note: These fields are ignored when a new selector value is loaded into a data segment register while the processor is in 64-bit Mode. Only the P bit is checked (and it must be set to 1 indicating that a valid segment descriptor was selected). This is necessary so the OS can preload the data and stack segment registers prior to performing a task switch to a legacy 16- or 32-bit application.

Figure 23-5: FS/GS Segment Descriptor Interpretation in 64-bit Mode

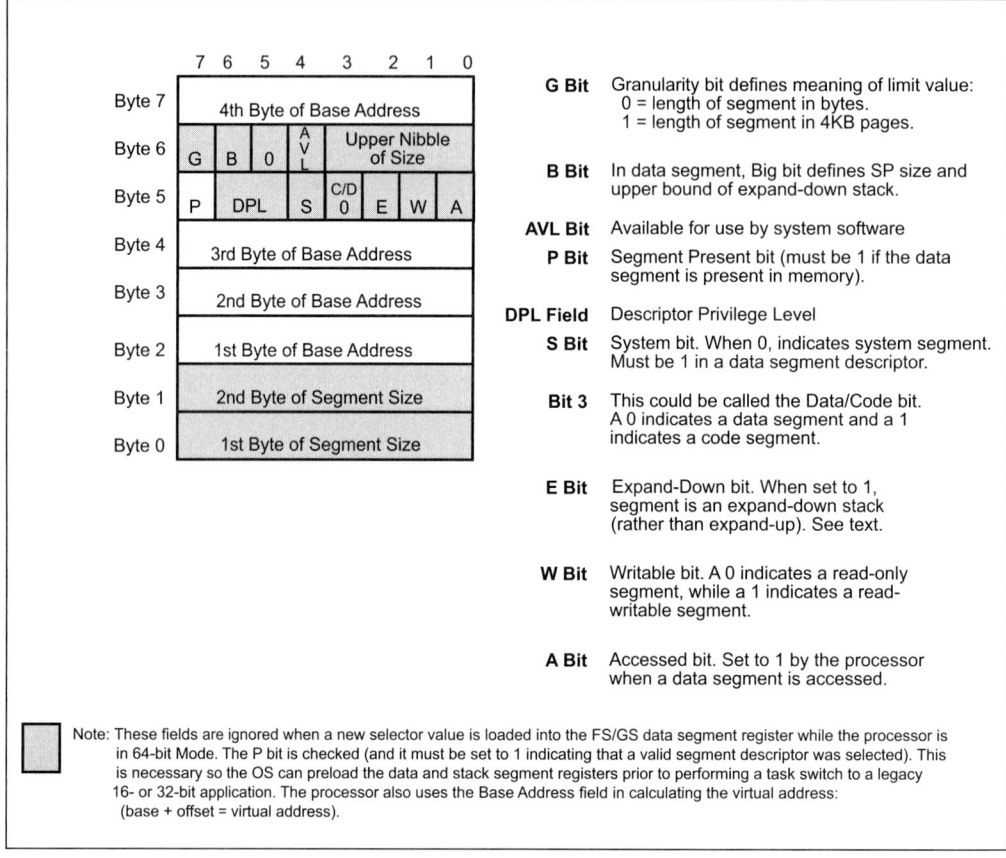

Note: These fields are ignored when a new selector value is loaded into the FS/GS data segment register while the processor is in 64-bit Mode. The P bit is checked (and it must be set to 1 indicating that a valid segment descriptor was selected). This is necessary so the OS can preload the data and stack segment registers prior to performing a task switch to a legacy 16- or 32-bit application. The processor also uses the Base Address field in calculating the virtual address: (base + offset = virtual address).

64-bit Mode: No Limit Checking = No Limits?

As highlighted earlier, when in 64-bit Mode the logical processor assumes that the CS, DS, ES, and SS segments start at virtual address 0 and that each of them are 2^{64} in length. Although the FS and GS segments may have a non-zero base address, they also have a length of 2^{64} locations.

In Protected Mode and Compatibility Mode, whenever a memory access is initiated the logical processor checks to ensure that the addressed location falls within the bounds of the target segment. Such a check is necessary to prevent the currently-running program from accessing areas of memory that don't belong to it. This check is not performed in 64-bit Mode, however, raising the question: how does the logical processor detect an attempt to access memory outside of the task's domain?

The answer: the address translation services. When the virtual memory access is submitted to the paging logic for translation, the logical processor uses it to perform a lookup in the task's address translation tables. If the address selects a PTE (Page Table Entry) wherein the Page Present bit = 0, it results in a Page Fault exception and the Page Fault exception handler is invoked. The handler then examines the virtual address (captured in CR2) to determine what action to take. There are two possibilities:

- **Case 1: Good address**. If it determines that the virtual address *is* within the bounds of the virtual address range assigned to the task, it will load the target page from disk into an available page in memory, fill in the physical start address in the PTE and set the PTE's Page Present bit to one, and then restart the memory access that caused the fault. The address translation will then succeed and the access will complete successfully.
- **Case 2: Bad address**. If, on the other hand, it determines that the virtual address is *not* within the bounds of the virtual address range assigned to the task, the handler will alert the kernel that an illegal access was attempted and the task will more than likely be aborted.

Table Limit Checks Are Performed

Although the logical processor does not perform a limit check when accesses are performed in 64-bit Mode, it does check to ensure that the limits of the special kernel tables—GDT, LDT, IDT and TSS—are not exceeded.

Stack Management

Stack Management in Compatibility Mode

In Compatibility Mode, stack accesses work precisely the same as they do in Protected Mode (see "Expand-Up Stack" on page 485). When a push is executed:

1. The logical processor decrements ESP by two or four (depending on whether it is in 16- or 32-bit Compatibility Mode).

2. It performs a limit check to ensure that the new ESP value (ESP -2, or ESP - 4) doesn't exceed the size of the stack specified in the descriptor.

3. It also checks to ensure that decrementing ESP by two or four doesn't decrement ESP below offset 00000000h in the stack. If this were the case, a Stack Exception (due to a stack underflow) would be generated.

4. The virtual address is formed by adding the current offset in the ESP register (ESP - 2, or ESP - 4) to the stack segment's base address.

5. The two or four bytes from the specified register are written into the two or four ascending virtual memory locations starting at ESP - 2 or ESP - 4.

When a pop is executed:

1. It performs a limit check to ensure that the ESP value (plus the size of the access—2 or 4 bytes) doesn't exceed the size of the stack specified in the descriptor.

2. The logical processor performs a two or four byte read from memory starting at the location currently pointed to by ESP + the stack segment's base address.

3. The two or four bytes from memory locations ESP through ESP + 2 or ESP + 4 are read, with the byte from location ESP (the lower location) placed in the LSB of the target register (e.g., BL) and the byte from location ESP + 2 or ESP + 4 placed in the MSB of the register.

4. The logical processor then increments ESP by two or four.

Stack Management in 64-bit Mode

Push/Pop Size is 64-bits. In 64-bit Mode, the default operation size for a push or pop operation is 64-bits (rather than 16- or 32-bits). RSP is decremented by eight for a push and incremented by eight for a pop. Prefacing a push or pop with the Operand Size Override prefix changes the operand size to 16-bits (but the reader should note that this may result in RSP not being aligned on an 8-byte address boundary).

Address Translation Replaces Limit Checking. As stated earlier, no stack limit checking is performed (for an underflow or an overflow) when the logical processor is in 64-bit Mode. Once again, it's the address translation logic that fills the void. When a push is executed:

1. The logical processor decrements the 64-bit RSP register by eight.

2. Since the flat model is in force, the stack segment base address is assumed to be 0. Adding the current contents of the RSP register (RSP - 8) to a segment base address of 0 yields the same value. This being the case, in 64-bit Mode the logical processor uses RSP as the virtual address.

3. The eight bytes from the specified register are written into the eight ascending virtual memory locations starting at RSP - 8.

4. The 64-bit virtual address is submitted to the paging logic for translation and the logical processor uses it to perform a lookup in the task's address translation tables. There are two possibilities:

   – **Good Translation**. In this case, the virtual address selects a valid PTE, the virtual address is successfully translated into a physical address, and the stack access completes successfully.

   – **Translation fails**. In this case, the virtual address selects an invalid PTE and the Page Fault exception handler is invoked. The handler then examines the offending virtual address (captured in CR2) to determine what action to take. There are two possibilities:

      – **Address is within the stack's assigned virtual address range, but a physical page has not yet been assigned**. In this case, it will locate a free page in memory, allocate it to the task's stack, fill in the physical start address in the PTE, set the PTE's Page Present bit to one, and then restart the stack access that caused the fault. The address translation and the access will then complete successfully.

      – **Address lies outside of the stack's assigned virtual address range**. In this case, there are two possibilities:

         – **Virtual address is available**. The handler can extend the virtual address range assigned to the stack by allocating one or more pages for stack use, fill in the appropriate PTEs to point to them, and then restart the stack access that caused the fault. The address translation the access will then complete successfully.

         – **Virtual address is unavailable**. If the necessary virtual address is already in use (i.e., it has already been assigned to the code or data associated with this task or to another task), then the kernel would likely choose to abort the task.

Segment Override Prefixes Other Than FS/GS Are Ignored

Since all segments other than FS and GS have a base address of 0, the CS/DS/ES/SS Segment Override prefixes are ignored if they are encountered when executing an instruction from a 64-bit code segment. If the FS or GS override is used, however, that segment's base address is used to calculate the virtual address (Base Address + offset = virtual address).

Protection Provided by Paging

Since the attributes in a segment descriptor are ignored when the logical processor is in 64-bit Mode, it may seem that protection has been lost. Don't forget, however, that the virtual address is submitted to the address translation logic for a lookup in the translation tables associated with the current task and the attribute bits in the selected table entries are used to perform the protection checks (see "IA-32e Address Translation" on page 983 for a detailed description).

Segment Registers Preserved On Mode Switch

Switching between 64-bit Mode and Compatibility Mode alters neither the 16-bit selector values in the segment registers nor the descriptor attributes cached in the invisible portions of them. There are two exceptions:

*   The CS register will be altered by the far jump or IRET.
*   The SS register may be changed due to a privilege level change on a Call, an interrupt, or an exception.

64-bit Instruction Pointer

Instruction Fetching

The virtual address in the Instruction Pointer register is used to fetch the next instruction to be executed. Which version of the register is used is dependent on the current mode of operation (see Figure 23-6 on page 939 and Table 23-5 on page 938).

Table 23-5: Instruction Pointer Usage

Mode	Version of Instruction Pointer Register Used
Real Mode	16-bit IP register.
System Management Mode	
VM86 Mode	

Table 23-5: Instruction Pointer Usage (Continued)

Mode	Version of Instruction Pointer Register Used
Protected Mode Compatibility Mode	There are two cases: • **286 Protected Mode**. When the logical processor is fetching code from a 286-compliant code segment, the 16-bit IP register is used. • **32-bit Protected Mode**. When the logical processor is fetching code from a 32-bit code segment, the 32-bit EIP register is used.
64-bit Mode	64-bit RIP register.

RIP-Relative Data Accesses

A new data operand memory addressing mode is available in 64-bit Mode. It permits the programmer to specify the address of a memory-based data operand as a signed 32-bit offset from the current value in the RIP register (i.e., from the position of the current instruction).

Figure 23-6: Instruction Pointer Register

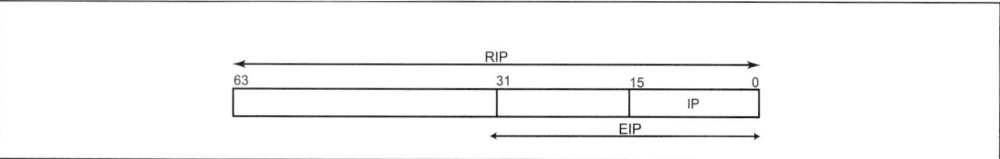

Changes To Kernel-Related Registers and Structures

Address Translation Mechanism

Basic Description

The 3rd generation virtual-to-physical address translation mechanism was introduced with the advent of IA-32e Mode and is required while in this mode.

- **1st Generation**. The 1st generation mechanism uses a two-level lookup and translates a 32-bit virtual address into a 32-bit physical address.
- **2nd Generation**. The 2nd generation mechanism (PAE mode) uses a three-level lookup and translates a 32-bit virtual address into a 36-bit physical address.
- **3rd Generation**. The 3rd generation mechanism uses a four-level lookup capable of translating a 48-bit virtual address into a 48-bit physical address (current implementations support translating the 48-bit virtual address into a 40-, 41-, or 48-bit physical address).

Top-Level Directory Placement

In all of the address translation mechanisms, the programmer creates the address translation tables in memory and then programs CR3 with the physical base address of the top-level directory. Prior to the initial switch into IA-32e Mode, CR3 is programmed while the logical processor is still in Protected Mode and CR3 is therefore still only 32-bits wide. This means that the initial top-level directory (the PML4 table) must reside in the lower 4GB of physical memory. Once the switch into IA-32e Mode has been accomplished, however, CR3 is expanded to 64-bits and the top-level directory may therefore be located anywhere within the physical memory space addressable by the logical processor.

Detailed Description

For a detailed description of the 3rd generation address translation mechanism, refer to "IA-32e Address Translation" on page 983.

GDT/LDT Descriptor Changes

Table 23-6 on page 941 and Table 23-7 on page 943 define the changes to the descriptors found in the GDT and the LDT when the logical processor is operating in IA-32e Mode.

Table 23-6: IA-32e GDT/LDT Descriptor Changes

Descriptor Type	Change
Task Gate	Since the hardware-based task switching mechanism is not supported in IA-32e Mode, the selection of Task Gate descriptors in the GDT or LDT is forbidden. If one is selected by a far jump or a far call, it results in a GP exception.
Call Gate	See Figure 23-7 on page 945. Call Gate descriptors are used to call OS services. Since the goal is a 64-bit OS kernel, 16- and 32-bit Call Gate descriptors are not allowed in the GDT or LDT when the logical processor is operating in IA-32e Mode. All Call Gate descriptors are now 16-bytes (rather than 8-bytes) in length and specify: • A 64-bit code segment (targeting a 16- or 32-bit code segment results in a GP exception). • The 64-bit virtual address of the kernel procedure entry point. This permits the kernel procedure to be located anywhere in the logical processor's addressable address space. Note: The base address of the target code segment (in the selected CS descriptor) is ignored (because the hardware-enforced flat model assumes a segment base address of 0).
LDT descriptor	See Figure 23-8 on page 946. In IA-32e Mode, LDT descriptors have been expanded from 8- to 16-bytes in length to accommodate a 64-bit LDT base address. This permits the LDT to be located anywhere in the logical processor's addressable address space.
TSS descriptor	See Figure 23-9 on page 947. In IA-32e Mode, TSS descriptors have been expanded from 8- to 16-bytes in length to accommodate a 64-bit TSS base address. This permits the TSS data structure to be located anywhere in the logical processor's addressable address space.

Table 23-6: IA-32e GDT/LDT Descriptor Changes (Continued)

Descriptor Type	Change

CS descriptor	• **In Compatibility Mode**: all CS descriptor fields have the same meaning as they do in legacy Protected Mode (see Figure 23-3 on page 922).
	• **In 64-bit Mode**:
	  – CS descriptors are still 8-bytes in length. They are not expanded to 16-bytes to accommodate a 64-bit base address because the hardware-enforced flat model assumes a segment base address of 0.
	  – Figure 23-3 on page 922 illustrates that a number of the CS descriptor fields are ignored by hardware when the logical processor is operating in 64-bit Mode.

Data Segment descriptors	• **In Compatibility Mode**: all data segment descriptor fields are interpreted just as they are in legacy Protected Mode (see Figure 15-3 on page 484).
	• **In 64-bit Mode**:
	  – Data segment descriptors are still 8-bytes in length. They are not expanded to 16-bytes to accommodate a 64-bit base address because the hardware-enforced flat model assumes a segment base address of 0.
	  – All but one of the descriptor fields (the Present bit) are ignored by hardware when the logical processor is operating in 64-bit Mode.
	It should be noted that, although the above statements are also true for the FS and GS data segments, the OS *can* specify a non-zero 64-bit segment base address for these segments by performing a WRMSR to the FS_Base or GS_ Base MSR registers.

Table 23-6: IA-32e GDT/LDT Descriptor Changes (Continued)

Descriptor Type	Change

SS descriptor	In both Protected Mode and IA-32e Mode there is no such thing as a stack segment descriptor per se. Rather, the stack segment is described by a data segment descriptor that defines a segment as read/writable.
	• **In Compatibility Mode**: the stack segment descriptor is interpreted just as it is in Protected Mode.
	• **In 64-bit Mode**:
	  – The stack segment descriptor is still 8-bytes in length. It is not expanded to 16-bytes to accommodate a 64-bit base address because the hardware-enforced flat model assumes a segment base address of 0.
	  – Figure 23-4 on page 933 illustrates that all but one of the descriptor fields (the Present bit) are ignored by hardware when the logical processor is operating in 64-bit Mode.

Table 23-7: GDT/LDT Descriptor Types in Protected Mode and IA-32e Mode

Type Field	Protected Mode (all 8-bytes in size)	IA-32e Mode (all 16-bytes in size)
0000b	Reserved (illegal).	Reserved (illegal).
0001b	16-bit, 286-compliant TSS descriptor (not busy).	Reserved (illegal).
0010b	LDT descriptor.	IA-32e LDT descriptor.
0011b	16-bit, 286-compliant TSS descriptor (busy).	Reserved (illegal).
0100b	16-bit, 286-compliant Call Gate descriptor.	Reserved (illegal).
0101b	Task Gate descriptor.	Reserved (illegal).
0110b	16-bit, 286-compliant Interrupt Gate descriptor.	Reserved (illegal).

Table 23-7: GDT/LDT Descriptor Types in Protected Mode and IA-32e Mode (Continued)

Type Field	Protected Mode (all 8-bytes in size)	IA-32e Mode (all 16-bytes in size)
0111b	16-bit, 286-compliant Trap Gate descriptor.	Reserved (illegal).
1000b	Reserved (illegal).	Reserved (illegal).
1001b	32-bit TSS descriptor (not busy).	IA-32e IA-32e TSS descriptor (not busy).
1010b	Reserved (illegal).	Reserved (illegal).
1011b	32-bit TSS descriptor (busy).	IA-32e TSS descriptor (busy).
1100b	32-bit Call Gate descriptor.	IA-32e Call Gate descriptor.
1101b	Reserved (illegal).	Reserved (illegal).
1110b	32-bit Interrupt Gate descriptor.	IA-32e Interrupt Gate descriptor.
1111b	32-bit Trap Gate descriptor.	IA-32e Trap Gate descriptor.

Figure 23-7: IA-32e Mode Call Gate Descriptor

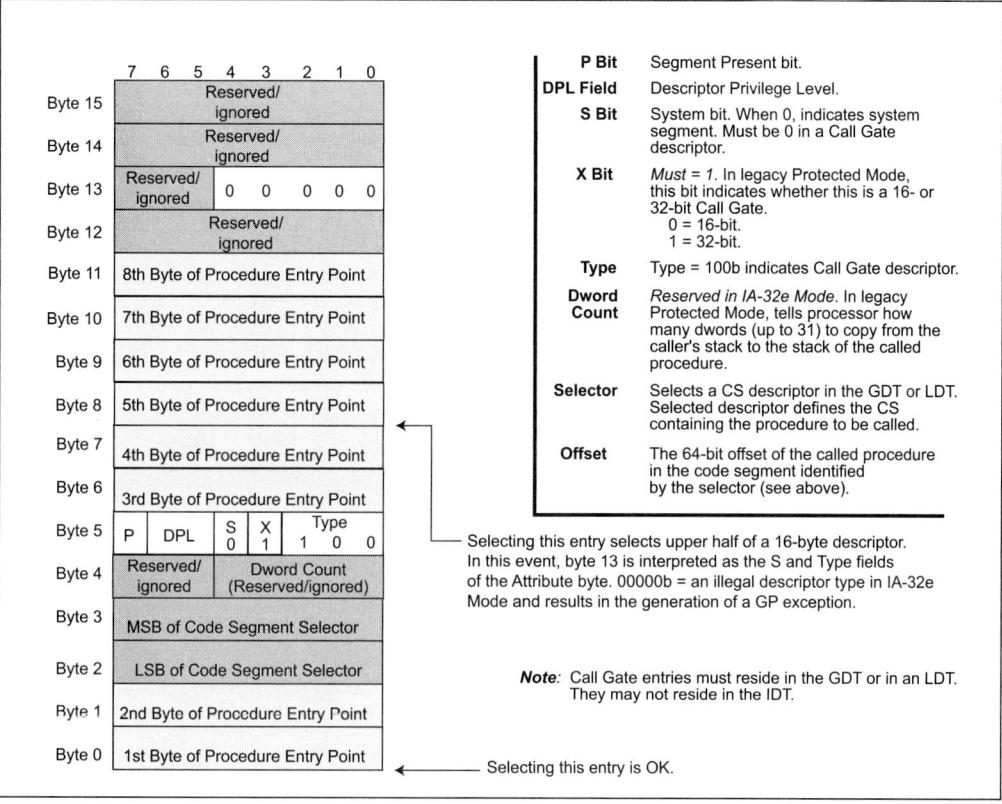

	7 6 5 4 3 2 1 0		
Byte 15	Reserved/ignored		
Byte 14	Reserved/ignored		
Byte 13	Reserved/ignored	0 0 0 0 0	
Byte 12	Reserved/ignored		
Byte 11	8th Byte of Procedure Entry Point		
Byte 10	7th Byte of Procedure Entry Point		
Byte 9	6th Byte of Procedure Entry Point		
Byte 8	5th Byte of Procedure Entry Point		
Byte 7	4th Byte of Procedure Entry Point		
Byte 6	3rd Byte of Procedure Entry Point		
Byte 5	P DPL S X Type		
Byte 4	Reserved/ignored Dword Count (Reserved/ignored)		
Byte 3	MSB of Code Segment Selector		
Byte 2	LSB of Code Segment Selector		
Byte 1	2nd Byte of Procedure Entry Point		
Byte 0	1st Byte of Procedure Entry Point		

P Bit	Segment Present bit.
DPL Field	Descriptor Privilege Level.
S Bit	System bit. When 0, indicates system segment. Must be 0 in a Call Gate descriptor.
X Bit	*Must = 1.* In legacy Protected Mode, this bit indicates whether this is a 16- or 32-bit Call Gate. 0 = 16-bit. 1 = 32-bit.
Type	Type = 100b indicates Call Gate descriptor.
Dword Count	*Reserved in IA-32e Mode.* In legacy Protected Mode, tells processor how many dwords (up to 31) to copy from the caller's stack to the stack of the called procedure.
Selector	Selects a CS descriptor in the GDT or LDT. Selected descriptor defines the CS containing the procedure to be called.
Offset	The 64-bit offset of the called procedure in the code segment identified by the selector (see above).

Selecting this entry selects upper half of a 16-byte descriptor. In this event, byte 13 is interpreted as the S and Type fields of the Attribute byte. 00000b = an illegal descriptor type in IA-32e Mode and results in the generation of a GP exception.

Note: Call Gate entries must reside in the GDT or in an LDT. They may not reside in the IDT.

Selecting this entry is OK.

Figure 23-8: LDT Descriptor in IA-32e Mode

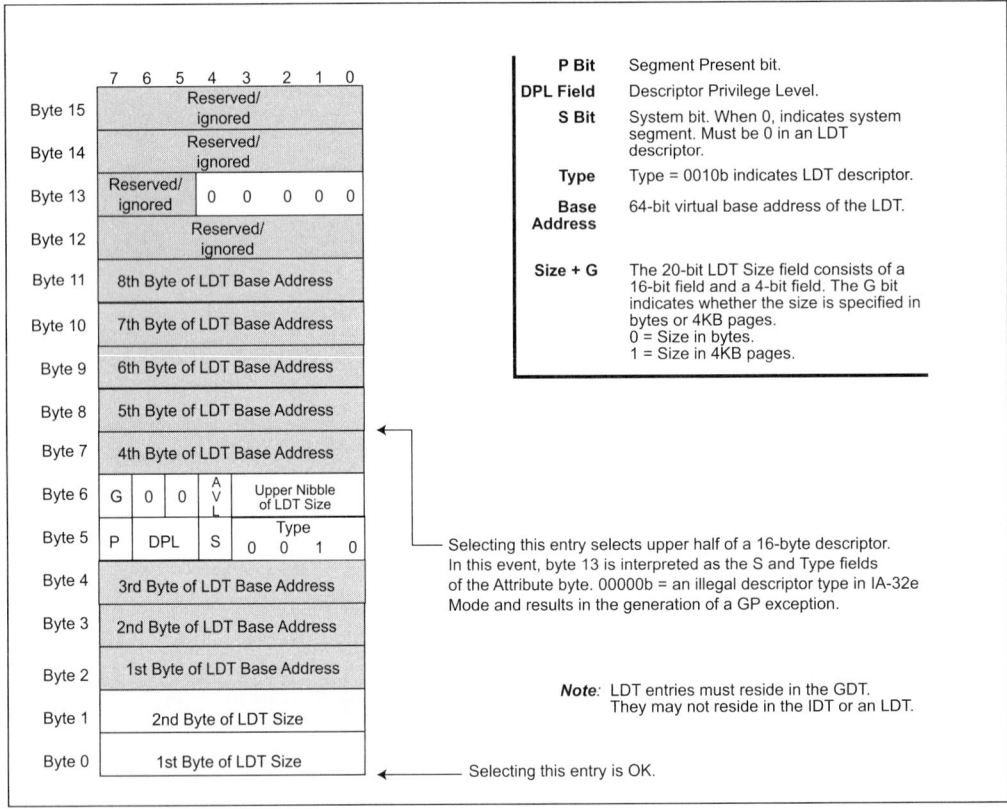

P Bit	Segment Present bit.
DPL Field	Descriptor Privilege Level.
S Bit	System bit. When 0, indicates system segment. Must be 0 in an LDT descriptor.
Type	Type = 0010b indicates LDT descriptor.
Base Address	64-bit virtual base address of the LDT.
Size + G	The 20-bit LDT Size field consists of a 16-bit field and a 4-bit field. The G bit indicates whether the size is specified in bytes or 4KB pages. 0 = Size in bytes. 1 = Size in 4KB pages.

Selecting this entry selects upper half of a 16-byte descriptor. In this event, byte 13 is interpreted as the S and Type fields of the Attribute byte. 00000b = an illegal descriptor type in IA-32e Mode and results in the generation of a GP exception.

Note: LDT entries must reside in the GDT. They may not reside in the IDT or an LDT.

Selecting this entry is OK.

Figure 23-9: TSS Descriptor in IA-32e Mode

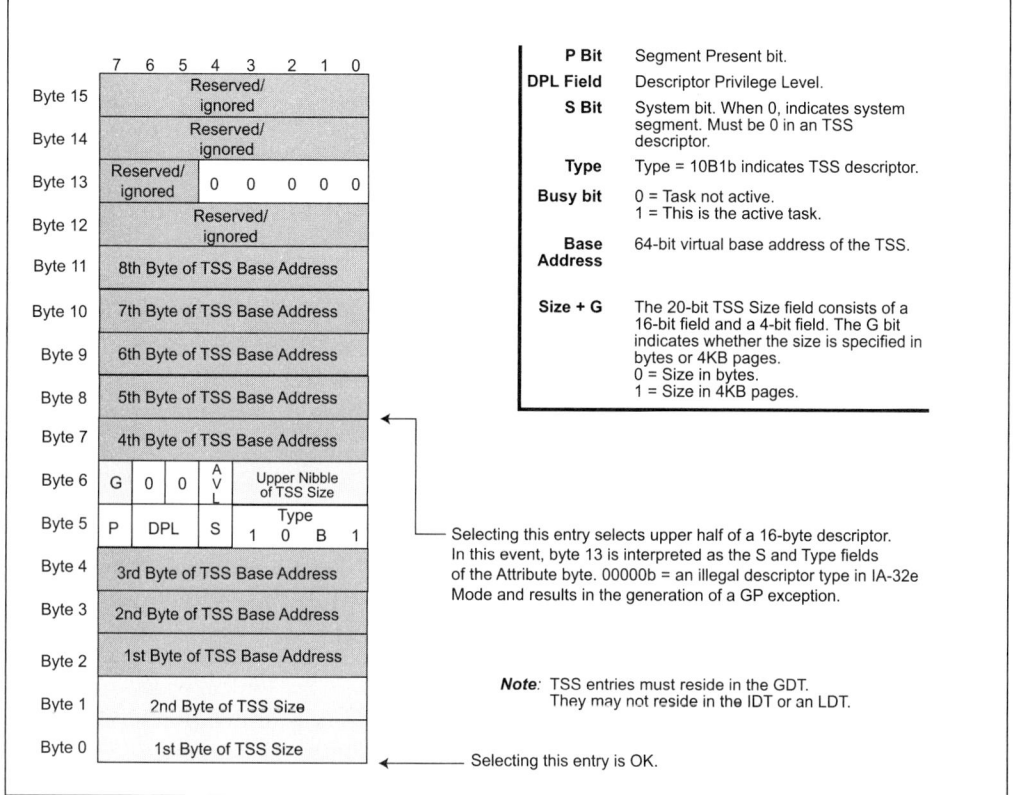

GDT and GDTR Changes

GDT Descriptor Types

In IA-32e Mode, the GDT is populated with the descriptor types shown in Table 23-8 on page 948.

Table 23-8: GDT Descriptor Types in IA-32e Mode

Descriptor Type	Size	Description
TSS descriptors	16-bytes	Contains the 64-bit virtual base address and 32-bit size of a TSS data structure. See Figure 23-9 on page 947.
LDT descriptors	16-bytes	Contains the 64-bit virtual base address and 32-bit size of an LDT. See Figure 23-8 on page 946.
CS descriptors	8-bytes	There are two types: • **Legacy CS descriptor**. See Figure 14-2 on page 421 and Figure 23-3 on page 922. When operating in Compatibility Mode, the logical processor utilizes all fields of the descriptor just as it would in Protected Mode. • **64-bit CS descriptor**. See Figure 23-3 on page 922. The hardware ignores most of the fields in a 64-bit CS descriptor. The segment base address is ignored and assumed to be 0 (and the descriptor therefore did not need to be expanded to 16-bytes to accommodate a 64-bit base address).
DS and ES data segment descriptors	8-bytes	• **In Compatibility Mode**, the logical processor utilizes all fields of the descriptor just as it would in Protected Mode. See Figure 15-3 on page 484. • **In 64-bit Mode**, the logical processor ignores all data segment descriptor fields with the exception of the segment *Present* bit. See Figure 23-4 on page 933.
FS and GS data segment descriptors	8-bytes	• **In Compatibility Mode**, the logical processor utilizes all fields of the descriptor just as it would in Protected Mode. See Figure 15-3 on page 484. • **In 64-bit Mode**, the logical processor ignores all data segment descriptor fields with the exception of the segment *Present* bit and the base address field. See Figure 23-5 on page 934.

Table 23-8: GDT Descriptor Types in IA-32e Mode (Continued)

Descriptor Type	Size	Description
SS descriptor	8-bytes	A stack segment descriptor is merely a data segment descriptor describing a read/writable data segment: • **In Compatibility Mode**, the logical processor utilizes all fields of the descriptor just as it would in Protected Mode. See Figure 15-6 on page 487. • **In 64-bit Mode**, the logical processor ignores all data segment descriptor fields with the exception of the segment *Present* bit. See Figure 23-4 on page 933.
Call Gates	16-bytes	See the description of the Call Gate in Table 23-6 on page 941. See Figure 23-7 on page 945.
Since hardware-based task switching is not supported in IA-32e Mode, Task Gate descriptors are forbidden.		

Executing LGDT in Compatibility Mode

When the LGDT instruction is executed in Compatibility Mode, the logical processor behaves exactly as it would in IA-32 Mode. It reads the GDT's virtual base address (32-bits) and size (16-bits) from memory into the lower 48-bits of the GDTR (see Figure 23-10 on page 950). The table size specified in the memory operand is always a 16-bit value. Regarding the GDT base address, there are two possibilities:

- **LGDT executed with 16-bit operand size**. If the LGDT instruction is executed when the operand size is 16-bits (because the LGDT instruction was fetched from a 16-bit code segment, or the instruction was fetched from a 32-bit code segment but was prefaced by the Operand Size Override prefix), the logical processor emulates the 286 by loading the GDTR with a 24-bit base address. In actuality, a 32-bit address is read from memory, but the logical processor forces the upper 8-bits to 0.
- **LGDT executed with 32-bit operand size**. If the LGDT instruction is executed when the operand size is 32-bits (because the LGDT instruction was fetched from a 32-bit code segment, or the instruction was fetched from a 16-bit code segment but was prefaced by the Operand Size Override prefix), the logical processor loads the GDTR with a 32-bit base address.

Figure 23-10: GDTR Contents After Loading in Compatibility Mode

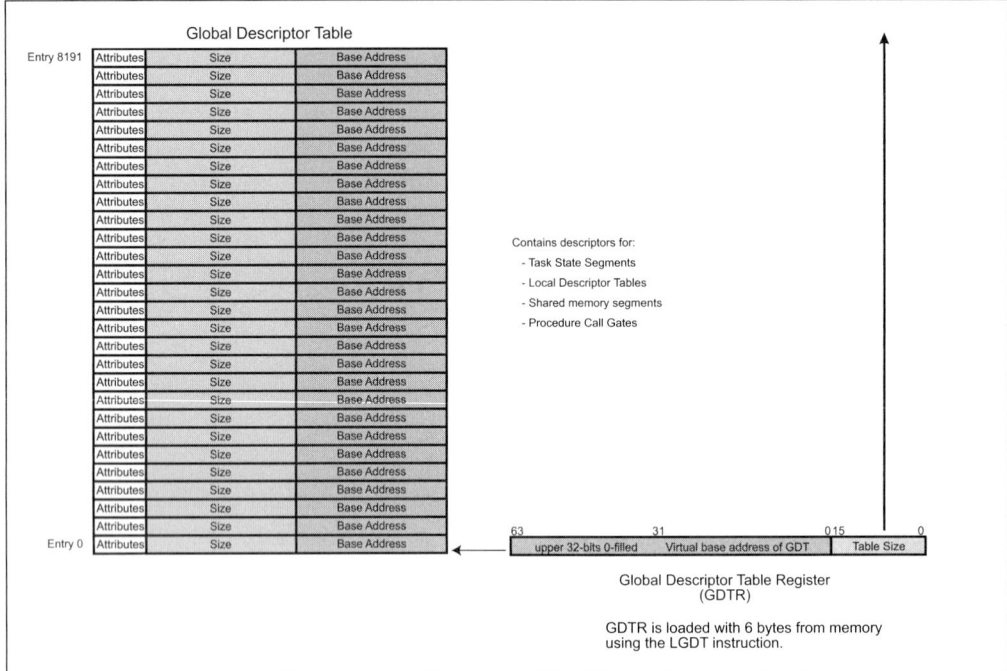

Executing LGDT in 64-bit Mode

When executed in 64-bit Mode, the LGDT instruction reads a 10-byte value from memory consisting of the 64-bit virtual base address of the GDT and the 16-bit GDT size and loads it into the GDTR. See Figure 23-11 on page 951.

Figure 23-11: GDTR Contents After Loading in 64-bit Mode

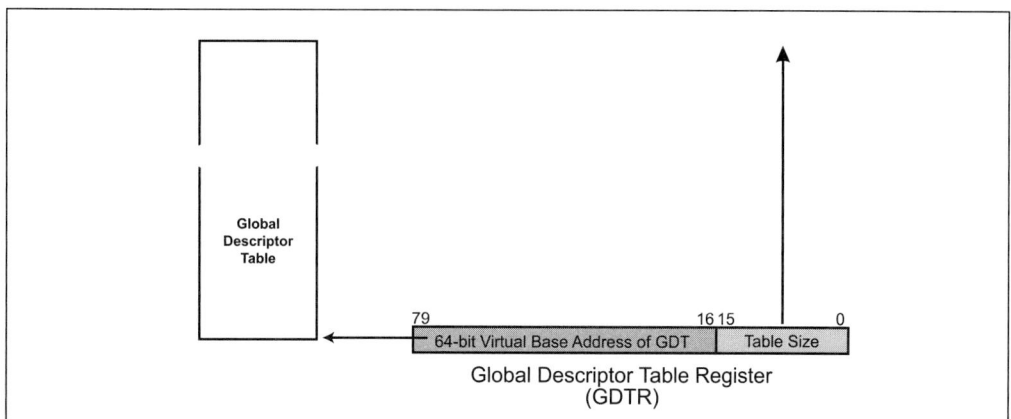

Unaligned Accesses to GDT or LDT

Refer to Figure 23-10 on page 950. In the IA-32 OS environment, the GDT and LDT have a homogeneous consistency: all descriptors are 8-bytes (64-bits) in size. When a 16-bit selector value loaded into a segment register selects the GDT or the LDT, the logical processor multiplies the selector's offset field by 8 to index into the table, adds the resultant offset to the GDT or LDT base address, and reads the selected 8-byte descriptor from the table into the invisible portion of the respective segment register.

Refer to Figure 23-12 on page 952. In the IA-32e OS environment, however, the GDT and LDT can contain a mixture of 8-byte and 16-byte descriptors. It is therefore possible to load a selector into a segment register that would select the second half (i.e., the upper half) of a 16-byte descriptor. In the illustration, the Table Index portion of the selector loaded into a segment register has selected the upper-half of a 16-byte Call Gate descriptor in the LDT. Obviously, this cannot be permitted. When the logical processor reads the selected descriptor into the hidden portion of the respective segment register, the all-zero settings of the S and Type fields (a descriptor type unsupported in IA-32e Mode) results in the generation of a GP exception.

Figure 23-12: GDT and LDT Can Contain Mix of 8- and 16-byte Descriptors

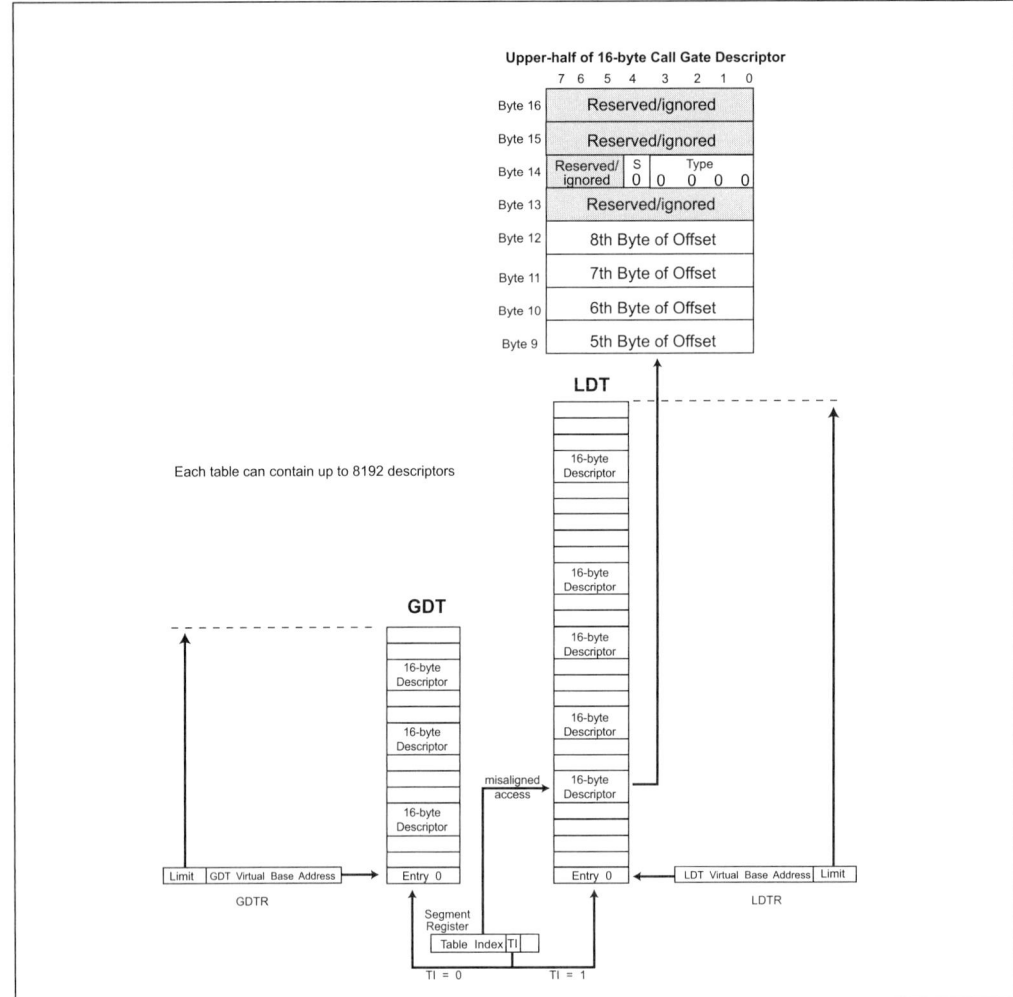

LDT and LDTR Changes

LDT Descriptor Types

In IA-32e Mode, the LDT is populated with the descriptor types listed in Table 23-9 on page 953.

Table 23-9: LDT Descriptor Types in IA-32e Mode

Descriptor Type	Size	Description
CS descriptors	8-bytes	Refer to the CS descriptor description in Table 23-8 on page 948.
DS and ES data segment descriptors	8-bytes	Refer to the DS/ES data segment descriptor description in Table 23-8 on page 948.
FS and GS data segment descriptors	8-bytes	Refer to the FS/GS data segment descriptor description in Table 23-8 on page 948.
SS descriptor	8-bytes	Refer to the SS descriptor description in Table 23-8 on page 948.
Call Gates	16-bytes	See the description of the Call Gate in Table 23-6 on page 941.
Since hardware-based task switching is not supported in IA-32e Mode, Task Gate descriptors are forbidden.		

LDTR Contents in IA-32e Mode

In legacy Protected Mode, execution of the LLDT instruction loads a 16-bit selector into the visible portion of the LDTR. It must select a GDT entry containing a legacy 8-byte LDT descriptor (see Figure 23-13 on page 954) that defines the 32-bit virtual base address and 16-bit size of the LDT. Execution of the LLDT instruction causes the logical processor to read the selected 8-byte descriptor into the invisible portion of the LDTR.

In IA-32e Mode, the LDT descriptor has been expanded from 8- to 16-bytes (see Figure 23-8 on page 946) in order to accommodate a 64-bit base address. Likewise, the size of the LDTR's invisible portion has been expanded in order to accommodate the 64-bit base address (see Figure 23-14 on page 955).

Unaligned Accesses to LDT

Refer to "Unaligned Accesses to GDT or LDT" on page 951.

Figure 23-13: Legacy 8-byte LDT Descriptor (see Figure 23-8 on page 946 for IA-32e Version)

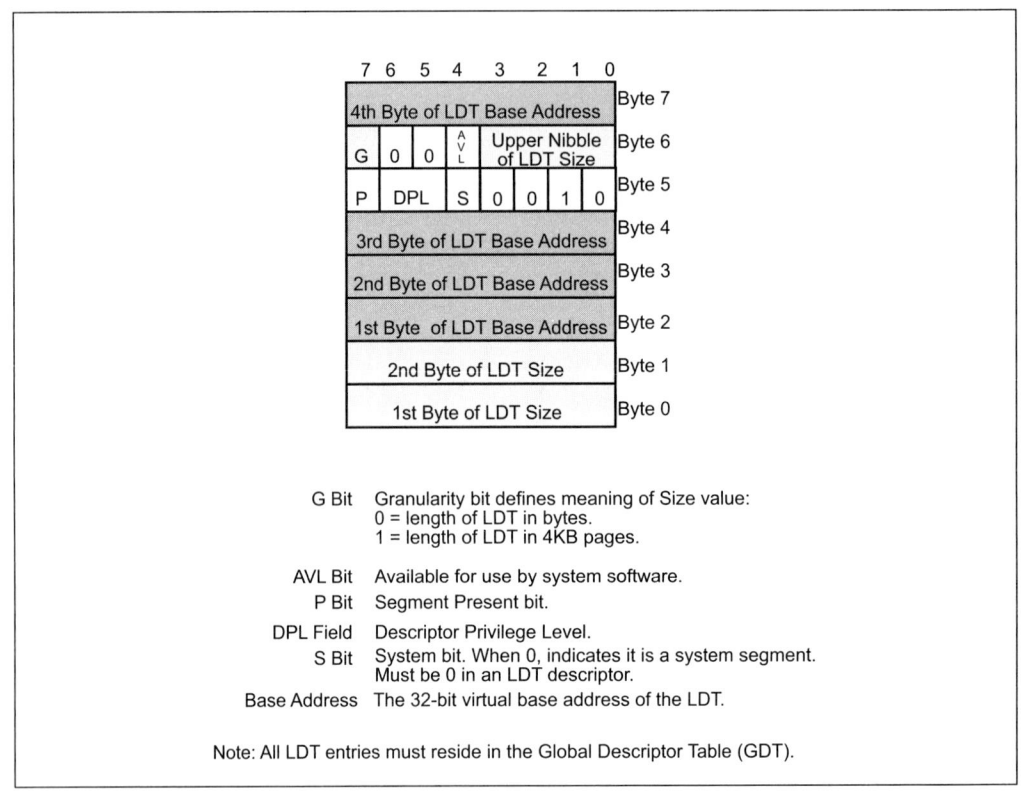

G Bit	Granularity bit defines meaning of Size value: 0 = length of LDT in bytes. 1 = length of LDT in 4KB pages.
AVL Bit	Available for use by system software.
P Bit	Segment Present bit.
DPL Field	Descriptor Privilege Level.
S Bit	System bit. When 0, indicates it is a system segment. Must be 0 in an LDT descriptor.
Base Address	The 32-bit virtual base address of the LDT.

Note: All LDT entries must reside in the Global Descriptor Table (GDT).

Figure 23-14: LDTR in IA-32e Mode

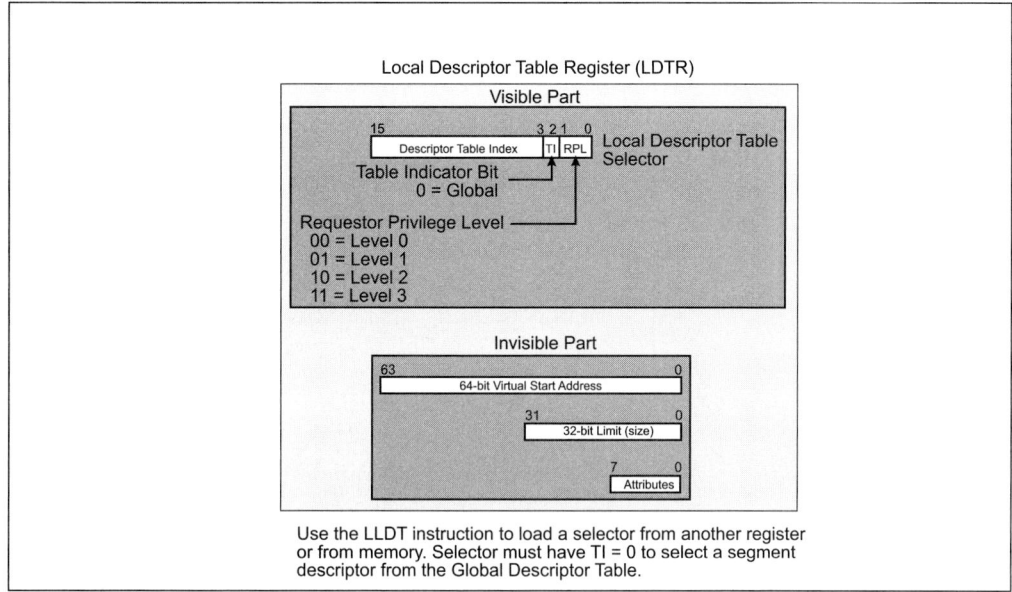

IDT/IDTR and Interrupt/Exception Changes

IDT Descriptor Types

In IA-32e Mode, all interrupt and exception handlers must reside in a 64-bit code segment. In order to support this constraint, all Interrupt and Trap Gate descriptors (see Figure 23-15 on page 957 and Figure 23-16 on page 958) must be 16-byte, 64-bit gates which support the specification of a full 64-bit handler entry point address.

In IA-32e Mode, the IDT is populated with the descriptor types shown in Table 23-10 on page 956.

Table 23-10: IDT Descriptor Types in IA-32e Mode

Descriptor Type	Size	Description

Interrupt Gate	16-bytes	See Figure 23-15 on page 957.
		• **Handler address** (offset field). Extended to 64-bits allowing OS to place handler anywhere in a 64-bit virtual address space.
		• **CS selector**. Selects the CS descriptor in the GDT or LDT that defines the characteristics of the code segment containing the handler. The selected descriptor must be a 64-bit CS descriptor.
		• **IST** field. See "Interrupt/Exception Stack Switch" on page 976.
		• **DPL**.
		  – When a hardware-initiated interrupt or a software exception is detected, the DPL is ignored.
		  – When a gate is selected due to the attempted execution of a software interrupt instruction (INT nn, INTO, BOUND, or INT3; *note: the INTO and BOUND instructions are not supported in 64-bit Mode*), a GP exception results if the CPL of the currently executing program isn't at least as privileged as the DPL of the selected gate.
		• **P**. Present bit must be one.
		• **S + Type**. 0 + 1110b.

Trap Gate	16-bytes	**S + Type = 0 + 1111b**. See Figure 23-16 on page 958.
Since hardware-based task switching is not supported in IA-32e Mode, Task Gate descriptors are forbidden.		

Figure 23-15: Interrupt Gate Descriptor in IA-32e Mode

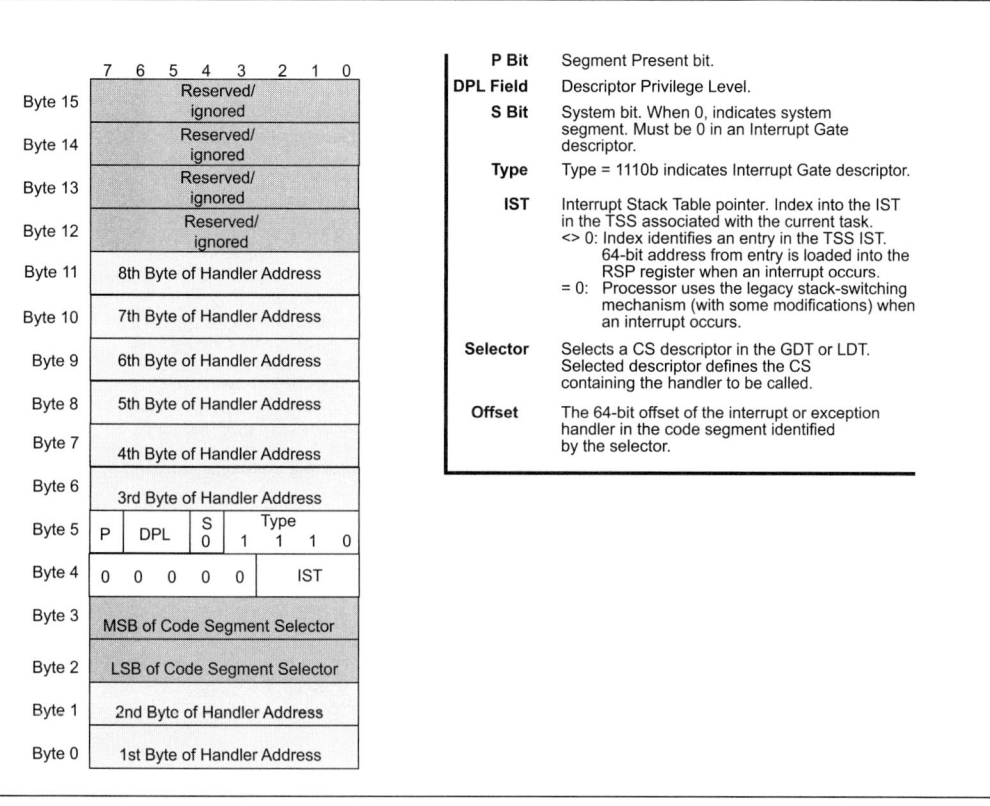

Figure 23-16: Trap Gate Descriptor in IA-32e Mode

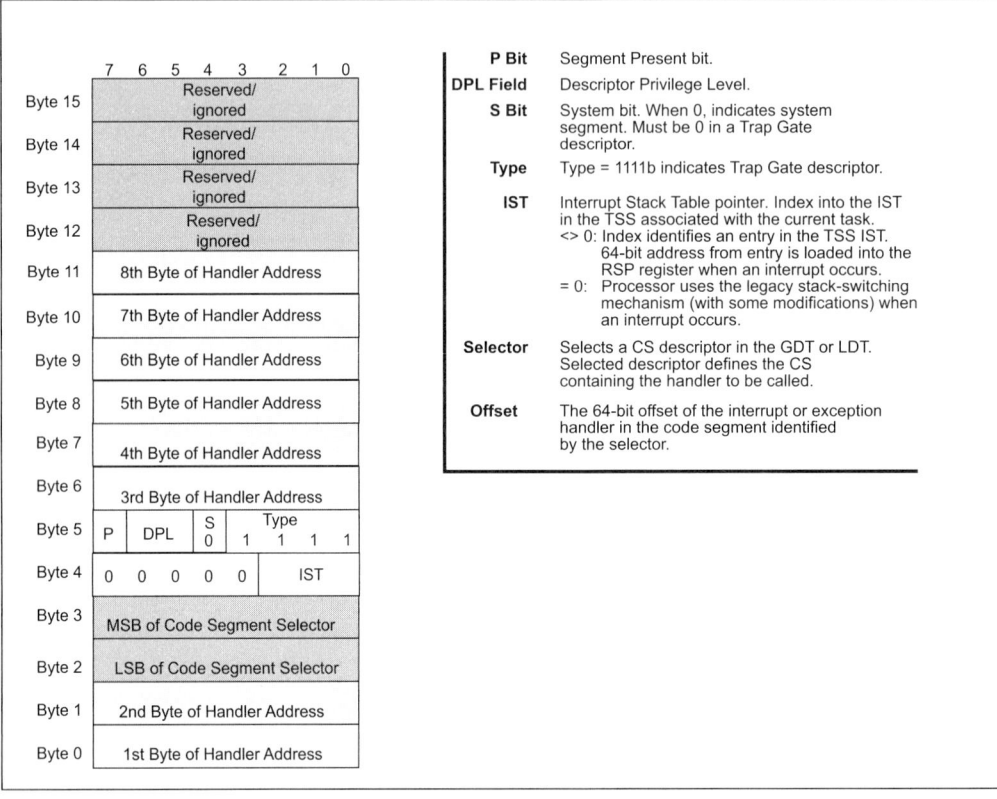

Interrupt/Trap Gate Operational Changes

General. The operation of Interrupt and Trap Gates changes as follows when the logical processor is in IA-32e Mode:

— **In Protected Mode**, the logical processor only switches to a new stack for the handler's use if the handler resides in a code segment more privileged than the interrupted program. In that case, it pushes the interrupted program's stack pointer (SS:ESP) onto the handler's stack along with CS:EIP and Eflags.

— **In IA-32e Mode**, an automatic stack switch can happen even if a privilege change does not occur. If the IST value in the selected IDT entry is non-zero, a new stack pointer is loaded from the TSS. Regardless of whether a new stack pointer was loaded, the processor always pushes the interrupted program's stack pointer (SS:RSP) onto the handler's stack along with CS:RIP and Rflags.

— In order to optimize performance when storing or loading 16-byte XMM registers from the stack while in a 64-bit handler, the logical processor automatically masks the handler's RSP stack pointer with the value FFFFFFFFFFFFFFF0h to adjust it downwards to the next lower 16-byte boundary before any pushes are performed. The handler can then use the MOVAPS instruction (which assumes 16-byte alignment) rather than the unaligned MOVUPS instruction.

— The CS:RIP, Rflags, and SS:SP stack pushes are 8-bytes each in IA-32e Mode.

— The stack switching mechanism has been enhanced. See "Interrupt/ Exception Stack Switch" on page 959.

Figure 23-17 on page 961 and Figure 23-18 on page 962 provide a detailed description of interrupt or exception handling in IA-32e Mode.

Interrupt/Exception Stack Switch.
In IA-32e Mode, the Interrupt and Trap Gate descriptors are redefined as 16-byte descriptors. Figure 23-15 on page 957 and Figure 23-16 on page 958 illustrate the layout of the IA-32e Interrupt and Trap Gate descriptors. They differ from IA-32 IDT descriptors (see Figure 19-5 on page 693 and Figure 19-6 on page 694) in the following ways:

— The offset field (i.e., the handler address field) has been expanded from 32- to 64-bits.

— The reserved bit field in bits 2:0 of byte 4 has been replaced by the 3-bit Interrupt Stack Table (IST) field.

When an interrupt or exception occurs, the logical processor multiplies the 8-bit vector by 16 (because each IDT entry is 16-bytes in size) and adds the resultant offset to the IDT base address to form the start virtual address of the selected IDT entry. It then reads the 16-byte descriptor to obtain, among other things, the 64-bit virtual entry point to the respective interrupt or exception handler. Before jumping to the handler, however, the logical processor must push the SS:RSP, Rflags, and CS:RIP registers (and, if it's an exception that reports an error code, the error code as well) onto the stack. The question is, **which stack will be used**?

— **Handler more privileged and Conforming**. If the handler resides in a more-privileged Non-Conforming code segment than the interrupted program, than the logical processor uses the same mechanism as it would for a far call that selects a Call Gate descriptor in the GDT or

LDT (see "Call Gate Stack Switch" on page 976). When the logical processor has switched to a new stack for the handler's use it pushes the pointer to the interrupted program's stack (SS:RSP) as well as Rflags, CS:RIP, and, if it's an exception with an error code, the error code to the new stack. Upon entry to the handler, the stack looks like Figure 23-19 on page 962.

— **Handler same privilege or in Conforming CS**. If, on the other hand, the handler has the same privilege level as the interrupted program or it resides in a Conforming code segment, there is no privilege level change. Normally, this would mean that the handler would use the interrupted program's stack:

  – **Non-zero IST selects new stack**. If, however, the IST field in the selected IDT descriptor contains a non-zero value, the logical processor uses it to select a new stack pointer from one of the seven IST fields in the TSS (see Figure 23-25 on page 971) associated with the currently-running task. When the logical processor has switched to the new stack for the handler's use it pushes the pointer to the interrupted program's stack (SS:RSP) as well as Rflags, CS:RIP, and, if it's an exception with an error code, the error code to the new stack. Upon entry to the handler, the stack looks like Figure 23-19 on page 962.

  – **IST = 0, no stack switch**. If the IST field in the gate = 000b, however, no stack switch occurs and the handler uses the same stack as the interrupted program.

Motivation for the IST. In the event of certain types of interrupts or exceptions (namely: a Machine Check exception, a Double-Fault exception, or an NMI hardware interrupt) generated as the result of catastrophic circumstances, the interrupted program's stack may be corrupted or otherwise invalid upon entry to the respective handler. In order to ensure that the respective handler is entered with a clean stack, the OS may preallocate a fresh stack, place a pointer to it in one of the TSS's IST fields, and set up the 3-bit IST field in the respective IDT descriptor to point to the respective TSS IST field.

IRET Behavior. In Protected Mode, the behavior of the IRET instruction is conditional upon whether the logical processor is returning to an interrupted program that resides at a less-privileged level than the handler (e.g. returning from a privilege level 0 handler to a privilege level 3 application):

— If returning to same privilege level, only CS:EIP and Eflags are restored from the stack and no stack switch occurs.

— If returning to a less-privileged level, a stack switch occurs. SS:ESP (the pointer to the interrupted program's stack) is restored from the handler's stack along with CS:EIP and Eflags.

In IA-32e Mode, the behavior of the IRET instruction is uniform regardless of a privilege level change on return to the interrupted program: SS:RSP is always restored from the handler's stack along with CS:RIP and Rflags.

Figure 23-17: Interrupt/Exception Flow in IA-32e Mode (1 of 2)

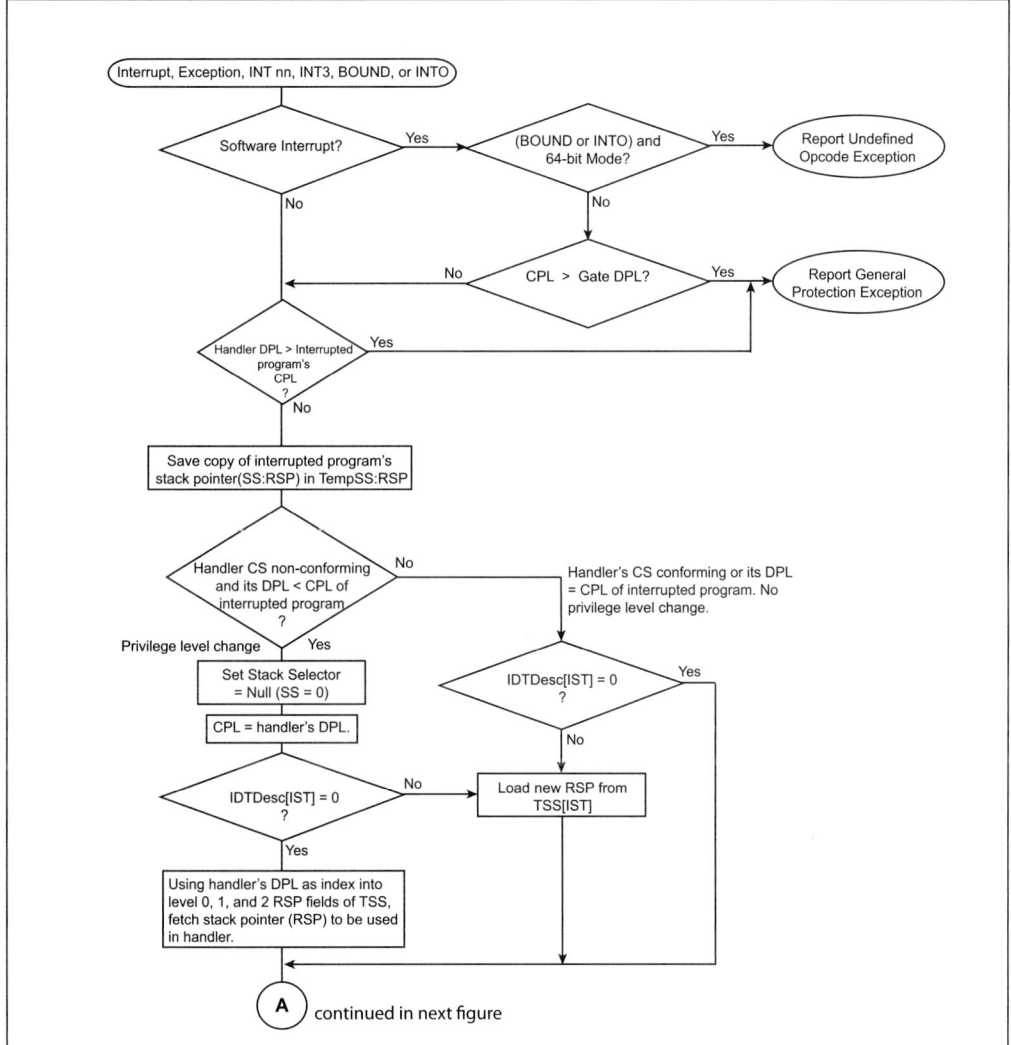

Figure 23-18: Interrupt/Exception Flow in IA-32e Mode (2 of 2)

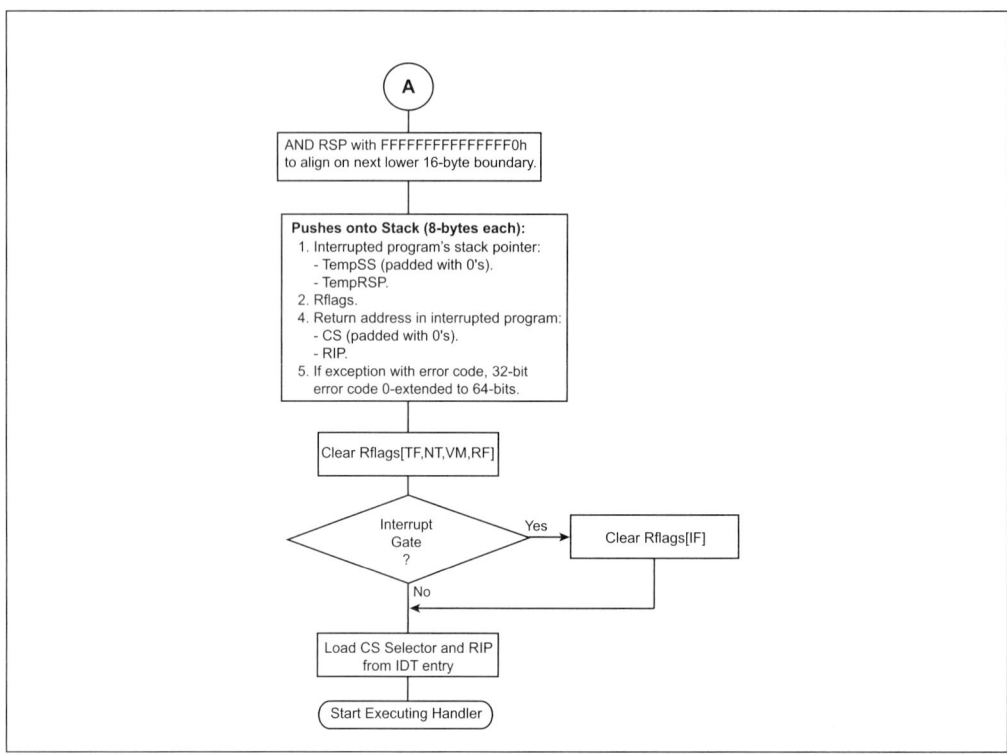

Figure 23-19: Handler's Stack After Pushes

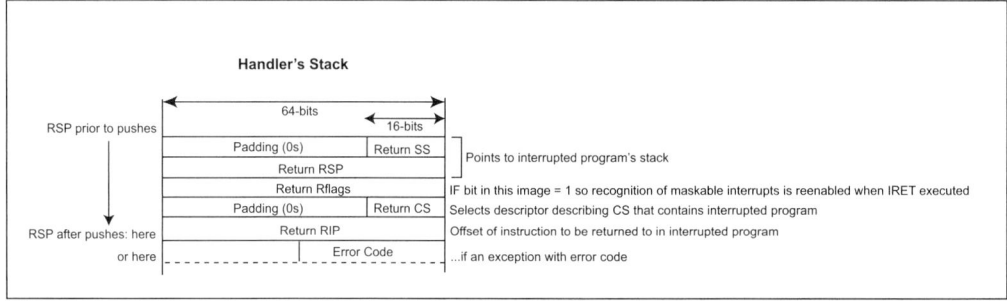

Executing LIDT in Compatibility Mode

When the LIDT instruction is executed in Compatibility Mode, the logical processor behaves exactly as it would in IA-32 Mode. It reads the IDT's virtual base address (32-bits) and size (16-bits) from memory into the IDTR (although the IDTR is 80-bits wide in IA-32e Mode, the logical processor only loads the lower 48 bits when the LIDT instruction is executed in Compatibility Mode; see Figure 23-20 on page 963). The table size specified in the memory operand is always a 16-bit value. Regarding the IDT base address, there are two possibilities:

- **LIDT executed with 16-bit operand size.** If the LIDT instruction is executed when the operand size is 16-bits (because the LIDT instruction was fetched from a 16-bit code segment, or the instruction was fetched from a 32-bit code segment but was prefaced by the Operand Size Override prefix), the logical processor emulates the 286 by loading the IDTR with a 24-bit base address. In actuality, a 32-bit address is read from memory, but the logical processor forces the upper 8-bits to 0.
- **LGDT executed with 32-bit operand size.** If the LIDT instruction is executed when the operand size is 32-bits (because the LIDT instruction was fetched from a 32-bit code segment, or the instruction was fetched from a 16-bit code segment but was prefaced by the Operand Size Override prefix), the logical processor loads the IDTR with a 32-bit base address.

Figure 23-20: IDTR Contents After Loading in Compatibility Mode

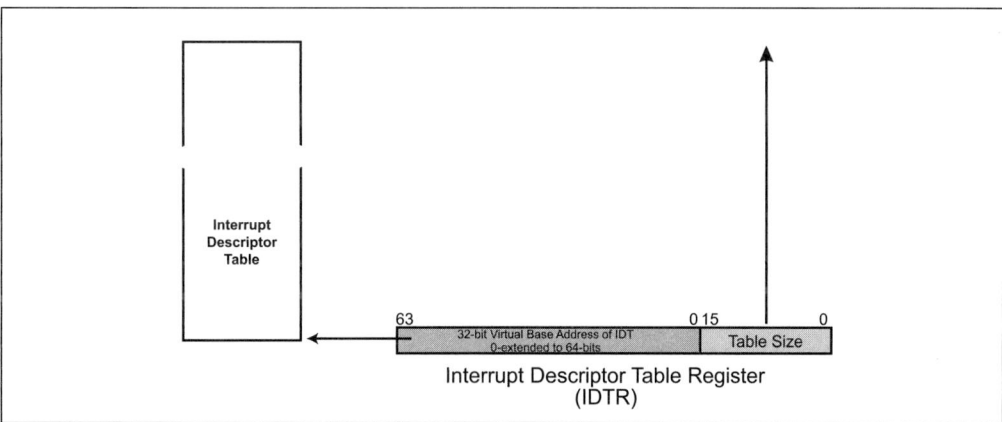

Executing LIDT in 64-bit Mode

When executed in 64-bit Mode, the LIDT instruction reads a 10-byte value from memory consisting of the 64-bit virtual base address of the IDT and the 16-bit IDT size and loads it into the IDTR. See Figure 23-21 on page 964.

Figure 23-21: IDTR Contents After Loading in 64-bit Mode

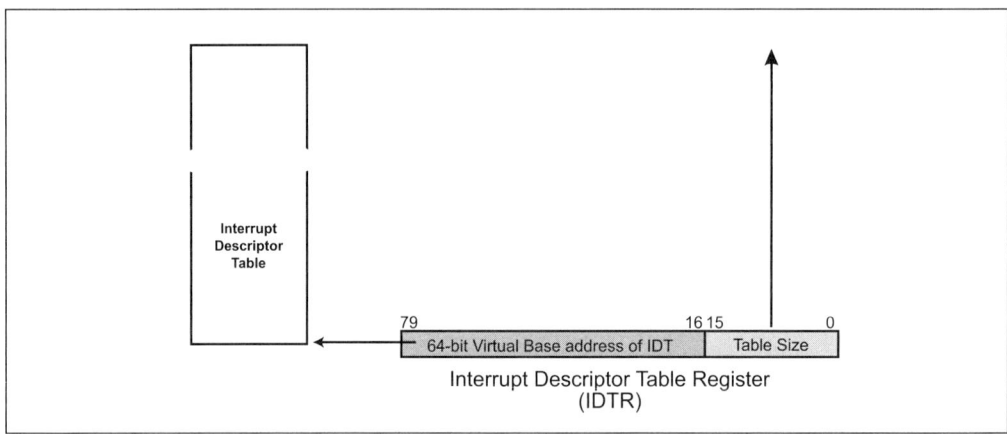

All Accesses to IDT Are Properly Aligned

Unlike the GDT and LDT which can contain a mix of 8- and 16-byte descriptors and care must be taken to avoid misaligned accesses, every entry in the IDT contains 16-byte descriptors. There is therefore no possibility of a misaligned access.

IA-32e Call Gate Operation

General

Refer to Figure 23-23 on page 968. In IA-32e Mode, the changes listed in Table 23-11 on page 964 are made to the Call Gate mechanism.

Table 23-11: IA-32e Call Gate Changes

Element	Change Description
Gate Size	The gate size is expanded to 16-bytes in order to accommodate a full 64-bit procedure entry point address.
Target Code Segment	The kernel procedure pointed to by the Call Gate must reside in a 64-bit code segment (or it results in a GP exception).

Table 23-11: IA-32e Call Gate Changes (Continued)

Element	Change Description
Parameter Count Field	Now reserved (no OSs used the parameter copy feature).
Gate Type	The 32-bit Call Gate type has been redefined as the IA-32e Call Gate descriptor.
16-bit Call Gate	Not permitted in IA-32e Mode.
Push Size	8-bytes rather than 4- or 2-bytes.
Stack Switching	See "IA-32e Call Gate Stack Switch" on page 966.

IA-32e Call Gate Detailed Operation

Figure 23-22 on page 966 provides a detailed description of IA-32e Call Gate Operation. Additional detail on the changes to the stack switching mechanism can be found in "IA-32e Call Gate Stack Switch" on page 966.

Figure 23-22: IA-32e Call Gate Operation

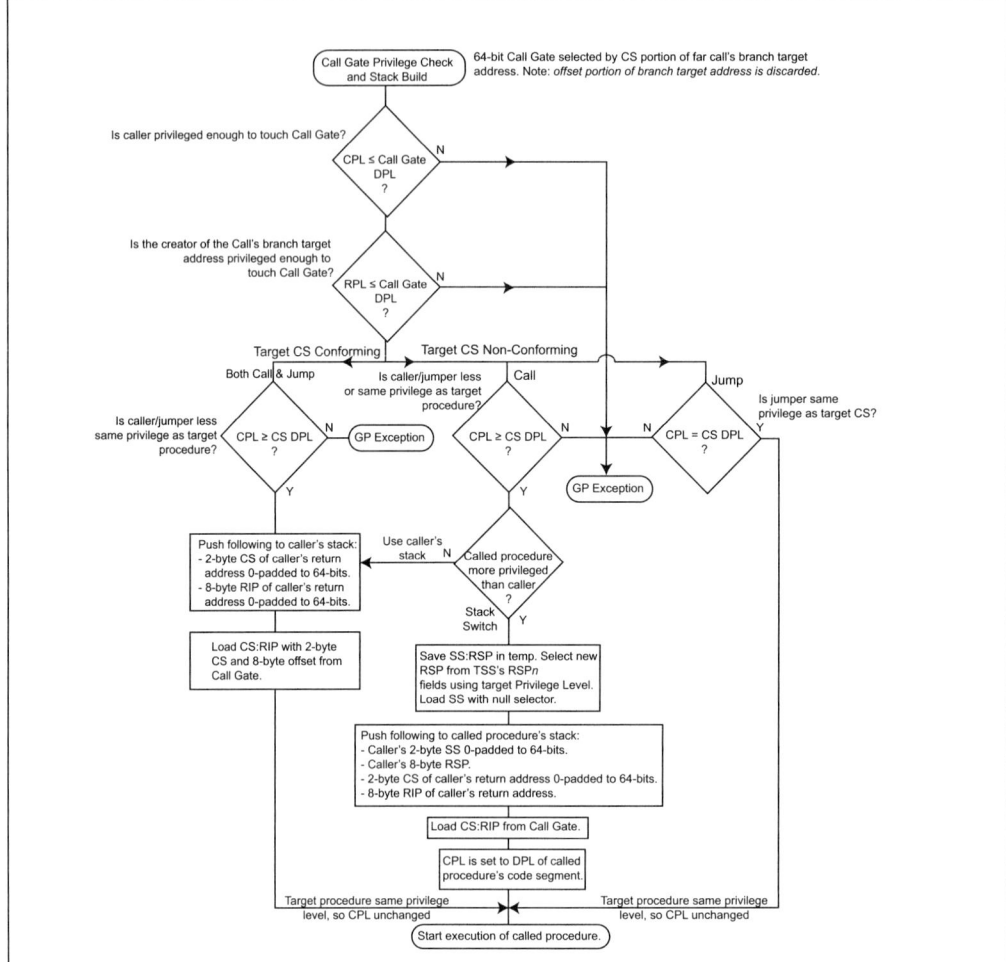

IA-32e Call Gate Stack Switch

With some minor modifications, the IA-32e Call Gate stack switching mechanism works the same as it does in Protected Mode (see "Automatic Stack Switch" on page 462). The differences are described in Table 23-12 on page 967. Examples of stack switching may be found in "Example Call/Return Operations" on page 1089.

Table 23-12: Call Gate Stack Switch Legacy/IA-32e Mode Differences

Deviation	Legacy Behavior	IA-32e Behavior
Stack push size	Each item pushed to stack is 4-bytes wide (refer to "Call Gate Example" on page 456).	Each item pushed to stack is 8-bytes wide (see Figure 23-19 on page 962): • Caller's SS is padded with 48 zeros. • Caller's RSP is pushed. If not a 64-bit caller, upper 32-bits of RSP is 0-filled. • Caller's CS is padded with 48 zeros and pushed. • Caller's RIP is pushed. If not a 64-bit caller, upper 32-bits of RIP is 0-filled.
Dword parameter copy eliminated	The legacy Call Gate descriptor contains a dword count field that can be used to specify the number of dword parameters (up to 31) to be copied to the new stack (on a privilege level change).	This feature is not supported in IA-32e Mode and the field is now reserved and ignored.
Target SS = Null on CPL change	When the called procedure resides at a higher level than the caller, SS is loaded with SS*n* field (where n = privilege level of called procedure) from legacy TSS (see Figure 23-29 on page 975).	SS is loaded with: • Table Index = 000000000b. • Table select = 0b (GDT). • RPL = privilege level of called procedure. This selects GDT entry 0 which contains a null descriptor consisting of all zeros.

Figure 23-23: IA-32e Call Gate

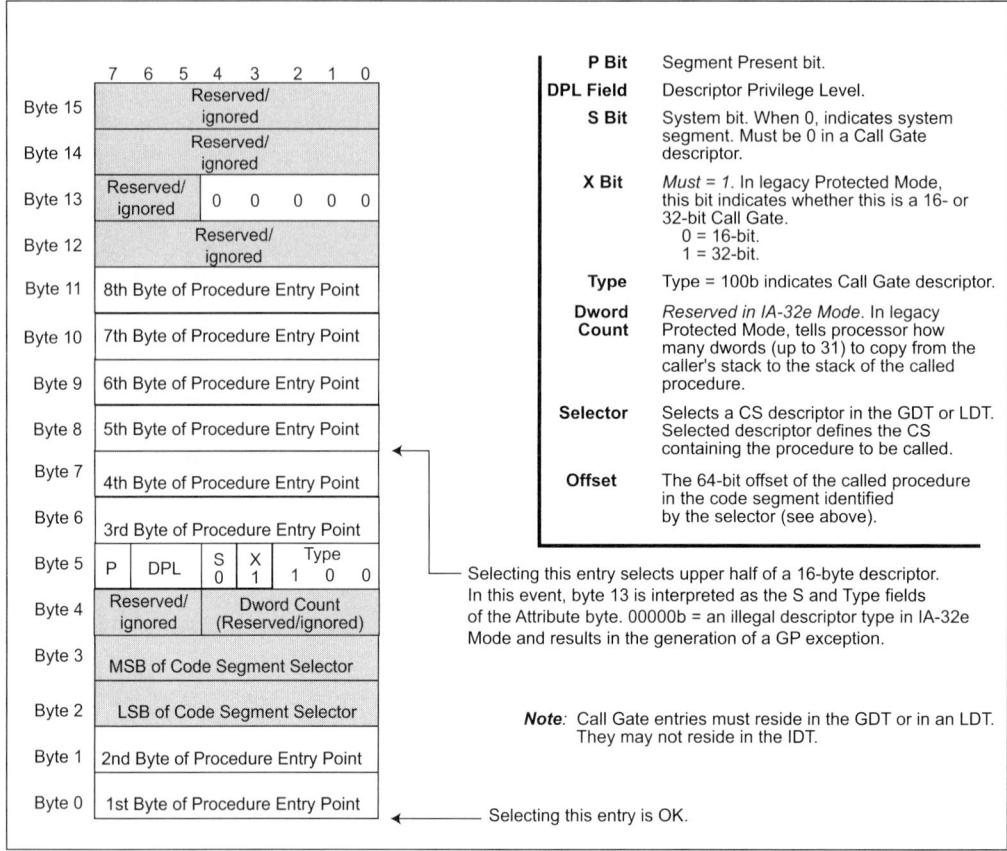

TR and TSS Changes

Real World TSS Usage

The original intent of the x86 designers was that the OS would create a separate TSS for each task. Since modern OSs do not use the hardware-based task switching mechanism, however, the register save/restore area of the legacy TSS (see Figure 23-29 on page 975) is not used. The only fields that are, in fact, used are:

- **IO Permission Bitmap**.
- The **three stack pointer fields** that point to the three areas of memory preal-located for use as stack memory to be used by privilege level 0, 1, and 2 programs.

As an example, Linux creates a single TSS to be used by all Protected Mode tasks executing on a logical processor. The IO Permission Bitmap defines the IO port access permissions for all tasks and the stack pointer fields are accessed whenever the logical processor invokes a more privileged interrupt/exception handler or executes a call through a Call Gate to a more privileged procedure.

The OS creates the following (refer to Figure 23-24 on page 970):

- The IA-32e TSS data structure in memory. Figure 23-25 on page 971 illustrates the IA-32e TSS.
- The IA-32e TSS descriptor in the GDT (see Figure 23-26 on page 972) containing (among other elements) the following:
  — The 64-bit virtual base address of the TSS data structure (in Protected Mode, it is a 32-bit base address). IA-32e TSS descriptors have been expanded to 16-bytes in order to accommodate the 64-bit TSS virtual base address.
  — The 32-bit size of the TSS in bytes.
  — A Busy bit indicating whether the task associated with the TSS is not currently running (Busy = 0), is suspended (due to a call to another task; Busy = 1), or is the currently-active task (Busy =1).

The task scheduler executes the LTR instruction specifying the GDT entry containing the task's TSS descriptor. In response, the logical processor:

- Reads the TSS's base address and size into the invisible portion of the TR (see Figure 23-27 on page 973).
- Executes a locked read/modify/write operation to set the Busy bit in the TSS descriptor to one indicating that the associated task is the currently-active one.

Figure 23-24: Relationship of TSS, GDT and TSS Descriptor

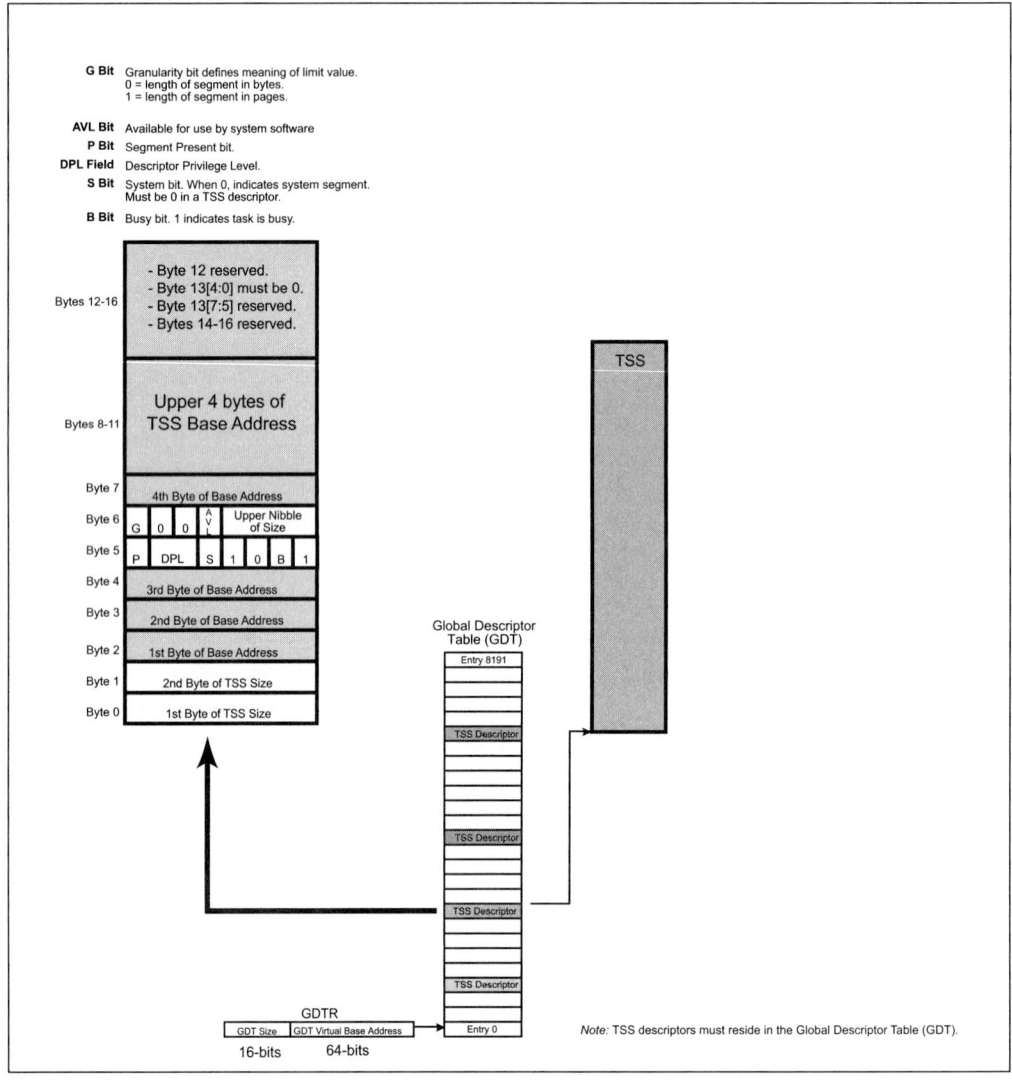

Figure 23-25: IA-32e TSS Data Structure

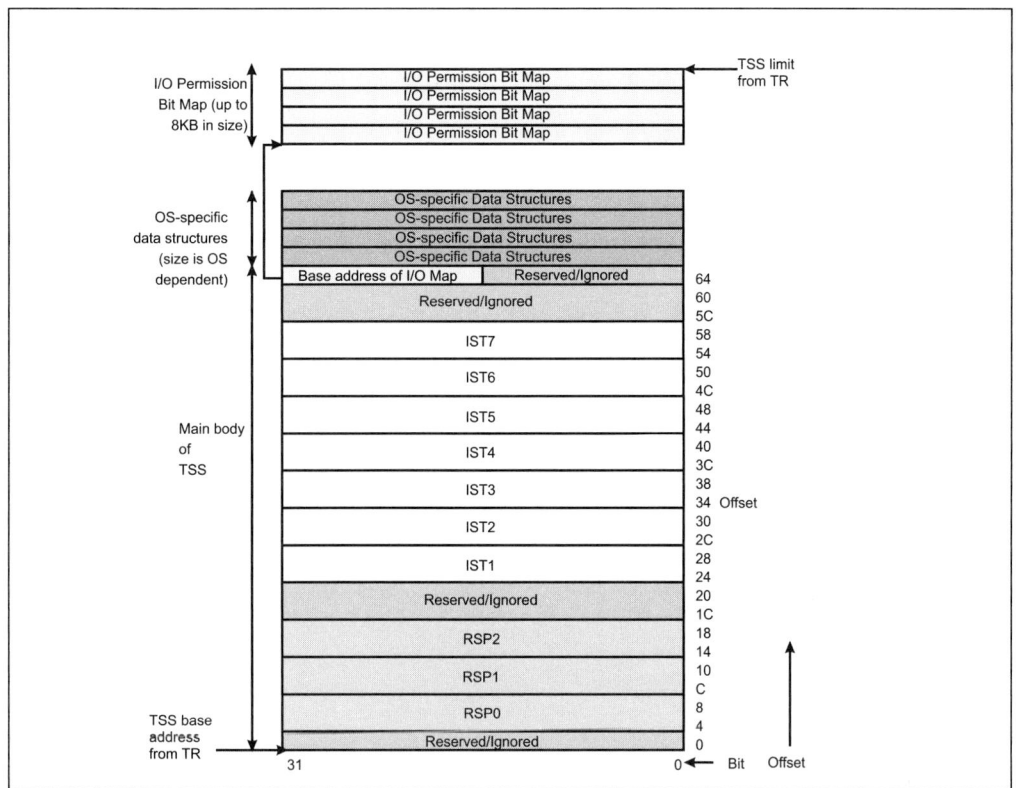

Figure 23-26: IA-32e Mode TSS Descriptor

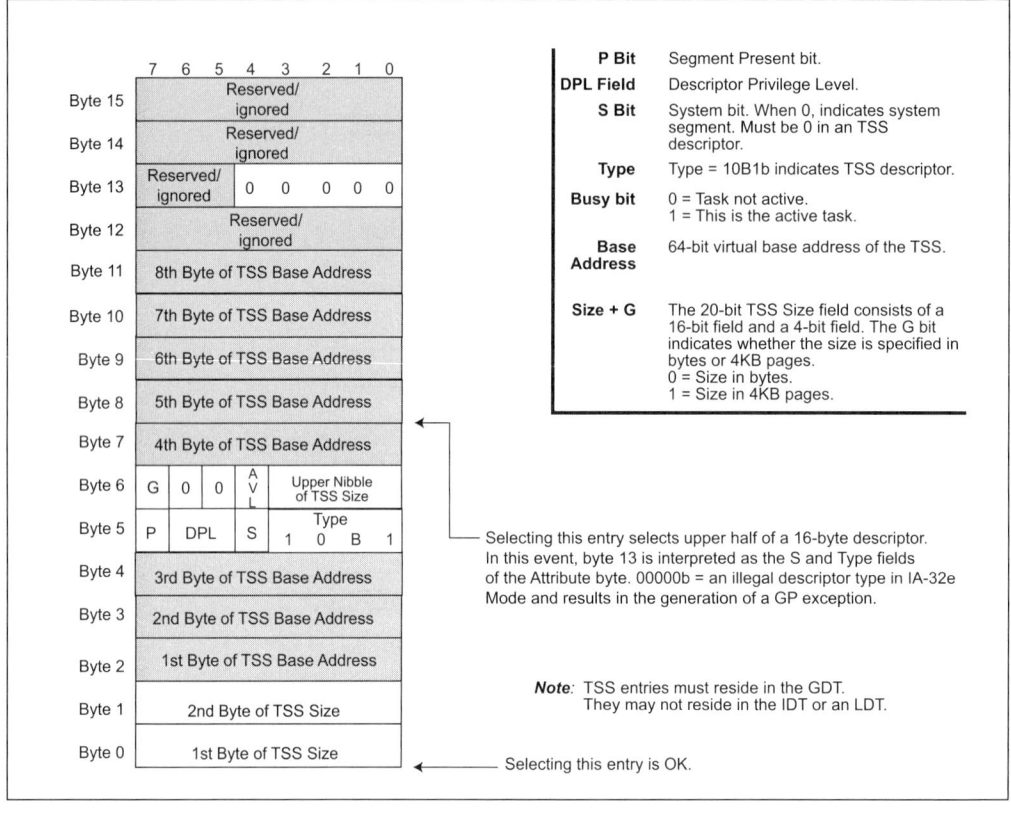

Figure 23-27: TR in IA-32e Mode

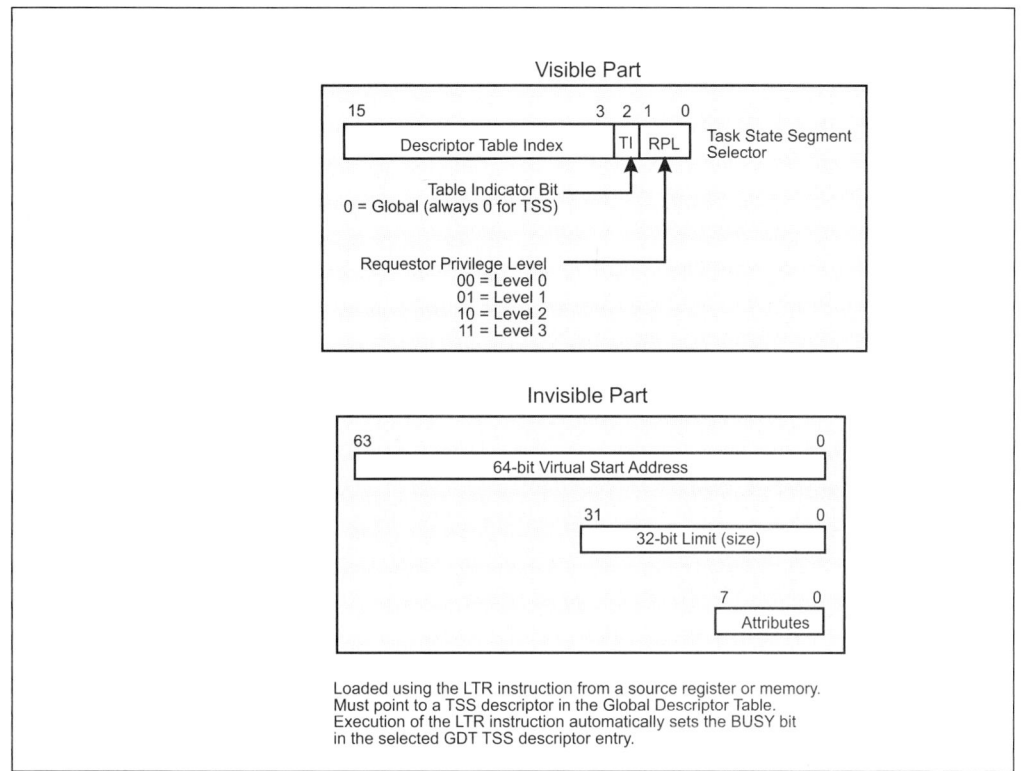

Illegal For Jump or Call To Select a TSS Descriptor

One way to trigger the x86 hardware-based task switching mechanism is to execute a far jump or a far call wherein the selector portion of the far address selects a TSS descriptor in the GDT. Since the hardware-based task switching mechanism is disabled in IA-32e Mode, this will result in a GP exception.

Executing LTR in Compatibility Mode

It doesn't make much sense to load the TR in Compatibility Mode as this should be a function of the OS kernel's task scheduler which will be implemented as 64-bit code. If, however, the LTR instruction were executed in Compatibility Mode, the logical processor behaves as it would in Protected Mode: the selected 8-byte descriptor (see Figure 23-28 on page 974; the lower 8-bytes of a 16-byte TSS selector) is read from the GDT and the 32-bit TSS virtual base address and 32-bit TSS size are stored in the invisible portion of the TR (see Figure 23-27 on page 973). The upper 32-bits of the TR's invisible base address field are not affected.

Figure 23-28: Lower 8-bytes of a 16-byte IA-32e TSS Descriptor

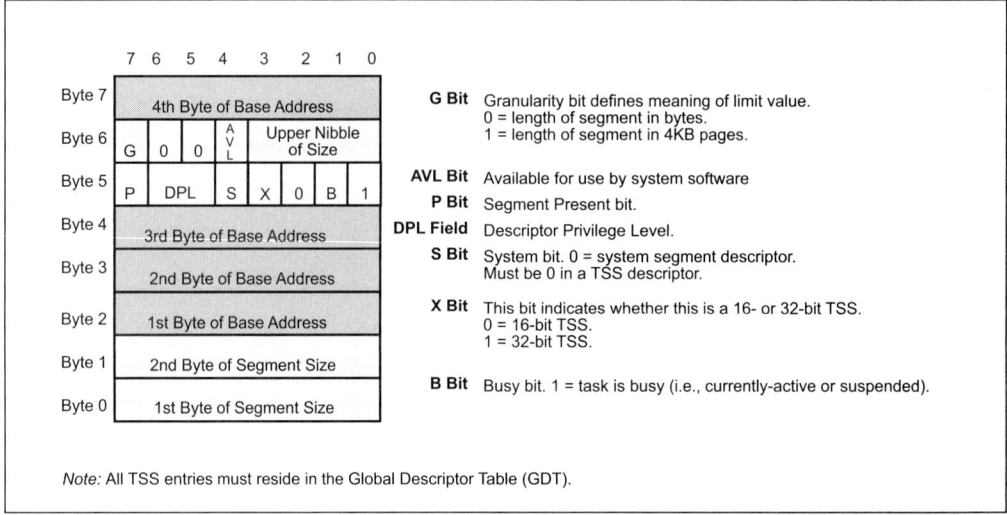

Executing LTR in 64-bit Mode

When the LTR instruction is executed in 64-bit Mode, the logical processor reads the selected 16-byte TSS descriptor (see Figure 23-26 on page 972) from the GDT and loads the 64-bit TSS base address and 32-bit size into the invisible portion of the TR (see Figure 23-27 on page 973).

Revised TSS Structure

Comparing the IA-32e TSS (Figure 23-25 on page 971) to the legacy TSS (see Figure 23-29 on page 975) reveals a number of changes:

*   **Link field** (refer to "Calling Another Task" on page 670) is now reserved because it's associated with the unsupported hardware-based task switching mechanism.
*   **SS*n*:ESP*n* Stack fields** (refer to "Automatic Stack Switch" on page 462). The three SS:ESP fields related to privilege levels 0, 1, and 2 have been replaced by the three 64-bit **RSP fields**.

- **Register save/restore area**. Because it was related to the now-unsupported hardware-based task switch mechanism, it has been replaced by the **Interrupt Stack Table (IST)**. See "Interrupt/Exception Stack Switch" on page 959 for more information.
- **Trap bit** [see "Debug Trap Bit (T)" on page 659] is now reserved because it's associated with the unsupported hardware-based task switch mechanism.
- **Interrupt Redirection Bitmap** (see "Software Interrupt Instruction Handling" on page 825) is no longer used because VM86 Mode is not supported in IA-32e Mode.

Figure 23-29: Legacy IA-32 TSS Data Structure

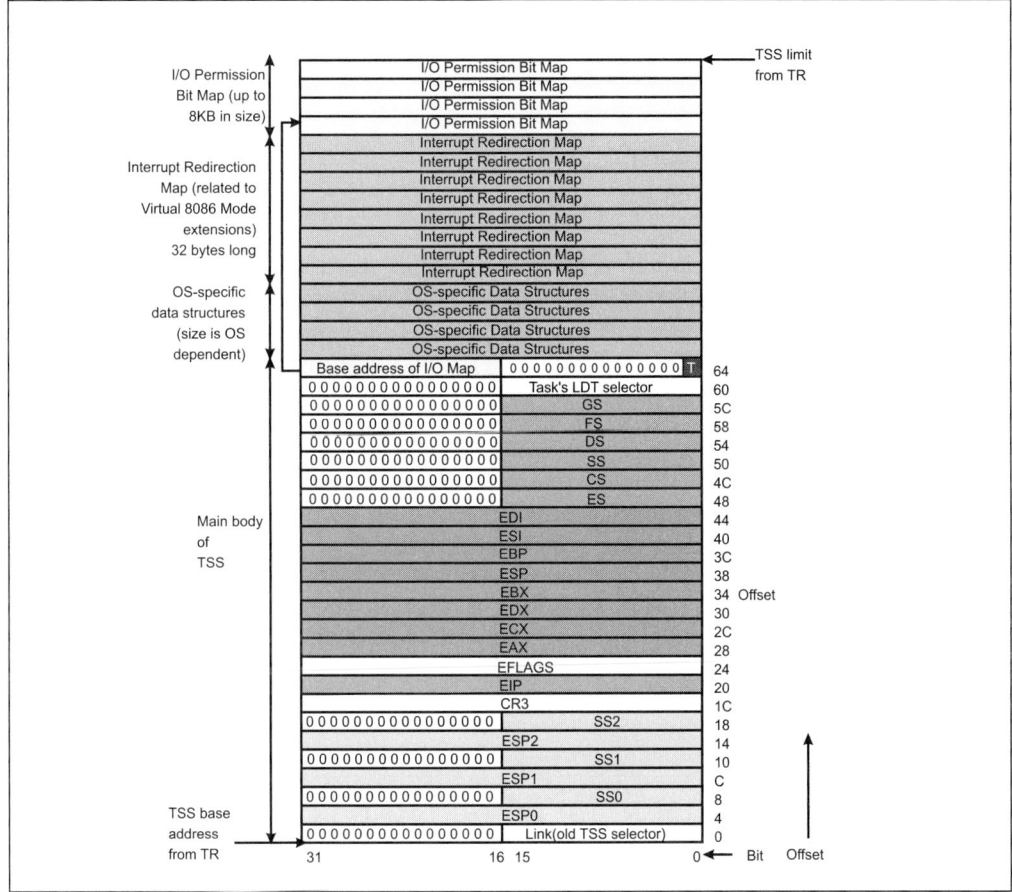

TSS Usage

General. Table 23-13 on page 976 describes the logical processor's usage of the TSS fields while it is operating in IA-32e Mode.

Table 23-13: TSS Usage in IA-32e Mode

Field(s)	Description
RSP[2:0]	Refer to "IA-32e Call Gate Stack Switch" on page 966 and "Interrupt/Trap Gate Operational Changes" on page 958.
IST[7:1]	Refer to "Interrupt/Trap Gate Operational Changes" on page 958.
IO Permission Bitmap	Utilized in the same manner as in IA-32 Mode. See "IO Permission in Protected Mode" on page 800.
OS-specific data structures	Can be utilized in the same manner as in IA-32 Mode. See "Optional Fields" on page 655.

Call Gate Stack Switch. If a far call is made to a 64-bit procedure in a more privileged CS through a Call Gate in IA-32e Mode, the logical processor, as it would in Protected Mode, will automatically switch to a fresh stack before making the call. There is a difference, however. Whereas the legacy TSS (see Figure 23-29 on page 975) defines six fields to hold the pointers to the privilege level 0, 1, and 2 stacks, the IA-32e TSS eliminates the SS fields (because the logical processor uses the flat memory model in 64-bit Mode) and implements instead three 64-bit RSP fields (see Figure 23-25 on page 971) to hold the respective stack pointers. A detailed description of their usage can be found in "IA-32e Call Gate Stack Switch" on page 966.

Interrupt/Exception Stack Switch. IA-32e Mode introduces an improved interrupt/exception stack switching mechanism. A detailed description can be found in "Interrupt/Trap Gate Operational Changes" on page 958.

Register Set Expansion (in 64-bit Mode)

When the logical processor is operating in 64-bit Mode, additional registers become available (these registers can only be addressed by prefacing an instruction with the REX prefix):

- 8 additional 64-bit GPR registers (R8 - R15).
- 8 additional 128-bit XMM registers (XMM8 - XMM15).
- 8 additional 64-bit Control registers (CR8 - CR15).
- 8 additional 64-bit Debug registers (DR8 - DR15).

In addition, the width of a number of legacy registers is expanded to 64-bits (note: the default operand size in 64-bit Mode is 32-bits; the expanded version of these registers can only be accessed by prefacing an instruction with the REX prefix). A detailed description of the registers available in 64-bit Mode can be found in the chapters entitled "64-bit Register Overview" on page 1023 and "64-bit Operands and Addressing" on page 1041.

Scheduler's Software-Based Task Switching Mechanism

Switching to a 64-bit Task

As previously covered in "Jumping from a Higher-to-Lesser Privileged Program" on page 441, it is not possible to jump from a privilege level 0 code segment to a privilege level 3 code segment (in order to launch or resume an application program). Instead, this is *accomplished by simulating a return from an exception handler.*

Prior to starting a user-level (i.e., privilege level 3) 64-bit task, the OS task scheduler takes the following actions. *Please note that this is intended as a simplified generic example not specific to any particular OS.*

The task switch code being executed resides in virtual page *n*. CR3 contains the start physical address of the top-level address translation table (PML4 Table) being used to translate the virtual addresses generated by the task switch code's memory accesses into physical addresses.

1. The application code to be started (or a portion of it) is loaded into one or more pages in physical memory.
2. The application's address translation tables are created in memory.
3. The start physical address of the new PML4 translation table is moved into CR3. This is accomplished using the task switch code's translation tables, so the **mov cr3** instruction is fetched from virtual page *n*.
4. The new translation tables must use the same mapping for virtual page *n* (i.e., accesses within virtual page *n* must be mapped to the physical page containing the task switch code).

5. Using CS:RIP, the next instruction is fetched from the next sequential location in virtual page *n* and is therefore mapped to next sequential instruction in the task switch code.

6. Execute a CLI to disable maskable interrupt recognition.

7. A note regarding the initialization of the data segment registers:
   — We're switching to a 64-bit task and the DS and ES segment registers aren't used (due to flat memory model enforcement). These two segment registers can be loaded with the null descriptor selector (GDT entry 0).
   — If the scheduler wishes to set a non-zero base address for the FS and/or GS data segment, it may do so in one of two ways:
       – If the base address is in the lower 4GB of memory, the FS or GS register may be loaded (using the MOV sreg or POP sreg instructions) with a value that selects a data segment descriptor. Assuming the P bit = 1, the logical processor will use the 32-bit base address obtained from the descriptor. All other elements of the selected descriptor are ignored.
       – If the programmer wishes to specify a 64-bit base address, the WRMSR instruction is used to write a 64-bit canonical address into the FS_Base or GS_Base MSR.

8. Allocate memory to be used as the stack for the application.

The steps that follow push the initial values for the application's stack pointer, Rflags value, and CS:RIP register values onto the stack (see Figure 23-30 on page 979) in preparation for executing the IRET instruction that will cause the task switch.

9. Push the application's stack pointer onto the stack. This consists of two 64-bit elements:
   — A 16-bit SS selector (i.e., selecting a GDT or LDT entry containing a data segment descriptor with the Present bit set to one) 0-extended to 64-bits (because interrupt/exception stack pushes are always 8-bytes each in 64-bit Mode).
   — The 64-bit RSP value points to the stack to be used by the task about to be started or resumed.

10. Create the 64-bit image to be loaded into the Rflags register when the application is initiated and push it onto the stack. Be sure and set the Rflags[IF] bit to 1 in the image so that when the Rflags register is loaded from the stack (on execution of the IRET instruction at the end of this sequence), recognition of maskable interrupts will be automatically reenabled.

11. Push the initial CS:RIP values onto the stack. This is the address of the application's first instruction. This actually consists of the 16-bit CS descriptor selector (0-extended to 64-bits) and the 64-bit RIP value and specifies the following:

- CS selector with an RPL value of 3 (assuming an application program is being started or resumed). In the CS descriptor chosen by the selector:
  - The DPL = 3.
  - The L bit = 1 indicating it is a 64-bit CS descriptor.
  - The D bit = 0 (this a requirement in a 64-bit CS descriptor).
- The RIP value specifies the initial entry point at which to start execution of the new task.

12. Execute the LTR instruction to load the TR with the base address and size of the application's TSS. Also see "Real World TSS Usage" on page 968.

13. Execute the IRET instruction. As a result:
- SS:RSP are loaded with the application's stack pointer.
- Rflags is loaded from the stack and, as a result, maskable interrupt recognition is reenabled.
- CS:RIP are loaded from the stack. The CPL changes to the application's privilege level (3).

14. Using the virtual address just loaded into the CS:RIP register pair, the first instruction of the application is fetched and executed. This virtual address could be either:
- The virtual address of the instruction immediately following the IRET in same virtual page (page *n*).
- An address in a different virtual page that contains the application's initial code.

Figure 23-30: Stack Contents When IRET Executed to Start Privilege Level 3, 64-bit Task

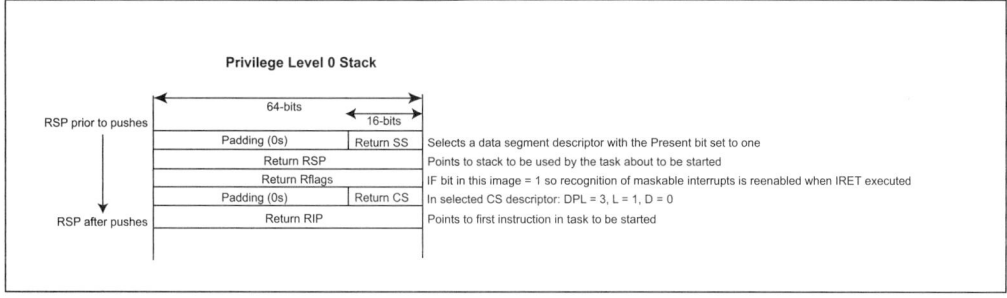

Switching to a Legacy Task

General

Similar to the discussion of "Switching to a 64-bit Task" on page 977, switching from the 64-bit scheduler to a legacy 16- or 32-bit task is *accomplished by simu-*

lating a return from an exception handler. While the stack frame created in preparation for execution of the IRET instruction uses the 64-bit format (Figure 23-31 on page 981 illustrates the stack frame created in preparation for switching to a 32-bit legacy task), the content of the register images it contains must adhere to those expected by the mode being switched to.

- RSP:
  — In a 16-bit task, only a 16-bit SP value is expected, so the upper 48-bits of the 64-bit RSP image are set to 0.
  — In a 32-bit task, only a 32-bit ESP value is expected, so the upper 32-bits of the 64-bit RSP image are set to 0.
- Rflags:
  — In a 16-bit task, only a 16-bit Flags value is expected, so the upper 48-bits of the 64-bit Rflags image are set to 0.
  — In a 32-bit task, only a 32-bit Eflags value is expected, so the upper 32-bits of the 64-bit Rflags image are set to 0.
- RIP:
  — In a 16-bit task, only a 16-bit IP value is expected, so the upper 48-bits of the 64-bit RIP image are set to 0.
  — In a 32-bit task, only a 32-bit EIP value is expected, so the upper 32-bits of the 64-bit RIP image are set to 0.

When the IRET is executed and the five 8-byte values are popped from the stack, the logical processor automatically masks out the upper portions that aren't used in the target mode (i.e., 16- or 32-bit Compatibility Mode).

Data Segment Register Initialization

The task switch code initializes the four data segment registers (DS, ES, FS, GS) with values that select the GDT or LDT entries describing the task's data segment(s). The RPL portion of the selector(s) = 3 if we switching to a level 3 application. *Note that, unlike 64-bit Mode, all elements of the selected data segment descriptors will be used by the logical processor once the switch to Compatibility Mode occurs.*

CS and Instruction Pointer Initialization

The two values (CS:IP or CS:EIP) to be restored to the register pair upon execution of the IRET consists of the 16-bit CS descriptor selector (0-extended to 64-bits) and the 16-bit IP or 32-bit EIP value (0-extended to 64 bits) and specifies the following:

- The CS value contains the target CS selector and an RPL value of 3.
- In the CS descriptor chosen by the selector:

— The DPL = 3.
— The L bit = 0 indicating it is a legacy CS descriptor.
— The D bit:
 – 0 if the task being started is a 16-bit task.
 – 1 if it's a 32-bit task.
— The segment base address, limit and other attributes must be valid.
• The 16-bit IP or 32-bit EIP value specifies the initial entry point at which to start execution of the new task in its code segment.

The Switch

The execution of the IRET instruction causes the SS:RSP, Rflags, and CS:RIP registers to be loaded from the stack. This has the following effects:

• The values loaded into the SS:RSP register pair points to the top of the stack pre-allocated by the OS for the use of the application program.
• Recognition of maskable interrupts is reenabled (because Rflags[IF] is set to one again).
• CPL is set to the DPL of the new code segment (3 if it's an application program).
• L = 0. This causes the logical processor to exit 64-bit Mode and enter Compatibility Mode.
• D bit:
 — 0 causes the logical processor to enter 16-bit Compatibility Mode.
 — 1 causes the logical processor to enter 32-bit Compatibility Mode.
• The new RIP value popped from the stack points to the first instruction of the task being started.

The logical processor then starts fetching code from the address pointed to by the CS:IP or CS:EIP register pair (the first instruction of the new task).

Figure 23-31: Stack Contents When IRET Executed to Start Legacy Task

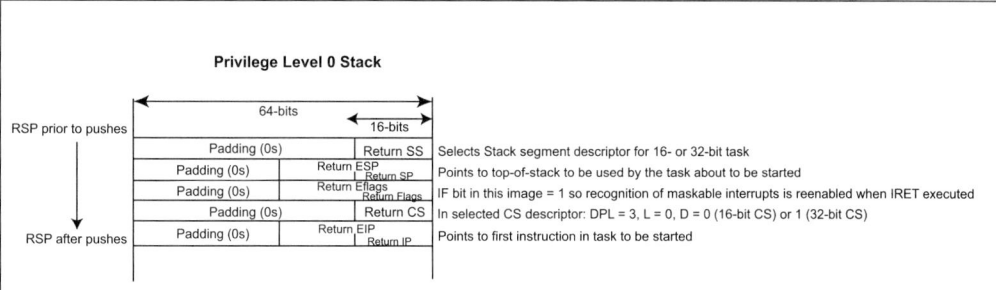

24 *IA-32e Address Translation*

The Previous Chapter

The previous chapter provided a detailed description of the IA-32e OS environment. The following topics were covered:

- Mode Switching Overview.
- Virtual Memory Addressing in IA-32e Mode.
- In 64-bit Mode, Hardware-Enforced Flat Model.
- 64-bit Instruction Pointer.
- Instruction Fetching.
- RIP-Relative Data Accesses.
- Changes To Kernel-Related Registers and Structures.
- Address Translation Mechanism.
- GDT/LDT Descriptor Changes.
- GDT and GDTR Changes.
- LDT and LDTR Changes.
- IDT/IDTR and Interrupt/Exception Changes.
- Interrupt/Trap Gate Operational Changes.
- IRET Behavior.
- IA-32e Call Gate Operation.
- TR and TSS Changes.
- Register Set Expansion (in 64-bit Mode).
- Scheduler's Software-Based Task Switching Mechanism.

This Chapter

This chapter provides a detailed description of the third generation address translation mechanism utilized in IA-32e Mode. This includes the following topics:

- Theoretical Address Space Size.
- Limitation Imposed by Current Implementation.
- Four-Level Lookup Mechanism.
  — Address Space Partitioning.
  — The Address Translation.
    - Initializing CR3.
    - Step 1: PML4 Lookup.
    - Step 2: PDPT Lookup.
    - Step 3: Page Directory Lookup.
    - Step 4: Page Table Lookup.
  — Page Protection Mechanisms in IA-32e Mode.
    - Page Protection in Compatibility Mode.
    - Page Protection in 64-bit Mode.
    - Don't Forget the Execute Disable Feature!
- TLBs Are More Important Than Ever.
- No 4MB Page Support.

The Next Chapter

The next chapter provides a detailed description of the Compatibility SubMode of IA-32e Mode.This includes the following topics:

- Initial Entry to Compatibility Mode.
- Switching Between Compatibility Mode and 64-bit Mode.
- Differences Between IA-32 Mode and Compatibility Mode.
- Memory Addressing.
- Register Set.
- Exception and Interrupt Handling.
- OS Kernel Calls.
- IRET Changes.
- Segment Load Instructions.

Theoretical Address Space Size

Theoretically, the 3rd generation address translation mechanism utilized in IA-32e Mode would support the translation of 64-bit virtual addresses to 52-bit physical addresses. This would provide the OS with the following virtual and physical memory space sizes:

- 2^{64} virtual addressing would permit the OS to assign virtual address ranges to applications within an 16EB (exabyte) virtual address space.

- 2^{52} physical addressing would permit the OS to map a 64-bit virtual address to any physical memory address in a 4PB (petabyte) physical memory address space.

Limitation Imposed by Current Implementations

Current implementations do not support the theoretical maximum virtual or physical address ranges, however:

- A 2^{48} (256TB—terabyte) virtual address space is currently supported.
- A 2^{40} (1TB) physical memory address space (and, in some high-end AMD products, 2^{48}) is currently supported.

In other words, in IA-32e Mode the 3rd generation address translation mechanism is presented with a 48-bit virtual address (sign-extended to 64-bits to form a 64-bit canonical address) which it translates into a 40-bit (or, in some high-end AMD products, a 41- or 48-bit) physical memory address.

Four-Level Lookup Mechanism

Address Space Partitioning

Refer to Figure 24-1 on page 987. In A-32e Mode, the partitioning of the 256TB virtual address space using a 48-bit address is viewed as follows:

- The overall 48-bit 256TB virtual space is divided into 512 blocks of 512GB each. Bits 47:39 identify the target 512GB block and selects the entry in the PML4 Directory associated with the addressed 512GB virtual address block (block 66 in the illustration). PML4 Entry 4 contains the physical base address of the Page Directory Pointer Table that catalogs the location of the 512 Page Directories (PDs) associated with the targeted 512GB block.
- Each 512GB block is sub-divided into 512 blocks of 1GB each. Bits 38:30 identify the target 1GB block and selects the entry in the Page Directory Pointer Table associated with the addressed 1GB virtual address block (block 97 in the illustration). Page Directory Pointer Table Entry 97 contains the physical base address of the Page Directory that catalogs the location of the 512 Page Tables associated with the targeted 1GB block.
- Each 1GB block is sub-divided into 512 blocks of 2MB each. Bits 29:21 identify the target 2MB block and selects the entry in the Page Directory associ-

ated with the addressed 2MB virtual address block (block 8 in the illustration). Page Directory Entry 8 contains either:

— The 4KB-aligned physical base address of the Page Table (PT) that catalogs the location of the 512 4KB pages in the targeted 2MB block;

— Or the physical base address of the targeted 2MB page in memory.

- Each 2MB block is sub-divided into 512 pages of 4KB each. Bits 20:12 identify the target 4KB page and selects the entry in the Page Table associated with the addressed 4KB virtual page (page 34 in the illustration). Page Table Entry 34 contains the physical base address of the target 4KB page.
- The lower 12-bits (11:0) identifies the target location within the page.

Figure 24-1: IA-32e 3rd Generation Address Translation Mechanism

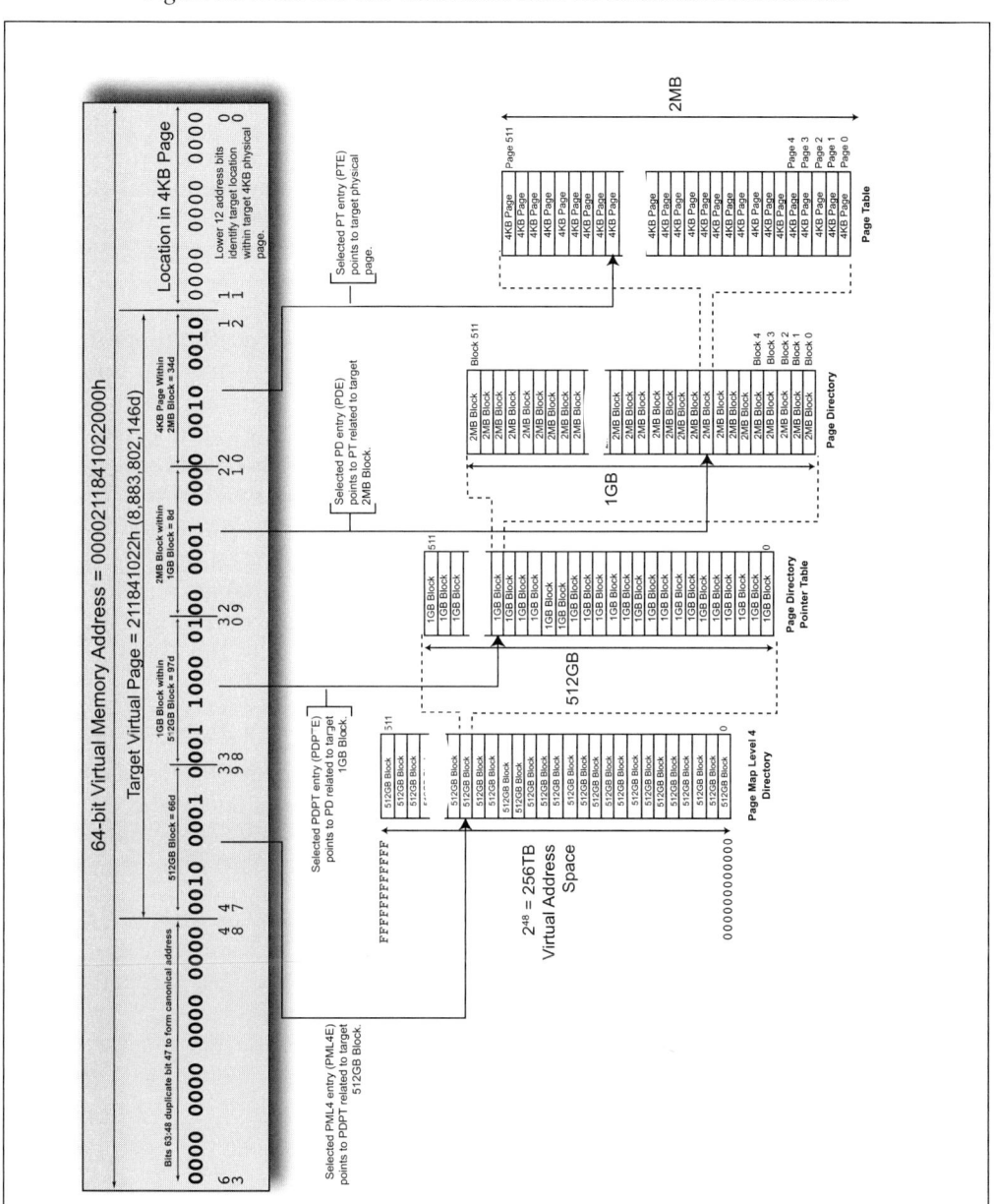

The Address Translation

Refer to Figure 24-2 on page 989.

Initializing CR3

Prior to starting or resuming the execution of a task, the task scheduler creates the set of memory-based address translation tables that the logical processor will use to translate the virtual memory addresses generated by the program into the appropriate physical memory addresses. It then loads CR3 with the base physical address of the top-level translation table.

When the logical processor is still in Protected Mode and the programmer is preparing to switch it into IA-32e Mode, the MOV CR3 instruction is executed to load CR3 with the base physical address of the top-level translation table (i.e., the Page Map Level 4—PML4—directory). Because the logical processor has not yet entered IA-32e Mode, however, only the lower 32-bits of CR3 are accessible. The top-level directory must therefore reside at a memory address in the lower 4GB of physical memory. Once the logical processor has completed the switch into IA-32e Mode and is executing OS kernel code from a 64-bit code segment, the programmer may relocate the address translation tables above the 4GB address boundary and then execute a MOV CR3 instruction to load the 64-bit physical start address of the top-level translation table (i.e., the PML4).

Step 1: PML4 Lookup

Refer to Figure 24-2 on page 989 and Figure 24-3 on page 990. Virtual address bits [47:39] identify the targeted 512GB block and selects one of the 512 entries in the PML4. The selected PML4 entry (PML4E) is 64-bits wide and, if valid, points to the 2nd-level Page Directory Pointer Table (PDPT) that catalogs the location of the 512 Page Directories (PDs) associated with the targeted 512GB block.

Figure 24-2: IA-32e Address Translation Step 1

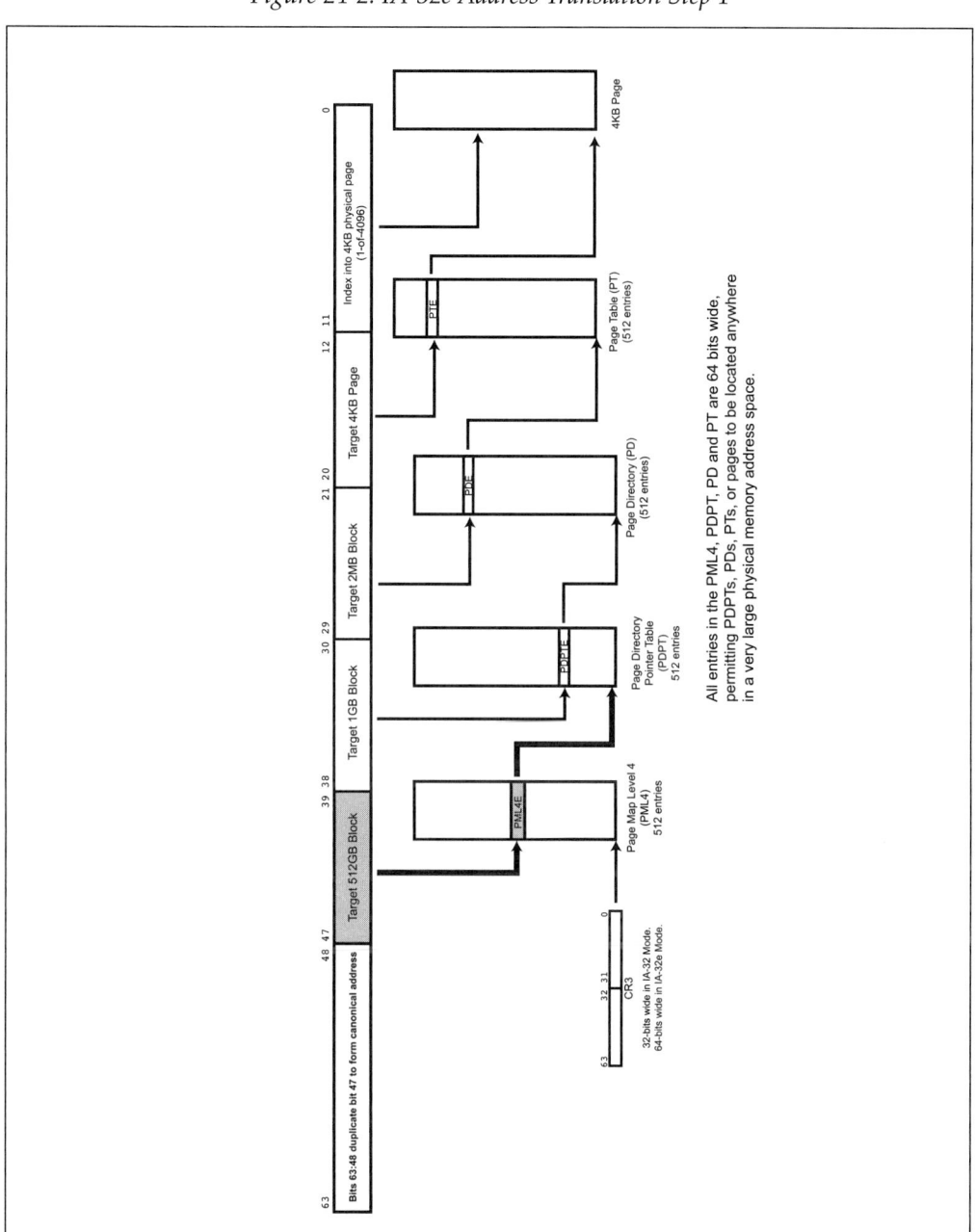

Figure 24-3: IA-32e Mode: PML4 Entry (PML4E) Format

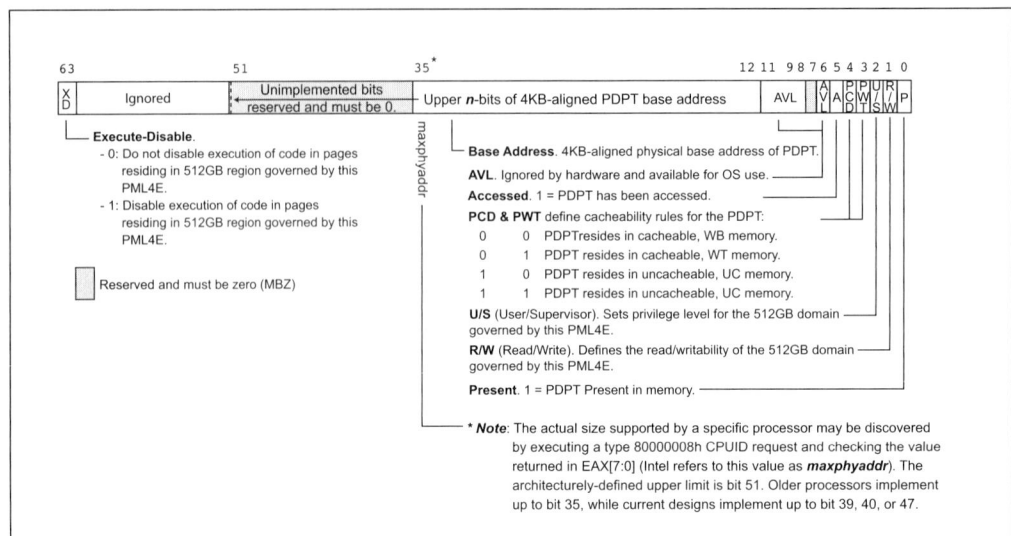

Step 2: PDPT Lookup

Refer to Figure 24-4 on page 991 and Figure 24-5 on page 992. Virtual address bits [38:30] identify the targeted 1GB block and selects one of the 512 entries in the PDPT. The selected PDPT entry (PDPTE) is 64-bits wide and, if valid, points to the 3rd-level Page Directory that catalogs the location of the 512 Page Tables associated with the targeted 1GB block.

Figure 24-4: IA-32e Address Translation Step 2

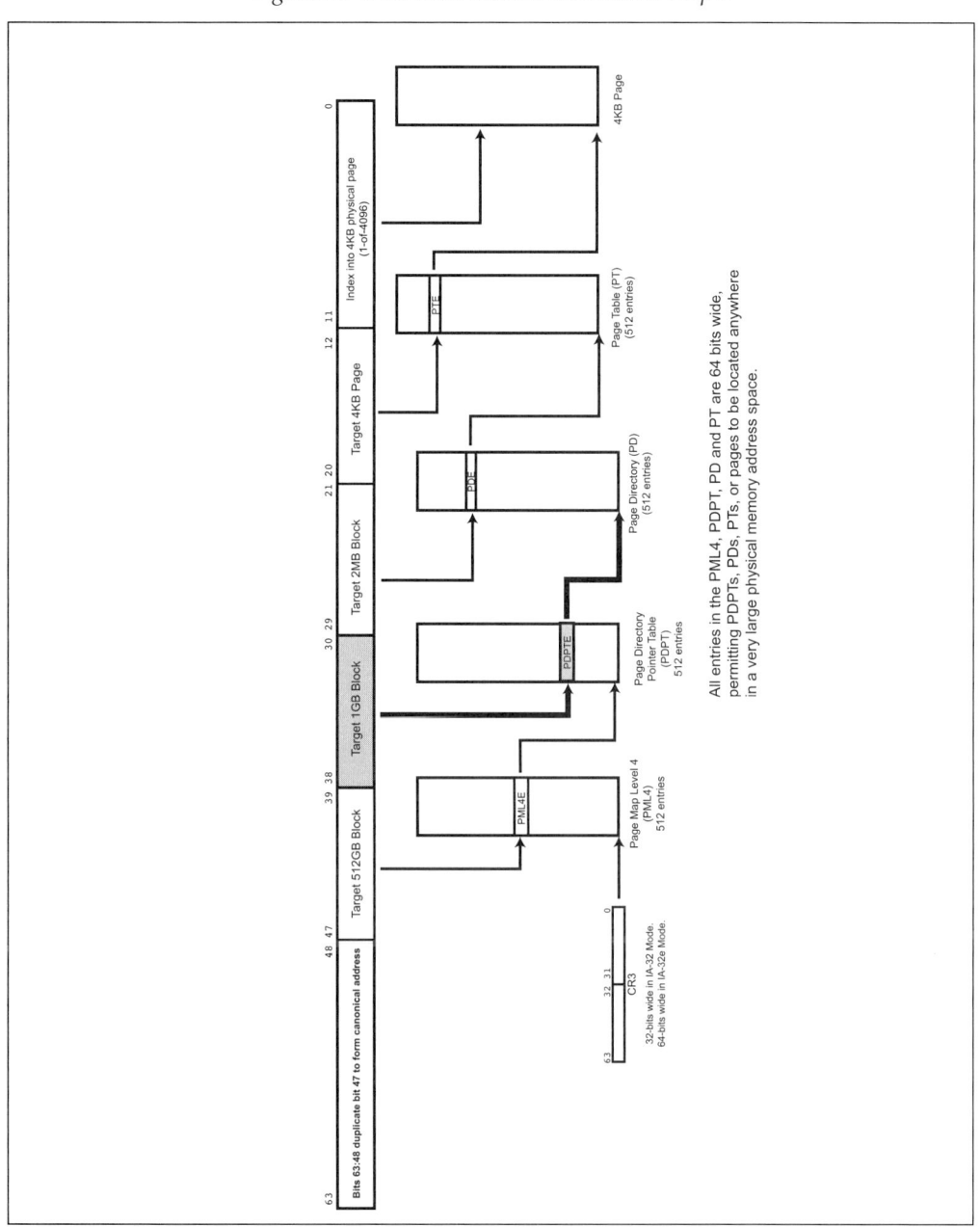

Figure 24-5: IA-32e Mode: PDPT Entry (PDPTE) Format

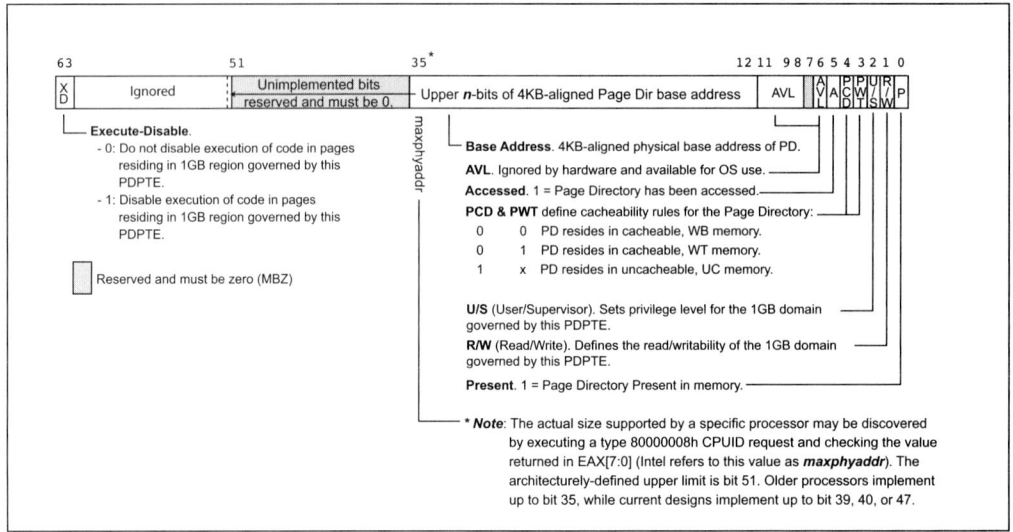

Step 3: Page Directory Lookup

Refer to Figure 24-6 on page 993. Virtual address bits [29:21] select 1-of-512 entries (PDEs) in the selected Page Directory. The selected PDE is associated with the targeted 2MB block:

- If the Present bit in the PDE = 0, the PDE is not valid and the PT or 2MB page is not currently in memory. This causes the logical processor to experience a Page Fault exception.
- If the Present bit in the selected PDE = 1, then the entry is valid and contains either:
  — The 4KB-aligned physical base address of the Page Table (PT) that catalogs the location of the 512 4KB pages in the targeted 2MB block;
  — Or the physical base address of the targeted 2MB page in memory.

Assuming the selected PDE is valid (i.e., PDE[P] = 1), it has one of the formats described in the next two sections.

Figure 24-6: IA-32e Address Translation Step 3

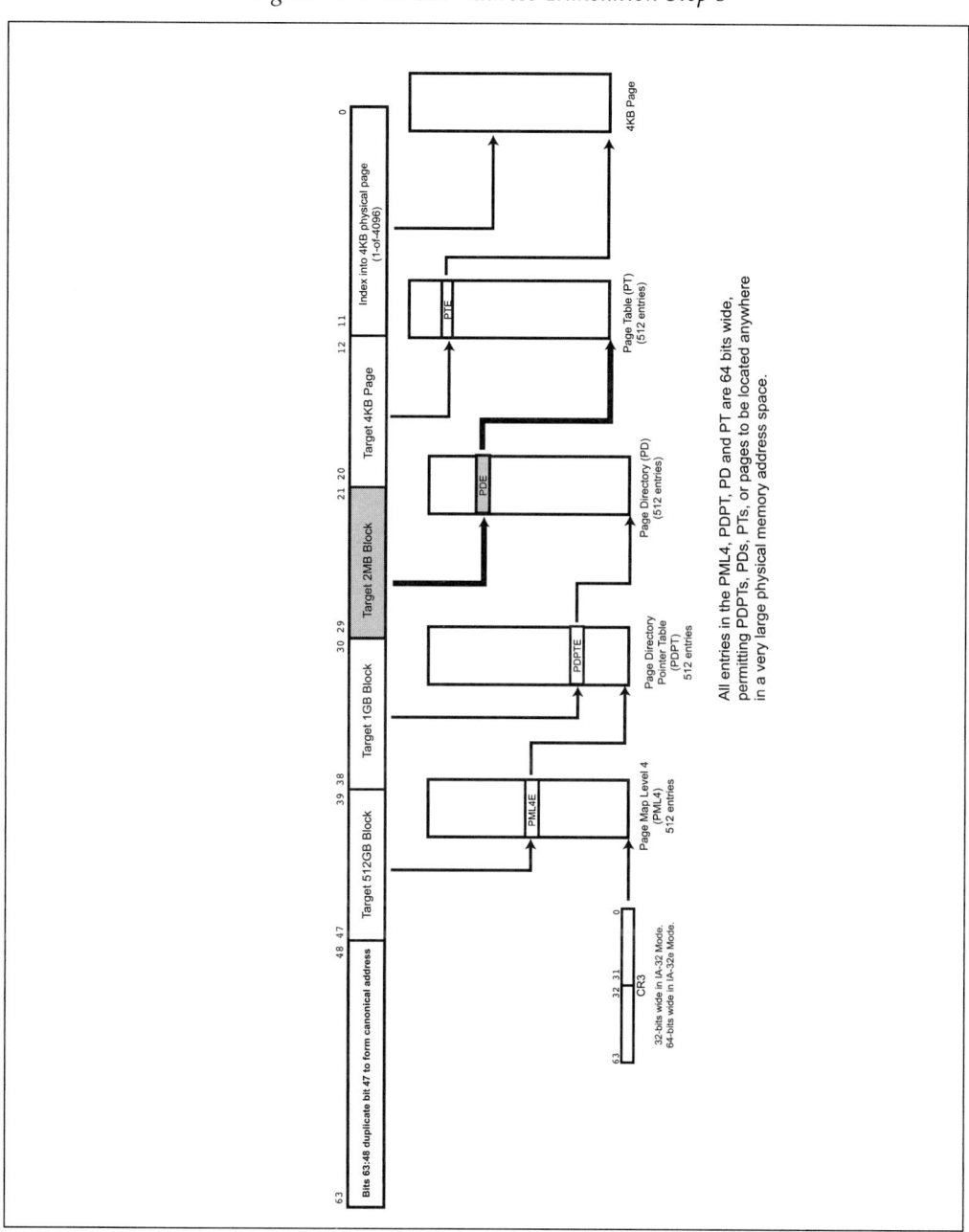

Step 3a: PDE Points to a Page Table. When PDE[PS] = 0 (see Figure 24-7 on page 994), the PDE contains the upper bits (the number of bits is implementation-specific) of the 4KB-aligned physical base address of the Page Table (PT) that catalogs the location of the 512 4KB pages in the selected 2MB block.

The final step in the address translation is described in "Step 4: Page Table Lookup" on page 997.

Figure 24-7: IA-32e Mode: PD Entry (PDE) Format (points to Page Table)

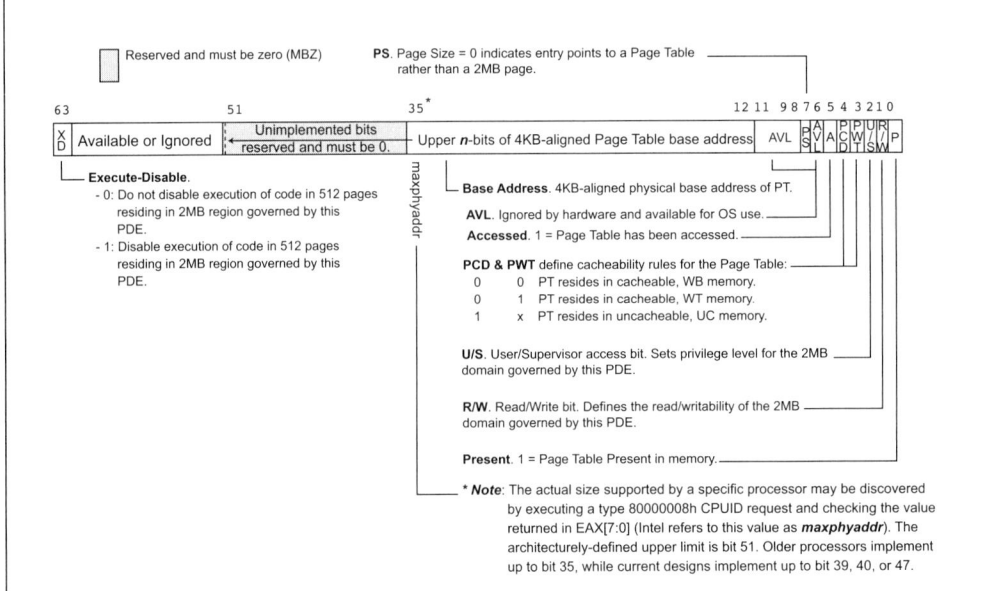

Step 3b: PDE Points to a 2MB Physical Page. When PDE[PS] = 1 (see Figure 24-8 on page 995), the PDE contains the 2MB-aligned physical base address of the targeted 2MB page (see Figure 24-9 on page 996). In this case, no 4th-level lookup is performed and the address translation is complete. The final physical memory address (its width is implementation-specific) is constructed as follows:

— The upper bits of the 2MB-aligned physical memory address are supplied from the PDE and
— The lower 21 bits are supplied by virtual address bits [20:0].

The PDE's PAT, PCD and PWT bits define the page's memory type (see "Defining a Page's Caching Rules" on page 585).

The reader should note that, when operating in IA-32e Mode, the logical processor ignores CR4[PSE] and 4MB pages are not supported.

Figure 24-8: IA-32e Mode: Page PD Entry (PDE) Format (points to 2MB page)

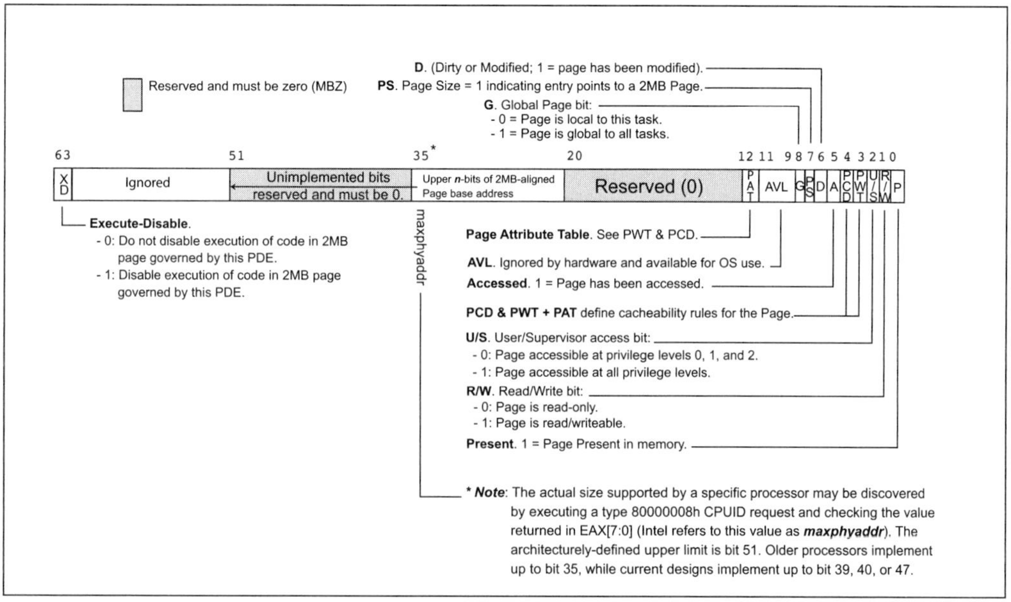

Figure 24-9: 2MB Physical Page Selected

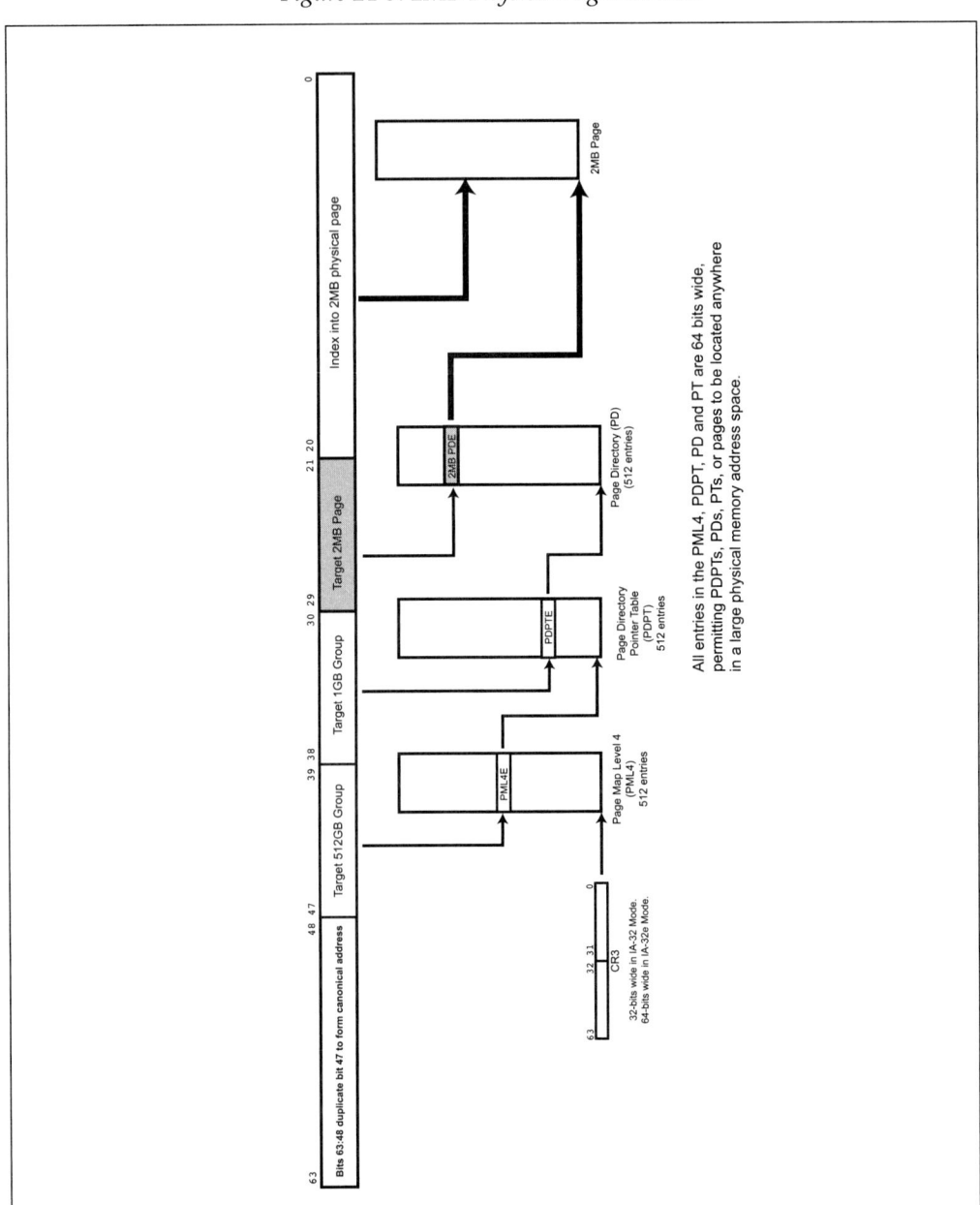

Step 4: Page Table Lookup

If the selected PDE is valid (i.e., PDE[P] = 1) and PDE[PS] = 0, then the PDE (see Figure 24-11 on page 998) points to the fourth and final lookup table, the Page Table. The paging unit uses virtual address bits [20:12] to index into the selected Page Table and the selected PTE has the format shown in Figure 24-10 on page 997. Finally, address bits [11:0] (which are never translated) are used to select the target location within the physical page.

The final physical memory address is constructed as follows:

- The upper bits of the physical memory address are supplied from the PTE's base address field.
- The lower 12 bits are supplied by virtual address bits [11:0].

The 3-bits consisting of PAT, PCD and PWT define the page's memory type (see "Defining a Page's Caching Rules" on page 585).

Figure 24-10: PT Entry (PTE) Format

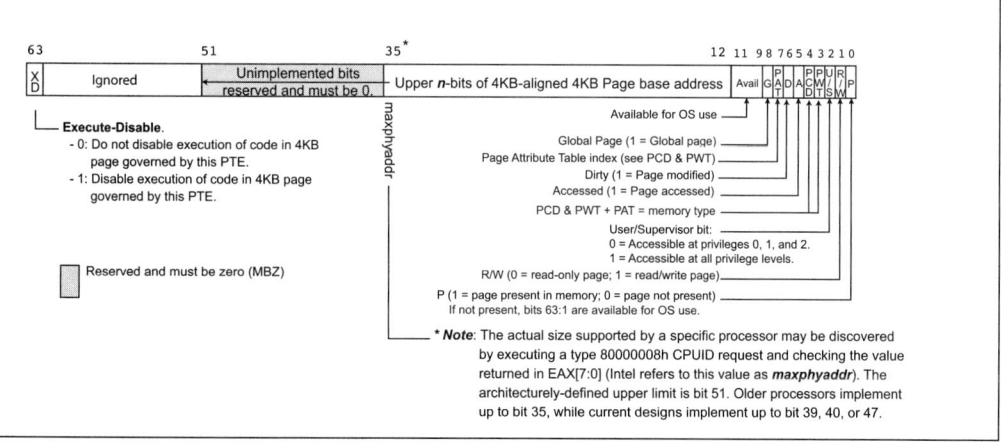

Figure 24-11: IA-32e Address Translation Step 4

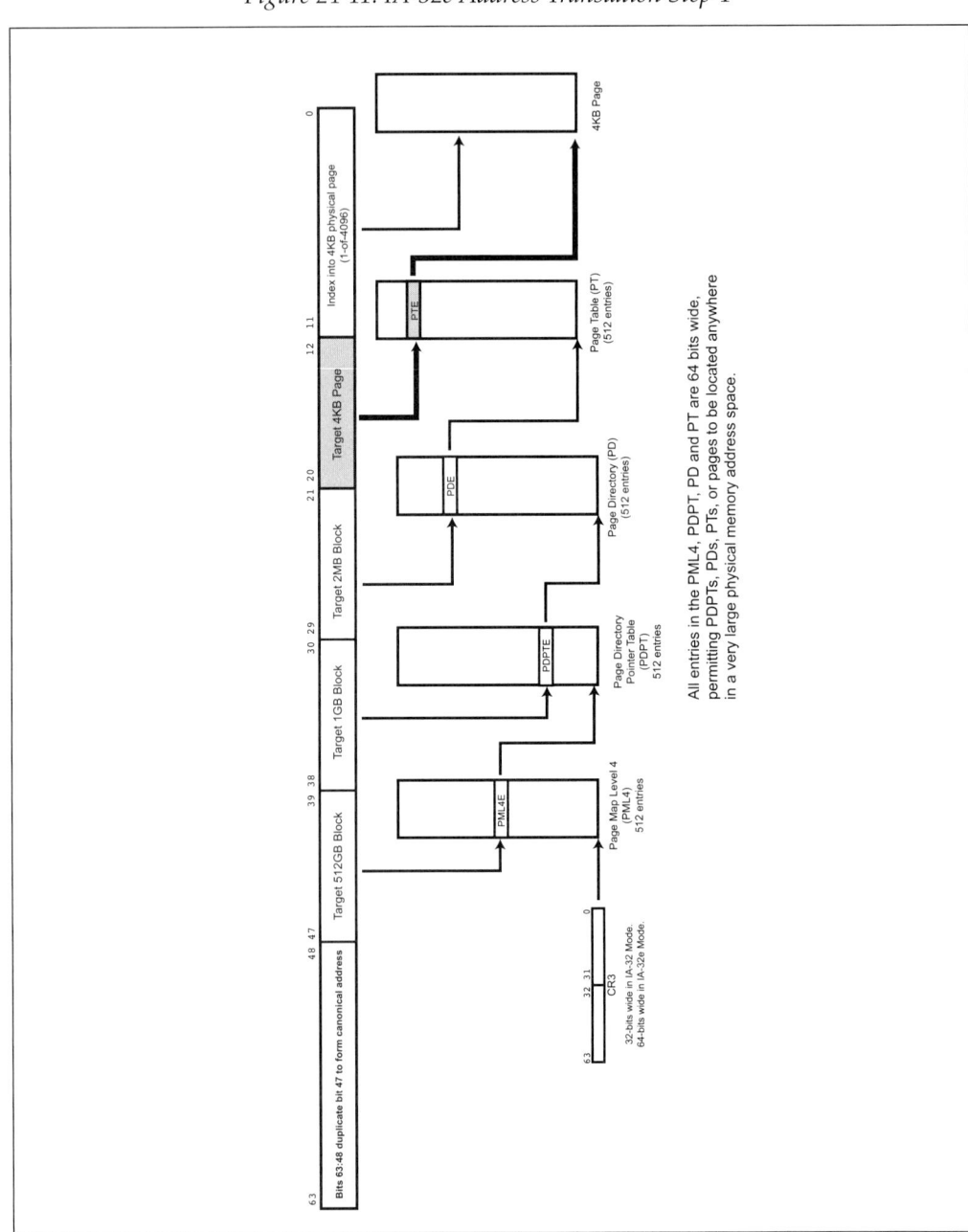

Page Protection Mechanisms in IA-32e Mode

Page Protection in Compatibility Mode

When the logical processor is operating in Compatibility Mode, page access permission determination operates just as it does in Protected Mode (see "Checking Page Access Permission" on page 535).

In Compatibility Mode, the logical processor first checks the access type against the respective segment descriptor's attributes. Assuming the access type is permitted by the segment attribute settings, the logical processor then checks the access type against the page attributes to determine if it will be permitted.

Page Protection in 64-bit Mode

When the logical processor is operating in 64-bit Mode, however, page access permission determination operates a little differently than in Compatibility Mode. The logical processor ignores:

- The code segment's R (Readable) bit.
- The data and stack segments' R/W, E and DPL checks.

One must also take into account the following statement from section 2.3 in AMD's Programmer's Manual Volume 2: System Programming:

> "Code and data segments used in 64-bit mode are treated as both readable and writable."

This is in direct contrast to Protected Mode and Compatibility Mode wherein a code segment is by definition not writable and any attempt to write to a code segment results in an exception. Read/Write protection for code areas must therefore be provided by the address translation attributes (R/W and U/S).

With one exception, access permission is based solely on the attributes associated with the address translation tables:

- **Data or Stack access permission check.** If an access targets a location in the stack or any of the data segments, the logical processor ignores all of the respective segment descriptor's attributes and makes a permission determination based solely on the address translation attributes.

- **Code segment access permission check**. If the access is a code fetch, before checking the address translation attributes, the logical processor first factors in the code segment's DPL:
  - If the DPL = 3, it is User-level code segment. In this case, the logical processor does go on to check the address translation attributes to determine the effective U/S permission.
  - If the DPL is not equal to 3, it is a Supervisor-level code segment. The logical processor ignores the state of the U/S bit in the address translation attributes and the effective U/S permission for the access is Supervisor.

Figure 24-12 on page 1001 and Figure 24-13 on page 1002 illustrate the logic used in 64-bit Mode to determine a page's effective R/W and U/S permissions, while Figure 24-14 on page 1003 (applies to Intel processors) and Figure 24-15 on page 1004 (applies to AMD processors) illustrate the logic used to determine whether a write to a page will be allowed to proceed or will result in an exception.

Don't Forget the Execute Disable Feature!

In addition to R/W and U/S protection, also keep in mind the Execute Disable feature. For a detailed description, refer to "Execute Disable Feature" on page 579.

Figure 24-12: Read/Write Permission Determination in 64-bit Mode

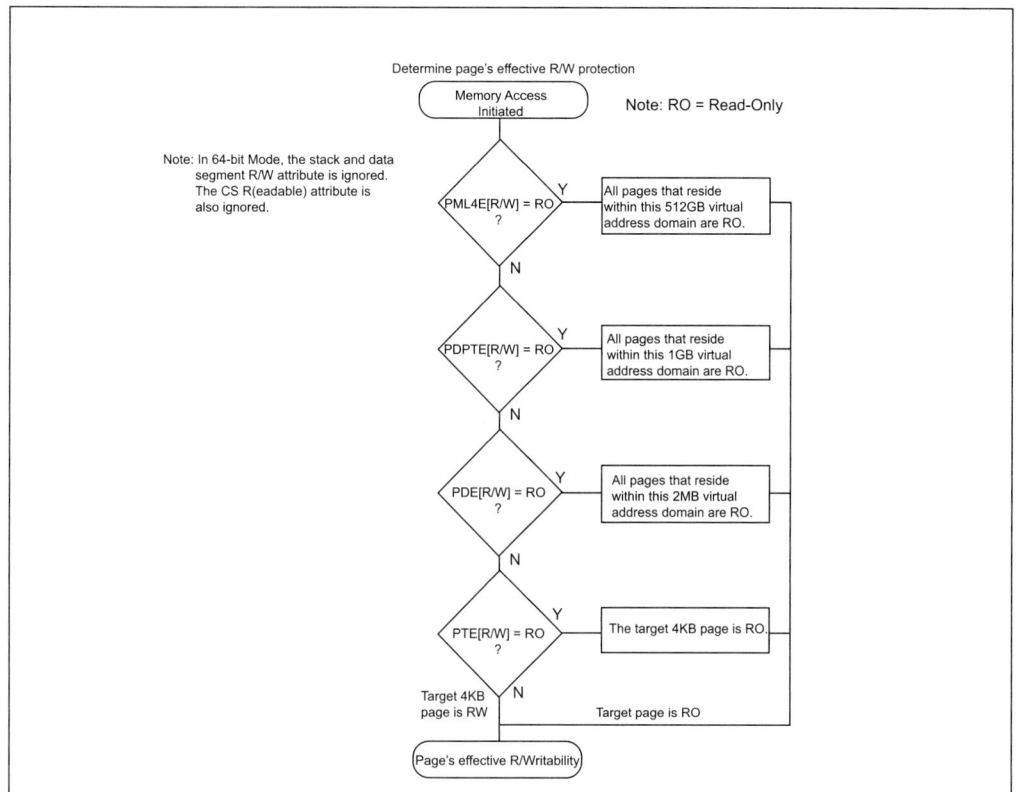

Figure 24-13: User/Supervisor Permission Determination in 64-bit Mode

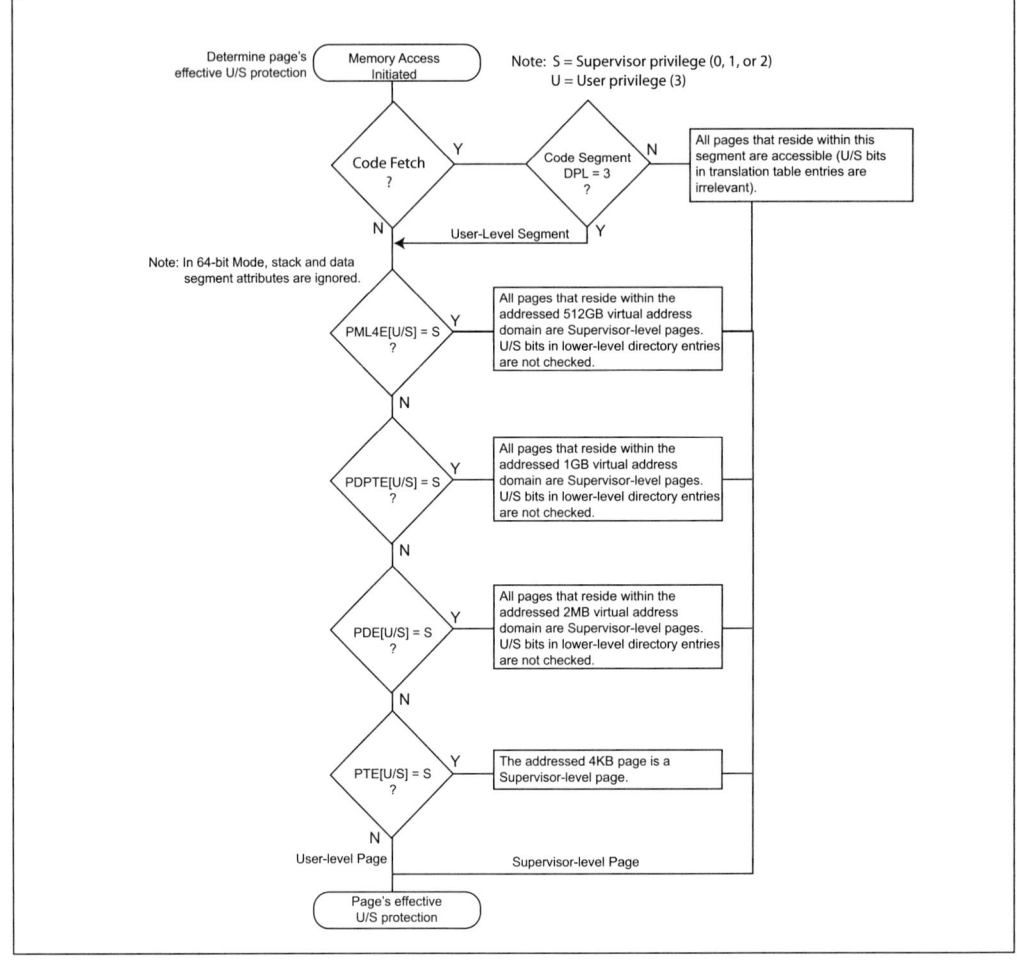

Figure 24-14: Write-Protection in 64-bit Mode (Intel)

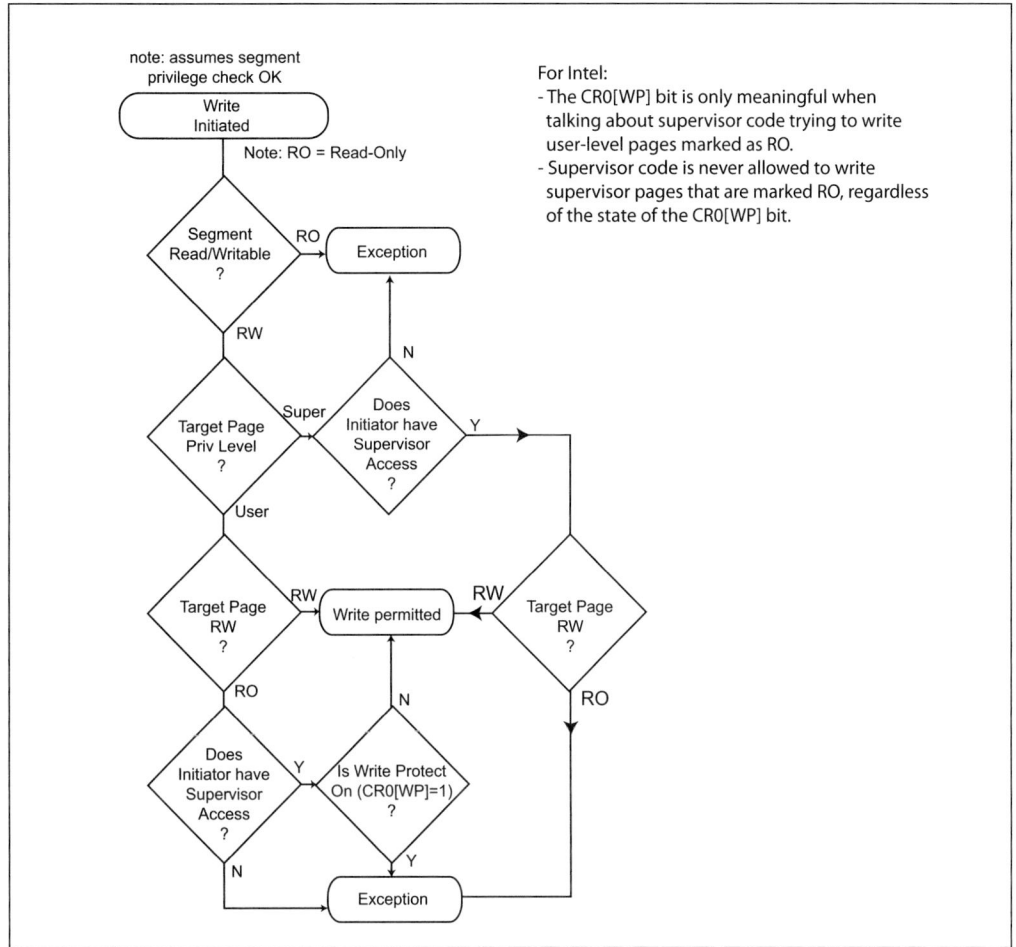

Figure 24-15: Write-Protection in 64-bit Mode (AMD)

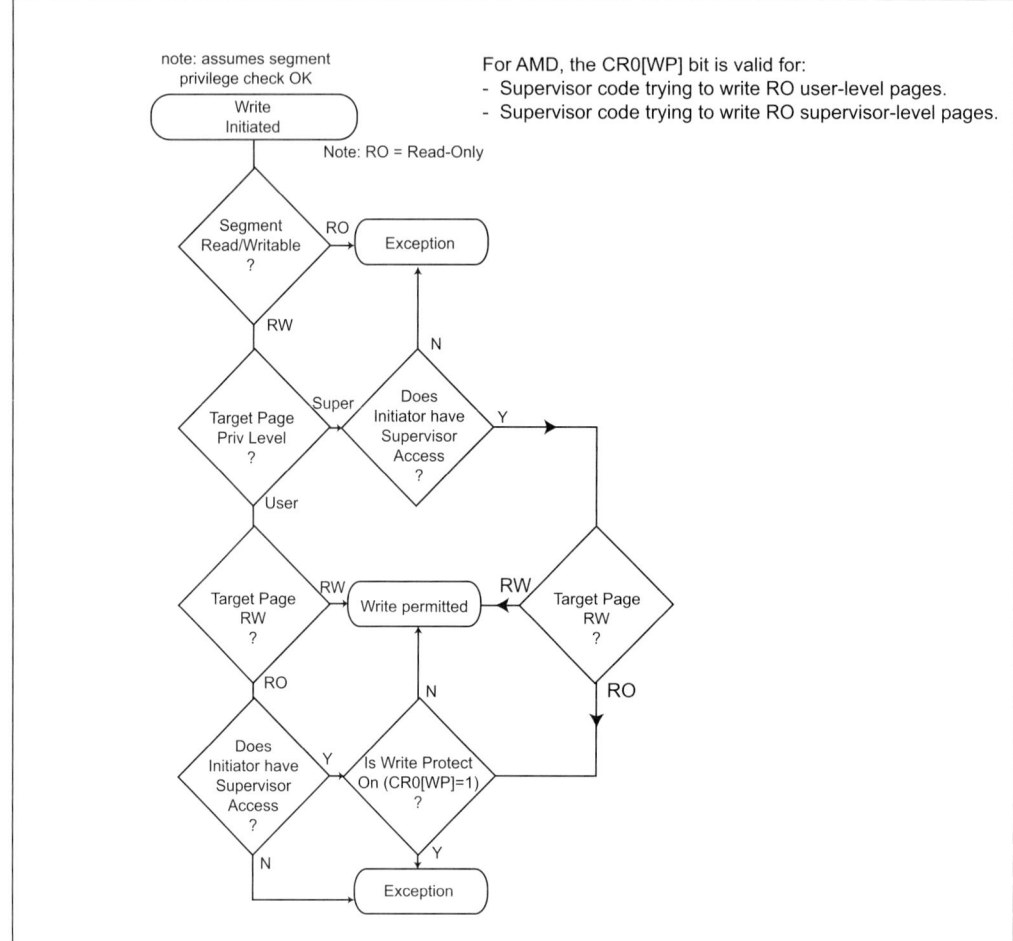

TLBs Are More Important Than Ever

As previously introduced in "3-Level Lookup—Increased TLB Size" on page 571, the four overhead memory reads performed by the 3rd generation translation mechanism can result in severe performance degradation. IA-32e-capable processors therefore implement larger TLBs (Translation Lookaside Buffers).

No 4MB Page Support

IA-32e Mode supports 4KB and 2MB pages. 4MB pages (see "4MB Pages" on page 550) are not supported.

Part 4:
Compatibility
Mode

The Previous Part

Part 3 provided a detailed description of the IA-32e OS kernel environment.

This Part

Part 4 provides a detailed description of the Compatibility submode of IA-32e Mode and consist of the following chapter:

- Chapter 25, entitled "Compatibility Mode," on page 1009.

The Next Part

Part 5 provides a detailed description of the 64-bit submode of IA-32e Mode.

25 *Compatibility Mode*

The Previous Chapter

The previous chapter provided a detailed description of the third generation address translation mechanism utilized in IA-32e Mode. This included the following topics:

- Theoretical Address Space Size.
- Limitation Imposed by Current Implementation.
- Four-Level Lookup Mechanism.
  — Address Space Partitioning.
  — The Address Translation.
    – Initializing CR3.
    – Step 1: PML4 Lookup.
    – Step 2: PDPT Lookup.
    – Step 3: Page Directory Lookup.
    – Step 4: Page Table Lookup.
  — Page Protection Mechanisms in IA-32e Mode.
    – Page Protection in Compatibility Mode.
    – Page Protection in 64-bit Mode.
    – Don't Forget the Execute Disable Feature!
- TLBs Are More Important Than Ever.
- No 4MB Page Support.

This Chapter

This chapter provides a detailed description of the Compatibility SubMode of IA-32e Mode. This includes the following topics:

- Initial Entry to Compatibility Mode.
- Switching Between Compatibility Mode and 64-bit Mode.
- Differences Between IA-32 Mode and Compatibility Mode.
- Memory Addressing.
- Register Set.

- Exception and Interrupt Handling.
- OS Kernel Calls.
- IRET Changes.
- Segment Load Instructions.

The Next Chapter

The next chapter provides an overview of the following:

- 64-bit Register Set.
- EFER (Extended Features Enable) Register.
- Sixteen 64-bit Control Registers.
- 64-bit Rflags Register.
- Sixteen 64-bit GPRs.
- Kernel Data Structure Registers in 64-bit Mode.
- SSE Register Set Expanded in 64-bit Mode.
- Debug Breakpoint Registers.
- Local APIC Register Set.
- x87 FPU/MMX Register Set.
- Architecturally-Defined MSRs.

Initial Entry to Compatibility Mode

This subject was introduced in "Initial Switch from IA-32 to IA-32e Mode" on page 917. A detailed description may be found in "Transitioning to IA-32e Mode" on page 1139.

Switching Between Compatibility Mode and 64-bit Mode

Once the logical processor has entered into IA-32e Mode, its mode of operation is controlled by the state of the D (Default) and L (Long Mode) bits in the current code segment's descriptor. Additional information about switching between Compatibility Mode and 64-bit Mode may be found in the following sections:

- "CS D and L Bits Control IA-32e SubMode Selection" on page 920.
- "Scheduler's Software-Based Task Switching Mechanism" on page 977.

Differences Between IA-32 Mode and Compatibility Mode

IA-32 Background

Except for those differences cited in this chapter, Compatibility Mode works exactly like 16- and 32-bit Protected Mode. Detailed descriptions of Protected Mode operation may be found in "Part 2: IA-32 Mode".

Unsupported IA-32 Features

The following IA-32 Mode features are not supported in IA-32e Mode (and are therefore not supported in Compatibility Mode):

- The hardware-based task switching mechanism. Due to this constraint, the following changes take effect:
  — Task Gates may not be selected in system tables (i.e., the GDT, LDTs and the IDT).
  — A far jump or a far call may not select:
    – A TSS descriptor in the GDT.
    – A Task Gate in the GDT or LDT.
    TSS descriptors are still used, however.
  — The TSS fields associated with automated task switching have been eliminated.
  — Execution of the IRET instruction when CR0[NT] = 1 does not cause a task switch.
- Real Mode.
- VM86 Mode.
- The 1st and 2nd generation address translation mechanisms.
- 4MB pages.

Changes to the OS Environment

As previously described in "IA-32e OS Environment" on page 913, the changes to the OS environment listed in Table 25-1 on page 1012 take effect in IA-32e Mode.

Table 25-1: OS Environment Changes in IA-32e Mode

Element	Description of Change
CS descriptor	A previously reserved bit, now defined as the L (Long Mode) bit, sets the logical processor's operating mode to 64-bit (L = 1) or Compatibility Mode (L = 0).
IDT	All entries in the IDT must consist of 16-byte Interrupt and Trap Gate descriptors that point to 64-bit handlers.
Call Gate	All Call Gate descriptors must be 16-byte descriptors that point to 64-bit OS services.
TSS descriptor	All TSS descriptors are 16-bytes long.
TSS	The TSS data structure format has been restructured to: • Support the IST mechanism (refer to "Interrupt/Exception Stack Switch" on page 976). • Eliminate the register save/restore area used by the automated task switch mechanism (because it is not supported). • Eliminate the Interrupt Redirection bitmap (because VM86 Mode is not supported). • Eliminate the Link field used by the automated task switch mechanism. • Eliminate the debug Trap bit.
LDT descriptor	All LDT descriptors are 16-bytes long.
Address Translation	• Only the 3rd generation translation mechanism is supported. • 4MB pages are not supported.
Virtual address	Although the virtual addresses generated by the legacy segmentation mechanism are 24- or 32-bits in length, they are zero-extended to form a 64-bit virtual address (in canonical form).
Physical address	Current implementations support a 2^{40} (1TB), 2^{41}, or 2^{48} physical address space.
CR3	CR3 is 64-bits wide enabling the top-level address translation table (the PML4) to be located anywhere in physical memory.

Table 25-1: OS Environment Changes in IA-32e Mode (Continued)

Element	Description of Change
GDTR, LDTR, IDTR and TR	The base address field of all of these registers has been extended to 64-bits enabling the system data structures to be located anywhere in virtual memory.
SS:RSP push on interrupt	On an interrupt or exception, the logical processor unconditionally pushes SS:RSP in addition to Rflags and CS:RIP to the stack.
SYSENTER/ SYSEXIT	Used to make a call to the OS services: • On Intel processors, the SYSENTER instruction can be executed in any mode. • On AMD processors, the SYSENTER instruction can only executed successfully in legacy Protected Mode. Otherwise it results in an Undefined Opcode exception.
SYSCALL/SYSRET	Used to make a call to the OS services: • On Intel processors, the SYSCALL instruction can only executed successfully by 64-bit applications. Otherwise it results in an Undefined Opcode exception. • On AMD processors, the SYSCALL instruction can be executed in any mode.

Memory Addressing

Segmentation

When the logical processor is operating in Compatibility Mode, the segmentation logic works precisely as it does in the 16- and 32-bit legacy Protected Modes:

• When the logical processor is operating in 16-bit Compatibility Mode (CS[D] = 0 and CS[L] = 0), the effective address is formed by adding the specified 16-bit offset to the segment's 24-bit base address. The resultant 24-bit virtual address is then 0-extended to 64-bits before being submitted to the address translation logic. If an instruction is prefaced by the Address Size Override prefix, the offset will be a 32-bit value.

- When the logical processor is operating in 32-bit Compatibility Mode (CS[D] = 1 and CS[L] = 0), the effective address is formed by adding the specified 32-bit offset to the segment's 32-bit base address. The resultant 32-bit virtual address is then 0-extended to 64-bits before being submitted to the address translation logic. If an instruction is prefaced by the Address Size Override prefix, the offset will be a 16-bit value.

FS/GS Segments

Although the base address fields in the invisible portion of the FS and GS segment registers are 64-bits wide in 64-bit Mode, the logical processor ignores the upper 32-bits of the base address when it is operating in Compatibility Mode.

Virtual Address

Also see "Segmentation" on page 1013:

- 16-bit legacy applications generate a 24-bit virtual address (0-extended to 64-bits) and are therefore capable of addressing a 16MB virtual address space.
- 32-bit legacy applications generate a 32-bit virtual address (0-extended to 64-bits) and are therefore capable of addressing a 4GB virtual address space.

Address Translation

The 64-bit virtual address produced by the segmentation logic is submitted to the address translation logic and is translated into the physical address of the target item in memory. Although 16- and 32-bits legacy applications are only capable of addressing 16MB or 4GB virtual address spaces, respectively, the IA-32e address translation mechanism can map those addresses to any location within the logical processor's addressable physical memory space:

- In current implementations, the addressable physical memory space is 2^{40} (1TB), 2^{41} (2TB), or 2^{48} (256TB) in size.
- Future implementations may be capable of addressing up to a 2^{52} of physical memory.

Register Set

Visible Registers

Figure 25-1 on page 1015 illustrates the register set as it appears when the logical processor is operating in Compatibility Mode. Pay particular attention to the notes regarding CR3, GDTR, LDTR, IDTR and the TR.

Figure 25-1: Register Set in Compatibility Mode

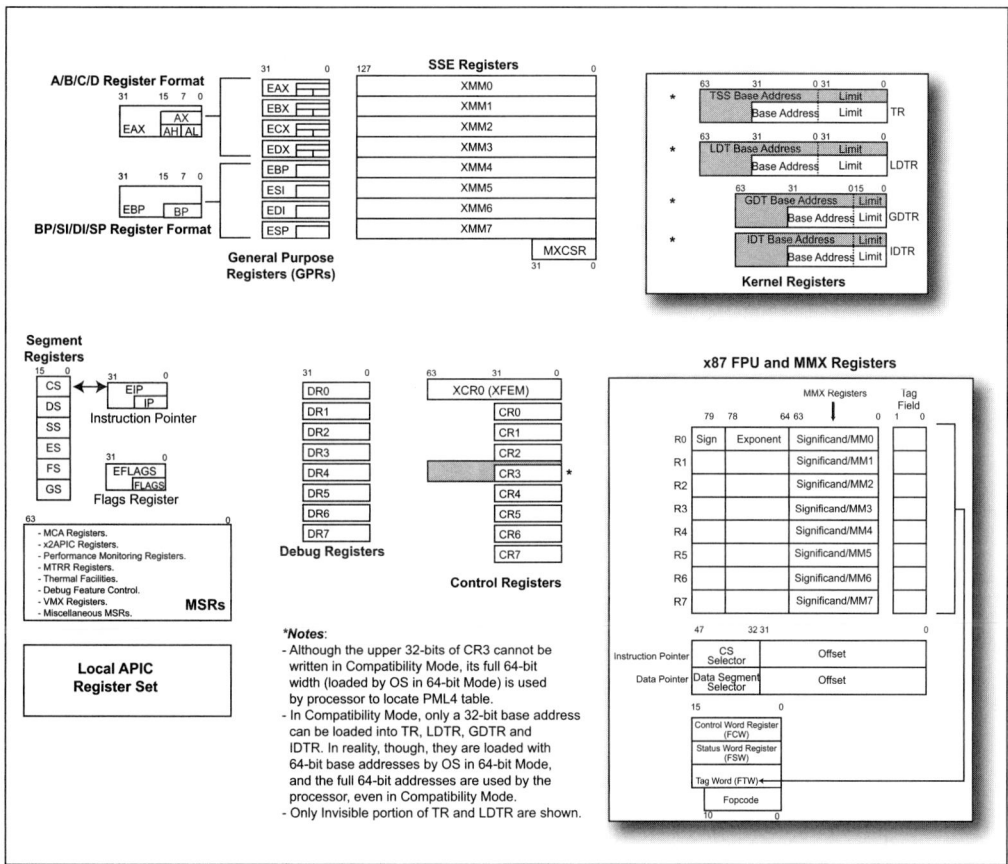

No Access to Additional or Extended Registers

While operating in Compatibility Mode, the following additional or extended registers cannot be accessed:

*   Upper half of the 64-bit Control registers.
*   Control registers CR8 - CR15. *An exception: on AMD processors, CR8 (the Task Priority register) can be accessed in modes other than 64-bit Mode by prefacing the MOV CR8 instruction with the LOCK prefix (F0h).*
*   XMM registers XMM8 - XMM15.
*   64-bit GPR registers R8 - R15 (or any subset of them).
*   RAX, RBX, RCX, RDX, RBP, RSI, RDI and RSP registers.
*   8-bit BPL, SIL, DIL and SIL registers.
*   Upper half of the RIP register.
*   Upper half of the Rflags register.
*   Upper half of Debug registers DR0 - DR7.
*   Debug registers DR8 - DR15.

Control Register Accesses

A write to a Control register accesses the lower 32-bits of the register and fills the upper 32-bits with zeros. A read only accesses the lower 32-bits. CR8 - CR15 are not accessible in Compatibility Mode. *An exception: on AMD processors, CR8 (the Task Priority register) can be accessed in modes other than 64-bit Mode by prefacing the MOV CR8 instruction with the LOCK prefix (F0h).*

Debug Register Accesses

A write to a Debug register (DR0 - DR7) accesses the lower 32-bits of the register and fills the upper 32-bits with zeros. A read only accesses the lower 32-bits. DR8 - DR15 are not accessible in Compatibility Mode.

Register Preservation Across Mode Switches

With the exception of the CS register which changes during the task switch, neither the initial entry into IA-32e Mode nor a transition between Compatibility Mode and 64-bit Mode alters the contents of the visible or invisible portions of the segment registers.

The upper 32 bits of the original 8 GPRs are not preserved when changing from 64-bit Mode to Compatibility Mode and back again.

The contents of R8 - R15 and XMM8 - XMM15 are preserved when transitioning back and forth between Compatibility Mode and 64-bit Mode. The contents are undefined, however, if software exits IA-32e Mode back to Protected Mode and then reenters IA-32e Mode.

Exception and Interrupt Handling

Interrupt/exception handling in Compatibility Mode differs from Protected Mode in the following ways:

- All of the entries in the IDT consists of 16-byte Interrupt or Trap Gate descriptors.
- Task Gate descriptors are not permitted in the IDT (because the automatic task switch mechanism is not used in IA-32e Mode).
- All IDT descriptors must point to handlers in 64-bit code segments.
- In Protected Mode, the logical processor only pushes SS:ESP onto the handler's stack if the handler and the interrupted program have different privilege levels. In IA-32e Mode, SS:RSP is unconditionally pushed onto the handler's stack.
- The Interrupt Stack Table (IST) in the TSS may be used to define a fresh stack to be used by a handler (even if there isn't a privilege level change). See "Interrupt/Exception Stack Switch" on page 976 for more information.
- Before SS:RSP, Rflags and CS:RIP are pushed onto the handler's stack, the logical processor masks the handler's RSP with FFFF_FFFF_FFFF_FFF0h to align the stack pointer to the next lower 16-byte address boundary.
- Each item pushed onto the stack consists of 8-bytes of information.
- Even though SS is not used in 64-bit Mode (because segmentation is disabled), it is still pushed onto the stack. After it has been saved to the handler's stack, SS is loaded with a null descriptor selector (i.e., one that selects entry 0 in the GDT).

OS Kernel Calls

Call Gates

The implementation and usage of Call Gates in IA-32e Mode differs from Protected Mode as follows:

- In IA-32e Mode, all selected Call Gate descriptors in the GDT and LDTs must be 16-byte descriptors.
- All Call Gates must point to OS services that reside in 64-bit code segments.
- Each item pushed onto the stack consists of 8-bytes of information.
- Even though SS is not used in 64-bit Mode (because segmentation is disabled), it is still pushed onto the stack. After it has been saved to the handler's stack:
  — If a privilege level change occurs, SS is loaded with a null descriptor selector (i.e., one that selects entry 0 in the GDT).
  — If there is no privilege level change, the contents of SS remains unchanged.

Kernel Call Instruction Usage

SysEnter Instruction

Support for the SYSENTER/SYSEXIT instruction pair differs on the Intel and AMD product lines:

- On Intel processors, the SYSENTER and SYSEXIT instructions can be executed in any mode.
- On AMD processors, the SYSENTER and SYSEXIT instructions can only executed successfully in legacy Protected Mode. Otherwise it results in an Undefined Opcode exception.

SysCall Instruction

Support for the SYSCALL/SYSRET instruction pair differs on the Intel and AMD product lines:

- On Intel processors, the SYSCALL and SYSRET instructions can only executed successfully by 64-bit applications. Otherwise it results in an Undefined Opcode exception.
- On AMD processors, the SYSCALL and SYSRET instructions can be executed in any mode.

Odds and Ends

IRET Changes

Table 25-2 on page 1019 details how the IRET instruction operates when the logical processor is in IA-32e Mode.

Table 25-2: IRET Characteristics in IA-32e Mode

When IRET executed in	Characteristics
Compatibility Mode	In order to properly emulate IRET execution in legacy Protected Mode, IRET pops SS:ESP from the stack only if there is a CPL change when returning to the interrupted program.
64-bit Mode	In 64-bit mode, IRET unconditionally pops SS:RSP from the stack (even if the CPL does not change). This is done because the original interrupt/exception always causes SS:RSP to be pushed to the stack. Because interrupt stack-frame pushes are always eight bytes in IA-32e Mode, an IRET from an IA-32e Mode interrupt handler (64-bit code) must pop eight-byte items off the stack. This is accomplished by preceding the IRET with a 64-bit REX operand-size prefix.
• Refer to "Example Call/Return Operations" on page 1089 for a description of IRET behavior.	

Segment Load Instructions

Although segmentation is not used when the logical processor is operating in 64-bit Mode, the OS kernel does have the ability to use the segment load instructions (MOV to Sreg, and POP Sreg). This permits the task scheduler to set up the segment registers in preparation for the initiation of or a return to a legacy application that will run in Compatibility Mode.

When a segment load instruction is executed, the descriptor is read from the selected GDT or LDT and is loaded into the hidden portion of the respective segment register. Since at this point the logical processor is still operating in 64-bit Mode, however, it does not validate any of the descriptor fields.

Part 5:
64-bit Mode

The Previous Part

Part 4 provided a detailed description of the Compatibility submode of IA-32e Mode.

This Part

Part 5 provides a detailed description of the 64-bit submode of IA-32e Mode and consists of the following chapters:

- Chapter 26, "64-bit Register Overview," on page 1023.
- Chapter 27, "64-bit Operands and Addressing," on page 1041.
- Chapter 28, "64-bit Odds and Ends," on page 1075.

The Next Part

Part 6 provides a detailed description of:

- Switching from Real Mode to Protected Mode.
- Switching from Protected Mode to IA-32e Mode.

26 *64-bit Register Overview*

The Previous Chapter

The previous chapter provided a detailed description of the Compatibility Sub-Mode of IA-32e Mode. This included the following topics:

- Initial Entry to Compatibility Mode.
- Switching Between Compatibility Mode and 64-bit Mode.
- Differences Between IA-32 Mode and Compatibility Mode.
- Memory Addressing.
- Register Set.
- Exception and Interrupt Handling.
- OS Kernel Calls.
- IRET Changes.
- Segment Load Instructions.

This Chapter

This chapter provides an overview of the following:

- 64-bit Register Set.
- EFER (Extended Features Enable) Register.
- Sixteen 64-bit Control Registers.
- 64-bit Rflags Register.
- Sixteen 64-bit GPRs.
- Kernel Data Structure Registers in 64-bit Mode.
- SSE Register Set Expanded in 64-bit Mode.
- Debug Breakpoint Registers.
- Local APIC Register Set.
- x87 FPU/MMX Register Set.
- Architecturally-Defined MSRs.

The Next Chapter

The next chapter describes the following topics:

- Switching to 64-bit Mode.
- The Defaults.
- The REX Prefix.
- Addressing Memory in 64-bit Mode.
    — 64-bit Mode Uses a Hardware-Enforced Flat Model.
    — Default Virtual Address Size (and overriding it).
    — Actual Address Size Support: Theory vs. Practice.
    — Canonical Address.
    — Memory-based Operand Address Computation.
    — RIP-relative Data Addressing.
    — Near and Far Branch Addressing.
- Immediate Data Values in 64-bit Mode.
- Displacements in 64-bit Mode.

Overview of 64-bit Register Set

Figure 26-1 on page 1025 illustrates the registers that are visible to the programmer when the logical processor is operating in the 64-bit SubMode of IA-32e Mode. A description of the registers may be found in this chapter. A description of segment register usage in 64-bit Mode can be found in "Segment Register Usage in 64-bit Mode" on page 927.

Figure 26-1: Intel 64 Register Set

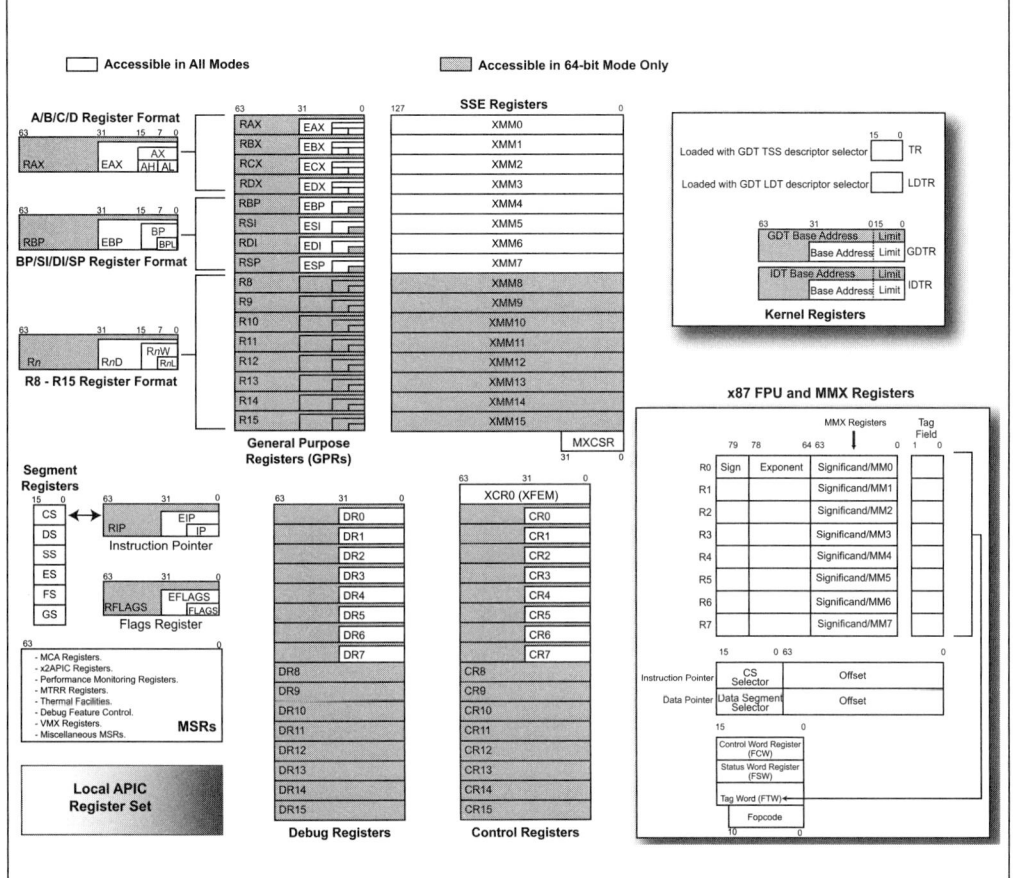

EFER (Extended Features Enable) Register

The EFER register (an MSR), pictured in Figure 26-2 on page 1026, plays a central role when switching a logical processor between legacy Protected Mode and IA-32e Mode. The bit critical to the switching process is the EFER[LME] bit (Table 26-1 on page 1026 describes the register's bit assignment).

Figure 26-2: EFER (Extended Features Enable) Register

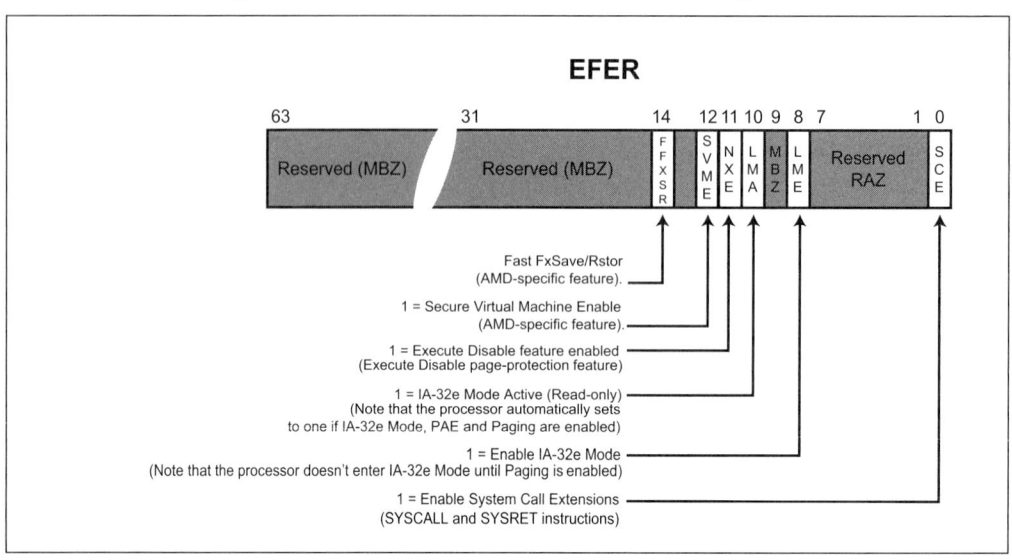

Table 26-1: EFER Register Bit Assignment

Bit	Description
SCE	**System Call Enable**. When set to one by the OS, enables the execution of the **SYSCALL** and **SYSRET** instructions which are used to make calls to the OS kernel. The OS sets this bit once it has set up the MSRs (STAR, LSTAR, CSTAR, SFMASK) used by these instructions: • Due to low overhead, these instructions provide applications a way to perform OS kernel calls very quickly. • Accomplished using predefined call/return points. The logical processor skips many of the normal type and limit checks when changing segments (CS and SS). • The call entry points and return info are defined in a set of MSRs: STAR, LSTAR, CSTAR and SFMASK. • Refer to "SysCall instruction" on page 1018 for more information.
LME	**Enable IA-32e Mode**. The OS kernel sets this bit before paging is enabled, but the logical processor doesn't actually enter IA-32e Mode until paging is subsequently turned on with physical address extensions enabled (CR0[PG] = 1 and CR4[PAE] = 1). As an interesting side-note, Intel uses AMD's acronym (Long Mode Enable, rather than IA-32e Mode Enable) for this bit.

Table 26-1: EFER Register Bit Assignment (Continued)

Bit	Description
LMA	**IA-32e Mode Active**. This read-only bit can be read by software to determine whether or not the logical processor is currently operating in IA-32e Mode. Intel uses AMD's acronym (Long Mode Active) for this bit.
NXE	**No-Execute Enable**. When set to one, the logical processor will not execute code from a page if its Execute Disable bit set to one. This feature was added to prevent data pages from being used by malicious software to execute code. Note that while Intel uses AMD's acronym for this EFER register bit (NXE), they actually refer to this feature as the Execute Disable feature rather than as the No Execute feature. For more information, refer to "Execute Disable Feature" on page 579.
SVME	**Secure Virtual Machine Enable**. *AMD-only feature.* When set to one, it enables the logical processor's ability to execute the following AMD-specific virtualization-related instructions: VMRUN, VMLOAD, VMSAVE, CLGI, VMMCALL, and INVLPGA (if SVME = 0, these instructions generate an Undefined Opcode exception).
FFXSR	**Fast FX Save/Restore**. *AMD-only feature.* If the OS has enabled the Fast FxSave/Restore feature by setting EFER[FFXSR] = 1, executing FXSAVE in 64-bit Mode at privilege level 0 causes the logical processor to complete the instruction more quickly by not saving the XMM registers.
MBZ	These bits are reserved and must be zero.

Sixteen 64-bit Control Registers

When operating in IA-32 Mode or Compatibility Mode, the architecture supports the implementation of up to eight 32-bit Control registers (CR0 - CR7). Current IA-32 and IA-32e processors implement four 32-bit Control Registers (five if the logical processor implements the optional, 64-bit XCR0 register). In Compatibility and Protected Modes, writes fill the lower 32-bits with data and the upper 32-bits with zeros, and reads return only the lower 32-bits.

As illustrated in Figure 26-1 on page 1025, when the logical processor is operating in 64-bit Mode:

- The set of addressable Control Registers is expanded from eight (CR0 - CR7) to sixteen (CR0 - CR15).

- Each Control Register is 64-bits wide (rather than 32-bits wide when the logical processor is operating in IA-32 Mode or Compatibility Mode).
- The registers are accessed using the MOV CRn instructions.
- The REX prefix is not necessary to access the full 64-bit register.

Table 26-2 on page 1028 describes the accessibility of the Control Registers when the logical processor is operating in the Compatibility and 64-bit Modes.

Table 26-2: Control Registers in Compatibility and 64-bit Modes

Register(s)	Description
CR0	Remains 32-bits in Compatibility Mode (see Figure 26-3 on page 1030), but expands to 64 bits in 64-bit Mode (see Figure 26-4 on page 1030). In 64-bit Mode, bits 63:32 are reserved and must be written with zeros. Writing a non-zero value to any of the upper 32-bits results in a GP exception.
CR1	Is still not implemented (but, if it were, it would be expanded to 64-bits in 64-bit Mode).
CR2 and CR3	Unlike the other Control registers which are 64-bits wide only when the logical processor is operating in 64-bit Mode, the paging-related Control registers, CR2 and CR3, are 64-bits wide when the logical processor is in IA-32e Mode. In other words, *these two registers are 64-bits wide in both Compatibility Mode and 64-bit Mode* (in Compatibility Mode, however, only the lower 32-bits are programmer accessible): • **CR2**. See Figure 26-5 on page 1030. In the event that a virtual address selects a PTE (or PDE, if a 2MB page is addressed) wherein the P bit = 0 indicating the page is not currently present in memory, CR2, the Page Fault Address Register, latches the 64-bit offending virtual address. CR2 may also be written by software. • **CR3**. See Figure 26-6 on page 1031 and Figure 26-7 on page 1031. While a task is executing and the logical processor is operating in Compatibility Mode or 64-bit Mode, CR3 contains the 52-bit, 4KB-aligned base physical address of the top-level address translation table (PML4). The logical processor does not check that addresses written to CR2 and CR3 are within the virtual or physical addressing limitations of the implementation.

Table 26-2: Control Registers in Compatibility and 64-bit Modes (Continued)

Register(s)	Description
CR4	Feature Enable register. Remains 32-bits wide in Compatibility Mode (see Figure 26-8 on page 1032), but expands to 64 bits in 64-bit Mode (see Figure 26-9 on page 1032). In 64-bit Mode, bits 63:32 are reserved and must be written with zeros. Writing a non-zero value to any of the upper 32-bits results in a GP exception.
CR5 through CR7	Not implemented at this time, but, if and when they are, they will be 32-bits wide in Compatibility Mode and 64-bits wide when the logical processor is operating in 64-bit Mode.
CR8	The Task Priority Register (TPR) is implemented as a 64-bit register (see Figure 26-10 on page 1033) and is only addressable in 64-bit Mode (using the REX prefix). The OS kernel uses the least-significant 4-bit field to set the threshold of interruptability for the currently-running task. See "CR8 (Alternative TPR)" on page 1308 for more information. *An exception: on AMD processors, CR8 (the Task Priority register) can be accessed in modes other than 64-bit Mode by prefacing the MOV CR8 instruction with the LOCK prefix (F0h).*
CR9 through CR15	Not implemented at this time, but, if and when they are, they will be 64-bits wide when the logical processor is operating in 64-bit Mode and will not be accessible in Compatibility Mode.

Figure 26-3: CR0 in IA-32 Mode and Compatibility Mode

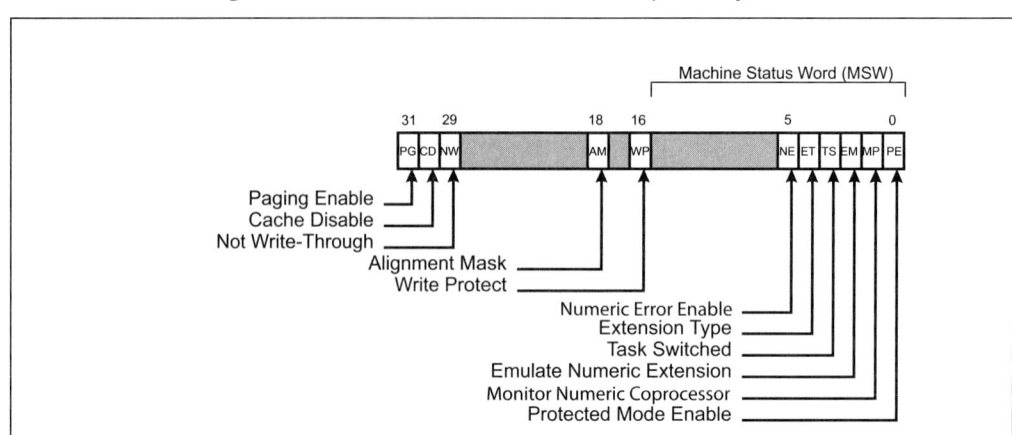

Figure 26-4: CR0 in 64-bit Mode

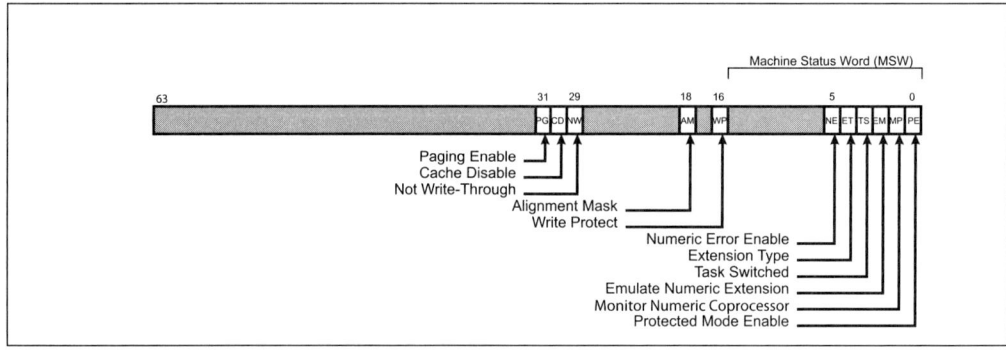

Figure 26-5: CR2 in IA-32e Mode

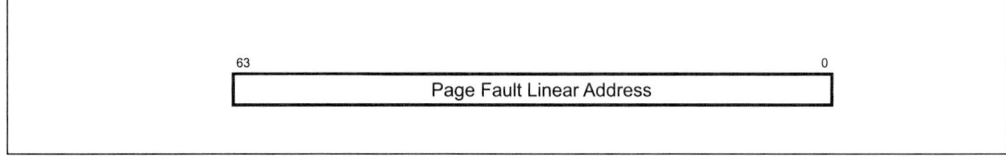

Figure 26-6: CR3 in IA-32e Mode

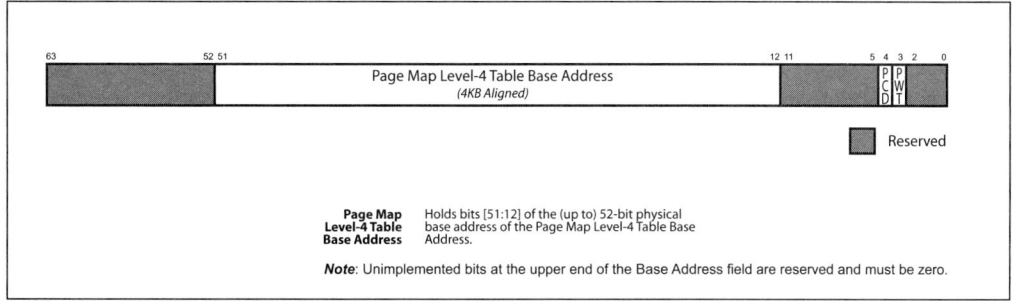

Figure 26-7: In IA-32e Mode, CR3 Points to Top-Level Paging Directory

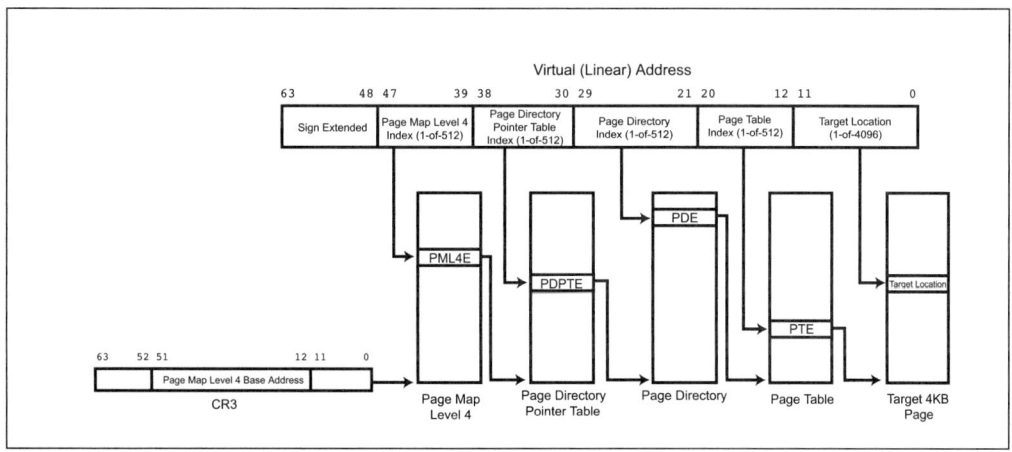

Figure 26-8: CR4 in IA-32 Mode and Compatibility Mode

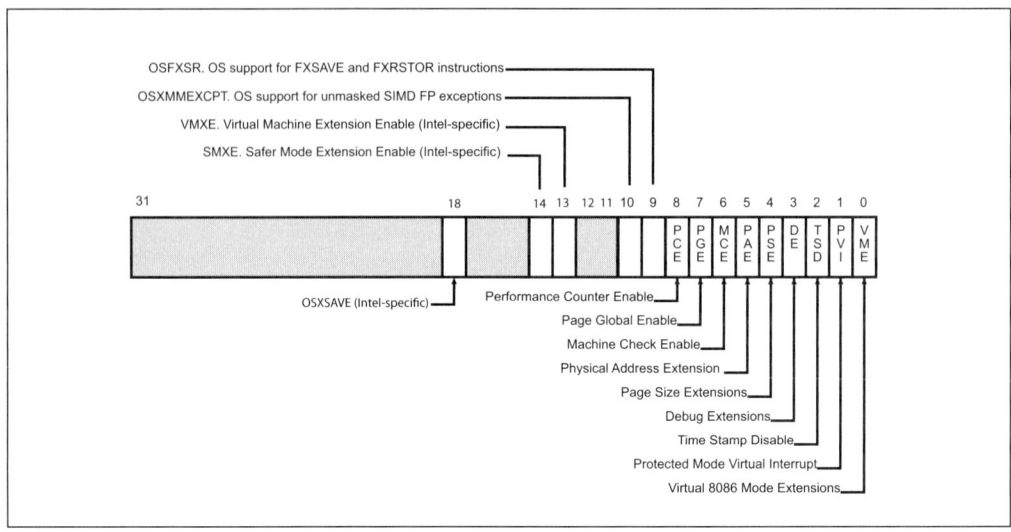

Figure 26-9: CR4 in 64-bit Mode

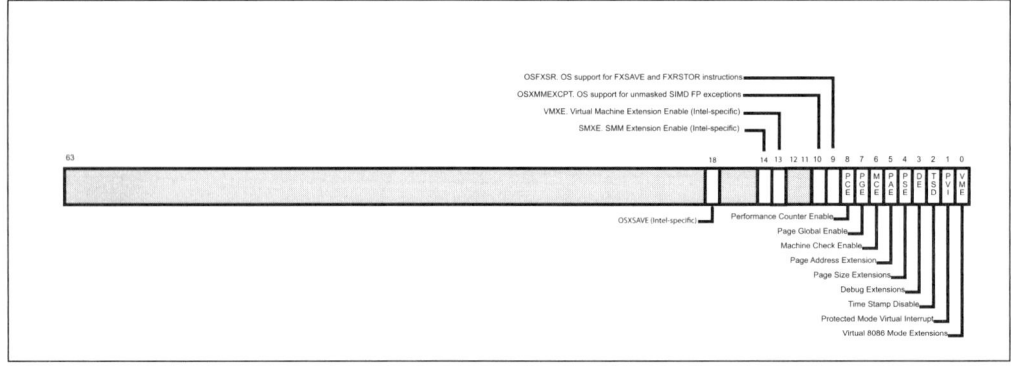

Figure 26-10: CR8 (Task Priority Register)

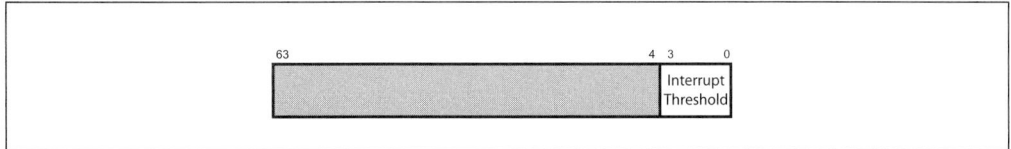

64-bit Rflags Register

In 64-bit Mode, the Eflags register is expanded to 64 bits (although no new bits are currently-defined) and is renamed Rflags (pictured in Figure 26-11 on page 1033). See "Flags Register" on page 251 for a description of the flag bits. The upper 32-bits are always read as zero and any attempt to set any of the upper 32-bits to a one is ignored by the logical processor.

Figure 26-11: Rflags Register (only in 64-bit Mode)

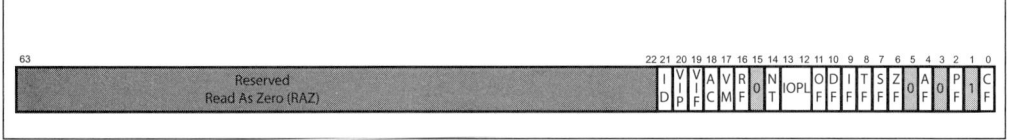

Sixteen 64-bit GPRs

Refer to Figure 26-1 on page 1025. When the logical processor is operating in 64-bit Mode:

- **IA-32 GPRs Extended**. 64-bit versions of the IA-32 Mode GPRs become available (referred to as RAX, RBX, RCX, RDX, RBP, RSI, RDI and RSP):
  — Figure 26-12 illustrates the format of the A, B, C and D registers.
  — Figure 26-13 on page 1034 illustrates the format of the BP, SI, DI and SP registers.
  The 64-bit versions of the GPRs are only addressable in 64-bit Mode when an instruction is prefaced by the REX prefix (which is used to address the new **R**egister Extensions).

- **New GPRs**. Eight new 64-bit GPRs (R8 - R15) become available. Figure 26-14 on page 1035 illustrates the format and characteristics of these registers. As with the other registers added with the advent of the 64-bit *register expansion*, these registers are only addressable in 64-bit Mode when an instruction is prefaced by the REX prefix (which is used to address the new Register Extensions).

- **Result Storage**. Figure 26-15 on page 1035 describes how the results of an operation are stored in the destination register when the logical processor is operating in 64-bit Mode.

- **Register preservation on mode switch**. Figure 26-16 on page 1036 illustrates that the upper 32-bits of the RAX, RBX, RCX, RDX, RBP, RSI, RDI and RSP registers are not preserved when the logical processor transitions to Compatibility Mode or Protected Mode and back again.

Figure 26-12: The A, B, C and D Registers (in 64-bit Mode)

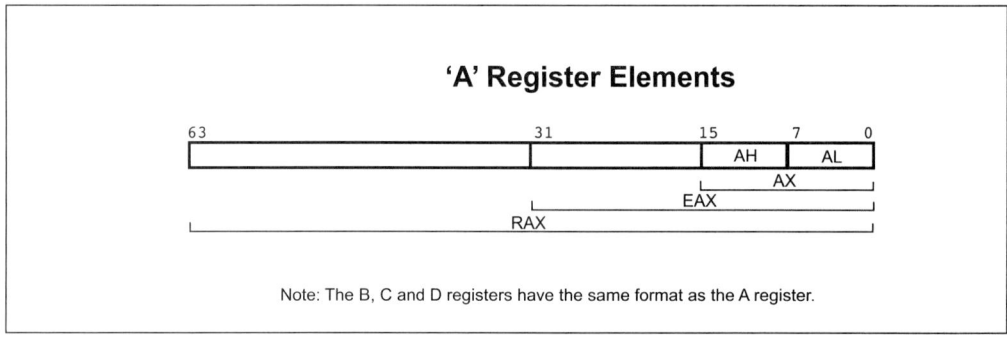

Figure 26-13: The BP, SI, DI and SP Registers (in 64-bit Mode)

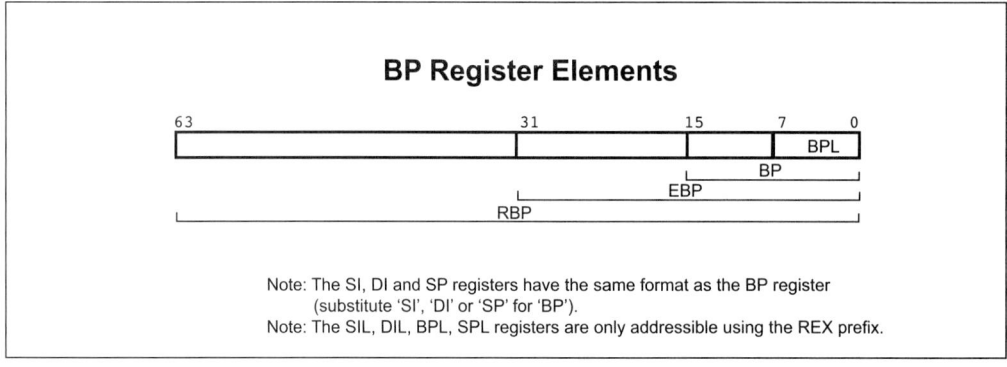

Figure 26-14: Registers R8 - R15 (only in 64-bit Mode)

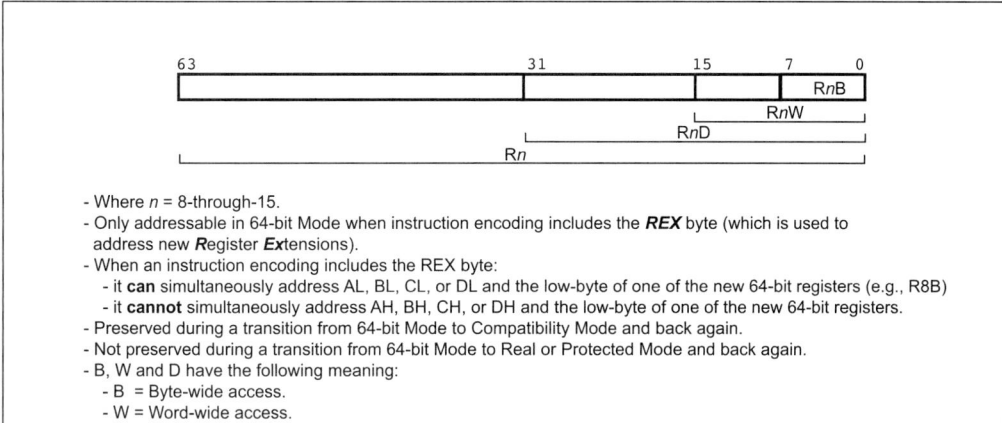

- Where *n* = 8-through-15.
- Only addressable in 64-bit Mode when instruction encoding includes the **REX** byte (which is used to address new **R**egister **Ex**tensions).
- When an instruction encoding includes the REX byte:
  - it **can** simultaneously address AL, BL, CL, or DL and the low-byte of one of the new 64-bit registers (e.g., R8B)
  - it **cannot** simultaneously address AH, BH, CH, or DH and the low-byte of one of the new 64-bit registers.
- Preserved during a transition from 64-bit Mode to Compatibility Mode and back again.
- Not preserved during a transition from 64-bit Mode to Real or Protected Mode and back again.
- B, W and D have the following meaning:
  - B = Byte-wide access.
  - W = Word-wide access.
  - D = Doubleword-wide access.

Figure 26-15: Result Storage in 64-bit Mode

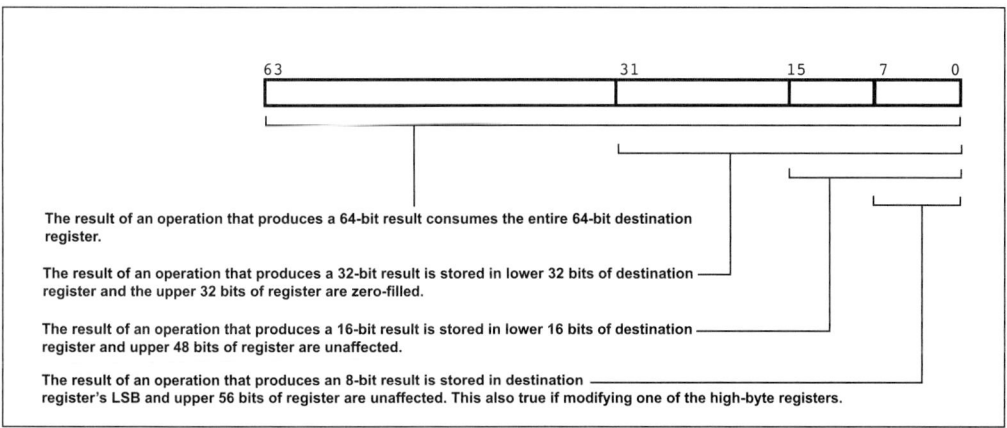

The result of an operation that produces a 64-bit result consumes the entire 64-bit destination register.

The result of an operation that produces a 32-bit result is stored in lower 32 bits of destination register and the upper 32 bits of register are zero-filled.

The result of an operation that produces a 16-bit result is stored in lower 16 bits of destination register and upper 48 bits of register are unaffected.

The result of an operation that produces an 8-bit result is stored in destination register's LSB and upper 56 bits of register are unaffected. This also true if modifying one of the high-byte registers.

Figure 26-16: Upper 32-bits of the First Eight GPRs Do Not Survive Mode Change

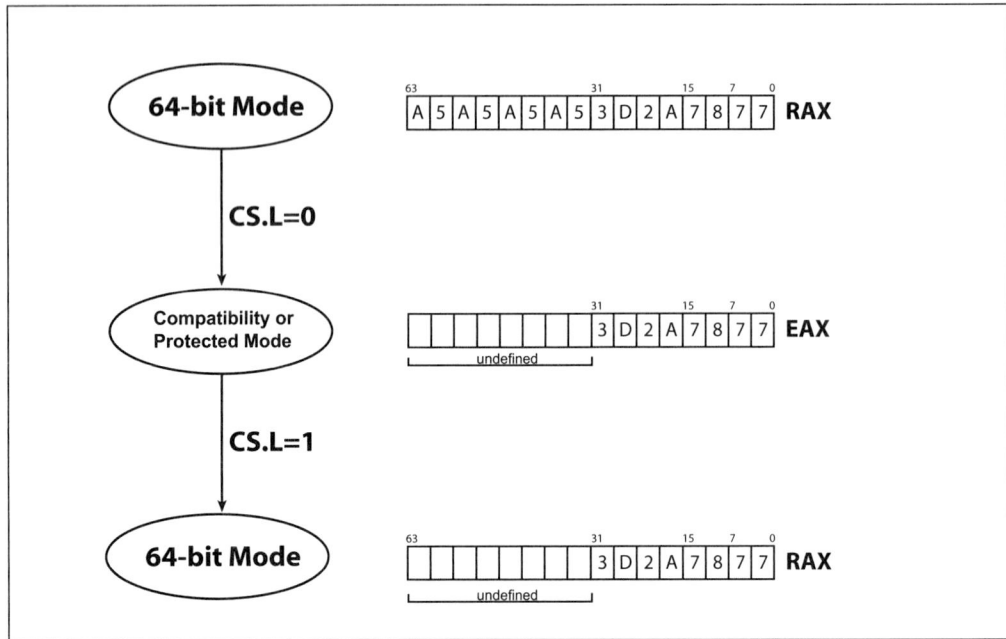

Kernel Data Structure Registers in 64-bit Mode

The base address field of the following kernel data structure-related registers are expanded to 64-bits in 64-bit Mode:

- TR. A detailed description can be found in "TR and TSS Changes" on page 968.
- GDTR. A detailed description can be found in "GDT and GDTR Changes" on page 947.
- LDTR. A detailed description can be found in "LDT and LDTR Changes" on page 952.
- IDTR. A detailed description can be found in "IDT/IDTR and Interrupt/Exception Changes" on page 955.

SSE Register Set Expanded in 64-bit Mode

Figure 26-17 on page 1037 illustrates the SSE register set as it appears in IA-32 and Compatibility Modes. In 64-bit Mode, the number of XMM data registers is expanded to sixteen (XMM0 - XMM15; see Figure 26-18 on page 1037). As with the other registers added with the advent of the 64-bit Mode *register expansion*, XMM8 - XMM15 are only addressable in 64-bit Mode (when an instruction is prefixed by the REX prefix; which, among other things, is used to address the new Register Extensions).

Figure 26-17: SSE Register Set in IA-32 and Compatibility Modes

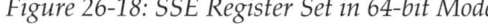

Figure 26-18: SSE Register Set in 64-bit Mode

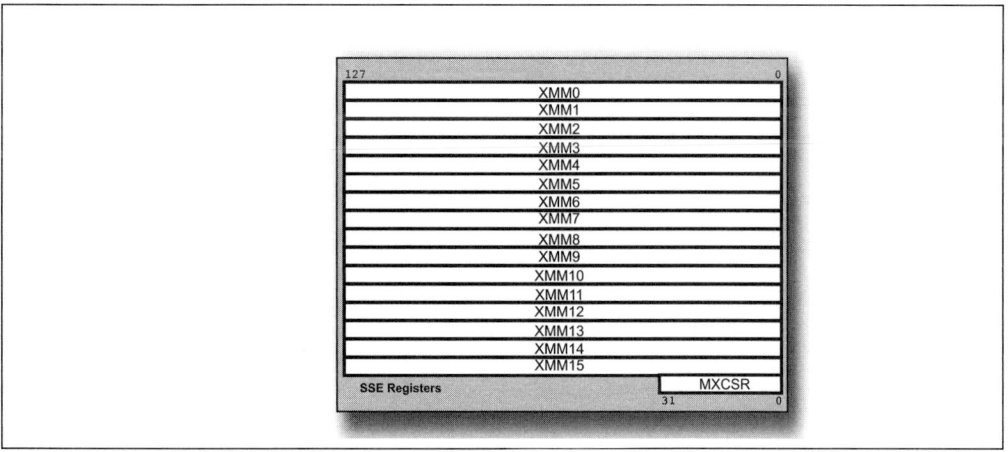

Debug Breakpoint Registers

The debug address breakpoint register set, introduced in"Debug Address Breakpoint Register Set" on page 262, has been enhanced in an Intel 64 processor (see Figure 26-19 on page 1038) in the following manner:

- All registers in this register set have increased in size from 32- to 64-bits.
- The upper 32-bits of DR6 and DR7 are currently reserved. DR8 - DR15, although not yet implemented, will only be accessible in 64-bit Mode (using the REX prefix).
- In DR7, the LEN field encoding has been enhanced in the following manner:
  — An encoding of 10b—reserved in earlier processor—can be used to specify a monitor address range length of 8-bytes.
- In Protected Mode and Compatibility Mode:
  — Writes to a debug register fill the upper 32-bits with zeros and reads return the lower 32-bits.
- In 64-bit Mode:
  — The full 64-bit register is accessed on both reads and writes (without the use of an Operand Size Override prefix).
  — The upper 32-bits of DR6 and DR7 are reserved. If any bit is set to one, a GP exception is generated.
- While all 64-bits of DR0 – DR3 are writable, hardware does not verify that the address is within the virtual address range supported by the specific processor implementation.

Figure 26-19: Debug Register Set (all modes in an Intel 64 Processor)

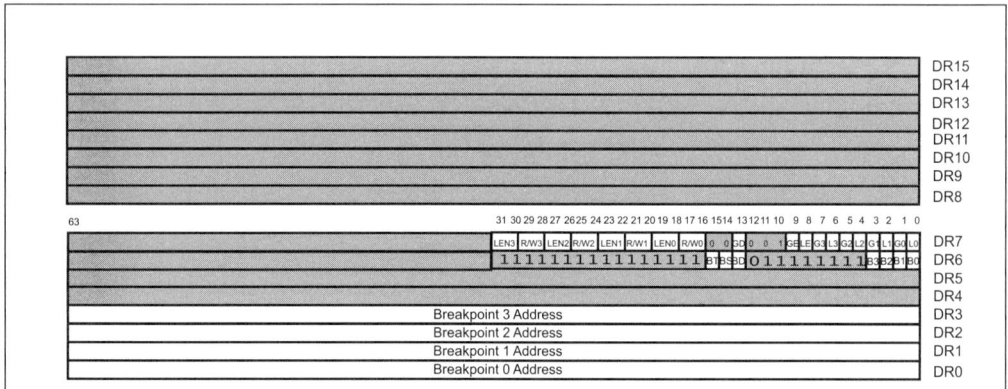

Local APIC Register Set

There is no change in the width or usage of the Local APIC registers in IA-32e Mode. A complete description of the Local APIC may be found in "The Local and IO APICs" on page 1239.

x87 FPU/MMX Register Set

There is no change in the width or usage of the x87 FPU/MMX registers in IA-32e Mode. A complete description of the x87 FPU may be found in "Legacy x87 FP Support" on page 339.

Architecturally-Defined MSRs

There is no change in the width or usage of the MSR register set in IA-32e Mode.

27 64-bit Operands and Addressing

The Previous Chapter

The previous chapter provided an overview of the following:

- 64-bit Register Set.
- EFER (Extended Features Enable) Register.
- Sixteen 64-bit Control Registers.
- 64-bit Rflags Register.
- Sixteen 64-bit GPRs.
- Kernel Data Structure Registers in 64-bit Mode.
- SSE Register Set Expanded in 64-bit Mode.
- Debug Breakpoint Registers.
- Local APIC Register Set.
- x87 FPU/MMX Register Set.
- Architecturally-Defined MSRs.

This Chapter

This chapter covers the following topics:

- Switching to 64-bit Mode.
- The Defaults.
- The REX Prefix.
- Addressing Memory in 64-bit Mode.
  — 64-bit Mode Uses a Hardware-Enforced Flat Model.
  — Default Virtual Address Size (and overriding it).
  — Actual Address Size Support: Theory vs. Practice.
  — Canonical Address.
  — Memory-based Operand Address Computation.
  — RIP-relative Data Addressing.
  — Near and Far Branch Addressing.
- Immediate Data Values in 64-bit Mode.
- Displacements in 64-bit Mode.

The Next Chapter

The next chapter describes the following 64-bit related topics:

- New Instructions.
- Enhanced Instructions.
- Invalid Instructions.
- Reassigned Instructions.
- Instructions That Default to a 64-bit Operand Size.
- Branching in 64-bit Mode.
- NOP Instruction.
- FXSAVE/FXRSTOR.
- The Nested Task Bit (Rflags[NT]).
- SMM Save Area.

Helpful Background

An understanding of the 32-bit instruction format (see "32-bit Machine Language Instruction Format" on page 155) provides the background necessary for a complete understanding of the subject matter in this chapter.

Switching to 64-bit Mode

This subject was covered earlier in "Mode Switching Overview" on page 916.

The Defaults

Unless overridden by instruction prefixes, while the logical processor is executing code from a 64-bit code segment (i.e., the L bit = 1 in the code segment descriptor), its default assumptions are set as follows:

- The default operand size = 32-bits.
- The default address size = 64-bits.

It should be noted that some instructions have a default operand size of 64-bits without the use of the REX prefix.

The REX Prefix

Problem 1: Addressing New Registers

The IA-32 instruction set's ability to specify a register as an operand is limited by the following:

- As described in "Explicit Register Specification in ModRM Byte" on page 196 (see Figure 27-1 on page 1044; please note that this figure describes the instruction format in IA-32 Mode and Compatibility Mode, *not* in 64-bit Mode), the Operand 1 (i.e., the RM field) and Operand 2 (i.e., the Reg field) fields in the ModRM byte are each three bits wide.
- As described in "Explicit Register Specification in Opcode" on page 196 (see Figure 27-2 on page 1044), the register specification field found in the primary opcode byte of some instructions is a 3-bit field.

Obviously, the constraint imposed by a 3-bit register selection field limits the selection to 1 of 8 possible registers. In 64-bit Mode, however, the programmer has the ability to specify any of 16:

- GPRs.
- XMM registers.
- Control Registers.
- Debug Registers.

This obviously requires that the Reg, RM and the primary opcode byte's register specification fields be expanded from 3- to 4-bits wide in order to address the new registers when the logical processor is in 64-bit Mode.

Refer to Figure 27-3 on page 1045. In addition:

- The Base field in the SIB (Scale/Index/Base) byte used to specify the register containing the base address of a memory-based data structure is only a 3-bit field.
- The Index field in the SIB byte used to specify the register containing the location (i.e., the index) within the data structure is only a 3-bit field.

In order to specify any of the upper eight of the sixteen GPRs as the Index and Base registers, both of these bit fields must also be expanded from 3- to 4-bits.

Figure 27-1: The ModRM Byte's Operand 1 and 2 Fields Are Each 3-bits Wide

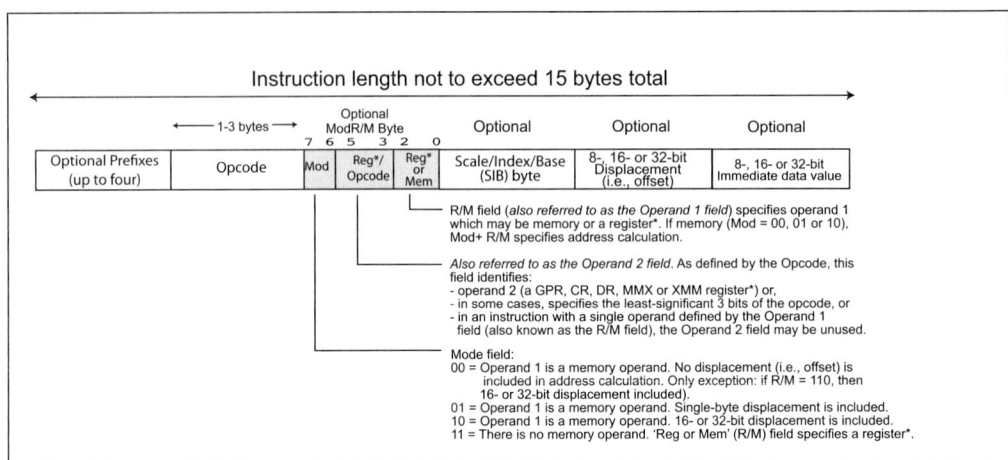

Figure 27-2: The Register Select Field in the Primary Opcode Byte Is 3-bits Wide

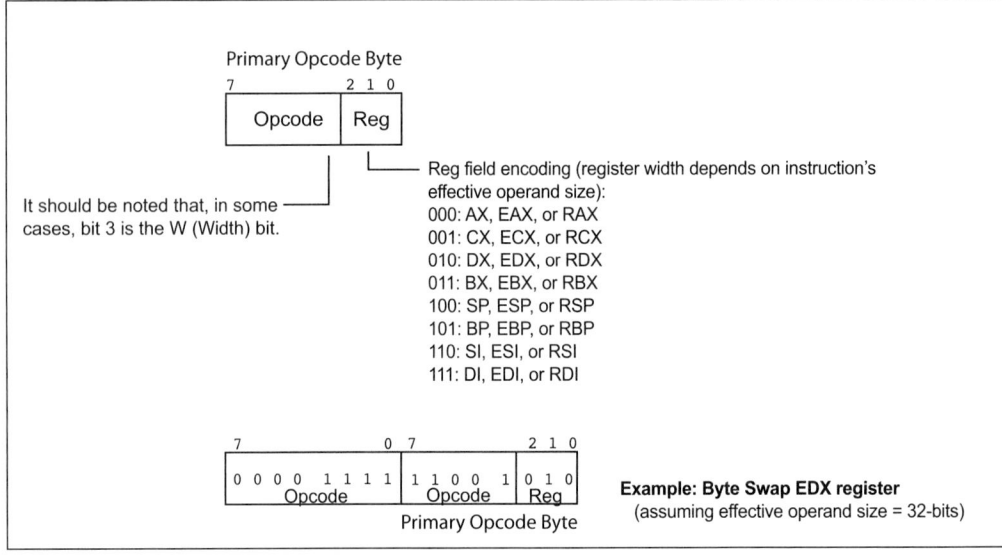

Figure 27-3: The Scale/Index/Base (SIB) Byte

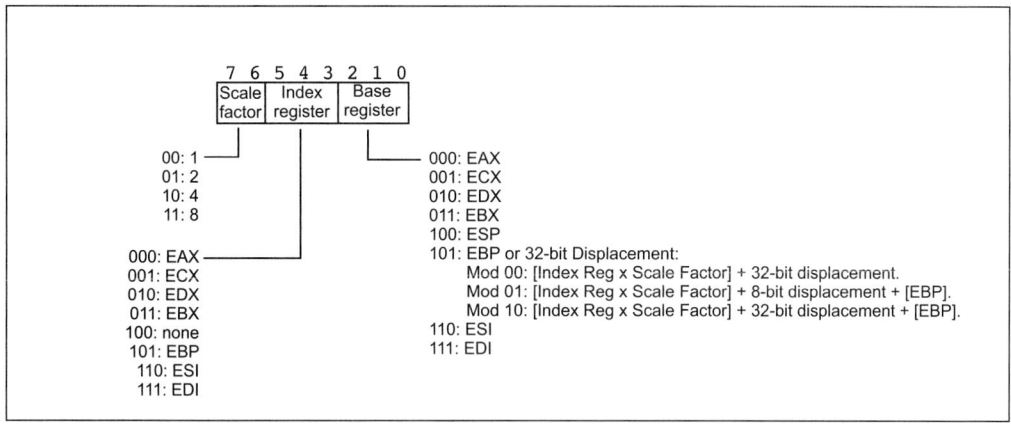

Problem 2: Using 16- and 64-bit Operands

It is mandatory that the D (Default Size bit) in a 64-bit code segment descriptor must be zero, thereby specifying a default operand size of 32-bits. In other words, unless instructed otherwise when executing an instruction, the logical processor defaults to using 32- rather than 64-bit registers, memory-based operands and and, if applicable, immediate data values. There must therefore be a way to instruct the logical processor to use a 64-bit operand size when executing an instruction.

In addition, the programmer must also have the ability to specify an operand size of 16-bits when necessary.

Solution: The Rex Prefix

The ability to select 1 of 16 registers and to specify an operand size of 64-bits are both addressed by the introduction of a new entity, the REX prefix (REX stands for *R*egister *EX*tensions). As will be seen in the upcoming sections, there are actually sixteen, one-byte variations on the REX prefix.

Making Room for REX

The assignment of a series of sixteen, one-byte opcodes (see Figure 7-2 on page 169) to the variations of the REX prefix required the reallocation of:

- The eight opcodes—40h through 47h—normally assigned to the IA-32 instructions used to increment a register (INC reg), which have the format 0100 0xxxb, where xxx selects the register to increment.
- And the eight opcodes—48h through 4Fh—normally assigned to the IA-32 instructions used to decrement a register (DEC reg), which have the format 0100 1xxxb, where xxx selects the register to decrement.

Since in 64-bit Mode the 16 variations on the REX prefix take the place of these 16 one-byte instructions, it should be fairly obvious that these forms of the IA-32 increment and decrement instructions do not exist in 64-bit Mode. However, the ability to increment and decrement a register still exists using the following 2-byte forms of the INC and DEC instructions wherein the one-byte opcode is accompanied by the ModRM byte:

- **Increment instruction**:
  - **Opcode**: 1111 111Wb, where the Width bit, W, indicates whether to increment only the one-byte or the full-width register specified in the ModRM byte.
  - **ModRM**:
    - Mod: 11b, indicating a register-only operation.
    - Reg: 000b. These bits are an extension of the opcode byte.
    - RM: xxxb, where xxx indicates the register to be incremented.
- **Decrement instruction**:
  - **Opcode**: 1111 111Wb, where the Width bit, W, indicates whether to decrement only the one-byte or the full-width register specified in the ModRM byte.
  - **ModRM**:
    - Mod: 11b, indicating a register-only operation.
    - Reg: 001b. These bits are an extension of the opcode byte.
    - RM: xxxb, where xxx indicates the register to be decremented.

REX Prefix Placement

Figure 27-4 on page 1047 highlights that the REX prefix must immediately precede the first byte of an instruction's opcode. As shown for the 3-byte opcode, this is true even if the instruction is normally preceded by a special instance of the F2h, F3h or 66h prefix (see "Special Use of Prefix Bytes" on page 177 for more information).

It should also be noted that the following restrictions still apply:

- Instruction size limit of 15 bytes still applies to instructions with a REX prefix.
- No more than 4 legacy prefixes plus one Rex prefix may preface any instruction.

Figure 27-4: Placement of REX Prefix

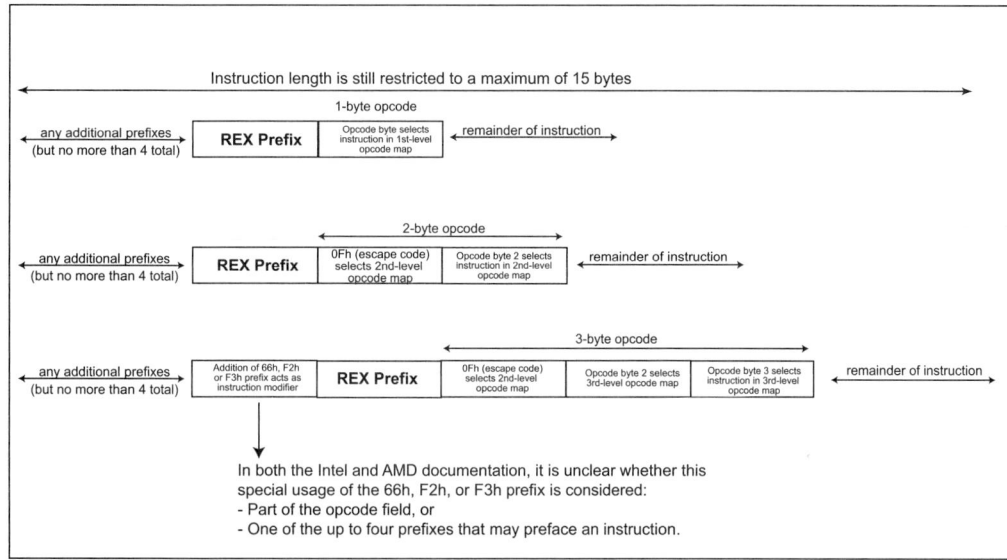

When You Need REX...

The REX prefix is only required under the following circumstances:

- When any of the following registers must be specified as operands:
  — XMM8 - XMM15.
  — The 64-bit, extended versions of the legacy GPRs (RAX, RBX, RCX, RDX, RBP, RSP, RSI and RDI).
  — The new one-byte SPL, BPL, SIL and DIL registers (which are only available in 64-bit Mode and only if the REX prefix is utilized).

— R8 - R15 (or any subset thereof; e.g., R8L, R8W, or R8D).
— Control Registers 8 - 15.
— Debug Registers 8 - 15.
- When a 64-bit operand must be specified. Note that there are some exceptions to this rule (see the next section).

...and when you don't

The REX prefix is not used under the following circumstances:

- You do not need the REX prefix if an instruction only operates on the legacy GPR registers.
- The legacy high-byte registers AH, BH, CH and DH cannot be addressed using the REX prefix.
- The REX prefix is not needed with near branch instructions or with instructions that implicitly reference the 64-bit stack pointer (RSP). These instructions are listed in Table 27-1 on page 1048 and default to a 64-bit operand size in 64-bit Mode.

Table 27-1: Instructions That Don't Require the REX Prefix

Near Branches
Jcc. Jump Conditional Near. JMP. Near Jump. CALL. Near Call. LOOP. Loop. LOOPcc. Loop Conditional.

Table 27-1: Instructions That Don't Require the REX Prefix (Continued)

Instructions That Implicitly Reference RSP
ENTER. Create Procedure Stack Frame. LEAVE. Delete Procedure Stack Frame. POP *reg/mem.* Pop Stack (to register or memory). POP *reg.* Pop Stack (to register). POP FS. Pop Stack into FS segment register. POP GS. Pop Stack into GS segment register. POPF, POPFD, POPFQ. Pop to Rflags register. PUSH *imm32.* Push onto Stack (sign-extended immediate dword). PUSH *imm8.* Push onto Stack (sign-extended immediate byte). PUSH *reg/mem.* Push onto Stack (register or memory). PUSH *reg.* Push onto Stack (register). PUSH FS. Push FS segment register onto Stack. PUSH GS. Push GS segment register onto Stack. PUSHF, PUSHFD, PUSHFQ. Push Rflags word, dword, or qword onto Stack.
Other instructions
LGDT. Load Global Descriptor Table register. LIDT. Load Interrupt Descriptor Table register. LLDT. Load Local Descriptor Table register. LTR. Load Task Register. MOV CRn. Move to a Control Register. MOV DRn. Move to a Debug Register. RET—Near Return.
Note: Due to the default 64-bit operand size used by these instructions, the REX prefix is not needed unless GPRs R8 - R15 (or any subset thereof; e.g., R8L, R8W or R8D) must be specified as operands. The REX prefix is then required in order to expand the instruction's register select fields from 3- to 4-bits.

Anatomy of a REX Prefix

General

Figure 27-5 on page 1050 illustrates the format of the REX prefix and Figure 27-6 on page 1051 provides greater detail. The upper hex digit is always 4h (identifying this as a REX prefix), while the lower hex digit is comprised of 4-bits, three of which (the B, X and R bits) are used to expand the 3-bit register select fields in the ModRM byte, the SIB byte and the primary opcode byte to four bits, thereby allowing them to select 1 of 16 registers rather than 1 of 8 (a detailed description can be found in "The Register Bit" on page 1053 and "The IndeX and Base Bits" on page 1055). The fourth bit, W, is described in the next section.

Figure 27-5: REX Prefix Format

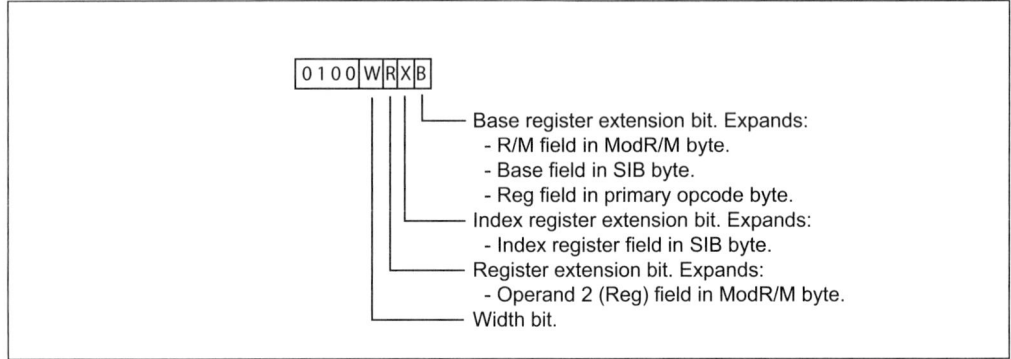

Figure 27-6: The REX Prefix

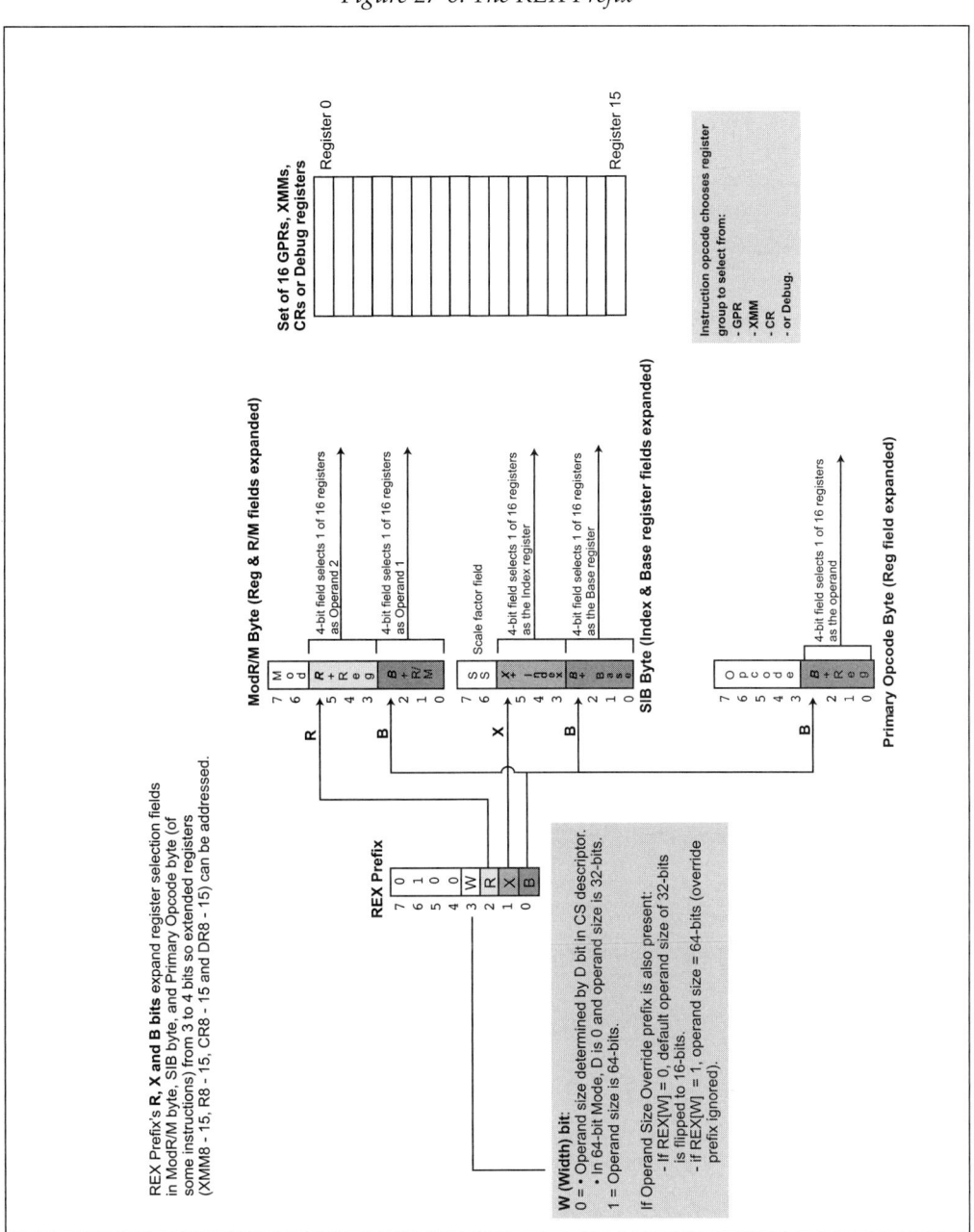

The *W*idth Bit

In conjunction with the optional Operand Size Override prefix (66h), the REX[W] bit selects an operand width of 16-, 32- or 64-bits (see Figure 27-6 on page 1051 and Table 27-2 on page 1052. It should be noted, however, that when a 66h acts as an opcode modifier rather than as an instruction prefix (see "Special Use of Prefix Bytes" on page 177), it has no relationship whatsoever with the REX[W] bit.

To clarify the relationship between the Operand Size Override prefix, the W bit in the REX prefix, and, if present, the W bit in an instruction's primary opcode byte (see Figure 7-14 on page 192):

- The instruction's effective operand size is selected using REX[W] and the Operand Size Override prefix,
- and then the W bit in the primary opcode byte selects whether this is a 1-byte or—based on the effective operand size—a full-width operation.

Table 27-2: Effective Operand Size in 64-bit Mode

Operand Size Override Prefix (66h) Present ?	REX[W]	Effective Operand Size
N	No REX prefix	32-bits
Y	No REX prefix	16-bits
N	0	32-bits
N	1	64-bits
Y	1	Operand size override prefix ignored. Effective operand size = 64-bits.
Y	0	16-bits.

The *R*egister Bit

Description. Figure 27-7 on page 1054 illustrates the encoding of the 3-bit Reg field (also referred to as the Operand 2 field) in the ModRM byte when the REX prefix does not preface an instruction. When the logical processor is operating in 64-bit Mode and an instruction is prefaced by the REX prefix, the REX[R] bit becomes the msb of the expanded 4-bit Reg field (see Table 27-3 on page 1054).

Note 1: REX[R] is ignored if ModRM[Reg] contains a 3-bit opcode extension [see "Opcode Micro-Maps (Groups)" on page 180] rather than a register designation.

Note 2: It should be noted that the four legacy high-byte registers—AH, BH, CH and DH—are nowhere to be found in Table 27-3 on page 1054. In 64-bit Mode, they cannot be addressed using the REX prefix.

An Example. Refer to Table 27-3 on page 1054. Assume an SSE instruction specifies XMM9 as an operand. Since one of the new extended registers is an operand, the REX prefix is required:

— The R bit in the REX prefix = 1 to select the second group of eight registers (XMM8 - XMM15).
— The ModRM Reg field = 001b to select register 1 within XMM8 - XMM15 (register 0 = XMM8, register 1 = XMM9, etc.)
— The operand size implied by the instruction opcode is a 128-bit XMM register.

Figure 27-7: The ModRM Byte

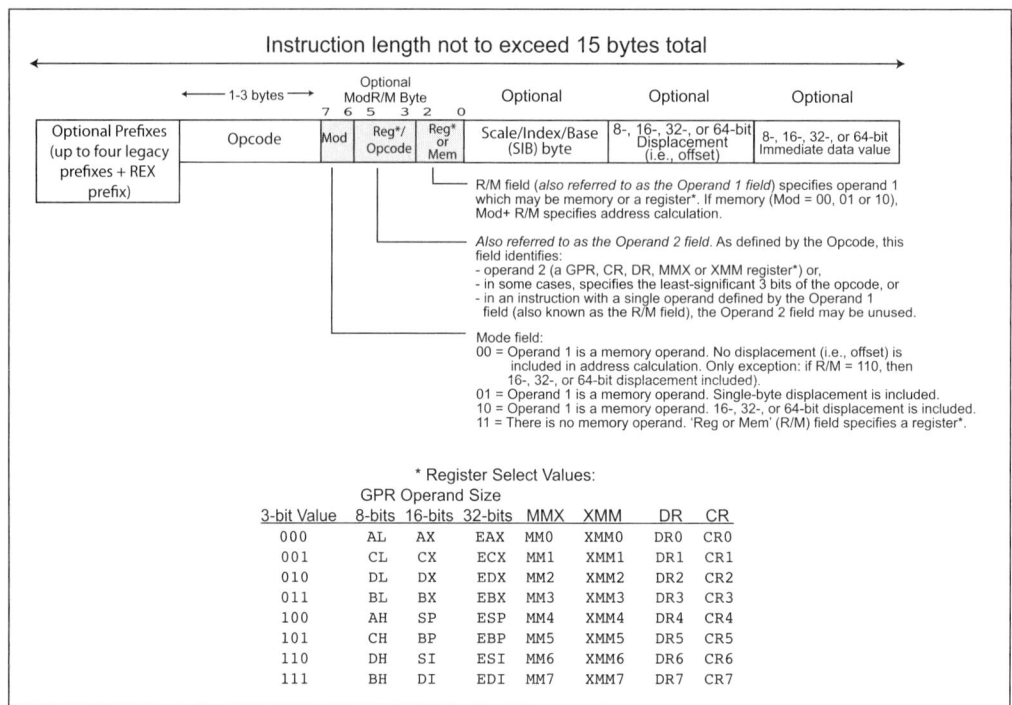

Table 27-3: REX[R] + ModRM[Reg], or REX[B] + Opcode[Reg],
or REX[B] + ModRM[RM] = 4-bit Register Select Field

REX R or B	ModRM Reg	Operand Size or Type (Opcode dictates group selected: GPR, MMX, XMM, CR or DR)							
		Reg8	Reg16	Reg32	Reg64	MMX	XMM	CR	DR
0	000	AL	AX	EAX	RAX	MM0	XMM0	CR0	DR0
0	001	CL	CX	ECX	RCX	MM1	XMM1	CR1	DR1
0	010	DL	DX	EDX	RDX	MM2	XMM2	CR2	DR2
0	011	BL	BX	EBX	RBX	MM3	XMM3	CR3	DR3

Table 27-3: REX[R] + ModRM[Reg], or REX[B] + Opcode[Reg],
or REX[B] + ModRM[RM] = 4-bit Register Select Field (Continued)

REX R or B	ModRM Reg	Operand Size or Type (Opcode dictates group selected: GPR, MMX, XMM, CR or DR)							
		Reg8	Reg16	Reg32	Reg64	MMX	XMM	CR	DR
0	100	SPL	SP	ESP	RSP	MM4	XMM4	CR4	DR4
0	101	BPL	BP	EBP	RBP	MM5	XMM5	CR5	DR5
0	110	SIL	SI	ESI	RSI	MM6	XMM6	CR6	DR6
0	111	DIL	DI	EDI	RDI	MM7	XMM7	CR7	DR7
1	000	R8L	R8W	R8D	R8	MM0	XMM8	CR8	DR8
1	001	R9L	R9W	R9D	R9	MM1	XMM9	CR9	DR9
1	010	R10L	R10W	R10D	R10	MM2	XMM10	CR10	DR10
1	011	R11L	R11W	R11D	R11	MM3	XMM11	CR11	DR11
1	100	R12L	R12W	R12D	R12	MM4	XMM12	CR12	DR12
1	101	R13L	R13W	R13D	R13	MM5	XMM13	CR13	DR13
1	110	R14L	R14W	R14D	R14	MM6	XMM14	CR14	DR14
1	111	R15L	R15W	R15D	R15	MM7	XMM15	CR15	DR15

The Inde*X* and *B*ase Bits

Description. When the Mod and RM fields in the ModRM byte indicate that an element within a memory-based data structure is being addressed as one of the operands, the SIB (Scale/Index/Base) byte (see Figure 27-3 on page 1045) is included in the instruction immediately following the ModRM byte (see Figure 27-7 on page 1054) and the address of the target data structure element is computed as follows (in 64-bit Mode):

— Data structure base address + (record number * record length in bytes), where:
  – The **base address** is contained in the register identified by the 4-bit value consisting of the REX[B] bit + the 3-bit Base field in the SIB byte.

- The target data structure **record number** is contained in the **index** register identified by the 4-bit value consisting of the REX[X] bit + the 3-bit Index field in the SIB byte.
- The **record length** (in bytes) is specified as 1, 2, 4 or 8 bytes by the 2-bit Scaling Factor field (the SIB[SS] field).

Table 27-4 on page 1056 illustrates the encoding of the three SIB byte fields (Scaling Factor, Index register, and Base register) when the logical processor is operating in 64-bit Mode and the REX prefix precedes an instruction.

As indicated in Note 2 of the table, when REX[X] = 0 and SIB[Index] = 100b, the effective memory address = the data structure's base address (contained in the Base register defined by the SIB[Base] field). In other words, the index value and the Scale Factor are not used in computing the address.

An Example. Refer to Table 27-4 on page 1056. Assume an instruction specifies that R12 acts as the Base register, R8 as the Index register and that the scaling factor = 4-bytes.

— The REX prefix is required with the B and X bits set to one:
  - B = 1 plus SIB[Base] field = 100b: 1100b selects R12 as the base register.
  - X = 1 plus SIB[Index] = 000b: 1000b selects R8 as the index register.
— Scaling factor of 10b specifies a scaling factor of 4-bytes.
— SIB byte therefore = 84h.

*Table 27-4: 64-bit Effective Address = Base + (Index * Scale Factor)*

If B + SIB[Base] (or if no REX) ==>		0000	0001	0010	0011	0100	0101	0110	0111
then Base Register ==>		RAX	RCX	RDX	RBX	RSP	note1	RSI	RDI
If B + SIB[Base] ==>		1000	1001	1010	1011	1100	1101	1110	1111
then Base Register ==>		R8	R9	R10	R11	R12	R13	R14	R15

SIB Index	Index Register Note3 + X=0 / X=1	Scale Factor (Index * SF)	Hex Value of SIB Byte							
000	[RAX] [R8]	00	00	01	02	03	04	05	06	07
001	[RCX] [R9]		08	09	0A	0B	0C	0D	0E	0F
010	[RDX] [R10]	Index + Base	10	11	12	13	14	15	16	17
011	[RBX] [R11]		18	19	1A	1B	1C	1D	1E	1F
100	note2 [R12]		20	21	22	23	24	25	26	27
101	[RBP] [R13]		28	29	2A	2B	2C	2D	2E	2F
110	[RSI] [R14]		30	31	32	33	34	35	36	37
111	[RDI] [R15]		38	39	3A	3B	3C	3D	3E	3F

*Table 27-4: 64-bit Effective Address = Base + (Index * Scale Factor) (Continued)*

000	[RAX]	[R8]	01	40	41	42	43	44	45	46	47
001	[RCX]	[R9]		48	49	4A	4B	4C	4D	4E	4F
010	[RDX]	[R10]	Index	50	51	52	53	54	55	56	57
011	[RBX]	[R11]	x 2	58	59	5A	5B	5C	5D	5E	5F
100	note2	[R12]	+	60	61	62	63	64	65	66	67
101	[RBP]	[R13]	Base	68	69	6A	6B	6C	6D	6E	6F
110	[RSI]	[R14]		70	71	72	73	74	75	76	77
111	[RDI]	[R15]		78	79	7A	7B	7C	7D	7E	7F
000	[RAX]	[R8]	10	80	81	82	83	84	85	86	87
001	[RCX]	[R9]		88	89	8A	8B	8C	8D	8E	8F
010	[RDX]	[R10]	Index	90	91	92	93	94	95	96	97
011	[RBX]	[R11]	x 4	98	99	9A	9B	9C	9D	9E	9F
100	note2	[R12]	+	A0	A1	A2	A3	A4	A5	A6	A7
101	[RBP]	[R13]	Base	A8	A9	AA	AB	AC	AD	AE	AF
110	[RSI]	[R14]		B0	B1	B2	B3	B4	B5	B6	B7
111	[RDI]	[R15]		B8	B9	BA	BB	BC	BD	BE	BF
000	[RAX]	[R8]	11	C0	C1	C2	C3	C4	C5	C6	C7
001	[RCX]	[R9]		C8	C9	CA	CB	CC	CD	CE	CF
010	[RDX]	[R10]	Index	D0	D1	D2	D3	D4	D5	D6	D7
011	[RBX]	[R11]	x 8	D8	D9	DA	DB	DC	DD	DE	DF
100	note2	[R12]	+	E0	E1	E2	E3	E4	E5	E6	E7
101	[RBP]	[R13]	Base	E8	E9	EA	EB	EC	ED	EE	EF
110	[RSI]	[R14]		F0	F1	F2	F3	F4	F5	F6	F7
111	[RDI]	[R15]		F8	F9	FA	FB	FC	FD	FE	FF

Note 1: SIB[Base] = 101b and *REX[X] = 0* provides the following address modes for the three memory-related values of ModRM[Mod]:

Mod	Effective Address
00	[Index Reg x Scale Factor] + 32-bit displacement.
01	[Index Reg x Scale Factor] + 8-bit displacement + [RBP].
10	[Index Reg x Scale Factor] + 32-bit displacement + [RBP].

Note 1 continued: SIB[Base] = 101b and *REX[X] = 1* provides the following address modes for the three memory-related values of ModRM[Mod]:

00	[Index Reg x Scale Factor] + 32-bit displacement.
01	[Index Reg x Scale Factor] + 8-bit displacement + [R13].
10	[Index Reg x Scale Factor] + 32-bit displacement + [R13].

*Table 27-4: 64-bit Effective Address = Base + (Index * Scale Factor) (Continued)*

Note 2: When SIB[Index] field = 100b and REX[X] = 0, the effective memory address = the address contained in the Base register defined by the SIB[Base] field. In other words, there is no index value and the Scale Factor is don't care.

Note 3: This column shows registers that can be selected as Index registers either when:
– There is a REX prefix and REX[X] = 0, or
– There is no REX prefix and 1 of 8 registers can be selected as the Index register using the 3-bit SIB[Index] field.

Addressing Registers Using REX[B] + Opcode[Reg]

Some instructions incorporate a 3-bit Reg field in the three lsbs of the primary opcode byte (see Figure 27-2 on page 1044 and "Explicit Register Specification in Opcode" on page 196). In all of these cases, the instructions target a single register operand identified by the PrimaryOpcode[Reg] field. In 64-bit Mode when any of these instructions are prefaced by the REX prefix, the REX[B] bit expands this field to four bits so the instruction can specify any of 16 possible registers. Table 27-3 on page 1054 defines the register encoding of this 4-bit field.

Addressing Registers Using REX[B] + ModRM[RM]

Expansion of RM field in ModRM byte. Rather than a memory-based operand, an instruction may specify a register in the 3-bit RM field of the ModRM byte (see "Explicit Register Specification in ModRM Byte" on page 196). In 64-bit Mode when such an instruction is prefaced by the REX prefix, the REX[B] bit expands this field to four bits so the instruction can specify any of 16 possible registers. Table 27-3 on page 1054 defines the register encoding of this 4-bit field.

Byte-Register Addressing Limitations

The legacy high-byte registers AH, BH, CH and DH cannot be addressed when an instruction includes the REX prefix. As a result, an instruction could not perform an operation on a legacy high-byte register and a register that is only accessible when using the REX prefix. As an example, it is not possible for an instruction to perform an operation on the AH and R9L registers (because one is only addressable without the REX prefix and the other only with it).

Sometimes, REX Fields Have No Effect

The REX prefix has no effect under the following circumstances:

*   Setting REX[W] to 1 specifies a 64-bit operand size. Like the Operand Size Override prefix, setting REX[W] to one has no effect on byte operations.
*   The REX[R] bit is ignored if the ModRM[Reg] field specifies a register other than a GPR, MMX, XMM, Control, or Debug register, or if an instruction uses ModRM[Reg] as 3-bit extension to the opcode rather than as a register select field.
*   When the operand specified is an immediate data value.
*   If both operands are MMX registers. There are only eight MMX registers and there is no need for an expansion of the register select field; they can be addressed with a 3-bit register select field.

Addressing Memory in 64-bit Mode

64-bit Mode Uses a Hardware-Enforced Flat Model

As described in "In 64-bit Mode, Hardware-Enforced Flat Model" on page 927, 64-bit Mode enforces the Flat Memory Model.

CS, DS, ES, and SS Segments Start at Virtual Address 0

In 64-bit Mode these four memory segments, by definition, start at virtual address 0. Furthermore, their size is assumed to be 2^{64} bytes. Since the segment base address is assumed to be 0, the segment base address is ignored in the calculation of a memory address. In the following two examples:

*   mov rdx, [offset]
*   mov r8, es:[offset]

the DS and ES base addresses are ignored and the 64-bit offset *is* the virtual address of the memory-based data operand being addressed.

Likewise, the CS and SS base addresses are also assumed to be zero:

*   The code fetch logic ignores the code segment base address and only uses the 64-bit virtual address in the RIP register when fetching the next instruction from memory.

- When storing data to (i.e., a push operation) or reading it from (a pop operation) stack memory, the logical processor ignores the stack segment base address and only uses the 64-bit virtual address in the RSP register.

CS/DS/ES/SS Segment Override Prefixes Ignored

Because all of these segments by definition start at virtual address 0, using any of the respective Segment Override prefixes with an instruction is treated as a "don't care".

FS and GS Segments Can Start at Non-Zero Base Addresses

Loading a new 16-bit segment descriptor selector into any of the data segment registers (DS, ES, FS or GS) causes the logical processor to read the selector segment descriptor into the invisible portion of the respective data segment register. While the logical processor ignores the attributes of the DS and ES data segments in 64-bit Mode, it does utilize the 32-bit segment virtual base address supplied by the FS or GS descriptor in computing the address of a memory operand. Since this only a 32-bit base address, however, it is by definition an address in the lower 4GB of virtual address space.

If the programmer wishes to specify an FS or GS segment base address above the 4GB virtual address boundary, this is accomplished when privilege level 0 software uses the WRMSR instruction to write a 64-bit base address into one of the following two MSR registers:

- The 64-bit FS base can be set by writing to the FS_Base MSR at address C000_0100h.
- The 64-bit GS base can be set by writing to the GS_Base MSR at address C000_0101h.

As an example, execution of:

- mov R13, fs:[offset]

results in the addition of the specified offset address to the 64-bit base address of the FS data segment to yield the 64-bit virtual address of the memory-based data operand.

FS/GS Segment Override Prefixes Matter

Because these two segments can start at a non-zero address, the logical processor does pay attention to these two prefixes in calculating the virtual address of a memory operand.

Default Virtual Address Size (and overriding it)

The default size of data operands and addresses assumed by the logical processor are dictated by the state of the D (Default) bit in the code segment descriptor. In a 64-bit code segment descriptor (see Figure 27-8 on page 1062), the only acceptable value of the D bit is 0 indicating:

- Default data operand size = 32-bits.
- Default virtual address size = 64-bits.

As previously described (see "The Width Bit" on page 1052), the default data operand size of 32-bits may be overriden to 16- or 64-bits by prefacing an instruction with the REX and/or Operand Size Override prefixes.

The default address size of 64-bits may be forced to 32-bits by prefacing an instruction with the Address Size Override prefix. 16-bit addresses are not supported in 64-bit Mode.

Figure 27-8: 64-bit Code Segment Descriptor

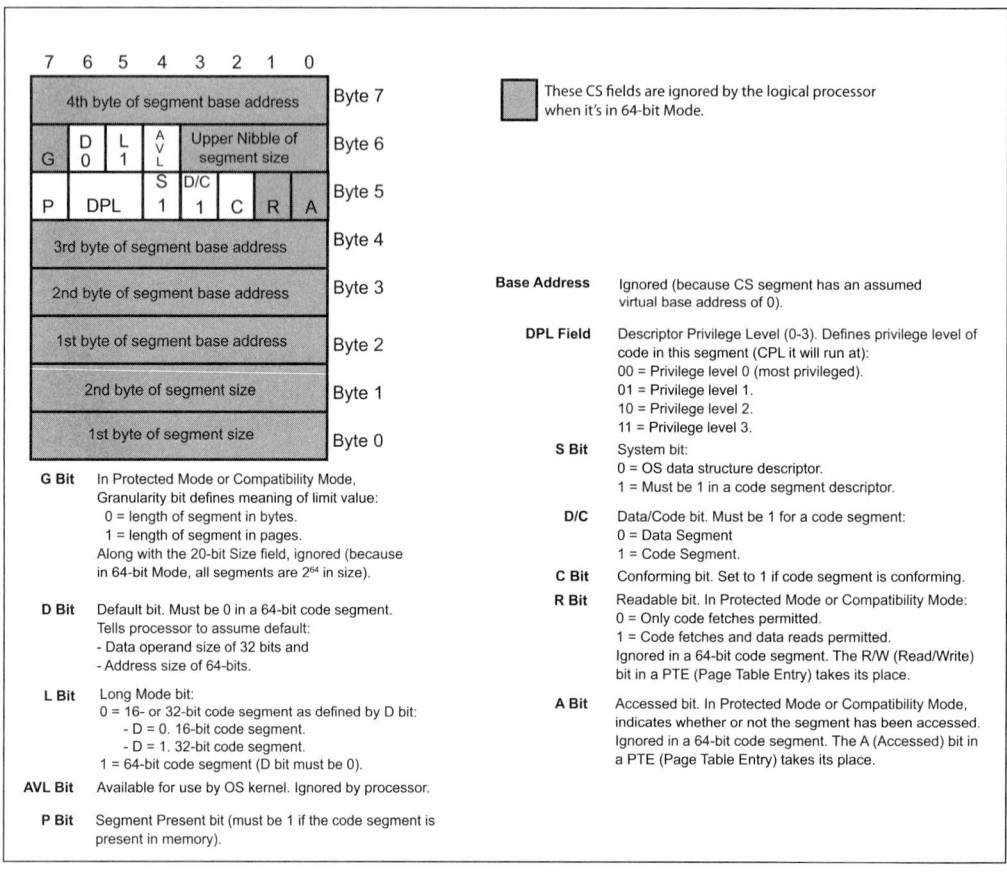

G Bit   In Protected Mode or Compatibility Mode,
Granularity bit defines meaning of limit value:
   0 = length of segment in bytes.
   1 = length of segment in pages.
Along with the 20-bit Size field, ignored (because
in 64-bit Mode, all segments are 2^{64} in size).

D Bit   Default bit. Must be 0 in a 64-bit code segment.
Tells processor to assume default:
- Data operand size of 32 bits and
- Address size of 64-bits.

L Bit   Long Mode bit:
0 = 16- or 32-bit code segment as defined by D bit:
   - D = 0. 16-bit code segment.
   - D = 1. 32-bit code segment.
1 = 64-bit code segment (D bit must be 0).

AVL Bit   Available for use by OS kernel. Ignored by processor.

P Bit   Segment Present bit (must be 1 if the code segment is
present in memory).

These CS fields are ignored by the logical processor
when it's in 64-bit Mode.

Base Address   Ignored (because CS segment has an assumed
virtual base address of 0).

DPL Field   Descriptor Privilege Level (0-3). Defines privilege level of
code in this segment (CPL it will run at):
00 = Privilege level 0 (most privileged).
01 = Privilege level 1.
10 = Privilege level 2.
11 = Privilege level 3.

S Bit   System bit:
0 = OS data structure descriptor.
1 = Must be 1 in a code segment descriptor.

D/C   Data/Code bit. Must be 1 for a code segment:
0 = Data Segment
1 = Code Segment.

C Bit   Conforming bit. Set to 1 if code segment is conforming.

R Bit   Readable bit. In Protected Mode or Compatibility Mode:
0 = Only code fetches permitted.
1 = Code fetches and data reads permitted.
Ignored in a 64-bit code segment. The R/W (Read/Write)
bit in a PTE (Page Table Entry) takes its place.

A Bit   Accessed bit. In Protected Mode or Compatibility Mode,
indicates whether or not the segment has been accessed.
Ignored in a 64-bit code segment. The A (Accessed) bit in
a PTE (Page Table Entry) takes its place.

Actual Address Size Support: Theory vs. Practice

Refer to Table 27-5 on page 1063.

Table 27-5: Theory vs. Practice

Theory	Current Practice
In theory, 64-bit Mode can support: • A **64-bit virtual memory address**, • which is translated into a **52-bit physical memory address** by the virtual-to-physical address translation services (i.e., the Paging logic). This would allow up to four petabytes of physical memory to be addressed.	Current implementations of the virtual-to-physical address translation services, however, are only capable of translating: • A **48-bit virtual memory address** • into a physical memory address up to 48-bits in width.

Please note that these limitations are imposed by the current implementation of the logical processor's Paging logic.

Canonical Address

General

As indicated under the previous topic, specific processor implementations may not support translation of the full, 64-bit virtual address into a physical memory address. Using today's processors as examples, only virtual address bits 47:0 are translated. It is a rule, however, that the virtual address bits above the most-significant implemented bit (which is bit 47 in today's implementations) must be filled with the state of the most-significant implemented bit (see Figure 27-9 on page 1065). In other words:

- If bit 47 is a 0, bits 63:48 must also be set to 0.
- If bit 47 is a 1, bits 63:48 must also be set to 1.

Addresses formatted in such a manner are said to be *canonical* in form (in other words, the address must adhere to this standard format because the specification writers command it to be so).

It is a rule that all implementations must check 64-bit virtual addresses to verify that they are, in fact, canonical in form and, if they're not, must generate either a Stack Fault exception (if an address accessing stack memory is badly-formed) or a General Protection exception (in all other cases).

x86 Instruction Set Architecture

32- (and 16-) bit Addressing Limited to Lower 4GB

32-bit Address Treatment in 64-bit Mode. In 64-bit Mode, prefacing an instruction with the Address Size Override prefix forces the size of a memory address to 32-bits rather than the default size of 64-bits. In this case, the logical processor:

— Fills the address bits above bit 31 with zeros to the full-width supported by the implementation (e.g., on today's processors, to bit 47)
— And then, adhering to the canonical address rule, fills bits 63:48 with zeros to reflect the state of bit 47 (continuing with the example of today's implementations).

Address Treatment in Compatibility Mode. Although this chapter is devoted to 64-bit Mode, 32- and 16-bit virtual addresses generated in Compatibility Mode must also be extended to a width of 64-bits and adhere to the canonical form. 32-bit addresses are treated as stated above and 16-bit addresses are treated similarly:

— A 16-bit address is formed by adding a 16-bit offset to the respective segment's virtual base address. A 16-bit segment has a 24-bit virtual base address.
— The logical processor fills the upper address bits with zeros to the full-width supported by the implementation (e.g., on today's processors, to bit 47)
— and then, adhering to the canonical address rule, fills bits 63:48 with zeros to reflect the state of bit 47 (continuing with the example of today's implementations).

As a result, in Compatibility Mode:

• 16-bit applications written for the 286 can only generate virtual addresses in a 16MB range (0000000000000000 - 0000000000FFFFFFh).
• and 32-bit applications can only address the lower 4GB of virtual address space (0000000000000000 - 00000000FFFFFFFFh).

Figure 27-9: Example of Canonical Address Formation

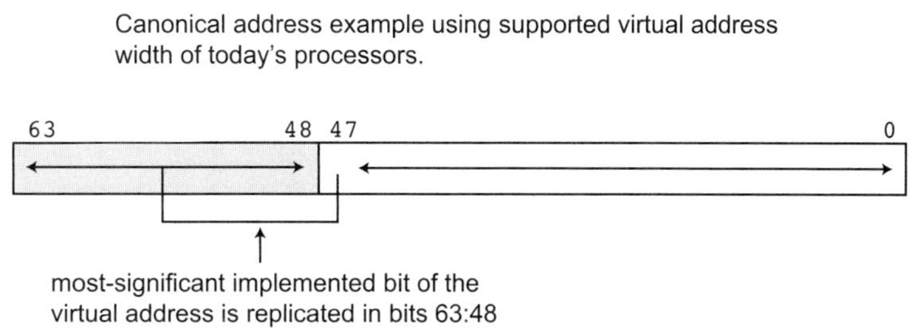

Memory-based Operand Address Computation

Table 27-6 on page 1066 appeared in "Addressing a Memory-Based Operand" on page 198 as a simplified summarization of the four memory operand addressing methods available in IA-32 Mode and Compatibility Mode. In 64-bit Mode, a fifth addressing mode—RIP-relative data operand addressing—is also available.

As described in "Addressing Memory Using the ModRM Byte" on page 200, any instruction that utilizes a memory-based operand includes the ModRM byte (see Figure 27-10 on page 1068) to instruct the logical processor regarding how to calculate the effective address (i.e., the offset) of the memory operand. The ModRM byte consists of three fields:

- 2-bit Mod field.
- 3-bit Register or Opcode field. This is also referred to as the Operand 2 field.
- 3-bit Register or Memory (RM) field. This is also referred to as the Operand 1 field.

If the addressing mode indicated by the ModRM[RM] field indicates that a fixed-length record is being addressed in a memory-based data structure (i.e., RM = 100b; see "Using the SIB Byte to Access a Data Structure" on page 203), then the SIB byte is included immediately following the ModRM byte. In all other cases, the formation of the memory address is defined by Table 27-7 on page 1068. Please note that the second column from the left defines the addressing modes available when the REX prefix is included and REX[B] = 0, *or when there is no REX prefix.*

As shown in the table, the REX[B] bit expands the RM field to four bits allowing eight more register selections than are available in IA-32 Mode or Compatibility Mode (see Table 7-22 on page 202).

Of special interest is a newly-introduced addressing method that is available only in 64-bit Mode (irrespective of the presence of the REX prefix) when:

- ModRM[Mod] = 00b, and
- ModRM[RM] = 101b.

This row is both bolded and italicized in the table to highlight its special nature. It is referred to as RIP-relative addressing and is described in detail in the next section.

Table 27-6: Summary of Memory Addressing Modes Available in 64-bit Mode

Method	Effective Address Computed?	Effective Address Derivation
1	No	Effective address is contained in the specified register. Symbolically shown as: *[reg]*. Referred to as a **register-indirect address**.
2	No	Effective address is **hard-coded** in the instruction as a 32-bit Displacement from the base address of a segment. Referred to as **direct addressing**.
3	Yes	Effective address = **[reg] ± a hard-coded 8- or 32-bit value** (i.e., an 8- or 32-bit, signed displacement).

Table 27-6: Summary of Memory Addressing Modes Available in 64-bit Mode (Continued)

Method	Effective Address Computed?	Effective Address Derivation
4	Yes	Target memory item resides in a **data structure** and the effective address computation is defined by one of four calculation methods: • [base] + [index * SF]. • [base] + [index * SF] ± hard-coded 8- or 32-bit value. • [index * SF] ± hard-coded 8- or 32-bit value. • [ebp] + [index * SF] ± hard-coded 8- or 32-bit value. Key: • Base = the register defined in the SIB byte that contains the data structure's base address. • Index = the register defined in the SIB byte that contains the target record number. • SF = the scaling factor (record length in bytes) to be multiplied by the value in the Index register. • The signed, 8- or 32-bit value is a Displacement that is hard-coded as part of the instruction. • [ebp] is the contents of the EBP register.
5	*Yes*	*RIP-relative data operand addressing.*

Figure 27-10: ModRM Byte

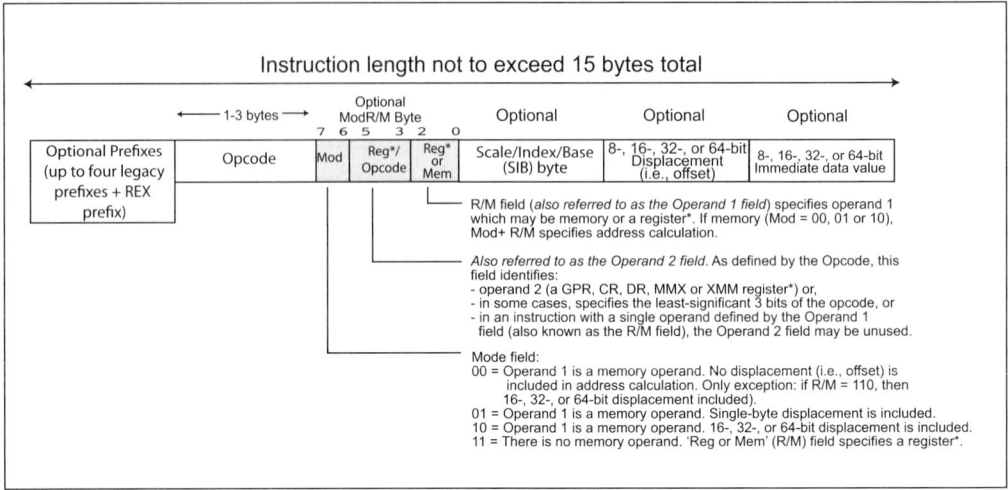

Table 27-7: Mod + RM Interpretation When Effective Address Size = 64-bits

RM	+ REX[B] = 0 (or there isn't a REX prefix)	+ REX[B] = 1
	Mod = 00b (Operand 1 = memory operand)	
000	[RAX]	[R8]
001	[RCX]	[R9]
010	[RDX]	[R10]
011	[RBX]	[R11]
100	address = SIB	address = SIB
101	**[RIP] + 32-bit Displacement**	**[RIP] + 32-bit Displacement**
110	[RSI]	[R14]
111	[RDI]	[R15]

Table 27-7: Mod + RM Interpretation When Effective Address Size = 64-bits (Continued)

Mod = 01b (Operand 1 = memory operand)	
000 `[RAX]+8-bit displacement`	`[R8]+8-bit displacement`
001 `[RCX]+8-bit displacement`	`[R9]+8-bit displacement`
010 `[RDX]+8-bit displacement`	`[R10]+8-bit displacement`
011 `[RBX]+8-bit displacement`	`[R11]+8-bit displacement`
100 `SIB + 8-bit displacement`	`SIB + 8-bit displacement`
101 `[RBP]+8-bit displacement`	`[R13]+8-bit displacement`
110 `[RSI]+8-bit displacement`	`[R14]+8-bit displacement`
111 `[RDI]+8-bit displacement`	`[R15]+8-bit displacement`
Mod = 10b (Operand 1 = memory operand)	
000 `[RAX]+32-bit displacement`	`[R8]+32-bit displacement`
001 `[RCX]+32-bit displacement`	`[R9]+32-bit displacement`
010 `[RDX]+32-bit displacement`	`[R10]+32-bit displacement`
011 `[RBX]+32-bit displacement`	`[R11]+32-bit displacement`
100 `SIB + 32-bit displacement`	`SIB + 32-bit displacement`
101 `[RBP]+32-bit displacement`	`[R13]+32-bit displacement`
110 `[RSI]+32-bit displacement`	`[R14]+32-bit displacement`
111 `[RDI]+32-bit displacement`	`[R15]+32-bit displacement`
Mod = 11b (Operands 1 and 2 are both register-based)	

- REX[B] + ModRM[RM] defines register containing operand 1.
- REX[R] + ModRM[Reg] defines register containing operand 2.

See Table 27-3 on page 1054 for encoding of these two 4-bit register select fields.

RIP-relative Data Addressing

In the x86 architecture it has always been possible to branch forward or backward relative to the position of the currently-executing branch instruction (i.e., relative to the address currently pointed to by the Instruction Pointer—IP—register). What has *not* been possible is the ability to access a memory-based data operand located backward or forward relative to the address of the currently-executing instruction. That ability does, however, exist when the logical processor is operating in 64-bit Mode (and has nothing whatsoever to do with the presence or absence of the REX prefix).

Refer to the highlighted row in Table 27-7 on page 1068. Irrespective of the presence or absence of a REX preface before an instruction, this newly-instituted addressing mode is active when:

- ModRM[Mod] = 00b, and
- ModRM[RM] = 101b.

Such an instruction includes a hard-coded, signed 32-bit displacement value which, when added to (or, if it's a negative value, subtracted from) the address currently resident in the 64-bit RIP register (i.e., the address of the next instruction), yields the address of a data operand up to 2GB forward or 2GB-1 backward from the current RIP address. Note that the 64-bit offset from the RIP register is *not* added to the CS base address (because, in 64-bit Mode, by definition, the CS, DS, ES and SS segments all start at virtual address 0).

Note: looking at Table 27-7 on page 1068, it may appear that it's not possible to address a memory operand using an indirect address in GPR R13 or RBP. It is, though; in order to do so, the instruction should use ModRM[Mod] = 01b and ModRM[RM] = 101b and specify an 8-bit, hard-coded displacement value of zero ([R13]or [RBP] + 0).

If the Address Size Override prefix prefaces an instruction, thereby setting the effective address size to 32-bits (rather than 64-bits), RIP-relative addressing can still be used. In that case, the 32-bit data operand address is extended to a width of 64 bits by filling address bits 63:32 with zeros and the signed, 32-bit displacement is then added to it to yield the virtual address of the data operand.

Near and Far Branch Addressing

In 64-bit Mode, branches come in a number of forms (see Table 27-8 on page 1071).

Table 27-8: Branch Forms in 64-bit Mode

Type	Branch Form
Conditional Branch	• **Short Jump**. Forward or backward from the virtual address in RIP register. Distance of up to 128 locations backward or 127 forward is specified via an 8-bit, signed displacement which is sign-extended to 64-bits in 64-bit Mode. • **Near Jump**. Forward or backward from the virtual address in RIP register. Signed 32-bit displacement (sign-extended to 64-bits) permits jump up to 2G backward or 2G-1 forward of address in RIP register.
Unconditional branch within same segment (i.e., a **near Jump**)	• **Short Jump, RIP-Relative**. Forward or backward from the virtual address in RIP register (RIP + 127 to RIP - 128), specified via an 8-bit, signed displacement sign-extended to 64-bits. • **Near Jump, RIP-Relative**. Forward or backward from the virtual address in RIP register (RIP + [2G-1] to RIP - 2G), specified via a 32-bit, signed displacement sign-extended to 64-bits. • **Near Jump, Register or Memory Indirect**. The 64-bit branch target address is specified in a 64-bit register or by a 64-bit address pointer stored in memory.

Table 27-8: Branch Forms in 64-bit Mode (Continued)

Type	Branch Form
Unconditional branch to different segment (i.e., a **far Jump**)	**Far Jump, Memory Indirect**. The new values to be placed in the CS:RIP register pair are specified in memory in one of three forms: • **To 16-bit CS**. When performing a far jump (preceded by the Operand Size Override prefix) to a legacy 16-bit code segment, four bytes are read from memory: a new 16-bit CS selector value and a new 16-bit IP value. • **To 32-bit CS**. When performing a far jump to a legacy 32-bit code segment, six bytes are read from memory: a new 16-bit CS selector value and a new 32-bit EIP value. • **To 64-bit CS**. When performing a far jump to a 64-bit code segment, ten bytes are read from memory: a new 16-bit CS selector value and a new 64-bit RIP value. This instruction requires the REX prefix with the W(idth) bit set to one.
Procedure Call within same segment (i.e., a **near Call**)	• **Near Call, RIP-Relative**. Forward or backward from the virtual address in RIP register (RIP + [2G-1] to RIP - 2G), specified via a 32-bit, signed displacement sign-extended to 64-bits. • **Near Call, Register or Memory Indirect**. The branch is preceded by the REX prefix and the 64-bit branch target address is specified in a 64-bit register or by a 64-bit address pointer stored in memory.

Table 27-8: Branch Forms in 64-bit Mode (Continued)

Type	Branch Form
Procedure Call to different segment (i.e., a **far Call**)	**Far Call, Memory Indirect**. The new values to be placed in the CS:RIP register pair are specified in memory in one of three forms: • **To 16-bit CS**. When performing a far call (preceded by the Operand Size Override prefix) to a legacy 16-bit code segment, four bytes are read from memory: a new 16-bit CS selector value and a new 16-bit IP value. • **To 32-bit CS**. When performing a far call to a legacy 32-bit code segment, six bytes are read from memory: a new 16-bit CS selector value and a new 32-bit EIP value. • **To 64-bit CS**. When performing a far jump to a 64-bit code segment, ten bytes are read from memory: a new 16-bit CS selector value and a new 64-bit RIP value. This instruction requires the REX prefix with the W(idth) bit set to one.

Immediate Data Values in 64-bit Mode

Rather than specifying a register or a memory location containing a data value to be used by an instruction, in some cases the programmer may explicitly specify (as part of the instruction itself) an 8-, 16-, 32- or 64-bit data value as the source operand. In this case, it is always encoded at the tail end of the instruction:

- In 16-bit Mode, it may be either 8- or 16-bits in length.
- In 32-bit Mode, it may be 8-, 16-, or 32-bits in length.
- In 64-bit Mode, it may be 8-, 16-, 32-, or 64-bits in length.

In 64-bit Mode, the only instruction that permits the specification of a full, 64-bit immediate data value is:

```
MOV  r64,imm64   ;where r64 is a 64-bit GPR and the
                 ;instruction is prefaced with a REX
                    ;prefix with REX[W] = 1.
```

In all other cases, immediate data values are 8-, 16-, or 32-bits in length and, if REX[W] = 1, the value is sign-extended to 64-bits before use.

Displacements in 64-bit Mode

When the logical processor is operating in 64-bit Mode, an instruction that addresses a memory-based operand can, just as it could in 32-bit Mode, specify an 8-, 16,- or 32-displacement (see the description of the Displacement Field in Table 7-5 on page 164). 8-, 16-, or 32-bit displacement values are sign-extended to 64-bits before being used in calculating a memory address.

A new form of the MOV instruction has been added that permits data to be read from or written to a 64-bit virtual address specified as a 64-bit displacement encoded within the body of the instruction itself. This register/memory operation implicitly specifies the AL, AX, EAX or RAX registers as one of the operands (the size of the register is defined by the operand size specified).

28 *64-bit Odds and Ends*

The Previous Chapter

The previous chapter described the following topics:

- Switching to 64-bit Mode.
- The Defaults.
- The REX Prefix.
- Addressing Memory in 64-bit Mode.
    - 64-bit Mode Uses a Hardware-Enforced Flat Model.
    - Default Virtual Address Size (and overriding it).
    - Actual Address Size Support: Theory vs. Practice.
    - Canonical Address.
    - Memory-based Operand Address Computation.
    - RIP-relative Data Addressing.
    - Near and Far Branch Addressing.
- Immediate Data Values in 64-bit Mode.
- Displacements in 64-bit Mode.

This Chapter

This chapter describes the following 64-bit related topics:

- New Instructions.
- Enhanced Instructions.
- Invalid Instructions.
- Reassigned Instructions.
- Instructions That Default to a 64-bit Operand Size.
- Branching in 64-bit Mode.
- NOP Instruction.
- FXSAVE/FXRSTOR.
- The Nested Task Bit (Rflags[NT]).
- SMM Save Area.

The Next Chapter

The next chapter describes the process of switching from Real Mode into Protected Mode. The following topics are covered:

- Real Mode Peculiarities That Affect the OS Boot Process.
- Typical OS Characteristics.
- Protected Mode Transition Primer.
- Example: Linux Startup.

New Instructions

General

Only two new instructions are defined when the logical processor is operating in 64-bit Mode:

- SwapGS.
- MOVSXD.

They are described in the next two sections.

SwapGS Instruction

The Problem

An application program may use the SysCall instruction to call the OS kernel services through a pre-defined entry point (the logical processor obtains the address from a special MSR register initialized by the OS). There is a problem, however. The kernel services must assume that the caller (i.e., the application program) expects the contents of the GPR registers to be preserved upon return from the kernel call. This being the case and considering that the kernel services will have to make use of one or more GPR registers in order to service the request, it will have to push the contents of one or more of the GPR registers to the stack. The problem lies in the following:

- With other system call mechanisms like Call Gates and software interrupts (INT nn), the switch to a new stack occurs automatically because there is a privilege level change occurring (unless the caller is a privilege level 0 entity). With SYSCALL, there is no automatic stack switch, so, without an instruction like this there is nowhere the called service can reliably save state information.

The SwapGS Solution

The SwapGS instruction may be used to solve this problem as shown in the following example. On entry to the kernel services, the following conditions are assumed to be true:

- The GS_Base MSR contains the 64-bit virtual base address of the caller's data area.
- The Kernel_GS_Base MSR contains the 64-bit virtual base address of a data structure within which the OS kernel stores critical information (e.g., a pointer to an empty stack area reserved for the kernel's use).

```
KernelServicesEntryPoint:
  SwapGS              ;swap KernelGSBase MSR and GSBase MSR
  mov gs:[SavedUserRSP], rsp;save caller's stack pointer
  mov rsp, gs:[KernelStackPtr]  ;set RSP = kernel stack ptr
  push rax        ;save caller's GPR(s) to kernel stack
  .
  .               ;perform requested service
  .
  pop ---         ;restore caller's GPR(s) and stack pointer
  mov rsp, gs:[SavedUserRSP];restore caller's stack pointer
  SwapGS          ; restore caller's GSBase and KernelGSBase
  ret
```

Although the stack problem doesn't exist for interrupt and exception handlers (see "Interrupt/Exception Stack Switch" on page 976), the SwapGS instruction can be used to quickly set the GS base address to point to the base address of a kernel-specific data structure that may contain information useful to the handler.

SwapGS has the following characteristics:

- SwapGS is a serializing instruction (see "Synchronizing Events" on page 618).
- The base address of the kernel-specific data structure is written to the KernelGSBase MSR (at MSR address C000_0102h) using the WRMSR instruction:
  — WRMSR may only be executed by privilege level 0 software.
  — The write will result in a GP exception if the address written to the register is not in canonical form.

- SwapGS uses a previously unused (and illegal) ModRM value accompanying the 2-byte opcode 0F01h (INVLPG; Invalidate Page Table Entry). Previously, only the memory forms (i.e., where the Mod field does not equal 11b) of this opcode were legal and the register forms (where the Mod field = 11b) were illegal. In 64-bit mode, when an 2-byte opcode of 0F01h is detected accompanied by a ModRM byte of 11 111 xxxb, the logical processor treats the xxxb bit field (i.e., the RM field) as an extension to the opcode which selects 1 of 8 instructions in a group of eight (see "Micro-Maps Associated with 2-byte Opcodes" on page 183). Currently, only RM = 000b is defined (as the SwapGS instruction) and the other seven values are currently undefined (and may be used to encode additional instructions in the future).

MOVSXD Instruction: Stretch It Out

In IA-32 and Compatibility Mode, the MOVSX instruction—Move and Sign-Extend—sign-extends a byte or word operand to a full 32-bit dword. In 64-bit Mode, the ARPL (Adjust RPL field of segment selector) is reassigned as a new instruction, MOVSXD (Move Dword and Sign Extend to 64-bits). When used with the REX prefix, it sign-extends a 32-bit value to a full 64-bits.

Enhanced Instructions

Table 28-1 on page 1078 lists instructions that support a 64-bit operand size when prefaced by the REX prefix with REX[W] = 1.

Table 28-1: Instructions Enhanced in 64-bit Mode With REX[W] = 1

Mnemonic	Opcode (hex)	Description
CDQE	98	RAX = sign-extended EAX.
CMPSQ	A7	String compare operation. Compares quadword at address RSI with quadword at address RDI and sets the Rflags status flags accordingly.

Table 28-1: Instructions Enhanced in 64-bit Mode With REX[W] = 1 (Continued)

Mnemonic	Opcode (hex)	Description
CMP XCHG16B	0F C7 /1	Compare and Exchange 16-bytes. Compares the 16-bytes contained in the RDX:RAX register pair with the specified 16-byte operand in memory. If equal, set ZF and load RCX:RBX into *m128*. Else, clear ZF and load *m128* into RDX:RAX.
LODSQ	AD	Load string operation. Load qword at address RSI into RAX.
MOVSQ	A5	String move operation. Move qword from address RSI to RDI.
MOVZX	0F B7 /*r*	Move 0-extended byte from the specified 8-bit register or memory location to the specified 64-bit register.
	0F B6 /*r*	Move 0-extended word from the specified 16-bit register or memory location to the specified 64-bit register.
STOSQ	AB	Using default address size of 64-bits: • Stores the qword in RAX into the memory location specified in the RDI register. Using Address Size Override prefix to select 32-bit address size: • Stores the qword in RAX into the memory location specified in the EDI register.

Invalid Instructions

When the logical processor is executing in 64-bit Mode, the instructions listed in Table 28-2 on page 1080 are considered invalid and result in the generation of the Invalid Opcode exception.

Table 28-2: Instructions Which Are Invalid In 64-bit Mode

Mnemonic	Opcode (hex)	Description
AAA	37	ASCII Adjust After Addition
AAD	D5	ASCII Adjust Before Division
AAM	D4	ASCII Adjust After Multiply
AAS	3F	ASCII Adjust After Subtraction
BOUND	62	Check Array Bounds
CALL (far)	9A	Procedure Call Far (absolute)
DAA	27	Decimal Adjust after Addition
DAS	2F	Decimal Adjust after Subtraction
INTO	CE	Interrupt to Overflow Vector
JMP (far)	EA	Jump Far (absolute)
LDS	C5	Load DS Segment Register
LES	C4	Load ES Segment Register
POP DS	1F	Pop Stack into DS Segment
POP ES	07	Pop Stack into ES Segment
POP SS	17	Pop Stack into SS Segment
POPA, POPAD	61	Pop All to GPR words or dwords
PUSH CS	0E	Push CS Segment Selector onto Stack
PUSH DS	1E	Push DS Segment Selector onto Stack
PUSH ES	06	Push ES Segment Selector onto Stack
PUSH SS	16	Push SS Segment Selector onto Stack
PUSHA, PUSHAD	60	Push All GPR words or dwords onto Stack

Table 28-2: Instructions Which Are Invalid In 64-bit Mode (Continued)

Mnemonic	Opcode (hex)	Description
Redundant Grp1 (undocumented)	82	Redundant encoding of group1 Eb,Ib opcodes
SALC (undocumented)	D6	Set AL According to CF
Attempted execution results in the generation of an Invalid Opcode exception.		

Reassigned Instructions

The opcodes listed in Table 28-3 on page 1081 are reassigned when the logical processor is in 64-bit Mode.

Table 28-3: Instructions Reassigned In 64-bit Mode

Mnemonic	Opcode (hex)	Description
ARPL	63	MOVSXD instruction in 64-bit mode. In all other modes, this is the Adjust Requester Privilege Level instruction opcode.
DEC	48-4F	The 1-byte versions of the INC and DEC instructions have been reassigned for use as the 16 possible versions of the REX prefix. The 2-byte versions of the INC and DEC are still valid in 64-bit Mode, however.
INC	40-47	

LAHF/SAHF Instruction Support

These two instructions are only supported in 64-bit Mode on some processor steppings. Support can be determined by executing CPUID with request type 80000001h and checking ECX[0] for a 1.

Instructions That Default to a 64-bit Operand Size

Stack Operations

All instructions that implicitly reference RSP default to a 64-bit operand size in 64-bit Mode (see Table 28-4 on page 1082) and do not require the REX prefix to select the 64-bit operand size. Pushes and pops of 32-bit stack values are not possible in 64-bit mode with these instructions (all pushes and pops are 8-byte operations), but they can be overridden to 16-bits (by prefacing the instruction with the Operand Size Override prefix).

Table 28-4: Instructions That Reference RSP (64-bit Mode) & Default to 64-bit Operand Size

Mnemonic	Opcode (hex)	Description
ENTER	C8	Create procedure stack frame.
LEAVE	C9	Delete procedure stack frame.
POP reg/ mem	8F/0	Pop top-of-stack into register or memory.
POP reg	58-5F	Pop top-of-stack into register.
POP FS	0F A1	Pop top-of-stack into FS segment register.
POP GS	0F A9	Pop top-of-stack into GS Segment Register.
POPF, POPFD, POPFQ	9D	Pop word, dword, or qword from top-of-stack to Rflags.
PUSH imm32	68	Push sign-extended immediate dword value onto stack.
PUSH imm8	6A	Push sign-extended immediate byte value onto stack.

Table 28-4: Instructions That Reference RSP (64-bit Mode) & Default to 64-bit Operand Size

Mnemonic	Opcode (hex)	Description
PUSH reg/mem	FF/6	Push contents of register or memory onto stack.
PUSH reg	50-57	Push contents of register onto stack.
PUSH FS	0F A0	Push FS segment register onto stack.
PUSH GS	0F A8	Push GS segment register onto stack.
PUSHF, PUSHFD, PUSHFQ	9C	Push Flags, Eflags or Rflags onto stack.

Near Branches

Refer to "Branching in 64-bit Mode" on page 1083.

Branching in 64-bit Mode

Short/Near Branches Default to 64-bit Operand Size

In 64-bit Mode, *all near branches default to a 64-bit operand size*; i.e., they do not require the REX prefix in order to update the entire 64-bit RIP register with a 64-bit branch target address:

- **To select a 16-bit operand size.** If a near branch is prefaced with the Operand Size Override prefix, the operand size is then 16-bits and the branch target address generated by the branch only updates the IP portion of the RIP register.
- **There is no 32-bit operand size**. In 64-bit mode, there is no way to override the default 64-bit short/near branch operand size in order to specify an operand size of 32-bits.

This is true for the near jump forms of the:

- Call instruction.
- Conditional Jump on ECX/RCX = Zero (JECXZ, JRCXZ) instructions.
- RET instruction.
- Unconditional jump (Jmp) instructions.
- Conditional jump (Jcc) instructions.
- LOOP instruction.
- LOOPcc instruction.

Unconditional Jumps in 64-bit Mode

Table 28-5 on page 1084 list the treatment of the various forms of unconditional Jump instructions in 64-bit Mode.

Table 28-5: Unconditional Branches in 64-bit Mode

Opcode	Instruction	Operand Size	Description
Valid Unconditional Short/Near Jump Forms in 64-bit Mode			
EB	JMP *rel8*	Defaults to 64-bit operand size. Doesn't require REX prefix.	• **Branch target address = RIP ± rel8** (where rel8 = 8-bit offset from current RIP value). • **Jump near** (within the current code segment) backwards or forwards relative to current RIP. RIP ± 8-bit displacement sign extended to 64-bits.
E9	JMP *rel32*	Defaults to 64-bit operand size. Doesn't require REX prefix.	• **Branch target address = RIP ± rel32** (where rel32 = 32-bit offset from current RIP value). • **Jump near** (within the current code segment) backwards or forwards relative to current RIP. RIP ± 32-bit displacement sign extended to 64-bits.

Table 28-5: Unconditional Branches in 64-bit Mode (Continued)

Opcode	Instruction	Operand Size	Description
FF /4	JMP r/m64	Defaults to 64-bit operand size. Doesn't require REX prefix.	• **Branch target address = 64-bit address specified in 64-bit register or memory.** • **Jump near** (within the current code segment), absolute indirect.
	Valid Unconditional Far Jump Forms in 64-bit Mode		
FF /5	JMP m16:16	16-bits	Operation when operand size = 16-bits: • **Jump far** (to a location within a different code segment), absolute indirect. • **Branch target address = 4-byte address (in CS:IP form) specified in memory.**
	JMP m16:32	32-bits	Operation when operand size = 32-bits: • **Jump far** (to a location within a different code segment), absolute indirect. • **Branch target address = 6-byte address (in CS:EIP form) specified in memory.**
	JMP m16:64	64-bits (requires REX prefix)	• **Jump far** (to a location within a different code segment), absolute indirect. • **Branch target address = 10-byte address (in CS:RIP form) specified in memory.**
	Invalid Unconditional Jump Forms in 64-bit Mode		
E9	JMP rel16	na	• Jump near (within the current code segment) backwards or forwards relative to current RIP. • Rel16 = 16-bit offset from current RIP value. • *Not supported in 64-bit mode.*

Table 28-5: Unconditional Branches in 64-bit Mode (Continued)

Opcode	Instruction	Operand Size	Description
FF /4	JMP *r/m16*	na	• Jump near (within the current code segment), absolute indirect. • Branch target address = current code segment base address + 16-bit offset specified in a 16-bit register or in a 16-bit memory operand. • *Not supported in 64-bit mode.*
FF /4	JMP *r/m32*	na	• Jump near (within the current code segment), absolute indirect. • Branch target address = current code segment base address + 32-bit offset specified in a 32-bit register or in a 32-bit memory operand. • *Not supported in 64-bit mode.*
EA cd	JMP *ptr16:16*	na	• Jump far (to a location within a different code segment), absolute. • Branch target address (in CS:IP form) is encoded in the instruction's displacement field. • *Not supported in 64-bit mode.*
EA cp	JMP *ptr16:32*	na	• Jump far (to a location within a different code segment), absolute. • Branch target address (in CS:EIP form) is encoded in the instruction's displacement field. • *Not supported in 64-bit mode.*

Note: FF /4 and /5 represent the 1-byte opcode FF wherein the ModRM byte's Operand 2 field (i.e., the REG field) = 4 (100b) or 5 (101b) and acts as a 3-bit extension of the opcode to select the instruction type. Refer to Figure 7-10 on page 182.

Calls/Ret/Iret in 64-bit Mode

Instruction Forms in 64-bit Mode

Table 28-6 on page 1087 describes the valid forms of the CALL, RET and IRET instructions when the logical processor is operating in 64-bit Mode.

Table 28-6: Calls, RET, and IRET in 64-bit Mode

Opcode	Instruction	Operand Size	Description
Calls in 64-bit Mode			
E8 cd	CALL *rel32*	Defaults to 64-bits	Call near, relative, ± displacement relative to next instruction. 32-bit displacement sign-extended to 64-bits.
FF /2	CALL *r/m64*	Defaults to 64-bits	Call near, absolute indirect, address specified in 64-bit register or in memory operand.
FF /3	CALL *m16:16*	16-bits	Call far, absolute indirect address specified in 4-byte memory operand in CS:IP form.
	CALL *m16:32*	32-bits	If selector selects a Call Gate: • **Then** RIP = 64-bit displacement specified in gate. 32-bit offset portion of far address is discarded. • **Else** RIP = 0-extended 32-bit offset specified in memory operand.
	CALL *m16:64*	64-bits	*Requires REX prefix with W bit = 1*. If selector selects a Call Gate: • **Then** CS:RIP = CS:RIP from gate. 64-bit offset portion of far address is discarded. • **Else** CS:RIP = CS:RIP specified in memory operand.

Table 28-6: Calls, RET, and IRET in 64-bit Mode (Continued)

Opcode	Instruction	Operand Size	Description
\multicolumn{4}{RET in 64-bit Mode}			

Opcode	Instruction	Operand Size	Description
C3	RET	Defaults to 64-bit operand size. Doesn't require REX prefix.	Near Return. Pops 8-bytes from stack to RIP.
CB	RET		Far Return to caller. **If caller at same privilege level**: • Restore CS:RIP from stack and resume caller's code. **If caller less-privileged**: • Restore caller's stack (SS:RSP) from called procedure's stack. • Restore CS:RIP from called procedure's stack. • Resume caller's code.
C2 *iw*	RET *imm16*		Near Return to caller: • Pops 8-bytes from stack into RIP. • Adjusts stack upward *n* bytes (*n* is specified by 16-bit immediate value—*iw*—in instruction) to release space in which caller passed parameters to called procedure.
CA *iw*	RET *imm16*		Far Return to caller. **If caller at same privilege level**: • Restore CS:RIP from stack. • Deallocate *n* bytes (space allocated for passed parameters) from stack (n = specified 16-bit value). • Resume caller's code. **If caller less-privileged**: • Restore CS:RIP from called procedure's stack. • Deallocate *n* bytes (space allocated for passed parameters) from stack (*n* = specified 16-bit value). • Restore caller's stack (SS:RSP; note SS will be null selector if 64-bit rather than Compatibility Mode caller) from called procedure's stack. • Resume caller's code.

Table 28-6: Calls, RET, and IRET in 64-bit Mode (Continued)

Opcode	Instruction	Operand Size	Description
IRET in 64-bit Mode			
CF	IRET	16-bits 32-bits 64-bits (requires REX prefix)	Return to interrupted program (or to caller if handler called using INT instruction). Actions taken depend on: • State of the NT bit in Rflags register. Depending on their state, the logical processor determines type of return: • Return from Protected Mode handler to interrupted Protected Mode program at same privilege level. • Return from Protected Mode handler to interrupted Protected Mode program at lesser privilege level. • Return from task acting as handler to interrupted task (note: this cannot happen in 64-bit Mode). Size of pops from stack are 8-bytes each in 64-bit Mode). Refer to "The IRET Instruction" on page 709 for a detailed description of the five variations on IRET execution.

Example Call/Return Operations

64-bit Near Call/Return. The operation proceeds as follows:
— On executing the Call, the logical processor pushes the 64-bit RIP to the current stack.
— It then loads the RIP register with the 64-bit branch target address specified by the instruction and begins to fetch and execute the called procedure.
— At the end of the called procedure, a near Ret is executed causing the logical processor to pop the 64-bit return address from the current stack into the RIP register after which it resumes execution at the instruction immediately following the Call.

32-bit Level 3 Code Calls 64-bit Level 3 Procedure. In this example, a Call Gate is used to pass control to the called procedure. It should be noted that although this works just fine, the called procedure has the same privilege level as the caller so the far call could also be accomplished without using a gate (i.e., the far address specified by the instruction could point directly to the called procedure's entry point). That method does impose a limitation, however. Since the offset portion of the far address is a 32-bit value, the target procedure's entry point would have to be in the lower 4GB of virtual address space. The operation proceeds as follows:

1. The logical processor is in Compatibility Mode executing code from a 32-bit code segment with a DPL of 3. The CPL is therefore 3.
2. The program executes a far Call and the branch target address selects an IA-32e Call Gate (see Figure 23-7 on page 945; 16- and 32-bit Call Gates are not supported in IA-32e Mode) in the GDT or LDT:
   a) Refer to Figure 23-22 on page 966.
   b) In the CS portion of the branch target address, CS[RPL] = 3 indicating that the far address of the called procedure was created by a privilege level 3 program.
   c) The offset portion of the branch target address is discarded.
   d) The gate points to a privilege level 3 Non-Conforming 64-bit procedure.
3. Since both the caller and the called procedure have the same privilege level, the logical processor uses the caller's stack to save the return address:
   a) CS is 0-extended to 64-bits and pushed to the caller's stack. The CS[RPL] value of 3 indicates the privilege level to return to when the far Ret instruction is executed at the completion of the called procedure.
   b) RIP is pushed to the caller's stack.
4. The logical processor reads the called procedure's start address from the Call Gate and loads it into the CS:RIP register pair.
5. The CPL remains at 3 as the logical processor begins to fetch and execute the level 3, 64-bit procedure.
6. At the completion of the called procedure, execution of the far Ret causes the logical processor to perform two 8-byte pops from the caller's stack:
   a) The 64-bit RIP value is placed in TempRIP.
   b) The 16-bit CS is placed in TempCS and the upper 48-bits (all 0s) are discarded.
7. The logical processor sets TempCPL = TempCS[RPL] (i.e., 3: the privilege level it's returning to).
8. It compares the CPL of the currently executing called procedure (3) to the value in TempCPL (3). They match, so the logical processor:
   a) Loads TempCS into CS.
   b) If the far Ret opcode = CAh, rather than CBh (see Table 28-6 on page 1087), the logical processor adds the instruction's 16-bit imme-

diate operand (sign-extended to 64-bits) to RSP. This is done to deallocate stack space allocated to pass parameters from the caller to the called procedure.

c) Copies TempRIP to the RIP register.

9. The logical processor then resumes execution of the caller's code at the instruction immediately following the far Call.

32-bit Level 3 Code Calls 64-bit Level 2 Procedure. The operation proceeds as follows:

1. The logical processor is in Compatibility Mode executing code from a 32-bit code segment with a DPL of 3. The CPL is therefore 3.

2. The program executes a far Call and the branch target address selects an IA-32e Call Gate (see Figure 23-7 on page 945; 16- and 32-bit Call Gates are not supported in IA-32e Mode) in the GDT or LDT.

   a) Refer to Figure 23-22 on page 966.

   b) In the CS portion of the branch target address, CS[RPL] = 3 indicating that the far address of the called procedure was created by a privilege level 3 program.

   c) The offset portion of the branch target address is discarded.

   d) The gate points to a privilege level 2 Non-Conforming 64-bit procedure.

3. The logical processor saves the caller's stack pointer (SS:RSP) in TempSS:RSP.

4. Accessing the CS descriptor selected by the CS portion of the branch target address specified in the Call Gate, the logical processor detects the L attribute bit = 1 indicating that the called procedure resides in a 64-bit code segment. Since it is a rule in IA-32e Mode that a Call Gate must point to a 64-bit code segment, a GP exception would have been generated if L = 0.

5. The logical processor places the CPL (3; the privilege level of the caller) in the CS[RPL] field.

6. The logical processor compares the CPL (i.e., the caller's privilege level: 3) to the DPL (2) of the CS descriptor selected by the CS portion of the branch target address specified in the Call Gate. Since there will be a jump to a more-privileged procedure, it will switch to the stack pre-allocated for privilege level 2 programs:

   a) Since the SS register isn't used in 64-bit Mode, the logical processor loads it with the null segment selector (0000h).

   b) The logical processor uses the target code segment's DPL (2) to index into the TSS data structure's RSPn fields (see Figure 23-25 on page 971) and loads the selected 64-bit stack pointer from the RSP2 field into the RSP register.

7. Using 8-byte pushes, the logical processor:
   a) 0-extends TempSS to 64-bits and pushes it onto the level 2 stack.
   b) Pushes TempRSP onto the level 2 stack.
   c) 0-extends CS to 64-bits and pushes it onto the level 2 stack. It's important to note here that the RPL field in the CS image on the stack contains 3, the privilege level of the caller.
   d) Pushes RIP onto the level 2 stack.
8. The logical processor loads CS:RIP with the start address of the called procedure obtained from the Call Gate. This switches it into 64-bit Mode (new CS descriptor's L bit = 1) and changes the CPL from 3 to 2 (the DPL from new CS descriptor).
9. At the completion of the called procedure, execution of the far Ret causes the logical processor to perform two 8-byte pops to read the caller's return address (CS:RIP) from the level 2 stack into TempCS:RIP.
10. If the far Ret opcode = CAh (see Table 28-6 on page 1087), the logical processor adds the instruction's 16-bit immediate operand (sign-extended to 64-bits) to RSP. This is done to deallocate stack space allocated to pass parameters from the caller to the called procedure.
11. The logical processor loads TempCPL with TempCS[RPL] so TempCPL now contains the value 3 (the privilege level we are about to return to).
12. Comparing TempCPL (3) to the current CPL (2), the logical processor determines that it must switch back to the caller's stack.
13. Performing two more 8-byte pops, the logical processor reads the caller's stack pointer (SS:RSP) from the level 2 stack into TempSS:RSP.
14. The logical processor restores the caller's CS by setting CS = TempCS. This causes it to read the selected 32-bit CS descriptor into the invisible portion of the CS register and switches the logical processor from 64-bit Mode back into 32-bit Compatibility Mode.
15. The logical processor sets CPL = TempCPL restoring the CPL to the caller's privilege level (3).
16. The logical processor restores the caller's stack pointer by loading TempSS:RSP into SS:RSP. If the far Ret instruction included a 16-bit immediate operand, it is sign-extended to 64-bits and added to RSP to deallocate stack space used to pass parameters from the caller to the called procedure.
17. For the four data segment registers, if their DPLs would prevent the caller from accessing any of them (because it has insufficient privilege), the logical processor loads the respective data segment registers with the null segment selector (0000h).
18. The logical processor restores the caller's return address by setting RIP = TempRIP.

19. The logical processor then resumes execution of the caller's code at the instruction immediately following the far Call.

Previous Example Plus Call to Level 0 Procedure. The operation proceeds as follows:

1. See steps 1-8 in previous example.
2. In the level 2 procedure, a far Call is executed that selects a Call Gate in the GDT or LDT and the gate points to a level 0 procedure in a 64-bit Non-Forming code segment. This will causes a switch from the level 2 stack to the level 0 stack and the level 2 stack pointer (SS:RSP; SS contains the null segment selector) is pushed onto the level 0 stack along with CS:RIP.
3. When the far Ret is executed at the completion of the level 0 procedure, the level 2 return address is popped off of the level 0 stack. A comparison of the CPL (0) and the CS[RPL] value (2) popped off the level 0 stack causes the logical processor to reload SS:RSP with the level 2 stack pointer popped off the level 0 stack. The logical processor returns to the level 2 procedure, completes it and executes the far Ret.
4. Continue with steps 9-17 of the previous example.

Conditional Branches in 64-bit Mode

Table 28-7 on page 1093 describes the valid forms of conditional branch instructions when the logical processor is operating in 64-bit Mode.

Table 28-7: Conditional Branches in 64-bit Mode

Opcode(s)	Instruction	Operand Size	Description
Conditional Short Jump Forms in 64-bit Mode			
E3 *cb*	JCXZ *rel8*	16-bits	*Invalid.* Jump short if CX register is 0 is invalid in 64-bit Mode.
	JECXZ *rel8*	32-bits	Jump short (RIP ± 8-bit signed displacement sign-extended to 64-bits) if ECX register is 0.
	JRCXZ *rel8*	64-bits	Jump short (RIP ± 8-bit signed displacement sign-extended to 64-bits) if RCX register is 0.

Table 28-7: Conditional Branches in 64-bit Mode (Continued)

Opcode(s)	Instruction	Operand Size	Description
70-7F Jcc Short	Jcc *rel8*	64-bits (operand size fixed at 64-bits.)	Branch target address = RIP ± 8-bit signed displacement sign-extended to 64-bits).
Conditional Near Jump Forms in 64-bit Mode			
0F80 - 0F8F Jcc Near	Jcc Near *rel16*	16-bits	*Invalid*. None of the Jcc Near forms support an operand size of 16-bits.
	Jcc Near *rel32*	32-bits	Branch target address = RIP ± 32-bit displacement sign-extended to 64-bits.
	Jcc Near rel64	64-bits	*Invalid*. No such form.

Table 28-7: Conditional Branches in 64-bit Mode (Continued)

Opcode(s)	Instruction	Operand Size	Description
		Loop instruction forms in 64-bit Mode	
E2 *cb*	LOOP *rel8*	32-bits	If address size = 32-bits: • ECX = ECX - 1. • If ECX != 0, branch to EIP ± 8-bit immediate value embedded in the instruction sign-extended to 32-bits. If address size = 64-bits (default): • RCX = RCX - 1. • If RCX != 0, branch to EIP ± 8-bit immediate value embedded in the instruction sign-extended to 32-bits.
		64-bits (default)	If address size = 32-bits: • ECX = ECX - 1. • If ECX != 0, branch to RIP ± 8-bit immediate value embedded in the instruction sign-extended to 64-bits. If address size = 64-bits (default): • RCX = RCX - 1. • If RCX != 0, branch to RIP ± 8-bit immediate value embedded in the instruction sign-extended to 64-bits.

Loop instruction forms in 64-bit Mode
- Note: count register width (EXC or RCX) is selected based on effective _address_ size.
- The default effective address size, 64-bits, can be overriden to 32-bits by prefixing the instruction with the Address Size Override prefix.
- 64-bit Mode does not support the 16-bit address size, *therefore the versions of the Loop instructions that utilize CX as the Count register are not supported.*
- Default operand size = 64-bits (does not require REX prefix). Can be overriden to 32-bits.

Table 28-7: Conditional Branches in 64-bit Mode (Continued)

Opcode(s)	Instruction	Operand Size	Description
E1 *cb*	LoopE *rel8*	32-bits	• Decrements zCX register (z = 'E' if address size = 32-bits, or 'R' if address size = 64-bits). If zCX != 0 and the ZF flag = 1, it branches back to the start of the loop. If zCX = 0 or the ZF flag = 0, it exits the loop and falls through to the next instruction. • 32-bit branch target address = EIP ± 8-bit immediate value embedded in the instruction sign-extended to 32-bits).
		64-bits (default)	• Decrements zCX register (z = 'E' if address size = 32-bits, or 'R' if address size = 64-bits). If zCX != 0 and the ZF flag = 1, it branches back to the start of the loop. If zCX = 0 or the ZF flag = 0, it exits the loop and falls through to the next instruction. • 64-bit branch target address = RIP ± 8-bit immediate value embedded in the instruction sign-extended to 64-bits.
E0 *cb*	LoopNE *rel8*	32-bits	• Decrements zCX register (z = 'E' if address size = 32-bits, or 'R' if address size = 64-bits). If zCX != 0 and the ZF flag = 0, it branches back to the start of the loop. If zCX = 0 or the ZF flag = 1, it exits the loop and falls through to the next instruction. • 32-bit branch target address = EIP ± 8-bit immediate value embedded in the instruction sign-extended to 32-bits).
		64-bits (default)	• Decrements zCX register (z = 'E' if address size = 32-bits, or 'R' if address size = 64-bits). If zCX != 0 and the ZF flag = 0, it branches back to the start of the loop. If zCX = 0 or the ZF flag = 1, it exits the loop and falls through to the next instruction. • 64-bit branch target address = RIP ± 8-bit immediate value embedded in the instruction sign-extended to 64-bits.

NOP Instruction

In legacy Protected Mode and Compatibility Mode, the logical processor treats the XCHG EAX, EAX instruction (opcode = 90h) as a 1-byte NOP (executing it has no effect on the logical processor's registers other than incrementing the instruction pointer). Since the default operand size in 64-bit Mode is 32-bits, however, after exchanging the 32-bit contents of the EAX register with itself, the logical processor would normally 0-fill the upper 32-bits of the RAX register (and altering the contents of any register other than the instruction pointer would mean it is not a true NOP). In order to maintain the integrity of opcode 90h as a true NOP, the logical processor treats it as if it had the REX prefix in front of it with the W bit set to one to choose a 64-bit operand size: it therefore executes as an XCHG RAX, RAX.

FXSAVE/FXRSTOR

General

Figure 28-1 on page 1098 illustrates the format in which the FXSAVE instruction saves the x87 FPU and SSE registers when it is executed in:

- 32-bit Protected Mode.
- 32-bit Compatibility Mode.
- 64-bit Mode using the default 32-bit operand size (i.e., without using the REX prefix with the W bit = 1).

Figure 28-2 on page 1099 illustrates the format used when FXSAVE is executed in 64-bit Mode and is prefaced with the REX prefix with REX[W] = 1.

Fast FxSave/Restore Feature (AMD-only)

Refer to Figure 28-3 on page 1100. If the OS has enabled the Fast FxSave/Restore feature by setting EFER[FFXSR] = 1, executing FXSAVE in 64-bit Mode at privilege level 0 causes the logical processor to complete the instruction more quickly by not saving the XMM registers (see Figure 28-4 on page 1101).

Figure 28-1: FXSAVE Structure Legacy Format

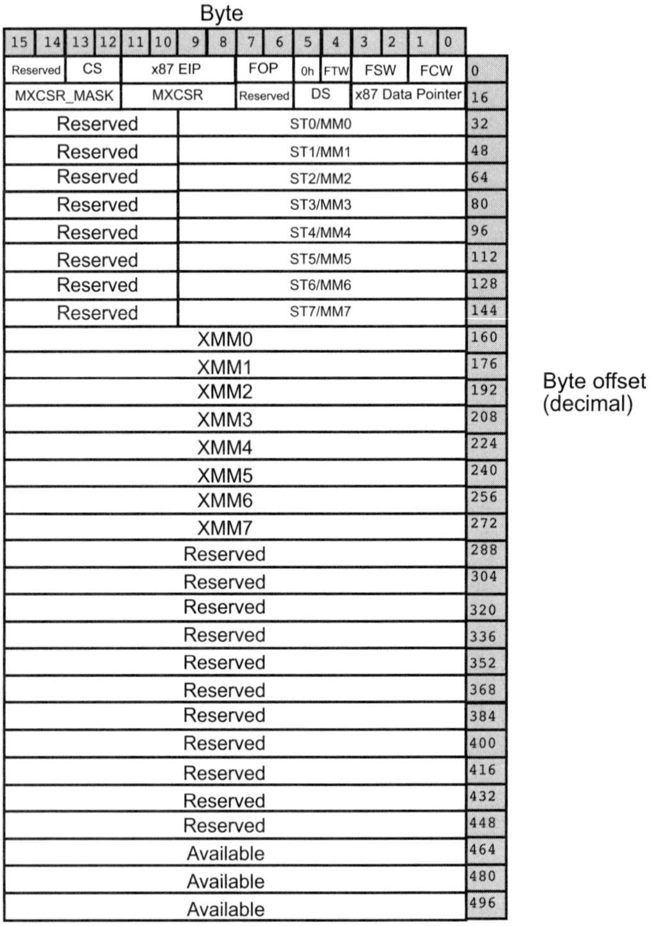

15	14	13	12	11	10	9	8	7	6	5	4	3	2	1	0	
Reserved	CS		x87 EIP		FOP		0h	FTW	FSW	FCW	0
MXCSR_MASK		MXCSR		Reserved	DS	x87 Data Pointer	16
Reserved		ST0/MM0		32
Reserved		ST1/MM1		48
Reserved		ST2/MM2		64
Reserved		ST3/MM3		80
Reserved		ST4/MM4		96
Reserved		ST5/MM5		112
Reserved		ST6/MM6		128
Reserved		ST7/MM7		144
XMM0		160
XMM1		176
XMM2		192
XMM3		208
XMM4		224
XMM5		240
XMM6		256
XMM7		272
Reserved		288
Reserved		304
Reserved		320
Reserved		336
Reserved		352
Reserved		368
Reserved		384
Reserved		400
Reserved		416
Reserved		432
Reserved		448
Available		464
Available		480
Available		496

Byte

Byte offset (decimal)

Figure 28-2: FXSAVE Structure in 64-bit Mode with REX[W] = 1

								Byte								
15	14	13	12	11	10	9	8	7	6	5	4	3	2	1	0	
64-bit RIP								FOP		0h	FTW	FSW		FCW		0
MXCSR_MASK			MXCSR					64-bit x87 Data Pointer								16
Reserved					ST0/MM0											32
Reserved					ST1/MM1											48
Reserved					ST2/MM2											64
Reserved					ST3/MM3											80
Reserved					ST4/MM4											96
Reserved					ST5/MM5											112
Reserved					ST6/MM6											128
Reserved					ST7/MM7											144
XMM0																160
XMM1																176
XMM2																192
XMM3																208
XMM4																224
XMM5																240
XMM6																256
XMM7																272
XMM8																288
XMM9																304
XMM10																320
XMM11																336
XMM12																352
XMM13																368
XMM14																384
XMM15																400
Reserved																416
Reserved																432
Reserved																448
Available																464
Available																480
Available																496

Byte offset
(decimal)

x86 Instruction Set Architecture

Figure 28-3: EFER Register

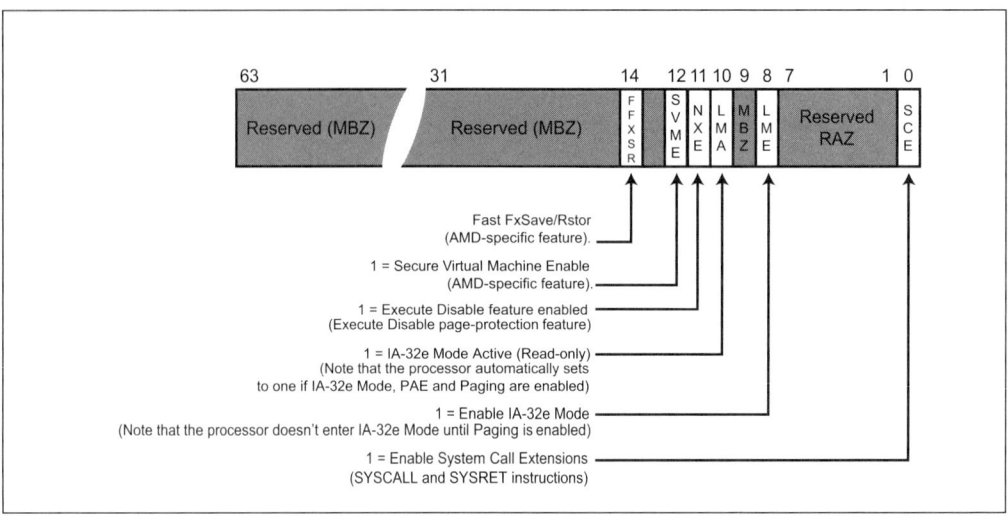

Figure 28-4: FXSAVE Format When EFER[FFXSR] = 1 in 64-bit Mode at Privilege Level 0

Byte																	
15	14	13	12	11	10	9	8	7	6	5	4	3	2	1	0		
		64-bit RIP						FOP		0h	FTW	FSW		FCW		0	
MXCSR_MASK			MXCSR					64-bit x87 Data Pointer								16	
Reserved								ST0/MM0								32	
Reserved								ST1/MM1								48	
Reserved								ST2/MM2								64	
Reserved								ST3/MM3								80	
Reserved								ST4/MM4								96	
Reserved								ST5/MM5								112	
Reserved								ST6/MM6								128	
Reserved								ST7/MM7								144	
Reserved																160	
Reserved																176	
Reserved																192	Byte offset (decimal)
Reserved																208	
Reserved																224	
Reserved																240	
Reserved																256	
Reserved																272	
Reserved																288	
Reserved																304	
Reserved																320	
Reserved																336	
Reserved																352	
Reserved																368	
Reserved																384	
Reserved																400	
Reserved																416	
Reserved																432	
Reserved																448	
Available																464	
Available																480	
Available																496	

The Nested Task Bit (Rflags[NT])

In Protected Mode, the logical processor automatically sets the NT bit whenever an interrupt, exception, or a software interrupt instruction selects a Task Gate descriptor in the IDT, or a Task Gate descriptor in the GDT or LDT, or a TSS descriptor in the GDT. In any of these cases, the descriptor selection triggers a task switch and the NT bit is set to one. When the IRET is subsequently executed at the completion of the handler or called task, the fact that the NT bit = 1 causes the logical processor to suspend the current task and switch back to the interrupted or calling task. In IA-32e Mode, however, the x86 automatic hardware-based task switching mechanism is completely disabled and the logical processor generates a GP exception if any attempt is made to trigger a task switch (including the execution of the IRET instruction while Rflags[NT] = 1). The logical processor itself therefore never sets the NT bit. It can be set by software, however, by executing the POPF, POPFD or POPFQ instructions.

SMM Save Area

IA-32 Processor SM Save Area

Figure 28-5 on page 1103 shows the default SMRAM memory map used by the logical processor immediately after a reset. The SM handler program can access up to 4GB of SM RAM address space. After a reset or a power-up, the logical processor's SM Base address is preset to address 00030000h and the logical processor determines the address of the following locations relative to the SM Base address:

- The entry point into the SM handler program = the SM Base address + 8000h. Since the default value of the SM Base address is 00030000h, this defines the default entry point address to be 00030000h + 8000h = 00038000h.
- The *end* address (*not* the start address) of the 512-byte State Save Area wherein the logical processor saves its register set on entry to SMM is calculated as follows:
  — The SM Base address (00030000h) + 8000h + 7FFFh = **0003FFFFh**. The 512-byte save area therefore consumes the area from location 3FE00h to 3FFFFh. 3FE00h is the default State Save Area start address. The SM Base address can be altered while the logical processor is executing the SM handler program. This topic is covered in "Relocating the SM RAM Base Address" on page 1204.

Table 28-8 on page 1104 defines the layout (*the format shown is Intel-specific; AMD uses a different format*) of the legacy SMM State Save Area. It should be noted that this format is used regardless of what mode the logical processor is in when the SMI (SM interrupt) is detected. Some of the fields are read-only while others are read-writable. Those marked read-writable can be altered while the logical processor is executing the SM handler. Additional information on the State Save Area can be found in "System Management Mode (SMM)" on page 1167.

As shown in the illustration, the true start address of SM RAM is memory address 00000000h. *Do not think of the SM Base address as defining the SM RAM start address. The address that Intel refers to as the SM Base address is the one used by the logical processor to calculate where the entry point of the SM handler and the start address of the State Save Area are within the 4GB SM RAM memory space.*

Additional information on the State Save Area can be found in "System Management Mode (SMM)" on page 1167.

Figure 28-5: Processor's SM RAM Memory Map

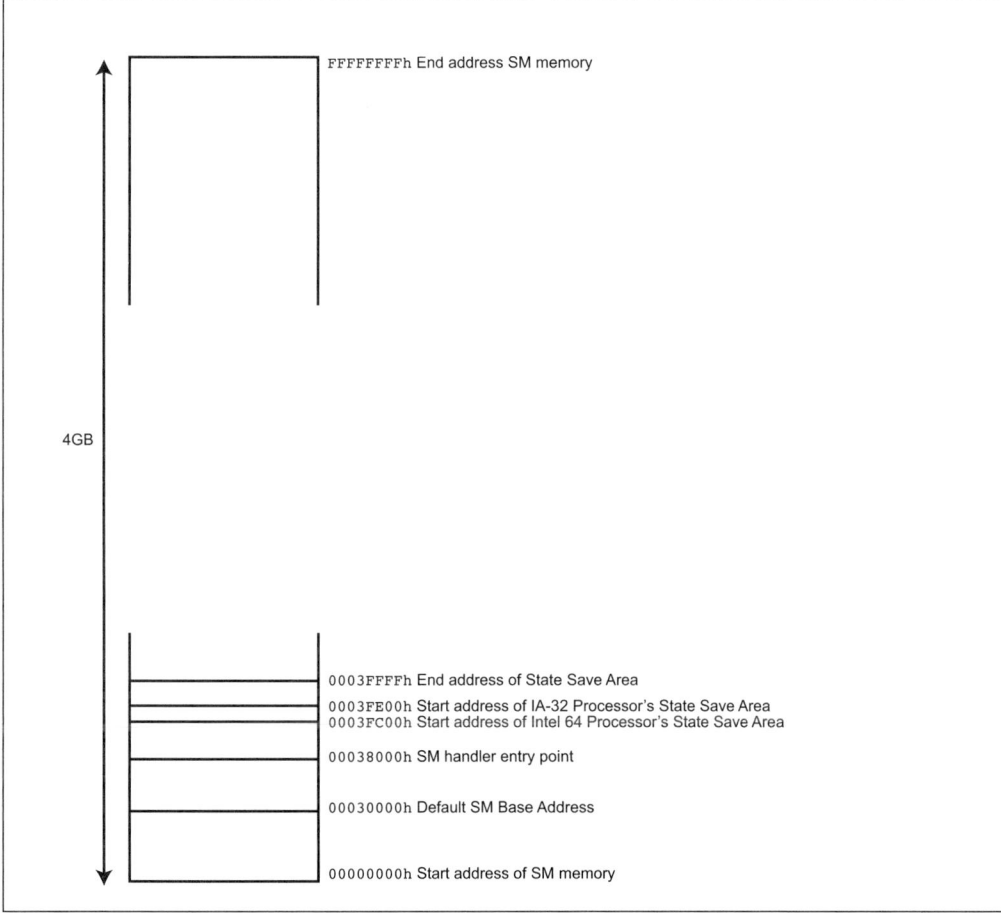

Table 28-8: IA-32 Processor SMRAM State Save Area (shown from top down)

Location in Save Area (SMBase + 8000h + the Offset shown)	Width (in bytes)	Register Image	Read/ Write?
7FFCh-7FFFh	4	CR0	No
7FF8h-7FFBh	4	CR3	No
7FF4h-7FF7h	4	Eflags	Yes
7FF0h-7FF3h	4	EIP	Yes
7FECh-7FEFh	4	EDI	Yes
7FE8h-7FEBh	4	ESI	Yes
7FE4h-7FE7h	4	EBP	Yes
7FE0h-7FE3h	4	ESP	Yes
7FDCh-7FDFh	4	EBX	Yes
7FD8h-7FDBh	4	EDX	Yes
7FD4h-7FD7h	4	ECX	Yes
7FD0h-7FD3h	4	EAX	Yes
7FCCh-7FCFh	4	DR6	No
7FC8h-7FCBh	4	DR7	No
7FC6h-7FC7h	2	Reserved	
7FC4h-7FC5h	2	TR. The Task Register register is only 2-bytes wide, but the logical processor saves a 4-byte image. The upper 2-bytes are reserved and are shown in the row prior to this one.	No
7FC0h-7FC3h	4	Reserved	No
7FBEh-7FBFh	2	Reserved	

Table 28-8: IA-32 Processor SMRAM State Save Area (shown from top down) (Continued)

Location in Save Area (SMBase + 8000h + the Offset shown)	Width (in bytes)	Register Image	Read/ Write?
7FBCh-7FBDh	2	GS. The segment registers are only 2-bytes wide, but the logical processor saves a 4-byte image. The upper 2-bytes are reserved and are shown in the row prior to this one.	No
7FBAh-7FBBh	2	Reserved	
7FB8h-7FB9h	2	FS. The segment registers are only 2-bytes wide, but the logical processor saves a 4-byte image. The upper 2-bytes are reserved and are shown in the row prior to this one.	No
7FB6h-7FB7h	2	Reserved	
7FB4h-7FB5h	2	DS. The segment registers are only 2-bytes wide, but the logical processor saves a 4-byte image. The upper 2-bytes are reserved and are shown in the row prior to this one.	No
7FB2h-7FB3h	2	Reserved	
7FB0h-7FB1h	2	SS. The segment registers are only 2-bytes wide, but the logical processor saves a 4-byte image. The upper 2-bytes are reserved and are shown in the row prior to this one.	No
7FAEh-7FAFh	2	Reserved	

Table 28-8: IA-32 Processor SMRAM State Save Area (shown from top down) (Continued)

Location in Save Area (SMBase + 8000h + the Offset shown)	Width (in bytes)	Register Image	Read/ Write?
7FACh-7FADh	2	CS. The segment registers are only 2-bytes wide, but the logical processor saves a 4-byte image. The upper 2-bytes are reserved and are shown in the row prior to this one.	No
7FAAh-7FABh	2	Reserved	
7FA8h-7FA9h	2	ES. The segment registers are only 2-bytes wide, but the logical processor saves a 4-byte image. The upper 2-bytes are reserved and are shown in the row prior to this one.	No
7FA4h-7FA7h	4	IO State field.	No
7FA0h-7FA3h	4	IO Memory Address field.	No
7F04h-7FBFh	156	This 39 dword area is Reserved.	No
7F02h-7F03h	2	Auto HALT Restart Field.	Yes
7F00h-7F01h	2	IO Instruction Restart Field.	Yes
7EFCh-7EFFh	4	SMM Revision Identifier Field.	No
7EF8h-7EFBh	4	SMBase Field.	Yes
7E00h-7EF7h	248	This 62 dword area is Reserved	No

Intel 64 Processor SM Save Area

On an Intel 64 processor, the SM Save area is expanded from 512- to 1024-bytes and the *end* address (*not* the start address) of the 1024-byte Save Area wherein the logical processor saves its register set on entry to SMM is calculated as follows:

- The SM Base address (00030000h) + 8000h + 7FFFh = **0003FFFFh**. The default 1024-byte save area therefore consumes the area from location 3FC00h to 3FFFFh. 3FC00h is the default State Save Area start address. The SM Base address (and therefore the Save Area end address) can be altered while the logical processor is executing the SM handler program. This topic is covered in "Relocating the SM RAM Base Address" on page 1204.

Table 28-9 on page 1107 shows the format (*the format shown is Intel-specific; AMD uses a different format*) of the State Save Area for an Intel 64 processor. It should be noted that this format is used regardless of what mode the logical processor is in when the SMI (SM interrupt) is detected. Some of the fields are read-only while others are read-writable. Those marked read-writable can be altered while the logical processor is executing the SM handler. Additional information on the State Save Area can be found in "System Management Mode (SMM)" on page 1167.

Table 28-9: Intel 64 Processor SMRAM State Save Area

Location in Save Area (SMBase + 8000h + the Offset shown)	Width (in bytes)	Register Image	Read/Write?
7FF8h-7FFFh	8	CR0	No
7FF0h-7FF7h	8	CR3	No
7FE8h-7FEFh	8	Rflags	Yes
7FE0h-7FE7h	8	EFER	Yes
7FD8h-7FDFh	8	RIP	Yes
7FD0h-7FD7h	8	DR6	No
7FC8h-7FCFh	8	DR7	No
7FC4h-7FC7h	4	TR selector (upper 2-bytes reserved).	No
7FC0h-7FC3h	4	LDTR selector (upper 2-bytes reserved).	No
7FBCh-7FBFh	4	GS selector (upper 2-bytes reserved).	No

Table 28-9: Intel 64 Processor SMRAM State Save Area (Continued)

Location in Save Area (SMBase + 8000h + the Offset shown)	Width (in bytes)	Register Image	Read/ Write?
7FB8h-7FBBh	4	FS selector (upper 2-bytes reserved).	No
7FB4h-7FB7h	4	DS selector (upper 2-bytes reserved).	No
7FB0h-7FB3h	4	SS selector (upper 2-bytes reserved).	No
7FACh-7FAFh	4	CS selector (upper 2-bytes reserved).	No
7FA8h-7FABh	4	ES selector (upper 2-bytes reserved).	No
7FA4h-7FA7h	4	IO_MISC.	No
7F9Ch-7FA3h	8	IO Memory Address field.	No
7F94h-7F9Bh	8	RDI	Yes
7F8Ch-7F93h	8	RSI	Yes
7F84h-7F8Bh	8	RBP	Yes
7F7Ch-7F83h	8	RSP	Yes
7F74h-7F7Bh	8	RBX	Yes
7F6Ch-7F73h	8	RDX	Yes
7F64h-7F6Bh	8	RCX	Yes
7F5Ch-7F63h	8	RAX	Yes
7F54h-7F5Bh	8	R8	Yes
7F4Ch-7F53h	8	R9	Yes
7F44h-7F4Bh	8	R10	Yes
7F3Ch-7F43h	8	R11	Yes

Table 28-9: Intel 64 Processor SMRAM State Save Area (Continued)

Location in Save Area (SMBase + 8000h + the Offset shown)	Width (in bytes)	Register Image	Read/ Write?
7F34h-7F3Bh	8	R12	Yes
7F2Ch-7F33h	8	R13	Yes
7F24h-7F2Bh	8	R14	Yes
7F1Ch-7F23h	8	R15	Yes
7F04h-7F1Bh	24	Reserved	No
7F02h-7F03h	2	Auto HALT Restart Field.	Yes
7F00h-7F01h	2	IO Instruction Restart Field.	Yes
7EFCh-7EFFh	4	SMM Revision Identifier Field.	No
7EF8h-7EFBh	4	SMBASE Field.	Yes
7EE4h-7EF7h	20	Reserved	No
7EE0h-7EE3h	4	Setting of Enable Extended Page Table (EPT) VM-execution control.	No
7ED8h-7EDFh	8	Value of Extended Page Table Pointer (EPTP) VM-execution control field.	No
7EA8h-7ED7h	48	Reserved	No
7EA4h-7EA7h	4	LDT Info.	No
7EA0h-7EA3h	4	LDT Limit	No
7E9Ch-7E9Fh	4	LDT Base (lower 32 bits). Upper 32-bits are in locations 7DD4h-7DD7h.	No
7E98h-7E9Bh	4	IDT Limit	No

Table 28-9: Intel 64 Processor SMRAM State Save Area (Continued)

Location in Save Area (SMBase + 8000h + the Offset shown)	Width (in bytes)	Register Image	Read/ Write?
7E94h-7E97h	4	IDT Base (lower 32 bits). Upper 32-bits are in locations 7DD8h-7DDBh.	No
7E90h-7E93h	4	GDT Limit	No
7E8Ch-7E8Fh	4	GDT Base (lower 32 bits). Upper 32-bits are in locations 7DD0h-7DD3h.	No
7E44h-7E8Bh	72	Reserved	No
7E40h-7E43h	4	CR4	No
7DF0h-7E3Fh	80	Reserved	No
7DE8h-7DEFh	8	IO_EIP.	Yes
7DDCh-7DE7h	12	Reserved	No
7DD8h-7DDBh	4	IDT Base (Upper 32 bits). Lower 32-bits are in locations 7E94h-7E97h.	No
7DD4h-7DD7h	4	LDT Base (Upper 32 bits). Lower 32-bits are in locations 7E9Ch-7E9Fh.	No
7DD0h-7DD3h	4	GDT Base (Upper 32 bits). Lower 32-bits are in locations 7E8Ch-7E8Fh.	No
7C00h-7DCFh	464	Reserved	No

Part 6:
Mode Switching
Detail

The Previous Part

Part 5 provided a detailed description of the 64-bit submode of IA-32e Mode.

This Part

Part 6 provides a detailed description of:

- Switching from Real Mode to Protected Mode. This topic is covered in Chapter 29, entitled "Transitioning to Protected Mode," on page 1113.
- Switching from Protected Mode to IA-32e Mode. This topic is covered in Chapter 30, entitled "Transitioning to IA-32e Mode," on page 1139.

The Next Part

Part 7 provides detailed descriptions of the following topics:

- Introduction to Virtualization Technology.
- System Management Mode (SMM).
- Machine Check Architecture (MCA).
- The Local and IO APICs.

29 *Transitioning to Protected Mode*

The Previous Chapter

The previous chapter described the following 64-bit related topics:

- New Instructions.
- Enhanced Instructions.
- Invalid Instructions.
- Reassigned Instructions.
- Instructions That Default to a 64-bit Operand Size.
- Branching in 64-bit Mode.
- NOP Instruction.
- FXSAVE/FXRSTOR.
- The Nested Task Bit (Rflags[NT]).
- SMM Save Area.

This Chapter

This chapter describes the process of switching from Real Mode into Protected Mode. The following topics are covered:

- Real Mode Peculiarities That Affect the OS Boot Process.
- Typical OS Characteristics.
- Protected Mode Transition Primer.
- Example: Linux Startup.

The Next Chapter

The next chapter describes the process of switching from Protected Mode into the Compatibility SubMode of IA-32e Mode. It then describes making the switch from Compatibility Mode into 64-bit Mode.

Real Mode Peculiarities That Affect the OS Boot Process

Immediately after the removal of reset, an x86 processor comes up in Real Mode and, to a goodly degree, emulates the 8086. Some of the logical processor's operational characteristics when operating in Real Mode are listed below:

- **It's a 16-bit world (unless overridden)**. Unless overriden by prefacing an instruction with the Address Size and/or Operand Size Override prefixes (67h and 66h, respectively), the default segment offset address size and the default data operand size are both 16-bits.
- **An addressing anomaly**:
  — **Segment wrap-around** (see "Accessing Extended Memory in Real Mode" on page 307). When executing code on an 8086, specifying a segment base address of FFFF0h and any offset address between 0010h and FFFFh resulted in segment wraparound to the bottom of memory (specifically, to locations 00000h - 0FFEFh). The 8086 only had twenty address lines (19:0) and was therefore incapable of addressing memory above the 1MB address boundary.
  — **The HMA**. Every x86 processor since the advent of the 286, however, is capable of addressing memory above the 1MB boundary (referred to as extended memory). When operating in Real Mode, adding any offset value between 0010h - FFFFh to a segment base address of FFFF0h generates a carry bit on address bit 20 permitting software to address extended memory locations 100000h - 10FFEFh (the area of memory referred to as the HMA, or High Memory Area) without switching the logical processor into Protected Mode.
  — **A20 Gate**. Refer to "Accessing Extended Memory in Real Mode" on page 307. In order to boot the OS kernel into memory (the kernel will consume a large amount of system RAM), the logical processor must have to have the ability to address memory above the 1MB address boundary. If the A20 Gate is disabled, however, the A20 address line will always be 0 and, as a result, the logical processor will be unable to correctly address extended memory (i.e., memory above the 1MB address boundary).

Example OS Characteristics

This discussion makes the following assumptions:

- In preparation for booting the OS kernel into memory, the logical processor will be transitioned from Real Mode to Protected Mode. This is necessary

because today's highly-complex kernels are very large and will not fit in the 1MB of memory addressable in Real Mode.
- The Protected Mode memory model utilized will be a Flat Memory Model (see "IA-32 Flat Memory Model" on page 409) using the first generation virtual-to-physical address translation mechanism (i.e., paging).
- Virtually all of today's modern OSs utilize software-based task switching rather than the x86 processor's hardware-based tasking switching mechanism.
- The OS kernel and device drivers will execute at privilege level 0 while application programs will execute at level 3.

Flat Model With Paging

The discussion that follows assumes we will boot an OS that uses the Flat Memory Model and the virtual-to-physical address translation mechanism. This means that in the course of switching from Real Mode to Protected Mode, we will have to set up an appropriately formatted GDT as well as a set of virtual-to-physical address translation tables.

Software-Based Task Switching

Since the OS will not utilize the x86 hardware-based task switching mechanism, neither the GDT, the LDT (if the OS uses LDTs), nor the IDT will utilize Task Gate descriptors.

To give it full access to all of the logical processor's facilities, the OS code will execute at privilege level 0 while application programs will run at level 3. Since the logical processor is incapable of executing a jump or a call from a more-privileged to a less-privileged program, the OS task scheduler (which is privilege level 0 code) will have to use the software-based task switching mechanism described in "Scheduler's Software-Based Task Switching Mechanism" on page 977 to launch or resume an application program.

In order to avoid possible stack overflows, the OS kernel will utilize the logical processor's automatic stack switching ability (see "Automatic Stack Switch" on page 462) when making calls from one level to another. This being the case, we will have to define a TSS data structure (most modern OSs use one TSS for *all* tasks—see "Real World TSS Usage" on page 968; the TSS contains the pointers to the level 2, 1, and 0 stacks preallocated by the OS) and the TR (Task Register) is loaded with the GDT entry selector for the TSS descriptor.

Protected Mode Transition Primer

GDT Must Be In Place Before Switch to Protected Mode

At a minimum, at least a rudimentary GDT must be created in memory (see Figure 29-1 on page 1117) prior to switching to Protected Mode. The location of this initial GDT is dictated by the current state of the A20 gate (see "Accessing Extended Memory in Real Mode" on page 307):

- If the A20 Gate has not been enabled by software yet, the logical processor cannot access memory above the first MB while in Real Mode. The initial GDT must therefore be created in the first MB of memory space.
- If, on the other hand, the A20 Gate has been enabled by software, the logical processor is not solely restricted to the first MB of memory space but can also access extended memory locations 00100000h - 0010FFEFh (the HMA). In this case, the GDT may be placed in the HMA.

Keeping in mind that the desired OS memory configuration is the Flat Memory Model, the structure of the initial minimalist GDT is as follows (see Figure 29-1 on page 1117):

- **GDT size**: 24 bytes (8 bytes/entry x 3 entries).
- **Entry 0**: Entry 0 must be a null descriptor consisting of all zeros.
- **Entry 1 = CS Descriptor**. Refer to Figure 29-2 on page 1118. Entry 1 will be a code segment descriptor with the following characteristics:
  — Segment base address: 00000000h.
  — Segment size: 4GB.
  — Segment DPL: 0.
  — Other characteristics: Present bit = 1, S bit = 1, C bit = 0 for a Non-Conforming code segment, and R bit = 1 defining the CS as accessible for both code fetches and data reads.
- **Entry 2 = DS Descriptor**. Refer to Figure 29-3 on page 1119. Entry 2 will be a data segment descriptor with the following characteristics:
  — Segment base address: 00000000h.
  — Segment size: 4GB.
  — Segment DPL: 0.
  — Other characteristics: Present bit = 1, S bit = 1, R/W bit = 1 indicating it is a read/writable data segment, E bit = 0 indicating it can be used as an expand-up stack.

After the initial GDT has been created in memory, the logical processor must be informed of its base address and size. This is accomplished as follows:

1. The 2-byte size and 4-byte base address are stored in six consecutive memory locations.
2. The programmer then executes the LGDT instruction to load the 6-byte memory-based operand into the GDTR:
   — It should be noted that the logical processor is still in Real Mode and the default operand size is therefore 16-bits.
   — If the LGDT instruction is executed without prefacing it by the Operand Size Override prefix (66h), the logical processor therefore emulates the 286 and loads a 16-bit limit and a *24-bit* base address into the GDTR (allowing the programmer to specify any address in the first 16MB of memory space).
   — Prefacing the LGDT instruction with the prefix, however, causes it to load a 16-bit limit and a 32-bit base address.

At this point, although the logical processor knows the location and size of the GDT, it is not yet in Protected Mode.

Figure 29-1: Initial Flat Model GDT

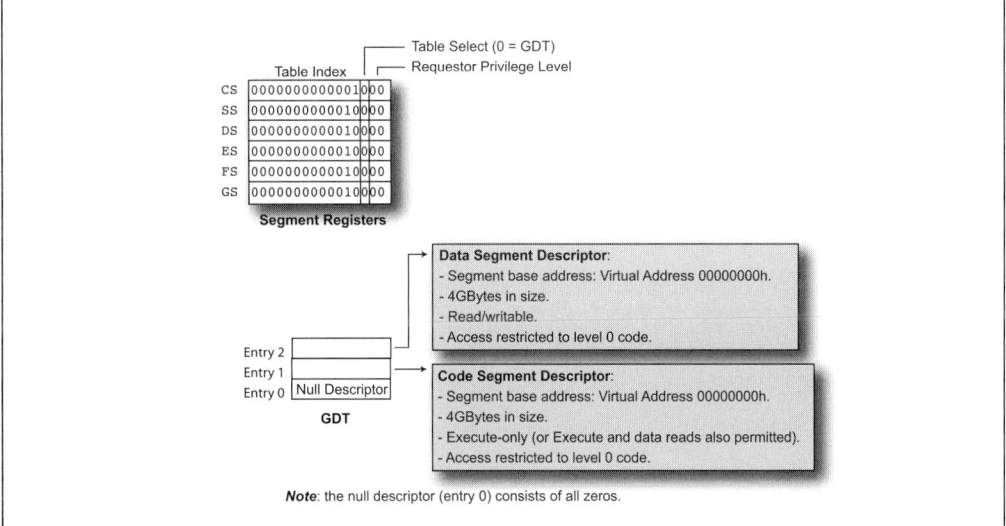

Figure 29-2: 32-bit CS Descriptor

	7	6	5	4	3	2	1	0	
	4th Byte of Base Address = 00h								Byte 7
	G 1	D 1	L 0	A V L	Upper Nibble of Size = FF				Byte 6
	P 1	DPL = 00		S 1	D/C 1	C 0	R 1	A 0	Byte 5
	3rd Byte of Base Address = 00h								Byte 4
	2nd Byte of Base Address = 00h								Byte 3
	1st Byte of Virtual Base Address = 00h								Byte 2
	2nd Byte of Segment Size = FFh								Byte 1
	1st Byte of Segment Size = FFh								Byte 0

G Bit Granularity bit defines interpretation of Size field.
0 = Segment size in bytes.
1 = Segment size in 4KB pages.

D Bit Default bit:
0 = 16-bit, 286 code segment. When fetching and executing code from this segment, processor assumes a default data operand size of 16 bits and an address (offset) size of 16 bits).
1 = 32-bit code segment. When fetching and executing code from this segment, processor assumes a default data operand size of 32 bits and an address (offset) size of 32 bits).

L Bit Long Mode bit. This bit is reserved and must be 0 in 16-bit and 32-bit code segment descriptors.

AVL Bit Available for use by OS kernel.

P Bit Segment Present bit (must be 1 if the code segment is present in memory).

DPL Field Descriptor Privilege Level (0-3). Defines privilege level of code in this segment (CPL it will run at).
00 = Privilege level 0 (most privileged).
01 = Privilege level 1.
10 = Privilege level 2.
11 = Privilege level 3.

S Bit System bit.
0 = OS data structure descriptor.
1 = Must be 1 in a code segment descriptor.

D/C Data/Code bit. Must be 1 for a code segment.
0 = Data Segment
1 = Code Segment.

C Bit Conforming bit. Set to 1 if code segment is conforming.

R Bit Readable bit.
0 = execute-only; Segment contains only code (no data).
1 = Segment contains code and data which may be read. No writes allowed.

A Bit Accessed bit. Set to 1 by the processor when a code segment is accessed.

Figure 29-3: 32-bit DS Descriptor

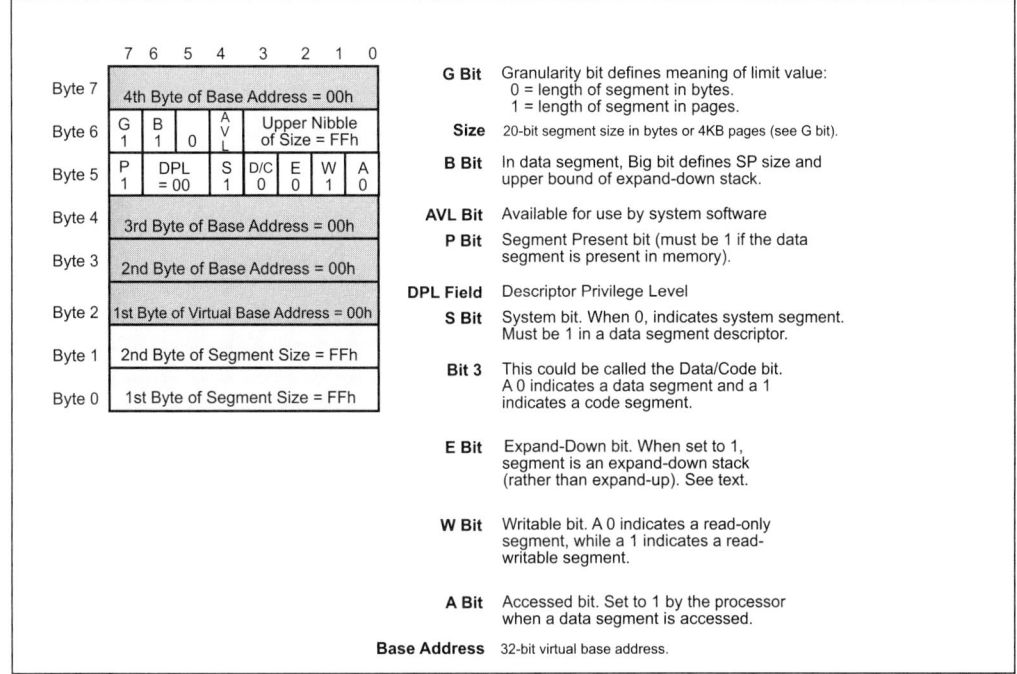

G Bit	Granularity bit defines meaning of limit value: 0 = length of segment in bytes. 1 = length of segment in pages.
Size	20-bit segment size in bytes or 4KB pages (see G bit).
B Bit	In data segment, Big bit defines SP size and upper bound of expand-down stack.
AVL Bit	Available for use by system software
P Bit	Segment Present bit (must be 1 if the data segment is present in memory).
DPL Field	Descriptor Privilege Level
S Bit	System bit. When 0, indicates system segment. Must be 1 in a data segment descriptor.
Bit 3	This could be called the Data/Code bit. A 0 indicates a data segment and a 1 indicates a code segment.
E Bit	Expand-Down bit. When set to 1, segment is an expand-down stack (rather than expand-up). See text.
W Bit	Writable bit. A 0 indicates a read-only segment, while a 1 indicates a read-writable segment.
A Bit	Accessed bit. Set to 1 by the processor when a data segment is accessed.
Base Address	32-bit virtual base address.

No Interrupts or Exceptions During Mode Switch

The programmer must ensure that the logical processor is not interrupted during the mode switching process. To this end, three conditions must be met:

- **Maskable interrupts**. The programmer must execute the CLI instruction to disable recognition of maskable hardware interrupts.
- **NMI**. The programmer must ensure that the platform's ability to deliver an NMI to the logical processor has been disabled. In a PC-compatible environment, this is accomplished by executing the following:
  — mov al, 80
  — out   70,al   ;performing an IO write to port 70h with bit 7 set to 1 will mask the platform's ability to deliver an NMI to the logical processor.
- **Exceptions**. The programmer must ensure that no instructions generate software exceptions during the switch.

Creation of Protected Mode IDT

As mentioned in the previous section, the programmer must ensure that the logical processor is not interrupted during the mode switch process. The Real Mode and Protected Mode IDTs have very different structures. The new, Protected Mode IDT (see Figure 29-4 on page 1121) may be created either before or after the switch to Protected Mode, but it must be in place and the IDTR register must have been programmed (using the LIDT instruction) with the IDT's base address and size *before* hardware interrupts are reenabled (i.e., maskable interrupts and NMI), software exceptions are permitted, or a software interrupt instruction is executed. Each IDT entry may contain either a Trap Gate (see Figure 19-6 on page 694) or Interrupt Gate (see Figure 19-5 on page 693), but, since we will not be using the x86 hardware-based task switching mechanism, none may contain Task Gate descriptors.

Once the IDT has been created and the appropriate Protected Mode interrupt and exception handlers have been loaded into memory, the programmer executes the STI instruction to reenable the logical processor's recognition of maskable interrupts and also performs the platform-specific actions necessary to reenable the platform's ability to generate NMI. It should be noted, however, that in our example:

- Since the event handlers have not, in fact, been loaded into memory yet, it would be premature to reenable interrupts at this point.
- SS:ESP must also be initialized with a valid stack pointer prior to the recognition of any type of interrupt/exception event (because the logical processor will automatically push the contents of several registers—e.g., CS:EIP and Eflags—onto the stack upon recognition of an interrupt or a software exception).

It should also be noted that the logical processor is still in Real Mode and the default operand size is therefore 16-bits. If the LIDT instruction is executed without prefacing it by the Operand Size Override prefix (66h), the logical processor emulates the 286 and loads a 16-bit limit and a *24-bit* IDT base address into the IDTR (allowing the programmer to specify any address in the first 16MB of memory space). Prefacing the LIDT instruction with the prefix, however, causes it to load a 16-bit limit and a 32-bit base address.

Figure 29-4: Protected Mode IDT

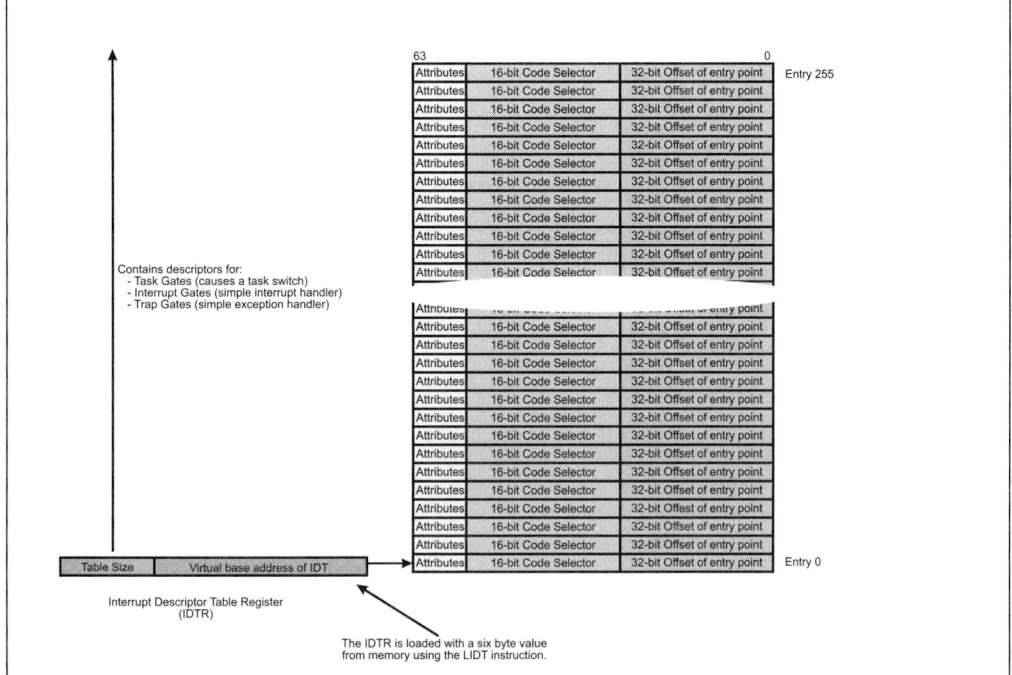

Other Protected Mode Structures

TSS

Once the OS kernel has been booted into memory and has completed initialization, the task scheduler will begin to initiate tasks. Typical modern OSs create a single TSS for all Protected Mode tasks (see "Real World TSS Usage" on page 968) and a corresponding TSS descriptor in the GDT. If any Real Mode tasks are to be run under VM86 Mode, it may create separate TSSs and TSS descriptors for each of them, as well. Although the OS will not be using the hardware-based task switching mechanism, the TSS is used under the following circumstances:

- **Stack Switch due to call to more-privileged procedure**. When a level 3 procedure calls a level 0 OS kernel service, the logical processor will automatically switch to the level 0 stack preallocated by the OS kernel. It obtains the level 0 stack pointer from the TSS.

- **Stack Switch due to Interrupt/Exception**. When a level 3 program (i.e., with a CS DPL of 3) is interrupted by a hardware interrupt or a software exception, the logical processor will automatically switch to the level 0 stack preallocated by the OS kernel. It obtains the level 0 stack pointer from the TSS.
- If the current task is a VM86 task and it attempts the execution of a software interrupt instruction (INT *nn*), the logical processor will interrogate the Interrupt Redirection Table in the current TSS.
- When the current task is either a level 3 Protected Mode task or a VM86 task attempting the execution of an IO read or write, the logical processor will use the port address(es) to index into the IO Permission Bitmap in the current TSS.

Address Translation Mechanism

Protected Mode Is a Prerequisite. The address translation mechanism can only be enabled (by setting CR0[PG] = 1; see Figure 29-5 on page 1123) when the logical processor is in Protected Mode:

— **Case 1**: **Both can be enabled simultaneously** by setting both CR0[PE] and CR0[PG] to one. In this case:
  – The initial set of address translation tables must have already been created in memory.
  – CR3 must have already been programmed with the start physical address of the top-level translation directory.
— **Case 2**: **Protected Mode can be enabled first** and the address translation mechanism afterwards. In this case:
  – The initial set of address translation tables may be created and CR3 programmed after Protected Mode has been entered.
  – This means that, for all memory accesses prior to the enabling of address translation, the addresses generated by adding the offset to a segment start address *are* the physical memory address (not virtual memory addresses).

Identity Mapping. The programmer must also keep in mind that right up until the execution of the MOV CR0 instruction that sets the PG bit to enable the paging mechanism, the logical processor has been fetching instructions from memory using physical memory addressing. The virtual address used to fetch the very next instruction (i.e., the instruction immediately following the MOV CR0), however, *will* be submitted to the address translation mechanism and translated into a physical memory address before the fetch from memory is performed. In order to successfully fetch the instruction that immediately follows the MOV CR0 in physical memory, the translation tables must be set up to translate that instruction's virtual address into the identical physical memory address; in other words it must be a 1-to-1 translation. This is commonly referred to as an *identity* mapping (in math, an *identity* operation is a transformation that leaves an object unchanged).

Which Translation Mechanism? While there are, in fact, three variations on the x86 address translation mechanism (first, second, and third generation), only two of them (first and second generation) are available in Protected Mode. The third generation mechanism is only available in IA-32e Mode:

— **First generation** mechanism (see "First-Generation Paging" on page 513). This mechanism utilizes a 2-level lookup during address translation and requires the creation of a top-level Page Directory (PD) and a series of one or more 2nd-level Page Tables (PTs) in memory. CR3 must be initialized with the start physical address of the Page Directory.

— **Second generation** mechanism (see "Second-Generation Paging" on page 553). This mechanism utilizes a 3-level lookup during address translation and requires the creation of a top-level Page Directory Pointer Table (PDPT), up to four 2nd-level Page Directories (PDs), and a series of one or more 3rd-level Page Tables (PTs) in memory. CR3 must be initialized with the start physical address of the Page Directory Pointer Table.

Figure 29-5: CR0

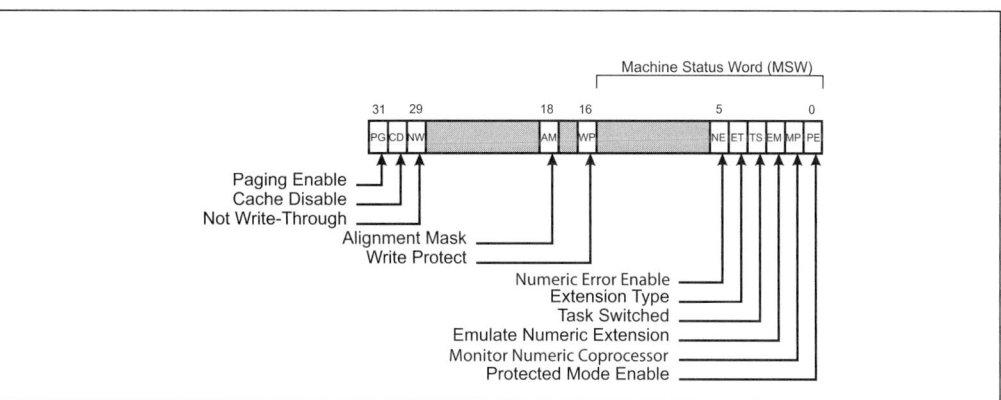

Optional Structure: LDT

At a minimum, the OS must create a GDT containing:

- One descriptor for each code or data segment that is **shared** among more than one task (i.e., a globally-accessible segment).
- **One or more TSS** (Task State Segment) **descriptors**. This descriptor defines the base address and size (as well as other attributes) of a task's TSS data structure. If the hardware-based task switch mechanism is used, the OS creates a separate TSS descriptor and TSS for each of them. Most modern OSs do use the hardware-based task switch mechanism, however, and create a single TSS descriptor and TSS for all tasks (see "Real World TSS Usage" on page 968).
- If an OS utilizes the optional Local Descriptor Table (LDT) to describe the segments of memory that are private (local) to a task, it will create an **LDT descriptor** for each task defining its LDT's base address and size (as well as other attributes).
- **Procedure Call Gates**. A Call Gate descriptor permits a lesser-privileged program to call a procedure in a more-privileged code segment (e.g., they permit an application to call services supplied by the OS kernel). A complete description can be found in "Indirect Procedure Far Call Through a Call Gate" on page 452.
- If the OS utilizes the x86 processor's hardware-based task switching mechanism (*note that none of the major OSs use it*), it may create (for each task) a **Task Gate descriptor** in the GDT. If a far jump or a far call is executed and the 16-bit segment selector portion of the branch target address selects a Task Gate descriptor or a TSS descriptor in the GDT, the logical processor's hardware-based task switching mechanism is triggered (and it switches to the task associated with the selected TSS descriptor).

Assuming the booted OS makes use of LDTs, they (like the TSS data structure) typically aren't created until a new task is created. Since this chapter assumes that we are switching the logical processor into Protected Mode in preparation for booting the OS, no LDTs are required yet. If and when an LDT is created, it contains:

- One descriptor for each code or data segment that is **local to the current task** (i.e., a private segment).
- **Procedure Call Gates**. Refer to "Indirect Procedure Far Call Through a Call Gate" on page 452.
- If the OS utilizes the x86 processor's hardware-based task switching mechanism (*note that none of the major OSs use it*), it may create one or more **Task**

Gate descriptors in a task's LDT. If a far jump or a far call is executed and the 16-bit segment selector portion of the far address selects a Task Gate descriptor in the current task's LDT, the logical processor's hardware-based task switching mechanism is triggered (and it switches to the task associated with the GDT-based TSS descriptor pointed to by the Task Gate descriptor).

Enable A20 Gate

As mentioned earlier (see "Accessing Extended Memory in Real Mode" on page 307), in order to correctly address extended memory (i.e., memory above the 1MB address boundary), the logical processor's A20 Gate must be enabled.

Load Initial Code and Handlers Into Memory

After the switch to Protected Mode, the OS loader will load the OS kernel into extended memory and, after doing so, will jump to the OS initialization code entry point. Before reenabling hardware interrupts, the Protected Mode interrupt and exception handlers must have been loaded into memory and the IDT initialized with Trap Gate and Interrupt Gate descriptors containing the handler entry points.

The Switch to Protected Mode

After ensuring that the appropriate data structures have been created in memory, software transitions the logical processor into Protected Mode by moving a value into CR0 that has bit 0, the PE bit, set to one.

Loading Segment Registers With GDT Descriptors

Although Protected Mode has now been activated, the six segment registers (both the visible and invisible parts) still retain the values they contained in Real Mode. In order to operate properly in Protected Mode, they must be loaded with 16-bit selectors that cause valid segment descriptors to be read from the GDT (or from the LDT if one has been created) and loaded into the invisible portions of the registers. Only then will the logical processor know the base address, size and attributes of the code, data, and stack segments. This is accomplished as indicated in Table 29-1 on page 1126.

Table 29-1: Segment Register Reload Procedure

Segment Register	Initialization Procedure
CS	**Background**: Though the logical processor is now in Protected Mode, the default address and operand sizes are still 16-bits. This is because a Protected Mode code segment descriptor has not yet been read from the GDT or LDT (if there is one) into the invisible part of the CS register. Only when a 32-bit CS descriptor has been loaded into the register will the D (Default) attribute bit in the invisible part of the register be set to one indicating that the default operand and address size is 32- rather than 16-bits. **Problem: operand size still = 16-bits**. In order to load a Protected Mode selector into the CS register, the programmer must execute a far jump or a far call instruction specifying a new 16-bit CS selector and the 32-bit offset of the branch target address within that CS. When it is executed, because the logical processor is still using a default operand size of 16-bits, it emulates a 286 in 16-bit Protected Mode and forces the upper 16-bits of the offset to zero (because, even in Protected Mode, the 286 had a maximum segment size of 64KB). This means the branch target address must be located in the lower 64KB of the target CS. **Solution: use prefix**. The programmer solves the problem by prefacing the far jump (or far call) with the Operand Size Override prefix (66h), thereby forcing the logical processor to use the entire, 32-bit offset address.
SS	**Initialize before interrupts/exceptions**. It should be stressed that the SS:ESP register pair must be initialized with valid stack parameters (i.e., base address, size, etc.) before hardware interrupts are reenabled, a software exception is permitted, or a software interrupt instruction is executed. At the risk of belaboring the obvious, this is because the logical processor will automatically push the contents of several registers (e.g., CS:EIP and Eflags) onto the stack upon recognition of an interrupt or a software exception.

Table 29-1: Segment Register Reload Procedure (Continued)

Segment Register	Initialization Procedure
DS, ES, FS, GS	At a minimum, the DS register should be loaded with a selector that selects a valid R/W data segment descriptor in the GDT (or LDT if there is one). Otherwise, software will not have R/W access to an area of memory in which to store data variables. Any of the data segment registers that will not be used should be loaded with a selector value of 0000h to select GDT entry 0 which should contain a null descriptor (i.e., one containing all zeros).

Load TSS Descriptor Into TR

Before launching the first task, the OS must initialize the Task Register (TR) with a 16-bit value that selects the a TSS descriptor in the GDT. This accomplishes two things:

- **Sets Busy bit**. Using a locked read/modify/write operation, the logical processor sets the Busy bit in the TSS descriptor to mark the task associated with this descriptor as currently busy (i.e., it is the currently-active task). For more information, refer to "Calling Another Task" on page 670.
- **Loads TSS Descriptor**. The logical processor loads the TSS descriptor from the GDT into the invisible part of the TR. From that point forward, it knows the base address and size of the current task's TSS data structure (in case it has to access any of its elements). For more information, see "TSS" on page 1121.
- Also refer to "Real World TSS Usage" on page 968.

Enable Interrupts

At this point, the Protected Mode IDT has been created and initialized with Trap Gate and Interrupt Gate descriptors containing the entry points of the various hardware and software event handlers. The LIDT instruction has also been executed so the logical processor knows the IDT base address and size. It is now safe to reenable hardware interrupts:

- Execute the STI instruction to reenable recognition of maskable hardware interrupts.

- Execute the appropriate code to reenable the platform's ability to generate NMI interrupts.

See "No Interrupts or Exceptions During Mode Switch" on page 1119 for more information.

Load Application Into Memory

Once the OS kernel has been loaded into memory and completed its initialization, it is now ready to start initiating tasks. Obviously, at least a portion of a task's code and data must be loaded into memory before it can be initiated.

Create Task's Address Translation Tables

In addition, after loading the task's startup code and data into memory, the OS kernel must create the set of address translation tables that the paging logic will use to translate the virtual memory addresses generated by the task into the appropriate physical memory addresses that will allow it to address its code and data in physical memory. Once it has done so, the kernel initializes CR3 with the start physical address of the top-level address translation directory.

Switching From OS Scheduler to First Task

The OS kernel's task scheduler (which is executing at privilege level 0) must now jump to the task being initiated. If it is a level 3 application, however, we have a problem. As described in "Jumping from a Higher-to-Lesser Privileged Program" on page 441, it isn't possible for code running at level 0 to jump to code in a level 3 code segment. This can only be accomplished by setting up the initial values in the registers, pushing the desired start address (in CS:EIP form) onto the level 0 stack along with the SS:ESP pointer to the stack to be used by the target task and the task's initial Eflags register image. Having done so, the scheduler then executes an IRET instruction. The detailed description can be found in "Jumping from a Higher-to-Lesser Privileged Program" on page 441 and in "Scheduler's Software-Based Task Switching Mechanism" on page 977.

Example: Linux Startup

This section uses Linux boot and initialization as an example to demonstrate the transition from Real Mode to Protected Mode. This discussion references the following Linux boot source files:

- linux/arch/i386/boot/bootsect.S
- linux/arch/i386/boot/setup.S
- Startup_32 in boot/compressed/head.s
- Startup_32 in kernel/head.s
- Start_kernel() in linux/init/main.c

1. Bootsect

The BIOS loads the 512-byte file Bootsect (boot sector; the source code may be found in linux/arch/i386/boot/bootsect.S) into Real Mode memory starting at location 07C00h and then executes a jump to 07C00h to execute it.

1. Bootsect.s copies itself (512-bytes) from 07C00h to 90000h and then jumps to the entry point of the *Go* procedure in the relocated image.
2. SS:SP is initialized so we have a stack to use.
3. A call is made to the BIOS to obtain the disk parameter table.
4. It obtains the number of sectors/track.
5. Reads the boot setup file—bsetup—(the source code may be found in linux/arch/i386/boot/setup.S) into memory right after bootsect (starting at 92000h).
6. Loads the kernel image into memory:
   — If it's an uncompressed kernel image, it's loaded into memory starting at 00100000h (i.e., the beginning of the 2nd MB of memory).
   — If it's a compressed kernel image, it's loaded into memory starting at 10000h.
7. Jump to Setup (see next section).

2. Setup

The source code may be found in linux/arch/i386/boot/setup.S. When executed, Setup performs the following actions:

1. Resets the disk controller. Recalibrates the head mechanism to cylinder 0 if necessary.
2. Sets DS = CS so we can access read-only data that resides in the code segment.
3. Checks for a good signature on the setup code.
4. Checks the boot loader type to ensure it can load a big kernel.
5. Get amount of extended memory using INT 15 bios call.
6. Max out the keyboard repeat rate.
7. Check for video adapter and allow user to browse through video modes.
8. Get characteristics of hard drive 0 (and 1, if present) from bios.
9. Use INT 11 bios call to see if mouse installed.

10. Use INT 15 bios call to initialize 32-bit Protected Mode APM (Advanced Power Management) bios.
11. Disable hardware interrupts in preparation for switch to Protected Mode:
    — Execute CLI to disable recognition of maskable interrupts.
    — Execute OUT 70, 80 to disable platform's ability to generate NMI.
12. Enable A20 Gate so we can properly address extended memory.
13. Execute LIDT to load the IDTR with an IDT base address of 0 and length of 0 [the IDT is null (i.e., empty) at this point]. It's OK, though, because interrupts are still disabled.
14. Execute LGDT to load the GDTR with the base address and length of the startup GDT. The startup GDT content is defined in Table 29-2 on page 1130.
15. Execute OUT F0, 00 and OUT F1, 00 to reset x87 FPU.
16. Mask all external hardware interrupts:
    — Execute an OUT A1, FF to the slave 8259A interrupt controller to mask out recognition of the IRQ8-15 hardware interrupt request signal lines.
    — And an OUT 21,FB to the master 8259A interrupt controller to mask out recognition of the IRQ0-7 hardware interrupt request signal lines.
17. *Execute LMSW (Load Machine Status Word; i.e., the lower 16-bits of CR0) instruction to set CR0[PE] = 1. At the conclusion of this instruction, the logical processor is in Protected Mode.*
18. Execute far jump to Startup_32 at:
    — 00010000h (if compressed kernel image was loaded). This procedure decompresses the kernel image and moves it to extended memory starting at location 00100000h. It then jumps to startup_32 at 00100000h. The source for this can be found in linux/arch/i386/boot/compressed/head.S. See "3a. Startup_32 in boot/compressed/head.s" on page 1131.
    — or 00100000h (if uncompressed kernel image was loaded). The source for this can be found in linux/arch/i386/kernel/head.S. See "3b. Startup_32 in kernel/head.s" on page 1132.
    — Note: The far jump must be prefaced by the Operand Size Override prefix (see the description of CS reload in Table 29-1 on page 1126).

Table 29-2: Startup GDT Content

Entry	Content	Description
0	0000000000000000h	Null descriptor.
1	0000000000000000h	This descriptor isn't used during Linux bootup.

Table 29-2: Startup GDT Content (Continued)

Entry	Content	Description
2	00CF9A000000FFFFh	**Kernel CS**: • Virtual base address: 00000000h. • Size: 4GB (G = 1 and Size = FFFFF, indicating 2^{20} 4KB pages in size). • DPL = 00b. Privilege level 0 CS. • S = 1. Not a special System descriptor (therefore, it's a CS or DS descriptor; see D/C). • D/C = 1. CS descriptor. • C = 0. Non-Conforming CS. • R = 1. Contains code and read-only data. • A = 0. Not accessed yet.
3	00CF92000000FFFFh	**Kernel DS**: • Virtual base address: 00000000h. • Size: 4GB (G = 1 and Size = FFFFF, indicating 2^{20} 4KB pages in size). • DPL = 00b. Privilege level 0 DS. • S = 1. Not a special System descriptor (therefore, it's a CS or DS descriptor; see D/C). • D/C = 0. DS descriptor. • E = 0. If used as stack memory, it behaves as an expand-up stack. • W = 1. Read/writable segment. • A = 0. Not accessed yet.

3a. Startup_32 in boot/compressed/head.s

When executed, Startup_32 performs the following actions:

1. Executes CLD to clear string Direction flag bit in Eflags.
2. Executes CLI to disable recognition of maskable hardware interrupts.
3. Sets all four data segment registers so they point to the kernel DS defined in entry 3 of GDT (see Table 29-2 on page 1130).
4. Initializes Protected Mode stack pointer (SS:ESP).
5. Test to ensure A20 Gate is enabled so we can properly address extended memory.
6. Decompress the kernel image and move it to extended memory starting at location 00100000h.

7. Execute far jump to Startup_32 at start of decompressed kernel image at location 00100000h (see next section).

3b. Startup_32 in kernel/head.s

On entry:

- ESI points to the parameter area created by the 16-bit Real Mode code. The parameters will be copied to *empty_zero_page* later.
- BX = the logical processor the boot code is running on. 0 = BSP (Boot Strap Processor).

When executed, Startup_32 performs the following actions:

1. Executes CLD to clear string Direction flag bit in Eflags.
2. Sets all four data segment registers so they point to the kernel DS defined in entry 3 of GDT (see Table 29-2 on page 1130).
3. Initializes the startup Page Directory and Page Tables. Ultimately, the kernel will be relocated to virtual memory starting at C0000000h (the 3GB address boundary). Any memory references generated by that code will be redirected to the kernel's actual location in lower physical memory by these Page Tables:
    — PDE 0 points to a Page Table (referred to by the rather confusing name of *pg0*) at location 00102000h that translates the 4MB virtual address range 00000000h - 003FFFFFh to physical addresses 00000000h - 003FFFFFh (in other words, identity mapping). All 1024 PTEs in the Page Table are marked as read/writable user pages (using the R/W and U/S bits; see Figure 16-18 on page 527).
    — PDE 1 points to a Page Table (referred to by the confusing name of *pg1*) at location 00103000h that translates the 4MB virtual address range from 00400000h - 007FFFFFh to physical addresses 00400000h - 007FFFFFh (in other words, identity mapping).
    — PDEs 2 - 767 are marked Not Present.
    — PDE 768 points to the same Page Table as PDE 0 and translates the 4MB virtual address range C0000000h - C03FFFFFh to physical addresses 00000000h - 003FFFFFh.
    — PDE 769 points to the same Page Table as PDE 1 and translates the 4MB virtual address range C0400000h - C07FFFFFh to physical addresses 00400000h - 007FFFFFh.
    — PDEs 770 - 1023 are marked Not Present.
    The final initialization of the Page Tables takes place later based on the actual amount of installed memory.

4. Sets CR3 = the physical base address of the top-level Page Directory.
5. Enables paging by setting CR[PG] = 1.
6. Initializes the stack pointer (SS:ESP).
7. Clears the *bss* (the common local variable storage area).
8. Initializes all 256 IDT entries so every entry contains a level 0 Trap Gate descriptor pointing to a do-nothing handler (i.e., it only contains the IRET instruction).
9. Copies the bootup parameters from Real Mode memory to extended memory.
10. Executes CPUID types 0 and 1 to obtain information about the processor and its capabilities.
11. Checks that the x87 is 387-compatible.
12. Executes the LGDT and LIDT instructions to load the base address and lengths of the GDT and IDT into the GDTR and IDTR. The content of the new GDT is defined in Table 29-3 on page 1133.
13. Since we've just switched to a new GDT, we need to reload the six segment registers so the logical processor will load the selected segment descriptors from the new GDT:
    — Performs a far jump to the very next instruction to load the CS descriptor from GDT entry 2 (kernel CS).
    — Initializes the four data segment registers with 0018h which selects GDT entry 3 (kernel data segment descriptor) in the new GDT.
14. Initializes SS:ESP with a fresh privilege level 0 stack pointer.
15. Executes the LLDT instruction to load the LDTR with 0000h to select GDT entry 0 (null descriptor) because there's no LDT yet (not until first task initiated).
16. Executes CLD to clear the string Direction flag bit in Eflags.
17. BSP calls Start_kernel() in linux/init/main.c
18. On return, the logical processor enters an idle loop.

Table 29-3: Startup_32 GDT Content

Entry	Content	Description
0	0000000000000000h	Null descriptor.
1	0000000000000000h	This descriptor isn't used during Linux bootup.

Table 29-3: Startup_32 GDT Content (Continued)

Entry	Content	Description
2	00CF9A000000FFFFh	**Kernel CS:** • P = 1. CS descriptor is present in memory. • S = 1. Not a special System descriptor (therefore, it's a CS or DS descriptor; see D/C). • D/C = 1. CS descriptor. • L = 0. Not a 64-bit CS. • D = 1. 32-bit descriptor. Default operand and address size = 32-bits. • Virtual base address: 00000000h. • Size: 4GB (G = 1 and Size = FFFFF, indicating 2^{20} 4KB pages in size). • DPL = 00b. Privilege level 0 CS. • C = 0. Non-Conforming CS. • R = 1. Contains code and read-only data. • A = 0. Not accessed yet.
3	00CF92000000FFFFh	**Kernel DS:** • P = 1. DS descriptor is present in memory. • S = 1. Not a special System descriptor (therefore, it's a CS or DS descriptor; see D/C). • D/C = 0. DS descriptor. • Virtual base address: 00000000h. • Size: 4GB (G = 1 and Size = FFFFF, indicating 2^{20} 4KB pages in size). • B = 1. 32-bit descriptor. 32-bit stack (rather than 16-bit). • DPL = 00b. Privilege level 0 DS. • E = 0. If used as stack memory, it behaves as an expand-up stack. • W = 1. Read/writable segment. • A = 0. Not accessed yet.

Table 29-3: Startup_32 GDT Content (Continued)

Entry	Content	Description
4	00CFFA000000FFFFh	**User CS**. • P = 1. Descriptor is present in memory. • S = 1. Not a special System descriptor (therefore, it's a CS or DS descriptor; see D/C). • D/C = 1. CS descriptor. • D = 1. 32-bit descriptor. Default operand and address size = 32-bits. • G = 1 and Limit = FFFFFh, indicating 2^{20} 4KB pages in size (4GB). • Virtual base address = 00000000h. • DPL = 11b. Privilege level 3 CS. • L = 0. Not a 64-bit CS. • C = 0. Non-Conforming CS. • R = 1. Contains code and read-only data. • A = 0. Not accessed yet.
5	00CFF2000000FFFFh	**User DS**. • P = 1. Descriptor is present in memory. • S = 1. Not a special System descriptor (therefore, it's a CS or DS descriptor; see D/C). • D/C = 0. DS descriptor. • B = 1. B = 1. 32-bit descriptor. 32-bit stack (rather than 16-bit). • G = 1 and Limit = FFFFFh, indicating 2^{20} 4KB pages in size (4GB). • Virtual base address = 00000000h. • DPL = 11b. Privilege level 3 DS. • E = 0. If used as stack memory, it's an expand-up stack. • W = 1. Read/writable segment. • A = 0. Not accessed yet.
6	0000000000000000h	This descriptor isn't used.
7	0000000000000000h	This descriptor isn't used.

Table 29-3: Startup_32 GDT Content (Continued)

Entry	Content	Description
		The following four entries define the APM (Advanced Power Management) segments. Their lengths have byte granularity (G = 0) and their base addresses and sizes will be set at run time.
8	0040920000000000h	APM data segment set up for bad BIOSs. • Descriptor is present in memory. • S = 1. Not a special System descriptor (therefore, it's a CS or DS descriptor; see D/C). • D/C = 0. DS descriptor. • B = 1. 32-bit descriptor. 32-bit stack (rather than 16-bit). • DPL = 00b. Privilege level 0 DS. • Base address = 00000000h. • G = 0 and Limit = 00000h, so size = 0 bytes. • E = 0. If used as stack memory, it behaves as an expand-up stack. • W = 1. Read/writable segment. • A = 0. Not accessed yet.
9	00409A0000000000h	32-bit APM CS. • P = 1. Descriptor is present in memory. • G = 0 and Limit = 00000h, so size = 0 bytes. • S = 1. Not a special System descriptor (therefore, it's a CS or DS descriptor; see D/C). • D/C = 1. CS descriptor. • D = 1. 32-bit CS descriptor. Default operand and address size = 32-bits. • L = 0. Not a 64-bit CS. • DPL = 00b. Privilege level 0 CS. • C = 0. Non-Conforming CS. • R = 1. Contains code and read-only data. • A = 0. Not accessed yet.

Table 29-3: Startup_32 GDT Content (Continued)

Entry	Content	Description
10	00009A0000000000h	16-bit APM CS. • P = 1. Descriptor is present in memory. • G = 0 and Limit = 00000h, so size = 0 bytes. • Base address = 00000000h. • S = 1. Not a special System descriptor (therefore, it's a CS or DS descriptor; see D/C). • D/C = 1. CS descriptor. • D = 0. 16-bit CS descriptor. Default operand and address size = 16-bits. • L = 0. Not a 64-bit CS. • DPL = 00b. Privilege level 0 CS. • C = 0. Non-Conforming CS. • R = 1. Contains code and read-only data. • A = 0. Not accessed yet.
11	0040920000000000h	APM DS segment descriptor. • P = 1. Descriptor is present in memory. • G = 0 and Limit = 00000h, so size = 0 bytes. • Base address = 00000000h. • S = 1. Not a special System descriptor (therefore, it's a CS or DS descriptor; see D/C). • D/C = 0. DS descriptor. • B = 1. 32-bit descriptor. 32-bit stack (rather than 16-bit). • DPL = 00b. Privilege level 0 DS. • E = 0. If used as stack memory, it behaves as an expand-up stack. • W = 1. Read/writable segment. • A = 0. Not accessed yet.
12-n	-------------------------	Reserved for TSS and LDT descriptors.

30 *Transitioning to IA-32e Mode*

The Previous Chapter

The previous chapter described the process of switching from Real Mode into Protected Mode. The following topics were covered:

- Real Mode Peculiarities That Affect the OS Boot Process.
- Typical OS Characteristics.
- Protected Mode Transition Primer.
- Example: Linux Startup.

This Chapter

This chapter describes the process of switching from Protected Mode into the Compatibility SubMode of IA-32e Mode. It then describes making the switch from Compatibility Mode into 64-bit Mode.

The Next Chapter

The next chapter provides a basic introduction to Virtualization Technology and covers the following topics:

- OS: I Am the God of All Things!
- Virtualization Supervisor: Sure You Are (:<)
- Root versus Non-Root Mode.
- Detecting VMX Capability.
- Entering/Exiting VMX Mode.
- Entering VMX Mode.
- Exiting VMX Mode.
- Virtualization Elements/Terminology.
- Introduction to the VT Instructions.

- Introduction to the VMCS Data Structure.
- Preparing to Launch a Guest OS.
- Launching a Guest OS.
- Guest OS Suspension.
- Resuming a Guest OS.
- Some Warnings Regarding VMCS Accesses.

No Need to Linger in Protected Mode

This chapter assumes that software will take the most efficient route possible from the removal of reset through Real Mode, Protected Mode, Compatibility Mode and, finally, to 64-bit Mode.

Entering Compatibility Mode

IA-32e Mode can only be entered by transitioning from legacy Protected Mode to Compatibility Mode. This transition is accomplished as follows:

1. Switch from Real Mode to legacy Protected Mode (this can be achieved using either 16- or 32-bit Protected Mode code). This topic was covered in "Transitioning to Protected Mode" on page 1113.
   — Note that there is no requirement that the address translation mechanism must be activated upon entering Protected Mode. Rather, the programmer may choose to immediately set up the 3rd generation address translation tables in preparation for the switch to the Compatibility SubMode of IA-32e Mode.

   Note: This discussion assumes the logical processor is now fetching code from a 32- rather than a 16-bit code segment. The default operand and address sizes are therefore 32-bits.

   DISABLE INTERRUPTS IN PREPARATION FOR SWITCH TO COMPATIBILITY MODE
2. Disable interrupts in preparation for switch from Protected Mode to IA-32e Mode:
   — Execute CLI to disable recognition of maskable hardware interrupts.
   — The programmer must ensure that the platform's ability to deliver an NMI has been disabled. In a PC-compatible environment, this is accomplished by executing the following:
     – mov al, 80
     – out 70,al   ;performing an IO write to port 70h with bit 7 set to 1 will mask the platform's ability to deliver an NMI to the logical processor.
   — The programmer also must ensure that no instructions generate software exceptions during the switch.

SET UP IA-32E COMPLIANT DATA STRUCTURES

3. Set up the 3rd generation address translation tables (see "IA-32e Address Translation" on page 983).

4. Point CR3 (see Figure 16-19 on page 528) to the top-level address translation table (i.e., the PML4 directory). Since CR3 is only 32-bits wide in Protected Mode, the PML4 directory's physical base address must be in the lower 4GB.

5. Create an IA-32e compliant IDT containing 16-byte Interrupt Gates and Trap Gates (and no Task Gates).

6. Create an IA-32e compliant GDT containing (in addition to Protected-/ Compatibility Mode-compliant data and stack segment descriptors):
   — An IA-32e compliant TSS descriptor (see Figure 23-9 on page 947).
   — An IA-32e compliant LDT descriptor (see Figure 23-8 on page 946).
   — IA-32e compliant Call Gate descriptors (see Figure 23-7 on page 945).
   — A 64-bit, privilege level 0 Non-Conforming code segment descriptor (see Figure 23-3 on page 922).

7. Create an IA-32e compliant LDT containing (in addition to Protected-/ Compatibility Mode-compliant data and stack segment descriptors) IA-32e compliant Call Gate descriptors (see Figure 23-7 on page 945).

8. Create an IA-32e compliant TSS data structure (see Figure 23-9 on page 947).

EXECUTE 3-STEP PROCESS TO ENABLE IA-32E MODE

9. Enable 2nd generation address translation by setting CR4[PAE] to 1. This is the first required precondition for the transition to IA-32e Mode. Note that although the PAE feature is now enabled, address translation itself has not yet been activated (CR0[PG] is still 0).

10. Set EFER[LME] = 1 to enable IA-32e Mode. This is the second required pre-condition for the transition to IA-32e Mode. IA-32e Mode is not yet active, however.

11. Set CR0[PG] = 1 to activate paging. This is the third and final precondition. Since all three preconditions for IA-32e Mode activation have now been met, **IA-32e Mode is now activated**. The three prerequisites are:
    — CR4[PAE] = 1.
    — EFER[LME] = 1.
    — CR0[PG] = 1.

12. The L bit in the currently-active CS descriptor = 0, so the logical processor is not in 64-bit Mode. Rather, based on the state of the D bit in the selected CS descriptor, it is now in either the 16- or 32-bit Compatibility SubMode of IA-32e Mode:
    — D = 0. The logical processor is in 16-bit Compatibility Mode.
    — D = 1. The logical processor is in 32-bit Compatibility Mode.

A Note Regarding Identity Address Mapping

Up until this moment, address translation was disabled. The memory address that the MOV CR0 instruction was fetched from was therefore treated as a physical rather than a virtual address. Address translation is now enabled, however, so the memory address used to fetch the next instruction (i.e., the one immediately following the MOV CR0 instruction which activated address translation) is treated as a virtual address and is therefore translated into a physical address. In order to fetch the instruction that immediately follows the MOV CR0 in physical memory, the address translation tables must translate this virtual address into the identical physical memory address (virtual = physical; referred to as identity address mapping).

After Switch to IA-32e Mode, Load System Registers

13. Execute the LIDT instruction to load the IDTR with the 16-bit size and 32-bit base address of the IA-32e compliant IDT.

14. Execute the LGDT instruction to load the GDTR with the 16-bit size and 32-bit base address of the IA-32e compliant GDT.

15. Execute the LLDT instruction to load the LDTR with the 16-bit GDT selector that points to the IA-32e compliant LDT descriptor in the GDT. In response, the logical processor loads the LDT descriptor into the invisible portion of the LDTR.

16. Execute the LTR instruction to load the TR with the 16-bit GDT selector that points to the 16-byte IA-32e compliant TSS descriptor in the GDT. In response, the logical processor loads the TSS descriptor into the invisible portion of the TR.

Switch to 64-bit Mode

1. Execute a far jump wherein the CS selector portion of the branch target address selects a 64-bit privilege level 0 Non-Conforming code segment descriptor in the GDT:

   — When the logical processor loads the CS descriptor into the invisible portion of the CS register, the one in the descriptor's L bit switches it into 64-bit Mode.

   — Segmentation is now disabled and the flat memory model is hardware-enforced: all segments (with the exception of the FS and GS data segments) have an assumed base address of 0 and a length of 2^{64} locations.

   — Since the far jump is executed while the logical processor is still in 32-bit Compatibility Mode, the offset portion of the branch target address is only 32-bits wide. The 64-bit RIP register is therefore loaded with the 32-bit address 0-extended to 64-bits. The target 64-bit code entry point must therefore reside in the lower 4GB of the 64-bit code segment.

Alternatively, the far jump could have selected a Call Gate descriptor in the GDT or LDT that contains the entry point of the 64-bit code anywhere in a 2^{64} address space.

POST-SWITCH HOUSEKEEPING

2. Initialize the pointer to the top-of-stack by moving a 64-bit virtual address into RSP.

3. The GDT currently pointed to by the GDTR is in the lower 4GB of memory. Do we need to switch to a new GDT? If the OS wishes to relocate the GDT above the 4GB address boundary, then the answer is yes. Otherwise, just leave it where it is.

4. At this point, the IA-32e address translation tables are located in the lower 4GB of memory. Since the logical processor is now operating in 64-bit Mode, if desired they can now be moved above the 4GB address boundary. If they are, a MOV CR3, RAX must then be executed to point CR3 to the relocated top-level directory (i.e., the PML4).

5. While the DS and ES data segments now adhere to the hardware-enforced flat model and start at virtual address 0, the FS and GS data segment base addresses that were loaded in IA-32e Mode are still valid and, because they are 32-bit addresses, are in the lower 4GB of address space:

   — Their base addresses can be changed to a different address in the lower 4GB by loading a data segment selector into the FS and/or GS segment registers that selects a data segment descriptor with a different 32-bit base address.

   — Alternatively, if the OS wishes to assign either data segment a 64-bit base address above the 4GB address boundary, it may do so by writing the 64-bit address to the FS_Base or GS_Base MSR using the WRMSR instruction.

6. At this point, it is safe to reenable maskable and NMI interrupts. The logical processor is also prepared to correctly handle software exception conditions or the execution of software interrupt instructions.

Part 7:
Other Topics

The Previous Part

Part 6 provided a detailed description of:

- Switching from Real Mode to Protected Mode.
- Switching from Protected Mode to IA-32e Mode.

This Part

Part 7 provides detailed descriptions of the following topics:

31 *Introduction to Virtualization Technology*

The Previous Chapter

The previous chapter described the process of switching from Protected Mode into the Compatibility SubMode of IA-32e Mode. It then described making the switch from Compatibility Mode into 64-bit Mode.

This Chapter

This chapter provides a basic introduction to Virtualization Technology and covers the following topics:

- OS: I Am the God of All Things!
- Virtualization Supervisor: Sure You Are (:<)
- Root versus Non-Root Mode.
- Detecting VMX Capability.
- Entering/Exiting VMX Mode.
- Entering VMX Mode.
- Exiting VMX Mode.
- Virtualization Elements/Terminology.
- Introduction to the VT Instructions.
- Introduction to the VMCS Data Structure.
- Preparing to Launch a Guest OS.
- Launching a Guest OS.
- Guest OS Suspension.
- Resuming a Guest OS.
- Some Warnings Regarding VMCS Accesses.

The Next Chapter

The next chapter provides a detailed description of System Management Mode (SMM). It includes the following topics:

- What Falls Under the Heading of System Management?
- The Genesis of SMM
- SMM Has Its Own Private Memory Space
- The Basic Elements of SMM
- A Very Simple Example Scenario
- How the Processor Knows the SM Memory Start Address
- Normal Operation, (Including Paging) Is Disabled
- The Organization of SM RAM
- Entering SMM
- Exiting SMM
- Caching from SM Memory
- Setting Up the SMI Handler in SM Memory
- Relocating the SM RAM Base Address
- SMM in an MP System
- SM Mode and Virtualization

Just an Introduction?

Yes, rather than a detailed description of every aspect of virtualization, this chapter provides an introduction. Complete coverage of all aspects of virtualization would entail the addition of several hundred additional pages to an already oversize book. As such, it warrants treatment as a separate topic.

Detailed Coverage of Virtualization

Comprehensive coverage of all aspects of virtualization is available in the following MindShare class offerings:

- Comprehensive PC Virtualization:
  - Instructor-led class. Duration: 4 days.
  - Instructor-led internet class. Duration: 5 days.
- Fundamentals of PC Virtualization:
  - Instructor-led class. Duration: 1 day.
  - Instructor-led internet class. Duration: 1 day.
- Introduction to Virtualization Technology:
  - Self-paced E-Learning Module.

- Introduction to PCI Express IO Virtualization:
  — Self-paced E-Learning Module.
- Comprehensive IO Virtualization:
  — Instructor-led class. Duration: 2 days.
  — Instructor-led internet class. Duration: 3 days.

Detailed information about MindShare's training classes and E-Learning modules may be found at www.mindshare.com.

The Intel Model

Although the basic concepts are the same, Intel and AMD have implemented vendor-specific approaches to virtualization. This chapter focuses on the Intel model.

OS: *I Am the God of All Things!*

A traditional OS (e.g., Windows XP, Windows 7, Mac OS X) has complete control of all of the logical processor's facilities:

- It executes at privilege level 0 and can therefore:
  — Access any register.
  — Control the logical processor's operational mode (i.e., whether it is in Real Mode, Protected Mode, IA-32e Mode, etc.).
  — Execute any instruction in the instruction set.
- It manages memory for all software (including itself).
- Under software control, it handles task switching among the various program's that are currently being executed.
- **Permission violation**. It manages all of the x86 protection mechanisms. If an application program attempts to touch something beyond its permission level (e.g., memory, an IO port, a Control Register, etc.), a software exception is generated which immediately returns control back to the OS kernel.
- **Action evaluation**. The kernel then evaluates the attempted action and determines how to handle it:
  — **Action permitted**. If the action would not prove detrimental to any other currently-suspended software entity, the OS may decide to permit it. In that case, the OS can execute the offending instruction itself (unlike the interrupted application program, it has sufficient privilege to do so) and then return to the interrupted program at the instruction immediately after the one that caused the exception.

— **Forbidden action**. If the attempted action is one that *would* prove detrimental to other currently-suspended software entities, the OS can handle it in either of two ways:

    – **Emulate attempted action**. The OS might choose to achieve the same goal by performing a set of actions that will not result in chaos for one or more other software entities that are currently-suspended.

    – **Abort the application**. If, in the OS's opinion, the attempted action cannot safely be permitted, it may choose to issue an alert message to the end user and then abort the errant application.

In a nutshell, the OS believes itself to be lord of all it surveys. While this *is* true under ordinary circumstances, it's *not* so when virtualization is enabled.

Virtualization Supervisor: *Sure You Are (:<)*

When the logical processor's Virtualization Technology (VT) feature (referred to as the *Virtual Mode Extensions, or VMX*) is enabled, the old gods (i.e., OSs) are subjugated to a new, all powerful God—the *Virtual Machine Monitor, or VMM* (otherwise referred to as the *hypervisor*). The hypervisor permits guest OSs to run under its guidance, allowing each to run either for a preallocated period of time (a *timeslice*) or until the guest OS attempts a sensitive operation that might prove harmful to another, currently-suspended guest OS or to the hypervisor itself (i.e., a *sensitive* operation).

Root versus Non-Root Mode

Refer to Figure 31-1 on page 1151. When the logical processor is executing the hypervisor code, it is said to be in VMX *Root Mode*. Conversely, it is in *VMX Non-Root Mode* when it is executing one of the guest OSs.

Figure 31-1: VMX Mode Transitions

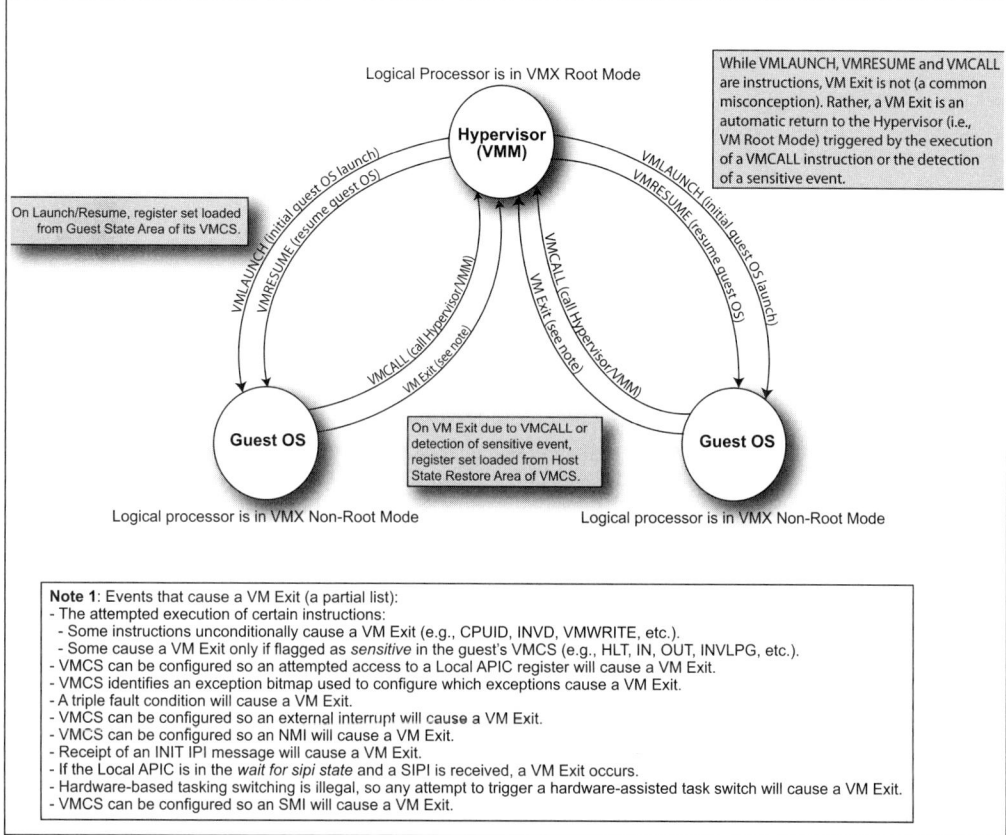

Detecting VMX Capability

A logical processor's support for VMX (Virtual Machine Extension) Mode is discovered by executing a CPUID request type 1. Additional information regarding a logical processor's VMX support may be found in the IA32_VMX_BASIC MSR (see Figure 31-2 on page 1152).

Figure 31-2: IA32_VMX_Basic MSR

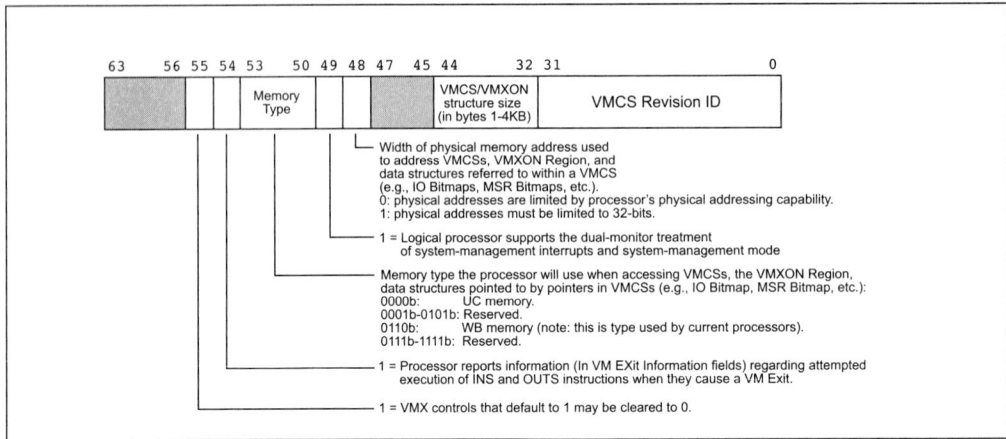

Entering/Exiting VMX Mode

Entering VMX Mode

A 2-step process:

1. Prior to entering VMX Mode, the programmer must first set CR4[13] to 1 (this is the VMX Enable—VMXE— bit).
2. VMX operation is then activated by executing the VMXON instruction.

The logical processor is then operating in VMX Root Mode.

Exiting VMX Mode

A 2-step process:

1. Execute the VMXOFF instruction.
2. Clear CR4[13] to 0. Note: this bit cannot be cleared before the VMXOFF instruction is executed.

Virtualization Elements/Terminology

There are a number of elements associated with the virtualization mechanism:

1. **Virtualization-related instructions**. A handful of new instructions have been added to the instruction set to support the virtualization feature (see Table 31-1 on page 1154).

2. **Hypervisor/VMM**. Frequently referred to as the hypervisor (Virtual Machine Monitor, or VMM), this top-level software entity is tasked with supervising the execution of multiple operating systems (referred to as guest OSs) and ensuring that they don't interfere with each other (or with the hypervisor itself). *A good analogy: the hypervisor is to the guest OSs running under its supervision what the OS task scheduler is to application programs running under its supervision.*

3. **Virtual Machine (VM)**. A guest OS running under the hypervisor's supervision and within the operating environment created by the hypervisor are collectively referred to as a *VM*.

4. **Monitor hardware**. Launching or resuming the execution of a guest OS causes the logical processor to transition from VMX Root Mode to VMX Non-Root Mode and automatically activates hardware-based logic that monitors for any guest OS attempt to perform a sensitive operation. When the hypervisor initiates or resumes the execution of a guest OS (i.e., a VM), this logic monitors the behavior of the guest OS and automatically triggers a transition (referred to as a *VM exit*) from Non-Root Mode back to Root Mode upon detection of an attempt to perform a sensitive operation. The hypervisor then evaluates the guest OS's attempted action and decides how to handle it in a manner that will, while achieving the guest OS's goal, not disturb the other guest OSs or the hypervisor itself.

5. **VMCS**. The hypervisor creates a customized, memory-based data structure—the Virtual Machine Control Structure—for each guest OS that will be run under its supervision. Among other things, the content of the VMCS defines the various event types (*sensitive* events) which trigger an automatic transition from Non-Root back to Root Mode operation (i.e., from the guest OS back to the hypervisor). The cause of the transition is also recorded in the VMCS so it can be evaluated by the hypervisor. The VMCS also contains information that instructs the logical processor regarding the operational environment under which the guest OS will run (Real Mode, Protected Mode, IA-32e Mode, paging on or off, etc.).

x86 Instruction Set Architecture

Introduction to the VT Instructions

Table 31-1 on page 1154 provides a basic description of the VMX-related instructions.

Table 31-1: VMX-related Instructions

Instruction	Basic Description
VMX Management Instructions	
VMLAUNCH	When executed by the hypervisor, causes the logical processor to launch (for the first time) the guest OS associated with the currently-active VMCS.
VMRESUME	When executed by the hypervisor, causes the logical processor to resume the execution of the guest OS associated with the currently-active VMCS.
VMXON	Enables VMX operation in Root Mode. The 4KB-aligned memory address specified as the operand identifies an area of memory (referred to as the VMXON area) that the hypervisor may use for temporary storage while the logical processor is in VMX Root Mode.
VMXOFF	Causes the logical processor to disable VMX operation and exit Root Mode. The logical processor returns to normal (non-VMX) operation.
VMCALL	A guest OS that is aware of the hypervisor's existence (an enlightened OS, indeed; one that has a personal relationship with God) can use the VMCALL instruction to trigger a VM exit back to the hypervisor. Prior to doing so, it would load a request and its associated parameters (if any) into the logical processor's register set. Upon interrogating the VMCS status area, the hypervisor would detect that the transition was caused by a VMCALL and would then determine the request type by examining the contents of the guest OS's registers.

Table 31-1: VMX-related Instructions (Continued)

Instruction	Basic Description
VMX Maintenance Instructions	
VMCLEAR	This instruction causes: • The logical processor to flush its internal copy of the VMCS out to memory in preparation for switching to the next guest's VMCS as part of the scheduling process. • The logical processor to initialize the VMCS whose base address is supplied as the instruction operand. It performs a series of memory writes to initialize some of the VMCS fields in memory. Which fields are written and how the logical processor uses them is processor design-specific. • The logical processor sets the memory-based VMCS's Clear/Launched indicator field to the Clear state (indicating that the associated guest OS has not yet been started). • If the specified VMCS base address = the address of the currently-active VMCS, the currently-active VMCS address in the logical processor is marked invalid (set to all Fs).
VMPTRLD	VM pointer Load. The 4KB-aligned VMCS base address specified as the operand is latched and marked as the currently-active VMCS.
VMPTRST	VM Pointer Store. Causes the logical processor to store the 64-bit base address of the currently-active VMCS into the specified memory location.

Table 31-1: VMX-related Instructions (Continued)

Instruction	Basic Description
VMREAD VMWRITE	Although the programmer specifies the 4KB-aligned base address of the VMCS associated with a guest OS, the placement and width of the various fields within the VMCS are processor-design specific. For this reason, they must be addressed indirectly using the VMREAD and VMWRITE instructions. The programmer specifies the following operands: • Identifies the target VMCS field using its identifier. • Identifies a memory or register operand as the other operand. • If it's a read, the target VMCS field is read and then written to the specified register or memory location. • If it's a write, the write data specified in memory or a register is written to the specified VMCS field. It should be noted that data written to the VMCS using the VMWRITE instruction may only update the logical processor's internal copy of the target VMCS field (and not the respective field in the memory-based copy of the VMCS). It may not actually be committed to memory until the VMCLEAR instruction is executed.
VMX TLB Management Instructions	
INVEPT	Invalidate TLB's copy of the virtual-to-physical translation (i.e., Page Table Entry or Page Directory Entry) obtained using the specified EPT (Extended Page Table).
INVVPID	Invalidate only the virtual-to-physical translations associated with the specified VPID (Virtual Processor ID).

Introduction to the VMCS Data Structure

The Virtual Machine Control Structure is subdivided into the regions introduced in Table 31-2 on page 1157. Its overall size as well as the fields it is comprised of, their width and their position within the VMCS is processor model-specific. For this reason, they must only be accessed indirectly using the VMREAD and VMWRITE instructions. The VMCS region consists of:

- The 32-bit VMCS Revision ID.
- The 32-bit VMX Abort indicator (contains the reason that the logical processor was forced to abort the execution of a guest OS).

- The body of the VMCS, the layout and size of which is processor model-specific (see Table 31-2 on page 1157).

Table 31-2: VMCS Regions

Region	Basic Description
Guest State Save / Restore Area	• **On initial launch**. When the hypervisor first launches a guest OS, the logical processor automatically loads the registers that control its operating mode (e.g., CR0, CR3, CR4, RSP, RIP, Rflags, segment registers, etc.) from this area. • **On a VM exit**. When the guest OS attempts to execute a sensitive instruction or detects some other sensitive condition (one that causes the guest to be suspended and control to be returned to the hypervisor), the logical processor automatically saves the registers that control its operational state in this area of the VMCS. It then reloads the registers that control its operational state from the Host State Restore Area of the VMCS (see the next row) and resumes execution of the hypervisor. • **On VM reentry**. When the hypervisor resumes a guest OS, the logical processor automatically reloads its operational state from this area.
Host State Restore Area	On a VM exit, after first saving the registers that control its operational state in the Guest State Area, the logical processor then reloads the registers that control its operational state from the Host State Restore Area before resuming execution of the hypervisor.

Table 31-2: VMCS Regions (Continued)

Region	Basic Description
VM-Execution Control fields	• **Pin-Based VM-Execution Controls** control how the logical processor responds to events that are asynchronous to program execution (e.g., external hardware interrupts, NMIs, exhaustion of the VMX preemption timer). • **Processor-Based VM-Execution Controls**. Defines how the logical processor handles program-synchronous events (for the most part, whether or not specific instruction types will cause a VM exit). Examples: hlt, invlpg, mwait, rdpmc, rdtsc, CR3 load/store, CR8 load/store, mov DR, all IO instructions, IO addresses defined by the IO bitmap, MSR accesses defined by the MSR bitmap, monitor, pause, Local APIC register accesses, kernel register accesses, wbinvd, etc. • **Exception Bitmap**. A 32-bit memory-based bitmap that defines which software exceptions will cause a VM exit. • **IO Bitmaps**. An 8-kilobit memory-based bitmap (it actually consists of two bit maps) that defines which IO addresses will cause a VM exit. • **MSR bitmaps**. Memory-based bitmaps that define which MSR addresses will cause a VM exit. • **Guest/Host Masks and Read Shadows for CR0 and CR4.** On a bit-by-bit basis, the bits in CR0 and CR4 can be designated as being *owned* by either the guest OS or by the hypervisor. A guest OS attempt to alter a bit it doesn't own results in a VM exit. • **CR3**. Whether or not an access to CR3 will cause a VM exit. • **TPR**. Whether or not an access to the Local APIC's TPR will cause a VM exit. • Other, miscellaneous fields.

Table 31-2: VMCS Regions (Continued)

Region	Basic Description
VM-Exit Control fields	These fields control VM exits.: • Whether or not to save DR7 and the DBGCTRL registers on a VM exit. • Defines the values to be loaded into EFER[LME], EFER[LMA] and CS[L] on a VM exit. • Whether or not the IA32_PERF_GLOBAL_CTRL MSR is loaded on VM exit. • If an external interrupt causes a VM exit, whether or not the logical processor obtains the interrupt vector from the interrupt controller before the VM exit. • Whether or not to save and/or load the IA32_PAT register on a VM exit. • Whether or not to save and/or load the EFER MSR on a VM exit. • Whether or not to save the value in the VMX Preemption Timer on a VM exit. • Optionally, a list of MSRs to be saved or loaded on a VM exit.
VM-Entry Control fields	These fields control the entry to a guest OS: • Whether or not to load DR7 and the DBGCTRL registers from the VMCS on a VM Entry. • Whether to enter or stay in IA-32c Mode on entry to guest OS. • Whether or not to enter or stay in SMM on entry to guest OS. • Whether or not IA32_PERF_GLOBAL_CTRL MSR is loaded from the VMCS on VM entry. • Whether or not IA32_PAT MSR is loaded from the VMCS on VM entry. • Whether or not to load EFER MSR from the VMCS on VM entry. • An optional list of MSRs to be loaded from the VMCS on VM entry. • Whether or not to generate a specified interrupt as the guest OS is resumed.

Table 31-2: VMCS Regions (Continued)

Region	Basic Description
VM-Exit Information fields	These fields are updated with information regarding the cause and nature of a VM exit: • The reason for a VM exit or the failure of a VM entry. • A virtual or physical memory address associated with the VM exit. • Information about the interrupt or exception that caused the VM exit. • If the VM exit was caused by a specific instruction, information regarding the instruction. They are read-only.

Preparing to Launch a Guest OS

In preparation for launching a guest OS, software must accomplish the following:

1. Obtain the following information (not a complete list) from the IA32_VMX_BASIC MSR (see Figure 31-2 on page 1152):
   — The logical processor's VMCS Revision ID.
   — The size of the memory areas the logical processor requires for its VMX scratchpad memory (i.e., the VMXON area) and for the VMCS data structure associated with each guest OS. It will be a value between 1-byte and 4KB.
2. Reserve a block of memory (aligned on a 4KB address boundary; the size was obtained in step 1) as scratchpad memory (the VMXON area) to be used by the logical processor in VMX Root Mode.
3. Initialize the first 4-bytes of the scratchpad memory (the VMXON area) with the VMCS Revision ID obtained in step 1.
4. Execute the VMXON instruction specifying the start address of the scratchpad memory (the VMXON area) as its operand. In response, the logical processor:
   — Latches the start address of the VMXON memory area.
   — Sets its current VMCS pointer to an invalid value (all ones).
   — Enters VMX Root Mode.
   — Instructs its Local APIC to ignore any incoming INIT (soft reset) IPIs (Inter-Processor Interrupt) messages.
   — Disables the A20 Mask signal (so it can address memory above the 1MB address boundary).

— If the MONITOR instruction has been executed, disables the logical processor's address range monitoring logic.

5. Reserve a block of memory for the guest OS's VMCS (aligned on a 4KB address boundary; the size was obtained in step 1).

6. Initialize the first 4-bytes of the VMCS with the VMCS Revision ID obtained in step 1.

7. Execute the VMCLEAR instruction. This causes the following:
   — The logical processor verifies that the VMCS pointer specified as the instruction operand is not the same the VMXON instruction's scratch-pad memory pointer.
   — The logical processor verifies that the VMCS Revision ID in the VMCS's first 4-bytes is the same as the logical processor's VMCS Revision ID.
   — The logical processor initializes some of the guest OS's VMCS fields in memory (which fields and what they are initialized to is processor model-specific).
   — The logical processor sets the Clear/Launched indicator in the VMCS to the Clear state (indicating the guest OS has not yet been launched).
   — If the VMCS pointer specified as the instruction operand is the same as the logical processor's current VMCS pointer (i.e., the last one loaded by the VMPTRLD instruction), it invalidates its current pointer by setting it to all ones.

8. Execute the VMPTRLD instruction specifying the guest OS's VMCS base address as the operand. In response:
   — The logical processor verifies that the VMCS pointer specified as the instruction operand is not the same as the VMXON instruction's scratchpad memory pointer.
   — The logical processor verifies that the VMCS Revision ID in the VMCS's first 4-bytes is the same as the logical processor's VMCS Revision ID.
   — The logical processor marks the guest OS's VMCS as the active VMCS (but the guest *has not yet been launched*).

9. Using the VMWRITE instruction, initialize the various fields of the VMCS.

Launching a Guest OS

With everything now in place, let's launch the guest OS:

1. One of the key elements that the programmer initialized in the guest OS's VMCS was the initial value in the 32-bit VMX Preemption Timer field. More on this in step 3.

2. Execute the VMLAUNCH instruction. It does not have any operands. Rather, the logical processor uses the current guest OS's VMCS pointer (the one loaded into the logical processor using the VMPTRLD instruction) as

the operand. In response to the execution of VMLAUNCH, the logical processor takes the following actions (note that this is not a complete list):

— Validates that the Clear/Launched indicator in the VMCS is currently in the Clear state (indicating the guest OS has not yet been launched).
— Validates the contents of the VMX Controls and Host State Areas of the VMCS.
— Loads the logical processor's operational state from the Guest State Area of the VMCS. Note that the CS and Instruction Pointer values obtained from this area point to the guest OS entry point.
— If the MONITOR instruction was executed earlier, disables the logical processor's address range monitoring logic.
— Loads MSRs specified in VM Entry Control fields with values specified in the VMCS.
— Sets the Clear/Launched indicator in the VMCS to the Launched state.
— Enters VMX Non-Root Mode.

3. The logical processor loads its VMX Preemption Timer with the initial value programmed into the VMCS's VMX Preemption Timer field. The hypervisor uses this timer to assign a *timeslice* to the guest OS.

4. The logical processor begins to fetch and execute the guest OS's start-up code.

5. As the logical processor proceeds to execute the guest OS code, it begins decrementing the Preemption Timer. If no other event causes it to exit back to the hypervisor (i.e., back to VMX Root Mode), timer exhaustion will cause a transition.

Guest OS Suspension

Once it is initially launched (or resumed following an earlier suspension), a guest OS will be automatically suspended (and the logical processor will return to VMX Root Mode) under the following circumstances:

• **Sensitive operation**. Detection of a guest OS attempt to perform a sensitive operation. Some of the sensitive operations are unconditional while others can be defined as sensitive in the guest OS's VMCS.

• **VMCALL**. A guest OS that is aware of the hypervisor's existence can trigger a return to VMX Root Mode by executing the VMCALL instruction (see the description of VMCALL in Table 31-1 on page 1154).

• **Timeslice expired**. Expiration of the VMX Preemption Timer.

This results in a VM exit and the logical processor takes the following actions:

- It saves the contents of the registers that control its operational state in the Guest State Save/Restore Area of the VMCS.
- It saves information regarding the cause of the VM exit in the VM exit Information Area of the VMCS.
- It loads the registers that control its operational state from the Host State Area of the VMCS.
- It switches from VMX Non-Root Mode to Root Mode.
- It resumes execution of the hypervisor.

Handling Timeslice Expiration

If the cause of the suspension was timeslice expiration, the hypervisor saves the contents of the logical processor's general registers in a data structure associated with the suspended guest OS. This discussion is continued in "Resuming a Guest OS" on page 1163.

Handling a Sensitive Operation or a VMCALL

If the VM exit was triggered by the detection of a sensitive operation or by a VMCALL, in addition to the actions listed in "Guest OS Suspension" on page 1162, the hypervisor handles the sensitive operation or the VMCALL, restores the general registers, and then executes the VMRESUME instruction to return control to the guest OS at the point of interruption. It should be noted that the logical processor ceased decrementing the OS's Preemption Timer field (i.e., the OS's remaining timeslice value) after the exit and resumes decrementing it after the resumption of guest OS execution.

Resuming a Guest OS

The hypervisor triggers a return to a previously-suspended guest OS under the following circumstances:

- **Return from VMM handler.** The hypervisor has handled a guest OS's attempt to perform a sensitive operation and is now ready to resume execution of the guest OS. In this case, the hypervisor uses the VMRESUME instruction to resume execution of the currently-active guest OS.
- **Scheduled resumption.** The guest OS was previously-suspended due to exhaustion of the VMX Preemption Timer (in other words, its timeslice had expired). The hypervisor then launched or resumed the execution of

another guest OS which, in turn, was suspended due to an attempted sensitive or a timer timeout. It is now ready to resume execution of a previously-suspended guest OS. In this case, the hypervisor uses the VMLAUNCH instruction to relaunch execution of the previously-suspended guest OS.

This example assumes the scheduled resumption of a previously-suspended guest OS:

1. Specifying the start memory address of the previously executing guest OS's VMCS as the operand, the hypervisor executes the VMCLEAR instruction to flush that guest OS's VMCS data to memory and set its Clear/Launched indicator to Clear.
2. It reinitializes the VMX Preemption Timer field in the VMCS of the guest OS about to be resumed.
3. The hypervisor then executes the VMPTRLD instruction specifying as its operand the start memory address of the VMCS associated with the guest OS to be resumed.
4. It restores the logical processor's general register set to its state at the point of earlier suspension.
5. It then executes the VMLAUNCH instruction to re-launch the previously suspended guest OS.
6. The logical processor validates that the Clear/Launched indicator in the VMCS is in the Clear state.
7. The logical processor validates the contents of the VMX Controls and Host State Restore Areas of the VMCS.
8. The logical processor loads the registers that govern its operational mode from the Guest State Area of the VMCS. Note that the CS and Instruction Pointer values obtained from this VMCS area point to the next instruction that would have been executed if a VM exit had not occurred.
9. If the MONITOR instruction was executed earlier, The logical processor disables the logical processor's address range monitoring logic.
10. The logical processor loads the MSRs specified in VM Entry Control fields with the values specified in the VMCS.
11. The logical processor exits VMX Root Mode and enters VMX Non-Root Mode.
12. The logical processor loads its VMX Preemption Timer with the initial value programmed into the VMCS's VMX Preemption Timer field. The hypervisor uses this timer to assign a *timeslice* to the guest OS.
13. The logical processor resumes the execution of the guest OS.
14. As the logical processor proceeds to execute the guest OS code, it begins decrementing the Preemption Timer (note: the timer is only decremented while the logical processor is in Non Root Mode). If no other event causes it to exit back to the hypervisor (i.e., back to VMX Root Mode), timer exhaustion will trigger a transition.

Some Warnings Regarding VMCS Accesses

Since the VMCS layout is processor model-specific (and is not published and can change from model to model!), software should never access the memory-based VMCS using direct memory reads and writes. It should only be accessed using the VMREAD and VMWRITE instructions (because only the processor knows the exact layout of its design-specific VMCS).

Accessing the VMCS data structure is solely the province of the hypervisor. The attempted execution of a VMWRITE or VMREAD by a guest OS triggers a VM exit back to the hypervisor.

32 *System Management Mode (SMM)*

The Previous Chapter

The previous chapter provided a basic introduction to Virtualization Technology and covered the following topics:

- OS: I Am the God of All Things!
- Virtualization Supervisor: Sure You Are (:<)
- Root versus Non-Root Mode.
- Detecting VMX Capability.
- Entering/Exiting VMX Mode.
- Entering VMX Mode.
- Exiting VMX Mode.
- Virtualization Elements/Terminology.
- Introduction to the VT Instructions.
- Introduction to the VMCS Data Structure.
- Preparing to Launch a Guest OS.
- Launching a Guest OS.
- Guest OS Suspension.
- Resuming a Guest OS.
- Some Warnings Regarding VMCS Accesses.

This Chapter

This chapter provides a detailed description of System Management Mode (SMM). It includes the following topics:

- What Falls Under the Heading of System Management?
- The Genesis of SMM

- SMM Has Its Own Private Memory Space
- The Basic Elements of SMM
- A Very Simple Example Scenario
- How the Processor Knows the SM Memory Start Address
- Normal Operation, (Including Paging) Is Disabled
- The Organization of SM RAM
- Entering SMM
- Exiting SMM
- Caching from SM Memory
- Setting Up the SMI Handler in SM Memory
- Relocating the SM RAM Base Address
- SMM in an MP System
- SM Mode and Virtualization

The Next Chapter

The next chapter provides a detailed description of the Machine Check Architecture (MCA):

- The MCA Elements.
- The Global Registers.
- The Composition of a Register Bank.
- The Error Code.
- Cache Error Reporting.
- MC Exception Is Generally Not Recoverable.

What Falls Under the Heading of System Management?

The types of operations that typically fall under the heading of System Management are power management and management of the system's thermal environment (e.g., temperature monitoring in the platform's various thermal zones and fan control). It should be stressed, however, that system management is not necessarily limited to these specific areas.

The following are some example situations that would require action by the SM handler program:

- A laptop chipset implements a timer that tracks how long it's been since the hard drive was last accessed. If this timer should elapse, the chipset generates an SMI (System Management Interrupt) to the processor to invoke the SM handler program. In the handler, software checks a chipset-specific status register to determine the cause of the SMI (in this case, a prolonged cessation of accesses to the hard drive). In response, the SM handler issues a command to the hard disk controller to spin down the spindle motor (to save on energy consumption).

- A laptop chipset implements a timer that tracks how long it's been since the keyboard and/or mouse was used. If this timer should elapse, the chipset generates an SMI to the processor to invoke the SM handler program. In the handler, software checks a chipset-specific status register to determine the cause of the SMI (in this case, a prolonged cessation of user interaction). In response, the SM handler issues a command to the display controller to dim or turn off the display's backlighting (to save on energy consumption).

- In a server platform, the chipset or system board logic detects that a thermal sensor in a specific zone of the platform is experiencing a rise in temperature. It generates an SMI to the processor to invoke the SM handler program. In the handler, software checks a chipset-specific status register to determine the cause of the SMI (in this case, a potential overheat condition). In response, the SM handler issues a command to the system board's fan control logic to turn on an exhaust fan in that zone.

The Genesis of SMM

Intel first implemented SMM in the 386SL processor and it has not changed very much since then. While it was not present in the earlier 486 models, it was implemented in all of the later models of the 486 and in all subsequent x86 processors. SMM is entered by generating an SMI (System Management Interrupt) to the processor. Prior to the P54C version of the Pentium, the chipset could only deliver the interrupt to the processor by asserting the processor's SMI# input pin. Starting with the P54C (which was the first IA-32 processor to incorporate the Local APIC) and up to and including the Pentium III, the chipset could also deliver the interrupt to the processor by sending an SMI IPI (Inter-Processor Interrupt) message to the processor over the 3-wire APIC bus. With the advent of the Pentium 4, the 3-wire APIC bus was eliminated and IPIs (including the SMI IPI) are sent to and from a logical processor by performing a special memory write transaction on the processor's external interface.

With the advent of the P54C processor, SMM was enhanced to include the IO Instruction Restart feature (described in this chapter).

The base address of the area of memory assigned to System Management Mode (SMM) has a default value of 30000h. While it could be reprogrammed on the earlier IA-32 processors, the newly-assigned address had to be aligned on an address that was evenly divisible by 32K. Starting with the Pentium Pro, this constraint was eliminated.

SMM Has Its Own Private Memory Space

Prior to the generation of an SMI to the logical processor, the chipset directs all memory accesses generated by the logical processor to system RAM memory:

- When interrupted by an SMI, the logical processor signals to the chipset that all subsequent memory accesses generated by the logical processor are to be directed to a special, separate area of memory referred to as SM RAM.
- Upon concluding the execution of the SM handler program, the logical processor signals to the chipset that all subsequent memory accesses generated by the logical processor are to be directed to system RAM memory rather than SM RAM.

The platform vendor's implementation of SM RAM can be up to 4GB in size.

The Basic Elements of SMM

The following is a list of the basic elements associated with SMM:

- The processor's SMI# input.
- The APIC SMI IPI message.
- The chipset/system board logic responsible for monitoring conditions within the platform that might require an invocation of the SM handler program.
- Chipset's ability to assert SMI# to invoke the SMI handler.
- The chipset's ability to send an SMI IPI message to the logical processor to invoke the SMI handler.
- The Resume (RSM) instruction which must always be the last instruction executed in the SM handler.
- The SM RAM area.
- The logical processor's context state save/restore area (i.e., data structure) in SM memory.
  — 512-bytes for an IA-32 processor.
  — 1024-bytes for an Intel 64 processor.
- The SMI Acknowledge message was added to the message repertoire of the Special transaction.
- On processors that utilize the FSB external interface, the processor's SMMEM# output (also referred to as the EFX4# output).
- The chipset's ability to discern when the processor is addressing regular RAM memory versus SM RAM memory. On processors that utilize the FSB external interface, it does this by monitoring for the processor's issuance of the SMI Acknowledge message and whether or not the processor is asserting the SMMEM# signal during a processor-initiated memory transaction.

A Very Simple Example Scenario

Assume that the platform logic (i.e., the chipset or the system board logic) detects a condition that requires management by the SM handler program (see "What Falls Under the Heading of System Management?" on page 1168 for some examples). In response, an SMI is generated to the logical processor. The following sequence of events occurs (this description assumes that the processor is a Pentium Pro or a subsequent IA-32 or Intel 64 processor; it also assumes that the processor utilizes the FSB external interface):

1. The logical processor recognizes the SMI on the next instruction boundary and suspends execution of the currently executing program.
2. The logical processor generates a Special transaction on its external interface and outputs the SMI Acknowledge message to inform the chipset that, until it generates another SMI Acknowledge message, all memory accesses generated by the logical processor are to be directed to SM memory rather than to regular RAM memory.
3. The logical processor then generates a series of memory write transactions on its external interface to store a snapshot of it registers in the State Save Area of SM memory. This is done so the logical processor can, at the conclusion of the execution of the SM handler program, resume execution of the interrupted program.
4. The logical processor then begins to execute the SM handler program.
5. The last instruction in the handler is the Resume (RSM) instruction. When executed, it causes the logical processor to automatically generate a series of memory read transactions on its external interface to reload its register set from the State Save Area of SM memory.
6. The logical processor generates a Special transaction on its external interface and outputs the SMI Acknowledge message to inform the chipset that, from this point forward, all memory accesses generated by the logical processor are to be directed to regular memory rather than to SM RAM memory.

How the Processor Knows the SM Memory Start Address

Although it's already been pointed out that the SM handler program and the SM State Save area are located in SM RAM, the question remains: What location contains the first instruction of the SMM handler?

After a reset or a power-up, the SM logic within the logical processor is initialized so that the first instruction of the SM handler will be fetched from memory address 38000h in SM RAM. As will be seen later (in "Relocating the SM RAM Base Address" on page 1204), this address can be altered while the logical processor is executing the SM handler program.

Normal Operation, (Including Paging) Is Disabled

As will be described in "The Register Settings on Initiation of the SM Handler" on page 1190, normal operation and virtual to physical address translation is disabled on entry to SMM handler. All memory addresses generated by the instruction fetch logic and as the result of instruction execution are therefore treated as physical memory accesses.

The Organization of SM RAM

General

Refer to Figure 32-1 on page 1174. As mentioned earlier, the SM handler program can access up to 4GB of SM memory address space. After a reset or power-up, the logical processor's SM Base address is preset to address 00030000h and it determines the address of the following locations relative to the SM Base address:

- The entry point into the SM handler program = the SM Base address + 8000h. Since the default value of the SM Base address is 00030000h, this defines the default entry point address to be 00030000h + 8000h = 00038000h.
- The *end* address (*not* the start address) of the State Save Area wherein the logical processor saves its register set on entry to SMM is calculated as follows:
  — The SM Base address (00030000h) + 8000h + 7FFFh = **0003FFFFh**. The default save area therefore consumes the area from:
    - **In an IA-32 processor**, locations 3FE00h to 3FFFFh. 3FE00h is the default start address of the 512-byte State Save Area.
    - **In an Intel 64 processor**, locations 3FC00h to 3FFFFh. 3FC00h is the default start address of the 1024-byte State Save Area.
  The SM Base address can be altered while the logical processor is executing the SM handler program. This topic is covered in "Relocating the SM RAM Base Address" on page 1204.

Do not think of the SM Base address as defining the SM memory start address. As shown in Figure 32-1 on page 1174, the true start address of SM memory is memory address 00000000h. *The address that Intel refers to as the SM Base address is the one used by the logical processor to calculate where the entry point of the SM handler and the start address of the State Save Area are within the 4GB SM memory space.* Remember that the SM Base address can be altered while the logical processor is executing the SM handler program (see "Relocating the SM RAM Base Address" on page 1204).

IA-32 Processor SM State Save Area

Whenever the logical processor enters SMM, it automatically saves its register set in the State Save Area. Table 32-1 on page 1174 defines the format of the 512-byte State Save Area for an IA-32 processor (*the format shown is Intel-specific; AMD uses a different format*). Some of the fields are read-only while others are read-writable. Those marked read-writable can be altered while the logical processor is executing the SM handler. Additional information on the State Save Area can be found in subsequent sections of this chapter.

Figure 32-1: SM RAM Memory Map

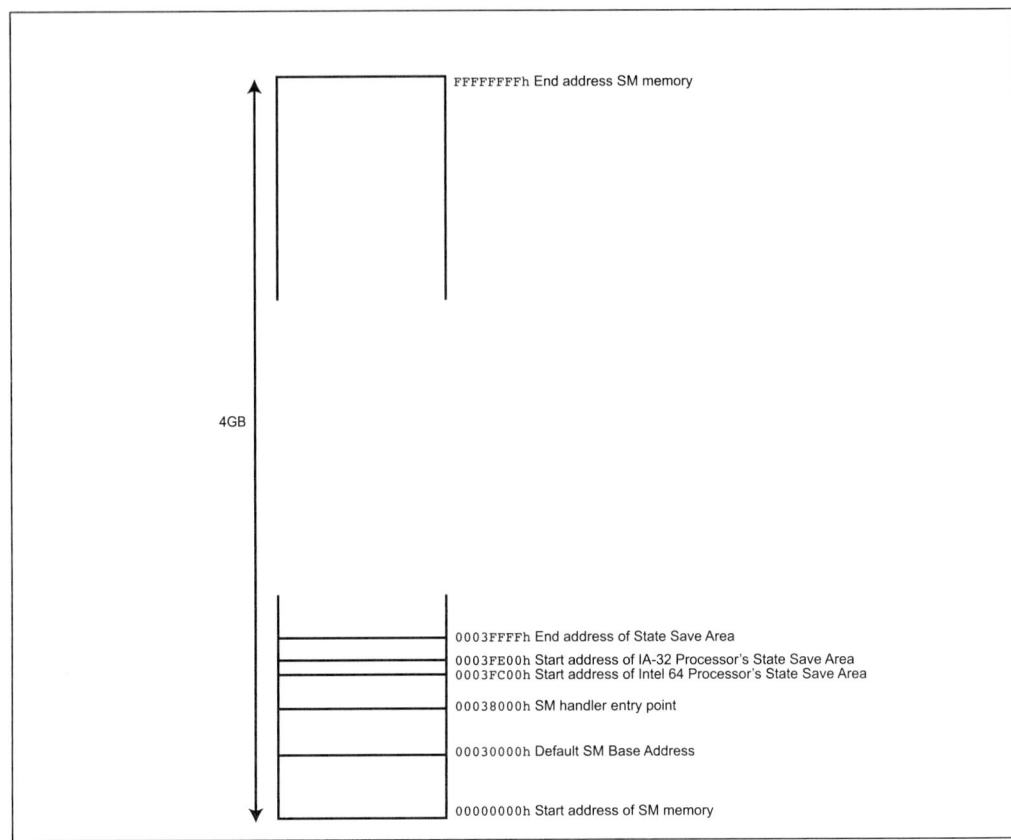

Table 32-1: IA-32 SM RAM State Save Area (shown from the top down)

Location in Save Area (SMBase + 8000h + the Offset shown)	Width (in bytes)	Register Image	Read/ Write?
7FFCh-7FFFh	4	CR0	No
7FF8h-7FFBh	4	CR3	No
7FF4h-7FF7h	4	Eflags	Yes

Table 32-1: IA-32 SM RAM State Save Area (shown from the top down) (Continued)

Location in Save Area (SMBase + 8000h + the Offset shown)	Width (in bytes)	Register Image	Read/ Write?
7FF0h-7FF3h	4	EIP	Yes
7FECh-7FEFh	4	EDI	Yes
7FE8h-7FEBh	4	ESI	Yes
7FE4h-7FE7h	4	EBP	Yes
7FE0h-7FE3h	4	ESP	Yes
7FDCh-7FDFh	4	EBX	Yes
7FD8h-7FDBh	4	EDX	Yes
7FD4h-7FD7h	4	ECX	Yes
7FD0h-7FD3h	4	EAX	Yes
7FCCh-7FCFh	4	DR6	No
7FC8h-7FCBh	4	DR7	No
7FC6h-7FC7h	2	Reserved	
7FC4h-7FC5h	2	TR. The Task Register register is only 2 bytes wide, but the logical processor saves a 4 byte image. The upper 2 bytes are reserved and are shown in the row prior to this one.	No
7FC0h-7FC3h	4	Reserved	No
7FBEh-7FBFh	2	Reserved	
7FBCh-7FBDh	2	GS. The segment registers are only 2 bytes wide, but the logical processor saves a 4 byte image. The upper 2 bytes are reserved and are shown in the row prior to this one.	No

Table 32-1: IA-32 SM RAM State Save Area (shown from the top down) (Continued)

Location in Save Area (SMBase + 8000h + the Offset shown)	Width (in bytes)	Register Image	Read/ Write?
7FBAh-7FBBh	2	Reserved	
7FB8h-7FB9h	2	FS. The segment registers are only 2 bytes wide, but the logical processor saves a 4 byte image. The upper 2 bytes are reserved and are shown in the row prior to this one.	No
7FB6h-7FB7h	2	Reserved	
7FB4h-7FB5h	2	DS. The segment registers are only 2 bytes wide, but the logical processor saves a 4 byte image. The upper 2 bytes are reserved and are shown in the row prior to this one.	No
7FB2h-7FB3h	2	Reserved	
7FB0h-7FB1h	2	SS. The segment registers are only 2 bytes wide, but the logical processor saves a 4 byte image. The upper 2 bytes are reserved and are shown in the row prior to this one.	No
7FAEh-7FAFh	2	Reserved	
7FACh-7FADh	2	CS. The segment registers are only 2 bytes wide, but the logical processor saves a 4 byte image. The upper 2 bytes are reserved and are shown in the row prior to this one.	No
7FAAh-7FABh	2	Reserved	

Table 32-1: IA-32 SM RAM State Save Area (shown from the top down) (Continued)

Location in Save Area (SMBase + 8000h + the Offset shown)	Width (in bytes)	Register Image	Read/ Write?
7FA8h-7FA9h	2	ES. The segment registers are only 2 bytes wide, but the logical processor saves a 4 byte image. The upper 2 bytes are reserved and are shown in the row prior to this one.	No
7FA4h-7FA7h	4	IO State field. See "Multiprocessor System Presents a Problem" on page 1196.	No
7FA0h-7FA3h	4	IO Memory Address Field. See "Multiprocessor System Presents a Problem" on page 1196.	No
7F04h-7FA7h	164	This 41 dword area is Reserved.	No
7F02h-7F03h	2	Auto HALT Restart Field. See "The Auto Halt Restart Feature" on page 1193.	Yes
7F00h-7F01h	2	IO Instruction Restart Field. See "The IO Instruction Restart Feature" on page 1195.	Yes
7EFCh-7EFFh	4	SMM Revision Identifier Field. See "The SMM Revision ID" on page 1191.	No
7EF8h-7EFBh	4	SMBase Field. See "Relocating the SM RAM Base Address" on page 1204.	Yes
7E00h-7EF7h	248	This 62 dword area is Reserved.	No

Intel 64 Processor SM Save Area

On an Intel 64 processor, the SM Save area is expanded from 512- to 1024-bytes and the *end* address (*not* the start address) of the 1024-byte Save Area wherein the logical processor saves its register set on entry to SMM is calculated in the same manner as it is on an IA-32 processor:

* The SM Base address (00030000h) + 8000h + 7FFFh = **0003FFFFh**. The default 1024-byte save area therefore consumes the area from location 3FC00h to 3FFFFh. 3FC00h is the default State Save Area start address. The SM Base address (and therefore the Save Area end address) can be altered while the logical processor is executing the SM handler program. This topic is covered in "Relocating the SM RAM Base Address" on page 1204.

Table 32-2 on page 1178 shows the format of the State Save Area for an Intel 64 processor (*the format shown is Intel-specific; AMD uses a different format*). It should be noted that this format is used *regardless of what mode the logical processor is in* when the SMI (SM interrupt) is detected. Some of the fields are read-only while others are read-writable. Those marked read-writable can be altered while the logical processor is executing the SM handler. Additional information on the State Save Area can be found in subsequent sections of this chapter.

Table 32-2: Intel 64 Processor SMRAM State Save Area

Location in Save Area (SMBase + 8000h + the Offset shown)	Width (in bytes)	Register Image	Read/ Write?
7FF8h-7FFFh	8	CR0	No
7FF0h-7FF7h	8	CR3	No
7FE8h-7FEFh	8	RFlags	Yes
7FE0h-7FE7h	8	IA32_EFER	Yes
7FD8h-7FDFh	8	RIP	Yes
7FD0h-7FD7h	8	DR6	No
7FC8h-7FCFh	8	DR7	No
7FC4h-7FC7h	4	TR selector (upper 2-bytes reserved).	No

Table 32-2: Intel 64 Processor SMRAM State Save Area (Continued)

Location in Save Area (SMBase + 8000h + the Offset shown)	Width (in bytes)	Register Image	Read/ Write?
7FC0h-7FC3h	4	LDTR selector (upper 2-bytes reserved).	No
7FBCh-7FBFh	4	GS selector (upper 2-bytes reserved).	No
7FB8h-7FBBh	4	FS selector (upper 2-bytes reserved).	No
7FB4h-7FB7h	4	DS selector (upper 2-bytes reserved).	No
7FB0h-7FB3h	4	SS selector (upper 2-bytes reserved).	No
7FACh-7FAFh	4	CS selector (upper 2-bytes reserved).	No
7FA8h-7FABh	4	ES selector (upper 2-bytes reserved).	No
7FA4h-7FA7h	4	IO State field. See "Multiprocessor System Presents a Problem" on page 1196.	No
7F9Ch-7FA3h	8	IO Memory Address Field. See "Multiprocessor System Presents a Problem" on page 1196.	No
7F94h-7F9Bh	8	RDI	Yes
7F8Ch-7F93h	8	RSI	Yes
7F84h-7F8Bh	8	RBP	Yes
7F7Ch-7F83h	8	RSP	Yes
7F74h-7F7Bh	8	RBX	Yes
7F6Ch-7F73h	8	RDX	Yes

Table 32-2: Intel 64 Processor SMRAM State Save Area (Continued)

Location in Save Area (SMBase + 8000h + the Offset shown)	Width (in bytes)	Register Image	Read/ Write?
7F64h-7F6Bh	8	RCX	Yes
7F5Ch-7F63h	8	RAX	Yes
7F54h-7F5Bh	8	R8	Yes
7F4Ch-7F53h	8	R9	Yes
7F44h-7F4Bh	8	R10	Yes
7F3Ch-7F43h	8	R11	Yes
7F34h-7F3Bh	8	R12	Yes
7F2Ch-7F33h	8	R13	Yes
7F24h-7F2Bh	8	R14	Yes
7F1Ch-7F23h	8	R15	Yes
7F04h-7F1Bh	24	Reserved	No
7F02h-7F03h	2	Auto HALT Restart Field. See "The Auto Halt Restart Feature" on page 1193.	Yes
7F00h-7F01h	2	IO Instruction Restart Field. See "The IO Instruction Restart Feature" on page 1195.	Yes
7EFCh-7EFFh	4	SMM Revision Identifier Field. See "The SMM Revision ID" on page 1191.	No
7EF8h-7EFBh	4	SMBASE Field. See "Relocating the SM RAM Base Address" on page 1204.	Yes
7EE4h-7EF7h	20	Reserved	No

Table 32-2: Intel 64 Processor SMRAM State Save Area (Continued)

Location in Save Area (SMBase + 8000h + the Offset shown)	Width (in bytes)	Register Image	Read/ Write?
7EE0h-7EE3h	4	Setting of enable Extended Page Table (EPT) VM-execution control.	No
7ED8h-7EDFh	8	Value of Extended Page Table Pointer (EPTP) VM-execution control field.	No
7EA8h-7ED7h	48	Reserved	No
7EA4h-7EA7h	4	LDT Info.	No
7EA0h-7EA3h	4	LDT Limit	No
7E9Ch-7E9Fh	4	LDT Base (lower 32 bits). Upper 32-bits are in locations 7DD4h-7DD7h.	No
7E98h-7E9Bh	4	IDT Limit	No
7E94h-7E97h	4	IDT Base (lower 32 bits). Upper 32-bits are in locations 7DD8h-7DDBh.	No
7E90h-7E93h	4	GDT Limit	No
7E8Ch-7E8Fh	4	GDT Base (lower 32 bits). Upper 32-bits are in locations 7DD0h-7DD3h.	No
7E44h-7E8Bh	72	Reserved	No
7E40h-7E43h	4	CR4	No
7DF0h-7E3Fh	80	Reserved	No
7DE8h-7DEFh	8	IO_EIP.	Yes
7DDCh-7DE7h	12	Reserved	No

Table 32-2: Intel 64 Processor SMRAM State Save Area (Continued)

Location in Save Area (SMBase + 8000h + the Offset shown)	Width (in bytes)	Register Image	Read/ Write?
7DD8h-7DDBh	4	IDT Base (Upper 32 bits). Lower 32-bits are in locations 7E94h-7E97h.	No
7DD4h-7DD7h	4	LDT Base (Upper 32 bits). Lower 32-bits are in locations 7E9Ch-7E9Fh.	No
7DD0h-7DD3h	4	GDT Base (Upper 32 bits). Lower 32-bits are in locations 7E8Ch-7E8Fh.	No
7C00h-7DCFh	464	Reserved	No

Protecting Access to SM Memory

If a processor supports the SM Range Register pair (see Figure 32-2 on page 1183), the programmer may protect access to the area of memory designated as SM memory by programming the register pair shown in Figure 32-3 on page 1183 (these registers may only be written to while the logical processor is in SM Mode; any attempt to write to them outside of SM Mode results in the generation of a GP exception). Refer to "Programming Variable-Range Register Pairs" on page 609 for examples of how to program this register pair.

Any attempt to write to the SM Range register pair on a processor that doesn't support this feature results in the generation of a GP exception. Assuming the logical processor supports this feature and that the register pair has been programmed and enabled, when an access attempt to SM memory is detected the logical processor reacts as follows:

- **Logical processor is in SM Mode**. The access is permitted using the memory type specified in SMRR_PhysBase register.
- **Logical processor is not in SM Mode**. Writes are ignored and reads return a fixed, processor design-specific value. The access is treated as one to UC memory.

These rules apply even if the address range accessed overlaps with one specified by the MTRRs.

Figure 32-2: MTRRCAP Register

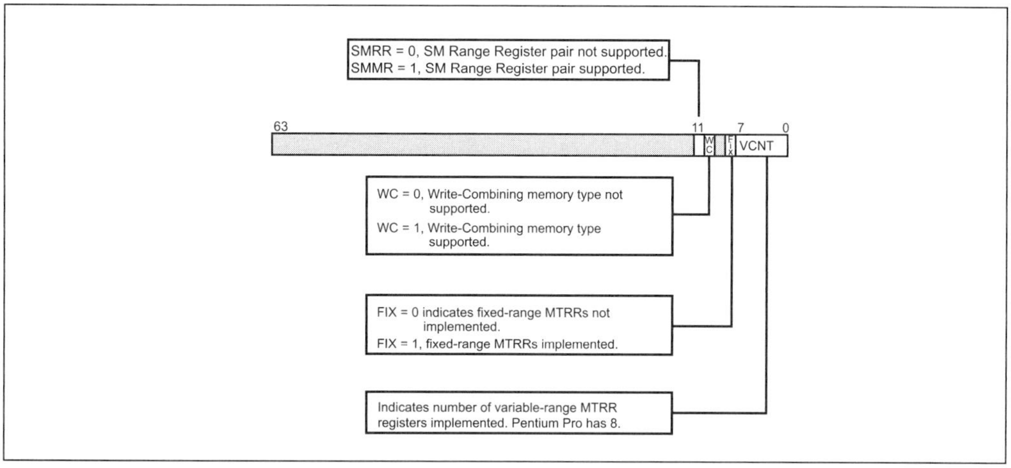

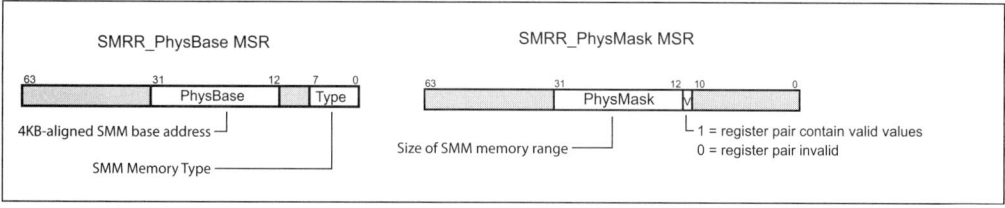

Figure 32-3: SM Range Register Pair

Entering SMM

The SMI Interrupt Is Generated

The chipset causes a logical processor to enter SMM by sending an SMI to it. The logical processor recognizes the interrupt on the next instruction boundary.

No Interruptions Please

General

When the SMI is recognized, the logical processor saves its register set to the State Save Area before proceeding. The logical processor will not recognize any hardware interrupts during the state save operation. Once the register set has been saved, it disables all hardware interrupts in the following manner:

- Eflags[IF] is cleared to 0, disabling the logical processor's ability to recognize external hardware interrupts delivered on the INTR (i.e., LINT0) input (or by the delivery of an Fixed Interrupt IPI to the logical processor's Local APIC).
- Eflags[TF] is cleared to 0, disabling single-step interrupts.
- DR7 (Debug Register 7, the Debug Control register) is cleared to all zeros, disabling the logical processor's breakpoint capability. This prevents the breakpoint recognition logic from inadvertently reporting an address match during an access to SM memory.
- The logical processor's ability to service Non-Maskable hardware interrupts (delivered on the processor's NMI input—i.e., its LINT1 input—or via an APIC NMI IPI message) is disabled. See "NMI Handling While in SMM" on page 1186 for more information.
- The logical processor will not recognize another SMI after entering SMM.
- The logical processor will not recognize the assertion of its INIT# (soft reset) input or the receipt of an INIT IPI message while it is in SMM.

Exceptions and Software Interrupts Permitted but Not Recommended

The execution of software interrupts (INT nn, INTO, INT 3, or BOUND instructions) and the generation of software exceptions are not disabled while in SMM, but Intel recommends that the SM handler should not execute software interrupt instructions or generate software exceptions. Intel does not provide the rationale behind this recommendation, but the author believes it is because the execution of an IRET instruction while in SMM causes NMI recognition to be re-enabled (see "How to Re-Enable NMI Recognition in the SM Handler" on page 1186). Assuming that the handler does use software initiated interrupts or that its execution can result in the generation of one or more types of software exceptions, then also refer to "If Interrupts/Exceptions Permitted, Build an IDT" on page 1185.

Servicing Maskable Interrupts While in the Handler

Although recognition of maskable hardware interrupts is automatically disabled upon entry into SMM, the handler can re-enable it by executing the STI instruction to set Eflags[IF] = 1. Assuming that the handler re-enables recognition of maskable hardware interrupts, then also refer to "If Interrupts/Exceptions Permitted, Build an IDT" on page 1185.

Single-Stepping through the SM Handler

Although single-step interrupts are automatically disabled upon entry into SMM, the handler can re-enable it by setting Eflags[TF] = 1. Assuming that the handler re-enables the single-step interrupt, then also refer to "If Interrupts/ Exceptions Permitted, Build an IDT" on page 1185.

If Interrupts/Exceptions Permitted, Build an IDT

It stands to reason that if any software interrupts, software-generated exceptions, or hardware interrupts are permitted while the SM handler is executing, then the designer of the handler must ensure that:

- The appropriate exception and/or interrupt handlers are present in SM RAM.
- An IDT must be set up in SM RAM and must be initialized with entries pointing to interrupt and/or exception handlers in SM RAM.
- The LIDT instruction is executed to load the logical processor's LDTR with the start address and length of the IDT in SM RAM.

The start address of the IDT must be SM RAM address 00000000h and must be formatted in the same manner as a Real Mode IDT (i.e., each entry is comprised of a 2-byte value to be loaded into the CS register, and a 2-byte value to be loaded into the IP register).

SMM Uses Real Mode Address Formation

When a memory access must be performed while the logical processor is operating in SMM, the address is formed in the same manner as in Real Mode:

1. Four 0 bits are appended to the lower end of the 16-bit value in the respective segment register to create the 20-bit segment base address.
2. The 16-bit offset of the target location is added to the 20-bit segment base address, resulting in the 20-bit physical memory address of the target location in SM RAM. The programmer may access any location in a 4GB address space by prefacing an instruction with the Address Size Override prefix and specifying a 32-bit offset in the desired segment.

This has several ramifications with respect to interrupts and exceptions:

- An interrupt or exception cannot transfer control to a handler that resides in a code segment with a base address of more that 20 bits. This means that the base address of the code segment that contains the target handler must be in the first megabyte of SM RAM memory space.
- An interrupt or exception can only transfer control to a location between 0000h and FFFFh (a 64K range) in the code segment that contains the target handler.

- When an exception or interrupt occurs, the logical processor pushes the CS value onto the stack but only pushes the 16-bit IP value onto the stack (rather than the 32-bit EIP value). This is the lower 16-bits of the 32-bit return address of the next instruction to be executed in the interrupted program (i.e., the SM handler). If the offset of the interrupted program location is greater than 64K (i.e., greater than a 16-bit value), it is not possible for the interrupt/exception handler to return control to the correct location in the interrupted program (because the logical processor only pops a 16-bit value from the stack into the IP register when the IRET instruction is executed at the end of the handler). This problem could be addressed by having the interrupt/exception handler adjust the return address on the stack.

- Assume that the SM Base address is altered (see "Relocating the SM RAM Base Address" on page 1204) from its default address of 00030000h to an address above the first megabyte of SM RAM address space (the SMM handler therefore resides in memory above the first megabyte of SM RAM address space). Also assume that the interrupt and/or exception handlers are located within the first megabyte of SM RAM address space. In this case, execution of the IRET instruction at the end of the exception/interrupt handler cannot cause a transfer back to the SM handler code residing above the first megabyte of SM RAM address space. The exception/interrupt handler could calculate a return address above 1 MB from the 16-bit return address on the stack and then use a 32-bit far Call to return to the interrupted program (i.e., the SM handler).

NMI Handling While in SMM

Default NMI Handling. The logical processor's ability to service Non-Maskable hardware interrupts (delivered on the processor's NMI input—i.e., its LINT1 input—or via an NMI IPI message) is automatically disabled upon recognition of an SMI.

If an NMI is detected during the execution of the SM handler, the NMI is latched but not serviced until after the Resume (RSM) instruction is executed at the end of the SM handler. The logical processor can only latch and remember one NMI during the execution of the SMI handler. If an NMI was latched during the SM handler's execution, when the RSM instruction has executed and restored the logical processor's register set from the State Save Area, the NMI is serviced before the next instruction of the program that was interrupted by the SMI is executed.

How to Re-Enable NMI Recognition in the SM Handler. Recognition of NMI can be re-enabled by executing an IRET/IRETD instruction. The SM handler should invoke a dummy interrupt service routine (using the INT instruction) and, in the dummy handler, execute an IRET/ IRETD instruction. This causes a return to the instruction after the INT instruction and also re-enables the logical processor's recognition of NMI. Of course, before re-enabling NMI recognition, the SM handler must first ensure that an NMI handler has been placed in SM RAM and that entry 2 in the IDT has been initialized to point to this NMI handler.

If an SMI Occurs within the NMI Handler. The following situation could occur:

— The logical processor is operating in IA-32 or IA-32e Mode.
— The chipset generates an NMI to the logical processor, causing it to execute the NMI handler that resides in normal memory (i.e., not an NMI handler that resides within SM RAM).
— The logical processor automatically disables recognition of additional NMIs upon entry to the NMI handler.
— While the logical processor is executing the "normal" NMI handler, the chipset generates an SMI to the logical processor.
— Before entering the SM handler, the logical processor saves its state (i.e., its register set contents) in the SM RAM State Save Area (so it can return to the interrupted program—the "normal" NMI handler—at the conclusion of the SM handler's execution). However, the saved information does not include the fact that the logical processor's ability to recognize NMI has been disabled.
— The chipset may or may not generate another NMI to the logical processor while the SM handler is being executed. If it does, the logical processor latches but does not service the NMI (unless the SM handler has re-enabled recognition of NMI—see "How to Re-Enable NMI Recognition in the SM Handler" on page 1186).
— Upon conclusion of the SM handler, the RSM instruction is executed causing the logical processor's register set to be reloaded from the State Save Area in SM RAM. Unfortunately, however, as stated earlier the logical processor's saved state does not *remember* that NMI recognition had been disabled upon entry to the *normal* NMI handler. As a result, NMI recognition is re-enabled before the logical processor resumes execution of the interrupted NMI handler.
— If a second NMI had been latched while the logical processor was executing the SM handler, the *normal* NMI handler (which was interrupted by the SMI and had not yet finished servicing the first NMI) begins execution again. In other words, the second execution of the *normal* NMI handler is nested within the first execution of the NMI handler.
— Even if a second NMI had not been latched during the execution of the SM handler, another NMI could occur after the return to the *normal*

NMI handler, but before it completed. It will be recognized and the NMI handler is again interrupted (this time by another NMI).

The designer of the NMI interrupt handler should take this possibility into consideration.

Informing the Chipset SM Mode Has Been Entered

This section decibels the actions taken by a processor that utilizes the FSB external interface. A processor with a different external interface implementation (e.g., Intel QPI) may take similar but different actions to accomplish the same goal.

General

Upon recognition of the SMI, the processor generates the Special transaction on its external interface and outputs the SMI Acknowledge message to inform the chipset (specifically the system memory controller) that, until informed otherwise, all memory accesses generated by the logical processor should be directed to SM memory rather than to normal memory.

A Note Concerning Memory-Mapped IO Ports

It should also be noted that, starting with the Pentium Pro, the processor asserts its SMMEM# signal (also referred to as EXF4#—Extended Function bit 4) in every memory transaction that it generates while in SMM. While most of these accesses should be directed to SM memory, it should be noted that the SM handler may need to communicate with one or more memory-mapped IO ports in order to check the status of a device or to issue a command or data to a device. Obviously, the chipset would need to direct these accesses to the correct memory-mapped IO ports.

The Context Save

General

Once SMI has been recognized, the logical processor performs a series of memory write transactions on its external interface to save the contents of its register set in the State Save Area of SM RAM (refer to "The Organization of SM RAM" on page 1172, Figure 32-1 on page 1174, Table 32-1 on page 1174, and Table 32-2 on page 1178.

Although Saved, Some Register Images Are Forbidden Territory

The Intel documentation states that the following registers are saved (but are not readable) upon entry to SMM and are restored upon exiting it:

- CR4. After being saved, CR4 is cleared to all 0s before beginning execution of the SM handler.
- The contents of the logical processor's hidden segment cache registers (see "Segment Register—Selects Descriptor Table and Entry" on page 386 and Figure 13-3 on page 389).

Special Actions Required on a Request for Power Down

If the chipset issues an SMI to the logical processor to prepare for a system power down, the values of all locations in the State Save Area, including the Reserved locations, must be saved to non-volatile memory. The following information is not automatically saved (on an SMI) or restored (on execution of the RSM instruction):

- Debug Registers DR0 through DR3.
- The x87 FPU register set.
- The MTRRs.
- CR2.
- The MSRs (for the P6 and subsequent processors) or TR3 - TR7 (for the Pentium and 486 processors; TR stands for Test Registers).
- The state of the trap controller.
- The MCA register set.
- The Local APIC's register set (ISR, IRR, etc.).
- The Microcode Update state.

On a power down request, the SM handler must read these registers and save them (along with the rest of RAM) in non-volatile storage (e.g., on disk). After the processor is powered up again, the SM handler must restore these registers (along with the rest of the system's state). On a general note, anytime the SM handler makes a change to any of these registers, it must first save the original contents and then restore it before returning to normal (i.e., non-SMM) operation.

Some of the MSRs (e.g., the TSC and Performance Monitoring Counters) are not writable and cannot be saved and restored. SMM-based power-down and restoration should therefore only be performed with OSs that do not use or rely on the values of these registers. OS developers must ensure that the OS power-down and restoration software will not be adversely affected by unexpected changes in these register values.

The Register Settings on Initiation of the SM Handler

After saving the logical processor's register set but before starting execution of the SM handler, the logical processor's registers are set to the values indicated in Table 32-3 on page 1190.

The PE (Protected Mode Enable) and PG (Paging Enable) bits in CR0 are cleared to 0, placing the logical processor in a mode similar to Real Mode. The differences between SMM and Real Mode are as follows:

- The addressable SM RAM address space is 4GB in size.
- The segment size in SMM is 4GB versus 64KB in Real Mode.
- The default operand and address size are both set to 16-bits, restricting the addressable SM RAM address space to the first megabyte of address space. The programmer, however, can use the Operand Size and Address Size Override prefixes to perform 32-bit data accesses and to address SM RAM above the first megabyte.

The first instruction of the SM handler is fetched from location 00038000h (unless the SM Base address field in the State Save Area was changed during an earlier execution of the SM handler).

The SM memory address space may be treated as a flat 4GB address space. A new value may be loaded into a segment register while in the SM handler. The new value has a lower hex digit of 0h appended as the least significant digit, yielding a new 20-bit segment base address. Changing the segment's base address, however, has no affect on the segment's limits and attributes.

Table 32-3: Register Set Values After Entering SMM

Register(s)	Initial Contents
GPRs	Undefined.
Eflags	00000002h. This value disables Single-Step interrupts, recognition of external maskable hardware interrupts, VM86 Mode, and the Alignment Check exception.

Table 32-3: Register Set Values After Entering SMM (Continued)

Register(s)	Initial Contents
EIP	00008000h. When added to the CS's base address of 30000h, the logical processor will fetch the first instruction of the SM handler from location 00038000h.
CS register	The CS register is loaded with the value 3000h which, with a lower hex digit of 0h appended as the least significant digit, yields a code segment start address of 30000h.
DS, ES, FS, GS, SS registers	0000h which, with a lower hex digit of 0h appended as the least significant digit, yields a segment start address of 00000h.
DS, ES, FS, GS, SS Limits	The segment length of all of these segments is set to 4GB (FFFFFFFFh).
CR0	The PE, EM, TS and PG bits are cleared to 0, while the other bits are unmodified.
DR6	The contents of the Debug Status register is undefined.
DR7	00000400h. This disables all four Debug Breakpoint address comparators.

The SMM Revision ID

When the logical processor enters SMM, in addition to saving its register set in the State Save Area, it also saves the following four items:

- The Auto Halt Restart Field. This field is described in "The Auto Halt Restart Feature" on page 1193.
- The IO Instruction Restart Field. This field is described in "The IO Instruction Restart Feature" on page 1195.
- The SMM Revision Identifier Field. This field is described below.
- The SM Base Field is described in "Relocating the SM RAM Base Address" on page 1204.

The SMM Revision ID field (pictured in Figure 32-4 on page 1192) is automatically deposited in the State Save Area on entry to SMM and contains the following information:

- The SMM Revision ID indicates the version of SMM that is supported by the logical processor.
- The IO Instruction Restart bit indicates whether or not the logical processor supports the IO Instruction Restart feature (see "The IO Instruction Restart Feature" on page 1195).
- The SM Base Relocation bit indicates whether or not the logical processor supports the SM Base Relocation feature (see "Relocating the SM RAM Base Address" on page 1204).

Figure 32-4: The SMM Revision ID

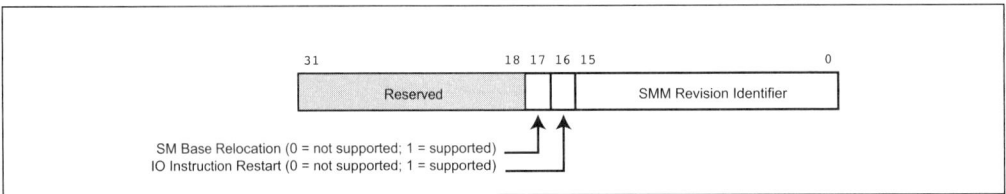

The Body of the Handler

After the logical processor's register set contents and the four additional fields mentioned in "The SMM Revision ID" on page 1191 are stored in the State Save Area, the logical processor begins execution of the SM handler.

Exiting SMM

The Resume Instruction

The last instruction executed in the SM handler is the Resume (RSM) instruction. Its execution causes the logical processor to reload its register set from the State Save Area (see Figure 32-1 on page 1174, Table 32-1 on page 1174, and Table 32-2 on page 1178) before resuming execution of the program interrupted by the SMI.

If the logical processor detects invalid state information during state restoration, it enters the Shutdown state (see "Shutdown Mode" on page 755). The following invalid information can cause a shutdown:

- If any reserved bits in CR4 are set to 1.
- If there is any illegal combination of bits in CR0 (e.g., Paging enabled and Protected Mode disabled, or NW = 1 and CD = 0).
- On the Pentium or the 486, if the address in the SM Base field is not aligned on an address that is evenly divisible by 32K.

The contents of the MSRs are not affected by a return from SMM.

Informing the Chipset That SMM Has Been Exited

When the logical processor has finished reloading its register set from the State Save Area, it generates the Special transaction on its external interface and outputs the SMI Acknowledge message to inform the chipset (specifically the system memory controller) that, until informed otherwise, all memory accesses generated by the logical processor should be directed to normal memory rather than to SM memory.

In addition, starting with the Pentium Pro, the processor deasserts its SMMEM# signal (also referred to as EXF4#—Extended Function bit 4) in every memory transaction that it generates after exiting SMM.

The Auto Halt Restart Feature

Upon entry to the SM handler, the logical processor has deposited the Auto Halt Restart field in the State Save Area (see Table 32-1 on page 1174, Table 32-2 on page 1178, and Figure 32-5 on page 1194). If the logical processor was in the Halt state (due to the prior execution of a HLT instruction) when it received the SMI, then the Auto Halt Restart bit will be set to one; otherwise, it will be cleared to 0. Assuming that the bit is set to one, the SM handler has two options:

- If it leaves the bit set to one, upon execution of the RSM instruction at the end of the handler the logical processor will re-execute the HLT instruction in the interrupted program. This causes it to reenter the Halt state.
- If it clears the bit to zero, upon execution of the RSM instruction at the end of the handler the logical processor will resume execution of the interrupted program at the instruction immediately following the HLT instruction.

Table 32-4 on page 1194 defines the action taken by the logical processor on execution of the RSM instruction based on the setting of the Auto Halt Restart bit on entry to and exit from the SM handler.

Table 32-4: Processor Actions on RSM Are Defined by the Bit Setting

Bit State on Entry to Handler	Bit State on Exit from Handler	On Exit from SMM
0	0	The logical processor resumes execution of the interrupted program at the next instruction.
0	1	The logical processor's actions are unpredictable.
1	0	The logical processor resumes execution of the interrupted program with the instruction immediately following the HLT instruction.
1	1	The logical processor resumes execution of the interrupted program by re-executing the HLT instruction.

Executing the HLT Instruction in the SM Handler

The HLT instruction must not be executed while the logical processor is in SMM unless recognition of external maskable hardware interrupts has been re-enabled by setting Eflags[IF] =1. If the HLT instruction is executed while the logical processor is in SMM, it halts and other than a hardware reset, the only event that can remove it from the halt state is a maskable hardware interrupt.

Figure 32-5: The Auto Halt Restart Field

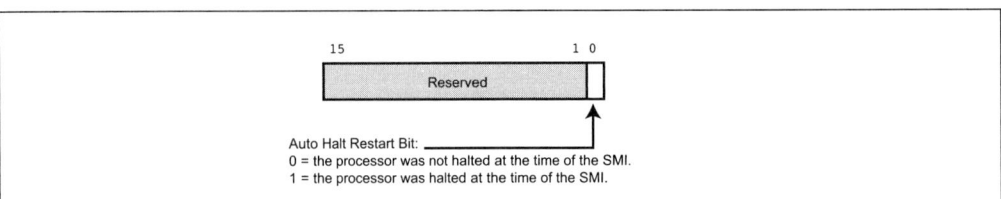

The IO Instruction Restart Feature

Introduction

This feature allows an IO instruction interrupted by an SMI from the chipset to be re-executed upon returning from SMM. Assuming that the logical processor supports the IO Instruction Restart feature (see "The SMM Revision ID" on page 1191), upon entry to the SM handler the logical processor has deposited the IO Instruction Restart field in the State Save Area (see Table 32-1 on page 1174 and Table 32-2 on page 1178.).

An Example Scenario

As an example scenario, an IO device may have been powered down earlier to save on power consumption. While the device is powered down, the device's driver executes an IO instruction (i.e., IN, OUT, INS, or OUTS) to access an IO port associated with the device. The chipset, recognizing that the IO device is powered down, responds to the IO transaction by sending an SMI to the logical processor. The SM handler is invoked, checks a chipset-specific status register to determine the cause of the SMI, and undertakes the actions necessary to power the device back up again. Upon returning from the SMI handler, the IO Instruction Restart mechanism can be used to successfully re execute the IO instruction.

The Detail

The IO Instruction Restart field in the State Save Area contains 0000h upon entry to the SM handler. It is up to the handler to determine that the cause of the SMI was an aborted IO instruction and, if it was, to take one of the following actions:

- **Leave the field set to 0000h.** In this case, when the RSM instruction is executed at the end of the handler, the logical processor resumes execution of the interrupted program at the instruction after the IO instruction that caused the SMI. This implies that the handler fixed the problem (e.g., powered the device up) and then performed the IO operation that was initially unsuccessful.
- **Set the field = 00FFh.** In this case, when the RSM instruction is executed at the end of the handler, the logical processor resumes execution of the interrupted program at the IO instruction that caused SMI. This time, however, the IO instruction's execution will not cause an SMI (because the handler fixed the problem that resulted in the SMI). The logical processor saves the

necessary machine state to insure that re-execution of the instruction is handled coherently. If a repeat prefix (REP) was used with the IO instruction (e.g., a REP INS), the next instruction will be the next iteration of the IO instruction in the repeat loop.

If an SMI is signaled on a non-IO instruction boundary and if the SM handler should set the IO Instruction Restart field to 00FFh prior to executing the RSM instruction, it will likely result in a program error.

Back-to-Back SMIs During IO Instruction Restart

An SMI could be received by the logical processor while it is servicing an SMI generated by the chipset due to an aborted IO instruction (see "An Example Scenario" on page 1195). In this case, upon executing the RSM instruction at the end of the handler, the logical processor will service the second SMI (i.e., it will re-invoke the SMI handler) before restarting the originally-interrupted IO instruction. If, prior to the execution of the RSM instruction at the conclusion of the second execution of the SM handler, the IO Instruction Restart field has been set to 00FFh (indicating that the IO instruction should be re-executed), the EIP register will contain the address of an instruction other than the IO instruction that caused the first execution of the handler. To avoid this situation, the SM handler must be able to recognize the occurrence of back-to-back SMIs when IO instruction restart is being used and ensure that the handler sets the restart field to 0000h prior to returning from the second execution of the SM handler.

Multiprocessor System Presents a Problem

As described earlier in this section—"The IO Instruction Restart Feature"—in a system with a single logical processor, the SM handler can easily determine if an SMI was generated due to an IO transaction intercepted by the chipset by checking the chipset's status. In a system with multiple programs simultaneously executing on multiple logical processors, however, determining whether an SMI was caused by an intercepted IO transaction associated with the logical processor that received an SMI can be problematic. To aid the SM handler running on a specific logical processor in determining whether an SMI was caused by an intercepted IO transaction, the following two fields were added to the information saved in the SM State Save Area:

- **IO State field** (32-bits). See locations 7FA4h-7FA7h in Table 32-2 on page 1178 and Table 32-1 on page 1174. Also see Figure 32-6 on page 1197. If the SMI was likely the result of an IO transaction (not a memory-mapped IO transaction) intercepted by the chipset, the IO port access type, length and the 16-bit IO port address are latched and saved in this field.

- **IO Memory Address** field (32-bits on an IA-32 processor; 64-bits on an Intel 64 processor). See locations 7F9Ch-7FA3h in Table 32-2 on page 1178, and 7FA0h-7FA3h in Table 32-1 on page 1174. If the SMI was likely the result of a memory-mapped IO transaction intercepted by the chipset:
  — The 32- or 64-bit memory-mapped IO address is recorded in this field;
  — The IO State field records the event by setting the IO SMI bit to one and recording the access length. In this case, the IO Type and IO Port Address fields are don't care.

The fact that the IO SMI bit is set to one does not necessarily indicate that the SMI is definitely associated with an IO instruction just completed by this logical processor. Purely by coincidence, the chipset may have generated an SMI to the logical processor immediately after a successful IO transaction to signal a platform event not associated with the just-completed IO transaction. When the IO SMI bit is set to one, however, it is a strong indication that the SMI may have been generated in response to the IO transaction. The SMI handler may gain additional insight by checking the chipset's status to determine the cause of the SMI.

Figure 32-6: IO State Field in SM State Save Area

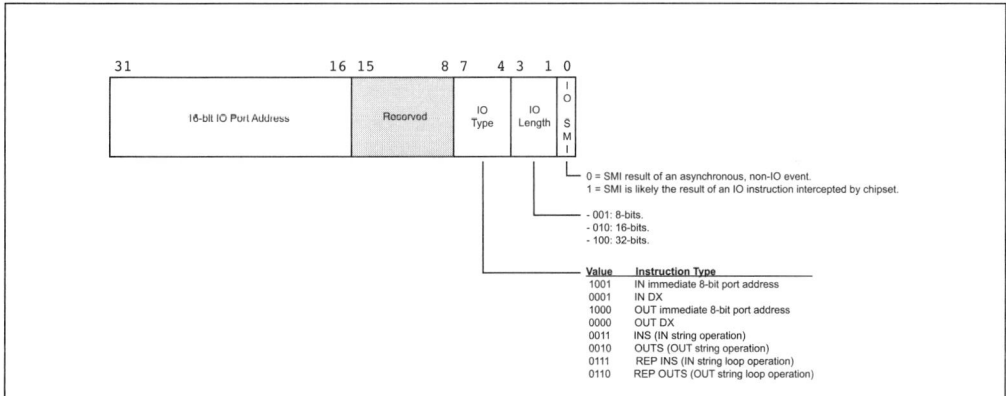

Caching from SM Memory

Background

It is important to note that to the processor's caches, a memory address is a memory address: the caches do not differentiate between accesses to SM memory versus regular system memory. This being the case, if the memory address range that is used to access SM memory (while the logical processor is in SMM) partially or fully overlaps an address range in system memory that holds OS and/or application information, then one of the following two strategies must be employed:

- The overlapping memory address range can be designated as UC (uncacheable) memory in the MTRRs. The logical processor will not cache any information from SM RAM or from regular system memory.
- The overlapping memory address range can be designated as cacheable memory (i.e., WP, WT or WB) in the MTRRs. The logical processor is then enabled to cache information from regular system memory when it is operating in IA-32 or IA-32e Mode, and from SM memory when it is operating in SMM. This can result in better performance while operating any of the three modes. There is a catch, however.

Consider the following scenario:

- Assume that SM memory overlaps with regular system memory in the A0000000h - A000FFFFh memory address range (any range could be used in the example).
- The overlapped address range has been marked cacheable (i.e., WP, WT or WB) in the MTRRs.
- The logical processor has been operating in IA-32 or IA-32e Mode and has cached some information (code and/or data) from the overlapped address range.
- An SMI occurs, switching the logical processor into SMM.
- While in SMM, the logical processor performs a read access from the overlapped address range for the first time since entering SMM. This should result in a cache miss, but instead, it hits on a line that was cached from that location in *regular* system memory. The requested information is sourced from the cache.
- This is *WRONG!* The logical processor should have performed the memory access on its external interface to fetch the line from SM memory. The SM

handler incorrectly receives data or code that was originally fetched from regular system memory and, as a result, it does not function correctly.

In this scenario, the cache must be flushed (execute WBINVD instruction) on entry to and exit from SMM. While this results in a big performance hit due to the resulting global cache flush and the subsequent cache misses, everything will work correctly.

The Physical Mapping of SM RAM Accesses

How the address ranges in SM memory address space are actually mapped to physical memory chips is system design-specific. Here are several examples:

1. Refer to **Figure 32-7 on page 1200**. The chipset can direct the entire range of SM RAM addresses to an area of system memory that will never be used by the OS and/or application programs. In this case, the entire range can be designated as cacheable memory (WP, WT or WB; *note that Intel documentation refers to WC as cacheable, but it is not*) in the MTRRs (so as to achieve the best possible performance by caching SM RAM information).
2. Refer to **Figure 32-8 on page 1201**. The chipset can direct the entire range of SM memory addresses to RAM storage that is implemented using totally separate and distinct RAM chips from the system RAM memory used by the OS and/or application programs. The address range may be an address range that is also used (by normal memory accesses) to access system memory. In this case, the entire range is designated as uncacheable memory (UC) in the MTRRs.
3. Refer to **Figure 32-9 on page 1201**. The chipset can direct any access within the SM memory address space to an area of system memory that is also used by the OS (but not at the same time, of course). This area would be designated as UC memory in the MTRRs.
4. Refer to **Figure 32-10 on page 1202**. The chipset can direct any access within the SM memory address space to the system memory that is also used by the OS and/or application programs and the MTRRs could designate the entire address range as cacheable (so as to achieve the best possible performance by caching OS/application information as well as SM memory information). However, the entire cache would have to be flushed upon entry to and exit from SMM (by executing the WBINVD instruction).
5. Refer to **Figure 32-11 on page 1202**. *This is the scenario recommended by Intel for all x86 processors starting with the Pentium Pro.* While part of the SM memory address range overlaps with regular memory used by the OS and applications, another part of the SM memory space is dedicated to SM RAM and is never used by the OS or applications. The overlapped portion of the

address space overlaps with video memory (which is usually in low memory) and is marked as UC memory in the MTRRs. The initial entry point to the SM handler is located in this shared area. Very soon after entering SMM, however, the SM handler code performs a jump to the main portion of the handler which is located in the memory range that is dedicated to SM memory and is never used by the OS and applications. This dedicated area can be designated as cacheable memory (i.e., WP, WT or WB) to achieve good performance while in SMM.

Figure 32-7: SM RAM Example One

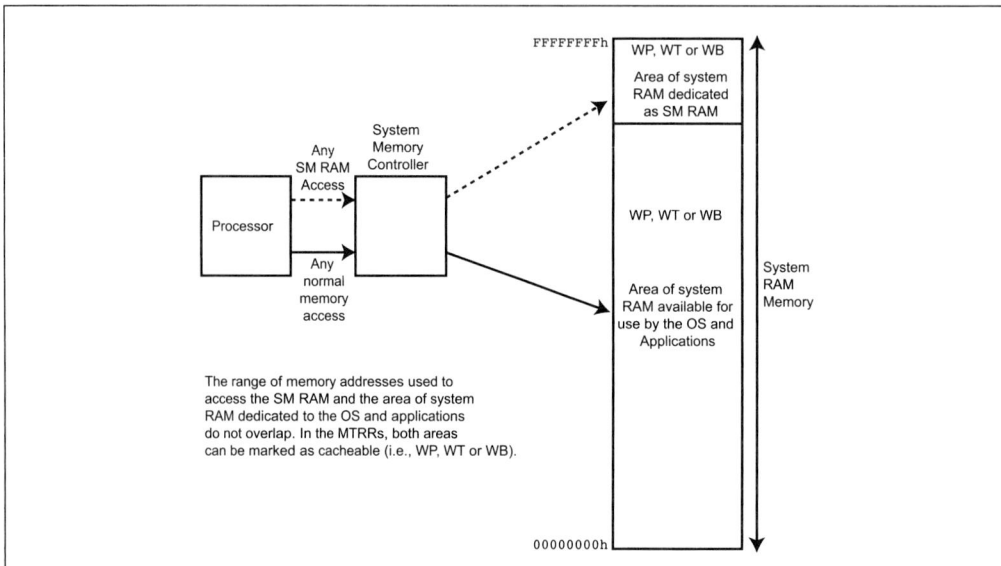

Figure 32-8: SM RAM Example Two

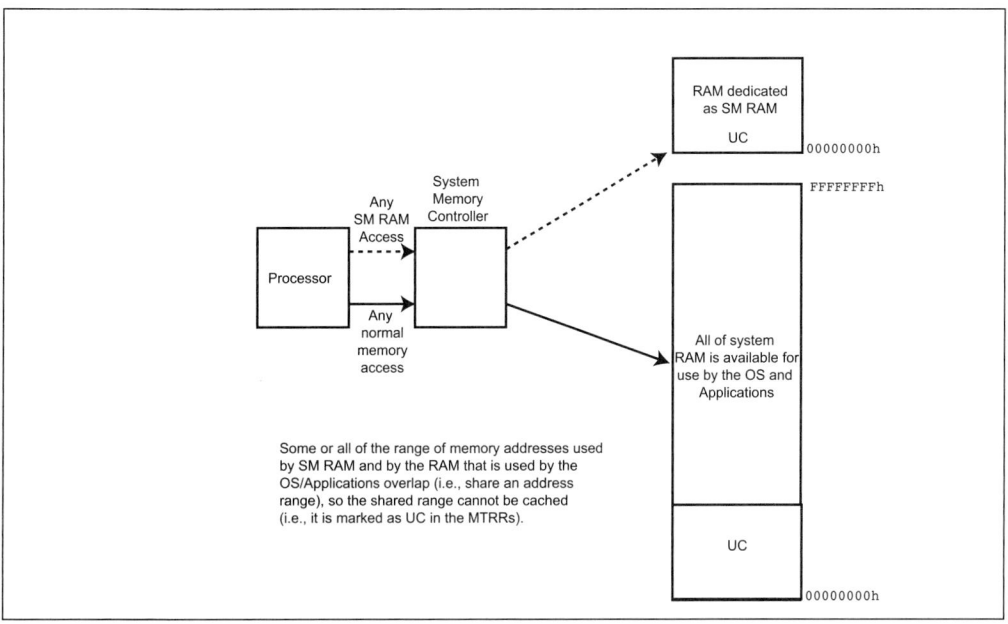

Figure 32-9: SM RAM Example Three

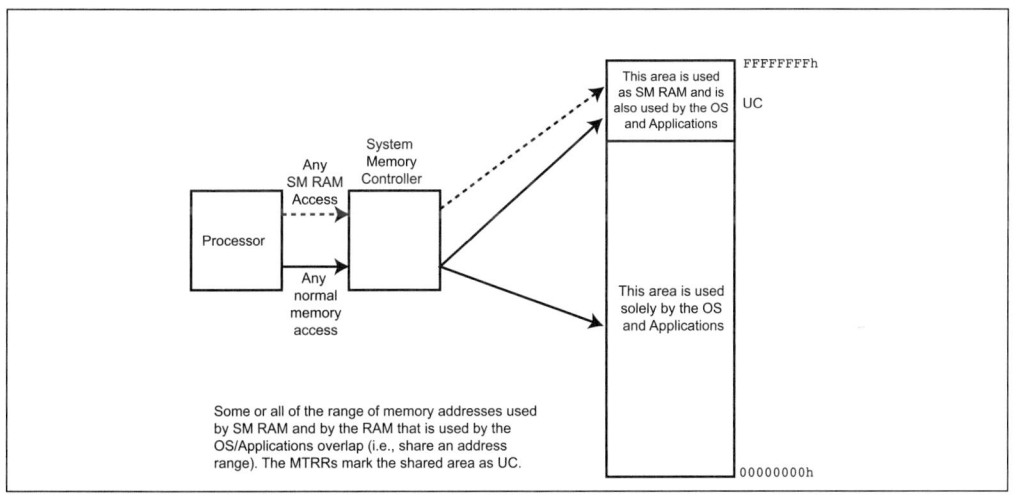

Figure 32-10: SM RAM Example Four

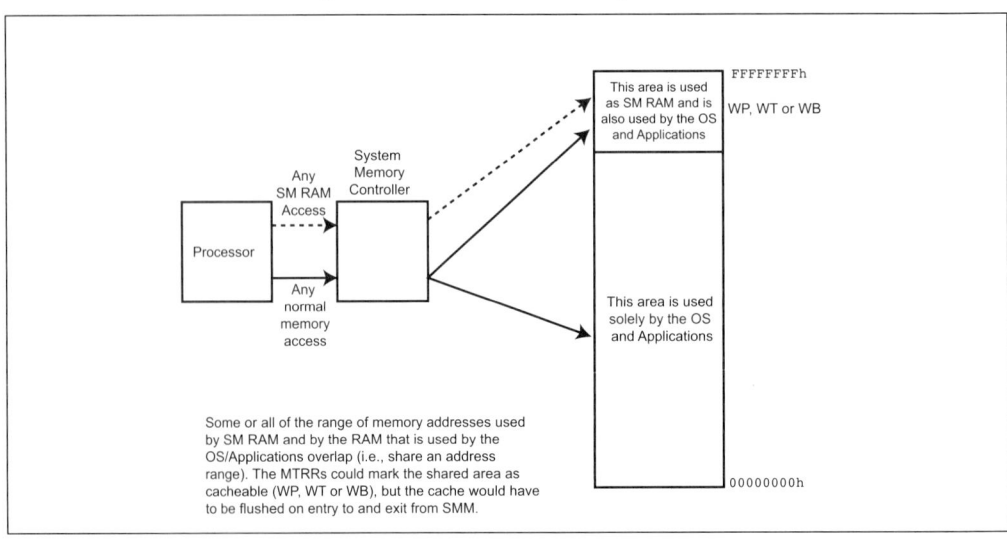

Figure 32-11: SM RAM Example Five

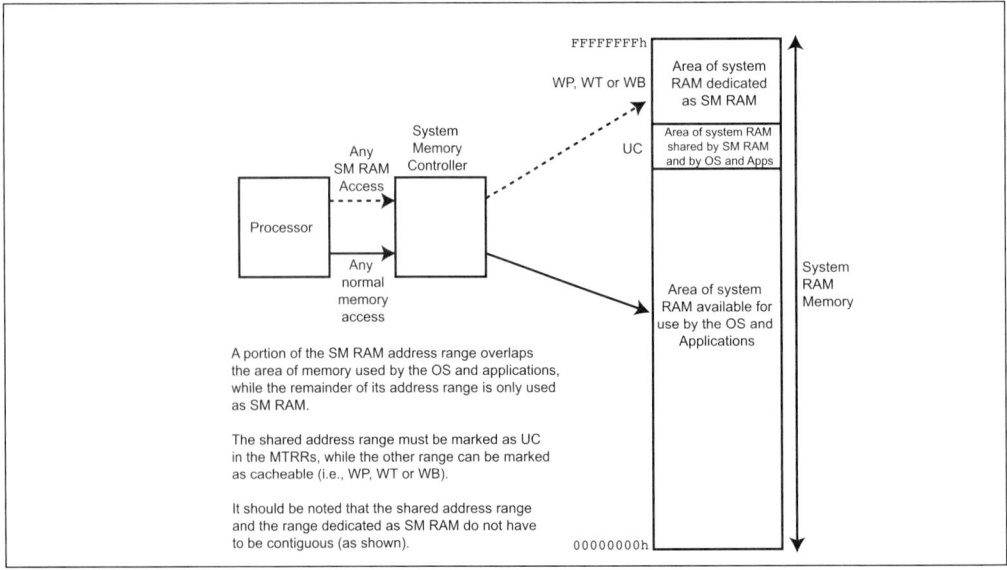

FLUSH# and SMI#

This discussion relates to the situation described in "Background" on page 1198. Prior to the advent of the Pentium 4, all IA-32 processors starting with the Pentium implemented the following two inputs:

- FLUSH#. When asserted by the chipset, it caused the processor to write back all of its modified lines to memory and then delete all of the lines in its caches. After completion of the cache flush, the processor would generate a Special transaction on its external interface and output the Flush Acknowledge message. This would inform the chipset that the flush had been completed.
- SMI#. When asserted by the chipset, it caused the logical processor to switch from Real Mode or Protected Mode into SMM.

Both of these inputs were treated as interrupts to the processor with FLUSH# having a higher priority than SMI#. A system could be designed so that it would assert SMI# and FLUSH# to the processor simultaneously. The processor would service the FLUSH# first, purging its caches of the information cached from regular system memory, and would then service the SMI# and enter SMM. The following timing constraints had to be met:

- In a system where FLUSH# and SMI# were synchronous and the set up and hold times were met, FLUSH# and SMI# could be asserted in the same clock.
- In asynchronous systems, FLUSH# had to be asserted at least one clock before SMI# to guarantee that FLUSH# was serviced first.

Before executing the RSM instruction to exit SMM, the SM handler would have to execute the WBINVD instruction to flush the information that had been cached from SM memory.

Setting Up the SMI Handler in SM Memory

In a system where the SM memory address range is separate and distinct from system memory, the SM handler must get loaded into SM RAM in some manner at startup time. In such a system, the system board logic must provide a programmable method of mapping the SM RAM into system memory space when the logical processor is not in SMM. This enables startup software to load the appropriate code and data into the SM RAM space before the chipset sends an SMI to the logical processor for the first time.

Relocating the SM RAM Base Address

Description

When the system is first powered up or when the processor receives a hard reset, the SM Base address is preset to a default value of 00030000h. Whenever an SMI is detected, the logical processor switches to SMM and, before beginning execution of the SM handler, performs a series of memory writes to SM RAM to save its register set and some additional values in the State Save Area (see Figure 32-1 on page 1174, Table 32-1 on page 1174, and Table 32-2 on page 1178). Among other things, one of the values deposited in the State Save Area is the SM Base field. Initially, the value placed in this field by the logical processor is 00030000h.

The programmer can determine if the logical processor supports changing the default SM Base address by checking the support bit in the SMM Revision ID field (which is also deposited in the State Save Area; see Figure 32-4 on page 1192). Assuming that this bit is a 1, the logical processor supports alteration of the SM Base address. In the SM handler, the programmer can write a new 32-bit value into the SM Base field (in the Pentium and 486, the new address had to be aligned on an address boundary evenly divisible by 32K; this constraint was eliminated with the advent of the Pentium Pro). When the RSM instruction is executed at the end of the SM handler, the logical processor automatically saves the new value in its internal SMBASE register (note that this register is not directly addressable by the programmer). For the remainder of the power-up session or until the processor should receive a hard reset (note that assertion of INIT#—soft reset—to the processor does not affect the SM Base address), the logical processor will use the new SM Base address in calculating the SM handler entry point as well as the start address of the State Save Area.

In an MP System, Each Processor Must Have a Separate State Save Area

In an MP system, the startup configuration software must adjust the SM Base address in each logical processor to ensure that the State Save Areas of the logical processors do not overlap.

Accessing SM Memory Above the First MB

As described in "SMM Uses Real Mode Address Formation" on page 1185, in SMM the segment registers operate in the same manner as in Real Mode. They permit the programmer to specify a 20-bit segment start address somewhere in the first megabyte of memory space. A start address above the first megabyte cannot be specified.

If SM memory is relocated to an address above the first megabyte, it can still be accessed by using the 32-bit Address Size Override prefix to generate an offset to the correct address. SM memory can be accessed by using 32-bit displacement registers, as in the following example:

```
mov esi,02AF4522      ;set esi = 32-bit offset of target location
mov ax,ds:[esi]       ;access the location
```

A stack located above the 1MB address boundary can be accessed in the same manner.

SMM in an MP System

The following should be noted when designing multiple-processor systems:

- Any logical processor in an MP system can respond to an SMI.
- The SM memory for different logical processors can be overlapped in the same memory space, but each logical processor must have its own State Save Area (see "In an MP System, Each Processor Must Have a Separate State Save Area" on page 1204) and its own dynamic data storage area. Code and static data can be shared among logical processors.
- At startup time the system configuration software must assign a different SM Base address for each logical processor; see "Relocating the SM RAM Base Address" on page 1204).
- The logical processors can receive SMIs through their SMI# pins or via SMI IPI messages received through the APIC interface. The APIC interface can distribute SMIs to different logical processors.
- Two or more logical processors can be executing in SMM at the same time.

SM Mode and Virtualization

This topic is not covered in this book. See "Just an Introduction?" on page 1148 and "Detailed Coverage of Virtualization" on page 1148.

33 *Machine Check Architecture (MCA)*

The Previous Chapter

The previous chapter provided a detailed description of System Management Mode (SMM). It included the following topics:

- What Falls Under the Heading of System Management?
- The Genesis of SMM
- SMM Has Its Own Private Memory Space
- The Basic Elements of SMM
- A Very Simple Example Scenario
- How the Processor Knows the SM Memory Start Address
- Normal Operation, (Including Paging) Is Disabled
- The Organization of SM RAM
- Entering SMM
- Exiting SMM
- Caching from SM Memory
- Setting Up the SMI Handler in SM Memory
- Relocating the SM RAM Base Address
- SMM in an MP System
- SM Mode and Virtualization

This Chapter

This chapter provides a detailed description of the Machine Check Architecture (MCA):

- The MCA Elements.
- The Global Registers.

- The Composition of a Register Bank.
- The Error Code.
- Cache Error Reporting.
- MC Exception Is Generally Not Recoverable.

The Next Chapter

The next chapter provides a complete description of the Local and IO APICs. It includes:

- A Short History of the APIC's Evolution.
- Before the APIC.
- MP Systems Need a Better Interrupt Distribution Mechanism.
- Detecting Presence/Version/Capabilities of Local APIC.
- Local APIC's Initial State.
- Enabling/Disabling the Local APIC.
- Mode Selection.
- The Local APIC Register Set.
- Local APIC ID Assignments and Addressing.
  — ID Assignment in xAPIC Mode.
  — ID Assignment in x2APIC Mode.
  — Local APIC Addressing.
  — Lowest-Priority Delivery Mode.
- Local APIC IDs Are Stored in the MP and ACPI Tables.
- Accessing the Local APIC ID.
- An Introduction to the Interrupt Sources.
- Introduction to Interrupt Priority.
- Task and Processor Priority.
- IO/Local APICs Cooperate on Interrupt Handling.
- Message Signaled Interrupts (MSI).
- Interrupt Delivery from Legacy 8259a Interrupt Controller.
- SW-Initiated Interrupt Message Transmission.
- x2APIC Mode's Self IPI Feature.
- Locally Generated Interrupts.
  — The Local Vector Table.
  — Local Interrupt 0 (LINT0).
  — Local Interrupt 1 (LINT1).
  — The Local APIC Timer.
  — The Performance Counter Overflow Interrupt.
  — The Thermal Sensor Interrupt.
  — Correctable Machine Check (CMC) Interrupt.
  — The Local APIC's Error Interrupt.

- The Spurious Interrupt Vector.
- Boot Strap Processor (BSP) Selection.
- How the APs are Discovered and Configured.

Why This Subject Is Included

When first introduced in x86 processors, the Machine Check Architecture error logging facility was not architecturally defined. Rather, it was a processor-specific addition to the Pentium and Pentium Pro processors with no guarantee that it would be implemented in subsequent processors or, if it was, that it would be implemented in the same manner. It was only with the advent of the Pentium 4 that it was defined as part of the x86 software architecture.

MCA = Hardware Error Logging Capability

The Machine Check Architecture facility consists of a set of error logging registers and the Machine Check exception. During a power up session, a logical processor may experience one or more hardware-related errors internally or on its external interface. Such errors can be divided into two basic categories:

- Soft errors that are automatically corrected by the processor hardware.
- Hard errors that cannot be automatically corrected.

It is expected that the OS will start a daemon that runs in background and periodically examines the MCA registers to determine if any soft errors have been logged since the last time the registers were examined. If so, the application snapshots the errors in a non-volatile storage medium (e.g., on the hard drive or in flash memory) and then clears the errors from the register set (the registers are then available to record any additional errors that may occur in the future).

If a hard error is detected and the Machine Check exception has been enabled, the logical processor records the error in the register set and also generates a Machine Check exception [see "Machine Check Exception (18)" on page 778 for a detailed description] to report it. In the Machine Check exception handler, the error recorded in the register set is read, recorded in the non-volatile storage medium, and possibly displayed on the console. Generally speaking, software cannot recover from most hard errors.

The MCA Elements

The Machine Check Architecture first appeared in the Pentium in rudimentary form (consisting of only two registers), but was greatly expanded with the advent of the Pentium Pro.

The MCA actually consists of two capabilities (detected by performing a CPUID request type 1 and checking the returned EDX capabilities bit mask): the ability to generate the Machine Check exception and the presence of the MCA register set.

The Machine Check Exception

Although it is optional whether or not a logical processor possesses the ability to generate a Machine Check exception when an uncorrectable hardware error has been detected, all current-day processors support this capability. Whether or not a processor supports this ability is indicated by executing a CPUID request type 1 and checking the EDX[MCE] bit. If it supports the generation of the Machine Check exception, this capability is enabled by setting CR4[MCE] = 1 (see Figure 33-1 on page 1210).

On the P6 processors, the Pentium 4 (and its Xeon and Celeron derivatives), and the Pentium M (and, to the author's knowledge, current-day processors), the Machine Check exception is not recoverable. The interrupted program cannot be safely resumed.

Figure 33-1: Machine Check Exception Enable/Disable Bit (CR4[MCE])

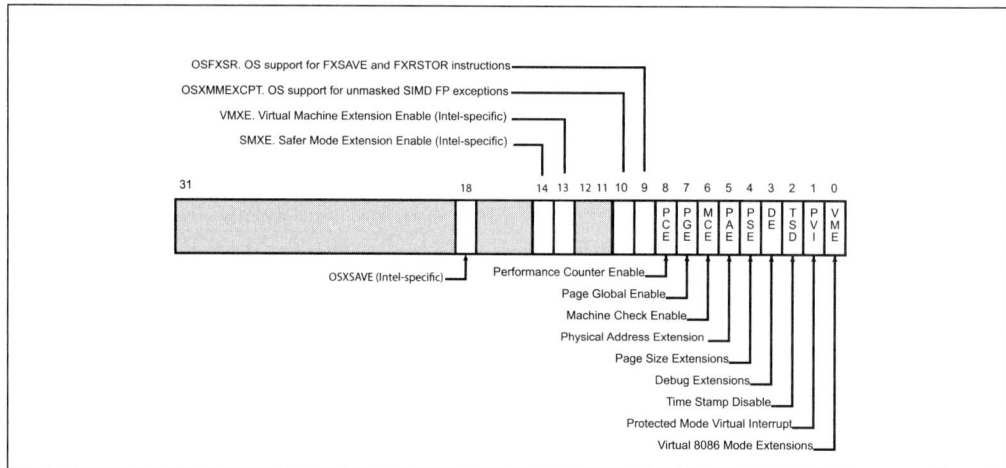

The MCA Register Set

The MCA register set (see Figure 33-2 on page 1211) is used to log both correctable and uncorrectable hardware errors associated with:

- The internal buses that interconnect units within the logical processor.
- The processor's external interface.
- Hard ECC (Error Correcting Code) errors associated with an access attempt to an internal processor memory array (e.g., a cache) or with the external interface.
- Parity errors detected on an attempt to access the processor's internal microcode ROM.
- Cache-related errors.
- TLB-related errors.

Whether or not a logical processor implements these registers is indicated by executing a CPUID request type 1 and checking the EDX[MCA] bit.

The MCA registers are implemented as MSRs and are accessed using the RDMSR and WRMSR instructions (the MSR addresses can be found in the appendices of the Intel manuals). The register set consists of:

- **Global registers**. A set of Global registers that provide information about the register set, high level status information and the ability to selectively enable or disable the recording of specific error types.
- **Error logging register banks**. A set of error logging register banks that record errors associated with a specific processor unit or units, or with a bus that provides the interconnect between processor units or between the processor and the external interface.

Figure 33-2: MCA Register Set

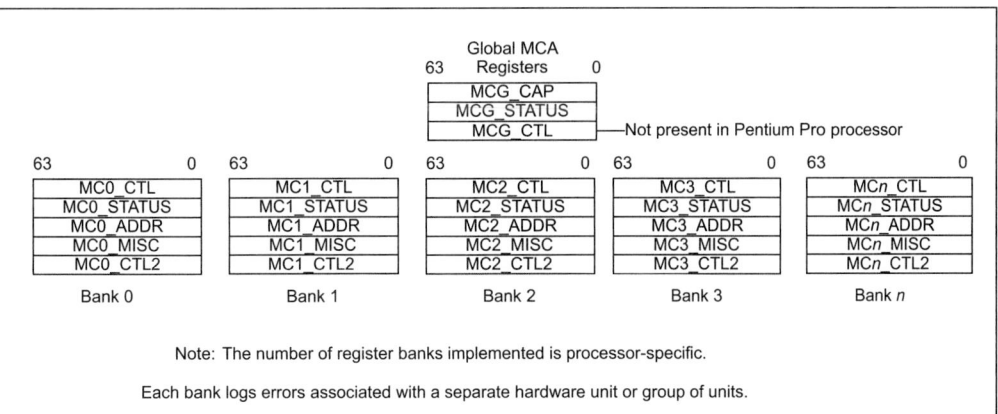

The Global Registers

Introduction

The MC Global registers provide information about the register set, high-level status information, and the ability to selectively enable or disable the recording of specific error types. The Global registers consists of:

- **MCG_CAP**. The MC Global Count and Present register (see "The Global Count and Present Register" on page 1212).
- **MCG_Status**. The MC Global Status register (see "The Global Status Register" on page 1213).
- **MCG_CTL**. The MC Global Control register (see "The Global Control Register" on page 1214).

The Global Count and Present Register

The IA32_MCG_CAP MSR (Global CAP = Count and Present) is a read-only register that provides information about the MCA implementation and contains the following (see Figure 33-3 on page 1213):

- **Count** field. Indicates the number of error logging register banks implemented in a logical processor. As an example, the P6 processors implemented five banks of MCA registers and the Pentium 4 implemented four.
- **CTL_P** (MC Global Control register Present). 1 indicates that the logical processor implements the IA32_MCG_CTL MSR.
- **EXT_P** (MC Extended registers Present). 1 indicates that the logical processor implements the extended MCA state registers (see "The Extended MC State MSRs" on page 1214).
- **EXT_CNT** field. Indicates the number of extended MCA state registers present (meaningful only when MCG_EXT_P = 1). As an example, the Pentium 4 implemented ten extended state registers. See "The Extended MC State MSRs" on page 1214.
- **CMCI_P**. Corrected MC Interrupt capability supported. Refer to "Interrupt On Soft Error Threshold Match" on page 1233.
- **TES_P**. Threshold-based Error Status capability present. Refer to "Green/ Yellow Cache Health Indicator" on page 1232.

Figure 33-3: MC Global Count and Present Register

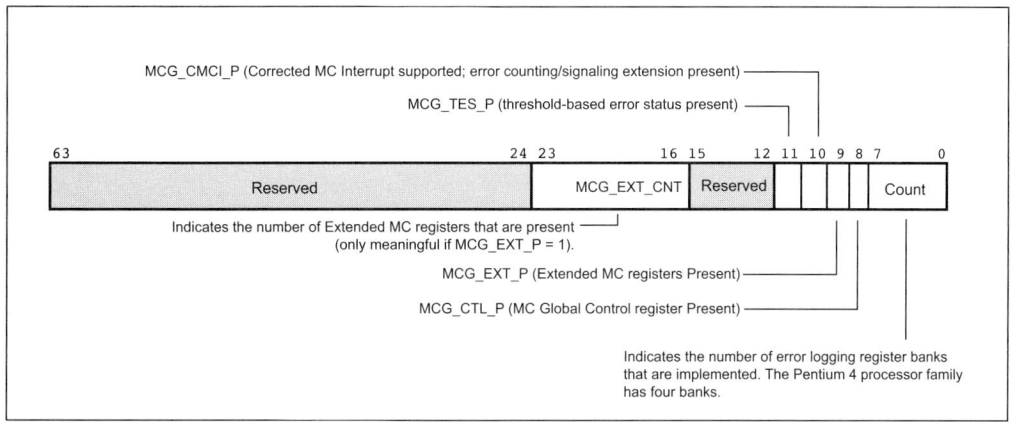

The Global Status Register

Figure 33-4 on page 1214 illustrates the Global Status register which contains the following status bits:

- **MCIP bit**. The **Machine Check In Progress** bit is automatically set to one by the logical processor when a MC exception is generated. If another MC exception should be generated while this bit is still set to one (i.e., it hasn't been cleared by the MC handler yet), the logical processor enters the Shutdown state (see "Shutdown Mode" on page 755). The MC exception handler should save sufficient processor state (i.e., register contents) to remember the current MC error and then clear the MCIP bit to zero. If another MC exception should subsequently be generated after MCIP has been cleared and the logical processor is still executing the MC exception handler, another MC exception is generated.
- **EIPV bit**. The **Error Instruction Pointer Valid** bit is set to one if the instruction pointer pushed onto the stack when the MC exception was generated is directly associated with the error.
- **RIPV bit**. The **Restart Instruction Pointer Valid** bit is set to one if the interrupted program can be safely resumed at the instruction that was pushed onto the stack when the MC exception was generated. *On the P6 processors, the Pentium 4 (and its Xeon and Celeron derivatives), and the Pentium M (and, to the author's knowledge, all current-day processors), the Machine Check exception is not recoverable. The interrupted program can not be safely resumed.*

Figure 33-4: MC Global Status Register

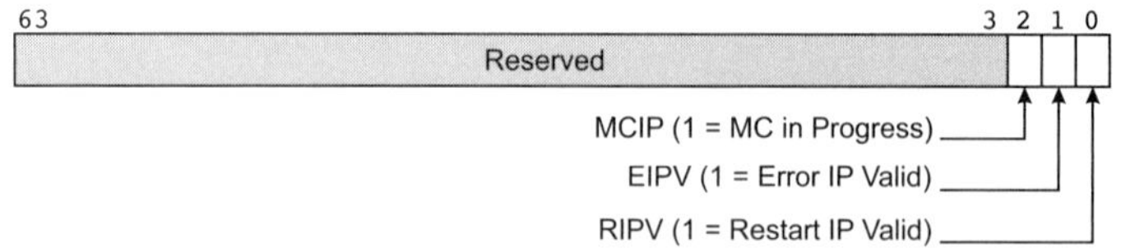

The Global Control Register

Whether or not a logical processor implements the MCG_CTL register is indicated by the state of the CTL_P bit in the MCG_CAP register (see Figure 33-3 on page 1213. If it is implemented:

- Writing all zeros to this register disables the MC feature.
- Writing all ones enables the MC feature.
- The specific meaning of each bit in this register is Intel confidential and implementation-specific.

The Extended MC State MSRs

These registers were added with the advent of the Pentium 4. Their presence or absence is indicated by the state of EXT_P bit in the MCG_CAP register (see Figure 33-3 on page 1213) and the number of registers is indicated by the Count field in the same register. When a Machine Check exception is generated, as an aid to the MC exception handler and/or a debugger the logical processor automatically creates a snapshot of a number of its registers in the extended MC state register set.

- Table 33-1 on page 1215 lists the extended state registers implemented in an IA-32 processor.
- Table 33-2 on page 1216 lists the extended state registers implemented in an Intel 64 processor.

Software can read the extended state registers but is only permitted to write zeros to them (or a GP exception is generated). They are cleared on reset or power-up, but are not cleared by a soft reset (i.e., an INIT).

Table 33-1: IA-32 Processor's Extended MC State MSRs

Register	is copied into this MC State Save MSR
EAX	IA32_MCG_EAX
EBX	IA32_MCG_EBX
ECX	IA32_MCG_ECX
EDX	IA32_MCG_EDX
ESI	IA32_MCG_ESI
EDI	IA32_MCG_EDI
EBP	IA32_MCG_EBP
ESP	IA32_MCG_ESP
Eflags	IA32_MCG_EFLAGS
EIP	IA32_MCG_EIP
-	IA32_MCG_MISC (see note at the end of this table).
-	The next 32 sequential MSR addresses are reserved for the addition of up to 32 additional state save registers in future implementations.

Note: The state save MSR registers shown in this table occupy sequential MSR addresses and are immediately followed by the IA32_MCG_MISC register. This 64-bit register currently contains just one unreserved bit, bit 0. It is the DS status bit and when set to one, it indicates that a Page Assist or Page Fault occurred while the Debug Store (DS) mechanism was attempting to store either a Branch Trace record or a PEBS record in the DS save area in memory (a complete description of the DS Store and PEBS mechanisms may be found in the MindShare book entitled *The Unabridged Pentium 4*). The logical processor enters the Shutdown state. This bit is set as an aid for debugging the DS handler code. Software must clear this bit to return the logical processor to normal DS operation.

Table 33-2: Intel 64 Processor's Extended MC State MSRs

Register	is copied into this MC State Save MSR
RAX	IA32_MCG_RAX
RBX	IA32_MCG_RBX
RCX	IA32_MCG_RCX
RDX	IA32_MCG_RDX
RSI	IA32_MCG_RSI
RDI	IA32_MCG_RDI
RBP	IA32_MCG_RBP
RSP	IA32_MCG_RSP
Rflags	IA32_MCG_RFLAGS
RIP	IA32_MCG_RIP
-	IA32_MCG_MISC (see footnote in Table 33-1 on page 1215).
-	Reserved
-	Reserved
-	Reserved
-	Reserved
-	Reserved
R8	IA32_MCG_R8
R9	IA32_MCG_R9
R10	IA32_MCG_R10
R11	IA32_MCG_R11
R12	IA32_MCG_R12
R13	IA32_MCG_R13

Table 33-2: Intel 64 Processor's Extended MC State MSRs (Continued)

Register	is copied into this MC State Save MSR
R14	IA32_MCG_R14
R15	IA32_MCG_R15
-	The next 19 sequential MSR addresses are reserved for the addition of up to 19 additional state save registers in future implementations.

The Composition of a Register Bank

Overview

Each MCA error logging register bank is associated with a specific internal processor unit or a group of internal processor units. The association of a specific bank with specific processor unit(s) is processor design-specific and is not published by Intel in the public domain. Each bank consists of the following registers:

- Control register.
- Status register.
- Address register (optional).
- Miscellaneous register (optional).
- Control 2 register. A description of this optional register can be found in "Interrupt On Soft Error Threshold Match" on page 1233.

A description of these registers can be found in the following sections.

The Bank Control Register

General

See Figure 33-5 on page 1218. The bank Control register is 64-bits wide and each bit acts as the Error Enable bit for a specific type of error associated with the error logging bank. Intel does not publish (in the public domain) a list relating each bit to a specific error type.

The Intel documentation states that setting an EE bit to one enables the logging of the error type associated with that bit, while clearing the bit to zero disables logging of that error type. However, this description is at odds with Intel's description of the EN bit in the Status register (see "Error Enabled Bit" on page 1221). It is the author's opinion that the correct description should be something along these lines:

- Setting an EE bit to zero causes the logical processor to log the respective error should it occur, but to mark it as one of lower precedence than an error with its EE bit set to one. For additional information, refer to "Error Enabled Bit" on page 1221.

Writing all ones to a bank's Control register marks all errors associated with that bank as high-precedence, while writing all zeros marks all errors associated with the bank as low-precedence.

P6 and Core Processors

For P6 family processors and processors based on Intel Core microarchitecture (excluding processors in family 06h from model 1Ah onward), the bank 0 Control register (MC0_CTL) is internally aliased to the logical processor's EBL_CR_POWERON MSR (see chapter 3 of the MindShare book entitled *Pentium Pro and Pentium II System Architecture*, Second Edition for more information) and therefore controls platform-specific error handling features. The BIOS is responsible for the initialization of the MC0_CTL MSR and the OS must not modify its contents.

Figure 33-5: MCi Control Register

The Bank Status Register

General

When a soft (correctable) or hard (uncorrectable) hardware error associated with an error logging bank occurs, the error is logged in the bank's Status register. A bank can only register one error at a time, so if another error related to that bank occurs before software has dealt with and cleared an earlier error associated with the same bank, the earlier error is lost (i.e., it is overwritten; there is one exception: see "Overflow Bit" on page 1220). Refer to Figure 33-6 on page 1220. The Bank Status register contains the following status bit fields:

- **VAL**. Error Valid bit. See "Error Valid Bit" on page 1220.
- **O**. Overflow bit. See "Overflow Bit" on page 1220.
- **UC**. Uncorrectable Error bit. See "Uncorrectable Error Bit" on page 1221.
- **EN**. Error Enabled bit. See "Error Enabled Bit" on page 1221.
- **MISCV**. Miscellaneous register Valid bit. See "Miscellaneous Register Valid Bit" on page 1221.
- **ADDRV**. Address register Valid bit. See "Address Register Valid Bit" on page 1221.
- **PCC**. Processor Context Corrupt bit. See "Processor Context Corrupt Bit" on page 1222.
- **MCA Error Code**. See "MCA Error Code and Model Specific Error Code" on page 1222.
- **Model Specific Error Code**. See "MCA Error Code and Model Specific Error Code" on page 1222.
- **Other Information**. See "MCA Error Code and Model Specific Error Code" on page 1222.
- **Corrected Error Count**. See "Interrupt On Soft Error Threshold Match" on page 1233.
- **TES** (Threshold Error Status). See "Green/Yellow Cache Health Indicator" on page 1232.

The subsections that follow describe each of these bits fields.

Figure 33-6: MCi Status Register Detail

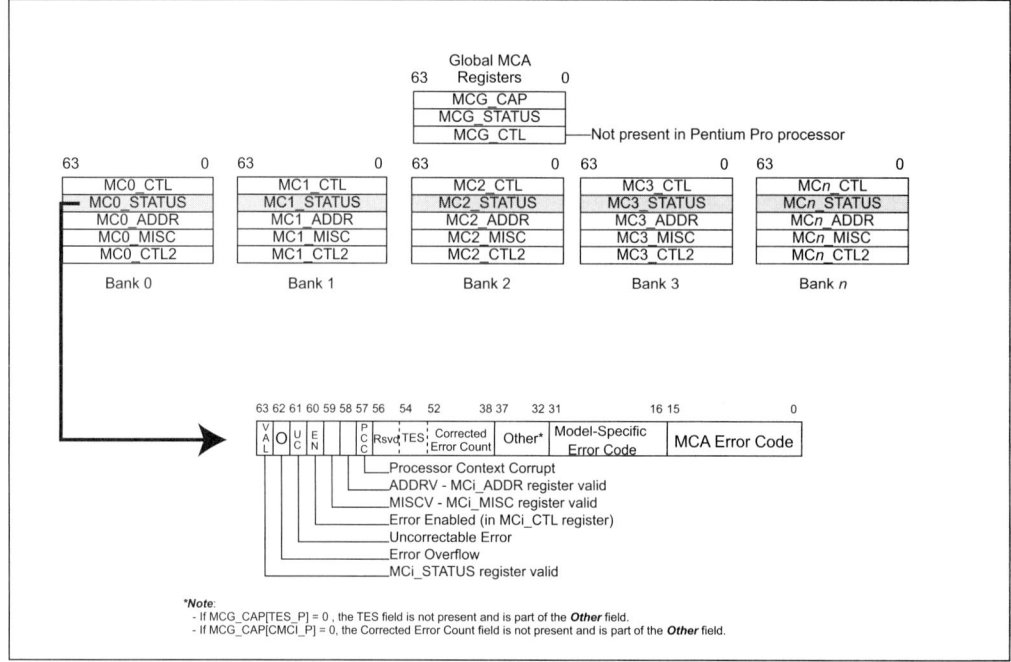

Error Valid Bit

The Error Valid bit is automatically set to one when an error has been logged in the bank's Status register. It is the responsibility of software to clear this bit back to zero:

- 0 = No error logged and the remaining information in the register is irrelevant.
- 1 = The Status register has logged an error and the remaining information in the register defines the error and any other relevant information associated with the error.

Overflow Bit

When set to one, indicates that a second error associated with the same bank was detected before an error logged earlier had been cleared by software. Whether or not the error information logged earlier is overwritten is defined by the following rules:

- A high-precedence error overwrites a low-precedence error (and the "O" bit is set to one to indicate that an overwrite occurred).
- An uncorrectable (i.e., hard) error overwrites a previously-logged correctable (i.e., soft) error (and the "O" bit is set to one to indicate that an overwrite occurred).
- A second uncorrectable error does not overwrite a previously-logged uncorrectable error.

Uncorrectable Error Bit

The logical processor sets this bit to one if the currently logged error is either one that can never be corrected, or that a correction was attempted and failed (e.g., a multi-bit failure that could not be corrected by a cache's ECC algorithm).

Error Enabled Bit

This bit is cleared to zero if the currently logged error is marked as low-importance (i.e., its respective EE bit in the bank Control register = 0), and is set to one if it is marked as high-importance (i.e., its respective EE bit in the bank Control register = 1). See "Overflow Bit" on page 1220.

Miscellaneous Register Valid Bit

If implemented, the bank's Miscellaneous register may contain additional information about the currently logged error. The interpretation of such information is error code specific. A logical processor may or may not implement the Miscellaneous register in each bank:

- 0. When this bit = 0, it means either that the bank does not implement a Miscellaneous register, or that the register may be implemented but does not contain any information associated with the currently logged error.
- 1. When this bit = 1, the bank does implement the Miscellaneous register and the register contains valid, error code-specific information related to the currently logged error.

Address Register Valid Bit

If the currently logged error was associated with an attempted code or data memory access, the memory address is logged in the bank's Address register and the ADDRV bit is set to one in the bank's Status register. If ADDRV = 0, it means either that the bank does not implement an Address register or that there is no memory address associated with the currently logged error.

The address logged is either a 32-bit offset into a memory segment, a 32-bit virtual memory address, or a 36-bit physical memory address. The proper interpretation is defined by the specific error type logged.

Processor Context Corrupt Bit

When set to one, indicates that the state of the logical processor's register set may have been corrupted by the error condition detected and that reliable restarting of the interrupted program (by executing the IRET instruction) may not be possible. When cleared to zero, indicates that the error did not affect the logical processor's state.

MCA Error Code and Model Specific Error Code

Refer to "The Error Code" on page 1223.

Other Information

The interpretation of the bits in this field are implementation-specific and are not part of the MCA specification. Software that is portable among x86 processors should not rely on the values in this field.

The Bank Address Register

See "Address Register Valid Bit" on page 1221.

The Bank Miscellaneous Register

See "Miscellaneous Register Valid Bit" on page 1221.

Control 2 Register

Refer to "Interrupt On Soft Error Threshold Match" on page 1233.

The Error Code

The Error Code Fields

Refer to Figure 33-6 on page 1220. The error code information is returned in MCi_STATUS[31:0] and is divided into two 16-bit error code fields:

- **MCA Error Code**. The 16-bit error code returned in bits [15:0] is guaranteed to be the same for all processors that implement the MCA. The MCA error codes fall into two categories: simple and compound. See "Simple MCA Error Codes" on page 1223 and "Compound MCA Error Codes" on page 1224 for more information.
- **Model-Specific Error Code**. Additional, processor design-specific error information is returned in this 16-bit field. This field contains the model-specific error code that uniquely identifies the Machine Check error condition that was detected. These error codes may differ among processors for the same Machine Check error condition and are Intel proprietary information. It should be noted that this error code is returned in addition to the non-zero MCA error code in the lower 16-bits of the MCi_STATUS register.

Simple MCA Error Codes

Simple MCA error codes indicate global error information. Table 33-3 on page 1223 describes the currently-defined simple MCA error codes.

Table 33-3: Simple MCA Error Codes

Error Type	Binary Encoding	Description
No Error	0000 0000 0000 0000	No error has been reported to this bank of error reporting registers.
Unclassified	0000 0000 0000 0001	This error has not been classified into the MCA error classes.
Microcode ROM Parity Error	0000 0000 0000 0010	There was a parity error in the internal microcode ROM.

Table 33-3: Simple MCA Error Codes (Continued)

Error Type	Binary Encoding	Description
External Error	0000 0000 0000 0011	The assertion of BINIT# by another processor caused this logical processor to generate a Machine Check exception.
FRC Error	0000 0000 0000 0100	An FRC (Functional Redundancy Check) master/slave error was detected. This only applied to the Pentium processor.
Internal Parity Error	0000 0000 0000 0101	Internal Parity Error.
Internal Timer Error	0000 0100 0000 0000	Internal Timer Error.
Internal Unclassified	0000 01xx xxxx xxxx	An internal unclassified error was detected (at least one of the *x* bits must be set to 1).

Compound MCA Error Codes

General

These error codes describe errors related to the TLBs, memory, caches, the external interface, the buses that interconnect internal processor units, or the internal timer (Intel documentation does not identify which timer is being referred to here). Compound errors take one of the forms listed in Table 33-4 on page 1225. As shown in this table, each error code form contains two or more named bit fields (e.g., the TT field). Table 33-5 on page 1226 through Table 33-9 on page 1228 define the meaning of each of these bit fields.

The standard error code name defined by the MCA specification is constructed by substituting the literal text selected in a table by the value of the respective bit field for the brace-delineated bit field within the error code. Text within the template that is not enclosed in braces (including the underscore) is used "as is" (i.e., no substitution). As an example, when applied to the appropriate template from Table 33-4 on page 1225, the error code value 0000 0001 0001 0001b yields the error code name ICACHEL1_RD_ERR, indicating a level 1 instruction cache read error.

Table 33-4: Compound Error Codes Forms

Error Type	Form (in binary)	Template
TLB Errors	000F 0000 0001 TTLL	{TT}TLB{LL}_ERR
Integrated Memory Controller Errors	000F 0000 1MMM CCCC	{MMM}_CHANNEL{CCCC}_ERR
Bus and Interconnect Errors	000F* 1PPT RRRR IILL	BUS{LL}_{PP}_{RRRR}_{II}_{T}_ERR
Generic Cache Hierarchy	000F 0000 0000 11LL	Generic cache hierarchy error.
Cache Hierarchy Errors	000F 0001 RRRR TTLL	{TT}CACHE{LL}_{RRRR}_ERR

*Note:
- The *F* notation in the Form column does not represent the hex character *F*. Rather, it represents the *F*iltering bit.
- Prior to the advent of the Core Duo processors, this bit was always 0.
- See "Correction Report Filtering Bit" on page 1225 for more information.

Correction Report Filtering Bit

Prior to the advent of the cache correction reporting feature in the Core Duo processors, the *F* bit was always 0. When set to one in the error code recorded in an MCA bank's status register, it indicates that the logical processor will not report some or all subsequent successful corrections to the affected cache line. This feature is present in a logical processor if the TES_P bit (Threshold Error Status) is set to one in the MCG_CAP register. Additional information on the TES feature can be found in "Green/Yellow Cache Health Indicator" on page 1232.

Table 33-5: Transaction Type Sub-Field (TT)

Transaction Type	Literal Text	Binary Value
Instruction	I	00b
Data	D	01b
Generic	G	10b
-	-	11b is reserved.
The transaction type field applies to the TLB, Cache, and Bus and Interconnect errors. Bus and Interconnect errors are primarily associated with P6 family and Pentium processors. The generic type is reported when the logical processor cannot determine the transaction type.		

Table 33-6: Memory Hierarchy Sub-Field (LL)

Hierarchy Level	Literal Text	Binary Value
Level 0	L0	00b
Level 1	L1	01b
Level 2	L2	10b
Generic	LG	11b
The Level field indicates the level in the integrated cache memory hierarchy where the error occurred. This field applies to the TLB, Cache, and Bus and Interconnect errors. The generic type is reported when the logical processor cannot determine the hierarchy level.		

Table 33-7: Request Sub-Field (RRRR)

Request Type	Literal Text	Binary Value
Generic error	ERR	0000b
Generic read	RD	0001b
Generic write	WR	0010b

Table 33-7: Request Sub-Field (RRRR) (Continued)

Request Type	Literal Text	Binary Value
Data read	DRD	0011b
Data write	DWR	0100b
Instruction fetch	IRD	0101b
Prefetch	PREFETCH	0110b
Eviction	EVICT	0111b
Snoop	SNOOP	1000b
-	-	1001b - 1111b are reserved.

The RRRR field indicates the action in progress when the error was detected: read and write operations, prefetches, cache line evictions, and cache snoops:
- The Generic error is returned when the error type cannot be determined.
- Generic read or write are indicated if the logical processor cannot determine the type of instruction or data request that caused the error.
- Eviction and snoop requests apply only to the caches.
- All of the other requests apply to TLBs, Caches and Bus and Interconnect-related errors.

Table 33-8: Definition of the Bus and Interconnect-related PP, T, and II Fields

Sub-Field	Transaction	Literal Text	Binary Value
PP (Participation)	Local processor originated request. SRC probably means that this logical processor was the Source (i.e., the originator) of the failed transaction.	SRC	00b
	Local processor responded (RES) to request.	RES	01b
	Local processor observed (OBS) error as 3rd party.	OBS	10b
	Generic.		11b

Table 33-8: Definition of the Bus and Interconnect-related PP, T, and II Fields (Continued)

Sub-Field	Transaction	Literal Text	Binary Value
T (Timeout)	Request timed out.	TIMEOUT	1b
	Request did not time out.	NOTIMEOUT	0b
II (Memory or IO)	Memory access.	M	00b
	Reserved.		01b
	IO access.	IO	10b
	Other transaction.		11b
A Bus (i.e., the processor's external interface) or Interconnect (the interconnect between the various levels of the processor's cache hierarchy) transaction consists of a request (e.g., a read or write) with an address, and the subsequent receipt of a response. The interpretation of the error conditions is independent of the processor-specific external interface implementation.			

Table 33-9: Definition of Integrated Memory Controller MMM and CCCC Fields

Sub-Field	Transaction	Literal Text	Binary Value
MMM	Generic undefined request.	GEN	000b
	Memory read error.	RD	001b
	Memory write error.	WR	010b
	Address/Command error.	AC	011b
	Memory scrubbing error. Refers to an attempted ECC correction.	MS	100b
	Reserved.	-	101b - 111b
CCCC	Channel number.	CHN	0000b - 1110b
	Channel not specified.	-	1111b

Table 33-9: Definition of Integrated Memory Controller MMM and CCCC Fields (Continued)

Sub-Field	Transaction	Literal Text	Binary Value
Errors associated with the integrated memory controller are defined by the memory transaction type (MMM), and the memory channel (CCCC) the error was detected on.			

Example External Interface Error Interpretation

Table 33-10 on page 1229 provides detailed information on the content of the MCA Error, Model-Specific Error, and Other fields of the MC*i*_STATUS register (see Figure 33-6 on page 1220) for an external interface-related error on a processor that implements the Front Side Bus (FSB) rather than the Intel QuickPath Interface (QPI).

Table 33-10: MCi_STATUS Breakdown for FSB-related Errors

Bit	Field	Description
1:0	MCA Error Code	Undefined.
3:2	"	Bit 2 = 1: Special transaction. Bit 3 = 1: Special transaction or IO transaction.
7:4	"	00WR, where W = 1 indicates write and R = 1 indicates read.
9:8	"	Undefined.
10	"	= 0 for all EBL (external bus logic) errors (i.e. FSB). = 1 for internal watchdog timer timeout. In this case, all other bits in the MCA error field are cleared to 0. A watchdog timer timeout only occurs if BINIT# driver enabled.
11	"	= 1 for EBL errors. = 0 for internal watchdog timer timeout.
15:12	"	Reserved.
18:16	Model-Specific Error Code	Reserved.

Table 33-10: MCi_STATUS Breakdown for FSB-related Errors (Continued)

Bit	Field	Description
24:19	"	Although Intel® doesn't define the following terms, the author believes that they have the following meaning: • **BQ**= Bus Queue (IOQ). • **DCU** = Data Cache Unit. • **IFU** = Instruction Fetch Unit. Where possible, the author has speculated on the meaning of the following error code fields. • 000000 = **BQ_DCU_READ_TYPE** error. Attempted read transaction. • 000010 = **BQ_IFU_DEMAND_TYPE** error. Attempted read line transaction generated by the Instruction Fetch Unit due to a miss on the instruction cache. • 000011 = **BQ_IFU_DEMAND_NC_TYPE** error. Attempted single-qword read from non-cacheable memory generated by the instruction fetcher. • 000100 = **BQ_DCU_RFO_TYPE** error. Request For Ownership = Memory Read and Invalidate transaction. • 000101 = **BQ_DCU_RFO_LOCK_TYPE** error. Locked Memory Read and Invalidate transaction. • 000110 = **BQ_DCU_ITOM_TYPE** error. Attempted memory read with intent to modify transaction (i.e., a Memory Read and Invalidate). May differ from the previous two entries by virtue of being for 0 bytes. • 001000 = **BQ_DCU_WB_TYPE** error. Attempted transaction to write a modified line back to memory. • 001010 = **BQ_DCU_WCEVICT_TYPE** error. Attempted transaction to write the contents of one of the processor's write-combining buffers back to memory. In this case, all 32 bytes don't have to be written, so it can be performed as a series of single-qword transfers. • 001011 = **BQ_WCLINE_TYPE** error. Attempted write line transaction to write the full 32 bytes in a write-combining buffer to memory. • 001100 = **BQ_DCU_BTM_TYPE** error. Branch Trace Message error. • 001101 = **BQ_DCU_INTACK_TYPE** error. Attempted Interrupt Acknowledge transaction. • 001110 = **BQ_DCU_INVALL2_TYPE** error. Attempted to invalidate one or more entries in the L2 cache. • 001111 = **BQ_DCU_FLUSHL2_TYPE** error. Attempted to flush the L2 cache. • 010000 = **BQ_DCU_PART_RD_TYPE** error. Attempted to read a qword (or a subset of a qword). • 010010 = **BQ_DCU_PART_WR_TYPE** error. Attempted to write a qword (or a subset of a qword). • 010100 = **BQ_DCU_SPEC_CYC_TYPE** error. Attempted Special transaction. • 011000 = **BQ_DCU_IO_RD_TYPE** error. Attempted IO read. • 011001 = **BQ_DCU_IO_WR_TYPE** error. Attempted IO write. • 011100 = **BQ_DCU_LOCK_RD_TYPE** error.Attempted locked memory read. • 011101 = **BQ_DCU_LOCK_WR_TYPE** error. Attempted locked memory write. • 011110 = **BQ_DCU_SPLOCK_RD_TYPE** error. Attempted locked memory read with Split Lock asserted.
27:25	"	• 000 = **BQ_ERR_HARD_TYPE** error. Transaction resulted in hard failure. • 001 = **BQ_ERR_DOUBLE_TYPE** error. ECC double-bit error detected on data read. • 010 = **BQ_ERR_AERR2_TYPE** error. Address parity error on 1st and 2nd transaction attempt. • 100 = **BQ_ERR_SINGLE_TYPE** error. ECC single-bit failure. • 101 = **BQ_ERR_AERR1_TYPE** error. Address parity error on 1st transaction attempt.
28	"	1 = FRCERR active.

Table 33-10: MCi_STATUS Breakdown for FSB-related Errors (Continued)

Bit	Field	Description
29	"	1 = BERR# asserted by this processor.
30	"	1 = BINIT# asserted by this processor.
31	"	Reserved.
34:32	Other Info	Reserved.
35	"	BINIT# sampled asserted.
36	"	Processor received a parity error on a response received from another agent.
37	"	Processor received a hard fail response from another agent.
38	"	**ROB timeout**. No μop has been retired for a pre-determined amount of time. Occurs when the 15-bit ROB Timeout Counter has a carry out of its high-order bit. The timer is cleared under the following circumstances: • When a μop retires. • When an exception is detected. • When RESET# is asserted. • When a ROB BINIT occurs. Each time that the 8-bit PIC timer has a carry, the ROB Timeout Counter is incremented by one. The PIC timer divides the FSB clock by 128.
41:39	"	Reserved.
42	"	This processor initiated a transaction that received a Hard Fail response.
43	"	The processor has experienced a failure that caused it to assert IERR#.
44	"	This processor initiated a transaction that received an AERR# during the request phase. Upon retrying the transaction, it again received an AERR# in the request phase.
45	"	Uncorrectable ECC error. Syndrome field is in bits 54:47.
46	"	Correctable ECC error. Syndrome field is in bits 54:47.
54:47	"	Contains the 8-bit ECC syndrome only if a correctable or uncorrectable ECC error occurred and there wasn't already a valid ECC syndrome in this field (indicated by bit 45 = 1). After processing an ECC error, the software must clear bit 45 to permit the logging of future ECC syndromes.
56:55	"	Reserved.

Cache Error Reporting

Green/Yellow Cache Health Indicator

Background

Some or all of the caches integrated onto the processor die (implementation-specific) may be protected by ECC (Error Correcting Code) logic. When a line (i.e., the line of data plus its associated cache tag) is written into an ECC-protected cache, the logical processor also stores an additional ECC code that is calculated using the information written into the line. Whenever the line is subsequently read from the cache the ECC bits are recalculated using the read data and are then compared to the ECC bits that were calculated and stored when the line (and its ECC bits) was first written into the cache. If there is a miscompare, then the line has been corrupted. If the ECC logic detects that a single data bit is incorrect, it corrects the error, logs it as a soft error in the MCA registers and continues operation. If two or more data bits have changed state, however, the ECC logic cannot reconstruct the original data. It is flagged as a hard failure, logged as such in the MCA error logging registers, and a MC exception is generated (if the MC exception has been enabled by the OS). This would be a red light condition.

TES (Threshold Error Status) Feature

Starting with the Intel Core Duo processors, a new feature referred to as the Threshold Error Status feature was implemented. Whether or not a logical processor implements this capability is indicated by the state of the TES_P bit (Threshold Error Status) in the MCG_CAP register (see Figure 33-3 on page 1213).

- **TES_P bit = 0**. The feature is not implemented and bits 56:53 of each bank's MCi_STAT register (see Figure 33-4 on page 1214) are part of the Other field (see "Other Information" on page 1222).
- **TES_P bit = 1**. The TES feature is implemented. When a soft (i.e., correctable) ECC cache error is detected, it is logged in the related MCA bank's MCi_STAT register:
  - MCiSTAT[56:55] are reserved.
  - MCiSTAT[54:53] represent the Green/Yellow light indicator (see Table 33-11 on page 1233).

Assuming that the TES feature is implemented and that a particular cache is monitored by the TES logic, the logic tracks the number of correctable ECC errors that have been detected. When a correctable ECC error is detected, the logical processor logs it as a soft error (the UC—Uncorrectable—error bit is cleared to 0) in the related MCA bank's MCi_STAT register (see Figure 33-6 on page 1220) and the TES logic also deposits the cache's TES status in bits [54:53] of the status register (see Table 33-11 on page 1233).

Table 33-11: Cache ECC Green/Yellow Light Indicator

MCi_STAT bits [54:53]	Cache Status
00	**No tracking**. No hardware status tracking is provided for the cache related to the logged soft error.
01	**Green**. Status tracking is provided for the cache related to the logged soft error and the number of correctable ECC errors detected for this cache has not yet risen above the threshold value*.
10	**Yellow**. Status tracking is provided for the cache related to the logged soft error and the number of correctable ECC errors detected for this cache has risen above the threshold value*. While the related cache has not yet incurred any hard (i.e., uncorrectable) ECC errors, Intel recommends that the processor be replaced within a reasonable amount of time.
11	Reserved.
*The design-specific threshold is chosen by Intel.	

Interrupt On Soft Error Threshold Match

Before CMCI, Soft Error Logging Required Periodic Scan

While a hard (i.e., uncorrectable) failure, in addition to being logged in a MC error logging bank, also generates a MC exception, the logging of a soft (i.e., correctable) error is a quiet event (i.e., it does not cause a MC exception). Prior to the advent of the CMCI feature, error logging software therefore had to periodically scan the MCi_STAT registers in each bank to detect whether or not any soft errors had been logged since the last scan. The errors would then be recorded in a non-volatile error log (e.g., on disk, or in flash memory) and zeros written to the respective MCi_STAT register to prepare it to record any future error.

CMCI Eliminates MC Register Scan

The addition of the CMCI (Corrected MC Interrupt) feature eliminates the need for error logging software to perform a periodic scan in order to record correctable errors. Its operation is very simple:

1. The error logging utility initializes a bank's CMCI logic as follows:
   — It programs a correctable error threshold count into the lower 15-bits of the bank's MCi_CTL2 register (see Figure 33-7 on page 1234).
   — It enables the bank's CMCI capability by setting the MCi_CTL2[CMCI_EN] bit to one (see Figure 33-7 on page 1234).
2. It sets up an Interrupt Gate or Trap Gate in the IDT to point to the CMCI interrupt handler.
3. It programs the Local APIC's CMCI LVT (Local Vector Table) register with the interrupt vector associated with CMCI interrupt and enables the interrupt. A detailed description of this LVT entry can be found in "Correctable Machine Check (CMC) Interrupt" on page 1372.

Each time that a correctable error is logged in any of the MC banks that support CMCI capability (and for which it has been enabled), the logical processor compares the Corrected Error Count field in the MCi_STAT register (see Figure 33-6 on page 1220) to the Threshold value specified in the bank's MCi_CTL2 register. When it matches, the CMCI interrupt (*not a Machine Check exception*) is generated to alert the error logging software. The software logs the error in non-volatile memory, clears the error (by writing all zeros to the bank's MCi_STAT register) and then returns to the interrupted program.

Figure 33-7: The MCi_CTL2 Register

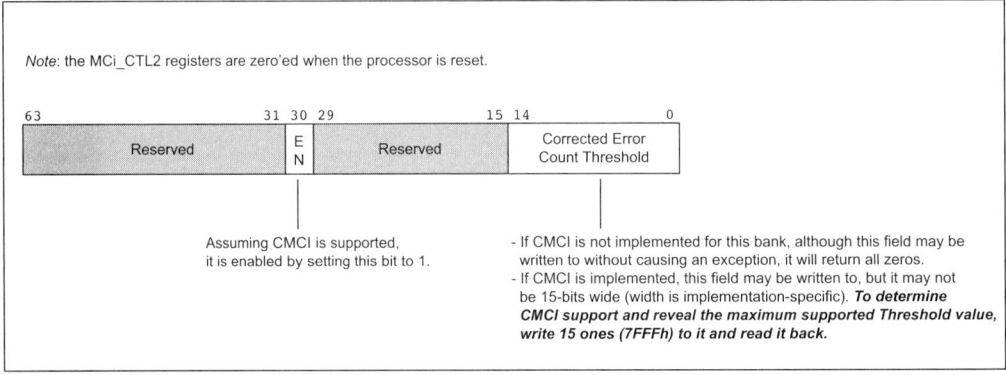

Determining Processor's CMCI Support

The programmer may determine whether or not a logical processor supports the CMCI feature by checking for a one in the MCG_CAP[CMCI_P] bit (see Figure 33-3 on page 1213). Whether or not a particular bank supports the feature, however, is determined as described in the next section.

Determining a Bank's CMCI Support

As described in Figure 33-7 on page 1234, the programmer may determine whether or not a specific bank supports the CMCI feature by writing all ones into the bank's Corrected Error Count Threshold field. If it returns all zeros, the bank does not support the feature. If it returns a non-zero value, the bank supports CMCI and the returned, non-zero value indicates the width of the programmable Threshold field.

CMCI Interrupt Is Separate and Distinct From MC Exception

The CMCI interrupt is separate and distinct from the MC exception and is unaffected by the state of the CR4[MCE] bit. It is also unaffected by the state of the bits in a bank's MCiCTL register.

CMC Interrupt May Affect Multiple Cores/Logical Processors

A cache shared by multiple cores (or by multiple logical processors if Hyper-Threading is enabled) may generate a correctable error and log it in a CMCI-enabled MC bank. If this results in a match between the MCi_STAT's Corrected Error Count field and the MCiCTL2's Threshold field, a CMC interrupt is sent to all of the Local APICs whose cores (or logical processors) are associated with the shared cache.

CMC Interrupt Should Only Be Serviced Once

While the CMC interrupt may be delivered to multiple cores or logical processors for servicing, just as with any other device it is important that it only be serviced by one of them. In order to ensure that this is the case, Intel documentation recommends following this procedure:

1. System software (i.e., the OS) should deposit an initialization procedure in memory and command each core/logical processor to execute it (by sending an IPI message to each of them). A semaphore should protect entry to the body of the procedure so that only one core or logical processor at a time can execute it. When executed by each core or logical processor, it causes the following actions to be taken.
2. The procedure will create a core/logical processor-specific data structure

with one field per MC bank initially indicating that the core/logical processor has not yet taken responsibility for handling CMC interrupts for any of the banks.

3. For each bank, check the state of the MCi_CTL2[EN] bit to see if any other core/logical processor has already taken responsibility for handling CMC interrupts for the bank:
   — If the EN bit = 1, another core/logical processor already owns this bank so skip to the next bank's MCi_CTL2 register.
   — If the EN bit = 0, determine if the bank supports CMCI capability (see "Determining a Bank's CMCI Support" on page 1235):
      – If it doesn't, skip to the next bank.
      – If it does, set the respective ownership (responsibility) bit in the data structure (to indicate that this logical processor has assumed responsibility for servicing CMC interrupts associated with this bank).
      – Then initialize the MCi_CTL2 register Threshold field with the correctable error threshold value.
      – Enable the bank's CMCI capability by setting MCi_CTL2[EN] = 1.

4. When the procedure has evaluated all of the banks, it should set up an Interrupt Gate or Trap Gate in the IDT to point to its CMCI interrupt handler.

5. Next, the procedure programs this core's/logical processor's Local APIC's CMCI LVT (Local Vector Table) register with the interrupt vector associated with its CMCI interrupt and enables the interrupt. A detailed description of the CMCI LVT entry can be found in "Correctable Machine Check (CMC) Interrupt" on page 1372.

6. Finally, the procedure logs and clears any correctable errors that have already been logged in the banks under its jurisdiction.

7. Having completed the bank scan, the procedure clears the semaphore (so another core/logical processor can run the procedure) and exits the procedure.

When a CMC interrupt is later generated, the CMC interrupt handler need only interrogate the MCi_STAT registers within the banks under its jurisdiction.

MC Exception Is Generally Not Recoverable

Generally speaking, after a Machine Check exception, the logical processor cannot reliably restart the interrupted program (by executing an IRET at the end of the MC handler). While certain Machine Check exception conditions in future processors may permit restart of the interrupted program, *to date, the Machine Check exception is not recoverable on any x86 processors. The interrupted program cannot be safely resumed.*

The state of the MCG_STATUS[RIPV], MCi_STATUS[O] and MCi_STATUS[PCC] bits (where i = the bank number) indicate whether or not the interrupted program may be safely resumed. If any of these bits are set to one, the interrupted program may not be safely resumed at the point of interruption.

Machine Check and BINIT#

To enable a logical processor's ability to generate a MC exception when it observes another agent (another processor or the chipset) asserts BINIT#, the BIOS must enable the processor's BINIT# drive as well as observation capabilities by writing to the processor's EBL_CR_POWERON MSR (see chapter 3 of the MindShare book entitled *Pentium Pro and Pentium II System Architecture*, Second Edition for more information).

Additional Error Logging Notes

Error Buffering Capability

The MCA permits a processor implementation to buffer up multiple Machine Check errors. It should be noted that the P6 processors, the Pentium 4 (and its Xeon and Celeron derivatives), and the Pentium M (and, to the author's knowledge, any current-day processors) do not support this capability. Error logging software should be written so as to be compatible with future processors. This is accomplished by reading each bank's MCi_STATUS register and then writing zeros to clear the O and V bits (see Figure 33-6 on page 1220). The software should then re-read the register to see if the V bit has, in fact, been cleared. Assuming that one or more additional errors have been buffered up for the bank, the logical processor loads the next error into the bank and sets the V bit again.

Additional Information for Each Log Entry

Additional information that should be stored by the error logging software includes:

- The logical processor's TSC (Time Stamp Counter register) value (can be used to determine the frequency of errors).
- In a system incorporating multiple processors, the ID of the logical processor.

34 *The Local and IO APICs*

The Previous Chapter

The previous chapter provided a detailed description of the Machine Check Architecture:

- The MCA Elements.
- The Global Registers.
- The Composition of a Register Bank.
- The Error Code.
- Cache Error Reporting.
- MC Exception Is Generally Not Recoverable.

This Chapter

This chapter provides a complete description of the Local and IO APICs. It includes:

- A Short History of the APIC's Evolution.
- Before the APIC.
- MP Systems Need a Better Interrupt Distribution Mechanism.
- Detecting Presence/Version/Capabilities of Local APIC.
- Local APIC's Initial State.
- Enabling/Disabling the Local APIC.
- Mode Selection.
- The Local APIC Register Set.
- Local APIC ID Assignments and Addressing.
  — ID Assignment in xAPIC Mode.
  — ID Assignment in x2APIC Mode.
  — Local APIC Addressing.
  — Lowest-Priority Delivery Mode.
- Local APIC IDs Are Stored in the MP and ACPI Tables.

- Accessing the Local APIC ID.
- An Introduction to the Interrupt Sources.
- Introduction to Interrupt Priority.
- Task and Processor Priority.
- IO/Local APICs Cooperate on Interrupt Handling.
- Message Signaled Interrupts (MSI).
- Interrupt Delivery from Legacy 8259a Interrupt Controller.
- SW-Initiated Interrupt Message Transmission.
- x2APIC Mode's Self IPI Feature.
- Locally Generated Interrupts.
  — The Local Vector Table.
  — Local Interrupt 0 (LINT0).
  — Local Interrupt 1 (LINT1).
  — The Local APIC Timer.
  — The Performance Counter Overflow Interrupt.
  — The Thermal Sensor Interrupt.
  — Correctable Machine Check (CMC) Interrupt.
  — The Local APIC's Error Interrupt.
- The Spurious Interrupt Vector.
- Boot Strap Processor (BSP) Selection.
- How the APs are Discovered and Configured.

APIC and the IA-32 Architecture

The APIC's (Advanced Programmable Interrupt Controller's) role has been central to the x86 platform's inter-device communication scheme for many years. In addition to providing a communication channel between device adapters and their respective drivers, the APICs allow program threads running on different logical processors to communicate with each other by passing IPI (Inter-Processor Interrupt) messages to each other. Until the advent of the x2APIC architecture, however, the Local APIC's register set and operational characteristics were considered design-specific and outside the scope of the IA-32 architecture. With the introduction of the x2APIC architecture (in the Core i7 processor), the Local APIC's register set is accessible as a set of architecturally-defined MSRs. Even prior to the introduction of the x2APIC feature, however, the Local and IO APICs played a central role in system design. For that reason, this chapter provides a detailed description of the Local and IO APIC operation in both x2APIC Mode as well as the earlier APIC modes of operation.

Definition of IO and Local APICs

Basic definitions of the Local and IO APICs may be found in "APIC" on page 19.

Hardware Context Is Essential

In order to adequately explain the genesis and functionality of the Local and IO APIC modules, it is necessary to have some understanding of their role within the hardware platform. Towards this end, this chapter, where applicable, describes the hardware ecosystem within which the Local and IO APICs fulfill such an important role.

A Short History of the APIC's Evolution

The following is a *very* short history of the APIC.

APIC Introduction

The APIC was first introduced as a separate, stand-alone chip, the 82489DX. The Local APIC was first introduced in the P54C version of the Pentium.

Pentium Pro APIC Enhancements

The Pentium Pro implemented the following improvements to the Local APIC:

- **Performance Counter Interrupt**. The APIC can be enabled to generate an interrupt if a Performance Counter generates an overflow when incremented. The Performance Counter Overflow entry (see "The Performance Counter Overflow Interrupt" on page 1368) was added to the Local APIC's Local Vector Table (LVT register set) to support this feature.
- **APIC Base MSR added**. While the memory address range associated with the Local APIC's register set was hardwired on the Pentium (the base address of the 4KB range was hardwired at FEE00000h), the APIC_BASE MSR added (see Figure 34-11 on page 1258) in the Pentium Pro permits the programmer to specify (in APIC_BASE[35:12]) the register set's base address starting on any 4KB-aligned address range in the logical processor's physical memory address space.

- **Software Enable/Disable added**. The Pentium processor's Local APIC could not be enabled or disabled under software control. This could only be accomplished via hardware when the processor sampled an input on the trailing-edge of reset. Starting with the Pentium Pro, the APIC_BASE[EN] bit can be used by software for this purpose.
- **BSP bit added**. The APIC_BASE[BSP] bit is a read-only bit that *remembers* whether the logical processor was selected as the Boot Strap Processor or as an Application Processor (AP) at startup time. See "Boot Strap Processor (BSP) Selection" on page 1378 for more information on the BSP selection process.
- **APIC access propagation deleted**. When software executing on a Pentium performed a load or a store targeting the processor's Local APIC register set, the memory access was also propagated out onto the processor's external interface. This was eliminated with the advent of the P6 processor family.
- **Illegal Register Address error bit added** to the Local APIC's Error Status register (see Figure 34-26 on page 1302).
- **Remote Register Read capability was eliminated**.
- **SMI delivery added**. The ability to deliver an SMI to a logical processor via an Inter-Processor Interrupt (IPI) message was added.

The Pentium II and Pentium III

No enhancements were made to the APIC architecture in the Pentium II and Pentium III processors.

Pentium 4 APIC Enhancements: xAPIC

To differentiate the revised APIC architecture introduced with the advent of the Pentium 4 from the old APIC architecture, it is referred to as the xAPIC architecture. For the remainder of this chapter, the earlier APIC architecture is referred to simply as the *APIC architecture*, or the *legacy APIC architecture*. The xAPIC architecture introduced the following improvements:

- **Thermal Sensor interrupt added** (see "The Thermal Sensor Interrupt" on page 1370).
- **APIC ID Register enhanced**. In the P6 and Pentium, the APIC ID field was 4-bits, and encodings 0h - Eh could be used to uniquely identify 15 different processors connected to the APIC bus. In the Pentium 4, the xAPIC spec extended the local APIC ID field to 8 bits which can be used to identify up to 255 logical processors in the system.

- **3-wire APIC bus eliminated** and interrupt messages take the form of memory-mapped IO write transactions performed on the FSB.
- **APIC Arbitration ID register eliminated** (because the APIC bus was eliminated).
- **Some error bits eliminated**. The following error bits became Reserved bits (see Figure 34-26 on page 1302): Receive Accept Error, Send Accept Error, Receive Checksum Error, and Send Checksum Error.
- **INIT message changed**. The INIT Level De-assert message was changed to the INIT message.
- **Lowest-Priority Delivery Mode enhanced**. In support of the Lowest-Priority Delivery Mode, a single-byte memory-mapped IO write transaction was added. The OS causes the logical processor to perform this write on the FSB to tell the chipset the relative importance of the task currently being executed on that logical processor (see "Lowest-Priority Delivery Mode" on page 1294).
- **Focus Processor Checking eliminated**.
- **MSI interrupt messages**. An MSI (Message-Signaled Interrupt) message generated by a PCI, PCI-X or PCI Express device can be sent directly to the logical processor(s) as a memory-mapped IO write transaction on the FSB.

The x2APIC Architecture

The latest batch of modifications to the APIC architecture (introduced with the advent of the Core i7 processor) is referred to as the x2APIC architecture and includes the following modifications:

- CPUID instruction enhanced to report whether or not a processor implements this feature (CPUID request type 1 returns a 1 in ECX[21]).
- If the x2APIC Architecture feature is available, it is enabled via a new bit in the APIC_Base MSR (see Figure 34-11 on page 1258).
- Enabling this feature disables the memory-mapped IO Local APIC registers and makes them available as MSRs instead. The 4KB memory range (or *hole*) normally consumed by the Local APIC registers is therefore available for assignment to system RAM memory.
- The Self IPI MSR was added (see Figure 34-58 on page 1359).
- The 64-bit Interrupt Command Register (ICR) can be written to using a single WRMSR operation versus two 32-bit memory-mapped IO accesses.
- Elimination of the Delivery Status bit in the ICR.
- Elimination of support for the Flat topology model and, as a result, elimination of the Destination Format Register (DFR).
- A new method for Local APIC ID assignment permits a significantly larger number of Local APICs (and therefore, logical processors) in the system.

- If support is indicated by a new read-only bit in the Local APIC's Version register, a new feature referred to as Directed EOI is available in both xAPIC and x2APIC modes (see "Broadcast Versus Directed EOI" on page 1338).
- Revised Error Status Register (ESR) layout in x2APIC mode (see Figure 34-67 on page 1375).

Before the APIC

Most x86 system chipsets incorporate an interrupt controller that receives interrupt requests from IO devices and passes them to the logical processor (or, in a multiprocessor system, to one or more of the logical processors). The Interrupt Controller typically consists of one of the following:

- In a single processor PC compatible machine, a pair of cascaded 8259A PICs (Programmable Interrupt Controllers). See Figure 34-2 on page 1246.
- In a multiprocessor system, an IO APIC module. See Figure 34-5 on page 1250.

Refer to Figure 34-1 on page 1245. In older chipsets, the interrupt controller was incorporated in the PCI-to-ISA Bridge (commonly referred to as the South Bridge), or in the ICH (IO Control Hub) in later chipsets. This was a strategically convenient location because the interrupt request signals from PCI and ISA devices could easily be connected to it.

Assuming that an older system was a single processor, PC-compatible machine (Figure 34-2 on page 1246 and Figure 34-1 on page 1245), the master 8259A asserts its INTR (Interrupt Request) output when it detects any interrupt requests from device adapters. This was connected to the processor's INTR pin (later referred to as the LINT0 pin). In response to its assertion, the processor would take the following actions:

1. Assuming that recognition of external interrupts was enabled (in other words, the programmer had not executed a CLI instruction), the processor recognized the request when it completed the execution of the current instruction.
2. The processor temporarily ceased execution of the interrupted program.
3. The processor generated an Interrupt Acknowledge transaction to obtain the 8-bit interrupt vector associated with the highest priority request from the Interrupt Controller.
4. The North Bridge passed the transaction to the PCI bus to make it visible to the chip that contains the interrupt controller (i.e., the South Bridge in the example system).

5. The interrupt controller supplied the 8-bit interrupt vector associated with the highest priority request to the North Bridge.
6. The North Bridge supplied the interrupt vector to the processor.
7. The processor used the 8-bit vector as an index into the IDT in memory and read the CS:EIP value from the selected entry. This CS:EIP value pointed to the entry point of the interrupt handler within the associated device's driver.
8. The processor pushed the contents of its CS, EIP and Eflags registers into stack memory (to mark its place in the interrupted program).
9. The processor then automatically disabled recognition of additional external hardware interrupts (i.e., it cleared Eflags[IF] to 0).
10. Using the new CS:EIP value obtained from the selected IDT entry, the processor started fetching the instructions that comprised the interrupt handler and executed it.

A detailed description of the dual 8259A PICs can be found in chapter 18 of the MindShare book entitled *ISA System Architecture, Third Edition*.

Figure 34-1: An External Hardware Interrupt Delivered to the Processor's INTR Pin

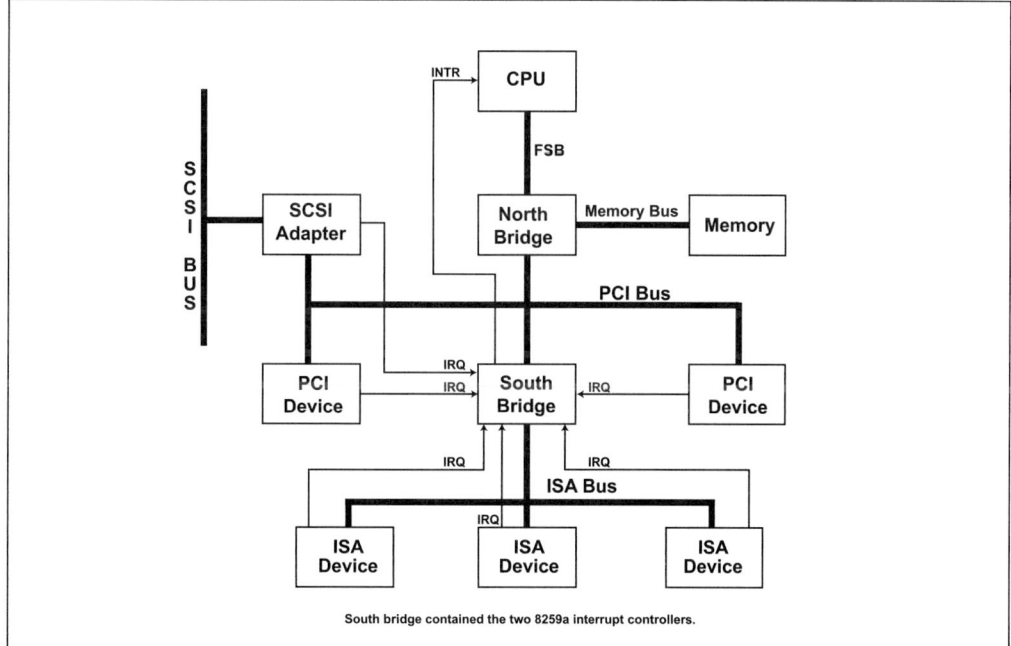

Figure 34-2: Legacy PC-AT Compatible Interrupt Controllers

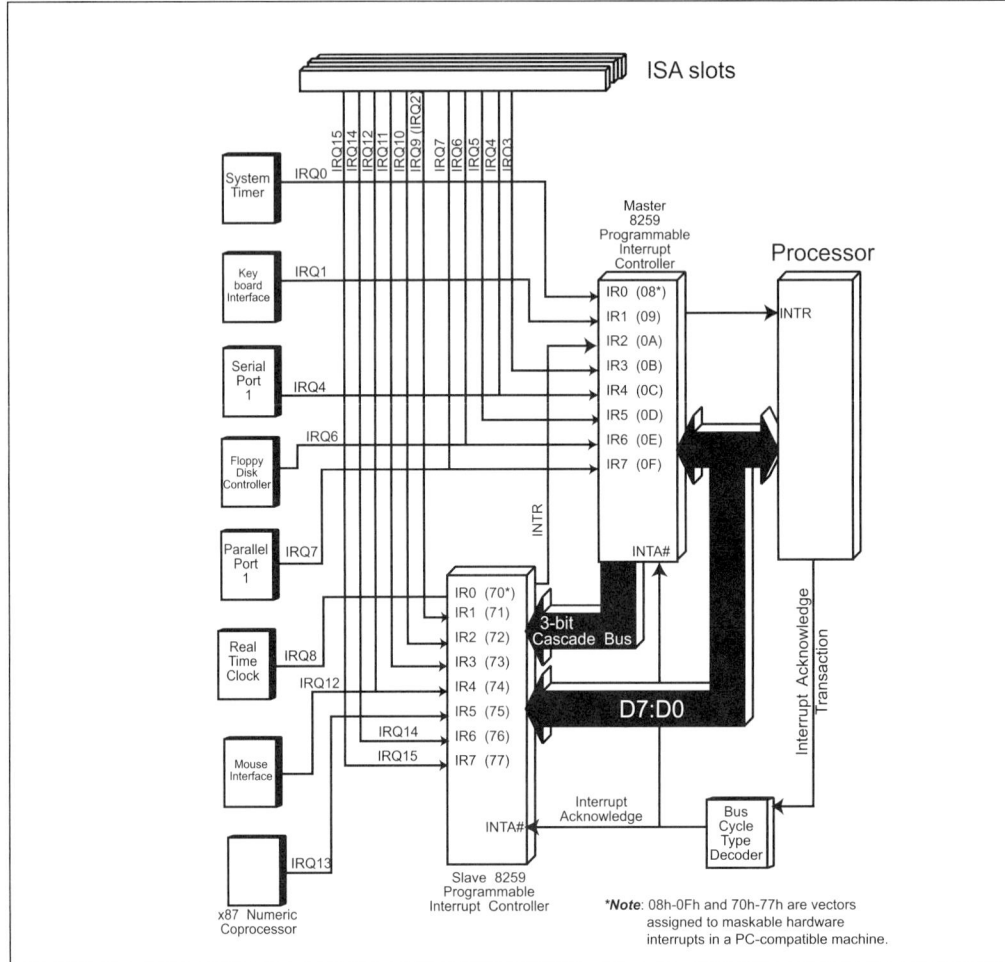

MP Systems Need a Better Interrupt Distribution Mechanism

Legacy Interrupt Delivery System Is Inefficient

As just described, the legacy interrupt delivery mechanism interrupts the processor by asserting the processor's INTR input signal. The processor recognizes the interrupt on the next instruction boundary and must then perform an Interrupt Acknowledge transaction on its external interface to obtain the interrupt vector from the interrupt controller. The legacy interrupt delivery system is inefficient in a number of ways (see Table 34-1 on page 1247).

Table 34-1: Legacy Interrupt Delivery Inefficiencies

Deficiency	Description
Single logical processor shoulders entire interrupt servicing load.	Refer to Figure 34-3 on page 1248. Using the INTR signal to deliver interrupts to the processors in a multiprocessor (MP) system is a poor approach. All of the interrupts would be delivered to one processor, the one connected to the output of the master 8259A PIC and that processor would have the burden of servicing *all* hardware interrupts. Placing such a burden on a single processor would yield an *asymmetric* processing model rather than one wherein the processing load could be more equally distributed across all of the processors. In an MP system, any processor should be capable of executing any program and of servicing interrupts initiated by any device adapter. The OS could then attempt to distribute the processing load more equally across all of the processors in order to achieve a *symmetric* rather than an asymmetric processing model. Delivering all of the interrupts to one processor would yield a system that supports asymmetric multiprocessing.
Two-step delivery process is inefficient.	The legacy interrupt delivery mechanism does not deliver the interrupt vector to the processor. The processor is forced to perform a transaction (the Interrupt Acknowledge transaction) on the external interface to obtain the vector. This consumes bus bandwidth and also increases the latency (i.e., the delay) in servicing an interrupt.
No ability for software to send an interrupt to another core or logical processor.	No method is provided for software running on one processor to transmit an interrupt to one or more of the other processors.

Table 34-1: Legacy Interrupt Delivery Inefficiencies (Continued)

Deficiency	Description
Inflexible delivery of NMI and SMI interrupts.	The chipset delivers NMI and SMI interrupts via hard-wired trace runs to a single processor in the system. It would be nice if the chipset had the ability to direct an NMI or SMI to any system processor under the guidance of system software.

Figure 34-3: Legacy Interrupt Delivery Mechanism Inefficient

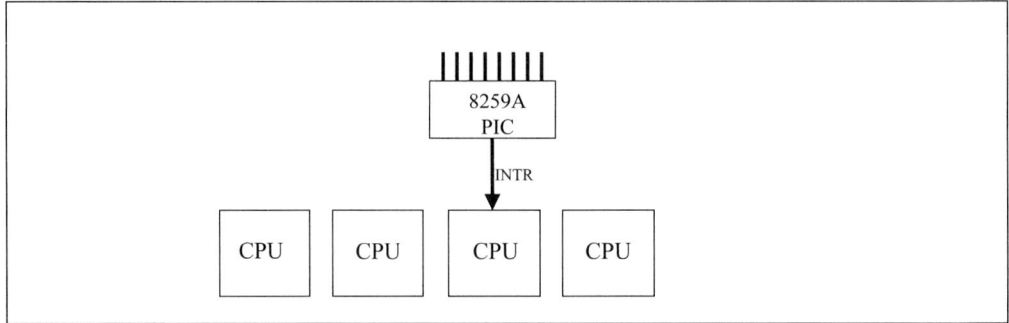

The APIC Interrupt Distribution Mechanism

Introduction

Refer to Figure 34-4 on page 1249. Starting with the P54C version of the Pentium, a Local APIC module was incorporated within all Intel x86 processors. In addition, the chipset incorporated an IO APIC module. When a device adapter generated an interrupt to the IO APIC, the IO APIC in turn transmitted an interrupt message to all of the Local APICs within the processor packages. The interrupt message contained the identity of the target Local APIC (or APICs) as well as the interrupt vector. An interrupt message could target one specific processor, multiple processors, or the processor that is currently executing the lowest-priority program (from the perspective of the OS).

Figure 34-4: The APIC Bus (Pentium and P6)

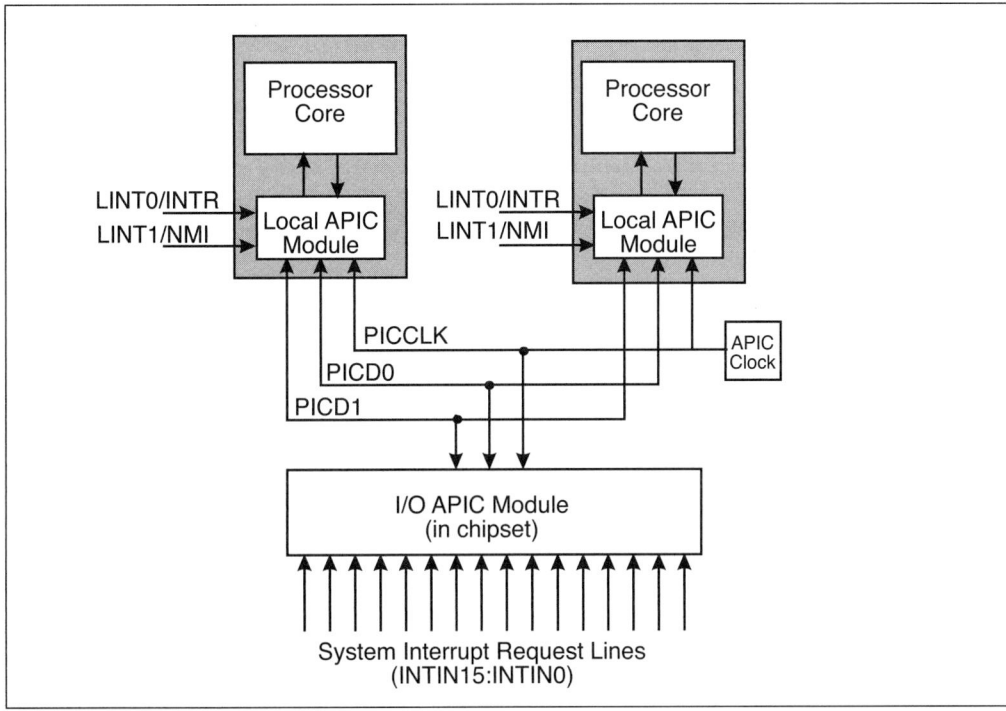

Message Types

Inter-Processor Interrupt (IPI) Messages. In addition to the IO APIC sending device adapter interrupt messages to the Local APICs within the processors, software executing on one logical processor can command its Local APIC to send an interrupt message to one or more of the other logical processors (or even to itself). It does so by writing a command into its Local APIC's ICR (Interrupt Command Register).

NMI, SMI and Init Messages. The IO APIC can translate a chipset generated NMI, SMI, or INIT (i.e., a soft reset) into an NMI, SMI, or INIT interrupt message and direct it to a specific logical processor or group of logical processors.

Legacy Interrupt Message. The IO APIC can translate an interrupt request received from the legacy 8259a interrupt controller into a legacy interrupt message and direct it to a specific logical processor.

Message Transfer Mechanism Prior to the Pentium 4

Refer to Figure 34-4 on page 1249. In systems based on the Pentium P54C/P55C and the P6 processor family, the IO APIC was connected to the Local APICs within the processors via a 3-wire APIC bus. The APIC bus consisted of two data lines and an APIC clock line. During each clock cycle, two bits of a message could be transmitted. Since all of the interrupt messages were considerably longer than two bits, it took multiple APIC clock cycles to transmit a message. Slow, to say the least.

Message Transfer Mechanism Starting with the Pentium 4

Starting with the Pentium 4, the APIC bus was eliminated. When the IO APIC within the chipset must send an interrupt message to the logical processors, it does so via the FSB (see Figure 34-5 on page 1250) by performing a memory write transaction to write the interrupt message to the Local APICs within the processors. The Local APICs are memory-mapped IO devices accessed via memory transactions. Likewise, when a message must be sent from the Local APIC of one logical processor to one or more of the Local APICs associated with other logical processors, it is sent by performing a memory write transaction on the FSB.

Figure 34-5: The Pentium 4 Eliminated the APIC Bus

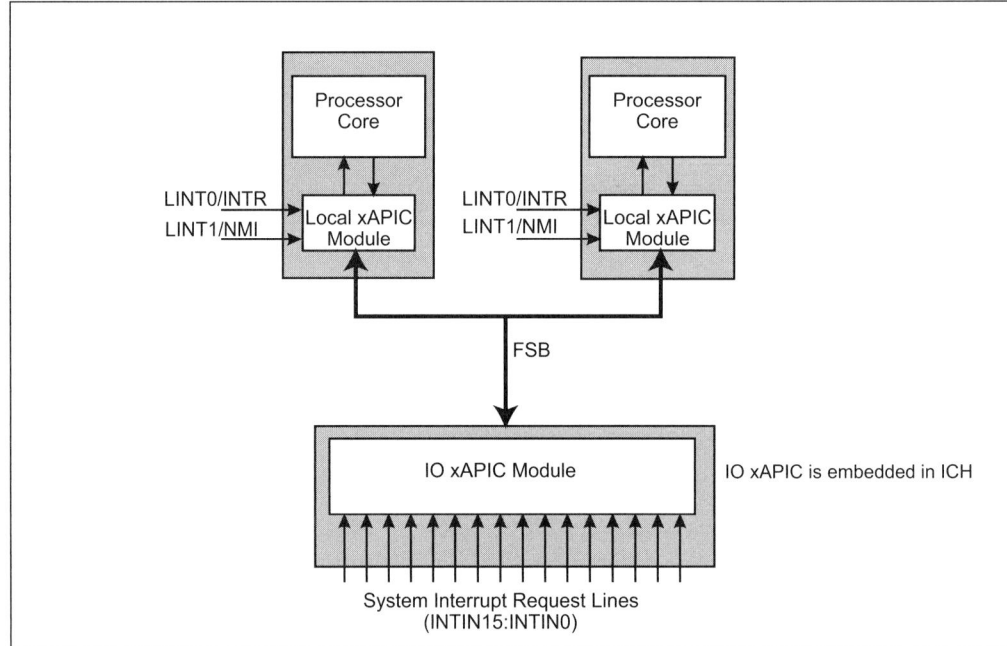

Message Transfer Mechanism in Intel QPI-based Systems

In systems wherein the processors communicate with each other and with the platform logic via the QPI (QuickPath Interconnect) external interface, interrupt messages are transferred over QPI as message packets. The series of three figures that follow illustrate single-, dual-, and quad-processor systems. Although they show multiple cores each with its own dedicated Local APIC, if Hyper-Threading is enabled, each core, in turn, contains multiple logical processors each with its own Local APIC. As illustrated in Figure 34-7 on page 1252, the ICH (IO Control Hub; what used to be called the South Bridge) contains both the legacy 8259A interrupt controllers as well as the IO APIC.

Figure 34-6: Intel QPI System With Single Physical Processor

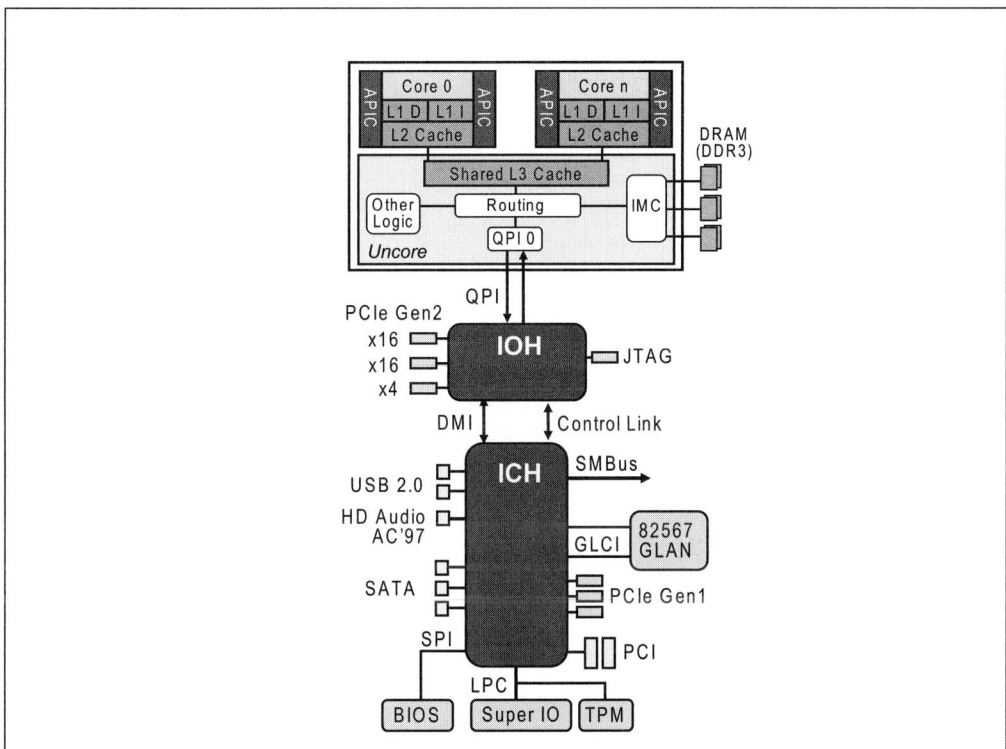

Figure 34-7: Intel QPI System With Dual Physical Processors

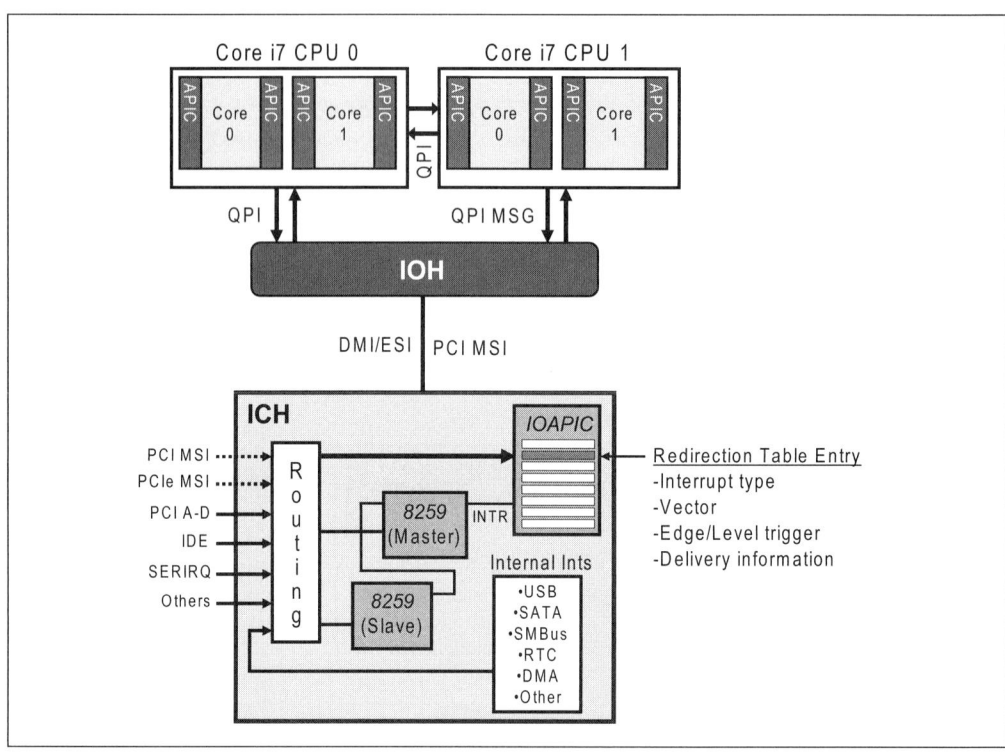

Figure 34-8: Intel QPI System With Four Physical Processors

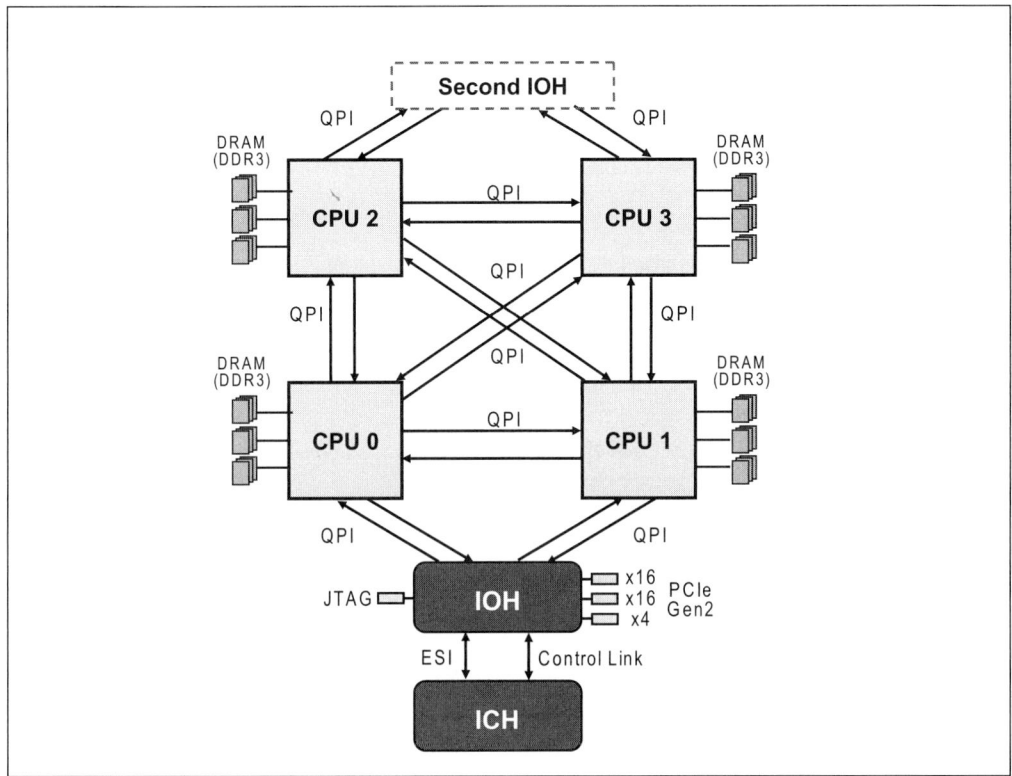

Processors Reside in Clusters

Figure 34-9 on page 1254 illustrates a system incorporating eight processors that utilize the FSB to communicate with each other and with the platform. A group of processors that reside on a specific FSB is referred to as a cluster. An MP system may incorporate one or more processor clusters. The illustration shows only four processor packages per FSB due to electrical loading constraints.

When the IO APIC sends a message to one or more of the logical processors (specifically, to their Local APICs), the interrupt message contains the ID of the target Local APIC within the target cluster. The processor hardware automatically assigns each Local APIC a unique APIC ID which includes the ID of the processor Cluster it resides within:

- When the Local APICs are operating in xAPIC Mode (rather than x2APIC

Mode), the cluster ID and unique Local APIC ID are automatically assigned at start-up time. After power-up, the OS can change the automatically assigned Local APIC IDs, but each of the Local APICs in the system must be assigned a unique ID.

- When the Local APICs are operating in x2APIC Mode, the Local APIC IDs are automatically assigned by hardware when x2APIC Mode is entered and software cannot change them.

Figure 34-9: The Big Picture

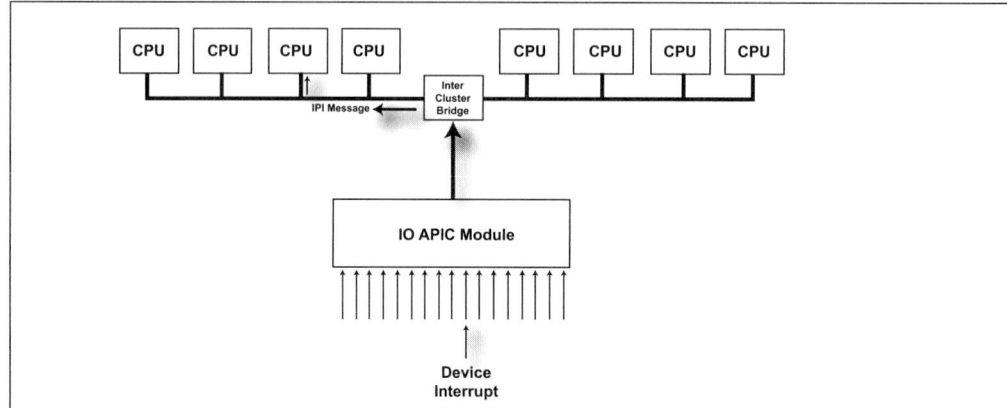

Each Core/Logical Processor Has a Dedicated Local APIC

A processor that implements multiple cores includes one Local APIC for each of the cores each with a unique APIC ID automatically assigned by hardware at start-up time. A processor or core that supports Hyper-Threading includes one Local APIC for each logical processor. As an example, if a processor package incorporates four cores, supports Hyper-Threading and Hyper-Threading is enabled, then the package implements eight Local APICs (two logical processors, each with a dedicated Local APIC, per core). This is necessary so that an interrupt can be directed to interrupt the program thread running on a specific core or logical processor.

Introduction to the Message Addressing Modes

Although an interrupt message takes the form of a specially-formatted memory-mapped IO write transaction, the address contained within the transaction consists of two components:

- The memory address FEE00000h which is recognized as the address of *all* Local APICs.
- The ID of the targeted Local APIC (or APICs).

There are two addressing modes:

- **Physical Destination Mode.** A message using this mode contains the unique address of the one and only target Local APIC. Although the message is received by all Local APICs, it is only accepted by the one whose APIC ID matches the one specified in the message. This method would be used under the following circumstances:
  — In an interrupt message packet generated as the result of a device adapter interrupt (because the interrupt handler should only be executed by one entity).
  — In an NMI or SMI interrupt message packet generated by the chipset (because the interrupt handler should only be executed by one entity).
  — In an interrupt message packet sent from one logical processor to another to command the target logical processor to run a program that has been placed in memory.
- **Logical Destination Mode.** This method is used if the OS kernel has placed a program in memory that it wishes a number of logical processors to execute. A message using this addressing mode contains either an 8-bit (when the Local APICs are operating in xAPIC Mode) or 16-bit (when the Local APICs are operating in x2APIC Mode) address field wherein each bit (if it is a one) can be used to select a Local APIC within a group of 8 or 16 Local APICs. In this way, the message can be sent to up to 8 or 16 Local APICs.

Detecting Presence/Version/Capabilities of Local APIC

Presence

The programmer can determine whether or not a processor supports the APIC architecture by executing a CPUID request type 1 and verifying that EDX[9] = 1. All processors introduced after the Pentium P54C include the Local APIC.

Version

Assuming the Local APIC is supported, additional information regarding the APIC implementation may be obtained from the read-only APIC Version register. It provides the information illustrated in Figure 34-10 on page 1256:

- The number of entries in the Local APIC's Local Vector Table (LVT). See "The Local Vector Table" on page 1360 for more information.

- The version (i.e., type of) the Local APIC implementation.
- A bit indicating whether or not the Directed EOI feature is supported (see "Broadcast Versus Directed EOI" on page 1338). If it is, this feature is available in both the xAPIC and x2APIC modes of operation.

x2APIC Capability Verification

The programmer may issue a CPUID request type 1 and check for a 1 in ECX[21] to determine whether or not a processor implements the x2APIC capabilities.

Figure 34-10: Local APIC Version Register

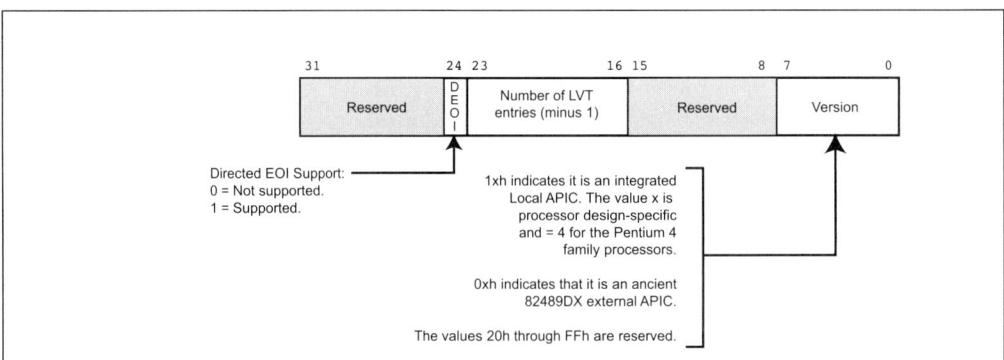

Local APIC's Initial State

When reset is removed from the processor, the Local APIC has the following operational characteristics:

- It is **enabled in xAPIC Mode** (EN = 1 and EXTD = 0 in the APIC Base MSR—Figure 34-11 on page 1258).
- **x2APIC Mode is disabled**.
- The Local APIC's register set resides in memory space starting at physical memory address **FEE00000h**. MSR access to the register set is disabled (because x2APIC Mode is disabled).
- In all of the LVT registers, all bits except the Mask bits are cleared to zero. The Mask bits are set to one to disable recognition of the respective local interrupt events.

- The Spurious Interrupt Vector register is set to 000000FFh. This has the following effects:
  - The EOI Broadcast feature is enabled (see "Broadcast Versus Directed EOI" on page 1338).
  - The spurious interrupt vector is set to FFh (see "The Spurious Interrupt Vector" on page 1376).
  - Although the APIC Software Enable bit is cleared to 0, the APIC is nonetheless enabled and is in xAPIC Mode. This condition is unique after a reset. Normally, clearing this bit to 0 disables the Local APIC.
- If this logical processor was selected as the Bootstrap Processor (BSP) by the hardware initialization process, the BSP bit in the APIC_Base MSR will be one. Otherwise it will be zero (indicating it's an Application Processor).
- The DFR (Destination Format Register) is set to all ones selecting the Flat topology model.
- The xAPIC ID register (see Figure 34-17 on page 1281) contains the ID assigned during the automatic hardware initialization that occurs on the removal of the reset signal.

Enabling/Disabling the Local APIC

General

On the Pentium, the processor's Local APIC could not be disabled or enabled by software. Rather, the processor sampled an input pin (on the removal of reset APIC data line 1 was treated as the APICEN signal) to determine whether to enable or disable the processor's Local APIC for the power-up session.

With the advent of the Pentium Pro processor, two mechanisms (see the next two sections) were added that permit software to enable or disable the Local APIC.

Disabling Local APIC for Remainder of Power-Up Session

Refer to Figure 34-11 on page 1258. Immediately following a power-up or reset, the xAPIC Global Enable/Disable bit in the IA32_APIC_BASE MSR is set to one, enabling the Local APIC in xAPIC Mode. By clearing this bit to zero, software can disable the Local APIC for the remainder of the current power up session. If a CPUID request type 1 is executed while this bit is 0, EDX[9] returns a 0 indicating the absence of a Local APIC. Once cleared by software, this bit can only be set again by a power-up or reset. When the Local APIC has been disabled in this manner, the logical processor operates as if it does not incorporate a Local APIC:

- All external hardware interrupts are delivered to the processor over its INTR (LINT0) and NMI (LINT1) input pins.
- SMIs are delivered to the processor on its SMI# input pin.
- The logical processor is incapable of sending or receiving interrupt messages.
- The logical processor can only receive an INIT (a soft reset) via its INIT# input pin.

Figure 34-11: IA32_APIC_BASE MSR

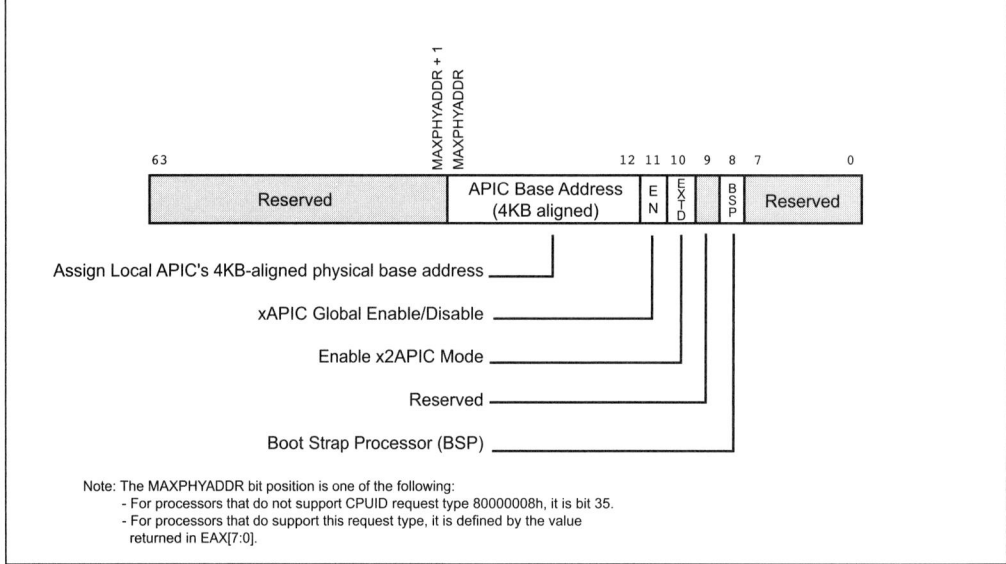

Dynamically Enabling/Disabling Local APIC

Assuming the xAPIC Global Enable/Disable bit in the IA32_APIC_BASE MSR has not been cleared to zero, software can dynamically enable/disable the Local APIC via the APIC Software Enable/Disable bit in the Spurious Vector register (see Figure 34-12 on page 1259). Although the default state of this bit after reset is 0 (which normally disables the Local APIC), the Local APIC is in fact enabled in xAPIC Mode immediately after a reset. It is only disabled if the programmer writes a zero into this bit. If software has temporarily disabled the Local APIC, the Local APIC's operational characteristics are as follows:

- It responds normally to the receipt of INIT, NMI, SMI, and SIPI [see "Boot Strap Processor (BSP) Selection" on page 1378] interrupt messages (more on these message types later in this chapter).
- It ignores inbound fixed interrupt messages and EXTInt messages, however.
- Pending interrupts in the Local APIC's IRR (Interrupt Request Register) and ISR (In-Service Register) are retained.
- If commanded to do so via its Interrupt Command Register (ICR), it can still issue IPI (Inter-Processor Interrupt) messages.
- If the reception or transmission of any IPIs are in progress when the Local APIC is disabled, the message transmission/reception is completed before the Local APIC enters the disabled state.
- The mask bits in all of the LVT (Local Vector Table) registers are set to one (thereby masking the recognition of the local events controlled by the LVT registers). Any attempt to clear these bits to zero is ignored.
- On the Pentium and P6 family processors, the Local APIC continues to monitor the flow of APIC bus messages in order to keep its APIC Arbitration ID synchronized with those of the other APICs connected to the APIC bus.

A CPU with a disabled APIC will not be used by an MP OS (because it cannot receive inbound fixed interrupt messages issued by the OS kernel running on another core or logical processor).

Figure 34-12: The Spurious Vector Register

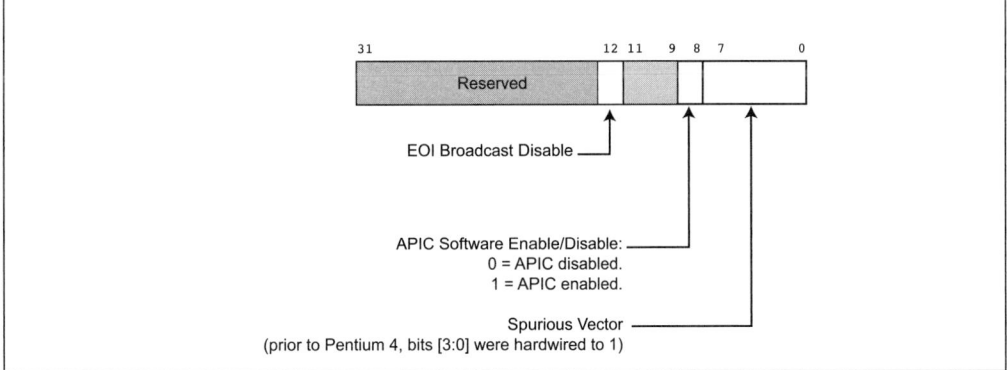

Mode Selection

Depending on its supported feature set, the Local APIC has either two or three modes of operation:

- **Disabled**.
- **xAPIC Mode**. This is the initial state after a power-up or reset.
- **x2APIC Mode**. This mode is only supported if a CPUID request type 1 returns a 1 in ECX[21].

Table 34-2 on page 1260 defines the Local APIC's operational state as specified by the EN and EXTD bits in the APIC_Base register (see Figure 34-11 on page 1258).

Table 34-2: Local APIC Operational Modes

EN	EXTD	Local APIC Mode
0	0	**Disabled**. Software disabled the Local APIC for the duration of the power-up session by clearing APIC_Base MSR[EN] to 0.
0	1	**Illegal** state.
1	0	**xAPIC Mode**. The Local APIC is in xAPIC Mode. This is the default state after a power-up or reset. While in this state, software can dynamically enable or disable the Local APIC using the Software Enable/Disable bit in the Spurious Vector register (see Figure 34-12 on page 1259). The Local APIC's registers set resides in memory space.
1	1	**x2APIC Mode**. The Local APIC is in x2APIC Mode. While in this state, software can dynamically enable or disable the Local APIC using the Software Enable/Disable bit in the Spurious Vector register (see Figure 34-12 on page 1259). The Local APIC's registers set are accessed as MSR registers using the RDMSR and WRMSR instructions.

The Local APIC Register Set

Register Access in xAPIC Mode: MMIO

General

When the Local APIC is operating in xAPIC Mode, its register set (with the exception of the APIC_Base MSR) is implemented as a memory-mapped IO (MMIO) register set occupying a 4KB memory address range starting at the address designated in the APIC_Base MSR (see Figure 34-11 on page 1258). The register set's default base address of FEE00000h may be changed to any desired 4KB-aligned address using this register.

Local and IO APIC xAPIC Register Areas Are Uncacheable

As with all areas of memory populated by memory-mapped IO registers, the memory areas within which the Local and IO APICs' register sets reside must be designated as uncacheable (UC) memory in the MTRRs (see "Memory Type Configuration" on page 599).

xAPIC Register Access Alignment

Refer to Figure 34-13 on page 1264. With the exception of the IRR, TMR, ISR and ICR registers, all of the Local APIC's memory-mapped IO registers are 32-bits wide and start on a 128-bit address boundary.

- The IRR, TMR and ISR registers, each consisting of 256-bits, are subdivided into a series of eight 32-bit registers each of which is aligned on a 128-bit address boundary.
- The ICR is a 64-bit register subdivided into two 32-bit register halves each of which is aligned on a 128-bit address boundary.

To modify a field (e.g., a bit or a byte) in any of the Local APIC's registers (with the exception of the APIC_Base MSR), the entire 32-bit register is read, the appropriate field(s) modified, and a 32-bit write is performed to update the register. Support for partial or non-aligned register access can vary from one implementation to another. 64-bit registers (i.e., the ICR) must be accessed as two, 32-bit registers, upper half first.

Register Access in x2APIC Mode: MSR

When the Local APIC is placed in x2APIC Mode, one of the major changes that occurs is the relocation of the Local APIC's register set from memory space to MSR space (i.e., the registers may no longer be accessed using loads and stores). In x2APIC Mode, the MSR address range from 00000800h through 00000BFFh is architecturally reserved for the Local APIC register set. This frees up the 4KB memory range normally occupied by the Local APIC for reassignment to system RAM (or another memory-mapped device).

Whereas the 64-bit Interrupt Command Register (ICR) must be accessed using two 32-bit memory accesses in xAPIC Mode, its entire width is accessed simultaneously using the RDMSR or WRMSR instructions in x2APIC Mode. Although all of the remaining registers are 64-bits wide (all MSRs are 64-bits wide), the upper 32-bits of each is reserved:

- To read from a Local APIC register in x2APIC Mode, preload the ECX register with the 32-bit MSR address and then execute the RDMSR instruction. The contents of the targeted 32-bit register is returned in the EAX register and, since all registers other than the ICR are 32-bit registers, the data returned in the EDX register is reserved. If the register being accessed is the 64-bit ICR, however, the lower 32-bits of the ICR are returned in the EAX register and the upper 32-bits in the EDX register.
- To write to a Local APIC register in x2APIC Mode, preload the ECX register with the 32-bit MSR address, the EAX:EDX register pair with the write data, and then execute the WRMSR instruction. If the target register is the 64-bit ICR, EAX is written to the register's lower half and EDX to its upper half. If the target register is a 32-bit register, EAX is written to the register and EDX is discarded.

Introduction to the Local APIC's Register Set

Figure 34-13 on page 1264 illustrates the Local APIC's register set and shows both the memory and MSR addresses. When first introduced in the Pentium, the memory-mapped IO register set occupied a 4KB memory address range starting at location FEE00000h and the address range could not be altered. This constraint disappeared with the addition of the APIC_BASE MSR in the Pentium Pro processor (see Figure 34-11 on page 1258; referred to as the IA32_APIC_BASE register starting with the Pentium 4). Using bits [35:12], the programmer can program the upper portion of the 4KB-aligned base address assigned to the register set. It should be noted that, although a 4KB address range is set aside for the register set, the register set currently only occupies the lower 1KB of the assigned address range. The remaining 3KB block is reserved for possible future expansion. In x2APIC Mode, the MSR base address of the Local APIC's MSR register set is 00000800h (and may not be changed).

Table 34-3 on page 1265 provides a brief description of each of the Local APIC registers. A comprehensive description of the registers can be found in the appropriate sections of this chapter.

Figure 34-13: Local APIC Register Set

Left Field	Right Field	Offset from base address (MMIO/MSR)
Reserved		0000 03F0h/3Fh
	Timer Divide Config Register	0000 03E0h/3Eh
Reserved		0000 03D0h/3Dh
		0000 03C0h/3Ch
		0000 03B0h/3Bh
		0000 03A0h/3Ah
Reserved	Timer Current Count Register	0000 0390h/39h
Reserved	Timer Initial Count Register	0000 0380h/38h
Reserved	LVT—Error	0000 0370h/37h
Reserved	LVT—LINT1	0000 0360h/36h
Reserved	LVT—LINT0	0000 0350h/35h
Reserved	LVT—Perf Counter OverFlow	0000 0340h/34h
Reserved	LVT—Thermal Sensor	0000 0330h/33h
Reserved	LVT—Timer	0000 0320h/32h
Reserved	Interrupt Command Register[63:32]	0000 0310h/**31h***
Reserved	Interrupt Command Register[31:0]	0000 0300h/**30h***
	LVT—CMC	0000 02F0h/2Fh
Reserved		0000 02E0h/2Eh
		0000 02D0h/2Dh
		0000 02C0h/2Ch
		0000 02B0h/2Bh
		0000 02A0h/2Ah
		0000 0290h/29H
Reserved	Error Status Register	0000 0280h/28h
		0000 0270h/27h
		0000 0260h/26h
		0000 0250h/25h
Reserved	Interrupt Request Register (IRR) 256 bits	0000 0240h/24h
		0000 0230h/23h
		0000 0220h/22h
		0000 0210h/21h
		0000 0200h/20h
		0000 01F0h/1Fh
		0000 01E0h/1Eh
		0000 01D0h/1Dh
Reserved	Trigger Mode Register (TMR) 256 bits	0000 01C0h/1Ch
		0000 01B0h/1Bh
		0000 01A0h/1Ah
		0000 0190h/19h
		0000 0180h/18h
		0000 0170h/17h
		0000 0160h/16h
		0000 0150h/15h
Reserved	In Service Register (ISR) 256 bits	0000 0140h/14h
		0000 0130h/13h
		0000 0120h/12h
		0000 0110h/11h
		0000 0100h/10h
Reserved	Spurious Interrupt Vector Register	0000 00F0h/0Fh
Reserved	Destination Format Register	0000 00E0h/0Eh
Reserved	Logical Destination Register	0000 00D0h/0Dh
Reserved	Remote Read Register	0000 00C0h/0Ch
Reserved	EOI Register	0000 00B0h/0Bh
Reserved	Processor Priority Register	0000 00A0h/0Ah
Reserved	Arbitration Priority Register	0000 0090h/09h
Reserved	Task Priority Register	0000 0080h/08h
Reserved		0000 0070h/07
		0000 0060h/06h
		0000 0050h/05h
		0000 0040h/04h
Reserved	Local APIC Version Register	0000 0030h/03h
Reserved	Local APIC ID Register	0000 0020h/02h
Reserved		0000 0010h/01h
Reserved		0000 0000h/00h

Byte: F E D C B A 9 8 7 6 5 4 3 2 1 0

***Note*: In x2APIC Mode, all registers are 32-bits except ICR. It is 64-bits at MSR address 30h.

Table 34-3: A Brief Description of the Local APIC Registers

Register Name	Width (bits)	R/W?	Offset from Base Address*	Description
Reserved	128	-	Memory: 00000000h MSR: 00000000h	Reserved.
Reserved	128	-	Memory: 00000010h MSR: 00000001h	Reserved.
Local APIC ID Register	32	RW or RO	Memory: 00000020h MSR: 00000002h	On the trailing-edge of reset, the Local APIC associated with each logical processor is assigned an APIC ID that is unique in the system. The ID is used as the address in an interrupt message to identify the Local APIC (and therefore logical processor) that is the sole target of the message. See "Local APIC ID Assignments and Addressing" on page 1277.
Local APIC Version Register	32	RO	Memory: 00000030h MSR: 00000003h	See Figure 34-10 on page 1256. This read-only register contains: • Local APIC version. • Number of entries (minus 1) that it implements in its LVT. • Whether or not it supports Directed EOI feature. See "Detecting Presence/Version/ Capabilities of Local APIC" on page 1255.

Table 34-3: A Brief Description of the Local APIC Registers (Continued)

Register Name	Width (bits)	R/W?	Offset from Base Address*	Description
Reserved	128	-	Memory: 00000040h MSR: 00000004h	Reserved.
Reserved	128	-	Memory: 00000050h MSR: 00000005h	Reserved.
Reserved	128	-	Memory: 00000060h MSR: 00000006h	Reserved.
Reserved	128	-	Memory: 00000070h MSR: 00000007h	Reserved.

Table 34-3: A Brief Description of the Local APIC Registers (Continued)

Register Name	Width (bits)	R/W?	Offset from Base Address*	Description
Task Priority Register (TPR)	32	RW	Memory: 00000080h MSR: 00000008h	This register allows the OS scheduler to prevent specific interrupts (generally low-priority interrupts) from disturbing high-priority work that the logical processor is doing. Whenever the OS scheduler instructs the logical processor to start executing a task, it also causes a value to be written into the Local APIC's TPR. This permits the scheduler to set a priority threshold for interrupting the logical processor. It services only those interrupts with a higher priority than that specified in the TPR. If the scheduler sets the task priority in the TPR to 0, the logical processor recognizes all interrupts, while setting it to 15 prevents the logical processor from handling all interrupts except NMI, SMI, INIT, ExtINT, INIT-deassert, and SIPI. See "Task and Processor Priority" on page 1305 for more information.

Table 34-3: A Brief Description of the Local APIC Registers (Continued)

Register Name	Width (bits)	R/W?	Offset from Base Address*	Description
Arbitration Priority Register (APR)	32	RO	Memory: 00000090h MSR: n/a	This read-only register was implemented in the Pentium and P6 processors, but eliminated starting with the Pentium 4 (because the 3-wire APIC bus was eliminated). When an interrupt message specifying Lowest-Priority delivery mode was received, the Local APICs compared their APR values on the APIC bus to determine which was currently executing the lowest-priority (and therefore the most interruptible) task. That Local APIC would then deliver the interrupt to its respective processor. See chapter 15 of the MindShare book entitled *Pentium Processor System Architecture, Second Edition* for more information.
Processor Priority Register (PPR)	32	RO	Memory: 000000A0h MSR: 0000000Ah	When interrupts are pending in the IRR and ISR registers, the Local APIC dispatches them to the logical processor one at a time, based on: • Their priority, • The priority of the current task (the TPR value), and • The processor priority (the PPR value). The PPR value represents the priority at which the logical processor is currently executing and is used to determine whether a pending interrupt can be dispensed to it. See "Task and Processor Priority" on page 1305 for more information.

Table 34-3: A Brief Description of the Local APIC Registers (Continued)

Register Name	Width (bits)	R/W?	Offset from Base Address*	Description
EOI Register	32	WO	Memory: 000000B0h MSR: 0000000Bh	After the body of an interrupt handler for any interrupt except NMI, SMI, INIT, ExtINT, SIPI, or INIT Deassert has completed servicing the interrupt request, the handler must perform a memory-mapped IO write of zero to the Local APIC's End-of-Interrupt register before executing the IRET instruction at the end of the handler. Upon receipt of the EOI, the Local APIC clears the highest-priority bit currently set to one in the ISR (this bit corresponds to the interrupt that was just serviced). It then clears the highest-priority bit that is currently set in the IRR, sets the corresponding bit in the ISR, and dispatches that interrupt to the logical processor for servicing. If the interrupt just serviced was a level-triggered interrupt, the Local APIC also broadcasts a memory-mapped IO EOI write to all IO APICs. See the following for more information: • "Overview of Edge-Triggered Interrupt Handling" on page 1316. • "Overview of Level-Sensitive Interrupt Handling" on page 1321 • "IO APIC EOI Register and Shared Interrupts" on page 1336.
Remote Read Register	32	-	Memory: 000000C0h MSR: n/a	Reserved since the advent of the Pentium Pro.

Table 34-3: A Brief Description of the Local APIC Registers (Continued)

Register Name	Width (bits)	R/W?	Offset from Base Address*	Description
Logical Destination Register (LDR)	32	see -->	Memory: 000000D0h MSR: 0000000Dh	When an interrupt message specifies Logical Destination Mode, the target Local APIC(s) are specified using an 8- or 32-bit Message Destination Address (MDA). Upon message receipt, the Local APIC(s) compare the MDA in the message with the values in their LDR and DFR (in xAPIC Mode), or just the LDR (in x2APIC Mode) to determine if they should accept and handle the message. See "Logical Addressing: Multiple Targets" on page 1288 for more information. *R/W in xAPIC Mode and RO in x2APIC Mode.*
Destination Format Register (DFR)	32	see -->	Memory: 000000E0h MSR: n/a	*Reserved in x2APIC Mode.* In xAPIC Mode: Bits [27:0] are read-only. Bits [31:28] are read/write and specify the system's APIC distribution model (Flat or Clustered Model). Upon receipt of a message that specifies Logical Destination Mode, the Local APIC uses the DFR value to properly interpret the message's MDA field (see the description of the LDR in this table). See "Logical Addressing: Multiple Targets" on page 1288 for more information.

Table 34-3: A Brief Description of the Local APIC Registers (Continued)

Register Name	Width (bits)	R/W?	Offset from Base Address*	Description
Spurious Interrupt Vector Register	32	see -->	Memory: 000000F0h MSR: 0000000Fh	Bits [8:0] are read/write and bits [31:9] are read-only. This register controls the following Local APIC features: • It contains a bit that permits software to temporarily enable or disable the Local APIC (see "Dynamically Enabling/Disabling Local APIC" on page 1258). • In the Pentium and the P6 processor family, it contains a bit that permits software to enable or disable Focus Processor checking (see "Additional Spurious Vector Register Features" on page 1377 for more information). This bit is reserved starting with the Pentium 4. • Permits software to specify the Spurious Interrupt Vector (see "The Spurious Interrupt Vector" on page 1376 for more information).
In-Service Register (ISR)	256	RO	Memory: 00000100h- 00000170h MSR: 00000010h - 00000017h	The bits that are set to one in the 256-bit, read-only ISR indicate all of the user-defined interrupts that are currently being serviced. As the servicing of each is completed, the associated ISR bit is cleared to 0 by an EOI. See "IO/Local APICs Cooperate on Interrupt Handling" on page 1313 for more information.

Table 34-3: A Brief Description of the Local APIC Registers (Continued)

Register Name	Width (bits)	R/W?	Offset from Base Address*	Description
Trigger Mode Register (TMR)	256	RO	Memory: 00000180h - 000001F0h MSR: 00000018h - 0000001Fh	The bits in this 256-bit, read-only register correspond to the user-defined interrupt vectors and indicate whether the respective interrupt is edge-triggered or level-sensitive: 0 = Edge-triggered. 1 = Level sensitive. See "IO/Local APICs Cooperate on Interrupt Handling" on page 1313 for more information.
Interrupt Request Register (IRR)	256	RO	Memory: 00000200h - 00000270h MSR: 00000020h - 00000027h	The bits in this 256-bit, read-only register correspond to the user-defined interrupt vectors. Upon receipt of an interrupt message containing a user-defined interrupt vector, the Local APIC sets the corresponding IRR bit to one. See "IO/Local APICs Cooperate on Interrupt Handling" on page 1313 for more information.
Error Status Register (ESR)	32	see -->	Memory: 00000280h MSR: 00000028h	When the Local APIC detects an error in a message to be sent or one that has been received, it sets the appropriate error bit in the ESR and, if enabled to do so (in the LVT Error register), generates an interrupt to invoke the Local APIC's error handler. This register is updated when a write is performed to it and cleared by two back-to-back writes. See "The Local APIC's Error Interrupt" on page 1373 for more information.

Table 34-3: A Brief Description of the Local APIC Registers (Continued)

Register Name	Width (bits)	R/W?	Offset from Base Address*	Description
Reserved	128	-	Memory: 00000290h MSR: 00000029h	Reserved.
Reserved	128	-	Memory: 000002A0h MSR: 0000002Ah	Reserved.
Reserved	128	-	Memory: 000002B0h MSR: 0000002Bh	Reserved.
Reserved	128	-	Memory: 000002C0h MSR: 0000002Ch	Reserved.
Reserved	128	-	Memory: 000002D0h MSR: 0000002Dh	Reserved.
Reserved	128	-	Memory: 000002E0h MSR: 0000002Eh	Reserved.

Table 34-3: A Brief Description of the Local APIC Registers (Continued)

Register Name	Width (bits)	R/W?	Offset from Base Address*	Description
Interrupt Command Register (ICR)	64	RW	Memory: 00000300h-00000310h MSR: 00000030h	This 64-bit register consists of upper and lower halves. The software executing on a logical processor can stimulate its Local APIC to send an IPI to another logical processor by writing to its Local APIC's ICR. The programmer first writes to the upper half and then writes the remaining information to the lower half. The write to the lower half of the ICR triggers the Local APIC to send the message defined by the information in the ICR. See "Sending a Message From the Local APIC" on page 1353.
Reserved	128	-	Memory: 000003A0h MSR: 0000003Ah	Reserved.
Reserved	128	-	Memory: 000003B0h MSR: 0000003Bh	Reserved.
Reserved	128	-	Memory: 000003C0h MSR: 0000003Ch	Reserved.
Reserved	128	-	Memory: 000003D0h MSR: 0000003Dh	Reserved.

Table 34-3: A Brief Description of the Local APIC Registers (Continued)

Register Name	Width (bits)	R/W?	Offset from Base Address*	Description
Reserved	128	-	Memory: 000003F0h MSR: 0000003Fh	Reserved.
Local Vector Table Registers				
LVT Timer Register		RW	Memory: 00000320h MSR: 00000032h	These registers control the programmable timer incorporated within the Local APIC. It can be programmed to generate a single interrupt after a programmed amount of time, or to generate an interrupt on a periodic basis at a programmed interval. See "The Local APIC Timer" on page 1366 for more information.
Initial Count Register (for Timer)	32	RW	Memory: 00000380h MSR: 00000038h	
Current Count Register (for Timer)	32	RO	Memory: 00000390h MSR: 00000039h	
Divide Configuration Register (for Timer)	32	RW	Memory: 000003E0h MSR: 0000003Eh	
LVT Thermal Sensor Register	32	RW	Memory: 00000330h MSR: 00000033h	This register is used to enable or disable the Thermal Sensor logic's ability to generate an interrupt when the core temperature rises above or drops below the thermal trip point. See "The Thermal Sensor Interrupt" on page 1370 for more information.

Table 34-3: A Brief Description of the Local APIC Registers (Continued)

Register Name	Width (bits)	R/W?	Offset from Base Address*	Description
LVT Performance Monitoring Counter Overflow Register	32	RW	Memory: 00000340h MSR: 00000034h	This register is used to enable or disable the Performance Counter logic's ability to generate an interrupt on counter overflow. See "The Performance Counter Overflow Interrupt" on page 1368 for more information.
LVT LINT0 Register	32	RW	Memory: 00000350h MSR: 00000035h	Defines an interrupt to be delivered to the logical processor when the processor's LINT0 pin is asserted. See "Local Interrupt 0 (LINT0)" on page 1362 for more information.
LVT LINT1 Register	32	RW	Memory: 00000360h MSR: 00000036h	Defines an interrupt to be delivered to the logical processor when the processor's LINT1 pin is asserted. See "Local Interrupt 1 (LINT1)" on page 1365 for more information.
LVT Error Status Register	32	RW	Memory: 00000370h MSR: 00000037h	Defines an interrupt to be delivered to the logical processor when the Local APIC detects an error condition. See "The Local APIC's Error Interrupt" on page 1373 for more information.
LVT CMC Register	32	RW	Memory: 000002F0h MSR: 0000002Fh	Correctable Machine Check interrupt register. Used to enable/disable and define the type of interrupt delivered to the logical processor when the number of correctable (soft) Machine Check errors matches a threshold value specified by the programmer. See "Correctable Machine Check (CMC) Interrupt" on page 1372.

Table 34-3: A Brief Description of the Local APIC Registers (Continued)

Register Name	Width (bits)	R/W?	Offset from Base Address*	Description
CR8	64	R/W	-	Refer to "CR8 (Alternative TPR)" on page 1308.

*Note: Local APIC register set base address:
- **x2APIC Mode**: MSR address 00000800h (hardwired and may not be changed).
- **xAPIC Mode**:
  - Default base memory address: FEE00000h.
  - Using APIC_Base MSR, may be configured on any 4KB-aligned base address.

Local APIC ID Assignments and Addressing

ID Assignment in xAPIC Mode

Introduction

On the trailing-edge of the reset signal (i.e., it's deassertion), the processor samples a processor design-specific set of inputs to determine:

- Cluster ID.
- Physical processor ID (also referred to as the processor package ID).
- Core IDs (if it's a multicore processor package).
- Logical processor IDs (if the processor supports Hyper-Threading).
- **Local APIC IDs**. Two addresses are assigned to the Local APIC:
  - **xAPIC ID** (Local APIC's unique physical ID). This is the address used in an interrupt message that targets a single Local APIC.
  - **Logical xAPIC ID**. This is the address used to determine if an interrupt message using logical rather than physical addressing has selected this Local APIC as one of the targets.

For processors that utilize the FSB external interface rather than Intel QPI, the IDs are assigned as described in the following sub-sections.

Cluster ID Assignment

The Cluster ID identifies what cluster of processors the physical processor (and therefore its encapsulated Local APICs) is a member of. The processor may be assigned a cluster number of 0, 1, 2, or 3. Address signal lines [12:11]# are sampled on the trailing-edge of reset to determine the cluster ID (see Figure 34-14 on page 1278):

- Sampled electrical value 00b = cluster 3.
- Sampled electrical value 01b = cluster 2.
- Sampled electrical value 10b = cluster 1.
- Sampled electrical value 11b = cluster 0.

Figure 34-14: Cluster ID Assignment

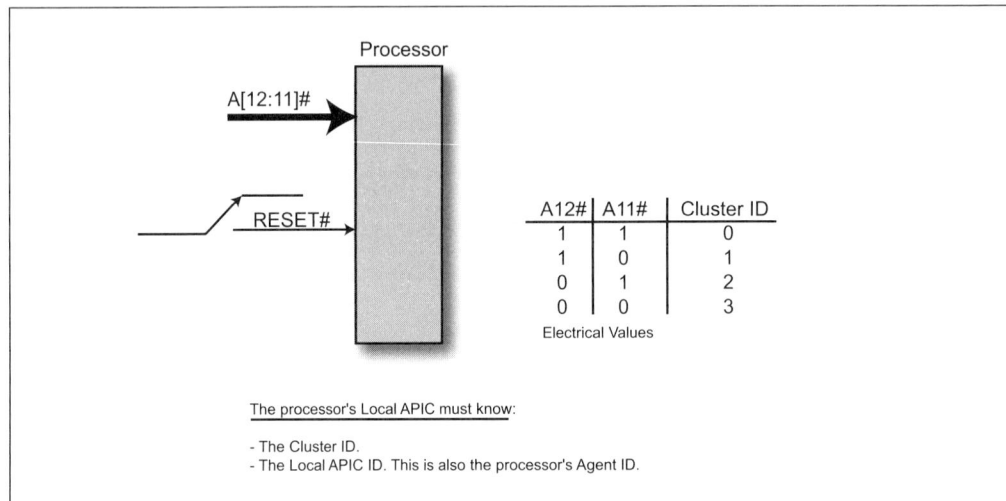

Physical/Logical Processor and Local APIC ID Assignment

Example Xeon MP System: Hyper-Threading Disabled. Figure 34-15 on page 1280 shows four Pentium 4 Xeon MP processors and assumes that Hyper-Threading is disabled. The signal lines BREQ0# through BREQ3# each has a pull-up resistor on the system board (not shown). While the chipset is still asserting reset to the processors, it is a rule that it must drive the BREQ0# signal line low (the chipset is labelled Central Agent in the illustration).

On the removal of reset, all of the processors sample their BR[3:1]# inputs to determine their Agent ID (physical processor ID) assignments. Remember that due to the pull-up resistors, the BREQ signal lines remain high unless driven low. The truth table in Table 34-4 on page 1279 shows the resultant Agent IDs assigned to the four processors.

Table 34-4: Quad Xeon MP System with Hyper-Threading Disabled

BR1#	BR2#	BR3#	Physical Processor ID
1	1	1	0
1	1	0	1
1	0	1	2
0	1	1	3

Example Xeon MP System: Hyper-Threading Enabled. If Hyper-Threading were enabled in the system shown in Figure 34-15 on page 1280, each of the physical processors shown has two logical processors within it. The ID assignments would be as shown in Table 34-5 on page 1279.

Table 34-5: Quad Xeon MP System with Hyper-Threading Enabled

BR1#	BR2#	BR3#	Physical Processor ID	ID of Logical Processor 0 and its Local APIC	ID of Logical Processor 1 and its Local APIC
1	1	1	0	0	1
1	1	0	1	2	3
1	0	1	2	4	5
0	1	1	3	6	7

Dual Processor System: Hyper-Threading Enabled. In a dual-processor system (see Figure 34-16 on page 1281), each of the processors only implements the BR0# and BR1# pins (and only BR1# is an input to the processor). The ID assignments are shown in Table 34-6 on page 1280.

Table 34-6: Dual Processor System with Hyper-Threading Enabled

BR1#	Physical Processor	ID of Logical Processor 0 and its Local APIC	ID of Logical Processor 1 and its Local APIC
1	0	0	1
0	1	2	3

A Single-Processor System: Hyper-Threading Enabled. In a single processor system, there are two possibilities:

— The processor is not a Celeron and can co-exist with another processor.
— The processor is a Celeron and therefore does not support multiple processors on the same FSB.

In either case, the processor only has a BR0# output pin and *knows* it's the only processor. Assuming Hyper-Threading is enabled, the two logical processors (and their Local APICs) are assigned IDs 0 and 1.

Figure 34-15: Assignment of Agent ID and Local APIC ID (Xeon MP System)

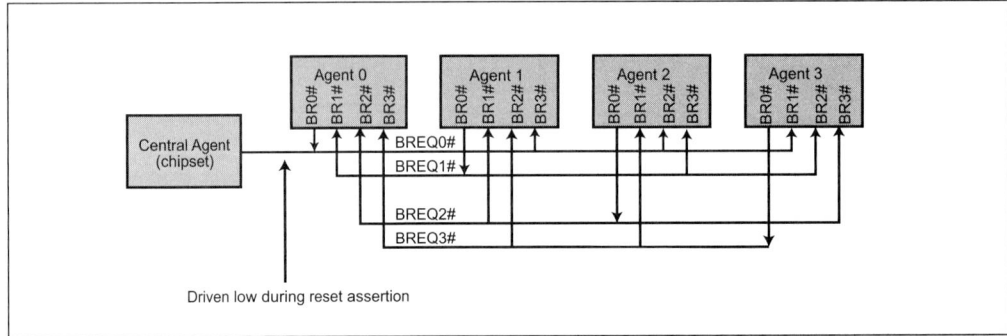

Figure 34-16: Assignment of Agent ID and Local APIC ID (Dual-Processor System)

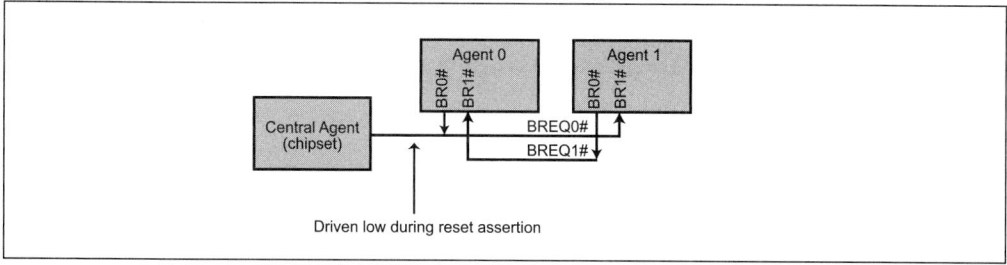

xAPIC ID Register

Refer to Figure 34-17 on page 1281. The automatically-assigned xAPIC ID is latched into the Local APIC's memory-mapped xAPIC ID register (at offset 00000020h from the Local APIC's base memory address; see Figure 34-13 on page 1264):

- In the P6 processor family, the Local APIC ID consisted of:
  — 2-bit Cluster ID.
  — 2-bit CPU ID.
- Starting with Pentium 4 processors that supported Hyper-Threading, the Local APIC ID consisted of:
  — 2-bit Cluster ID.
  — 2-bit CPU ID.
  — 1-bit Logical Processor ID.

Figure 34-17: The xAPIC ID Register

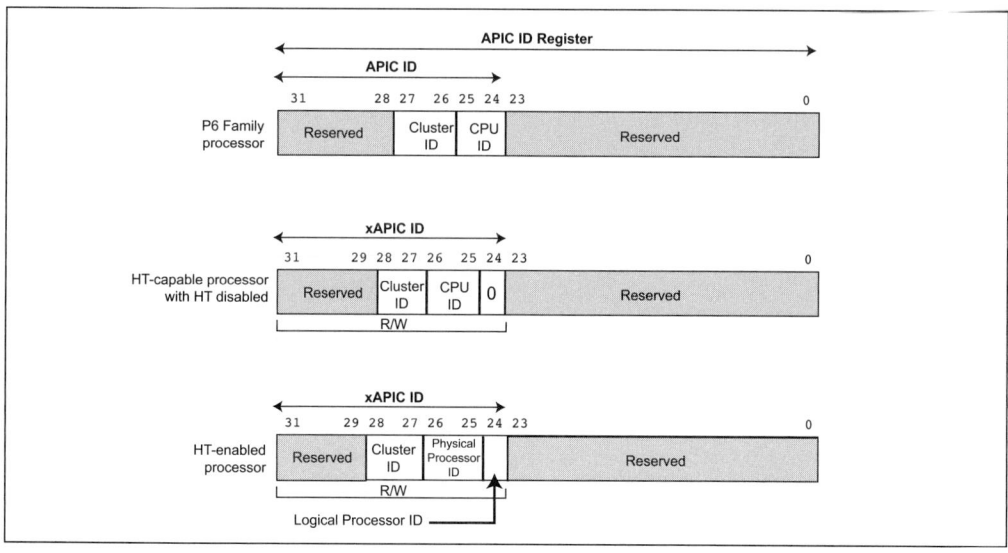

BIOS/OS Reassignment of xAPIC ID

The BIOS and/or the OS can change the xAPIC ID at any time after the initial IDs are automatically assigned at startup time. Software must ensure, however, that the xAPIC ID for each Local APIC is unique.

In an HT-capable processor, the Local APIC associated with each logical processor is automatically assigned a unique xAPIC ID. It should be noted, however, that when a CPUID request type 1 is executed, only the xAPIC ID of the primary logical processor (logical processor 0) is returned in the EBX register (see Figure 34-18 on page 1282).

Logical xAPIC Address Assignment

In legacy processors (Pentium and P6) and in xAPIC Mode, a Local APIC's 8-bit logical address is assigned by software (see Figure 34-19 on page 1286). "xAPIC Logical Addressing Background" on page 1285 describes the legacy and xAPIC addressing mechanism.

Figure 34-18: EBX Contents After a CPUID Request Type 1

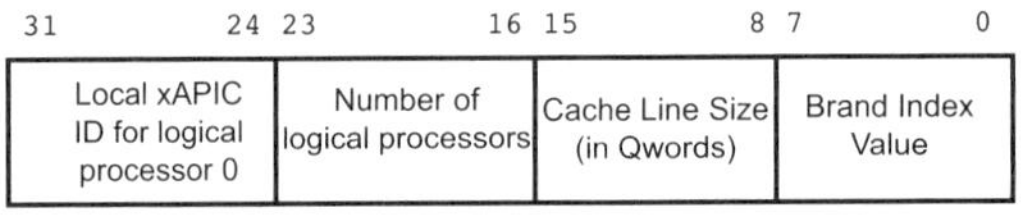

31	24 23	16 15	8 7	0
Local xAPIC ID for logical processor 0	Number of logical processors	Cache Line Size (in Qwords)	Brand Index Value	

Maximum Number of xAPICs

As shown in Figure 34-17 on page 1281, in the P6 and Pentium processor families the APIC ID field in the APIC ID register is 4-bits wide. The values 0h - Eh can be used (the value Fh is reserved for a message broadcast operation) to uniquely identify 15 different processors.

Starting with the advent of the Pentium 4, the xAPIC specification expanded the APIC ID field from four bits to eight bits (it is referred to as the xAPIC ID). This is not evident when looking at Figure 34-17 on page 1281 because bits [31:29] are shown as Reserved. They are only reserved when the processor automatically assigns the Cluster ID, Physical Processor ID and Logical Processor ID on the trailing-edge of reset. At any time after this, the BIOS and/or the OS can write a new 8-bit xAPIC ID into bits [31:24] of the APIC ID register. The values 0h - FEh can be used to identify up to 255 logical processors in the system (the value FFh is reserved for a message broadcast operation).

ID Assignment in x2APIC Mode

Two Hardware-Assigned Local APIC IDs

When software switches the Local APIC from xAPIC Mode to x2APIC Mode (see "Mode Selection" on page 1260), the logical processor hardware automatically:

- Expands the *xAPIC ID* field in the APIC ID register from 8- to a full 32-bits. The expanded field is then referred to as the *x2APIC ID* and is guaranteed to contain a unique physical ID that can be used to target the Local APIC when it is the sole target of a message using Physical Destination addressing.
- Makes the APIC ID register read-only.
- Using information from the 32-bit x2APIC ID, it replaces the programmable 8-bit *logical xAPIC ID* in the Logical Destination Register (LDR) with a hardware-assigned 32-bit, read-only *logical x2APIC ID*. This is the Local APIC's logical address which is used to address it in Logical Destination address mode.

The following two sections describe the *x2APIC ID* and *logical x2APIC ID*.

x2APIC ID (Physical Local APIC ID)

General. The unique 32-bit Local APIC ID (i.e., the x2APIC ID) automatically created by hardware upon entry to x2APIC Mode cannot be changed by software. Bits [7:0] in the register are the same as the 8-bit xAPIC ID (see Figure 34-17 on page 1281). The number of and the width of any additional automatically-created bit fields in bits [31:8] are processor design-specific. Taken together, the content of the bit fields that comprise the x2APIC ID defines the position the Local APIC and its associated logical processor occupy within the physical processor's internal hierarchy. As an example, software might read the x2APIC ID of the Local APIC associated with a logical processor and obtain the following information:

— Cluster ID = 22.
— Physical Processor ID (also referred to as Processor Package ID) = 3.
— Core number = 6.
— Logical Processor = 1.

Some Interesting Questions. This raises a couple of interesting questions:

— How does software know the number of and the width of each of the ID bit fields that comprise the x2APIC ID? These values are processor design-specific.
— How can software discover the number of cores and logical processors implemented in a processor (and, in future processors, other processing unit levels that may reside above or below the core level)?
— How can software discover which cores or logical processors share processor resources (e.g., caches)?

CPUID Provides the Answers. The answer lies in the CPUID instruction:

— **Number of Logical Processors**. A CPUID request type 1h returns the information shown in Figure 34-18 on page 1282. The nearest power-of-2 integer that is not smaller than EBX[23:16] is the number of unique initial APIC IDs reserved for addressing different logical processors in a physical package.
— **Number of Logical Processors that share each cache**. A CPUID request type 4h returns this information.
— **Number of cores within the package**. A CPUID request type 4h returns this information.
— **Enumeration of processing units**. CPUID request type Bh (11d; introduced with the advent of the Core i7 processor) is used to learn all of the processing unit levels (e.g., core, logical processor, etc.) implemented within a particular processor implementation. The following are two examples of the processing unit hierarchy that might exist within a socket:
    – **Example 1**: Package, Core, Logical Processor.
    – **Example 2**: Multi-Chip Module (MCM), Package, Core, Logical Processor.
    Using Request types 1h, 4h, and Bh, the programmer may acquire and use this information to parse the unique x2APIC ID of each Local APIC, discover the width of each sub-ID field within the x2APIC ID, and the obtain the ID stored in each field.

Refer to the Intel 64 and IA-32 Architectures Software Developer's Manual Volume 3A: System Programming Guide, Part 1 for a complete description of the CPUID instruction.

x2APIC ID and Physical Destination Mode. Refer to "Introduction to the Message Addressing Modes" on page 1254. Delivering an interrupt message to one target Local APIC obviously requires the use of that Local APIC's unique ID. The x2APIC ID is the address that is used.

Obtaining the x2APIC ID. The programmer may obtain the x2APIC ID of a Local APIC in the following ways:

— Execute the RDMSR instruction to read the ID from the APIC ID register.
— Execute a CPUID request type B (11d) and the x2APIC ID is returned in the EDX register.
— Obtain it from the Local APIC's record in the MP or ACPI table that was constructed by the BIOS at startup time (see "How the APs are Discovered and Configured" on page 1381).

Logical x2APIC ID

xAPIC Logical Addressing Background. As previously described in "Introduction to the Message Addressing Modes" on page 1254, the Logical Destination addressing mode is used if an interrupt message is to be sent to a group of two or more Local APICs in the system. In xAPIC Mode, the message's address (known as the Message Destination Address, or MDA) consists of an 8-bit selector field wherein each of the eight bits corresponds to a Local APIC within a logical group of up to eight Local APICs. Upon receipt of the message, each Local APIC ANDs the MDA with the bit mask programmed into the 8-bit field in its Logical Destination Register (LDR; see Figure 34-19 on page 1286). If the result is non-zero, a Local APIC is selected as one of the targets and it accepts the message. If the result is 0, it is not one of the targets and it discards the message. As an example:

— Inbound message's logical address contains 5Ah.
— Local APIC's 8-bit Logical Address (in LDR) contains 20h.
— ANDing 5Ah and 20h yields 0, so the Local APIC discards the message.
— A logical address of 5Ah (0101 1010b) is addressing Local APICs with logical addresses of 02h, 08h, 10h, and 40h.

Figure 34-19: Logical Destination Register (LDR) in xAPIC Mode

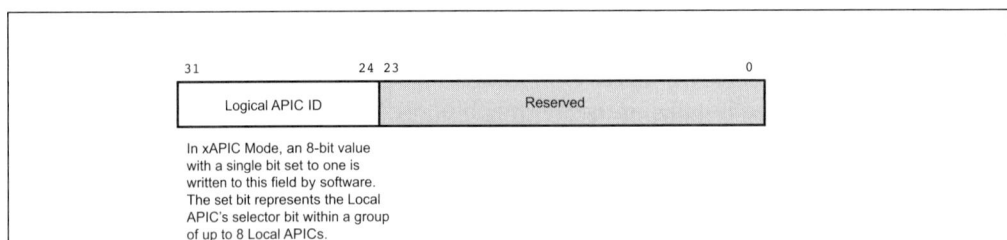

Logical x2APIC ID Formation. In x2APIC Mode, the address field in the LDR is 32-bits wide rather than 8-bits and, unlike xAPIC Mode, it is not programmable. Like the Local APIC's x2APIC ID, the Logical x2APIC ID is automatically generated by logical processor hardware upon entry to x2APIC Mode and is deposited in the read-only Logical Destination Register (LDR; see Figure 34-20 on page 1287). The content of the LDR's Cluster and Logical x2APIC ID fields are derived from the x2APIC ID (in the APIC ID register) as follows (see Figure 34-20 on page 1287):

— **Assumptions**:
  – It is assumed that each cluster will be populated by up to 16 logical processors (and therefore up to 16 Local APICs). It should be noted that the definition of the logical cluster ID discussed here is not necessarily the same as the cluster number within which a physical processor resides. See **LDR Address Formation** below.
  – Bits [3:0] of the Local APIC's unique x2APIC ID identify the logical address of the Local APIC within a cluster.
  – Bits [19:4] of the Local APIC's unique x2APIC ID represent the 16-bit address of the cluster the Local APIC resides in.
— **LDR address formation**:
  – The 16-bit cluster address in the LDR is formed by copying bits [19:4] of the x2APIC ID into the LDR's Cluster ID field.
  – The binary-weighted value encoded in Bits [3:0] of the Local APIC's unique x2APIC ID is used to select which bit in the LDR's Logical x2APIC ID field to set to one.

Figure 34-20: Logical Address in LDR Is Formed From x2APIC ID

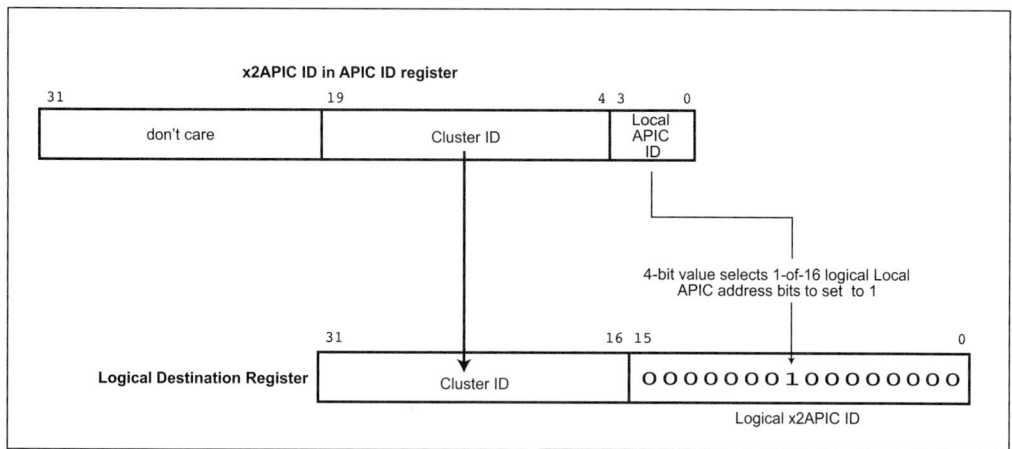

Logical x2APIC ID Usage. In x2APIC Mode, an interrupt message that uses Logical Destination addressing can address up to 16 Local APICs that reside in the same physical cluster (1 of 64K-1 possible clusters; cluster address FFFFh indicates a message broadcast to all Local APICs). As an example:

— An inbound message's logical address contains 02B329F7h. The following example breaks it down into the cluster address plus the 16 logical selector bits:
  – Cluster 691 (02B3) is the target cluster.
  – Within cluster 691, the Local APICs with Logical x2APIC IDs of 0001h, 0002h, 0004h, 0010h, 0020h, 0040, 0080h, 0100h, 0800h, and 2000h are being addressed.

Local APIC Addressing

Physical Addressing: Single Target

If an inbound message indicates physical addressing (the Destination Mode bit in the message = 0), the target of the message is specified by:

- In xAPIC Mode: the 8-bit xAPIC ID in the message.
- In x2APIC Mode: the 32-bit x2APIC ID in the message.

The interrupt message is accepted only by the Local APIC whose xAPIC ID or x2APIC ID matches the ID in the message.

Logical Addressing: Multiple Targets

Additional information on logical addressing can be found in:

- "Logical xAPIC Address Assignment" on page 1282.
- "Logical x2APIC ID" on page 1285.
- Table 34-7 on page 1292.

Introduction. If an inbound message indicates logical addressing (the Destination Mode bit in the message = 1), the targets of the message are specified by:

— In xAPIC Mode: the 8-bit logical address in the message.
— In x2APIC Mode: the 32-bit logical address in the message.

Upon receipt of the message, the Local APICs interpret the address as follows:

— **xAPIC Mode**. The Local APICs interpret the message's logical address based on the topology model indicated in their Destination Format Registers (DFRs; see Figure 34-24 on page 1292).
  – 0000b indicates **Flat model** addressing (see"Flat Model" on page 1289).
  – 0001b indicates **Cluster model** addressing (see "Flat Cluster Model" on page 1290 and "Hierarchical Cluster Model" on page 1291.
— **x2APIC Mode**. The Local APICs interpret the message's logical address as described in "x2APIC Cluster Model" on page 1288.

x2APIC Cluster Model. Since the Flat model is not supported in x2APIC Mode, there is no need for the Destination Format Register (DFR) to select the Flat or Cluster addressing model. Only the Cluster model is used. Refer to the example in "Logical x2APIC ID Usage" on page 1287 as well as the one shown in Figure 34-21 on page 1289.

Figure 34-21: x2APIC Logical Address Compare

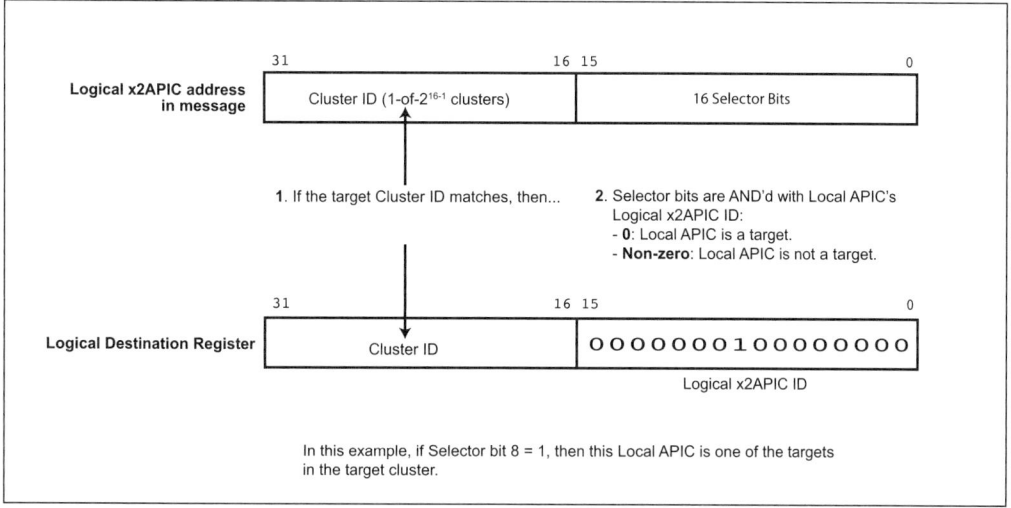

Flat Model. *Not supported in x2APIC Mode.* In the Flat Model, each of the eight bits in the message's logical address field acts as a selector bit permitting the message to select up to 8 Local APICs on the 3-wire APIC bus (Pentium or P6) or the FSB (processors supporting xAPIC Mode) by setting the appropriate bits to one in the message's logical address. In each of the Local APICs, the Logical APIC ID field in each of their respective LDRs (see Figure 34-19 on page 1286) is programmed as follows (references to Local APIC 0, Local APIC 1, etc. refers to a Local APIC's ID number, or software-assigned bit position, within the logical group):

— 00000001b is stored in Local APIC 0's LDR Logical APIC ID field.
— 00000010b is stored in Local APIC 1's LDR Logical APIC ID field.
— 00000100b is stored in Local APIC 2's LDR Logical APIC ID field.
— 00001000b is stored in Local APIC 3's LDR Logical APIC ID field.
— 00010000b is stored in Local APIC 4's LDR Logical APIC ID field.
— 00100000b is stored in Local APIC 5's LDR Logical APIC ID field.
— 01000000b is stored in Local APIC 6's LDR Logical APIC ID field.
— 10000000b is stored in Local APIC 7's LDR Logical APIC ID field.

In the following example, the message sender transmits a message to 5 of the 8 processors in a logical group. Upon message receipt, the Local APIC with the value 20h in the Logical APIC ID field of its LDR performs a logical AND operation between the value received in the message's logical address

(B3h in this case) and the contents of the Logical APIC ID field of its LDR (20h). A non-zero result indicates it *is* one of the selected destination Local APICs:

```
10110011b  Address selects Local APICs 0, 1, 4, 5 and 7
00100000b  Contents of Local APIC 5's LDR
00100000b  Local APIC 5 receives the message, ANDs
           the address and its Local APIC ID, yielding
           a non-zero result, so APIC 5 is a member of
           the targeted group
```

Flat Cluster Model. *This addressing scheme is only supported on the Pentium and P6 processors.* Using this model, all of the Local APICs are assumed to be connected through the 3-wire APIC bus. Refer to Figure 34-22 on page 1291. The high-order four bits of the message's logical address contains the target Cluster ID (1-of-15; valid cluster IDs are 0h through Eh; Cluster ID Fh is reserved for a message broadcast), while the lower four bits are used as select bits to select up to four Local APICs within the target cluster as targets of the message.

Upon message receipt, a potential target Local APIC compares the upper 4-bits of the message's logical address with bits [31:28] of the Logical APIC ID field in its LDR to determine if it's a member of the target logical cluster. Assuming it is, the Local APIC ANDs bits [27:24] of the message's logical address with bits [27:24] of the Logical APIC ID field in its LDR and, if the result is non-zero, the Local APIC accepts the message.

Although it may appear that this addressing mode would support addressing up to 60 Local APICs (15 clusters x 4 Local APICs per cluster), the Pentium and P6 APIC bus arbitration mechanism only supported a maximum of 15 APIC agents, so the total number of processors supported in this mode is limited to 15. A message broadcast to all local APICs is achieved by setting the message's logical address field to FFh, thereby addressing all Local APICs in all clusters.

Figure 34-22: xAPIC Logical Address Compare When Using Flat or Hierarchical Cluster Model

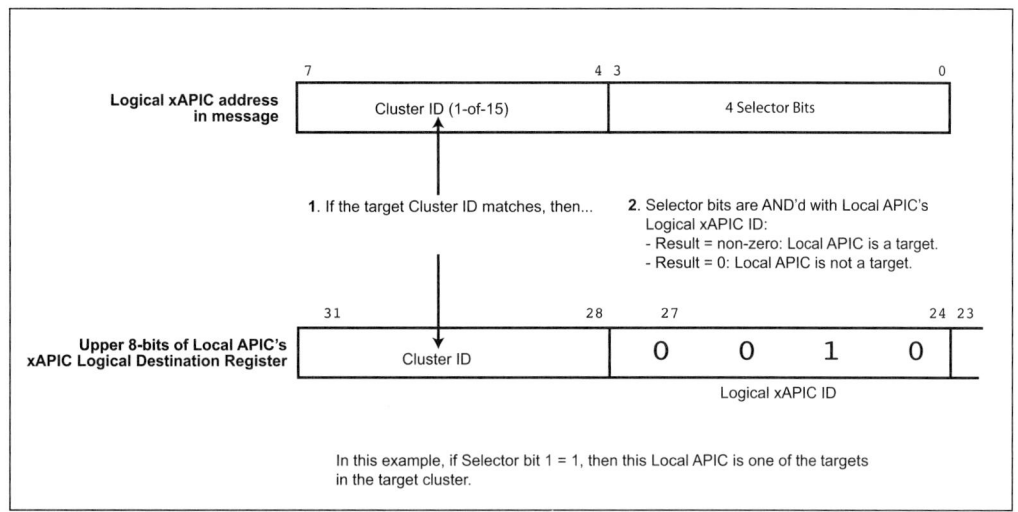

Hierarchical Cluster Model. *This is the only logical addressing model supported in x2APIC Mode (see "x2APIC Cluster Model" on page 1288).* This model can be used with members of current generation processor families, the Pentium 4 family, the P6 family, or Pentium processors (starting with the P54C). While the Flat Cluster model (see "Flat Cluster Model" on page 1290) is limited to no more than 15 Local APICs due to electrical loading constraints (because all of the Local APICs reside on a single APIC bus), *this* model assumes that up to four Local APICs reside on each, separate 3-wire APIC bus or FSB. A hierarchical network is created by including a Cluster Routing Device on each external interface (3-wire APIC bus, FSB, or Intel QPI). The Cluster Routing Device uses the target cluster ID in the message's logical address (see Figure 34-22 on page 1291) to route the message to the target cluster's 3-wire APIC bus, FSB, or QPI. The Cluster Routing Device is not an off-the-shelf Intel part. Rather, it is system design-specific.

Upon message receipt, a potential target Local APIC compares the upper 4-bits of the message's logical address with bits [31:28] of the Logical xAPIC ID field in its LDR to determine if it's a member of the target logical cluster. Assuming it is, the Local APIC ANDs bits [27:24] of the message's logical address with bits [27:24] of the Logical xAPIC ID field in its LDR and, if the result is non-zero, the Local APIC accepts the message.

Figure 34-23: Logical Destination Register (LDR) in xAPIC Mode

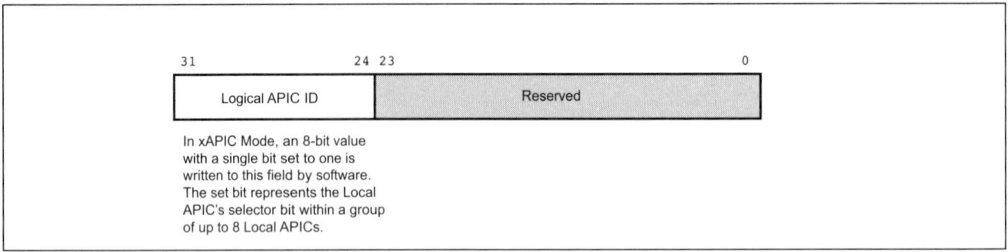

Figure 34-24: Destination Format Register (DFR) in xAPIC Mode

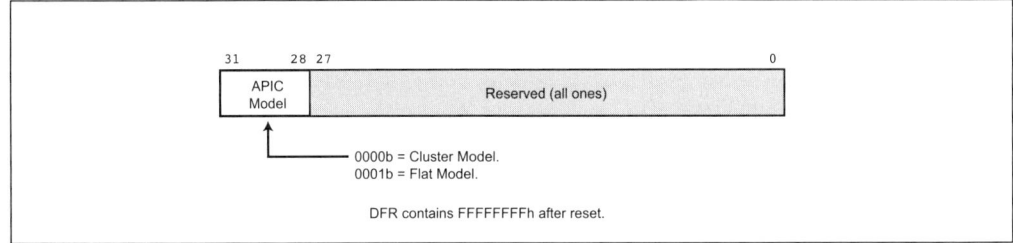

Message Addressing Summary

Table 34-7 on page 1292 summarizes both physical and logical addressing in legacy (Pentium and P6), xAPIC, and x2APIC Modes.

Table 34-7: Addressing Summary Table

Processor Family	Addressing Mode	Description
P6, Pentium	Legacy Physical	• Addresses 0h - Eh are used to address of 1-of-15 Local APICs connected to the 3-wire APIC bus. • Address Fh is used to broadcast a message to all Local APICs (up to 15) connected to the 3-wire APIC bus.

Table 34-7: Addressing Summary Table (Continued)

Processor Family	Addressing Mode	Description
P6, Pentium	Legacy Logical	• Using the **Flat distribution model** (DFR[31:28] = 0001b), the 8-bit address can select up to 8 Local APICs connected to the 3-wire APIC bus as the destination(s). • Using the **Cluster distribution model** (DFR[31:28] = 0000b), there are **two possibilities**: — **Flat cluster model** (assumes all APICs in all clusters are connected to the same 3-wire APIC bus; the arbitration scheme only supports up to 15 APICs). Upper 4-bits of 8-bit address identifies 1-of-15 possible clusters (Fh is reserved for a broadcast operation). Lower 4-bits are used as selector bits to select up to 4 Local APICs within the target cluster. — **Hierarchical cluster model** (assumes there are multiple APIC buses each with up to four logical processors—and therefore APICs—attached to it). It requires a cluster router to route a message to the correct cluster. Upper 4-bits of 8-bit address identifies 1-of-15 possible clusters (Fh is reserved for a broadcast operation). Lower 4-bits are used as selector bits to select up to 4 Local APICs within the target cluster. Supports up to 60 Local APICs. Address of FFh specifies a broadcast to all Local APICs in all clusters.
Pentium 4	xAPIC Physical	• Addresses 00h - FEh are used to address 1-of-255 Local APICs. • Address FFh is used to broadcast a message to all Local APICs.

Table 34-7: Addressing Summary Table (Continued)

Processor Family	Addressing Mode	Description
Pentium 4	xAPIC Logical	• Using the **Flat distribution model** (DFR[31:28] = 0001b), the 8-bit address can select up to 8 Local APICs on the FSB as the destination(s). • **Hierarchical cluster model** (DFR[31:28] = 0000b). Assumes there are multiple FSBs each with up to four logical processors—and therefore APICs—attached to it. Requires a cluster router to route a message to the correct cluster. Upper 4-bits of 8-bit address identifies 1-of-15 possible clusters (Fh is reserved for a broadcast operation). Lower 4-bits are used as selector bits to select up to 4 Local APICs within the target cluster. Supports up to 60 Local APICs. Address of FFh specifies a broadcast to all Local APICs in all clusters.
Processors supporting x2APIC	x2APIC Physical	• Addresses 00000000h-FFFFFFFEh are used to address any one of 4G-1 Local APICs. • Address FFFFFFFFh is used to broadcast a message to all Local APICs (up to a maximum of 4G-1).
Processors supporting x2APIC	x2APIC Logical	Refer to Figure 34-20 on page 1287: • Bits [31:16] of the address identifies the target cluster (1 of 2^{16}-1 clusters; Cluster address FFFFh is reserved to indicate a broadcast). • Bits [15:0] of the address identifies up to 16 possible Local APICs within the targeted cluster. • Address FFFFFFFFh is used to broadcast a message to all Local APICs in all clusters.

Lowest-Priority Delivery Mode

Intel does not recommend this mode of operation for the Pentium 4 processor family or later processors because receipt of a message indicating Lowest-Priority Delivery Mode results in multiple Local APICs issuing interrupt messages that consume external interface bandwidth (and therefore can degrade system performance). This was not a problem on the P6 or the Pentium processor families because the interrupt mes-

sages were transmitted over the 3-wire APIC bus and did not consume any external interface bandwidth.

General

When this Delivery Mode is specified in a message, the message also specifies one of the following:

- Logical Destination Mode.
- *All Including Self* destination shorthand.
- *All Excluding Self* destination shorthand.

The group of Local APICs targeted by the message all arbitrate for ownership of the external interface (FSB or Intel QPI for the Pentium 4 family or later), or the APIC bus (for the P6 or Pentium families):

- On the Pentium 4 and later processor families, Local APICs associated with the targeted group of logical processors then exchange interrupt messages in order to determine which of them is currently executing the lowest-priority program (as specified in their respective TPRs).
- On the Pentium and P6 family processors, the Local APICs associated with each processor compare their TPR values bit-by-bit over the 3-wire APIC bus to determine which of them is currently executing the lowest-priority program.

The logical processor executing the lowest-priority program then accepts the original interrupt message and is interrupted.

Warnings Related to Lowest-Priority Delivery Mode

- Support for Local APIC handling of messages that specify the All Including Self destination shorthand addressing as well as Lowest-Priority Delivery Mode is model-specific.
- A broadcast message (bits [31:28] of the message's physical address = 1111b) specifying physical addressing originated under software control by a Local APIC, or an interrupt message originated by the IO APIC specifying physical addressing and Lowest-Priority Delivery Mode is not supported and must not be configured by software.
- In order to guarantee proper handling of non-broadcast messages originated by a Local APIC or the IO APIC that specify Lowest-Priority Delivery Mode, software must ensure that all of the targeted Local APICs exist and have been enabled to receive interrupts.

- Broadcast messages initiated by either a Local APIC or the IO APIC using Lowest-Priority Delivery Mode and specifying the Cluster address model are not supported.
- An OS may permit the IO APIC or PCI devices using MSI to initiate messages specifying Lowest-Priority Delivery Mode. After updating a Local APIC's Task Priority Register (TPR), however, the OS may neglect to perform a memory-mapped IO write to update the chipset's copy of that Local APIC's task priority. In this case, the chipset may deliver interrupt messages specifying Lowest-Priority Delivery Mode to the wrong logical processor (i.e., one that is not actually executing the lowest-priority program).

Chipset-Assisted Lowest-Priority Delivery

As mentioned in the previous section, use of the Lowest-Priority Delivery Mode is not recommended for the Pentium 4 processor family or later. This section describes an alternative implementation of this mode, but it only applies to user-defined interrupts being delivered to the processors by the chipset (it does not apply to NMI, INIT, or SMI).

Assume that a device adapter asserts an IRQ signal to request service from the interrupt handler within its device driver:

1. The IRQ is received on one of the inputs of the chipset's IO APIC.
2. The IO APIC consults the Redirection Table register associated with the respective IRQ input pin and determines that this IRQ is to be sent to the logical processor that is currently executing the lowest-priority (and therefore the most interruptible) program.
3. The chipset consults a set of memory-mapped IO registers (within the chipset). Each one of these registers is associated with a logical processor. Whenever the OS writes a new value into a Local APIC's TPR, the OS also performs a memory-mapped IO write to the chipset register associated with that logical processor. In this way, the chipset is aware of the priority of the programs currently being executed on the various logical processors.
4. After consulting the chipset-specific, memory-mapped IO register set, the chipset arbitrates for ownership of the processors' external interface (e.g., FSB or Intel QPI) and initiates an interrupt message transaction directing the device adapter's interrupt to the logical processor executing the lowest-priority program. It uses Physical Destination Mode in the message.

It must be stressed that it is chipset-specific whether or not this method is supported. Also, the memory-mapped IO addresses at which the chipset's logical processor/task priority registers are implemented is chipset-specific. The OS must be aware of the chipset's support and must know the chipset memory-mapped IO port addresses to which the task priority for each logical processor must be written.

Alternatively, the device adapter may generate an interrupt by performing an MSI memory write [see "Message Signaled Interrupts (MSI)" on page 1345] rather than by asserting an IRQ signal. In this case, the message delivered to the chipset by the MSI memory write may specify Lowest-Priority Delivery Mode. If it does, the chipset performs steps 3 and 4 to select the target logical processor and deliver the interrupt to it. Additional information can be found in "Direct-Delivery of an MSI" on page 1346.

Just as a note of interest, in Intel's Itanium processor documentation, the optional, chipset-specific memory-mapped IO ports into which the OS writes the task priority for each processor are referred to as the XTP (External Task Priority) registers.

Local APIC IDs Are Stored in the MP and ACPI Tables

- AP stands for Application Processor.
- BSP stands for Bootstrap Processor.

During system startup, the BIOS detects the presence of any APs (see "How the APs are Discovered and Configured" on page 1381 for a detailed description) and causes the BSP and the APs to create entries for themselves in both the Multiprocessing Table and the ACPI (Advanced Configuration and Power Interface) namespace (the term used for the ACPI table) in memory. Each logical processor's capabilities and the APIC ID assigned to its Local APIC are stored in these tables. When the BIOS boots the OS into memory and yields control to the OS startup code, the OS will consult one of these tables (the table consulted is OS design-specific) to discover what processor resources it has to work with.

While only the APIC IDs of the primary logical processors (logical processor 0) in each physical processor package are included in the MP table, entries are included in the ACPI table for all of the logical processors in the system (and each entry includes the APIC ID for that logical processor's Local APIC).

More information can be found in "Boot Strap Processor (BSP) Selection" on page 1378.

Accessing the Local APIC ID

Software (e.g., the OS) can access the APIC IDs in any of the following ways:

- Read the Local APIC's APIC ID register:
    — In xAPIC Mode, by executing a MOV instruction to read the contents of the register.
    — In x2APIC Mode, by executing the RDMSR instruction.
- Read the logical processor entries from the ACPI or MP table (the BIOS creates an ACPI table and an MP table as part of the MP initialization protocol).
- On a Pentium 4 or subsequent processor, execute a CPUID request type 1. The primary logical processor's (logical processor 0's) xAPIC ID is returned in the most-significant byte of the EBX register (see Figure 34-18 on page 1282).
- On a processor that supports x2APIC Mode, execute a CPUID request type Bh (11d). The x2APIC ID is returned in the EDX register.

An Introduction to the Interrupt Sources

A logical processor can receive interrupts from local as well as from remote sources. The following two sections provide a list and a basic description of the local and remote interrupt sources.

Local Interrupts

As well as receiving interrupt messages initiated by device adapters, a logical processor's Local APIC can receive interrupts from a number of local sources (see Figure 34-25 on page 1299):

1. **Local Interrupt pin 0 (LINT0)**. When the Local APIC is disabled, this processor input acts as the INTR input from the legacy 8259A interrupt controllers (see Figure 34-2 on page 1246). Alternatively, the LINT0 input can be used to generate an interrupt when an event local to the processor occurs. For example, a thermal sensor in the machine (external to but in close proximity to the processor) might monitor the thermal envelope immediately surrounding the processor and generate an interrupt to the processor if the temperature in the processor's immediate vicinity rises too much.

2. **Local Interrupt pin 1 (LINT1)**. When the Local APIC is disabled, this processor input acts as the NMI input from the system board logic. Alterna-

tively, the LINT1 input can be used to generate an interrupt when an event local to the processor occurs.

3. **Timer.** A timer within the Local APIC can be programmed to generate a single interrupt after a programmed amount of time, or an interrupt on a periodic basis at a programmed interval.

4. **Performance Counters.** The logical processor's Performance Counters can be programmed to generate an interrupt when a counter overflows.

5. **Internal Thermal Sensor.** The logical processor's internal Thermal Sensor can be programmed to generate an interrupt either when the core temperature rises above a programmed trip point, when the temperature drops below the programmed trip point, or both.

6. **CMC logic.** The logical processor's Correctable Machine Check (CMC) logic can be programmed to generate an interrupt when the number of correctable (i.e., soft) errors have reached a programmed threshold value.

7. **Local APIC Error logic.** The Local APIC can generate an interrupt if it encounters an error while performing its duties.

Figure 34-25: Local Interrupt Sources

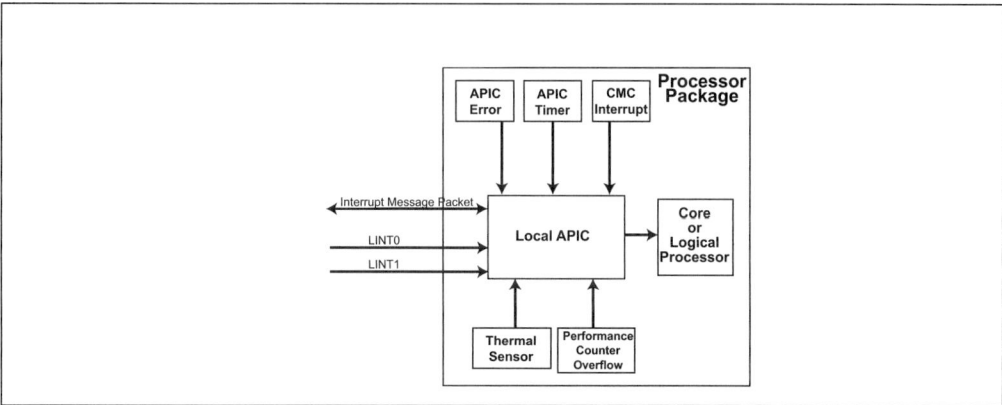

Remote Interrupt Sources

A logical processor's Local APIC can also receive interrupts in the form of interrupt messages from the outside world. These remote sources would include:

1. IPIs (Inter Processor Interrupt) messages received from the Local APICs associated with other logical processors (or that the Local APIC might send to itself).

2. Interrupt messages received from the IO APIC due to a device adapter's assertion of an IRQ (Interrupt Request) signal line to the IO APIC.

3. An ExtINT (external interrupt) message received from the IO APIC due to the generation of an interrupt request by the legacy 8259a interrupt controller.

4. Interrupt messages received due to a device adapter generating an MSI (Message Signaled Interrupt). See "Message Signaled Interrupts (MSI)" on page 1345 for more information.

5. Special interrupt messages sent to the processor by the chipset. The chipset uses special messages to deliver an NMI, SMI, or INIT to a logical processor.

Introduction to Interrupt Priority

General

Table 34-8 on page 1301 is a subset of Table 19-10 on page 739 and shows the priority relationship of the various types of interrupts to each other in the event that multiple interrupt types are received by the Local APIC simultaneously. As an example, if the logical processor were to simultaneously receive an SMI and an NMI interrupt, the SMI would be serviced first followed by the NMI (when the logical processor has completed servicing the SMI).

Table 34-8: Interrupt Priorities

Class	Class Description	Ranking Within Class (highest shown first)	Handled by APIC?
3 Highest Priority	Special external hardware interrupts	**Flush**. The chipset asserts the FLUSH# signal to the processor to force a cache flush (e.g., on a switch to SMM). Starting with the Pentium 4, the FLUSH# signal is no longer implemented.	No
		Stop Clock. The chipset asserts the STP-CLK# signal to the processor, commanding it to turn off its internal clock (as a power conservation measure).	No
		SMI. The chipset sends an SMI to the logical processor to switch it into SMM.	Yes
		INIT. The chipset sends an INIT to the logical processor. This is a soft reset [see "286 DOS Extender Programs" on page 311 for more information].	Yes
5	External Interrupts.	**NMI**. The chipset sends a Non-Maskable Interrupt to the logical processor, typically to report that a serious problem was detected in the platform.	Yes
		An interrupt message containing a **user-defined interrupt** vector value between 32 and 255.	Yes

Definition of a User-Defined Interrupt

Interrupt vector values 0 - 31 are reserved for architecturally-defined interrupts and exceptions (see Table 19-8 on page 729). As noted in Table 19-5 on page 715, in a PC-compatible machine the interrupt vector values in the 8 - 15 range are shared by software exceptions and hardware interrupts.

A user-defined interrupt is one that is not generated by the logical processor (it is delivered by the chipset, by a source local to the logical processor—e.g., a Thermal Sensor interrupt—or by the OS to the logical processor's Local APIC) and one that has an interrupt vector value in the 32 to 255 range.

When an interrupt message containing a vector in the range of 0 - 15 is sent or received through the Local APIC, it sets the Received Illegal Vector or Send Illegal Vector bit in its Error Status Register (see Figure 34-26 on page 1302). Note that although the vectors 16 - 31 are reserved for processor exceptions, the Local APIC will not generate an error on the send or receive of an interrupt message using one of these vectors.

Figure 34-26: Local APIC Error Status Register

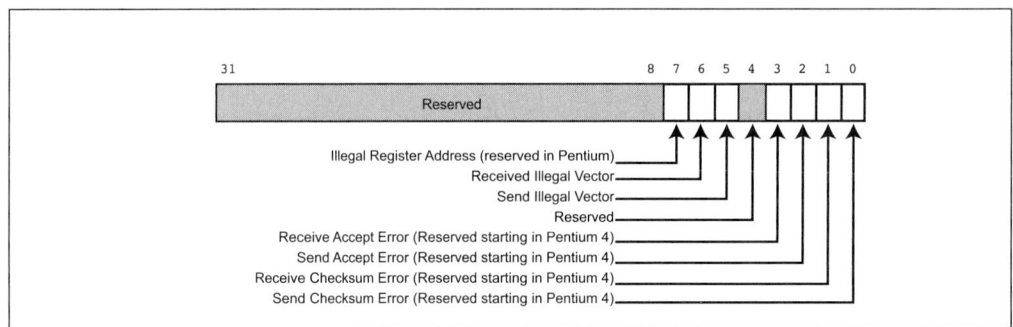

User-Defined Interrupt Priority

Consider a scenario wherein none of the higher-priority interrupts (SMI, INIT or NMI) are pending and the Local APIC receives multiple interrupt messages containing user-defined (i.e., fixed) interrupt vectors (in the 32 to 255 range). In what order does the Local APIC dispatch these interrupts to the logical processor (in other words, what is the priority scheme)?

Refer to Table 34-9 on page 1303. The 256 possible interrupt vectors are divided into 16 groups, or classes, of 16 interrupt vectors each. The vectors in classes 0 (vectors 00h - 0Fh) and 1 (vectors 10h - 1Fh) are not considered user-defined interrupts because they are reserved for software exception conditions (see Table 19-10 on page 739) and NMI. The user-defined vectors within interrupt priority class 15 (vectors F0h - FFh) have the highest priority, while those within interrupt priority class 2 (vectors 20h - 2Fh) have the lowest priority. Although the Local APIC can send or receive an interrupt message with a vector in the 10h to 1Fh range (interrupt class 1) without generating an error, this would be ill-advised as those 16 vectors, like those in class 0, are dedicated for software exceptions (see Table 19-10 on page 739). Priority classes 0 and 1 are shaded in Table 34-9 on page 1303 because they are not user-defined interrupt vectors.

Within each group of 16 user-defined vectors, the lowest numbered vector has the lowest priority while the highest numbered one has the highest priority.

Table 34-9: User-Defined Interrupt Priority Scheme

Interrupt Class	Vector Number (decimal)	Priority
0. Class 0 is not included because these 16 vectors are dedicated for software exceptions (see Table 19-10 on page 739)	0 - 15	
1. Although an interrupt message could be sent or received with a vector in the 16 to 31 range without causing the Local APIC to generate an error, this would be ill-advised because these 16 vectors are dedicated for software exceptions (see Table 19-10 on page 739).	16 - 31	Within this class, 16 is the lowest and 31 is the highest priority. Note: Technically-speaking, this is the lowest-priority user-defined priority class, but as noted in the left column, these 16 vectors are not user-defined interrupts.
2 is the lowest user-defined priority class and 15 is the highest.	32 - 47	Within this class, 32 is the lowest and 47 is the highest priority.
3	48 - 63	Within this class, 48 is the lowest and 63 is the highest priority.
4	64 - 79	Within this class, 64 is the lowest and 79 is the highest priority.
5	80 - 95	Within this class, 80 is the lowest and 95 is the highest priority.

Table 34-9: User-Defined Interrupt Priority Scheme (Continued)

Interrupt Class	Vector Number (decimal)	Priority
6	96 - 111	Within this class, 96 is the lowest and 111 is the highest priority.
7	112 - 127	Within this class, 112 is the lowest and 127 is the highest priority.
8	128 - 143	Within this class, 128 is the lowest and 143 is the highest priority.
9	144 - 159	Within this class, 144 is the lowest and 159 is the highest priority.
10	160 - 175	Within this class, 160 is the lowest and 175 is the highest priority.
11	176 - 191	Within this class, 176 is the lowest and 191 is the highest priority.
12	192 - 207	Within this class, 192 is the lowest and 207 is the highest priority.
13	208 - 223	Within this class, 208 is the lowest and 223 is the highest priority.
14	224 - 239	Within this class, 224 is the lowest and 239 is the highest priority.
15 is the highest priority user-defined class and 2 is the lowest.	240 - 255	Within this class, 240 is the lowest and 255 is the highest priority.

Definition of Fixed Interrupts

The user-defined interrupts are frequently referred to as fixed interrupts in the APIC documentation. When an interrupt message is received and it specifies the Fixed Delivery Mode, this instructs the Local APIC to use the 8-bit vector that was delivered in the message and to prioritize the interrupt as a user-defined interrupt (see "User-Defined Interrupt Priority" on page 1302).

When an interrupt message is received that specifies the NMI, SMI, INIT, ExtINT, SIPI, or INIT-deassert Delivery Mode, the Local APIC ignores the 8-bit vector delivered in the message.

Masking User-Defined Interrupts

While each of the interrupts associated with the LVT (see "Locally Generated Interrupts" on page 1360) has its own Mask bit, the user-defined interrupts cannot be individually masked in the Local APIC. Rather, executing the CLI instruction mass disables recognition of all user-define interrupts, while executing the STI instruction mass enables recognition of all of them.

Task and Processor Priority

Introduction

The Local APIC uses two register values to determine in what order to dispatch user-defined interrupts to the logical processor:

*   **Task Priority Register (TPR)**. The value written to the TPR by the OS represents the relative importance of the currently running program from the OS's point of view.
*   **Processor Priority Register (PPR)**. The PPR derives its contents from:
    — The TPR and,
    — If a user-defined interrupt is currently being serviced, the priority of that interrupt.

In order to determine the eligibility of a user-defined interrupt to interrupt the executing program or the currently executing user-defined interrupt handler, the Local APIC compares the pending user-defined interrupt's priority to the logical processor's priority. The following sections describe the TPR, the PPR and the eligibility test.

The Task Priority Register (TPR)

As described in "User-Defined Interrupt Priority" on page 1302, the user-defined interrupts (32 - 255) are divided into 14 classes with class 15 having the highest priority and class 2 having the lowest. Within each class, the numerically lowest-numbered interrupt has the lowest priority and the highest numbered has the highest priority.

When the OS instructs a logical processor to start executing a task, it also programs the Local APIC's Task Priority Register (TPR; see Figure 34-27 on page 1306) with a threshold value consisting of the 4-bit priority Class and a 4-bit priority SubClass. At a given moment in time, the value in the TPR reflects the relative importance of the program currently being executed (from the OS's point of view).

As described in the next section, the priority class specified in TPR[7:4] is used in deciding whether or not a pending user-defined interrupt will be allowed to interrupt the currently-executing program (*TPR[3:0] are not considered when making this decision*). Rather, TPR[3:0], the Priority SubClass is used to break a priority Class tie when Lowest-Priority Delivery Mode is specified in an interrupt message (refer to "Lowest-Priority Delivery Mode" on page 1294) targeting multiple Local APICs.

Figure 34-27: Task Priority Register (TPR)

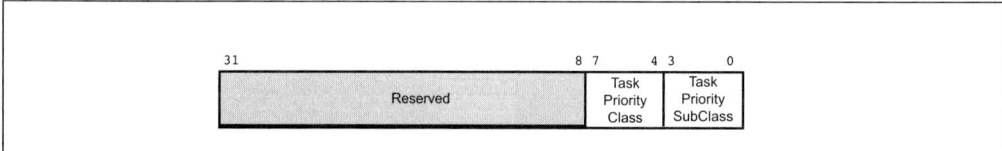

The Processor Priority Register (PPR)

At a given moment in time, the program priority Class specified in TPR[7:4] reflects the relative importance of the program currently being executed (from the OS's point of view). Consider the following scenario:

- The logical processor is currently executing a program (*not* a user-defined interrupt handler) and the TPR contains the value 93h, indicating that the currently executing program will not be interrupted by any user-defined interrupt unless the interrupt's priority Class > 9h.
- A user-defined interrupt of A2h is received and dispatched to the logical processor for execution (because Ah is > 9h).

The User-Defined Interrupt Eligibility Test

When a user-defined interrupt is pending (i.e., its respective bit has been set to one in the IRR), its user-defined interrupt class is compared to the value in the Processor Priority Register (PPR; see Figure 34-28 on page 1308) to determine if it will be dispatched to the logical processor to interrupt the currently-running program or handler. The PPR is a read-only register and its content is automatically updated by the logical processor hardware under either of two circumstances:

- Whenever a new value is written into the TPR, or
- When a user-defined interrupt is dispatched to the logical processor for servicing.

The logical processor hardware updates the PPR value based on the following criteria:

- **If a handler is executing**. If the logical processor is currently executing an interrupt handler, it is because the handler has a higher priority Class than that of the interrupted program's. In other words, the user-defined interrupt's priority Class (see Table 34-9 on page 1303) is greater than the priority Class of the interrupted program (i.e., the value in TPR[7:4]). In this case, the logical processor hardware sets PPR[7:4] = the priority class of the user-defined interrupt currently being handled. PPR[3:0] is set to 0h.
- **If the program is executing**. The program (and *not* a handler) is executing because either:
  — No fixed interrupts are currently pending, or,
  — One or more fixed interrupts *are* pending (their respective IRR bits are set), but they have not been dispatched to the logical processor because the priority Class of the program specified in TPR[7:4] is greater than the priority Class of the pending fixed interrupts.
  In this case, the logical processor hardware sets PPR[7:0] = TPR[7:0] (i.e., the priority of the program).

Figure 34-28: Processor Priority Register (PPR)

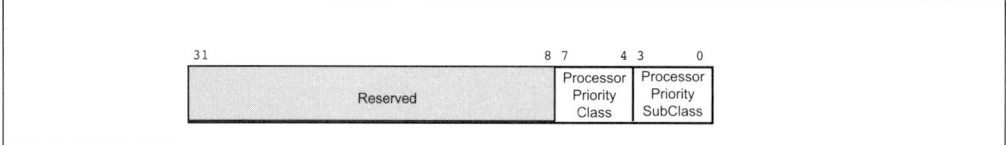

CR8 (Alternative TPR)

The Local APIC architecture is not considered part of the IA-32 or Intel 64 architecture. This being the case, the design of the integrated interrupt controller is subject to possible change in the future. CR8 (see Figure 34-29 on page 1308) was added to the Intel 64 architecture in order to provide to the OS an architecturally-guaranteed mechanism for defining the priority (and therefore the interruptibility) of the currently-running program. CR8 is one of the extended control registers (CR8 - CR15) added in the Intel 64 architecture and is only accessible (using the MOV CR8 instruction) when the logical processor is operating in 64-bit Mode:

• Writes into the priority Class field of CR8 are aliased into the priority Class field of the TPR (see Figure 34-27 on page 1306) and vice versa. A write to CR8 sets the TPR's priority Class and clears TPR[3:0] to zero.
• A read from the 64-bit CR8 register returns TPR[7:4] (program's priority Class) in CR8[3:0] and CR8[63:4] contain zeros.

An exception: on AMD processors, CR8 (the Task Priority register) can be accessed in modes other than 64-bit Mode by prefacing the MOV CR8 instruction with the LOCK prefix (F0h).

Figure 34-29: CR8

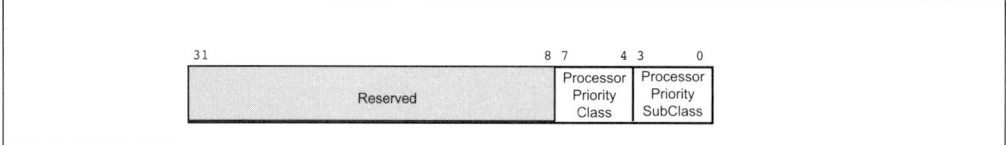

Interrupt Message Format

When an interrupt transaction is performed on the processor's external interface, it takes the form of a memory-mapped IO write transaction. As indicated in Table 34-10 on page 1309, the address used in the transaction takes the form:

```
FEExx00yh
```

where:

- FEEh is the signature that instructs the processor to deliver the message content to all of the Local APICs within the physical processor package.
- xx = the Destination ID of the Local APIC or group of Local APICs.
- If the Local APICs have been programmed in x2APIC Mode, the 00h field can be used as an extension of the Destination ID field.
- y = Hint bit + Destination Mode bit + 00b.

Table 34-11 on page 1311 describes the information output as the write data in the interrupt transaction.

Table 34-10: Interrupt Message Address Format

Bit(s)	Description
63:32	If the device adapter implements a 64-bit MSI Address register, these address bits must be all zeros.
31:20	Must be FEEh.
19:12	Destination ID.
11:4	Extended Destination ID (used in x2APIC Mode).

Table 34-10: Interrupt Message Address Format (Continued)

Bit(s)	Description
3	**Redirection Hint bit.** The message's Delivery Mode is delivered as part of the write data (see Table 34-11 on page 1311) and is not present in the message's address (i.e., the information shown in this table). If the message's Delivery Mode is the Lowest-Priority Delivery Mode, however, the Redirection Hint bit is set to one in the transaction's address phase to alert the MCH (or IOH). The message address also contains a Destination Mode bit (see the next row in this table). There are three possible combinations of these two bits: **Hint Destination** **Bit Mode Bit** 0 — na 1 — 0 — **Lowest-Priority Delivery Mode and Physical Destination Mode.** All of the logical processors in the cluster are considered for redirection of that interrupt. 1 — 1 — **Lowest-Priority Delivery Mode and Logical Destination Mode.** The redirection is limited to only those logical processors that are part of the logical group specified in the Destination ID field. In the latter two cases, the Hint bit is an alert to the MCH (or IOH) that this interrupt message uses the Lowest-Priority Delivery Mode. The MCH (or IOH) is therefore to use the method described in "Chipset-Assisted Lowest-Priority Delivery" on page 1296 to select the logical processor that is currently executing the lowest-priority program within the cluster or the logical group. The MCH (IOH) then modifies the message to indicate Fixed Delivery Mode (see Table 34-11 on page 1311), changes the message's Destination field value to that of the target logical processor's unique Local APIC ID, and alters the Destination Mode from Logical to Physical. The message is then forwarded onto the processor's external interface.
2	**Destination Mode.** This bit only has meaning if the Redirection Hint bit is set to 1: • 0 = **Physical** Destination Mode. • 1 = **Logical** Destination Mode. See the description of the Redirection Hint bit in this table.
1:0	Must be 00b.

Table 34-11: Interrupt Message Data Format

Bit(s)	Description
31:16	Must be 0000h.
15	**Trigger Mode**: • 0 = Edge. • 1 = Level.
14	**Delivery Status**. • If this is an edge-triggered interrupt, this bit is always 1. • If this is an level-sensitive interrupt, this bit indicates the state of the interrupt input: - 1 = Asserted. - 0 = Deasserted.
13:11	Must be 00b.

Table 34-11: Interrupt Message Data Format (Continued)

Bit(s)	Description
10:8	**Delivery Mode.** This is the same as the corresponding bits in the Redirection Table registers (see Figure 34-34 on page 1318) for that interrupt. • **000b = Fixed**. Delivers the vector in the Vector field (see below) to all of the Local APICs listed in the Destination field. The Trigger Mode can be either edge-triggered or level-sensitive. • **001b = Lowest-Priority**. Deliver the interrupt to the logical processor that is executing the lowest-priority program of all the logical processors listed in the Destination field. The Trigger Mode can be either edge-triggered or level-sensitive. • **010b = SMI**. The Delivery Mode must be edge-triggered. The Vector is ignored but must be programmed to all zeroes for future compatibility. • 011b = Reserved. • **100b = NMI**. Delivers the interrupt to all of the Local APICs listed in the Destination field. The Vector is ignored. Regardless of the Trigger Mode setting, NMI is an edge-triggered interrupt. • **101b = INIT (soft reset)**. Delivers the interrupt to all of the Local APICs listed in the Destination field. The Vector is ignored. Regardless of the Trigger Mode setting, INIT is an edge-triggered interrupt. • 110b = Reserved. • **111b = ExINT**. Note that the spec says it delivers the interrupt to all of the Local APICs listed in the Destination field (as an interrupt that originated from an 8259A compatible interrupt controller). It should state that *it is delivered to the single Local APIC specified in the message's Destination field.* That logical processor then issues an Interrupt Acknowledge transaction on the processor's external interface to request the vector from the 8259A-compatible interrupt controller. ExtINT is an edge-triggered interrupt.
7:0	**Vector.** This field is only used when the Delivery Mode = Fixed. In that case, it contains one of the valid user-defined interrupts vectors (i.e., 20h through FFh). Otherwise, this field must contain 00h.

IO/Local APICs Cooperate on Interrupt Handling

The Purpose of the IO APIC

When a device adapter issues an interrupt request to a logical processor, it is usually issued in one of two forms:

- By asserting one of the IRQ signal lines.
- By performing an MSI write transaction in the form of a memory-mapped IO write [see "Message Signaled Interrupts (MSI)" on page 1345].

The IO APIC is incorporated within the chipset and its inputs are connected to the IRQ lines (and possibly to the chipset's SMI# and NMI# signal lines). When a device adapter asserts an IRQ line or when the system board logic asserts the SMI# or NMI# signal, the IO APIC converts this into an interrupt message and transmits it to the logical processors:

- Over the 3-wire APIC bus (for the Pentium and P6 processors families; see Figure 34-30 on page 1314).
- Over the FSB (for the Pentium 4 family processors or later; see Figure 34-31 on page 1315).
- Over Intel QPI (for the latest processors; see Figure 34-32 on page 1315).

The number of IRQ inputs implemented on an IO APIC is design-specific, but 24 is a very common number. For each of the IRQ inputs (and the SMI# input, if the IO APIC has one), the IO APIC implements a register that is programmed by the BIOS or the OS with:

- Information regarding the IRQ signal's characteristics (whether an interrupt is signaled by the rising-edge of the signal or by a static voltage level, and if by a static voltage level, whether a static high or low should be recognized as a valid interrupt).
- Information necessary to compose the interrupt message to be sent to the logical processors.

This register set is referred to as the Redirection Table, or RT, register set.

As mentioned at the beginning of this section, device adapters may also generate an interrupt request by performing an MSI write transaction in the form of a memory-mapped IO write. This memory write transaction targets one of the following:

- **Special IO APIC port** (see "IRQ Pin Assertion Register" on page 1335). The IO APIC implements a special memory-mapped IO port dedicated to the receipt of MSI writes from device adapters. The OS may program a device adapter's MSI register set with the address of this port as well as the data to be written to it. When the device generates an interrupt request, it does so by generating a memory write to the special IO APIC port. Upon receipt of such a message, the IO APIC generates an interrupt message on the 3-wire APIC bus (for the Pentium and P6 processors), or on the external interface (for later processors).

- **A specific Local APIC** (see "Direct-Delivery of an MSI" on page 1346). In a Pentium 4-based system or one based on later processors, the OS may program a device adapter's MSI register set with the address of a logical processor's Local APIC (i.e., its xAPIC or x2APIC ID) as well as the interrupt message to be delivered to the Local APIC. When the device generates an interrupt request, it does so by generating a memory write to the Local APIC's memory-mapped IO default base address (FEE00000h). Upon chipset receipt of such a message, the IO APIC is bypassed. The ICH (see Figure 34-31 on page 1315 and Figure 34-32 on page 1315) passes the MSI write to the MCH (in Intel QPI-based systems, the MCH is renamed the IOH) and the MCH (or IOH) passes it to the processor's external interface (FSB or QPI) without modification. Refer to "Direct-Delivery of an MSI" on page 1346.

Figure 34-30: IO APIC and Pentium/P6 Processors Communicate Via 3-Wire APIC Bus

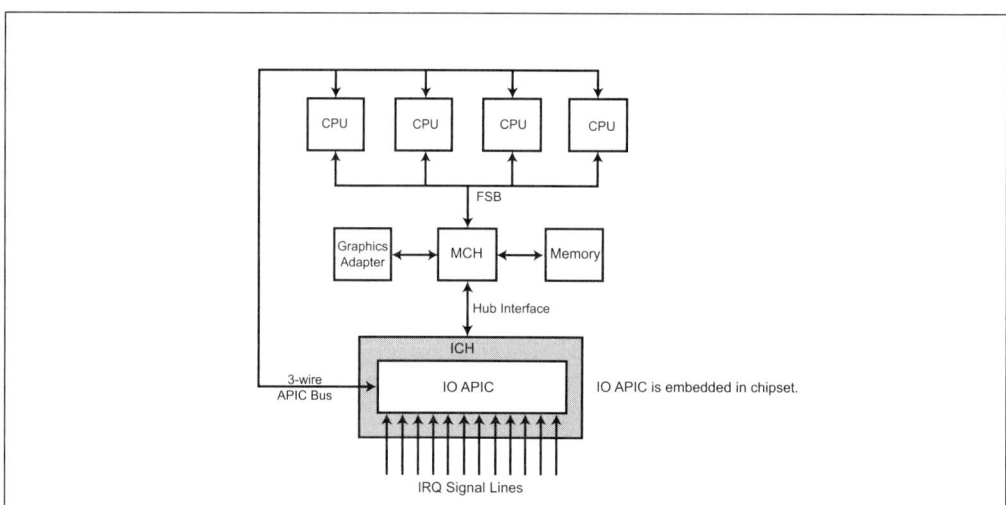

Figure 34-31: IO APIC and Pentium 4 & Later Processors Communicate Via FSB

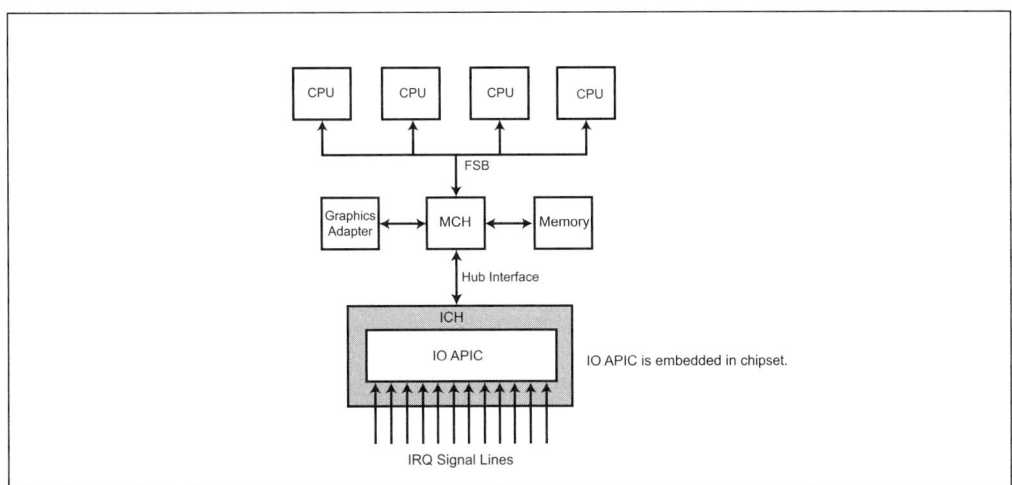

Figure 34-32: IO APIC & Latest Processors Communicate Via Intel QPI

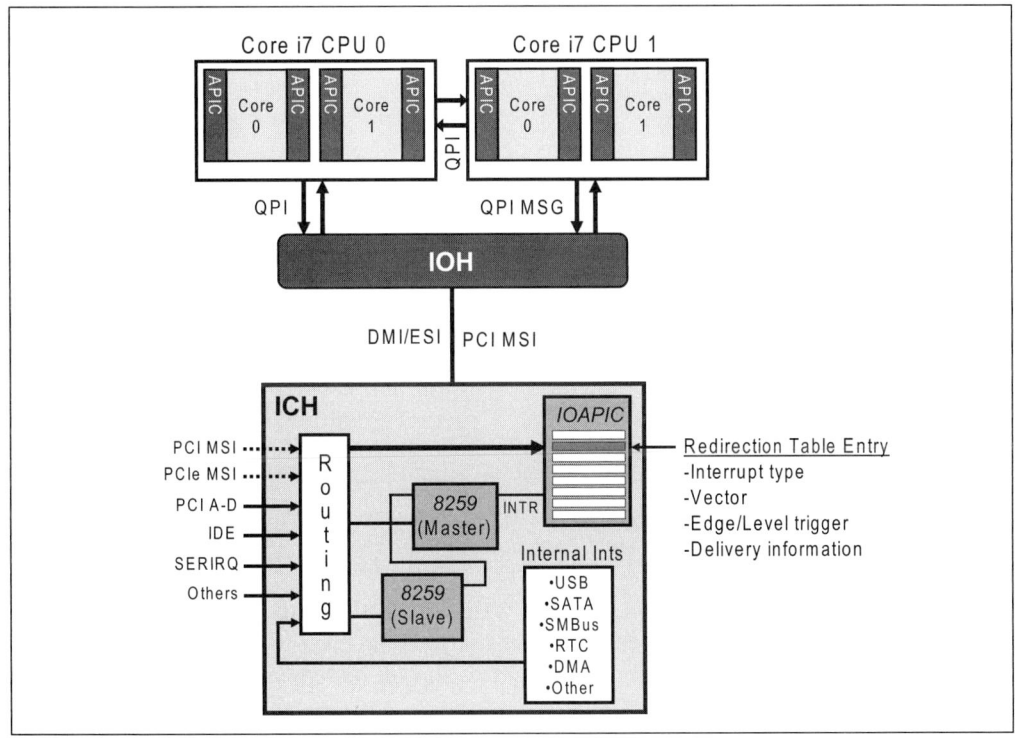

Overview of Edge-Triggered Interrupt Handling

Assumptions

This overview makes the following assumptions:

- Initially, no fixed (i.e., user-defined) interrupts have been received by the Local APIC (see Figure 34-33 on page 1317).
- The device adapter is connected to the IO APIC's input number 3 (RT register 0 is associated with input 1, RT register 1 is associated with input 2, etc.).
- The device adapter issues an interrupt request by generating a low-to-high transition on its IRQ signal line.
- Input 3 has been programmed (via RT register 2 in the IO APIC; see Figure 34-34 on page 1318) as follows:
  — It is an edge-triggered input.
  — It specifies Physical Destination Mode and targets the Local APIC that has been assigned a Local APIC ID of 23h.
  — It uses Fixed Delivery Mode and specifies a user-defined (i.e., fixed) interrupt vector of 20h (32d).
- It also assumes that the system is based on processors that communicate via the FSB (see Figure 34-31 on page 1315).

Description

1. The device adapter issues an interrupt request by generating a low-to-high transition on its IRQ signal line.
2. On detection of the low-to-high transition (i.e., the positive-going edge) on input 3, the IO APIC sets the Delivery Status bit = 1 in RT register 2 (see Figure 34-34 on page 1318), indicating that the message has not yet been accepted by the logical processors (at this point, it hasn't even been sent).
3. Using the information programmed into RT register 2, the IO APIC formulates the interrupt message as a memory-mapped IO write to the Local APICs within the processors on the FSB. *Note: they all respond to the same address—FEExxxxxh (this is derived from memory address FEE00000h, the default base address of the Local APIC's memory-mapped IO register set). Refer to "Interrupt Message Format" on page 1309 for a detailed description of the IPI message format.*
4. The ICH forwards the memory write across the Hub Link to the MCH.
5. The MCH determines from the memory address (i.e., the address of the Local APICs) that the memory write should be forwarded to the FSB.

6. The MCH initiates the memory write transaction representing the interrupt message.
7. All of the processors latch the transaction request, decode the target memory address (FEExxxxxh) and deliver the interrupt message to all of the Local APICs within the processor package.
8. This example assumes that the message specifies Physical Destination Mode targeting Local APIC 23h. Local APIC 23h recognizes that it is the target of the message, while the other Local APICs ignore the message. Continued on page 1319.

Figure 34-33: No User-Defined (Fixed) Interrupts Pending

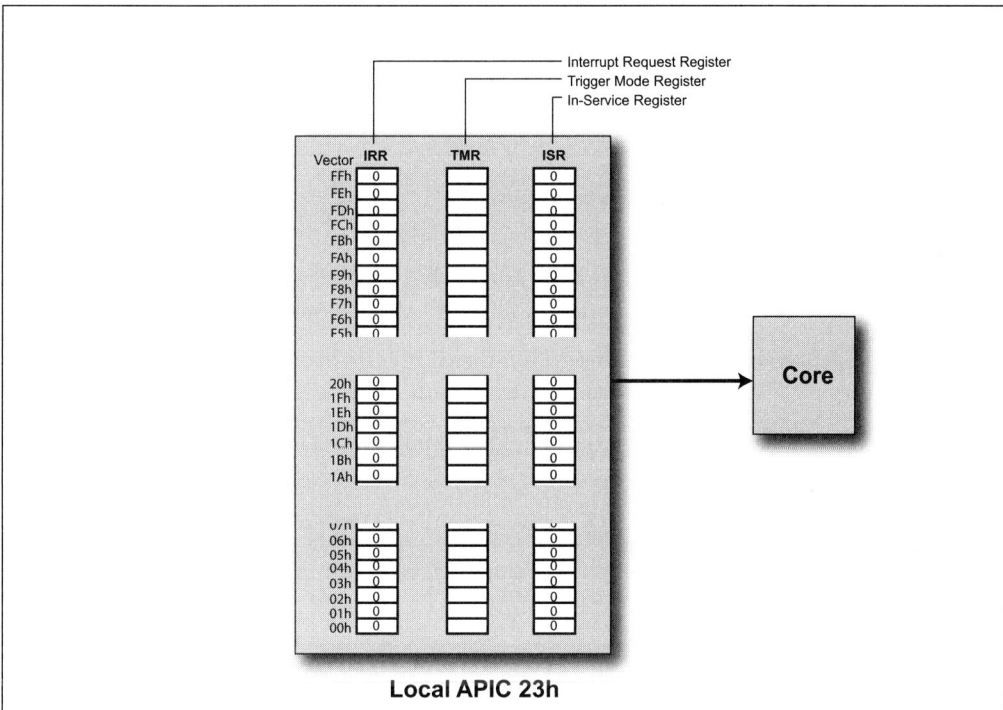

Figure 34-34: RT Entry Format

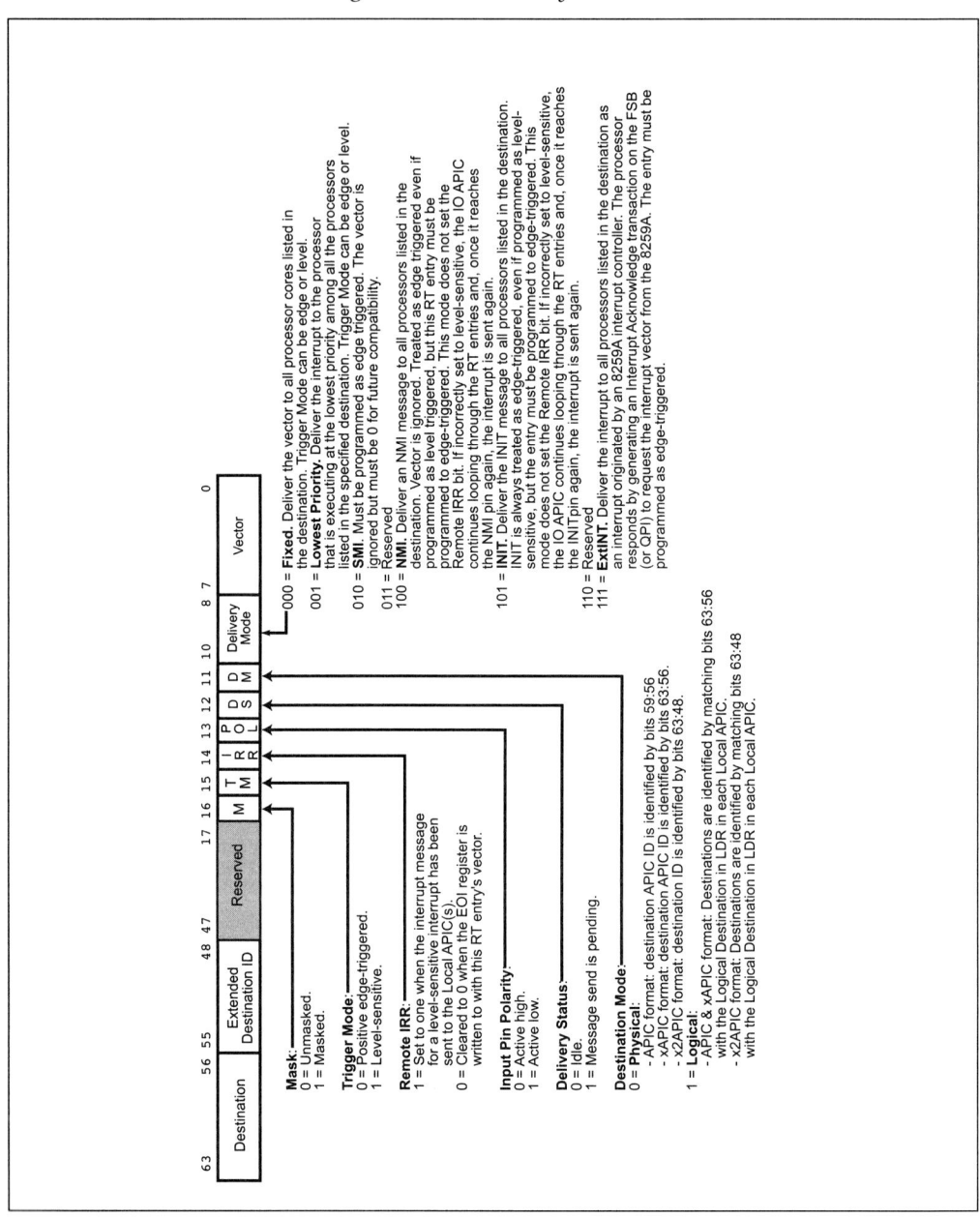

Figure 34-35: Fixed Interrupt 20h (32d) Received

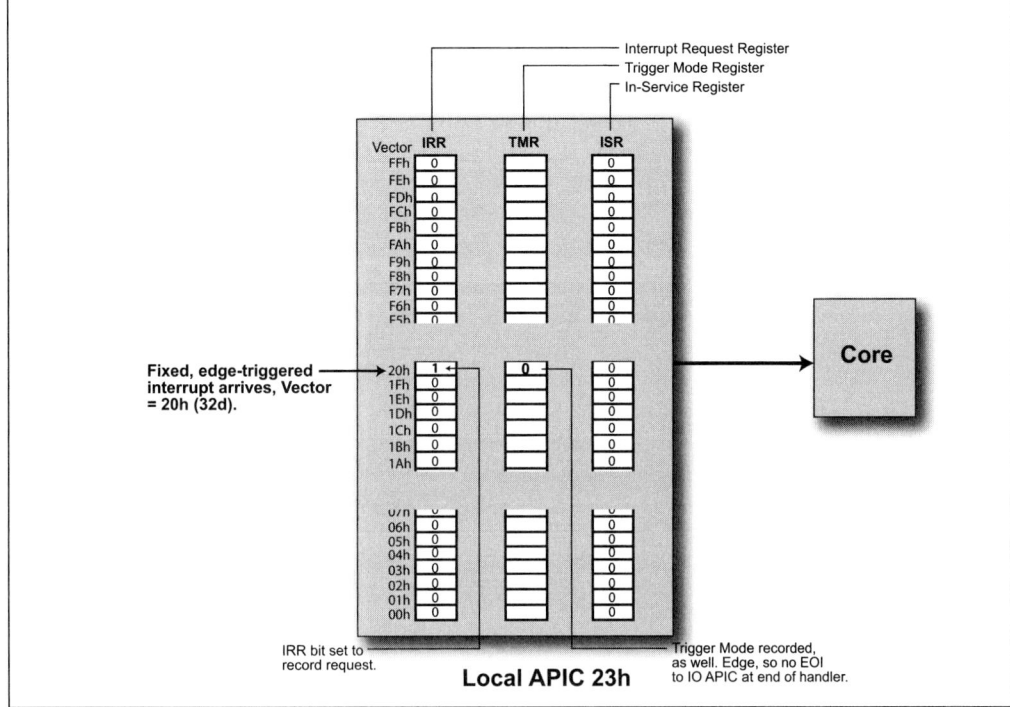

9. Figure 34-35 on page 1319. Local APIC 23h sets bit 20h/32d in its Interrupt Request Register (IRR); the bit is selected by the user-defined vector delivered in the message. In this example, it sets bit IRR[20h] to one to indicate that vector $20h/32_d$ has an interrupt request pending delivery to the logical processor.

10. When the edge-triggered message is received, the target Local APIC clears Trigger Mode Register (TMR) bit[20h] to 0.

11. Having accepted the message, the processor allows the FSB memory write transaction to end normally (i.e., without error). *Note*: the Local APIC may have previously accepted an earlier message with a vector of 20h/32d and IRR[20h] would therefore have already been set to one. In this case, the new message is accepted and IRR[20h] remains set to one.

12. Upon receipt of the Normal Response to the memory write transaction, the MCH sends an acknowledgement of successful message transmission to the ICH over the Hub Link interface.

13. The IO APIC in the ICH clears the Delivery Status bit in RT register 2 to 0. The IO APIC can not accept another edge-triggered interrupt on input 3 until this bit has been cleared.

Figure 34-36: Fixed Interrupt 20h (32d) Forwarded to Logical Processor and Handler Starts Execution

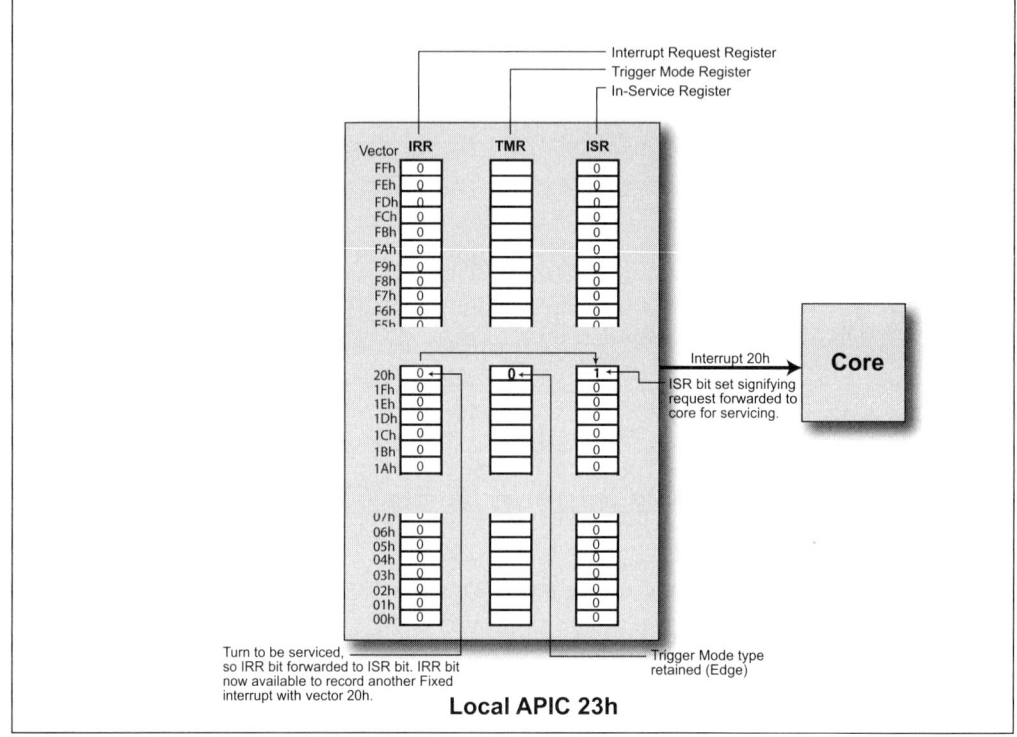

14. Figure 34-36 on page 1320. Within the target logical processor, the Local APIC dispatches user-defined interrupt 20h to the logical processor (see "User-Defined Interrupt Priority" on page 1302). When it does so, IRR[20h] is cleared and ISR[20h] is set to indicate that the interrupt is now being serviced.

Figure 34-37: Handler 20h (32d) Issues EOI to Local APIC

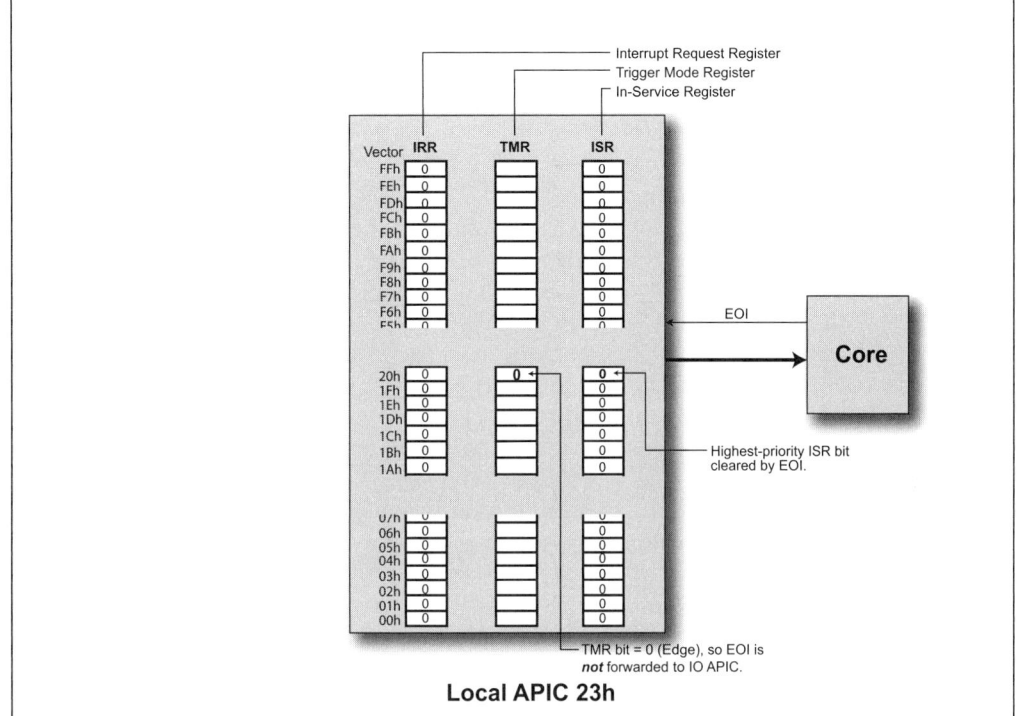

Local APIC 23h

15. Figure 34-37 on page 1321. The interrupt handler is executed. Towards the end of the handler, the handler performs a memory-mapped IO write to the Local APIC's EOI (End-of-Interrupt) register. This causes the Local APIC to clear ISR[20h] (signifying that the level 20h interrupt has been serviced).

16. Since TMR[20h] = 0, this is an edge-triggered interrupt. An EOI therefore does not be sent to the external IO APIC.

Overview of Level-Sensitive Interrupt Handling

Assumptions

This overview makes the following assumptions:

- Initially, no fixed (i.e., user-defined) interrupts have been received by the Local APIC (see Figure 34-33 on page 1317).

- The device adapter is connected to the IO APIC's input number 3 (RT register 0 is associated with input 1, RT register 1 is associated with input 2, etc.).
- The device adapter issues an interrupt request by driving input 3 low and it will continue to drive it low until it has been serviced by the interrupt handler within its device driver.
- Input 3 has been programmed (via RT register 2 in the IO APIC) as follows:
  — It is a level-sensitive input.
  — It recognizes an electrical low as a valid interrupt request.
  — It specifies Physical Destination Mode and targets the Local APIC that has been assigned a Local APIC ID of 23h.
  — It uses Fixed Delivery Mode and specifies a user-defined (fixed) interrupt vector of 20h/32d.
- It also assumes that the system is based on processors that communicate via the FSB (see Figure 34-31 on page 1315).

Description

1. The device adapter issues an interrupt request by driving a low on its IRQ signal line.
2. On detection of the electrical low on input 3, the IO APIC sets the Remote IRR bit (Interrupt Request Register) and the Delivery Status bit = 1 in RT register 2:
   — Setting the Remote IRR bit in RT register 2 indicates a level-sensitive request has been received, but that it has not yet been serviced by the interrupt handler.
   — Setting the Delivery Status bit in RT register 2 indicates that the message has not yet been accepted by the logical processors (at this point, it hasn't been sent yet).
3. Using the information programmed into RT register 2, the IO APIC formulates the interrupt message as a memory-mapped IO write to the Local APICs within the processors on the FSB. *Note: they all respond to the same address—FEExxxxxh (this is derived from memory address FEE00000h, the default base address of the Local APIC's memory-mapped IO register set). Refer to "Interrupt Message Format" on page 1309 for a detailed description of the IPI message format.*
4. The ICH forwards the memory write across the Hub Link interface to the MCH.
5. The MCH determines from the memory address (i.e., the address of the Local APICs: FEE00000h) that the memory write should be forwarded to the FSB.
6. The MCH initiates the memory write transaction that represents the interrupt message.

7. All of the processors latch the transaction request, decode the target memory address (FEExxxxh) and deliver the interrupt message to their Local APICs.

8. This example assumes that the message specifies Physical Destination Mode targeting Local APIC 23h. Local APIC 23h recognizes that it is the target of the message, while the other Local APICs ignore the message.

Figure 34-38: Fixed Interrupt 20h (32d) Received

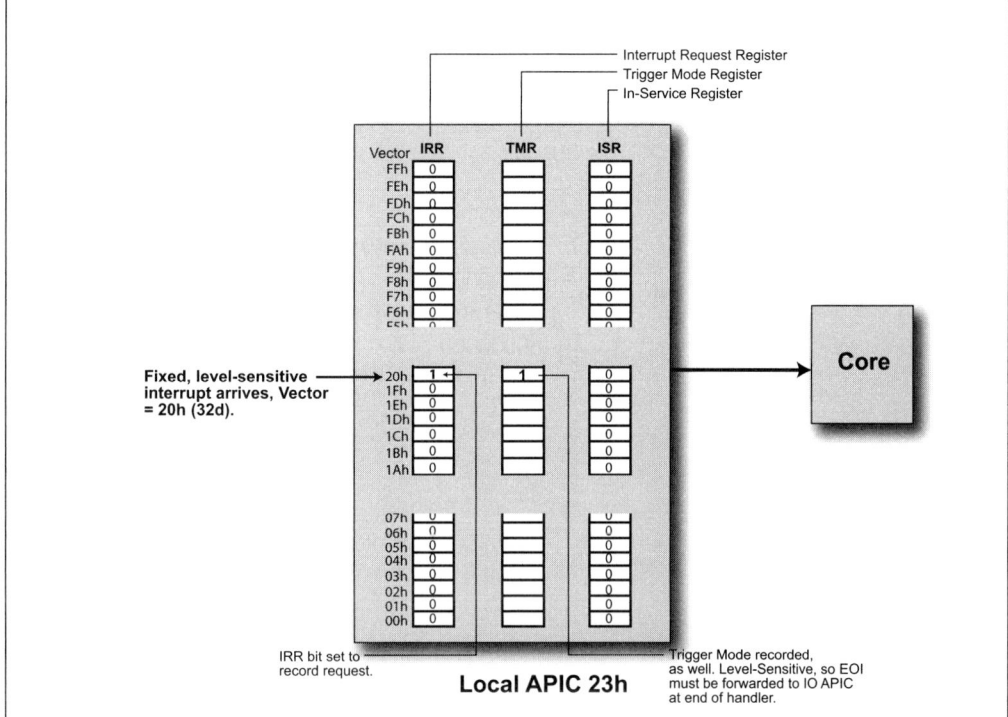

9. Figure 34-38 on page 1323. Local APIC 23h sets the bit in its IRR selected by the user-defined vector delivered in the message. In this example, its sets IRR[20h] to one to indicate that vector $20h/32_d$ has an interrupt request pending delivery to the logical processor.

10. When a level-sensitive message is received, the target Local APIC sets the respective TMR bit (TMR[20h] in this case) to one.

11. Having accepted the message, the processor allows the FSB memory write transaction to end normally (without error). *Note*: the Local APIC may have previously accepted an earlier message with a vector of 20h and IRR[20h]

may have already been set to one. In this case, the new message is accepted and IRR[20h] remains set to one.

12. Upon receipt of the Normal Response to the memory write transaction, the MCH sends an acknowledgement of successful message transmission to the ICH over the Hub Link interface.

13. The IO APIC clears the Delivery Status bit in RT register 2 to 0. The IO APIC cannot send another interrupt message for interrupt input 3 until this bit has been cleared.

14. The IO APIC sets the Remote IRR bit in RT register 2 to indicate that the interrupt has been accepted by the logical processor but has not yet been serviced. The IO APIC cannot accept another interrupt request on input 3 until this bit is cleared by the Local APIC.

Figure 34-39: Fixed Interrupt 20h (32d) Forwarded to Logical Processor and Handler Starts Execution

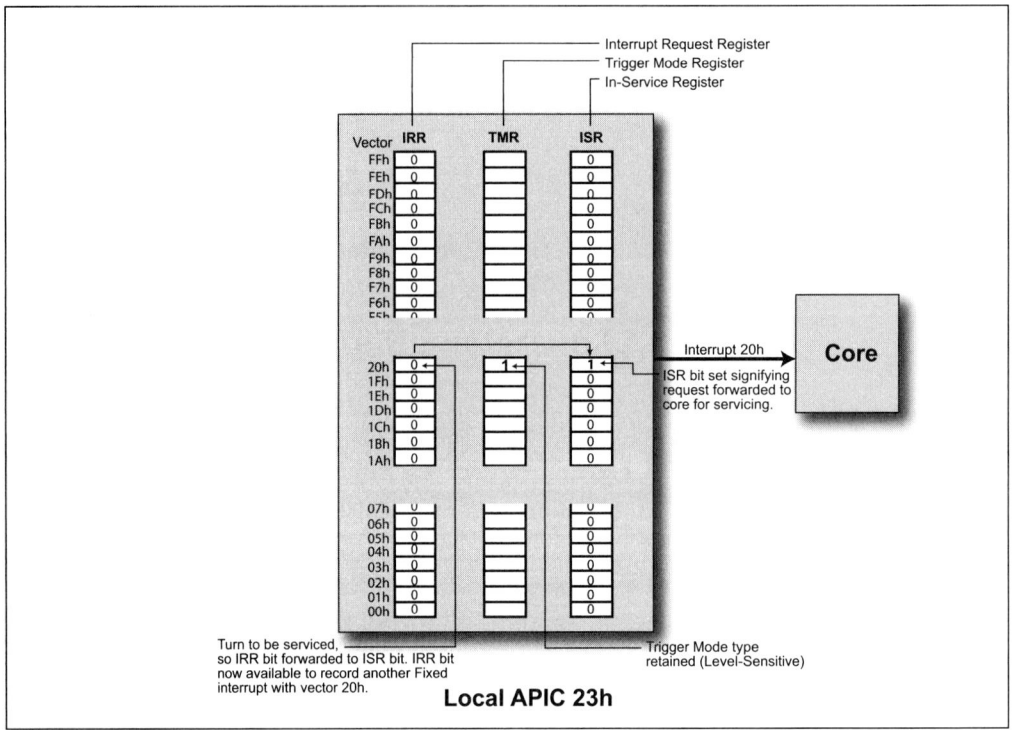

Local APIC 23h

15. Figure 34-39 on page 1324. The target logical processor's Local APIC dispatches user-defined interrupt 20h/32d to the logical processor (see "User-Defined Interrupt Priority" on page 1302). When it does so, IRR[20h] is cleared and ISR[20h] is set to indicate the interrupt is now being serviced.

Chapter 34: The Local and IO APICs

Figure 34-40: Handler 20h (32d) Issues EOI to Local APIC

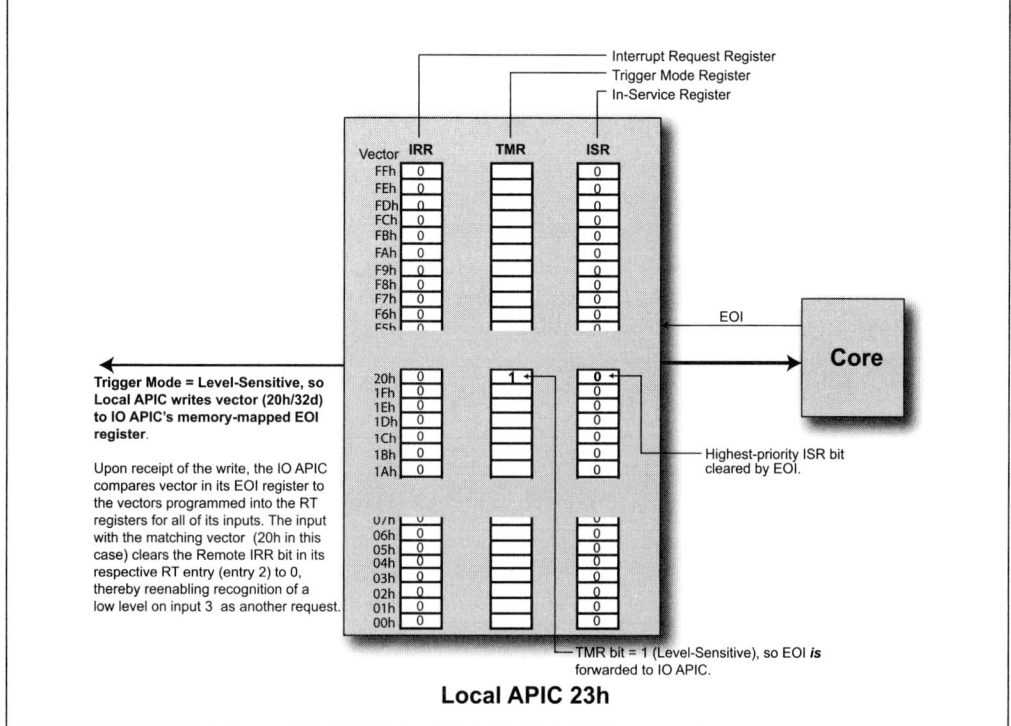

Local APIC 23h

16. Figure 34-40 on page 1325. The interrupt handler is executed. Towards the end of the handler, the handler performs a memory-mapped IO write to the Local APIC's EOI (End-of-Interrupt) register. This causes the Local APIC to clear ISR[20h].

17. When an interrupt handler writes to the Local APIC's EOI register to clear a request, the Local APIC consults the respective TMR bit (bit 20h/32d in this case) to determine whether or not the EOI needs to be forwarded to the external IO APIC, as well. In this case, since TMR[20h] = 1 indicating this is a level-sensitive interrupt, the Local APIC not only clears ISR[20h], but also performs a memory-mapped IO write transaction on the FSB to write the interrupt vector (20h/32d in this case) to the IO APIC's EOI register. This is referred to as a *Broadcast EOI* because it doesn't target the EOI register in a specific IO APIC. If there were more than one IO APIC in the system, they would all receive the write to their EOI registers. For more information, refer to "Broadcast Versus Directed EOI" on page 1338.

18. Upon receipt of the write to its EOI register, the IO APIC compares the vector in the EOI register to the vectors programmed into the RT registers for all of its inputs. The input with the matching vector (input 3 in this case) clears the Remote IRR bit in its respective RT register (register 2) to 0, thereby reenabling recognition of active low, level-sensitive interrupts received on input 3.

Additional information can be found in "IO APIC EOI Register and Shared Interrupts" on page 1336.

Higher-Priority Fixed Interrupt Preempts Handler

The following series of illustrations describes Local APIC handling of multiple fixed (user-defined) interrupts.

Figure 34-41: Fixed Interrupt 20h/32d Received and Registered

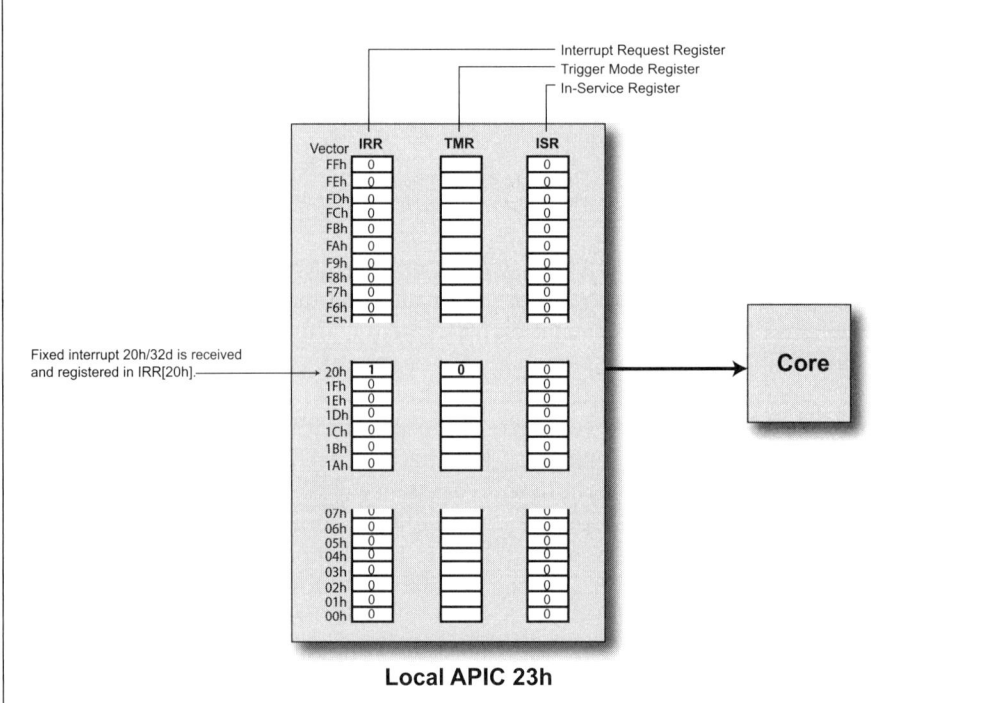

In the illustration above, the Local APIC receives a fixed, edge-triggered interrupt message containing fixed interrupt vector 20h/32d. The request is latched into IRR[20h] and the Trigger Mode (0 = Edge) is latched into TMR[20h].

Figure 34-42: Highest-Priority, So Shifted to ISR and Delivered to Logical Processor

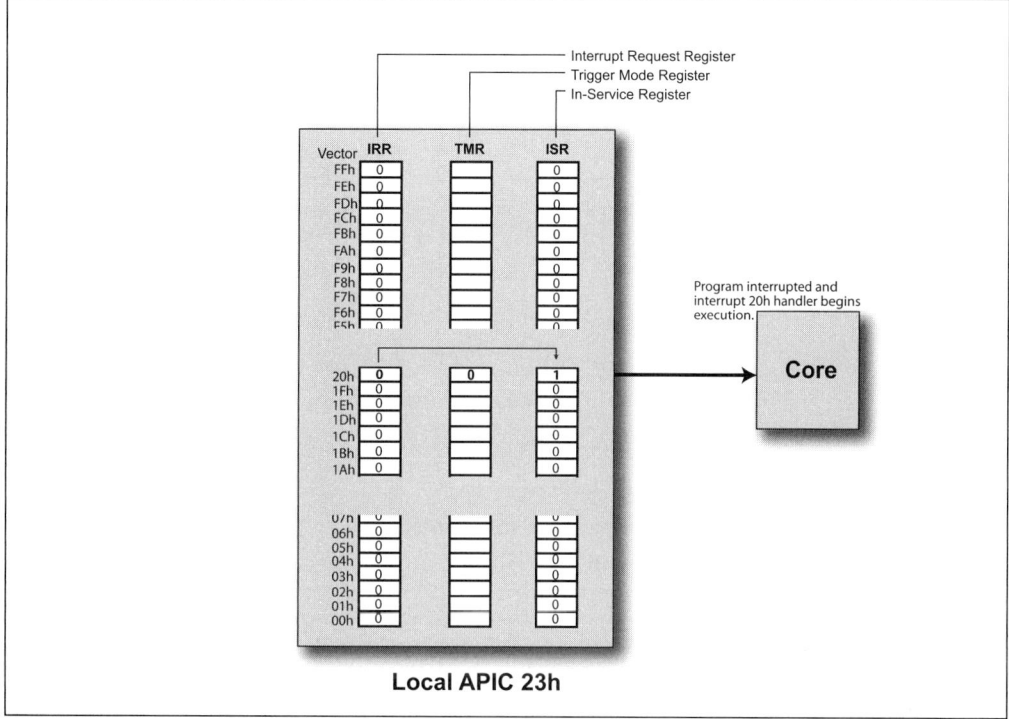

This discussion assumes recognition of external fixed interrupts (i.e. maskable hardware interrupts) is currently enabled (Eflags[IF] = 1). Since no other fixed interrupt requests are currently pending, fixed interrupt 20h is, by definition, the highest priority request. As such, the request is immediately forwarded to ISR[20h], the interrupt is delivered to the logical processor. The currently-running program is interrupted and suspended, and the contents of CS:EIP and Eflags are pushed onto the stack. The logical processor then obtains the start address of handler 20h from IDT entry 20h, loads it into CS:EIP, and begins execution of the 20h handler. This discussion assumes that handler 20h does not disable recognition of external fixed interrupts (i.e., maskable hardware interrupts).

Figure 34-43: Fixed Interrupt FBh/251d Received and Registered

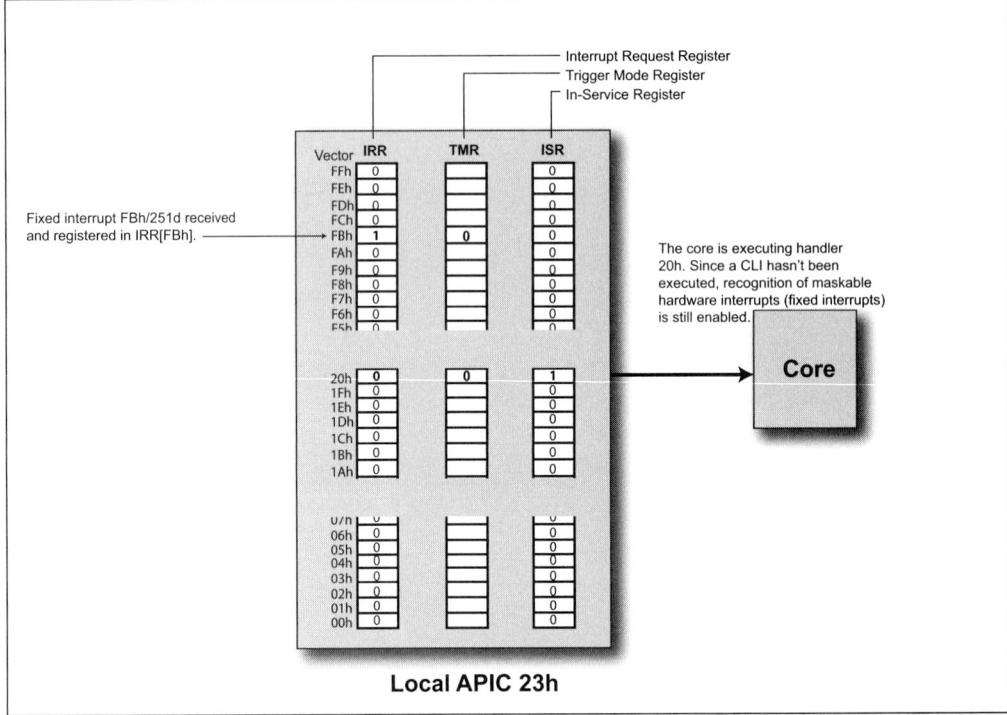

While handler 20h is executing, another fixed, edge-triggered interrupt message containing fixed interrupt vector FBh/251d is received, accepted into IRR[FBh], and the Trigger Mode (0 = Edge) is latched into TMR[FBh].

Figure 34-44: Handler 20h/32d Interrupted by Fixed Interrupt FBh/251d

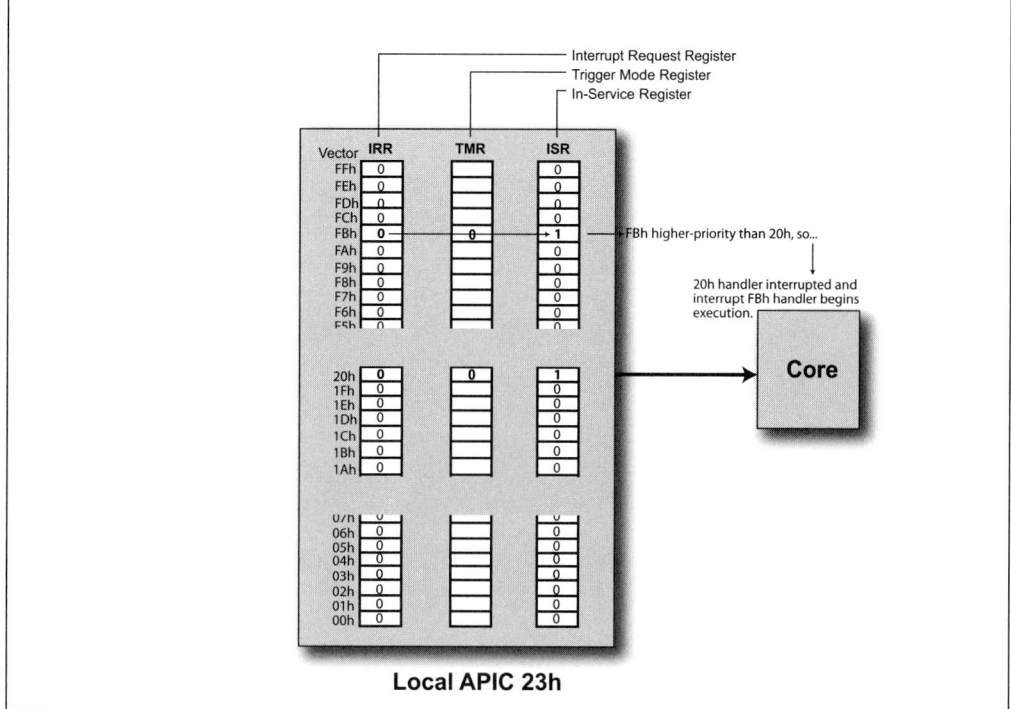

A CLI hasn't been executed in handler 20h, so recognition of maskable hardware interrupts (fixed interrupts) is still enabled (Eflags[IF] = 1). Determining that the interrupt just received (FBh) is a higher priority than the interrupt currently being serviced (20h), the Local APIC shifts IRR[FBh] into ISR[FBh], clears IRR[FBh], and forwards interrupt FBh to the logical processor. Handler 20h is interrupted and suspended, and the contents of CS:EIP and Eflags are pushed onto the stack. The logical processor then obtains the start address of handler FBh from IDT entry FBh, loads it into CS:EIP, and begins execution of the FBh handler. Note that ISR[20h] and ISR[FBh] are now both set to one.

Figure 34-45: FBh Handler Issues EOI to Local APIC

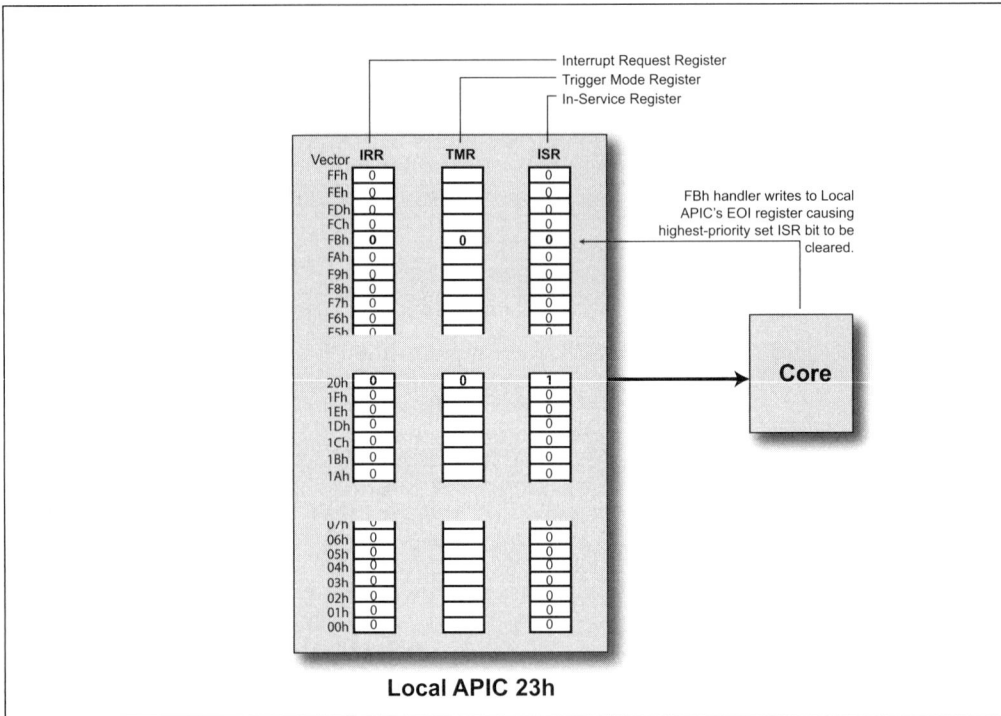

Local APIC 23h

At the end of the FBh handler, the handler performs a memory-mapped IO write to the Local APIC's EOI register. As a result, the Local APIC clears the highest ISR bit that is currently set to one (ISR[FBh]) signifying that request FBh has been serviced. The IRET instruction at the end of handler FBh is then executed causing the logical processor to pop CS:EIP and Eflags from the stack back into the registers. The logical processor then resumes execution of handler 20h at the point of interruption.

Figure 34-46: 20h Handler Issues EOI to Local APIC

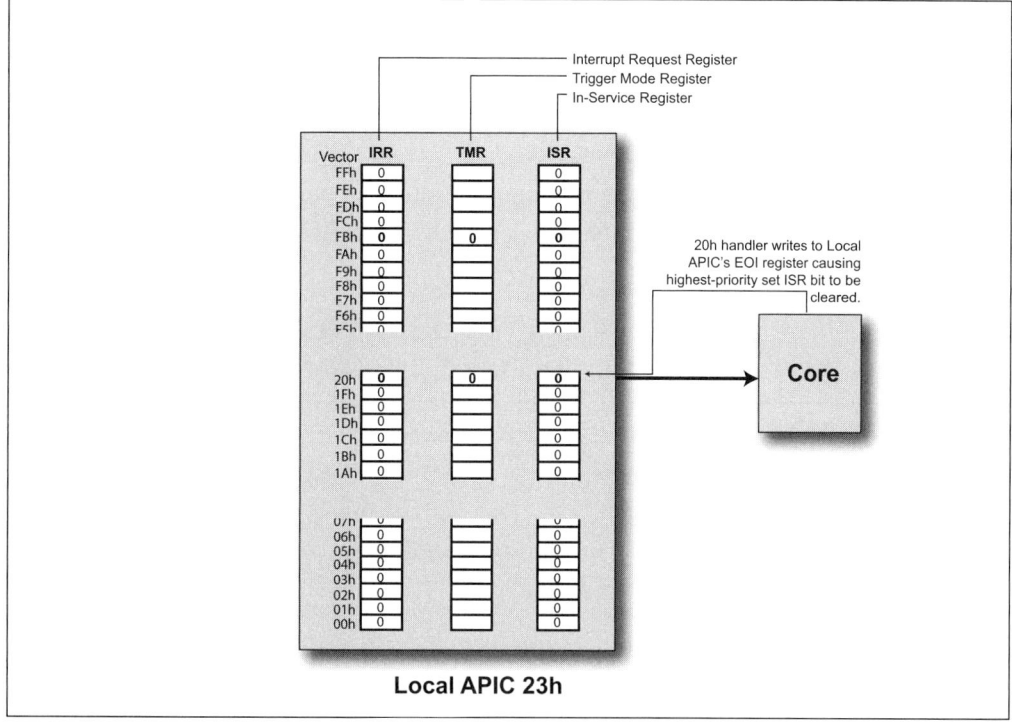

At the end of the 20h handler, the handler performs a memory-mapped IO write to the Local APIC's EOI register. As a result, the Local APIC clears the highest ISR bit that is currently set to one (ISR[20h]) signifying that request 20h has been serviced. The IRET instruction at the end of handler 20h is then executed causing the logical processor to pop CS:EIP and Eflags from the stack back into the registers. The logical processor then resumes execution of the interrupted program.

IO APIC Register Set

IO APIC Register Set Base Address

The default base address of the IO APIC's memory-mapped IO register set is FEC00000h. Depending on the chipset, the base address may or may not be programmable. If it is programmable, the register that is used to reprogram the base address is typically called the APICBASE register and the register address is chipset design-specific.

IO APIC Register Set Description

The IO APIC's register set consists of the memory-mapped IO registers listed in Table 34-12 on page 1332. While the Index Register, Data Register, IRQ Pin Assertion Register, and the EOI register are directly-addressable, the remainder of the registers are indirectly-addressable and are accessed by first writing the 8-bit Index value of the desired register into the Index Register to select the desired register. A subsequent read from or write to the Data Register accesses the desired register.

Table 34-12: The IO APIC Register Set

Register	Start Address or Index	Width (in bits)	R/W	Description
Directly-Addressable Registers				
Index Register	FEC00000h	8	R/W	Name: IND. To access any of the indirectly-accessed registers, the programmer first writes the register's index value into this register. This selects the desired register. A subsequent read from or write to the Data Register accesses the desired register.
Data Register	FEC00010h	32	R/W	Name: DAT. See the description in the previous row.
IRQ Pin Assertion Register	FEC00020h	32	WO	Name: IRQPA. This is a special, memory-mapped IO register device adapters may write to (using an MSI memory write) in order to issue an interrupt request. See "IRQ Pin Assertion Register" on page 1335.

Table 34-12: The IO APIC Register Set (Continued)

Register	Start Address or Index	Width (in bits)	R/W	Description
EOI Register	FEC00040h	32	WO	Name: EOIR. The End-of-Interrupt register is only used if any of the IO APIC's inputs are designated as level-sensitive (rather than positive edge-triggered) inputs. At the end of the interrupt handler associated with a level-sensitive user-defined interrupt, the programmer performs a write to the EOI register in the Local APIC. This causes the Local APIC to clear the ISR bit (In-Service Register) associated with this interrupt. In addition, the Local APIC, after consulting the corresponding TMR bit and determining it is a level-sensitive interrupt, automatically issues an EOI message to the IO APIC's EOI register (in the form of a memory write containing the vector to be cleared). In response, the IO APIC clears the Remote IRR bit in the RT register that contains the matching interrupt vector. See "IO APIC EOI Register and Shared Interrupts" on page 1336. Also refer to "Broadcast Versus Directed EOI" on page 1338.
Indirectly-Accessed Registers (accesses to these registers must be 32-bit accesses)				
Identification Register	Index 00h	32	R/W	Name: ID. This register contains the unique APIC ID assigned to the IO APIC module. See "IO APIC ID Register" on page 1340.

Table 34-12: The IO APIC Register Set (Continued)

Register	Start Address or Index	Width (in bits)	R/W	Description
Version Register	Index 01h	32	RO	Name: VER. This read-only register contains the following information: • The IO APIC's version. • The number of RT registers. • A bit that indicates whether or not the IO APIC implements the IRQ Pin assertion Register (see "IRQ Pin Assertion Register" on page 1335). See "IO APIC Version Register" on page 1340.
Reserved	Index 02h-0Fh	-	RO	
Redirection Table Register 0	Index 10h-11h	64	R/W RO	Name: REDIR_TBL0. This is the first entry in the Redirection Table register set and is associated with IRQ input 1. See "IO APIC Redirection Table (RT) Register Set" on page 1341.
Redirection Table Register 1	Index 12h-13h	64	R/W RO	Name: REDIR_TBL1. This is the second entry in the Redirection Table and is associated with IRQ input 2.
Redirection Table Register n	Index 14h onwards	64	R/W RO	Name: REDIR_TBLn. This is the nth entry in the Redirection Table and is associated with IRQ input n+1. The number of table entries (and input pins) is IO APIC design-specific.

Table 34-12: The IO APIC Register Set (Continued)

Register	Start Address or Index	Width (in bits)	R/W	Description
Reserved	Index values through FFh	-	RO	

IRQ Pin Assertion Register

This is a special, write-only, memory-mapped IO port (at memory address FEC00020h) which device adapters can write to (using an MSI write) in order to deliver an interrupt request to the IO APIC (in the form of a virtual IRQ pin assertion). To generate an interrupt request, the device adapter writes a 32-bit value into this register (see Figure 34-47 on page 1335). Register bits [4:0] contain the IRQ pin number associated with this interrupt. Since currently-available IO APICs only implement 24 IRQ inputs, the only valid values are 0 – 23. The IO APIC ignores bits [31:5]. To provide for future expansion, device adapters must always write a value of 0 into bits [31:5].

On receipt of an IRQ pin number in this register, the IO APIC uses the RT register associated with the specified pin to format an interrupt message and sends it to the logical processors [see "IO APIC Redirection Table (RT) Register Set" on page 1341 for more information]. It should be noted that the Intel ICH5 Data Sheet specifies that the selected IRQ pin's RT register must be programmed as an edge-triggered interrupt.

Figure 34-47: The IRQ Pin Assertion Register

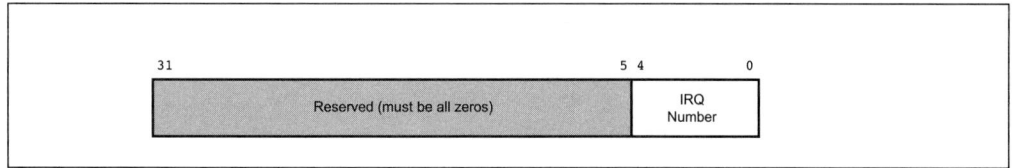

x86 Instruction Set Architecture

IO APIC EOI Register and Shared Interrupts

Non-Shareable IRQ Lines. In the early days of the PC, very few IRQ lines were available to the designers of device adapters (see Figure 34-2 on page 1246). This was further complicated by the type of signaling device adapters used to signal an interrupt request. The 8259A interrupt controller only recognized the positive-edge (i.e., the rising-edge) of the IRQ signal as representing a valid request for service. Two or more adapters could not share an IRQ because each would drive the signal line high (an illegal electrical operation) to indicate a request for service.

Shareable IRQ Lines. Later, the IBM PS/2 and the PCI specification defined active-low, level-sensitive IRQ lines that could be shared among multiple device adapters. Refer to Figure 34-49 on page 1339. Each shareable IRQ signal line has a pull-up resistor that maintains the IRQ line in the deasserted (electrically-high) state when no adapters are driving it low to request service.

When one or more adapters require service, each of them gates an electrical low onto the signal line. A logic low on a shared IRQ line indicates that one or more adapters require servicing. When the interrupt controller detects a low on a shared input, it generates an interrupt to the logical processor and supplies it with the vector associated with that IRQ line. The logical processor uses the vector to index into the IDT and jumps to the interrupt handler pointed to by the selected entry.

Linked List of Interrupt Handlers. That raises a question: When multiple devices share an IDT entry, which adapter's interrupt handler does the entry point to? Earlier in time, the OS loaded the device drivers associated with the installed devices. When a driver is loaded into memory by the OS, the OS then calls the driver's initialization code entry point to finish the setup of the device. As part of this process, assuming that the device uses a shared IRQ line, the driver's initialization code reads the pointer already stored in the respective IDT entry and stores *that* pointer within the body of the driver. It then writes the pointer to its own interrupt handler into this IDT entry. The next driver whose adapter uses the same IRQ line is then loaded by the OS and its initialization code is called. It reads the IDT entry (which contains the pointer to the previously-loaded driver's interrupt handler) and saves *that* pointer in the body of its driver. It then replaces the IDT entry with the pointer to its own interrupt handler. A linked-list of interrupt handlers that share this vector is therefore dynamically created.

How It Works. Refer to Figure 34-49 on page 1339 (ignore the Interrupt Router; it's chipset-specific and permits the OS to choose to which of the interrupt controller's inputs the signal is routed) and assume that both adapters generate an interrupt by placing a low on the shared IRQ line. The IO APIC (labelled *Interrupt Controller* in the figure) sets a bit to register the fact that an adapter attached to this line needs to be serviced. Using the respective RT register, the IO APIC formulates an interrupt message and sends it to a logical processor. On receipt of the message, the Local APIC passes the interrupt vector to the logical processor. The logical processor uses it to index into the IDT and jumps to the interrupt handler associated with the driver that hooked that IDT entry last during the driver load process. That handler executes and the first thing the handler does is to read the Interrupt Pending bit from an adapter-specific port to determine if its adapter is really generating an interrupt. Assuming the bit is set, the body of the handler is executed, thereby servicing the adapter associated with that handler. The act of servicing the adapter causes the adapter to clear its Interrupt Pending bit and to cease driving the IRQ line low. However, the line remains low if another adapter that has not yet been serviced is still driving it low.

Although servicing the first adapter cleared the request from the adapter's perspective, the IO APIC doesn't know that it has been serviced. At the end of the interrupt handler, the programmer performs a memory-mapped IO write (of 0) to the Local APIC's EOI register. This causes the Local APIC to clear the highest-priority ISR bit currently set to one thereby signifying that the interrupt has completed servicing. If the interrupt was defined as an active-low, level-sensitive interrupt (as indicated by a 1 in its respective TMR bit), however, the Local APIC must also inform the IO APIC that the interrupt has completed servicing. It does this by automatically performing a memory-mapped IO write to the IO APIC's (write-only) EOI register (see Figure 34-48 on page 1338). The data written to the register is the vector for the interrupt that just completed servicing. Upon receipt of the vector write to the EOI register, the IO APIC compares the vector to the Vector field in all of its RT registers. It clears the Remote IRR bit in the RT register that has a vector match (signifying that the first adapter has been serviced). For more information regarding the EOI, refer to "Broadcast Versus Directed EOI" on page 1338.

If the IRQ line is still low, however, the IO APIC sets the RT register's Remote IRR bit again and generates another interrupt message to the logical processor with the same interrupt vector. The process just described is repeated until all pending requests on that IRQ line have been serviced after which the pull-up resistor pulls the line back up to the deasserted state.

Broadcast Versus Directed EOI. When an interrupt handler performs a write to the Local APIC's EOI register, the Local APIC clears the highest-priority bit currently set to one in the ISR. It also consults the associated bit in the TMR and, if it is set to one indicating it's a level-sensitive interrupt, it also performs a *Broadcast EOI write* on the processor's external interface to send the interrupt vector to the EOI register of all of the IO APICs in the system (most systems would have one IO APIC, but some might implement more than one). In response, the IO APIC(s) compares the vector to the Vector field in all of its RT registers. It clears the Remote IRR bit in the RT register that has a vector match.

Broadcasting the vector to the EOI registers in all of the system's IO APICs is the Local APIC's default mode of operation. In some systems, however, the IO APICs may each implement the EOI register at a unique memory-mapped IO address. In this case, the system programmer would want to turn off (i.e., disable) the Broadcast EOI feature:

— Whether or not this feature is supported is indicated by a one in bit 24 of the Local APIC Version register (see Figure 34-50 on page 1339). If it is supported, it is available in both xAPIC and x2APIC modes.
— If it is supported, Broadcast of the EOI to all IO APICs is disabled by setting bit 12 of the Spurious Vector register (see Figure 34-51 on page 1340) to one.

Once the Broadcast feature is disabled, the OS would have to ensure that, at the end of each level-sensitive interrupt handler, a *Directed EOI* is performed to the EOI register of the specific IO APIC that handled the interrupt request.

Figure 34-48: The IO APIC's EOI Register

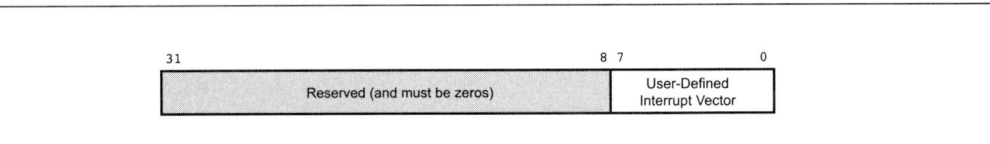

Figure 34-49: Shareable IRQ Line

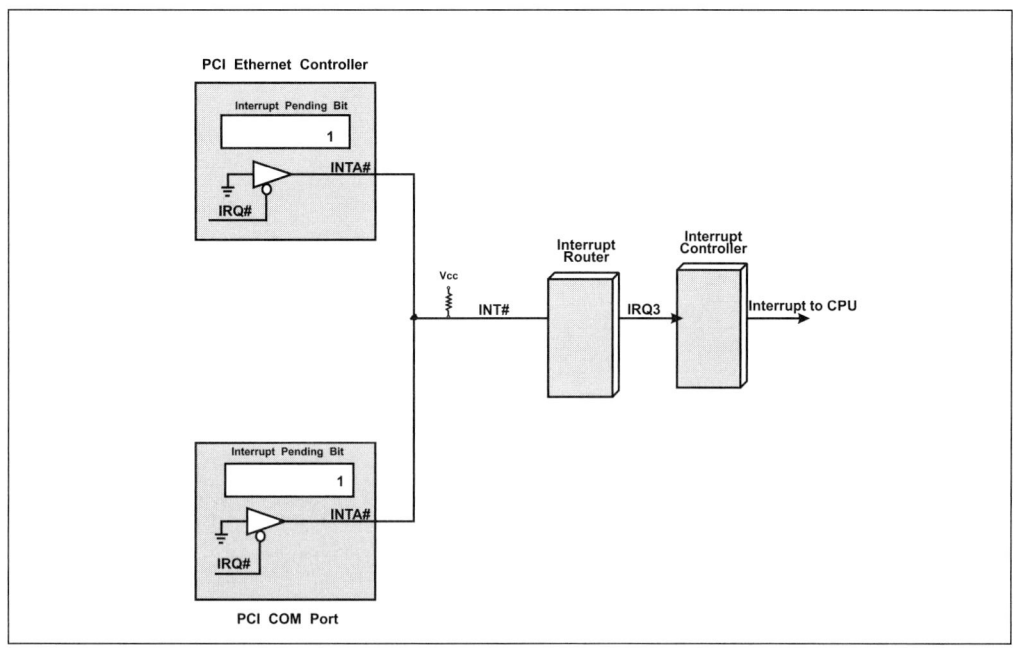

Figure 34-50: Local APIC Version Register

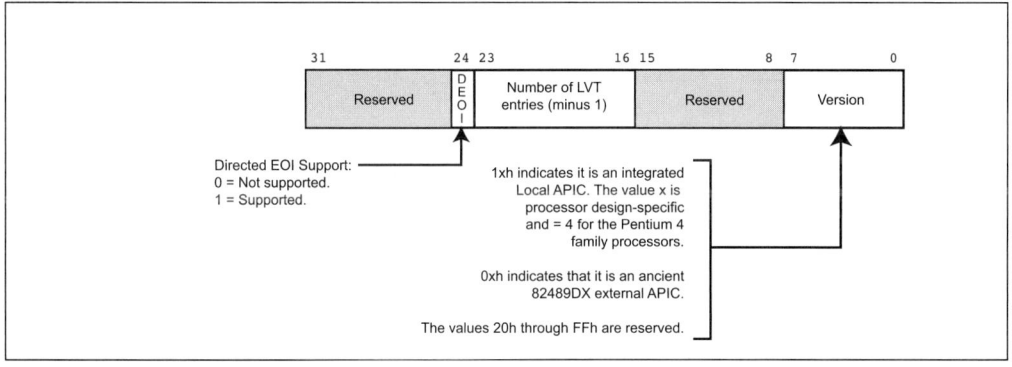

Figure 34-51: The Spurious Vector Register

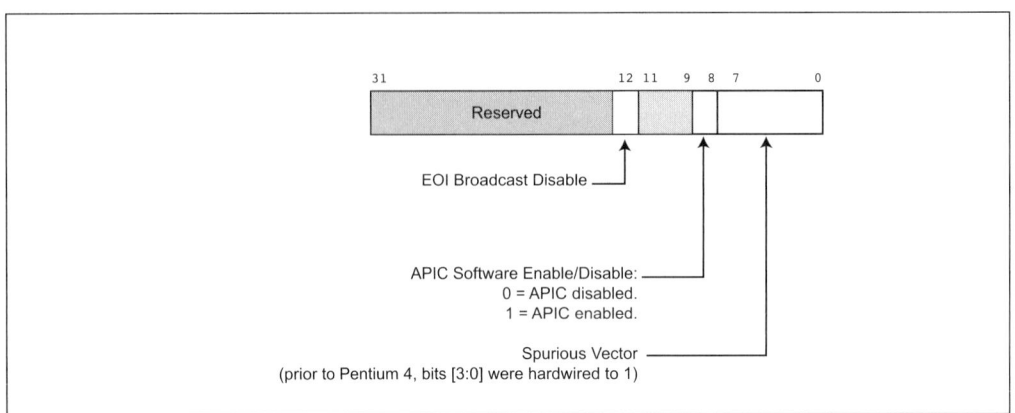

IO APIC ID Register

Unique IO APIC IDs are automatically assigned to each Local APIC by hardware when the system is first powered up. Once the OS has booted, it may assign new IDs by writing to this 32-bit read/write register.

IO APIC Version Register

See Figure 34-52 on page 1340. This read-only register contains the following information:

- The number of IRQ input pins implemented and therefore the number of entries in the Redirection Table (RT) register set.
- A bit that indicates whether or not the IO APIC implements the IRQ Pin Assertion Register.
- The version number of the IO APIC implementation.

Figure 34-52: The IO APIC's Version Register

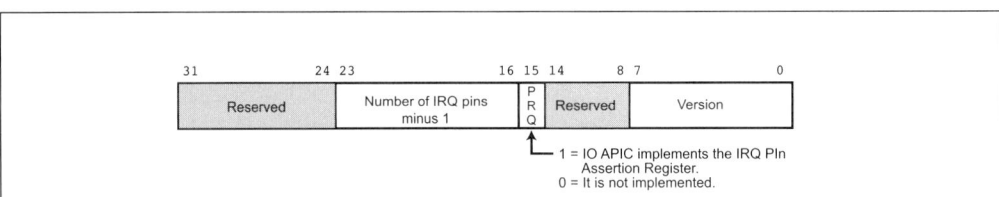

IO APIC Redirection Table (RT) Register Set

As mentioned earlier, the IO APIC implements a configuration register for each of the IRQ input pins implemented on the IO APIC (and the number of IRQ input pins is IO APIC design-specific). This register set is referred to as the Redirection Table, or RT. Each register is 64-bits wide and has the format shown in Figure 34-53 on page 1342 and described in Table 34-13 on page 1343.

When an edge-triggered interrupt is detected, the respective RT register's Delivery Status bit is set to one to indicate that the message has not yet been sent to the logical processor(s). Once the message has been sent, the Delivery Status bit is cleared and only then can the IO APIC recognize a new interrupt request on that input pin.

Figure 34-53: RT Entry Format

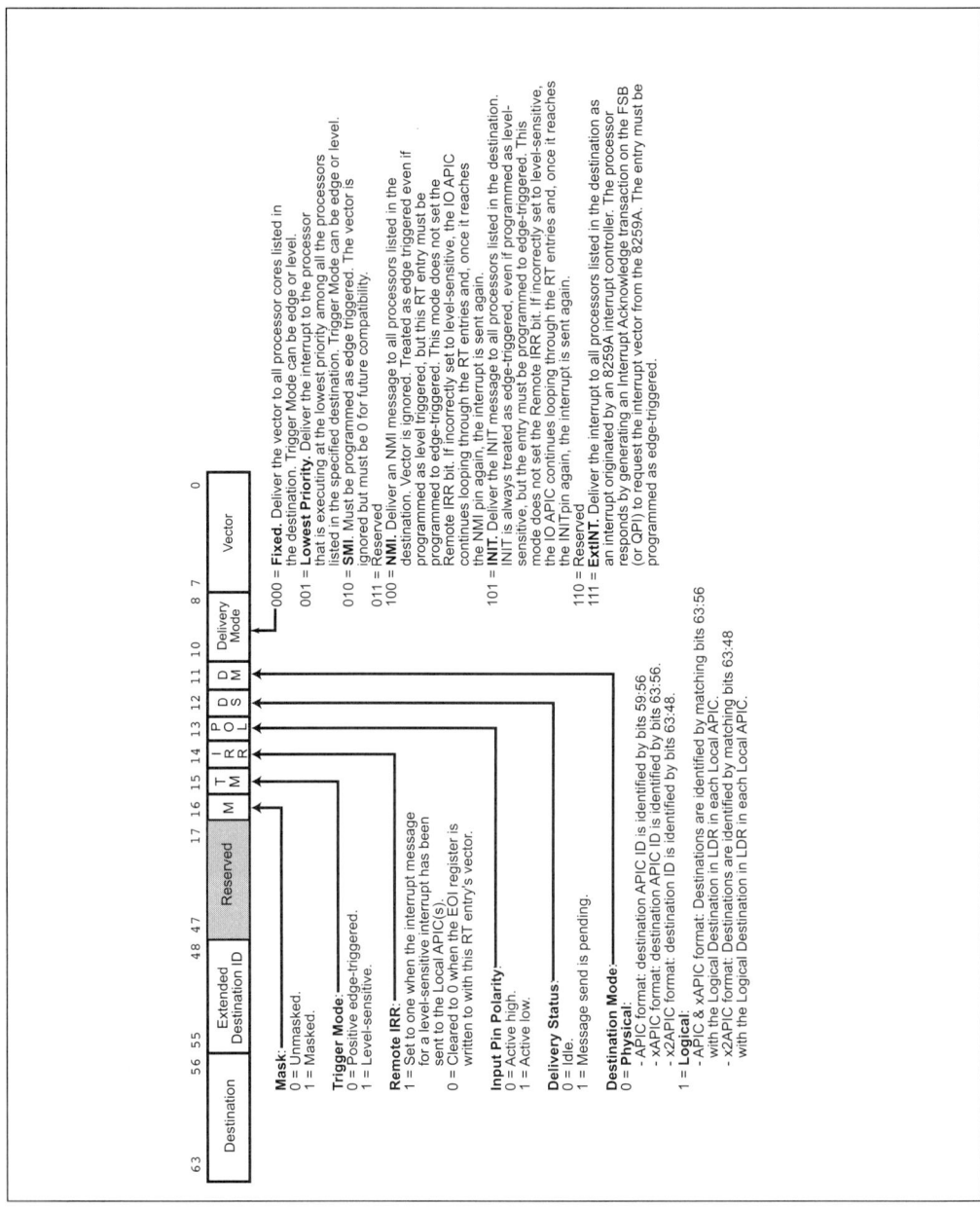

Table 34-13: RT Register Format

Bit(s)	Description

63:56	**Destination field**. R/W.
	• If this register's Destination Mode bit = 0 designating Physical Destination Mode, then:
	  - If the system uses Pentium or P6 processors, bits [59:56] specifies the target APIC ID and bits [63:60] must be 0.
	  - If the system uses Pentium 4 family processors or later, bits [63:56] specifies the target APIC ID.
	• If this register's Destination Mode bit = 1 designating Logical Destination Mode, then bits [63:56] specify the logical address of a set of eight logical processors. See "Logical Addressing: Multiple Targets" on page 1288.
	• See the next row regarding Destination field width when x2APIC addressing is used.

55:48	• Reserved when xAPIC ID formatting is used. • When x2APIC ID formatting is used, the Destination field is expanded to 32-bits (bits [63:48]).
47:17	Reserved.
16	**Mask bit**. R/W. • 0 = Unmasked. • 1 = Masked. Interrupts are neither latched nor are they delivered. Setting this bit after an interrupt has been accepted by a Local APIC doesn't affect the interrupt. It is software's responsibility to deal with the case wherein the Mask bit is set after the interrupt message has been accepted by a Local APIC but before the interrupt is dispatched to the logical processor.
15	**Trigger Mode**. R/W. This field indicates the type of signal on the interrupt pin that is recognized as a valid interrupt request: • 0 = Edge-triggered. • 1 = Level-sensitive.

Table 34-13: RT Register Format (Continued)

Bit(s)	Description
14	**Remote IRR** (Interrupt Request Register). R/W. This bit only applies to level-sensitive interrupts. Its meaning is undefined for edge-triggered interrupts: • Set when the Local APIC(s) accept a level-sensitive interrupt sent by the IO APIC. • Cleared when an EOI message containing this pin's vector has been received from a Local APIC.
13	**Interrupt Input Pin Polarity**. R/W. This bit only applies if this pin is defined as a level-sensitive interrupt. It specifies whether a valid interrupt request is signified by an electrical low or high: • 0 = high. • 1 = low.
12	**Delivery Status**. RO. Indicates the current delivery status of this interrupt: • 0 = **Idle**. No activity for this interrupt. • 1 = **Send Pending**. The interrupt message has not yet been accepted by the Local APIC(s).
11	**Destination Mode**. R/W. This field determines the target Local APIC's interpretation of the Destination field: • 0 = **Physical**. The interrupt is delivered to the sole Local APIC specified in this register's Destination field. See "Physical Addressing: Single Target" on page 1287. • 1 = **Logical**. The destination Local APICs are identified by the content of this register's Destination field using the Logical Destination Register in each Local APIC. See "Logical Addressing: Multiple Targets" on page 1288.
10:8	**Delivery Mode**. R/W. See Figure 34-53 on page 1342 for description.
7:0	**Vector**. R/W. This field is only used if the Destination Mode = Fixed. It contains the user-defined (fixed) interrupt vector associated with this pin. Valid values range between 20h and FFh (32 - 255).

IO APIC Interrupt Delivery Order Is Rotational

Unlike the Local APIC, the IO APIC does not implement a priority scheme to determine the order in which interrupt messages associated with each of its inputs are delivered to the logical processors. Rather, the IO APIC constantly scans through its RT registers and, if the Delivery Status bit in the currently-selected register is set to one, it sends the message associated with that RT register to the logical processors.

Message Signaled Interrupts (MSI)

General

The PCI specification permits a PCI function to generate an interrupt in one of three ways:

1. **Signal assertion**. The method defined in the earlier versions of the PCI specification. Required the PCI function to assert an interrupt pin connected to a trace that delivers the interrupt request to an input on the interrupt controller.
2. **MSI**. The later versions of the PCI specification defined the Message Signaled Interrupt (MSI) method.
3. **MSI-X**. The 3.0 PCI spec defined the MSI-X method (an enhanced form of MSI).

The MSI and MSI-X methods are also supported in PCI-X and in PCI Express. In order to support the MSI method, an adapter must implement the following PCI configuration registers:

- The MSI Address register.
- The MSI Data register.
- The MSI Control register.

In order to support the MSI-X method, an adapter must implement the following PCI configuration registers:

- The MSI-X Control register.
- The Message Upper Address register.
- The Table Offset register.

In addition, the device adapter must also implement the MSI-X Table that software programs with the message address and data (among other things, the data associated with each address defines an interrupt vector assigned to the adapter). Each of these table entries also contains a vector-specific Mask bit and an Interrupt Pending bit.

During system configuration, the BIOS or the OS programs a device's MSI Address and Data registers and then enables the capability by setting the enable bit in the Control register.

To issue an interrupt request via MSI, the adapter performs a memory write transaction to write the contents of the MSI Data register to the dword-aligned memory address specified in the MSI Address register. To issue an interrupt request via MSI-X, the adapter performs a memory write to the address specified in the device event-specific MSI-X Table entry and writes the data specified in that entry.

The remainder of this discussion is outside the scope of the PCI specification and describes the possible values programmed as the address and data and how they might be handled by the chipset.

Using the IO APIC as a Surrogate Message Sender

This topic was described in "IRQ Pin Assertion Register" on page 1335.

Direct-Delivery of an MSI

As described earlier (see "IRQ Pin Assertion Register" on page 1335), an adapter's MSI registers could be programmed to write an IO APIC input number (i.e. an IRQ pin number) to the IO APIC's IRQ Pin Assertion register. The IO APIC would then use the RT register associated with that input number to create an interrupt message to send to the logical processors.

Alternatively, the BIOS or OS (more likely the OS) can program an adapter's MSI Address register with the address of the Local APICs within the processors (FEExxxxxh). When the adapter issues a request by performing a memory write to this address, it is ignored by the IO APIC (because it is not being addressed). Rather, the ICH (see Figure 34-31 on page 1315) treats the memory write as an interrupt message and passes the memory write to the MCH (or IOH) over the Hub Link interface. The MCH (IOH) can either pass the memory write directly to the processor's external interface without modification, or, if the message specifies Lowest-Priority Delivery mode, it can take the actions described in "Chipset-Assisted Lowest-Priority Delivery" on page 1296 and in the description of the Redirection Hint bit in Table 34-10 on page 1309.

"Interrupt Message Format" on page 1309 describes the information output as the memory-mapped IO address and the write data in an interrupt transaction performed on the processor's external interface. It should be noted that section

8.11.2 in the Intel manual entitled *IA32 Intel Architecture Software Developer's Manual Volume 3: System Programming Guide* indicates that this is the information that must be programmed into a device adapter's MSI Address and Data registers when using the direct-delivery method. It should also be noted that while this method is supported if a device adapter implements MSI-X capability, a device adapter that only supports MSI capability cannot be programmed in this manner via its MSI Data register. It should also be noted that the PCI Express specification only supports edge-triggered (see bit 15 in Table 34-11 on page 1311) interrupts.

Memory Already Sync'd When Interrupt Handler Entered

The Problem

Assume that a PCI device performs one or more memory write transactions to write data into system memory. If there are any bridges between the device and system memory, the writes are posted within the bridge and are actually performed at some later time. Assume that the writes have not yet arrived at system memory and the device now generates an interrupt request to inform its driver that the data is in memory ready to be processed. The device generates its request using its interrupt request pin rather than MSI. The hardware interrupt request is delivered to the processor over the INTR signal line, the APIC bus (in the Pentium and P6 processor families), the FSB (in the Pentium 4 family), or Intel QPI in later processors, and does not cause bridges between the device adapter and system memory to flush their posted write buffers towards memory. The currently-executing program is suspended and the logical processor executes the interrupt handler within the device driver. The driver then reads the data from system memory and processes it. **Oops!** All of the memory writes may not have arrived in system memory yet, so **the driver may not be processing the correct data**.

Old Solution

The driver can solve this problem by **performing** a **read from** a **location within its device** adapter **before processing** the **data**. To get to the device adapter, the read has to traverse the same bridge (or bridges) that the memory writes from the device have to traverse to get to system memory. The ordering rules for bridges dictate that the bridge must flush its posted write buffers in both directions before permitting a read to traverse the bridge. As a result, by the time the read data is returned to the driver, all of the posted writes have been flushed to memory. Performing this extra read from the device increases interrupt servicing latency and is an awkward extra step that it would be nice to eliminate.

How MSI Solves the Problem

Once again assume that a PCI device performs one or more memory write transactions to write data into system memory. If there are any bridges between the device and system memory, the writes are posted within the bridges and are actually performed at some later time. Assume that the writes have not yet arrived at system memory and the device generates an interrupt request to inform its driver that the data is in memory ready to be processed. However, this time the device generates its request using MSI. In other words, it performs a memory write to write the interrupt message data to the address specified in the MSI Message Address register. Also keep in mind that the MCH (or IOH) is the gateway to system memory. This means that the interrupt message memory write is in the posted write buffers and was posted *after* the writes that the device previously performed to update the buffer in main memory. A *key ingredient* here is that it's a rule that *bridges must perform posted writes in the same order that they were received*. This means that, by the time the write to the MSI memory address arrives at the MCH (or IOH), system memory has already received all of the writes to the device's buffer in system memory. Upon receipt of the MSI write, the MCH (or IOH) then generates the interrupt request to the logical processor, the currently-executing program is suspended and the logical processor executes the interrupt handler within the device driver. The driver then reads the data from system memory and processes it—*and it's the correct data*. The programmer doesn't have to perform the artificial extra step of reading from the device to force the posted writes to be flushed to memory.

Interrupt Delivery from Legacy 8259a Interrupt Controller

Two methods are defined for the delivery of interrupts from the legacy 8259a interrupt controllers. They are referred to as:

- Virtual Wire Mode A (see Figure 34-54 on page 1349).
- Virtual Wire Mode B (see Figure 34-55 on page 1351).

Virtual Wire Mode A

Refer to Figure 34-54 on page 1349. This is an archaic method for delivering interrupts from the legacy 8259a interrupt controllers to a core or a logical processor. In the example, the following conditions would be true:

- In physical processor 0:
  — The Mask bit in the LINT0 LVT register associated with core 1 would be set to one (masking the processor's LINT0 pin).
  — The Mask bit in the LINT0 LVT register associated with core 0 would be cleared to zero (unmasking the processor's LINT0 pin).
- Core 0's LINT0 LVT would be configured to detect an edge-triggered interrupt and to deliver an ExtINT (i.e., 8259a interrupt) to core 0.

In response to the assertion of INTR:

1. Core 0 would cause physical processor 0 to generate an Interrupt Acknowledge transaction on the FSB to request the highest-priority interrupt vector from the legacy interrupt controllers.
2. The MCH would pass the request to the ICH.
3. In response, the legacy interrupt controllers would return the interrupt vector which would be passed back to the requesting processor.
4. Upon receipt of the vector, the interrupt is delivered to core 0 for servicing.

Figure 34-54: Virtual Wire Mode A

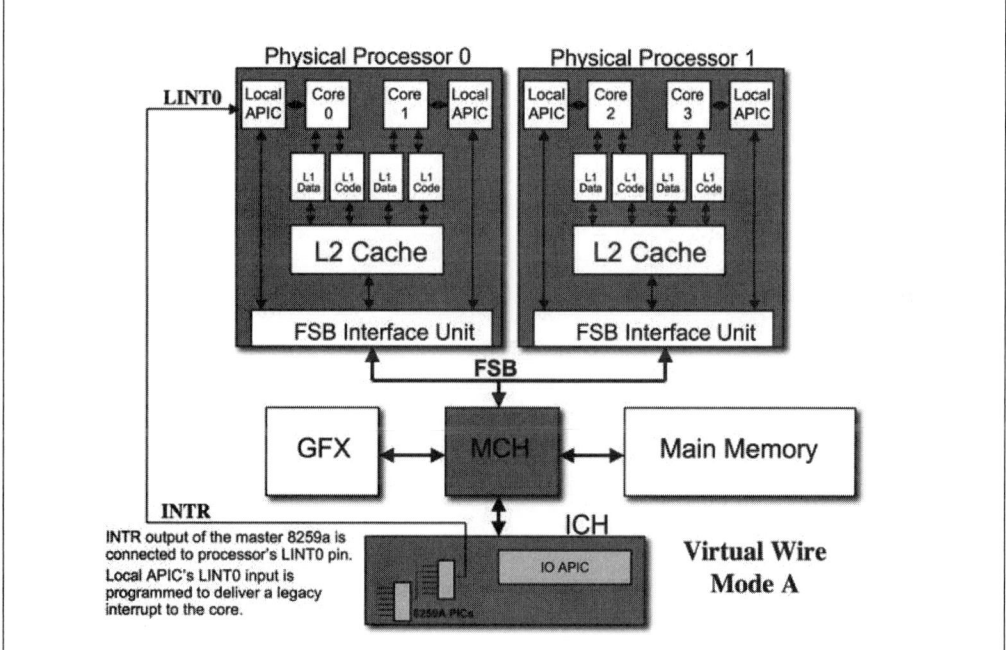

Virtual Wire Mode B

In the configuration shown in Figure 34-55 on page 1351, the following conditions would be true:

- The INTR output of the master 8259a legacy interrupt controller is connected to one of the input pins on the IO APIC.
- The RT (Redirection Table) register associated with that pin is configured as follows:
  — To detect an edge-triggered interrupt on the input pin.
  — To deliver an ExtINT message to a specific core.

In response to the assertion of INTR:

1. The IO APIC would send the ExtINT interrupt message upstream onto the FSB.
2. The Local APIC addressed in the message's Destination field accepts the message and the other Local APICs discard it.
3. The targeted core would cause the processor to generate an Interrupt Acknowledge transaction on the FSB to request the highest-priority interrupt vector from the legacy interrupt controllers.
4. The MCH would pass the request to the ICH.
5. In response, the legacy interrupt controllers would return the interrupt vector which would be passed back to the requesting processor.
6. Upon receipt of the vector, the interrupt is delivered to the requesting core for servicing.

Figure 34-55: Virtual Wire Mode B

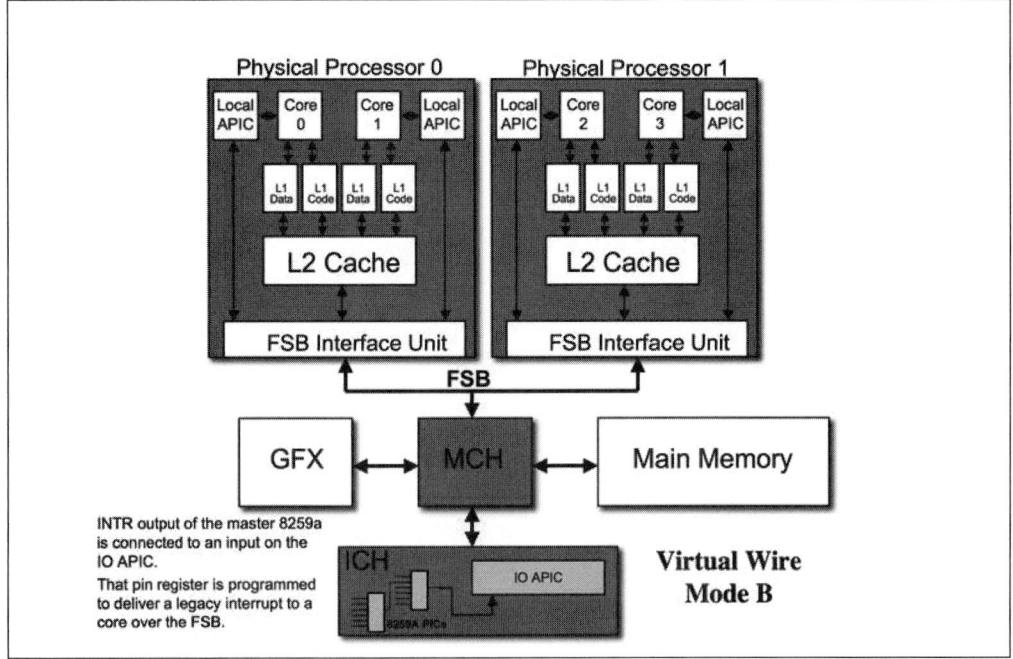

SW-Initiated Interrupt Message Transmission

Introduction

Interrupt messages can be categorized as follows:

1. **Inter-Processor Interrupt (IPI) messages** sent from the Local APIC of one logical processor to the Local APIC of one or more other logical processors under software control, or sent by a Local APIC to itself (under software control). The following are IPI messages:
   — On a system incorporating multiple P6 family processors on the FSB, the processors exchange a series of **BIPI and FIPI messages** at startup time to determine which of them will be the BootStrap Processor (BSP). See chapter 4 of the MindShare book entitled *Pentium Pro and Pentium II System Architecture*, Second Edition for more information. These messages were eliminated in the Pentium 4 and subsequent processor families.

- — The **Startup Inter-Processor Interrupt (SIPI) message**. The BIOS commands the BSP's Local APIC to send this message to the APs (Application Processors) in a multiprocessor system during the boot process. It commands each of them to execute an initialization program that has been placed in memory by the BIOS code. See "How the APs are Discovered and Configured" on page 1381 for more information.
- — **INIT message**. See "Soft Reset" on page 73.
- — **Task Dispatch Message**. Once the OS has been booted, the OS scheduler assigns a task to a logical processor by placing the task in memory and issuing a user-defined interrupt to the target core or logical processor's Local APIC. Upon message receipt, the target logical processor executes the user-defined interrupt handler, causing it to begin execution of the task.
- — One **logical processor forwards an interrupt to another logical processor**. A logical processor's Local APIC may receive an interrupt and dispatch it to its logical processor. Rather than servicing the interrupt, the invoked interrupt handler may decide to pass the interrupt to another logical processor for servicing by causing the Local APIC to forward the interrupt in an interrupt message to another logical processor's Local APIC.
2. **Interrupt messages originated by device adapters**. A device adapter that requires servicing may generate an interrupt by:
   - — Asserting an **IRQ** signal to the IO APIC module in the chipset. Upon detection of the IRQ, the IO APIC formulates an interrupt message and sends it to one or more logical processors for handling.
   - — Generating a **Message Signaled Interrupt (MSI)**. The MSI takes the form of a memory write. Assuming that the system is based upon a Pentium 4 family processor (or later), the chipset receives the memory-mapped IO write (i.e., the MSI) and forwards the memory write to the processor's external interface. This interrupt message commands one or more logical processors to handle the interrupt (see "Message Signaled Interrupts (MSI)" on page 1345).
3. An interrupt **message originated by the legacy 8259a interrupt controller**. This is referred to as an **ExtINT message** (see "Interrupt Delivery from Legacy 8259a Interrupt Controller" on page 1348).
4. **Interrupt Messages Originated by the Chipset**. Under platform design-specific circumstances, the chipset may send one of the following types of interrupt messages to one or more of the logical processors to be handled:
   - — SMI.
   - — INIT.
   - — NMI.

Sending a Message From the Local APIC

Software executing on a core or a logical processor can instruct its Local APIC to send a message to one or more other Local APICs by writing to its Local APIC's Interrupt Command Register (ICR).

ICR in xAPIC Mode

The ICR (as it appears in xAPIC Mode) is shown in Figure 34-56 on page 1354 and its bit fields are described in Table 34-14 on page 1355. To transmit most types of interrupt messages in xAPIC Mode, the programmer must perform two memory writes to the 64-bit ICR:

1. The first 32-bit write is to the upper half of the ICR to set the Destination field.
2. The second 32-bit write is to the lower half of the ICR. This write provides the remaining information related to the message and triggers the Local APIC to transmit the message defined by the ICR content.

If a message is to be transmitted only to the source Local APIC (i.e., a loopback operation), to all Local APICs except the source Local APIC, or to all Local APICs including the source Local APIC, the programmer need only perform one 32-bit memory write to the lower half of the ICR. In this case, the Destination Shorthand field must be set to a value other than 00b.

ICR in x2APIC Mode

The ICR (as it appears in x2APIC Mode) is shown in Figure 34-57 on page 1354. Three changes differentiate it from xAPIC Mode:

- The destination field is expanded from 8- to 32-bits permitting a significantly larger number of Local APICs to be addressed.
- In xAPIC Mode, before writing a new command into the ICR software is required to wait for the Delivery Status bit (bit 12) to clear (indicating that a previous message transmission has been completed). Since this requirement does not exist in x2APIC Mode, the Delivery Status bit (bit 12) has been eliminated.
- Whereas the 64-bit Interrupt Command Register (ICR) must be accessed using two 32-bit memory-mapped IO accesses in xAPIC Mode, in x2APIC Mode its entire width is accessed simultaneously using the RDMSR or WRMSR instructions.

Figure 34-56: xAPIC Interrupt Command Register (ICR)

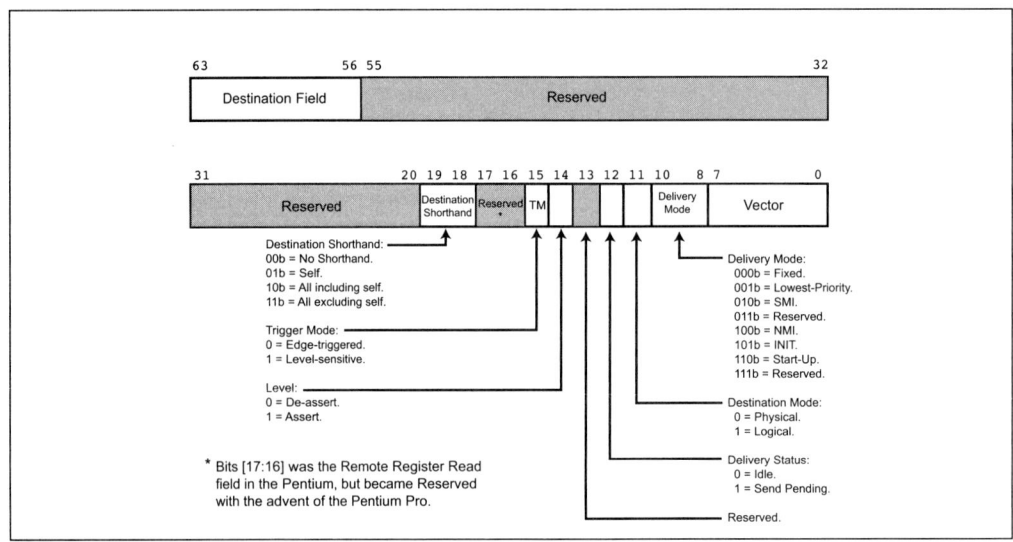

Figure 34-57: x2APIC Interrupt Command Register (ICR)

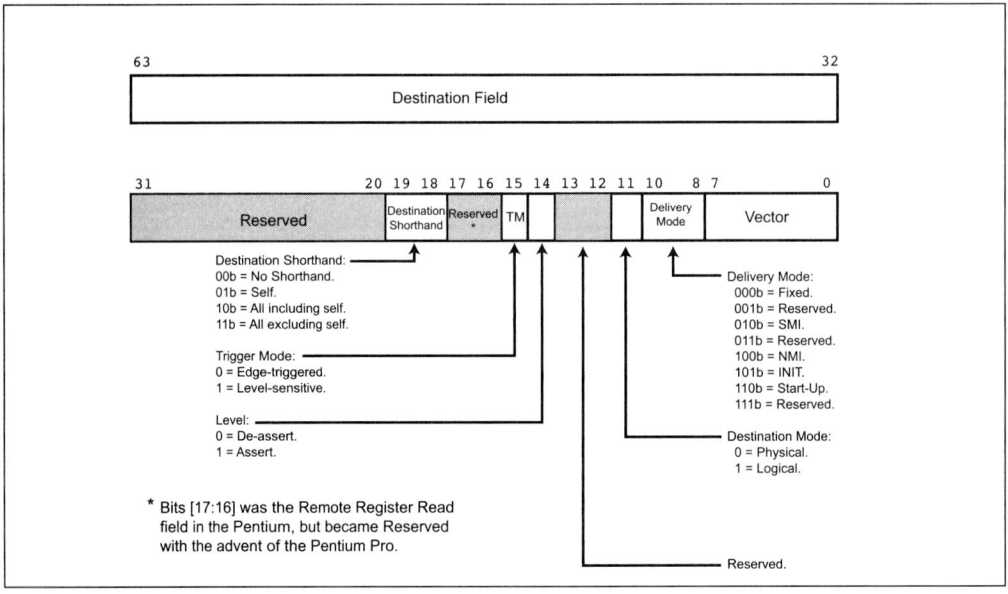

Table 34-14: ICR Bit Assignment

Bit Field	Field Width in bits	Description
Destination Field	4, 8, or 32	The destination field contents is referred to as the Message Destination Address (MDA). **Width**: • 4-bits in legacy APICs (Pentium and P6). • 8-bits in xAPIC Mode. • 32-bits in x2APIC Mode. Specifies the target logical processor(s). In x2APIC Mode, this field is only used when Destination Shorthand isn't used (see the next row in this table): • **Destination Mode = Physical**: — **Pentium and P6**. ICR[59:56] specifies the 4-bit physical address of the target Local APIC. — **xAPIC Mode**. ICR[63:56] specifies the 8-bit physical address of the target Local APIC. — **x2APIC Mode**. ICR[63:32] specifies the 32-bit physical address of the target Local APIC. • **Destination Mode = Logical**: — **Pentium/P6/xAPIC Mode**: ICR[63:56] specifies the logical address of up to eight target Local APICs. Logical address interpretation by the target(s) is defined by the settings of the DFR and LDR registers of the Local APICs in all of the system processors. — **x2APIC Mode**. ICR[63:32] specifies the 32-bit logical address of up to 16 target Local APICs in 1 of 2^{16}-1 clusters. See "Physical Addressing: Single Target" on page 1287 and "Logical Addressing: Multiple Targets" on page 1288 for more information.

Table 34-14: ICR Bit Assignment (Continued)

Bit Field	Field Width in bits	Description
Destination Shorthand	2	A Destination Shorthand can be used in place of the 8- or 32-bit Destination field. When this is the case in xAPIC Mode, software can send a message by performing a single 32-bit memory write to the lower half of the ICR (in x2APIC Mode, a single WRMSR instruction delivers all message-related information to the ICR). The currently-defined shorthand values are: • **00b = No Shorthand**. The destination is specified in the ICR's 8- or 32-bit Destination field. • **01b = Self**. The issuing Local APIC is the one and only target of the IPI. This allows software to interrupt the logical processor on which it is executing. A specific Local APIC implementation could be designed to deliver the message internally, or it could issue the message to the APIC bus (P6) or the external interface (Pentium 4 or later) and then detect it like any other IPI message. • **10b = All Including Self**. The IPI is sent to all logical processors in the system including the logical processor sending the IPI. The Local APIC broadcasts the IPI message with the Destination field = Fh for the Pentium and P6, FFh for the Pentium 4 processor family (or later), and FFFFFFFFh for logical processors whose Local APICs are in x2APIC Mode. • **11b = All Excluding Self**. The IPI is sent to all logical processors in the system with the exception of the logical processor sending the IPI. The sender's Local APIC broadcasts the message using the Physical Destination Mode with the Destination field = Fh for the Pentium and P6, FFh for the Pentium 4 processor family (or later), and FFFFFFFFh for logical processors whose Local APICs are in x2APIC Mode. On Pentium 4 family processors (or later), when this shorthand setting is used in conjunction with the Lowest-Priority Delivery Mode, the IPI may be redirected back to the issuing logical processor (if it is running the lowest priority program).
Trigger Mode	1	When using the INIT Level De-assert Delivery Mode, this bit selects the Trigger Mode: • 0 = Edge-triggered. • 1 = Level-sensitive. It is ignored for all other delivery modes. *This bit has no meaning in Pentium 4 family processors or later and is always 0.*

Table 34-14: ICR Bit Assignment (Continued)

Bit Field	Field Width in bits	Description
Level	1	For the INIT Level De-assert Delivery Mode, this bit must be set to 0. For all other Delivery Modes it must be set to 1. *This bit has no meaning in Pentium 4 family processors or later and is always 1.*
Delivery Status	1	*This bit is reserved in x2APIC Mode:* • **0 = Idle**. There is currently no IPI activity for this Local APIC, or the previous IPI sent from this local APIC completed transmission without error. It is therefore safe for software to write a new message transmission command into the ICR. • **1 = Send Pending**. Indicates that the last IPI sent from this Local APIC has not yet completed transmission. It is therefore *not* yet safe for software to write a new message transmission command into the ICR yet.
Destination Mode	1	Selects either: • 0 = **Physical Delivery Mode**. In this case, the message is delivered only to the Local APIC specified in the Destination field. • 1 = **Logical Delivery Mode**. In this case, the message is delivered to one or more Local APICs (see "Logical Addressing: Multiple Targets" on page 1288 for more information).

Table 34-14: ICR Bit Assignment (Continued)

Bit Field	Field Width in bits	Description
Delivery Mode	3	Also referred to as the **IPI Message Type** field. Specifies the type of IPI message to be sent: • **000b = Fixed**. Delivers the user-defined (fixed) interrupt specified in the ICR's Vector field to the target logical processor(s). • **001b = Lowest-Priority** *(reserved in x2APIC Mode)*. Same as Fixed, but the interrupt is delivered to the logical processor executing at the lowest priority among the set of logical processors specified in the destination field. *Use of this mode is not recommended for Pentium 4 family processors (or later). It will cause IPIs to be sent by all of the Local APICs specified in the destination,* consuming external interface bandwidth and degrading performance. • **010b = SMI**. Delivers an SMI interrupt to the target logical processor(s). The vector field must be programmed to 00h for future compatibility. • 011b = Reserved. • **100b = NMI**. Delivers an NMI interrupt to the target logical processor(s). The vector field is ignored. • **101b = INIT**. Delivers an INIT (i.e., a soft reset; see "Soft Reset" on page 73) to the target logical processor(s). The Vector field must be programmed to 00h for future compatibility. • **101b = INIT Level De-assert**. *Not supported by the Pentium 4 family or later.* Sends a synchronization message to all system Local APICs to set their Arbitration IDs (stored in their Arb ID registers) to the values of their APIC IDs. The Level bit must = 0 and Trigger Mode = 1. Software must specify the *All Including Self* shorthand. The IPI is sent to all logical processors, regardless of the value in the Destination field. • **110b = Start-Up**. Sends a Start-up IPI (a SIPI) to all Local APICs in the system. The Vector field specifies the 4KB-aligned start address of a start-up routine that is part of the BIOS boot strap code. All other message types target entities (Local APICs) known to the sender and are therefore automatically retried if they don't receive a valid completion. A SIPI, on the other hand, is a broadcast to discover if any other Local APICs exist. Because the sender may, in fact, be the only Local APIC in the system, SIPIs are not automatically retried if the source Local APIC doesn't receive a valid completion. Software must determine if the SIPI was not successfully transmitted and reissue the SIPI if necessary. See "How the APs are Discovered and Configured" on page 1381 for more information.
Vector	8	If the ICR's Delivery Mode is set to Fixed, this field contains the 8-bit user-defined (fixed) interrupt vector to be delivered to the target logical processor(s).

x2APIC Mode's Self IPI Feature

Code running on a logical processor may stimulate its Local APIC to deliver an interrupt solely to its associated logical processor in any of the following ways:

1. **Any Local APIC mode**: Execute the INT xx software interrupt instruction, where xx designates the 8-bit interrupt vector to be delivered to the logical processor.

2. **xAPIC or x2APIC Mode**: Issue a message transmission request to the Local APIC by writing the following to the ICR (see Figure 34-56 on page 1354):
   — Set the Destination Shorthand field to 01b indicating the generation of a Self IPI (Inter-Processor Interrupt). This is also referred to as a Self Interrupt.
   — Trigger Mode 0 (Edge-triggered).
   — Level = 1 for all Delivery Modes on logical processors starting with the Pentium 4.
   — Destination Mode = 0 (Physical).
   — Delivery Mode = 000b (Fixed).
   — Vector = desired 8-bit vector.

3. **x2APIC Mode only**: Write the desired 8-bit vector to the write-only Self IPI MSR (see Figure 34-58 on page 1359). This is the functional equivalent of method 2.

In response to method 2 or 3, the Local APIC behaves exactly as if an edge-triggered Fixed interrupt message was received:

- The Vector selects the IRR bit to set.
- The Vector selects the TMR bit and clears it to 0 (Edge-Triggered interrupt request).
- The sequence of actions taken by the Local APIC are described in "Overview of Edge-Triggered Interrupt Handling" on page 1316.

The Self IPI register is cleared to zero by reset. Writing an illegal vector (00h - 0Fh) into the Self IPI register does not result in an interrupt and the Local APIC's ESR[SendIllegalVector] error bit is set to one.

Figure 34-58: x2APIC Self IPI MSR Register

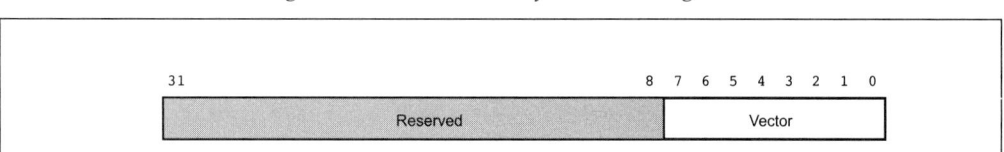

Locally Generated Interrupts

Introduction

Refer to Figure 34-59 on page 1360. The Local APIC can receive an interrupt from any of the following local sources:

- The physical processor's Local Interrupt pin 0 (LINT0).
- The physical processor's Local Interrupt pin 1 (LINT1).
- The programmable timer incorporated within the Local APIC.
- The logical processor's Performance Counters.
- The logical processor's internal Thermal Sensor.
- The logical processor's CMC Interrupt logic.
- The Local APIC's error detection logic.

The sections that follow provide a detailed description of each of the local interrupt sources.

Figure 34-59: Local Interrupt Sources

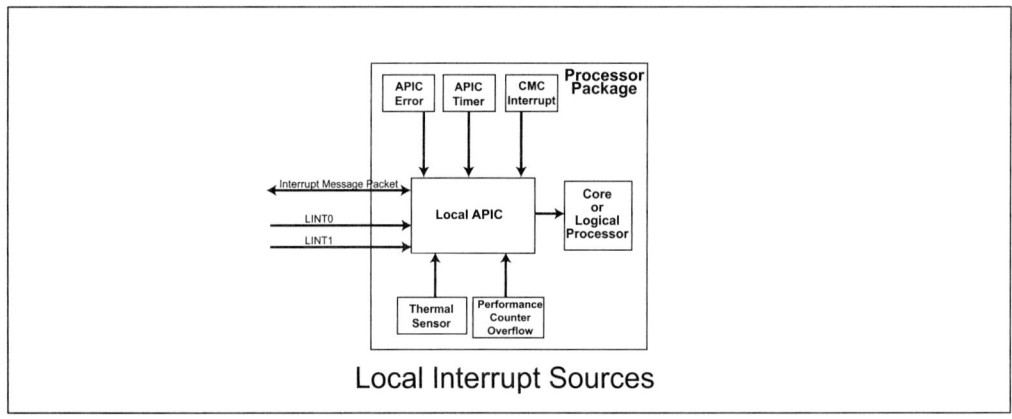

The Local Vector Table

The Local APIC's register set includes a set of registers (referred to as the Local Vector Table—LVT) used to configure it to handle each type of local interrupt event. The number and types of local interrupt sources are design-specific. The programmer can determine the number of local interrupt types by reading the Local APIC's Version Register (see "Detecting Presence/Version/Capabilities of Local APIC" on page 1255).

The Pentium Family's LVT

The Pentium processor family's LVT consisted of the following registers:

- The LINT0 register.
- The LINT1 register.
- The Timer registers.
- The Error register.

The P6 Family's LVT

The P6 processor family's LVT consisted of the following registers:

- The LINT0 register.
- The LINT1 register.
- The Timer registers.
- The Error register.
- The Performance Counter register.

The Pentium 4 Family's LVT

The Pentium 4 processor family's LVT consists of the following registers:

- The LINT0 register.
- The LINT1 register.
- The Timer registers.
- The Error register.
- The Performance Counter register.
- The Thermal Sensor register.

Core Processor's LVT

The Core processor and subsequent processor families' LVT consists of the following registers:

- The LINT0 register.
- The LINT1 register.
- The Timer registers.
- The Error register.
- The Performance Counter register.
- The Thermal Sensor register.
- The CMCI register.

LVT Register State After Reset, INIT, or Software Disable

Table 34-15 on page 1362 defines the basic state of a logical processor's LVT registers:

- Immediately after a power-up or hard reset.
- Immediately after a soft reset (receipt of an INIT).
- Immediately after software disables the Local APIC.

Table 34-15: State of LVT Registers

After	State of LVT Registers
Power-up or Hard Reset	Mask bits are set to one and all other bit fields are cleared to 0. The net effect is that the ability of any local event to generate an interrupt is disabled.
Soft Reset (INIT)	
Software Disable	Mask bits are set to one while all other bit fields are unaffected. The net effect is that the ability of any local events to generate an interrupt is disabled.

Local Interrupt 0 (LINT0)

Figure 34-60 on page 1366 illustrates the format of the LINT0 and LINT1 LVT registers.

The Mask Bit

Software uses this bit to enable or disable recognition of the LINT0 input:

- 0 = Enable recognition.
- 1 = Disable recognition.

The Trigger Mode and the Input Pin Polarity

The processor must be told what it is to recognize as a valid interrupt presented on its LINT0 input. There are two choices:

- If the Trigger Mode is cleared to 0, the processor will recognize a low-to-high transition on the LINT0 pin as a valid interrupt request.
- If the Trigger Mode is set to 1, the processor will recognize a static electrical low or electrical high on the LINT0 pin as a valid interrupt request. In this case, the value programmed into the Input Pin Polarity bit defines which level is recognized as a valid interrupt request.

The Trigger Mode only has meaning when the Delivery Mode is Fixed (i.e., the message contains a user-defined interrupt vector):

- If the Delivery Mode (see the next section) is NMI, SMI, or INIT, the Trigger Mode is always positive edge-triggered.
- If the Delivery Mode is ExtINT, the Trigger Mode is always level-sensitive.

The Delivery Mode

The value placed in this field by software defines the type of interrupt to be sent to the logical processor if a valid interrupt request is detected on the LINT0 input. The permissible Delivery Modes are defined in Table 34-16 on page 1363.

Table 34-16: Permissible Delivery Modes for the LINT Inputs

Value	Delivery Mode	Description
000b	Fixed	The interrupt is treated as a user-defined interrupt. The 8-bit value programmed into the register's Vector field is used as the vector. The interrupt is submitted to the Local APIC for prioritization as a user-defined interrupt.
001b		Reserved
010b	SMI	The interrupt is treated as an SMI and is delivered directly to the logical processor (unless a higher-priority interrupt is pending). The value programmed into the register's Vector field must be 0 (for future compatibility) and it is ignored.
011b		Reserved

Table 34-16: Permissible Delivery Modes for the LINT Inputs (Continued)

Value	Delivery Mode	Description
100b	NMI	The interrupt is treated as an NMI and is delivered directly to the logical processor (unless a higher-priority interrupt is pending). The value programmed into the register's Vector field is ignored.
101b	INIT	The interrupt is treated as an INIT (a soft reset) and is delivered directly to the logical processor (unless a higher-priority interrupt is pending). The value programmed into the register's Vector field must be 0 (for future compatibility) and it is ignored.
110b		Reserved
111b	ExtINT	The interrupt was delivered by an 8259A interrupt controller (e.g., in a PC-AT compatible machine). The value programmed into the register's Vector field is ignored. The processor responds as it would if the Local APIC were disabled and it had detected its INTR input asserted. It suspends the currently executing program and generates an Interrupt Acknowledge transaction on its external interface to request the interrupt vector from the 8259A interrupt controller in the chipset. Upon receipt of the Interrupt Acknowledge transaction, the 8259A determines the highest priority IRQ input currently pending and returns the vector associated with that input. Upon receipt of the vector, the logical processor uses it as an index into the IDT and jumps to the interrupt handler associated with that IRQ line.

The Vector Field

The 8-bit value programmed into the Vector field is only used if the Delivery Mode defines this as a Fixed (i.e., a user-defined) interrupt. In this case, the interrupt is submitted to the Local APIC for prioritization as a user-defined interrupt.

The Remote IRR Bit

This read-only bit is only valid if the LINT0 input is programmed as a level-sensitive interrupt and for Fixed Delivery Mode (i.e., it is a user-defined interrupt).

It is automatically set to 1 when the Local APIC accepts the interrupt and is cleared to 0 when the interrupt handler issues an EOI at the end of the handler. This bit is undefined for edge-triggered interrupts and for Delivery Modes other than Fixed.

The Delivery Status

This read-only bit indicates the status of the delivery of this interrupt to the logical processor:

- 0 = Idle. This indicates one of the following:
  — There is currently no activity for the LINT0 pin.
  — The previous interrupt on LINT0 was delivered to the logical processor and was accepted.
- 1 = Send Pending. This indicates that an interrupt from LINT0 has been delivered to the logical processor, but has not yet been accepted.

Local Interrupt 1 (LINT1)

The LINT1 LVT register is programmed in the same manner as the LINT0 LVT register [see "Local Interrupt 0 (LINT0)" on page 1362].

Figure 34-60: LVT LINT0 or LINT1 Register

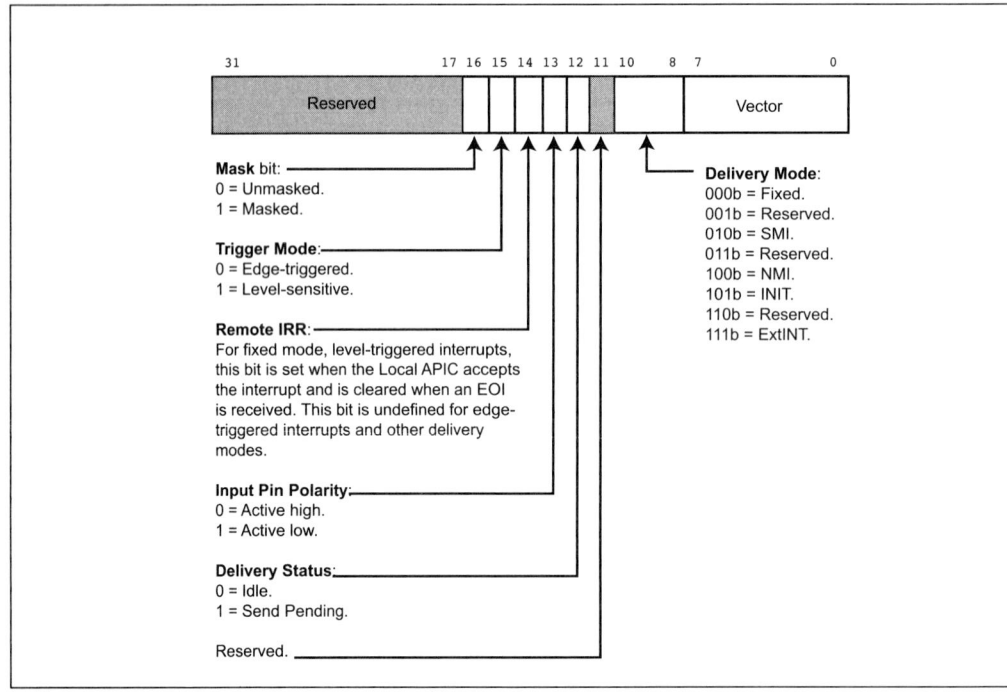

The Local APIC Timer

General

A timer within the Local APIC can be programmed to either generate a single interrupt after a programmed amount of time, or to generate interrupts on a periodic basis at a programmed interval. The timer's register set is shown in Figure 34-61 on page 1368 and the register addresses are shown in Table 34-3 on page 1265 and in Figure 34-13 on page 1264.

The LVT Timer register supplies the vector number delivered to the logical processor when the timer count reaches zero. The Mask bit is used to mask (i.e., disable recognition of) or unmask (enable recognition of) the timer interrupt. Also see "The Delivery Status" on page 1365.

The Initial Count register is a read-write register while the Current Count register is read-only.

The Divide Configuration Register

The clock frequency used by the timer is derived from the external interface's clock frequency. The 3-bit value programmed into the Divide Configuration Register is used as the frequency divisor.

One Shot Mode

In one-shot mode, the timer is triggered by writing to its Initial Count register. Upon completion of the write, the value in the Initial Count register is automatically copied into the Current Count register and the count-down begins. When the Current Count register reaches zero, a timer interrupt is generated and the timer remains at 0 until it is reprogrammed.

Periodic Mode

In periodic mode, the Current Count register is automatically reloaded from the Initial Count register when the count reaches 0 and the timer interrupt is generated. The count-down is then repeated. If a new value is written into the Initial Count register while a count-down is in progress, counting is immediately restarted using the new Initial Count value.

Figure 34-61: Local APIC Timer Register Set

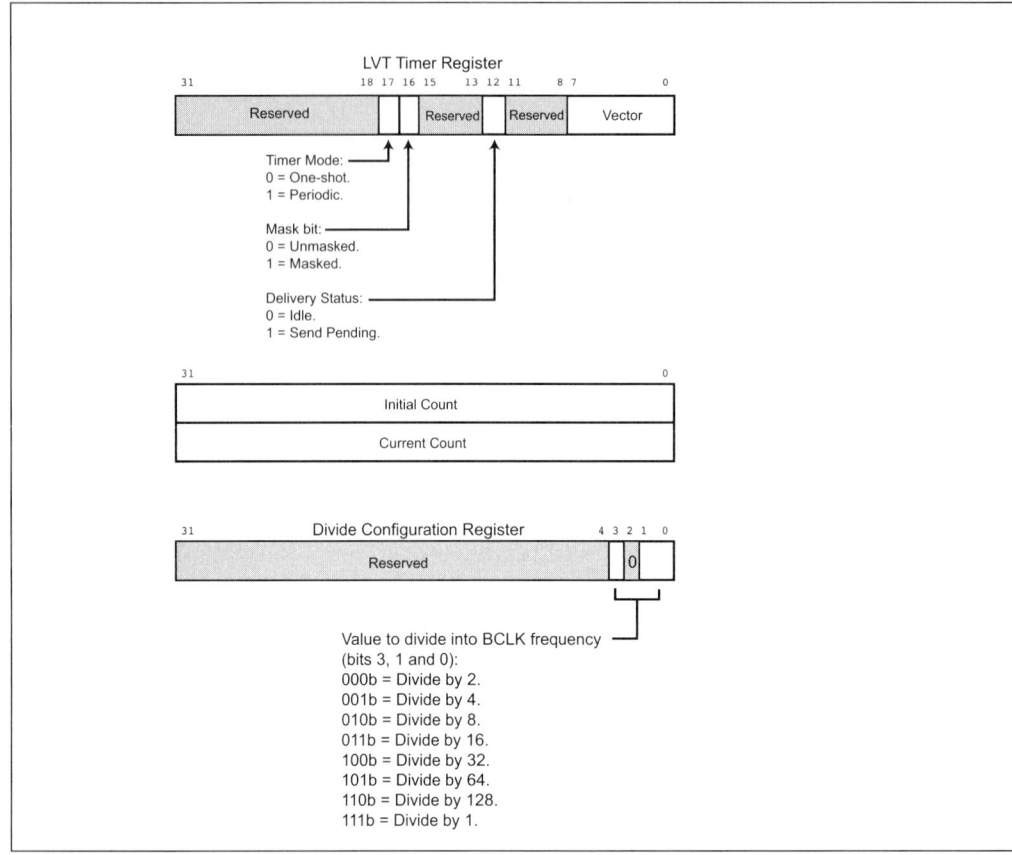

The Performance Counter Overflow Interrupt

Although the Pentium processor implemented Performance Counters, it did not implement the ability to generate an interrupt on counter overflow. This feature was first implemented on the Pentium Pro and is implemented on all subsequent x86 processors. The number of counters implemented is processor design-specific. The types of events the counters can be configured to count are typically those related to the execution of micro-op instructions (see "IA Instructions vs. Micro-ops" on page 15). Some examples:

- Cache hits and misses.
- TLB hits and misses.

- Correctly predicted and mispredicted branches.
- Packed SP FP operations.
- Packed DP FP operations.
- and many, many more.

Basically, these counters operate as follows:

- A counter is set up to count one or more event types.
- It is preset with an initial count.
- It is enabled to generate a Performance Counter interrupt when the counter has an overflow condition.
- When the counter overflows, an interrupt is delivered to the Local APIC and the handler is called.
- The interrupt handler records the Return Instruction Pointer (RIP), resets the count to its initial programmed value, restarts the counter, and returns to the interrupted program.

The Performance Counter Overflow LVT register is illustrated in Figure 34-62 on page 1370. When a counter overflow interrupt is generated on a Pentium 4 family or subsequent processor, the Mask bit in its LVT register is automatically set to one (thereby masking the recognition of any additional counter overflow interrupts). It remains set until it is cleared by software (typically, by the counter overflow interrupt handler).

Three actions are necessary in order to enable the counter overflow interrupt:

1. Set up an Interrupt or Trap Gate in the IDT to point to the counter overflow interrupt handler.
2. The interrupt on overflow enable bit in a Counter Control register must be set to one. A detailed description of the Performance Counter facility can be found in the chapter entitled *Pentium 4 Software Enhancements* in the Mind-Share book entitled *The Unabridged Pentium 4.*
3. The counter overflow LVT register must be configured:
   — The Mask bit must be cleared to 0.
   — The type of interrupt to deliver to the logical processor is defined in the Delivery Mode field (see "The Delivery Mode" on page 1363).
   — If the Delivery Mode is defined as Fixed, the Vector field is programmed with the IDT vector associated with the event.

Figure 34-62: Performance Counter Overflow, Thermal Sensor & CMC LVT Registers

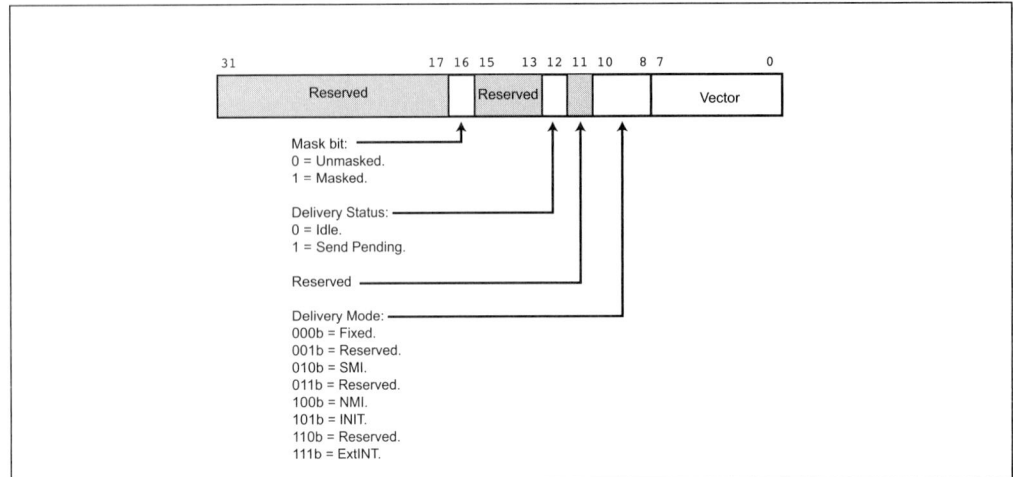

The Thermal Sensor Interrupt

The hardware-based Automatic Thermal Monitoring facility was introduced in the Pentium 4. This thermal sensor is factory calibrated to a trip temperature somewhat lower than the temperature trip point used by the catastrophic shut-down detector. The Automatic Thermal Monitoring facility is enabled by setting IA32_Misc_Enable[3] (Thermal Monitor Enable) to 1. The default setting of this bit is 0 after a power-up or reset, disabling the facility.

When enabled, the internal Stop Clock circuitry slows down the logical processor (to cool the core) whenever the core temperature exceeds the trip point and returns the logical processor to full speed (by setting the internal Stop Clock signal to a steady high state) when the temperature drops below the trip point. It should be noted that this clock throttling has no effect on the Time Stamp Counter register.

The IA32_Therm_Status MSR (see Figure 34-63 on page 1371) contains two bits that reflect the status of the clock throttling logic:

- **Thermal Status bit** (read-only):
    — 1 = The core temperature is currently above the trip point and the Stop Clock duty cycle is being modulated to reduce the core temperature.

— 0 = The core temperature is currently below the trip point and the Stop Clock duty cycle is not being modulated.

- **Thermal Status Log bit** (this is a sticky bit):
  — 1 = The thermal sensor has tripped since the last power-up or reset, or since the last time software cleared this bit.
  — Once this bit is set to one, it remains set until it is cleared by software, or until a power-up or reset.
  — The default state of this bit after a power-up or reset is 0.
  — After the sensor trips, the thermal monitor maintains a 50% Stop Clock duty cycle for at least 1ms, or until the core temperature drops below the trip point (hysteresis is taken into account).

Figure 34-63: The IA32 Thermal Status MSR

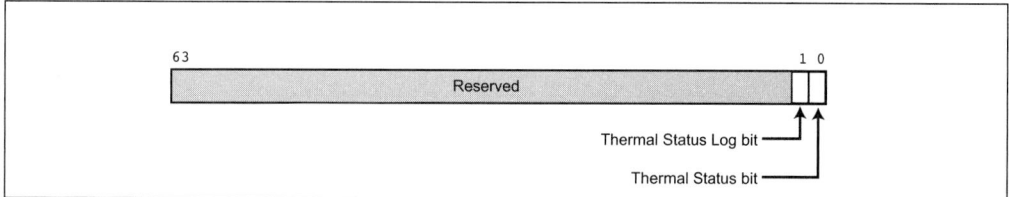

The thermal monitor logic can be programmed to generate an interrupt when the trip point is crossed in either direction. The two bits illustrated in Figure 34-64 on page 1372 (the IA32_Therm_Interrupt MSR) are used as follows:

- If the Low-Temperature Interrupt Enable bit is set to one, the logical processor will generate a thermal interrupt when the core temperature drops below the trip-point.
- If the High-Temperature Interrupt Enable bit is set to one, the logical processor will generate a thermal interrupt when the core temperature elevates above the trip-point.
- If both bits = 1, the logical processor will generate a thermal interrupt when the core temperature crosses the trip-point in either direction.

Three actions are necessary in order to enable the Thermal Sensor interrupt:

1. Set up an Interrupt or Trap Gate in the IDT to point to the Thermal Sensor interrupt handler.
2. One or both of the enable bits in the Thermal Interrupt MSR must be set to one.
3. The Thermal Sensor LVT register (see Figure 34-62 on page 1370) must be configured:

— The Mask bit must be cleared to 0.
— The type of interrupt to deliver to the logical processor is defined in the Delivery Mode field (see "The Delivery Mode" on page 1363).
— If the Delivery Mode is defined as Fixed, the Vector field is programmed with the IDT vector associated with the event.

This interrupt should be handled either by the OS or SMM code.

Figure 34-64: The IA32 Thermal Interrupt MSR

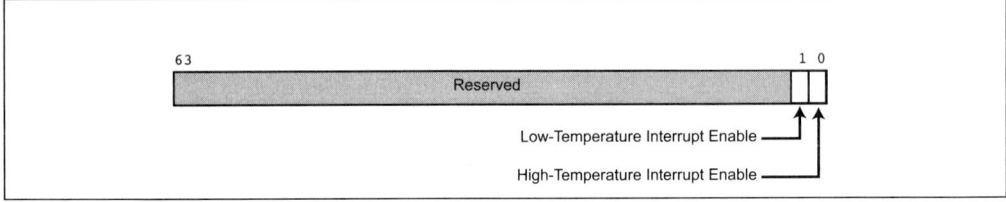

Correctable Machine Check (CMC) Interrupt

Refer to "Interrupt On Soft Error Threshold Match" on page 1233. Three actions are necessary in order to enable the CMC interrupt:

1. The error logging utility initializes a bank's CMCI logic as follows:
   — It programs a correctable error threshold count into the lower 15-bits of the bank's MCi_CTL2 register (see Figure 33-7 on page 1234).
   — It enables the bank's CMCI capability by setting the MCi_CTL2[CMCI_EN] bit to one (see Figure 33-7 on page 1234).
2. It sets up an Interrupt or Trap Gate in the IDT to point to the CMC interrupt handler.
3. The CMC LVT register (see Figure 34-62 on page 1370) must be configured:
   — The Mask bit must be cleared to 0.
   — The type of interrupt to deliver to the logical processor is defined in the Delivery Mode field (see "The Delivery Mode" on page 1363).
   — If the Delivery Mode is defined as Fixed, the Vector field is programmed with the IDT vector associated with the event.

The Local APIC's Error Interrupt

Local APIC Error LVT Register

Using the Local APIC's LVT Error Register (see Figure 34-65 on page 1374) it can be programmed to generate an interrupt if it detects an error related to sending or receiving interrupt messages:

- **Mask bit**. When set to one, the Mask bit prevents the generation of the Local APIC Error interrupt. It also prevents new errors from being recorded in the ESR, but the ESR retains its previous contents.
- **Delivery Status bit**:
  — 0: The previous Local APIC error interrupt (if there was one) was successfully sent to the logical processor.
  — 1: The Local APIC has not yet completed sending the previous Local APIC error interrupt to the logical processor.
- **Vector field**. Defines the user-defined (fixed) interrupt (a value between 20h and FFh) sent to the logical processor when a Local APIC error interrupt occurs.

The error is recorded by setting the appropriate bit in the Error Status Register (ESR).

Error Status Register (ESR) Operation in xAPIC Mode

The ESR (see Figure 34-66 on page 1374 and Table 34-17 on page 1375) is a write/read register. A write (of any value) must be done to the ESR before reading it. This forces the Local APIC to update the ESR with the latest error status. Back-to-back writes clears the register. After an error bit is set, it remains set until the register is cleared. Setting the Mask bit in the LVT Error register (see Figure 34-65 on page 1374) prevents new errors from being recorded in the ESR, but the ESR retains its previous contents.

Error Status Register Operation in x2APIC Mode

In x2APIC Mode, the ESR has the format illustrated in Figure 34-67 on page 1375. Like the other Local APIC registers in x2APIC Mode, the ESR is accessed using the RDMSR and WRMSR instructions. Only zeros may be written to it in x2APIC Mode. Using any other value will result in the generation of a GP exception. Miscellaneous behavior notes:

- Writing an illegal vector (00h - 0Fh) to the Self IPI register (see "x2APIC Mode's Self IPI Feature" on page 1359) causes the ESR[SendIllegalVector] bit to be set.
- Commanding the Local APIC to transmit a message using Lowest-Priority Delivery Mode results in the following:
  — The ESR[Redirectable IPI] bit is set to one.
  — The interrupt message will not be sent.
  — If the command included an illegal vector (00h - 0Fh), the ESR[SendIllegalVector] bit is not set (because the message was not sent).
- Commanding the Local APIC to transmit a message containing an illegal vector (00h - 0Fh) using Lowest-Priority Delivery Mode results in the following:
  — The ESR[Redirectable IPI] bit is set to one.
  — The interrupt message will not be sent.

Figure 34-65: LVT Error Register

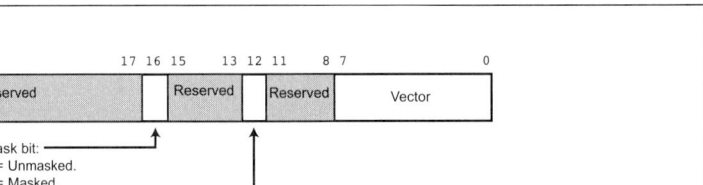

Figure 34-66: Local APIC Error Status Register (ESR) in xAPIC Mode

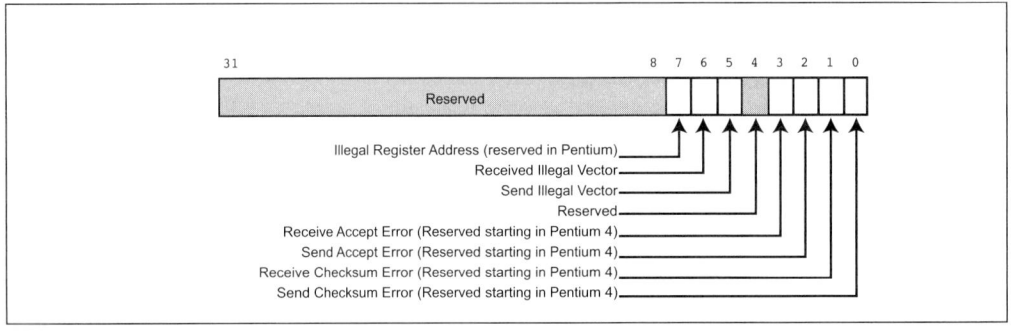

Figure 34-67: Local APIC Error Status Register (ESR) in x2APIC Mode

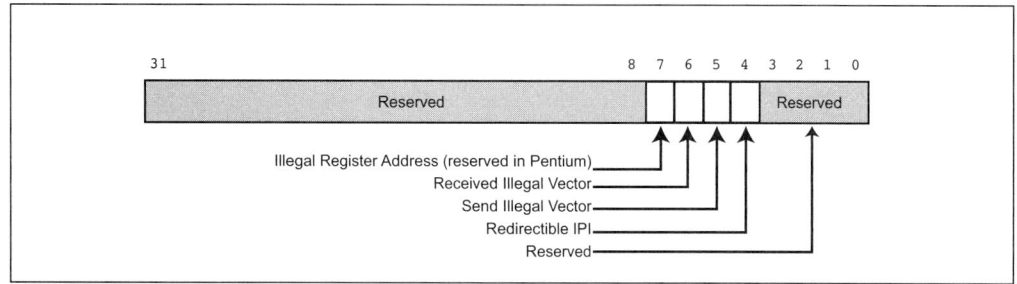

Table 34-17: Local APIC Error Status Register

Bit	Bit Implemented?			Description
	P5	**P6**	**Pentium 4 or later**	
Illegal Register Address	N	Y	Y	The logical processor attempted to access an unimplemented register within the Local APIC's 4KB memory address space (or MSR space in x2APIC Mode).
Received Illegal Vector	Y	Y	Y	Set if the Local APIC detects an illegal vector (0 through 15) in an interrupt message it received, or in one of its LVT registers.
Send Illegal Vector	Y	Y	Y	Set when the Local APIC detects an illegal vector (0 through 15) in an interrupt message that it is sending (i.e., in its ICR).
Redirectible IPI	N	N	Y	This bit is set to one if the ICR is commanded to send an IPI message using Lowest Priority Delivery Mode.

Table 34-17: Local APIC Error Status Register (Continued)

Bit	Bit Implemented?			Description
	P5	**P6**	**Pentium 4 or later**	
Receive Accept Error	Y	Y	N	Set when the Local APIC detects that the message it received was not accepted by any APIC on the APIC bus, including itself.
Send Accept Error	Y	Y	N	Set when the Local APIC detects that a message it sent was not accepted by any APIC on the APIC bus.
Receive Checksum Error	Y	Y	N	Set when the Local APIC detects a checksum error in a message that it received on the APIC bus.
Send Check-sum Error	Y	Y	N	Set when the Local APIC detects a checksum error in a message that it sent on the APIC bus.

The Spurious Interrupt Vector

The Problem

Assume that the Local APIC detects a user-defined interrupt and, as a result, generates an interrupt to the logical processor. As a result, the logical processor will request the interrupt vector from the Local APIC. A special situation arises, however, if software raises the logical processor's task priority [see "The Task Priority Register (TPR)" on page 1306] to be greater than or equal to the level of the interrupt for which the logical processor is being interrupted. Technically speaking then, the logical processor should not be interrupted. It already has, however, and a vector must be returned. The question is: what vector will be returned?

Solution

The Local APIC handles this by returning the Spurious Interrupt Vector programmed into the Spurious Interrupt Vector register (see the Spurious Vector field in Figure 34-68 on page 1378). This selects an IDT entry that has been programmed (by system software) with a pointer to a dummy handler that contains only the IRET instruction (i.e., a *do nothing* handler is executed):

- In the Pentium and P6 processor families, bits [7:4] are programmable by software and bits [3:0] are hardwired to ones. Software writes to bits 0 through 3 have no effect.
- In the Pentium 4 processor family and subsequent processors, bits [7:0] are programmable by software.

This register is initialized to 000000FFh after reset. Since no bit is set in the Local APIC's ISR when the spurious interrupt vector is returned to the logical processor, the spurious interrupt handler does not need to write to the Local APIC's EOI register.

Additional Spurious Vector Register Features

In addition to the Spurious Vector field, the Spurious Interrupt Vector register also contains the following bit fields:

- **APIC Global Enable/Disable** bit. If the APIC Global Enable/Disable bit in the IA32_APIC_BASE MSR has not been cleared to zero, software can enable/disable the Local APIC by writing to the APIC Software Enable/Disable bit in the Spurious Vector register (see Figure 34-68 on page 1378). The default state of this bit after reset is 0 (indicating that the Local APIC is disabled). *Although the APIC Software Enable bit is cleared to 0, the APIC is nonetheless enabled and is in xAPIC Mode. This condition is unique after a reset. Normally, clearing this bit to 0 disables the Local APIC.*
- **Focus Processor Check** bit. Selects whether Focus Processor Checking is enabled (0) or disabled (1) when using the Lowest-Priority Delivery Mode. *This bit is reserved in Pentium 4 family and later processors and must be cleared to 0.* In P6 and Pentium family processors, if a focus processor exists, it may accept an interrupt that uses Lowest-Priority Delivery Mode regardless of the processor's current priority.

Figure 34-68: Local APIC's Spurious Vector Register

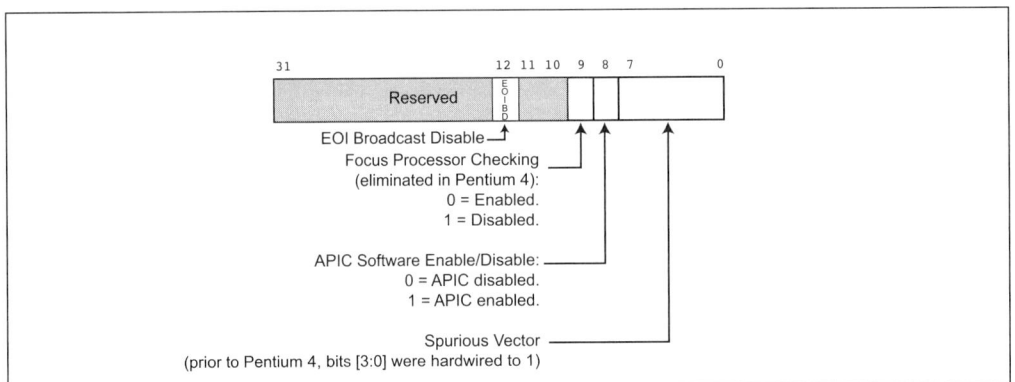

Boot Strap Processor (BSP) Selection

The following discussion describes the process utilized to select the logical processor (BootStrap Processor—BSP) which will be responsible for system topology discovery, configuration, and for booting the OS. This description pertains to systems wherein the processor(s) communicate with each other and with the system via the Front-Side Bus (FSB) external interface. Systems wherein the processor(s) communicate with each other and with the system via the Intel Quick-Path Interconnect (QPI) utilize a different methodology. Intel has not yet released documentation on this process in the public domain, but has announced that a book describing this process, *Weaving High Performance Multi-processor Fabric*, will be released by Intel Press in Q3 of 2009.

Introduction

Refer to Figure 34-31 on page 1315. Upon the deassertion of reset (and, if it was started, the completion of a processor's BIST—Built-In Self-Test), the logical processors within the cluster must negotiate amongst themselves to select the logical processor that will wake up and start fetching, decoding and executing the POST code from ROM memory. This logical processor is referred to as the BootStrap Processor, or BSP. After the BSP is selected, the other logical processors—referred to as the Application Processors, or APs—remain dormant (in the halted, low-power state) until they subsequently receive a startup interrupt message (SIPI) from the BSP. The following section provides a detailed description of the BSP selection process.

The BSP Selection Process

Pre-QPI BSP Selection Process

The BSP selection process utilized by the Pentium 4 family and later FSB-oriented processors is extremely simple when compared to the method used in the P6 processor family (refer to chapter 4 of the MindShare book entitled *Pentium Pro and Pentium II System Architecture*, Second Edition for a detailed description of the P6 process).

Many of today's processors contain multiple cores and, if the processor supports Hyper-Threading, each core contains two or more logical processors each of which is capable of executing a separate program thread:

- If a processor does not support Hyper-Threading, each core has its own, dedicated Local APIC.
- If a processor supports Hyper-Threading but it is disabled, each core has its own, dedicated Local APIC.
- If a processor supports Hyper-Threading and it is enabled, each logical processor has its own, dedicated Local APIC.

This discussion assumes that the Hyper-Threading feature is enabled in each of four Xeon physical processors (in a multi-core environment, each core has its own Local APIC). Refer to Figure 34-31 on page 1315. The selection of the BSP is actually performed by the Local APICs associated with logic processor 0 within core 0 of each of the physical processors. The other logical processors within each physical processor clear the BSP bit in their IA32_APIC_BASE MSRs (see Figure 34-70 on page 1381).

Refer to Figure 34-69 on page 1380:

1. The Local APIC associated with logical processor 0 in each of the processors cause the processors to simultaneously request ownership of the FSB. They are in a race to see which of them can initiate a Special transaction and send the NOP message first.
2. Based on the rotational FSB arbitration scheme used by the processors, the physical processor with the highest-numbered Physical Processor ID (in a quad Xeon MP system with Hyper-Threading enabled, this is physical processor 3) wins the arbitration. As demonstrated in the subsequent steps, in a properly operating quad Xeon MP system with Hyper-Threading enabled, logical processor 0 in physical processor 3 becomes the BSP.
3. The winning physical processor initiates a Special transaction and outputs the NOP message. Each of the other physical processors start the same type of transaction, one-after-the-other, based on the rotational scheme.

4. When each of the other physical processors receives the first NOP message from a physical processor other than itself, all of the logical processors within each of them clears the BSP bit in their respective IA32_APIC_BASE MSRs to zero (see Figure 34-70 on page 1381), thereby identifying themselves as APs.

5. When the physical processor that started the first transaction receives the NOP message from itself first, it sets the BSP bit in logical processor 0's IA32_APIC_BASE MSR (see Figure 34-70 on page 1381) to one, thereby identifying itself as the BSP. The BSP bits of all of the other logical processors within the winning physical processor clear the BSP bit in their respective IA32_APIC_BASE MSRs (marking themselves as APs).

Once the BSP selection process has completed, the BSP initiates fetch, decode and execution of the ROM POST code starting at the power-on restart address. This discussion continues in "How the APs are Discovered and Configured" on page 1381.

Figure 34-69: Pentium 4 BSP Selection Process

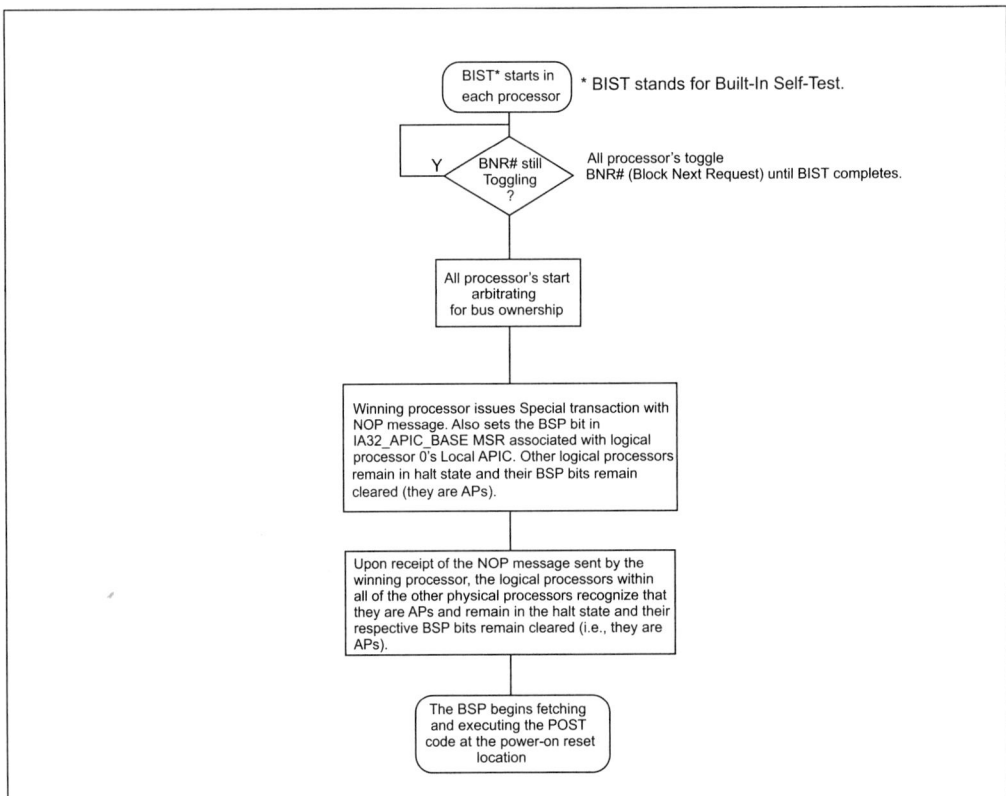

Figure 34-70: The IA32_APIC_BASE MSR

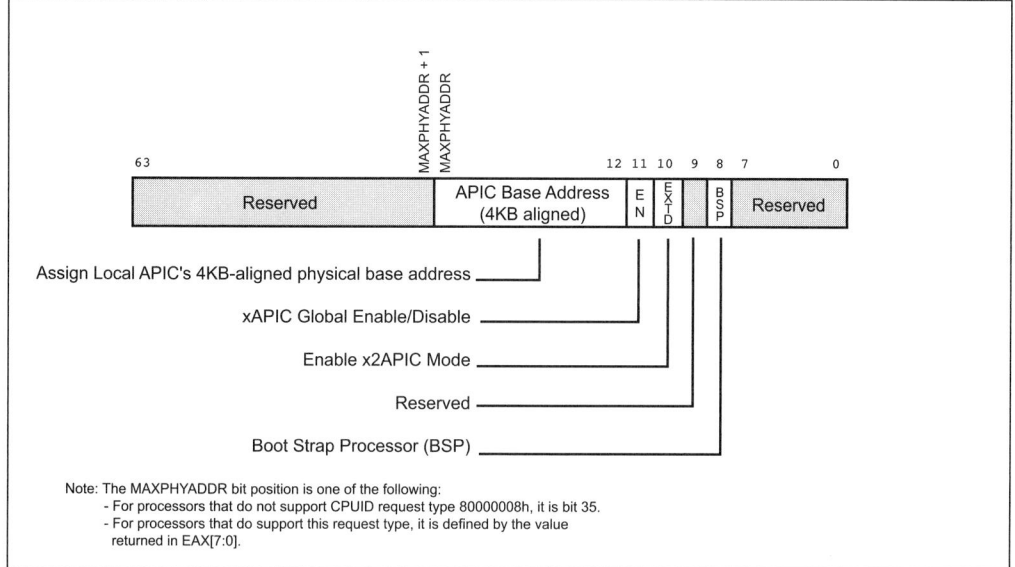

Intel QPI BSP Selection Process

Systems wherein the processor(s) communicate with each other and with the system via the Intel QuickPath Interconnect (QPI) utilize a different methodology. Immediately after reset removal and before initiating code fetches from the boot ROM, each of the physical processors must first execute the internal microcode responsible for:

- Configuring their integrated memory controllers and transaction routing devices. This includes determination of the path to the chipset, the boot ROM, and to the remainder of the system.
- Determining the number of logical processors present and configuration of the QPI paths that permit them to communicate with each other.
- Selection of the logical processor that will play the role of the BSP.

How the APs are Discovered and Configured

The Intel MultiProcessing (MP) 1.4 specification (available for download at the Intel developers' web site) states that the startup code executed by the BSP is responsible for detecting the presence of logical processors other than the BSP.

x86 Instruction Set Architecture

As part of this process, two tables are dynamically created by the BIOS code: the MP (Multi-Processing) Table and the ACPI (Advanced Configuration and Power Management Interface) table. When an MP-aware OS is booted, it consults one or the other of these tables to discover how many and what type of logical processors it has to work with.

AP Detection and Configuration

According to the Multiprocessor Specification, the BIOS/POST code is responsible for detecting the presence of and initializing the APs. Intel recommends that this be accomplished as shown in the flowchart in Figure 34-71 on page 1385 (continued in Figure 34-72 on page 1386). The flowchart assumes that Hyper-Threading is enabled in each of the processors.

Introduction

Under program control, a startup message (i.e., a SIPI—Startup Inter-Processor Interrupt message) will be broadcast by the BSP's Local APIC to the Local APICs associated with all of the APs (assuming any are present). The vector field in this message is not actually an interrupt vector. Rather, it represents the upper 8-bits of the 4KB-aligned 20-bit start address of the FindAndInitAllCPUs routine (which must reside in the first megabyte of memory). Upon receipt of this message, all of the APs simultaneously begin fetching and executing the FindAndInitAllCPUs routine. To prevent all of the logical processors from simultaneously executing the body of this routine, a semaphore (i.e., a spin-lock) is tested upon entry into the routine to determine if any other logical processor has already claimed ownership of the body of the routine. The first AP that is successful in testing and setting the semaphore executes the body of the routine, while the other APs go into a program spin loop waiting for the winning logical processor to clear the semaphore. In this way, each of the logical processors in succession gets to execute the body of the routine.

BIOS AP Discovery Procedure

The following is a slightly expanded version of the flowchart. The BIOS code executing on the BSP:

1. If necessary (to fix processor errata), loads a microcode update into the BSP (see the chapter entitled *Microcode Update Feature* in the MindShare book entitled *The Unabridged Pentium 4* for a detailed description).
2. Initializes the MTRRs (see "Memory Type Configuration" on page 599) and defines the 4KB address range assigned to the logical processor's memory-mapped IO Local APIC register set as UC (Uncacheable) memory.
3. Enables caching by clearing the CR0[CD] and CR0[WT] bits to zero.

4. Executes a CPUID request type 0 to determine if the BSP is "GenuineIntel."
5. Executes a CPUID request type 1 and saves the logical processor capability information returned in the EAX, EBX and EDX registers in the ACPI and MP tables and optionally in system configuration RAM.
6. Loads the AP start-up code (the Intel Multiprocessing Specification refers to it as the FindAndInitAllCPUs routine) into the first MB of memory on a 4KB-aligned address boundary.
7. Switches the BSP into Protected Mode. This is necessary because some of the steps that follow necessitate accessing the Local APIC's register set (which is in high memory and cannot be accessed in Real Mode).
8. Reads the BSP's Local APIC ID from its Local APIC ID register and saves it in the ACPI and MP tables and optionally in system configuration RAM.
9. Converts the 4KB-aligned base address of the AP startup program into an 8-bit vector (e.g., a vector of BDh specifies a start memory address of 000BD000h).
10. Enables the Local APIC by setting Spurious Vector Register (SVR) bit 8 = 1 (see Figure 34-73 on page 1387).
11. Sets up the Local APIC's LVT (Local Vector Table) Error register. It sets the register's vector field = a vector that selects an IDT entry which points to the error handler for the Local APIC. See "The Local APIC's Error Interrupt" on page 1373.
12. Clears the memory semaphore that each AP will check in order to gain entry to the body of the AP start-up program.
13. Sets a CPU count variable in RAM = 1, the current count of known logical processors (so far, only the BSP is known to exist).
14. Broadcast a command to all APs in the system to execute the AP start-up program that was placed in memory. The code running on the BSP accomplishes this as follows:
    — Commands its Local APIC to broadcast the INIT (soft reset) message to all Local APICs in the system.
    — Wait for 10 milliseconds.
    — Commands its Local APIC to broadcast a SIPI (Startup IPI) message to all Local APICs within all physical processors (including itself). This SIPI contains the vector that represents the 4KB-aligned start address of the AP start-up program.
    — Wait for 200 microseconds.
    — Repeat the broadcast of the SIPI message again.
    — Wait for 200 microseconds.
    — This is commonly referred to as the *INIT-SIPI-SIPI sequence*.
15. Start a 100ms timer (using the BSP Local APIC's integrated timer). This is more than enough time for all of the logical processors that may be present in the system to have completed execution of the AP startup program.

16. When the 100ms timer expires an interrupt to the BSP is generated and the BIOS checks the CPU counter location in RAM to see if it still contains the value 1. If it doesn't, then the counter was incremented by one or more APs in the system. If it is still = 1, then there are no APs.

When the BSP has completed execution of the POST/BIOS code and has configured and enabled the devices necessary to read the OS startup code from a mass storage device, it executes the OS boot to begin the process of reading the OS startup code into memory and, after doing so, passes control to the OS startup code.

The OS startup code is responsible for reading the remainder of the OS kernel into memory. Assuming that the OS is MP-aware, it consults either the MP table or the ACPI table (OS-design specific) to determine how many and what type of logical processors it has to work with.

Uni-Processor OS and the APs

If the booted OS (e.g., DOS) is not capable of recognizing the existence of the APs, they remain dormant and are never used (in other words, they suck power and are a waste of money).

MP OS and the APs

If the booted OS is a Multi-Processing (MP) OS, it must:

- Consult either the MP table (earlier OSs) or ACPI table (later OSs) in memory to determine the presence (or absence) of the other logical processors (the APs).
- Place tasks in memory for them to execute.
- Point IDT entries to these programs and issue APIC IPI messages to each logical processors' Local APICs containing the respective IDT vector numbers.

Figure 34-71: BIOS's AP Discovery Procedure Part 1

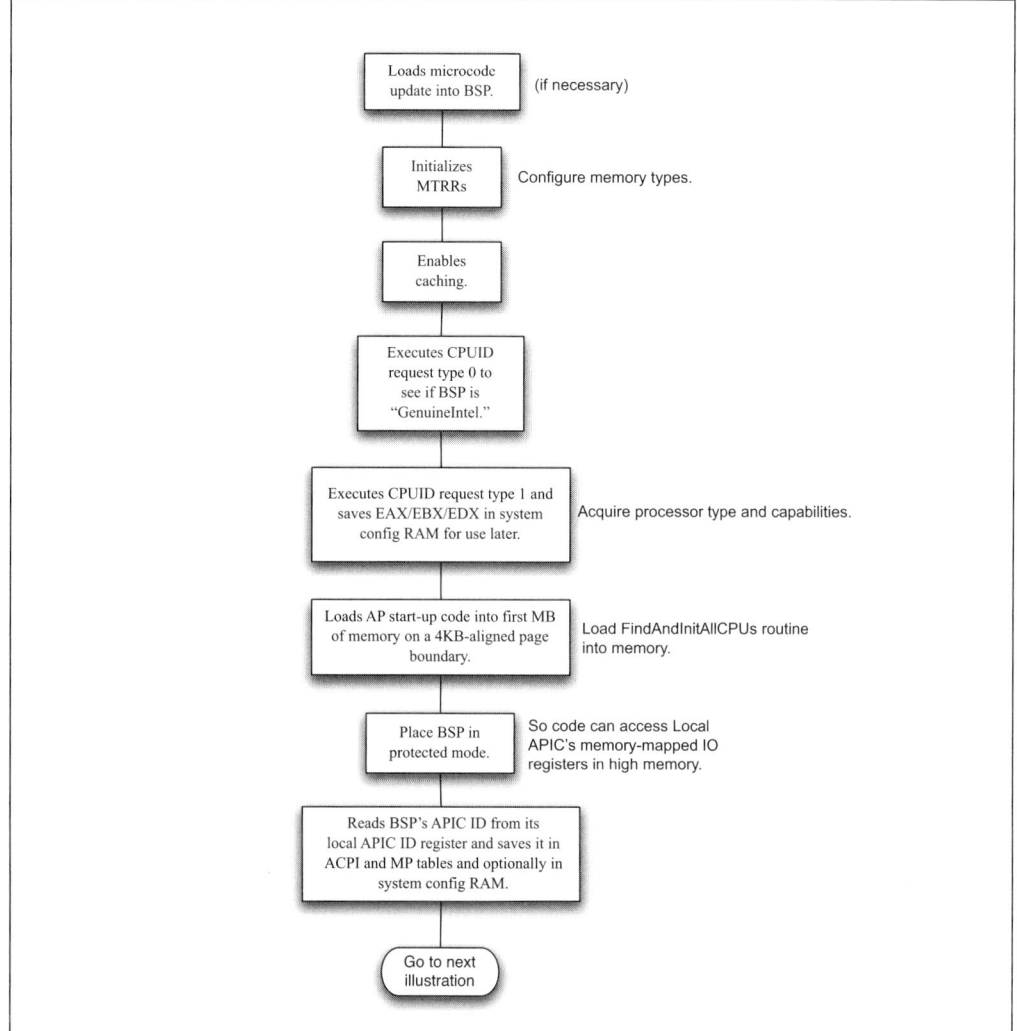

Figure 34-72: BIOS's AP Discovery Procedure Part 2

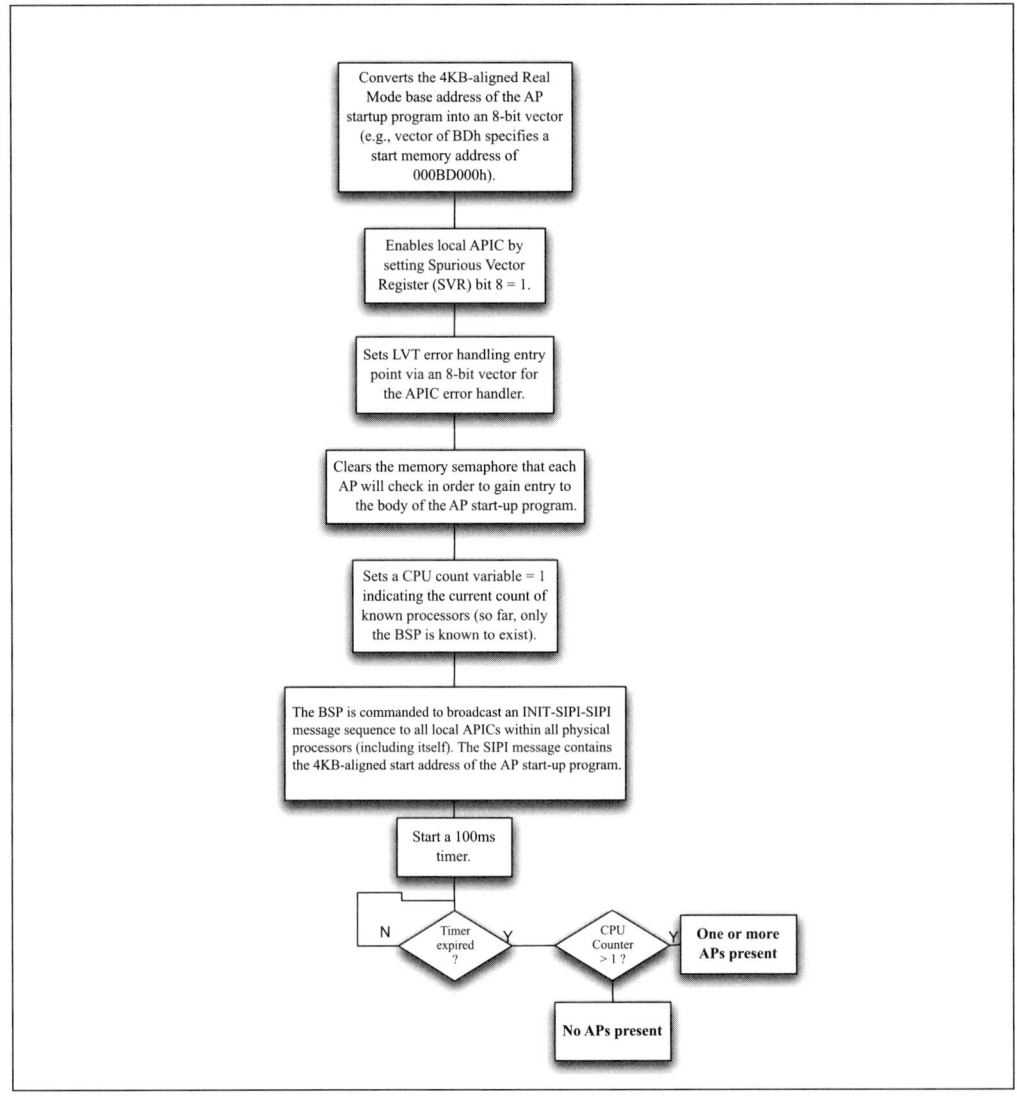

Figure 34-73: The Local APIC's Spurious Vector Register

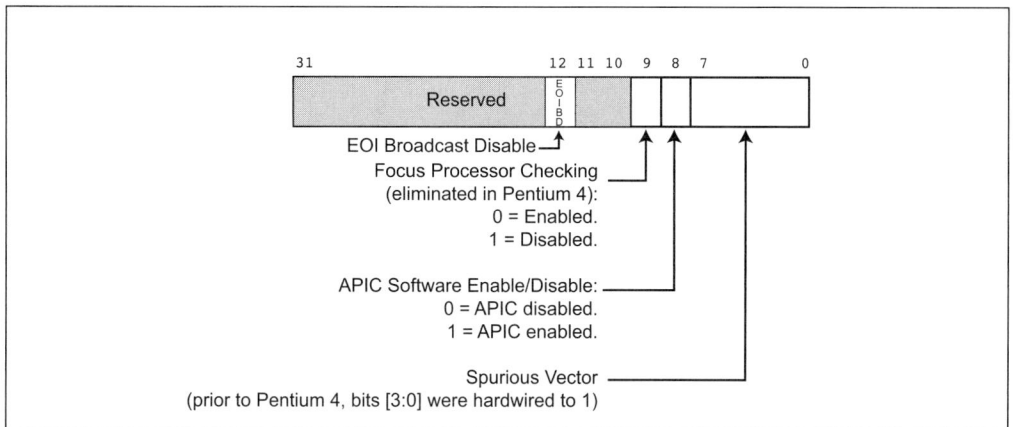

The FindAndInitAllCPUs Routine

Upon receipt of the startup message (SIPI) issued by the BSP's Local APIC under the control of the BIOS code, each of the APs simultaneously begin to fetch and execute the FindAndInitAllCPUs routine. This routine performs the functions shown in the flowcharts in Figure 34-74 on page 1389 (continued in Figure 34-75 on page 1390):

1. The first AP that executes the semaphore test at the start of the FindAnd InitAllCPUs routine determines that the semaphore is clear (the BIOS code cleared it to 00h before issuance of the startup message). It sets the semaphore to FFh, thereby indicating that it owns the body of the FindAndInit AllCPUs routine until it completes its execution and clears the semaphore. The following is an example of the semaphore test and set operation (note that an x86 processor, in order to prevent another device from accessing the semaphore location in between its memory read and subsequent write, automatically asserts its LOCK# output when performing the memory read and write transactions associated with an exchange instruction):

```
    moval,FFh
TestLock:
    xchgbyte ptr [Semaphore],al      ;read and set semaphore
    cmpal,FFh                         ;test value read
    jzTestLock                        ;spin if already set
;execute body of FindAndInitAllCPUs routine (see step 2)
```

2. When each of the remaining logical processors reads the semaphore, it has already been set by the winner, so each of them enters a spin loop waiting for the semaphore to be cleared. The winning logical AP executes the body of the routine which accomplishes the tasks outlined in the steps that follow.
3. If necessary, the routine loads a microcode update into the processor.
4. It initializes the MTRRs with the same settings as in the BSP.
5. It enables the caches by clearing the CR0[CD] and CR0[WT] bits to zero.
6. It executes a CPUID request type 0 to determine if the AP is *GenuineIntel*.
7. It executes a CPUID request type 1 and saves the logical processor capability information returned in the EAX, EBX and EDX registers in the MP and ACPI tables and optionally to the system configuration information in RAM.
8. It switches the AP into Protected Mode. This is necessary because some of the steps that follow necessitate accessing the Local APIC's register set (which is in high memory and cannot be accessed in Real Mode).
9. It reads the AP's Local APIC ID from its Local APIC ID register, and adds it to the MP and ACPI tables and optionally to the system configuration information in RAM.
10. It enables the Local APIC by setting Spurious Vector Register bit 8 = 1 (see Figure 34-73 on page 1387).
11. It sets up the Local APIC's LVT (Local Vector Table) Error register. It sets the register's vector field = a vector that selects an IDT entry which points to the error handler for the Local APIC. See "Locally Generated Interrupts" on page 1360.
12. It configures the AP's SMI execution environment (each AP and the BSP must have a different SM Base address). See "System Management Mode (SMM)" on page 1167 for more information.
13. It increments the CPU counter variable by 1.
14. Using a locked read/modify/write operation, it clears the semaphore, thereby permitting the other APs to execute the body of the AP start-up program. The following is an example of the semaphore clear operation:

```
ReleaseLock:
   moval,00h
   xchgbyte ptr[Semaphore],al        ;clear semaphore to 00h
                                      ;go to next step
```

15. It executes a CLI instruction to disable recognition of external hardware interrupts, and a HLT instruction to place the AP in low-power mode while it awaits the pleasure of the MP OS.
16. It awaits the receipt of an INIT IPI. This will be sent later by the MP OS (after it has been booted).

Figure 34-74: AP Setup Program Part 1

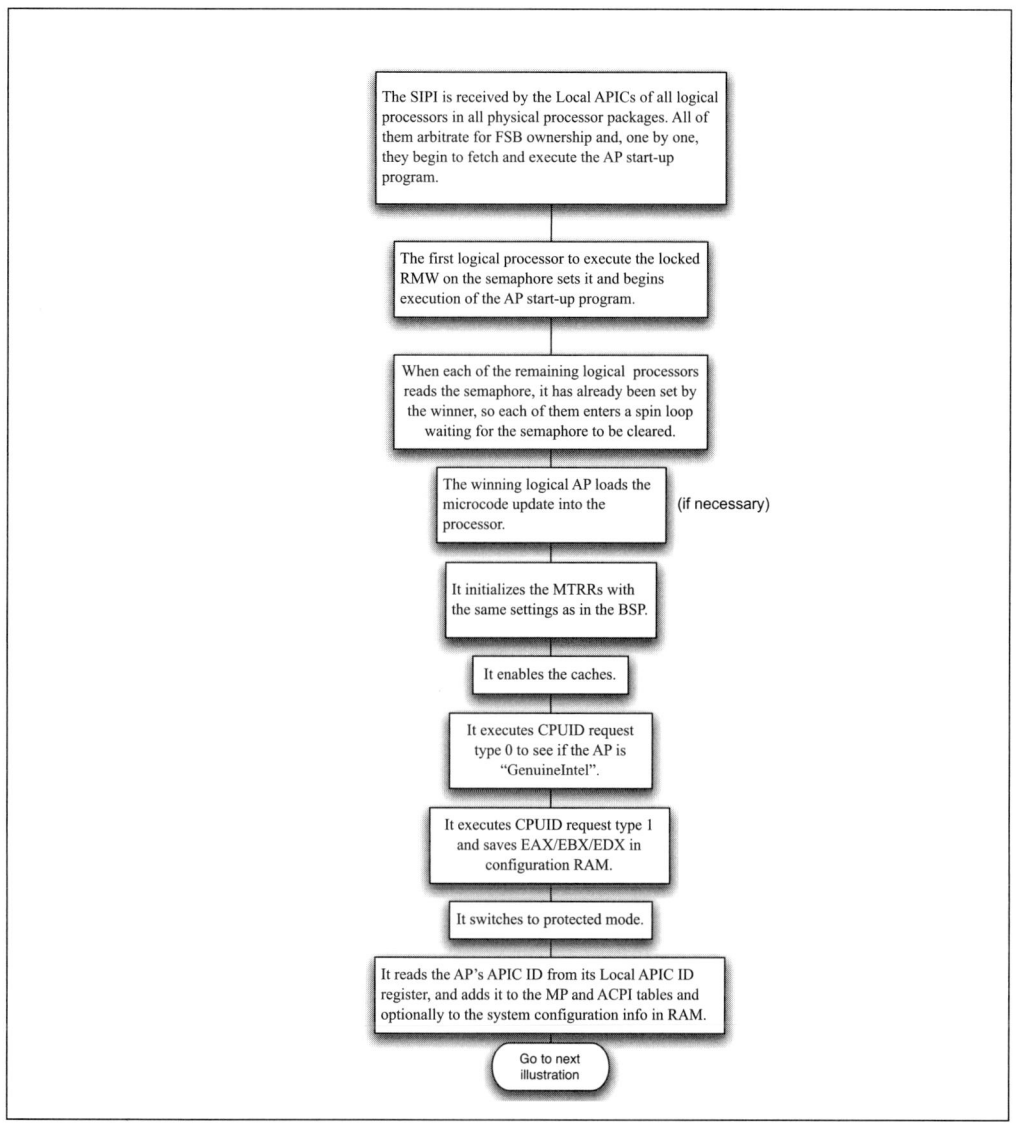

Figure 34-75: AP Setup Program Part 2

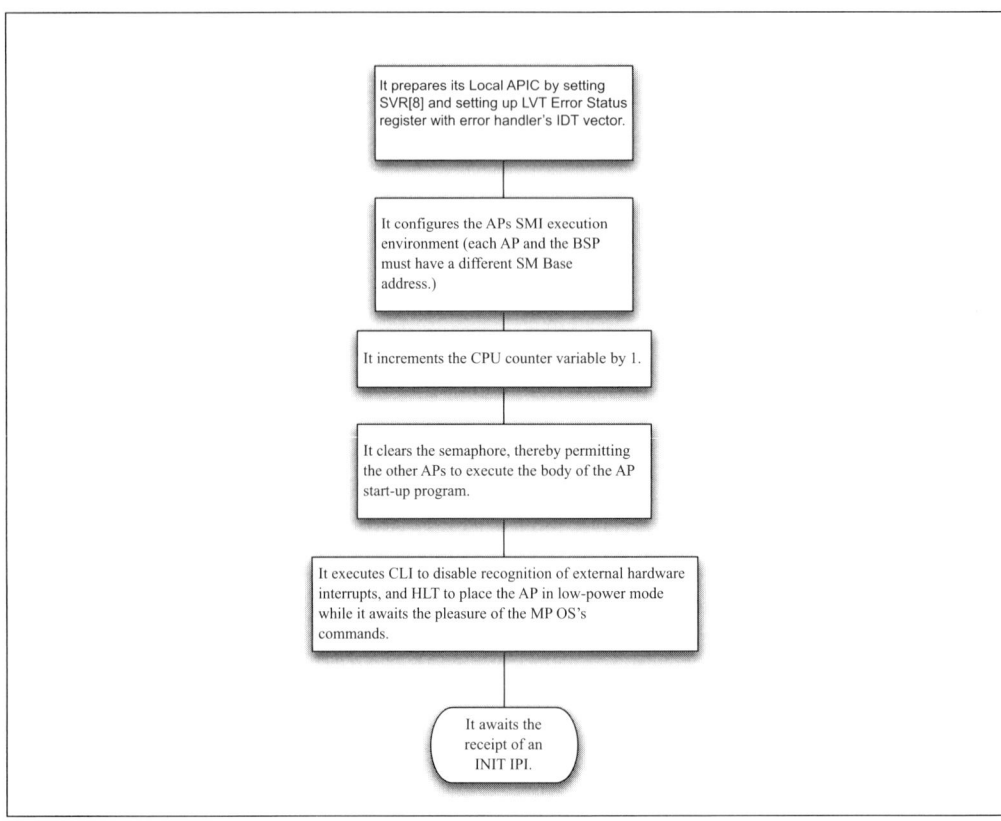

Term	Description
16-bit Compatibility SubMode	The logical processor is in Compatibility Mode executing code from a 286-compliant code segment (i.e., the code segment descriptor's L [Long Mode] and D [Default] bits are both 0).
286 DOS Extender	A procedure that: • Sets up a simple GDT. • Switches the 286 into Protected Mode. • Accesses extended memory for the DOS application that called it. • Commands the chipset to assert Reset or Soft Reset (INIT) to the processor to switch it back into Real Mode. • Resumes execution of the DOS application at the instruction immediately following the DOS extender call.
32-bit Compatibility SubMode	The logical processor is in Compatibility Mode and is executing code from a 32-bit code segment (i.e., the code segment descriptor's L [Long Mode] bit = 0 and D [Default] bit = 1).
64-bit Mode	The logical processor is executing code from a 64-bit code segment (i.e., the code segment descriptor's L (Long Mode] bit = 1).
8259A Interrupt Controller	The legacy external interrupt controller used in the original IBM PC and PC-AT. For legacy compatibility, it is still present in the ICH or IOH chipset member.
A20 Gate	Originally (i.e., prior to the advent of the 486), this external gate either propagated or blocked the A20 address line from the processor. Starting with the 486, it is embedded on the processor.
Abort	A class of software exception wherein the interrupted code cannot be reliably resumed.

Term	Description
Absolute Address	Also referred to as direct addressing. An unsigned, 16- (when using 16-bit addressing) or 32-bit (when using 32-bit addressing) value can be specified as the one and only addressing component of a memory-based operand. In other words, the programmer specifies a hard-coded address (as an offset from a segment base address) which is encoded as part of the instruction itself.
AC	The Alignment Check bit in the Eflags register. Assuming CR0[AM] = 1: • AC = 0: The logical processor will not generate an Alignment Check exception when it detects a mis-aligned multi-byte transfer attempt. • AC = 1: The logical processor will generate an Alignment Check exception when it detects a mis-aligned multi-byte transfer attempt.
ACPI	See Advanced Configuration and Power Management specification.
ACPI table	A resource table built by the BIOS and consulted by the OS to determine what resources (e.g., processor types) it has to work with.
Address Size Override Prefix	When this 1-byte prefix (67h) precedes an instruction, the default address size for the currently-active code segment is overriden. See "Address Size Override Prefix (67h)" on page 214.
Address Translation Tables	The lookup tables used by the logical processor to convert a virtual address into a physical address.
ADDRV	The Address Register Valid bit in the Status register of an MCA error-logging register bank. When set to one, it indicates that the respective bank's Address register contains the address of a memory-based operand associated with the error logged in the respective bank.

Term	Description
Advanced Configuration and Power Interface specification	Defines platform-independent interfaces for hardware discovery, configuration, power management and monitoring. The specification is central to OS-directed configuration and Power Management (OSPM) (a term used to describe a system implementing ACPI), which removes device management responsibilities from legacy firmware interfaces.
AF	**Auxiliary Carry Flag bit in Eflags**. This bit is used in binary-coded decimal (BCD) arithmetic: • AF = 1 if a BCD arithmetic operation generates a carry or a borrow out of bit 3 of the result. • Otherwise, AF = 0.
Alignment Check feature	This feature was added as an aid in performance tuning. A performance tuning software tool enables this feature by setting CR0[AM] to one and can then choose during which applications alignment checking is actually performed by setting the Eflags[AC] bit to one while an application is executing. While activated, this feature checks to ensure that any multi-byte load or store is aligned on a natural address boundary (i.e., word accesses are on an address boundary divisible by two, dword accesses on an address boundary divisible by four, etc. When a misaligned access attempt is detected, an AC exception (exception 17) is generated and the AC handler in the performance tuning software tool is called. The programmer is alerted regarding the misalignment of the data operand in memory.
AM	**Alignment Mask** (AM) bit in CR0. The alignment mask bit enables or disables alignment checking: • If AM = 0, Eflags[AC] is ignored and alignment checking isn't performed. • If AM = 1, allows Eflags[AC] to control alignment checking. See "Alignment Check Exception (17)" on page 774 for more information.

Term	Description
AP	See Application Processor.
APIC	Advanced Programmable Interrupt Controller. • See Local APIC. • See IO APIC.
APIC Bus	Beginning with the advent of the Local APIC in the Pentium P54C processor and continuing through the Pentium III product line, the IO APIC in the chipset and the Local APICs associated with each processor communicated by sending IPI messages over the 3-wire APIC bus.
Application Processor	Immediately after the removal of reset, a processor design-specific set of actions are automatically performed to select which logical processor will assume the role of the BSP to perform the initial machine configuration and boot the OS into memory. All of the other logical processors, referred to as Application Processors, remain in a low-power Halt state until the OS is given control.
APR register	See Arbitration Priority register.
Arbitration Priority register	This read-only register was implemented in the Pentium and P6-based products and was then eliminated along with the 3-wire APIC bus. When an interrupt message specifying Lowest-Priority Delivery Mode was received, the Local APICs displayed their APR values on the APIC bus to determine which of the processors was currently executing the lowest-priority (and therefore the most interruptible) task. That selected Local APIC would then deliver the interrupt to its respective processor core.
Atomic Operation	A locked RMW operation where no other entity is permitted to access memory until the locked memory read and write have both been completed.

Term	Description
Base Pointer register	Can be used for any of the following purposes: • General purpose data register. • To address locations in a memory-based data structure by placing the base address in the BP or EBP register and specifying an offset from the base address. In response, the logical processor forms the memory address by adding the specified operand offset to the base address in the BP or EBP register. • When loaded with the stack frame pointer, it can be used to address the variables, register images, and dynamically-allocated buffers associated with the calling procedure.
Big Real Mode	See Real Big Mode.
BIST	See Built-In Self-Test.
Blue Screen Compositing	See Chroma-Keying.
BootStrap Processor	The logical processor that is selected to perform the initial system configuration and OS boot. The other logical processors, referred to as Application Processors, remain halted until the OS has been booted and it chooses to make use of them.
BOS	Bottom-of-Stack. The base address of the stack. Specified in the SS register.
Branch	A general reference to any form of a jump or call instruction.

Term	Description
Branch Hint Prefixes	The first time that a conditional branch enters the instruction pipeline, the branch prediction logic (a special form of cache) has no history on its previous execution and must therefore make a prediction based on default assumptions (which may prove incorrect). The programmer or compiler can increase the odds that the path taken by a conditional branch the first time it's executed will be correctly predicted by prefacing the conditional branch with one of the two Branch Hint prefixes: • **2Eh: Predict** the branch as **not taken** and assume that the instructions immediately following the conditional branch are to be executed. • **3Eh: Predict** the branch as **taken** and assume that the instructions fetched from the branch target address are to be executed.
Branch Target Buffer cache	The Branch Target Buffer maintains history on branches that have been executed (whether they were taken or not taken).
Broadcast EOI	When an interrupt handler writes to the Local APIC's EOI register to clear a request, the Local APIC consults the respective TMR bit to determine whether or not the EOI needs to be forwarded to the IO APIC, as well. If the selected TMR bit = 1 indicating this is a level-sensitive interrupt, the Local APIC not only clears the corresponding ISR bit, but also performs a memory-mapped IO write transaction to write the interrupt vector to the IO APIC's EOI register. This is referred to as a *Broadcast EOI* because it doesn't target the EOI register in a specific IO APIC. If there were more than one IO APIC in the system, they would all receive the write to their EOI registers. Also see Directed EOI.
BSP	See BootStrap Processor.
BTB	See Branch Target Buffer cache.

Term	Description
Buffer Overflow Exploit	Malicious code that takes advantage when procedures don't check the number of characters input into a stack-oriented buffer against the length of the buffer.
Built-In Self-Test (BIST)	If commanded to do so by the system board logic at startup time, the processor executes a BIST implemented in microcode to validate that it appears to be operating properly.
Byte	8-bits of information.
Call Gate	Gates that permit indirect calls to OS kernel procedures.
Canonical Address	In IA-32e Mode, all memory addresses must be in canonical form. If the address is less than 64-bits in width, it is extended to a 64-bit virtual address in canonical form. Virtual address bits above the most-significant implemented bit must be filled with the state of the most-significant implemented bit.
CD	Cache Disable bit in CR0.
CF	**Carry Flag bit in Eflags:** • This bit is set to one if an arithmetic operation generates a carry or a borrow out of the msb of the result; • otherwise, it is cleared.
Chroma-Keying	The weather person on TV in front of the weather map is really the result of the real-time merging of two video frame buffers: one contains the data received from a camera pointing at the map, while the other contains the data received from a camera pointing at the person walking around in front of a blue background. The program is constantly studying the buffer containing the person pixels and, wherever a blue pixel is detected, it is replaced with the same pixel from the map video buffer.

Term	Description
CISC	See Complex Instruction Set Computer.
CLI	Two definitions: • Clear Interrupt Instruction. Clears Interrupt Flag bit in Eflags register, disabling recognition of maskable interrupts. • With reference to an OS, refers to the Command Line Interface program used by the admin.
Cluster Model	See Flat Cluster Model and Hierarchical Cluster Mode.
Cluster, Processor	A group of logical processors (their Local APICs, actually) that reside within the same addressable domain.
CMC	Corrected Machine Check. See Corrected Machine Check Interrupt.
CMCI	See Corrected Machine Check Interrupt.
Code Segment	A region of memory that contains code (and, perhaps, read-only data associated with the program).
Code Segment Descriptor	An 8-byte descriptor in the GDT or LDT that describes a region memory containing code (and, perhaps, read-only data associated with the program).
Code Segment register (CS)	See EIP.
Command Line Interface	The OS kernel utility that permits the operator to issue commands to the OS (e.g., *Terminal* in Unix).
Compatibility Mode	One of the two IA-32e submodes (the other is 64-bit Mode). While in Compatibility Mode, with some few exceptions the logical processor operates as if it is in Protected Mode.

Term	Description
Complex Instruction Set Computer (CISC)	Unlike a RISC processor which implements a set of fixed-length primitive instructions and simple execution units, a CISC processor's instruction set includes highly-complex, variable-length instructions that are executed by equally complex execution units. This yields more compact code to accomplish the same programmatic goal.
Compositing	See Chroma-Keying.
Conditional Branch	Any form of a Jump or Loop instruction that tests the state of one or more of the Condition Code bits in the lower part of the Eflags register in order to determine whether or not to take the jump or fall through to the next instruction.
Conforming Code Segment	A code segment's descriptor may define it as a *conforming code segment*. In that case, when a procedure within that code segment is called by code in another code segment, the logical processor executes the called procedure at the caller's assigned privilege level rather than that assigned to the target code segment.
Coprocessor	Before the x87 FPU was integrated onto the processor die, it was referred to as a numeric coprocessor.

x86 Instruction Set Architecture

Term	Description
Copy-on-Write Strategy	The Unix copy-on-write strategy saves memory space and time by mapping the child task's (i.e., the new task's) segments and pages to the same segments and pages used by the parent task. As long as the two tasks only perform read accesses to a page, they are accessing the same physical page in memory. The OS only creates a copy of a page that is private to a task when one of the tasks attempts to write to the page. By setting CR0[WP] and marking the shared pages as read-only, a Page Fault exception is generated when the currently executing program (no matter its privilege level) attempts to write to the page. The OS can then make a private copy of that page (for the use of the cloned copy of the task) upon detection of the Page Fault exception, and may then permit the write to the private page.
Core	A physical processor may include a single core or multiple cores and each core, in turn, may include one or more logical processors (and their associated Local APICs). If a processor does not implement Hyper-Threading or if Hyper-Threading has been disabled, then each core consists of a single logical processor and its associated Local APIC.

Term	Description
Corrected Machine Check Interrupt	While a hard (i.e., uncorrectable) failure, in addition to being logged in a MC error logging bank, also generates a MC exception, the logging of a soft (i.e., correctable) error is a quiet event (i.e., it does not cause a MC exception). Prior to the advent of the CMCI feature, error logging software therefore had to periodically scan the MCi_STAT registers in each bank to detect whether or not any soft errors had been logged. The errors would then be recorded in a non-volatile error log (e.g., on disk) and zeros written to the respective MCi_STAT register to prepare it to record any future soft error. The addition of the CMCI feature eliminates the need for error logging software to perform a periodic scan. Each time that a correctable error is logged in any of the MC banks, the logical processor compares the Corrected Error Count field in the MCi_STAT register to the Threshold value specified in the bank's MCi_CTL2 register. When it matches, the CMCI interrupt is generated to alert the error logging software which then logs the error in non-volatile memory, clears the error and then returns to the interrupted program.
CPL	See Current Privilege Level.
CPUID instruction	When executed, returns various types of information regarding the logical processor's capabilities. The value in the EAX register indicates the type of information being requested.
CR	Control Register.
CS	Code Segment. CS is sometimes used in this book as shorthand for CS register. Also see EIP.
CSDesc	Shorthand for Code Segment Descriptor. For example, CSDesc[D] refers to the D (Default) bit in a Code Segment descriptor.

Term	Description
Current Privilege Level	When a far jump or far call is performed, the new value loaded into the 16-bit CS register selects a segment descriptor in either the GDT or the LDT. The 2-bit DPL (Descriptor Privilege Level) field in the selected code segment descriptor becomes the logical processor's CPL.
DTLB	Data Translation Lookaside Buffer. See Translation Lookaside Buffer.
DAZ Mode	See Denormal-As-Zeros Mode.
DE	Debug Extensions bit in CR4.
Debug registers	Refers to DR0 - DR7, the breakpoint detection register set.
Default/Big bit	• In a code segment descriptor, the state of the D (Default) bit defines it as a 16- or 32-bit code segment (0 = 16-bit; 1 = 32-bit). • In a data segment descriptor, if the segment will be used as a stack segment, the state of the B (Big) bit defines whether it is a 16- or 32-bit stack (0 = 16-bit stack; 1 = 32-bit stack).
Delivery Mode	In an interrupt message, this field defines the type of interrupt (SMI, NMI, INIT, user-defined, etc.).
Demand-Mode Paging	See Paging.
Denormal Number	Numbers (irrespective of their sign, either positive or negative) that are less than 1 but greater than 0 (e.g., +0.1242, +0.98, -0.548, -0.13, etc.). These are also referred to as *tiny* numbers.

Term	Description
Denormals-As-Zeros Mode	This performance enhancement tool enhances performance by not invoking the exception 19 handler when a denormal operand is detected. When the DAZ bit in the MXCSR register is set to one, the logical processor converts all denormal source operands to a zero with the sign of the original operand before performing any computations on them. It does not set the Denormal Operand Exception (DE) status bit to one, regardless of the setting of the Denormal Operand mask bit (DM), and does not generate a Denormal Operand exception if the exception is unmasked.
DEP	Refers to an 80-bit Double Extended Precision FP number.
Destination Format register	*Reserved in x2APIC Mode.* In xAPIC Mode: Bits [27:0] are read-only. Bits [31:28] are read/write and specify the system's APIC distribution model (Flat or Clustered Model). Upon receipt of a message that specifies Logical Destination Mode, the Local APIC uses the DFR value to properly interpret the message's MDA field.
Destination Mode	The addressing mode specified in an IPI message is either: • Physical destination mode, addressing a single Local APIC using its unique physical address. • Logical destination mode, addressing a group of Local APICs.
DF	The Direction Flag bit in the Eflags register: • Eflags[DF] = 0 causes string instructions to process strings of information in memory starting at the start address and ascending through memory (i.e., ascending from the start address). • Eflags[DF] = 0, the logical processor descends rather than ascends through memory.
DFR register	See Destination Format register.

Term	Description
Direct Address	See Absolute Address.
Directed EOI	Also refer to Broadcast EOI. In a system with multiple IO APICs, each of them may implement the EOI register at a unique memory-mapped IO address. In this case, the system programmer would want to turn off (i.e., disable) the Broadcast EOI feature. EOI Broadcast is disabled by setting bit 12 of the Spurious Vector register to one. Once it is disabled, the OS would have to ensure that, at the end of each level-sensitive interrupt handler, a *Directed EOI* is performed to the EOI register of the specific IO APIC that handled the interrupt request.
Dirty	This bit in a Page Table Entry indicates whether or not any modifications have been made within the associated page.
Displacement	An optional instruction field used in calculating the address of a memory operand. It can take one of two forms: • See Absolute Address. • A signed, 8-, 16-, or 32-bit value that is encoded in the instruction and is added to (or subtracted from) the other components specified as part of the memory address calculation.
DOS Extender	See 286 DOS Extender.

Term	Description
Double Extended Precision (DEP) FP number	All memory-based FP numeric operands that the x87 FPU deals with are stored in the 80-bit Double Extended Precision (DEP) format. When instructed to operate upon an 80-bit DEP memory-based FP numeric value as a 64-bit DP FP number, it reads the 80-bit value from memory and converts it into the 64-bit DP format before performing an operation on it. Likewise, when instructed to treat an 80-bit DEP memory-based FP numeric value as a 32-bit SP FP number, it reads the 80-bit value from memory and converts it into the 32-bit SP format before performing an operation on it. Conversely, when a FP number must be stored in memory, it automatically converts it (if necessary) into the 80-bit DEP format before storing it to memory.
DP	Refers to a 32-bit Double Precision FP number.
DPL	Descriptor Privilege Level.
DS	Refers to the Data Segment, or to the Data Segment register.
DT index	Refers to the Descriptor Table Index field in a segment register (when the logical processor is operating in Protected Mode, Compatibility Mode, or 64-bit Mode).
DTLB	Data Translation Lookaside Buffer. See TLB.
Dword or DW	4-bytes (32-bits) of information.
ECC	See Error Correcting Code.
Edge-Triggered Interrupt	A hardware interrupt recognized by a low-to-high transition on a signal line.
EFER	See Extended Functions Enable register.

Term	Description
Effective Address	**Effective address = offset**. Defined as the 16-bit (if the logical processor is operating in Real Mode, 286 Protected Mode, VM86 Mode, or SM Mode) or 32-bit (if it is operating in 386 Protected Mode) offset portion of the address that selects a location within a code, data or stack segment.
Eflags register	The bit fields within the Eflags register may be categorized as follows: • **Status bits**. A series of status bits (referred to as *Condition Code—or cc—bits*) that indicate the results of the previously-executed instruction. These bits are tested by the Jcc (i.e., conditional jump) instructions to determine whether to jump to the branch target address or fall through to the next instruction.They are also tested by some other types of instructions. • **Control bits**. A series bits that control various aspects of the logical processor's operation (e.g., the IF bit—set and cleared by the STI and CLI instructions, respectively—enables or disables the logical processor's ability to recognize interrupt requests from external devices). • **Miscellaneous bits**. A series of miscellaneous bits related to other logical processor behaviors.
EIP register	32-bit Extended Instruction Pointer register. Together, the CS:EIP register pair tells the logical processor where to fetch the next instruction from (CS supplies the code segment base address and the Instruction Pointer register supplies the offset within the code segment).
EIPV	EIP Valid bit in an MCA bank's Status register. • If EIPV = 1, the CS:EIP value saved on the stack is directly associated with the error that caused the exception. • If EIPV = 0, the CS:EIP value on the stack may or may not be associated with the error.

Term	Description
EM	Emulate x87 FPU. 1 = indicates the x87 FPU is not present. If it is present, its ability to execute FP instructions is disabled. When an x87 FP instruction is detected, a DNA exception is generated. If the logical processor is MMX-capable, the detection of an MMX instruction causes an invalid opcode exception. If the logical processor is SSE-capable, the detection of an SSE instruction causes an invalid opcode exception. A few SSE instructions aren't affected by the EM bit.
EM64T	Extended Memory 64-bit Technology. An early name for IA-32e Mode.
EOI	End-of-Interrupt. See Broadcast EOI.
EOI register	End-of-Interrupt register. Refers to a register in the Local APIC or the IO APIC. See Broadcast EOI.
Error Correcting Code (ECC)	Refers to ECC-protected RAM. When data is written to memory, the memory control logic computes an ECC based on the data being written and stores it into the target location along with the data. When data is read from a location, the ECC logic computes a new ECC code based on the data read and compares it to the actual ECC read from the location: • If they are the same, no data corruption has occurred. • If they are different, the ECC logic attempts to re create the original data using the ECC. Typical implementations can detect and correct single-bit failures but not multi-bit failures.
Error Status Register (ESR)	Local APIC's status register.
ES	Refers to the ES data segment or the ES data segment register.
ESP register	The 32-bit Extended Stack Pointer register (points to the current TOS).

Term	Description
ESR register	Error Status register. Local APIC's status register.
ET	Extension Type bit in Eflags register: • 0 = 287 FPU installed. • 1 = 387-compatible FPU installed.
Event	As used in this book, refers to an interrupt or exception event which interrupts the currently-running program and calls the event handler selected by the 8-bit vector associated with the event.
Event Queue	Refers to the OS-specific queue that tracks which events are associated with each task.
Exabyte (EB)	2^{60} memory locations.
Exception	An error detected during the attempted execution of an instruction. As a result, the logical processor uses the specific error's assigned vector to index into the IDT and select an entry. It then calls the handler pointed to be the selected entry.
Execute Disable feature	The logical processor's ability to fetch and execute exploit code from the stack (which is a read/write data segment) can be prevented by designating the stack as no-execute memory. An OS can implement that capability by enabling and using the Execute-Disable feature.
Expand-Down Stack	A stack segment with E = 1 in its descriptor is defined as an expand-down stack. As with an expand up stack, the stack still grows downward towards its floor as items are pushed into the stack. The only real difference is that the stack now has an artificial floor which, when needed, can be adjusted downwards towards its actual floor.

Term	Description
Expand-Up Stack	The most common form of stack used by x86 software. As each item is pushed onto the stack, the Stack Pointer register is adjusted downward and the item is then written into stack memory. Conversely, as each item is popped from the stack, it is read from the stack using the address in the Stack Pointer register and the Stack Pointer is then adjusted upwards to point to the next item.
Extended Functions Enable register (EFER)	Among other bit fields, this register contains the IA-32e Mode enable bit (referred to by the AMD name Long Mode enable bit).
Extended Instruction Pointer	See EIP.
Extended Memory	Memory above the 1MB address boundary.
Far Call	An instruction that calls a procedure residing in a different code segment than the caller. As such, the branch target address must specify both a new 16-bit CS value as well as the offset within the target code segment.
Far Jump	An unconditional branch to a location in a different code segment.
Fault	A class of exception. Before being pushed onto the stack, the logical processor first rewinds CS:EIP (which had already been incremented to point to the next instruction) to point to the instruction that caused the error event. This permits the instruction to be restarted (i.e., all registers are restored to their original state prior to the attempted execution of the instruction) when the IRET is executed at the end of the exception handler.

Term	Description
Fence instruction	Any instruction which restricts the logical processor's ability to execute instructions that reside beneath the fence until all instructions up to and including the fence have completed execution. Some fences affect all instructions beyond the fence while others (e.g., LFENCE) only restrict the execution of certain types of instructions.
FFXSR	AMD-only feature. If the OS has enabled the Fast FxSave/Restore feature by setting EFER[FFXSR] = 1, executing FXSAVE in 64-bit Mode at privilege level 0 causes the logical processor to complete the instruction more quickly by not saving the XMM registers to memory.
Fixed Interrupt	See User-Defined Interrupt.
Flags register	The lower 16-bits of the Eflags (or Rflags) register. The portion of the flags register accessible in Real Mode, 286 Protected Mode, or 16-bit Compatibility Mode.
Flat Cluster Model	*Not supported in x2APIC Mode.* In the Flat Cluster addressing model, each of the eight bits in the IPI message's logical address field acts as a selector bit permitting the message to select up to 8 Local APICs on the 3-wire APIC bus (Pentium or P6) or the FSB (processors supporting xAPIC Mode) by setting the appropriate bits to one in the message's logical address.
Flat Memory Model	The memory model supported by virtually all modern OSs wherein segmentation is disabled and memory is viewed as a single linear address space.
Flat Real Mode	See Real Big Mode.

Term	Description
Flush-to-Zero Mode	A performance enhancement tool enabled by setting MXCSR[FTZ] = 1. At the cost of a slight precision loss, faster execution can be achieved for applications where underflows are common and rounding the underflow result to zero can be tolerated.
Fopcode register	When an x87 FP error is encountered, the logical processor latches the lower 11-bits of the FP instruction's 2-byte opcode in this register.
FP	Floating-Point. Refers to math operations on numbers with decimal places.
FPU	Floating-Point Unit. The FP math execution unit (e.g., the x87 FPU).
Front-Side Bus	The shared bus that connects processors and the chipset.
FS	The FS data segment register.
FSB	See Front-Side Bus.
FSW register	x87 FP Status Word register.
FTW register	x87 FP Tag Word register contains eight bit fields corresponding to the eight x87 FP data registers. Each bit field indicates whether or not the corresponding data register currently contains valid data.
FTZ Mode	See Flush-to-Zero Mode.

Term	Description
GDT	Global Descriptor Table. There is only one GDT and it contains the following types of descriptors: • One descriptor for each code or data segment that is **shared** among more than one task (i.e., it is a globally-accessible segment). • **TSS descriptor(s):** – If the hardware-based task switch mechanism is used, there will be a separate TSS descriptor for each task. – Most modern OSs create a single TSS descriptor and TSS to be used by all tasks. • If an OS utilizes an optional Local Descriptor Tables (LDT) to describe the segments of memory that are private (local) to the task, it will create an **LDT descriptor** defining its base address and size (as well as other attributes). • **Procedure Call Gates.** Permit calls to OS kernel procedures. • If the OS utilizes the x86 processor's hardware-based task switching mechanism (*note that none of the major OSs use it*), it may create (for each task) a **Task Gate descriptor** in the GDT.
GDTR register	Global Descriptor Table register. Contains the base address and size of the GDT in memory.
General Detect condition	The logical processor generates a Debug exception indicating a General Detect condition when software attempts to use one of the Debug address breakpoint registers that is already in use by an external tool (e.g., an In-Target Probe tool).
General Protection exception	This exception is generated if an error not associated with any other type of exception is detected. An error code is pushed onto the stack to aid in problem determination.
Global Page	A page that is accessible by multiple tasks.
GP	See General Protection exception.

Glossary of Terms

Term	Description
Granularity bit	In a segment descriptor, the Granularity bit tells the processor how to interpret the descriptor's segment size field: • 0 = size in bytes. • 1 = size in 4KB pages.
Group	Refers to an instruction wherein the opcode identifies a group of eight instructions and the middle 3-bits of the ModRM byte act as an extension to the opcode, identifying 1 of 8 possible instructions in the group.
GS	The GS data segment register.
Guest OS	An OS hosted by a VT hypervisor (e.g., by VMWare).
Guest State	The area of the VMCS where the contents of a number of the logical processor's registers are saved when a guest OS is suspended and from which they are reloaded on the launch or resumption of a guest OS.
Handler	Refers to an interrupt or exception handler that handles a device- or instruction-specific event.
Hierarchical Cluster Model	Using this addressing model, the address field in the IPI message contains an 8-bit Cluster ID field and a 4-bit selector field. This allows an IPI message to be delivered to up to four Local APICs within any of 256 possible clusters.
High Memory Area	Memory locations 100000h - 10FFEFh at the start of the second MB of memory space.
HMA	See High Memory Area.
Host State	The area of a VMCS from which some of the logical processor's registers are loaded on a VMCALL or a VM Exit.

Term	Description
Hot Reset	Software can issue a command to the chipset to assert INIT (Soft reset) to the processor by writing a FEh to the Keyboard/Mouse interface's command port at IO port 0064h. In response, the Keyboard/Mouse interface pulses its Hot Reset output one time, causing the system board hardware to generate a soft reset to the processor.
Hypervisor	The Root Mode program which supervises the execution of multiple guest OSs.
IA-32 Architecture	Refers to the architecture of a 32-bit x86 processor that supports IA-32 Mode but not IA-32e Mode.
IA-32 Mode	The mode the logical processor is in when it is operating in Real Mode, Protected Mode, VM86 Mode, or SM Mode.
IA-32e Mode	The Intel 64 processor supermode within which 64-bit and 16- and 32-bit Compatibility Mode applications are run.
ICH	IO Control Hub member of the chipset. Sometimes referred to as the South Bridge.
ICR register	A Local APIC register. See Interrupt Command register.
ID	If the programmer can change the state of this Eflags bit to a one, the logical processor supports the CPUID instruction.
Identity Mapping	Translating a virtual address into the identical physical memory address (a 1-for-1 translation) is referred to as identity mapping.
IDT	See Interrupt Descriptor Table.

Term	Description
IF	Interrupt Flag bit in the Eflags register: • 0 = Disables recognition of maskable hardware interrupts. • 1 = Enables recognition of maskable hardware interrupts.
Immediate Data	A data operand hard-coded within the body of an instruction.
Imprecise Error Reporting	An error that is not reported to software (via an exception or interrupt) at the exact moment when the error is detected. When the execution of a computational FP instruction results in the detection of an unmasked error, the x87 FPU sets the appropriate error bit in the FSW and also sets the FSW[ES] bit. An exception or interrupt is not generated immediately, however. Rather, the generation of the exception or interrupt is deferred until one of the following occurs: • The execution of the next WAIT/FWAIT instruction. • The detection of another computational FP instruction. Before executing the instruction, the x87 FPU first tests the state of the FSW[ES] bit and generates an exception or interrupt if FSW[ES] = 1. In other words, an exception or interrupt is generated if the execution of the previous computational FP instruction caused an unmasked error to be generated and the FSW[ES] bit to be set to one.
Index registers	Refers to the SI and DI, ESI and EDI, or RSI and RDI registers which, in addition to being used as general-purpose data registers, are used as parameter registers when string operations are performed.
INIT	When received by a logical processor, the INIT IPI message acts as a soft reset. See Soft Reset.

Term	Description
In-Service register	A 256-bit Local APIC register that tracks which user-defined interrupts have already been dispatched to the logical processor and are in the process of being serviced by their respective handlers.
Instruction Pipeline	The series of stages in a logical processor that handle the decode, dispatch and execution of the instructions that comprise the currently-running program.
Instruction Set Architecture	The Instruction Set Architecture, or ISA, is defined as that part of the processor architecture related to programming, including the native data types, instructions, registers, addressing modes, memory architecture, interrupt and exception handling, and external IO.
Intel 64 Architecture	Refers to the architecture of a 64-bit x86 processor that supports IA-32e Mode as well as IA-32 Mode.
Interrupt Command register	A 64-bit Local APIC register that software uses to command the Local APIC to transmit an IPI message to one or more other Local APICs in the system.
Interrupt Descriptor Table	The 256-entry memory-based table containing the start addresses of the various hardware interrupt and software event handlers.

Term	Description
Interrupt Gate	In modes other than Real Mode and SM Mode, the IDT contains a series of gates that contain the start addresses of the various hardware interrupt and software event handlers. When an interrupt or exception selects an IDT entry containing an Interrupt or Trap Gate, before calling the specified event handler the logical processor first pushes the program pointer and flags register contents onto the stack: • If it's an Interrupt Gate, the logical processor then clears Eflags[IF] to 0 to disable recognition of maskable hardware interrupts before calling the handler. • If it's a Trap Gate, the logical processor then calls the handler (without clearing Eflags[IF] to zero).
Interrupt Redirection Bitmap	Only used when all of the following circumstances are true: • The logical processor is executing a VM86 task (i.e., when Eflags[VM] = 1). • The VM86 Extensions are enabled (CR4[VME] = 1). • The logical processor is executing a software interrupt instruction (i.e., INT nn, BOUND, INT3, or INTO). The logical processor uses the vector supplied by the instruction to consult the respective bit in the TSS's Interrupt Redirection Bitmap. The state of the selected bit indicates whether the respective Real Mode or Protected Mode IDT entry will be used to call the handler.
Interrupt Request register	A 256-bit Local APIC register that registers user-defined interrupt requests as they are received. Based on the interrupt priority scheme, they are then forwarded to the logical processor one at a time.
Interrupt Service Routine	See Handler.

Term	Description
Interrupt Stack Table (IST)	Refers to the IST section of an IA-32e-compatible TSS. In the event of certain types of interrupts or exceptions (namely: a Machine Check exception, a Double-Fault exception, or an NMI hardware interrupt) generated as the result of catastrophic circumstances, the interrupted program's stack may be corrupted or otherwise invalid upon entry to the respective handler. In order to ensure that the respective handler is entered with a clean stack, the OS may preallocate a fresh stack, place a pointer to it in one of the TSS's IST fields, and set up the 3-bit IST field in the respective IDT descriptor to point to the respective TSS IST field.
IO APIC	One or more IO APICs (the number is platform design-specific) are external to the processors (typically, integrated into the chipset). The IO APIC: • Receives interrupt requests from device adapters (e.g., network adapters, disk controllers, etc.) and from the chipset (e.g., SMIs—System Management Interrupts, NMIs—Non-Maskable Interrupts, etc.). • Formulates interrupt message packets. • Delivers interrupt message packets to the Local APICs associated with the targeted logical processors.
IOH	IO Hub. This bridge chip provides the interface between the processor's Intel QPI interface and the ICH chip.

Term	Description
IO Permission Bitmap	In Protected Mode: • If the CPL of the currently executing program is numerically <= the IOPL (i.e., program's privilege level is the same as or better than the IOPL), no exception is generated and the IO instruction is executed. • If the CPL is numerically > the IOPL (i.e., the program's privilege level is not as privileged as the threshold value specified in the IOPL field) and the instruction is one of the IO instructions (IN, OUT, INS, or OUTS), then the logical processor uses the target port address to index into the current task's IO Permission Bitmap (in the TSS) to determine if the current application is permitted to access the addressed IO port(s). If the bit(s) selected by the IO port address (see "IO Permission Bit Map" on page 661) indicate the task is permitted to access the indicated IO port(s), no exception is generated and the IO instruction is executed. Otherwise, a GP exception is generated. In VM86 Mode: • The IOPL is not checked at all (VM86 tasks by definition operate at privilege level 3). • The logical processor checks the current task's IO Permission Bitmap (in the TSS) to determine if the current application is permitted to access the addressed IO port(s). If the bit map indicates that the task is permitted to access the indicated IO port(s), no exception is generated and the IO instruction is executed. Otherwise, a GP exception is generated.
IOH	IO HUB. Member of the chipset. In systems wherein the processor(s) incorporate an integrated memory controller, the IOH takes the places of the North Bridge (i.e., the MCH or Memory Control Hub). It provides the interface between the Intel QPI interface and the ICH chip.

Term	Description
IOPL	See IO Privilege Level.
IPI Message	See Inter-Processor Interrupt message.
IP-relative Branch	A conditional or unconditional branch (jump) wherein the branch target address is specified as a positive or negative offset from the address currently in the Instruction Pointer register (IP, EIP, or RIP).
IRQ Pin Assertion register	A special, write-only, memory-mapped IO port device adapters can write to (using an MSI write) in order to deliver an interrupt request to the IO APIC (in the form of a virtual IRQ pin assertion). On receipt of an IRQ pin number in this register, the IO APIC uses the RT entry associated with the specified pin to format an interrupt message to send to the logical processors.
IRR register	See Interrupt Request register.
ISA	See Instruction Set Architecture.
ISR	Interrupt Service Routine. See Handler.
ISR register	See In-Service Register.
IST	See Interrupt Stack Table.
ITLB	Instruction Translation Lookaside Buffer. See Translation Lookaside Buffer.
Jump	Refers to any form of conditional or unconditional branch instruction that conditionally or unconditionally alters program flow.
Kernel	Refers to the critical portion of the OS that is used on an on-going basis and, for this reason, is pinned (see Pin) in memory.

Term	Description
Kernel registers	The x86 registers specifically associated with the OS kernel-related memory-based data structures: • **GDTR**. Global Descriptor Table register specifies the base address and size of the GDT in memory. • **LDTR**. Selects an LDT descriptor in the GDT that describes the base address and size of the LDT. • **IDTR**. Interrupt Descriptor Table register specifies the base address and size of the IDT in memory. • **TR**. Selects a TSS descriptor in the GDT that describes the base address and size of the current task's TSS in memory.
LDR register	See Logical Destination register.
LDT	See Local Descriptor Table.
LDT descriptor	The descriptor in the GDT that defines the following characteristics of the current task's LDT: • Its base address. • Its size. • Its Privilege Level.
LDTR register	See Local Descriptor Table register.
Level-Sensitive Interrupt	A device adapter may generate an interrupt request by driving its respective interrupt request signal line low.
LINT0 pin	Local Interrupt Pin 0. An external processor pin that connects to the LINT0 input on every Local APIC within the processor package. Each Local APIC contains a LINT0 LVT register that software uses to enable or disable LINT0 recognition and to assign an interrupt type to be delivered to the respective logical processor.

Term	Description
LINT1 pin	Local Interrupt Pin 1. An external processor pin that connects to the LINT1 input on every Local APIC within the processor package. Each Local APIC contains a LINT1 LVT register that software uses to enable or disable LINT1 recognition and to assign an interrupt type to be delivered to the respective logical processor.
LME	Long Mode Enable bit in the EFER MSR.
Load	Refers to a memory data operand read.
Local APIC	Each core (or logical processor if Hyper-Threading is implemented and enabled) incorporates a dedicated Local APIC that receives interrupt messages from: • IO APIC(s). • The Local APICs associated with other cores or logical processors. • From internal sources (e.g., thermal interrupts, Local APIC Timer interrupts, etc.). Upon receipt of one or more types of interrupts, the Local APIC prioritizes them and delivers them to its associated core or logical processor.
Local Descriptor Table register	When starting or resuming a task, the kernel's task scheduler programs this register with a 16-bit selector. This value selects an LDT descriptor in the GDT that contains the base address and size of the memory-based LDT that describes the areas of memory that are private to the currently-running task.
Local Vector Table	A series of registers (LVT registers) associated with each Local APIC that are used to configure the treatment of events that are local to its associated logical processor.

Term	Description
Lock Prefix	When an instruction that performs a back-to-back memory read and write (e.g., a CMPXCHG instruction) with a memory operand is prefaced by the Lock prefix byte (F0h), the logical processor prevents any other entity from accessing the memory operand until it has completed both the read and the subsequent write.
Logical Destination Mode	An IPI message addressing mode that permits the message to be delivered to a logical group of Local APICs.
Logical Destination register	A Local APIC register that contains the Local APIC's logical (as opposed to physical) address.
Logical x2APIC ID	See x2APIC ID.
Logical xAPIC ID	When a Local APIC is operating in xAPIC Mode (rather than x2APIC Mode), this address is used to determine if an inbound IPI message using logical rather than physical addressing has selected this Local APIC as one of the targets.
Long Mode	AMD's name for IA-32e Mode.
Lowest-Priority Delivery Mode	When Lowest-Priority Delivery Mode is specified in an inbound IPI message, the Local APICs associated with the targeted group of logical processors then exchange interrupt messages in order to determine which of them is currently executing the lowest-priority program (as specified in their respective TPRs).
LVT	See Local Vector Table.
Machine Check Architecture registers	A set of architecturally-defined MSRs that record hardware-related errors that occur internally or on a processor's external interfaces (e.g., its FSB, Intel QPI, or integrated DRAM controller's RAM interface).

Term	Description
Machine Check Exception	Automatically generated whenever a logical processor detects an uncorrectable internal or external hardware-related error. The logical processor's ability to generate it is controlled by CR4[MCE].
Machine Language	Refers to the processor's native code that is fetched from system memory.
Machine Status Word register	Refers to the lower 16-bits of CR0. This was its name in the 286 processor.
Malloc	Refers to the OS kernel's memory allocation facility.
Mantissa	The fractional portion of a number to the right of the decimal point. Also referred to as the significand.
Maskable Interrupt	Refers to the class of hardware interrupts that can be masked by clearing the Eflags[IF] bit to zero.
MB	Megabyte of memory (2^{20} locations).
MCA	See Machine Check Architecture registers.
MCE	See Machine Check Exception.
MCG_CAP register	Machine Check Global Count and Present register.
MCG_CTL register	Machine Check Global Control register.
MCG_Status register	Machine Check Global Status register.
MCH	Memory Control Hub. This bridge chip provides the interface between the processor's FSB interface, the ICH chip, and system RAM.

Term	Description
MCIP	Machine Check In Progress bit in MCG_Status register. Automatically set to one when a MC exception is generated. If another MC exception should be generated while this bit is still set to one (i.e., it hasn't been cleared by the MC handler yet), the logical processor enters the Shutdown state. The MC exception handler should save sufficient processor state (i.e., register contents) to remember the current MC error and then clear the MCIP bit to zero. If another MC exception should subsequently be generated after MCIP has been cleared and the logical processor is still executing the MC exception handler, another MC exception is generated.
MDA	See Message Destination Address.
Memory Segment	A region of memory containing: • Code. • Data. • Stack. • TSS data structure. • Local Descriptor Table.
Memory-Mapped IO	Refers to device adapter control, status, or data ports that are implemented in memory rather than IO space. They are therefore accessed using load and store instructions rather than IO instructions (i.e., IN, OUT, INS, or OUTS).

Term	Description

MESI	Refers to the caching model wherein a line from memory may be in any of the following states in a cache:
	• **M** = Modified state. One or more locations have been modified since the line was read from memory but the updates have not been written through to memory. No other physical processor has a copy of the line.
	• **E** = Exclusive state. No other physical processor has a copy of the line and code running on this processor has not made any modification to the line. The line is therefore still identical to the one in memory.
	• **S** = Shared state. Two possible meanings:
	  – WP or WT memory: One or more processors have a copy of the line in their caches and the copy (or copies) are still the same as the one in memory).
	  – WB memory: More than one processor contains a copy of the line in its caches and all copies are the same as the one in memory.

Message Destination Address	The field in an IPI message that contains the address of the target Local APIC(s).
Message Signaled Interrupt	A hardware interrupt that takes the form of a specially-formatted memory write transaction. When received by the MCH or IOH, it is converted into an IPI message and transmitted to the target Local APIC[s] over the FSB or Intel QPI.
Microarchitecture	Refers to the specific hardware implementation of an ISA instruction execution engine (e.g., the P6, Net-Burst, Nehalem, etc.).

Term	Description
Microcode ROM	Contains (among other things): • The series of one or more fixed-length micro-ops that each variable-length x86 instruction translates into. • The Built-In Self-Test microcode that the processor executes (when commanded to do so at start-up time) to determine its health. • In an Intel QPI-based processor, the microcode that is automatically run at startup time to configure the processor's internal fabric and resources and to determine which logical processor will act as the BSP.
Microcode Update feature	Introduced with the advent of the Pentium Pro, this feature permits the programmer to check the processor's silicon stepping and, if it is not up to date and an applicable Microcode Update image has been supplied by Intel, to command the processor to load the update into itself to patch its Microcode ROM.
Micro-Op	Refers to the fixed-length RISC instructions into which the variable-length x86 instructions are translated before execution.
MISCV	The Miscellaneous Register Valid bit in the Status register of an MCA error-logging register bank. When set to one, it indicates that the respective bank's Miscellaneous register contains additional information associated with the error just logged.
MM registers	The 64-bit MMX data registers MM0 - MM7.
MMIO	See Memory-Mapped IO.
MMX	Much speculation, none of it ever substantiated by Intel. It's the author's opinion that it stands for Matrix Math eXtensions.

Term	Description
Mod	Refers to the 2-bit Mod field in an instruction's ModRM byte. The ModRM byte is most-often used to specify the method for calculating the address of a memory-based operand: • If Mod = 00b, 01b, or 10b, then one of the operands is memory-based and the Mod value stipulates the address calculation method. • If Mod = 11b, then one or both of the instruction's operands are register-based and there is no memory operand.
Model-Specific Register	Originally, these registers were truly model-specific. While some of them still are, the names of many of them are now prefaced with *IA32* indicating that they are part of the x86 ISA (e.g., the full name of the EFER register is IA32_EFER MSR).
ModRM Byte	The ModRM byte is used to explicitly specify the memory and/or register-based operands of an instruction.
MP	This acronym has the following meanings: • MultiProcessing or multiprocessor. • When used in the context of the x87 FPU, it refers to the CR0[MP] bit which, in conjunction with CR0[EM] defines the presence or absence of the x87 FPU.
MP table	Multiprocessing Table. Defined by the Intel 1.4 MP specification, this table is created by the BIOS code and contains a list of all of the logical processors and their capabilities.
MSI	See Message Signaled Interrupt.
MSI-X	An enhanced version of the MSI interrupt mechanism.
MSR	See Model-Specific Register.
MSW register	See Machine Status Word register.

Term	Description
MTRR registers	Memory Type and Range Registers. A group of architecturally-defined MSRs initialized by the BIOS to define the types of memory (and therefore the caching-related rules the logical processor must follow) that occupy each area of memory space.
MTRRdefType register	The MTRR Default Type register.
MTRRPhysBase register MTRRPhysMask register	Assuming a processor implements one or more sets of variable-range MTRR registers pairs, each pair consists of a Base address register and a Mask register that specifies the size of a memory region. The base address register also defines the type of memory residing within the specified memory range.
MXCSR register	SSE Control/Status register: • Controls the generation of SSE FP exceptions (via six FP exception masking bits). • Records the status of SSE FP operations (via six FP exception error status bits). • Enables/disables two SSE FP performance enhancement modes (FTZ and DAZ modes).

Term	Description
NaN	Not-a-Number. FP values that are not real numbers (referred to as *NaNs*). They are categorized as follows: • **SNaN (Signaling NaN)**. A SNaN is a NaN with the most significant fraction bit cleared to zero. SNaNs generally signal an FP Invalid Operation exception whenever they appear as operands in arithmetic operations. SNaNs are typically used to cause a FP exception. The logical processor never generates an SNaN as a result of a FP operation. Rather, software would insert a SNaN operand to cause a FP exception. • **QNaN (Quiet NaN)**. A QNaN is a NaN with the most significant fraction bit set to one. The logical processor's FP execution units allow QNaNs to propagate through most arithmetic operations without causing a FP exception.
NE	CR0[NE]. CR0[NE] = 0 disables the logical processor's ability to generate an exception 16 if an x87 FP exception occurs. Instead, the logical processor signals the event using the DOS-compatible method (i.e., by asserting the processor's FERR# output which causes the assertion of IRQ13 to the 8259A interrupt controller).
Near Call	An instruction that calls a procedure residing in the same code segment as the caller.
Near Jump	An instruction that jumps to a location in the same code segment. As such, the branch target address need only specify a new value to be placed in the Instruction Pointer register.

Term	Description
Nested Task	The logical processor automatically sets the Eflags[NT] bit to one when an automatic task switch occurs due to one of the following: • A far call selects a Task Gate in the GDT or LDT thereby causing the processor to switch to and call another task as if it were a called procedure. • An interrupt, exception, or software interrupt selects an IDT entry containing a Task Gate. As a result, the logical processor switches to and call another task as if it were an event handler.
NMI	See Non-Maskable Interrupt.
Non-Conforming Code Segment	A code segment's descriptor may define it as a *non-conforming code segment*. In that case, procedures within that code segment can only be called by programs with the same privilege level.
Non-Maskable Interrupt (NMI)	Unlike maskable hardware interrupts, if an NMI is delivered to a logical processor, its recognition cannot be masked by software. NMI is issued to the logical processor by the chipset to signal that a serious hardware condition has been detected on the system board.
Non-Root Mode	The virtualization mode the logical processor is in when it is executing a guest OS.
Non-Temporal Store	A special store instruction used by the programmer when he or she is storing to an operand in WB memory that will not be accessed any time in the near future. The logical processor will treat it as a store to WC memory: • The store address and data are recorded in a WCB buffer. • A lookup is performed in the caches and, if the line is present in the cache, it is marked Invalid (note that, if it is marked Modified, it is first flushed to memory).

Term	Description
NOP message	On a system wherein the processors communicate with each other and the system via a shared FSB, immediately after the removal of reset, they all arbitrate for ownership of the FSB in order to perform what is referred to as the Special transaction. This transaction does not contain an address. Rather a message (NOP, Halt, or Shutdown) is broadcast over the Byte Enable signals. The primary logical processor in the first physical processor to gain ownership of the FSB and broadcast the NOP message becomes the BSP while all of the other logical processors are marked as Application Processors.
North Bridge	The informal name for the MCH or IOH member of the chipset.
NT	The Nested Task bit in the Eflags register. The logical processor automatically sets it to one in either of the circumstances cited in Nested Task (in this table).
Null Descriptor	Entry 0 in the GDT must contain what is referred to as a null descriptor containing 64-bits of all zeros.
NW	In combination with CR0[CD] (the Cache Disable bit), the Not Write-Through bit in CR0 controls the logical processor's ability to cache from memory.
NXE	The No Execute Enable bit in the EFER register enables or disable the Execute Disable feature.
OF	The Overflow Flag bit in the Eflags register. Tested by the INTO instruction.
Opcode	That portion of an instruction that defines the instruction type.
Operand	The object upon which an instruct acts (a register, a pair or registers, or a register and a memory-based operand). It can also consist of an immediate data value encoded within the instruction.

Term	Description
Operand Size Override Prefix	• When executing code from a 16-bit code segment, inclusion of the Operand Size Override prefix before an instruction flips the effective operand size from 16- to 32-bits. As an example, a move instruction would move 32-bits (a dword) between a 32-bit register (e.g., EAX) and a word-aligned address in memory. • When executing code from a 32-bit code segment, inclusion of the Operand Size Override prefix before the instruction flips the effective operand size from 32- to 16-bits. As an example, a move instruction would move 16-bits (a word) between a 16-bit register (e.g., AX) and a dword-aligned address in memory.
OSFXSR	OS FX Save/Restore instruction pair support bit in CR4. Setting CR4[OSFXSR] to one: • Enables the logical processor to execute the SSE instruction set. *The following SSE instructions are always enabled: PREFETCHh or SFENCE. On any x86 processor starting with the Pentium 4, the following SSE2 instructions are always enabled: PAUSE, LFENCE, MFENCE, MOVNTI, and CLFLUSH.* • Enables the FXSAVE and FXRSTOR instructions to save and restore the contents of the SSE register set along with the contents of the FPU/MMX register set.
OSXMMEXCPT	**OS XMM Exception support bit in CR4.** SSE SIMD FP exceptions are only generated by SSE SIMD FP instructions: • The OS will set CR4[OSXMMEXCPT] to one if it implements an SSE FP SIMD exception handler (i.e., the exception 19 handler). • If CR4[OSXMMEXCPT] is cleared to zero, the logical processor generates an Invalid Opcode exception whenever it detects an unmasked (i.e., enabled) SIMD FP exception.

Term	Description
OSXSAVE	When set to one by the OS kernel, this bit in CR4 **has three effects**: 1. Indicates the kernel supports the use of the XGETBV, XSAVE and XRSTOR instructions by applications. 2. Enables the XSAVE and XRSTOR instructions to save and restore the x87 FPU/MMX register set, SSE register set, and any other register sets enabled in XCR0. 3. Enables the logical processor's ability to read and write the XCR0 register using the XGETBV and XSETBV instructions.
PAE	**Physical Address Extension bit in CR4**. Also referred to as PAE-36 Mode: • 0: The Paging mechanism can only map a 32-bit linear/virtual address to a 32-bit physical memory address in the first 4GB of memory space. • 1: The Paging mechanism can map a 32-bit linear/virtual memory address to a 36-bit physical memory address in the first 64GB of memory space. Refer to "Second-Generation Paging" on page 553 for a detailed description.
PAE-36 Mode	See PAE.
Page	A 4KB, 2MB, or 4MB block of memory space aligned on a 4KB, 2M, or 4MB address boundary.
Page Attribute Table	Each Page Table Entry (PTE) contains a 3-bit field consisting of PCD, PWT, and PAT which selects 1 of 8 fields in the IA32_CR_PAT MSR (this register *is* the PAT table). The value in the selected entry defines the type of memory that occupies that page of memory space (and therefore the logical processor's rules of conduct when performing reads and writes within the page).

Term	Description
Page Directory	Each valid entry (PDE) in the Page Directory contains one of two things: • The base address and attributes of a 4KB Page Table. • The base address and attributes of a 2MB or 4MB page.
Page Directory Pointer Table	Each valid entry (each PDPTE) in the PDPT contains the base address and attributes of a Page Directory.
Page Fault	The logical processor generates a Page Fault exception under the following conditions: • The selected PDE's P bit = 0, indicating that the selected Page Table is not present in memory. • The selected PTE's P bit = 0, indicating that the target page is not present in memory. • An attempt to write to a read-only page. • Code running in user mode (privilege level 3) attempts to write to a read-only page. • If CR0[WP] = 1, a Page Fault also occurs on an attempt by code with supervisor privilege (0, 1, or 2) to write to a user page (i.e., PTE[U/S] = 1). • Insufficient page-level privilege to access the Page Table or the page. • A reserved bit is set to one in the PDE or PTE.
Page Map Level 4	The PML4 table is the top-level address translation table used by the virtual-to-physical address translation mechanism when the logical processor is in IA-32e Mode.
Page Table	Each valid entry (PTE) in a Page Table contains the base address and attributes of a 4KB page.
Page Table Entry	See Page Table.
Paging	A name frequently used for the virtual-to-physical address translation mechanism. Also referred to as demand mode paging.

x86 Instruction Set Architecture

Term	Description
Paragraph	16-bytes of information stored in memory starting at an address divisible by 16.
PAT feature	See Page Attribute Table.
PCC	The Processor Context Corrupt bit in the Status register of a MCA error-logging register bank. When set to one, indicates that the state of the logical processor's register set may have been corrupted by the error condition detected and that reliable restarting of the interrupted program (by executing the IRET instruction) may not be possible. When cleared to zero, indicates that the error did not affect the logical processor's state.
PCD	Page Cache Disable bit. Together with the PWT bit and, in some cases, the PAT bit, it defines the memory type for a page or an address translation table. This bit is found in: • CR3. • PTE. • PDE. • PDPTE.
PCE	**RDPMC (Read Performance Counter) instruction permission**. The RDPMC instruction, if permitted by the state of CR4[PCE], can be used to read the contents of a performance counter: • When CR4[PCE] = 0, the RDPMC instruction can only be successfully executed (without causing a GP exception) by programs executing at privilege level 0. • When CR4[PCE] = 1, the RDPMC instruction can be successfully executed by programs executing at any privilege level. Refer to the MindShare book entitled *The Unabridged Pentium 4* for a detailed description of the Performance Monitoring logic.
PD	See Page Directory.

Glossary of Terms

Term	Description
PDBR register	Page Directory Base Address register. Also known as CR3. Contains the base address of the top-level address translation table for the current task. Also contains the PCD and PWT bits that define the memory type for the top-level address translation table.
PDE	Page Directory Entry. See Page Directory.
PDPT	See Page Directory Pointer Table.
PDPTE	Page Directory Pointer Table Entry. See Page Directory Pointer Table.
Performance Monitoring registers	The performance monitoring facility is invaluable when tuning or profiling program code to yield the best possible performance. It permits the programmer to obtain an accurate profile of how efficiently the processor and memory are utilized by a program. The performance monitoring counters can be programmed independently of each other to take one of two types of measurements: • A measure of the duration of a specific event type. • A count of the number of occurrences of a specific event type. The event types that can be measured are processor-dependent and include a large number of types such as cache hits, cache misses, TLB hits and misses, etc.
Petabyte (PB)	2^{50} memory locations.
PF	The Parity Flag bit in the Eflags register: • If the LSB of the result contains an even number of one bits, PF = 1; • Otherwise, PF = 0.
PG	Paging Enable bit in CR0. When set to one, it enables the logical processor's virtual-to-physical address translation mechanism.
PGE	Global Page feature enable bit in CR4.

Term	Description
Physical Address	The actual address of an operand in memory.
Physical Address Extension	See PAE.
Physical Destination Mode	An IPI message addressing mode that permits the message to be delivered to a single, specific Local APIC.
Pin	A page pinned in memory by the OS kernel will remain in memory and not be swapped out.
Pipeline	See Instruction Pipeline.
PML4	See Page Map Level 4. The top-level virtual-to-physical address translation table in IA-32e Mode.
PML4E	Page Map Level 4 Entry. Contains the base address and attributes of a Page Directory Pointer Table (PDPT) address translation table.
PMWB	See Posted Memory Write Buffer.
Pop operation	A stack operation that first reads the data operand currently pointed to by the Stack Pointer and then increments the Stack Pointer by 2, 4, or 8 (depending on the effective operand size in force at the time).
Port	Refers to a device adapter's command, status or data register.
Posted Memory Write Buffer	All memory writes (stores) performed in UC, WP, and WT memory are posted in the logical processor's PMWB and are later performed in strict program order.
PPR register	See Processor Priority register.
Precise Error Reporting	An error that is reported to software (via an exception or interrupt) at the exact moment when the error is detected.

Term	Description
Preemptive Multitasking	An OS/hardware environment wherein the currently-running program can be preempted by the detection of a higher-priority event (such as a high priority interrupt).
Prefix	A 1-byte prefix added before an instruction's opcode that in some way amends the action performed by the instruction. Examples would be: • Repeat prefixes. • Segment Override prefixes. • Operand Size Override prefix. • Address Size Override prefix. • Lock prefix. • Branch Hint prefixes. • REX prefix.
Procedure Call, Direct	A procedure call instruction that directly specifies the branch target address of the procedure.
Procedure Call, Indirect	A far procedure call instruction that indirectly specifies the branch target address of the procedure. The CS portion of the branch target address selects a GDT or LDT entry contains a Call Gate which, in turn, contains the address of the called procedure in CS/Instruction Pointer format. The offset portion of the specified the branch target address is discarded.
Processor	In the context of this book, refers to the physical processor package which may contain a number of cores and logical processors.
Processor Priority register	The PPR value represents the priority at which the logical processor is currently executing and is used to determine whether a pending interrupt has sufficient priority to be dispensed to the logical processor.

Term	Description
Protected Mode Virtual Interrupt feature	Controlled by CR4[PVI]. When CR4[PVI] = 1, if a Protected Mode application (i.e., with a CPL of 3) attempts the execution of a CLI or an STI instruction it is handled in the same manner as would a VM86 task's attempted execution of CLI or STI.
PS	The Page Size bit in a PDE: • 0 = PDE contains the base address and attributes of a 4KB Page Table. • 1 = PDE contains the base address and attributes of a 2MB or 4MB page.
PSE-36 Mode	When set to one, CR4[PSE] activates PSE-36 Mode. While permitting a 32-bit virtual address to be translated into a 36-bit physical memory address, PSE-36 Mode does not require a major rewrite of the paging portion of the OS kernel. It uses the same 2-level directory structure as the first-generation paging mechanism and each entry in the Page Directory and the Page Tables is still 32-bits in width. However, it is neither as elegant as, nor as flexible as PAE-36 Mode.
PT	See Page Table.
PTE	Page Table Entry. See Page Table.
Push operation	A stack operation that first decrements the Stack Pointer by 2, 4, or 8 (depending on the effective operand size in force at the time) and then writes the contents of the specified register into stack memory.
PVI	See Protected Mode Virtual Interrupt feature.
PWT	Page Write-Through bit. See PCD.
QNaN	A quiet NaN. When a FP operation results in a QNaN, it does not cause an exception. See NaN.
QPI, Intel	See QuickPath Interconnect.

Term	Description
QuickPath Interconnect, Intel	The network fabric-based interconnect utilized by Intel processors and chipsets starting with the advent of the Nehalem-class processors.
Qword or QW	8-bytes (64-bits) of information.
R/W	The Read/Write bit is found in: • PTEs. Designate the 4KB page as read-writable or read-only. • PDEs. Designates the address domain covered by the PDE as read-writable or read-only. • DR7. The four R/W bits in the Debug Control register defines whether the breakpoint monitoring logic should monitor for read or write accesses. • Page Fault error code. The R/W bit in the error code pushed onto the stack indicates whether the offending access was a read or a write attempt. • Segment Descriptor. The R/W bit in a data or stack segment descriptor defines the data segment as read-writable or read-only.
Read/Modify/Write	Refers to an instruction that performs three operations: • Reads an operand from memory. • Unconditionally or conditionally modifies the value read. • Writes the resultant value back into the same memory location. Also see Lock.
Real Big Mode	All x86 processors subsequent to the 286 can address up to 4GB of memory space in Real Mode, as long as they have (at least once) been switched to Protected Mode and back to Real Mode since the last reset. This is sometimes referred to as *Big Real Mode, Flat Real Mode, Real Big Mode* and *UnReal Mode*. For more information, refer to "Big Real Mode" on page 310.

Term	Description
Real Mode	The initial mode entered immediately after the removal of reset. Emulates the operational characteristics of the 8086 processor.
Redirection Table registers	A register set in the IO APIC. Each register is associated with an interrupt request input pin and is used to configure: • What condition the IO APIC will recognize as an interrupt request on the respective pin. • The format of the IPI message that will be forwarded to one or more of the logical processors when an interrupt is recognized on the respective interrupt request input pin.
Reduced Instruction Set Computer	RISC (Reduced Instruction Set Computer) ISAs define an instruction set wherein each instruction is the same length. In its purest form, the instruction set consists of a limited number of simple instructions that perform primitive operations and which the compiler can use as the building blocks to accomplish complex operations. On the plus side, the execution units are fairly simple. On the minus side, when compared to a CISC processor, it typically takes a greater number of primitive instructions to achieve the same programmatic goal as would a single CISC instruction.

Term	Description
Remote IRR	Remote Interrupt Request Register. Belying its name, this is a single bit found in each of the IO APIC's Redirection Table registers. Setting the Remote IRR bit in an RT register indicates a level-sensitive request has been received, but that it has not yet been serviced by the interrupt handler. While it remains set, the respective input pin is masked. At the end of the interrupt handler, the write to the Local APIC's EOI register causes the processor to perform a memory-mapped IO write of the respective interrupt vector to the IO APIC's EOI register. Upon receipt, the vector is compared to the vectors in the Redirection Table registers and the Remote IRR bit in the register with a match is cleared. This causes the IO APIC to unmask the respective input pin.
Remote Read register	A Local APIC register that was eliminated with the advent of the Pentium Pro.
ReOrder Buffer (ROB)	After the variable-length instructions are translated into fixed-length micro-ops, they are placed in the ROB in strict program order. They are then visible to the dispatch logic and are dispatched to the various execution units for out of order execution.
Repeat Prefixes	Placing the REP prefix (F2h or F3h) before a string-oriented instruction tells the logical processor to loop on the instruction until the count specified in the C register (CX or ECX) has been exhausted, at which time it will fall through to the instruction immediately following the string instruction.

Term	Description
Requester Privilege Level	The RPL (Requester Privilege Level) consists of the lower 2-bits in the CS portion of a far branch target address and serves two purposes: • It is used in the privilege level check to determine if the call or jump is allowed. • It is also checked when a RET or IRET is executed. The RPL indicates the privilege level of the software that originated the far branch target address.
REX Prefix	In 64-bit Mode, prefacing some instructions with the REX prefix permits: • Up to 16 GPRs, Debug registers, Control registers, or XMM registers to be addressed. • In combination with the Operand Size Override prefix, an operand size of 16-, 32-, or 64-bits to be selected.
RF	The Resume Flag bit in the Eflags register (Eflags[RF]). When the Resume Flag bit is set to one by the debugger, the subsequent execution of the IRETD instruction prevents the logical processor from generating a debug exception again when it returns to an instruction that already caused a debug exception.
Rflags register	The 64-bit version of the Eflags register. Only used in 64-bit Mode.
RIP register	The 64-bit version of the Instruction Pointer register.
RIP-relative data addressing	The ability to access a memory-based data operand located backward or forward relative to the address of the currently-executing instruction. Only available in 64-bit Mode.
RIPV	The Return Instruction Pointer Valid bit in the Machine Check Global Status register. Set to one if the interrupted program can be safely resumed at the instruction pointed to by the pointer pushed on the stack when the MC exception was generated.

Term	Description
RISC	See Reduced Instruction Set Computer.
RM	The *Register or Memory* field in the ModRM byte. If the Mod field contains 00b, 01b, or 10b, a memory operand is specified and Mod + RM (and possibly the SIB byte) defines the method used to calculate its memory address.
RMW	See Read/Modify/Write.
ROB	See ReOrder Buffer.
ROM	Read-Only Memory device.
Root Mode	The virtualization mode the logical processor is in when it is executing the hypervisor rather than a guest OS.
RPL	See Requester Privilege Level.
RSP register	The 64-bit version of the Stack Pointer register. Only used in 64-bit Mode.
RT registers	See Redirection Table registers.

Term	Description
Saturated Math	**Signed, saturated math**. Using signed, saturated math, out-of-range results are automatically clamped to the representable range of signed integers for the integer size being operated on. Two examples: • If an operation on signed word integers results in a positive overflow, the result is clamped (i.e., *saturated*) to 7FFFh, the largest positive integer that can be represented in 16-bits. • If in the same scenario a negative overflow occurs, the result is saturated to 8000h. **Unsigned, saturated math**. Using unsigned, saturated math, out-of-range results are automatically clamped to the representable range of unsigned integers for the integer size being operated on. Positive overflow when operating on unsigned byte integers results in FFh being returned and negative overflow results in 00h being returned.
Scalar Operation	Definition of scalar: a single number (as opposed to a matrix of numbers). As an example, scalar multiplication refers to the operation of multiplying one number (one scalar value) by another and the term scalar is used to differentiate this from matrix (i.e., SIMD) math operations.
Scaling Factor	A 2-bit field in the SIB byte that specifies the size of the records in the data structure and therefore the number to multiply the Index value (i.e., the record number) by to calculate the offset of the target record's start address from the structure's base address.
SCE	The System Call Enable bit in the EFER register. When set to one by the OS, enables the execution of the SYSCALL and SYSRET instructions which are used to make calls to the OS kernel. The OS sets this bit once it has set up the MSRs (STAR, LSTAR, CSTAR, SFMASK) used by these instructions.

Term	Description
Scheduler	Refers to the OS kernel's task scheduler.
Segment	A region of memory.
Segment Override Prefixes	An optional Segment Override prefix appended to an instruction in order to access a segment other than the default DS data segment defined by the DS register.
Segment Wraparound	If an 8088/8086 processor were to execute an instruction wherein the segment base address were FFFF0h and the offset a value between 0010h and FFFFh, address bit A[20] would not be high (because the 8088/8086 processors did not implement address lines above A[19]). The net result, therefore, would be that the 8088/8086 would produce an address between 00000000h-0000FFEFh. This is called address or segment wraparound.
Semaphore	A flag in memory used by multiple software entities to determine the availability of a shared resource.
Sensitive Operation	• In VM86 Mode when the Eflags[IOPL] threshold is set to a value lower than 3 (the privilege level of a VM86 task), the logical processor is sensitive to any attempt to execute CLI, STI, PUSHF, POPF, INT, or IRET (a GP exception is generated). • When Virtualization Mode is enabled and a guest OS attempts any operation defined as sensitive, it triggers a switch from Non-Root Mode to Root Mode (i.e., the guest OS is suspended and the hypervisor is invoked).
Serializing Event	Any event that causes the logical processor to temporarily cease out-of-order program execution.

Term	Description
SF	There are two definitions: • Sign Flag bit in the Eflags register. SF = the value (1 or 0) of the result's msb (i.e., the sign bit of a signed integer): − 0 = a positive value. − 1 = a negative value. • The 2-bit Scaling Factor field in the SIB byte. See Scaling factor.
Shared Resource	A device or memory buffer accessed by multiple software entities and protected by a semaphore.
Short Jump	A jump to an instruction within the same code segment. The distance and direction of the jump is specified by a signed displacement encoded within the jump instruction.
SIB Byte	The Scale, Index, Base byte is used to calculate the start address of a fixed-length record within a memory-based data structure: • The Base field specifies which register contains the base address of the data structure. • The Scaling Factor field specifies the length of each record in bytes. • The Index field specifies which register contains the record number of the target record in the data structure. The logical processor calculates the target record's start address by multiplying the record length by the scaling factor and adding the result to the data structure's base address.
Significand	The fractional portion of a FP number. See Mantissa.
Single Precision FP number	32-bit FP number.
SIPI	Startup Inter-Processor Interrupt message. Specifies the 4KB-aligned start address of a program to be executed in the first MB of memory space.

Term	Description
SMXE	Safer Mode Extension Enable bit in CR4 register.
Snarf	Slang term referring to an action taken, typically by a cache. Upon detection of a memory write by another entity, it captures the write data and uses it to keep its copy of a line up-to-date.
SNaN	A Signaling NaN. When a FP operation results in an SNaN, it causes an exception. See NaN.
Soft Reset	A hard reset completely initializes the logical processor and its Local APIC, and clears its caches. A soft reset (known as an INIT) has the same effect but preserves the contents of the caches, MSRs, MTRRs, and the x87 FPU state (the contents of the BTB and the TLBs are cleared, however). A soft reset may be delivered to a logical processor in one of two ways: • The chipset can be commanded to assert the INIT# signal (or to send an INIT IPI message) to the processor. See "286 DOS Extenders on Post-286 Processors" on page 313 for additional information. • Software (typically kernel code) running on a logical processor may command its Local APIC to transmit an INIT IPI (Inter-Processor Interrupt) message to one or more other Local APICs in the system.
Software Exception	See Exception.

Term	Description
Software Interrupt Instruction	An instruction that calls an interrupt handler: • INT nn. Calls the handler pointed to by IDT entry nn. • BOUND. Calls the handler pointed to be IDT entry 5 if the specified array index is not within the bounds of the specified memory array. • INTO. Calls the handler pointed to by IDT entry 4 if Eflags[OF] = 1. Useful because the signed and unsigned arithmetic instructions cannot detect a result overflow. • INT3. Also referred to as the **Breakpoint** instruction. Unlike the 2-byte INT *03* instruction, it is one byte long.
South Bridge	The informal name for the ICH member of the chipset.
SP	The 16-bit version of the Stack Pointer register.
Special Transaction	On a system wherein the processors communicate with each other and the system via a shared FSB, a logical processor causes the Special transaction to be generated on the FSB under the following circumstances: • To select which logical processor will assume the role of the BSP immediately after the removal of reset. • To signal to the chipset that it has executed a Halt instruction and has therefore ceased program execution. • To signal to the chipset that it has experienced a fatal software condition and entered the Shutdown state. The Special transaction has the following characteristics: • There is no address. • The message type is encoded on the processor's eight Byte Enable signals.

Term	Description
Speedstep Technology	Earlier x86 processors designed for mobile applications implemented a basic form of the SpeedStep technology. Essentially, the processor only had two operating modes: • Lowest Frequency Mode (LFM). While in this mode, the processor operated at a lower clock speed and core voltage. • Highest Frequency Mode (HFM). While in this mode, the processor operated at the full clock speed and core voltage. Rather than just two operational modes, Enhanced SpeedStep implements multiple operational voltage and frequency combinations, ranging from the Lowest Frequency Mode (LFM; LFM speed on all processors is 600MHz) to the Highest Frequency Mode (HFM; the processor is operating at full speed). The processor is capable of automatically performing real-time dynamic switching of the voltage and frequency based on CPU demand. This is accomplished by switching the BCLK-to-core clock ratio and the core operating voltage (without resetting the system). In addition, software can control both the operational voltage and frequency. Whether the operational mode is being switched automatically or under software control, the time to transition from one frequency/voltage setpoint to another is very low. Later multi-core processors also implement Turbo Boost Mode wherein the processor can power-down unused cores (when they aren't being used) and then increase the operating speed of those still executing code.
Spin-Lock	Refers to a piece of code that tests the state of a semaphore and, if it is set (indicating that a shared resource is still busy), spins back to retest the semaphore again.

Term	Description
SS	Stack Segment register. Sometimes used as shorthand for Stack Segment.
SSE	Streaming SIMD Extensions. Sometimes used as a general reference to the entire SSE environment consisting of all SSE instructions, the XMM data registers, and the MXCSR Control/Status register. In some contexts, refers to the original SSE1 instruction set.
SSE2	144 new instructions added in the 140nm Pentium 4.
SSE3	13 new instructions added in the 90nm Pentium 4.
SSSE3	32 new instructions added in the Core 2 Duo.
SSE4.1	47 new instructions added in 45nm Core 2 Duo.
SSE4.2	7 new instructions added in Nehalem-based Core i7.
Stack	See Stack Segment.
Stack Frame	The area of the stack containing the variables, register images, and dynamically-allocated buffers associated with a procedure.
Stack Overflow	The condition wherein an attempt is made to push one-too-many items onto the stack and, as a result, a Stack exception is generated.
Stack Segment	The area of RAM memory allocated to temporarily hold (among other things): • Register images. • Return addresses for procedure calls, interrupts and exceptions. • Exception error codes. • Dynamically-allocated buffers to be used by procedures.
Stack Underflow	The condition wherein an attempt is made to pop one-too-many items from the stack and, as a result, a Stack exception is generated.

Term	Description
Store	A write to a memory data operand.
Streaming SIMD Extensions	See SSE.
Streaming Store	Stores (memory data writes) to WC memory or non-temporal stores to WB memory are queued up in the logical processor's WCBs. When a WCB becomes full, the processor performs a full-line memory write (i.e., a burst or streaming write) to dump the buffer's contents to memory.
String Operation	A string instruction is one that, based on an initial count loaded into the CX or ECX register and the memory addresses in the Source Index and Destination Index registers, processes a string of bytes, words or dwords.
Supervisor	Supervisor privilege level refers to privilege level 0, 1, and 2 code associated with the OS kernel. Also see R/W.
SVME	Secure Virtual Machine Enable bit in the EFER register. *AMD-only feature.* When set to one, it enables the logical processor's ability to execute the following AMD-specific virtualization-related instructions: VMRUN, VMLOAD, VMSAVE, CLGI, VMMCALL, and INVLPGA. If SVME = 0, these instructions generate an Undefined Opcode exception.
SVR	Acronym for Spurious Interrupt Vector register.
Synchronizing Event	A synchronizing event forces all posted writes within the logical processor to be flushed to external memory before executing the next instruction. This ensures that all updates to UC, WC, WP, and WT memory have been propagated to memory.

Term	Description
System Segment descriptors	A general term that refers to special descriptors related to the OS kernel: • TSS descriptor. • Task Gate descriptor. • Call Gate descriptor. • LDT descriptor. • Interrupt Gate descriptor. • Trap Gate descriptor.
Task Data Structure	A general, processor-independent term (not x86-specific) referring to the data structure that a task scheduler associates with a task. In the x86 architecture, some of this functionality is fulfilled by the TSS.
Task Gate	If an interrupt or exception, or a far jump or a far call selects descriptor table entry containing a Task Gate descriptor, the logical processor's hardware-based task switching mechanism is triggered. The logical processor suspends the interrupted task, switches to and executes the task which will handle the event, and, if the switch occurred due to a far call, an interrupt, or an exception, then switches back to the interrupted task.
Task Priority register	This mechanism enables the OS scheduler to prevent specific interrupts (generally low-priority interrupts) from disturbing high-priority code the logical processor is executing. Whenever the OS scheduler instructs the logical processor to start executing a task, the OS also causes a value to be written into the Local APIC's TPR. This permits the scheduler to set a priority threshold for the interruption of a task. The logical processor only services only interrupts that have a priority higher than that specified in the TPR. If the scheduler sets the task priority in the TPR to 0, the logical processor recognizes all interrupts, while setting it to 15 prevents the logical processor from handling any interrupts except NMI, SMI, INIT, ExtINT, INIT-deassert, and SIPI.

Term	Description
Task Queue	An OS kernel-specific data structure in which the task scheduler maintains a queue of the currently-active task and those that are currently suspended.
Task Register (TR)	The Task Register is programmed with a 16-bit selector which selects a GDT entry containing a TSS descriptor. The selected TSS descriptor defines the base address and size of the TSS data structure to be used by the current task.
Task Scheduler	Refers to the OS kernel's task scheduler.
TDS	Acronym for Task Data Structure (see this table). Also see "Concept" on page 363.
Temporal Store	A memory data write to an operand in WB memory that may be accessed again in the near-term (see also Non-Temporal Store).
Terabyte	2^{40} memory locations.
TES	Refers to the Threshold Error Status feature. Tracks the number of correctable ECC errors that have been detected in a processor cache. When a correctable ECC error is detected, the logical processor logs it as a soft error (the UC—Uncorrectable—error bit is cleared to 0) in the related MCA bank's MCi_STAT register and the TES logic also deposits the cache's TES status in bits [54:53] of the bank's Status register.
TF	The Trap Flag bit in the Eflags register. When set to one, it enables Single-Step Mode as a program debug aid.
Thermal Monitor feature	When enabled, it slows down the logical processor whenever the core temperature exceeds a factory-calibrated trip point and returns the logical processor to full speed when the temperature drops below the trip point.
Threshold Error Status	See TES.

Term	Description
TI	In Protected Mode or IA-32e Mode, the Table Indicator bit in a segment register selects either the GDT or LDT and the 13-bit Table Index field identifies a descriptor in the selected table.
Time Stamp Counter	A 64-bit MSR that is initialized to zero by reset after which it increments once for each processor clock cycle. A *very* accurate timepiece.
TLB	See Translation Lookaside Buffer.
TMR register	When an inbound maskable hardware interrupt is received, the Local APIC's 256-bit Trigger Mode Register latches the state of the Trigger Mode bit (edge-triggered or level-sensitive) delivered in the IPI message. The TMR bit is selected by the 8-bit interrupt vector delivered in the message.
TOS	Top-of-Stack. The address currently contained in the Stack Pointer register.
TP or TPR register	See Task Priority register.
TR register	See Task Register.
Translation Lookaside Buffer	A special-purpose, high-speed lookaside cache that caches PTEs that point to 4KB pages and PDEs that point to 2MB or 4MB pages. A processor design-specific feature that speeds up the virtual-to-physical address translation mechanism. Frequently divided into two TLBs: one to cache code (instruction) page translations (the ITLB), and the other to cache data page translations (the DTLB).

Term	Description
Trap	Type of exception (also see Fault and Abort). CS:EIP pushed onto the stack points to the instruction following the one that caused the error event. If the trap occurs during execution of an instruction that alters program flow (e.g., a jump), the return address on the stack points to the branch target address (e.g., the address being jumped to). If the instruction is a string instruction and has a repeat prefix and the count has not been exhausted, the return address points to the same instruction and the values in the other registers related to the instruction contain the values for the next iteration.
Trap bit	The Trap bit in a task's TSS. Causes a debug exception when an automatic task switch occurs to a task with this bit (the T bit) set to one.
Trap Gate	See Interrupt Gate.
Trigger Mode register	See TMR.

Term	Description
TS	Refers to the Task Switch bit in CR0. CR0[TS] = 1 indicates: • A task switch has occurred since the last time an x87, MMX, or SSE instruction was executed, • but the contents of the x87 FPU's registers and the SSE register set (the XMM registers and the MXCSR register) were not saved when the task switch occurred. When CR0[TS] = 1 and CR0[EM] = 0, the logical processor generates a DNA exception when an x87, MMX, or SSE instruction is encountered (with some exceptions). The DNA exception handler saves the x87 FPU registers, the XMM registers, and the MXCSR register in the Task Data Structure associated with the task that last performed x87, MMX, or SSE operations. The exception handler then clear CR0[TS] to 0 and returns to the instruction in the current task that caused the DNA exception. The x87, MMX, or SSE instruction encountered in the current task then executes without causing a DNA exception (because CR0[TS] = 0).
TSC	See Time Stamp Counter.
TSD	The Time Stamp Disable bit in CR4. When the logical processor is in Protected Mode or VM86 Mode, CR4[TSD] restricts use of the RDTSC (Read Time Stamp Counter) instruction as follows: • CR4[TSD] = 0, RDTSC can be executed at any privilege level. • CR4[TSD] = 1, RDTSC can only be executed by programs executing with a privilege level of 0. The RDTSC instruction can be executed when the logical processor is in Real Mode.

Term	Description
TSS	Task State Segment: • If the hardware-based task switch mechanism is used, the OS kernel creates one TSS per task which contains: – IO Permission Bitmap. – Interrupt Redirection Bitmap. – Trap bit. – Register save/restore area. – Pointers to pre-allocated stacks. – Trap debug bit. – Link to calling task's TSS descriptor. • Most modern OSs create a single TSS to be used by all tasks (see "Real World TSS Usage" on page 968).
TSS descriptor	A special descriptor in the GDT that contains: • Base address of a TSS. • Size of TSS. • Task Busy bit. • TSS DPL.
U/S	The User/Supervisor attribute bit is found in: • PTE that points to a 4KB page. • PDE that points to a 2MB or 4MB page. • PDE that points to a Page Table. The state of the U/S bit in a PTE or PDE defines the privilege level the currently executing program must have in order to successfully access the address domain covered by the PTE or PDE. • 0 = Supervisor access only (privilege levels 0, 1, or 2). • 1 = Can be accessed by any program.
UC memory	Uncacheable memory type.
Unconditional Branch	When executed, causes the logical processor to unconditionally jump to the specified branch target address.
UnReal Mode	See Real Big Mode.

Term	Description
User	See U/S.
User-Defined Interrupt	Also referred to as a Fixed Interrupt. Interrupt vector values 0 - 31 are reserved for architecturally-defined interrupts and exceptions. A user-defined interrupt is one that has an interrupt vector value in the 32 - 255 range.
Vector	The 8-bit value associated with an interrupt or exception event. The logical processor uses it to select the IDT entry containing the pointer to the corresponding event handler.
VIF	Virtual Interrupt Flag bit in the Eflags register. **VM86 Mode**. If the IOPL for a Real Mode task is set to a value < 3 and the logical processor is in VM86 Mode, any attempt to execute the CLI, STI, POPF or PUSHF instructions has no effect on the Eflags[IF] bit. Instead, the change (if any) is made to Eflags[VIF]: • As always, the state of Eflags[IF] is what controls the logical processor's ability to recognize a maskable hardware interrupt. • The state of Eflags[VIF], on the other hand, merely notes the preference of the Real Mode task to be disturbed (VIF = 1) or not (VIF = 0) by maskable interrupts during a given period of time. **Protected Mode**. If the logical processor is executing a privilege level 3 Protected Mode task, the PVI feature is enabled, and Eflags[IOPL] < 3, any attempt to execute the STI or CLI instruction alters VIF rather than IF.

Term	Description

VIP	The Virtual Interrupt Pending bit in the Eflags register is never set or cleared automatically by the logical processor. Rather, the VMM software controls it:
	• The VMM clears Eflags[VIP] to 0 if it has not deferred the servicing of any maskable hardware interrupts during a period when:
	  – IF = 1 (interrupt recognition is enabled),
	  – but VIF = 0 (the Real Mode task has indicated that it prefers not to be interrupted).
	• The VMM sets Eflags[VIP] = 1 if it has deferred the servicing of one or more maskable hardware interrupts during a period when:
	  – IF = 1 (interrupt recognition is enabled),
	  – but VIF = 0 (the Real Mode task has indicated that it prefers not to be interrupted).

Virtual Address	The information (both code and data) associated with the currently-running task frequently occupies widely-fragmented areas of physical memory. In order to simplify a task's view of memory, the OS kernel's memory manager assigns it a contiguous range of memory addresses that it uses to access its code and data. This is referred to as a virtual memory address range. When a logical processor is operating in 32-bit Protected Mode or IA-32e Mode, the virtual memory addresses generated by the instruction fetcher or by an execution unit when a load or store must be performed are first submitted to the logical processor's address translation services (commonly referred to as the Paging unit) which translates the virtual address into the actual physical address before the memory read or write is performed.
Virtual Machine	A guest OS running under the hypervisor's supervision and within the operating environment created by the hypervisor are collectively referred to as a *VM*.

Term	Description
Virtual Machine Control Structure	When Virtualization is enabled, the hypervisor creates a VMCS for each guest OS running under its supervision. Among other things, the content of the VMCS defines the various event types (*sensitive* events) which trigger an automatic transition from Non-Root back to Root Mode operation (i.e., from the guest OS back to the hypervisor). The cause of the transition is also recorded in the VMCS so it can be evaluated by the hypervisor.
Virtual Machine Monitor (VMM)	This term is used in two different contexts in the ISA specification: • The VMM is a special OS kernel facility that handles attempts by a Real Mode program running under VM86 Mode to execute sensitive instructions. • The hypervisor that supervises the execution of multiple guest OSs is frequently referred to as the VMM.
Virtual Wire Mode A	A system design wherein legacy interrupts from the 8259A interrupt controllers in the chipset are delivered to a physical processor by a hard-wired connection to the processor's INTR input pin (i.e., its LINT0 or LINT1 pin).
Virtual Wire Mode B	A system design wherein legacy interrupts from the 8259A interrupt controllers in the chipset are first delivered to the IO APIC in the chipset which, in turn, transmits an ExtInt IPI message to a logical processor.
Virtualization Technology (VT)	Feature that permits an executive (the VMM or hypervisor) with super-privileges to multi-task multiple guest OSs.
VM	See Virtual Machine.

Term	Description
VM86 Mode	When the scheduler switches to a Real Mode application, it flips a bit in the Eflags register (Eflags[VM]) to activate a logical processor mechanism (the VM86 logic). This logic monitors the behavior of the application on an instruction-by-instruction basis and intercepts any action (referred to as a *sensitive* operation) which might prove destabilizing to the overall multitasking environment.
VM86 Task	A Real Mode application running under VM86 Mode.
VMCS	See Virtual Machine Control Structure.
VME	VM86 Mode Extensions bit in CR4. If it is enabled, the following elements come into play when a Real Mode task is executing: • Eflags[VIF] and Eflags[VIP] bits. • Interrupt redirection bitmap consultation. Provides two improvements to VM86 Mode: • Improved handling of the INT *nn* instruction using the Interrupt Redirection Bitmap in the Real Mode task's TSS. • Improved handling of CLI/STI/POPF/PUSHF instructions using the VIF and VIP bits in the Eflags register.
VMM	See Virtual Machine Monitor.
VMX Mode	Virtualization Mode. The mode the logical processor is in when the Virtualization Technology feature is enabled. It permits a hypervisor to supervise the execution of multiple guest OSs.
VMXE	VMX Mode Enable. When set to one, the VT enable bit in CR4 enables the VT feature.
VT	See Virtualization Technology.
WB memory	Write Back memory type.

Term	Description
WC memory	Write Combining memory type.
WCB	Write Combining Buffer. Stores (memory data writes) to WC memory or non-temporal stores to WB memory are queued up in the logical processor's WCBs. When a WCB becomes full, the processor performs a full-line memory write (i.e., a burst or streaming write) to dump the buffer's contents to memory.
Word	2-bytes (16-bits) of information.
WP	The Write Protect bit is found in CR0. When set to one, it protects read-only memory pages from supervisor (i.e., OS kernel) write access: • WP = 0 permits the OS to write to write-protected pages. • WP = 1. An exception is generated when the OS attempts to write to a write-protected memory page.
WP memory	Write Protect memory type.
Wraparound Math	Using wraparound math, a true out-of-range result is truncated; the carry or overflow is ignored and only the lsbs of the result are stored in the destination. Wraparound math can be used in applications that control the range of operands to prevent out-of-range results. Care should be taken, however; if the range of operands is not controlled, wraparound math can result in large errors (e.g., adding two large, signed numbers can result in positive overflow and produce a negative result).
Write-Combining Buffer	See WCB.
WT memory	Write Through memory type.

Term	Description
x2APIC Architecture	The latest batch of modifications to the APIC architecture (introduced with the advent of the Core i7 processor) is referred to as the x2APIC architecture and includes (among other things) the following modifications: • If the x2APIC architectural feature is available, it is enabled via a new bit in the APIC_Base MSR. • Enabling it disables the memory-mapped IO Local APIC registers and makes them available as MSRs instead. The 4KB memory range (or *hole*) normally consumed by the Local APIC registers therefore becomes available for assignment to system RAM memory. • The Self IPI MSR is available. • A new method for Local APIC ID assignment permits a significantly larger number of Local APICs (and therefore, logical processors) in the system.
x2APIC ID	When software switches the Local APIC from xAPIC Mode to x2APIC Mode, the logical processor hardware automatically: • Expands the xAPIC ID field in the APIC ID register from 8- to a full 32-bits. The expanded field is then referred to as the x2APIC ID and is guaranteed to contain a unique physical ID that can be used to target the Local APIC when a message uses Physical Destination addressing. • Makes the APIC ID register read-only. • Using information from the 32-bit x2APIC ID, it replaces the programmable 8-bit logical xAPIC ID in the Logical Destination Register (LDR) with a hardware-assigned 32-bit, read-only logical x2APIC ID. This is the Local APIC's logical address which is used to address it in Logical Destination address mode.

Term	Description
xAPIC Architecture	To differentiate the revised APIC architecture introduced with the advent of the Pentium 4 from the old APIC architecture, it is referred to as the xAPIC architecture.
XCR0 register	Also known as the XFEM—Extended Feature Enable Mask—register. If implemented, it can only be accessed if CR4[OSXSAVE] = 1. Each defined bit in XCR0 corresponds to a specific register set and is initialized by the OS kernel to reflect whether or not it supports saving the respective register set to the data structure in memory used by the XSAVE instruction. Prior to executing the XSAVE instruction, the programmer sets up a bit mask in the EDX:EAX register pair to indicate which register set(s) he or she wishes to save to the data structure in memory. Upon execution of XSAVE, the logical processor ANDs the request bits specified in EDX:EAX with the support bits in XCR0 and only saves the requested register sets if the respective request and support bits are both one.
XD	The eXecute Disable bit is found in: • Each PDPTE that points to a Page Directory. • Each PDE that points to a Page Table. • Each PDE that points to a 2MB page. • Each PTE that points to a 4KB page. Assuming that the Execute-Disable feature is enabled (EFER[NXE] = 1), if the currently-running program should attempt to perform a code fetch from a page with the XD bit set to one, the logical processor generates a Page Fault exception and the I/D status bit is set to one in the error code pushed onto the stack.
XFEM register	See XCR0 register.

Term	Description
XMM registers	SSE data registers. Each is 128-bits wide. XMM0 - XMM15 are accessible in 64-bit Mode (using the REX prefix to access XMM8 - XMM15), while only XMM0 - XMM7 are accessible in other modes.
ZF	The Zero Flag bit in the Eflags register. Reflects the result of the instruction just executed: • ZF = 1 if the result is zero. • Otherwise, ZF = 0.

Index

Index

Index

Index

Index

Index

Index

Index

Index

Index

Index

Index

Index

www.mindshare.com

Live Training Courses on the x86 Architecture

 ## Comprehensive x86 Architecture (32/64-bit)

This lecture-based course describes the entire x86 architecture; everything from Real Mode addressing to 64-bit Mode interrupt handling. This course focuses on the architectural elements of x86, like segmentation, interrupt/exception handling, paging, etc. After completing this course, you will have a much deeper understanding of the x86 architecture.

Topics covered in this course:
- Instruction Set
- Register Sets
- Operating Modes
- Segmentation
- Task Management
- Interrupts and Exceptions
- Paging
- Memory Types
- Virtualization

 ## System Programming for the x86 Architecture

This course teaches the x86 architecture (both 32-bit and 64-bit) through a mix of lectures and hands-on programming labs. All topics are explained in lecture format first and then the students are given programming labs in assembly to reinforce the concepts and to get hands-on experience working with x86 processors at a very low level. This course focuses mainly on the behavior of legacy Protected Mode, Compatibility Mode and 64-bit Mode as these are the modes most commonly used in modern operating systems.

The lab exercises range from printing to the screen using the flat memory model in legacy Protected Mode to setting up an interrupt driven, multitasking 64-bit Mode environment, with paging turned on.

You Will Learn:
- x86 programming basics like an overview of the instruction set, register set and operating modes
- The behavior of segmentation, how it was originally intended to be used and how it is actually used by operating systems today
- How to setup system calls using multiple methods (and benefits / side-effects of each)
- How to setup interrupt service routines for both software and hardware interrupts and implement a rudimentary scheduler
- How to implement paging in both the 32-bit environments as well as the 64-bit environments including using various page sizes

www.mindshare.com

eLearning Course on the x86 Architecture

 ## Intro to 32/64-bit x86 Architecture

MindShare's Intro to x86 eLearning course provides a great overview of the x86 instruction set architecture. It describes the concepts and implementation of the major architectural elements of x86 (paging, interrupt handling, protection, register set, address spaces, operating modes, virtualization, etc.).

You Will Learn:
- The different groupings of x86 instructions and basic instruction formats
- The different address spaces available in x86 and how each can be accessed
- The registers defined in x86 and how they have grown over time
- All the operating modes that x86-based processors can run in and characteristics of each
- The concepts of paging and its base implementation in x86
- How interrupts and exceptions are handled inside the core
- What virtualization is and about the hardware extensions that companies like Intel are adding their processors

What's Included:
- Unlimited access to the x86 eLearning modules for 90 days
- PDF of the course slides (yours to keep, does not expire)
- Q&A capability with the instructor

Benefits of MindShare eLearning:

- *Cost Effective* - Get the same information delivered in a live MindShare class at a fraction of the cost
- *Available 24/7* - MindShare eLearning courses are available when and where you need them
- *Learn at Your Pace* - MindShare eLearning courses are self-paced, so you can proceed when you're ready
- *Access to the Instructor* - Ask questions to the MindShare instructor that taught the course